ISBN 978-1-5281-0606-1
PIBN 10915368

English
Français
Deutsche
Italiano
Español
Português

www.forgottenbooks.com

Mythology Photography **Fiction**
Fishing Christianity **Art** Cooking
Essays Buddhism Freemasonry
Medicine **Biology** Music **Ancient
Egypt** Evolution Carpentry Physics
Dance Geology **Mathematics** Fitness
Shakespeare **Folklore** Yoga Marketing
Confidence Immortality Biographies
Poetry **Psychology** Witchcraft
Electronics Chemistry History **Law**
Accounting **Philosophy** Anthropology
Alchemy Drama Quantum Mechanics
Atheism Sexual Health **Ancient History**
Entrepreneurship Languages Sport
Paleontology Needlework Islam
Metaphysics Investment Archaeology
Parenting Statistics Criminology
Motivational

Air University Library Index

to
Military Periodicals

CUMULATIVE ISSUE
JANUARY-DECEMBER 1976
Volume 27 Number 4

Ipsa scientia potestas est

Air University Library
Maxwell Air Force Base, Alabama

Air University Library Index
to
Military Periodicals

Volume 27   **Number 4**

Cumulative Issue

January-December 1976

Frances B. Rucks, Editor

Air University Library   **Maxwell Air Force Base, Ala.**

This is a cumulative issue. It includes all indexing since the beginning of the current volume. No further reference to Issues Nos. 1-3 is necessary.

Preface

The *Air University Library Index to Military Periodicals* is a subject index to significant articles, news items and editorials appearing in 72 English language military and aeronautical periodicals not indexed in readily available commercial indexing services. The *Index* originated with 23 titles as a quarterly publication in 1949, and has continued on a quarterly basis superseded by annual cumulations; triennial cumulative issues were published from 1952 through 1967. From 1949 to 1962 the *Index* was issued as *Air University Periodical Index*. Staff members in the Reader Services Division and Editing Section of Air University Library index the periodicals with the exception of six titles which other Air Force, Army, and Navy libraries index. *Air University Library Index to Military Periodicals* serves primarily the educational and research programs of Air University. The *Index* is available to other libraries upon request.

This publication has been reviewed and approved by competent personnel of the preparing command in accordance with current directives on doctrine, policy, essentiality, propriety, and quality.

ROBERT B. LANE
Director
Air University Library

PERIODICALS INDEXED

Aerosp Hist--Aerospace Historian (q) $20.00. Department of History, Kansas State University, Manhattan, Kans, 66506.

Aerosp Intl--Aerospace International (bim) $18.00. P.O.Box 87, D-53, Bonn-Duisdorf, Germany.

Aerosp Safety--Aerospace Safety - AFRP 127-2 (m) $10.35. Superintendent of Documents, U.S. Government Printing Office, Washington, DC, 20402.

*Air Def Mag--Air Defense Magazine (q) $4.00. U.S. Army Air Defense Artillery Museum Historical Assoc, USAADS Box 5240, Fort Bliss, Tex, 79916.

AF Compt--The Air Force Comptroller - AFRP 170-2 (q) $3.90. Superintendent of Documents, U.S. Government Printing Office, Washington, DC, 20402.

AF Engrg & Svcs Qtr--Air Force Engineering and Services Quarterly - AFRP CE 85-1 (q) $3.00. Superintendent of Documents, U.S. Government Printing Office, Washington, DC, 20402.

AF Law Rev--Air Force Law Review - AFRP 110-1 (q) $5.55. Superintendent of Documents, U.S. Government Printing Office, Washington, DC, 20402.

AF Mag--Air Force Magazine (m) $10.00. Air Force Assoc, Suite 400, 1750 Pennsylvania Ave, NW, Washington, DC, 20006.

AF Plcy Ltr for Comdrs: Sup--Air Force Policy Letter for Commanders: Supplement - AFRP 190-2 (m) No price given. Internal Information Division, SAFOII, Pentagon, Washington, DC, 20330.

AF Times--Air Force Times (Eastern Edition) (w) $21.00. Army Times Publishing Co, 475 School St, SW, Washington, DC, 20024.

Air Pict--Air Pictorial (m) $20.00. Profile Books Limited, Dept APS, Coburg House, Sheet St, Windsor, Berks., SL4 1EB, England.

Air Reservist - AFRP 30-1 (10 nos. a year) $4.30. Superintendent of Documents, U.S. Government Printing Office, Washington, DC, 20402.

AU Rev--Air University Review, the Professional Journal of the United States Air Force (bim) $11.60. Superintendent of Documents, U.S. Government Printing Office, Washington, DC, 20402.

Airman, Official Magazine of the U.S. Air Force - AFRP 30-15 (m) $18.20. Superintendent of Documents, U.S. Government Printing Office, Washington, DC, 20402.

Am Avn Hist Soc J--American Aviation Historical Society Journal (q) $12.50. American Aviation Historical Society, P.O. Box 99, Garden Grove, Calif, 92642.

Approach, the Naval Aviation Safety Review - NavAir 00-75-510 (m) $11.70. NAVSAFECEN, NAS, Norfolk, Va, 23511.

Armed Forces & Soc--Armed Forces and Society (q) $16.00. Social Science Building, University of Chicago, Chicago, Ill, 60637.

Armed Forces Compt--Armed Forces Comptroller (q) $7.00. The Armed Forces Comptroller, 206 James Thurber Court, Falls Church, Va, 22046.

Armed Forces J Intl--Armed Forces Journal International (m) $12.00. Army and Navy Journal, Inc, 1710 Connecticut Ave, NW, Washington, DC, 20009.

Armor (bim) $6.50. Armor, P.O. Box O, Fort Knox, Ky, 40121.

Army (m) $10.00. Assoc of the U.S. Army Fulfillment Manager, 1529 - 18th St, NW, Washington, DC, 20036.

Army Log--Army Logistician (bim) $7.65. Superintendent of Documents, U.S. Government Printing Office, Washington, DC, 20402.

Army Qtr--Army Quarterly and Defence Journal (q) $20.00. West of England Press, Publishers, Ltd, 1, West Street, Tavistock, Devon, England.

Aviation, Space & Envmt Med--Aviation, Space, and Environmental Medicine (m) $35.00. Aerospace Medical Assoc, Washington National Airport, Washington, DC, 20001.

Combat Crew - SACRP 127-1 (m) No price given. Editor, Combat Crew, Hq SAC (DOSE), Offutt AFB, Nebr, 68113.

Comdrs Dig--Commanders Digest (biw) $17.00. American Forces Press Service, 1117 N. 19th St., Arlington, Va, 22209; for sale by Superintendent of Documents, U.S. Government Printing Office, Washington, DC, 20402.

Contact - AFITRP 35-1 (bim) No price given. AFIT(CI), Wright-Patterson AFB, Ohio, 45433.

*Countermeasures (m) $15.00. Electronic Defense Assoc, 2065 Martin Ave, Ste 104, Santa Clara, Calif, 95050.

Def & For Aff Dig--Defense & Foreign Affairs Digest (m) $50.00. Copley & Associates, 266 World Trade Center, San Francisco, Calif, 94111.

Def Mgt J--Defense Management Journal (q) $4.85. Superintendent of Documents, U.S. Government Printing Office, Washington, DC, 20402.

*Def Monitor--Defense Monitor (m) No price given. Center for Defense Information, 122 Maryland Ave NE, Washington, DC, 20002.

Def Trans J--Defense Transportation Journal (bim) $20.00. National Defense Transportation Assoc, 1612 K St, NW, Washington, DC, 20006.

*Educ J--Education Journal - AFROTCRP 53-1 (3 nos. a year) No price given. Air Force ROTC, AFROTC/SDEP, Bldg 500, Maxwell AFB, Ala, 36112.

Elect Warfare--Electronic Warfare (bim) $15.00. EW Communications, Inc., 3921 E. Bayshore Road, Palo Alto, Calif, 94303.

Fld Arty J--Field Artillery Journal (bim) $6.00. Field Artillery Historical Assoc, Fort Sill, Okla, 73503.

Forum (changed to National Security Affairs Forum with Fall 1975 issue)

Govt Exec--Government Executive (m) $15.00. 1725 K St, NW, Washington, DC, 20006.

Hawk, the Independent Journal of the Royal Air Force Staff College (a) $1.25 (est). Royal Air Force Staff College, Bracknell, Berkshire, England.

*Added titles since the 1975
Cumulative Issue

**Titles ceased indexing since the
1975 Cumulative Issue

***Titles changed since the 1975
Cumulative Issue

Infantry (bim) $5.95. Editor, Infantry Magazine, Box 2005, Fort Benning, Ga, 31905.

Interavia (m) $25.00. Interavia U.S.A., 275 Madison Ave, New York, NY, 10017.

Interceptor - ADCRP 127-2 (m) No price given. Editor, Interceptor, Hq ADCOM/SEOD, Peterson AFB, Colo, 80914.

Intl Def Rev--International Defense Review (bim) $24.00. Interavia U.S.A., 295 Madison Ave, New York, NY, 10017.

*Intl Sec--International Security (q) $12.00. Program for Science and International Affairs, Harvard University, 9 Divinity Ave, Cambridge, Mass, 02138.

J Pol & Mil Sociol--Journal of Political and Military Sociology (sa) $8.50. Department of Sociology, Northern Illinois University, DeKalb, Ill, 60115.

Log Spectrum--Logistics Spectrum (q) $10.00. Society of Logistics Engineers, 3322 South Memorial Parkway, Suite 65, Huntsville, Ala, 35801.

MAC Flyer - MACRP 127-5 (m) $7.90. Superintendent of Documents, U.S. Government Printing Office, Washington, DC, 20402.

MarCor Gaz--Marine Corps Gazette (m) $10.00. P.O. Box 1775, MCB, Quantico, Va, 22134.

Mil Engr--Military Engineer (bim) $15.00. Society of American Military Engineers, 740 - 15th St, NW, Washington, DC, 20005.

Mil Rev--Military Review (m) $8.00. Military Review, USACGSC, Fort Leavenworth, Kans, 66027.

NATO's Fifteen Nations (bim) $15.00. Jules Perel's Publishing Co, Post Box 366, Amstelveen, The Netherlands.

Natl Def--National Defense (bim) $12.00. American Defense Preparedness Assoc, Union Trust Bldg, Washington, DC, 20005.

Natl Guardsman--National Guardsman (11 nos. a year) $3.00. National Guard Assoc of the U.S., 1 Massachusetts Ave, NW, Washington, DC, 20001.

***Natl Sec Aff Forum--National Security Affairs Forum (formerly Forum) (3 nos. a year) No price given. National War College, Fort Lesley J.McNair, DC, 20319.

Nav War Col Rev--Naval War College Review (q) No price given. Editor, Naval War College Review, U.S. Naval War College, Newport, RI, 02840.

Navigator - AFRP 50-3 (3 nos. a year) $3.00. Superintendent of Documents, U.S. Government Printing Office, Washington, DC, 20402.

Officer (m) $5.00. Reserve Officers Assoc of the U.S., 1 Constitution Ave, NE, Washington, DC, 20002.

Parameters, the Journal of the Army War College (sa) No price given. Editor, Parameters, U.S. Army War College, Carlisle Barracks, Pa, 17013.

Persp in Def Mgt--Perspectives in Defense Management (irregular) No price given. Editor, Perspectives in Defense Management, Industrial College of the Armed Forces, Fort Lesley J. McNair, Washington, DC, 20319.

RUSI J for Def Studies--RUSI, Journal of the Royal United Services Institute for Defence Studies (q) $20.00. Secretary, Royal United Services Institute for Defence Studies, Whitehall, London, SWIA 2, ET, England.

Review (bim) $10.00. American Logistics Assoc, 1000 Connecticut Ave, NW, Washington, DC, 20036.

Royal Air Forces Qtr--Royal Air Forces Quarterly (q) $5.50 (est). Portland Road, Malvern, Worchestershire WR14 2TA, England.

Sea Power (m) $5.00. Navy League of the U.S., 818-18th St, NW, Washington, DC, 20006.

Signal (10 nos. a year) $11.00. Armed Forces Communications and Electronics Assoc, 5205 Leesburg Pike, Falls Church, Va, 22041.

Soldiers, Official U.S. Army Magazine (m) $18.80. Superintendent of Documents, U.S. Government Printing Office, Washington, DC, 20402.

Soviet Mil Rev--Soviet Military Review (m) $7.00. Soviet Military Review, 2, Marshal Biryuzov St, Moscow 123298, USSR. (Available from Victor Kamkin Agency, 1410 Columbia Rd, Washington, DC, 20009)

Spaceflight (m) $25.00. British Interplanetary Society, 12, Bessborough Gardens, London, SWIV 2JJ, England.

Strat Rev--Strategic Review (q) $25.00. United States Strategic Institute, 20 Memorial Drive, Cambridge, Mass, 02142.

TAC Attack - TACRP 127-1 (m) No price given. Editor, TAC Attack, Hq TAC(SEPP), Langley AFB, Va, 23665.

TIG Brief--The Inspector General Brief - AFRP 11-1 (biw) No price given. Editor, TIG Brief, AF/IGEP, Hq USAF, Washington, DC, 20330. Limited to AF offices.

Translog (m) $9.85. Superintendent of Documents, U.S. Government Printing Office, Washington, DC, 20402.

USAF Ftr Wpns Rev--USAF Fighter Weapons Review (q) No price given. 57th Fighter Weapons Wing (DON), Nellis AFB, Nev, 89191.

USA Avn Dig--United States Army Aviation Digest (m) $15.70. Superintendent of Documents, U.S. Government Printing Office, Washington, DC, 20402.

US Nav Inst Proc--United States Naval Institute Proceedings (m) $15.00. U.S. Naval Institute, Annapolis, Md, 21402.

The following abbreviations are used to denote frequency of issue:

a	annual	bim	every two months
biw	every two weeks	and/or	twice a month
m	monthly	q	quarterly
sa	twice a year	w	weekly

ARRANGEMENT

The subject entries are constructed on the direct entry principle. Most sponsor agency entries under U.S. have been eliminated and entry is directly under subject agency, e.g., STRATEGIC AIR COMMAND, not U.S. AIR FORCE. STRATEGIC AIR COMMAND. Specific military services of various countries are entered under their name, followed by the name of their country, e.g., AIR FORCE--Great Britain; ARMY--United States.

Material on United States military aircraft by name has been entered under the headings AIRPLANE TYPE; HELICOPTER TYPE; MISSILE TYPE. United States space vehicles by name have been entered under the heading SPACE PROJECT.

AERONAUTICS here embraces the technical and technological aspects of aviation and aircraft; AVIATION the art of flying, both military and civilian; and AIRLINES the commercial transportation companies; FLYING popular, nontechnical articles on the pleasures of flying.

Government departments are listed alphabetically by department title, e.g., DEFENSE DEPT--United States, not DEPARTMENT OF DEFENSE.

Author entries are included for admirals, generals, Dept of Defense officials, and others who are prominent in some field of Index interest.

An organization's abbreviation, if it is a national term, is used not only as a cross reference (e.g., NATO see NORTH ATLANTIC TREATY ORGANIZATION) but also as geographic subdivision (e.g., DEFENSES--NATO). Abbreviations and acronyms are listed at the beginning of their alphabetical section. However, the artificial words LASERS and LORAN are accepted as normal words and are so listed alphabetically.

Reviews of books are grouped under BOOK REVIEWS; military poetry is listed under POEMS.

KEY TO ABBREVIATIONS

+ (after paging)	continuation of article not	Jun	June
	paged consecutively	Mar	March
Apr	April	Nov	November
Aug	August	No.	number
bibliog	bibliography	obit	obituary
biog	biography	Oct	October
chart	organizational chart	por	portrait(s)
Dec	December	Sep	September
Feb	February	sup	supplement
illus	illustration(s)	tab	table(s)
Jan	January	trans	translated
Jul	July	vol	volume

EXPLANATION

Sample entry: PROFESSIONALISM

Professionalism. LtGen Raymond B. Furlong.
TIG Brief 28:2 Mar 12 '76

Explanation: Under the subject PROFESSIONALISM an article
entitled "Professionalism" by LtGen Raymond
B. Furlong appears in the magazine TIG Brief,
volume 28, on page 2, the March 12, 1976 issue.

A

ACCELERATION

Bradycardia induced by negative acceleration. (Test for standard lap belt) James A. Kennealy and others. illus Aviation, Space & Envmt Med 47: 483-484 May '76

Cardiac pathology associated with high sustained $+G_z$. I: Subendocardial hemorrhage. R. R. Burton and W. F. MacKenzie. illus tabs Aviation, Space & Envmt Med 47:711-717 Jul '76

Cardiac pathology associated with high sustained $+G_z$. II: Stress cardiomyopathy. W. F. MacKenzie and others. illus tab Aviation, Space & Envmt Med 47:718-725 Jul '76

ACCELERATION - Continued

Cardiovascular function during sustained $+G_z$ stress. Howard H. Erickson and others. illus tabs Aviation, Space & Envmt Med 47:750-758 Jul '76

Changes in clinical cardiologic measurements associated with high $+G_z$ stress. Kent K. Gillingham and Phelps P. Crump. illus tabs Aviation, Space & Envmt Med 47:726-733 Jul '76

Disorienting effects of aircraft catapult launchings. II: Visual and postural contributions. Malcolm M. Cohen. tabs Aviation, Space & Envmt Med 47:39-41 Jan '76

Heart biochemical responses 14 days after $+G_z$ acceleration. R. T. Dowell and others. illus tab Aviation, Space & Envmt Med 47:1171-1173 Nov '76

Human response to buffeting in an all-terrain vehicle. T. M. Fraser and others. tabs Aviation, Space & Envmt Med 47:9-16 Jan '76

Instrumentation for the rhesus monkey as a cardiovascular analog for man during air-combat maneuvering acceleration. Howard H. Erickson and John R. Ritzman. illus tabs Aviation, Space & Envmt Med 47:1153-1158 Nov '76

Prolonged visual loss and bradycardia following deceleration from $+6 G_z$ acceleration: A case report. John S. Kirkland and James A. Kennealy. illus Aviation, Space & Envmt Med 47:310-311 Mar '76

That (pull of gravity) machine. LtCol Lee Crock. illus tabs Interceptor 18:8-13 Aug '76

Vestibular habituation in flightcrew. P. Pialoux and others. illus Aviation, Space & Envmt Med 47: 302-307 Mar '76

ACCIDENT PREVENTION

See also
Safety Programs

A-4 spoilers. illus Approach 21:24-25 May '76

A-7 emergency brake problems. LT Carl Tankersley. illus Approach 21:15 Jan '76

The accident that should have happened. LCDR G. L. Forsberg. illus Approach 22:1-3 Sep '76

Air controllers hit on safety (by National Transportation Safety Board). AF Times 36:14 Apr 26 '76

(Airborne collision avoidance system announced) Signal 30:75 Feb '76

Aircraft accident prevention. TIG Brief 28:7 Feb 27 '76

Aircraft corrosion control. TIG Brief 28:14 Aug 27 '76

An aircraft engine container can be a bomb. TIG Brief 28:4 Dec 17 '76

The Aircraft Structural Integrity Program (ASIP). TIG Brief 28:17 Feb 13 '76

Anatomy of a TCTO (Time Compliance Technical Order). Capt Marty Steere. illus TAC Attack 16: 20-21 Sep '76

Another big vote for NATOPS (Naval Air Training and Operating Procedures Standardization). CAPT I. Patch. illus Approach 21:12-13 Feb '76

Approaches are for navigators, too. ENS S. W. Braisted. illus Approach 21:20-22 Feb '76

A long 30 minutes (after engine cowling damage and necessary fuel jettisoning for a safe landing). illus Aerosp Safety 32:4-5 Jan '76

Low altitude wind shear. illus Aerosp Safety 32:10-13 Sep '76

Machiavellian safety. TIG Brief 28:7 Mar 26 '76

Mishap potential. TIG Brief 28:5 Dec 3 '76

NTSB (National Transportation Safety Board): The target is modal balance. Frank McGuire. Govt Exec 8:25-26+ Jul '76

Near miss! Capt Marty Steere. illus TAC Attack 16: 24-25 Jun '76

Night flight. Capt Richard P. Keida. illus Aerosp Safety 32:18-19 Apr '76

"No joy." Maj Jack Spey. illus Aerosp Safety 32 10-11 Jun '76

No new causes. Capt James P. Bloom. illus Aerosp Safety 32:8-9 Jun '76

NonNuclear Munitions Safety Group (NNMSG). TIG Brief 28:15 Sep 24 '76

Nuclear weapon system safety rules. TIG Brief 28:6 Apr 23 '76

Of empty cockpits, storage space, and things. Maj Lawrence E. Wagy. illus Aerosp Safety 32:6-7 May '76

On a night mission. (Pilot's courage and skill helped to save a supersonic missile-carrying plane) LtCol A. Sorokin. illus Soviet Mil Rev No. 1:36-38 Jan '76

One of the finest pilots in the squadron. illus Approach 22:16-18 Aug '76; Combat Crew 27:8-10 Oct '76

Operation of vehicles loaded with or towing nuclear weapons. TIG Brief 28:15-16 Sep 24 '76

Out-of-control aircraft losses (precipitate conference under sponsorship of Naval Safety Center). Approach 21:14 Jan '76

Overcontrol: Commanded or uncommanded? Col Neil L. Eddins. illus tabs TAC Attack 16:10-14 Sep '76

The peanut approach. LT Cameron B. Place. illus Approach 22:8-10 Aug '76

Pilots: Be suspicious! illus Approach 22:10-11 Sep '76

Power cables too short on MD-3 generators. TIG Brief 28:3-4 Jul 16 '76

Prior planning prevents ... Capt Marty Steere. illus TAC Attack 16:20-22 May '76

Problem egress accident items. TIG Brief 28:6 Jul 16 '76

Raindrops keep falling. MAC Flyer 23:11 Feb '76

Realistic training at any price? Arnold R. Lambert. illus USA Avn Dig 22:35-36 Jun '76

Rendezvous at FL 350. illus MAC Flyer 23:16-17 Aug '76

Safe and on time. Capt Bruce L. Gumble. illus MAC Flyer 23:6-9 Sep '76

Safety is everyone's responsibility. BrigGen George C. Cannon, Jr. illus Interceptor 18:14-15 May '76

Safety planning: Protection of workers. TIG Brief 28:8 Mar 26 '76

Scope interpretation. Sgt Edward A. Ranzenbach. illus tabs Combat Crew 27:14-17 Jul '76

Seeking failure-free systems. MajGen Richard E. Merkling. illus tab AU Rev 27:41-50 Jul-Aug '76

"Sinking to ten ..." MAC Flyer 23:11 Jan '76

Situation awareness: One key to safety. Capt Larry Kanaster. illus Aerosp Safety 32:14-15 Dec '76

Small arms: Big problems. TIG Brief 28:6 May 21 '76

So now you're an instructor pilot! Maj Donald E. Yarbrough. illus Aerosp Safety 32:2-4 Aug '76

Static electricity during winter months. TIG Brief 28:6 Feb 27 '76

"Super troop." (Pressure on the men who repair airplanes) Capt Milton G. Schellhase. illus MAC Flyer 23:8-9 Dec '76

Take ten (seconds to evaluate)! LT Richard L. Marquis. illus Approach 21:15 Mar '76

Things that go bump in the flight. Maj Joe Tillman. illus TAC Attack 16:26-28 Aug '76

Thirty ways to crunch an A-7 (or any other type of carrier aircraft). LCDR Jim White. illus Approach 22:16-17 Sep '76

Tuning in the (crew member) awareness frequency. 1stLt Alfred Nickerson. illus MAC Flyer 23:8-9 Apr '76

Twelve o'clock low. Maj Orlen L. Brownfield. illus MAC Flyer 23:18-19 Mar '76

Two perceptions. Maj Thomas L. Sutton. illus Aerosp Safety 32:18-20 May '76

Unapproved aircraft appliances. TIG Brief 28:15 Jul 2 '76

Unqualified passengers (who have never been briefed about the hazards in and around helicopter operations). Arnold R. Lambert. illus USA Avn Dig 22: 40-43 Apr '76

Upside down! And out of ideas? Maj Anthony Helbling, Jr. illus Aerosp Safety 32:21 Mar '76

Use of captive adapter plugs on AIM-9 missiles. TIG Brief 28:8 Dec 17 '76

Validation of aircraft accident recommendations. TIG Brief 28:5 Dec 3 '76

Water/glycol: Fire hazard. Donald Gwynne. illus Aerosp Safety 32:7 Sep '76

The way we were. WO1 Burton E. Crockett. illus USA Avn Dig 22:35-37 Feb '76

Weapons range trespassers. Gordon S. Taylor. illus Aerosp Safety 32:20 Jun '76 .

What are you (squadron commanders and supervisors) doing for Green 16? LtCol Murphy Neal Jones. illus Aerosp Safety 32:2-4 Jun '76

What do you hear? Capt Jerry E. Walker. Aerosp Safety 32:5 Aug '76

What every pilot should know about PFC (Porous Friction Course). Capt Richard E. Simmons. illus MAC Flyer 23:10-11 Nov '76

ACCIDENT PREVENTION - Continued

What's a cubit? Maj R.B.Bateman. illus Aerosp
Safety 32:1-4 Nov '76

What's your viewpoint (when you're trying to land an
airplane)? illus MAC Flyer 23:7-8 Oct '76

When it's reeley cold. 1stLt Don Pierson. illus
Aerosp Safety 32:20-21 Oct '76

When you gotta bingo, you gotta go! illus Approach
21:5 May '76

Wild FIGAT (FiberGlass Aerial Target). illus Approach 21:22-23 Jun '76

The wings of a helicopter. Maj Robert L.Gardner.
illus Aerosp Safety 32:8-9 Mar '76

Wings, wizards and wisdom. Sammy Mason. (Reprinted from Flight Operations, March 1976) illus
USA Avn Dig 22:41-45 Dec '76

Wire act (helicopter hazard). illus Aerosp Safety 32:5
Jun '76

You and your toolbox. Sgt1C Jerry E.Mills. illus
USA Avn Dig 22:30-35 Dec '76

Your signal is bingo! LCDR K.E.Hughes. illus Approach 21:10-11 Nov '75

ACCIDENTS

Accidents and public information responsibilities.
TIG Brief 28:15 Jun 18 '76

Attitudes and accidents aboard an aircraft carrier.
John B. Levine and others. tabs Aviation, Space &
Envmt Med 47:82-85 Jan '76

(Automobile) crash: Then what? (Reprinted from
Family Safety, Fall 1974) illus TAC Attack 16:
18-19 Mar '76

Chlorine hazard. TIG Brief 28:5 Feb 27 '76; Addendum: Use of protective masks for chlorine maintenance. TIG Brief 28:7 Jun 18 '76

$825,000 paid in mid-air crash (of) jet and private
plane (and other accident claims settled). AF
Times 36:32 May 24 '76

The Feres doctrine after twenty-five years. (Military
member's cause of action under the Federal Tort
Claims Act) Capt Robert L.Rhodes. AF Law Rev
18:24-44 Spring '76

Lifting device accidents. TIG Brief 28:9-10 Jan 16 '76

Potential hazards of a nuclear weapon accident. TIG
Brief 28:8 Feb 13 '76; Correction. TIG Brief 28:8
Jul 2 '76

Problem egress accident items. TIG Brief 28:6
Jul 16 '76

Revised procedures for nuclear accident, incident,
deficiency reporting. (AFR 127-4) TIG Brief 28:5
Mar 12 '76

A supervisor's responsibility. TIG Brief 28:4
Jan 30 '76

Texaco Oklahoma: Another Bermuda Triangle victim?
LT Michael R.Adams. illus map US Nav Inst Proc
102:109-110 Mar '76

Costs

Cutting the accident bill. Maj Thomas R.Allocca.
illus Aerosp Safety 32:25-27 Nov '76

ACCIDENTS - Continued

Investigations

Accident investigation board training. TIG Brief 28:6
Oct 8 '76
Industrial accident investigations. TIG Brief 28:14

ACCIDENTS, AIR

Crash rules out small (aircraft) trainer (BD-5J). AF
Times 36:41 Jan 5 '76

$825,000 paid in mid-air crash (of) jet and private
plane (and other accident claims settled). AF
Times 36:32 May 24 '76

FAA acts to cut down on near misses in air. AF
Times 36:10 Jan 5 '76

Seeking failure-free systems. MajGen Richard E.
Merkling. illus tab AU Rev 27:41-50 Jul-Aug '76

Survival. illus Approach 21:22-23 Jan '76

The will to live. (From address, 1975 SAC Safety
Conference, Carswell AFB, Tex) BrigGen William
W.Spruance. illus Combat Crew 26:16-21 Jan '76

Causes

See also
Pilot Error

The ABC (Actions, Briefings, Coordination) for flying professionals. Col Richard C.Jones. illus
TAC Attack 16:12-15 Dec '76

The accident that should have happened. LCDR G.L.
Forsberg. illus Approach 22:1-3 Sep '76

Airframe icing takes its toll. illus Approach 21:
16-17 Dec '75

Are biorhythms a waste of time? Maj John H.Wolcott
and others. (Reprinted from TAC Attack, Nov
1975) illus tabs MAC Flyer 23:11-15 Mar '76

Attitude. LtCol Robert J.Brun. illus Aerosp Safety
32:8-9 Apr '76

Autorotation. illus MAC Flyer 23:11-14 May '76

Bird strike avoidance--what's been done? Capt Don
A.Mynard. illus USA Avn Dig 22:40-42 Jun '76

Birdstrikes ... and the ejection seat. Michael R.
Grost. illus TAC Attack 16:4-6 Jan '76

The "brakes" of naval air. illus Approach 21:19
Feb '76

Breakaway after tanking. illus Approach 22:16-17
Oct '76

Carelessness, incapacity, or neglect. illus MAC
Flyer 23:9-11 Jun '76

A Christmas story. (Plain of Jars, Dec 1970) Capt
Craig W.Duehring. illus TAC Attack 16:18-19
Dec '76

Cockpit UNs (UNaccountables). illus Approach 22:
24-25 Oct '76

Complacency: What it is, what we can do about it.
Maj T.R.Allocca. Aerosp Safety 32:9 Aug '76

Control & supervision and flying. Col Paul M.Davis.
illus Aerosp Safety 32:19-21 Aug '76

Cutting the accident bill. Maj Thomas R.Allocca.
illus Aerosp Safety 32:25-27 Nov '76

DI (Decision Irreversibility). LtCol Gerald B.Hurst.
illus TAC Attack 16:12-14 Feb '76

Causes - Cont'd

Danger area--look out. Maj Jack Spey. illus Aerosp
Safety 32:8-9 Sep '76

Death at the ramp. illus Approach 21:26-27 Feb '76

The depths of distraction. LtCol Robert J. Brun. illus
Aerosp Safety 32:3 Jul '76

Disastrous bingo! illus Approach 21:18-21 Jan '76

Ego trip or hidden message? Maj Lowell A. Schuk-
necht. MAC Flyer 23:20-21 Mar '76

Eliminating the wife error. Jackie Starmer. (Adapted
from MATS Flyer, Aug 1963) illus Interceptor 18:
5-7 Apr '76; Adaptation. Approach 21:24-26
Nov '75

Fatigue. LtCol David H. Karney and Patsy Thompson.
illus tabs USA Avn Dig 22:28-34 Feb '76

Feedback and USAF accident board recommendations.
Maj T. R. Allocca. illus Aerosp Safety 32:18-19
Jun '76

Fire and rain. (An inoperative radar, a revised
weather forecast, a communications breakdown)
illus MAC Flyer 23:13-15 Dec '76

The 5C recipe for inadvertent soup. Capts Michael E.
Herndon and Kent N. Graham. illus USA Avn Dig
22:30-31 Oct '76

Flight limits and crew rest. LtCol David H. Karney.
illus tab USA Avn Dig 22:38-39 Dec '76

Fly smart! Capt Donald K. Fenno. illus Aerosp Safety
32:26-27 Dec '76

For light plane flyers--winter wisdom. Capt Philip
M. McAtee. illus Aerosp Safety 32:8-10 Oct '76

He hit a what? Maj Thomas R. Allocca. illus Aerosp
Safety 32:12-13 Feb '76

Hey blue four, I need help. Maj Charles Barr. (Reprinted from Aerospace Safety, Sep 1975) illus
USA Avn Dig 22:37-39 Sep '76

Hold the ice, please. Maj Philip M. McAtee. illus
Aerosp Safety 32:23-25 Dec '76

Hypoxia. Maj Brian C. Bernet. Aerosp Safety 32:25
Mar '76

Is Danny O'Keefe qualified ... yet? Capt Richard L.
Cecil. illus MAC Flyer 23:18-21 Dec '76

Just a simple error. (Change in altimeter setting)
illus MAC Flyer 23:23 Mar '76

Landing ... or getting it down. LtCol John P. Heffernan. illus Aerosp Safety 32:4-5 Feb '76

The launch. (Complacency in the cockpit) LCDR Bob
Jones. illus Approach 22:24-25 Dec '76

Learning by doing. Capt Robert M. Hail. illus Aerosp
Safety 32:10-13 Dec '76

Look out Johnathan! illus Interceptor 18:14-15
Oct '76

Low altitude wind shear. illus Aerosp Safety 32:10-13
Sep '76

Low-level wind shear. Maj Shirley M. Carpenter.
illus TAC Attack pt 1, 16:4-8 Sep '76; pt 2, Wind
shear on final approach. 16:18-22 Oct '76; pt 3,
Detecting and coping with wind shear. 16:8-13
Nov '76

Causes - Cont'd

Mishaps with a moral. Regular feature in some issues
of MAC Flyer

Mountain flying. illus Approach 21:16-17 Nov '75

Near miss! Capt Marty Steere. illus TAC Attack 16:
24-25 Jun '76

No letup (in unintentional wheels-up landings). illus
tab Approach 21:10-12 Jan '76

No new causes. Capt James P. Bloom. illus Aerosp
Safety 32:8-9 Jun '76

Not up to par. illus Approach 21:12-13 Mar '76

Nugget nightmare. illus Approach 22:18-20 Nov '76

Objects in motion: A look at the mechanics of wind
shear. illus MAC Flyer 23:12-15 Sep '76

One problem too many. illus Approach 21:24-26
Jan '76

Out-of-control aircraft losses (precipitate conference
under sponsorship of Naval Safety Center). Approach 21:14 Jan '76

"P" stands for practice, not prang. Maj Robert L.
Gardner. illus Aerosp Safety 32:20-22 Jul '76

Penetration and landing, company business only.
Capt Jim Jenchura. illus Combat Crew 27:16-17
May '76

A problem with ice. (Engine inlet icing) LtCol
Charles R. Barr. illus Aerosp Safety 32:26-27
Mar '76

Rendezvous at FL 350. illus MAC Flyer 23:16-17
Aug '76

Ricochets. LtCol Jim Learmonth. illus tab Aerosp
Safety 32:16-17 Jan '76

Safe and on time. Capt Bruce L. Gumble. illus MAC
Flyer 23:6-9 Sep '76

"Sinking to ten ..." MAC Flyer 23:11 Jan '76

Situation awareness: One key to safety. Capt Larry
Kanaster. illus Aerosp Safety 32:14-15 Dec '76

Talking of safety. Douglas H. Chopping. illus tabs
Interavia pt 1, 31:1074-1075 Nov '76

They said it couldn't be done! (Multiple emergency:
Single-engine failure and utility hydraulic loss)
illus Approach 22:14-15 Jul '76

To see or not to see: Visual acuity of pilots involved
in midair collisions. Leonard C. Ryan and others.
illus Combat Crew 27:8-10 Sep '76

Too late, too hot to survive. LCDR C. J. Sutherland.
illus Approach 21:18-19 May '76

A trace of disaster. LtCol Robert J. Brun. illus
Aerosp Safety 32:17 Feb '76

Twelve o'clock low. Maj Orlen L. Brownfield. illus
MAC Flyer 23:18-19 Mar '76

2 in the space for 1. Maj Brian C. Bernet. illus tabs
Aerosp Safety 32:2-4 May '76

The way we were. WO1 Burton E. Crockett. illus
USA Avn Dig 22:35-37 Feb '76

Weather report. illus MAC Flyer 23:10-12 Aug '76

ACCLIMATIZATION - Continued

Simple reaction time during exercise, heat exposure, and heat acclimation. E.Shvartz and others. tabs Aviation, Space & Envmt Med 47:1168-1170 Nov '76

ACCOUNTING

AFSC's cost accounting system. Gary W.Amlin. tab illus AF Compt 10:8-9 Jan '76

Directorate of Accounting & Finance. MajGen L. Theus. illus chart AF Compt 10:20-21 Jan '76

Directorate of Accounting & Finance. MajGen Lucius Theus. illus chart AF Compt 10:16-17 Apr '76

Directorate of Accounting & Finance. MajGen Lucius Theus. illus chart AF Compt 10:16-17 Oct '76

Notes from the Director of Accounting & Finance. MajGen Lucius Theus. illus AF Compt 10:16-17 Jul '76

Review of travel vouchers. TIG Brief 28:13 Mar 26 '76

Review, surveillance and self-examination: A special interview on Army funding problems. Hadlai A. Hull. illus Armed Forces Compt 21:2-5 Jan '76

History

Luca Pacioli. 1stLt William A.Bernstein. illus AF Compt pt 1, The father of accounting. 10:44-45 Apr '76; pt 2, The accounting writer. 10:42-44 Jul '76; pt 3, The method of Venice. 10:44-46 Oct '76

ACES

The ace. (The first American fighter ace of World War II relives his Aug 27, 1941, mission with RAF No.71 Eagle Sq) LtCol William R.Dunn, Ret. illus AF Mag 59:76-78+ Sep '76

An Air Force almanac: The United States Air Force in facts and figures. tabs AF Mag 59:132-143 May '76

The Experten and the Flying Tiger: World War II aces in Arizona. Robert C.Sullivan. illus Aerosp Hist 23:148-149+ Sep '76

ACKER, William P.

Bending the Chief's ear. (AF Personnel Management Teams (PMT Air Staff teams) discuss the AF life with members, and then work with the Chief of Staff to solve problems) MSgt Fred Harrison. Airman 20:36-37 Jan '76

ACOUSTICS

Acoustic countermeasures in the undersea environment. Owen Flynn. illus tabs Elect Warfare 8: 62-64+ Sep-Oct '76

Project Kiwi One--new dimensions in underwater sound. David G.Browning and Richard W.Bannister. illus maps US Nav Inst Proc 102:104-105 Jan '76

ADAMS, Lawrence E.

The evolving role of C^3 in crisis management. BrigGen Lawrence E.Adams. Signal 30:59-61 Aug '76

WWMCCS in transition. (Panel discussion, AFCEA, Washington, June 8, 1976) BrigGen Lawrence E. Adams and others. por Signal 30:58-73 Aug '76

ADAMS, Ranald T., Jr

Air Force Inspection and Safety Center. por AF Mag 59:95-96 May '76

ADJUTANT GENERAL

Army

People with a capital P. MajGen Paul T.Smith. illus Army 26:123-124+ Oct '76

Directories

State Adjutants General. Army 26:143 Oct '76

National Guard--Armed Forces

Adjutants General Association Conference (Williamsburg, Va, April 1976). Natl Guardsman 30:34-36 Jun '76

ADMINISTRATION

See also
Management
Management, Military
Personnel Administration

ADMINISTRATIVE SERVICES--AIR FORCE

The Administrative Center: Air Force makes it (word processing) work! John F.Judge. illus Govt Exec 8:39+ Sep '76

ADMIRALS see Flag Officers

ADOPTION see Children, Military

ADVANCED AIRBORNE COMMAND POST

AFSC's Electronic Systems Division (ESD). illus AF Mag 59:51-57 Jul '76

The E-4 airborne command post. W.L.Shockley. illus (Also cutaway) Countermeasures 2:34-36 Jul '76

ADVANCED LOGISTICS SYSTEMS CENTER

(USAF) switch to computer logistics. AF Times 36:41 Jan 5 '76

ADVANCED MANNED STRATEGIC AIRCRAFT

See also
Airplane Type--B-1

ADVANCED MEDIUM SHORT TAKEOFF AND LANDING TRANSPORT

Lockheed doubts AMST value, proposes stretched Hercules. illus Interavia 31:202 Mar '76

Military airlift and the future. (Excerpt from address, 57th Defense Preparedness Meeting, American Defense Preparedness Assoc, Los Angeles, Oct 15, 1975) Gen Paul K.Carlton. Natl Def 60: 288 Jan-Feb '76

New kid on the flight line. (YC-14 and YC-15 compete for the USAF AMST program) illus Airman 20: inside front cover Nov '76

Short takeoff and landing aircraft. (Remarks, YC-14 rollout ceremony, Seattle, June 11, 1976) James W.Plummer. AF Plcy Ltr for Comdrs: Sup No.9: 22-24 Sep '76

Why its contestants think AMST is a good deal for the government. (Interview with AF program manager, LtCol Dave Englund) illus Govt Exec 8:43-44+ Apr '76

AERONAUTICAL ENGINEERS

History

Charles Willard: The creative years. Martin Cole and H.L.Schreiner. illus tab Am Avn Hist Soc J 21:62-70 Spring '76

Duel of designers. (Development of Soviet aviation equipment before and during the Great Patriotic War) Mikhail Arlazorov. illus Soviet Mil Rev No. 1:50-52 Jan '76

AERONAUTICAL INSTRUMENTS

See also specific types of instruments, e.g., Altimeters

Big instrument. Regular feature in issues of Combat Crew

Don't take everything at face value. LtCol Gary R. Tompkins. illus TAC Attack 16:12-13 Jul '76

Flight deck design--technology--money. illus Interavia 31:640-642 Jul '76

Hey blue four, I need help. Maj Charles Barr. (Reprinted from Aerospace Safety, Sep 1975) illus USA Avn Dig 22:37-39 Sep '76

Planning a tactical instrument flight. Capt Lewis D. Ray. illus USA Avn Dig 22:11-13 Jan '76

A revolutionary all-weather HUD (Head-Up Display). (Thomson-CSF TC 125) Douglas Chopping. illus Interavia 31:548-549 Jun '76

AERONAUTICAL LABORATORIES

New (altitude) chamber (Carter P.Luna Physiological Training Center) at Pete(rson AFB, Colo). Capt David V.Frochlich. illus Interceptor 18:5-7 Nov '76

AERONAUTICAL RATINGS

Air Force moves to counter rated turbulence. Ed Gates. tab AF Mag 59:56-59 Apr '76

Fliers assured on-time top rates (under pending changes to AFR 35-13). AF Times 36:5 Mar 29 '76

Nonrated officers get Reg(ular) AF break. AF Times 36:4 Jul 26 '76

100-250 pilots (rated supplement withdrawals) going back to flying status. Lee Ewing. AF Times 37:12 Nov 22 '76

Rated--nonrated distribution by grade. Table only. AF Times 36:52 Mar 1 '76

Rated supplement list issued. tabs AF Times 37:26+ Nov 15 '76

2 plans aim at cutting flight time. Lee Ewing. AF Times 36:3 Jun 21 '76

Statistics

Air Force moves to counter rated turbulence. Ed Gates. tab AF Mag 59:56-59 Apr '76

AERONAUTICAL RESEARCH

United States

Air commerce: Stimulated or damned. A.Scott Crossfield. illus tabs Govt Exec 8:31-32+ Dec '76

U.S. aeronautical R&D: Seeking effective policies and leadership. A.Scott Crossfield. illus tabs Govt Exec 8:38-39+ Nov '76

AERONAUTICAL SYSTEMS DIVISION

Directories

Who's who in ASD EW, Wright-Patterson AFB, Ohio. Table only. Elect Warfare 7:49-51 May-Jun '75

AERONAUTICS

This heading is used for articles on technical and technological aspects of aviation and aircraft, both military and civilian; Airlines is used for articles on commercial air transportation companies; Flying is used for popular, nontechnical articles on the pleasures of flying.

See also

All-Weather Flying	Instrument Flying
Altitude Flying	Night Flying
Aviation	Visual Flying
Flight, Low-Altitude	

History

Flying myths and legends, balloons, blimps and dirigibles: A quest for relevancy. Capt Lawrence Pace. Educ J 19:13-18 Fall '76

United States

NASA's goal: Keeping the U.S. Number One in aeronautics. Alan M.Lovelace. illus AF Mag 59:36-40 Feb '76

AEROSPACE DEFENSE COMMAND

See also
Aerospace Force, 14th

Aerospace defense. (Remarks, American Defense Preparedness Assoc, Los Angeles, Oct 15, 1975) Gen Daniel James, Jr. AF Plcy Ltr for Comdrs: Sup No.1:2-10 Jan '76; Condensation. Natl Def 60: 289 Jan-Feb '76

Aerospace Defense Command. illus chart AF Mag 59:54-55 May '76

Coming: William.Tell 1976 (Tyndall AFB, Fla, Oct 31-Nov 21).tabs Interceptor 18:6-7 Aug '76

The competitive spirit of '76. (Aerospace Defense Command 1976 Weapons Loading Competition, Tyndall AFB, Fla) Capt Robert J.Perry. illus Interceptor 18:5-9 Jul '76

The number '1' team (in 1976 William Tell Weapons Loading Competition). illus Air Reservist 28:11 Aug-Sep '76

On the Santa Fe Trail. (Operating Location Alpha Bravo, a high-frequency radio site in eastern Colorado, operated by Aerospace Defense Command) SMSgt Harold Newcomb. illus Airman 20: 11-14 Nov '76

30th anniversary of the combat commands. illus AF Mag 59:123-125 Mar '76

The Voodoo (Oregon's 142d Fighter Interceptor Gp) revenge (wins the 1976 Aerospace Defense Command's Weapons Loading Competition). illus Natl Guardsman 30:4-5 Jul '76

AEROSPACE DEFENSE DIVISION see Aerospace Force, 14th

AEROSPACE FORCE, 14th

History

The Chinese-American Composite Wing (CACW). LtCol Kenneth Kay, Ret. illus AF Mag 59:60-65 Feb '76

AEROSPACE INDUSTRY AND TRADE

See also
Aircraft Industry and Trade
Electronic Industry and Trade
Missile Industry and Trade
Space--Commercial Applications

Aerospace review. Regular feature in issues of
Aerospace International

Aerospace world. Regular feature in issues of Air
Force Magazine

Industrial periscope: A business, technological &
scientific news bulletin. Regular feature in some
issues of NATO's Fifteen Nations

Jane's aerospace review 1975/76. John W.R.Taylor.
illus AF Mag 59:22-29 Jan '76

The world of aerospace. Regular feature in issues of
Interavia

Economic Aspects

Aerospace: Capital shortage--artificial environment.
Paul Thayer. illus Govt Exec 8:36-37 Feb '76

Exhibitions

1976 Aerospace Development Briefings and Displays.
illus AF Mag 59:44-46 Nov '76

Pentagon suppliers squeezed to exhibit at NASA's
Disneyworld. (Bicentennial science and technology
exhibit at Cape Canaveral) Benjamin F.Schemmer.
illus Armed Forces J Intl 113:31+ Mar '76

International Aspects

Foreword to 'Jane's All the World's Aircraft,
1975-76.' John W.R.Taylor. Royal Air Forces
Qtr 16:25-32 Spring '76

Where is the German (Hanover) Air Show going? illus
tab Interavia 31:505-510 Jun '76

Europe, Western

The space business--has Europe a chance? Dan
Boyle. illus tab Interavia 31:647-650 Jul '76

France

A profile of Aerospatiale. John Marriott. illus
NATO's Fifteen Nations 20:80-84 Dec '75-Jan '76

Germany (Federal Republic)

Where is the German (Hanover) Air Show going? illus
tab Interavia 31:505-510 Jun '76

Great Britain

Aerospace (equipment). John Marriott. illus tabs
NATO's Fifteen Nations 21:35-39+ Apr-May '76

British aerospace: End of a chapter--or the book?
tab illus Air Pict 38:345-348+ Sep '76

Nationalizing the British aerospace industry: When,
how and for how long? Derek Wood. illus Interavia
31:799-800 Sep '76

What's happening in British aerospace? illus Spaceflight 18:42-46 Feb '76

Statistics

The British aerospace industry in figures and tables.
illus tabs Interavia 31:825-830 Sep '76

Japan

The Japanese aerospace industry: In a tight squeeze.
illus tabs Interavia 31:965-968+ Oct '76

AEROSPACE INDUSTRY AND TRADE - Continued

United States

Aerospace sales gains are more illusory than real.
F.Clifton Berry, Jr. illus Armed Forces J Intl
113:10 Jan '76

Defense industry: Is the foundation crumbling? tab
Govt Exec 8:19 Mar '76

AEROSPACE MEDICAL ASSOCIATION

(Annual directory of members, corporate members,
allied organizations, fellows, constitution and by-
laws, 1976 index) Aviation, Space & Envmt Med
47: entire issue Dec '76

Med society (Aerospace Medical Assoc) confers
awards (at 47th annual Scientific Meeting, Bal
Harbour, Fla, May 10-13, 1976). illus AF Times
36:27 May 31 '76

Minutes of 1976 Business Meeting, Aerospace Medical Association (Bal Harbour, Fla, May 11, 1976).
illus Aviation, Space & Envmt Med 47:1130-1134
Oct '76

1976 award winners of the Aerospace Medical Association. illus Aviation, Space & Envmt Med 47:572-
576 May '76

Directories

(Annual directory of members, corporate members,
allied organizations, fellows, constitution and by-
laws, 1976 index) Aviation, Space & Envmt Med
47: entire issue Dec '76

AEROSPACE MEDICINE see Aviation Medicine; Space
Medicine

AEROSPACE POWER

See also
Air Defenses

Air power: A perspective on fighting aircraft. David
Harvey and Gregory Copley. illus Def & For Aff
Dig No.4:14-18+ '76

A call from the wilderness. Maj Donald J.Alberts.
illus AU Rev 28:35-45 Nov-Dec '76

Some thoughts about air power. ACM Andrew Humphrey. illus Hawk No.37:5-7+ Jul '76

The threat. (Keynote address, Royal Air Forces
Assoc Annual Conference, Eastbourne, Eng,
May 15-16, 1976) ACM Andrew Humphrey. Royal
Air Forces Qtr 16:203-207 Autumn '76

China (People's Republic)

Communist China's aerospace forces. Col Angus M.
Fraser, Ret. tab AF Mag 59:74-77 Nov '76

Germany (Federal Republic)

The West German Air Force re-equips for the 1980s.
Rudi Meller. illus tab Interavia pt 1, Combat
strength increases under cost pressures. 31:320-
322+ Apr '76; pt 2, 31:459-461 May '76

Great Britain

Defence cuts continue. (Points from Britain's 1976
Defence White Paper) illus tabs Air Pict 38:174-
177 May '76

History

The RAF and counter-force strategy before World
War II. Malcolm Smith. RUSI J for Def Studies
121:68-73 Jun '76

AEROSPACE POWER - Continued

NATO

Air power and NATO options. (1st prize, Gordon Shephard Memorial Trophy Essay Competition, 1975) Air Commodore M.J.Armitage. Royal Air Forces Qtr 16:17-23 Spring '76

The viability of offensive air support in the next decade. Gary Tobin. illus Intl Def Rev 9:361-364 Jun '76

Russia

The ever-expanding umbrella. LtCol Arthur D. McQueen. tab illus Air Def Mag, pp 8-17, Jul-Sep '76

Soviet aerospace almanac. illus charts tabs map AF Mag 59:37-51+ Mar '76

Soviet aerospace forces: Continuity and contrast. Col William F.Scott, Ret. illus charts AF Mag 59:38-47 Mar '76

United States

The Air Force story. MSgt Dave Sylva. illus Aerosp Safety 32:4-9 Jul '76

Air interdiction in a European future war: Doctrine or dodo? WgComdr Alan Parkes. AU Rev 27:16-18 Sep-Oct '76

Flexibility--a state of mind. Gen Richard H.Ellis and LtCol Frank B.Horton III. illus Strat Rev 4: 26-36 Winter '76

Forces for the future. (Remarks, Lancaster Chamber of Commerce, Lancaster, Calif, Feb 6, 1976) Thomas C.Reed. AF Plcy Ltr for Comdrs: Sup No.4:16-20 Apr '76

The future and Tactical Air Command. (Remarks, American Defense Preparedness Assoc Meeting, Los Angeles, Oct 15, 1975) Gen Robert J.Dixon. AF Plcy Ltr for Comdrs: Sup No.2:10-21 Feb '76; Condensation. Natl Def 60:285 Jan-Feb '76

Future concepts of air power. (Excerpt from address, 57th Defense Preparedness Meeting, American Defense Preparedness Assoc, Los Angeles, Oct 15, 1975) LtGen John W.Pauly. Natl Def 60: 284 Jan-Feb '76

Secretary of the Air Force's Air Force authorization request. (Statement before House Committee on Armed Services, Washington, Jan 29, 1976) Thomas C.Reed. tabs AF Pley Ltr for Comdrs: Sup No.3:2-23 Mar '76

A tactical triad for deterring limited war in Western Europe. LtCol Thomas C.Blake, Jr. illus AU Rev 27:8-15 Sep-Oct '76

Who needs nuclear tacair? Col David L.Nichols. illus AU Rev 27:15-25 Mar-Apr '76

Warsaw Pact

The air attack potential of the Warsaw Pact. Peter Borgart. illus tabs Intl Def Rev 9:193-197 Apr '76

AEROSPACE RESCUE AND RECOVERY SERVICE

Readiness. (Remarks, Jolly Green Pilots Assoc reunion, Eglin AFB, Fla, April 24, 1976) MajGen Billy J.Ellis. AF Plcy Ltr for Comdrs: Sup No.7: 2-6 Jul '76

AFRICA

Sports in Africa: A U.S. grass roots involvement. illus Govt Exec 8:50+ Sep '76

AFRICA - Continued

Politics and Government

Revolution and tradition in the Middle East, Africa, and South Asia. Marcus W.Franda. illus Natl Sec Aff Forum No.24:23-31 Spring-Summer '76

Strategic Importance

Africa strategy. Gregory Copley. illus Def & For Aff Dig No.3:6-9+ '76

AFRICA, NORTH

The Green March (1975). C.G.White. Army Qtr 106: 351-358 Jul '76

AFRICA, SOUTH
Here are entered articles on the southern region of Africa. For the country of South Africa see South Africa (Republic).

Strategic Importance

The vulnerability of the West in the Southern Hemisphere. Patrick Wall. illus tab Strat Rev 4:44-50 Winter '76

AGENCY FOR INTERNATIONAL DEVELOPMENT

Guatemala: Helping hand. SSgt Zack Richards. illus Soldiers 31:14-17 Aug '76

AGRICULTURE

Azores

It began with cows. (USAF veterinarians from Lajes AB have worked with the people of Terceira in the Azores since 1949 to improve dairy and other farm production) Maj Angelo Cerchione, Ret. illus Airman 20:34-38 Aug '76

Russia

The food weakness. (State of the Soviets) Ellis Tenant. illus tabs Def & For Aff Dig No.6:11-14 '76

A note on wheat and the Soviet Armed Forces. Harriet Fast Scott. (Reprinted from Strategic Review, Fall 1975) Mil Rev 56:33-35 May '76

(USSR) farming prospects (under the 10th five-year plan). G.Alexeyev. illus Soviet Mil Rev No.7:6-7 Jul '76

United States

Agricultural freedom and national strength. Earl L. Butz. Persp in Def Mgt No.24:13-18 Winter '75-'76

AGRICULTURE DEPT

Now, a way to get at those grants and loans. (Federal Domestic Assistance Program Retrieval Systems) Spencer B.Child. illus Govt Exec 8:26+ Mar '76

AIDES

'Dogrobber' flap (about enlisted aides) nothing new. AF Times 37:31 Sep 13 '76

Hill raids cut aides to 396. AF Times 36:40 Jun 21 '76

Which generals have how many aides and where. Table only. AF Times 36:40 Jun 21 '76

White gloves and the aide's aide. Elizabeth B.Libbey. illus Army 26:33-36 Jul '76

AIR ASSAULT CONCEPT

The artillery raid, air assault style. LtCol Albert E. Wolfgang and Capt Ronald E. Spears. illus Fld Arty J 44:22-28 May-Jun '76

101st Aviation Group night flying. Capt Peter L. Wyro. illus USA Avn Dig 22:8-10 Jan '76

NATO views on employment of airborne assault forces. Col M. Belov. (Trans from a Russian publication. Reprinted in part from Translations on USSR Military Affairs, No. 1181, Sep 16, 1975) illus USA Avn Dig 22:4-5+ Apr '76

The threat to air assault operations. Capt Daniel W. Henk. illus USA Avn Dig 22:6-7+ Feb '76

AIR BASE DEFENSE

See also
Disaster Control
Vietnamese Conflict, 1957-1975--Security Operations

Airfield defense--the British approach. R. Pengelley. illus Intl Def Rev 8:832-834 Dec '75

The forgotten mission. Col William V. Kennedy. illus charts Armor 85:37-40 Sep-Oct '76

Spang(dahelm AB, Germany) SPs test skills under 'fire.' TSgt Bill Zink. illus AF Times 37:21 Aug 9 '76

Study and Teaching

The enemy fired needles. (Security police from NM ANG and USAF's 4900th Security Police Sq, Kirtland AFB, NM, complete Corona Lock, AF's Combat Air Base Defense Course) illus Natl Guardsman 30:37 Jan '76

AIR BASES

See also
Air Bases, Naval
Inactivation of Installations and Units--Air Force Tenant Units

Construction

See also
Bare Base Concept

Contemporary forum of cooperative planning. (Air Installation Compatible Use Zone) Gary D. Vest. illus maps AF Engrg & Svcs Qtr 17:9-12 Aug '76

Europe, Western

Airfield defense--the British approach. R. Pengelley. illus Intl Def Rev 8:832-834 Dec '75

United States

Air bases are entered by name and location as given by the U.S. Organization Chart Service's U.S. Military and Government Installation Directory.

(AF) libraries held vital to bases. AF Times 36:18 Mar 29 '76

Political campaigning on Air Force bases. TIG Brief 28:15 Jun 18 '76

Directories

Guide to USAF bases (and stations) at home and abroad. map AF Mag 59:144-152 May '76

Andrews AFB, Md

Bolling (AFB, DC), Andrews (AFB, Md) join MAC. AF Times 36:27 Jul 19 '76

AIR BASES - Continued

United States - Cont'd

Biggs AFB, Tex--History

From whence we came: Biggs Field, Texas, circa 1920-22. Pictorial. Aerosp Safety 32:14-16 Feb '76

Bolling AFB, DC

Bolling (AFB, DC), Andrews (AFB, Md) join MAC. AF Times 36:27 Jul 19 '76

Bolling (AFB, DC) EM rooms valued at $50. Ron Sanders. AF Times 37:21 Nov 29 '76

Dobbins AFB, Ga

Dobbins AFB (Ga) pays the Air Force Reserves. Chris J. Scheer. illus AF Compt 10:32-33 Apr '76

Eglin AFB, Fla

Toward a new land and life. (Resettlement for many Vietnamese began at Eglin AFB, Fla: A report from a year later) Robert K. Ruhl. illus Airman 20:24-30 Aug '76

Lackland AFB, Tex

Lackland (AFB, Tex) Reception Center. TIG Brief 28:3 Jun 18 '76

Luke AFB, Ariz

The Luftwaffe + twenty. (German pilots train at Luke AFB, Ariz) LtCol Fred A. Meurer. illus Airman 20:2-8 Aug '76

Maxwell AFB, Ala

Rebuilt Wright. (Volunteers from Squadron Officer School at Maxwell AFB, Ala, build a replica of the Wright brothers' 1910 hangar) Irene P. Barrett. illus Airman 20:20 Nov '76

Maxwell AFB, Ala--History

The great naval battle of Maxwell Field (Ala), 11 November 1929. MajGen John W. Sessums, Ret. illus Aerosp Hist 22:210-211 Dec '75

Moody AFB, Ga

A new home for TAC fighters ... Moody AFB (Ga). LtCol Bill Ardern. illus TAC Attack 16:10-11 Feb '76

Scott AFB, Ill--History

The great flying game. (Flying training at Scott Field, Ill, 1917-18) Isobel Bryant. illus MAC Flyer 23:18-20 Jul '76

Shemya AS, Alas

Shemya (AS, Alas, home of 2064th Communications Sq, 1931st Communications Gp) fights wind, weather. Paul M. Turkheimer. illus AF Times 36:47 Jul 12 '76

Sparrevohn AFS, Alas

Living in the ice age. (Remote duty at Sparrevohn AFS, Alas) TSgt Tom Dwyer. illus Airman 20:2-7 Apr '76

Vandenberg AFB, Calif

The space shuttle and Vandenberg Air Force Base. MajGen R. C. Henry and Maj Aubrey B. Sloan. illus map AU Rev 27:19-26 Sep-Oct '76

AIR BASES, AMERICAN

Directories

USAF's major bases overseas. AF Mag 59:152 May '76

Azores

It began with cows. (USAF veterinarians from Lajes AB have worked with the people of Terceira in the Azores since 1949 to improve dairy and other farm production) Maj Angelo Cerchione, Ret. illus Airman 20:34-38 Aug '76

Europe, Western

Maintenance and Repair

Base maintenance contracts: A different approach. Capt George E. Ehnert. illus AF Engrg & Svcs Qtr 17:15-17 May '76

Germany (Federal Republic)

Bernkastel's Burgermeister. (The major of a nearby town is a friend to Americans based at Hahn AB, Germany) MSgt Yuen-Gi Yee. illus Airman 20: 17-19 Oct '76

Friends are for the making. (1stLt William Baird teaches unique and useful human relations course for German employees at Bitburg AB, Germany) MSgt Yuen-Gi Yee. illus Airman 20:16-17 Nov '76

Japan

Out front by being responsive. (Prime BEEF in PACAF) Harry A. Davis. illus AF Engrg & Svcs Qtr 17:21+ Aug '76

Marianas

Marianas commonwealth status approved; DOD eyes air base. AF Times 36:20 Mar 8 '76

Philippines (Republic)

The night the world died (at Clark AB, RP). illus Approach 22:6-7 Oct '76

Puerto Rico

History

The Battle of Borinquen (PR, 1941). LtGen Harry E. Goldsworthy, Ret. illus Aerosp Hist 22:185-187 Dec '75

Spain

The Spanish connection: A wider U.S. commitment in the making. maps tabs Def Monitor 5: entire issue Feb '76

AIR BASES, NAVAL

Great Britain

History

Those magnificent men 'mid the bathing machines: The story of RNAS Westgate. Geoffrey Williams. illus Air Pict 38:361-363 Sep '76

United States

Naval air bases are entered by name and location as given by the U.S. Organization Chart Service's U.S. Military and Government Installation Directory.

North Island NAS, Calif

Naval Air Rework Facility, North Island (NAS, Calif). William M. Powers. illus US Nav Inst Proc 102: 62-71 Jun '76

AIR CABIN CREWS see Cabin Crews

AIR CARGO

See also
Hazardous Substances--Transportation

Air cargo market undergoing major changes. Siegfried Koehler. illus tabs Interavia 31:929-930 Oct '76

Air cargo's problem areas. (Interview with Stanley F. Wheatcroft, 8th International Forum for Air Cargo, London, May 10-12, 1976) illus Interavia 31:671 Jul '76

Bringing air freight into the intermodal age. Russell T. Daly. illus Def Trans J 32:18-20+ Jun '76

GAO: 'Lift ability is overestimated. AF Times 36:40 Jul 12 '76

It's tough at the top, but that's the way Seaboard's Richard Jackson likes it. (Interview with Richard Jackson) Arthur Wallis. illus Interavia 31:529 Jun '76

North Atlantic air cargo: A time for re-assessment. Arthur J. Wallis. illus Interavia 31:527-528 Jun '76

Preparation of 463L pallet and net control report. TIG Brief 28:11 Mar 12 '76

AIR CAVALRY

Forward ho! The Delta Troop myth. LtCol William P. Gillette. tab Armor 85:45-46 Jan-Feb '76

Hangar talk for aeroscouts. CW2 Homer E. Shuman. illus Armor 85:48-49 May-Jun '76

The "Real Cav" (4th Sq, 9th Cavalry). MSgt Wayne E. Hair. illus USA Avn Dig 22:24-25 Mar '76

AIR COMMAND AND STAFF COLLEGE

ACSC Associate Programs revision. TIG Brief 28:6 Aug 27 '76

AIR COMMANDOS

TAC navigators: Meeting the challenge. Maj Ronald E. Schulz. illus Navigator 23:10-14 Spring '76

AIR CONDITIONINO

See also
Airplanes--Heating and Ventilation

Costs

Computers cut energy costs in buildings. Phil Deakin. illus tab Govt Exec 8:33+ May '76

AIR CREWS

See also
Cabin Crews
    also specific kinds of crew members, e.g.,
Flight Engineers
Navigators
Pilots

Aircrew medical standards and their application in the Royal Australian Air Force. Roy L. DeHart and others. tabs Aviation, Space & Envmt Med 47: 70-76 Jan '76

(Combat crew officers' careers) Gen Russell E. Dougherty. illus Combat Crew 27:3+ Jul '76; TIG Brief 28:2-4 Aug 13 '76

Crew rest. illus Approach 21:24-25 Jun '76

AIR CREWS - Continued

Critical 11 minutes. (Takeoff plus 3 and landing minus 8) Maj John R.Dockendorff. illus Combat Crew 27:4-7 May '76; Aerosp Safety 32:2-5 Sep '76

Evaluating the ability of aircrew personnel to hear speech in their operational environments. C.E. Williams and others. tabs Aviation, Space and Envmt Med 47:154-158 Feb '76

Fatigue. LtCol David H.Karney and Patsy Thompson. illus tabs USA Avn Dig 22:28-34 Feb '76

Flight-induced changes in human amino acid excretion. James P.Ellis, Jr and others. tabs Aviation, Space & Envmt Med 47:1-8 Jan '76

Flight limits and crew rest. LtCol David H.Karney. illus tab USA Avn Dig 22:38-39 Dec '76

Flying EM closer to career status: Mixed blessing. Bruce Callander. AF Times 36:2 May 17 '76

Hawkeye (E-2C) crew coordination. LCDR Richard J. Malla. illus Approach 21:8 Mar '76

Logging flying time. TIG Brief 28:19 Jul 16 '76

One last word on discipline. LtGen R.M.Hoban. illus Combat Crew 27:3+ Oct '76

Psychomotor test performance and sleep patterns of aircrew flying transmeridional routes. Leslie Buck. illus tabs Aviation, Space & Envmt Med 47: 979-986 Sep '76

Psychotherapy and return to flying duties. Carl B. Steinbacher and Carlos J.G.Perry. tabs Aviation, Space & Envmt Med 47:770-772 Jul '76

A study of crew workload in low-level tactical fighter aircraft. WgComdr W.J.Wratten. Royal Air Forces Qtr 16:119-121+ Summer '76

Tuning in the (crew member) awareness frequency. 1stLt Alfred Nickerson. illus MAC Flyer 23:8-9 Apr '76

Vestibular habituation in flightcrew. P.Pialoux and others. illus Aviation, Space & Envmt Med 47: 302-307 Mar '76

(The winners of SAC's) Giant Voice ('76). LtCol Richard W.Blatter. illus tabs Combat Crew 27: 4-7+ Dec '76

The "young" professional SAC crew force. MajGen A.B.Anderson, Jr. illus Combat Crew 26:3+ Feb '76

Education and Training

Aircrew ground training (by ISD, Instructional System Development). TIG Brief 28:3 Mar 12 '76

Back to basics: Planning & execution of pop-up patterns. Capt James P.Feighny, Jr. illus tab TAC Attack 16:4-9 Dec '76

Incidence of decompression sickness in Navy low-pressure chambers. R.Bason and others. tabs Aviation, Space & Envmt Med 47:995-997 Sep '76

Lomcevak (46th Flying Training Sq, Peterson Fld, Colo). Capt Eugene W.Bricker. illus Interceptor 18:8-12 Feb '76

'Plan' lists simulator data. (Air Force Master Plan Simulators for Aircrew Training, issued by Aeronautical Systems Division) AF Times 36:30 Apr 5 '76

Who are you calling student? Capt Charles E.Bailey. illus Combat Crew 27:8-10 Dec '76

AIR CUSHION VEHICLES

Booster shot for the high speed Navy: Technological successes, and a 3K green light from DOD. James D.Hessman. illus Sea Power 19:23-25 Jun '76

Men o'war. Joseph Fama. illus Def & For Aff Dig No. 6:26-31 '76

The small ships. James D.Hessman. illus Sea Power 19:13-16 Sep '76

Strategic mobility: Impetus for a Southwest Passage. Col Jack W.Dindinger, Ret. illus map tabs US Nav Inst Proc 102:33-37 Apr '76

Surface effect vehicles: A perspective. J.F.Sladky, Jr. illus (Also cutaway) US Nav Inst Proc 102; 101-105 Apr '76

AIR DEFENSE COMMAND see Aerospace Defense Command

AIR DEFENSES

See also
Missile Defense
Warning Systems

"Above the best" but below the threat. Capt Lewis D. Ray. illus USA Avn Dig 22:19-23 Feb '76

Air defense: Protecting the power centers. David Harvey. illus Def & For Aff Dig No. 11:4-5+ '76

New data handling technology in air defence. J.W. Sutherland. illus Intl Def Rev 9:616-618 Aug '76

Roving AA (Anti-Aircraft) subunits and ambushes. Col V.Subbotin. Soviet Mil Rev No.2:24-25 Feb '76

The threat to air assault operations. Capt Daniel W. Henk. illus USA Avn Dig 22:6-7+ Feb '76

History

History of air defense. Regular feature in issues of Air Defense Magazine

Europe, Western

Vietnam in Europe? (Sir Robert Brooke-Popham Prize Essay) WgComdr R.W.D.C.Holliday. illus Hawk No.37:15-20 Jul '76

Germany (Democratic Republic)

Threat scenario: German Democratic Republic. illus Elect Warfare 8:66 Mar-Apr '76

Great Britain

CINCUKAIR (Commander-IN-Chief United Kingdom AIR Forces): ACE's new one. illus NATO's Fifteen Nations 20:53-60 Dec '75-Jan '76

Defence cuts continue. (Points from Britain's 1976 Defence White Paper) illus tabs Air Pict 38:174-177 May '76

More efficient use of the RAF Phantom force. (Sir Robert Brooke-Popham Prize Essay) SqLdr R.D. Arnott. illus Hawk No.37:23-28 Jul '76

SACEUR's subcommanders take the floor: United Kingdom Air Forces. ACM Denis Smallwood. illus NATO's Fifteen Nations 21:96-103 Feb-Mar '76

"Small is not beautiful--but still may be useful.' ' ACM Christopher Foxley-Norris. Army Qtr 106 271-276 Jul '76

The threat. (Keynote address, Royal Air Forces Assoc Annual Conference, Eastbourne, Eng, May 15-16, 1976) ACM Andrew Humphrey. Royal Air Forces Qtr 16:203-207 Autumn '76

AIR DEFENSES - Continued

Great Britain - Cont'd

History

Anticipating air attack--in defence of Britain. Alfred Gollin. illus Aerosp Hist 23:197-201 Dec '76

Iran

The Rapier & mace: Air defense & the art of grand strategy; a study of the Iranian example. Gregory Copley. illus Def & For Aff Dig No.4:6-11 '76

NATO

Air defense in Reforger. LtCol Joseph J.Heinlein, Jr. illus Air Def Mag, pp 16-21, Apr-Jun '76

CINCUKAIR (Commander-IN-Chief United Kingdom AIR Forces): ACE's new one. illus NATO's Fifteen Nations 20:53-60 Dec '75-Jan '76

Effective use of NATO air resources. WgComdr A.E.G.Woods, Ret. Royal Air Forces Qtr 16: 109-117 Summer '76

SACEUR's subcommanders take the floor: United Kingdom Air Forces. ACM Denis Smallwood. illus NATO's Fifteen Nations 21:96-103 Feb-Mar '76

"Small is not beautiful--but still may be useful." ACM Christopher Foxley-Norris. Army Qtr 106: 271-276 Jul '76

Tac air, member of the (combined arms) team supporting the supersoldier. LtCol William H.Rees. illus Infantry 66:16-23 May-Jun '76

Russia

At maximum range. A.Polyakov. Soviet Mil Rev No.1:21-22 Jan '76

The ever-expanding umbrella. LtCol Arthur D. McQueen. tab illus Air Def Mag, pp 8-17, Jul-Sep '76

The growing threat: New challenges for the EW community. Ronald T.Pretty. illus Elect Warfare 8: 43+ Mar-Apr '76

Ship air defence. Capt B.Orestov. illus Soviet Mil Rev No.1:23-24 Jan '76

Soviet air defense concepts. LtCol Thomas E.Bearden, Ret. illus Air Def Mag, pp 6-11, Jan-Mar '76

The Soviet juggernaut: Racing faster than ever. Edgar Ulsamer. illus tabs AF Mag 59:56-58+ Mar '76

Sweden

The Swedish Air Force: An official history. illus Aerosp Hist 22:218-230 Dec '75

United States

See also
North American Air Defense Command

ALCM (Air-Launched Cruise Missile). Govt Exec 8:16 Jun '76

Aerospace defense. (Remarks, American Defense Preparedness Assoc, Los Angeles, Oct 15, 1975) Gen Daniel James, Jr. AF Plcy Ltr for Comdrs: Sup No.1:2-10 Jan '76; Condensation. Natl Def 60: 289 Jan-Feb '76

AIR DEFENSES - Continued

United States - Cont'd

Air defense: The Excalibur of the corps and division commanders. Col Russell W.Parker and LtCol Joseph W.House. illus Air Def Mag, pp 29-33, Apr-Jun '76

Army aircraft survivability. Maj N.I.Patla. illus tab USA Avn Dig 22:7+ Nov '76

Divisional air defense--how much is enough? LtCol William O.Staudenmaier. illus map Air Def Mag, pp 34-37, Jul-Sep '76

An eagle in the sky. Bill Walsh. map illus (Also cutaway) Countermeasures 2:30+ Jul '76

The future and Tactical Air Command. (Remarks, American Defense Preparedness Assoc Meeting, Los Angeles, Oct 15, 1975) Gen Robert J.Dixon. AF Plcy Ltr for Comdrs: Sup No.2:10-21 Feb '76; Condensation. Natl Def 60:285 Jan-Feb '76

The future of tactical Air Forces. (Remarks, Graduation Ceremonies, 82d Flying Training Wg, Williams AFB, Ariz, June 12, 1976) LtGen Sanford K.Moats. AF Plcy Ltr for Comdrs: Sup No.8: 17-22 Aug '76

Modernizing the strategic bomber force without really trying: A case against the B-1. Archie L.Wood. Intl Sec 1:98-116 Fall '76

"Our" Air Force and its future. (Remarks, ROA National Convention, Bal Harbour, Fla, June 29-July 2, 1976) Gen Robert J.Dixon. illus Air Reservist 28:4-6 Aug-Sep '76

A place in the sun (for 31st Air Defense Artillery Brigade, Homestead AFB, Fla). SSgt Zack Richards. illus Soldiers 31:36-38 Jun '76

Radar application within the USAF. BrigGen Phillip N.Larsen. illus Signal 31:46-47+ Oct '76

Roland meets the challenge. Robert L.Roderick. illus Natl Def 61:39-42 Jul-Aug '76

Strategic Force modernization. (Remarks, Air Force Assoc luncheon, Washington, Sep 22, 1976) Thomas C.Reed. AF Plcy Ltr for Comdrs: Sup No.11: 2-8 Nov '76

Study and Teaching

The role of air defense. BrigGen Sinclair L.Melner. illus Air Def Mag, pp 24-25, Apr-Jun '76

Vietnam (Democratic Republic)

What really happened in the air defense battle of North Vietnam. LtCol Thomas E.Bearden, Ret. illus tab Air Def Mag, pp 8-15, Apr-Jun '76

Warsaw Pact

Effective use of NATO air resources. WgComdr A.E.G.Woods, Ret. Royal Air Forces Qtr 16: 109-117 Summer '76

AIR DROP see Airdrop

AIR EXPRESS see Air Cargo

AIR FORCE

Air Forces of the world--1976. Tables only. Interavia 31:165-176 Feb '76

AIR FORCE - Continued

Divisions, Wings, Groups, etc

See also specific types of units, e.g.,
Aeromedical Evacuation Units
Airlift Units
Bomber Units
Fighter Units
Missile Units
Refueling Units
Transportation Units

Statistics

Average strength of military formations. London's
International Institute for Strategic Studies. Table
only. AF Mag 59:97 Dec '76

Great Britain

The story of the "Ginger" Mitchell Flight (No.226
Sq, RAF, 1944). Christopher Shores and G.E.T.
Nichols. illus Air Pict 38:237 Jun '76

Strike's silent targets. (Flying with the RAF today,
no.5) Roger Lindsay. illus Air Pict 38:86-89
Mar '76

United States

ABCCC (AirBorne Command and Control Center): A
capsule view of the men and machines of the 7th
Airborne Command & Control Squadron. TSgt Fred
C.McCaslin, Jr. illus Signal 31:26-29 Nov-Dec '76

Diversity our specialty--the 55th Strategic Reconnaissance Wing reports. Capt Sid R.Howard. illus
Combat Crew 27:16-17 Oct '76

Lomcevak (46th Flying Training Sq, Peterson Fld,
Colo). Capt Eugene W.Bricker. illus Interceptor
18:8-12 Feb '76

A place in the sun (for 31st Air Defense Artillery
Brigade, Homestead AFB, Fla). SSgt Zack Richards. illus Soldiers 31:36-38 Jun '76

Reservist to join active unit in (347th Tactical
Fighter Wg) test. AF Times 36:28 Jun 21 '76

United States--History

From bailing wire to the SR-71: 1st Strategic Recon
Sq one of oldest air units. illus AF Times 36:42
May 17 '76

Brunei

Brunei (British North Borneo)--the military scene.
Paul A.Thompson. illus tab Air Pict 38:256-257
Jul '76

China (People's Republic)

Communist China's aerospace forces. Col Angus M.
Fraser, Ret. tab AF Mag 59:74-77 Nov '76

Germany (Federal Republic)

The Luftwaffe 1976. Gen Johannes Steinhoff, Ret. tab
illus chart AF Mag 59:68-74 Sep '76

The Luftwaffe + twenty. (German pilots train at Luke
AFB, Ariz) LtCol Fred A.Meurer. illus Airman
20:2-8 Aug '76

The West German Air Force re-equips for the 1980s.
Rudi Meller. illus tab Interavia pt 1, Combat
strength increases under cost pressures. 31:320-
322+ Apr '76; pt 2, 31:459-461 May '76

AIR FORCE - Continued

Germany (Federal Republic) - Cont'd

History

The Experten and the Flying Tiger: World War II
aces in Arizona. Robert C.Sullivan. illus Aerosp
Hist 23:148-149+ Sep '76

Organization

Command structure of the German Air Force. Chart
only. AF Mag 59:71 Sep '76

Statistics

Today's Luftwaffe at a glance. Table only. AF Mag
59:72 Sep '76

Great Britain

Airfield defense--the British approach. R.Pengelley.
illus Intl Def Rev 8:832-834 Dec '75

Battle flight Gutersloh. (RAF's Mark 2A Lightnings
in Germany) Trevor Tarr. illus tab NATO's Fifteen Nations 21:84-88 Apr-May '76

CINCUKAIR (Commander-IN-Chief United Kingdom
AIR Forces): ACE's new one. illus NATO's Fifteen Nations 20:53-60 Dec '75-Jan '76

Defence cuts continue. (Points from Britain's 1976
Defence White Paper) illus tabs Air Pict 38:174-
177 May '76

Flight engineer on a Short Belfast. (Flying with the
RAF today, no.6) Philip J.Birtles. illus Air Pict
38:144-149 Apr '76

Flying Dutchman (Commodore J.E. van der Kop) in
the Royal Air Force: Surabaya--2d TAF (Tactical
Air Force). Humphrey Wynn. illus Royal Air
Forces Qtr 16:51-56 Spring '76

Ground attack in a Jaguar. (Flying with the RAF today, no.9) Dagmar Heller. illus Air Pict 38:397-
400 Oct '76

More efficient use of the RAF Phantom force. (Sir
Robert Brooke-Popham Prize Essay) SqLdr R.D.
Arnott. illus Hawk No.37:23-28 Jul '76

'Offshore tapestry'--co-ordination and control.
FltLt J.A.Cowan. Royal Air Forces Qtr 16:41-44
Spring '76

The Royal Air Force, 1976. John W.R.Taylor. illus
AF Mag 59:50-59 Feb '76

SAC wins Blue Steel Trophy in Giant Strike VI (Royal
Air Force Strike Command's Bombing and Navigation Competition). LtCol Richard W.Blatter. illus
tab Combat Crew 27:8-10 Jun '76

SACEUR's subcommanders take the floor: United
Kingdom Air Forces. ACM Denis Smallwood.
illus NATO's Fifteen Nations 21:96-103 Feb-
Mar '76

Strike's silent targets. (Flying with the RAF today,
no.5) Roger Lindsay. illus Air Pict 38:86-89
Mar '76

Word processing in the RAF. SqLdr D.J.Silk. Royal
Air Forces Qtr 16:259-263 Autumn '76

History

Air operations and the Dieppe raid. John P.Campbell.
illus maps Aerosp Hist 23:10-20 Mar '76

The RAF and counter-force strategy before World
War II. Malcolm Smith. RUSI J for Def Studies
121:68-73 Jun '76

AIR FORCE - Continued

Great Britain - Cont'd

History - Cont'd

The RAF and the Warsaw uprising. Richard C. Lukas. illus Aerosp Hist 22:188-194 Dec '75

Royal Air Force--Day 1: Activities on the Western Front, 1st April 1918. Norman L.R. Franks. illus tabs Air Pict 38:474-479 Dec '76

The Royal Air Force: Its origin and history, 1918-1970. Humphrey Wynn. illus Aerosp Hist 23:154-167 Sep '76

The Royal Air Force, 1976. John W.R. Taylor. illus AF Mag 59:50-59 Feb '76

Iran

F-16: Fighter procurement essential to Iranian Air Force modernization. Robert Ellsworth. illus (Also cutaway) Comdrs Dig 19: entire issue Oct 21 '76

Israel

Air war: Middle East--a report from the International Symposium on the Military Aspects of the Arab-Israeli Conflict, Jerusalem, 12-17 October 1975. Jeffrey Greenhut. illus Aerosp Hist 23:21-23 Mar '76

The Israeli Air Force. Zeev Schiff. illus map AF Mag 59:31-38 Aug '76

Italy

History

Bell Aircobra in the Italian service. Tullio Marcon. illus Am Avn Hist Soc J 21:200-201 Fall '76

NATO

Battle flight Gutersloh. (RAF's Mark 2A Lightnings in Germany) Trevor Tarr. illus tab NATO's Fifteen Nations 21:84-88 Apr-May '76

SACEUR's subcommanders take the floor: United Kingdom Air Forces. ACM Denis Smallwood. illus NATO's Fifteen Nations 21:96-103 Feb-Mar '76

Poland

History

The operational doctrine of the Polish Air Force in World War II: A thirty-year perspective. Michael A. Peszke. illus chart Aerosp Hist 23:140-147 Sep '76

Rhodesia

History

An outline history of the Rhodesian Air Force. illus Aerosp Hist 23:36-42 Mar '76

Russia

The growing threat: New challenges for the EW community. Ronald T. Pretty. illus Elect Warfare 8: 43+ Mar-Apr '76

The Northern Theater: Soviet capabilities and concepts. John Erickson. map Strat Rev 4:67-82 Summer '76

Soviet aerospace forces: Continuity and contrast. Col William F. Scott, Ret. illus charts AF Mag 59:38-47 Mar '76

AIR FORCE - Continued

Russia - Cont'd

History

Soviet aerospace forces: Continuity and contrast. Col William F. Scott, Ret. illus charts AF Mag 59:38-47 Mar '76

Sweden

History

Flygvapnet is fifty: The Swedish Air Force in its jubilee year surveyed. Paul A. Thompson. illus map tab Air Pict 38:298-306 Aug '76

The Swedish Air Force: An official history. illus Aerosp Hist 22:218-230 Dec '75

United States

(AF) ability to fight given careful scrutiny (by AF Readiness Initiative Group (AFRIG)). AF Times 36:3 Apr 26 '76

(AF) Secretary (John L.) McLucas's farewell message. AF Mag 59:21 Jan '76

An Air Force almanac: The United States Air Force in facts and figures. tabs AF Mag 59:132-143 May '76

The Air Force and national security: 1976 and beyond. (Remarks, Air Force Assoc, Mobile Chapter, Mobile, Ala, March 27, 1976) LtGen John W. Pauly. AF Plcy Ltr for Comdrs: Sup No. 6:10-18 Jun '76

Air Force Chief of Staff's FY 1977 Posture Statement. (Statement before House Committee on Armed Services, Washington, Jan 29, 1976) Gen David C. Jones. AF Plcy Ltr for Comdrs: Sup No. 3:23-40 Mar '76

The Air Force since 1952. (Remarks, University of Maryland Air Force ROTC Commissioning Ceremony, College Park, May 15, 1976) MajGen Charles C. Blanton. AF Plcy Ltr for Comdrs: Sup No. 9:25-29 Sep '76

BrigGen Marks retires; served as Ass't Sec'y, Air Force (Financial Management). AF Compt 10:7 Oct '76

Collateral mission support (agreement between U.S. Navy and Air Force): An economic and operational necessity. LCDR Brent Baker. illus US Nav Inst Proc 102:93-95 Feb '76

The cutting edge: Combat capability. Gen David C. Jones. illus tab AF Mag 59:48-50+ May '76

Ex-USAF officer back as Secretary. (Thomas C. Reed confirmed to replace John L. McLucas as Secretary of the Air Force) Officer 52:22 Feb '76

Flexibility--a state of mind. Gen Richard H. Ellis and LtCol Frank B. Horton III. illus Strat Rev 4: 26-36 Winter '76

The future of tactical Air Forces. (Remarks, Graduation Ceremonies, 82d Flying Training Wg, Williams AFB, Ariz, June 12, 1976) LtGen Sanford K. Moats. AF Plcy Ltr for Comdrs: Sup No. 8: 17-22 Aug '76

International law and the Air Force. (Address, Society of International Law, New York, Oct 29, 1975) John L. McLucas. AF Law Rev 18:76-80 Summer '76

Lead on, Mr Secretary! (SecAF Thomas C. Reed discusses his job and the Air Force as a whole) Interview. illus Airman 20:2-7 Jun '76

18

United States - Cont'd

Manpower aide named. (Juanita Ashcraft to be Asst SecDef AF for Manpower and Reserve Affairs) illus AF Times 37:8 Aug 2 '76

New Air Force Secretary: Thomas C. Reed is well qualified to meet the current problems. illus Natl Def 60:428-429 May-Jun '76

New leadership for a new Air Force. Col Harold P. Knutty. illus AU Rev 27:78-84 Jan-Feb '76

"Our" Air Force and its future. (Remarks, ROA National Convention, Bal Harbour, Fla, June 29-July 2, 1976) Gen Robert J. Dixon. illus Air Reservist 28:4-6 Aug-Sep '76

Ours is an honorable profession. Gen Russell E. Dougherty. (Reprinted from Combat Crew, May 1975) illus Combat Crew 27:8-11 Mar '76

People come first, says (SecAF) Reed on tour. AF Times 36:10 Feb 9 '76

The promised land. Thomas C. Reed. illus tab AF Mag 59:45-47 May '76

Readiness. (Remarks, Jolly Green Pilots Assoc reunion, Eglin AFB, Fla, April 24, 1976) MajGen Billy J. Ellis. AF Plcy Ltr for Comdrs: Sup No.7: 2-6 Jul '76

SAF/FM organization. (SecAF/Financial Management) illus chart AF Compt 10:29 Jan '76

SAF/FM organization. (SecAF/Financial Management) Chart only. AF Compt 10:10 Apr '76

SAF/FM organization. (SecAF/Financial Management) Chart only. AF Compt 10:7 Oct '76

(SecAF Thomas C.) Reed calls for 'people' aid. Lee Ewing. AF Times 36:3 Feb 9 '76

(SecAF Thomas C. Reed lists 5 conclusions about the Air Force in recent news conference at the Pentagon) illus Air Reservist 28:13 May '76; AF Compt 10:24-25 Jul '76

(SecAF Thomas C.) Reed slaps at congressional critic (of B-1). (From address, Air Force Assoc National Convention, Washington, Sep 19-22, 1976) illus AF Times 37:21 Oct 4 '76

Secretary of the Air Force's Air Force authorization request. (Statement before House Committee on Armed Services, Washington, Jan 29, 1976) Thomas C. Reed. tabs AF Plcy Ltr for Comdrs: Sup No.3:2-23 Mar '76

Setting reasonable rules. Interview. Gen David C. Jones. illus AF Times 36:4 May 3 '76

Thomas C. Reed, USAF's new Secretary. Claude Witze. illus AF Mag 59:32-34 Feb '76

The thread of doctrine. LtGen John W. Pauly. illus AU Rev 27:2-10 May-Jun '76

USAF EW program matrix. Table only. Elect Warfare 7:41 May-Jun '75

USAF in the forefront of the C^3 revolution. Thomas C. Reed. illus AF Mag 59:62-65 Jul '76

USAF's new Soviet awareness program. Edgar Ulsamer. AF Mag 59:38-42 May '76

The U.S. Air Force--systems of the future. (Excerpts from talks, Luncheon and Seminar Sessions, 57th Defense Preparedness Meeting, American Defense Preparedness Assoc, Los Angeles, Oct 15, 1975) illus Natl Def 60:283-290 Jan-Feb '76

United States - Cont'd

History

The Air Corps' 1926 Pan American flight. LtGen Ira C. Eaker, Ret. illus map AF Mag 59:114+ Sep '76

The Air Force since 1952. (Remarks, University of Maryland Air Force ROTC Commissioning Ceremony, College Park, May 15, 1976) MajGen Charles C. Blanton. AF Plcy Ltr for Comdrs: Sup No. 9:25-29 Sep '76

The Air Force story. MSgt Dave Sylva. illus Aerosp Safety 32:4-9 Jul '76

The great flying game. (Flying training at Scott Field, Ill, 1917-18) Isobel Bryant. illus MAC Flyer 23:18-20 Jul '76

The Logistics Command job. (Remarks, Iron Gate Chapter, Air Force Assoc, New York, Sep 29, 1976) Gen F. Michael Rogers. AF Plcy Ltr for Comdrs: Sup No. 12:2-8 Dec '76

The ordeal of Lieutenants (Harold G.) Peterson and (Paul H.) Davis (Army Air Service Border Patrol, 1919). Stacy Hinkle. illus Am Avn Hist Soc J 21:219-224 Fall '76

Sources in aerospace history: The USAF oral history collection (at Albert F. Simpson Historical Research Center, Maxwell AFB, Ala). James C. Hasdorff. illus Aerosp Hist 23:103-104 Jun '76

Those days of the leather helmet. MSgt Dave Sylva. illus Aerosp Safety 32:14-17 May '76

Unit history ("corporate memory"). TIG Brief 28:8 Aug 13 '76

Organization

(Photocharts of structure of the Office of the Secretary of the Air Force, the USAF Air Staff, the Deputy Chiefs of Staff, the major commands, and the separate operating agencies as of Aug 25, 1976) AF Mag 59:60-67 Sep '76

26 wings (AF) goal: 1700 planes needed. Len Famiglietti. AF Times 36:19 May 3 '76

Statistics

An Air Force almanac: The United States Air Force in facts and figures. tabs AF Mag 59:132-143 May '76

The cutting edge: Combat capability. Gen David C. Jones. illus tab AF Mag 59:48-50+ May '76

USAF force modernization sees 125 new planes FY 77. tabs Armed Forces J Intl 113:10 Apr '76

(USAF) strength in Europe to increase with F-15, F-111 moves. Len Famiglietti. AF Times 37:2 Nov 8 '76

AIR FORCE, 8th

Strategic Air Command. illus charts AF Mag 59:74-76 May '76

AIR FORCE, 9th

Tactical Air Command. illus charts AF Mag 59:77-79 May '76

AIR FORCE, 12th

Tactical Air Command. illus charts AF Mag 59:77-79 May '76

AIR FORCE, 13th

History

13th at Clark (AB, RP) marks 33 years. AF Times 36:27 Jan 26 '76

The United States Air Force in West New Guinea 1962-1963--help for the United Nations. LtCol Nick P. Apple. illus Aerosp Hist 22:212-217 Dec '75

AIR FORCE, 14th see Aerospace Force, 14th

AIR FORCE, 15th

Strategic Air Command. illus charts AF Mag 59:74-76 May '76

AIR FORCE, 21st

Military Airlift Command. tab illus charts AF Mag 59:69-71 May '76

AIR FORCE, 22d

Military Airlift Command. tab illus charts AF Mag 59:69-71 May '76

AIR FORCE ACADEMY

The (AF) Academy honor system. Gen T.R. Milton, Ret. AF Mag 59:86 Jul '76

Air Force Academy. illus AF Mag 59:107-108 May '76

(Air Force) Academy Athletic Association: Investment losses held high. Andy Plattner. AF Times 36:29 May 17 '76

Air Force Academy solar energy program. Maj M.W. Nay, Jr and Lt W.A. Tolbert. illus tab AF Engrg & Svcs Qtr 17:23-27 Feb '76

(Cadet 1C Luckey M.) Dunn tops '76 (AF Academy) class (and others win awards). illus AF Times 36:26 Jun 21 '76

Enlisted women have route to (Air Force) Academy (Preparatory School). Contact, p 6, Winter '76

Favor curried on Hill for athletes: (AF Academy Athletic) Assocation spent thousands recruiting for Academy. Andy Plattner. AF Times 36:33 May 24 '76

First 10 women enroll at (AF) Academy Prep School. illus AF Times 36:11 Jan 26 '76

Four officers' daughters nominated for (AF) Academy. AF Times 36:8 Feb 23 '76

The Honor Code. (Statement, Subcommittee on Manpower and Personnel, Committee on Armed Services, U.S. Senate, June 22, 1976) LtGen James R. Allen. AF Plcy Ltr for Comdrs: Sup No. 10: 27-31 Oct '76

The new cadets. (Women enter the USAF Academy as part of the class of 1980) Capt John B. Taylor. illus Airman 20:2-9 Dec '76

Probe of 'theft ring' still on at (AF) Academy. AF Times 37:12 Sep 20 '76

Rocky Mountain high. (Soaring program at U.S. AF Academy) Capt John B. Taylor. illus Airman 20: 2-6 May '76

Solar home saves on gas (in test at (AF) Academy). AF Times 37:37 Aug 9 '76

Staff women fill model role at the (AF) Academy. illus AF Times 36:41 Jul 12 '76

AIR FORCE ACADEMY - Continued

The USAF Academy B-6700 management decision. LtCol Jerry B. Smith. illus tabs AF Compt 10:44-47 Jul '76

USAFA prepares for first women cadets. James R. Patterson. illus AF Mag 59:50-54 Apr '76

USAFA (U.S. Air Force Academy)'s liaison officers. illus AF Mag 59:62-63 Jan '76

AIR FORCE ACCOUNTING AND FINANCE CENTER

Air Force Accounting and Finance Center. illus AF Mag 59:92 May '76

Audit finds many paid wrong rent. AF Times 36:2 Jun 28 '76

Directorate of Accounting & Finance. MajGen L. Theus. illus chart AF Compt 10:20-21 Jan '76

Directorate of Accounting & Finance. MajGen Lucius Theus. illus chart AF Compt 10:16-17 Apr '76

Directorate of Accounting & Finance. MajGen Lucius Theus. illus chart AF Compt 10:16-17 Oct '76

EFTS (Electronic Funds Transfer System)--alive and well at the USAF Accounting & Finance Center. Thomas D. Kronoveter. illus Armed Forces Compt 21:6-7 Apr '76

Monument to people oriented construction (Air Force Accounting and Finance Center, Lowry AFB, Colo). Maj Peter LoPresti and William L. Kollman. illus AF Engrg & Svcs Qtr 17:7-10 Nov '76

Notes from the Director of Accounting & Finance. MajGen Lucius Theus. illus AF Compt 10:16-17 Jul '76

AIR FORCE ASSOCIATION

(AFA Convention, Washington, Sep 19-21, 1976: 30th anniversary highlights) illus Air Reservist 28: 16-17 Nov '76

AFA's committees, councils, and advisers. illus AF Mag 59:76-77 Feb '76

AFA's Statement of Policy for 1976-77 (and 2 policy papers adopted at the 30th National Convention, Washington, Sep 20, 1976). AF Mag 59:26-33 Nov '76

AFA's thirtieth anniversary. James H. Straubel. AF Mag 59:13-15 Feb '76

AFA's Thirtieth Anniversary Convention (Washington, Sep 19-23, 1976). Don Steele. illus AF Mag 59:56-63 Nov '76

AFA's 30th Anniversary Convention (Washington, Sep 19-23, 1976): A window on USAF's new challenges. Edgar Ulsamer. illus AF Mag 59:22-25 Nov '76

Awards at the 1976 Air Force Association National Convention (Washington, Sep 19-23, 1976). illus AF Mag 59:42-43 Nov '76

Block unionizing, AFA demands. AF Times 36:10 Jun 14 '76

A blueprint for safeguarding the strategic balance.. (2d report on AFA's Symposium on "Tomorrow's Strategic Options," Vandenberg AFB, Calif, April 28-29, 1976) Edgar Ulsamer. illus tabs AF Mag 59:68-74 Aug '76

(Military) 'Bill of Rights' backed to protect benefits; (Gen David C.) Jones warns on Soviets (at Air Force Assoc National Convention, Washington, Sep 19-22, 1976). Lee Ewing. illus AF Times 37:21 Oct 4 '76

AIR FORCE ASSOCIATION - Continued

1976 Aerospace Development Briefings and Displays. illus AF Mag 59:44-46 Nov '76

Outstanding Airmen for 1976. illus AF Times 37:19+ Sep 27 '76

Outstanding Airmen (of 1976). illus Airman 20:11-14 Dec '76

SALT II's gray-area weapon systems. (Report on AFA's Symposium on "Tomorrow's Strategic Options," Vandenberg AFB, Calif, April 28-29, 1976 Edgar Ulsamer. illus AF Mag 59:80-82+ Jul '76

2 captains (Donald R. Blacklund and Roland W. Purser) top AFA awards list. AF Times 37:8 Sep 20 '76

USAF's finest. (12 Outstanding Airmen for 1976) Maj Terry A. Arnold. illus AF Mag 59:47-49 Nov '76

Unionization of the military: AFA position paper. AF Mag 59:88-89 Jul '76

AIR FORCE AUDIT AGENCY

Air Force Audit Agency. illus AF Mag 59:92-93 May '76

Auditing tomorrow's Air Force today. Capt Allen J. Spinka. illus AF Compt 10:8-9 Oct '76

Auditor General. BrigGen T. G. Bee. chart illus AF Compt 10:28-29 Jan '76

Auditor General. BrigGen Thomas G. Bee. illus chart AF Compt 10:18-19 Apr '76

Auditor General. BrigGen Joseph B. Dodds. illus chart AF Compt 10:18-19 Oct '76

Notes from the Auditor General. BrigGen Joseph B. Dodds. illus AF Compt 10:18-19 Jul '76

AIR FORCE AVIONICS LABORATORY

Scope detects space objects by sun glints. illus AF Times 36:38 May 17 '76

AIR FORCE COMMUNICATIONS SERVICE

AFCS and AF resource management. BrigGen Rupert H. Burris. illus AF Compt 10: back cover Jan '76

AFCS creates mobile PME. AF Times 37:29 Nov 22 '76

Air Force C-E: A brief history. Louis B. Jones. illus Signal 30:14-16+ Jul '76

Air Force Communications Service. illus chart AF Mag 59:56-57 May '76

Comptroller activities at major commands: Air Force Communications Service. Col R. G. Maynard. illus AF Compt 10:12-14 Jan '76

Impact of AFCS move (from Richards-Gebaur AFB, Mo, to Scott AFB, Ill). Ron Sanders. AF Times 36:21 Jul 19 '76

AIR FORCE DATA AUTOMATION AGENCY

Air Force Data Automation Agency. illus AF Mag 59: 93-94 May '76

AIR FORCE INSPECTION AND SAFETY CENTER

Air Force Inspection and Safety Center. illus AF Mag 59:95-96 May '76

AIR FORCE INSTITUTE OF TECHNOLOGY

See also
Minuteman Education Program

538 officers picked for AFIT programs. AF Times 36:8 Mar 22 '76

I think that next I'd like to go to AFIT. Maj Barry W. Bullard. illus AF Engrg & Svcs Qtr 17:16-17+ Aug '76

New colonels offered procurement training. AF Times 37:6 Oct 25 '76

99 degrees awarded at AFIT School (of Systems and Logistics). AF Times 36:18 Jul 19 '76

AIR FORCE INTELLIGENCE SERVICE

Air Force Intelligence Service. illus AF Mag 59:94-95 May '76

AIR FORCE LOGISTICS COMMAND

See also
Advanced Logistics Systems Center

AFLC: A delicate balance. Gen Felix M. Rogers. illus Review 55:39+ Jan-Feb '76

AFLC: Lifeline of the electronic warfare team. LtCol William F. Eaton. illus Elect Warfare 7:30-31+ May-Jun '75

AFLC steps up USAF's combat readiness. Edgar Ulsamer. illus AF Mag 59:63-67 Jun '76

Air Force Logistics Command. illus chart AF Mag 59:58-59 May '76

The Logistics Command job. (Remarks, Iron Gate Chapter, Air Force Assoc, New York, Sep 29, 1976) Gen F. Michael Rogers. AF Pley Ltr for Comdrs: Sup No. 12:2-8 Dec '76

Logistics Command keeps AF flying: An industrial operation. illus AF Times 36:32 Feb 23 '76

A new horizon for Integrated Logistics Support (ILS). TIG Brief 28:18 Sep 10 '76

Waste removal shared (by Defense Property Disposal Service and Air Force Logistics Command). AF Times 36:42 Jan 5 '76

We service what we sell. (USAF Logistics Command gives assistance and advice to foreign purchasers of U.S.-made military aircraft) Capt John B. Taylor. illus Airman 20:10-12 May '76

Statistics

AFLC steps up USAF's combat readiness. Edgar Ulsamer. illus AF Mag 59:63-67 Jun '76

AIR FORCE MILITARY PERSONNEL CENTER

Air Force Military Personnel Center. illus AF Mag 59:97-98 May '76

Human side of assignment making: Computers just a tool. MSgt Freddie K. Harrison. illus AF Times 36:20+ Jan 12 '76

MPC withdraws control of SEIs (Special Experience Identifiers) from commands. AF Times 37:8 Dec 6 '76

AIR FORCE OFFICE OF SPECIAL INVESTIGATIONS
see Office of Special Investigations

AIR FORCE SATELLITE COMMUNICATIONS SYSTEM

AFSC's Electronic Systems Division (ESD). illus AF Mag 59:51-57 Jul '76

USAF in the forefront of the C^3 revolution. Thomas C. Reed. illus AF Mag 59:62-65 Jul '76

AIR FORCE SECURITY SERVICE

Comptroller activities at major commands: Air Force Security Service. Col David H. Brockett. illus AF Compt 10:26-29 Apr '76

The EW Center and the Air Force. BrigGen Kenneth D. Burns. TIG Brief 28:2 Nov 5 '76

USAF Security Service. illus AF Mag 59:82 May '76

AIR FORCE SERGEANTS ASSOCIATION

(Air Force) Sergeants (Assoc) opposes two state taxes. AF Times 37:21 Sep 20 '76

New AFSA president (MSgt John P. May of Gunter AFS, Ala) youngest chief yet. AF Times 37:10 Aug 30 '76

(Pres-elect Jimmy) Carter still studying draft pardon ... groups against it. AF Times 37:14 Dec 20 '76

AIR FORCE SPACE AND MISSILE TEST CENTER see Space and Missile Test Center

AIR FORCE SPECIALTY CODE see Personnel Classification--Air Force--U.S.

AIR FORCE SYSTEMS COMMAND

See also agencies by name, e.g.,
Aeronautical Systems Division
Electronic Systems Division
Foreign Technology Division
Space and Missile Systems Command
Space and Missile Test Center

AFSC's cost accounting system. Gary W. Amlin. tab illus AF Compt 10:8-9 Jan '76

Affordability + performance: USAF's R&D goal. Edgar Ulsamer. illus AF Mag 59:31-36 Mar '76

Air Force Systems Command. illus chart AF Mag 59: 60-61 May '76

Auditing tomorrow's Air Force today. Capt Allen J. Spinka. illus AF Compt 10:8-9 Oct '76

Meet BrigGen Hans H. Driessnack, DCS/Comptroller, Hq Air Force Systems Command. illus AF Compt 10:11 Apr '76

USAF's crusade to streamline industrial production. Edgar Ulsamer. illus AF Mag 59:62-67 Oct '76

AIR FORCE TEST AND EVALUATION CENTER

Air Force Test and Evaluation Center. illus AF Mag 59:96-97 May '76

AIR FORCE WEAPONS LABORATORY

Propellent recovery nets $145,000 savings. AF Times 36:32 Feb 2 '76

The Trading Post (Kans) event. (AF Weapons Laboratory studies the effect of simulated nuclear explosions on different types of soil) MSgt Harold Newcomb. illus Airman 20:14-17 Mar '76

AIR FORCES IN EUROPE

Prime BEEF in Europe. Maj Charles F. Kreis. illus AF Engrg & Svcs Qtr 17:28-30 May '76

AIR FORCES IN EUROPE - Continued

United States Air Forces in Europe. illus tab chart AF Mag 59:80-81 May '76

United States Air Forces in Europe and the beginning of the Cold War. Walton S. Moody. illus tab Aerosp Hist 23:75-85 Jun '76

AIR FREIGHT see Air Cargo

AIR-GROUND TRAINING

New training center. (Marine Corps Air-Ground Combat Training Center, 29 Palms, Calif) MarCor Gaz 60:4 Jan '76

The role of air defense. BrigGen Sinclair L. Melner. illus Air Def Mag, pp 24-25, Apr-Jun '76

AIR-LAND FORCES APPLICATION

Air-Land Forces Application (ALFA). Air Def Mag, p 37, Apr-Jun '76

AIR LAW

General Flight Rules (AFR 60-16). TIG Brief 28: 13-14 Dec 3 '76

International law and the Air Force. (Address, Society of International Law, New York, Oct 29, 1975) John L. McLucas. AF Law Rev 18:76-80 Summer '76

AIR LOGISTICS CENTERS

The San Antonio Air Logistics Center financial management. Col Ralph Law. illus AF Compt 10:32-33 Oct '76

AIR MAIL SERVICE see Postal Service

AIR MOBILITY

See also
Air Assault Concept
Air Cavalry
Close Air Support

ATCA (Advanced Tanker Cargo Aircraft)--key to global mobility. Edgar Ulsamer. illus (Also cutaway) map AF Mag 59:20-25 Apr '76

101st (Airborne Division (Air Assault)) in Reforger 76. Col Larry J. Baughman and Maj Robert E. Jones, Jr. illus maps USA Avn Dig 22:2-3+ Dec '76

The airborne division and a strategic concept. Col Fletcher K. Ware. illus tabs Mil Rev 56:23-33 Mar '76

Airlift problems pose threat to our security. Editorial. Officer 52:6+ Jan '76

Airmobility for air defense. Capt Bob Messmore. illus Air Def Mag, pp 28-31, Jul-Sep '76

The British Army and the battlefield aerial vehicle: The way ahead. Col S. M. W. Hickey. illus RUSI J for Def Studies 121:53-62 Jun '76

Helicopters and land force tactics. Col M. Belov. illus Soviet Mil Rev No. 12:22-24 Dec '76

AIR NATIONAL GUARD see National Guard--Air Force

AIR NAVIGATION see Navigation, Air

AIR POLICE see Military Police

AIR POLLUTION see Pollution

AIR POWER see Aerospace Power

AIR RACES see Airplanes--Races

AIR RESERVE PERSONNEL CENTER

    Administrative transfer orders. TIG Brief 28:16
Oct 22 '76

    Air Reserve Personnel Center. illus AF Mag 59:104
May '76

    NCO job review starting (for) 5000 senior Reserves.
AF Times 37:3 Aug 2 '76

AIR ROUTES see Airways

AIR-SEA RESCUE see Search and Rescue

AIR SHOWS see Aviation--Exhibitions

AIR-SPEED

    Low altitude wind shear. illus Aerosp Safety 32:10-13
Sep '76

    Low-level wind shear. Maj Shirley M.Carpenter.
illus TAC Attack pt 1, 16:4-8 Sep '76; pt 2, Wind
shear on final approach. 16:18-22 Oct '76; pt 3,
Detecting and coping with wind shear. 16:8-13
Nov '76

    Objects in motion: A look at the mechanics of wind
shear. illus MAC Flyer 23:12-15 Sep '76

    On speed: 245-265 KIAS (Knots Indicated Air Speed).
Capt Dwayne Hicks. illus Combat Crew 27:12-13
Mar '76

    Wind shear: The mystery of the vanishing airspeed.
Capt Barry Schiff. (Reprinted from AOPA Pilot,
Nov 1975) illus Combat Crew 26:12-15 Feb '76;
Interceptor 18:8-13 Jun '76

AIR STAFF

    The Air Staff--a view from the top. Interview. Gen
William V.McBride. illus AF Mag 59:26-29
Apr '76

    (Air) Staff TRAining plan (ASTRA) open. AF Times
37:33 Sep 27 '76

    Bending the Chief's ear. (AF Personnel Management
Teams (PMT Air Staff teams) discuss the AF life
with members, and then work with the Chief of
Staff to solve problems) MSgt Fred Harrison.
illus Airman 20:36-37 Jan '76

    How does the (AF) Chief (of Staff) keep on target?
Management by objectives. Lee Ewing. AF Times
36:10 Jan 26 '76

AIR STRATEGY see Strategy, Air

AIR SURVEILLANCE see Surveillance

AIR TACTICS see Tactics, Air

AIR TAXI SERVICE see Airlines, Local Service;
Helicopters, Local Service

AIR TRAFFIC CONTROL

    See also
    Ground-Controlled Approach

    ATC systems for tomorrow. Dale Milford. illus
Aerosp Intl 12:26-28+ Mar-Apr '76

    Air commerce: Stimulated or damned. A.Scott Cross-
field. illus tabs Govt Exec 8:31-32+ Dec '76

    Air traffic control automation (in Italy, Sweden,
Netherlands). Dan Boyle. illus Interavia 31:155-
159 Feb '76

AIR TRAFFIC CONTROL - Continued

    Air traffic management and tactical instruments.
Capt Lewis D.Ray. illus USA Avn Dig 22:22-23+
Mar '76

    (Airborne collision avoidance system announced) Sig-
nal 30:75 Feb '76

    The art of listening. illus MAC Flyer 23:3-5 Oct '76

    C-E/ATC (Communications-Electronics/Air Traffic
Control) service from a user's point of view. TIG
Brief 28:8 Aug 13 '76

    Energy savings: The FAA. (Automation of environ-
mental control in 20 Air Route Traffic Control
Centers) illus Govt Exec 8:15+ Mar '76

    FAA acts to cut down on near misses in air. AF
Times 36:10 Jan 5 '76

    Flight over Africa. (MAC survey team reports on
African airfields) LtCol John W.Ray. MAC Flyer
23:6-7 Feb '76

    Flight violation! LT Dave McPherson. illus Approach
22:12-13 Jul '76

    Latest FAA innovations (Radar Beacon Code System,
Conflict Alert System) for safety, convenience.
illus MAC Flyer 23:22-23 Apr '76

    Near miss! Capt Marty Steere. illus TAC Attack 16:
24-25 Jun '76

    New horizons for radar. John L.McLucas. illus Sig-
nal 31:65-67 Oct '76

    No evidence of (military pilot) intercepts (on civilian
planes), says FAA. Ron Sanders. AF Times 36:11
Feb 16 '76

    'Offshore tapestry'--co-ordination and control.
FltLt J.A.Cowan. Royal Air Forces Qtr 16:41-44
Spring '76

    Radar capabilities for the USAF air traffic control
system. Frederick A.Spencer. illus Signal 31:30-
34 Oct '76

    Radar-directed routing and terminal arrival depic-
tion. LT Daniel E.Graham. illus maps Approach
21:1-4 May '76

    Rendezvous at FL 350. illus MAC Flyer 23:16-17
Aug '76

    Roger means everything but negative. Capt Gregory
Ulrich. illus Aerosp Safety 32:5 May '76

    Severe weather avoidance. illus Combat Crew 27:
8-10 Nov '76

    There are no dragons. (Landing at Taipei, Hong
Kong, or Manila) Maj Jack Spey. illus Aerosp
Safety 32:14-15 Oct '76

    What do you hear? Capt Jerry E.Walker. Aerosp
Safety 32:5 Aug '76

Equipment

    The U.S. air traffic control and navigation equipment
market--continuing growth foreseen. tabs Interavia 31:462-463 May '76

Study and Teaching

    Clearing the air. (Air Traffic Control School, Fort
Rucker, Ala) Janet Hake. illus Soldiers 31:6-9
Aug '76

    Fort Rucker (Ala) ATC school trains Fort Campbell
(Ky) controllers. Sgt1C Keith A.Ellefson and John
C.Smith. illus USA Avn Dig 22: back cover Sep '76

AIR TRAFFIC CONTROL - Continued

Study and Teaching - Cont'd

Volk-Alpena connection. (Air Traffic Control (ATC) training programs at ANG bases in Michigan and Wisconsin) Capt D. T. Davis. illus Air Reservist 27:10-11 Feb '76

Terminology

What the captain really means. (Glossary of terms used by pilots and controllers) MAC Flyer 23:5-6 Oct '76

AIR TRAFFIC CONTROLLERS

Air controllers hit on safety (by National Transportation Safety Board). AF Times 36:14 Apr 26 '76

Air Traffic Controller of the Year for 1976 (SSgt Steven A. Lewis). illus USA Avn Dig 22:28+ Sep '76

Big mother can kill you. Capt Marshall Hydorn. illus TAC Attack 16:10-11 Jan '76

Control aircraft or scrape paint? AC2 L. F. Press. illus Approach 21:10-11 Feb '76

The controller and weather. David D. Thomas. illus MAC Flyer 23:18-20 Jan '76

Fly your own jet! LTJG D. A. Abner. illus Approach 21:29 Dec '75

Like the real thing--almost. illus Aerosp Safety 32: 8-9 May '76

Radar keeps watch. (Det 2, 51st Composite Wg (Tactical), Mangilsan, Korea) Sgt Larry Finney. illus AF Times 36:34 Jan 19 '76

Stress in air traffic controllers: Effects of ARTS-III. C. E. Melton and others. illus tabs Aviation, Space & Envmt Med 47:925-930 Sep '76

AIR TRAINING COMMAND

ATC, SAC split gun honors (in Worldwide Security Police Marksmanship matches at Vandenberg AFB, Calif). Ron Sanders. AF Times 37:24 Oct 18 '76

Air Training Command. illus chart AF Mag 59:62-63 May '76

Contract KP--ATC (Air Training Command)'s asset. James L. Skiles. illus AF Engrg & Svcs Qtr 17: 23-24 Aug '76

One love. (Sgt Tom Theobald of Chanute AFB, Jll, is ATC's Instructor of the Year) Milene Wells. illus Airman 20:41-42 Oct '76

Plan and coordinate (with ATC) before you buy off-the-shelf systems. TIG Brief 28:8 Sep 10 '76

Quality control is everybody's business. TIG Brief 28:13 Jun 18 '76

Reimbursement of travel expenses involving ATC TDY-to-school funds. TIG Brief 28:17 Nov 19 '76

Safety awards (presented to Alaskan Air Command and Air Training Command in recognition of the most effective accident prevention programs during 1975). TIG Brief 28:10 Apr 9 '76

AIR UNIVERSITY

See also
Air Command and Staff College
Air Force Institute of Technology
Air War College
Squadron Officer School

AIR UNIVERSITY - Continued

Air University. illus chart AF Mag 59:64-65 May '76

Curricula

Air Force Air University adds new units (USAF Leadership and Management Development Center, located at Maxwell AFB, Ala, and the Air Force Logistics Management Center, located at Gunter AFS, Ala). Review 55:9 Nov-Dec '75

Air University gets two new units (USAF Leadership and Management Development Center, Maxwell AFB, Ala, and Air Force Logistics Management Center, Gunter AFS, Ala). Contact, p 6, Winter '76

New Air University units (USAF Leadership and Management Development Center, Maxwell AFB, Ala, and Air Force Logistics Management Center, Gunter AFS, Ala). AF Pley Ltr for Comdrs: Sup No. 2:26 Feb '76

Notes from the Director of the Professional Military Comptroller Course (at Air University, Maxwell AFB, Ala). Col Hugh S. Austin. illus AF Compt 10: 20-22 Jul '76

PMCC--now or later? LCDR D. T. Waggoner. illus AF Compt 10:40-42 Oct '76

Professional Military Comptroller Course (at Air University, Maxwell AFB, Ala). Col Hugh S. Austin. illus AF Compt 10:20-21 Oct '76

Professional Military Comptroller Course (at Institute for Professional Development, Air University, Maxwell AFB, Ala). Col Hugh S. Austin. illus AF Compt 10:22-23 Apr '76

Professional Military Comptroller Course (at Institute for Professional Development, Air University, Maxwell AFB, Ala). Maj Jackson E. Rendleman. tabs illus AF Compt 10:30-32 Jan '76

AIR WAR COLLEGE

Air War College training 170 CAP officers. AF Times 36:10 Jun 21 '76

AIR WARFARE

Air electronic warfare. RADM Julian S. Lake, Ret and LCDR Richard V. Hartman, Ret. illus US Nav Inst Proc 102:42-49 Oct '76

Is TacAir dead? CAPT Gerald G. O'Rourke, Ret. illus US Nav Inst Proc 102:34-41 Oct '76

The RAF and counter-force strategy before World War II. Malcolm Smith. RUSI J for Def Studies 121:68-73 Jun '76

Weather and war. John F. Fuller. illus Aerosp Hist 23:24-27 Mar '76

Study and Teaching

Dissimilar aircraft engagements. Capt Maurice B. Johnston, Jr. (Reprinted from USAF Fighter Weapons Newsletter, March 1968) illus USAF Ftr Wpns Rev, pp 14-17+, Summer '76

The enemy is a man who (will try to kill you before you see him). Capt Nelson Cobleigh. illus USAF Ftr Wpns Rev, pp 23-30, Fall '76

(F-15) Eagle makes bow (during Red Flag III). AF Times 36:38 Mar 29 '76

Realistic Red Flag (VIII). Capt John V. Alexander. illus AF Times 37:43 Oct 25 '76

Red Flag. illus USAF Ftr Wpns Rev, p 17, Spring '76

AIR WARFARE - Continued

Study and Teaching - Cont'd

Red Flag. MSgt Robert Foster. illus Air Reservist 28:10 Jun '76

Red Flag VI. AF Times 37:30 Aug 23 '76

Red Flag: Getting caught in a washer. T.J.Coats. AF Times 37:35 Nov 22 '76

AIRBORNE EARLY WARNING

ALR-59 passive detection system (for the E-2C). illus Countermeasures 2:23-25 Apr '76

The eyes of the fleet. Thomas A.Guarino and Charle. F.Muller, Jr. illus US Nav Inst Proc 102:117-120 Oct '76

AIRBORNE FORCES

See also
Paratroops

France

The myth and reality of the paratrooper in the Algerian War. John E.Talbott. Armed Forces & Soc 3:69-86 Fall '76

Russia

Soviet airborne forces: Increasingly powerful factor in the equation. Graham H.Turbiville. illus Army 26:18-24+ Apr '76

United States

AFJ's bum dope on LBJ's farewell. Col John G. Jameson, Jr. illus Armed Forces J Intl 113:20-21 Apr '76

Airborne--and then some. (Airborne School, Fort Benning, Ga, has first female instructors) LtCol Floyd A.Frost. illus Soldiers 31:30 Dec '76

101st (Airborne Division (Air Assault)) in Reorger 76. Col Larry J.Baughman and Maj Robert E. Jones, Jr. illus maps USA Avn Dig 22:2-3+ Dec '76

The airborne division and a strategic concept. Col Fletcher K.Ware. illus tabs Mil Rev 56:23-33 Mar '76

The day the President got conned: (Lyndon Johnson) saying goodbye to the wrong troops (at Fort Bragg, NC, Feb 16, 1968). Benjamin F.Schemmer. illus Armed Forces J Intl 113:26-28 Feb '76

Ready & waiting. (82d Airborne Division, Fort Bragg, NC) SSgt John Savard. illus Soldiers 31: 6-10 Nov '76

Return to airborne country. (SecArmy Martin R. Hoffmann visits Fort Bragg, NC) SP4 Jack Frear. illus Soldiers 31:52-53 Jan '76

AIRBORNE OPERATIONS

Communications in a tactical airborne force. Col S.Vasilyev. map Soviet Mil Rev No.4:26-28 Apr '76

NATO views on employment of airborne assault forces. Col M.Belov. (Trans from a Russian publication. Reprinted in part from Translations on USSR Military Affairs, No.1181, Sep 16, 1975) illus USA Avn Dig 22:4-5+ Apr '76

Ready & waiting. (82d Airborne Division, Fort Bragg, NC) SSgt John Savard. illus Soldiers 31: 6-10 Nov '76

AIRBORNE OPERATIONS - Continued

Study and Teaching

Cooperation in an airborne force. Col A.Bykov. illus Soviet Mil Rev No.6:26-27 Jun '76

AIRBORNE WARNING AND CONTROL SYSTEM

AFSC's Electronic Systems Division (ESD). illus AF Mag 59:51-57 Jul '76

AWACS: Can it cut out ground clutter on Capitol Hill? illus tab Govt Exec 8:16-17 Mar '76

Airborne navonics. illus tab Countermeasures 2:43-44+ Feb '76

Airborne warning--it's worth the price. LtCol Lowell Davis. illus (Also cutaway) Natl Def 60:374-377 Mar-Apr '76

An eagle in the sky. Bill Walsh. map illus (Also cutaway) Countermeasures 2:30+ Jul '76

Gallery of Soviet aerospace weapons: Reconnaissance, ECM, and early warning aircraft. illus AF Mag 59:99 Mar '76

New AWACS proposals to NATO. Intl Def Rev 9:709 Oct '76

USAF's new Soviet awareness program. Edgar Ulsamer. AF Mag 59:38-42 May '76

XM-1, Leopard II stakes raised; AWACS hostage? illus Armed Forces J Intl 113:14 Apr '76

AIRBUS see Airplanes, Transport (Jet)

AIRCRAFT see specific kinds of aircraft, e.g,
Airplanes   Helicopters, Military
Airplanes, Military   Missiles
Helicopters   Rockets

AIRCRAFT, EXPERIMENTAL

See also
Air Cushion Vehicles

Russia

Gallery of Soviet aerospace weapons: Experimental aircraft. illus AF Mag 59:102 Mar '76

United States

The Advanced Short/Medium Range project: Will it become a reality? illus maps tabs Interavia 31: 1176-1178 Dec '76

Bell's new YAH-63 (AAH) Advanced Attack Helicopter. illus tab Interavia 31:251-254 Mar '76

Flight Research Center (Edwards AFB, Calif). Mike Howard. illus Spaceflight 18:190-191 May '76

McDonnell Douglas YC-15. (Design profile, no.29) Maurice Allward. illus tab Air Pict 38:484-487 Dec '76

Northrop's YF-17 and F-18 fighters. (Design profile, no.22) Maurice Allward. illus tab Air Pict 38:129-134 Apr '76

History

The Republic XR-12 Rainbow. Lin Hendrix. illus tab Am Avn Hist Soc J 21:282-285 Winter '76

AIRCRAFT, REMOTELY PILOTED see Remotely Piloted Vehicles

AIRCRAFT CARRIERS

Aboard the USS "John F. Kennedy." Brian M. Service. illus tab Air Pict 38:168-173 May '76

The antisubmarine cruiser "Kiev." illus Soviet Mil Rev No. 11:22-23 Nov '76

Attitudes and accidents aboard an aircraft carrier. John B. Levine and others. tabs Aviation, Space & Envmt Med 47:82-85 Jan '76

Backfire problems and the Aegis mix. L. Edgar Prina. illus Sea Power 19:19-21 Sep '76

Black nights and glassy seas. LCDR Bill Roop. illus Approach 22:28-29 Dec '76

The carrier. CAPT Stephen T. DeLaMater, Ret. illus tab US Nav Inst Proc 102:66-74 Oct '76

DLC (Direct Lift Control) is here, finally! LCDR George Webb. tab illus Approach 21:1-3 Jun '76

"Kiev" and her aircraft. illus Air Pict 38:342-343 Sep '76

Kiev and the U.S. carrier controversy. Henry T. Simmons. illus tabs Intl Def Rev 9:741-744 Oct '76

Kiev--latest photos reveal new Russian V/STOL aircraft. illus Intl Def Rev 9:536-538 Aug '76

MOVLAS (Manually Operated Visual Landing Aid System) technique for pilots and LSOs. LCDR Mike Mears. illus Approach 22:26-27 Sep '76

Paddles to pilots, what now? LT Randy Leddy. illus tab Approach 22:18-19 Dec '76

The peanut approach. LT Cameron B. Place. illus Approach 22:8-10 Aug '76

The role of the Kiev in Soviet naval operations. LCDR William R. Hynes. illus Nav War Col Rev 29:38-46 Fall '76

Something new for the LAMPS program. (GSI, Glide Slope Indicator) illus Approach 22:10-11 Nov '76

The Soviet aircraft carrier. Norman Polmar. illus US Nav Inst Proc 102:138-141 Oct '76

V/STOL goes to sea. John S. Phillip. illus tab Aerosp Intl 12:24-26+ Jul-Aug '76

The Viking at home in the fleet. LT John P. Richman. illus Approach 22:12-14 Dec '76

The Vosper Thornycroft Harrier Carrier proposal. illus Intl Def Rev 8:853-854 Dec '75

What's a good carrier aviator? LCDR Michael N. Matton. illus Approach 21:20-21 May '76

Characteristics

The carrier. CAPT Stephen T. DeLaMater, Ret. illus tab US Nav Inst Proc 102:66-74 Oct '76

History

Cinderella carriers. (Conversion of merchant ships into aircraft carriers in WW II) Robert L. Evans, Ret. illus US Nav Inst Proc 102:52-61 Aug '76

The Navy and the Brodie (high-wire landing gear). RADM George van Deurs, Ret. illus US Nav Inst Proc 102:88-90 Oct '76

The old indispensables. (Four "jeep" carriers, the first American escort carriers to be involved in combat in WW II, in the North African campaign) CAPT Fitzhugh L. Palmer, Ret. illus US Nav Inst Proc 102:61-63 Aug '76

AIRCRAFT CARRIERS - Continued

Safety Measures

A-7 emergency brake problems. LT Carl Tankersley. illus Approach 21:15 Jan '76

The air wing duty safety officer. LCDR L. G. Mullin, Jr. illus Approach 22:10-11 Dec '76

CV safety organization--reality or lip service. CDR H. A. Petrich. illus tab Approach 21:1-4 Jan '76

CV safety problems: (USS) America's approach. CDR S. P. Dunlap. illus Approach 21:12-15 May '76

The "in-close" waveoff: An LSO's (Landing Signal Officer) point of view. LCDR George Webb and others. illus Approach 21:6-9 Feb '76

The LSO Phase One School. LCDR Mick Sumnick. illus Approach 22:14 Sep '76

Midnight mass divert. LT John Stevenson. illus Approach 22:2-5 Dec '76

Nugget nightmare. illus Approach 22:18-20 Nov '76

The saga of the Humble Hummer (E-2). LT Cam Place. illus Approach 22:6-8 Dec '76

"Stand by for high winds and heavy seas!" illus Approach 22:18-21 Oct '76

Thirty ways to crunch an A-7 (or any other type of carrier aircraft). LCDR Jim White. illus Approach 22:16-17 Sep '76

AIRCRAFT CONTROLLERS see Air Traffic Controllers

AIRCRAFT INDUSTRY AND TRADE

See also
Aerospace Industry and Trade
Helicopter Industry and Trade
Missile Industry and Trade

Aerospace world. Regular feature in issues of Air Force Magazine

Aircraft manufacturing in the developing nations: A question of policy and politics. illus Interavia 31: 1155-1157 Dec '76

Avionics: General aviation sets the trend. Dan Boyle. illus Interavia 31:884-885 Sep '76

Farnborough (Air Show, Sep 1976): General aviation was there too. illus Interavia 31:1055-1056 Nov '76

Farnborough International '76: A second report. illus Interavia 31:1039-1046 Nov '76

Farnborough report. (Highlights, 30th S. B. A. C. Show, 5th-12th Sep 1976) illus Air Pict 38:390-395 Oct '76

The 5th Japanese Aerospace Show (Iruma AFB, Oct 16-24, 1976). illus Interavia 31:1121-1122 Dec '76

Industrial periscope: A business, technological & scientific news bulletin. Regular feature in some issues of NATO's Fifteen Nations

Industrial roundup. Regular feature in some issues of Interavia

Jane's aerospace review 1975/76. John W. R. Taylor. illus AF Mag 59:22-29 Jan '76

The world of aerospace. Regular feature in issues of Interavia

Economic Aspects

Airline deregulation: Will it make the dominos fall faster? C. W. Borklund. illus tabs Govt Exec 8: 38-40+ Jul '76

AIRCRAFT INDUSTRY AND TRADE - Continued

Economic Aspects - Cont'd

The economics of light aircraft production. Rolf H. Wild. illus tabs Interavia 31:224-226 Mar '76

U.S. general and business aviation strides ahead in difficult economic climate. Marc Grangier. illus tabs Interavia 31:219-223 Mar '76

History

The Handley Page agreement, 1918. John Bagley. illus tabs Am Avn Hist Soc J 21:38-45 Spring '76

International Aspects

The Advanced Short/Medium Range project: Will it become a reality? illus maps tabs Interavia 31: 1176-1178 Dec '76

The Airbus in the West Indies. Arthur Wallis. illus Interavia 31:298 Apr '76

Alpha Jet series (Franco-German) production starts for 1978 deliveries: Sales campaign intensifies. Michael Brown. illus tabs Interavia 31:120-122 Feb '76

Atlantic cooperation or European surrender? Negotiations continue on future transport aircraft projects. Interavia 31:609-610 Jul '76

Boeing's views of the aircraft market and European cooperation. J.Philip Geddes. illus tab Interavia 31:850-851 Sep '76

Britain-Europe-America: Cooperation, but with whom? Derek Wood. illus Interavia 31:800-801 Sep '76

British aerospace: End of a chapter--or the book? tab illus Air Pict 38:345-348+ Sep '76

CFM56 engine still looking for an aircraft. Michael Brown. illus tabs Interavia 31:847-849 Sep '76

The F-16 connection. George W.Deskin. illus tabs Elect Warfare pt 1, The backgrounder. 8:83-85+ Jul-Aug '76; pt 2, Marconi-Elliott HUDsight chosen for F-16. 8:101+ Sep-Oct '76

The Handley Page agreement, 1918. John Bagley. illus tabs Am Avn Hist Soc J 21:38-45 Spring '76

Jaguar Juggernaut: Flying Europe's new strike fighter. Gregory Copley. illus Def & For Aff Dig No. 11:7-9 '76

Lynx joins up. illus Air Pict 38:430 Nov '76

MRCA development tempo quickens. Douglas H. Chopping. illus tabs Intl Def Rev 8:828-831 Dec '75

MRCA (Multi-Role Combat Aircraft): Meeting its targets. John S.Phillip. illus Aerosp Intl 12:6-7+ Mar-Apr '76

Poor European productivity plagues U.S. purchases. F.Clifton Berry, Jr. tabs Armed Forces J Intl 113:32-33 Mar '76

Postwar use of Handley Page in U.S. John Underwood. illus Am Avn Hist Soc J 21:46-49 Spring '76

Ten-ton (jet engine) competition. Mark E.Berent. tab illus Aerosp Intl 12:36+ Jul-Aug '76

Tornado programme slowed by engine delays. illus Interavia 31:1062 Nov '76

Transall C-160. (Design profile, no.26) Maurice Allward. illus tabs Air Pict 38:316-319 Aug '76

AIRCRAFT INDUSTRY AND TRADE - Continued

International Aspects - Cont'd

The West German aerospace industry: State control or free enterprise? illus tabs Interavia 31:315-319 Apr '76

Where is the German (Hanover) Air Show going? illus tab Interavia 31:505-510 Jun '76

Statistics

The uncertain market for commercial aircraft to 1990: A McDonnell Douglas survey. J.Philip Geddes. illus tabs Interavia 31:350-354 Apr '76

Australia

The Australian aircraft industry--can the decline be halted? Henry Krug. illus Interavia 31:729-730 Aug '76

Introducing the N24 Nomad. illus Interavia 31:378 Apr '76

Brazil

Embraer Bandeirante. (Design profile, no.24) Maurice Allward. illus tab Air Pict 38:218-222 Jun '76

Canada

The Canadian aerospace industry--towards a promising future? John F.Brindley. illus tabs Interavia 31:1127-1134 Dec '76

The Lockheed JetStar II and the Canadair LearStar 600--aiming for the long-range market. Marc Grangier. illus tab Interavia 31:662-663 Jul '76

China (People's Republic)

The Shenyang F-9 combat aircraft. Nikolai Cherikov. illus tab Intl Def Rev 9:714-716 Oct '76; Interavia 31:1160-1162 Dec '76

Europe, Western

Poor European productivity plagues U.S. purchases. F.Clifton Berry, Jr. tabs Armed Forces J Intl 113:32-33 Mar '76

Tornado programme slowed by engine delays. illus Interavia 31:1062 Nov '76

France

The Dassault-Breguet Falcon 50 programme: First flight in November 1976. Marc Grangier. tabs illus (Also cutaways) Interavia 31:383-385 Apr '76

Dassault-Breguet Super Etendard: Twelve months to first flight of production model. Michael Brown. illus tab Interavia 31:974-975 Oct '76

Transair France: Business aviation in action. illus Interavia 31:1004-1005 Oct '76

Germany (Federal Republic)

The West German aerospace industry: State control or free enterprise? illus tabs Interavia 31:315-319 Apr '76

Where is the German (Hanover) Air Show going? illus tab Interavia 31:505-510 Jun '76

Great Britain

Aerospace (equipment). John Marriott. illus tabs
NATO's Fifteen Nations 21:35-39+ Apr-May '76

Bristol Buckingham. Michael J.F.Bowyer. tabs illus
(Also cut short) Air Pict 38:446-453 Nov '76

British aerospace: End of a chapter--or the book?
tab illus Air Pict 38:345-348+ Sep '76

British aerospace--the future. tab Air Pict 38:267
Jul '76

The British equipment industry. Derek Wood. illus
Interavia 31:824 Sep '76

De Havilland Flamingo: The airliner whose career
was cut short by the war. Philip J.Birtles. illus
tabs Air Pict 38:438-442 Nov '76

The HS.125-700: The bizjet is alive and well. Derek
Wood. illus tabs Interavia 31:707-708 Aug '76

Hawker Siddeley Hawk entering service this year.
Derek Wood. illus (Also cutaway) tabs Interavia
31:116-119 Feb '76

Hawker Siddeley's fanjet HS 125-700. (Design profile, no.25) Maurice Allward. illus tabs Air Pict
38:258-263 Jul '76

Nationalizing the British aerospace industry: When,
how and for how long? Derek Wood. illus Interavia
31:799-800 Sep '76

Rolls-Royce pushing for RB.211 orders. illus tabs
Interavia 31:177-180 Feb '76

Rolls-Royce status report. Derek Wood. illus Interavia 31:804 Sep '76

UK aerospace--a U.S. view. Philip Gadeside. illus
Air Pict 38:231 Jun '76

The UK airframe industry. Derek Wood. illus Interavia 31:802-803 Sep '76

Statistics

The British aerospace industry in figures and tables.
illus tabs Interavia 31:825-830 Sep '76

Israel

Introducing the 1124 N Westwind to the military.
illus (Also cutaway) NATO's Fifteen Nations 21:
93 Jun-Jul '76

Why Bedek (Aviation Division of Israel Aircraft Industries) is bidding for U.S. government aircraft
service contract work. illus Govt Exec 8:31-32
May '76

Japan

The Japanese aerospace industry: In a tight squeeze.
illus tabs Interavia 31:965-968+ Oct '76

Netherlands

The Fokker-VFW recipe for success: Slow but sure.
John F.Brindley. illus tab Interavia 31:422-423
May '76

Russia

Duel of designers. (Development of Soviet aviation
equipment before and during the Great Patriotic
War) Mikhail Arlazorov. illus Soviet Mil Rev
No.1:50-52 Jan '76

Sweden

Swedish industry looks ahead. Dan Boyle. illus Interavia 31:131-134 Feb '76

History

The Swedish Air Force: An official history. illus
Aerosp Hist 22:218-230 Dec '75

Switzerland

Air Maintenance: At the crossroads of Europe. Marc
Grangier. illus Interavia 31:660-661 Jul '76

United States

The Boeing 7N7 and 7X7 families. illus tabs Interavia
31:1057-1059 Nov '76

The Boeing 727 goes on ... and on. John F.Brindley.
illus tabs Interavia 31:1143-1145 Dec '76

Century III series (of six new Learjets). Richard S.
Page. illus Aerosp Intl 12:28-29 May-Jun '76

The Cessna Citation spread its wings. illus tab Interavia 31:1033 Nov '76

(Collier Trophy awarded by National Aeronautic
Assoc to David S.Lewis, chief executive officer
of General Dynamics Corp, and to USAF-industry
team that produced the F-16) illus Natl Def 61:
102-103 Sep-Oct '76

From the Cub to the Cheyenne: Interavia talks to
Piper's J.Lynn Helms (on the current situation
and the prospects for general aviation). illus
Interavia 31:674-675 Jul '76

Grumman eyes new markets for the E-2C and F-14.
John F.Brindley. illus tabs Interavia 31:976-978
Oct '76

I dreamed we went nowhere in our solid gold airplane. (Based upon remarks, National Security Industrial Assoc, Absecon, NJ, June 23, 1975) O.C.
Boileau. Def Mgt J 12:5-9 Jan '76

The Lockheed JetStar II and the Canadair LearStar
600--aiming for the long-range market. Marc
Grangier. illus tab Interavia 31:662-663 Jul '76

Lockheed's ASW market. (Modernization of P-3 Orion
and current status of S-3A Viking) J.Philip Geddes.
illus tabs Interavia 31:444-447 May '76

NBAA business aviation showcase. (29th Annual
Meeting, Denver, Sep 14-16, 1976) J.Philip
Geddes. illus Interavia 31:1095-1097 Nov '76

Rockwell International's Shuttle Orbiter. (Design
profile, no.28) Maurice Allward. illus tab Air
Pict 38:432-436 Nov '76

The story of a Beechcraft dynasty--from the King
Air 90 to the King Air 400. Marc Orangier. illus
tab Interavia 31:135-138 Feb '76

The uncertain market for commercial aircraft to
1990: A McDonnell Douglas survey. J.Philip Geddes. illus tabs Interavia 31:350-354 Apr '76

U.S. general and business aviation strides ahead in
difficult economic climate. Marc Grangier. illus
tabs Interavia 31:219-223 Mar '76

The U.S. general aviation market--a decade of solid
growth is forecast. illus tabs Interavia 31:567-569
Jun '76

AIRCRAFT INDUSTRY AND TRADE - Continued

United States - Cont'd

History

The Air Kings of Lomax. Paul D. Stevens. illus tabs
Am Avn Hist Soc J 21:263-268 Winter '76

Charles Willard: The creative years. Martin Cole
and H. L. Schreiner. illus tab Am Avn Hist Soc J
21:62-70 Spring '76

The Errett Lobban Cord story. Robert Fabris. illus
Am Avn Hist Soc J 21:214-218 Fall '76

The Republic XR-12 Rainbow. Lin Hendrix. illus tab
Am Avn Hist Soc J 21:282-285 Winter '76

AIRCRAFT MAINTENANCE

See also
Missile Maintenance
also subdivision Maintenance and Repair under
specific subjects

The accident that should have happened. LCDR G. L.
Forsberg. illus Approach 22:1-3 Sep '76

Air Maintenance: At the crossroads of Europe. Marc
Grangier. illus Interavia 31:660-661 Jul '76

Aircraft corrosion control. TIG Brief 28:14
Aug 27 '76

Aircraft empathy. illus Aerosp Safety 32:10-12
Aug '76

Aircraft maintenance scheduling. TIG Brief 28:9
May 21 '76

The Aircraft Structural Integrity Program (ASIP).
TIG Brief 28:17 Feb 13 '76

(The aircraft was in the hangar awaiting work when)
the canopy was jettisoned. illus Approach 22:21
Nov '76

Aircraft washing versus touchup painting. TIG Brief
28:20 Dec 3 '76

Aircraft weight and balance. Maj John E. Freitas.
illus TAC Attack 16:10-12 Aug '76

Anatomy of a TCTO (Time Compliance Technical
Order). Capt Marty Steere. illus TAC Attack 16:
20-21 Sep '76

(Army) Guard aviation logistics. Capt Arthur W.
Ries. illus Army Log 8:8-11 Nov-Dec '76

Bolts from the blue. Regular feature in some issues
of Interceptor

A challenge to logistics managers. LtGen Robert E.
Hails. TIG Brief 28:2 Jul 2 '76

Chock talk--incidents and incidentals with a maintenance slant. Regular feature in issues of TAC
Attack

Compressed gas cylinders: Are you sure of the contents? TIG Brief 28:5 Jul 16 '76

Condition status reporting. TIG Brief 28:4 Apr 9 '76

Effective plans and scheduling: Cure for most panic
situations. TIG Brief 28:7 Aug 13 '76

FOD: A management problem. Col Samuel Huser.
illus tabs TAC Attack 16:24-27 Sep '76

The fastest hose in the West. (Transient maintenance
and services at Richards-Gebaur AFB, Mo) illus
Interceptor 18:12-15 Mar '76

AIRCRAFT MAINTENANCE - Continued

Flight safety. (Trans from a Russian publication)
illus USA Avn Dig 22:40-41 Mar '76

Foreign Object Damage (FOD). TIG Brief 28:6
Sep 10 '76

General aviation fuel--which is right? Maj Philip M.
McAtee. illus tab Aerosp Safety 32:6-7 Nov '76

Health Indication Test (HIT). Clarence J. Carter.
USA Avn Dig 22:35 Mar '76

Improved maintenance inspection (with neutron-radiography). Maj Vincent G. Ripoll. illus USA Avn
Dig 22:44-45 Mar '76

Maintenance management procedures. TIG Brief 28:
9-10 Mar 12 '76

Maintenance/operations liaison. TIG Brief 28:4
Sep 24 '76

Naval Air Rework Facility, North Island (NAS, Calif).
William M. Powers. illus US Nav Inst Proc 102:
62-71 Jun '76

Night aircraft maintenance. Maj Ted A. Cimral. illus
Army Log 8:36-37 Jan-Feb '76

Night aircraft maintenance. Maj Ted A. Cimral and
Capt L. Allyn Noel. illus USA Avn Dig 22:8-10
Apr '76

O-ring know how. Capt Jon New. (Reprinted from
Aerospace Safety, July 1975) tab illus USA Avn
Dig 22:39-43 Jan '76

One problem too many. illus Approach 21:24-26
Jan '76

The positive side. (Battery problems) Ted Kontos.
illus USA Avn Dig 22:32-35 Oct '76

Reliability centered maintenance. TIG Brief 28:8
Jun 4 '76

Spotlight on maintenance. Ted Kontos. illus USA Avn
Dig 22:5+ Nov '76

Sub-zero defects. illus MAC Flyer 23:8-10 Nov '76

"Super troop." (Pressure on the men who repair airplanes) Capt Milton G. Schellhase. illus MAC Flyer 23:8-9 Dec '76

The team: Operations and maintenance. Majs James
D. Stetson, III and Warren D. Johnson. illus Navigator 23:29-30 Winter '76

Tech order versus quick checks. TIG Brief 28:16
Apr 23 '76

(Temperature) going up! Ted Kontos. illus USA Avn
Dig 22:34-37 May '76

Things that go bump in the flight. Maj Joe Tillman.
illus TAC Attack 16:26-28 Aug '76

Those tenacious trouble-shooters at (maintenance
branch of) ALC (Aviation Logistics Center, Edgewood Arsenal, Md). Bruce P. Hargreaves. illus
tab Natl Guardsman 30:22-25 Apr '76

To his credit. (A1C Bert Jackson has the best air-
craft maintenance record at RAF Lakenheath,
Eng) Maj Mark R. Foutch. illus Airman 20:32-34
Apr '76

Transair France: Business aviation in action. illus
Interavia 31:1004-1005 Oct '76

Trust (aircraft forms and the Exceptional Release
(ER)). Capt Philip M. McAtee. illus Aerosp Safety
32:6 Sep '76

AIRCRAFT MAINTENANCE - Continued

Two-man team qualification. TIG Brief 28:3 Apr 9 '76

Two perceptions. Maj Thomas L. Sutton. illus Aerosp Safety 32:18-20 May '76

Use of captive adapter plugs on AIM-9 missiles. TIG Brief 28:8 Dec 17 '76

Vital life fluid. (Oil analysis program) Patsy Thompson. illus USA Avn Dig 22:36-40 Aug '76

We service what we sell. (USAF Logistics Command gives assistance and advice to foreign purchasers of U.S.-made military aircraft) Capt John B. Taylor. illus Airman 20:10-12 May '76

Weapons release systems inspections. TIG Brief 28:5 May 21 '76

What's a national maintenance point? Robert T. Grothe. illus Army Log 8:6-9 May-Jun '76

Why Bedek (Aviation Division of Israel Aircraft Industries) is bidding for U.S. government aircraft service contract work. illus Govt Exec 8:31-32 May '76

X-ray for FOD. TIG Brief 28:13 Aug 27 '76

You and F-4 depot maintenance. Capt Lawrence H. Hoffman, Jr. illus TAC Attack 16:22-23 Jun '76

You and your toolbox. Sgt1C Jerry E. Mills. illus USA Avn Dig 22:30-35 Dec '76

AIRCRAFT MECHANICS see Ground Crews

AIRDROP

'Drop in' troops: Fast and flexible. Maj James K. McCollum, Ret. illus Army 26:40-44 Sep '76

Study and Teaching

The great Minnesota/Arizona cactus caper. Capt Neal Gendler. illus Natl Guardsman 30:30-31 May '76

AIRLIFT

See also
Berlin Airlift
Mercy Missions
Vietnamese Conflict, 1957-1975--Airlift Operations

ATCA (Advanced Tanker Cargo Aircraft)--key to global mobility. Edgar Ulsamer. illus (Also cutaway) map AF Mag 59:20-25 Apr '76

101st (Airborne Division (Air Assault)) in Reforger 76. Col Larry J. Baughman and Maj Robert E. Jones, Jr. illus maps USA Avn Dig 22:2-3+ Dec '76

Airlift is key to commuter Army (in Reforger 75). Translog 7:16-17 Mar '76; Mil Engr 68:308 Jul-Aug '76

Airlift problems pose threat to our security. Editorial. Officer 52:6+ Jan '76

(Airlift) transportation in support of American embassies. TIG Brief 28:9 Jun 4 '76

Airlifts to Turkish quake victims end. illus AF Times 37:22 Dec 13 '76

Angola--a last look? John Wegg. illus Air Pict 38: 96-98 Mar '76

AIRLIFT - Continued

Earthquake! (USAF aids Guatemala with airlift, reconnaissance, and communications) MSgt Harold Newcomb and SSgt Ken Peterson. illus Airman 20: 8-13 Jun '76

Flexibility--a state of mind. Gen Richard H. Ellis and LtCol Frank B. Horton III. illus Strat Rev 4: 26-36 Winter '76

GAO: 'Lift ability is overestimated. AF Times 36:40 Jul 12 '76

GAO slams strategic airlift "requirements" and programs. Armed Forces J Intl 113:14 Jul '76

Guatemala: 210th Aviation Battalion comes through again in disaster relief. CW2 Larry R. Santure. illus USA Avn Dig 22:4-5+ Jul '76

Joint ops: An exercise in frustration. Capt J. T. Reynolds. illus Aerosp Safety 32:16-19 Oct '76

In the barrel. (Military airlift managers, referred to as barrelmasters, respond to worldwide demands) TSgt Tom Dwyer. illus Airman 20:36-39 Jun '76

Korea: Proving ground in combat air transportation. Col Ray L. Bowers. illus map Def Mgt J 12:62-66 Jul '76

MAC 'new look' ORI. BrigGen Edward J. Nash. tab TIG Brief 28:3-4 Aug 27 '76

MAC's (Gen Paul K.) Carlton asks 'airlift partnership.' AF Times 37:36 Dec 6 '76

Military airlift and the future. (Excerpt from address, 57th Defense Preparedness Meeting, American Defense Preparedness Assoc, Los Angeles, Oct 15, 1975) Gen Paul K. Carlton. Natl Def 60: 288 Jan-Feb '76

Operation Wagonmaster. ("D" Company (Wagonmasters), 34th Support Battalion, 6th Cavalry Brigade (Air Combat), in disaster relief operation in Guatemala) Maj Terry N. Rosser. illus USA Avn Dig 22:6-7+ Jul '76

The other side of the coin. (Many non-flying personnel were necessary for Operation Coin Alaska, airlift supply operation from Elmendorf AFB to AF and Navy installations on the North Slope) TSgt Tom Dwyer. illus Airman 20:38-42 May '76

Priority of nuclear logistic movement support. TIG Brief 28:10 Nov 19 '76

Raven on the 'cap. (109th Tactical Airlift Group of the Air National Guard flies resupply missions to DEW-Line sites in Greenland) Maj Terry A. Arnold. illus Airman 20:2-8 Nov '76

Reforger 76 is history. illus Translog 7:7 Dec '76

"Return the forces to Germany"--(Reforger) 76. LtCol Gary Sorensen. illus Def Trans J 32:6-8+ Oct '76

Special assignment airlift mission. TIG Brief 28:15 Feb 27 '76

Supply airlift after quake (in) Guatemala. illus AF Times 36:26 Mar 8 '76

Costs

House panel (Appropriations Committee) scores 9.7-billion dollar airlift hodge-podge. tab Armed Forces J Intl 113:14-15 Jul '76

Why airlift isn't free. Gen Paul K. Carlton. tab illus Army Log 8:2-6 Jan-Feb '76

AIRLINES - Continued

Europe, Eastern

Eastern European air transport: McDonnell Douglas' view. illus tabs Interavia 31:1075-1077 Nov '76

Europe, Western

Integration in the European air tourism industry. André Perrault. illus tabs Interavia pt 1, 31:140-143 Feb '76; pt 2, 31:235-237 Mar '76; pt 3, 31:435-437 May '76

Fiji

Airlines of the world. (African Cargo Airways Ltd, Cathay Pacific Airways Ltd, Fiji Air Ltd) Günter G. Endres. illus tabs Air Pict 38:225 Jun '76

History

Air Pacific. F.G. Barnes. illus tab Air Pict 38:366-370 Sep '76

Germany (Federal Republic)

Airlines of the world. (Hapag-Lloyd Fluggesellschaft mbH, Malév Hungarian Airlines, Royal Brunei Airlines) Günter G. Endres. illus tabs Air Pict 38:266 Jul '76

Lufthansa guardedly optimistic even in difficult times. (Interview with Hans Süssenguth) Klaus Höhle. illus Interavia 31:534 Jun '76

Lufthansa looks toward the 1980s. (Interview with Reinhardt Abraham) illus tabs Interavia 31:346-349 Apr '76

History

Half a century of Lufthansa. John Stroud. illus Air Pict 38:142-143 Apr '76

Great Britain

Air Anglia: Local airline makes good. Chris Bulloch. map illus tab Interavia 31:1078 Nov '76

Autoland starts to pay off for British Airways. Don Craig. illus Interavia pt 1, 31:721-724 Aug '76; pt 2, 31:863-867 Sep '76

UK independent airlines and their relation to the national airline. K.W. Clark. illus tabs Interavia 31:715-717 Aug '76

Hong Kong

Airlines of the world. (African Cargo Airways Ltd, Cathay Pacific Airways Ltd, Fiji Air Ltd) Günter G. Endres. illus tabs Air Pict 38:225 Jun '76

Hungary

Airlines of the world. (Hapag-Lloyd Fluggesellschaft mbH, Malév Hungarian Airlines, Royal Brunei Airlines) Günter G. Endres. illus tabs Air Pict 38:266 Jul '76

Iceland

Airlines of the world. (Aerovias Quisqueyana, Flugfélag Nordurlands h.f., Zambia Airways Corporation) Günter G. Endres. illus tabs Air Pict 38:482 Dec '76

Israel

Airlines of the world. (Kanaf-Arkia Airlines and Aviation Services Ltd, Skystream Airlines Inc, Trans Mediterranean Airways SAL) Günter G. Endres. tabs illus Air Pict 38:181 May '76

AIRLINES - Continued

Italy

Airlines of the world. (Air Nauru, Avio Ligure S.p.A., Syrian Arab Airlines) Günter G. Endres. illus tabs Air Pict 38:309 Aug '76

Japan

Airlines of the world. (Command Airways Incorporated, Japan Asia Airways Company, Yemen Airways Corporation) Günter G. Endres. illus Air Pict 38:357 Sep '76

Lebanon

Airlines of the world. (Kanaf-Arkia Airlines and Aviation Services Ltd, Skystream Airlines Inc, Trans Mediterranean Airways SAL) Günter G. Endres. tabs illus Air Pict 38:181 May '76

Morocco

Airlines of the world. (Alaska International Air, Inc, Royal Air Maroc, Transporte Aéreo Rioplatense S.A.) Günter G. Endres. illus tabs Air Pict 38:443 Nov '76

Nauru

Airlines of the world. (Air Nauru, Avio Ligure S.p.A., Syrian Arab Airlines) Günter G. Endres. illus tabs Air Pict 38:309 Aug '76

Netherlands

Airlines of the world. (NLM Dutch Airlines, Safe Air Ltd, Thai Airways International Ltd) Günter G. Endres. illus Air Pict 38:99 Mar '76

New Zealand

Airlines of the world. (NLM Dutch Airlines, Safe Air Ltd, Thai Airways International Ltd) Günter G. Endres. illus Air Pict 38:99 Mar '76

Russia

See Aeroflot

Saudi Arabia

Saudia: Saudi Arabian Airlines. John Wegg. illus map tabs Air Pict 38:102-106 Mar '76

Syria

Airlines of the world. (Air Nauru, Avio Ligure S.p.A., Syrian Arab Airlines) Günter G. Endres. illus tabs Air Pict 38:309 Aug '76

Thailand

Airlines of the world. (NLM Dutch Airlines, Safe Air Ltd, Thai Airways International Ltd) Günter G. Endres. illus Air Pict 38:99 Mar '76

United States

Airline deregulation: Will it make the dominos fall faster? C.W. Borklund. illus tabs Govt Exec 8:38-40+ Jul '76

Airlines of the world. (Command Airways Incorporated, Japan Asia Airways Company, Yemen Airways Corporation) Günter G. Endres. illus Air Pict 38:357 Sep '76

Airlines of the world. (Kanaf-Arkia Airlines and Aviation Services Ltd, Skystream Airlines Inc, Trans Mediterranean Airways SAL) Günter G. Endres. tabs illus Air Pict 38:181 May '76

AIRLINES - Continued

United States - Cont'd

Bringing air freight into the intermodal age. Russell T. Daly. illus Def Trans J 32:18-20+ Jun '76

Is PanAm seeing the end of the tunnel? Klaus Höhle. illus tab Interavia 31:619-621 Jul '76

It's tough at the top, but that's the way Seaboard's Richard Jackson likes it. (Interview with Richard Jackson) Arthur Wallis. illus Interavia 31:529 Jun '76

Planning for growth at Continental Airlines. J. Philip Geddes. illus tab map Interavia 31:53-54+ Jan '76

Transportation career forecast. Chester Levine and others. tab Def Trans J pt 1, Outlook. 32:18-20+ Oct '76

United Airlines also in the red. Klaus Höhle. illus tabs Interavia 31:621-622 Jul '76

History

The aircraft history of Northwest Airlines. David Galbraith. illus map tabs Am Avn Hist Soc J 21: 241-256 Winter '76

The aircraft history of United Airlines. Barrett Tillman and Matthew Edward Rodina, Jr. illus tabs Am Avn Hist Soc J 21:169-184 Fall '76

The aircraft history of Western Air Lines. William T. Larkins. illus tabs Am Avn Hist Soc J 21:9-23 Spring '76

The Errett Lobban Cord story. Robert Fabris. illus Am Avn Hist Soc J 21:214-218 Fall '76

Super Electra: Lockheed's model 14. Thomas M. Emmert and William T. Larkins. illus tabs Am Avn Hist Soc J 21:101-111 Summer '76

Yemen

Airlines of the world. (Command Airways Incorporated, Japan Asia Airways Company, Yemen Airways Corporation) Günter G. Endres. illus Air Pict 38:357 Sep '76

Zambia

Airlines of the world. (Aerovias Quisqueyana, Flugfélag Nordurlands h.f., Zambia Airways Corporation) Günter G. Endres. illus tabs Air Pict 38:482 Dec '76

AIRLINES, LOCAL SERVICE

Air Anglia: Local airline makes good. Chris Bulloch. map illus tab Interavia 31:1078 Nov '76

Trans-Australia Airlines: Waiting for the upswing. tab Interavia 31:410 May '76

AIRMAN COMMISSIONING PROGRAM see Airman Education and Commissioning Program

AIRMAN EDUCATION AND COMMISSIONING PROGRAM

(AF) personnel program best in Pentagon, (SecAF) Reed says (in news conference). AF Times 36:3 Mar 8 '76

Bootstrappers lose school breaks (and some tighter controls may be coming for students under DANTES). Len Famiglietti. AF Times 37:12 Nov 29 '76

AIRMAN EDUCATION AND COMMISSIONING PROGRAM - Continued

Degree-holding EM can vie for AECP. AF Times 37:10 Nov 15 '76

Return of AECP? AF Times 36:4 Jun 21 '76

Some officials expect a new life for AECP. AF Times 36:27 Jul 26 '76

AIRMAN PERFORMANCE REPORTS

APR rating controls eyed as inflation check. AF Times 36:2 Jan 26 '76

Correction of officer and airman evaluation reports. TIG Brief 28:21 Jan 16 '76

Testing

15 bases to test new APR plan. AF Times 36:9 Feb 2 '76

AIRMEN

AFROTC airman scholarship and commissioning program. TIG Brief 28:6 Aug 13 '76

Admin EM conversion Jan 1. AF Times 37:12 Dec 6 '76

Airmen already overseas added to 'home-basing.' Bruce Callander. AF Times 36:2 Feb 16 '76

Airmen can choose o'seas tour sites--year longer required. Bruce Callander. AF Times 36:24 Mar 15 '76

Airmen home basing assignments. TIG Brief 28:17 Feb 27 '76

Basics quizzed at Lackland (AFB, Tex) reveal ideas on prevailing issues. Bruce Callander. AF Times 37:10 Sep 6 '76

Community College of the Air Force registrations: Getting the word out! TIG Brief 28:3 Nov 19 '76

Degree-holding EM can vie for AECP. AF Times 37:10 Nov 15 '76

E-3s promoted Oct 1975 eligible for BTZ hike. AF Times 37:2 Nov 15 '76

E-4 sergeant 'ranks' senior airman in E-4. AF Times 37:32 Dec 13 '76

EM early outs extended a year--surplus first termers eligible. Bruce Callander. AF Times 36:2 Apr 26 '76

EM exit options changed. AF Times 36:11 May 24 '76

EM grade overhaul begins June 1. AF Times 36:6 Apr 26 '76

EM hikes--changes, impact. Bruce Callander. tabs AF Times 37:3 Aug 30 '76

EM must solve re-up equation. Bruce Callander. AF Times 37:14 Nov 29 '76

Early outs end; some not okayed. Bruce Callander. AF Times 36:2 Jun 14 '76

Early outs limited to first termers. AF Times 36:2 Jan 19 '76

Early release skills for May identified. AF Times 36:21 Feb 23 '76

Enlisted force structure changes. AF Plcy Ltr for Comdrs: Sup No. 5:34-36 May '76

Extra hike cycles reduced for airmen. AF Times 36:6 Jul 19 '76

AIRMEN - Continued

Fewer EM face hike delays. AF Times 37:9 Sep 6 '76

First-term airman recruiter assistance program. TIG Brief 28:15 Nov 5 '76

1st termers must plan ahead for retraining bonus. AF Times 36:16 Jun 21 '76

Flying EM closer to career status: Mixed blessing. Bruce Callander. AF Times 36:2 May 17 '76

Ford signs 120-day notice order (for) grounded EM fliers. AF Times 37:10 Aug 9 '76

Help ahead for lower EM: New budget said to include funds for travel. Randy Shoemaker. AF Times 37:3 Dec 13 '76

Hike activity getting back on track. Bruce Callander. AF Times 36:3 Jun 21 '76

Hikes open to Reserve EM. AF Times 37:2 Dec 27 '76

Horror stories! (AF enlisted personnel job placement explained) Capt John B. Taylor. illus Airman 20: 24-28 Apr '76

Job reservation no guarantee: Warning to airmen. AF Times 37:46 Sep 13 '76

Junior E-3s due below-zone hikes. Bruce Callander. AF Times 36:50 Feb 2 '76

Low AQE (Airman Qualifying Examination) scorers urged to try again. Bruce Callander. AF Times 36:3 Jul 5 '76

Lower-grade insignia: Who's what? AF Times 36:6 Jun 14 '76

MPC (Military Personnel Center) withdraws control of SEIs (Special Experience Identifiers) from commands. AF Times 37:8 Dec 6 '76

Major career overhaul set for EM. AF Times 36:6+ Mar 15 '76

NCO status: 'Must' before E-5 hike. AF Times 36:8 Jun 21 '76

New factor ("special experience identifiers") added in EM assignments. Bruce Callander. AF Times 36:6 Jul 12 '76

New 2-step E-4 plan begins June 1. Bruce Callander. AF Times 36:16 Feb 23 '76

Not all first-term EM to get early outs. AF Times 36:8 Mar 1 '76

OTS age limit raised. AF Times 36:20 May 24 '76

Outstanding Airmen for 1976. illus AF Times 37:19+ Sep 27 '76

Outstanding Airmen (of 1976). illus Airman 20:11-14 Dec '76

Personnel must meet prerequisite qualifications before retraining is approved. TIG Brief 28:15 Jul 16 '76

Quotas issued for below-zone hikes: 1242 to make E-4. AF Times 36:6 Feb 16 '76

Reconsideration of favorable selective reenlistment program decisions. TIG Brief 28:6 Sep 10 '76

Rules preclude 3-tier 'slips.' Bruce Callander. AF Times 36:25 Jun 14 '76

Senior airman: New E-4 title. Bruce Callander. AF Times 36:3 Jan 12 '76

Special Experience Identifiers (SEIs). TIG Brief 28:3 Sep 10 '76

AIRMEN - Continued

Switch to three-tier (system) includes cushioners. Bruce Callander. AF Times 36:1+ Jun 7 '76

10,000 EM get 'job reservations.' AF Times 36:23 Mar 1 '76

3000 EM may leave early. AF Times 36:4 Jan 12 '76

3-tier structure: New EM lineup begins June 1. AF Times 36:3 Mar 1 '76

1200 making special E-4. Bruce Callander. AF Times 36:3 Jan 5 '76

USAF's finest. (12 Outstanding Airmen for 1976) Maj Terry A. Arnold. illus AF Mag 59:47-49 Nov '76

AIRMEN'S CLUBS see Servicemen's Clubs

AIRPLANE HIJACKING

Entebbe and after. ACM Christopher Foxley-Norris. Army Qtr 106:397-401 Oct '76

Israel solves a hijacking. LtGen Ira C. Eaker, Ret. AF Times 36:13-14 Jul 26 '76

MAC not joking about security. TIG Brief 28:15 May 7 '76

Punishment of aerial piracy--a new development. Robert-Louis Perret. illus Interavia 31:545 Jun '76

Prevention

A total system for aviation security. Fred Dorey. illus Interavia 31:543-544 Jun '76

AIRPLANE TYPE
Only U.S. military airplanes are entered under type. For airplanes of other countries see entries under specific categories, e.g., Airplanes, Military-- Great Britain.

A-4

A-4 spoilers. illus Approach 21:24-25 May '76

A-5

Death at the ramp. illus Approach 21:26-27 Feb '76

A-6

(The aircraft was in the hangar awaiting work when) the canopy was jettisoned. illus Approach 22:21 Nov '76

Not up to par. illus Approach 21:12-13 Mar '76

TRAM (Target Recognition Attack Multi-sensor) makes A-6E world's most advanced EO aircraft. illus Elect Warfare 8:75-76+ May-Jun '76

A-7

A-7 emergency brake problems. LT Carl Tankersley. illus Approach 21:15 Jan '76

The A-7: One aircraft or two? LCDR Ken Sanger. illus Approach 21:10-11 Jun '76

Nugget nightmare. illus Approach 22:18-20 Nov '76

Thirty ways to crunch an A-7 (or any other type of carrier aircraft). LCDR Jim White. illus Approach 22:16-17 Sep '76

A-10

The A-10. Col Craig Powell, Ret. illus Army 26:43-47 Mar '76

AIRPLANE TYPE - Continued

A-10 - Cont'd

A-10 accepted formally by TAC at Langley (AFB, Va). illus AF Times 36:17 Apr 5 '76

A-10, close air support stone. Maj Michael L. Ferguson. illus Infantry 66:24-28 May-Jun '76

The A-10 does it better. Maj John F. Gulick. illus tab AF Mag 59:75-79 Jul '76

A-10 progress report: We're slightly confused. illus Armed Forces J Intl 113:30 Mar '76

Fairchild's A-10 is entering service: The return of the Flying Can-Opener. John F. Brindley. illus tab Interavia 31:1089-1090 Nov '76

Open letter to A-10 drivers. LtCol Dale Tabor. illus TAC Attack 16:4-7 Aug '76

Say hello to the Wart Hog (A-10). Maj Jack Stitzel. illus TAC Attack 16:26-28 Apr '76

TAC 30th birthday party celebrates A-10 acceptance. Bobbe Lindland. illus Armed Forces J Intl 113:22 Apr '76

Tank killer team (Air Force A-10 ground-attack aircraft mounting the powerful GAU-8/A 30-mm gun system). Col Robert G. Dilger. illus Natl Def 61: 190-191 Nov-Dec '76

A titanium bathtub with wings. illus Natl Guardsman 30:58 Aug-Sep '76

A-18

Flexible multimission avionics. illus Countermeasures 2:25-26+ Nov '76

AC-130

Hours of terror. Maj John O'Connor. illus MAC Flyer 23:3-5 Feb '76

AV-8

Advanced Harrier program. illus MarCor Gaz 60:9 Oct '76

Alpha, Beta, and Theta Jay. (Problems in the new aerodynamics of the Harrier) LtComdr John Leng. illus Approach 21:1-3 Nov '75

Marine Aviation: Looking up (straight up). John Rhea. illus Sea Power 19:9-13 Nov '76

A step forward with Harrier. Capt A. H. Boquet. illus MarCor Gaz 60:59-61 Apr '76

A Yank in the RAF. (AF exchange officer flies the V/STOL Harrier) Capt Dennis A. Guyitt. illus Airman 20:38-41 Mar '76

Albatross
See HU-16

B-1

ALCM (Air-Launched Cruise Missile). Govt Exec 8:16 Jun '76

Air Chief (Gen David C. Jones) tells aides B-1 is vital. illus Officer 52:18 May '76

The Air Force and national security: 1976 and beyond. (Remarks, Air Force Assoc, Mobile Chapter, Mobile, Ala, March 27, 1976) LtGen John W. Pauly. AF Plcy Ltr for Comdrs: Sup No. 6:10-18 Jun '76

AIRPLANE TYPE - Continued

B-1 - Cont'd

Artful dodger of the 1980s. Bill Walsh. illus Countermeasures 2:42-43+ Nov '76

The attempt to kill the B-1. LtGen Ira C. Eaker, Ret. AF Times 36:13+ Jun 21 '76

The B-1: A national imperative. Francis P. Hoeber. Strat Rev 4:111-117 Summer '76

(The B-1 debate: Authors' responses) Archie L. Wood and John F. McCarthy, Jr. Intl Sec 1:117-122 Fall '76

The B-1 strategic bomber: A necessary weapons system. Maj R. O'Mara. illus tab Royal Air Forces Qtr 16:236-242 Autumn '76

The B-1: Strategic deterrence into the twenty-first century. MajGen Abner B. Martin. illus tabs AU Rev 27:2-14 Mar-Apr '76

The B-1: The right solution. (Remarks, Council of World Affairs, Dallas, April 15, 1976) Thomas C. Reed. AF Plcy Ltr for Comdrs: Sup No. 6:2-9 Jun '76

The case for the B-1 bomber. John F. McCarthy, Jr. illus tabs Intl Sec 1:78-97 Fall '76

Congress okays B-1 go-ahead. AF Times 36:3 Jul 12 '76

Congress views B-1 delay, new ship mix as major hardware issues in new budget. Armed Forces J Intl 113:5 Jun '76

Defense Appropriations Bill moves: House votes money for comstores, B-1. AF Times 36:4 Jun 28 '76

(DefSec Donald) Rumsfeld gives go-ahead on B-1: Carter could block it. Lee Ewing. AF Times 37:4 Dec 13 '76

The fate of the B-1 bomber. LtGen Ira C. Eaker, Ret. AF Times 37:13-14 Oct 11 '76

First impressions (of the B-1). Maj George W. Larson. illus Combat Crew 26:4-7+ Jan '76

Flying the B-1: A pilot's view. Maj George W. Larson, Jr. illus tab AF Mag 59:22-27 Jun '76

Forces for the future. (Remarks, Lancaster Chamber of Commerce, Lancaster, Calif, Feb 6, 1976) Thomas C. Reed. AF Plcy Ltr for Comdrs: Sup No. 4:16-20 Apr '76

Modernizing the strategic bomber force without really trying: A case against the B-1. Archie L. Wood. Intl Sec 1:98-116 Fall '76

(SecAF Thomas C.) Reed slaps at congressional critic (of B-1). (From address, Air Force Assoc National Convention, Washington, Sep 19-22, 1976) illus AF Times 37:21 Oct 4 '76

(Sen William) Proxmire: 41 for B-1, 26 against. AF Times 36:14 Mar 1 '76

Costs

The B-1: Strategic deterrence into the twenty-first century. MajGen Abner B. Martin. illus tabs AU Rev 27:2-14 Mar-Apr '76

Equipment

B-1: A view from the aft station. MajGen Richard N. Cody. illus Combat Crew 27:4-7+ Sep '76

AIRPLANE TYPE - Continued

B-1 - Cont'd

Equipment - Cont'd

A test nav looks at the B-1. LtCol Kenneth W. Brotnov. illus tab Navigator 23:5-11 Winter '76

Testing

The B-1: First flight plus one year. Maj Mike Butchko. illus Aerosp Safety 32:10-14 Mar '76

B-1 gets 'clean' (environmental) rating. AF Times 37:18 Oct 18 '76

The B-1: Strategic deterrence into the twenty-first century. MajGen Abner B. Martin. illus tabs AU Rev 27:2-14 Mar-Apr '76

B-1 tests. Contact, p 5, Winter '76

Second B-1 joins flight test programme. illus Interavia 31:205 Mar '76

A test nav looks at the B-1. LtCol Kenneth W. Brotnov. illus tab Navigator 23:5-11 Winter '76

B-25

AAF's flying artillery--the 75-mm Baker two-five. LtCol Jim Beavers, Ret. illus AF Mag 59:65-69 Apr '76; Fld Arty J 44:25-29 Jul-Aug '76

B-25s over Tokyo, 18 April 1942. MSgt Dave Sylva. illus Aerosp Safety 32:14-17+ Apr '76

B-36

Double stall. Meyers K. Jacobsen. illus Aerosp Hist 23:207-213 Dec '76

B-52

(The B-1 debate: Authors' responses) Archie L. Wood and John F. McCarthy, Jr. Intl Sec 1:117-122 Fall '76

B-52 in-flight emergency. Capt Stephen R. Schmidt. illus Combat Crew 27:16-17 Sep '76

B-52 nuclear weapon system safety study completed. TIG Brief 28:10 Aug 27 '76

B-52--20th anniversary in SAC. illus Aerosp Hist 22:198-200 Dec '75

Modernizing the strategic bomber force without really trying: A case against the B-1. Archie L. Wood. Intl Sec 1:98-116 Fall '76

SRAM (Short Range Attack Missile): A potent weapons system and a lot more! Capt Stephen M. Ray. illus Combat Crew 27:7+ Aug '76

Equipment

Window to the world: EVS (Electro-optical Viewing System) and the navigator. 1stLt James R. McDonald. illus Navigator 23:25-26 Summer '76

History

Twenty years on the line. Capts Stephen O. Manning III and Len Brady. illus Airman 20:2-7 Jan '76

Maintenance and Repair

In Guam they rust. Capt John B. Taylor. illus Airman 20:8 Jan '76

AIRPLANE TYPE - Continued

C-5

C-5 flaws (largely wing modification) to cost $1.5 billion. (GAO report) AF Times 36:35 Jan 19 '76

High speed aircraft fueling project. (Largest fuel storage tank and biggest single piece of cargo airlifted to Incirlik, Turkey) Walter Will. illus AF Engrg & Svcs Qtr 17:28-29 Feb '76

Maintenance and Repair

Triple Deuce leads the way. (Two C-5's at Dover AFB, Del, compete in a Lead the Force program of accelerated use of the planes in order to prepare for maintenance needs in other C-5's) Maj Jim Gibson. illus Airman 20:20-23 Aug '76

C-12

A new member of the team (C-12A Huron). LtCol Robert F. Forsyth. tabs illus (Also cutaway) USA Avn Dig 22:24-27 Jul '76

C-47

Incident at Foul Bay. (C-47 beached on the west coast of the Red Sea) John F. Ohlinger. illus Aerosp Hist 23:71-74 Jun '76

C-130

The C-130: Talented tactical transport. Capt Peter W. Lindquist. illus AF Mag 59:69-73 Nov '76

Doing it by 'rote.' (Rotational units of AF's Military Airlift Command, flying C-130s, perform routine and emergency missions) SSgt Ken Peterson. illus Airman 20:36-39 Nov '76

Lockheed doubts AMST value, proposes stretched Hercules. illus Interavia 31:202 Mar '76

Raven on the 'cap. (109th Tactical Airlift Group of the Air National Guard flies resupply missions to DEW-Line sites in Greenland) Maj Terry A. Arnold. illus Airman 20:2-8 Nov '76

C-141

C-141 still OK for female pilots. AF Times 37:32 Sep 6 '76

Inertial navigation means help is on the way. illus MAC Flyer 23:9-10 Mar '76

Canberra
See EB-57

Corsair II
See A-7

Delta Dart
See F-106

E-1

One of those days. illus Approach 21:6-7 Jun '76

E-2

ALR-59 passive detection system (for the E-2C). illus Countermeasures 2:23-25 Apr '76

AWACS: Can it cut out ground clutter on Capitol Hill? illus tab Govt Exec 8:16-17 Mar '76

Airborne navonics. illus tab Countermeasures 2:43-44+ Feb '76

AIRPLANE TYPE - Continued

E-2 - Cont'd

The eyes of the fleet. Thomas A. Guarino and Charles F. Muller, Jr. illus US Nav Inst Proc 102:117-120 Oct '76

Grumman eyes new markets for the E-2C and F-14. John F. Brindley. illus tabs Interavia 31:976-978 Oct '76

Hawkeye (E-2C) crew coordination. LCDR Richard J. Malla. illus Approach 21:8 Mar '76

Israel buys four E-2C Hawkeyes. illus Armed Forces J Intl 113:14 Feb '76

The saga of the Humble Hummer (E-2). LT Cam Place. illus Approach 22:6-8 Dec '76

E-3

AFSC's Electronic Systems Division (ESD). illus AF Mag 59:51-57 Jul '76

AWACS: Can it cut out ground clutter on Capitol Hill? illus tab Govt Exec 8:16-17 Mar '76

An eagle in the sky. Bill Walsh. map illus (Also cutaway) Countermeasures 2:30+ Jul '76

New AWACS proposals to NATO. Intl Def Rev 9:709 Oct '76

E-4

AFSC's Electronic Systems Division (ESD). illus AF Mag 59:51-57 Jul '76

The E-4 airborne command post. W.L. Shockley. illus (Also cutaway) Countermeasures 2:34-36 Jul '76

EB-57

Canberras to Europe. 1stLt Norman B. Hutcherson. illus Interceptor 18:8-9 Dec '76

EC-121

Airborne warning--it's worth the price. LtCol Lowell Davis. illus (Also cutaway) Natl Def 60:374-377 Mar-Apr '76

EF-111

EF-111A (tactical jamming aircraft) designated 'major system.' illus Elect Warfare 8:19 Jul-Aug '76

Eagle

See F-15

F-4

Back to basics: Planning & execution of pop-up patterns. Capt James P. Feighny, Jr. illus tab TAC Attack 16:4-9 Dec '76

Disastrous bingo! illus Approach 21:18-21 Jan '76

Don't let your Phantom blow its top. Capt Terryl J. Schwalier. illus TAC Attack 16:4-6 May '76

Drag, weight, and G in ACM (Air Combat Maneuvering). LT Ross Burgess. illus Approach 21:12-14 Dec '75

F-4 BLC (Boundary Layer Control)--blessing or burden? LtCol J.P. Cline. illus Aerosp Safety 32:17-19 Sep '76

AIRPLANE TYPE - Continued

F-4 - Cont'd

Let's get serious about dive toss. Capt Robert H. Baxter. (Reprinted from USAF Fighter Weapons Newsletter, Sep 1970) illus tab USAF Ftr Wpns Rev, pp 28-34, Summer '76

Linked pairs. Capts Daniel J. Gibson and John G. Swanson. illus USAF Ftr Wpns Rev, pp 31-36, Fall '76

More efficient use of the RAF Phantom force. (Sir Robert Brooke-Popham Prize Essay) SqLdr R.D. Arnott. illus Hawk No.37:23-28 Jul '76

Overcontrol: Commanded or uncommanded? Col Neil L. Eddins. illus tabs TAC Attack 16:10-14 Sep '76

Sync-z-turn (intercept technique). Maj Milan Zimer. illus tabs USAF Ftr Wpns Rev, pp 26-30, Spring '76

They said it couldn't be done! (Multiple emergency: Single-engine failure and utility hydraulic loss) illus Approach 22:14-15 Jul '76

What's a good carrier aviator? LCDR Michael N. Matton. illus Approach 21:20-21 May '76

Maintenance and Repair

To his credit. (A1C Bert Jackson has the best aircraft maintenance record at RAF Lakenheath, Eng) Maj Mark R. Foutch. illus Airman 20:32-34 Apr '76

Where were the inspectors? (F-4 loss-of-control accidents) TIG Brief 28:8 Mar 12 '76

You and F-4 depot maintenance. Capt Lawrence H. Hoffman, Jr. illus TAC Attack 16:22-23 Jun '76

Study and Teaching

Until the Aggressors come! Capt Neil McCoy. illus USAF Ftr Wpns Rev, pp 9-13, Fall '76

F-14

DLC (Direct Lift Control) is here, finally! LCDR George Webb. tab illus Approach 21:1-3 Jun '76

F-14 Tomcat. William M. Powers. illus US Nav Inst Proc 102:75-87 Oct '76

F-14--weapon system in search of its engine. RADM John S. Christiansen, Ret. illus US Nav Inst Proc 102:103-105 Dec '76

GCA slow roll. illus Approach 21:5 Jun '76

Grumman eyes new markets for the E-2C and F-14. John F. Brindley. illus tabs Interavia 31:976-978 Oct '76

F-15

(F-15) Eagle makes bow (during Red Flag III). AF Times 36:38 Mar 29 '76

F-15 fuel gravity transfer system. Glenn Harper. illus tabs TAC Attack 16:20-22 Nov '76

F-15 gear limit switch. Capt Dan Brown. TAC Attack 16:26-27 Jul '76

The F-15A Eagle program: A reliability case history. Donald Malvern. tabs Def Mgt J 12:40-45 Apr '76

Faith restored--the F-15 program. Maj Gilbert B. Guarino and others. illus AU Rev 27:63-77 Jan-Feb '76

AIRPLANE TYPE - Continued

F-15 - Cont'd

McDonnell-Douglas USAF F-15 air superiority fighter. illus tab NATO's Fifteen Nations 20:98 Dec '75-Jan '76

(USAF) strength in Europe to increase with F-15, F-111 moves. Len Famiglietti. AF Times 37:2 Nov 8 '76

Testing

F-15 passes latest tests. AF Times 37:30 Aug 23 '76

F-16
See also YF-16

(Collier Trophy awarded by National Aeronautic Assoc to David S.Lewis, chief executive officer of General Dynamics Corp, and to USAF-industry team that produced the F-16) illus Natl Def 61: 102-103 Sep-Oct '76

F-16. Capt George S.Gennin. illus (Also cutaways) tab USAF Ftr Wpns Rev, pp 1-8, Spring '76

F-16 ACF pilot report. Neil R.Anderson. illus tabs NATO's Fifteen Nations 21:24-32 Aug-Sep '76

The F-16 connection. George W.Deskin. illus tabs Elect Warfare pt 1, The backgrounder. 8:83-85+ Jul-Aug '76; pt 2, Marconi-Elliott HUDsight chosen for F-16. 8:101+ Sep-Oct '76

F-16: Fighter procurement essential to Iranian Air Force modernization. Robert Ellsworth. illus (Also cutaway) Comdrs Dig 19: entire issue Oct 21 '76

F-16 programme heads for December first flight. Michael Brown. illus (Also cutaways) tab Interavia 31:104-106 Feb '76

F-16: Swing-force fighter for the '80s. Capt Robert G.H.Carroll. illus AF Mag 59:30-35 Apr '76

Westinghouse starts full-scale development of the F-16 radar. illus NATO's Fifteen Nations 21:42-43+ Aug-Sep '76

Maintenance and Repair

The F-16 fighter--marvel of maintainability. Maj C.G.Kincaid and G.A.Cude. illus Natl Def 61: 116-117 Sep-Oct '76

F-18

The F-18. CAPT Hank L.Halleland, Ret. illus (Also cutaway) US Nav Inst Proc 102:123-127 Oct '76

F.18 multimission fighter/attack. illus tab NATO's Fifteen Nations 21:91-92 Jun-Jul '76

Flexible multimission avionics. illus Countermeasures 2:25-26+ Nov '76

Land-based F-18 programme firms up. illus tab Interavia 31:1060-1061 Nov '76

Northrop's YF-17 and F-18 fighters. (Design profile, no.22) Maurice Allward. illus tab Air Pict 38:129-134 Apr '76

The U.S. Navy's F-18 programme gathers momentum. tabs illus (Also cutaway) Interavia 31:627-629 Jul '76

F-101

Wahoo. illus Interceptor 18:5-9 Mar '76

AIRPLANE TYPE - Continued

F-104
Study and Teaching

The Luftwaffe + twenty. (German pilots train at Luke AFB, Ariz) LtCol Fred A.Meurer. illus Airman 20:2-8 Aug '76

F-105

Attack T(hunder)-stick style. Capt John C.Morrissey. (Reprinted from Fighter Weapons Newsletter, Dec 1967) illus USAF Ftr Wpns Rev, pp 21-27, Summer '76

Emergency situation training, F-105. Maj Al Adams. illus TAC Attack 16:28 Jun '76

Readiness through realism. LtCol James Glaza. illus Air Reservist 28:8-9 Aug-Sep '76

F-106

Air superiority tactics training. Capt Keith R.Talladay. illus tab Interceptor 18:20-23 Jan '76

F-111

F-111 nacelle fire analysis; Why the bold face emergency procedure was changed. LtCol Malcolm F. Bolton. illus Aerosp Safety 32:20-22 Apr '76

F-111 terrain following radar. Maj John Phillips. (Reprinted from USAF Fighter Weapons Newsletter, March 1969) illus USAF Ftr Wpns Rev, pp 11-13, Summer '76

(USAF) strength in Europe to increase with F-15, F-111 moves. Len Famiglietti. AF Times 37:2 Nov 8 '76

Galaxy
See C-5

HU-16

Airman gallery. Photo only. Airman 20: back cover Nov '76

Harrier
See AV-8

Hawkeye
See E-2

Hercules
See C-130; LC-130; WC-130

Huron
See C-12

Intruder
See A-6

KC-135

And now, a navigator in a box. (The Palletized Inertial Navigation System (PINS) is adding flight course accuracy to some AF tanker flights) MSgt Harold Newcomb. illus Airman 20:16-18 Jun '76

From props to jets. illus Air Reservist 28:8-9 Apr '76

LC-130

"Hercules unchained." CDR W.S.Kosar. illus map US Nav Inst Proc 102:151-153 Oct '76

Mitchell
See B-25

38

Mohawk
See OV-1

OV-1

The Hawk performs in Europe. Capt Michael F. Blacker. illus USA Avn Dig 22:6-7 Aug '76

OV-10

Picture day. LtCol William H. Rees. illus Interceptor 18:5-7 Sep '76

Ride the foam. illus Aerosp Safety 32:2-4 Apr '76

Orion
See P-3

P-3

ASW: The deterrent. F. Glenn Peters. illus Elect Warfare 8:49-50+ Jul-Aug '76

Lockheed's ASW market. (Modernization of P-3 Orion and current status of S-3A Viking) J. Philip Geddes. illus tabs Interavia 31:444-447 May '76

Look what's new! (Performance card) LTJG Bruce Arnold. illus Approach 22: inside back cover Sep '76

Phantom II
See F-4

RF-4

Don't let your Phantom blow its top. Capt Terryl J. Schwalier. illus TAC Attack 16:4-6 May '76

S-3

ASW: The deterrent. F. Glenn Peters. illus Elect Warfare 8:49-50+ Jul-Aug '76

DLC (Direct Lift Control) is here, finally! LCDR George Webb. tab illus Approach 21:1-3 Jun '76

Lockheed's ASW market. (Modernization of P-3 Orion and current status of S-3A Viking) J. Philip Geddes. illus tabs Interavia 31:444-447 May '76

New advances in doppler radar. Charles N. Bates. illus tabs Countermeasures 2:34-37 Apr '76

The S-3A Viking. CDR Rosario Rausa. illus US Nav Inst Proc 102:131-134 Oct '76

The Viking at home in the fleet. LT John P. Richman. illus Approach 22:12-14 Dec '76

SR-71

SR-71. illus Combat Crew 27:4-7 Oct '76

SR-71: 6 records. illus AF Times 37:3 Aug 9 '76

SR-71 takes aim at MIG-25 speed mark. AF Times 36:4 Jul 26 '76

Sabreliner
See T-39

Shooting Star
See T-33

Skyhawk
See A-4

Spectre
See AC-130

Starlifter
See C-141

Stratofortress
See B-52

Stratotanker
See KC-135

T-28

Unscheduled road recce. illus Approach 21:24-26 Mar '76

T-33

Egress news for the T-bird (T-33). LtCol Everett R. Patterson. illus Interceptor 18:5-7 Feb '76

Fond farewell to Lockheed's racer (T-33). Maj Tim Kline. illus Aerosp Hist 23:7-9 Mar '76

T-bird sweepstakes. LtCol William H. Rees. illus Interceptor 18:10-11 Dec '76

T-38

T-38 outfitted with minigun may take on new mission. AF Times 36:41 Jan 5 '76

T-39

Did I do something wrong, coach? WgComdr Mark Perrett. illus Aerosp Safety 32:13 May '76

T-43

Catching up with today. (New methods and equipment for training USAF navigators at Mather AFB, Calif) Ted R. Sturm. illus Airman 20:39-43 Apr '76

TFX
See F-111

Talon
See T-38

Thunderchief
See F-105

Tomcat
See F-14

Tracer
See E-1

Trojan
See T-28

U-2
See WU-2

V-1
See OV-1

V-10
See OV-10

VFX
See F-14

VSX
See S-3

Vigilante
See A-5

Viking
See S-3

AIRPLANE TYPE - Continued

Voodoo

See F-101

WC-130

The AWRS (Air Weather Reconnaissance Sq) nav(igation) subsystem. Maj Thomas R. Roll. illus Navigator 23:20-21 Summer '76

WU-2

Learning to land the U-2(CT). Capt Glenn Perry II. illus tab AF Mag 59:42-45 Jan '76

The view from a U-2. (The 349th Strategic Reconnaissance Sq from Davis-Monthan AFB, Ariz, flies over Guatemala to survey and describe earthquake damage) Capt Robert W. Gaskin. illus Airman 20:14-15 Jun '76

YC-14

Boeing unveils first YC-14 short field transport aircraft. illus Def Trans J 32:53-54 Aug '76

New kid on the flight line. (YC-14 and YC-15 compete for the USAF AMST program) illus Airman 20: inside front cover Nov '76

Short takeoff and landing aircraft. (Remarks, YC-14 rollout ceremony, Seattle, June 11, 1976) James W. Plummer. AF Pley Ltr for Comdrs: Sup No. 9: 22-24 Sep '76

Why its contestants think AMST is a good deal for the government. (Interview with AF program manager, LtCol Dave Englund) illus Govt Exec 8:43-44+ Apr '76

Testing

YC-14 put through paces. illus AF Times 37:28 Aug 23 '76

YC-15

McDonnell Douglas YC-15. (Design profile, no. 29) Maurice Allward. illus tab Air Pict 38:484-487 Dec '76

New kid on the flight line. (YC-14 and YC-15 compete for the USAF AMST program) illus Airman 20: inside front cover Nov '76

Why its contestants think AMST is a good deal for the government. (Interview with AF program manager, LtCol Dave Englund) illus Govt Exec 8:43-44+ Apr '76

YF-16

See also F-16

YF-16 pilot report. LtCol James G. Rider. illus tab AF Mag 59:32-37 Oct '76

YF-17

Northrop's YF-17 and F-18 fighters. (Design profile, no. 22) Maurice Allward. illus tab Air Pict 38:129-134 Apr '76

ZF-14

See F-14

AIRPLANES

See also
Aircraft, Experimental

Jane's aerospace review 1975/76. John W. R. Taylor. illus AF Mag 59:22-29 Jan '76

AIRPLANES - Continued

Accidents

See Accidents, Air; Accidents, Ground (Aircraft)

Air Conditioning

See Airplanes--Heating and Ventilation

Cabins

Study of the microbiological environment within long- and medium-range Canadian Forces aircraft. A. J. Clayton and others. illus tabs Aviation, Space & Envmt Med 47:471-482 May '76

Characteristics

Jane's All the World's Aircraft Supplement. Regular feature in issues of Aerospace International; some issues of Air Force Magazine

Cockpits

Flight deck design--technology--money. illus Interavia 31:640-642 Jul '76

Optimization of crew effectiveness in future cockpit design: Biomedical implications. Siegfried J. Gerathewohl. illus tab Aviation, Space & Envmt Med 47:1182-1187 Nov '76

Control

See Flight Control Systems

Cost of Operation

Civil transport technology up to 2000: NASA believes fuel consumption is the major consideration. J. Philip Geddes. illus tabs Interavia 31:419-421 May '76

De-icing

See Airplanes--Ice Prevention

Design

Canadair CL-215. (Design profile, no. 21) Maurice Allward. illus tabs Air Pict 38:90-95 Mar '76

Electronic Equipment

See Electronic Equipment (Aircraft)

Emergency Procedures

Escape. LtCol Charles L. Pocock, Jr. illus Aerosp Safety 32:10-11 Jul '76

Incapacitation. Capt Luther R. Wilson. illus tab Combat Crew 26:8-11 Feb '76

Night flight. Capt Richard P. Keida. illus Aerosp Safety 32:18-19 Apr '76

Engines

See also
Gas Turbines (Aircraft)
Jet Engines

General aviation fuel--which is right? Maj Philip M. McAtee. illus tab Aerosp Safety 32:6-7 Nov '76

Fires and Fire Prevention

Making headway with aircraft fire fighting: A report on the 1st International Seminar on Aircraft Rescue and Fire Fighting (Geneva, Sep 13-17, 1976). illus tab Interavia 31:1098-1099 Nov '76

AIRPLANES - Continued

Fuels

Civil transport technology up to 2000: NASA believes fuel consumption is the major consideration. J. Philip Geddes. illus tabs Interavia 31:419-421 May '76

General aviation fuel--which is right? Maj Philip M. McAtee. illus tab Aerosp Safety 32:6-7 Nov '76

Heating and Ventilation

Study of the microbiological environment within long- and medium-range Canadian Forces aircraft. A. J. Clayton and others. illus tabs Aviation, Space & Envmt Med 47:471-482 May '76

Ice Prevention

A trace of disaster. LtCol Robert J. Brun. illus Aerosp Safety 32:17 Feb '76

Inspection

See also
Preflight Inspections

Instruments
See Aeronautical Instruments

Interception

No evidence of (military pilot) intercepts (on civilian planes), says FAA. Ron Sanders. AF Times 36:11 Feb 16 '76

International Incidents

See also
Airplane Hijacking

Landing and Takeoff

See also
Automatic Landing Systems
Catapults
Ground-Controlled Approach
Hydroplaning
Microwave Landing Systems

Cold weather clues: Super slide. illus MAC Flyer 23: 10-11 Dec '76

Night flight. Capt Richard P. Keida. illus Aerosp Safety 32:18-19 Apr '76

Raindrops keep falling. MAC Flyer 23:11 Feb '76

A revolutionary all-weather HUD (Head-Up Display). (Thomson-CSF TC 125) Douglas Chopping. illus Interavia 31:548-549 Jun '76

"Sinking to ten ..." MAC Flyer 23:11 Jan '76

Turbulence technique. John B. Clark. illus tabs Combat Crew 27:10-15+ Aug '76

Wind shear: The mystery of the vanishing airspeed. Capt Barry Schiff. (Reprinted from AOPA Pilot, Nov 1975) illus Combat Crew 26:12-15 Feb '76; Interceptor 18:8-13 Jun '76

Launching
See Catapults

Maintenance and Repair
See Aircraft Maintenance

Manufacture
See Aircraft Industry and Trade

AIRPLANES - Continued

Modifications

More seats on (aircraft) charters seen as saving millions. AF Times 37:3 Nov 1 '76

Races

History

A long trail with no dust. (Dole Race to Honolulu, 1927) VADM W. V. Davis, Jr, Ret. illus Aerosp Hist 22:181-184 Dec '75

The racing Curtiss triplanes. Thomas G. Foxworth. illus Am Avn Hist Soc J 21:32-37 Spring '76

Refueling

See also
In-Flight Refueling

Restoration

Guarding the victory at Silver Hill (Md, the Smithsonian's National Air and Space Museum Preservation and Restoration Facility). Lawrence Noriega and Ronald Carriker. illus Aerosp Hist 23:28-35 Mar '76

Safety Measures

See also
Flying Safety

Escape. LtCol Charles L. Pocock, Jr. illus Aerosp Safety 32:10-11 Jul '76

Stability

Turbulence technique. John B. Clark. illus tabs Combat Crew 27:10-15+ Aug '76

Stalling

Attitude. LtCol Robert J. Brun. illus Aerosp Safety 32:8-9 Apr '76

Takeoff
See Airplanes, Military--Landing and Takeoff

Windshields

Low-cost panoramic vision. illus Aerosp Intl 12:58 Mar-Apr '76

Great Britain

History

Avro 536 K-105. (Aeroplane biography, no. 8) Peter W. Moss. illus Air Pict 38:179 May '76

The CHW (Charles Horace Watkins) monoplane. Acting Pilot Officers T. M. Winn-Morgan and M. A. Barker. illus tab Royal Air Forces Qtr 16:264-271 Autumn '76

United States

History

The Air Kings of Lomax. Paul D. Stevens. illus tabs Am Avn Hist Soc J 21:263-268 Winter '76

The aircraft history of Northwest Airlines. David Galbraith. illus map tabs Am Avn Hist Soc J 21: 241-256 Winter '76

American birdmen in the Philippines, 1912-1913. Enrique B. Santos. illus Am Avn Hist Soc J 21: 26-30 Spring '76

AIRPLANES, AMPHIBIOUS

See also
Airplanes, Ski-Equipped
Seaplanes

Canada

Canadair CL-215. (Design profile, no.21) Maurice Allward. illus tabs Air Pict 38:90-95 Mar '76

AIRPLANES, BOMBER

Characteristics

Gallery of Soviet aerospace weapons: Bombers and maritime. illus AF Mag 59:94-95 Mar '76

Gallery of USAF weapons: Bombers. illus AF Mag 59:111-112 May '76

The threat: Badger TU-16. illus tab Interceptor 18: 20-21 Jun '76

The threat: Bear TU-95. illus tab Interceptor 18: 20-21 Aug '76

The threat: Bison M-4. illus tab Interceptor 18:20-21 Jul '76

History

The Handley Page agreement, 1918. John Bagley. illus tabs Am Avn Hist Soc J 21:38-45 Spring '76

Postwar use of Handley Page in U.S. John Underwood. illus Am Avn Hist Soc J 21:46-49 Spring '76

The three victories of the bomber offensive (WW II). Marshal Arthur T. Harris, Ret. AF Mag 59:36+ Dec '76

Great Britain

History

Bristol Buckingham. Michael J. F. Bowyer. tabs illus (Also cutaway) Air Pict 38:446-453 Nov '76

Recover one Skua. (The story of L2940) Elfan ap Rees. illus Air Pict 38:279-280 Jul '76

Russia

Gallery of Soviet aerospace weapons: Bombers and maritime. illus AF Mag 59:94-95 Mar '76

The threat: Badger TU-16. illus tab Interceptor 18: 20-21 Jun '76

The threat: Bear TU-95. illus tab Interceptor 18: 20-21 Aug '76

The threat: Bison M-4. illus tab Interceptor 18:20-21 Jul '76

United States

ATCA (Advanced Tanker Cargo Aircraft)--key to global mobility. Edgar Ulsamer. illus (Also cutaway) map AF Mag 59:20-25 Apr '76

B-52--20th anniversary in SAC. illus Aerosp Hist 22:198-200 Dec '75

Gallery of USAF weapons: Bombers. illus AF Mag 59:111-112 May '76

History

AAF's flying artillery--the 75-mm Baker two-five. LtCol Jim Beavers, Ret. illus AF Mag 59:65-69 Apr '76; Fld Arty J 44:25-29 Jul-Aug '76

AIRPLANES, BOMBER (SUPERSONIC)

Characteristics

The B-1: Strategic deterrence into the twenty-first century. MajGen Abner B. Martin. illus tabs AU Rev 27:2-14 Mar-Apr '76

Backfire. illus tabs Interceptor 18:8-12 Apr '76

The threat: Blinder TU-22. illus tab Interceptor 18: 12-13 May '76

Russia

Backfire. illus tabs Interceptor 18:8-12 Apr '76

Backfire (Tu-V-G, new Soviet supersonic bomber): Strategic implications. Gerard K. Burke. illus tabs Mil Rev 56:85-90 Sep '76

The threat: Blinder TU-22. illus tab Interceptor 18: 12-13 May '76

United States

The B-1: First flight plus one year. Maj Mike Butchko. illus Aerosp Safety 32:10-14 Mar '76

The B-1 strategic bomber: A necessary weapons system. Maj R. O'Mara. illus tab Royal Air Forces Qtr 16:236-242 Autumn '76

The B-1: Strategic deterrence into the twenty-first century. MajGen Abner B. Martin. illus tabs AU Rev 27:2-14 Mar-Apr '76

The B-1: The right solution. (Remarks, Council of World Affairs, Dallas, April 15, 1976) Thomas C. Reed. AF Plcy Ltr for Comdrs: Sup No.6:2-9 Jun '76

Second B-1 joins flight test programme. illus Interavia 31:205 Mar '76

AIRPLANES, CARGO see
Airplanes, Military Transport
Airplanes, Military Transport (Jet)
Airplanes, Transport
Airplanes, Transport (Jet)

AIRPLANES, EXPERIMENTAL see Aircraft, Experimental

AIRPLANES, FAMOUS AND HISTORIC

Air circus. SSgt Zack Richards. illus Soldiers 31: 22-24 May '76

The CHW (Charles Horace Watkins) monoplane. Acting Pilot Officers T. M. Winn-Morgan and M. A. Barker. illus tab Royal Air Forces Qtr 16:264-271 Autumn '76

Caproni triplanes. Malcolm B. Passingham. Pictorial. Air Pict 38:264-265 Jul '76

Flying the early birds: The Curtiss Hawks. BrigGen Ross G. Hoyt, Ret. illus tab AF Mag 59:68-69 Oct '76

Guarding the victory at Silver Hill (Md, the Smithsonian's National Air and Space Museum Preservation and Restoration Facility). Lawrence Noriega and Ronald Carriker. illus Aerosp Hist 23:28-35 Mar '76

The P-26 (forerunner of the fighter-bomber). Ross G. Hoyt. illus Aerosp Hist 23:62-64 Jun '76

Piper Cub goes to war. Devon Francis. illus Am Avn Hist Soc J 21:72-79 Spring '76

AIRPLANES, FAMOUS AND HISTORIC - Continued

The racing Curtiss triplanes. Thomas G.Foxworth. illus Am Avn Hist Soc J 21:32-37 Spring '76

Rebels over the Rockies. Capt David V.Froehlich. illus Interceptor 18:16-19 Aug '76

Rebels with a cause. (Confederate Air Force is dedicated to finding, restoring, preserving and flying World War II airplanes) LtCol Fred A.Meurer. illus Airman 20:24-31 Feb '76

Reservists restore a rare one (Martin B-10 bomber). illus AF Times 37:55 Dec 13 '76

A Sandringham returns. Peter J.Bish. illus Air Pict 38:444-445 Nov '76

The search for Leon Klink (Lindbergh's barnstorming partner). Jack Keasler. illus map Am Avn Hist Soc J 21:92-100 Summer '76

The Wright brothers. Charles H.Gibbs-Smith. Royal Air Forces Qtr 15:311-316 Winter '75

AIRPLANES, FIGHTER

A study of crew workload in low-level tactical fighter aircraft. WgComdr W.J.Wratten. Royal Air Forces Qtr 16:119-121+ Summer '76

Armament

Air superiority (F-4) GIB (WSO, Weapon Systems Officer). Capt Roger E.Rosenberg. illus Navigator 23:18-19 Summer '76

Characteristics

Dassault-Breguet Super Etendard: Twelve months to first flight of production model. Michael Brown. illus tab Interavia 31:974-975 Oct '76

F-16. Capt George S.Gennin. illus (Also cutaways) tab USAF Ftr Wpns Rev, pp 1-8, Spring '76

F-16 programme heads for December first flight. Michael Brown. illus (Also cutaways) tab Interavia 31:104-106 Feb '76

F.18 multimission fighter/attack. illus tab NATO's Fifteen Nations 21:91-92 Jun-Jul '76

Fitter C--link between 2d and 3d generation Soviet attack aircraft. illus tabs Intl Def Rev 9:167-169 Apr '76; Condensation. Interavia 31:557-558 Jun '76

Gallery of Soviet aerospace weapons: Attack aircraft. illus AF Mag 59:98-99 Mar '76

Gallery of Soviet aerospace weapons: Fighters. illus AF Mag 59:96-98 Mar '76

Gallery of USAF weapons: Fighters. illus AF Mag 59: 112-114 May '76

Israel introduces the Kfir-C2. illus (Also cutaway) Interavia 31:782 Sep '76

Jaguar--new claws for the RAF. Richard E.Gardner. Royal Air Forces Qtr 15:305-309 Winter '75

McDonnell-Douglas USAF F-15 air superiority fighter. illus tab NATO's Fifteen Nations 20:98 Dec '75-Jan '76

Orao--detail changes for the production model. Nikolai Cherikov. illus tabs Intl Def Rev 9:343-344 Jun '76

The Orao Yugoslav-Romanian combat aircraft. Nikolai Cherikov. illus tabs Interavia 31:739-740 Aug '76

AIRPLANES, FIGHTER - Continued

Characteristics - Cont'd

The real story behind Foxbat. (The arrival of Soviet Air Force Lt Viktor Belenko in a MIG-25 Foxbat interceptor at the Hakodate air terminal on Japan's Hokkaido Island in Sep) illus AF Mag 59:34 Dec '76

The SU-19 Fencer--threat to Western Europe. Georg Panyalev. illus map tabs Intl Def Rev 9:67-69 Feb '76

The Shenyang F-9 combat aircraft. Nikolai Cherikov. illus tab Intl Def Rev 9:714-716 Oct '76; Interavia 31:1160-1162 Dec '76

Sukhoi Su-7B. Mark Lambert. (Condensed from Flight International, March 13, 1975) illus Air Def Mag, pp 26-27, Jul-Sep '76

The threat: Flogger MIG-23. Capt David V.Froehlich. illus tab Interceptor 18:20-21 Nov '76

The threat (MIG-25 Foxbat). Capt David V.Froehlich. illus tab Interceptor 18:5-7 Dec '76

The threat (Mikoyan MIG 17, 19, and 21). Capt David V.Froehlich. illus tab Interceptor 18:20-23 Oct '76

Design

F-16 programme heads for December first flight. Michael Brown. illus (Also cutaways) tab Interavia 31:104-106 Feb '76

Northrop's YF-17 and F-18 fighters. (Design profile, no.22) Maurice Allward. illus tab Air Pict 38:129-134 Apr '76

Engines

F-14--weapon system in search of its engine. RADM John S.Christiansen, Ret. illus US Nav Inst Proc 102:103-105 Dec '76

SNECMA M.53 status report. Marc Grangier. illus Interavia 31:409 May '76

Tornado programme slowed by engine delays. illus Interavia 31:1062 Nov '76

Performance

Drag, weight, and G in ACM (Air Combat Maneuvering). LT Ross Burgess. illus Approach 21:12-14 Dec '75

Open letter to A-10 drivers. LtCol Dale Tabor. illus TAC Attack 16:4-7 Aug '76

Piloting

A mistake in flight. Col V.Pokrovsky. Soviet Mil Rev No.1:28-29 Jan '76

Open letter to A-10 drivers. LtCol Dale Tabor. illus TAC Attack 16:4-7 Aug '76

Wahoo. illus Interceptor 18:5-9 Mar '76

Study and Teaching

Top Gun--the Navy's "MIG-killing" school. (Navy Fighter Weapons School, Miramar NAS, Calif) CAPT Andrew Hamilton, Ret. illus US Nav Inst Proc 102:95-97 Jan '76

China (People's Republic)

The Shenyang F-9 combat aircraft. Nikolai Cherikov. illus tab Intl Def Rev 9:714-716 Oct '76; Interavia 31:1160-1162 Dec '76

AIRPLANES, FIGHTER - Continued

Egypt

Sukhoi Su-7B. Mark Lambert. (Condensed from Flight International, March 13, 1975) illus Air Def Mag, pp 26-27, Jul-Sep '76

Europe, Eastern

Orao--detail changes for the production model. Nikolai Cherikov. illus tabs Intl Def Rev 9:343-344 Jun '76

The Orao Yugoslav-Romanian combat aircraft. Nikolai Cherikov. illus tabs Interavia 31:739-740 Aug '76

Europe, Western

Jaguar Juggernaut: Flying Europe's new strike fighter. Gregory Copley. illus Def & For Aff Dig No. 11:7-9 '76

MRCA development tempo quickens. Douglas H. Chopping. illus tabs Intl Def Rev 8:828-831 Dec '75

MRCA (Multi-Role Combat Aircraft): Meeting its targets. John S. Phillip. illus Aerosp Intl 12:6-7+ Mar-Apr '76

Tornado programme slowed by engine delays. illus Interavia 31:1062 Nov '76

France

Dassault-Breguet Super Etendard: Twelve months to first flight of production model. Michael Brown. illus tab Interavia 31:974-975 Oct '76

SNECMA M.53 status report. Marc Orangier. illus Interavia 31:409 May '76

Great Britain

Battle flight Gutersloh. (RAF's Mark 2A Lightnings in Germany) Trevor Tarr. illus tab NATO's Fifteen Nations 21:84-88 Apr-May '76

Ground attack in a Jaguar. (Flying with the RAF today, no. 9) Dagmar Heller. illus Air Pict 38:397-400 Oct '76

Jaguar--new claws for the RAF. Richard E. Gardner. Royal Air Forces Qtr 15:305-309 Winter '75

Israel

Israel introduces the Kfir-C2. illus (Also cutaway) Interavia 31:782 Sep '76

Russia

And how good is the MIG-25? LtGen Ira C. Eaker, Ret. AF Times 37:13-14 Oct 4 '76

Fitter C--link between 2d and 3d generation Soviet attack aircraft. illus tabs Intl Def Rev 9:167-169 Apr '76; Condensation. Interavia 31:557-558 Jun '76

Gallery of Soviet aerospace weapons: Attack aircraft. illus AF Mag 59:98-99 Mar '76

Gallery of Soviet aerospace weapons: Fighters. illus AF Mag 59:96-98 Mar '76

How good is the MIG-21? Mark Lambert. illus (Also cutaway) US Nav Inst Proc 102:98-101 Jan '76

The real story behind Foxbat. (The arrival of Soviet Air Force Lt Viktor Belenko in a MIG-25 Foxbat interceptor at the Hakodate air terminal on Japan's Hokkaido Island in Sep) illus AF Mag 59:34 Dec '76

AIRPLANES, FIGHTER - Continued

Russia - Cont'd

The SU-19 Fencer--threat to Western Europe. Georg Panyalev. illus map tabs Intl Def Rev 9:67-69 Feb '76

The Shenyang F-9 combat aircraft. Nikolai Cherikov. illus tab Intl Def Rev 9:714-716 Oct '76; Interavia 31:1160-1162 Dec '76

The threat: Flogger MIG-23. Capt David V. Froehlich. illus tab Interceptor 18:20-21 Nov '76

The threat (MIG-25 Foxbat). Capt David V. Froehlich. illus tab Interceptor 18:5-7 Dec '76

The threat (Mikoyan MIG 17, 19, and 21). Capt David V. Froehlich. illus tab Interceptor 18:20-23 Oct '76

What we learned from MIG (25). LtGen Ira C. Eaker, Ret. AF Times 37:13-14 Oct 25 '76

History

Duel of designers. (Development of Soviet aviation equipment before and during the Great Patriotic War) Mikhail Arlazorov. illus Soviet Mil Rev No. 1:50-52 Jan '76

United States

F-16: Fighter procurement essential to Iranian Air Force modernization. Robert Ellsworth. illus (Also cutaway) Comdrs Dig 19: entire issue Oct 21 '76

Faith restored--the F-15 program. Maj Gilbert B. Guarino and others. illus AU Rev 27:63-77 Jan-Feb '76

Gallery of USAF weapons: Fighters. illus AF Mag 59: 112-114 May '76

Is EW still a Pentagon stepchild? Harry F. Eustace. illus Elect Warfare 8:28-29+ Jul-Aug '76

History

Douglas F4D-1 Skyray record flights. Nicholas M. Williams. illus map tab Am Avn Hist Soc J 21: 50-60 Spring '76

The P-26 (forerunner of the fighter-bomber). Ross G. Hoyt. illus Aerosp Hist 23:62-64 Jun '76

AIRPLANES, GUNSHIP see Gunships

AIRPLANES, JET-PROPELLED

See also
Airplanes, Military Transport (Jet)
Airplanes, Transport (Jet)

Jacks of all trades (modern jet trainers). Stefan Geisenheyner. illus tab Aerosp Intl 12:4-7+ Jan-Feb '76

Piloting

Fly your own jet! LTJG D. A. Abner. illus Approach 21:29 Dec '75

United States

Century III series (of six new Learjets). Richard S. Page. illus Aerosp Intl 12:28-29 May-Jun '76

AIRPLANES, LIGHT

See also
Airplanes in Agriculture
Airplanes in Business

AIRPLANES, LIGHT - Continued

The economics of light aircraft production. Rolf H. Wild. illus tabs Interavia 31:224-226 Mar '76

Farnborough (Air Show, Sep 1976): General aviation was there too. illus Interavia 31:1055-1056 Nov '76

Performance

Flying the Rockwell Turbo Commander 690A. Douglas H.Chopping. illus tab Interavia 31:231-232 Mar '76

Piloting

Light aircraft flying can be fun. Capt Marty Steere. illus TAC Attack 16:6-7 Jul '76

Safety is no accident--the first commandment: Guidelines for light aircraft pilots. tab illus Interavia 31:233-234 Mar '76

Great Britain

Evans VP-1. Air Commodore Christopher Paul. tab illus (Also cutaway) Air Pict 38:110-112 Mar '76

Jurca M. J.2A Tempête. Air Commodore Christopher Paul. illus tab Air Pict 38:194-196 May '76

United States

The U.S. general aviation market--a decade of solid growth is forecast. illus tabs Interavia 31:567-569 Jun '76

History

Piper Cub goes to war. Devon Francis. illus Am Avn Hist Soc J 21:72-79 Spring '76

AIRPLANES, MILITARY

See also specific categories of military airplanes, e.g.,
Airplanes, Bomber   Airplanes, Trainer
Airplanes, Fighter   Gunships
Airplanes, Reconnaissance   Targets, Aerial
also entries on U.S. military planes by model designation under the specific type, e.g.,
Airplane Type--B-1

Air power: A perspective on fighting aircraft. David Harvey and Gregory Copley. illus Def & For Aff Dig No.4:14-18+ '76

Born to fly. LtCol Robert T.Howard, Ret. illus Combat Crew 26:4-7 Feb '76

The military aircraft scene. illus Interavia 31:115 Feb '76

Accidents
See Accidents, Air; Accidents, Ground (Aircraft)

Armament

History

AAF's flying artillery--the 75-mm Baker two-five. LtCol Jim Beavers, Ret. illus AF Mag 59:65-69 Apr '76; Fld Arty J 44:25-29 Jul-Aug '76

Arresting Gear

Stopping on the runway. Capt Gary A.Voellger. illus tab Aerosp Safety 32:6-8 Feb '76

Brakes

A-7 emergency brake problems. LT Carl Tankersley. illus Approach 21:15 Jan '76

AIRPLANES, MILITARY - Continued

Brakes - Cont'd

The "brakes" of naval air. illus Approach 21:19 Feb '76

Runway surface hazards. Capt Dannie O.Burk. illus tabs Aerosp Safety 32:8-11 Nov '76

Stopping on the runway. Capt Gary A.Voellger. illus tab Aerosp Safety 32:6-8 Feb '76

Canopies

(The aircraft was in the hangar awaiting work when) the canopy was jettisoned. illus Approach 22:21 Nov '76

Don't let your Phantom blow its top. Capt Terryl J. Schwalier. illus TAC Attack 16:4-6 May '76

Characteristics

The A-10 does it better. Maj John F.Gulick. illus tab AF Mag 59:75-79 Jul '76

Gallery of USAF weapons: Attack and observation aircraft. illus AF Mag 59:114-115 May '76

Jane's All the World's Aircraft Supplement. Regular feature in issues of Aerospace International; some issues of Air Force Magazine

Coatings

Aircraft washing versus touchup painting. TIG Brief 28:20 Dec 3 '76

Cockpits

Crew protection (from birdstrikes which penetrate some portion of the cockpit enclosure). LtCol Frank B.Pyne. illus Aerosp Safety 32:24-25 Mar '76

Head-up displays. Stefan Geisenheyner. illus Aerosp Intl 12:8+ Jul-Aug '76

"No joy." Maj Jack Spey. illus Aerosp Safety 32: 10-11 Jun '76

Of empty cockpits, storage space, and things. Maj Lawrence E.Wagy. illus Aerosp Safety 32:6-7 May '76

Physiological effects of solar heat load in a fighter cockpit. Sarah A.Nunneley and Loren G.Myhre. illus tabs Aviation, Space & Envmt Med 47:969-973 Sep '76

Radar electro-optical display improvements. L.Wesley Hopper. illus tabs Countermeasures 2:96+ Sep '76

Combat Evaluation

Joint Technical Coordinating Group on Aircraft Survivability. Maj William A.Allen. illus USA Avn Dig 22:38-39 Jul '76

Control
See Flight Control Systems

De-icing
See Airplanes, Military--Ice Prevention

Design

The design and development of a military combat aircraft. B.R.A.Burns. illus tabs Interavia pt 1, Design for performance. 31:241-246 Mar '76; pt 2, Sizing the aircraft. 31:448-450 May '76; pt 3, Longitudinal stability and control. 31:553-556 Jun '76; pt 4, Lateral stability and control. 31:643-646 Jul '76

AIRPLANES, MILITARY - Continued

Design - Cont'd

History

Duel of designers. (Development of Soviet aviation equipment before and during the Great Patriotic War) Mikhail Arlazorov. illus Soviet Mil Rev No.1:50-52 Jan '76

(Pavel O.) Sukhoi: Pioneer Soviet aircraft designer. Jean P. Alexander. illus tab Air Pict 38:136-139 Apr '76

Detection and Recognition
See Airplanes, Military--Identification

Electrical Systems

Unscheduled road recce. illus Approach 21:24-26 Mar '76

Water/glycol: Fire hazard. Donald Gwynne. illus Aerosp Safety 32:7 Sep '76

Electronic Equipment
See Electronic Equipment (Aircraft)

Emergency Procedures

About aborts. Capt Dick Morrow. illus tab Aerosp Safety 32:6-7 Oct '76; TAC Attack 16:4-6 Oct '76

The accident that should have happened. LCDR G.L. Forsberg. illus Approach 22:1-3 Sep '76

B-52 in-flight emergency. Capt Stephen R. Schmidt. illus Combat Crew 27:16-17 Sep '76

Be prepared! SqLdr Mark Perrett. Aerosp Safety 32:3 Jan '76

A "bearing" on safety. LT Bob Fritsch. illus Approach 22:9 Sep '76

Birdstrikes ... and the ejection seat. Michael R. Grost. illus TAC Attack 16:4-6 Jan '76

Blacked out at 390. illus Approach 22:8-9 Oct '76

Critical 11 minutes. (Takeoff plus 3 and landing minus 8) Maj John R. Dockendorff. illus Combat Crew 27:4-7 May '76; Aerosp Safety 32:2-5 Sep '76

The decision. LtCol James A. Learmonth. Aerosp Safety 32:5 Oct '76

Disastrous bingo! illus Approach 21:18-21 Jan '76

Do you have a blown tire? Maj Dick Henderson. illus Interceptor 18:14-15 Sep '76

Dry lake landing (with faulty landing gear). Capt John E. Hemmer. illus Combat Crew 27:16-19 Aug '76

Engine hot, reaction cool. LCDR P. L. Leum. illus Approach 22:26-27 Dec '76

F-111 nacelle fire analysis: Why the bold face emergency procedure was changed. LtCol Malcolm F. Bolton. illus Aerosp Safety 32:20-22 Apr '76

GCA slow roll. illus Approach 21:5 Jun '76

Ground-to-air advice during aircraft emergencies. TIG Brief 28:6 Jun 18 '76

Hangar flying. Maj John R. Spey. illus Aerosp Safety 32:10-11 Feb '76

Hey blue four, I need help. Maj Charles Barr. (Reprinted from Aerospace Safety, Sep 1975) illus USA Avn Dig 22:37-39 Sep '76

AIRPLANES, MILITARY - Continued

Emergency Procedures - Cont'd

Hours of terror. Maj John O'Connor. illus MAC Flyer 23:3-5 Feb '76

Incapacitation. Capt Luther R. Wilson. illus tab Combat Crew 26:8-11 Feb '76

It couldn't happen to me ... LtCol Brooks G. Bays and others. illus Interceptor 18:24-27 Sep '76

Learning by doing. Capt Robert M. Hail. illus Aerosp Safety 32:10-13 Dec '76

A long 30 minutes (after engine cowling damage and necessary fuel jettisoning for a safe landing). illus Aerosp Safety 32:4-5 Jan '76

Midnight mass divert. LT John Stevenson. illus Approach 22:2-5 Dec '76

The night the world died (at Clark AB, RP). illus Approach 22:6-7 Oct '76

Nugget nightmare. illus Approach 22:18-20 Nov '76

On a night mission. (Pilot's courage and skill helped to save a supersonic missile-carrying plane) LtCol A. Sorokin. illus Soviet Mil Rev No.1:36-38 Jan '76

One of those days. illus Approach 21:6-7 Jun '76

One problem too many. illus Approach 21:24-26 Jan '76

Passenger assistance in emergencies. LtCol Robert J. Brun. illus Aerosp Safety 32:9 Feb '76

Ride the foam. illus Aerosp Safety 32:2-4 Apr '76

Runway foaming ... an extinct species. CDR R.C. Gibson. illus tab Approach 22:3-5 Aug '76

They said it couldn't be done! (Multiple emergency: Single-engine failure and utility hydraulic loss) illus Approach 22:14-15 Jul '76

Too late, too hot to survive. LCDR C.J. Sutherland. illus Approach 21:18-19 May '76

Two perceptions. Maj Thomas L. Sutton. illus Aerosp Safety 32:18-20 May '76

Unscheduled road recce. illus Approach 21:24-26 Mar '76

Upside down! And out of ideas? Maj Anthony Helbling, Jr. illus Aerosp Safety 32:21 Mar '76

What's a cubit? Maj R.B. Bateman. illus Aerosp Safety 32:1-4 Nov '76

When it rains. Capt Guy P. Sumpter. illus Aerosp Safety 32:12-13 Apr '76

Yaw, roll, and drag. (Outboard engine loss during or after liftoff) Maj Albert R. Barbin, Jr. illus tabs MAC Flyer 23:20-23 Feb '76

Your signal is bingo! LCDR K. E. Hughes. illus Approach 21:10-11 Nov '75

Study and Teaching

Emergency situation training, F-105. Maj Al Adams. illus TAC Attack 16:28 Jun '76

The instructor pilot. Capt Frank B. Mercy. illus Aerosp Safety 32:26-27 Jul '76

NATOPS (Naval Air Training and Operating Procedures Standardization) training: A total approach. LT Frederick D. Hansen. illus Approach 21:18-21 Dec '75

AIRPLANES, MILITARY - Continued

Emergency Procedures - Cont'd

Study and Teaching - Cont'd

Simulator emergency procedure training. Capt Bernard R.Smith, Jr. TAC Attack 16:8-9 Oct '76

Engines

See also
Gas Turbines (Aircraft)
Jet Engines

Aerospace (equipment). John Marriott. illus tabs NATO's Fifteen Nations 21:35-39+ Apr-May '76

Recovery of parts and teardown deficiency report exhibits. (Accident investigation) TIG Brief 28:5-6 Jul 16 '76

Maintenance and Repair

An aircraft engine container can be a bomb. TIG Brief 28:4 Dec 17 '76

Corrosion control of reciprocating aircraft engines. TIG Brief 28:8 Jun 18 '76

Did I do something wrong, coach? WgComdr Mark Perrett. illus Aerosp Safety 32:13 May '76

Engine installation. TIG Brief 28:10 May 21 '76

Foreign Object Damage (FOD). TIG Brief 28:6 Sep 10 '76

(Maintenance) records are dollars. TIG Brief 28:14 Nov 5 '76

O-ring know how. Capt Jon New. (Reprinted from Aerospace Safety, July 1975) tab illus USA Avn Dig 22:39-43 Jan '76

Equipment

Unapproved aircraft appliances. TIG Brief 28:15 Jul 2 '76

Fires and Fire Prevention

F-111 nacelle fire analysis: Why the bold face emergency procedure was changed. LtCol Malcolm F. Bolton. illus Aerosp Safety 32:20-22 Apr '76

Runway foaming ... an extinct species. CDR R.C. Gibson. illus tab Approach 22:3-5 Aug '76

Water/glycol: Fire hazard. Donald Gwynne. illus Aerosp Safety 32:7 Sep '76

Equipment

The P-15--soon to be the largest production crash-fire vehicle in existence. illus tab AF Engrg & Svcs Qtr 17:24-25 May '76

Fuel Systems

F-15 fuel gravity transfer system. Glenn Harper. illus tabs TAC Attack 16:20-22 Nov '76

Inflight failure of fuel boost pumps. TIG Brief 28:7 Sep 10 '76

Fuel Tanks

Potluck lubrication. TIG Brief 28:3 Jan 16 '76

Maintenance and Repair

Fuel tank Foreign Object Damage (FOD). TIG Brief 28:11-12 Jul 2 '76

Uncommanded drop tank droppings. TIG Brief 28:9 Aug 27 '76

AIRPLANES, MILITARY - Continued

Fuels

Costs

Only a couple of hundred pounds. (Fuel conservation) Capt Thomas F.King. illus Combat Crew 26:19-21 Feb '76

Where to go when fuel gets low. Maj Orlen L.Brownfield. illus tab MAC Flyer 23:22-24 May '76

Ground-Support Equipment

Did I do something wrong, coach? WgComdr Mark Perrett. illus Aerosp Safety 32:13 May '76

GSE (Ground Support Equipment): From yellow to dark green. TIG Brief 28:13 Apr 23 '76

Ice Prevention

Airframe icing takes its toll. illus Approach 21:16-17 Dec '75

Hold the ice, please. Maj Philip M.McAtee. illus Aerosp Safety 32:23-25 Dec '76

Ice and airfoils. (Reprinted from F-5 Technical Digest, Jan 1976) illus Aerosp Safety 32:26-27 Feb '76

"The ice man cometh." Capt David V.Froehlich. illus tabs Interceptor 18:8-11 Nov '76

A problem with ice. (Engine inlet icing) LtCol Charles R.Barr. illus Aerosp Safety 32:26-27 Mar '76

Identification

USN & USMC units and their identification codes. Duane A.Kasulka. illus tabs Am Avn Hist Soc J pt 1, 21:129-143 Summer '76; pt 2, 21:185-198 Fall '76

Insignia

Bicentennial parade. (Aircraft in commemorative markings) Gerald Markgraf. Pictorial. Am Avn Hist Soc J 21:290-296 Winter '76

Inspection

See also
Preflight Inspections

Anatomy of a TCTO (Time Compliance Technical Order). Capt Marty Steere. illus TAC Attack 16:20-21 Sep '76

Improved maintenance inspection (with neutron-radiography). Maj Vincent G.Ripoll. illus USA Avn Dig 22:44-45 Mar '76

Weapons release systems inspections. TIG Brief 28:5 May 21 '76

Instruments
See Aeronautical Instruments

Interception

Sync-z-turn (intercept technique). Maj Milan Zimer. illus tabs USAF Ftr Wpns Rev, pp 26-30, Spring '76

Target detected ... lock-on! Col D.Sulyanov. Soviet Mil Rev No.5:34-35 May '76

AIRPLANES, MILITARY - Continued

Landing and Takeoff

See also
Automatic Landing Systems
Catapults
Ground-Controlled Approach
Hydroplaning
Microwave Landing Systems

A-4 spoilers. illus Approach 21:24-25 May '76

About aborts. Capt Dick Morrow. illus tab Aerosp
Safety 32:6-7 Oct '76; TAC Attack 16:4-6 Oct '76

Airframe icing takes its toll. illus Approach 21:
16-17 Dec '75

Approaches are for navigators, too. ENS S.W.
Braisted. illus Approach 21:20-22 Feb '76

An audiovisual approach to strange (air) fields. illus
MAC Flyer 23:16-17 Mar '76

Comprehensive (formerly master) Plan Tabs and
TERminal instrument Procedures (TERPs). TIG
Brief 28:13 Nov 19 '76

Critical 11 minutes. (Takeoff plus 3 and landing
minus 8) Maj John R.Dockendorff. illus Combat
Crew 27:4-7 May '76; Aerosp Safety 32:2-5 Sep '76

DLC (Direct Lift Control) is here, finally! LCDR
George Webb. tab illus Approach 21:1-3 Jun '76

Danger area--look out. Maj Jack Spey. illus Aerosp
Safety 32:8-9 Sep '76

Death at the ramp. illus Approach 21:26-27 Feb '76

Descent decisions. Capt Mike C.Kostelnik. illus tabs
TAC Attack 16:12-14 Oct '76

Disastrous bingo! illus Approach 21:18-21 Jan '76

Dry lake landing (with faulty landing gear). Capt John
E.Hemmer. illus Combat Crew 27:16-19 Aug '76

Fear of the first brick (on a wet runway). LtCol Jim
Learmonth. illus Aerosp Safety 32:1 Aug '76

Flight violation! LT Dave McPherson. illus Approach
22:12-13 Jul '76

Fly your own jet! LTJG D.A.Abner. illus Approach
21:29 Dec '75

GCA slow roll. illus Approach 21:5 Jun '76

Getting it off the ground. illus Interceptor 18:5-7
Jun '76

How to prevent taxi accidents. TIG Brief 28:7-8
Dec 17 '76

How to prevent undershoot or landing short accidents. TIG Brief 28:9 Oct 22 '76

The "in-close" waveoff: An LSO's (Landing Signal
Officer) point of view. LCDR George Webb and
others. illus Approach 21:6-9 Feb '76

Just a simple error. (Change in altimeter setting)
illus MAC Flyer 23:23 Mar '76

The LSO Phase One School. LCDR Mick Sumnick.
illus Approach 22:14 Sep '76

Landing ... or getting it down. LtCol John P.Heffer-
nan. illus Aerosp Safety 32:4-5 Feb '76

Lost ... on a circling approach. Maj Brian C.Ber-
net. illus Aerosp Safety 32:22-23 Mar '76

AIRPLANES, MILITARY - Continued

Landing and Takeoff - Cont'd

Low-level wind shear. Maj Shirley M.Carpenter.
illus TAC Attack pt 1, 16:4-8 Sep '76; pt 2, Wind
shear on final approach. 16:18-22 Oct '76; pt 3,
Detecting and coping with wind shear. 16:8-13
Nov '76

MOVLAS (Manually Operated Visual Landing Aid
System) technique for pilots and LSOs. LCDR
Mike Mears. illus Approach 22:26-27 Sep '76

Maintaining aircraft control during takeoff/landing
emergencies. TIG Brief 28:11 Sep 24 '76

Midnight mass divert. LT John Stevenson. illus Approach 22:2-5 Dec '76

A mistake in flight. Col V.Pokrovsky. Soviet Mil
Rev No.1:28-29 Jan '76

The Navy and the Brodie (high-wire landing gear).
RADM George van Deurs, Ret. illus US Nav Inst
Proc 102:88-90 Oct '76

No letup (in unintentional wheels-up landings). illus
tab Approach 21:10-12 Jan '76

Nugget nightmare. illus Approach 22:18-20 Nov '76

Paddles to pilots, what now? LT Randy Leddy. illus
tab Approach 22:18-19 Dec '76

The peanut approach. LT Cameron B.Place. illus
Approach 22:8-10 Aug '76

Penetration and landing, company business only.
Capt Jim Jenchura. illus Combat Crew 27:16-17
May '76

Reviewing the fine print. Capt M.C.Kostelnik. illus
TAC Attack 16:22-24 Jul '76

Ride the foam. illus Aerosp Safety 32:2-4 Apr '76

Runway foaming ... an extinct species. CDR R.C.
Gibson. illus tab Approach 22:3-5 Aug '76

Runway surface hazards. Capt Dannie O.Burk. illus
tabs Aerosp Safety 32:8-11 Nov '76

The second time around. Maj Jack Spey. illus Aerosp
Safety 32:16-18 Aug '76

Stopping on the runway. Capt Gary A.Voellger. illus
tab Aerosp Safety 32:6-8 Feb '76

Surveillance radar approach Minimum Descent Altitude (MDA) for circling approaches. TIG Brief
28:8 Nov 19 '76

There are no dragons. (Landing at Taipei, Hong
Kong, or Manila) Maj Jack Spey. illus Aerosp
Safety 32:14-15 Oct '76

Thirty ways to crunch an A-7 (or any other type of
carrier aircraft). LCDR Jim White. illus Approach 22:16-17 Sep '76

Thrice is nice. (Crosswind corrections) Capt M.C.
Kostelnik. illus TAC Attack 16:28-30 Dec '76

'Unclear' clear zone. TIG Brief 28:3 Feb 13 '76

Unscheduled road recce. illus Approach 21:24-26
Mar '76

The Viking at home in the fleet. LT John P.Richman.
illus Approach 22:12-14 Dec '76

AIRPLANES, MILITARY - Continued

Landing and Takeoff - Cont'd

Visibility--to land or not to land. Capt John L. Wilson. illus Combat Crew pt 1, 27:22-23 Aug '76; pt 2, The runway environment. 27:18-20 Sep '76; pt 3, The rules. 27:26-27 Oct '76; pt 4, Going visual. 27:20-21 Nov '76; pt 5, Techniques. 27: 14-15 Dec '76

What do you hear? Capt Jerry E. Walker. Aerosp Safety 32:5 Aug '76

What every pilot should know about PFC (Porous Friction Course). Capt Richard E. Simmons. illus MAC Flyer 23:10-11 Nov '76

What's a good carrier aviator? LCDR Michael N. Matton. illus Approach 21:20-21 May '76

What's your approach plate IQ? LT Bob Harler. illus Approach 22:10-12 Oct '76

What's your viewpoint (when you're trying to land an airplane)? illus MAC Flyer 23:7-8 Oct '76

Yaw, roll, and drag. (Outboard engine loss during or after liftoff) Maj Albert R. Barbin, Jr. illus tabs MAC Flyer 23:20-23 Feb '76

Your signal is bingo! LCDR K.E. Hughes. illus Approach 21:10-11 Nov '75

Landing Gear

Dry lake landing (with faulty landing gear). Capt John E. Hemmer. illus Combat Crew 27:16-19 Aug '76

F-15 gear limit switch. Capt Dan Brown. TAC Attack 16:26-27 Jul '76

Ride the foam. illus Aerosp Safety 32:2-4 Apr '76

Launching
See Catapults

Lighting

ILSAA: Improved Lighting System for Army Aircraft Silas G. Garrett. illus USA Avn Dig 22:18-20 Jan '76

"No joy." Maj Jack Spey. illus Aerosp Safety 32: 10-11 Jun '76

Load Distribution

Aircraft weight and balance. Maj John E. Freitas. illus TAC Attack 16:10-12 Aug '76

Loading and Unloading

The competitive spirit of '76. (Aerospace Defense Command 1976 Weapons Loading Competition, Tyndall AFB, Fla) Capt Robert J. Perry. illus Interceptor 18:5-9 Jul '76

The number '1' team (in 1976 William Tell Weapons Loading Competition). illus Air Reservist 28:11 Aug-Sep '76

The Voodoo (Oregon's 142d Fighter Interceptor Gp) revenge (wins the 1976 Aerospace Defense Command's Weapons Loading Competition). illus Natl Guardsman 30:4-5 Jul '76

Maintenance and Repair
See Aircraft Maintenance and subdivision Maintenance and Repair under specific Airplane Types

AIRPLANES, MILITARY - Continued

Manufacture
See Aircraft Industry and Trade

Markings
See Airplanes, Military--Insignia

Modifications

The A-7: One aircraft or two? LCDR Ken Sanger. illus Approach 21:10-11 Jun '76

Look what's new! (Performance card) LTJG Bruce Arnold. illus Approach 22: inside back cover Sep '76

Unapproved aircraft appliances. TIG Brief 28:15 Jul 2 '76

Performance

The A-10 does it better. Maj John F. Gulick. illus tab AF Mag 59:75-79 Jul '76

Piloting

Aircraft empathy. illus Aerosp Safety 32:10-12 Aug '76

Cockpit UNs (UNaccountables). illus Approach 22: 24-25 Oct '76

Danger area--look out. Maj Jack Spey. illus Aerosp Safety 32:8-9 Sep '76

GCA slow roll. illus Approach 21:5 Jun '76

Hangar flying. Maj John R. Spey. illus Aerosp Safety 32:10-11 Feb '76

Keep your eyes on the road! LT Gary W. Garland. illus Approach 22:6-7 Sep '76

Lost ... on a circling approach. Maj Brian C. Bernet. illus Aerosp Safety 32:22-23 Mar '76

Low-level wind shear. Maj Shirley M. Carpenter. illus TAC Attack pt 1, 16:4-8 Sep '76; pt 2, Wind shear on final approach. 16:18-22 Oct '76; pt 3, Detecting and coping with wind shear. 16:8-13 Nov '76

The new abort pop-up criteria. Capt Marty Steere. tab TAC Attack 16:24-26 Oct '76

One problem too many. illus Approach 21:24-26 Jan '76

Radar-directed routing and terminal arrival depiction. LT Daniel E. Graham. illus maps Approach 21:1-4 May '76

Safety razor's edge? Maj Robert P. Bateman. illus Aerosp Safety 32:2-4 Mar '76

The second time around. Maj Jack Spey. illus Aerosp Safety 32:16-18 Aug '76

Situation awareness: One key to safety. Capt Larry Kanaster. illus Aerosp Safety 32:14-15 Dec '76

The story of G. CDR A. F. Wells. illus Approach 22: 22-23 Nov '76

They said it couldn't be done! (Multiple emergency: Single-engine failure and utility hydraulic loss) illus Approach 22:14-15 Jul '76

Thrice is nice. (Crosswind corrections) Capt M. C. Kostelnik. illus TAC Attack 16:28-30 Dec '76

(What is cockpit discipline?) What it isn't. Maj Albert R. Barbin, Jr. illus MAC Flyer 23:14-15 Apr '76

AIRPLANES, MILITARY - Continued

Piloting - Cont'd

Where to go when fuel gets low. Maj Orlen L. Brownfield. illus tab MAC Flyer 23:22-24 May '76

Wing low--sweet chariot. Capt Ron Langenfeld. illus Combat Crew 27:4-5+ Nov '76

Power Plants

See also
Airplanes, Military--Engines

Protection

Hurevac (hurricane evacuation) No. 1 and subsequent. CDR Harry Fremd. illus Approach 22:6-7 Jul '76

Recognition
See Airplanes, Military--Identification

Refueling

See also
In-Flight Refueling

Power cables too short on MD-3 generators. TIG Brief 28:3-4 Jul 16 '76

Reliability

The F-15A Eagle program: A reliability case history. Donald Malvern. tabs Def Mgt J 12:40-45 Apr '76

Reliability centered maintenance. TIG Brief 28:8 Jun 4 '76

Restoration

Guarding the victory at Silver Hill (Md, the Smithsonian's National Air and Space Museum Preservation and Restoration Facility). Lawrence Noriega and Ronald Carriker. illus Aerosp Hist 23:28-35 Mar '76

Rebels over the Rockies. Capt David V. Froehlich. illus Interceptor 18:16-19 Aug '76

Rebels with a cause. (Confederate Air Force is dedicated to finding, restoring, preserving and flying World War II airplanes) LtCol Fred A. Meurer. illus Airman 20:24-31 Feb '76

Reservists restore a rare one (Martin B-10 bomber). illus AF Times 37:55 Dec 13 '76

Safety Measures

See also
Flying Safety

(The aircraft was in the hangar awaiting work when) the canopy was jettisoned. illus Approach 22:21 Nov '76

Build your own safety system. LCDR Charles D. Shields, Jr. illus Approach 21:10-11 Dec '75

F-15 fuel gravity transfer system. Glenn Harper. illus tabs TAC Attack 16:20-22 Nov '76

Hold the ice, please. Maj Philip M. McAtee. illus Aerosp Safety 32:23-25 Dec '76

Hurricane in a barrel. LtCol Robert J. Brun. illus Aerosp Safety 32:24-25 May '76

Of empty cockpits, storage space, and things. Maj Lawrence E. Wagy. illus Aerosp Safety 32:6-7 May '76

AIRPLANES, MILITARY - Continued

Safety Measures - Cont'd

Out-of-control aircraft losses (precipitate conference under sponsorship of Naval Safety Center). Approach 21:14 Jan '76

The saga of the Humble Hummer (E-2). LT Cam Place. illus Approach 22:6-8 Dec '76

Special assignment airlift mission. TIG Brief 28:15 Feb 27 '76

Sunday afternoon cu(mulonimbus). Maj Orlen L. Brownfield. illus MAC Flyer 23:3-5 Apr '76

Thirty ways to crunch an A-7 (or any other type of carrier aircraft). LCDR Jim White. illus Approach 22:16-17 Sep '76

Trust (aircraft forms and the Exceptional Release (ER)). Capt Philip M. McAtee. illus Aerosp Safety 32:6 Sep '76

Unapproved aircraft appliances. TIG Brief 28:15 Jul 2 '76

Water/glycol: Fire hazard. Donald Gwynne. illus Aerosp Safety 32:7 Sep '76

Seats

Egress news for the T-bird (T-33). LtCol Everett R. Patterson. illus Interceptor 18:5-7 Feb '76

What's your viewpoint (when you're trying to land an airplane)? illus MAC Flyer 23:7-8 Oct '76

Spare Parts

We service what we sell. (USAF Logistics Command gives assistance and advice to foreign purchasers of U.S.-made military aircraft) Capt John B. Taylor. illus Airman 20:10-12 May '76

Stability

Aircraft weight and balance. Maj John E. Freitas. illus TAC Attack 16:10-12 Aug '76

Low altitude wind shear. illus Aerosp Safety 32:10-13 Sep '76

Low-level wind shear. Maj Shirley M. Carpenter. illus TAC Attack pt 1, 16:4-8 Sep '76; pt 2, Wind shear on final approach. 16:18-22 Oct '76; pt 3, Detecting and coping with wind shear. 16:8-13 Nov '76

Objects in motion: A look at the mechanics of wind shear. illus MAC Flyer 23:12-15 Sep '76

Overcontrol: Commanded or uncommanded? Col Neil L. Eddins. illus tabs TAC Attack 16:10-14 Sep '76

Wahoo. illus Interceptor 18:5-9 Mar '76

Stalling

A new look at aerodynamic coupling. 1stLt Mark N. Brown. illus Aerosp Safety 32:21-23 May '76

Upside down! And out of ideas? Maj Anthony Helbling, Jr. illus Aerosp Safety 32:21 Mar '76

What's a cubit? Maj R. B. Bateman. illus Aerosp Safety 32:1-4 Nov '76

Yaw, roll, and drag. (Outboard engine loss during or after liftoff) Maj Albert R. Barbin, Jr. illus tabs MAC Flyer 23:20-23 Feb '76

AIRPLANES, MILITARY - Continued

Takeoff
See Airplanes, Military--Landing and Takeoff

Testing

Test flight: The arena of truth. Grover Tate. illus Aerosp Safety 32:16-19 Nov '76

Tires

Aircraft tire damage due to grooved runways. illus Approach 21:16-17 Mar '76

Do you have a blown tire? Maj Dick Henderson. illus Interceptor 18:14-15 Sep '76

Maintenance and Repair

Tires and team work. TIG Brief 28:10 Mar 26 '76

Tracking
See Airplanes, Military--Identification

Weight

Aircraft weight and balance. Maj John E.Freitas. illus TAC Attack 16:10-12 Aug '76

Build your own safety system. LCDR Charles D. Shields, Jr. illus Approach 21:10-11 Dec '75

Wheels

A "bearing" on safety. LT Bob Fritsch. illus Approach 22:9 Sep '76

Maintenance and Repair

Unsatisfactory wheel bearing grease. TIG Brief 28:7 Oct 8 '76

Windshields

Crew protection (from birdstrikes which penetrate some portion of the cockpit enclosure). LtCol Frank B.Pyne. illus Aerosp Safety 32:24-25 Mar '76

Wings

A-4 spoilers. illus Approach 21:24-25 May '76

Great Britain

Aerospace (equipment). John Marriott. illus tabs NATO's Fifteen Nations 21:35-39+ Apr-May '76

Army Air Corps up to date. J.D.R.Rawlings. illus Air Pict 38:184-185 May '76

CINCUKAIR (Commander-IN-Chief United Kingdom AIR Forces): ACE's new one. illus NATO's Fifteen Nations 20:53-60 Dec '75-Jan '76

RAF front-line aircraft and missiles, 1st April 1976. Table only. Air Pict 38:175 May '76

Strike's silent targets. (Flying with the RAF today, no.5) Roger Lindsay. illus Air Pict 38:86-89 Mar '76

Israel

The Israeli Air Force. Zeev Schiff. illus map AF Mag 59:31-38 Aug '76

Italy

History

Bell Aircobra in the Italian service. Tullio Marcon. illus Am Avn Hist Soc J 21:200-201 Fall '76

AIRPLANES, MILITARY - Continued

Russia

Military production in the USSR. (Basic facts on each type of Russian weapon) Tables only. NATO's Fifteen Nations 21:46-47 Jun-Jul '76

Sukhoi's Su-19 Fencer combat aircraft. Georgiy Panyalev. illus tabs Interavia 31:255-256 Mar '76

History

(Pavel O.) Sukhoi: Pioneer Soviet aircraft designer. Jean P.Alexander. illus tab Air Pict 38:136-139 Apr '76

United States

Department of the Air Force Fiscal Years 1977 and 1978 aircraft procurement estimates. Table only. AF Plcy Ltr for Comdrs: Sup No.5;26 May '76

Gallery of USAF weapons: Attack and observation aircraft. illus AF Mag 59:114-115 May '76

New aircraft and missiles. (Presentation, Senate Appropriations Committee, Washington, March 18, 1976) LtGen Alton D.Slay. tabs AF Plcy Ltr for Comdrs: Sup No.5:10-28 May '76

The planes we (ANG/AFR) fly. Pictorial. Air Reservist 27:12-13 Dec '75-Jan '76

Tac air--history's most potent fighting machine. Edgar Ulsamer. illus AF Mag 59:22-26 Feb '76

USN & USMC units and their identification codes. Duane A.Kasulka. illus tabs Am Avn Hist Soc J pt 1, 21:129-143 Summer '76; pt 2, 21:185-198 Fall '76

History

Flying the early birds: The Curtiss Hawks. BrigGen Ross G.Hoyt, Ret. illus tab AF Mag 59:68-69 Oct '76

Flying the early birds: The SE-5. BrigGen Ross G. Hoyt, Ret. illus tab AF Mag 59:110-111 Sep '76

The Republic XR-12 Rainbow. Lin Hendrix. illus tab Am Avn Hist Soc J 21:282-285 Winter '76

Statistics

USAF force modernization sees 125 new planes FY 77. tabs Armed Forces J Intl 113:10 Apr '76

AIRPLANES, MILITARY TRANSPORT

Characteristics

Gallery of Soviet aerospace weapons: Transports. illus AF Mag 59:100-101 Mar '76

Gallery of USAF weapons: Transports and tankers. illus AF Mag 59:117-119 May '76

Europe, Western

Transall C-160. (Design profile, no.26) Maurice Allward. illus tabs Air Pict 38:316-319 Aug '76

Great Britain

Flight engineer on a Short Belfast. (Flying with the RAF today, no.6) Philip J.Birtles. illus Air Pict 38:144-149 Apr '76

History

De Havilland Flamingo: The airliner whose career was cut short by the war. Philip J.Birtles. illus tabs Air Pict 38:438-442 Nov '76

AIRPLANES, MILITARY TRANSPORT - Continued

Russia

Gallery of Soviet aerospace weapons: Transports.
illus AF Mag 59:100-101 Mar '76

United States

Gallery of USAF weapons: Transports and tankers.
illus AF Mag 59:117-119 May '76

The planes we (ANG/AFR) fly. Pictorial. Air Reservist 27:12-13 Dec '75-Jan '76

Costs

House panel (Appropriations Committee) scores 9.7-
billion dollar airlift hodge-podge. tab Armed
Forces J Intl 113:14-15 Jul '76

AIRPLANES, MILITARY TRANSPORT (JET)

Characteristics

Gallery of Soviet aerospace weapons: Transports.
illus AF Mag 59:100-101 Mar '76

Gallery of USAF weapons: Transports and tankers.
illus AF Mag 59:117-119 May '76

Landing and Takeoff

Fine tuning your INS (Inertial Navigation System).
LtCol Wallace E. Beebe and Capt Gerald R. J.
Heuer. illus Navigator 23:16-20 Winter '76

Takeoff

See Airplanes, Military Transport (Jet)--
Landing and Takeoff

Wings

C-5 flaws (largely wing modification) to cost $1.5
billion. (GAO report) AF Times 36:35 Jan 19 '76

Russia

Gallery of Soviet aerospace weapons: Transports.
illus AF Mag 59:100-101 Mar '76

United States

ATCA (Advanced Tanker Cargo Aircraft)--key to
global mobility. Edgar Ulsamer. illus (Also cutaway) map AF Mag 59:20-25 Apr '76

GAO: 'Lift ability is overestimated. AF Times 36:40
Jul 12 '76

Gallery of USAF weapons: Transports and tankers.
illus AF Mag 59:117-119 May '76

AIRPLANES, MODEL

At home air force. (SSgt Dave H. Donnelly builds
model airplanes which are specific and detailed)
TSgt Jim Schmidt. illus Airman 20:31 Dec '76

AIRPLANES, RECONNAISSANCE

Characteristics

Gallery of Soviet aerospace weapons: Reconnaissance,
ECM, and early warning aircraft. illus AF Mag
59:99 Mar '76

Gallery of USAF weapons: Reconnaissance and spe-
cial-duty aircraft. illus AF Mag 59:116-117
May '76

Hawker Siddeley's Coastguarder. (Design profile,
no. 27) Maurice Allward. illus tab Air Pict 38:
411-414 Oct '76

AIRPLANES, RECONNAISSANCE - Continued

Characteristics - Cont'd

Introducing the 1124 N Westwind to the military.
illus (Also cutaway) NATO's Fifteen Nations 21:
93 Jun-Jul '76

Great Britain

Hawker Siddeley's Coastguarder. (Design profile,
no. 27) Maurice Allward. illus tab Air Pict 38:
411-414 Oct '76

Israel

Introducing the 1124 N Westwind to the military.
illus (Also cutaway) NATO's Fifteen Nations 21:
93 Jun-Jul '76

Russia

Gallery of Soviet aerospace weapons: Reconnaissance,
ECM, and early warning aircraft. illus AF Mag
59:99 Mar '76

United States

Gallery of USAF weapons: Reconnaissance and spe-
cial-duty aircraft. illus AF Mag 59:116-117
May '76

The Hawk performs in Europe. Capt Michael F.
Blacker. illus USA Avn Dig 22:6-7 Aug '76

History

The Republic XR-12 Rainbow. Lin Hendrix. illus tab
Am Avn Hist Soc J 21:282-285 Winter '76

AIRPLANES, SKI-EQUIPPED

United States

"Hercules unchained." CDR W.S. Kosar. illus map
US Nav Inst Proc 102:151-153 Oct '76

Raven on the 'cap. (109th Tactical Airlift Group of
the Air National Guard flies resupply missions to
DEW-Line sites in Greenland) Maj Terry A. Arnold. illus Airman 20:2-8 Nov '76

AIRPLANES, SUBMERSIBLE see Submersible Vehicles

AIRPLANES, SUPERSONIC

See also
Airplanes, Bomber (Supersonic)
Airplanes, Transport (Supersonic)

United States

The technological case for a supersonic cruise aircraft. (Advanced Supersonic Technology/Super-
sonic Cruise Aircraft Research (AST/SCAR) program) Edgar Ulsamer. illus AF Mag 59:34-39
Jun '76

AIRPLANES, TANKER

United States

ATCA (Advanced Tanker Cargo Aircraft)--key to
global mobility. Edgar Ulsamer. illus (Also cutaway) map AF Mag 59:20-25 Apr '76

Gallery of USAF weapons: Transports and tankers.
illus AF Mag 59:117-119 May '76

Tanker task force operations (at Loring AFB, Me).
Col Kenneth M. Patterson. illus map Combat Crew
27:4-7+ Jul '76

AIRPLANES, TARGET see Targets, Aerial

AIRPLANES, TRAINER

Characteristics

Gallery of Soviet aerospace weapons: Trainers. illus AF Mag 59:101-102 Mar '76

Gallery of USAF weapons: Trainers. illus AF Mag 59: 119-120 May '76

Jacks of all trades (modern jet trainers). Stefan Geisenheyner. illus tab Aerosp Intl 12:4-7+ Jan-Feb '76

Europe, Western

Alpha Jet series (Frahco-German) production starts for 1978 deliveries: Sales campaign intensifies. Michael Brown. illus tabs Interavia 31:120-122 Feb '76

Great Britain

Dominie--trainer for the backroom boys. (No.6 Flying Training School, RAF Finningley) (Flying with the RAF today, no.8) Philip J.Birtles. illus Air Pict 38:358-360 Sep '76

Hawker Siddeley Hawk entering service this year. Derek Wood. illus (Also cutaway) tabs Interavia 31:116-119 Feb '76

Vickers Valetta WJ465. (Aeroplane biography, no.9) Peter W.Moss. illus Air Pict 38:278 Jul '76

Italy

Aermacchi's MB.326K. (Design profile, no.23) Maurice Allward. illus (Also cutaways) tabs Air Pict 38:188-191 May '76

Russia

Gallery of Soviet aerospace weapons: Trainers. illus AF Mag 59:101-102 Mar '76

United States

Crash rules out small (aircraft) trainer (BD-5J). AF Times 36:41 Jan 5 '76

Fond farewell to Lockheed's racer (T-33). Maj Tim Kline. illus Aerosp Hist 23:7-9 Mar '76

Gallery of USAF weapons: Trainers. illus AF Mag 59: 119-120 May '76

Greater emphasis placed on use of flight trainers. AF Times 36:22 May 10 '76

T-38 outfitted with minigun may take on new mission. AF Times 36:41 Jan 5 '76

AIRPLANES, TRANSPORT

Characteristics

A new member of the team (C-12A Huron). LtCol Robert F.Forsyth. tabs illus (Also cutaway) USA Avn Dig 22:24-27 Jul '76

History

Still going strong: The (DC-3) Dakotas of Lydd, Kent. Michael Hingston. Royal Air Forces Qtr 16:155-157 Summer '76

Australia

Introducing the N24 Nomad. illus Interavia 31:378 Apr '76

AIRPLANES, TRANSPORT - Continued

Great Britain

History

De Havilland Flamingo: The airliner whose career was cut short by the war. Philip J.Birtles. illus tabs Air Pict 38:438-442 Nov '76

Netherlands

The Fokker-VFW recipe for success: Slow but sure. John F.Brindley. illus tab Interavia 31:422-423 May '76

United States

History

The aircraft history of United Airlines. Barrett Tillman and Matthew Edward Rodina, Jr. illus tabs Am Avn Hist Soc J 21:169-184 Fall '76

Super Electra: Lockheed's model 14. Thomas M. Emmert and William T.Larkins. illus tabs Am Avn Hist Soc J 21:101-111 Summer '76

AIRPLANES, TRANSPORT (JET)

Atlantic cooperation or European surrender? Negotiations continue on future transport aircraft projects. Interavia 31:609-610 Jul '76

Farnborough (Air Show, Sep 1976): General aviation was there too. illus Interavia 31:1055-1056 Nov '76

The 1976 Reading (Pa) Show--better than ever. Howard Levy. illus Interavia 31:703-706 Aug '76

Characteristics

The Boeing 7N7 and 7X7 families. illus tabs Interavia 31:1057-1059 Nov '76

Design

Civil transport technology up to 2000: NASA believes fuel consumption is the major consideration. J.Philip Geddes. illus tabs Interavia 31:419-421 May '76

Ground-Support Equipment

Aircraft ground towing: Current advantages and potential technology. Robert W. and John P.Forsyth. illus tabs Interavia 31:725-728 Aug '76

Ground time costs money: Handling problems at airports. Klaus Höhle. illus tab Interavia 31:1148-1150 Dec '76

Piloting

Rendezvous at FL 350. illus MAC Flyer 23:16-17 Aug '76

Turbulence technique. John B.Clark. illus tabs Combat Crew 27:10-15+ Aug '76

Brazil

Embraer Bandeirante. (Design profile, no.24) Maurice Allward. illus tab Air Pict 38:218-222 Jun '76

Canada

The Lockheed JetStar II and the Canadair LearStar 600--aiming for the long-range market. Marc Grangier. illus tab Interavia 31:662-663 Jul '76

AIRPLANES, TRANSPORT (JET) - Continued

Europe, Western

The Airbus in the West Indies. Arthur Wallis. illus Interavia 31:298 Apr '76

Britain-Europe-America: Cooperation, but with whom? Derek Wood. illus Interavia 31:800-801 Sep '76

British aerospace: End of a chapter--or the book? tab illus Air Pict 38:345-348+ Sep '76

France

The Dassault-Breguet Falcon 50 programme: First flight in November 1976. Marc Grangier. tabs illus (Also cutaways) Interavia 31:383-385 Apr '76

Great Britain

The HS.125-700: The bizjet is alive and well. Derek Wood. illus tabs Interavia 31:707-708 Aug '76

Hawker Siddeley's fanjet HS 125-700. (Design profile, no.25) Maurice Allward. illus tabs Air Pict 38:258-263 Jul '76

Netherlands

The Fokker-VFW recipe for success: Slow but sure. John F.Brindley. illus tab Interavia 31:422-423 May '76

United States

The Advanced Short/Medium Range project: Will it become a reality? illus maps tabs Interavia 31: 1176-1178 Dec '76

The Boeing 7N7 and 7X7 families. illus tabs Interavia 31:1057-1059 Nov '76

The Boeing 727 goes on ... and on. John F.Brindley. illus tabs Interavia 31:1143-1145 Dec '76

Bringing air freight into the intermodal age. Russell T.Daly. illus Def Trans J 32:18-20+ Jun '76

The Cessna Citation spread its wings. illus tab Interavia 31:1033 Nov '76

The Lockheed JetStar II and the Canadair LearStar 600--aiming for the long-range market. Marc Grangier. illus tab Interavia 31:662-663 Jul '76

McDonnell Douglas YC-15. (Design profile, no.29) Maurice Allward. illus tab Air Pict 38:484-487 Dec '76

Rockwell Sabre 75A--flight report. Douglas Chopping. illus tabs Interavia 31:1087-1088 Nov '76

History

The Convair 880. Jonathan Proctor. tabs illus (Also cutaway) Am Avn Hist Soc J 21:202-213 Fall '76

The Convair 990. Jonathan Proctor. tabs illus (Also cutaway) Am Avn Hist Soc J 21:274-281 Winter '76

AIRPLANES, TRANSPORT (SUPERSONIC)

Europe, Western

British aerospace: End of a chapter--or the book? tab illus Air Pict 38:345-348+ Sep '76

Concorde enters service to good reviews: "New York is the key." (Interviews with Jean-Claude Martin, Alan Beaves and Doug Shore) illus Interavia 31: 424-426+ May '76

AIRPLANES, V/STOL

See also
Advanced Medium Short Takeoff and Landing Transport

V/STOL goes to sea. John S.Phillip. illus tab Aerosp Intl 12:24-26+ Jul-Aug '76

Why V/STOL? CAPT Gerald G.O'Rourke, Ret. illus US Nav Inst Proc 102:39-45 Jan '76

Characteristics

Alpha, Beta, and Theta Jay. (Problems in the new aerodynamics of the Harrier) LtComdr John Leng. illus Approach 21:1-3 Nov '75

Gallery of Soviet aerospace weapons: Experimental aircraft. illus AF Mag 59:102 Mar '76

Why its contestants think AMST is a good deal for the government. (Interview with AF program manager, LtCol Dave Englund) illus Govt Exec 8:43-44+ Apr '76

Great Britain

Harrier--the horizon widens. Derek Wood. illus tab Intl Def Rev 8:849-853 Dec '75

The need for a tactical VSTOL fighter. SqLdr J.D. Rust. illus Hawk No.37:41-45 Jul '76; Royal Air Forces Qtr 16:273-277 Autumn '76

The Vosper Thornycroft Harrier Carrier proposal. illus Intl Def Rev 8:853-854 Dec '75

Russia

Gallery of Soviet aerospace weapons: Experimental aircraft. illus AF Mag 59:102 Mar '76

An initial assessment of the Yak-36. illus Intl Def Rev 9:739-740 Oct '76

Kiev and the U.S. carrier controversy. Henry T. Simmons. illus tabs Intl Def Rev 9:741-744 Oct '76

Kiev--latest photos reveal new Russian V/STOL aircraft. illus Intl Def Rev 9:536-538 Aug '76

United States

(ADM James L.) Holloway discusses future needs; VTOL, Tomahawk head weapons list. L.Edgar Prina. illus Sea Power 19:9-10 May '76

Marine Aviation: Looking up (straight up). John Rhea. illus Sea Power 19:9-13 Nov '76

NASA's goal: Keeping the U.S. Number One in aeronautics. Alan M.Lovelace. illus AF Mag 59:36-40 Feb '76

V/STOL close air support in the U.S. Marine Corps. Col Stanley P.Lewis. illus US Nav Inst Proc 102: 113-116 Oct '76

V/STOL progress. Pictorial. US Nav Inst Proc 102: 148-149 Oct '76

Why V/STOL? CAPT Gerald G.O'Rourke, Ret. illus US Nav Inst Proc 102:39-45 Jan '76

AIRPLANES IN AGRICULTURE

Agricultural aviation in Brazil and India: A sharp contrast. illus tab Interavia 31:1158-1159 Dec '76

Sudanese sprayers at Southend. illus tab Air Pict 38: 415 Oct '76

AIRPLANES IN BUSINESS

Century III series (of six new Learjets). Richard S. Page. illus Aerosp Intl 12:28-29 May-Jun '76

The Cessna Citation spread its wings. illus tab Interavia 31:1033 Nov '76

The Dassault-Breguet Falcon 50 programme: First flight in November 1976. Marc Grangier. tabs illus (Also cutaways) Interavia 31:383-385 Apr '76

Flying the Rockwell Turbo Commander 690A. Douglas H.Chopping. illus tab Interavia 31:231-232 Mar '76

From the Cub to the Cheyenne: Interavia talks to Piper's J.Lynn Helms (on the current situation and the prospects for general aviation). illus Interavia 31:674-675 Jul '76

The HS.125-700: The bizjet is alive and well. Derek Wood. illus tabs Interavia 31:707-708 Aug '76

Hawker Siddeley's fanjet HS 125-700. (Design profile, no.25) Maurice Allward. illus tabs Air Pict 38:258-263 Jul '76

The Lockheed JetStar II and the Canadair LearStar 600--aiming for the long-range market. Marc Grangier. illus tab Interavia 31:662-663 Jul '76

NBAA business aviation showcase. (29th Annual Meeting, Denver, Sep 14-16, 1976) J.Philip Geddes. illus Interavia 31:1095-1097 Nov '76

The '75 NBAA (National Business Aircraft Assoc) show (New Orleans, Oct 29-31, 1975). illus Interavia 31:75-78 Jan '76

Rockwell Sabre 75A--flight report. Douglas Chopping. illus tabs Interavia 31:1087-1088 Nov '76

The story of a Beechcraft dynasty--from the King Air 90 to the King Air 400. Marc Grangier. illus tab Interavia 31:135-138 Feb '76

Transair France: Business aviation in action. illus Interavia 31:1004-1005 Oct '76

U.S. general and business aviation strides ahead in difficult economic climate. Marc Orangier. illus tabs Interavia 31:219-223 Mar '76

Exhibitions

NBAA business aviation showcase. (29th Annual Meeting, Denver, Sep 14-16, 1976) J.Philip Geddes. illus Interavia 31:1095-1097 Nov '76

AIRPLANES IN FIRE FIGHTING

Canadair CL-215. (Design profile, no.21) Maurice Allward. illus tabs Air Pict 38:90-95 Mar '76

AIRPLANES IN SCIENTIFIC RESEARCH

"Hercules unchained." CDR W.S.Kosar. illus map US Nav Inst Proc 102:151-153 Oct '76

AIRPORTS

Planning an airport disaster drill. Marvin B.Hays and others. Aviation, Space & Envmt Med 47:556-560 May '76

Design

Ground time costs money: Handling problems at airports. Klaus Höhle. illus tab Interavia 31:1148-1150 Dec '76

AIRPORTS - Continued

Equipment

Ground time costs money: Handling problems at airports. Klaus Höhle. illus tab Interavia 31:1148-1150 Dec '76

A total system for aviation security. Fred Dorey. illus Interavia 31:543-544 Jun '76

Landing Aids

An audiovisual approach to strange (air) fields. illus MAC Flyer 23:16-17 Mar '76

How to prevent undershoot or landing short accidents. TIG Brief 28:9 Oct 22 '76

Reviewing the fine print. Capt M.C.Kostelnik. illus TAC Attack 16:22-24 Jul '76

Visibility--to land or not to land. Capt John L.Wilson. illus Combat Crew pt 1, 27:22-23 Aug '76; pt 2, The runway environment. 27:18-20 Sep '76; pt 3, The rules. 27:26-27 Oct '76; pt 4, Going visual. 27:20-21 Nov '76; pt 5, Techniques. 27:14-15 Dec '76

Statistics

The world's principal airports: Traffic results 1974/1975. Table only. Interavia 31:500 Jun '76

Africa

Flight over Africa. (MAC survey team reports on African airfields) LtCol John W.Ray. MAC Flyer 23:6-7 Feb '76

China (Republic)

There are no dragons. (Landing at Taipei, Hong Kong, or Manila) Maj Jack Spey. illus Aerosp Safety 32:14-15 Oct '76

Hong Kong

There are no dragons. (Landing at Taipei, Hong Kong, or Manila) Maj Jack Spey. illus Aerosp Safety 32:14-15 Oct '76

Kenya

Nairobi: Safari gateway. P.J.Cooper. illus tabs Air Pict 38:268-274 Jul '76

Philippines (Republic)

There are no dragons. (Landing at Taipei, Hong Kong, or Manila) Maj Jack Spey. illus Aerosp Safety 32:14-15 Oct '76

Sweden

Bromma visited. John Stroud. illus Air Pict 38:310-314 Aug '76

United States

History

Round Hill (Mass) Airport. Wallace L.Smith. illus Am Avn Hist Soc J 21:126-127 Summer '76

AIRSHIPS

See also
Balloons

History

Dr August Greth and the first airship flight in the United States (Oct 18, 1903). Douglas H.Robinson. illus Am Avn Hist Soc J 21:84-91 Summer '76

AIRSICKNESS see Motion Sickness

AIRSPACE

Military Operating Area (MOA) spillouts. TIG Brief 28:12 Sep 24 '76

No evidence of (military pilot) intercepts (on civilian planes), says FAA. Ron Sanders. AF Times 36:11 Feb 16 '76

AIRSPEED see Air-Speed

AIRWAYS

Concorde enters service to good reviews: "New York is the key." (Interviews with Jean-Claude Martin, Alan Beaves and Doug Shore) illus Interavia 31: 424-426+ May '76

High-speed, low-level training routes. TIG Brief 28:8 May 21 '76

AKERS, Albert B.

Firepower. (Address, V Corps Artillery Firepower Conference, Giessen, Germany, March 19, 1976) BrigGen Albert B.Akers. Fld Arty J 44:17-21+ May-Jun '76

ALASKA

North to Nome. (TSgt Steve Fee represents Elmendorf AFB, Alas, in the Iditarod dog sled race) SSgt Joe Cardoza. illus Airman 20:30-34 May '76

Realistic exercise (Jack Frost 76) tests Alaska pipeline defense. Armed Forces J Intl 113:28 Jan '76

The village armories in Alaska. LtCol W.F.Gabella and SP5 Byron Wooten. illus Natl Guardsman 30: 26-27 Feb '76

Strategic Importance

Alaska's North Slope oil fields: Energy asset or defense liability? Col Lewis L.Simpson. illus map Mil Rev 56:33-44 Sep '76

ALASKAN AIR COMMAND

Alaskan Air Command. illus chart AF Mag 59:66-67 May '76

An operations cost index: Answer to the question "how much more?" (CONUS vs overseas cost differences) Capt Willard L.Mason. illus tabs AU Rev 27:61-71 Mar-Apr '76

The other side of the coin. (Many non-flying personnel were necessary for Operation Coin Alaska, airlift supply operation from Elmendorf AFB to AF and Navy installations on the North Slope) TSgt Tom Dwyer. illus Airman 20:38-42 May '76

Safety awards (presented to Alaskan Air Command and Air Training Command in recognition of the most effective accident prevention programs during 1975). TIG Brief 28:10 Apr 9 '76

ALASKAN COMMAND

14,000 taking part in Alaska Exercise Jack Frost. illus AF Times 36:38 Feb 2 '76

ALCOHOL AND ALCOHOLISM

Alcohol abuse and deglamorization. TIG Brief 28:12 Oct 8 '76

Alcohol abuse battle. AF Times 37:28 Sep 27 '76

Alcohol abuse efforts pushed (by House Appropriations Committee). AF Times 36:4 Jun 21 '76

ALCOHOL AND ALCOHOLISM - Continued

Alcohol awareness at the bases. MSgt Dave Sheeder and others. illus AF Times 37:23+ Nov 29 '76

Alcohol consultant (National Council on Alcoholism) hired (by AF). AF Times 36:10 Jul 5 '76

Alcohol countermeasures Screening Breath Tester (SBT) demonstration program (AFR 125-14). TIG Brief 28:17 Oct 8 '76

Alcohol in aviation: A problem of attitudes. Capt J.A. Pursch. illus USA Avn Dig 22:30-33 Nov '76

Alcohol inaction charged (by General Accounting Office). AF Times 36:31 May 3 '76

The alcohol problem and what the Army is doing about it. E.A.Lawrence. illus Army 26:23-27 Aug '76

Alcohol won't push drug program aside. AF Times 37:61 Oct 4 '76

Alcoholism today. AVM P.J.O'Connor. Royal Air Forces Qtr 15:319-320 Winter '75

Andrews (AFB, Md) gets Alcohol (Treatment) Center. AF Times 36:4 Jun 14 '76

Bars to jobs eliminated (for prior alcohol abuse). AF Times 37:26 Oct 18 '76

Belligerence mark of drunk driver. AF Times 36:38 Apr 12 '76

Bottled in booze. Darryl D.McEwen. illus Soldiers 31:47-48 Aug '76

Civilian drug and alcohol abuse control program. TIG Brief 28:10-11 Sep 10 '76

Dealing with drinking nonalcoholics. Maj W.D.Benner. MarCor Gaz 60:57-58 Dec '76

Don't ignore the problem drinker--lessons learned. TIG Brief 28:3-4 Jun 4 '76

Effect of ethyl alcohol on ionic calcium and prolactin in man. Jerry M.Earll and others. tab Aviation, Space & Envmt Med 47:808-810 Aug '76

The enlightened species: The emergence of a new image for aircrew members. LtCol Rich Pilmer and SSgt Joe Denhof. illus Combat Crew 26:28-29 Feb '76

Evaluation of Alcohol Safety Action Projects (ASAP) (AFR 125-14). TIG Brief 28:17-18 Oct 8 '76

Experts to examine alcohol problem. Len Famiglietti. AF Times 36:2 May 10 '76

Major new push (by AF) aimed at drinker. Len Famiglietti. AF Times 37:2 Nov 1 '76

Marines and alcohol. Maj H.J.Sage. MarCor Gaz 60:32-39 Dec '76

Moody maze saves lives (at Moody AFB, Ga). Capt Bob Revell. illus tab TAC Attack 16:12-13 Mar '76

New alcohol abuse control measures implemented. TIG Brief 28:5-6 Oct 22 '76

Pot still tops drugs in use. AF Times 36:8 Jan 5 '76

Putting the brakes on drinkers: New get-tough policy urged. AF Times 37:22 Nov 29 '76

Recovered alcoholics get help: Discrimination fought. Len Famiglietti. AF Times 37:61 Sep 20 '76

Reg (AFR 215-1, v.16) to discourage heavy drinking: Frowns on happy hours. AF Times 37:8 Nov 8 '76

ALCOHOL AND ALCOHOLISM - Continued

SPs planning alcohol tests (for drivers). AF Times
37:4 Aug 9 '76

Laws and Regulations

Taxation of Federal instrumentalities incident to
state regulation of intoxicants: The Mississippi
Tax Commission case. Capt Edward C. Hooks.
AF Law Rev 18:1-23 Spring '76

ALERT SYSTEMS

See also
Warning Systems

ALGERIA

The Green March (1975). C.G.White. Army Qtr 106:
351-358 Jul '76

The myth and reality of the paratrooper in the Algerian War. John E.Talbott. Armed Forces & Soc
3:69-86 Fall '76

ALIENS

See also
Foreign Nationals in the Armed Forces

ALL-TERRAIN VEHICLES

Goer--a comer to the inventory. Edward F. Young.
illus Army Log 8:24-25 May-Jun '76

Human response to buffeting in an all-terrain vehicle.
T. M. Fraser and others. tabs Aviation, Space &
Envmt Med 47:9-16 Jan '76

New Swedish cross-country logistics vehicles. Colin
E.Howard. illus tab Intl Def Rev 9:826-828 Oct '76

Wheels and tracks. M. G. Bekker. illus tabs Armor
85:15-20 May-Jun '76

ALL-WEATHER FLYING

The gap that must be bridged. (Tactical instrument
flight--will you be ready?) CW2 Alvin T.Kyle, Jr.
illus USA Avn Dig 22:4-5+ Aug '76

No time to gamble. map illus Interceptor 18:5-9
May '76

A review of helicopter IFR (Instrument Flight Rules)
operational considerations: The U.S. viewpoint.
Glen A.Gilbert. illus maps tabs Interavia 31:709-
713 Aug '76

A revolutionary all-weather HUD (Head-Up Display).
(Thomson-CSF TC 125) Douglas Chopping. illus
Interavia 31:548-549 Jun '76

ALLEN, James R.

Air Force Academy. por AF Mag 59:107-108
May '76

The Honor Code. (Statement, Subcommittee on Manpower and Personnel, Committee on Armed Services, U.S. Senate, June 22, 1976) LtGen James
R. Allen. AF Plcy Ltr for Comdrs: Sup No. 10:
27-31 Oct '76

ALLIANCES see Treaties and Alliances

ALLIED AIR FORCES, CENTRAL EUROPE see Allied
Forces, Central Europe

ALLIED AIR FORCES, SOUTHERN EUROPE see Allied
Forces, Southern Europe

ALLIED COMMAND ATLANTIC

Defence of North Sea energy sources: The military
aspects of the problem. Patrick Wall. illus map
NATO's Fifteen Nations 21:78-83 Apr-May '76

ALLIED COMMAND CHANNEL

The Channel Command, sea highway to Europe.
Comdr Joseph M.Palmer, Ret. illus map chart
US Nav Inst Proc 102:176-189 May '76

ALLIED COMMAND EUROPE

See also
Allied Forces, Central Europe
Allied Forces, Northern Europe
Allied Forces, Southern Europe
Supreme Headquarters Allied Powers in Europe

Allied Command Europe--25 years of a new military
tradition. Adm of the Fleet Peter Hill-Norton.
illus NATO's Fifteen Nations 21:35 Feb-Mar '76

CINCUKAIR (Commander-IN-Chief United Kingdom
AIR Forces): ACE's new one. illus NATO's Fifteen Nations 20:53-60 Dec '75-Jan '76

(Exercise) Atlas Express runs its chilly course. AF
Times 36:38 Mar 29 '76

Former SACEURs: The 25th anniversary of SHAPE
and Allied Command Europe. Gen Matthew B.
Ridgway and others. illus NATO's Fifteen Nations
21:36-39 Feb-Mar '76

SACEUR's subcommanders take the floor: The ACE
Mobile Force. MajGen John Groven. illus NATO's
Fifteen Nations 21:106-113 Feb-Mar '76

ALLIED FORCES, CENTRAL EUROPE

Allied team. (Brigade 76 will deploy to Europe to gain
combat proficiency in its North Atlantic Treaty
Organization role) MSgt Dick Larsen. illus map
Soldiers 31:6-10 Mar '76

Apprehension without fear. Interview. Gen Alexander
M.Haig, Jr. illus NATO's Fifteen Nations 21:
18-21+ Feb-Mar '76

SACEUR's subcommanders take the floor: The central region of ACE. Gen Karl Schnell. illus
NATO's Fifteen Nations 21:76-82+ Feb-Mar '76

ALLIED FORCES, NORTHERN EUROPE

Apprehension without fear. Interview. Gen Alexander
M.Haig, Jr. illus NATO's Fifteen Nations 21:
18-21+ Feb-Mar '76

NATO's tender watery flanks. Joseph Palmer. illus
Sea Power 19:34-39 Mar '76

SACEUR's subcommanders take the floor: Northern
European Command after 25 years. Gen John
Sharp. illus NATO's Fifteen Nations 21:68-74
Feb-Mar '76

ALLIED FORCES, SOUTHERN EUROPE

Apprehension without fear. Interview. Gen Alexander
M.Haig, Jr. illus NATO's Fifteen Nations 21:
18-21+ Feb-Mar '76

Red runs the Rubicon: Turbulent Italy faces new
troubles, NATO could lose its Mediterranean anchor. Lawrence Griswold. illus map Sea Power
19:20-24 Mar '76

SACEUR's subcommanders take the floor: The southern region. ADM Stansfield Turner. illus chart
NATO's Fifteen Nations 21:86-94 Feb-Mar '76

ALLIED FORCES, SOUTHERN EUROPE - Continued

The southern flank of NATO: Problems of the south-
ern region in the post-1973 October War period.
ADM Means Johnston, Jr. illus Mil Rev 56:22-29
Apr '76

ALLIED LAND FORCES, SOUTHEASTERN EUROPE
see Allied Forces, Southern Europe

ALLIED MILITARY IN THE U.S.

See also
Exchange Programs, Military

DOD lowers charges for foreign trainees. AF Times
37:10 Nov 1 '76

The Experten and the Flying Tiger: World War II
aces in Arizona. Robert C.Sullivan. illus Aerosp
Hist 23:148-149+ Sep '76

The Luftwaffe + twenty. (German pilots train at Luke
AFB, Ariz) LtCol Fred A.Meurer. illus Airman
20:2-8 Aug '76

ALLOYS

Working titanium alloys. Aerosp Intl 12:56 Mar-
Apr '76

ALTIMETERS

AF 209, wind 270° at 600 kts. LtCol Roland R.Robin-
son. illus Interceptor 18:14-15 Apr '76

Just a simple error. (Change in altimeter setting)
illus MAC Flyer 23:23 Mar '76

ALTITUDE, INFLUENCE OF

See also
Aviation--Physiological Aspects

Amelioration of the symptoms of acute mountain sickness by staging and acetazolamide. Wayne O.Ev-
ans and others. tabs Aviation, Space & Envmt Med
47:512-516 May '76

Pulmonary gas exchange in acute mountain sickness.
John R.Sutton and others. tabs Aviation, Space &
Envmt Med 47:1032-1037 Oct '76

Responses of the autonomic nervous system during
acclimatization to high altitude in man. M.S.Mal-
hotra and others. tabs Aviation, Space & Envmt
Med 47:1076-1079 Oct '76

ALTITUDE FLYING

See also
Flight, Low-Altitude

IFR minimum altitudes. Capt John L.Wilson. illus
Combat Crew pt 1, 27:26-27 May '76; pt 2, 27:
22-24 Jun '76

ALUMINUM see Metals

AMBUSH see Surprise in Warfare

AMERICAN FORCES RADIO AND TELEVISION SERVICE

Air Force AFRT (Air Force Radio and Television)
Broadcast Management: Inspection Guide D-1. TIG
Brief 28:2p addendum Feb 27 '76

DOD broadcasts in Iran to go off air Oct 25. AF
Times 36:8 Jul 19 '76

AMERICAN LOGISTICS ASSOCIATION

ALA's 29th Annual Convention (Miami Beach,
Sep 13-15, 1976): Member participation--key to
success. illus Review 56:21-36 Sep-Oct '76

Association news. Regular feature in some issues of
Review

Convention scrapbook. (28th Annual Meeting, Washington, Nov 11-12, 1975) illus Review 55:59-61
Nov-Dec '75

A look at the budget: What's ahead for ALA members.
Tony Upton. tab Review 55:16-18 Jan-Feb '76

AMERICAN MANAGEMENT ASSOCIATION

Management training: AMA (American Management
Associations) courses show results. illus Govt
Exec 8:38-39 Mar '76

AMERICAN SOCIETY OF MILITARY COMPTROLLERS

(American Society of Military Comptrollers National
Symposium, Arlington, Va, May 25-26, 1976) illus
Armed Forces Compt 21: entire issue Jul '76

AMERICANS IN FOREIGN COUNTRIES

See also
People-to-People Program

Americans & overseas law. illus Comdrs Dig 19:
entire issue Feb 12 '76

86 in jail abroad on drugs. Fred Reed. AF Times
37:16 Dec 6 '76

Making the most of it. (Dr (LtCol) Jaroslav K.Rich-
ter of MacDill AFB, Fla, likes to be where the
action is) 1stLt Katie Cutler. illus Airman 20:
20-23 Oct '76

Nonduty travel to Communist-controlled countries by
USAF civilian and military members. TIG Brief
28:8 Oct 22 '76

On going native: A discussion. Maj Robert V.Bran-
son. illus tab Mil Rev 56:13-25 Jan '76

AMMUNITION

Ammo supply in rapid deployment. LtCol Robert P.
Jones. illus Army Log 8:30-32 Jan-Feb '76

Demilitarization facility. Frits H.Fenger. illus tab
Mil Engr 68:86-87 Mar-Apr '76

Long-term storage of ammunition. Howard M.
Weiner. illus Army Log 8:34-36 Jul-Aug '76

A new ball game: Arms shipment security rules.
Capt Paul L.Govekar, Jr. tabs Translog 7:16-17+
Oct '76

Ricochets. LtCol Jim Learmonth. illus tab Aerosp
Safety 32:16-17 Jan '76

The up-load exercise. (Planning for combat battalion
ammunition supply points in the European environment) Capt Keith E.Predmore. illus Fld Arty J 44:
33-36 May-Jun '76

Whatever happened to mutual trust and respect?
Clyde A.Parton. illus Natl Def 60:268-270 Jan-
Feb '76

When ammo goes to sea. Eric R.Jackson and William
F.Ernst. illus tab Translog 7:6+ Nov '76

History

Antipersonnel shrapnel rounds. Capt John R.deTre-
ville. illus (Also cutaways) Fld Arty J 44:24-28
Mar-Apr '76

AMNESTY

Best and worst clemency records revealed. Ann Gerow. AF Times 36:12 Jan 26 '76

Clemency people victims of misfortune, (Presidential Clemency) Board says. AF Times 36:49 Feb 9 '76

Deserter discharges could be upgraded (by AF Discharge) Review Board. AF Times 36:12 Jan 26 '76

(Former Clemency Board chairman, Charles) Goodell would extend clemency indefinitely. AF Times 36:25 Feb 2 '76

(Jimmy) Carter scored on pardon (at) Legionnaire convention. AF Times 37:24 Sep 6 '76

On pardons for draft dodgers. LtGen Ira C. Eaker, Ret. AF Times 37:13-14 Sep 27 '76

(Pres-elect Jimmy) Carter affirms blanket pardon. Fred Reed. AF Times 37:2 Nov 29 '76

(Pres-elect Jimmy) Carter still studying draft pardon ... groups against it. AF Times 37:14 Dec 20 '76

Social implications of the clemency discharge. William A. Pearman. tabs J Pol & Mil Sociol 4:309-316 Fall '76

Views on amnesty: Panel (sponsored by an education organization called Fund for New Priorities in America) explores 'unconditional' issue. AF Times 36:26 Mar 22 '76

AMPHIBIOUS FORCES

Foreign policy and the Marine Corps. Maj W. Hays Parks. illus US Nav Inst Proc 102:18-25 Nov '76

The Marine Corps in 1985. Peter A. Wilson. illus US Nav Inst Proc 102:31-38 Jan '76

The Marine Corps today: Asset or anachronism? Gen Robert E. Cushman, Jr, Ret. Intl Sec 1:123-129 Fall '76

Today's Marine Corps: Stepping out smartly. James W. Canan. illus Sea Power 19:14-18 Nov '76

Vital tool for our nation. (Amphibious forces) Capt Wayne S. Keck. MarCor Gaz 60:50-51 Aug '76

AMPHIBIOUS OPERATIONS

Assault by sea. Frank Uhlig, Jr. illus MarCor Gaz 60:18-20 Jun '76

A battalion in a seaborne landing. Col A. Akimov. illus maps Soviet Mil Rev No. 3:22-24 Mar '76

Defence of a sea coast. (Actions of an artillery battalion) Col V. Saksonov. Soviet Mil Rev No. 11: 20-21 Nov '76

A flexible military posture. Gen Louis H. Wilson. illus Strat Rev 4:7-13 Fall '76

Manoeuvre with forces, weapons and fire. Col A. Akimov. (Adapted from Soviet Military Review, July 1975) illus map MarCor Gaz 60:45-48 Dec '76

Operation Chromite: A study of generalship. (Korea, 1950) Capt James P. Totten. illus Armor 85:33-38 Nov-Dec '76

Return to a maritime-based national strategy for the Marine Corps. E. W. Girard. illus tabs MarCor Gaz 60:38-45 Nov '76

Warsaw Pact amphib ops in Northern Europe. Graham H. Turbiville. illus MarCor Gaz 60:20-27 Oct '76

AMPHIBIOUS OPERATIONS - Continued

History

The daring sloop Providence. Charles R. Smith. illus MarCor Gaz 60:25-28 Jul '76

The destiny of Pete Ellis. Col David H. Wagner. illus MarCor Gaz 60:50-55 Jun '76

Our pre-colonial experience. Col Brooke Nihart, Ret. illus MarCor Gaz 60:29-34 Jul '76

Royal Marines: Soldiers from the sea. Col T. J. Saxon, Jr, Ret. illus MarCor Gaz 60:35-42 Oct '76

Study and Teaching

Amphibious mission (training). Capt Dennis R. Blankenship and Capt Ross Brown. illus Infantry 66:31-35 May-Jun '76

AMPHIBIOUS VEHICLES

The Marine Corps in 1985. Peter A. Wilson. illus US Nav Inst Proc 102:31-38 Jan '76

The new West German Luchs (Armored Reconnaissance Scout Vehicle). Capt Edwin W. Besch, Ret. illus Armor 85:16-17 Nov-Dec '76

The Radspähpanzer Luchs--a new reconnaissance vehicle for the Bundeswehr. tab illus (Also cutaway) Intl Def Rev 8:893-894 Dec '75

History

The tank that was ahead of its time. illus Armor 85: 35 Jan-Feb '76

AMPHIBIOUS WARFARE see Amphibious Operations

AMPHIBIOUS WARFARE SHIPS

Best ship in the business. (LHA (Landing Helicopter Assault) general purpose amphibious assault ship) LtCol Angelo Fernandez. illus tabs Infantry 66:36-41 May-Jun '76

First military landing. (A CH-46 lands on a LHA-1, Tarawa, first in a new class of amphibious assault ships) illus MarCor Gaz 60:8 Feb '76

Navy shipbuilding problems reach critical stage. illus Sea Power 19:13-14 Jul '76

Today's Marine Corps: Stepping out smartly. James W. Canan. illus Sea Power 19:14-18 Nov '76

USS Tarawa joins fleet. illus MarCor Gaz 60:2 Jul '76

ANDERSON, Andrew B., Jr

The future and the strategic mission. (Excerpt from address, 57th Defense Preparedness Meeting, American Defense Preparedness Assoc, Los Angeles, Oct 15, 1975) MajGen Andrew B. Anderson, Jr. Natl Def 60:286 Jan-Feb '76

The "young" professional SAC crew force. MajGen A. B. Anderson, Jr. por Combat Crew 26:3+ Feb '76

ANGOLA

Angola--a last look? John Wegg. illus Air Pict 38: 96-98 Mar '76

Cuba: Russia's foreign legion. Col Robert Debs Heinl, Jr, Ret. illus Sea Power 19:44-45 Mar '76

Foreign Relations

Russia

The Soviet intervention in Angola: Intentions and implications. Peter Vanneman and Martin James. tabs Strat Rev 4:92-103 Summer '76

60

ANTISUBMARINE WARFARE - Continued

Huff-Duff vs the U-boat. illus Elect Warfare 8:71+
May-Jun '76

In VS (air antisubmarine squadron), the enemy has
been found and the enemy is us. LCDR Stephen L.
Chappell. illus US Nav Inst Proc 102:120-122
Oct '76

Lockheed's ASW market. (Modernization of P-3 Orion
and current status of S-3A Viking) J. Philip Geddes.
illus tabs Interavia 31:444-447 May '76

New advances in doppler radar. Charles N. Bates.
illus tabs Countermeasures 2:34-37 Apr '76

The role of the Kiev in Soviet naval operations.
LCDR William R. Hynes. illus Nav War Col Rev
29:38-46 Fall '76

Soviet Naval Aviation. Norman Polmar. illus chart
tab AF Mag 59:69-75 Mar '76

Sub detection. Bill Walsh. illus Countermeasures 2:
6-7+ Apr '76

Tactical ASW: Let's fight fire with fire. LCDR A.
Van Saun. illus US Nav Inst Proc 102:99-101
Dec '76

Thinking about Soviet ASW. Norman Polmar. illus
map US Nav Inst Proc 102:108-129 May '76

ANTITANK WEAPONS see
Armored Warfare
Artillery, Antitank
Missiles, Antitank

ANTONELLI, Theodore

American industrial mobilization during World
War I. MajGen Theodore Antonelli. Def Mgt J
12:40-46 Jul '76

APPROPRIATIONS AND EXPENDITURES

Air Force--Great Britain

Defence cuts continue. (Points from Britain's 1976
Defence White Paper) illus tabs Air Pict 38:174-
177 May '76

Air Force--U.S.

Air Force Chief of Staff's FY 1977 Posture State-
ment. (Statement before House Committee on
Armed Services, Washington, Jan 29, 1976) Gen
David C.Jones. AF Plcy Ltr for Comdrs: Sup
No.3:23-40 Mar '76

The Air Force FY 77 budget. Maj Scott S.Pinckney.
illus tabs AF Compt 10:7-10 Apr '76

Appropriated funds for Morale, Welfare, and Recreation (MWR) activities. TIG Brief 28:15 Nov 19 '76

Department of the Air Force Fiscal Years 1977 and
1978 aircraft procurement estimates. Table only.
AF Plcy Ltr for Comdrs: Sup No.5:26 May '76

Department of the Air Force Fiscal Years 1977 and
1978 missile procurement estimates. Table only.
AF Plcy Ltr for Comdrs: Sup No.5:27 May '76

Force modernization highlights budget. Len Famiglietti. tab AF Times 36:2 Feb 2 '76

Forecasting the impact of base level programs. LtCol
Norbert W.Frische. illus tabs AF Compt 10:34-37
Jul '76

APPROPRIATIONS AND EXPENDITURES - Continued

Air Force--U.S. - Cont'd

New aircraft and missiles. (Presentation, Senate Appropriations Committee, Washington, March 18,
1976) LtGen Alton D.Slay. tabs AF Plcy Ltr for
Comdrs: Sup No.5:10-28 May '76

An operations operating budget. LtCol Michael L.
Hinnebusch. illus AF Compt 10:37-38 Jul '76

Personnel cuts linked to (buying) arms (and doing research). AF Times 36:22 Mar 1 '76

The promised land. Thomas C.Reed. illus tab AF
Mag 59:45-47 May '76

(SecAF Thomas C.) Reed calls for 'people' aid. Lee
Ewing. AF Times 36:3 Feb 9 '76

(SecAF Thomas C.Reed lists 5 conclusions about the
Air Force in recent news conference at the Pentagon) illus Air Reservist 28:13 May '76; AF Compt
10:24-25 Jul '76

Secretary of the Air Force's Air Force authorization
request. (Statement before House Committee on
Armed Services, Washington, Jan 29, 1976)
Thomas C.Reed. tabs AF Plcy Ltr for Comdrs:
Sup No.3:2-23 Mar '76

TDY funding for short course students: Try centralized control! LtCol Norman E.Qualtrough. illus
AF Compt 10:30-31 Apr '76

Armed Forces

Comparisons of defence expenditures 1973-76. London's International Institute for Strategic Studies.
Table only. AF Mag 59:95 Dec '76

Armed Forces--Great Britain

Britain's Armed Forces after the defence cuts. Michael Cary. RUSI J for Def Studies 121:1-6 Mar '76

British defence policy--a critical analysis. George
Younger. RUSI J for Def Studies 121:15-22 Mar '76

Armed Forces--Russia

Estimates of Soviet defense spending: What they
mean. (Message to major commands, March 22,
1976) MajGen George J.Keegan, Jr. AF Plcy Ltr
for Comdrs: Sup No.6:26-27 Jun '76

Military economics in the USSR. William T.Lee.
illus AF Mag 59:48-51 Mar '76

The Soviet military machine: Morale, muscles, and
megatons. Col Robert D.Heinl, Jr, Ret. illus Sea
Power 19:31-34 May '76

Armed Forces--U.S.

Authorization, money bills give--and take away.
(Congress OK's B-1, carrier, small ROTC units)
Officer 52:4+ Aug '76

Building budget shrinks. AF Times 36:23 Mar 29 '76

Commissary store operations appropriated fund support. Table only. Review 55:16 Jan-Feb '76

Congress okays B-1 go-ahead. AF Times 36:3
Jul 12 '76

Congress told shortages, cuts hurting readiness (by
Gen George S.Brown). AF Times 36:6 Mar 1 '76

Defense Authorization Bill: House-passed measure
calls for high spending. AF Times 36:3 Apr 26 '76

APPROPRIATIONS AND EXPENDITURES - Continued

Armed Forces--U.S. - Cont'd

Defense Authorization Bill: Senate Panel (Armed Services Committee) votes deep benefits cuts. Phil Stevens. AF Times 36:3 Apr 26 '76

Defense budget moving smoothly. F.Clifton Berry, Jr. tab Armed Forces J Intl 113:15-17 Apr '76

Defense budget, 1977: A 'serious effort' at restraint. illus tabs Eric C.Ludvigsen. Army 26:12-17 Mar '76

Defense Department report--FY 77. (Statement before House Armed Services Committee, Washington, Jan 27, 1976) Donald H.Rumsfeld. AF Plcy Ltr for Comdrs: Sup No.4:2-12 Apr '76

The FY 77 Defense budget: Adding teeth to the Navy, reducing tail in the Air Force. F.Clifton Berry, Jr. tabs Armed Forces J Intl 113:16-17+ Feb '76

FY 77 proposed Defense budget. illus tabs Comdrs Dig 19: entire issue Feb 26 '76

Hill Budget Office asks $ for arms. AF Times 36:12 Apr 5 '76

Hill fight: People, weapons. Phil Stevens. AF Times 36:3 Jun 14 '76

(House Armed Services Committee) members scold (SecDef) Rumsfeld. Phil Stevens. AF Times 36:25 Feb 9 '76

House Armed Services (Committee) restores budget cuts. tab Officer 52:4+ May '76

House money bill rejects most 'people' cuts. Officer 52:18+ Jul '76

House panel (Armed Services Committee) again supports stores. AF Times 36:2 Mar 29 '76

House panel (Armed Services Committee) rejects extra $$ for Navy. AF Times 37:6 Sep 20 '76

How to look at the U.S. military budget: Major issues for President Carter. tab Def Monitor 5: entire issue Dec '76

Key (military) $$ bills still in works. AF Times 37:3 Sep 20 '76

Many congressional actions impact on Services. Officer 52:5+ Jun '76

Many details surface in passage of military construction legislation. Officer 52:5+ Aug '76

Move to erase store $$ wins (by) 45-44 Senate vote. Phil Stevens. AF Times 37:2 Aug 16 '76

The next budget and the new Congress: Changes in both. L.Edgar Prina. illus Sea Power 19:8-9 Dec '76

'76 money bill goes to (Pres) Ford. AF Times 36:4 Feb 9 '76

(Pres) Ford nixes junior EM aid; phaseout of store subsidies asked. Randy Shoemaker. AF Times 37:3 Dec 27 '76

(Pres) Ford signs DOD (FY 1977 Defense Authorization) Bill; stores question open. AF Times 36:8 Jul 26 '76

(Pres) Ford signs $104 billion defense bill. AF Times 37:9 Oct 4 '76

Senate curbs commissaries in passing money bill-- many other Congress actions. Officer 52:4+ Sep '76

APPROPRIATIONS AND EXPENDITURES - Continued

Armed Forces--U.S. - Cont'd

Senate OKs money bill, comstore fund fight set. tab AF Times 37:6 Aug 23 '76

Senate unit (Appropriations Committee) okays full stores funding. Phil Stevens. AF Times 37:4 Aug 2 '76

Stores: DOD must cut costs--Authorization Bill goes to President. AF Times 36:3 Jul 12 '76

U.S. EO (Electro-Optics) and IRCM (InfraRed CounterMeasures) budget outlined. Tables only. Elect Warfare 7:24+ Nov-Dec '75

Army--U.S.

The Army: Electronics vs dwindling budgets. illus Govt Exec 8:37+ Jan '76

Professionalism in Army Aviation and budgetary constraints. BrigGen Charles E.Canedy. illus USA Avn Dig 22:1-3 Jun '76

Review, surveillance and self-examination: A special interview on Army funding problems. Hadlai A. Hull. illus Armed Forces Compt 21:2-5 Jan '76

TDY funding for short course students: Try centralized control! LtCol Norman E.Qualtrough. illus AF Compt 10:30-31 Apr '76

Defense Dept--Germany (Federal Republic)

A new self-confidence in the Bundeswehr. Richard Cox. RUSI J for Def Studies 120:58-61 Dec '75

Defense Dept--Great Britain

British policy for defence procurement. G.H.Green. RUSI J for Def Studies 121:20-28 Sep '76

Sights lowered: The United Kingdom's defense effort 1975-84. (1974 Defence Review) David Greenwood. (Reprinted from Royal Air Forces Quarterly, Autumn 1975) illus Mil Rev 56:34-46 Mar '76

Defense Dept--Russia

CIA says Soviet defense spending is double earlier estimates. tab Armed Forces J Intl 113:8 Jul '76

Former DIA (Defense Intelligence Agency) director (Daniel O.Graham) speaks out. F.Clifton Berry, Jr. Armed Forces J Intl 113:15 Mar '76

Russia's space budget. Spaceflight 18:98 Mar '76

The Soviet military budget controversy. LtGen Daniel O.Graham, Ret. AF Mag 59:33-37 May '76

Defense Dept--U.S.

Airpower in the news. Regular feature in issues of Air Force Magazine

The artificial crisis of American security. illus tabs Def Monitor pt 1 (Military balance between U.S. and USSR) 5: entire issue May '76; pt 2, How much for defense? 5: entire issue Jun '76

Bicentennial tories. (Speech, Army Aviation Assoc of America, Williamsburg, Va, March 1976) Barry Goldwater. illus Natl Guardsman 30:28-29 May '76

Budget keeps (DefSec Donald H.) Rumsfeld busy. AF Times 36:10 Jan 12 '76

APPROPRIATIONS AND EXPENDITURES - Continued

Defense Dept--U.S. - Cont'd

The budget process vs national defense. (Excerpts from address, American Defense Preparedness Assoc, Washington, Nov 11, 1975) Strom Thurmond. Natl Guardsman 30:18-19 Jan '76

Budget ups hardware but degrades personnel. tabs Officer 52:4+ Mar '76

Building budget shrinks. AF Times 36:23 Mar 29 '76

Commissaries OK for now. AF Times 36:3 Jul 5 '76

Compensation situation: Many developments. Officer 52:10 Jan '76

Congress split on money bill. Phil Stevens. AF Times 36:2 Jun 7 '76

Congress views B-1 delay, new ship mix as major hardware issues in new budget. Armed Forces J Intl 113:5 Jun '76

Controversy and politics mark start of FY '77 Defense debate: Dollar-rich, ship-poor budget plan pleases few; Naval Reserve slashed. James D. Hessman and Vicki Smithson. illus tabs Sea Power 19:21-28 Feb '76

DOD budget for FY 76 hung up in Congress. AF Times 36:10 Feb 9 '76

DOD spending hard to cut. (Brookings Institution study, "Setting National Priorities") Randy Shoemaker. AF Times 37:14 Oct 4 '76

Defense Appropriations Bill moves: House votes money for comstores, B-1. AF Times 36:4 Jun 28 '76

Defense Appropriations Bill moves: Senate committee (Appropriations Defense Subcommittee) makes major cuts. Phil Stevens. AF Times 36:4 Jun 28 '76

Defense Authorization Bill: House-passed measure calls for high spending. AF Times 36:3 Apr 26 '76

Defense Authorization Bill: Senate Panel (Armed Services Committee) votes deep benefits cuts. Phil Stevens. AF Times 36:3 Apr 26 '76

Defense budget moving smoothly. F.Clifton Berry, Jr. tab Armed Forces J Intl 113:15-17 Apr '76

Defense budget, 1977: A 'serious effort' at restraint. illus tabs Eric C.Ludvigsen. Army 26:12-17 Mar '76

The Defense budget: The price of freedom. L.Edgar Prina. illus tabs Natl Guardsman 30:8-13 Mar '76

Defense Department report--FY 77. (Statement before House Armed Services Committee, Washington, Jan 27, 1976) Donald H.Rumsfeld. AF Plcy Ltr for Comdrs: Sup No.4:2-12 Apr '76

Defense expenditures and the survival of American capitalism: A note. Clark Nardinelli and Gary B. Ackerman. tabs Armed Forces & Soc 3:13-16 Fall '76

Defense hearings underway: Rumsfeld details plans for new weapons. tabs Officer 52:5+ Mar '76

Explaining the 'A' (authorization and appropriations) bills: Setting limits, supplying funds. tab AF Times 36:4 Jun 21 '76

The FY 77 Defense budget: Adding teeth to the Navy, reducing tail in the Air Force. F.Clifton Berry, Jr. tabs Armed Forces J Intl 113:16-17+ Feb '76

APPROPRIATIONS AND EXPENDITURES - Continued

Defense Dept--U.S. - Cont'd

The FY 1977 Federal budget. Col Edmund W.Edmonds, Jr. tabs AF Compt 10:3-6 Apr '76

FY 77 proposed Defense budget. illus tabs Comdrs Dig 19: entire issue Feb 26 '76

Force modernization highlights budget. Len Famiglietti. tab AF Times 36:2 Feb 2 '76

A force second to none: The FY 1977 Defense budget. Terence E.McClary. illus tab Armed Forces Compt 21:16-19 Apr '76

Hardware outweighs people (in) budget tradeoff. AF Times 36:3 Feb 2 '76

Hill group (Members of Congress for Peace through Law) would slash manpower $$. Andy Plattner. AF Times 36:23 Jun 7 '76

Hill made few major DOD cuts: 6-year budget review. AF Times 37:25 Nov 1 '76

House Armed Services (Committee) restores budget cuts. tab Officer 52:4+ May '76

How to look at the U.S. military budget: Major issues for President Carter. tab Def Monitor 5: entire issue Dec '76

Industry and defense. (Excerpt from address, 57th Defense Preparedness Meeting, American Defense Preparedness Assoc, Los Angeles, Oct 15, 1975) R.Anderson. Natl Def 60:287 Jan-Feb '76

A look at the budget: What's ahead for ALA members. Tony Upton. tab Review 55:16-18 Jan-Feb '76

Managing for Defense. Robert S.McNamara. Def Mgt J 12:67-73 Jul '76

Military procurement: Still an unsolved problem. tabs Def Monitor 5: entire issue Oct '76

More housing funds to go for repairs. Ron Sanders. AF Times 36:18 Jun 28 '76

'76 money bill goes to (Pres) Ford. AF Times 36:4 Feb 9 '76

Old, new budgets affect Reserves, Defense. Officer 52:4+ Feb '76

People programs get boost from House (Appropriations) Committee. AF Times 36:4 Jun 21 '76

People savings (in the fiscal 1977 Defense budget request): Good, bad news. AF Times 36:22 Feb 16 '76

People vs hardware: Tough nut for Carter (administration). AF Times 37:6 Dec 6 '76

Political prelude to a no-win scenario. James D. Hessman and Vincent C.Thomas. illus Sea Power 18:23-24 Dec '75

President (Ford) accuses Congress of driving up defense costs. AF Times 37:4 Sep 6 '76

(Pres) Ford signs $104 billion defense bill. AF Times 37:9 Oct 4 '76

Resource management: A view from the top. (Panel discussion, American Society of Military Comptrollers National Symposium, Arlington, Va, May 26, 1976) Fred P.Wacker and others. illus Armed Forces Compt 21:20-26 Jul '76

Senate, House votes combine to assure new CHAMPUS cuts. Officer 52:8 Jan '76

APPROPRIATIONS AND EXPENDITURES - Continued

Defense Dept--U.S. - Cont'd

Senate panel (Armed Services Committee) OKs DOD (FY 1977 Defense Authorization) Bill. Phil Stevens. AF Times 36:3 May 24 '76

Senate votes 5-year stageout of commissary staff subsidy. Officer 52:8 Jan '76

Stores: DOD must cut costs--Authorization Bill goes to President. AF Times 36:3 Jul 12 '76

"The United States should possess a military capability second to none." Donald H. Rumsfeld. illus Comdrs Dig 19:2-4 Jan 8 '76

What we get for our DOD telecommunications $. LtGen Lee M. Paschall. illus Signal 30:6-8 Jan '76

With pen, purse and sword. (Process of getting the Defense budget approved by Congress) Ted R. Sturm. illus tab Airman 20:24-29 Jan '76

Marine Corps--U.S.

Spirit of '76: 'The troops are looking good.' (A briefing to Congress) Gen Louis H. Wilson. illus tabs MarCor Gaz 60:11-22 Mar '76

National Aeronautics and Space Administration--U.S.

The NASA budget--FY 1977. David Baker. illus tabs Spaceflight 18:351-355 Oct '76

National Guard--Armed Forces--U.S.

The budget--a grim outlook. MajGen Francis S. Greenlief, Ret. tab Natl Guardsman 30:15 Jan '76

Reserve projects voted big boost. tab Officer 52:4+ May '76

Navy--U.S.

Controversy and politics mark start of FY '77 Defense debate: Dollar-rich, ship-poor budget plan pleases few; Naval Reserve slashed. James D. Hessman and Vicki Smithson. illus tabs Sea Power 19:21-28 Feb '76

House panel (Armed Services Committee) increases SCN (Ship Construction, Navy) funding: Nuclear power advocates gain ground. L. Edgar Prina. illus Sea Power 19:7-11 Apr '76

House panel (Armed Services Committee) rejects extra $$ for Navy. AF Times 37:6 Sep 20 '76

House/Senate conferees set for bitter battle (over naval ship construction for FY 1977). tab Sea Power 19:12-13 Jun '76

New five-year shipbuilding plan. tab Sea Power 19:29 Feb '76

Next year: $7.8 billion for shipbuilding. James D. Hessman. illus Sea Power 19:33-36 Nov '76

(Pres) Ford signs procurement bill: Hits Congress for shipbuilding cuts. L. Edgar Prina. illus Sea Power 19:7-10 Aug '76

The small ships. James D. Hessman. illus Sea Power 19:13-16 Sep '76

Reserve Forces--Armed Forces--U.S.

Authorization, money bills give--and take away. (Congress OK's B-1, carrier, small ROTC units) Officer 52:4+ Aug '76

APPROPRIATIONS AND EXPENDITURES - Continued

Reserve Forces--Armed Forces--U.S. - Cont'd

Budget ups hardware but degrades personnel. tabs Officer 52:4+ Mar '76

Many details surface in passage of military construction legislation. Officer 52:5+ Aug '76

Old, new budgets affect Reserves, Defense. Officer 52:4+ Feb '76

Reserve projects voted big boost. tab Officer 52:4+ May '76

Reserves fare well in both construction bills. tab Officer 52:5+ Aug '76

United States

The Bicentennial challenge: The management revolution. Donald Ogilvie. illus Armed Forces Compt 21:10-14 Jul '76

200 years of financial management. Allen Schick. Armed Forces Compt 21:4-7 Jul '76

ARAB-ISRAELI CONFLICT, 1967-

See also
Middle East War, 1973

Conflict in the Middle East. (Conclusions, lessons and opinions) K. Vologdin. Soviet Mil Rev No. 6: 44-46 Jun '76

Crisis decisionmaking in Israel: The case of the October 1973 Middle East War. Maj Robert H. McKenzie-Smith. illus Nav War Col Rev 29:39-52 Summer '76

Doomed to peace. Béchir Ben Yahmed. (Digested from Foreign Affairs, Oct 1975) Mil Rev 56:39-44 Feb '76

Israel and the Fedayeen: Persistence or transformation. Maj Bard E. O'Neill. illus Strat Rev 4:89-101 Spring '76

The Israeli Air Force. Zeev Schiff. illus map AF Mag 59:31-38 Aug '76

Middle East oil and military balance of power. Col Irving Heymont, Ret. illus Mil Rev 56:70-76 Jul '76

Naked racism. (Zionism) V. Dmitrovsky. Soviet Mil Rev No. 4:47-48 Apr '76

The psychology of Middle East peace. Nahum Goldmann. (Digested from Foreign Affairs, Oct 1975) Mil Rev 56:31-39 Feb '76

The safety of the Republic: Can the tide be turned? Eugene V. Rostow. illus Strat Rev 4:12-25 Spring '76

ARABIAN PENINSULA

Economic Conditions

Arabesque. (The Arabian Peninsula) Leigh Johnson. illus Def & For Aff Dig No. 4:32-38+ '76

Strategic Importance

Arabesque. (The Arabian Peninsula) Leigh Johnson. illus Def & For Aff Dig No. 4:32-38+ '76

ARCHITECTURE

Toward flexible definitive designs. Capt Michael J. Burrill. illus AF Engrg & Svcs Qtr 17:26-31 Nov '76

ARCHITECTURE - Continued

Great Britain

The restoration of York Minster. J.A.Lord. illus tab Mil Engr 68:432-436 Nov-Dec '76

United States

Monument to people oriented construction (Air Force Accounting and Finance Center, Lowry AFB, Colo). Maj Peter LoPresti and William L.Kollman. illus AF Engrg & Svcs Qtr 17:7-10 Nov '76

The National Air and Space Museum. Gyo Obata. illus Mil Engr 68:279-281 Jul-Aug '76

New approaches to office design. illus AF Engrg & Svcs.Qtr 17:6-10 Feb '76

History

American architectural heritage. Edward M.Tower. illus Mil Engr 68:207-209 May-Jun '76

ARCHIVES

United States

Flying saucers (AF's investigation of UFOs, Project Blue Book) land at (National) Archives. illus AF Times 37:21 Aug 9 '76

ARCTIC REGIONS

For conquering the Arctic. LtCol N.Yelshin. Soviet Mil Rev No.10:41-42 Oct '76

Living in the ice age. (Remote duty at Sparrevohn AFS, Alas) TSgt Tom Dwyer. illus Airman 20:2-7 Apr '76

Navigation North of Seventy. 1stLt David J.Haney. illus map Navigator 23:5-10 Summer '76

PINS (Palletized Inertial Navigation System) in Alaska. Capt William T.Nuzum and Lt Christopher G. Knowles. illus Combat Crew 27:28-29 Nov '76

Raven on the 'cap. (109th Tactical Airlift Group of the Air National Guard flies resupply missions to DEW-Line sites in Greenland) Maj Terry A.Arnold. illus Airman 20:2-8 Nov '76

With the Byrd North Pole expedition. E.J. "Pete" Demas. illus Am Avn Hist Soc J 21:4-8 Spring '76

ARCTIC RESEARCH

Searching for icebergs. (Coast Guard and International Ice Patrol work to prevent another Titanic disaster) Marianne Lester. illus AF Times, Times Magazine sup:10-14+ Jul 12 '76

Ship of ice. LCDR Brian H.Shoemaker. illus maps US Nav Inst Proc 102:103-106 Feb '76

ARCTIC TRAINING

Realistic exercise (Jack Frost 76) tests Alaska pipeline defense. Armed Forces J Intl 113:28 Jan '76

Supersoldiers of the North. (172d ("Arctic Light")) Infantry Brigade) BrigGen James G.Boatner. illus Army 26:27-30 Nov '76

Training at -70° F. (Army's Northern Warfare Training Center (NWTC), Fort Greely, Alas) Sgt1C Floyd Harrington. illus Soldiers 31:46-48 Nov '76

AREA SPECIALIST PROGRAMS

Fiction reading in the Foreign Area Speciality Program. Maj Kenneth M.Taggart. illus Mil Rev 56: 71-78 Sep '76

ARMAMENT

See also
Artillery
Munitions
Ordnance
  also subdivision under specific subjects, e.g.,
Airplanes, Military--Armament
Helicopters, Military--Armament
Ships--Armament
Tanks, Military--Armament

A new ball game: Arms shipment security rules. Capt Paul L.Govekar, Jr. tabs Translog 7:16-17+ Oct '76

ARMED FORCES

See also
General Purpose Forces
Interservice Cooperation
Strategic Forces
Unification of the Armed Forces
  also subdivision under specific subjects, e.g.,
Appropriations and Expenditures--Armed Forces--U.S
Officers--Armed Forces--U.S.
Promotion--Armed Forces--U.S.

Statistics

Comparative strengths of armed forces 1955-75. London's International Institute for Strategic Studies. Table only. AF Mag 59:97 Dec '76

Comparisons of military manpower 1972-76. London's International Institute for Strategic Studies. Table only. AF Mag 59:96 Dec '76

The Military Balance: 1975/76. London's International Institute for Strategic Studies. illus tabs Aerosp Intl 11:6-64+ Nov-Dec '75

The Military Balance: 1976/77. London's International Institute for Strategic Studies. illus tabs AF Mag 59:41-107 Dec '76

Afghanistan

Statistics

Afghanistan. London's International Institute for Strategic Studies. Tables only. AF Mag 59:81 Dec '76

Africa

African elements in Portugal's armies in Africa (1961-1974). Douglas L.Wheeler. tab Armed Forces & Soc 2:233-250 Winter '76

Africa's future armies: Age of experiment. Maj P.G. Francis. Army Qtr 106:324-332 Jul '76

Africa, Sub-Saharan

Statistics

Sub-Saharan Africa. London's International Institute for Strategic Studies. illus tabs AF Mag 59:75-78 Dec '76

Albania

Statistics

Albania. London's International Institute for Strategic Studies. Tables only. AF Mag 59:62 Dec '76

Algeria

Statistics

Algeria. London's International Institute for Strategic Studies. Tables only. AF Mag 59:68 Dec '76

ARMED FORCES - Continued

Angola

Statistics

Angola. London's International Institute for Strategic Studies. Tables only. AF Mag 59:75 Dec '76

Argentina

Statistics

Argentina. London's International Institute for Strategic Studies. Tables only. AF Mag 59:88-89 Dec '76

Asia

Statistics

Other Asian countries and Australasia. London's International Institute for Strategic Studies. illus tabs AF Mag 59:81-87 Dec '76

Australia

Statistics

Australia. London's International Institute for Strategic Studies. Tables only. AF Mag 59:82 Dec '76

Austria

Statistics

Austria. London's International Institute for Strategic Studies. Tables only. AF Mag 59:62 Dec '76

Bangladesh

Statistics

Bangladesh. London's International Institute for Strategic Studies. Tables only. AF Mag 59:82 Dec '76

Belgium

Syndicalism in the Belgian Armed Forces. Victor Werner. (Trans by Gwen Harries-Jenkins) tab Armed Forces & Soc 2:477-494 Summer '76

Statistics

Belgium. London's International Institute for Strategic Studies. Tables only. AF Mag 59:56 Dec '76

Bolivia

Statistics

Bolivia. London's International Institute for Strategic Studies. Tables only. AF Mag 59:89 Dec '76

Brazil

Statistics

Brazil. London's International Institute for Strategic Studies. Tables only. AF Mag 59:89 Dec '76

Bulgaria

Statistics

Bulgaria. London's International Institute for Strategic Studies. Tables only. AF Mag 59:51-52 Dec '76

Burma

Efficiency, responsibility, and equality in military staffing: The ethnic dimension in comparative perspective. (Demography of military institutions in Burma and Malaysia) James F.Guyot. Armed Forces & Soc 2:291-304 Winter '76

ARMED FORCES - Continued

Burma - Cont'd

Statistics

Burma. London's International Institute for Strategic Studies. Tables only. AF Mag 59:82-83 Dec '76

Cambodia

Statistics

Kampuchea (Cambodia). London's International Institute for Strategic Studies. Tables only. AF Mag 59:84 Dec '76

Canada

Officer career profile in the Canadian forces. LtCol Robert S.Riley. illus tabs Mil Rev 56:45-55 Feb '76

Professionalism and the Canadian military. LtCol J.H.Pocklington. AU Rev 27:34-40 Mar-Apr '76

Statistics

Canada. London's International Institute for Strategic Studies. Tables only. AF Mag 59:57-58 Dec '76

Ceylon

Statistics

Sri Lanka (Ceylon). London's International Institute for Strategic Studies. Tables only. AF Mag 59:87 Dec '76

Chile

Statistics

Chile. London's International Institute for Strategic Studies. Tables only. AF Mag 59:89-90 Dec '76

China (People's Republic)

U.S. General Purpose Forces: A need for modernization. Gen George S.Brown. illus tab Comdrs Dig 19: entire issue May 27 '76

Statistics

China. London's International Institute for Strategic Studies. illus tabs AF Mag 59:79-80 Dec '76

China (Republic)

Statistics

China: Republic of (Taiwan). London's International Institute for Strategic Studies. Tables only. AF Mag 59:83 Dec '76

Colombia

Statistics

Colombia. London's International Institute for Strategic Studies. Tables only. AF Mag 59:90 Dec '76

Congo (Brazzaville)

Statistics

People's Republic of Congo. London's International Institute for Strategic Studies. Tables only. AF Mag 59:75 Dec '76

66

ARMED FORCES - Continued

Cuba

Racial and ethnic relations in the Cuban Armed
Forces: A non-topic. Jorge I. Dominguez. tabs
Armed Forces & Soc 2:273-290 Winter '76

History

Guarding the gains of socialism. (20th anniversary of
the Revolutionary Armed Forces of Cuba) Maj I.
Garbuzov. illus Soviet Mil Rev No. 12:43-45
Dec '76

Statistics

Cuba. London's International Institute for Strategic
Studies. Tables only. AF Mag 59:90 Dec '76

Czechoslovakia

Statistics

Czechoslovakia. London's International Institute for
Strategic Studies. Tables only. AF Mag 59:52
Dec '76

Denmark

Statistics

Denmark. London's International Institute for Strategic Studies. Tables only. AF Mag 59:58 Dec '76

Dominican Republic

Statistics

Dominican Republic. London's International Institute
for Strategic Studies. Tables only. AF Mag 59:90
Dec '76

Ecuador

Statistics

Ecuador. London's International Institute for Strategic Studies. Tables only. AF Mag 59:90 Dec '76

Egypt

Statistics

Egypt. London's International Institute for Strategic
Studies. Tables only. AF Mag 59:68 Dec '76

Ethiopia

Statistics

Ethiopia. London's International Institute for Strategic Studies. Tables only. AF Mag 59:75-76 Dec '76

Europe

Statistics

Other European countries. London's International Institute for Strategic Studies. tabs illus AF Mag
59:62-64 Dec '76

The theatre balance between NATO and the Warsaw
Pact. London's International Institute for Strategic
Studies. tabs AF Mag 59:98-106 Dec '76

Finland

Statistics

Finland. London's International Institute for Strategic Studies. Tables only. AF Mag 59:63 Dec '76

ARMED FORCES - Continued

France

France. Def & For Aff Dig No. 10:29-31+ '76

Syndicalism and the French military system. (Excerpted from paper, British Inter-University Seminar, Manchester, Eng, 1976) Lucien Mandeville.
Armed Forces & Soc 2:539-552 Summer '76

Statistics

France. London's International Institute for Strategic
Studies. Tables only. AF Mag 59:58-59 Dec '76

Germany

The current implications of German military excellence (in WWs I and II). Col Trevor N. Dupuy,
Ret. illus tabs Strat Rev 4:87-94 Fall '76

Germany (Democratic Republic)

Invasion in Europe--a scenario. (Soviet forces in
East Germany) Graham H. Turbiville. illus maps
Army 26:16-21 Nov '76

Statistics

German Democratic Republic. London's International
Institute for Strategic Studies. Tables only. AF
Mag 59:52 Dec '76

Germany (Federal Republic)

The military and labor union organizations in Germany. Bernhard Fleckenstein. Armed Forces &
Soc 2:495-515 Summer '76

Union in Germany (Public Service, Transport and
Traffic Workers Union, the OTV): Many setbacks.
David Cortright and Boykin Reynolds. AF Times
36:30 Jan 19 '76

Youth information officers of the Federal Armed
Forces. Capt Jürgen Conze. illus NATO's Fifteen
Nations 21:49-56 Aug-Sep '76

Statistics

Germany: Federal Republic of. London's International Institute for Strategic Studies. Tables only.
AF Mag 59:59-60 Dec '76

A new self-confidence in the Bundeswehr. Richard
Cox. RUSI J for Def Studies 120:58-61 Dec '75

Ghana

Army in a multi-ethnic society: The case of Nkrumah's Ghana, 1957-1966. (Condensed from paper,
African Studies Assoc 17th Annual Meeting, Chicago, Oct 30-Nov 2, 1974) J. 'Bayo Adekson. tab
Armed Forces & Soc 2:251-272 Winter '76

The military in Ghanaian politics. S. J. Baynham.
Army Qtr 106:428-439 Oct '76

Statistics

Ghana. London's International Institute for Strategic
Studies. Tables only. AF Mag 59:76 Dec '76

Great Britain

Britain's Armed Forces after the defence cuts. Michael Cary. RUSI J for Def Studies 121:1-6 Mar '76

Guarding Britain's liquid gold. (North Sea oil) Stefan
Geisenheyner. illus AF Mag 59:31-33 Jan '76

Manpower trends in the British all-volunteer force.
LtCol Thomas A. Fabyanic. tabs Armed Forces &
Soc 2:553-572 Summer '76

ARMED FORCES - Continued

Great Britain - Cont'd

Statistics

Britain. London's International Institute for Strategic Studies. Tables only. AF Mag 59:56-57 Dec '76

Greece

Statistics

Greece. London's International Institute for Strategic Studies. Tables only. AF Mag 59:59-60 Dec '76

Honduras

Statistics

Honduras. London's International Institute for Strategic Studies. Tables only. AF Mag 59:90 Dec '76

Hungary

Statistics

Hungary. London's International Institute for Strategic Studies. Tables only. AF Mag 59:52-53 Dec '76

India

Statistics

India. London's International Institute for Strategic Studies. Tables only. AF Mag 59:83 Dec '76

Pakistan rearmed? Ravi Rikhye. illus Armed Forces J Intl 113:12-13 Jan '76

Indonesia

Statistics

Indonesia. London's International Institute for Strategic Studies. Tables only. AF Mag 59:83 Dec '76

Iran

Statistics

Iran. London's International Institute for Strategic Studies. Tables only. AF Mag 59:68-69 Dec '76

Iraq

Statistics

Iraq. London's International Institute for Strategic Studies. Tables only. AF Mag 59:69 Dec '76

Ireland

Statistics

Eire. London's International Institute for Strategic Studies. Tables only. AF Mag 59:62-63 Dec '76

Ireland, Northern

Northern Ireland's volunteer force (Ulster Defence Regiment). James B.Deerin. illus Natl Guardsman 30:6-8 Nov '76

Israel

Two years after: The Israel Defence Forces (IDF), 1973-75. Martin van Creveld. RUSI J for Def Studies 121:29-34 Mar '76

ARMED FORCES - Continued

Israel - Cont'd

Statistics

Israel. London's International Institute for Strategic Studies. Table only. AF Mag 59:69-70 Dec '76

Italy

Statistics

Italy. London's International Institute for Strategic Studies. Tables only. AF Mag 59:60 Dec '76

Japan

The U.S.-Japanese alliance and stability in Asia. Col Angus M.Fraser, Ret. illus tabs AF Mag 59:34-39 Jan '76

Statistics

Japan. London's International Institute for Strategic Studies. Tables only. AF Mag 59:83-84 Dec '76

Jordan

Statistics

Jordan. London's International Institute for Strategic Studies. Tables only. AF Mag 59:70 Dec '76

Kenya

Statistics

Kenya. London's International Institute for Strategic Studies. Tables only. AF Mag 59:76 Dec '76

Korea (Democratic People's Republic)

Korea and U.S. policy in Asia. illus tabs Def Monitor 5: entire issue Jan '76

Statistics

Korea: Democratic People's Republic (North). London's International Institute for Strategic Studies. Tables only. AF Mag 59:84 Dec '76

Korea (Republic)

Korea and U.S. policy in Asia. illus tabs Def Monitor 5: entire issue Jan '76

Statistics

Korea: Republic of (South). London's International Institute for Strategic Studies. Tables only. AF Mag 59:84 Dec '76

Kuwait

Statistics

Kuwait. London's International Institute for Strategic Studies. Tables only. AF Mag 59:70 Dec '76

Laos

Statistics

Laos. London's International Institute for Strategic Studies. Tables only. AF Mag 59:84-85 Dec '76

Latin America

Statistics

Latin America. London's International Institute for Strategic Studies. illus tabs AF Mag 59:88-91 Dec '76

ARMED FORCES - Continued

Lebanon

Statistics

Lebanon. London's International Institute for Strategic Studies. Tables only. AF Mag 59:70 Dec '76

Libya

Statistics

Libya. London's International Institute for Strategic Studies. Tables only. AF Mag 59:70-71 Dec '76

Luxembourg

Statistics

Luxembourg. London's International Institute for Strategic Studies. Tables only. AF Mag 59:60 Dec '76

Malaysia

Efficiency, responsibility, and equality in military staffing: The ethnic dimension in comparative perspective. (Demography of military institutions in Burma and Malaysia) James F. Guyot. Armed Forces & Soc 2:291-304 Winter '76

Statistics

Malaysia. London's International Institute for Strategic Studies. Tables only. AF Mag 59:85 Dec '76

Mediterranean Region

Statistics

The Middle East and the Mediterranean. London's International Institute for Strategic Studies. illus tabs AF Mag 59:67-72 Dec '76

Mexico

Statistics

Mexico. London's International Institute for Strategic Studies. Tables only. AF Mag 59:91 Dec '76

Middle East

Statistics

The Middle East and the Mediterranean. London's International Institute for Strategic Studies. illus tabs AF Mag 59:67-72 Dec '76

Mongolia

Statistics

Mongolia. London's International Institute for Strategic Studies. Tables only. AF Mag 59:85-86 Dec '76

Morocco

Statistics

Morocco. London's International Institute for Strategic Studies. Tables only. AF Mag 59:71 Dec '76

Mozambique

Statistics

Mozambique. London's International Institute for Strategic Studies. Table only. AF Mag 59:76 Dec '76

ARMED FORCES - Continued

NATO

Hell on wheels. (Air Force and Army's 2d Armored Division (Brigade 75) train in West Germany for NATO support) MSgt Harold D. Newcomb. illus Airman 20:8-12 Apr '76

The MBFR (Mutual Balanced Force Reduction) talks--problems and prospects. Axel Hörhager. illus tab map Intl Def Rev 9:189-192 Apr '76

A status report on Mutual and Balanced Forced Reductions (MBFRs). Rembert van Delden. NATO's Fifteen Nations 21:20-21 Aug-Sep '76

Statistics

The North Atlantic Treaty. London's International Institute for Strategic Studies. illus tabs AF Mag 59:54-61 Dec '76

The theatre balance between NATO and the Warsaw Pact. London's International Institute for Strategic Studies. tabs AF Mag 59:98-106 Dec '76

Nepal

Statistics

Nepal. London's International Institute for Strategic Studies. Tables only. AF Mag 59:86 Dec '76

Netherlands

The successful case of military unionization in the Netherlands. Ger Teitler. Armed Forces & Soc 2:517-528 Summer '76

Statistics

Netherlands. London's International Institute for Strategic Studies. Tables only. AF Mag 59:60-61 Dec '76

New Zealand

Statistics

New Zealand. London's International Institute for Strategic Studies. Tables only. AF Mag 59:86 Dec '76

Nigeria

Nigeria: African super-state. Leigh Johnson. illus maps tabs Def & For Aff Dig No.8-9:44-45+ '76

Statistics

Nigeria. London's International Institute for Strategic Studies. Tables only. AF Mag 59:76 Dec '76

Norway

Statistics

Norway. London's International Institute for Strategic Studies. Tables only. AF Mag 59:61 Dec '76

Oman

Statistics

Oman. London's International Institute for Strategic Studies. Tables only. AF Mag 59:71 Dec '76

Pakistan

Statistics

Pakistan. London's International Institute for Strategic Studies. Tables only. AF Mag 59:86 Dec '76

Saudi Arabia

Statistics

Saudi Arabia. London's International Institute for Strategic Studies. Tables only. AF Mag 59:71-72 Dec '76

Senegal

Statistics

Senegal. London's International Institute for Strategic Studies. Tables only. AF Mag 59:77 Dec '76

Singapore

The Singapore military/industrial scene. R.B.Pengelley. illus tab Intl Def Rev 9:657-660 Aug '76

Statistics

Singapore. London's International Institute for Strategic Studies. Tables only. AF Mag 59:87 Dec '76

Somali Democratic Republic

Statistics

Somali Democratic Republic. London's International Institute for Strategic Studies. Tables only. AF Mag 59:77-78 Dec '76

South Africa (Republic)

South Africa: NATO's unwelcome ally. Charles Latour. illus map tab NATO's Fifteen Nations 21: 58-64+ Jun-Jul '76

Statistics

South Africa. London's International Institute for Strategic Studies. Tables only. AF Mag 59:78 Dec '76

Spain

Statistics

Spain. London's International Institute for Strategic Studies. Tables only. AF Mag 59:63-64 Dec '76

Sudan

Statistics

Sudan. London's International Institute for Strategic Studies. Tables only. AF Mag 59:72 Dec '76

Sweden

Military trade unionism in Sweden. Annika Brickman. tabs Armed Forces & Soc 2:529-538 Summer '76

National defense and citizen participation in Sweden: The citizen army in an open society. William J. Stover. Nav War Col Rev 28:97-99 Fall '75

Statistics

Sweden. London's International Institute for Strategic Studies. Tables only. AF Mag 59:64 Dec '76

Switzerland

Statistics

Switzerland. London's International Institute for Strategic Studies. Tables only. AF Mag 59:64 Dec '76

Syria

Statistics

Syria. London's International Institute for Strategic Studies. Tables only. AF Mag 59:72 Dec '76

Tanzania

Statistics

Tanzania. London's International Institute for Strategic Studies. Tables only. AF Mag 59:78 Dec '76

Thailand

Statistics

Thailand. London's International Institute for Strategic Studies. Tables only. AF Mag 59:87 Dec '76

Tunisia

Statistics

Tunisia. London's International Institute for Strategic Studies. Tables only. AF Mag 59:72 Dec '76

Turkey

Statistics

Turkey. London's International Institute for Strategic Studies. Tables only. AF Mag 59:61 Dec '76

Uganda

Statistics

Uganda. London's International Institute for Strategic Studies. Tables only. AF Mag 59:78 Dec '76

United States

Assault on military institutions. Gen T.R.Milton, Ret. AF Mag 59:30 Jan '76

Countering the Pentagon line. (Center for Defense Information) Interview. RADM Gene La Rocque, Ret. AF Times 36:28+ Jan 26 '76

Detente and reality. R.J.Rummel. illus tabs Strat Rev 4:33-43 Fall '76

Forces for the future. (Remarks, Lancaster Chamber of Commerce, Lancaster, Calif, Feb 6, 1976) Thomas C.Reed. AF Plcy Ltr for Comdrs: Sup No.4:16-20 Apr '76

The military and national purpose. (Farewell remarks, Pentagon, Nov 10, 1975) James R.Schlesinger. illus AF Mag 59:13-14 Jan '76; Nav War Col Rev 28:57-59 Fall '75

The military and the media. (Remarks, Air War College Media-Military Symposium '76, Maxwell AFB, Ala, March 29, 1976) LtGen Raymond B. Furlong. AF Plcy Ltr for Comdrs: Sup No.6:19-21 Jun '76

Public confidence in the U.S. military. David R. Segal and John D.Blair. tabs Armed Forces & Soc 3:3-11 Fall '76

The role of the Services in support of foreign policy. J.K.Holloway, Jr. illus tabs US Nav Inst Proc 102:65-81 May '76

U.S. General Purpose Forces: A need for modernization. Gen George S.Brown. illus tab Comdrs Dig 19: entire issue May 27 '76

ARMED FORCES ∴ Continued

United States - Cont'd

What does the nation want of its military? (Remarks, 1976 Air Force Sergeants Assoc Convention, Kansas City, Mo, July 25, 1976) Gen Russell E. Dougherty. AF Plcy Ltr for Comdrs: Sup No. 11:20-30 Nov '76

History

Economy before preparedness. (Jefferson's policy) Forrest C. Pogue. illus Def Mgt J 12:14-18 Jul '76

Honor America. (Armed Forces Week, May 8-15, 1976) illus Comdrs Dig 19: entire issue Apr 1 '76

Statistics

Active personnel and forces. Table only. Officer 52:5 Mar '76

Are 2 million members enough? Bruce Callander. AF Times 37:14 Sep 27 '76

FY 77 proposed Defense budget. illus tabs Comdrs Dig 19: entire issue Feb 26 '76

The military numbers game: An analysis. Lee Ewing. AF Times 36:14 Feb 9 '76

(Pres) Ford asks AF cut of 13,000. tab AF Times 36:4 Feb 2 '76

Some statistics on manpower. tabs AF Times 37:26 Sep 13 '76

Soviet Armed Forces: Facts and figures. (Relative capabilities of U.S. and Soviet aerospace forces, and recent trends in defense funding on both sides) tabs AF Mag 59:108-109 Mar '76

The United States. London's International Institute for Strategic Studies. illus tabs AF Mag 59:45-47 Dec '76

The United States and the Soviet Union. London's International Institute for Strategic Studies. illus tabs AF Mag 59:44-50 Dec '76

U.S.-USSR military balance. Table only. Govt Exec 8:25 Dec '76

Uruguay

Statistics

Uruguay. London's International Institute for Strategic Studies. Tables only. AF Mag 59:91 Dec '76

Venezuela

Statistics

Venezuela. London's International Institute for Strategic Studies. Tables only. AF Mag 59:91 Dec '76

Vietnam (Democratic Republic)

Statistics

Vietnam: Democratic Republic. London's International Institute for Strategic Studies. Tables only. AF Mag 59:87 Dec '76

Warsaw Pact

The MBFR (Mutual Balanced Force Reduction) talks--problems and prospects. Axel Hörhager. illus tab map Intl Def Rev 9:189-192 Apr '76

A status report on Mutual and Balanced Forced Reductions (MBFRs). Rembert van Delden. NATO's Fifteen Nations 21:20-21 Aug-Sep '76

ARMED FORCES - Continued

Warsaw Pact - Cont'd

Statistics

The theatre balance between NATO and the Warsaw Pact. London's International Institute for Strategic Studies. tabs AF Mag 59:98-106 Dec '76

The Warsaw Pact. London's International Institute for Strategic Studies. illus tabs AF Mag 59:51-53 Dec '76

Yemen

Statistics

Yemen Arab Republic (North). London's International Institute for Strategic Studies. Tables only. AF Mag 59:72 Dec '76

Yemen (People's Democratic Republic)

Statistics

Yemen: People's Democratic Republic (South). London's International Institute for Strategic Studies. Tables only. AF Mag 59:72 Dec '76

Yugoslavia

Statistics

Yugoslavia. London's International Institute for Strategic Studies. Tables only. AF Mag 59:64 Dec '76

Zaire Republic

Statistics

Zaire Republic. London's International Institute for Strategic Studies. Tables only. AF Mag 59:78 Dec '76

Zambia

Statistics

Zambia. London's International Institute for Strategic Studies. Tables only. AF Mag 59:78 Dec '76

ARMED FORCES COMMUNICATIONS AND ELECTRONICS ASSOCIATION

AFCEA Chapter Man of the Month (Maj Phillip J. Lurie, DCS/Communications-Electronics, Air University, Maxwell AFB, Ala). illus Signal 30:50 Feb '76

(AFCEA's 30th Annual Convention Program, Washington, June 8-10, 1976) illus Signal 30:10-15 May-Jun '76

(30th Annual AFCEA Convention Report, Washington, June 8-10, 1976) illus Signal 30: entire issue Aug '76

Directories

AFCEA's new directors, class of 1980. illus Signal 31:45-47 Nov-Dec '76

The 1976 APGEA sustaining and group member capabilities directory. illus Signal 30:54-111 Jan '76

ARMED FORCES IN EUROPE

Congressional demands for American troop withdrawals from Western Europe: The past as prologue. Phil Williams and Scott D. Sagan. RUSI J for Def Studies 121:52-56 Sep '76

Dove in the cockpit: Peace in today's Europe. Maj Edd D. Wheeler. illus tabs AU Rev 27:36-44 Jan-Feb '76

ARMORED VEHICLES - Continued

History

A Yankee inventor (J. Walter Christie) and the military establishment. George F. Hofmann. (Reprinted in part from Military Affairs, Feb 1975) illus Armor 85:13-17+ Mar-Apr '76

ARMORED WARFARE

See also
Missiles, Antitank

An antiaircraft tank. Robert E. Stone. Armor 85:29 Jul-Aug '76

The armoured forces of the future. Col R. Trofimov. Soviet Mil Rev No. 9:21-23 Sep '76

Beehive: An innovative approach to employment. Maj Eugene D. Colgan. illus tabs Armor 85:20-22 Sep-Oct '76

The blitzkrieg: A premature burial? Colin S. Gray. illus Mil Rev 56:15-18 Oct '76

Combined arms: A look ahead. Capts Joseph R. Inge and James P. Isenhower, Jr. illus tabs Armor 85:9-12 Jul-Aug '76

Destroying armor. Edited by Infantry Magazine Staff. illus Infantry 66:35-42 Sep-Oct '76

Fighting tanks. Col A. Akimov. illus Soviet Mil Rev No. 10:10-13 Oct '76

Hell on wheels. (Air Force and Army's 2d Armored Division (Brigade 75) train in West Germany for NATO support) MSgt Harold D. Newcomb. illus Airman 20:8-12 Apr '76

Hold off the tank fight for a while, Ivan, until we build up. F. Clifton Berry, Jr. tab Armed Forces J Intl 113:8 Apr '76

How to defend outnumbered and win. LtCol David L. Tamminen. (Reprinted from Armor, Nov-Dec 1975) illus tabs Fld Arty J 44:39-43 Mar-Apr '76

Meeting engagements of tank armies (1941-45). Col Z. Shutov. map Soviet Mil Rev No. 12:51-53 Dec '76

More bangs for fewer buck$. Col Robert J. Icks, Ret. illus Armor 85:35-39 Mar-Apr '76

Needed now: An antiarmor doctrine. Capt Timothy R. O'Neill. illus Armor 85:18-24 Jan-Feb '76

Night tactical evaluation. Col John H. Weckerling. illus Armor 85:45-46 May-Jun '76

The October War: Burying the blitzkrieg. Jeffrey Record. illus Mil Rev 56:19-21 Apr '76

An overview (of mechanized Infantry). Col Zeb B. Bradford. (Condensed from Infantry, Nov-Dec 1975) illus Infantry 66:15-18 Sep-Oct '76

Psychological steeling of tankmen. Maj M. Rudachenko. Soviet Mil Rev No. 1:30-31 Jan '76

The Soviet antitank debate. Phillip A. Karber. (Reprinted from Survival, May-June 1976) illus Mil Rev 56:67-76 Nov '76; Armor 85:10-14 Nov-Dec '76

The Soviet Manchurian campaign, August 1945: Prototype for the Soviet offensive. Capt Eugene D. Bétit. illus map Mil Rev 56:65-73 May '76

A tank Army in the offensive (in WW II). Col N. Kobrin. illus Soviet Mil Rev No. 1:47-49 Jan '76

ARMORED WARFARE - Continued

Tank company FMF (Fleet Marine Force). Capt Maxwell O. Johnson. illus MarCor Gaz 60:33-38 Jun '76

A tank myth or a missile mirage? Charles Wakebridge. illus Mil Rev 56:3-11 Aug '76

Tank, supertank, or no tank at all. Maj L. D. Holder. illus Armor 85:41-44 Jan-Feb '76

Tank warrior in the Golan. BrigGen S. L. A. Marshall, Ret. illus Mil Rev 56:3-12 Jan '76

Tanks in the Middle East. Jac Weller. illus Mil Rev 56:11-23 May '76

Equipment

Future combat vehicles. William F. Banks. Natl Def 60:274-275 Jan-Feb '76

History

Craftsmen in armor: The hobo (MajGen Percy Hobart) and der schnelle Heinz (Gen Heinz Guderian). Kenneth Macksey. illus Armor 85:36-40 Jan-Feb '76

(Field Marshall Erich von) Manstein's winter miracle (Jan-March 1943). Capt Ronald J. Brown. illus maps Armor 85:18-21 Nov-Dec '76

French antitank doctrine, 1940: The antidote that failed. Maj Robert A. Doughty. illus Mil Rev 56:36-48 May '76

A good tank misused. (The French Char B) Raymond Surlémont. illus tab Armor 85:41-43 Jul-Aug '76

The nemesis of the Panzer armies. (Russian T-34 tanks in WW II) Robert P. Arnoldt. illus tab Armor 85:44-47 Sep-Oct '76

Study and Teaching

Bringing the battlefield to class. Maj Donald L. Cummings. illus Armor 85:39-40 Jul-Aug '76

Forward ho! The Delta Troop myth. LtCol William P. Gillette. tab Armor 85:45-46 Jan-Feb '76

Friend or foe? (Armored vehicle recognition) Robert K. Bauer. illus Armor 85:27-29 Nov-Dec '76

Gaining the edge (in the armor situation). LtCol John C. Bahnsen. tabs Armor 85:49-52 Jan-Feb '76

The making of a tanker. Capt Robert E. Laird. illus Armor 85:23-26 May-Jun '76

Mini-ranges pay big dividends. SP5 Jeffrey Stark. Armor 85:24 Nov-Dec '76

Reduce your (fire control system) budget, yet buy more. Capt Edward A. Bryla. tab Armor 85:15 Nov-Dec '76

Revive the telescope. Capt Everette L. Roper, Jr. illus tabs Armor 85:23-24 Sep-Oct '76

Structuring a combat maneuver battalion. Kenneth J. Ayers. illus Armor 85:50-51 May-Jun '76

Tank crew proficiency testing. LtCol Eric L. Prall. illus tab Armor 85:13-15 Sep-Oct '76

Training tankers to think. (1st Cav Div, Fort Hood, Tex) Richard C. Barnard. illus AF Times, Times Magazine sup:4-8 Jun 14 '76

'We didn't come just to qualify.' (Tank Crew Qualification Course (TCQC)) Capt Robert E. Harry. illus Armor 85:30-34 Mar-Apr '76

ARMORIES

The village armories in Alaska. LtCol W.F.Gabella and SP5 Byron Wooten. illus Natl Guardsman 30: 26-27 Feb '76

ARMS CONTROL

See also
Disarmament

Air Force Chief of Staff's FY 1977 Posture Statement. (Statement before House Committee on Armed Services, Washington, Jan 29, 1976) Gen David C.Jones. AF Plcy Ltr for Comdrs: Sup No.3:23-40 Mar '76

Arms control and world order. Hedley Bull. Intl Sec 1:3-16 Summer '76

The B-1 strategic bomber: A necessary weapons system. Maj R.O'Mara. illus tab Royal Air Forces Qtr 16:236-242 Autumn '76

Backfire (Tu-V-G, new Soviet supersonic bomber): Strategic implications. Gerard K.Burke. illus tabs Mil Rev 56:85-90 Sep '76

A comprehensive test ban: Everybody or nobody. Donald G.Brennan. Intl Sec 1:92-117 Summer '76

The cruise missile: A weapon in search of a mission. illus (Also cutaway) Def Monitor 5: entire issue Sep '76

Foreign policy and national security. (From address, World Affairs Council and Southern Methodist University, Dallas, March 22, 1976) Henry A.Kissinger. Intl Sec 1:182-191 Summer '76

A holocaust for Happy Valley? Henry Young. illus US Nav Inst Proc 102:52-61 Nov '76

Military concepts for political objectives. LtCol Joel J.Snyder, Ret. illus AU Rev 27:55-62 Jan-Feb '76

The new SecDef: Donald H.Rumsfeld. L.Edgar Prina. Sea Power 18:17-18 Dec '75

New threats to the nuclear balance: A challenge for arms control. (Remarks, Town Hall of California, Los Angeles, Aug 31, 1976) Fred C.Ikle. AF Plcy Ltr for Comdrs: Sup No.11:14-20 Nov '76

Nuclear non-proliferation: U.S. Defense policy today. Donald R.Cotter. illus Comdrs Dig 19: entire issue Nov 25 '76

Nuclear strategy: The debate moves on. Colin S.Gray. RUSI J for Def Studies 121:44-50 Mar '76

On the objectives of arms control. Bernard Brodie. Intl Sec 1:17-36 Summer '76

A program guide to SALT II. Colin S.Gray. (Reprinted from Survival, Sep-Oct 1975) Mil Rev 56: 82-89 Apr '76

Problems of nuclear free zones--the Nordic example. LtCol Jay C.Mumford. illus Mil Rev 56:3-10 Mar '76

SALT on the eagle's tail. William R.Van Cleave. illus Strat Rev 4:44-55 Spring '76

SALT: Time to quit. Colin S.Gray. illus Strat Rev 4:14-22 Fall '76

SALT II's gray-area weapon systems. (Report on AFA's Symposium on "Tomorrow's Strategic Options," Vandenberg AFB, Calif, April 28-29, 1976) Edgar Ulsamer. illus AF Mag 59:80-82+ Jul '76

ARMS CONTROL - Continued

Senator (Henry M.) Jackson declassifies Schlesinger SALT testimony, awaits Kissinger reply to August letter (concerning Soviet deployment of the SS-19 missile). Armed Forces J Intl 113:8 Jan '76

Strategic missile forces. Gen George S.Brown. illus Natl Def 61:36-38+ Jul-Aug '76

Strategic nuclear balance is not enough. Interview. Gen George Brown. illus tab Govt Exec 8:24-26+ Dec '76

ARMS RACE

A blueprint for safeguarding the strategic balance. (2d report on AFA's Symposium on "Tomorrow's Strategic Options," Vandenberg AFB, Calif, April 28-29, 1976) Edgar Ulsamer. illus tabs AF Mag 59:68-74 Aug '76

Nearing the climacteric 1976. A.H.S.Candlin. Army Qtr 106:194-203 Apr '76

On the objectives of arms control. Bernard Brodie. Intl Sec 1:17-36 Summer '76

The Soviet juggernaut: Racing faster than ever. Edgar Ulsamer. illus tabs AF Mag 59:56-58+ Mar '76

Soviet R&D at "critical mass": "Sobering assessment" troubles DOD research chief (Malcolm R. Currie). Benjamin F.Schemmer. tabs Armed Forces J Intl 113:12-13 Mar '76

Strategic Forces: How America & the Soviets compare. Gen George S.Brown. illus tabs Comdrs Dig 19: entire issue Apr 15 '76

Strategic nuclear balance is not enough. Interview. Gen George Brown. illus tab Govt Exec 8:24-26+ Dec '76

(U.S./USSR military balance) illus tabs Armed Forces J Intl pt 1, U.S./USSR military balance shifts in favor of Russia. Benjamin F.Schemmer. 113:18+ Mar '76; pt 2, Scope of and reasons behind U.S./USSR force asymmetries. 113:23-26+ Apr '76; pt 3 (Summary) 113:24-28 May '76

ARMS SALES

Aerospace sales gains are more illusory than real. F.Clifton Berry, Jr. illus Armed Forces J Intl 113:10 Jan '76

Affordability + performance: USAF's R&D goal. Edgar Ulsamer. illus AF Mag 59:31-36 Mar '76

Coming: A North Atlantic Common Defense Market. Thomas A.Callaghan, Jr. illus map Countermeasures 2:24+ Aug '76

Defense industry: Is the foundation crumbling? tab Govt Exec 8:19 Mar '76

Exporting & importing: A two sided view. Wallace W. Orr. tabs Countermeasures 2:50-51+ Aug '76

F-16: Fighter procurement essential to Iranian Air Force modernization. Robert Ellsworth. illus (Also cutaway) Comdrs Dig 19: entire issue Oct 21 '76

FMS (Foreign Military Sales) is only one export control. (Interview with Maurice Mountain) Govt Exec 8:20-21 Dec '76

FMS (Foreign Military Sales): "No more giving it away." Interview. LtGen Howard Fish. illus tabs Govt Exec 8:19+ Dec '76

ARMS SALES - Continued

Foreign arms sales: 2 sides to the coin. LtCol David L. Morse. illus tabs Army 26:14-21 Jan '76

Foreign military sales: An $11 billion market for the U.S. Charles De Vore. illus Signal 30:38-43 Jan '76

Israeli defense capability. Irvine J. Cohen. Natl Def 60:271-273 Jan-Feb '76

Keeping foreign military sales in perspective. John F. Loosbrock. AF Mag 59:4-5 Feb '76

Large-scale changes coming in military trade legislation. F. Clifton Berry, Jr. Armed Forces J Intl 113:12 Feb '76

Latin Americans shift from U.S. to foreign arms suppliers, now pay more cash. F. Clifton Berry, Jr. illus Armed Forces J Intl 113:14-15 Jun '76

Market data report: Foreign military sales orders (FY 1974 and FY 1975). Table only. Review 55:38 Nov-Dec '75

Military assistance program and foreign military sales. (Statement before House Committee on International Relations, Nov 11, 1975) William P. Clements, Jr. AF Pley Ltr for Comdrs: Sup No. 2:27-31 Feb '76

Military sales abroad. Philip A. Phalon. Natl Def 61: 129-130 Sep-Oct '76

Military sales overseas. S. Stanley Katz. illus Natl Def 60:446-448 May-Jun '76

New duty in Defense (Deputy SecDef): Robert Ellsworth will supervise intelligence and foreign operations. illus Natl Def 60:346-347 Mar-Apr '76

Poor European productivity plagues U.S. purchases. F. Clifton Berry, Jr. tabs Armed Forces J Intl 113:32-33 Mar '76

Savings realized through foreign military sales. tabs Armed Forces J Intl 113:9 Jun '76

The Security Assistance Program. (Statement before Committee on International Relations, House of Representatives, Nov 12, 1975) LtGen H. M. Fish. AF Pley Ltr for Comdrs: Sup No. 1:18-22 Jan '76

U.S. arms sales: Congress steps on the brake. Henry T. Simmons. illus Interavia 31:987-988 Oct '76

U.S. military assistance and sales to Korea (1971-76). Table only. Def Monitor 5:7 Jun '76

Value of U.S. helicopter exports continues to increase. illus tab Armed Forces J Intl 113:11 Jan '76

We service what we sell. (USAF Logistics Command gives assistance and advice to foreign purchasers of U.S.-made military aircraft) Capt John B. Taylor. illus Airman 20:10-12 May '76

XM-1, Leopard II stakes raised; AWACS hostage? illus Armed Forces J Intl 113:14 Apr '76

History

United States-Soviet naval relations in the 1930's: The Soviet Union's efforts to purchase naval vessels. Thomas R. Maddux. illus Nav War Col Rev 29:28-37 Fall '76

ARMY

See also
Armor
Artillery
Infantry
Quartermaster Corps
   also subdivision under specific subjects, e.g., Education and Training--Army--U.S.

ARMY - Continued

Biography

America's first Chief Engineer (Col Richard Gridley). Raleigh B. Buzzaird. (Reprinted from Military Engineer, Dec 1947) illus map Mil Engr 68:31-36 Jan-Feb '76

Washington's last Chief Engineer, Etienne Bechet, Sieur de Rochefontaine. Raleigh B. Buzzaird. (Reprinted from Military Engineer, March-April 1953) illus map Mil Engr 68:452-455 Nov-Dec '76

Corps, Divisions, etc

See also
Transportation Units

Statistics

Average strength of military formations. London's International Institute for Strategic Studies. Table only. AF Mag 59:97 Dec '76

Great Britain

British Army Infantry. (1st Battalion of the Staffordshire Regiment) MSgt Dick Larsen. illus Infantry 66:42-46 May-Jun '76

United States

AFJ's bum dope on LBJ's farewell. Col John G. Jameson, Jr. illus Armed Forces J Intl 113:20-21 Apr '76

Air defense in the 2d Infantry Division. (Fit-to-fight (Pro-Life) program) illus Air Def Mag, pp 20-23, Jan-Mar '76

The day the President got conned: (Lyndon Johnson) saying goodbye to the wrong troops (at Fort Bragg, NC, Feb 16, 1968). Benjamin F. Schemmer. illus Armed Forces J Intl 113:26-28 Feb '76

Financial management--division to battalion contracts. LtCol Thomas W. Cassada. illus Mil Rev 56:42-46 Jan '76

Hell on wheels. (Air Force and Army's 2d Armored Division (Brigade 75) train in West Germany for NATO support) MSgt Harold D. Newcomb. illus Airman 20:8-12 Apr '76

Ready & waiting. (82d Airborne Division, Fort Bragg, NC) SSgt John Savard. illus Soldiers 31: 6-10 Nov '76

The "Real Cav" (4th Sq, 9th Cavalry). MSgt Wayne E. Hair. illus USA Avn Dig 22:24-25 Mar '76

Supersoldiers of the North. (172d ("Arctic Light") Infantry Brigade) BrigGen James G. Boatner. illus Army 26:27-30 Nov '76

Training tankers to think. (1st Cav Div, Fort Hood, Tex) Richard C. Barnard. illus AF Times, Times Magazine sup:4-8 Jun 14 '76

United States--History

History + symbolism = morale. (Organizational History Branch, Center of Military History) Robert K. Wright, Jr. Translog 7:14-15+ Aug-Sep '76

United States--Organization

Smaller, more 'agile' but more units in new division. Officer 52:11 Oct '76

Africa

History

African armies in historical and contemporary perspectives: The search for connections. Rene Lemarchand. J Pol & Mil Sociol 4:261-275 Fall '76

France

New automated command and control systems for the French Army. H.-J. Jung. illus Intl Def Rev 9: 453-457 Jun '76

Germany

History

The Hutier legend. Laszlo M. Alfoldi. illus Parameters 5, No. 2:69-74 '76

Seeckt and the Führerheer. Maj L. D. Holder. illus Mil Rev 56:71-79 Oct '76

The Waffen SS: A social psychological perspective. George M. Kren and Leon H. Rappoport. Armed Forces & Soc 3:87-102 Fall '76

Germany (Democratic Republic)

The effect of detente on professionalism and political control in the East German Army. Dale R. Herspring. illus Nav War Col Rev 28:10-20 Winter '76

National People's Army of the GDR (German Democratic Republic). illus Soviet Mil Rev No. 2:58-59 Feb '76

Great Britain

The British Army today. LtGen William Scotter. RUSI J for Def Studies 121:16-21+ Jun '76

Change--but not decay. MajGen J. D. Lunt. Army Qtr 106:394-396 Oct '76

The corporals' war: Internal security operations in Northern Ireland. Col Norman L. Dodd, Ret. illus Mil Rev 56:58-68 Jul '76

Northern Ireland's 'Twilight War': Frustrating duty for British troops. Col James B. Deerin, Ret. illus map Army 26:14-21 Dec '76

Ptarmigan--a secure area communications system for the British Army. illus tabs Intl Def Rev 9: 458-461 Jun '76

A visit with Queen Elizabeth's own Sixth Gurkhas. LtCol Kimbale R. Wakefield. illus MarCor Gaz 60:27-31 Dec '76

History

The Army of Lord Cornwallis: A study of logistics inadequacies. James L. Carpenter, Jr. illus map Log Spectrum 10:5-13 Fall '76

Organization--History

The contested evolution of the line. Gregory Blaxland. tab RUSI J for Def Studies 121:23-29 Mar '76

Hungary

The Hungarian People's Army. F. Rubin. chart RUSI J for Def Studies 121:59-66 Sep '76

History

Army for defence of socialism. Col P. Topolev. illus Soviet Mil Rev No. 9:59-60 Sep '76

Organization

The Hungarian People's Army. F. Rubin. chart RUSI J for Def Studies 121:59-66 Sep '76

Ireland

History

The Royal Irish in U.S. War of Independence. Maj H. E. D. Harris. Army Qtr 106:488-491 Oct '76

Italy

The Italian Army: Some notes on recruitment. Gianfranco Pasquino. tabs Armed Forces & Soc 2:205-217 Winter '76

Russia

A capsule assessment of Soviet Army capabilities. tabs Mil Rev 56:94-95 Jun '76

The growing threat: New challenges for the EW community. Ronald T. Pretty. illus Elect Warfare 8: 43+ Mar-Apr '76

New method of comparing (U.S.-Soviet strength) advised (by Defense Manpower Commission). AF Times 36:38 May 31 '76

The regulations and commander's initiative. MajGen A. Zyryanov. illus Soviet Mil Rev No. 2:26-27 Feb '76

Soviet ground forces and the conventional mode of operations. John Erickson. RUSI J for Def Studies 121:45-49 Jun '76

The Soviet Land Forces today. (Interview with I. G. Pavlovsky) illus Soviet Mil Rev No. 9:2-7 Sep '76

The Soviet soldier. Maj Joseph C. Liberti. illus Infantry 66:37-41 Jan-Feb '76

Threat scenario: German Democratic Republic. illus Elect Warfare 8:66 Mar-Apr '76

History

Bolshevik ideas on the military's role in modernization. William E. Odom. Armed Forces & Soc 3: 103-120 Fall '76

Experience in organisation and recruitment. Col A. Babakov and LtCol A. Pastukhov. Soviet Mil Rev No. 9:12-14 Sep '76

Ideas are the first to engage the enemy. (Interview with Marshal Ivan Khristoforovich Bagramyan) Soviet Mil Rev No. 9:16-18 Sep '76

Switzerland

Military service and social change in Switzerland. Hanspeter Kriesi. tabs Armed Forces & Soc 2: 218-226 Winter '76

Thailand

The tasks for Thailand's Army and an assessment of its ability. E. Stuart Kirby. RUSI J for Def Studies 121:50-53 Mar '76

United States

See also
Army Materiel Command
Forces Command
Military Traffic Management Command
Signal Corps
Training and Doctrine Command
Transportation Corps

America and its Army: A Bicentennial look at posture and goals. Gen Fred C. Weyand. illus Parameters 6, No. 1:2-11 '76

Army meets the fuel crisis. LtCol Robert R. Bachmann. illus tabs Natl Def 60:436-438 May-Jun '76

Basil Liddell Hart: Much to say to the 'Army of '76. MajGen George B. Pickett, Jr, Ret. illus Army 26:29-33 Apr '76

Coalition warfare. Robert W. Komer. illus Army 26: 28-32 Sep '76

ARMY - Continued

United States - Cont'd

Cohesion and disintegration in the American Army (in Vietnam): An alternative perspective. Paul L. Savage and Richard A. Gabriel. tabs Armed Forces & Soc 2:340-376 Spring '76

Combat readiness on a shoestring. (Army augmentation units) Anthony J. Daniels. illus Army 26: 49-51 Apr '76

'Great progress in very difficult circumstances.' Interview. Gen Fred C. Weyand. illus Army 26: 14-16+ Oct '76

In Guard, Army partnership, the key is mutual respect. LtCol Raymond E. Bell, Jr. illus Army 26: 24-26 Jan '76

MTMC and the total Army. Dan Hall. illus Translog 7:3-5 Dec '76

The military ethic. Col William L. Hauser. illus Strat Rev 4:76-86 Fall '76

New method of comparing (U.S.-Soviet strength) advised (by Defense Manpower Commission). AF Times 36:38 May 31 '76

(1976 Green Book: Status reports, command and staff directory, weapons and equipment) illus Army 26: entire issue Oct '76

The present role of the American soldier. Maj Robert F. Helms II. illus Mil Rev 56:12-18 Apr '76

Self-moving test seen in jeopardy. AF Times 37:4 Aug 16 '76

Tough and ready--"to keep the peace ... to deter war." Interview. Army Chief of Staff, Gen Fred C. Weyand. illus Soldiers 31:31-34 Feb '76

The U.S. Army after the fall of Vietnam: A contemporary dilemma. Maj Marc B. Powe. illus Mil Rev 56:3-17 Feb '76

Directories

(Army) command and staff (1976 directory). pors Army 26:131-143 Oct '76

History

Army almanack: Highlights in the growth of a nation. tabs Soldiers 31:55 Jun '76

Challenging the logistics status quo during the Civil War. James A. Huston. illus Def Mgt J 12:25-33 Jul '76

Continental Army logistics: An overview. illus Army Log 8:12-13 Jul-Aug '76

Continental Army logistics: Food supply. illus Army Log 8:24-28 Jan-Feb '76

Continental Army logistics: Transportation. (Reprinted from Army Logistician, Nov-Dec 1975) illus map Def Trans J 32:28-31 Aug '76

Doomed to fail: The first Federal Army. LtCol Gordon Taylor Bratz. Mil Rev 56:56-57 Jun '76

Forty miles a day on beans & hay. (Soldier's life on the 1876 frontier) LtCol Wilfred L. Ebel. illus Soldiers 31:36-39 Jul '76

The gasoline brigade. (Excerpts from Forging the Thunderbolt) Mildred Gillie. illus Armor 85:30-35 May-Jun '76

(George) Washington builds an Army. James B. Deerin. illus Natl Guardsman 30:6-9 Jan '76

United States - Cont'd

History - Cont'd

George Washington's first generals. James B. Deerin. illus Natl Guardsman 30:2-6 Apr '76

Management of the "mixed multitude" in the Continental Army. BrigGen James L. Collins, Jr. illus Def Mgt J 12:7-13 Jul '76

The militia in the Revolutionary War. James B. Deerin. map illus Natl Guardsman 30:32p sup opposite p 12 Aug-Sep '76

National Guard Heritage Encampment (Washington, Aug 28-Sep 1, 1976). Paul Lyter. illus Air Reservist 28:12-13 Jul '76

Order: (Baron Friedrich Wilhelm von) Steuben's contribution to the patriot cause. Maj David A. Armstrong. illus Mil Rev 56:58-68 Jun '76

Organize a mechanized force. Col H.H.D. Heiberg, Ret. illus Armor 85:8-11+ Sep-Oct '76

The private (Nathanael Greene)'s strategy. LtCol Fred Grenier. illus Soldiers 31:42-43 May '76

Taking stock of the Army on nation's Bicentennial. Martin R. Hoffmann. illus Army 26:8-9+ Oct '76

They would endure. (Life in the Continental Army, based on the diary of an enlisted man, Aaron Barlow) Capts Duncan A. Carter and Michael S. Lancaster. illus Soldiers 31:6-9 Jul '76

Washington's most brilliant engineer (Chevalier Louis Le Bègue Du Portail). Raleigh B. Buzzaird. illus maps Mil Engr 68:104-110 Mar-Apr '76

Organization

Another mission for the CSC (Combat Support Company) commander. Capt William F. Greer. illus Armor 85:47-48 Nov-Dec '76

Combined arms: A look ahead. Capts Joseph R. Inge and James P. Isenhower, Jr. illus tabs Armor 85: 9-12 Jul-Aug '76

Four men and a lion. (Science of the organization of armies) Capt John R. Wallace. illus Armor 85:40-42 Mar-Apr '76

Structuring a combat maneuver battalion. Kenneth J. Ayers. illus Armor 85:50-51 May-Jun '76

Tooth-to-tail: A conceptual void. illus tab Army Log 8:33-37 Mar-Apr '76

Total force. LtCol James E. Witek. tab Soldiers 31: 43-46 Aug '76

Statistics

Army almanack: Highlights in the growth of a nation. tabs Soldiers 31:55 Jun '76

Readiness of all total force jumps. tabs Officer 52:19 Feb '76

Vietnam (Democratic Republic)

Vietnam summary: Military operations after the cease-fire agreement. MajGen Charles J. Timmes, Ret. illus tab maps Mil Rev pt 1, 56:63-75 Aug '76; pt 2, 56:21-29 Sep '76

Vietnam (Republic)

Vietnam summary: Military operations after the cease-fire agreement. MajGen Charles J. Timmes, Ret. illus tab maps Mil Rev pt 1, 56:63-75 Aug '76; pt 2, 56:21-29 Sep '76

ARMY, 7th

War with Russia in Europe would find U.S. sorely
outnumbered. Col Robert D.Heinl, Jr, Ret. illus
Sea Power 19:33-34 Aug '76

ARMY, 8th

In Korea, 'single-minded emphasis on deterrence.'
Gen Richard G.Stilwell. illus Army 26:68-70+
Oct '76

Plastic police (ration control card). Sgt1C Floyd
Harrington. illus tab Soldiers 31:37-40 Nov '76

Directories

Eighth Army. Army 26:139 Oct '76

ARMY, ALASKA

Supersoldiers of the North. (172d ("Arctic Light") Infantry Brigade) BrigGen James G.Boatner. illus
Army 26:27-30 Nov '76

ARMY, EUROPE

See also
Army, 7th

Allied team. (Brigade 76 will deploy to Europe to gain
combat proficiency in its North Atlantic Treaty
Organization role) MSgt Dick Larsen. illus map
Soldiers 31:6-10 Mar '76

11th Aviation Group (Combat) aviation training in
USAREUR. Capt Eric R.Kunz. illus USA Avn Dig
22:2-3+ Aug '76

Charlie's place. (SSgt Charles R.Reed, NCOIC of
Wackernheim Range near Mainz, West Germany)
Lt Michael A.Bartell and SP4 Kregg P.J.Jorgen-
son. illus Army 26:22-25 Nov '76

"Interoperability"--the now challenge in Europe. Maj
Gary F.Ramage. illus USA Avn Dig 22:26-29
Aug '76

Land beyond the moon (Grafenwoehr, Germany, Ar-
my Europe and 7th Army's Training Center). SP4
Kathleen E.Murray. illus Soldiers 31:37-38
Dec '76

Making Kontakt. (Strengthening German-American
relations) Capt Larry J.Myers. illus Soldiers 31:
10-13 Aug '76

The new short war strategy. Gen James H.Polk, Ret.
(Reprinted from Strategic Review, Summer 1975)
Mil Rev 56:58-64 Mar '76

Putting it together with R-S-1 in U.S. Army, Europe.
Gen George S.Blanchard. illus Army 26:52-54+
Oct '76

Showdown at (Grafenwoehr's) Range 32 (Army Europe
and 7th Army's Training Center). Capt Larry
Brainerd. illus Soldiers 31:34-36 Dec '76

U.S. Army Europe ... 'Sense of excitement.' Interview. Gen George S.Blanchard. illus Army 26:13+
Aug '76

Directories

U.S. Army, Europe. Army 26:139 Oct '76

ARMY, JAPAN

Directories

U.S. Army, Japan. Army 26:139 Oct '76

ARMY AEROMEDICAL RESEARCH LABORATORY

U.S. Army Aeromedical Research Laboratory. Col
Robert W.Bailey. illus USA Avn Dig 22:4-5+
Oct '76

ARMY AIR DEFENSE SCHOOL

Major General (Robert J.) Lunn is new Fort Bliss
commander. illus Air Def Mag, pp 4-5, Apr-
Jun '76

ARMY AND AIR FORCE EXCHANGE SERVICE see
Exchanges--Air Force--U.S.; Exchanges--Armed
Forces--U.S.; Exchanges--Army--U.S.

ARMY ARTILLERY AND MISSILE SCHOOL see Army
Field Artillery School

ARMY AVIATION

Great Britain

Army Air Corps up to date. J.D.R.Rawlings. illus
Air Pict 38:184-185 May '76

The British Army and the battlefield aerial vehicle:
The way ahead. Col S.M.W.Hickey. illus RUSI J
for Def Studies 121:53-62 Jun '76

History

The evolution of British Army Aviation. Col S.M.W.
Hickey. RUSI J for Def Studies 120:15-18+ Dec '75

United States

101st (Airborne Division (Air Assault)) in Reforg-
er 76. Col Larry J.Baughman and Maj Robert E.
Jones, Jr. illus maps USA Avn Dig 22:2-3+
Dec '76

Army aircraft survivability. Maj N.I.Patla. illus tab
USA Avn Dig 22:7+ Nov '76

(Army) Guard aviation logistics. Capt Arthur W.
Ries. illus Army Log 8:8-11 Nov-Dec '76

Attack. (4th Battalion (Attack Helicopter), 77th Field
Artillery) Capts Michael E.Sloniker and Gary R.
Sosnowski. illus USA Avn Dig 22:4-5+ Dec '76

Aviation as a specialty. LtCol B.H.Freeman. USA
Avn Dig 22:16-18 Oct '76

101st Aviation Group night flying. Capt Peter L.
Wyro. illus USA Avn Dig 22:8-10 Jan '76

A commander speaks to his aviators on aviation safety. MajGen Eivind H.Johansen. illus USA Avn Dig
22:2-4 Nov '76

A doctor looks at Army Aviation. MajGen Spurgeon
Neel. illus USA Avn Dig 22:1+ Oct '76

Increased responsibility for Army aviators. BrigGen
Charles E.Canedy. illus USA Avn Dig 22:1+
Nov '76

"Interoperability"--the now challenge in Europe. Maj
Gary F.Ramage. illus USA Avn Dig 22:26-29
Aug '76

Professionalism in Army Aviation and budgetary constraints. BrigGen Charles E.Canedy. illus USA
Avn Dig 22:1-3 Jun '76

Realistic training at any price? Arnold R.Lambert.
illus USA Avn Dig 22:35-36 Jun '76

Terrain flight international. (Survey of 9 NATO nations and 3 Army agencies) Capt Don A.Mynard.
illus USA Avn Dig 22:30-34 Aug '76

ARMY AVIATION - Continued

United States - Cont'd

Those tenacious trouble-shooters at (maintenance
branch of) ALC (Aviation Logistics Center, Edgewood Arsenal, Md). Bruce P.Hargreaves. illus
tab Natl Guardsman 30:22-25 Apr '76

Training points the way. LtGen Robert M.Shoemaker.
illus USA Avn Dig 22:2-3+ Jul '76

U.S. Army Aviation Center Tactics Laboratory.
Capt Charles E.Taylor. illus tab USA Avn Dig 22:
8-12 Feb '76

History

The Army Aviation story. illus USA Avn Dig pt 10,
The early 1960s. Maj David H.Price. 22:4-5+
Jun '76; pt 11, The mid-1960s. 22:8-11 Jul '76;
pt 12, The late 1960s. 22:20-22 Aug '76; Outlook.
22:10-11 Sep '76

Those days of the leather helmet. MSgt Dave Sylva.
illus Aerosp Safety 32:14-17 May '76

When flying was up in the air. (Military aviation got
its start in 1909 at what became known as the Army Aviation School, College Park, Md) TSgt Tom
Dwyer. illus Airman 20:18-22 Nov '76

Organization

11th Aviation Group (Combat) aviation training in
USAREUR. Capt Eric R.Kunz. illus USA Avn Dig
22:2-3+ Aug '76

Divisional air defense--how much is enough? LtCol
William O.Staudenmaier. illus map Air Def Mag,
pp 34-37, Jul-Sep '76

ARMY AVIATION CENTERS AND SCHOOLS

Clearing the air. (Air Traffic Control School, Fort
Rucker, Ala) Janet Hake. illus Soldiers 31:6-9
Aug '76

Fort Rucker (Ala) ATC school trains Fort Campbell
(Ky) controllers. Sgt1C Keith A.Ellefson and John
C.Smith. illus USA Avn Dig 22: back cover Sep '76

Hail and farewell. (MajGen James C.Smith succeeds
MajGen William J.Maddox, Jr, as commander of
Army Aviation Center, Fort Rucker, Ala) illus USA
Avn Dig 22:48-49 Jul '76

U.S. Army Aviation Center Tactics Laboratory.
Capt Charles E.Taylor. illus tab USA Avn Dig 22:
8-12 Feb '76

History

When flying was up in the air. (Military aviation got
its start in 1909 at what became known as the Army Aviation School, College Park, Md) TSgt Tom
Dwyer. illus Airman 20:18-22 Nov '76

ARMY AVIATION HALL OF FAME

See also
Aviation Hall of Fame

CW4 Michael J.Novosel (in) Army Aviation Hall of
Fame. illus USA Avn Dig 22:15 Sep '76

(Col) J.Elmore Swenson (in) Army Aviation Hall of
Fame. illus USA Avn Dig 22:15 Feb '76

(LtGen John J.Tolson in) Army Aviation Hall of
Fame. illus USA Avn Dig 22:30 Mar '76

ARMY AVIATION HALL OF FAME - Continued

(Maj Charles L.Kelly in) Army Aviation Hall of
Fame. illus USA Avn Dig 22:23 Dec '76

(MajGen) Spurgeon Neel elected to Army Aviation
Hall of Fame for pioneering aeromedevac. illus
Aviation, Space & Envmt Med 47:799 Jul '76

ARMY FIELD ARTILLERY SCHOOL

View from the blockhouse. (Notes from the School)
Regular feature in issues of Field Artillery
Journal

Organization

USAFAS reorganization. chart Fld Arty J 44:57-59
Mar-Apr '76

ARMY FORCES COMMAND see Forces Command

ARMY FOREIGN SCIENCE AND TECHNOLOGY CENTER

U.S. Army Foreign Science and Technology Center.
David Latt. illus USA Avn Dig 22:24-27 Feb '76

ARMY GENERAL STAFF

Gen (Bernard W.) Rogers named to succeed (Gen
Fred C.) Weyand as Army Chief of Staff. Army
26:9-10 Sep '76

New (Army) Chief of Staff (Gen Bernard W.Rogers).
illus Soldiers 31:2 Oct '76

New Army Chief of Staff: General (Bernard W.) Rogers brings vision and experience to this high office. illus Natl Def 61:186-187 Nov-Dec '76

Directories

(Army) command and staff (1976 directory). pors
Army 26:131-143 Oct '76

History

The evolution of the general staff concept. MajGen
James Murphy. illus Def Mgt J 12:34-39 Jul '76

ARMY HEALTH SERVICES COMMAND

HSC (Health Services Command) outlines cutbacks in
medical care. tabs AF Times 37:28 Dec 13 '76

ARMY LOGISTICS CENTER

Managing logistics in the field. LtCol William C.
Banze and Miles S.Abbott. illus Army Log 8:2-5
May-Jun '76

ARMY MATERIEL COMMAND see Army Materiel Development and Readiness Command

ARMY MATERIEL DEVELOPMENT AND READINESS
COMMAND

See also subcommands by name, e.g.,
Army Foreign Science and Technology Center
Aviation Systems Command
Missile Command

AMC schools--the other Army school system. illus
Army Log 8:10-14 Jan-Feb '76

Combat oriented general support: A conceptual view
of how the general support of the Army in the field
can be operated. LtCols James R.Stivison and
Richard M.Wangenheim. illus Army Log 8:20-23
Jan-Feb '76

Evaluating nonmajor procurements. Robert F.Wil-
liams. Army Log 8:33-35 May-Jun '76

ARMY MATERIEL DEVELOPMENT AND READINESS
COMMAND - Continued

New aviation testing concept. (Collocation of TRA-
DOC's operational test activity (Army Aviation
Test Board) and DARCOM's aviation developmen-
tal test organization (Army Aircraft Development
Test Activity) at U.S. Army Aviation Center, Fort
Rucker, Ala) Maj David M. Mabardy. charts USA
Avn Dig 22:24-25 Jun '76

A new way of doing business. Interview. Gen John R.
Deane, Jr. illus Soldiers 31:21-24 Jun '76

PROMS (PROcurement Management System). Robert
F. Williams and Capt Robert J. Walker. tabs Army
Log 8:2-6 Nov-Dec '76

Progress in the midst of change: From AMC to
DARCOM. Gen John R. Deane, Jr. illus Army
26:78-80+ Oct '76

Directories

Material Development and Readiness Command. Army 26:135 Oct '76

Organization

AMC reorganizes. charts Army Log 8:7-9 Jan-
Feb '76

ARMY MILITARY PERSONNEL CENTER

(Army personnel problems) Interview. MajGen Robert Gard. Fld Arty J 44:35-37 Nov-Dec '76

Organization

Managing your logistics career: Here's how OPMD
(Officer Personnel Management Directorate) does
it. Maj Frank Cunningham III. Army Log 8:12-13
Nov-Dec '76

ARMY POSTS

Maintenance and Repair

The Army's facilities engineering operations.
BrigGen Walter O. Bachus. illus tabs chart Mil
Engr 68:94-97 Mar-Apr '76

United States

Army posts are entered by name and location as given
by the U. S. Organization Chart Service's U.S. Military and Government Installation Directory.

History

(Military) posts from the past. Capt John D. Anderson. illus Soldiers 31:47-51 Jan '76

The rock (Alcatraz). Capt John D. Anderson. illus
Soldiers 31:45-48 Apr '76

Fort Chaffee, Ark

Refugee boom town to ghost town (Fort Chaffee, Ark).
Capt Phil E. Raschke and Jane Moorer. illus Soldiers 31:45-49 Mar '76

Fort McClellan, Ala

'They flat love the MPs in this town': Fort McClellan
and Anniston, Ala and the Army's only law enforcement academy. LtCol Tom Hamrick, Ret.
illus Army 26:34-39 Dec '76

Fort Ord, Calif

As it is. (Basic training today) Darryl D. McEwen.
illus Soldiers 31:49-51 Jul '76

ARMY POSTS - Continued

United States - Cont'd

Fort Rucker, Ala

Capstone (Warrant Officer Senior Course (WOSC),
Fort Rucker, Ala) is back. Sgt1C Floyd Harrington. illus Soldiers 31:11-13 Jun '76

Fort Rucker reorganization. chart USA Avn Dig 22:
inside back cover Mar '76

WOC (Warrant Officer Candidates) to chopper jock.
(Rotary Wing School, Fort Rucker, Ala) Sgt1C
Floyd Harrington. illus Soldiers 31:17-21 May '76

Fort Sill, Okla--History

An Army wife remembers. (Fort Sill at the turn of
the century) Grace Paulding. illus Soldiers 31:40-
41 Jul '76

ARMY TRAINING AND DOCTRINE COMMAND see
Training and Doctrine Command

ARMY WAR COLLEGE

History

George S. Patton's student days at the Army War College. Martin Blumenson. illus Parameters 5,
No. 2:25-32 '76

ARNOLD, Benedict

Crime does not pay. Lynn L. Sims. Mil Rev 56:56-57
Jan '76

ARSENALS

Rocky Mountain haven. (Rocky Mountain Arsenal
(RMA)) Darryl D. McEwen. illus Soldiers 31:49-
51 Aug '76

ART

Air Force Art (Collection). Capt Robert W. Nicholson, Jr. Pictorial. Airman 20:42-47 Mar '76

Cover reproductions. (14 Continental Marine scenes
to commemorate the Bicentennial) Maj Charles
Waterhouse. MarCor Gaz no. 1, "The First Re-
cruits, December 1775." 59: outside covers
Jan '75; no. 2, "Landing at New Providence,
3 March 1776." 59: outside covers Feb '75; no. 3,
"A Marine Lieutenant Dies, 6 April 1776." 59:
outside covers Mar '75; no. 4, "Defeat on Lake
Champlain, 13 October 1776." 59: outside covers
Apr '75; no. 5, "Marines with Washington at
Princeton, 3 January 1777." 59: outside covers
May '75; no. 6, "The Evacuation of Billingsport,
2 October 1777." 59: outside covers Jun '75; no. 7,
"Flag Raising at New Providence, 28 January
1778." 59: outside covers Jul '75; no. 8, "Willing's Marine Expedition, February 1778." 59:
outside covers Aug '75; no. 9, "Launching of the
Whitehaven Raid, 22 April 1778." 59: outside covers Sep '75; no. 10, "John Adams Reviews Jones'
Marines, 13 May 1779." 59: outside covers
Oct '75; no. 11, "Fighting Tops." 59: outside covers Nov '75; no. 12, "Assault at Penobscot." 59:
outside covers Dec '75; no. 13, "Ohio River Row
Galley, Summer 1782." 60: outside covers Jan '76;
no. 14, "Mustering Out, 1 April 1783." 60: outside
covers Feb '76

ART - Continued

In the Tricentennial year 2076. (Artist Robert T. McCall illustrates possible items of the future and creates space mural for the new National Air and Space Museum) Robert K.Ruhl. illus Airman 20: 24-33 Jul '76

Poster war. S.Michael Schnessel. illus Army 26: 40-45 Jul '76

The Spirit of '76. (How an Ohio militiaman's crayon drawing became a famous symbol of the colonial spirit of America) Capt Clint Tennill, Jr. illus Natl Guardsman 30:2-4 Jan '76

Worth a thousand words. (Drawings by former POW Navy LCDR John M.McGrath illustrate what he and others suffered) illus Airman 20:27 Nov '76

ARTIFICIAL RESPIRATION

CPR (CardioPulmonary Resuscitation) ... it could save your life or that of someone else! Chris Scheer. illus Air Reservist 28:15 Nov '76

ARTILLERY

See also
Guns

History

The theoretical evaluation of artillery after World War I. Fred K.Vigman. (Reprinted from Military Affairs, Fall 1952) Fld Arty J 44:21-23+ Jan-Feb '76

Army--Brazil

Brazilian Army artillery rockets. Ronaldo S.Olive. illus Intl Def Rev 9:435-436 Jun '76

Army--France

The Sirocco meteorological sounding station. illus tab Intl Def Rev 9:433-435 Jun '76

Army--Great Britain

The Royal Artillery shows its paces. Col Norman L. Dodd, Ret. Army Qtr 106:459-462 Oct '76

Army--Israel

The Tampella 155 mm gun-howitzer. LtCol P.Crèvecoeur, Ret. illus tabs Intl Def Rev 9:662-663 Aug '76

Army--NATO

Artillery projects of the future. Karl Heinz Bodlien. (Trans from Soldat und Technik, Aug 1974) illus tabs Fld Arty J 44:10-15 Jan-Feb '76

Army--U.S.

Counterfire! illus tabs Fld Arty J pt 1, 43:14-21 Nov-Dec '75; pt 2, 44:32-38 Jan-Feb '76

Heavy artillery: Who needs it? Capt John C.Abshier. illus tabs Fld Arty J 44:31-33 Sep-Oct '76

The rotary forge--revolution in cannon making. Robert E.Weigle. illus tabs Natl Def 60:459-462 May-Jun '76

Track back, smack back. Bill Walsh. illus tab Countermeasures 2:18-21+ Aug '76

ARTILLERY - Continued

Army--U.S. - Cont'd

U.S. field artillery in Vietnam. MajGen David E.Ott. (Extracts from "Field Artillery Monograph") illus tabs maps Fld Arty J pt 1, The field artillery adviser. 43:23-29 Jan-Feb '75; pt 2, In order to win. 43:39-45 Mar-Apr '75; pt 3, Field artillery mobility. 43:15-22 May-Jun '75; pt 4, The buildup. 43: 9-16 Jul-Aug '75, 43:46-51 Sep-Oct '75; pt 4, The field artillery buildup: 1967 combat operations. 43:29-34 Nov-Dec '75; pt 5, The hot war: 1968, the Tet offensive. 44:27-31 Jan-Feb '76; pt 5, The hot war: The Battle of Khe Sanh. 44:44-48 Mar-Apr '76; pt 5, The hot war: 1968-69, A Shau Valley. 44:53-57 May-Jun '76; pt 5, The hot war: Operations and raids. 44:37-43 Jul-Aug '76; pt 6, Vietnamization: FA assistance programs. 44: 10-17 Sep-Oct '76; pt 6, Vietnamization: Operations into Cambodia. 44:13-18 Nov-Dec '76

History

Cantankerous commander (artillery officer John Lamb during the American Revolution). Fairfax Downey. illus Natl Def 61:214-216 Nov-Dec '76

Winning the West. Col Robert M.Stegmaier, Ret. maps illus Fld Arty J pt 1, 44:52-54 Mar-Apr '76; pt 2, 44:37-39 May-Jun '76; pt 3, 44:53-54 Jul-Aug '76; pt 4, 44:38-41 Sep-Oct '76; pt 5, 44:58-61 Nov-Dec '76

Army--Vietnam (Republic)

U.S. field artillery in Vietnam. MajGen David E.Ott. (Extracts from "Field Artillery Monograph") illus tabs maps Fld Arty J pt 1, The field artillery adviser. 43:23-29 Jan-Feb '75; pt 2, In order to win. 43:39-45 Mar-Apr '75; pt 3, Field artillery mobility. 43:15-22 May-Jun '75; pt 4, The buildup. 43: 9-16 Jul-Aug '75, 43:46-51 Sep-Oct '75; pt 4, The field artillery buildup: 1967 combat operations. 43:29-34 Nov-Dec '75; pt 5, The hot war: 1968, the Tet offensive. 44:27-31 Jan-Feb '76; pt 5, The hot war: The Battle of Khe Sanh. 44:44-48 Mar-Apr '76; pt 5, The hot war: 1968-69, A Shau Valley. 44:53-57 May-Jun '76; pt 5, The hot war: Operations and raids. 44:37-43 Jul-Aug '76; pt 6, Vietnamization: FA assistance programs. 44: 10-17 Sep-Oct '76; pt 6, Vietnamization: Operations into Cambodia. 44:13-18 Nov-Dec '76

Marine Corps--U.S.

Track back, smack back. Bill Walsh. illus tab Countermeasures 2:18-21+ Aug '76

ARTILLERY, ANTI-AIRCRAFT

The BT39 anti-aircraft gun fire simulator. illus Intl Def Rev 9:101-102 Feb '76

Repulsing "enemy" air strikes. LtCol K.Myznikov. Soviet Mil Rev No.9:38-39 Sep '76

Roving AA (Anti-Aircraft) subunits and ambushes. Col V.Subbotin. Soviet Mil Rev No.2:24-25 Feb '76

Self-propelled antiaircraft gun: The ZSU-23-4. LtCol V.Strelkov. (Trans from a Russian publication) illus USA Avn Dig 22:18-21 Mar '76

Ship air defence. Capt B.Orestov. illus Soviet Mil Rev No.1:23-24 Jan '76

The threat to air assault operations. Capt Daniel W. Henk. illus USA Avn Dig 22:6-7+ Feb '76

ARTILLERY, ANTITANK

Fighting tanks. Col A.Akimov. illus Soviet Mil Rev No.10:10-13 Oct '76

A role for the uncommitted Reserve? LtCol Michael Burkham. RUSI J for Def Studies 121:43-45 Sep '76

Tank killer team (Air Force A-10 ground-attack aircraft mounting the powerful GAU-8/A 30-mm gun system). Col Robert G.Dilger. illus Natl Def 61: 190-191 Nov-Dec '76

True magic for the artilleryman. (A shell homing in automatically on a target with the help of laser technology devices) John S.Phillip. illus Aerosp Intl 12:22-24 Jan-Feb '76

The U.S. Army's cannon launched guided projectile. R.D.M.Furlong. illus tab Intl Def Rev 9:117-119 Feb '76

ARTILLERY, FIELD

Artillery projects of the future. Karl Heinz Bodlien. (Trans from Soldat und Technik, Aug 1974) illus tabs Fld Arty J 44:10-15 Jan-Feb '76

Counterfire! MajGen David E.Ott and Col Donald M. Rhea. illus Army 26:22-26 Jul '76

Decisive lateral repositioning. Col Howard R.Guffey. illus Fld Arty J 44:6-10 Mar-Apr '76

Destruction of artillery batteries. Col V.Rudakov. Soviet Mil Rev No.10:22-23 Oct '76

FIST (FIre Support Team)! Responses. LtCol William F.Muhlenfeld and others. illus Fld Arty J 44: 16-21+ Jul-Aug '76

Heavy artillery: Who needs it? Capt John C.Abshier. illus tabs Fld Arty J 44:31-33 Sep-Oct '76

The Tampella 155 mm gun-howitzer. LtCol P.Crevecoeur, Ret. illus tabs Intl Def Rev 9:662-663 Aug '76

U.S. field artillery in Vietnam. MajGen David E.Ott. (Extracts from "Field Artillery Monograph") illus tabs maps Fld Arty J pt 1, The field artillery adviser. 43:23-29 Jan-Feb '75; pt 2, In order to win. 43:39-45 Mar-Apr '75; pt 3, Field artillery mobility. 43:15-22 May-Jun '75; pt 4, The buildup. 43: 9-16 Jul-Aug '75, 43:46-51 Sep-Oct '75; pt 4, The field artillery buildup: 1967 combat operations. 43:29-34 Nov-Dec '75; pt 5, The hot war: 1968, the Tet offensive. 44:27-31 Jan-Feb '76; pt 5, The hot war: The Battle of Khe Sanh. 44:44-48 Mar-Apr '76; pt 5, The hot war: 1968-69, A Shau Valley. 44:53-57 May-Jun '76; pt 5, The hot war: Operations and raids. 44:37-43 Jul-Aug '76; pt 6, Vietnamization: FA assistance programs. 44: 10-17 Sep-Oct '76; pt 6, Vietnamization: Operations into Cambodia. 44:13-18 Nov-Dec '76

The vanishing yellow helmet. LtCol Jon Porter. illus tab Fld Arty J 44:12-17 Mar-Apr '76

View from the blockhouse. (Notes from the Army Field Artillery School) Regular feature in issues of Field Artillery Journal

Win the first battle! MajGen David E.Ott. illus tab Natl Def 60:276-278 Jan-Feb '76

Maintenance and Repair

Mobility versus maintenance. LtCol William L. Hughes. illus Fld Arty J 44:18-20 Mar-Apr '76

ARTILLERY, FIELD - Continued

Study and Teaching

Battalion FDC--Cav style. Capt Eric C.Deets. illus Fld Arty J 44:38-40 Nov-Dec '76

Consumer notice: Please read FAAO (Field Artillery Aerial Observer) team article thoroughly prior to entering combat. Fld Arty J 44:50-54 Nov-Dec '76

Forging the main link. LtCol Serge P.C.Demyanenko. illus Fld Arty J 44:40-44 May-Jun '76

Forward observer effectiveness. Col Paul F.Pearson. tab Fld Arty J 44:24-26 Jan-Feb '76

Necessity--the mother of ... (Direct fire training against moving targets) LtCol Frank A.Partlow, Jr and Capt Richard A.Snow. illus Fld Arty J 44: 49-51 Mar-Apr '76

The new gunnery sergeant. SGM Harvey M.McBride. illus Fld Arty J 44:8-9 Sep-Oct '76

Operation Redleg. Capt Bruce A.Olson. illus Fld Arty J 44:29-31 Mar-Apr '76

Red Team AO (Aerial Observer) training. Capt Gary N.Grubb. illus Fld Arty J 44:22-23 Nov-Dec '76

ARTILLERY RANGES see Bombing and Gunnery Ranges

ASHCRAFT, Juanita

Manpower aide named. (Juanita Ashcraft to be Asst SecDef AF for Manpower and Reserve Affairs) por AF Times 37:8 Aug 2 '76

ASIA

Lasting peace and security for Asia. Y.Lugovskoi. Soviet Mil Rev No.7:56-58 Jul '76

Strategic Importance

U.S. policy alternatives in Asia. Robert A.Scalapino. illus Parameters 5, No.2:14-24 '76

ASIA, EASTERN

Foreign Relations

United States

Our stake in Asia. William V.Kennedy. illus Army 26:19-21+ Sep '76

Strategic Importance

The geostrategic triangle of North-East Asia. Niu Sien-chong. NATO's Fifteen Nations 21:68+ Aug-Sep '76

The scrambled geometry of the new Pacific: West of the Dateline and East of India. Lawrence Griswold. illus Sea Power 19:24-29 Apr '76

ASIA, SOUTH

China 'cross the bay: The Burmese hub of Asia. illus Def & For Aff Dig No.10:22-23+ '76

Politics and Government

Revolution and tradition in the Middle East, Africa, and South Asia. Marcus W.Franda. illus Natl Sec Aff Forum No.24:23-31 Spring-Summer '76

ASIA, SOUTHEASTERN

Sidelight on post-détente Southeast Asia. WgComdr Maharaj K.Chopra, Ret. Mil Rev 56:11-22 Mar '76

ASIA, SOUTHEASTERN - Continued

South East Asia now. Brig F. W. Speed. Army Qtr 106:226-235 Apr '76

The USSR-DRV-PRC triangle in Southeast Asia. Donald E. Weatherbee. illus Parameters 6, No. 1: 71-86 '76

Foreign Relations

China (People's Republic)

Sidelight on post-détente Southeast Asia. WgComdr Maharaj K. Chopra, Ret. Mil Rev 56:11-22 Mar '76

ASPIN, Les

Aspin bills would overhaul pay. Phil Stevens. AF Times 37:4 Oct 18 '76

Comparing Soviet and American defense efforts. Les Aspin. NATO's Fifteen Nations 21:34-36+ Jun-Jul '76

Debate on TV: (Rep Les) Aspin vs (Col George) Hennrikus. por AF Times 37:16+ Dec 13 '76

In the (military pay) crunch it'll be up to Congress. Bruce Callander. AF Times 37:4 Oct 18 '76

(Rep Les) Aspin continues attack on retiree pay. AF Times 37:10 Dec 20 '76

Retired pay reform: Aspin answers critics again. AF Times 37:11 Oct 11 '76

'Salary' bill readied for Hill (by Rep Les Aspin). AF Times 37:4 Nov 29 '76

Why (Rep Les) Aspin wants to change (military retirement) system. AF Times 37:28-29 Sep 6 '76

ASSIGNMENTS, MILITARY

See also
Tours of Duty

(AF) recruits could get nuclear jobs. Ron Sanders. AF Times 37:4 Oct 18 '76

Base-choice program succeeded too well. AF Times 37:10 Nov 15 '76

CMC lists (general officer) reassignments. MarCor Gaz 60:2 May '76

'Dogrobber' flap (about enlisted aides) nothing new. AF Times 37:31 Sep 13 '76

Don't broaden careers by PCS, commands told. (Use base-level cross-training) AF Times 36:3 Jan 19 '76

"The easiest job in the squadron." (Safety Officer) LCDR L. E. Gardiner. illus Approach 21:26-27 Dec '75

General officer changes. Regular feature in News Call section of some issues of Army

Generals on the move. (Title varies) Regular feature in some issues of Air Force Times

Guide due on 1stSgt manning. Len Famiglietti. AF Times 37:6 Oct 18 '76

High-risk jobs listed in reg (AFR 35-99). AF Times 37:21 Dec 13 '76

Human side of assignment making: Computers just a tool. MSgt Freddie K. Harrison. illus AF Times 36:20+ Jan 12 '76

Location called key job factor. AF Times 37:16 Aug 23 '76

ASSIGNMENTS, MILITARY - Continued

(Maj)Gen (Richard) Bodycombe new AFR Vice Cmdr; other officers receive new assignments. illus Officer 52:19 Dec '76

NCO job review starting (for) 5000 senior Reserves. AF Times 37:3 Aug 2 '76

New steps taken to match people, jobs. AF Times 37:2 Nov 8 '76

Retirements, reassignment. MarCor Gaz 60:2 Jun '76

SAC chief (Gen Russell E. Dougherty) extended a year (and other general officer news announced). AF Times 37:3 Aug 16 '76

SEIs (Special Experience Identifiers) to match members, jobs. Lee Ewing. AF Times 37:2 Oct 25 '76

Senior Army officers in special assignments. Army 26:138 Oct '76

Senior staff changes. Regular feature in issues of Air Force Magazine

Special Experience Identifiers (SEIs). TIG Brief 28:3 Sep 10 '76

Star status: Army, Navy, Air Force, Marines. Regular feature in some issues of Armed Forces Journal International

ASSOCIATION OF THE U.S. ARMY

AUSA delegates approve 19 resolutions (at 1976 Annual Meeting). Army 26:50-54 Nov '76

AUSA opposes Selective Service cuts. illus Army 26: 60-61 Mar '76

Frank Pace, former Army Secretary, is named to receive (George Catlett) Marshall Medal. illus Army 26:11 Jun '76

(MajGen Robert F.) Cocklin to be new executive vice-president (of AUSA). illus Army 26:9 May '76

(Maj)Gen (Winant) Sidle named AUSA executive. illus Army 26:8 Jan '76

The 1975 Association of the U.S. Army Show (Washington, Oct 20-22). illus Intl Def Rev 8:927-929 Dec '75

President's report (1976). LtGen John J. Tolson, Ret. illus Army 26:48-49 Nov '76

6,000 attend AUSA event: World power balance gets major attention at '76 Annual Meeting (Washington, Oct 11-13, 1976) illus Army 26:36-38+ Nov '76

'Some concerns about this country we love.' (Condensed from address upon acceptance of the George C. Marshall Medal, AUSA 1976 Annual Meeting) Frank Pace, Jr. Army 26:46-47 Nov '76

ASTRONAUTICS see Space Flight

ASTRONAUTS

Astronaut positions open for space shuttle flights. illus AF Times 37:18 Sep 20 '76

The cosmonauts. Gordon R. Hooper. illus Spaceflight pt 1, 17:58-59 Feb '75; pt 2, 17:116-117 Mar '75; pt 3, 17:129-130 Apr '75; pt 4, 17:189-190 May '75; pt 5, 17:236-237 Jun '75; pt 6, 17:274-275 Jul '75; pt 7, 17:333-334 Aug-Sep '75; pt 8, 17:365 Oct '75; pt 9, 17:403-404 Nov '75; pt 10, 17:443-445 Dec '75; pt 11, 18:26-27 Jan '76

ASTRONAUTS - Continued

Help wanted: Astronaut! (Qualifications and possible careers for the new space shuttle astronauts needed by NASA in 1978) Capt John B. Taylor. illus Airman 20:46-48 Oct '76

Make way for the women astronauts! Mitchell R. Sharpe. illus Spaceflight 18:418-421 Dec '76

Education and Training

Sport in the life of a cosmonaut. MajGen G. Beregovoi. illus Soviet Mil Rev No. 2:63-65 Feb '76

ASTRONOMICAL RESEARCH

See also
Satellites, Artificial--Astronomical Applications

Calling M13 on 12.6 cm: Do you read? A. T. Lawton. illus Spaceflight 18:10-12 Jan '76

A 'red giant' opens its eyes. (USSR's radio-telescope, RATAN 600) Anthony T. Lawton and Kenneth W. Gatland. illus map Spaceflight 18:268-272 Jul-Aug '76

ASTRONOMY

See also
Radio Astronomy

ATKESON, Edward B.

Hemispheric denial: Geopolitical imperatives and Soviet strategy. BrigGen Edward B. Atkeson. por Strat Rev 4:26-36 Spring '76

Precision guided munitions: Implications for detente. BrigGen Edward B. Atkeson. Parameters 5, No. 2: 75-87 '76

The relevance of civilian-based defense to U.S. security interests. BrigGen Edward B. Atkeson. por Mil Rev pt 1, 56:24-32 May '76; pt 2, 56:45-55 Jun '76

ATLANTIC COMMAND, ALLIED see Allied Command Atlantic

ATLANTIC COMMUNITY

Cohesion and competition in the Atlantic Community: Implications for security. Col William F. Burns. illus Parameters 6, No. 1:35-47 '76

ATLANTIC REGION

Strategic Importance

The South Atlantic: A new order emerging. Richard E. Bissell. illus Sea Power 19:11-13 Oct '76

ATMOSPHERE

Atmospheric transmissometer for military system performance evaluation. Frederic M. Zweibaum and Thomas F. McHenry. tabs illus Countermeasures 2:27-29+ Jun '76

The future environment. LCDR Jacob D. Dumelle. Mil Engr 68:304-305 Jul-Aug '76

The Global Atmospheric Research Programme (GARP): GARP Atlantic Tropical Experiment (GATE). B. J. Mason. Royal Air Forces Qtr 16: 35-40 Spring '76

The Sirocco meteorological sounding station. illus tab Intl Def Rev 9:433-435 Jun '76

ATMOSPHERE, UPPER

High-altitude carbon monoxide. (First microwave observations of carbon monoxide in upper atmospheres of Earth, Venus and Mars) Spaceflight 18:196 May '76

Holloman (AFB, NM) balloonists end Project Ashcan (with the successful recovery of their fifth atmospheric sampling package of radioactive waste). AF Times 36:40 May 17 '76

Interrelation of atmospheric ozone and cholecalciferol (vitamin D_3) production in man. J. F. Leach and others. illus tabs Aviation, Space & Envmt Med 47:630-633 Jun '76

Viking: Orbiter science equipment. David Baker. illus (Also cutaway) Spaceflight 18:124-125 Apr '76

ATMOSPHERIC RESEARCH see Atmosphere, Upper

ATOMIC ENERGY COMMISSION see Energy Research and Development Administration

ATTACK AND DEFENSE (MILITARY SCIENCE)

The armoured forces of the future. Col R. Trofimov. Soviet Mil Rev No. 9:21-23 Sep '76

An army in the offensive. (Soviet Armed Forces in WW II) MajGen M. Kiryan. map Soviet Mil Rev No. 8:53-55 Aug '76

Assault by sea. Frank Uhlig, Jr. illus MarCor Gaz 60:18-20 Jun '76

A battalion in the second echelon. Col V. Zhukov. map Soviet Mil Rev No. 4:16-18 Apr '76

The blitzkrieg: A premature burial? Colin S. Gray. illus Mil Rev 56:15-18 Oct '76

Counterencirclement. Maj James L. Estep. Infantry 66:47-48 Jan-Feb '76

Counterfire! illus tabs Fld Arty J pt 1, 43:14-21 Nov-Dec '75; pt 2, 44:32-38 Jan-Feb '76

Counterfire! MajGen David E. Ott and Col Donald M. Rhea. illus Army 26:22-26 Jul '76

Decisive lateral repositioning. Col Howard R. Guffey. illus Fld Arty J 44:6-10 Mar-Apr '76

Defence of a sea coast. (Actions of an artillery battalion) Col V. Saksonov. Soviet Mil Rev No. 11: 20-21 Nov '76

Defense against mechanized forces. Capt C. M. Lohman. MarCor Gaz 60:52-53 Oct '76

Destroying armor. Edited by Infantry Magazine Staff. illus Infantry 66:35-42 Sep-Oct '76

Destruction of artillery batteries. Col V. Rudakov. Soviet Mil Rev No. 10:22-23 Oct '76

Fighting tanks. Col A. Akimov. illus Soviet Mil Rev No. 10:10-13 Oct '76

The final coordination line. Maj M. R. Janay. MarCor Gaz 60:50-51 Jan '76

Firepower. (Address, V Corps Artillery Firepower Conference, Giessen, Germany, March 19, 1976) BrigGen Albert B. Akers. Fld Arty J 44:17-21+ May-Jun '76

How to defend outnumbered and win. LtCol David L. Tamminen. (Reprinted from Armor, Nov-Dec 1975) illus tabs Fld Arty J 44:39-43 Mar-Apr '76

ATTACK AND DEFENSE (MILITARY SCIENCE) - Continued

Ideas are the first to engage the enemy. (Interview with Marshal Ivan Khristoforovich Bagramyan) Soviet Mil Rev No. 9:16-18 Sep '76

In the depth of defences. LtCol A. Tkalenko. map Soviet Mil Rev No. 4:22-23 Apr '76

MOBA (Military Operations in Built-up Areas): Why? What? How? LtCols Robert L. Graham and Ray M. Franklin. illus tabs maps USA Avn Dig 22:1+ Feb '76

Manoeuvre in an offensive battle. Col V. Savelyev. Soviet Mil Rev No. 2:16-17 Feb '76

Manoeuvre with forces, weapons and fire. Col A. Akimov. (Adapted from Soviet Military Review, July 1975) illus map MarCor Gaz 60:45-48 Dec '76

Manoeuvre with reserves. (Combat actions of First Byelorussian and First Ukrainian fronts, 1944-45) Col Z. Shutov. maps Soviet Mil Rev No. 4:54-56 Apr '76

Meeting engagements of tank armies (1941-45). Col Z. Shutov. map Soviet Mil Rev No. 12:51-53 Dec '76

Needed now: An antiarmor doctrine. Capt Timothy R. O'Neill. illus Armor 85:18-24 Jan-Feb '76

The nuclear land battle. Col Marc Geneste, Ret. illus Strat Rev 4:79-85 Winter '76

The October War: Burying the blitzkrieg. Jeffrey Record. illus Mil Rev 56:19-21 Apr '76

Reflections of fire. illus tab Infantry 66:19-28 Sep-Oct '76

Speed in attack. Col V. Ustyuzhnikov. Soviet Mil Rev No. 2:20-21 Feb '76

Strong point defense. illus Infantry 66:43-51 Sep-Oct '76

A tank Army in the offensive (in WW II). Col N. Kobrin. illus Soviet Mil Rev No. 1:47-49 Jan '76

The threat. illus Infantry 66:29-34 Sep-Oct '76

(Water barriers in combination with obstructions considerably influence the character of combat operations of attacking subunits) 1. Crossing a water obstacle; 2. Dash to a river; 3. Supporting motorised Infantry; 4. Air defence of an advanced detachment; 5. Pontoniers; 6. Raising offensive enthusiasm; 7. Exploit at crossing; 8. An Army forces a crossing. illus maps Soviet Mil Rev No. 7: 17-41 Jul '76

When time is short: Organisation of defence by a motorised Infantry battalion. Col I. Podgorny. map Soviet Mil Rev No. 8:19-21 Aug '76

ATTITUDES

Alcohol in aviation: A problem of attitudes. Capt J.A. Pursch. illus USA Avn Dig 22:30-33 Nov '76

Alienation and participation: A replication comparing leaders and the "mass." D. Duane Braun. tabs J Pol & Mil Sociol 4:245-259 Fall '76

The American volunteer soldier: Will he fight? A provisional attitudinal analysis. Col Charles W. Brown and Charles C. Moskos, Jr. illus tabs Mil Rev 56:8-17 Jun '76

Attitude. LtCol Robert J. Brun. illus Aerosp Safety 32:8-9 Apr '76

ATTITUDES - Continued

Attitudes and accidents aboard an aircraft carrier. John B. Levine and others. tabs Aviation, Space & Envmt Med 47:82-85 Jan '76

Fighting mood. Capt A. Stolyarenko. Soviet Mil Rev No. 10:39-40 Oct '76

A military elite in transition: Air Force leaders in the 1980s. (Research undertaken at Air Command and Staff College) LtCol Franklin D. Margiotta. tabs Armed Forces & Soc 2:155-184 Winter '76

Mobilizing people for collective political action. (Paper, American Sociological Assoc, San Francisco, Aug 1975) Kenneth L. Wilson and Anthony M. Orum. J Pol & Mil Sociol 4:187-202 Fall '76

Occupational mobility and political behavior: Some unresolved issues. Joseph Lopreato and others. J Pol & Mil Sociol 4:1-15 Spring '76

ROTC cadet attitudes: A product of socialization or self-selection? James E. Dorman. tabs J Pol & Mil Sociol 4:203-216 Fall '76

So now you're an instructor pilot! Maj Donald E. Yarbrough. illus Aerosp Safety 32:2-4 Aug '76

Some ideas about influencing attitudes. Capt Lee G. Borts. Educ J 19:21-23 Winter '76

Status inconsistency and Democratic Party preference: A replication and critique. Phillip A. Salopek and Christopher K. Vanderpool. tab J Pol & Mil Sociol 4:29-38 Spring '76

Wings, wizards and wisdom. Sammy Mason. (Reprinted from Flight Operations, March 1976) illus USA Avn Dig 22:41-45 Dec '76

AUDIO-VISUAL AIDS

Air Force Bicentennial slide production wins gold medal (at the 18th Annual International Film and Television Festival, New York City). TIG Brief 28:16 Jan 30 '76

An audiovisual approach to strange (air) fields. illus MAC Flyer 23:16-17 Mar '76

Audio-visual transfer (to civilian contractors) weighed. AF Times 36:13 Jun 14 '76

How about a modern safety program? LCDR Russ Harrison. illus Approach 22:24-25 Nov '76

Increased use of available audiovisual aids. TIG Brief 28:7 Apr 9 '76

AUDIO-VISUAL INSTRUCTION

ILC (Instructional Learning Center): A success story. (Unique application of audio-visual techniques, personalized additional instruction and assistance and a practical field application, all in one package, to improve readiness of Reserve Component units in Army Readiness Region I) Col Edward P. Metzner. Fld Arty J 44:53-54 Jul-Aug '76

Training: A new concept. (Caramate II audiovisual teaching machine) Capt Robert S. Klinger. illus tab Combat Crew 27:16-19 Mar '76

AUDITING

See also
Air Force Audit Agency

Auditing tomorrow's Air Force today. Capt Allen J. Spinka. illus AF Compt 10:8-9 Oct '76

Auditor General. BrigGen T.G. Bee. chart illus AF Compt 10:28-29 Jan '76

AUDITING - Continued

Auditor General. BrigGen Thomas G.Bee. illus chart AF Compt 10:18-19 Apr '76

Auditor General. BrigGen Joseph B.Dodds. illus chart AF Compt 10:18-19 Oct '76

Notes from the Auditor General. BrigGen Joseph B. Dodds. illus AF Compt 10:18-19 Jul '76

Report of patients: Workload audits. TIG Brief 28:16 Dec 17 '76

Using simulation models in operational auditing. Capt James R.Crockett. illus tabs AF Compt 10:10-11+ Jan '76

AUSTIN, Charles E.

Learning--despite the instructor. Capt Charles Austin. AU Rev 27:72-78 Mar-Apr '76

AUSTIN, Hugh S.

Notes from the Director of the Professional Military Comptroller Course (at Air University, Maxwell AFB, Ala). Col Hugh S.Austin. por AF Compt 10: 20-22 Jul '76

Professional Military Comptroller Course (at Air University, Maxwell AFB, Ala). Col Hugh S.Austin. por AF Compt 10:20-21 Oct '76

Professional Military Comptroller Course (at Institute for Professional Development, Air University, Maxwell AFB, Ala). Col Hugh S.Austin. por AF Compt 10:22-23 Apr '76

AUSTRALIA

Economic Conditions

The vulnerability of Australia's maritime trade. A.W.Grazebrook. illus tabs NATO's Fifteen Nations 20:40-45+ Dec '75-Jan '76

Foreign Policy

Australia: Defence planner's teaser. Brig F.V.Speed. map Army Qtr 106:359-365 Jul '76

Australia's defence dilemma. Brig F.W.Speed. tab Army Qtr 106:92-100 Jan '76

New look down under as (Malcolm) Fraser backs U.S./Australian naval cooperation. L.Edgar Prina. illus Sea Power 19:37-38 Feb '76

Foreign Relations

United States

New look down under as (Malcolm) Fraser backs U.S./Australian naval cooperation. L.Edgar Prina. illus Sea Power 19:37-38 Feb '76

AUTOMATIC LANDING SYSTEMS

See also
Microwave Landing Systems

ATC systems for tomorrow. Dale Milford. illus Aerosp Intl 12:26-28+ Mar-Apr '76

Autoland starts to pay off for British Airways. Don Craig. illus tabs Interavia pt 1, 31:721-724 Aug '76; pt 2, 31:863-867 Sep '76

Terminal Precision Approach Control Program (TPACP). TIG Brief 28:12 Aug 27 '76

There are no dragons. (Landing at Taipei, Hong Kong, or Manila) Maj Jack Spey. illus Aerosp Safety 32:14-15 Oct '76

AUTOMATIC VOICE NETWORK

Abuse of AUTOVON precedence system. TIG Brief 28:20 Jan 16 '76

Use of AUTOVON for graphics, facsimile, and data service. TIG Brief 28:10 Jun 18 '76

AUTOMATION

See also
Electronic Data Processing Systems

Air traffic control automation (in Italy, Sweden, Netherlands). Dan Boyle. illus Interavia 31:155-159 Feb '76

Automation in military air traffic control. Bill Walsh. illus Countermeasures 2:40-41 Apr '76

The computer: The computer: The comp; triumph or terror for transportation manager. Col Alan D. Wheeler. illus Def Trans J 32:12-18+ Feb '76

Energy monitoring control systems. Capt Robert E. Dant. illus tab AF Engrg & Svcs Qtr 17:25-28 Aug '76

Energy savings: The FAA. (Automation of environmental control in 20 Air Route Traffic Control Centers) illus Govt Exec 8:15+ Mar '76

Exploitation of computers. TIG Brief 28:13-14 Feb 27 '76

Managing logistics in the field. LtCol William C. Banze and Miles S.Abbott. illus Army Log 8:2-5 May-Jun '76

Men, myths, and machines, or, "All the ships at sea." Douglas M.Johnston. illus tabs Def Mgt J 12:17-22 Oct '76

New horizons for radar. John L.McLucas. illus Signal 31:65-67 Oct '76

SP automation would speed (AF) file retrieval. AF Times 37:12 Nov 1 '76

Technical telecommunications forces and trends that have affected and are affecting the confluence of automatic data processing and telecommunications. Thomas Yium and others. illus tabs Signal 30:28-35 Feb '76

AUTOMOBILES

(Automobile) crash: Then what? (Reprinted from Family Safety, Fall 1974) illus TAC Attack 16: 18-19 Mar '76

Key points in shipping your car. Don Hirst. AF Times 37:36 Aug 30 '76

Making a military move: 10-cents a mile rate OK'd for those using own car. Randall Shoemaker. AF Times 36:4 Mar 1 '76

SP gate search right limited. AF Times 36:49 Feb 23 '76

SPs issued warning on searching cars (at gates). Ron Sanders. AF Times 36:4 Mar 8 '76

Use of rental cars. TIG Brief 28:14 May 7 '76

You and the 'other guy.' (A discussion of auto insurance) LtCol Harry A.Grab, Jr. illus Airman 20: 30-34 Mar '76

Drivers and Driving
See Motor Vehicles--Drivers and Driving

AUTOMOBILES - Continued

Engines

Maintenance and Repair

Synthetic oil? SGM Nat Dell. illus Soldiers 31:19-22
Oct '76

Equipment

Car devices cut (electrically ignited crash) fires,
tests show. AF Times 36:25 Mar 1 '76

Catalytic converter confusion. Tory Billard. illus
Translog 7:13-15 May '76

POVs face tough controls in Japan (because of emission standards). Don Hirst. AF Times 36:16
Jul 5 '76

Laws and Regulations

Restrictions (on POVs) vary in host countries. Translog 7:16 May '76

Maintenance and Repair

Violations of the public trust in connection with contractor-operated parts stores. TIG Brief 28:6-7
Jan 30 '76

AUXILIARY SHIPS

See also
Icebreakers

AVIATION
For articles on commercial air transportation companies see Airlines; for articles on technical and technological aspects of aviation and aircraft see Aeronautics; for popular, nontechnical articles on the
pleasures of flying see Flying.
See also
Flights, Famous and Historic

Aerospace world. Regular feature in issues of Air
Force Magazine

The world of aerospace. Regular feature in issues of
Interavia

Exhibitions

Germany (Federal Republic)

Hanover photo report. Brian M.Service. illus Air
Pict 38:214-217 Jun '76

Where is the German (Hanover) Air Show going? illus
tab Interavia 31:505-510 Jun '76

Great Britain

Avionic developments steal Farnborough Air Show.
illus tab Elect Warfare 8:19-20+ Nov-Dec '76

Farnborough (Air Show, Sep 1976): General aviation
was there too. illus Interavia 31:1055-1056 Nov '76

Farnborough International '76: A second report. illus
Interavia 31:1039-1046 Nov '76

Farnborough International '76: The biggest SBAC
show ever. illus Interavia 31:912-914 Oct '76

Farnborough report. (Highlights, 30th S.B.A.C.
Show, 5th-12th Sep 1976) illus Air Pict 38:390-395
Oct '76

AVIATION - Continued

Exhibitions - Cont'd

Japan

The 5th Japanese Aerospace Show (Iruma AFB,
Oct 16-24, 1976). illus Interavia 31:1121-1122
Dec '76

United States

Air circus. SSgt Zack Richards. illus Soldiers 31:
22-24 May '76

The '75 NBAA (National Business Aircraft Assoc)
show (New Orleans, Oct 29-31, 1975). illus Interavia 31:75-78 Jan '76

The 1976 Helicopter Assoc of America meeting (and
exhibition). J.Philip Geddes. illus Interavia 31:
207-210 Mar '76

The 1976 Reading (Pa) Show--better than ever. Howard Levy. illus Interavia 31:703-706 Aug '76

History

Folklore of aviation. (Based on oral history record-
ings, Imperial War Museum, London) David Lance
illus RUSI J for Def Studies 121:62-68 Mar '76

International Aspects

International law and the Air Force. (Address, Society of International Law, New York, Oct 29, 1975)
John L.McLucas. AF Law Rev 18:76-80 Summer '76

Laws and Regulations
See Air Law

Physiological Aspects
See also specific conditions, e.g.,
Decompression   Hypoxia
Hyperventilation   Motion Sickness

Air operations and circadian performance rhythms.
Karl E.Klein and others. illus tabs Aviation,
Space & Envmt Med 47:221-230 Mar '76

Bradycardia induced by negative acceleration. (Test
for standard lap belt) James A.Kennealy and
others. illus Aviation, Space & Envmt Med 47:
483-484 May '76

Cardiovascular function during sustained +G$_z$ stress.
Howard H.Erickson and others. illus tabs Aviation, Space & Envmt Med 47:750-758 Jul '76

Changes in clinical cardiologic measurements asso-
elated with high +G$_z$ stress. Kent K.Gillingham
and Phelps P.Crump. illus tabs Aviation, Space
& Envmt Med 47:726-733 Jul '76

Changes in pulmonary volumes with relocation to
1,600 m following acute translocation to 4,300 m.
J.G.Dramise and others. tabs Aviation, Space &
Envmt Med 47:261-264 Mar '76

A Christmas story. (Plain of Jars, Dec 1970) Capt
Craig W.Duehring. illus TAC Attack 16:18-19
Dec '76

Crew rest. illus Approach 21:24-25 Jun '76

Dear Joe. (Requirements of a career in Naval Aviation) Willie E.Cumbie. illus Approach 21:1-5
Mar '76

Effects of rapid round trips against time displacement on adrenal cortical-medullary circadian
rhythms. Chiharu Sekiguchi and others. tabs Aviation, Space & Envmt Med 47:1101-1106 Oct '76

AVIATION - Continued

Physiological Aspects - Cont'd

Effects of time zone changes on performance and physiology of airline personnel. F.S. Preston and others. illus tabs Aviation, Space & Envmt Med 47:763-769 Jul '76

Ethnic variations in psychological performance under altitude stress. V.M.Sharma and M.S.Malhotra. illus tabs Aviation, Space & Envmt Med 47:248-251 Mar '76

Fatigue, a tiring subject. Maj Lowell A.Schuknecht, Jr. illus MAC Flyer 23:12-13 Jan '76

Flight-induced changes in human amino acid excre-. tion. James P.Ellis, Jr and others. tabs Aviation, Space & Envmt Med 47:1-8 Jan '76

The four horsemen of the apocalypse (illness, bore-dom, fatigue, unfitness). CDR A.F.Wells. illus Approach 21:10-11 May '76

Hazy daze. (Altitude myopia: Visual deception in the air) illus MAC Flyer 23:9-10 Feb '76; Interceptor 5:18-19 May '76

Heat and simulated high altitude: Effects on biochemi-cal indices of stress and performance. Ralph P. Francesconi and others. tabs Aviation, Space & Envmt Med 47:548-552 May '76

Incapacitation. Capt Luther R.Wilson. illus tab Com-bat Crew 26:8-11 Feb '76

Of heart attacks and belly aches (for pilots only). An-chard F. Zeller. Aerosp Safety 32:20-21 Feb '76

Physiological index as an aid in developing airline pilot scheduling patterns. Stanley R.Mohler. illus map tabs Aviation, Space & Envmt Med 47:238-247 Mar '76

Phyz-biz. Regular feature in some issues of TAC Attack

The story of G. CDR A.F.Wells. illus Approach 22: 22-23 Nov '76

That (pull of gravity) machine. LtCol Lee Crock. illus tabs Interceptor 18:8-13 Aug '76

Use of pilot heart rate measurement in flight evalua-tion. Alan H.Roscoe. illus tabs Aviation, Space & Envmt Med 47:86-90 Jan '76

Study and Teaching

New (altitude) chamber (Carter P.Luna Physiologi-cal Training Center) at Pete(rson AFB, Colo). Capt David V.Froehlich. illus Interceptor 18:5-7 Nov '76

Psychological Aspects

Complacency: What it is, what we can do about it. Maj T.R.Allocca. Aerosp Safety 32:9 Aug '76

Dear Joe. (Requirements of a career in Naval Avia-tion) Willie E.Cumbie. illus Approach 21:1-5 Mar '76

Ego trip or hidden message? Maj Lowell A.Schuk-necht. MAC Flyer 23:20-21 Mar '76

Ethnic variations in psychological performance under altitude stress. V.M.Sharma and M.S.Malhotra. illus tabs Aviation, Space & Envmt Med 47:248-251 Mar '76

Fatigue, a tiring subject. Maj Lowell A.Schuknecht, Jr. illus MAC Flyer 23:12-13 Jan '76

Psychological Aspects - Cont'd

Flying steels will. LtCol Y.Besschyotnov. Soviet Mil Rev No. 12:30-31 Dec '76

The four horsemen of the apocalypse (illness, bore-dom, fatigue, unfitness). CDR A.F.Wells. illus Approach 21:10-11 May '76

The launch. (Complacency in the cockpit) LCDR Bob Jones. illus Approach 22:24-25 Dec '76

A mistake in flight. Col V.Pokrovsky. Soviet Mil Rev No.1:28-29 Jan '76

Time bomb (stress). Capt Allan R.Sweeny. illus Aerosp Safety 32:26-28 Jun '76

Terminology

Handbook of MAC aviator terms and other neat say-ings (for unofficial use only). Maj Garnett C. Brown, Jr. MAC Flyer 23:16-17 Jun '76

Africa

Civil aviation training facilities and manpower needs in Africa. R.E.Owusu. illus tabs Interavia 31: 963-964 Oct '76

Flight over Africa. (MAC survey team reports on African airfields) LtCol John W.Ray. MAC Flyer 23:6-7 Feb '76

Africa, East

Civil aviation in East Africa. Chris Bulloch. illus tab map Interavia 31:530-533 Jun '76

Great Britain

University (of London Air Squadron) cadet in a bull-dog. (Flying with the RAF today, no.7) J.D.R. Rawlings. illus tab Air Pict 38:320-322 Aug '76

History

Alex Henshaw (sporting and racing pilot of the 1930s, and one of the outstanding test-pilots of WW II). A.M.Spong. illus Air Pict 38:232-236 Jun '76

The CHW (Charles Horace Watkins) monoplane. Act-ing Pilot Officers T.M.Winn-Morgan and M.A. Barker. illus tab Royal Air Forces Qtr 16:264-271 Autumn '76

A short account of the East Midlands Universities Air Squadron. Col G.J.Eltringham, Ret. Royal Air Forces Qtr 15:325-330 Winter '75

Philippines

History

American birdmen in the Philippines, 1912-1913. Enrique B.Santos. illus Am Avn Hist Soc J 21: 26-30 Spring '76

United States

U.S. aeronautical R&D: Seeking effective policies and leadership. A.Scott Crossfield. illus tabs Govt Exec 8:38-39+ Nov '76

U.S. general and business aviation strides ahead in difficult economic climate. Marc Grangier. illus tabs Interavia 31:219-223 Mar '76

History

Air passenger--1928 style. Carl Weeks. Am Avn Hist Soc J 21:83 Summer '76

AVIATION - Continued

United States - Cont'd

History - Cont'd

'Early Birds' recall pioneer flight days. TSgt Jim Denney. illus AF Times 37:45-46 Nov 15 '76

Flight training marks 65 years of growth. AF Times 36:24 Apr 12 '76

Flying--simple and unsophisticated (in the 1920s and 1930s). Capt Duke Nauton. illus Aerosp Hist 22: 195-197 Dec '75

From bailing wire to the SR-71: 1st Strategic Recon Sq one of oldest air units. illus AF Times 36:42 May 17 '76

The great flying game. (Flying training at Scott Field, Ill, 1917-18) Isobel Bryant. illus MAC Flyer 23:18-20 Jul '76

Jimmy Doolittle--the first 80 years. Barrett Tillman. illus Am Avn Hist Soc J 21:297-306 Winter '76

Memories of Grover Loening. Robert E.McMinn. illus Aerosp Hist 23:202-206 Dec '76

Orville (Wright) lost the toss but won the flight. illus AF Times 37:21 Dec 20 '76

President OKs (BrigGen Charles E.) Yeager medal (for) breaking the sound barrier. AF Times 36:11 Jan 12 '76

Rebuilt Wright. (Volunteers from Squadron Officer School at Maxwell AFB, Ala, build a replica of the Wright brothers' 1910 hangar) Irene P.Barrett. illus Airman 20:20 Nov '76

The search for Leon Klink (Lindbergh's barnstorming partner). Jack Keasler. illus map Am Avn Hist Soc J 21:92-100 Summer '76

Super Electra: Lockheed's model 14. Thomas M. Emmert and William T.Larkins. illus tabs Am Avn Hist Soc J 21:101-111 Summer '76

Those days of the leather helmet. MSgt Dave Sylva. illus Aerosp Safety 32:14-17 May '76

The Wright brothers. Charles H.Gibbs-Smith. Royal Air Forces Qtr 15:311-316 Winter '75

AVIATION, COMMERCIAL

Here are entered general articles on transportation of personnel and/or cargo by commercial aircraft.

See also
Air Cargo
Airlines
Airports

Atlantic cooperation or European surrender? Negotiations continue on future transport aircraft projects. Interavia 31:609-610 Jul '76

Boeing's view of future air transport growth. illus tabs Interavia 31:626 Jul '76

Lockheed world air traffic report, 1976-1985. J.Philip Geddes. illus map tabs Interavia 31: 623-625 Jul '76

Economic Aspects

Air cargo market undergoing major changes. Siegfried Koehler. illus tabs Interavia 31:929-930 Oct '76

Air cargo's problem areas. (Interview with Stanley F.Wheatcroft, 8th International Forum for Air Cargo, London, May 10-12, 1976) illus Interavia 31:671 Jul '76

AVIATION, COMMERCIAL - Continued

Economic Aspects - Cont'd

Air commerce: Stimulated or damned. A.Scott Crossfield. illus tabs Govt Exec 8:31-32+ Dec '76

Airline deregulation: Will it make the dominos fall faster? C.W.Borklund. illus tabs Govt Exec 8: 38-40+ Jul '76

Airlines walk the financing tightrope--not always successfully. Nicolas Travers. tabs Interavia 31: 60-63 Jan '76

Changing pattern of scheduled airline operations. G.P.Khare. illus tabs Interavia 31:927-928 Oct '76

The concept of the aircraft lease. Robert S.Sowter. tabs Interavia 31:546-547 Jun '76

Financial data for 12 leading airlines. Table only. Interavia 31:62-63 Jan '76

Is PanAm seeing the end of the tunnel? Klaus Höhle. illus tab Interavia 31:619-621 Jul '76

It's tough at the top, but that's the way Seaboard's Richard Jackson likes it. (Interview with Richard Jackson) Arthur Wallis. illus Interavia 31:529 Jun '76

North Atlantic air cargo: A time for re-assessment. Arthur J.Wallis. illus Interavia 31:527-528 Jun '76

Report cites DOD for lack of commercial air support. AF Times 37:25 Nov 22 '76

The state of the air transport industry--by some of its leading personalities. illus Interavia 31:923-926+ Oct '76

United Airlines also in the red. Klaus Höhle. illus tabs Interavia 31:621-622 Jul '76

Upholding the IATA tariff structure: The long arm of the compliance law. illus Interavia 31:1146-1147 Dec '76

International Aspects

See also
Airplane Hijacking

Concorde enters service to good reviews: "New York is the key." (Interviews with Jean-Claude Martin, Alan Beaves and Doug Shore) illus Interavia 31: 424-426+ May '76

Integration in the European air tourism industry. André Perrault. illus tabs Interavia pt 1, 31:140-143 Feb '76; pt 2, 31:235-237 Mar '76; pt 3, 31: 435-437 May '76

Tempair International--the airlines' airline. John F. Brindley. illus Interavia 31:438-439 May '76

Upholding the IATA tariff structure: The long arm of the compliance law. illus Interavia 31:1146-1147 Dec '76

Laws and Regulations
See Air Law

Statistics

The uncertain market for commercial aircraft to 1990: A McDonnell Douglas survey. J.Philip Geddes. illus tabs Interavia 31:350-354 Apr '76

France

Transair France: Business aviation in action. illus Interavia 31:1004-1005 Oct '76

AVIATION, COMMERCIAL - Continued

Great Britain

CSE Aviation: One of the world's leading FBOs (Fixed-Base Operators). Marc Grangier. illus Interavia 31:1167-1169 Dec '76

Kenya

Nairobi: Safari gateway. P.J.Cooper. illus tabs Air Pict 38:268-274 Jul '76

Russia

Aeroflot today and tomorrow. (Interview with ColGen A.N.Katrich) illus Soviet Mil Rev No.8:9-12 Aug '76

United States

Air commerce: Stimulated or damned. A.Scott Crossfield. illus tabs Govt Exec 8:31-32+ Dec '76

Airline industry in jeopardy. LtGen Ira C.Eaker, Ret. AF Times 36:17-18 Jul 12 '76

MAC's (Gen Paul K.) Carlton asks 'airlift partnership.' AF Times 37:36 Dec 6 '76

AVIATION CLUBS see Aero Clubs

AVIATION HALL OF FAME

See also
Army Aviation Hall of Fame

(Eight aviation pioneers (Clarence D.Chamberlin, John H.Glenn, Jr, George W.Goddard, Albert F. Hegenberger, Edwin A.Link, Sanford A.Moss, William A.Patterson, Nathan F.Twining) to be enshrined in Aviation Hall of Fame, July 24, 1976) illus AF Mag 59:29-30 Jul '76

New names for Aviation Hall of Fame. illus AF Times 36:27 May 31 '76

AVIATION MATERIEL COMMAND see Aviation Systems Command

AVIATION MEDICINE

See also
Space Medicine

Aeromedical safety operations: A new concept in aviation accident prevention and investigation. CDR A.F.Wells. illus Approach 21:18-21 Jun '76

Application of hyperbaric oxygen therapy in a case of prolonged cerebral hypoxia following rapid decompression. Paul J.Sheffield and Jefferson C.Davis. tab Aviation, Space & Envmt Med 47:759-762 Jul '76

Death in a flyer due to acute epiglottitis and septicemia caused by Haemophilus influenza type B. Leonard W.Johnson, Jr. tab Aviation, Space and Envmt Med 47:187-191 Feb '76

A doctor looks at Army Aviation. MajGen Spurgeon Neel. illus USA Avn Dig 22:1+ Oct '76

Phyz-biz. Regular feature in some issues of TAC Attack.

Sopite syndrome: A sometimes sole manifestation of motion sickness. Ashton Graybiel and James Knepton. tabs Aviation, Space & Envmt Med 47: 873-882 Aug '76

AVIATION MEDICINE - Continued

Study of the microbiological environment within long- and medium-range Canadian Forces aircraft. A.J. Clayton and others. illus tabs Aviation, Space & Envmt Med 47:471-482 May '76

Transportation in commercial aircraft of passengers having contagious diseases. Michel Perin. Aviation, Space & Envmt Med 47:1109-1113 Oct '76

U.S. Army Aeromedical Research Laboratory. Col Robert W.Bailey. illus USA Avn Dig 22:4-5+ Oct '76

Research

See also
Aviation--Physiological Aspects

AVIATION RECORDS
Here are entered articles on record flying time for a given distance. For articles on time spent in flying by an individual pilot to maintain his proficiency rating see Flying Time. For articles on logs and reports of a flight see Flight Records.

American birdmen in the Philippines, 1912-1913. Enrique B.Santos. illus Am Avn Hist Soc J 21: 26-30 Spring '76

Douglas F4D-1 Skyray record flights. Nicholas M. Williams. illus map tab Am Avn Hist Soc J 21: 50-60 Spring '76

President OKs (BrigGen Charles E.) Yeager medal (for) breaking the sound barrier. AF Times 36:11 Jan 12 '76

SR-71. illus Combat Crew 27:4-7 Oct '76

SR-71: 6 records. illus AF Times 37:3 Aug 9 '76

SR-71 takes aim at MIG-25 speed mark. AF Times 36:4 Jul 26 '76

AVIATION SYSTEMS COMMAND

What's a national maintenance point? Robert T. Grothe. illus Army Log 8:6-9 May-Jun '76

AVIONICS

AH-1S avionics. Peter Boxman. illus USA Avn Dig 22:42-45 Nov '76

Artful dodger of the 1980s. Bill Walsh. illus Countermeasures 2:42-43+ Nov '76

Avionic developments steal Farnborough Air Show. illus tab Elect Warfare 8:19-20+ Nov-Dec '76

Avionics equipment reliability: An elusive objective. LtGen Robert T.Marsh. illus tabs Def Mgt J 12: 24-29 Apr '76

Avionics: General aviation sets the trend. Dan Boyle. illus Interavia 31:884-885 Sep '76

Avionics proliferation: A life cycle cost perspective. Russell M.Genet and Thomas D.Meitzler. tabs Def Mgt J 12:60-64 Jan '76

B-1: A view from the aft station. MajGen Richard N. Cody. illus Combat Crew 27:4-7+ Sep '76

DAIS (Digital Avionics Information System) computers developed. illus Countermeasures 2:54 Jul '76

Electronics, pivot of USAF's technological strength: A new era in electronic warfare. Edgar Ulsamer. illus AF Mag 59:46-50 Jul '76

AVIONICS - Continued

Fiber optics and Naval Aviation. William M.Powers. illus US Nav Inst Proc 102:135-136 Oct '76

Flexible multimission avionics. illus Countermeasures 2:25-26+ Nov '76

Liquid crystals: The daylight survivable display. Glen F.Ingle. illus tabs Elect Warfare 8:55-56+ Sep-Oct '76

A test nav looks at the B-1. LtCol Kenneth W. Brotnov. illus tab Navigator 23:5-11 Winter '76

The U.S. general aviation market--a decade of solid growth is forecast. illus tabs Interavia 31:567-569 Jun '76

Who's who in helicopter avionics? illus Interavia 31: 48-50 Jan '76

Maintenance and Repair

Avionics maintenance. TIG Brief 28:13-14 Jan 16 '76

AVIONICS LABORATORY see Air Force Avionics Laboratory

AWARDS, DECORATIONS, ETC

Germany (Federal Republic)

Uncommon medals, uncommon feats. (USAF MSgt Lois R.Dextraze earns the Bundeswehr Achievement Badge) Katie Wiley. illus Airman 20:37 May '76

Great Britain

SAC wins Blue Steel Trophy in Giant Strike VI (Royal Air Force Strike Command's Bombing and Navigation Competition). LtCol Richard W. Blatter. illus tab Combat Crew 27:8-10 Jun '76

United States

See also
Legion of Merit
Medal of Honor

ALA salutes the National Restaurant Association on the Hennessy (Trophy) at 20. illus Review 55:33-34+ Mar-Apr '76

An Air Force almanac: The United States Air Force in facts and figures. tabs AF Mag 59:132-143 May '76

Air Force Bicentennial slide production wins gold medal (at the 18th Annual International Film and Television Festival, New York City). TIG Brief 28:16 Jan 30 '76

Air.Traffic Controller of the Year for 1976 (SSgt Steven A.Lewis). illus USA Avn Dig 22:28+ Sep '76

Awards & citations. Regular feature in issues of Air Force Times

Awards at the 1976 Air Force Association National Convention (Washington, Sep 19-23, 1976). illus AF Mag 59:42-43 Nov '76

Blanchard Trophy winner: Malmstrom (AFB, Mont, 341st Strategic Missile) Wing top SAC unit (in 1976 Missile Combat Competition). illus AF Times 36:34 May 17 '76

Broken Wing Awards given (to CWOs Tommy P.Hall and Harold A.Mulherin). Translog 7: inside back cover Feb '76

AWARDS, DECORATIONS, ETC - Continued

United States - Cont'd

(Ch(Maj) Loren Dale Pugh nominated as ROA's Chaplain of the Year) illus Officer 52:21 Jan '76

Chief of Staff Individual Safety Award (presented to Stancil R.Hardison, art director of TAC Attack). illus TAC Attack 16:25 Jul '76

(Collier Trophy awarded by National Aeronautic Assoc to David S.Lewis, chief executive officer of General Dynamics Corp, and to USAF-industry team that produced the F-16) illus Natl Def 61: 102-103 Sep-Oct '76

(Col) J.Elmore Swenson (in) Army Aviation Hall of Fame. illus USA Avn Dig 22:15 Feb '76

The competitive spirit of '76. (Aerospace Defense Command 1976 Weapons Loading Competition, Tyndall AFB, Fla) Capt Robert J.Perry. illus Interceptor 18:5-9 Jul '76

Conquering the world with ribbon. LtCol W.D.Fitts. illus MarCor Gaz 60:68-70 Nov '76

318th FIS (Fighter Interceptor Sq) Hughes Trophy winners. illus Interceptor 18:10-11 Mar '76

Fairchild Trophy winners (1948-76). Table only. Combat Crew 27:19 Dec '76

Food service--200 years of advancement. Lt Dennis A.Bossen. illus AF Engrg & Svcs Qtr 17:14-16 Feb '76

For extraordinary heroism ... (USAF recipients of medals of heroism for action during Mayaguez incident) illus Airman 20:44-45 Feb '76

Frank Pace, former Army Secretary, is named to receive (George Catlett) Marshall Medal. illus Army 26:11 Jun '76

Freedoms (Foundation) Awards honor ROA, ROTC members. Officer 52:31 Jul '76

Freedoms Foundation honors Guard writers, doers. Natl Guardsman 30:37 Apr '76

Giant Sword '76: Best of the best. (Strategic Air Command's Munitions Loading Competition) illus tab Combat Crew 27:11-13 Dec '76

Giant Sword '76 (Ellsworth AFB, SD, Sep 27-Oct 6, 1976). illus Combat Crew 27:12-15 Sep '76

John Philip Sousa is enshrined (by Hall of Fame for Great Americans). MarCor Gaz 60:6 Nov '76

(Koren Kolligian Trophy for 1975 awarded to Capt Robert C.Helt) AF Times 36:28 Jul 12 '76

Looking forward to new horizons (161st Air Refueling Group, Phoenix, Ariz, receives Spaatz Trophy and AFA's Outstanding Unit Award). SMSgt Louis M. Nicolucci. illus Air Reservist 28:8-9 Nov '76

(MTMC Awards) for Excellence in Traffic Management (made during NDTA's 31st Annual Forum, 1976). illus Translog 7:1-3 Oct '76

(Maj Betty Vierra the recipient of) first annual E.A. Hoefly Award. illus Aviation, Space & Envmt Med 47:798 Jul '76

(MajGen) Spurgeon Neel elected to Army Aviation Hall of Fame for pioneering aeromedevac. illus Aviation, Space & Envmt Med 47:799 Jul '76

(Maj Robert W.) Undorf wins Mackay Trophy for role in Mayaguez rescue. AF Times 37:31 Oct 25 '76

AWARDS, DECORATIONS, ETC - Continued

United States - Cont'd

Med society (Aerospace Medical Assoc) confers awards (at 47th annual Scientific Meeting, Bal Harbour, Fla, May 10-13, 1976). illus AF Times 36:27 May 31 '76

(NDTA) military unit awards. illus Def Trans J 32: 65-69+ Oct '76

NGAUS awards program: Criteria for selection. illus Natl Guardsman 30:18-20 Feb '76

(21st NORAD Region/Air) Division recaptures (Gen Frederic H.) Smith Trophy. illus Interceptor 18:13 Feb '76

Never a 'Question Mark.' (Spaatz Trophy, given to SAC by TAC to be awarded to best tanker unit each year, in honor of historic flight of the Question Mark in 1929, which stayed in the air nearly 7 days and proved that in-flight refueling was practical) Maj Jay B.Welsh. illus Airman 20: 24-29 Mar '76

New awards for procurement research. AF Times 36:11 Jan 5 '76

1976 award winners of the Aerospace Medical Association. illus Aviation, Space & Envmt Med 47:572-576 May '76

The number '1' team (in 1976 William Tell Weapons Loading Competition). illus Air Reservist 28:11 Aug-Sep '76

Olympic Arena 76: Competition highlights. Maj Don Green. illus Combat Crew 27:4-7+ Jun '76

Olympic Arena trophy winners. illus tab Combat Crew 27:28-29 Jun '76

One love. (Sgt Tom Theobald of Chanute AFB, Ill, is ATC's Instructor of the Year) Milene Wells. illus Airman 20:41-42 Oct '76

Outstanding (Air Force Reservists) Mobilization Augmentees. illus Air Reservist 28:8-9 May '76

Outstanding Airmen for 1976. illus AF Times 37:19+ Sep 27 '76

Outstanding Airmen (of 1976). illus Airman 20:11-14 Dec '76

Practice makes perfect. (Marksmanship matches, clubs, and awards) Sgt1C Floyd Harrington. illus Soldiers 31:42-44 Jun '76

(Pres) Ford okays new medal for superior service (Defense Superior Service Medal). AF Times 36:2 Feb 23 '76

President OKs (BrigGen Charles E.) Yeager medal (for) breaking the sound barrier. AF Times 36:11 Jan 12 '76

'Question Mark' 'refuelers' honored: Two Air Force pioneers (BrigGens Ross G.Hoyt, Ret, and Joseph G.Hopkins, Ret) awarded DFCs nearly half a century after their key role in a world record endurance flight. illus AF Mag 59:22 Jul '76

RAF Chicksands (Eng), Kadena AB (Okinawa) take firsts in Hennessy contest. illus AF Engrg & Svcs Qtr 17:22 Aug '76

ROA honors a staunch friend. (F.Edward Hébert chosen Minute Man of the Year) Officer 52:8-9 Nov '76

(Report on NGAUS 98th General Conference, Washington, Aug 30-Sep 1, 1976) illus Air Reservist 28:8-9+ Oct '76

Rules for V (valor device) consolidated. AF Times 37:8 Dec 27 '76

AWARDS, DECORATIONS, ETC - Continued

United States - Cont'd

Safety awards: Chief of Staff Individual Safety Award to TSgt Ricardo N.Guerra; Koren Kolligian, Jr Trophy to Capt Robert C.Helt. illus Combat Crew 27:11 Oct '76

Safety awards (presented to Alaskan Air Command and Air Training Command in recognition of the most effective accident prevention programs during 1975). TIG Brief 28:10 Apr 9 '76

Safety awards: USAF Nuclear Safety Certificates. TIG Brief 28:6 Jun 4 '76

Secretary (of the Army Martin R.) Hoffmann joins (Field Artillery OCS) Hall of Fame. illus Fld Arty J 44:45-46 May-Jun '76

(Sen John C.) Stennis receives Truman Award. illus Natl Guardsman 30:30 Mar '76

(SSgt Herman J.) Kokojan sweeps contest (as Military Photographer of the Year, 1975). illus AF Times 36:34-35 Apr 19 '76

'Some concerns about this country we love.' (Condensed from address upon acceptance of the George C.Marshall Medal, AUSA 1976 Annual Meeting) Frank Pace, Jr. Army 26:46-47 Nov '76

Three words or less. (Adapted from speech, Outstanding Airman banquet, Air Force Assoc Convention, Washington, Sep 15, 1975) Gen William V.McBride. illus Airman 20:9-10 Jan '76

Two Air Force Olympians know the glint of gold. (Capt Phillip G.Boggs and Amn Darrell O.Pace win gold medals in the 1976 Montreal Olympics; seven other AF men compete) Capt John B.Taylor. illus Airman 20:42-48 Dec '76

2 at Shaw (AFB, SC, TSgt Gerald C.Arruda and SSgt Billy J.Peterson) win Cheney (Award). AF Times 36:30 Jan 12 '76

2 captains (Donald R.Blacklund and Roland W.Purser) top AFA awards list. AF Times 37:8 Sep 20 '76

USAF safety trophies (and) safety awards, 1975. illus Aerosp Safety 32:32-33 Jul '76

USAF's finest. (12 Outstanding Airmen for 1976) Maj Terry A.Arnold. illus AF Mag 59:47-49 Nov '76

VMFA-323 wins 2d Hanson Award (for best Fighter Attack Sq of the Year). MarCor Gaz 60:4 Dec '76

The Voodoo (Oregon's 142d Fighter Interceptor Gp) revenge (wins the 1976 Aerospace Defense Command's Weapons Loading Competition). illus Natl Guardsman 30:4-5 Jul '76

Weyand: Full circle. (Gen Fred C.Weyand accepts "Minute Man Hall of Fame" award at ROA National Convention, Bal Harbour, Fla, June 29-July 2, 1976) Officer 9:21+ Sep '76

(The winners of SAC's) Giant Voice ('76). LtCol Richard W.Blatter. illus tabs Combat Crew 27: 4-7+ Dec '76

History

The Armor Leadership Award. 1stLt Joseph T.Martin. illus Armor 85:27-29 Sep-Oct '76

AZORES

Another Army "Navy" game (Azores). SSgt Virgil L. Laning. illus Translog 7:16-20 Jan '76

B

The Army's facilities engineering operations.
BrigGen Walter O.Bachus. Mil Engr 68:94-97
Mar-Apr '76

BACTERIOLOGICAL WARFARE see Chemical-Biological
Warfare

BAGLEY, Worth H.

Superpowers at sea: A debate. ADM Worth H.Bagley,
Ret and RADM Gene R.LaRocque, Ret. Intl Sec
1:56-76 Summer '76

BAILOUTS see Parachute Jumping

BAINBRIDGE, William G.

Quality, training and motivation. SMA William G.
Bainbridge. por Army 26:27-29 Oct '76

BAKER, Milton G.

LtGen Milton G.Baker: 'A man of infinite personal
power and inner strength.' por obit Army 26:10
Nov '76

BAKER, Royal N.

(LtGen) Royal N.Baker, 58. por obit AF Times 36:24
May 3 '76

BALANCE OF PAYMENTS

Balance of payments tables. Regular feature in some
issues of Defense & Foreign Affairs Digest

BALANCE OF POWER

After the Bicentennial: The end of an era? Maj Barry
M.Meuse. illus tab AU Rev 27:2-12 Jul-Aug '76

The Air Force and national security: 1976 and beyond. (Remarks, Air Force Assoc, Mobile Chapter, Mobile, Ala, March 27, 1976) LtGen John W.
Pauly. AF Plcy Ltr for Comdrs: Sup No.6:10-18
Jun '76

Air Force Chief of Staff's FY 1977 Posture State-
ment. (Statement before House Committee on
Armed Services, Washington, Jan 29, 1976) Gen
David C.Jones. AF Plcy Ltr for Comdrs: Sup
No.3:23-40 Mar '76

American maritime strategy and Soviet naval expansion. J.William Middendorf II. illus tabs Strat
Rev 4:16-25 Winter '76

Arms control and world order. Hedley Bull. Intl Sec
1:3-16 Summer '76

Arms, men, and military budgets: Some grim facts
and sobering conclusions about the present military 'balance.' James D.Hessman. tabs Sea Power
19:14-16 May '76

The artificial crisis of American security. illus tabs
Def Monitor pt 1 (Military balance between U.S.
and USSR) 5: entire issue May '76; pt 2, How much
for defense? 5: entire issue Jun '76

Backfire (Tu-V-G, new Soviet supersonic bomber):
Strategic implications. Gerard K.Burke. illus
tabs Mil Rev 56:85-90 Sep '76

Being Number One nation: Primacy and detente. Col
Anthony L.Wermuth, Ret. illus tabs Parameters
5, No.2:54-68 '76

A blueprint for safeguarding the strategic balance.
(2d report on AFA's Symposium on "Tomorrow's
Strategic Options," Vandenberg AFB, Calif, April
28-29, 1976) Edgar Ulsamer. illus tabs AF Mag
59:68-74 Aug '76

BALANCE OF POWER - Continued

Capabilities and courage. Robert F.Ellsworth. Natl
Def 61:29-31 Jul-Aug '76

A capsule assessment of Soviet Army capabilities.
tabs Mil Rev 56:94-95 Jun '76

Comparing American & Soviet defense: How does
U.S. technology stack up with USSR? Malcolm R.
Currie. illus tab Comdrs Dig 19: entire issue
Jun 17 '76

Comparing Soviet and American defense efforts. Les
Aspin. tabs NATO's Fifteen Nations 21:34-36+
Jun-Jul '76

Conventional forces as deterrent. LtGen Daniel O.
Graham, Ret. illus Army 26:18-22 Jun '76

Defence cuts continue. (Points from Britain's 1976
Defence White Paper) illus tabs Air Pict 38:174-
177 May '76

Detente and reality. R.J.Rummel. illus tabs Strat
Rev 4:33-43 Fall '76

The dimensions of current U.S. military strategy.
LtCol C.R.Nelson. illus tabs Mil Rev 56:88-92
Aug '76

European security: Helsinki to Vienna. Colin Gordon.
RUSI J for Def Studies 121:34-36+ Sep '76

(Excerpt from) Keynote Address (57th Defense Preparedness Meeting, American Defense Preparedness Assoc, Los Angeles, Oct 15, 1975). Gen
William J.Evans. Natl Def 60:283 Jan-Feb '76

A force second to none: The FY 1977 Defense budget.
Terence E.McClary. illus tab Armed Forces
Compt 21:16-19 Apr '76

Forces for the future. (Remarks, Lancaster Cham-
ber of Commerce, Lancaster, Calif, Feb 6, 1976)
Thomas C.Reed. AF Plcy Ltr for Comdrs: Sup
No.4:16-20 Apr '76

A forecast for the 70's and 80's. Anthony J.Wiener.
Persp in Def Mgt No.24:1-12 Winter '75-'76

The foreword to Jane's (Fighting Ships 1976-77).
Capt John Moore, Ret. Sea Power 19:24-32 Sep '76

Former DIA (Defense Intelligence Agency) director
(Daniel O.Graham) speaks out. F.Clifton Berry,
Jr. Armed Forces J Intl 113:15 Mar '76

Future tactical missiles. Malcolm R.Currie. illus
Natl Def 61:32-35 Jul-Aug '76

(Gen Alexander) Haig paints bleak picture of European situation. Col Robert D.Heinl, Jr, Ret. illus
Sea Power 19:22-24 Dec '76

A holocaust for Happy Valley? Henry Young. illus US
Nav Inst Proc 102:52-61 Nov '76

Inflexibility in NATO's flexible response. Maj Donald
F.Borden. illus maps Mil Rev 56:26-41 Jan '76

JCS Chairman's Posture Statement. (Statement before House Armed Services Committee, Washington, Jan 27, 1976) Gen George S. Brown. tabs AF
Plcy Ltr for Comdrs: Sup No.4:13-15 Apr '76

Jane's aerospace review 1975/76. John W.R.Taylor.
illus AF Mag 59:22-29 Jan '76

Keynote luncheon address (AFCEA, Washington,
June 8, 1976). Thomas C.Reed. illus Signal 30:
19-23 Aug '76

Kissinger's grand design: Peace without risk ... the
promise cannot be fulfilled. G.Warren Nutter.
illus Sea Power 18:19-22 Dec '75

BALANCE OF POWER - Continued

Technological investment and payoff. (Remarks, AFA/SAC 9th Annual Missile Combat Competition, Vandenberg AFB, Calif, April 29, 1976) Gen William J. Evans. AF Plcy Ltr for Comdrs: Sup No. 7: 7-14 Jul '76

The theatre balance between NATO and the Warsaw Pact. London's International Institute for Strategic Studies. tabs AF Mag 59:98-106 Dec '76

Tides and currents in the Pacific: Long-term maritime implications. ADM James L. Holloway III. illus Strat Rev 4:33-39 Summer '76

Trends in Soviet military technology. Charles De-Vore. illus tabs Signal 30:47-50 Jul '76

USAF's new Soviet awareness program. Edgar Ulsamer. AF Mag 59:38-42 May '76

The United States: A military power second to none? Gen Maxwell D. Taylor, Ret. Intl Sec 1:49-55 Summer '76

U.S. defense perspectives. Donald H. Rumsfeld. illus tabs Comdrs Dig 19: entire issue Aug 26 '76

U.S. General Purpose Forces: A need for modernization. Gen George S. Brown. illus tab Comdrs Dig 19: entire issue May 27 '76

U.S.-USSR military balance. Table only. Govt Exec 8:25 Dec '76

(U.S./USSR military balance) illus tabs Armed Forces J Intl pt 1, U.S./USSR military balance shifts in favor of Russia. Benjamin F. Schemmer. 113:18+ Mar '76; pt 2, Scope of and reasons behind U.S./USSR force asymmetries. 113:23-26+ Apr '76; pt 3 (Summary) 113:24-28 May '76

War with Russia in Europe would find U.S. sorely outnumbered. Col Robert D. Heinl, Jr, Ret. illus Sea Power 19:33-34 Aug '76

Will the Soviets wage war in space? Edgar Ulsamer. illus AF Mag 59:30-33+ Dec '76

BALLISTIC MISSILE EARLY WARNING SYSTEM

RAF Fylingdales and the USAF spacetrack system. SqLdr D. J. Nicholson. illus Royal Air Forces Qtr 15:333-336 Winter '75

BALLISTIC MISSILES see Missiles

BALLOONS

And now--the (parachuting) balloon. Capt Marshall L. Helena. Infantry 66:13-14 May-Jun '76

Balloonists sample food and air aloft. AF Times 37:23 Sep 6 '76

Balloons tested for containership offload. Dan Hall. illus Translog 7:1-4 Apr '76

Food samples slated for balloon journey--taste tests to reveal flight effects. Ron Sanders. illus AF Times 36:24 Feb 23 '76

Holloman (AFB, NM) balloonists end Project Ashcan (with the successful recovery of their fifth atmospheric sampling package of radioactive waste). AF Times 36:40 May 17 '76

The silent bombers. (Japanese free balloons in WW II) LtCol Joseph P. Frankoski. illus Air Def Mag, pp 34-36, Apr-Jun '76

The Sirocco meteorological sounding station. illus tab Intl Def Rev 9:433-435 Jun '76

BALLOONS - Continued

Up, up and away. (Hot air ballooning then and now) SSgt Zack Richards. illus Soldiers 31:14-18 Jun '76

History

The air role in the War between the States. (The Civil War balloon activities of Professor Thaddeus S. C. Lowe) Capt Daniel T. Davis. illus AU Rev 27: 13-29 Jul-Aug '76

The first aerial voyage in America. (A Frenchman, Jean Pierre Blanchard, Philadelphia, Jan 9, 1793) Douglas H. Robinson. Am Avn Hist Soc J 21:3 Spring '76

Flying myths and legends, balloons, blimps and dirigibles: A quest for relevancy. Capt Lawrence Pace. Educ J 19:13-18 Fall '76

My beautiful balloon: Evolution--the FO. Ronald W. Shin. illus Fld Arty J 44:9-12 Nov-Dec '76

My forty-fifth ascension: The first aerial voyage in America (Philadelphia, Jan 9, 1793). Jean Pierre Blanchard. Translog 7:7-8+ Mar '76

BALTIC SEA REGION

Strategic Importance

NATO's tender watery flanks. Joseph Palmer. illus Sea Power 19:34-39 Mar '76

BANDS (MUSIC)

What band? SqLdr J. W. Martindale. Royal Air Forces Qtr 16:57-59 Spring '76

History

John Philip Sousa is enshrined (by Hall of Fame for Great Americans). MarCor Gaz 60:6 Nov '76

BANGLADESH

Economic Conditions

Bangladesh. Stefan T. Possony and Leigh Johnson. illus Def & For Aff Dig No. 11:18-23+ '75

Foreign Relations

Bangladesh. Stefan T. Possony and Leigh Johnson. illus Def & For Aff Dig No. 11:18-23+ '75

History

Bangladesh. Stefan T. Possony and Leigh Johnson. illus Def & For Aff Dig No. 11:18-23+ '75

Politics and Government

Bangladesh. Stefan T. Possony and Leigh Johnson. illus Def & For Aff Dig No. 11:18-23+ '75

Strategic Importance

Bangladesh. Stefan T. Possony and Leigh Johnson. illus Def & For Aff Dig No. 11:18-23+ '75

BANKS AND BANKING

See also
Electronic Funds Transfer System

The Automated Clearing House (ACH)--a new delivery system. James H. Jarrell. illus Armed Forces Compt 21:4-5 Apr '76

Checks To Financial Organizations (CTFO) program and innocent NonSufficient Funds (NSF) checks. TIG Brief 28:18 Feb 13 '76; Correction. 28:12 Mar 26 '76

BANKS AND BANKING - Continued

O'seas banks (for American servicemen) cost U.S. $$.
Andy Plattner. AF Times 36:4 Jan 5 '76

Panel (House Banking Subcommittee) charges Trea-
sury balks overseas banking. AF Times 36:10
Mar 29 '76

Recurring Federal payments and EFTS (Electronic
Funds Transfer System) at the U.S. Treasury.
Les W.Plumly. illus Armed Forces Compt 21:
2-3 Apr '76

Retirees to get option (to have pay sent directly to
banks electronically). AF Times 36:33 Apr 12 '76

Unintended bad check not actionable. AF Times 36:6
Mar 8 '76

Voting, banking off (military) privacy list. Ann
Gerow. AF Times 36:2 Mar 1 '76

What do you know about military banks? BrigGen
John A.Seitz, Ret. illus Armed Forces Compt 21:
8-9 Apr '76

BARE BASE CONCEPT

Prime BEEF in Europe. Maj·Charles F.Kreis. illus
AF Engrg & Svcs Qtr 17:28-30 May '76

BARGES

"LASH" (Lighter-Aboard SHip) shipment to Egypt:
Unit of 30 barges towed between New York & Alba-
ny; largest grain shipment in U.S. by LASH. illus
Def Trans J 32:6-7 Dec '76

BARNES, Frank G.

Requiem for an engineer, MajGen Frank G.Barnes.
obit por AF Engrg & Svcs Qtr 17:13+ Nov '76

BARRACKS AND QUARTERS

See also
Housing

Air Force--U.S.

Airmen home basing assignments. TIG Brief 28:17
Feb 27 '76

Audit finds many paid wrong rent. AF Times 36:2
Jun 28 '76

Civilian use of government quarters. TIG Brief 28:13
Dec 17 '76

Is (new) base housing (at Bolling AFB, DC) burglar-
proof? Ron Sanders. AF Times 36:4 Apr 12 '76

New family housing: None (for AF) in FY 77. AF
Times 36:18 Feb 23 '76

Plan to improve dorms outlined. AF Times 37:29
Nov 8 '76

Rental charges for inadequate quarters. TIG Brief
28:16 Jun 18 '76

Rental charges for inadequate quarters. TIG Brief
28:4 Sep 10 '76

3-bedroom homes in view (for) master sergeants.
Ron Sanders. AF Times 36:6 Feb 9 '76

Use of government facilities during Temporary DutY
(TDY). TIG Brief 28:20-21 Apr 9 '76

Equipment

Interior design with people satisfaction in mind. Wil-
liam A.Brown, Sr. illus AF Engrg & Svcs Qtr 17:
2-5 Feb '76

BARRACKS AND QUARTERS - Continued

Air Force--U.S. - Cont'd

Maintenance and Repair

Homes, dorms due new look. AF Times 36:2
Jul 26 '76

Renovations cause (military) housing shortages. AF
Times 37:25 Sep 6 '76

Armed Forces--U.S.

DOD reviewing fair-rental idea. Fred Reed. AF
Times 37:12 Nov 22 '76

(DefSec Donald) Rumsfeld to evaluate rental proposal.
Randy Shoemaker. AF Times 37:4 Sep 27 '76

Fair market rental favored. Randy Shoemaker. AF
Times 37:3 Nov 1 '76

Rental won't include meters (for utilities). AF Times
37:3 Oct 4 '76

History

Old quarters that never die. Marianne Lester. illus
AF Times, Times Magazine sup:6-14+ Jul 26 '76

Maintenance and Repair

More housing funds to go for repairs. Ron Sanders.
AF Times 36:18 Jun 28 '76

Army--U.S.

Barracks thieves. MSgt Nat Dell. illus Soldiers 31:
22-24 Jan '76

Marine Corps--U.S.

History

CMC house now a landmark. illus MarCor Gaz 60:11
Oct '76

BARRIERS (MILITARY SCIENCE) see Obstacles (Mili-
tary Science)

BASE EXCHANGES see Exchanges

BASE OPERATIONS

The fastest hose in the West. (Transient maintenance
and services at Richards-Gebaur AFB, Mo) illus
Interceptor 18:12-15 Mar '76

Operations: Inspection Guide F. TIG Brief pt 1, Sec-
tions I-VI. 28:6p addendum Aug 13 '76; pt 2, Sec-
tions VII-IX. 28:7p addendum Aug 27 '76; Supple-
ment 1. 28:2p addendum Oct 8 '76

Ops topics. Regular feature in issues of Aerospace
Safety

·Maintenance/operations liaison. TIG Brief 28:4
Sep 24 '76

Supervisor Of Flying (SOF) program. (AFR 60-2)
TIG Brief 28:14 Dec 3 '76

The team: Operations and maintenance. Majs James
D.Stetson, III and Warren D.Johnson. illus Navi-
gator 23:29-30 Winter '76

BATTERIES

Don't melt the battery. Walter B.Orr. illus USA Avn
Dig 22:20-21 Jun '76

Lithium batteries. TIG Brief 28:7 Mar 12 '76

The positive side. (Battery problems) Ted Kontos.
illus USA Avn Dig 22:32-35 Oct '76

BATTERIES - Continued

Maintenance and Repair

Nickel cadmium battery thermal runaway. TIG Brief 28:3 Oct 8 '76

BATTLEFIELD SURVEILLANCE see Surveillance

BATTLES

See also subdivision Campaigns and Battles under specific wars, e.g.,
Korean War, 1950-1953--Campaigns and Battles
Vietnamese Conflict, 1957-1975--Campaigns and Battles
World War I--Campaigns and Battles
World War II--Campaigns and Battles

The battle at Moore's Creek Bridge (NC). James D. Deerin. illus Natl Guardsman 30:2-5 Feb '76

The Battle of Fort Washington: One of the worst American defeats of the Revolutionary War. Bruce P. Hargreaves. illus map Natl Guardsman 30:2-5 Nov '76

Bunker Hill. Col John H. Mason and Walter F. Mackie. illus Mil Engr 68:166-170 May-Jun '76

Coalition warfare--relieving the Peking legations, 1900. (Boxer Rebellion) Col James B. Agnew. illus map Mil Rev 56:58-70 Oct '76

Colenso: The first battle of the early Tugela River Campaign (1899). 1stLt David M. Crane. maps illus Mil Rev 56:77-91 Feb '76

The first Battle of Charleston. James B. Deerin. map illus Natl Guardsman 30:2-6 Jun '76

Forgotten victory: The Sullivan Expedition of 1779. Col John B. B. Trussell, Jr, Ret. illus map Parameters 5, No. 2:40-53 '76

The ultimate battle. (French Foreign Legion action at Camerone, Mexico, 1863) SP4 Robert G. Fuller. illus Soldiers 31:50-53 Sep '76

Valentine's Day at Kettle Creek, Georgia, 1779. Capt Emory A. Burton. Mil Rev 56:56-57 May '76

BAYNE, Marmaduke G.

The National Defense University: A strategic asset. VADM Marmaduke G. Bayne. por Strat Rev 4:23-32 Fall '76

BEE, Thomas G.

Air Force Audit Agency. por AF Mag 59:92-93 May '76

Auditor General. BrigGen T. G. Bee. por AF Compt 10:28-29 Jan '76

Auditor General. BrigGen Thomas G. Bee. por AF Compt 10:18-19 Apr '76

BEHAVIORISM (PSYCHOLOGY)

Arousing environmental stresses can improve performance, whatever people say. E. C. Poulton. tabs Aviation, Space & Envmt Med 47:1193-1204 Nov '76

Attitudes and accidents aboard an aircraft carrier. John B. Levine and others. tabs Aviation, Space & Envmt Med 47:82-85 Jan '76

Complacency: What it is, what we can do about it. Maj T. R. Allocca. Aerosp Safety 32:9 Aug '76

Conflict in organizations: Good or bad? LtCol Russell Pierre, Jr and Maj Jerome G. Peppers, Jr, Ret. AU Rev 28:69-79 Nov-Dec '76

BEHAVIORISM (PSYCHOLOGY) - Continued

Eliminating the wife error. Jackie Starmer. (Adapted from MATS Flyer, Aug 1963) illus Interceptor 18: 5-7 Apr '76; Adaptation. Approach 21:24-26 Nov '75

Occupational mobility and political behavior: Some unresolved issues. Joseph Lopreato and others. J Pol & Mil Sociol 4:1-15 Spring '76

Psychologic and psychophysiologic response to 105 days of social isolation. Don A. Rockwell and others. illus tabs Aviation, Space & Envmt Med 47: 1087-1093 Oct '76

Psychological steeling of tankmen. Maj M. Rudachenko. Soviet Mil Rev No. 1:30-31 Jan '76

Survival: Your way out. SSgt Robert J. Paetz. illus Aerosp Safety 32:12-13 Jun '76

Why pilots make errors. William C. McDaniel. illus USA Avn Dig pt 1, 22:32-34 Mar '76; pt 2, 22:30-32 Apr '76; pt 3, 22:38-39 May '76; pt 4, 22:32-34 Jun '76

BENEFITS see
Bonuses   Survivors Rights and Benefits
Fringe Benefits   Veterans Benefits

BENNETT, John J.

(John J.) Bennett and (David R.) Macdonald join Navy Secretariat. Ellen R. Davis. por Sea Power 19:14 Oct '76

BERGQUIST, Robert L.

A firearms treasure. (Collection of Col Farley L. Berman, Ret, Anniston, Ala) BrigGen Robert L. Bergquist. Natl Def 60:378-381 Mar-Apr '76

BERLIN

Description and Travel

Berlin: A tale of two cities. Capt Larry J. Myers. illus Soldiers 31:14-17 Nov '76

BERLIN AIRLIFT

Airlift on trial: Maj Orlen L. Brownfield. illus MAC Flyer 23:5-7 Jul '76

BICYCLES see Motorcycles and Bicycles

BIOGRAPHY see subdivision under specific subjects, e.g.,
Army--Biography
Marine Corps--Biography

BIOLOGICAL RESEARCH

See also
Space Biology

BIOLOGICAL RHYTHMS

Air operations and circadian performance rhythms. Karl E. Klein and others. illus tabs Aviation, Space & Envmt Med 47:221-230 Mar '76

Are biorhythms a waste of time? Maj John H. Wolcott and others. (Reprinted from TAC Attack, Nov 1975) illus tabs MAC Flyer 23:11-15 Mar '76

Changes in glucose, insulin, and growth hormone levels associated with bedrest. Joan Vernikos-Danellis and others. tabs Aviation, Space & Envmt Med 47:583-587 Jun '76

Effects of rapid round trips against time displacement on adrenal cortical-medullary circadian rhythms. Chiharu Sekiguchi and others. tabs Aviation, Space & Envmt Med 47:1101-1106 Oct '76

BLOOD - Continued

Blood viscosity in man following decompression: Correlations with hematocrit and venous gas emboli. Tom S. Neuman and others. illus tab Aviation, Space & Envmt Med 47:803-807 Aug '76

Effect of sequential anti-G suit inflation on pulmonary capillary blood flow in man. Raymond Begin and others. illus tabs Aviation, Space & Envmt Med 47:937-941 Sep '76

Free amino acids in human blood plasma during space flights. A.S. Ushakov and T.F. Vlasova. tabs Aviation, Space & Envmt Med 47:1061-1064 Oct '76

Hematologic changes in man during decompression: Relations to overt decompression sickness and bubble scores. Robert F. Goad and others. tabs Aviation, Space & Envmt Med 47:863-867 Aug '76

Keep the blood flowing. (Blood Bank Center, Fort Knox, Ky) Sgt Robert DeVoe. illus Soldiers 31: 50-51 Apr '76

Measurement of change in plasma volume during heat exposure and exercise. M.H. Harrison and R.J. Edwards. tabs Aviation, Space & Envmt Med 47: 1038-1045 Oct '76

BLUE ANGELS

Flying for show: A look at six aerobatic teams from five nations--they're all good, but different. Richard F. Lord. illus AF Times, Times Magazine sup:10-15 May 31 '76

BOATNER, James G.

Supersoldiers of the North. (172d ("Arctic Light") Infantry Brigade) BrigGen James G. Boatner. Army 26:27-30 Nov '76

BOATS

Are Coast Guard small boats small enough? LCDR Paul Hureau. illus US Nav Inst Proc 102:96-98 Jun '76

BODY ARMOR

Body armor today. Martin J. Miller, Jr. illus Natl Def 61:217-220 Nov-Dec '76

BODYCOMBE, Richard

(Maj)Gen Bodycombe new AFR Vice Cmdr; other officers receive new assignments. por Officer 52:19 Dec '76

BOLIVIA

Economic Policy

Andean tract. A. Ranney Johnson. illus Def & For Aff Dig No. 3:20-23 '76

Foreign Relations

Argentina

Andean tract. A. Ranney Johnson. illus Def & For Aff Dig No. 3:20-23 '76

Chile

Andean tract. A. Ranney Johnson. illus Def & For Aff Dig No. 3:20-23 '76

La Paz lament. (Need for sovereign access to the Pacific) Leigh Johnson. Def & For Aff Dig No. 3: 14-19 '76

BOMBER UNITS

Giant Sword '76: Best of the best. (Strategic Air Command's Munitions Loading Competition) illus tab Combat Crew 27:11-13 Dec '76

(The winners of SAC's) Giant Voice ('76). LtCol Richard W. Blatter. illus tabs Combat Crew 27: 4-7+ Dec '76

History

B-25s over Tokyo, 18 April 1942. MSgt Dave Sylva. illus Aerosp Safety 32:14-17+ Apr '76

Memories of a U.S. 8th AF Bomb Group. 1stLt Tony Fairbairn. illus Air Pict 38:238-240 Jun '76

"Old Leatherface's" bombers. (Chennault's forces included the 308th Bombardment Gp (Heavy) which saw much action in China during WW II) Capt Stephen O. Manning III. illus Airman 20:8-14 Jul '76

Pacific Privateers: VPB-121 in World War II. Joseph C. Woolf. illus Am Avn Hist Soc J 21:118-125 Summer '76

BOMBING

Attack T(hunder)-stick style. Capt John C. Morrissey. (Reprinted from Fighter Weapons Newsletter, Dec 1967) illus USAF Ftr Wpns Rev, pp 21-27, Summer '76

(Day and night bombing accuracy) Signal 30:146 Jan '76

Initial pipper position and tracking. Capt Alexander H.C. Harwick. (Reprinted from USAF Fighter Weapons Review, Fall 1972) illus tab USAF Ftr Wpns Rev, pp 2-10, Summer '76

Let's get serious about dive toss. Capt Robert H. Baxter. (Reprinted from USAF Fighter Weapons Newsletter, Sep 1970) illus tab USAF Ftr Wpns Rev, pp 28-34, Summer '76

The new abort pop-up criteria. Capt Marty Steere. tab TAC Attack 16:24-26 Oct '76

When do I turn? (Planning bomb releases) Maj Robert P. Reisinger. illus tabs Combat Crew 27:10-11 May '76

Study and Teaching

Prior planning prevents ... Capt Marty Steere. illus TAC Attack 16:20-22 May '76

What are the hazards of practice bombs? TIG Brief 28:11 Jan 16 '76

BOMBING AND GUNNERY RANGES

Charlie's place. (SSgt Charles R. Reed, NCOIC of Wackernheim Range near Mainz, West Germany) Lt Michael A. Bartell and SP4 Kregg P.J. Jorgenson. illus Army 26:22-25 Nov '76

Land beyond the moon (Grafenwoehr, Germany, Army Europe and 7th Army's Training Center). SP4 Kathleen E. Murray. illus Soldiers 31:37-38 Dec '76

Mini-ranges pay big dividends. SP5 Jeffrey Stark. Armor 85:24 Nov-Dec '76

Ricochets. LtCol Jim Learmonth. illus tab Aerosp Safety 32:16-17 Jan '76

Showdown at (Grafenwoehr's) Range 32 (Army Europe and 7th Army's Training Center). Capt Larry Brainerd. illus Soldiers 31:34-36 Dec '76

Weapons range trespassers. Gordon S. Taylor. illus Aerosp Safety 32:20 Jun '76

BOMBING AND GUNNERY RANGES - Continued

Maintenance and Repair

Home on the range. Maj John N.P.Reisbick. illus TAC Attack 16:8-9 Jan '76

BOMBING, NAVIGATION, ETC

Competitions

Air Force

Giant Voice '76. illus Combat Crew 27:20-21 Oct '76

SAC wins Blue Steel Trophy in Giant Strike VI (Royal Air Force Strike Command's Bombing and Navigation Competition). LtCol Richard W.Blatter. illus tab Combat Crew 27:8-10 Jun '76

(The winners of SAC's) Giant Voice ('76). LtCol Richard W.Blatter. illus tabs Combat Crew 27: 4-7+ Dec '76

BOMBINGS, TERRORIST see Terrorism

BOMBS

See also
Nuclear Bombs

Bombs and bomb beaters. LtCol S.G.Styles, Ret. illus tabs Intl Def Rev 9:817-819 Oct '76

The silent bombers. (Japanese free balloons in WW II) LtCol Joseph P.Frankoski. illus Air Def Mag, pp 34-36, Apr-Jun '76

What are the hazards of practice bombs? TIG Brief 28:11 Jan 16 '76

Guidance and Control

A case for smart weapons. LtCol Frank C.Regan, Jr. illus tabs MarCor Gaz 60:31-35 May '76

Modern weapons employment. Capt Arthur Fowler. illus Aerosp Safety 32:5 Nov '76

History

German remotely piloted bombs (WW II). Charles H. Bogart. illus US Nav Inst Proc 102:62-68 Nov '76

BONUSES

Advocate of people programs. Interview. David P. Taylor. AF Times 37:14 Nov 15 '76

Be choosy on special pay, manpower group (Defense Manpower Commission) says. AF Times 36:27 May 10 '76

Broader power asked on bonus (by DOD). Andy Plattner. AF Times 36:8 Jun 14 '76

Cutback in government Dr benefits asked. AF Times 37:31 Nov 15 '76

Debate growing over doctor bonus. Phil Stevens. AF Times 37:12 Aug 9 '76

EM must solve re-up equation. Bruce Callander. AF Times 37:14 Nov 29 '76

Early out means bonus payback (when reenlisting). AF Times 37:10 Sep 20 '76

1st termers must plan ahead for retraining bonus. AF Times 36:16 Jun 21 '76

BONUSES - Continued

In cash & in kind. Bruce Callander. illus tabs AF Times pt 1, 36:22 Jul 19 '76; pt 2, 36:26 Jul 26 '76; pt 3, 37:38 Aug 2 '76; pt 4, 37:34 Aug 9 '76; pt 5, Marrieds and singles: How much to pay them. 37:28 Aug 16 '76; pt 6, BAS: How rates were developed. 37:26 Aug 23 '76; pt 7, Benefits mean cutting costs. 37:34 Aug 30 '76; pt 8, Retirement: Benefits good despite Congress. 37:28 Sep 6 '76; pt 9, File of personal papers should be kept current. 37:45 Sep 13 '76; pt 10, Can system be changed? 37:28 Sep 20 '76

Many first termers can't get re-up $ $. AF Times 36:30 Jul 5 '76

NCO retrainees due $ $. AF Times 37:8 Aug 16 '76

N. Dakota extends Vietnam deadline--14 others paying bonuses. AF Times 36:26+ Mar 1 '76

SRBs cut, retrainees protected. Bruce Callander. AF Times 36:4 Mar 8 '76

Self-movers can get $ bonus. AF Times 36:3 Mar 29 '76

Some bonus skills dropped, a few added. AF Times 36:3 Jun 7 '76

Some can retrain for 2d re-up $ $. Bruce Callander. AF Times 36:5 Mar 29 '76

Some can seek bonuses earlier. AF Times 36:2 Apr 26 '76

Some 1st termers to miss re-up $ $. AF Times 37:10 Sep 20 '76

Supreme Court to rule on Navy VRB (Variable Reenlistment Bonuses) suit. AF Times 37:45 Dec 20 '76

3 big changes in SRB eyed: Two would ease, one would tighten, rules. Bruce Callander. AF Times 36:2 Apr 12 '76

27 skills set for Zone-B (6-10 years' service) bonuses. Bruce Callander. tabs AF Times 36:8 Apr 19 '76

BOOK REVIEWS

The Accountability of Power, by W.F.Mondale. Parameters 6, No.1:97-99 '76

Adolph Hitler, by J.Toland. Natl Def 61:236 Nov-Dec '76; AF Mag 59:124-125 Dec '76

The Advisors: Oppenheimer, Teller, and the Superbomb, by H.F.York. Mil Rev 56:98 Jul '76

Against the Tide: An Argument in Favor of the American Soldier, by P.B.Petersen. Armor 85:60 May-Jun '76

Aircraft Versus Submarine, by A.Price. Nav War Col Rev 28:104-105 Winter '76

An American First: John T.Flynn and the America First Committee, by M.F.Stenehjem. Mil Rev 56:107-108 Aug '76

The American Heritage History of the Thirteen Colonies, by L.B.Wright. Mil Rev 56:101-102 Apr '76

The American Intellectual Elite, by C.Kadushin. Armor 85:59-60 May-Jun '76

The American Soldier in Fiction, 1880-1963: A History of Attitudes Toward Warfare and the Military Establishment, by P.Aichinger. Mil Rev 56:103-104 Apr '76; Nav War Col Rev 28:96-97 Spring '76

The American Way of War: A History of United
States Military Strategy and Policy, by R.F.
Weigley. Armed Forces & Soc 2:595-599
Summer '76

The Americas in a Changing World, including the
Report of the Commission on United States-Latin
American Relations, with a Preface by S.M.
Linowitz. Mil Rev 56:101-102 Jan '76

America's Maritime Heritage, by E.Engle and A.S.
Lott. MarCor Gaz 60:18 Jan '76

The Armed Services and Society: Alienation, Management and Integration, edited by J.N.Wolfe and
J.Erickson. J Pol & Mil Sociol 4:321-323 Fall '76

Armies of the American Revolution, by I.V.Hogg
and J.H.Batchelor. Armor 85:59 May-Jun '76

Arming America: How the U.S. Buys Weapons, by
J.R.Fox. Persp in Def Mgt No.24:107-108
Winter '75-'76

Arms and African Development--Proceedings of the
First Pan-African Citizens' Conference, edited
by F.S.Arkhurst. Armed Forces & Soc 2:333-336
Winter '76

Arms, Defense Policy, and Arms Control, edited by
F.A.Long and G.W.Rathjens. Mil Rev 56:107
Oct '76

The Arms Trade with the Third World, revised and
abridged edition, by Stockholm International Peace
Research Institute. Nav War Col Rev 29:133-134
Summer '76

The Art of Psychological Warfare: 1914-1945, by
C.Roetter. Armor 85:59 Jul-Aug '76

Asia and the Road Ahead: Issues for the Major Powers, by R.A.Scalapino. Mil Rev 56:100 Jun '76

Assault in Norway, by T.Gallagher. Army Qtr 106:
373 Jul '76

The Atlantic Wall: Hitler's Defenses in the West,
1941-1944, by A.F.Wilt. Mil Rev 56:99 May '76

Baa Baa Black Sheep, by G.Boyington. MarCor Gaz
60:15 Dec '76

The Battle for Berlin, by J.Strawson. Soviet Mil Rev
No.1:55-56 Jan '76

The Battle for North Africa, 1940-43, by W.G.F.
Jackson. Mil Rev 56:108-109 Aug '76

The Battles for Cassino, by E.D.Smith. Royal Air
Forces Qtr 15:349-350 Winter '75

Becoming Modern: Individual Change in Six Developing Countries, by A.Inkeles and D.H.Smith. J Pol
& Mil Sociol 4:174-176 Spring '76

Behind the Middle East Conflict: The Real Impasse
Between Arab and Jew, by G.C.Alroy. Mil Rev
56:106-107 Apr '76

The Bermuda Triangle Mystery--Solved, by L.D.
Kusche. AU Rev 27:82-83 Mar-Apr '76

Beyond Kissinger: Ways of Conservative Statecraft,
by G.Liska. Nav War Col Rev 29:127-129 Summer '76

The Bitter Years: The Invasion and Occupation of
Denmark and Norway April 1940-May 1945, by
R.Petrow. RUSI J for Def Studies 120:72-73
Dec '75

The Black Soldier and Officer in the United States
Army, 1891-1917, by M.E.Fletcher. Infantry 66:
57-58 Jan-Feb '76

Blue Skies and Blood: The Battle of the Coral Sea,
by E.P.Hoyt. Mil Rev 56:107 Mar '76

Bodyguard of Lies, by A.C.Brown. Parameters 5,
No.2:93-94 '76; Mil Rev 56:97-98 May '76; Air
Def Mag, p 44, Jan-Mar '76; Strat Rev 4:103-104
Spring '76; RUSI J for Def Studies 121:87-88
Sep '76; Royal Air Forces Qtr 16:223-226
Autumn '76

Born on the Fourth of July, by R.Kovic. AF Times
37:16 Dec 20 '76; MarCor Gaz 60:14-15 Dec '76

Brazil since 1964: Modernisation under a Military
Regime, by G.-A.Fiechter. RUSI J for Def
Studies 121:96-97 Jun '76

Bringing Down America, by L.Grathwohl. MarCor
Gaz 60:16 Oct '76

Bringing the War Home: The American Soldier in
Vietnam and After, by J.Helmer. Armed Forces
& Soc 2:435-467 Spring '76; J Pol & Mil Sociol 4:
176-177 Spring '76

Britain and the People's Republic of China, 1949-
1974, by R.Boardman. RUSI J for Def Studies
121:98 Jun '76

Broadcasting to the Soviet Union, by M.Lisann.
J Pol & Mil Sociol 4:177-179 Spring '76

The Buffalo War: The History of the Red River Indian
Uprising of 1874, by J.L.Haley. MarCor Gaz 60:
16-17 Oct '76

Bureaucratic Politics & Foreign Policy, by M.H.
Halperin. Armed Forces & Soc 2:326-332 Winter '76

Can America Win the Next War? by D.Middleton. AF
Mag 59:60 Jan '76; Mil Rev 56:100-101 Feb '76;
Nav War Col Rev 28:91-96 Spring '76; AU Rev 27:
108-109 Jul-Aug '76; Armor 85:61 Sep-Oct '76

Canada and the American Presence: The U.S. Interest in an Independent Canada, by J.S.Dickey. Nav
War Col Rev 28:97-98 Spring '76

The Chetnik Movement and the Yugoslav Resistance,
by M.J.Milazzo. Armed Forces & Soc 2:604-609
Summer '76

The Chetniks, by J.Tomasevich. Armed Forces &
Soc 2:604-609 Summer '76

Chile: The Balanced View, edited by F.O.Vicuna.
Mil Rev 56:102-103 Jun '76

China and Japan--Emerging Global Powers, by P.G.
Mueller and D.A.Ross. Mil Rev 56:108 Mar '76;
RUSI J for Def Studies 121:98-99 Jun '76

The China Hands: America's Foreign Service Officers and What Befell Them, by E.J.Kahn, Jr.
Mil Rev 56:102-103 Apr '76

China's Uninterrupted Revolution: From 1840 to the
Present, edited by V.Nee and J.Peck. Mil Rev
56:105 Jul '76

The Chinese Calculus of Deterrence: India and Indochina, by A.S.Whiting. Mil Rev 56:103-104
May '76; Nav War Col Rev 29:135-137 Summer '76

Clausewitz and the State, by P.Paret. Mil Rev 56:
102-103 Sep '76

Code of Honor, by J.Dramesi. Nav War Col Rev 28:
102-103 Winter '76; Infantry 66:58 May-Jun '76

BOOK REVIEWS - Continued

The Coming Breakpoint, by B.Goldwater. Parameters 6, No.1:97-99 '76

The Communist Parties of Western Europe, by N.McInnes. RUSI J for Def Studies 120:74 Dec '75

The Concorde Conspiracy, by J.Costello and T.Hughes. Natl Def 61:75 Jul-Aug '76; Air Pict 38:247 Jun '76

Conflict in Africa: Concepts and Realities, by A.B. Bozeman. Mil Rev 56:70 Dec '76

Contemporary Strategy: Theories and Policies, by J.Baylis and others. Royal Air Forces Qtr 16:77-78 Spring '76; Mil Rev 56:100-101 Apr '76; RUSI J for Def Studies 121:98 Mar '76

Coups and Army Rule in Africa: Studies in Military Style, by S.Decalo. Mil Rev 56:72 Dec '76

Crisis in the West: American Leadership and the Global Balance, by L.Gelber. RUSI J for Def Studies 120:73-74 Dec '75

Critical Choices for Americans, prepared for the Commission on Critical Choices for Americans. Sea Power 19:39-40 Nov '76

The Crucial Years, 1939-1941: The World at War, by H.W.Baldwin. Army 26:62-63 Apr '76; Mil Rev 56:106-107 Jun '76

The Cultural Contradictions of Capitalism, by D.Bell.. Mil Rev 56:105-106 Jun '76

Cunningham the Commander, by S.W.C.Pack. US Nav Inst Proc 102:83 Jan '76

The Cybernetic Theory of Decision: New Dimensions of Political Analysis, by J.D.Steinbruner. Nav War Col Rev 28:105-106 Winter '76; Armed Forces & Soc 2:326-332 Winter '76

Cyprus: The Tragedy and the Challenge, by P.G. Polyviou. J Pol & Mil Sociol 4:157-160 Spring '76

Dachau: The Official History 1933-1954, by P.Berben. RUSI J for Def Studies 120:79-80 Dec '75

The Deception Game: Czechoslovak Intelligence in Soviet Political Warfare, by L.Bittman. AF Plcy Ltr for Comdrs: Sup No.5:29-33 May '76

Decisions in Israel's Foreign Policy, by M.Brecher. Nav War Col Rev 28:101-102 Winter '76

Decisive Battles of the 20th Century: Land-Sea-Air, edited by N.Frankland and C.Dowling. Mil Rev 56:109 Nov '76

Defense Policy Formulation: A Comparative Analysis of the McNamara Era, by C.A.Murdock. J Pol & Mil Sociol 4:328-330 Fall '76

Defense: Promises and Pitfalls, by G.L.Steibel. Armor 85:60-61 Jul-Aug '76

Destination Berchtesgaden: The Story of the United States Seventh Army in World War II, by J.F. Turner and R.Jackson. Mil Rev 56:103 Jun '76

Detente: Promises and Pitfalls, by G.L.Steibel. Mil Rev 56:105 Jan '76

Deterrence in American Foreign Policy: Theory and Practice, by A.L.George and R.Smoke. Strat Rev 4:94-96 Winter '76

The Discarded Army: Veterans after Vietnam, by P.Starr. Armed Forces & Soc 2:435-467 Spring '76

Documents in the History of NASA, edited by M.D. Wright. Spaceflight 18:183-184 May '76

BOOK REVIEWS - Continued

Duel Between the First Ironclads, by W.C.Davis. US Nav Inst Proc 102:84-85 Aug '76

Eagle and Sword: The Federalists and the Creation of the Military Establishment in America, 1783-1802, by R.H.Kohn. Nav War Col Rev 28:103-104 Spring '76; Infantry 66:58-59 May-Jun '76

East Asia and US Security, by R.N.Clough. RUSI J for Def Studies 120:70 Dec '75

The Eastern Front, 1914-1917, by N.Stone. Army 26:58 Mar '76

Ecological Consequences of the Second Indochina War, by the Stockholm International Peace Research Institute. Mil Rev 56:101-102 Nov '76

The Economic Structure of the Middle East, by Z.Y. Hershlag. RUSI J for Def Studies 121:92 Sep '76

The Economics of Defence, by G.Kennedy. RUSI J for Def Studies 120:84 Dec '75

The Economics of Detente and U.S./Soviet Grain Trade, by M.M.Costick. Def & For Aff Dig No.3:32 '76

The Economics of Peacetime Defense, by M.L. Weidenbaum. Mil Rev 56:108-109 Jan '76; Armed Forces Compt 21:27 Jan '76

The Electronic Battlefield, by P.Dickson. Sea Power 19:32 Aug '76; Mil Rev 56:104-105 Sep '76

Electronics and Sea Power, by A.Hezlet. US Nav Inst Proc 102:91-92 Apr '76

Embassy at War, by H.J.Noble. Mil Rev 56:98 May '76

Energy Policy and Naval Strategy, by H.Bucknell III. Nav War Col Rev 29:110-111 Fall '76; AU Rev 27: 68-72 Sep-Oct '76

The Escape of the Goeben: "Prelude to Gallipoli," by R.McLaughlin. MarCor Gaz 60:10 Feb '76

The Face of Battle, by J.Keegan. Army Qtr 106:506-507 Oct '76

Families in the Military System, edited by H.I. McCubbin and others. Nav War Col Rev 29:121-123 Fall '76; Mil Rev 56:104-105 Oct '76

The Fate of the Atlantic Community, by E.R.Goodman. Mil Rev 56:103 Feb '76; RUSI J for Def Studies 121:105-106 Jun '76

Fighter Pilot: A Self-Portrait, by G.Barclay, edited by H.Winn. Royal Air Forces Qtr 16:287 Autumn '76

Fire over the Islands, by D.C.Horton. Royal Air Forces Qtr 15:353-354 Winter '75

The First Casualty: From the Crimea to Vietnam; the War Correspondent as Hero, Propagandist, and Myth Maker, by P.Knightley. Mil Rev 56:98-99 Apr '76; MarCor Gaz 60:14 May '76; AU Rev 27:75-77 May-Jun '76

Flight Before Flying, by D.W.Wragg. Aerosp Hist 22:237 Dec '75

Foreign Policy and National Defense: The Liberal Democracy in World Affairs, by L.I.Radway. AF Plcy Ltr for Comdrs: Sup No.7:25 Jul '76

The Foreign Policy Process in Britain, by W.Wallace. RUSI J for Def Studies 121:94-95 Sep '76

The Four Days of Mayaguez, by R.Rowan. MarCor Gaz 60:19 Jan '76; US Nav Inst Proc 102:81-83 Jan '76

BOOK REVIEWS - Continued

Frontiers in the Americas: A Global Perspective, by J.Mañach. Mil Rev 56:107 Apr '76

The G.I.'s: The Americans in Britain, 1942-1945, by N.Longmate. Mil Rev 56:107 Sep '76

Germany and the Politics of Nuclear Weapons, by C.M.Kelleher. Mil Rev 56:109-110 Jul '76

Ghana under Military Rule, 1966-1969, by R.Pinkney. Armed Forces & Soc 2:333-336 Winter '76

Giai Phong! The Fall and Liberation of Saigon, by T.Terzani. Army 26:64-66 Jun '76

The Glider War, by J.E.Mrazek. Mil Rev 56:106 Jan '76; Royal Air Forces Qtr 15:347-348 Winter '75; Armor 85:61 Jul-Aug '76

Goebbels: The Man Who Created Hitler, by V.Reimann. Trans by S.Wendt. Air Def Mag, p 60, Apr-Jun '76

The Good Guys, the Bad Guys, and the First Amendment, by F.W.Friendly. AF Mag 59:21 Sep '76

The Great Détente Disaster: Oil and the Decline of American Foreign Policy, by E.Friedland and others. Mil Rev 56:107-108 Jan '76; Parameters 5, No.2:100 '76; AU Rev 27:68-72 Sep-Oct '76

The Great Tanks, by C.Ellis and P.Chamberlain. Armor 85:57-58 Nov-Dec '76

The Great War and Modern Memory, by P.Fussell. Infantry 66:58-59 Jan-Feb '76

Greece 1940-1941, by C.Cruikshank. Army Qtr 106:250-251 Apr '76

The Grumman Story, by R.Thruelsen. Mil Rev 56:109 Nov '76

Guerrillas in History, by L.H.Gann. AF Plcy Ltr for Comdrs: Sup No.8:31 Aug '76

Handling Narcotic and Drug Cases, by F.L.Bailey and H.B.Rothblatt. AF Law Rev 17:92-93 Winter '75

Harry H.Woodring: A Political Biography of FDR's Controversial Secretary of War, by K.McFarland. AU Rev 27:84-85 Mar-Apr '76

The History of Assassination, by B.McConnell. MarCor Gaz 60:74 Jun '76

Hitler's Decision To Invade Russia 1941, by R.Cecil. RUSI J for Def Studies 121:88 Mar '76; Army Qtr 106:132 Jan '76

Hitler's Naval War, by C.Bekker. MarCor Gaz 60:19-20 Jan '76

Home from the War: Vietnam Veterans, Neither Victims nor Executioners, by R.J.Lifton. Armed Forces & Soc 2:435-467 Spring '76

How Much Is Enough: Shaping the Defense Program, 1961-1969, by A.C.Enthoven and K.W.Smith. J Pol & Mil Sociol 4:328-330 Fall '76

How We Won the War, by V.Nguyen Giap and V.Tien Dung. Mil Rev 56:71-72 Dec '76

The Influence of Law on Sea Power, by D.P.O'Connell. RUSI J for Def Studies 121:106 Jun '76; Nav War Col Rev 29:124-125 Fall '76

An Inquiry into the Human Prospect, by R.L.Heilbroner. Armed Forces Compt 21:31 Apr '76

Interest and Ideology: The Foreign Policy Beliefs of American Businessmen, by B.M.Russett and E.C.Hanson. Nav War Col Rev 29:129-130 Summer '76

BOOK REVIEWS - Continued

International Terrorism: A New Mode of Conflict, by B.Jenkins. Mil Rev 56:69 Dec '76

International Terrorism and World Security, edited by D.Carlton and C.Schaerf. Mil Rev 56:69 Dec '76

International Terrorism: National, Regional, and Global Perspectives, edited by Y.Alexander. RUSI J for Def Studies 121:103 Sep '76; Natl Def 61:75 Jul-Aug '76

Intervention: External Involvement in Civil Wars, by R.Little. RUSI J for Def Studies 121:105 Jun '76

Intervention or Abstention: The Dilemma of American Foreign Policy, edited by R.Higham. Educ J 19:42 Fall '76; Armor 85:57 Nov-Dec '76

The Invisible Soldier: The Experience of the Black Soldier, World War II, edited by M.P.Motley. Mil Rev 56:101-102 May '76

Ireland in the War Years 1939-1945, by J.T.Carroll. RUSI J for Def Studies 121:94-95 Jun '76

The Israeli Army, by E.Luttwak and D.Horowitz. Nav War Col Rev 28:101-102 Winter '76; Army Qtr 106:375-376 Jul '76

Japan Today: People, Places, Power, by W.H.Forbis. Parameters 5, No.2:96-97 '76

Japan's Nuclear Option: Political, Technical and Strategic Factors, by J.E.Endicott. Army Qtr 106:503 Oct '76

Justice and the Military, by H.E.Moyer, Jr. Armed Forces & Soc 2:468-472 Spring '76

Justice in Jeopardy, by A.B.Logan. AF Law Rev 17:91-92 Winter '75

Justice under Fire: A Study of Military Law, by J.W.Bishop, Jr. AF Law Rev 17:85-90 Winter '75; Armed Forces & Soc 2:468-472 Spring '76

KCB: The Secret Work of Soviet Secret Agents, by J.Barron. AF Plcy Ltr for Comdrs: Sup No.5:29-33 May '76

The Last Chance: Nuclear Proliferation and Arms Control, by W.Epstein. Mil Rev 56:108-109 Sep '76

The Last Chopper: The Denouement of the American Role in Vietnam, 1963-1975, by W.A.Brown. Mil Rev 56:100-101 Oct '76

The Last European War, by J.Lukacs. AF Mag 59:98 Jul '76; AU Rev 28:103-104 Nov-Dec '76

Latin American Foreign Policies: An Analysis, by H.E.Davis and L.C.Wilson. Mil Rev 56:108-109 Feb '76

Law and Responsibility in Warfare: The Vietnam Experience, by P.D.Trooboff. Armor 85:60 Sep-Oct '76

The Law of War, edited by R.I.Miller. Mil Rev 56:108 May '76

Lessons of Ulster, by T.E.Utley. RUSI J for Def Studies 121:96 Jun '76

Letters and Papers of Alfred Thayer Mahan, edited by R.Seager II and D.D.Maguire. Nav War Col Rev 29:47-60 Fall '76; Natl Def 61:236+ Nov-Dec '76

Limited Nuclear Options: Deterrence and the New American Doctrine, by L.E.Davis. Def & For Aff Dig No.3:32 '76

Living in Outer Space, by G.S.Robinson. Spaceflight 18:377 Oct '76

BOOK REVIEWS - Continued

Living with Terrorism, by R.Clutterbuck. Army Qtr
106:373-374 Jul '76; Mil Rev 56:69-70 Dec '76

Logistics and the Failure of the British Army in
America 1775-1783, by R.A.Bowler. Nav War
Col Rev 29:106-108 Fall '76

The Lusitania Disaster: An Episode in Modern War-
fare and Diplomacy, by T.A.Bailey and P.B.
Ryan. US Nav Inst Proc 102:93-94 Apr '76; Mil
Rev 56:101-102 Jul '76

A Man Called Intrepid: The Secret War, by W.Ste-
venson. Mil Rev 56:99-100 Jun '76; Sea Power
19:39 Jul '76; RUSI J for Def Studies 121:93-94
Sep '76; AU Rev 27:81-82 Sep-Oct '76; Army Qtr
106:383 Jul '76

Man in Space. Spaceflight 18:377 Oct '76

The Management of Organization: A System and Hu-
man Resources Approach, 2d edition, by H.G.
Hicks. AF Pley Ltr for Comdrs: Sup No.1:30-31
Jan '76

Management of Organizational Behavior, 2d edition,
by P.Hersey and K.H.Blanchard. AF Pley Ltr for
Comdrs: Sup No.1:31-32 Jan '76

Management: Tasks, Responsibilities, Practices, by
P.F.Drucker. Nav War Col Rev 29:120-122 Summer '76

The Maquis: A History of the French Resistance
Movement, by C.Chambard. Trans by E.P.Hal-
perin. Mil Rev 56:105-106 Sep '76

A Marine Named Mitch, by M.Paige. MarCor Gaz
60:16 Oct '76

Marines in the Revolution: A History of Continental
Marines in the American Revolution, 1775-1783,
by C.R.Smith. MarCor Gaz 60:15-16 Apr '76

Mass Political Violence: A Crossnational Causal
Analysis, by D.A.Hibbs, Jr. Armed Forces &
Soc 3:147-160 Fall '76

Masters of the Art of Command, by M.Blumenson
and J.L.Stokesbury. Parameters 5, No.2:
92-93 '76; AF Mag 59:70 Apr '76; Nav War Col
Rev 29:104-105 Fall '76

Memoirs of My Services in the World War, 1917-
1918, by G.C.Marshall. Army 26:63-64 Nov '76

The Messenger's Motives, by J.L.Hulteng. AF Mag
59:21 Sep '76

The Military and American Society, by M.B.Hick-
man. AF Plcy Ltr for Comdrs: Sup No.2:31-32
Feb '76

The Military and the Problem of Legitimacy, edited
by G.Harries-Jenkins and J.van Doorn. Nav War
Col Rev 29:112-115 Fall '76

Military Conflict: Essays in the Institutional Analysis
of War and Peace, by M.Janowitz. Mil Rev 56
101-102 Aug '76

Military Elites: Special Fighting Units in the Modern
World, by R.A.Beaumont. MarCor Gaz 60:18-19
Jan '76

Military Force and American Society, edited by
B.M.Russett and A.Stepan. J Pol & Mil Sociol
4:171-172 Spring '76; Nav War Col Rev 29:130-131
Summer '76

The Military in Chilean History: Essays on Civil-
Military Relations, 1810-1973, by F.M.Nunn.
Mil Rev 56:101-102 Sep '76

BOOK REVIEWS - Continued

Military Lessons of the Yom Kippur War: Historical
Perspectives, by M.van Creveld. AU Rev 28:104-
105 Nov-Dec '76

Military Power and Potential, by K.Knorr. AF Pley
Ltr for Comdrs: Sup No.6:31 Jun '76

Military Role and Rule, by C.E.Welch, Jr and A.K.
Smith. Mil Rev 56:107-108 Jun '76

Military Roles in Modernization: Civil-Military Relations in Thailand and Burma, by M.Lissak. Mil
Rev 56:103-104 Sep '76

Military Rule in Africa--Dahomey, Ghana, Sierra
Leone and Mali, by A.Bebler. Armed Forces &
Soc 2:333-336 Winter '76

Mr Roosevelt's Navy: The Private War of the U.S.
Atlantic Fleet, 1939-1942, by P.Abbazia. Nav
War Col Rev 28:100-101 Winter '76; Mil Rev 56:
104 May '76

The Modern Japanese Military System, edited by
J.H.Buck. Nav War Col Rev 29:108-110 Fall '76;
RUSI J for Def Studies 121:99 Jun '76

Modernizing the Strategic Bomber Force: Why and
How, by A.H.Quanbeck and A.L.Wood. Nav War
Col Rev 29:122-126 Summer '76; AU Rev 27:79-80
Sep-Oct '76

Montgomery at Alamein, by A.Chalfont. Army 26:
60-61 Sep '76; RUSI J for Def Studies 121:85-86
Sep '76; Mil Rev 56:105-106 Nov '76

The My Lai Massacre and Its Cover-Up: Beyond the
Reach of Law? The Peers Commission Report,
edited by J.Goldstein and others. Mil Rev 56:98-
100 Oct '76

The Mythical World of Nazi War Propaganda 1939-
1945, by J.W.Baird. RUSI J for Def Studies 120:
75-76 Dec '75

The Myths of National Security: The Peril of Secret
Government, by A.M.Cox. Parameters 5, No.2:
90-91 '76

National Security and Detente, by members of the
Faculty, U.S. Army War College. Parameters 5,
No.2:90 '76

Naval Wargames: World War I and World War II, by
B.J.Carter. US Nav Inst Proc 102:131 Mar '76

Neither Peace nor Honor: The Politics of American
Military Policy in Vietnam, by R.L.Gallucci.
J Pol & Mil Sociol 4:165-166 Spring '76; Nav War
Col Rev 28:100-101 Spring '76

The Neutralization of South-East Asia, by D.Wilson.
RUSI J for Def Studies 121:97 Jun '76

A New Age Now Begins: A People's History of the
American Revolution, by P.Smith. Nav War Col
Rev 29:113-117 Summer '76

The New Muckrakers, by L.Downie, Jr. AF Mag
59:21 Sep '76

The New Oil Stakes, by J.-M.Chevalier. Trans by
I.Rock. RUSI J for Def Studies 121:92 Mar '76

The Newest Whore of Babylon: The Emergence of
Technocracy, a Study in the Mechanization of
Man, by J.L.Reed. Mil Rev 56:108 Jun '76

The Night Will End, by H.Frenay. Trans by D.Hof-
stadter. Mil Rev 56:109-110 May '76; RUSI J for
Def Studies 121:94 Sep '76; Army Qtr 106:504
Oct '76

No More Heroes--the Royal Navy in the Twentieth
Century: Anatomy of a Legend, by C.Owen. US
Nav Inst Proc 102:86-87 Jun '76

No Second Place Winner, by W.H.Jordan. MarCor
Gaz 60:16 Apr '76

The Notebooks of Sologdin, by D.Panin. Trans by
J.Moore. Mil Rev 56:108-109 May '76

Nuclear Threat in the Middle East, by R.J.Pranger
and D.R.Tahtinen. Strat Rev 4:92-93 Winter '76

The Nuremberg Fallacy: Wars and War Crimes since
World War II, by E.Davidson. AF Law Rev 18:97-
100 Spring '76

Oil: A Plain Man's Guide to the World's Energy Crisis, by P.Windsor. RUSI J for Def Studies 120:72
Dec '75

Old Wars Remain Unfinished: The Veteran Benefit
System, by S.A.Levitan. Armed Forces & Soc 2:
435-467 Spring '76

On War: Political Violence in the International System, by M.I.Midlarsky. Aerosp Hist 22:236
Dec '75; Mil Rev 56:104-105 Apr '76; Armor 85:
60 Sep-Oct '76; Armed Forces & Soc 3:147-160
Fall '76

On Watch: A Memoir, by E.R.Zumwalt, Jr. US Nav
Inst Proc 102:85-86 Jul '76; Parameters 6, No.1:
99-100 '76; AF Mag 59:132 Sep '76; Strat Rev 4:
121-124 Summer '76; Mil Rev 56:100-101 Nov '76;
Natl Def 61:236 Nov-Dec '76

One Man's Jungle, by R.Barker. RUSI J for Def
Studies 120:76-77 Dec '75

Operation 'Menace': The Dakar Expedition and the
Dudley North Affair, by A.Marder. US Nav Inst
Proc 102:94 Dec '76

The Organizational Politics of Defense, by W.A.
Lucas and R.H.Dawson. Nav War Col Rev 28:105-
106 Fall '75

The Other Arms Race: New Technologies and Nonnuclear Conflict, edited by G.Kemp and others.
Parameters 5, No.2:98-99 '76; RUSI J for Def
Studies 121:100-101 Jun '76; Nav War Col Rev 29:
119-121 Fall '76

The Papers of General Lucius D.Clay: Germany,
1945-1949, edited by J.E.Smith. Armed Forces &
Soc 2:610-612 Summer '76

The Paralysis of International Institutions and the
Remedies: A Study of Self-Determination, Concord
among the Major Powers, and Political Arbitra-
tion, by I.Bibo. Mil Rev 56:107-109 Nov '76

The Partisans of Europe in World War II, by
K.Macksey. RUSI J for Def Studies 121:89-90
Mar '76; Army Qtr 106:129-130 Jan '76

Patton, by H.Essame. Armor 85:58 May-Jun '76

Peace Is Not at Hand: The American Position in the
Post-Vietnam World and the Strategic Weakening
of the West, by R.Thompson. Parameters 5,
No.2:99-100 '76

Peace Soldiers: The Sociology of a United Nations
Military Force, by C.C.Moskos, Jr. J Pol & Mil
Sociol 4:154-155 Spring '76; Mil Rev 56:108-109
Jul '76

The People's Liberation Army: Communist China's
Armed Forces, by A.M.Fraser. Armor 85:60
Mar-Apr '76

The Persian Gulf and Indian Ocean in International
Politics. Army Qtr 106:510-511 Oct '76

The Peruvian Experiment: Continuity and Change
under Military Rule, edited by A.F.Lowenthal.
Mil Rev 56:100-101 Jul '76

The Philosophical Heritage of V.I.Lenin and Problems of Contemporary War, a Soviet View, edited
by A.S.Milovidov and V.G.Kozlov. (Trans and
published under the auspices of the USAF) AF Plcy
Ltr for Comdrs: Sup No.11:30-32 Nov '76

The Point of No Return, by R.Fisk. RUSI J for Def
Studies 121:96 Jun '76

The Political Implications of North Sea Oil and Gas,
edited by M.Saeter and I.Smart. Royal Air
Forces Qtr 16:78-80 Spring '76

The Political Police in Britain, by T.Bunyan. Army
Qtr 106:508-509 Oct '76

Political Terrorism, by P.Wilkinson. Parameters
5, No.2:98 '76; Mil Rev 56:68-69 Dec '76

Political Violence and Insurgency, edited by B.E.
O'Neill and others. Nav War Col Rev 28:103-104
Winter '76

Politics and Oil: Moscow in the Middle East, by
L.Landis. AU Rev 27:68-72 Sep-Oct '76

The Politics and Strategy of the Second World War:
Greece, 1940-1941, by C.Cruickshank. RUSI J for
Def Studies 121:100 Sep '76

The Politics of Defense Analysis, by R.Sanders.
Persp in Def Mgt No.24:108-110 Winter '75-'76;
J Pol & Mil Sociol 4:328-330 Fall '76

The Poverty of Power: Energy and the Economic
Crisis, by B.Commoner. AU Rev 27:68-72 Sep-
Oct '76

Power and Policy in China, by P.H.Chang. Mil Rev
56:100 Jul '76

Precarious Security, by M.D.Taylor. AF Times 36:
33 Jan 28 '76; Army 26:56+ Jul '76; Mil Rev 56:
99-100 Nov '76

Prelude to Disaster: The American Role in Vietnam,
1940-1963, by W.A.Brown. Mil Rev 56:108-109
Jun '76

Presidents, Bureaucrats and Foreign Policy, by
I.M.Destler. Armed Forces & Soc 2:326-332
Winter '76

Prisoner of War: Six Years in Hanoi, by J.M.
McGrath. Nav War Col Rev 28:102-103 Winter '76

Problems of Modern Strategy, edited by A.Buchan.
AF Plcy Ltr for Comdrs: Sup No.10:26 Oct '76

Project Cancelled, by D.Wood. Royal Air Forces
Qtr 15:339 Winter '75

Pursuing the American Dream: White Ethnics and the
New Populism, by R.Krickus. J Pol & Mil Sociol
4:330-333 Fall '76

The Raid, by B.F.Schemmer. Mil Rev 56:71 Dec '76

Reason and Violence, edited by S.M.Stanage. J Pol
& Mil Sociol 4:180-181 Spring '76

Rebellion, Revolution, and Armed Force: A Com-
parative Study of Fifteen Countries with Special
Emphasis on Cuba and South Africa, by D.E.H.
Russell. Armed Forces & Soc 3:147-160 Fall '76

106

Rebels under Sail: The American Navy During the Revolution, by W.M.Fowler. Nav War Col Rev 29:111-112 Fall '76

Red Star Rising at Sea, by S.G.Gorshkov. Mil Rev 56:103-104 Mar '76

A Responsible Congress, by A.Frye. Strat Rev 4: 96-98 Winter '76

Revolution in the Middle East and Other Case Studies, edited by P.J.Vatikiotis. Armed Forces & Soc 3: 147-160 Fall '76

The Revolutionary Party: Essays in the Sociology of Politics, by F.Gross. MarCor Gaz 60:18 Nov '76

Revolutionary Warfare in the Middle East: The Israelis vs the Fedayeen, by B.O'Neill. MarCor Gaz 60:14 Apr '76

Riot Control, by A.Deane-Drummond. Royal Air Forces Qtr 15:352-353 Winter '75

The Rise and Fall of British Naval Mastery, by P.M. Kennedy. Sea Power 19:41 Oct '76

The Rise of the Luftwaffe, 1918-1940, by H.M.Mason. Royal Air Forces Qtr 16:81-82 Spring '76

The Road to Ramadan, by M.Heikal. RUSI J for Def Studies 120:71-72 Dec '75; Mil Rev 56:106-107 May '76

The Road to Stalingrad: Stalin's War with Germany, by J.Erickson. Nav War Col Rev 28:98-100 Spring '76

The Rockets' Red Glare, by W.von Braun and F.I. Ordway III. Mil Rev 56:103-104 Oct '76

Roosevelt and Churchill: Their Secret Wartime Correspondence, edited by F.L.Loewenheim and others. RUSI J for Def Studies 120:69-70 Dec '75; Mil Rev 56:102-103 Jan '76; US Nav Inst Proc 102: 129-130 Mar '76

Russia: The People and the Power, by R.G.Kaiser. AF Mag 59:60 Jun '76; Natl Def 61:72 Jul-Aug '76

The Russians, by H.Smith. AF Mag 59:60 Jun '76

SALT: The Moscow Agreements and Beyond, edited by M.Willrich and J.B.Rhinelander. RUSI J for Def Studies 121:97-98 Sep '76

School for Soldiers: West Point and the Profession of Arms, by J.Ellis and R.Moore. Army 26:66-67 May '76

Sea Power in the 1970s, edited by G.H.Quester. Mil Rev 56:102 Feb '76; Nav War Col Rev 29:125-126 Fall '76

Security in the Nuclear Age: Developing U.S. Strategic Arms Policy, by J.Kahan. AU Rev 27:103-107 Jul-Aug '76; Nav War Col Rev 29:122-126 Summer '76; Intl Sec 1:130-146 Fall '76

The Seven Sisters: The Great Oil Companies and the World They Made, by A.Sampson. RUSI J for Def Studies 121:92 Mar '76

Seventy Days to Singapore, by S.L.Falk. Mil Rev 56:110 Mar '76; AF Mag 59:61 Jun '76

Shadow Government, by D.Guttman and B.Willner. Mil Rev 56:100-101 Sep '76

Shark Attack, by H.D.Baldridge. US Nav Inst Proc 102:85-86 Jan '76

The Shark: Splendid Savage of the Sea, by J.-Y. and P.Cousteau. US Nav Inst Proc 102:85-86 Jan '76

Sharks: The Silent Savages, by T.W.Brown. US Nav Inst Proc 102:85-86 Jan '76

Ships and the Sea: A Chronological Review, by D. Haws. MarCor Gaz 60:15 Dec '76

A Short History of Guerrilla Warfare, by J.Ellis. RUSI J for Def Studies 121:103 Sep '76

Silent Victory, by C.Blair, Jr. Infantry 66:58 May-Jun '76

Silk Glove Hegemony: Finnish-Soviet Relations, 1944-1974, by J.P.Vloyantes. Mil Rev 56:106 Sep '76

Sizing Up the Soviet Army, by J.Record. AF Mag 59:60-61 Jan '76; Mil Rev 56:108-110 Mar '76

Social Origins and Political Orientations of Officer Corps in a World Perspective, by G.A.Kourvetaris and B.A.Dobratz. J Pol & Mil Sociol 4:169-171 Spring '76

The Soldier and Social Change: Comparative Studies in the History and Sociology of the Military, by J.Van Doorn. Mil Rev 56:110 May '76

A Soldier Reports, by W.C.Westmoreland. Armed Forces J Intl 113:9 Jan '76; AF Times 36:30 Mar 1 '76; Parameters 5, No.2:88-90 '76; Army 26:56-58 Jan '76; AF Mag 59:70-71 Apr '76; Natl Def 60:477 May-Jun '76; MarCor Gaz 60:13-15 Jul '76; Armor 85:60-61 Sep-Oct '76; US Nav Inst Proc 102:87-88 Sep '76; Strat Rev 4:104-106 Spring '76; AU Rev 28:98-102 Nov-Dec '76

Soldiers in Revolt, by D.Cortright. MarCor Gaz 60:17 Jan '76

South Asian Crisis: India, Pakistan, Bangladesh, by R.Jackson. RUSI J for Def Studies 121:90-91 Mar '76; Army Qtr 106:123-124 Jan '76

The Soviet-American Arms Race, by C.S.Gray. RUSI J for Def Studies 121:100-101 Jun '76

Soviet Arms Aid in the Middle East, by R.F.Pajak. Def & For Aff Dig No.4:64 '76

Soviet Foreign Policy 1962-73: The Paradox of Super Power, by R.Edmonds. RUSI J for Def Studies 120:77-78 Dec '75

Soviet Naval Policy--Objectives and Constraints, edited by M.MccGwire and others. RUSI J for Def Studies 120:64-66 Dec '75; US Nav Inst Proc 102: 85-86 Feb '76

Soviet Military Strategy, 3d edition, by V.D.Sokolovsky, edited by H.F.Scott. RUSI J for Def Studies 120:77 Dec '75; MarCor Gaz 60:20 Jan '76; AF Mag 59:67 Feb '76; Armor 85:58-59 May-Jun '76; AU Rev 27:78-85 May-Jun '76; Army Qtr 106:131-132 Jan '76

The Soviet Naval Offensive, by E.Wegener. Nav War Col Rev 29:134-135 Summer '76; MarCor Gaz 60:14 Dec '76

The Soviet Navy Today, by J.Moore. RUSI J for Def Studies 121:85-86 Mar '76; US Nav Inst Proc 102: 85-86 Jun '76

Soviet Penetration of Latin America, by L.Gouré and M.Rothenberg. MarCor Gaz 60:15 Apr '76

Soviet Policy Toward the Middle East since 1970, by R.O.Freedman. RUSI J for Def Studies 121:100 Jun '76

The Soviet Presence in Latin America, by J.D. Theberge. MarCor Gaz 60:14-15 Jun '76

The Soviet Soldier: Soviet Military Management at the Troop Level, by H.Goldhamer. AF Mag 59: 61-62 Jun '76; Nav War Col Rev 28:101-103 Spring '76; RUSI J for Def Studies 121:102 Sep '76; Strat Rev 4:110-112 Fall '76; Armor 85:57 Nov-Dec '76; J Pol & Mil Sociol 4:324-326 Fall '76

Soviet Sources of Military Doctrine and Strategy, by W.F.Scott. AU Rev 27:84-85 May-Jun '76

Soviet Strategy in Europe, edited by R.Pipes. Natl Def 61:236 Nov-Dec '76

The Soviet Union and the October 1973 Middle East War: The Implications for Detente, by F.D.Kohler and others. Armor 85:59-60 Jul-Aug '76

The Soviet View of War, Peace and Neutrality, by P.H.Vigor. Mil Rev 56:106-107 Mar '76; RUSI J for Def Studies 121:84-85 Mar '76; Strat Rev 4: 107-108 Spring '76; Army Qtr 106:133 Jan '76

Spandau, the Secret Diaries, by A.Speer. (Trans by R. and C.Winston) AU Rev 28:103 Nov-Dec '76

Special Envoy to Churchill and Stalin, 1941-1946, by W.A.Harriman and E.Abel. US Nav Inst Proc 102: 86-87 Jul '76; Strat Rev 4:125-126 Summer '76; Nav War Col Rev 29:115 Fall '76

Spoils of War, by C.J.Levy. Armed Forces & Soc 2:435-467 Spring '76

Stalin as Military Commander, by A.Seaton. Mil Rev 56:102-103 Oct '76; RUSI J for Def Studies 121:101 Sep '76

The Story of Changi, Singapore, by D.Nelson. RUSI J for Def Studies 121:88-89 Mar '76

Strategic Air Command, by D.A.Anderton. Royal Air Forces Qtr 16:179-180 Summer '76; Mil Rev 56:106-107 Nov '76

Strategic Bombing in World War II: A Study of the United States Strategic Bombing Survey, by D. MacIsaac. AU Rev 27:73-76 Sep-Oct '76; Strat Rev 4:108-110 Fall '76

Strategic Weapons: An Introduction, by N.Polmar. AU Rev 27:76-79 Sep-Oct '76

Strategy for Tomorrow, by A.Beaufre. AU Rev 27: 102-108 Jan-Feb '76; Armor 85:60 Jan-Feb '76

The Strategy of Social Protest, by W.A.Gamson. J Pol & Mil Sociol 4:167-169 Spring '76

The Struggle for Cyprus, by C.Foley and W.I.Scobie. J Pol & Mil Sociol 4:152-154 Spring '76; Mil Rev 56:105-106 Aug '76

The Struggle for Greece 1941-1949, by C.M.Wood-house. RUSI J for Def Studies 121:100-101 Sep '76

The Superwarriors--the Fantastic World of Pentagon Superweapons, by J.W.Canan. Nav War Col Rev 28:102-104 Fall '75

Survivors, by Z.Grant. AU Rev 27:86 Mar-Apr '76

Swords into Plowshares: Our G.I. Bill, by S.A. Levitan. Armed Forces & Soc 2:435-467 Spring '76

Technology and International Politics: The Crisis of Wishing, by W.R.Kintner and H.Sicherman. Mil Rev 56:105 May '76

Tell It to the Dead: Memories of a War, by D.Kirk. Mil Rev 56:105-106 Feb '76; Natl Def 61:156 Sep-Oct '76

A Theory of Conflict, by B.Crozier. MarCor Gaz 60:16-17 Jan '76

Those Who Served, by M.K.Taussig. Armed Forces & Soc 2:435-467 Spring '76

The Thresher Disaster: The Most Tragic Dive in Submarine History, by J.Bentley. MarCor Gaz 60:20 Jan '76

Through Russian Eyes: American-Chinese Relations, by S.Sergeichuk. AU Rev 28:106-107 Nov-Dec '76

Titans of the Seas: The Development and Operations of Japanese and American Carrier Task Forces During World War II, by J.H. and W.M.Belote. US Nav Inst Proc 102:107-108 Oct '76

Twenty Years and Twenty Days, by Nguyen Cao Ky. US Nav Inst Proc 102:89 Sep '76

The UFO Controversy in America, by D.M.Jacobs. AU Rev 27:79-82 Mar-Apr '76

UFOs Explained, by P.J.Klass. Aerosp Hist 23:233-234 Dec '76

The United States and Saudi Arabia: A Policy Analysis, by E.A.Nakhleh. Def & For Aff Dig No.2: 36 '76

The United States Army in Transition, by Z.B.Bradford, Jr and F.J.Brown. J Pol & Mil Sociol 4: 317-318 Fall '76

The U.S. Camel Corps: An Army Experiment, by O.B.Faulk. Mil Rev 56:104 Aug '76

United States Foreign Policy and World Order, by J.A.Nathan and J.K.Oliver. Nav War Col Rev 29:123-124 Fall '76

The United States Marines: The First Two Hundred Years, 1775-1975, by E.H.Simmons. MarCor Gaz 60:10 Sep '76

U.S. Policy and Strategic Interests in the Western Pacific, by Y.Wu. Mil Rev 56:105-106 Mar '76; RUSI J for Def Studies 121:97-98 Jun '76

U.S. Power and the Multinational Corporation: The Political Economy of Foreign Direct Investment, by R.Gilpin. Parameters 5, No.2:97-98 '76

The Unknown War, by M.Lindsay. Army Qtr 106: 252-253 Apr '76

Urban Terrorism: Theory, Practice and Response, by A.Burton. Royal Air Forces Qtr 16:82-83 Spring '76; RUSI J for Def Studies 121:92-93 Mar '76

Vain Hopes, Grim Realities, by R.W.Stevens. Nav War Col Rev 29:129-131 Fall '76; RUSI J for Def Studies 121:92-93 Sep '76

The Vietnam Drug User Returns, by L.N.Robins. Armed Forces & Soc 2:435-467 Spring '76

The Vietnam Legacy: The War, American Society and the Future of American Foreign Policy, edited by A.Lake. Mil Rev 56:100 Oct '76

Vietnam Studies: Allied Participation in Vietnam, by S.R.Larsen and J.L.Collins, Jr. Natl Def 61:238 Nov-Dec '76

Vietnam Studies: The Role of Military Intelligence, 1965-1967, by J.A.McChristian. Natl Def 61:156 Sep-Oct '76

The Vietnam War and International Law. Vol 4: The Concluding Phase, edited by R.A.Falk. Mil Rev 56:104-105 Nov '76

WW II: A Chronicle of Soldiering, by J.Jones. Parameters 5, No.2:94 '76; Mil Rev 56:100-101 Jan '76; MarCor Gaz 60:11 Feb '76

BOOK REVIEWS - Continued

WW2: Readings on Critical Issues, edited by T.A.
Wilson. MarCor Gaz 60:10-11 Feb '76

War and Christian Ethics, edited by A.F.Holmes.
Mil Rev 56:101-102 Feb '76

War and Politics, by B.Brodie. J Pol & Mil Sociol
4:165-166 Spring '76

War and Society, edited by B.Bond and I.Roy. Nav
War Col Rev 29:105-106 Fall '76

War in the Next Decade, edited by R.A.Beaumont
and M.Edmonds. AU Rev 27:102-108 Jan-Feb '76;
Infantry 66:57-58 May-Jun '76

War in the Shadows, by R.B.Asprey. AU Rev 28:91-
97 Nov-Dec '76

The War Lords, edited by M.Carver. Army Qtr 106:
507-508 Oct '76

The War of Atonement, by C.Herzog. RUSI J for Def
Studies 120:70-71 Dec '75; Parameters 5, No.2:
91-92 '76; Mil Rev 56:100-101 May '76; Strat Rev
4:126-128 Summer '76

The Wars in Vietnam, 1954-1973, by E.O'Ballance.
Mil Rev 56:102 May '76

The Wartime Alliance and the Zonal Division of Germany, by T.Sharp. Nav War Col Rev 29:126-127
Fall '76

The Way of the Fox: American Strategy in the War
for America, 1775-1783, by D.R.Palmer. Armor
85:61 Jul-Aug '76; Army 26:58-59 Aug '76

We Came To Help, by M.Schwinn and B.Diehl. Mil
Rev 56:108-109 Oct '76

The Week France Fell, by N.Barber. Mil Rev 56:
107-108 Oct '76

Where Does the Marine Corps Go from Here, by
M.Binkin and J.Record. MarCor Gaz 60:7-9
Mar '76; Nav War Col Rev 29:117-119 Summer '76

Whither NATO: Problems of West European Defence,
by J.Steinhoff. RUSI J for Def Studies 121:98
Sep '76

Why Nations Go to War, by J.G.Stoessinger. MarCor
Gaz 60:18-19 Nov '76

Wings over Kabul: The First Airlift, by A.Baker and
R.Ivelaw-Chapman. Royal Air Forces Qtr 16:83+
Spring '76

Winston S.Churchill. Vol 4. 1917-1922, by M.Gil-
bert. RUSI J for Def Studies 120:66-67 Dec '75

The Witness and I, by O.E.Clubb. Armor 85:59
Mar-Apr '76

A World Destroyed: The Atomic Bomb and the Grand
Alliance, by M.J.Sherwin. Educ J 19:40-41
Fall '76; Nav War Col Rev 29:127-129 Fall '76;
Mil Rev 56:102-103 Nov '76

World Politics and International Economics, edited
by C.F.Bergsten and L.B.Krause. Mil Rev 56:104
Apr '76

World Power Assessment: A Calculus of Strategic
Drift, by R.S.Cline. AF Mag 59:67-68 Feb '76;
Mil Rev 56:101-102 Jun '76

World War II Fighter Conflict, by A.Price. Royal
Air Forces Qtr 15:343 Winter '75

The Years of MacArthur. Vol 2. 1941-1945, by D.C.
James. Parameters 5, No.2:94-95 '76; RUSI J for
Def Studies 121:106-107 Jun '76

The Zambesi Salient: Conflict in South Africa, by
A.J.Venter. MarCor Gaz 60:15 Jun '76

BOOKS AND READING

Fiction reading in the Foreign Area Specialty Program. Maj Kenneth M.Taggart. illus Mil Rev 56:
71-78 Sep '76

Notable naval books of 1975. Jack Sweetman. illus
US Nav Inst Proc 102:87-90 Jan '76

Soviet military thought. Joseph D.Douglass, Jr. illus
AF Mag 59:88-91 Mar '76

BOOSTERS

Ariane: ESA (European Space Agency) heavy launcher.
Robert Edgar. tabs illus Spaceflight 18:87-91
Mar '76

Ariane programme on schedule for July 1979 launch.
Michael Brown. illus Interavia 31:972-973 Oct '76

Comparative description of ISAS (Institute of Space
and Aeronautical Science, University of Tokyo)
satellite launch vehicles. Table only. Spaceflight
18:106 Mar '76

Gallery of Soviet aerospace weapons: Launch vehicles. AF Mag 59:107 Mar '76

Gallery of USAF weapons: Launch vehicles. illus AF
Mag 59:127-128 May '76

Soviet rocket engines--some new details. Anthony
Kenden. illus tabs Spaceflight 18:223-226 Jun '76

BOOTSTRAP COMMISSIONING PROGRAM see Airman
Education and Commissioning Program

BOUNDARY LAYER CONTROL

F-4 BLC (Boundary Layer Control)--blessing or
burden? LtCol J.P.Cline. illus Aerosp Safety
32:17-19 Sep '76

BOWEN, Thomas W.

Vietnam ... lest we forget. MajGen Thomas W.Bow-
en. Army 26:8-9 Apr '76

BOWMAN, Richard C.

NATO: Standardization for improved combat capability. MajGen Richard C.Bowman. Comdrs Dig 19:
entire issue Sep 9 '76

BOYD, Albert

Gen Boyd, 'father' of test flying. obit AF Times
37:24 Oct 4 '76

BOYES, Jon L.

A Navy satellite communications system. VADM Jon
L.Boyes. por Signal 30:5+ Mar '76

WWMCCS in transition: A Navy view. VADM Jon L.
Boyes. Signal 30:72-73 Aug '76

BRAIN

Alpha index and personality traits of pilots. Jan
Terelak. tab Aviation, Space and Envmt Med 47:
133-136 Feb '76

What EEG criteria for diving fitness? J.Corriol and
others. illus tabs Aviation, Space & Envmt Med
47:868-872 Aug '76

BRAKES

See also
Airplanes, Military--Brakes

BREHM, William K.

Morale shifts worry (Asst SecDef William) Brehm.
AF Times 36:11 Feb 23 '76

BREZHNEV, Leonid I.

The balancing of L.I.Brezhnev. Lawrence Griswold.
por Sea Power 18:11-16 Dec '75

The Brezhnev report (to the 25th CPSU Congress):
The meaning of words. Charles T.Baroch. Strat
Rev 4:118-120 Summer '76

Distinguished party leader and statesman. por Soviet
Mil Rev No. 12:2-7 Dec '76

Fighter for peace and communist ideals. (Bronze
bust unveiled at Dneprodzerzhinsk, May 8, 1976)
Soviet Mil Rev No. 7:2-3 Jul '76

BRIDGES

Bridging the generations. (Replicas of the famous
bridge at Concord, Mass, are spanning the Anacostia River in Washington to the new Children's
Islands Park) Sgt Deb Notah. illus Soldiers 31:
18-21 Dec '76

The French PAA (Pont Automoteur d'Accompagnement) self-propelled bridging vehicle. illus tab
Intl Def Rev 9:302-305 Apr '76

The medium girder bridge. LtCol C.Hartington, Ret.
illus Mil Engr 68:306-307 Jul-Aug '76

History

The bridge at kilometer 111 (China). Bonnie Baker
Quinby and Capt G.William Quinby. illus Mil Engr
68:88-90 Mar-Apr '76

BRIEFING and BRIEFING TEAMS

Briefing & debriefing techniques. Maj Les Alford.
illus USAF Ftr Wpns Rev, pp 9-16, Spring '76

Talk talk--a series of ideas to improve your presentations. Laurence E. Olewine. illus Armed Forces
Compt pt 1, 17:14-15+ Fall '72; pt 2, 18:30-31
Winter '73; pt 3, 18:8-9+ Spring '73; pt 4, 18:
28-29 Summer '73; pt 5, 18:24-25+ Fall '73; pt 6,
19:20-21 Winter '74; pt 7, 19:18-19 Spring '74;
pt 8, 19:16-17 Summer '74; pt 9, 19:14-15 Fall '74;
pt 10, 20:22-23 Winter '75; pt 11, 20:26-27 Apr '75;
pt 12, 20:24-25 Fall '75; pt 13, 21:24-25 Jan '76

Unqualified passengers (who have never been briefed
about the hazards in and around helicopter operations). Arnold R.Lambert. illus USA Avn Dig 22:
40-43 Apr '76

BRITISH INTERPLANETARY SOCIETY

A report of the discussions at the 31st Annual General
Meeting (London, June 24, 1976). Spaceflight 18:
375-376 Oct '76

BROWN, George S.

Congress told shortages, cuts hurting readiness (by
Gen George S.Brown). AF Times 36:6 Mar 1 '76

(JSC Chairman Gen George S.) Brown criticizes
Times newspapers (in testimony before House
Armed Services Committee). AF Times 36:3
Feb 9 '76

JCS Chairman's Posture Statement. (Statement before House Armed Services Committee, Washington, Jan 27, 1976) Gen George S. Brown. AF Plcy
Ltr for Comdrs: Sup No. 4:13-15 Apr '76

A military force in a democracy. (Address, Twin
Cities Federal Executive Board Bicentennial Cele-
bration, Twin Cities, Minn, July 1, 1976) Gen
George S.Brown. AF Plcy Ltr for Comdrs: Sup
No. 9:2-5 Sep '76

BROWN, George S. - Continued

Narrow vote confirms JCS chief for 2d term. por AF
Times 36:26 Jul 19 '76

Strategic Forces: How America & the Soviets compare. Gen George S.Brown. por Comdrs Dig 19:
entire issue Apr 15 '76

Strategic missile forces. Gen George S. Brown. Natl
Def 61:36-38+ Jul-Aug '76

Strategic nuclear balance is not enough. Interview.
Gen George Brown. por Govt Exec 8:24-26+
Dec '76

TROA views benefits issue; (Gen) Brown decries
'contract attitude' (at TROA 23d Biennial Convention, Philadelphia, Sep 14-17, 1976). Bruce Callander. AF Times 37:25 Oct 4 '76

U.S. General Purpose Forces: A need for modernization. Gen George S.Brown. Comdrs Dig 19: entire
issue May 27 '76

BUCKINGHAM, Charles E.

Air Force comptroller objectives. LtGen Charles E.
Buckingham. por Armed Forces Compt 21:20-22
Apr '76

BXs, comstores: Credit cards (and) centralized control. Interviews. LtGen Charles E. Buckingham
and MajGen Daniel L.Burkett. por AF Times
37:19+ Nov 8 '76

A message from the Comptroller of the Air Force.
LtGen C.E.Buckingham. por AF Compt 10:2-4
Jan '76

BUDGET

For budgets of the military services and other agencies see Appropriations and Expenditures.

Directorate of Budget. MajGen C.C.Blanton. chart
illus AF Compt 10:16-17 Jan '76

Directorate of Budget. MajGen C.C.Blanton. illus
chart AF Compt 10:12-13 Apr '76

Directorate of Budget. MajGen C.C.Blanton. illus
chart AF Compt 10:12-13 Oct '76

Notes from the Director of Budget. MajGen C.C.
Blanton. illus AF Compt 10:12-13 Jul '76

United States

The budget process vs national defense. (Excerpts
from address, American Defense Preparedness
Assoc, Washington, Nov 11, 1975) Strom Thurmond. Natl Guardsman 30:18-19 Jan '76

Congress & budgets: The computer takes hold. illus
Govt Exec 8:60-61 May '76

The Congressional Budget Office: The logistics of
budget, program, and finance. Ronald G.Bishop.
illus tab charts Log Spectrum 10:26-32 Winter '76

The Defense budget: The price of freedom. L.Edgar
Prina. illus tabs Natl Guardsman 30:8-13 Mar '76

The FY 1977 Federal budget. Col Edmund W.Ed-
monds, Jr. tabs AF Compt 10:3-6 Apr '76

How GAO assists the Congress on budgetary matters.
Ellsworth H.Morse, Jr. illus Armed Forces
Compt 21:6-10 Jan '76

Lawton Chiles and spending reforms: Is it for real
this time? (Interview with chairman, Senate Subcommittee on Federal Spending Practices) C.W.
Borklund. illus Govt Exec 8:12+ Feb '76

BUDGET - Continued

United States - Cont'd

Political prelude to a no-win scenario. James D. Hessman and Vincent C. Thomas. illus Sea Power 18:23-24 Dec '75

200 years of financial management. Allen Schick. Armed Forces Compt 21:4-7 Jul '76

BUETER, Arnold G.

SAF/FM organization. (SecAF/Financial Management) por AF Compt 10:29 Jan '76

BUILDING AND CONSTRUCTION

See also
Air Bases--Construction

Arkansas Nuclear One. Harlan T. Holmes. illus Mil Engr 68:287-289 Jul-Aug '76

The Bethesda project (National Naval Medical Center and Uniformed Services University of the Health Sciences). RADM A. R. Marschall. illus Mil Engr 68:14-17 Jan-Feb '76

The bridge at kilometer 111 (China). Bonnie Baker Quinby and Capt G. William Quinby. illus Mil Engr 68:88-90 Mar-Apr '76

Bridging the generations. (Replicas of the famous bridge at Concord, Mass, are spanning the Anacostia River in Washington for the new Children's Islands Park) Sgt Deb Notah. illus Soldiers 31: 18-21 Dec '76

Building bill passed by House restricts civilian cuts. AF Times 36:25 May 24 '76

Building budget shrinks. AF Times 36:23 Mar 29 '76

Computers cut energy costs in buildings. Phil Deakin. illus tab Govt Exec 8:33+ May '76

Construction bill veto tied to closing limit. AF Times 36:6 Jul 19 '76

Corrosion control features for Air Force facilities. TIG Brief 28:4 Dec 3 '76

Dining in style. (Army's new facilities) Sgt JoAnn Mann. illus Soldiers 31:34-35 Jun '76

Easy access for handicapped urged: Changes proposed in building law. AF Times 37:46 Sep 13 '76

Five flats per minute. (Housing construction in the USSR) G. Alexeyev. illus Soviet Mil Rev No. 10: 5-6 Oct '76

GAO finds Reserves building needlessly. AF Times 37:57 Nov 29 '76

Gabions control erosion. illus Mil Engr 68:28-29 Jan-Feb '76

Geotechnical engineering in the coastal zone. CDR Gordon W. Callender, Jr. illus tabs Mil Engr 68: 366-370 Sep-Oct '76

High speed aircraft fueling project. (Largest fuel storage tank and biggest single piece of cargo airlifted to Incirlik, Turkey) Walter Will. illus AF Engrg & Svcs Qtr 17:28-29 Feb '76

Interior design with people satisfaction in mind. William A. Brown, Sr. illus AF Engrg & Svcs Qtr 17: 2-5 Feb '76

Law to increase (civilian) housing (around military bases) never used. AF Times 36:4 Mar 29 '76

Many details surface in passage of military construction legislation. Officer 52:5+ Aug '76

BUILDING AND CONSTRUCTION - Continued

Medical school (Uniformed Services University of the Health Sciences) cancels plans for third building. AF Times 36:21 Mar 22 '76

(Military) construction bill passes Senate. AF Times 36:36 Jun 14 '76

Monument to people oriented construction (Air Force Accounting and Finance Center, Lowry AFB, Colo). Maj Peter LoPresti and William L. Kollman. illus AF Engrg & Svcs Qtr 17:7-10 Nov '76

More decisions affect Medicare. Officer 52:4+ Aug '76

The National Air and Space Museum. Gyo Obata. illus Mil Engr 68:279-281 Jul-Aug '76

New approaches to office design. illus AF Engrg & Svcs Qtr 17:6-10 Feb '76

New facilities for Air Force working dogs. TIG Brief 28:18 Dec 3 '76

New family housing: None (for AF) in FY 77. AF Times 36:18 Feb 23 '76

Out front by being responsive. (Prime BEEF in PACAF) Harry A. Davis. illus AF Engrg & Svcs Qtr 17:21+ Aug '76

Passing 200 and still climbing. (Army Corps of Engineers) LtGen William C. Gribble, Jr. illus Mil Engr 68:6-10 Jan-Feb '76

The pipe (line, Exercise Jack Frost). Sgt1C Floyd Harrington. illus Soldiers 31:30-34 Nov '76

Plan to improve dorms outlined. AF Times 37:29 Nov 8 '76

Preparing site plans for explosives facilities. TIG Brief 28:13-14 May 7 '76

Renovations cause (military) housing shortages. AF Times 37:25 Sep 6 '76

Reserve projects voted big boost. tab Officer 52:4+ May '76

Reserves fare well in both construction bills. tab Officer 52:5+ Aug '76

The restoration of York Minster. J. A. Lord. illus tab Mil Engr 68:432-436 Nov-Dec '76

Site plans for explosives facilities. TIG Brief 28:7 Nov 5 '76

Toward flexible definitive designs. Capt Michael J. Burrill. illus AF Engrg & Svcs Qtr 17:26-31 Nov '76

Varied challenges for Coast Guard engineers. RADM Malcolm E. Clark. illus map Mil Engr 68:18-21 Jan-Feb '76

Work begins on solar energy BX at Kirtland (AFB, NM). AF Times 37:4 Nov 8 '76

Zero base management system. CDR Walter E. Peterson. Mil Engr 68:371-373 Sep-Oct '76

History

American architectural heritage. Edward M. Tower. illus Mil Engr 68:207-209 May-Jun '76

Development of our construction industry. S. Peter Volpe. Mil Engr 68:202-203 May-Jun '76

BUOYS

ASW: The deterrent. F. Glenn Peters. illus Elect Warfare 8:49-50+ Jul-Aug '76

BUREAU OF THE BUDGET see Office of Management and Budget

BURIAL

Mortuary affairs. TIG Brief 28:8 Apr 9 '76

BURKE, Arleigh A.

Dissidence is not a virtue. ADM Arleigh A. Burke, Ret. por US Nav Inst Proc 102:78-79 Apr '76

BURKETT, Daniel L.

(Air Force Commissary Service) Interview. MajGen Daniel L. Burkett. por Review 56:15-16 Jul-Aug '76

Air Force commissary system (Air Force Commissary Service) begins to take shape under (MajGen Daniel L.) Burkett. Review 55:23 Mar-Apr '76

BXs, comstores: Credit cards (and) centralized control. Interviews. LtGen Charles E. Buckingham and MajGen Daniel L. Burkett. por AF Times 37:19+ Nov 8 '76

(Gen) Burkett on AFCOMS (Air Force COMmissarieS). por Review 56:39-40+ Sep-Oct '76

(Major) General (Daniel L.) Burkett heads new (Air Force) Commissary Service. AF Times 36:3 Feb 23 '76

Stores 'here to stay,' AFCOMS chief says. Interview. MajGen Daniel L. Burkett. AF Times 37:2 Sep 6 '76

A talk with the commander of AFCOMS. Interview. MajGen Daniel L. Burkett. por AF Engrg & Sves Qtr 17:14-17 Nov '76

BURKHART, John W.

Olympic Arena '76. MajGen John W. Burkhart. Combat Crew 27:4-5 Apr '76

BURMA

Foreign Policy

China 'cross the bay: The Burmese hub of Asia. illus Def & For Aff Dig No. 10:22-23+ '76

BURMA - Continued

Politics and Government

China 'cross the bay: The Burmese hub of Asia. illus Def & For Aff Dig No. 10:22-23+ '76

Strategic Importance

China 'cross the bay: The Burmese hub of Asia. illus Def & For Aff Dig No. 10:22-23+ '76

BURNS, Kenneth D.

The EW Center and the Air Force. BrigGen Kenneth D. Burns. TIG Brief 28:2 Nov 5 '76

USAF Security Service. por AF Mag 59:82 May '76

BURRIS, Rupert H.

AFCS and AF resource management. BrigGen Rupert H. Burris. por AF Compt 10: back cover Jan '76

Air Force Communications Service. por AF Mag 59: 56-57 May '76

BUSINESS

See also
Small Business

How private enterprise is committing "subtle suicide." illus Govt Exec 8:56-57 May '76

Industry in the U.S.: The facts don't match the image. illus Govt Exec 8:30+ Feb '76

Rockwell's (Donn L.) Williams: "We do it to ourselves." illus Govt Exec 8:29+ Feb '76

BUTZ, Earl L.

Agricultural freedom and national strength. Earl L. Butz. Persp in Def Mgt No. 24:13-18 Winter '75-'76

BUYING see Purchasing

BYRD, Richard E.

With the Byrd North Pole expedition. E.J. "Pete" Demas. por Am Avn Hist Soc J 21:4-8 Spring '76

C

C A B see Civil Aeronautics Board

C A P see Civil Air Patrol

C A T (Clear Air Turbulence) see Turbulence

C B W see Chemical-Biological Warfare

C E M A see Council of Mutual Economic Assistance

C E N T O see Central Treaty Organization

C H A M P U S (Civilian Health And Medical Program of the Uniformed Services) see Medicare

C O M E C O N see Council of Mutual Economic Assistance

C O S T A R see Combat Support of the Army

C R A F see Civil Reserve Air Fleet

CABIN CREWS

Effect of physical activity of airline flight attendants on their time of useful consciousness in a rapid decompression. Douglas E. Busby and others. tabs Aviation, Space and Envmt Med 47;117-120 Feb '76

Pregnant stewardess--should she fly? Paul Scholten. Aviation, Space & Envmt Med 47;77-81 Jan '76

Protection of airline flight attendants from hypoxia following rapid decompression. Douglas E. Busby and others. illus tabs Aviation, Space & Envmt Med 47;942-944 Sep '76

CABLES

Power cables too short on MD-3 generators. TIG Brief 28:3-4 Jul 16 '76

Wild FIGAT (FiberGlass Aerial Target). illus Approach 21:22-23 Jun '76

Maintenance and Repair

Underground electrical system testing: A review. Capt Michael A. Aimone. illus tabs AF Engrg & Svcs Qtr 17:33-35 May '76

CALIBRATION

Maintenance data reporting for Precision Measurement Equipment (PME). TIG Brief 28:3 Oct 22 '76

Precision Measurement Equipment (PME) calibration support. TIG Brief 28:9-10 Sep 24 '76

CALKINS, Ronald R.

Can academic management research be profitable? LtCol Ronald R. Calkins. AU Rev 27:47-55 Mar-Apr '76

CAMBODIA

Political change in wartime: The Khmer Krahom revolution in southern Cambodia, 1970-1974. Kenneth M. Quinn. illus maps charts Nav War Col Rev 28: 3-31 Spring '76

CAMBODIA - Continued

U.S. field artillery in Vietnam. MajGen David E. Ott. (Extracts from "Field Artillery Monograph") illus tabs maps Fld Arty J pt 1, The field artillery adviser. 43:23-29 Jan-Feb '75; pt 2, In order to win. 43:39-45 Mar-Apr '75; pt 3, Field artillery mobility. 43:15-22 May-Jun '75; pt 4, The buildup. 43: 9-16 Jul-Aug '75, 43:46-51 Sep-Oct '75; pt 4, The field artillery buildup: 1967 combat operations. 43:29-34 Nov-Dec '75; pt 5, The hot war: 1968, the Tet offensive. 44:27-31 Jan-Feb '76; pt 5, The hot war: The Battle of Khe Sanh. 44:44-48 Mar-Apr '76; pt 5, The hot war: 1968-69, A Shau Valley. 44:53-57 May-Jun '76; pt 5, The hot war: Operations and raids. 44:37-43 Jul-Aug '76; pt 6, Vietnamization: FA assistance programs. 44: 10-17 Sep-Oct '76; pt 6, Vietnamization: Operations into Cambodia. 44:13-18 Nov-Dec '76

CAMBODIAN CONFLICT, 1973-

The Air Force, the courts, and the controversial bombing of Cambodia. 1stLt Stephen M. Millett. illus AU Rev 27:80-88 Jul-Aug '76

CAMERAS

Determination of regional pulmonary mechanics using a scintillation camera. R.C.Brown and others. illus tabs Aviation, Space & Envmt Med 47:231-237 Mar '76

CAMOUFLAGE

The Hawk and the clamshell. Capt Dave Hawkins. illus Air Def Mag, pp 18-22, Jul-Sep '76

Principles of passive defense. Capt C.A.Parlier. MarCor Gaz 60:62 May '76

Supply base camouflage. Capt John M.Forbes, Jr. illus Army Log 8:20-22 May-Jun '76

CAMPING see Recreation

CAMPS, MILITARY see Army Posts

CANAL ZONE

TAC sets up (USAF Southern Air Division (USAFSO)) in Canal Zone (territory formerly covered by Southern Command). AF Times 36:2 Jan 12 '76

CANALS see Waterways

CANEDY, Charles E.

Increased responsibility for Army aviators. BrigGen Charles E.Canedy. USA Avn Dig 22:1+ Nov '76

Professionalism in Army Aviation and budgetary constraints. BrigGen Charles E.Canedy. USA Avn Dig 22:1-3 Jun '76

CANNON, George C., Jr

Safety is everyone's responsibility. BrigGen George C.Cannon, Jr. por Interceptor 18:14-15 May '76

CARBON MONOXIDE

High-altitude carbon monoxide. (First microwave observations of carbon monoxide in upper atmospheres of Earth, Venus and Mars) Spaceflight 18:196 May '76

CAREER PROGRAM

Here are entered materials on career specialization
and professional development. Specific occupations
may be found under their own headings, e.g.,
Engineers.

Bars to stars. Regular feature in issues of Air Defense Magazine.

Career information (Signal Corps and Air Force personnel). Regular feature in some issues of Signal

Career patterns for field artillery company grade officers. LtCol Richard L. Reynard. illus Fld Arty J
44:42-44 Nov-Dec '76

Career transition course (offered by Catholic University) teaches retirees to survive. M.L. Craver.
AF Times 37:12 Nov 8 '76

Changed admin(istration) field to groom 1st shirts.
Len Famiglietti. AF Times 37:6 Oct 11 '76

(Combat crew officers' careers) Gen Russell E. Dougherty. illus Combat Crew 27:3+ Jul '76; TIG
Brief 28:2-4 Aug 13 '76

Dear Joe. (Requirements of a career in Naval Aviation) Willie E. Cumbie. illus Approach 21:1-5
Mar '76

Desk to desk. (USAR Research and Development Officer Career Program) Col James L. Wohlfahrt.
illus Army Log 8:6-7 Jul-Aug '76

Don't broaden careers by PCS, commands told. (Use
base-level cross-training) AF Times 36:3
Jan 19 '76

EM career notes. Regular feature in issues of
Infantry

EPMS (Enlisted Personnel Management System):
What it's all about. SGM Nat Dell. illus Soldiers
31:8-11 Sep '76

Enhance your potential through PME. LtCol Marvin
T. Howell. illus tabs AF Engrg & Svcs Qtr 17:33-
37 Nov '76

Enlisted career news. Regular feature in issues of
Air Defense Magazine

Human factor is paramount. (Defense Manpower Commission report) Eric C. Ludvigsen. illus Army 26:
38-40 Jun '76

Introspection (on professional development)--and
some reflections on the way it was. Col Gustav J.
Gillert, Jr. illus Mil Rev 56:36-41 Nov '76

Low AQE (Airman Qualifying Examination) scorers
urged to try again. Bruce Callander. AF Times
36:3 Jul 5 '76

Making the mark with missiles. Capt Robert G.H.
Carroll. illus tab AF Mag 59:50-54 Jun '76

Managerial careers of Air Force generals: A test of
the Janowitz convergence hypothesis. Arnold Kanter. tabs J Pol & Mil Sociol 4:121-133; Comment.
Kurt Lang. 4:141-143; Comment. Thomas C. Padgett. 4:145-146; Reply to comments by Lang and
Padgett. Arnold Kanter. 4:147-149 Spring '76

Managing your logistics career: Here's how OPMD
(Officer Personnel Management Directorate) does
it. Maj Frank Cunningham III. Army Log 8:12-13
Nov-Dec '76

NCO job review starting (for) 5000 senior Reserves.
AF Times 37:3 Aug 2 '76

New guide for officers: Reg (AFR 36-23) answers
many career questions. AF Times 36:32 Jul 12 '76

CAREER PROGRAM - Continued

Notes from the Chief of Palace Dollar. LtCol Thomas
D. Scanlon. illus tab AF Compt 10:26-27 Jul '76

O-5s can cross-train in new fields. AF Times 37:26
Sep 20 '76

Officer career management directory. Contact,
pp 7-8, Winter '76

Officers career notes. Regular feature in issues of
Infantry

Officers get choice of when to update career statement. AF Times 36:4 Mar 29 '76

Officers who apply for CRS (Career Reserve Status)
must qualify for retirement. AF Times 37:3
Dec 6 '76

Palace Blueprint: Six years later. LtCol Marvin T.
Howell. illus tabs AF Engrg & Svcs Qtr 17:31-32+
May '76

Palace Dollar (comptroller career counseling) today.
Capt Benjamin Lester, Jr. illus AF Compt 10:33
Jan '76

Palace Dollar today. Capt Al Yanik. illus AF Compt 10:21
Apr '76

Palace Dollar today: The importance of career broad-
ening. LtCol Joseph Farrell. illus AF Compt 10:
26-27 Oct '76

Reg (AFR 39-4) gives details on job switching. AF
Times 37:26 Nov 1 '76

Remote assignments: On the decline. Maj Richard L.
Brown. illus tabs AF Engrg & Svcs Qtr 17:22-25
Nov '76

Strength, skill, top EM problems: Pieces in TOPCAP
puzzle. Bruce Callander. AF Times 36:6 Jan 26 '76

10,000 EM get 'job reservations.' AF Times 36:23
Mar 1 '76

Transportation career forecast. Chester Levine and
others. tab Def Trans J pt 1, Outlook. 32:18-20+
Oct '76

CAREY, Richard E.

Frequent Wind. MajGen Richard E. Carey and Maj
D.A. Quinlan. MarCor Gaz pt 1, Organization and
assembly (of 9th Marine Amphibious Brigade). 60:
16-24 Feb '76; pt 2, Planning. 60:35-45 Mar '76;
pt 3, Execution. 60:35-45 Apr '76

CARGO

See also
Air Cargo
Hazardous Substances--Transportation

Balloons tested for containership offload. Dan Hall.
illus Translog 7:1-4 Apr '76

Cargo preference: Prescription for an ailing industry. Donald C. Leavens. illus tabs Sea Power 19:
26-30 Jun '76

Cargo security conferees stress industry/shipper
controls (at National Cargo Security Conference,
Washington, March 30-31, 1976). Col H.I. Pitchford. Translog 7:6-7 May '76

DISREP (Discrepency In Shipment REPort, SF 361)
system is ITO's 'Man Friday.' LtCol B.E. Greenfield. Translog 7:5 Oct '76

Intermodal technology as seen by Lykes Brothers.
illus Def Trans J 32:28+ Jun '76

CARGO - Continued

Keeping cargo secure. Tory Billard. illus Translog 7:13-15 Feb '76

MOTBY (Military Ocean Terminal, BaYonne) security forces: Unique. Arthur Stewart. illus Translog 7:1-2+ Nov '76

New support for cargo preference. L.Edgar Prina. illus Sea Power 19:30-33 Mar '76

Outport insight. Debbi Dunstan and Donna Orsini. illus Translog 7:1-3+ Jan '76

Pressure builds for (Merchant Marine) 'fair share' legislation. James D.Hessman. illus Sea Power 19:19-22 Aug '76

The role of intermodality. Alfred E.Perlman. Def Trans J 32:6-11 Feb '76

"Send in the special team." (Port Pilferage Prevention and Detection Team) Capt William C.Fluty. illus Translog 7:6+ Dec '76

CARIBBEAN REGION

Strategic Importance

The Caribbean: Pirates to politics. Leigh Johnson. illus Def & For Aff Dig No.7:12-13+ '76

CARICATURES AND CARTOONS

Bringing up Beetle. (Interview with Mort Walker) Capt John D.Anderson. illus Soldiers 31:19-23 Feb '76

Is there really an Uncle Sam? illus Armor 85:44-45 Jul-Aug '76

Son of a ruddy duck. (Fleagle, an accident-prone bird drawn by Stan Hardison, teaches safety to TAC Attack readers) MSgt Harold Newcomb. illus Airman 20:12-16 Aug '76

CARLTON, Paul K.

MAC's (Gen Paul K.) Carlton asks 'airlift partnership.' AF Times 37:36 Dec 6 '76

Military airlift and the future. (Excerpt from address, 57th Defense Preparedness Meeting, American Defense Preparedness Assoc, Los Angeles, Oct 15, 1975) Gen Paul K.Carlton. Natl Def 60: 288 Jan-Feb '76

Military Airlift Command. por AF Mag 59:69-71 May '76

Perceiving the challenge. (Remarks, 3d Annual Reunion, B-58 Hustler Assoc, Fort Worth, Tex, July 3, 1976) Gen Paul K.Carlton. AF Pley Ltr for Comdrs: Sup No.10:8-15 Oct '76

System safety--expanding the user's role. Gen Paul K.Carlton. TIG Brief 28:2 Jun 4 '76

Why airlift isn't free. Gen Paul K.Carlton. Army Log 8:2-6 Jan-Feb '76

CARTER, James E.

Carter (administration) on MIAs: Policy wait. AF Times 37:10 Dec 6 '76

A change of command: Signing up the new CinC. Army 26:4+ Dec '76

(DefSec Donald) Rumsfeld gives go-ahead on B-1: Carter could block it. Lee Ewing. AF Times 37:4 Dec 13 '76

How to look at the U.S. military budget: Major issues for President Carter. Def Monitor 5: entire issue Dec '76

CARTER, James E. - Continued

How's (President-elect Jimmy) Carter on defense? Bruce Callander. AF Times 37:4 Nov 15 '76

(Jimmy) Carter: 1st Naval (Academy) graduate elected president. Bill Kreh. por AF Times 37:20 Nov 15 '76

(Jimmy) Carter scored on pardon (at) Legionnaire convention. AF Times 37:24 Sep 6 '76

No panic at Pentagon over (President-elect Jimmy) Carter's victory. Paul Smith. AF Times 37:20 Nov 15 '76

People vs hardware: Tough nut for Carter (administration). AF Times 37:6 Dec 6 '76

(Pres-elect Jimmy) Carter affirms blanket pardon. Fred Reed. AF Times 37:2 Nov 29 '76

(Pres-elect Jimmy) Carter still studying draft pardon ... groups against it. AF Times 37:14 Dec 20 '76

(Pres-elect Jimmy) Carter, (VP-elect Walter) Mondale bring new direction to defense. por Officer 52:22+ Dec '76

CARTOGRAPHY see Maps and Mapping

CARTOONS see Caricatures and Cartoons

CASTINGS

Foundries and the OSHA Act: Problems and some solutions. Debbie C.Tennison. illus Natl Def 61:56-59 Jul-Aug '76

Foundries in dilemma. Debbie C.Tennison. illus tabs Natl Def 60:453-458 May-Jun '76

The foundry industry--Achilles' heel of defense? Debbie C.Tennison. illus tab Natl Def 60:366-369 Mar-Apr '76

Laws to aid foundries. Debbie C.Tennison. illus Natl Def 61:131-134 Sep-Oct '76

Light metal castings. Hans-G.Lülfing. illus Aerosp Intl 12:40-41 May-Jun '76

CASUALTIES

See also subdivision under specific wars, e.g., Vietnamese Conflict, 1957-1975--Casualties

Civilian combat casualties: Our moral and legal responsibilities. Maj S.P.Mehl. illus MarCor Gaz 60:43-46 Oct '76

Long wait seen on accounting for war dead (from Vietnamese Conflict and French-Indochinese War). Ann Gerow. AF Times 36:17 Apr 19 '76

Nuclear war--the life-and-death issues. Edgar Ulsamer. illus AF Mag 59:57-59 Jan '76

Radiation battlefield casualties--credible!! Capt Arnold S.Warshawsky. illus tabs Mil Rev 56:3-10 May '76

Taking care of our dead. Capt Al Rawls, Jr. MarCor Gaz 60:56 Sep '76

CATAPULTS

The "brakes" of naval air. illus Approach 21:19 Feb '76

Build your own safety system. LCDR Charles D. Shields, Jr. illus Approach 21:10-11 Dec '75

Disorienting effects of aircraft catapult launchings. II: Visual and postural contributions. Malcolm M. Cohen. tabs Aviation, Space & Envmt Med 47:39-41 Jan '76

CAVALRY

See also
Air Cavalry

CELEBRATIONS

Air Force Bicentennial slide production wins gold medal (at the 18th Annual International Film and Television Festival, New York City). TIG Brief 28:16 Jan 30 '76

Airmen of foot. (A volunteer troupe at Offutt AFB, Nebr, modeled after the 2d Maryland Regiment of Foot, reenacts battles of the Revolutionary War) MSgt Harold Newcomb. illus Airman 20:42-47 Jan '76

America gets it on. Pictorial. Soldiers 31:10-14 Dec '76

Annual Navy Day report (1975). illus Sea Power 18: 35 Dec '75

Bicentennial parade. (Aircraft in commemorative markings) Gerald Markgraf. Pictorial. Am Avn Hist Soc J 21:290-296 Winter '76

Centennial. (America's 1st 100-year celebration) Marc J. Epstein. illus Soldiers 31:33-35 Jul '76

Honor America. (Armed Forces Week, May 8-15, 1976) illus Comdrs Dig 19: entire issue Apr 1 '76

Military (Bicentennial) events set for DC area. AF Times 36:24 May 10 '76

Military Bicentennial exhibits move by truck. illus Translog 7:6-8 Jul '76

A nautical observance of the Bicentennial from sea to shining sea; a monumental itinerary. (Operation Sail and the International Naval Review) Col Brooke Nihart, Ret. illus Sea Power 19:21-28 May '76

Nostalgia rides the rails for the Bicentennial. (American Freedom Train) Dan Hall. illus tab Translog 7:14-18 Jul '76

"One nation, indivisible ..." (The American Freedom Train builds unity and patriotism within its visitors) Ted R. Sturm. illus Airman 20:18-23 Jul '76

Proud heritage. (U.S. flag) Betty Woolley. illus Countermeasures 2:51 Jul '76

Putting the us in U.S. (The small town of Preston, Ga, has a Bicentennial festival aided by the Armed Forces Bicentennial Caravan) Robert K. Ruhl. illus Airman 20:42-47 Jul '76

When the (Armed Forces Bicentennial) Caravan comes to town. Robert K. Ruhl. illus Airman 20: 48 Jul '76

CELESTIAL NAVIGATION see Navigation, Celestial

CEMETERIES, NATIONAL

Arlington burials to expand? Larry Carney. AF Times 37:11 Aug 9 '76

New national cemetery (at Otis AFB, Mass). MarCor Gaz 60:3 Jan '76

Quantico (Va Marine Corps Base) opening to relieve national cemetery crowding. Army 26:8 Mar '76

VA to open new cemeteries. AF Times 36:8 Feb 2 '76

CENTER FOR NAVAL ANALYSES

"Captive think tanks" revisited: Rebuttal to rebuttal. James R. Craig. Armed Forces J Intl 113:42+ Mar '76

Setting the record straight about CNA. (Comments on "Captive 'think tanks'--DOD's $265-million hobby horse?" by James R. Craig, Armed Forces J Intl, Dec 1975) Arnold B. Moore. tab Armed Forces J Intl 113:26-27 Jan '76

CENTRAL TREATY ORGANIZATION

The Middle East and the Mediterranean. London's International Institute for Strategic Studies. illus tabs AF Mag 59:67-72 Dec '76

CENTRIFUGES

That (pull of gravity) machine. LtCol Lee Crock. illus tabs Interceptor 18:8-13 Aug '76

CEREMONIES, MILITARY see Military Ceremonies, Honors and Salutes

CHAMBERLIN, Clarence D.

(Eight aviation pioneers (Clarence D. Chamberlin, John H. Glenn, Jr, George W. Goddard, Albert F. Hegenberger, Edwin A. Link, Sanford A. Moss, William A. Patterson, Nathan F. Twining) to be enshrined in Aviation Hall of Fame, July 24, 1976) por AF Mag 59:29-30 Jul '76

CHANNEL COMMAND see Allied Command Channel

CHAPELS AND CHURCHES

Chapel management personnel. TIG Brief 28:16 Jul 16 '76

Lay involvement in chapel programs. TIG Brief 28:21 Sep 10 '76

Maintenance and Repair

The restoration of York Minster. J. A. Lord. illus tab Mil Engr 68:432-436 Nov-Dec '76

CHAPLAINS

Air Force--U.S.

Air Force Chaplain Service: Inspection Guide H. TIG Brief 28:2p addendum Dec 3 '76

Air Force Chaplain Service inspection model. TIG Brief 28:10 Dec 3 '76

Chaplain OERs now controlled. AF Times 36:31 Apr 12 '76

Chaplain visitations. TIG Brief 28:13 Aug 13 '76

Chaplains' goal: Stronger families. AF Times 37:10 Nov 22 '76

Strengthening Air Force family life. Ch(MajGen) Henry J. Meade. TIG Brief 28:2 Dec 17 '76

What's (Ch(Maj)) Gordy Johnson up to? TSgt Tom Dwyer. illus Airman 20:34-38 Feb '76

Armed Forces--U.S.

Groome on marriage breakdowns. Interview. Ch(BrigGen) Thomas M. Groome, Jr. illus AF Times 36:12 Jul 26 '76

Army--U.S.

(Ch(Maj) Loren Dale Pugh nominated as ROA's Chaplain of the Year) illus Officer 52:21 Jan '76

Sunday every day. Janet Hake. illus Soldiers 31:28-31 Oct '76

CHAPLAINS - Continued

National Guard--Air Force--U.S.

'The people business.' Chris Scheer. illus Air Reservist 27:4-5 Mar '76

Reserve Forces--Air Force--U.S.

'The people business.' Chris Scheer. illus Air Reservist 27:4-5 Mar '76

CHARITIES

AF Assistance Fund seeks new ideas. AF Times 36:12 May 24 '76

CHARTER AIR SERVICE see Airlines--Nonscheduled Operations

CHARTS

See also
Aeronautical Charts

CHASE, John D.

U.S. Merchant Marine--for commerce and defense. RADM John D.Chase. US Nav Inst Proc 102:130-145 May '76

CHEMICAL-BIOLOGICAL WARFARE

A CB (Chemical and Biological) primer: Looking at the chemical and biological warfare scenarios. C.Bruce Sibley. illus tab Def & For Aff Dig No.10:6-9+ '76

History

A sword undrawn: Chemical warfare and the Victorian Age. J.B.Poole. Army Qtr pt 1, 106:463-469 Oct '76

CHEMICAL RESEARCH

Chemical engineering aids solar energy. Talbot A. Chubb. illus tab Mil Engr 68:456-458 Nov-Dec '76

CHENNAULT, Claire L.

The Chinese-American Composite Wing (CACW). LtCol Kenneth Kay, Ret. por AF Mag 59:60-65 Feb '76

"Old Leatherface's" bombers. (Chennault's forces included the 308th Bombardment Gp (Heavy) which saw much action in China during WW II) Capt Stephen O.Manning III. Airman 20:8-14 Jul '76

CHILDREN, MILITARY

See also
Education (Dependents)
Project--CHAP

CHAMPUS clears up child abuse cases. Ann Gerow. AF Times 36:20 Jun 21 '76

Child abuse: Reporting is critical. M.L.Craver. illus AF Times 37:46 Oct 18 '76

Child problem can lead to involuntary discharge. AF Times 37:8 Aug 16 '76

Child support push starting. AF Times 36:8 Mar 8 '76

Children are due full SBP annuity. AF Times 37:61 Oct 18 '76

Children homicides (among AF families) decline. AF Times 36:13 Jun 14 '76

CHILDREN, MILITARY - Continued

Day care: Babysitting or more? Task Force (for Child Care in the Military) scores shortcomings of base nurseries. Donna Peterson. illus AF Times 36:35+ Mar 1 '76

Handicapped getting help in infancy (at Vandenberg AFB, Calif). Donna Peterson. illus AF Times 37:37+ Dec 6 '76

Mothers in army green. Martha Falls. illus Soldiers 31:45-46 Oct '76

Sex ratio in offspring of pilots: A contribution to stress research. H.P.Goerres and K.Gerbert. tabs Aviation, Space & Envmt Med 47:889-892 Aug '76

When Daddy comes home: How to cope with children who are hurt and angry because Daddy's been away. Marianne Lester. illus AF Times, Times Magazine sup:8-11 Sep 20 '76

CHILE

Politics and Government

Chile: Fascism and militarism. G.Spersky. Soviet Mil Rev No.7:59-60 Jul '76

CHINA

History

Coalition warfare--relieving the Peking legations, 1900. (Boxer Rebellion) Col James B.Agnew. illus map Mil Rev 56:58-70 Oct '76

Sun Pin: China's other master of war. Maj W.H.P.J. Fitzsimons. Army Qtr 106:287-290 Jul '76

CHINA (PEOPLE'S REPUBLIC)

Economic Conditions

China at the economic crossroads. A.Ranney Johnson. tabs Def & For Aff Dig No.6:32-34 '76

China's oil trade in the 1980s: A closer look. Col Sidney Klein. illus Mil Rev 56:52-55 Oct '76

Mao Tse-tung and original sin. Richard Clutterbuck. Army Qtr 106:142-148 Apr '76

Economic Policy

China at the economic crossroads. A.Ranney Johnson. tabs Def & For Aff Dig No.6:32-34 '76

Foreign Policy

CCIS (Communist Chinese Intelligence Services). David Harvey. illus Def & For Aff Dig pt 1, No.11: 14-16+ '75; pt 2, No.12-No.1:16-17+ '75-'76

China: Friend or enemy? Richard Clutterbuck. Army Qtr 106:17-22 Jan '76

Dangerous doctrine. G.Apalin. Soviet Mil Rev No.1: 44-45 Jan '76

The Peking NATO fans. Y.Lugovskoi. Soviet Mil Rev No.6:47-48 Jun '76

The scrambled geometry of the new Pacific: West of the Dateline and East of India. Lawrence Griswold. illus Sea Power 19:24-29 Apr '76

U.S. policy alternatives in Asia. Robert A.Scalapino. illus Parameters 5, No.2:14-24 '76

CHINA (PEOPLE'S REPUBLIC) - Continued

Foreign Relations

Asia, Southeastern

The USSR-DRV-PRC triangle in Southeast Asia. Donald E. Weatherbee. illus Parameters 6, No. 1: 71-86 '76

China (Republic)

Trouble in the Far East: Quemoy still waging war of words; the domino theory--alive and well. Fred Reed. AF Times 36:10-11 Mar 1 '76

Europe, Western

The Sino-West European connection. Maj Alfred Biegel. illus Mil Rev 56:68-78 Jan '76

Hong Kong

The Crown Colony of Hong Kong. Col Norman L. Dodd, Ret. illus Mil Rev 56:37-46 Oct '76

India

Border war: China vs India. RADM Ben Eiseman. illus MarCor Gaz 60:19-25 Sep '76

NATO

The Peking NATO fans. Y. Lugovskoi. Soviet Mil Rev No. 6:47-48 Jun '76

Russia

Peking and Soviet-Chinese relations. I. Alexandrov. Soviet Mil Rev No. 9:55-58 Sep '76

Tanzania

Inroads into East Africa: The People's Republic of China and Tanzania. Maj Michael E. Dash. illus map Mil Rev 56:58-64 Apr '76

United States

China's nuclear strategy and U.S. reactions in the "post-détente" era. William T. Tow. illus Mil Rev 56:80-90 Jun '76

Politics and Government

China's evolving national security requirements. R. D. M. Furlong. illus map tab Intl Def Rev 9: 557-562+ Aug '76

Mao Tse-tung and original sin. Richard Clutterbuck. Army Qtr 106:142-148 Apr '76

The politics of the Chinese People's Republic Navy. LT David G. Muller, Jr. illus Nav War Col Rev 28:32-51 Spring '76

History

Republican China. Jerry Kamstra. illus Countermeasures pt 1, The death of a dynasty. 2:24-26+ Jul '76; pt 2, Birth of modern China. 2:22-23 Aug '76

Social Conditions

Mao Tse-tung and original sin. Richard Clutterbuck. Army Qtr 106:142-148 Apr '76

CHINA (REPUBLIC)

Foreign Policy

The geostrategic triangle of North-East Asia. Niu Sien-chong. NATO's Fifteen Nations 21:68+ Aug-Sep '76

CHINA (REPUBLIC) - Continued

Strategic Importance

Asia. Philip Paisley and Leigh Johnson. illus tab Def & For Aff Dig No. 5:18-19+ '76

CHRISTIANSEN, John S.

F-14--weapon system in search of its engine. RADM John S. Christiansen, Ret. por US Nav Inst Proc 102:103-105 Dec '76

CHRONOLOGY

See also subdivision Chronology under specific subjects

CHURCHES see Chapels and Churches

CIPHERS see Cryptography

CIRCADIAN RHYTHMS see Biological Rhythms

CITIES AND TOWNS

Russia

City of courage and glory (Novorossiisk). LtCol G. Nikolayev. illus Soviet Mil Rev No. 12:9-11 Dec '76

Fortress on the Bug (Brest, Belorussia). LtCol N. Yelshin. illus Soviet Mil Rev No. 6:39-41 Jun '76

Hero city of Sevastopol. (Interview with Viktor Makarenko) Capt A. Kontiyevsky. illus Soviet Mil Rev No. 10:7-9 Oct '76

Volgograd--a hero-city. LtCol L. Rakovsky. illus Soviet Mil Rev No. 2:8-10 Feb '76

United States

Are the cities saveable? illus Govt Exec 8:18-20+ Nov '76

Crime fighting in Oceanside (Calif). Richard C. Barnard. illus AF Times, Times Magazine sup:6-10 Mar 22 '76

Crisis in relocation planning. (Denver NDTA chapter undertaking emergency evacuation planning exercises) John W. Billheimer. Def Trans J 32:20+ Apr '76

The end of the disposable city. Stephen D. Julias. illus Govt Exec 8:44-45+ May '76

Jacksonville (Fla): Consolidation is no panacea. illus chart Govt Exec 8:24-26+ Nov '76

Logistics management in municipalities. (Burbank, Calif) Robert N. Carlton. illus chart Log Spectrum 10:22-25+ Summer '76

Off-base buying: What impact does this have on the town? Capt Randall B. King. illus tabs AF Compt 10:26-27 Jan '76

San Diego: Navy town. illus US Nav Inst Proc 102: 109-113 Apr '76

Small cities (like Redondo Beach, Calif) & computers: It can be done. illus Govt Exec 8:55-56+ Dec '76

UMTA (Urban Mass Transportation Administration): Controlling the costs. John F. Judge. illus Govt Exec 8:18-20 Jul '76

CITIZENS BAND RADIO see Citizens Radio Service

CITIZENS RADIO SERVICE

Break for a CB update! Sgt1C Floyd Harrington. tabs Soldiers 31:27-29 Dec '76

CB held asset in traffic. AF Times 36:32 May 24 '76

Citizens Band (CB) operations. TIG Brief 28:11 Dec 17 '76

CIVIC ACTION PROGRAM

See also
Defense Community Service Program

Earthquake! (USAF aids Guatemala with airlift, reconnaissance, and communications) MSgt Harold Newcomb and SSgt Ken Peterson. illus Airman 20: 8-13 Jun '76

Sports in Africa: A U.S. grass roots involvement. illus Govt Exec 8:50+ Sep '76

CIVIL AERONAUTICS BOARD

CAB studies airline overbooking. Don Hirst. AF Times 36:25 May 31 '76

CAB wants to end 'champagne flights.' AF Times 37:8 Nov 1 '76

Charter flights might reimburse bumped fares. (Rule change recently proposed by Civil Aeronautics Board's consumer advocate) AF Times 36:9 Jul 5 '76

CIVIL AFFAIRS

History

Civil affairs: Civil War style. Capt James T. Currie. illus Mil Rev 56:19-25 Dec '76

CIVIL AIR PATROL

United States

Air War College training 170 CAP officers. AF Times 36:10 Jun 21 '76

CAP marks 35th. AF Times 37:26 Dec 13 '76

Little Charlie Hill is missing! (Idaho CAP aids in search for lost 20-month-old child) Laura Tangley. illus Airman 20:22-23 Apr '76

CIVIL DEFENSE

See also
Evacuation, Civilian

Russia

Soviet Civil Defense--upsetting the strategic balance. Editorial. John L. Frisbee. AF Mag 59:4 Aug '76

War survival in Soviet strategy. Foy D. Kohler. AF Mag 59:90-92+ Sep '76

United States

See also
Defense Civil Preparedness Agency

DNA's (Defense Nuclear Agency) business: Thinking the unthinkable. Edgar Ulsamer. illus AF Mag 59: 50-54 Sep '76

MOBDES (MOBilization DESignee): Modern Minutemen. LtCol John X. Loughran III. illus Air Reservist 28:18 Nov '76

The new nuclear strategy: Battle of the dead? maps Def Monitor 5: entire issue Jul '76

CIVIL DEFENSE - Continued

Our neglected civil defenses. BrigGen Lynn D. Smith, Ret. illus Army 26:12-20 Jul '76

Relocation plan drafted in case of nuclear war. M.L. Craver. AF Times 37:18 Nov 15 '76

U.S. on dangerous course. (Interview with Sidney D. Drell) M.L. Craver. AF Times 37:11 Dec 27 '76

War survival in Soviet strategy. Foy D. Kohler. AF Mag 59:90-92+ Sep '76

CIVIL ENGINEERING

The Army's facilities engineering operations. BrigGen Walter O. Bachus. illus tabs chart Mil Engr 68:94-97 Mar-Apr '76

Emergency power generators. TIG Brief 28:11 Nov 19 '76

Facility engineering in the 1970's--a challenge. (Remarks, Society of American Military Engineers, San Antonio, May 18, 1976) Joe F. Meis. tab AF Plcy Ltr for Comdrs: Sup No. 8:23-29 Aug '76

Gabions control erosion. illus Mil Engr 68:28-29 Jan-Feb '76

Geotechnical engineering in the coastal zone. CDR Gordon W. Callender, Jr. illus tabs Mil Engr 68: 366-370 Sep-Oct '76

Make service your profession. (Address, Air Force Engineering and Services Conference, Homestead AFB, Fla, Dec 1975) Gen Russell E. Dougherty. illus AF Engrg & Svcs Qtr 17:6-12 May '76

Monument to people oriented construction (Air Force Accounting and Finance Center, Lowry AFB, Colo). Maj Peter LoPresti and William L. Kollman. illus AF Engrg & Svcs Qtr 17:7-10 Nov '76

Never a dull moment. (USAF Reserve Civil Engineers work at restoring the Fort Jefferson National Monument 65 miles west of the Florida coast) TSgt Dan Doherty. illus Airman 20:42-47 Aug '76

Palace Blueprint: Six years later. LtCol Marvin T. Howell. illus tabs AF Engrg & Svcs Qtr 17:31-32+ May '76

Passing 200 and still climbing. (Army Corps of Engineers) LtGen William C. Gribble, Jr. illus Mil Engr 68:6-10 Jan-Feb '76

Preparing site plans for explosives facilities. TIG Brief 28:13-14 May 7 '76

Zero base management system. CDR Walter E. Peterson. Mil Engr 68:371-373 Sep-Oct '76

History

Coast Guard public works. Jeffrey P. High. illus Mil Engr 68:194-197 May-Jun '76

Engineering for people: 200 years of Army public works. Roy Gordon. illus Mil Engr 68:180-185 May-Jun '76

Navy public works--1776-1976. Judith Johnston. illus Mil Engr 68:186-193 May-Jun '76

CIVIL RESERVE AIR FLEET

Military airlift and the future. (Excerpt from address, 57th Defense Preparedness Meeting, American Defense Preparedness Assoc, Los Angeles, Oct 15, 1975) Gen Paul K. Carlton. Natl Def 60: 288 Jan-Feb '76

CIVILIAN EMPLOYEES - Continued

United States - Cont'd

145,000 are 'double dippers.' AF Times 37:3 Nov 8 '76

142,000 retirees hold Federal jobs. AF Times 37:2 Nov 15 '76

(Pension) funds 'time bomb' cited by (Sen Thomas) Eagleton. AF Times 36:3 Jan 26 '76

Personal liability for official acts. LtCol Garrett W. Palmer. AF Law Rev 18:85-100 Fall '76

Salaries and Wages

Bill would thaw top pay--boost to civilian workers. AF Times 36:16 Mar 8 '76

Board (Commission on Executive, Legislative and Judicial Salaries) expected to ask for big VIP raise. Don Mace. AF Times 37:4 Nov 22 '76

CSC sets new cost-of-living rates in U.S. areas o'seas. AF Times 37:12 Dec 6 '76

Comparing pay, examining benefits--fringes under fire in House harangue. tab AF Times 36:16 Mar 8 '76

Compensation situation: Many developments. Officer 52:10 Jan '76

Council (Advisory Committee on Federal Pay) urges (Pres) Ford to OK 6% raise. AF Times 37:3 Sep 27 '76

DOD to appeal 'bag-boy' minimum (wages). AF Times 37:4 Dec 6 '76

Davis: Pay comparable to civilian. Interview. MajGen B.L.Davis. AF Times 36:4 Mar 1 '76

(Federal employee) unions attack raise methods. Randy Shoemaker. AF Times 37:2 Aug 30 '76

Federal wage regulations and service contracts. Capt Derrick R.Franck. AF Law Rev 18:17-34 Summer '76

5.16% Oct 1 raise studied. AF Times 36:3 Jul 19 '76

4.83% raise Oct 1 sure(?). AF Times 37:3 Sep 13 '76

Future pay boosts face fight. Randall Shoemaker. illus AF Times 36:3 Feb 2 '76

House panel (Civil Service Committee) opposes 5% cap. Randy Shoemaker. AF Times 36:4 Mar 8 '76

Military $ $ called better than civilian. AF Times 37:8 Nov 15 '76

Move to pay bag boys could hike store costs. Randy Shoemaker. AF Times 37:2 Nov 15 '76

New pay raise indexes sought. Randy Shoemaker. AF Times 36:3 Apr 19 '76

No pay hike cap, but ... Randy Shoemaker. AF Times 37:3 Aug 16 '76

Pay: Freeze or 16% raise? Randy Shoemaker. AF Times 36:3 Mar 29 '76

Pay panel (President's Panel on Federal Compensation) submits changes; far-reaching effects seen. Randy Shoemaker. AF Times 36:2 Jan 5 '76

Pay raise: Only 4.83 percent seen. Randy Shoemaker. AF Times 37:4 Aug 23 '76

Rocky: 5% cap (on pay increases for federal and military workers) OK at present. Donna Peterson. illus AF Times 36:39 Feb 9 '76

CIVILIAN EMPLOYEES - Continued

Salaries and Wages - Cont'd

Senior officials lose (pay) raise (this year). Phil Stevens. AF Times 37:3 Sep 27 '76

Services hit salary plan. Randy Shoemaker. AF Times 37:3 Oct 25 '76

6.7% October raise urged. Don Mace and Randy Shoemaker. AF Times 37:4 Aug 2 '76

State order on garnishment backed. Lee Ewing. AF Times 36:4 Mar 29 '76

Sticky court suit could affect raise (for civilian workers and the military). AF Times 36:2 Jan 19 '76

3 members (of the Federal Employees Pay Council) walk out: Pay distributing plan hit. Don Mace. AF Times 37:4 Aug 23 '76

What's going on about pay--COLA trouble. AF Times 36:3 May 24 '76

X factor vs comparability: Comparison with civilian pay ignores hazards. Randy Shoemaker. AF Times 36:3 Mar 15 '76

CIVILIAN HEALTH AND MEDICAL PROGRAM OF THE UNIFORMED SERVICES see Medicare

CLAIMS

See also
Court of Claims
Liability

CHAMPUS appeal procedures ordered. Andy Plattner. AF Times 37:4 Sep 20 '76

CHAMPUS delay hits Southwest. Andy Plattner. AF Times 37:2 Oct 18 '76

CHAMPUS reg outlines claim appeal procedure. AF Times 37:3 Nov 8 '76

DISREP (Discrepency In Shipment REPort, SF 361) system is ITO's 'Man Friday.' LtCol B.E.Greenfield. Translog 7:5 Oct '76

$825,000 paid in mid-air crash (of) jet and private plane (and other accident claims settled). AF Times 36:32 May 24 '76

The Feres doctrine after twenty-five years. (Military member's cause of action under the Federal Tort Claims Act) Capt Robert L.Rhodes. AF Law Rev 18:24-44 Spring '76

It's your move and your money. Sgt1C Floyd Harrington. illus tab Soldiers 31:6-11 Apr '76

(Medical) malpractice claims seen at high level. AF Times 26:26 Jun 14 '76

Motor vehicle claims. Capt David G.Darugh. AF Law Rev 18:103-107 Summer '76

PCS claim revision due. AF Times 36:4 May 10 '76

Southwest contractor changed: CHAMPUS developments. AF Times 37:20 Dec 6 '76

CLARK, Malcolm E.

Varied challenges for Coast Guard engineers. RADM Malcolm E.Clark. Mil Engr 68:18-21 Jan-Feb '76

CLASSIFICATION see Personnel Classification; Security Classification

CLAUSEWITZ, Karl von

Clausewitz and Soviet politico-military strategy. BrigGen Antonio Pelliccia. NATO's Fifteen Nations 20:18-21+ Dec '75-Jan '76; Digest. Mil Rev 56:23-33 Aug '76

Scharnhorst to Schlieffen: The rise and decline of German military thought. Herbert Rosinski. Nav War Col Rev 29:83-103 Summer '76

CLEMENTS, William P., Jr

(Deputy DefSec William P.) Clements on pay, benefits: Restraints could encourage unions. AF Times 36:10 Feb 2 '76

(Deputy DefSec William P.) Clements speaks on NCOs. Gene Famiglietti. AF Times 36:61 May 24 '76

Military assistance program and foreign military sales. (Statement before House Committee on International Relations, Nov 11, 1975) William P. Clements, Jr. AF Pley Ltr for Comdrs: Sup No. 2:27-31 Feb '76

Naval Academy faculty called 'worst' (of the three by DepSecDef William P. Clements). AF Times 36:12 Apr 5 '76

CLIMATIC RESEARCH

The Global Atmospheric Research Programme (GARP): GARP Atlantic Tropical Experiment (GATE). B.J.Mason. Royal Air Forces Qtr 16: 35-40 Spring '76

CLOSE AIR SUPPORT

The A-10. Col Craig Powell, Ret. illus Army 26:43-47 Mar '76

A-10, close air support stone. Maj Michael L. Ferguson. illus Infantry 66:24-28 May-Jun '76

A-10 progress report: We're slightly confused. illus Armed Forces J Intl 113:30 Mar '76

Alpha Jet series (Franco-German) production starts for 1978 deliveries: Sales campaign intensifies. Michael Brown. illus tabs Interavia 31:120-122 Feb '76

A case for smart weapons. LtCol Frank C.Regan, Jr. illus tabs MarCor Gaz 60:31-35 May '76

Cooperation of aviation with land forces (in WW II). Col Y.Veraksa. illus Soviet Mil Rev No. 10:54-56 Oct '76

The ever-expanding umbrella. LtCol Arthur D. McQueen. tab illus Air Def Mag, pp 8-17, Jul-Sep '76

Forward air control in the Korean War. Maj Tim Cline. illus Am Avn Hist Soc J 21:257-262 Winter '76

Modern weapons employment. Capt Arthur Fowler. illus Aerosp Safety 32:5 Nov '76

Open letter to A-10 drivers. LtCol Dale Tabor. illus TAC Attack 16:4-7 Aug '76

Tac air, member of the (combined arms) team supporting the supersoldier. LtCol William H.Rees. illus Infantry 66:16-23 May-Jun '76

Tally on the FAC (Forward Air Controller). Capt Duane Tway. illus TAC Attack 16:4-6 Nov '76

V/STOL close air support in the U.S. Marine Corps. Col Stanley P.Lewis. illus US Nav Inst Proc 102: 113-116 Oct '76

CLOSE AIR SUPPORT - Continued

The WX-50 close air support radar. illus tab Intl Def Rev 9:287-288 Apr '76

Who needs nuclear tacair? Col David L.Nichols. illus AU Rev 27:15-25 Mar-Apr '76

CLOTHING

See also
Clothing, Protective
Personal Equipment
Uniforms

Military clothing sales stores under new management. TIG Brief 28:12 Nov 19 '76

CLOTHING, PROTECTIVE

See also
Helmets
Pressure Suits

Antiexposure: Then and now. (Cold water exposure protection) illus Approach 22:1-5 Nov '76

Don't get caught with your long johns down--or winter weather woes. Capt Marty Steere. illus TAC Attack 16:24-26 Nov '76

Effectiveness of four water-cooled undergarments and a water-cooled cap in reducing heat stress. George F.Fonseca. tabs Aviation, Space & Envmt Med 47:1159-1164 Nov '76

Facility and a method for evaluation of thermal protection. A.M.Stoll and others. illus tab Aviation, Space & Envmt Med 47:1177-1181 Nov '76

Good news for aircrews. (Nomex winter-weight flight jacket (CWU/45/P)) Capt Kenneth M.Lewis. illus MAC Flyer 23:20 Aug '76

How strongly do you feel about life? Your survival gear and SAR preparation will probably tell. LTJG Kim A.King. illus Approach 21:18-21 Nov '75; Aerosp Safety 32:22-24 Jan '76

Identification of an apprehension effect on physiological indices of thermal strain. M.H.Harrison and C.Saxton. tabs Aviation, Space & Envmt Med 47: 950-953 Sep '76

Nomex protection, a 50-50 proposition. Capt Michael E.Humphreys. illus MAC Flyer 23:7-8 Jan '76

Super-search progress report. (Another look at life support equipment development) LtCol Lee Crock. illus Interceptor 18:8-11 Sep '76

The Ventile antiexposure suit: It's great! LCDR Gary Smith and LT Bob Brich. illus tab Approach 22: 1-5 Oct '76

Winter flying ... seasonal work. Capt John E.Richardson. Aerosp Safety 32:9 Dec '76

CLOTHING ALLOWANCES

Clothing allowance drops Oct 1. Ron Sanders. AF Times 37:46 Sep 13 '76

Defense (Dept) to reduce EM clothing pay. AF Times 36:2 Jan 5 '76

EM clothing allowances to vary by Service. AF Times 37:39 Oct 4 '76

CLOUDS

Sunday afternoon cu(mulonimbus). Maj Orlen L. Brownfield. illus MAC Flyer 23:3-5 Apr '76

Thunderstorm? Cumulonimbus? Maj Herbert Weigl, Jr. illus Aerosp Safety 32:1 Sep '76

COLOR - Continued

New approaches to office design. illus AF Engrg &
Svcs Qtr 17:6-10 Feb '76

Military Applications

GSE (Ground Support Equipment): From yellow to
dark green. TIG Brief 28:13 Apr 23 '76

COLORADO

On the Santa Fe Trail. (Operating Location Alpha
Bravo, a high-frequency radio site in eastern
Colorado, operated by Aerospace Defense Command) SMSgt Harold Newcomb. illus Airman 20:
11-14 Nov '76

COMBAT

Decisive lateral repositioning. Col Howard R.Guffey.
illus Fld Arty J 44:6-10 Mar-Apr '76

A method for conceptualizing combat theory. Chantee
Lewis. illus tabs Nav War Col Rev 28:45-56
Fall '75

Would women fight like men in combat? Fred Reed.
AF Times 37:8 Dec 27 '76

Study and Teaching

(AF) women to begin combat courses. Ron Sanders.
AF Times 37:42 Nov 15 '76

Real training now for combat. Maj Gary E.Todd.
MarCor Gaz 60:52-55 Sep '76

COMBAT CONTROL CENTERS
This term is used to include organizations whose
missions are like: Tactical Air Control Centers,
Tactical Control Centers, Combat Operations
Centers, Combat Information Centers.

Navy

Fleet commanders: Afloat or ashore? VADM Ray
Peet, Ret and Michael E.Melich. illus US Nav
Inst Proc 102:25-33 Jun '76

The Naval Command and Control System (NOCS).
CAPT Frank R.Fahland. illus Signal 30:79-83
Aug '76

COMBAT EVALUATION

See also subdivision under specific subjects,
e.g.,
Helicopters, Military--Combat Evaluation
Weapon Systems--Combat Evaluation

The EW Center and the Air Force. BrigGen Kenneth
D.Burns. TIG Brief 28:2 Nov 5 '76

COMBAT INFORMATION see Intelligence, Military

COMBAT READINESS

See also
Operational Readiness

(AF) ability to fight given careful scrutiny (by AF
Readiness Initiative Group (AFRIG)). AF Times
36:3 Apr 26 '76

AFLC steps up USAF's combat readiness. Edgar Ulsamer. illus AF Mag 59:63-67 Jun '76

AFRES/ANG--best shape ever. Interviews. MajGens
John J.Pesch and William Lyon. illus AF Mag 59:
55-59 Jun '76

Bold Eagle '76. illus USAF Ftr Wpns Rev, p 17,
Spring '76

COMBAT READINESS - Continued

Bold thinking is needed to revitalize the Ready Reserve. Col T.G.Westerman and LtCol Wayne C.
Knudson. illus Army 26:34-38 May '76

Can the Reserve Components make it? LtCol Benjamin L.Abramowitz. illus tab Mil Rev 56:58-64
May '76

Combat alert duty. Col Y.Gridasov. Soviet Mil Rev
No.11:37-39 Nov '76

Combat readiness on a shoestring. (Army augmentation units) Anthony J.Daniels. illus Army 26:
49-51 Apr '76

Congress told shortages, cuts hurting readiness (by
Gen George S.Brown). AF Times 36:6 Mar 1 '76

The cutting edge: Combat capability. Gen David C.
Jones. illus tab AF Mag 59:48-50+ May '76

The DOC (Designed Operational Capability) and UCMS
(Unit Capability Measurement System). TIG Brief
28:7 Jun 4 '76

The EW Center and the Air Force. BrigGen Kenneth
D.Burns. TIG Brief 28:2 Nov 5 '76

Exercise Bold Eagle (76). AF Times 36:31 Mar 1 '76

FORSCOM engineers: The first 1,000 days. Col Alvin G.Rowe. illus tab Mil Engr 68:445-447 Nov-
Dec '76

Fighting mood. Capt A.Stolyarenko. Soviet Mil Rev
No.10:39-40 Oct '76

A flexible military posture. Gen Louis H.Wilson.
illus Strat Rev 4:7-13 Fall '76

GAO report: O'seas aid causes U.S. arms shortage.
AF Times 36:10 Jan 19 '76

'Great progress in very difficult circumstances.' Interview. Gen Fred C.Weyand. illus Army 26:
14-16+ Oct '76

In U.S. Forces Command: 'Total Army' readiness.
Gen Bernard W.Rogers. illus Army 26:30-32+
Oct '76

MAC Associates ... a vital role. MSgt Gerald H.
Smith. illus Air Reservist 28:12-13 Nov '76

A new way of doing business. (Army Materiel Development and Readiness Command) Interview. Gen
John R.Deane, Jr. illus Soldiers 31:21-24 Jun '76

"Our" Air Force and its future. (Remarks, ROA National Convention, Bal Harbour, Fla, June 29-
July 2, 1976) Gen Robert J.Dixon. illus Air Reservist 28:4-6 Aug-Sep '76

Prime BEEF in Europe. Maj Charles F.Kreis. illus
AF Engrg & Svcs Qtr 17:28-30 May '76

Readiness. (Remarks, Jolly Green Pilots Assoc reunion, Eglin AFB, Fla, April 24, 1976) MajGen
Billy J.Ellis. AF Plcy Ltr for Comdrs: Sup No.7:
2-6 Jul '76

Readiness of all total force jumps. tabs Officer 52:19
Feb '76

Readiness through realism. LtCol James Glaza. illus
Air Reservist 28:8-9 Aug-Sep '76

Ready & waiting. (82d Airborne Division, Fort
Bragg, NC) SSgt John Savard. illus Soldiers 31:
6-10 Nov '76

COMBAT READINESS - Continued

(SecAF Thomas C.Reed lists 5 conclusions about the Air Force in recent news conference at the Pentagon) illus Air Reservist 28:13 May '76; AF Compt 10:24-25 Jul '76

Ship's inspections and reviews. Capt K.Antonov. Soviet Mil Rev No. 4:20-21 Apr '76

Stability for an urgent mission: Army Reserve looks ahead. MajGen Henry Mohr. illus Army 26:39-40+ Oct '76

Strategy and readiness. Gen John J.Hennessey. illus Strat Rev 4:44-48 Fall '76

Total force. LtCol James E.Witek. tab Soldiers 31: 43-46 Aug '76

Tough and ready--"to keep the peace ... to deter war." Interview. Army Chief of Staff, Gen Fred C.Weyand. illus Soldiers 31:31-34 Feb '76

Training (cost-reducing) study ordered by C/S (Gen David C.Jones). AF Times 36:2 May 31 '76

UCMS (Unit Capability Measurement System) reporting. TIG Brief 28:11 Aug 13 '76

Unit Capability Measurement System (UCMS). TIG Brief 28:10 Oct 22 '76

U.S. Army Europe ... 'Sense of excitement.' Interview. Gen George S.Blanchard. illus Army 26:13+ Aug '76

Study and Teaching

Brave Shield XIV. illus Air Reservist 28:6 Oct '76

ILC (Instructional Learning Center): A success story. (Unique application of audio-visual techniques, personalized additional instruction and assistance and a practical field application, all in one package, to improve readiness of Reserve Component units in Army Readiness Region I) Col Edward P. Metzner. Fld Arty J 44:53-54 Jul-Aug '76

COMBAT SUPPORT OF THE ARMY

Achilles' heel. (ASL, Authorized Stockage List, immobility) Maj Walter A.Bawell. illus Army Log 8:17-19 Sep-Oct '76

Another mission for the CSC (Combat Support Company) commander. Capt William F.Greer. illus Armor 85:47-48 Nov-Dec '76

The dynamism of Army combat logistics. MajGen Erwin M.Graham, Jr. illus Mil Rev 56:65-75 Apr '76

FORSCOM engineers: The first 1,000 days. Col Alvin G.Rowe. illus tab Mil Engr 68:445-447 Nov-Dec '76

The Infantry-artillery team. illus Fld Arty J 44:54-58 Sep-Oct '76

A maintenance perspective. LtCols Clifford L.Wollard and Garry A.Scharberg. illus Army Log 8: 17-19 Nov-Dec '76

Supply base camouflage. Capt John M.Forbes, Jr. illus Army Log 8:20-22 May-Jun '76

Tooth-to-tail: A conceptual void. illus tab Army Log 8:33-37 Mar-Apr '76

COMBAT SURVEILLANCE see Surveillance

COMBINED FORCES
This term applies to the forces among two or more allied countries. For information on forces of one country only see Joint Forces.

See also
North American Air Defense Command

Coalition warfare. Robert W.Komer. illus Army 26: 28-32 Sep '76

COMBINED OPERATIONS
This term applies to operations among two or more allied countries. For operations of one country only see Joint Operations.

Airdrop tops (three-nation (Australia, New Zealand, U.S.) Exercise) Triad. AF Times 36:38 Mar 29 '76

(Exercise) Atlas Express runs its chilly course. AF Times 36:38 Mar 29 '76

"Interoperability"--the now challenge in Europe. Maj Gary F.Ramage. illus USA Avn Dig 22:26-29 Aug '76

Reforger 76: A MTMC first. illus Translog 7:2-4 Aug-Sep '76

SAREX 76: Canada versus U.S. illus AF Times 37:28 Nov 1 '76

COMMAND

See also
Leadership

ACE (Accelerated Co-pilot Enrichment) grooms co-pilots for commander slots. AF Times 37:36 Aug 9 '76

The art of command. Maj Roger F.Pemberton. Army Qtr 106:451-458 Oct '76

Battalion command. LtCol George C.Wallace. illus Army Log 8:26-29 Sep-Oct '76

Command at sea--the ultimate specialty. CAPT William J.Holland, Jr. illus US Nav Inst Proc 102: 18-23 Dec '76

Competence in method--the commander: A pedagogue and educator. LtGen L.Kuznetsov. Soviet Mil Rev No. 11:17-19 Nov '76

Decisions and disaster. Norman F.Dixon. illus RUSI J for Def Studies 121:50-53 Jun '76

Management and command--possible confusion today? LtGen John W.Roberts. TIG Brief 28:2 Jul 16 '76

Principles of command, guidelines of conduct: First report on ADM Hyland's endorsement to the Pueblo inquiry (1969). DeWitt James Griffin. Sea Power 19:31-36 Feb '76

The regulations and commander's initiative. MajGen A.Zyryanov. illus Soviet Mil Rev No. 2:26-27 Feb '76

Revitalizing a beaten unit. (Story of MajGen John Pope of the Union Army shows what not to do; Field Marshal Montgomery's command of British 8th Army in Africa, 1942, demonstrates what should be done) LtGen Phillip B.Davidson, Jr, Ret. illus Army 26:43-45 Jan '76

Unity of command and commander's responsibility. I.Garbuzov. Soviet Mil Rev No.4:14-15 Apr '76

What are you (squadron commanders and supervisors) doing for Green 16? LtCol Murphy Neal Jones. illus Aerosp Safety 32:2-4 Jun '76

COMMAND - Continued

Your opinion counts. Darryl D.McEwen. illus Soldiers 31:6-9 Dec '76

Study and Teaching

CATTS (Combined Arms Tactical Training Simulator)--a new approach to command training. R.E. Sansom and LtCol R.C.Dickson. illus Countermeasures 2:24+ Jun '76

COMMAND AND CONTROL SYSTEMS

See also

Air Force Satellite Communications System
Combat Control Centers
National Military Command System
Worldwide Military Command and Control System

ABCCC (AirBorne Command and Control Center): A capsule view of the men and machines of the 7th Airborne Command & Control Squadron. TSgt Fred C.McCaslin, Jr. illus Signal 31:26-29 Nov-Dec '76

AFSC's Electronic Systems Division (ESD). illus AF Mag 59:51-57 Jul '76 .

ALR-59 passive detection system (for the E-2C). illus Countermeasures 2:23-25 Apr '76

A better horse for Paul Revere: National command and control communications. Thomas C.Reed. illus Strat Rev 4:25-32 Summer '76

C^3 for tactical RPVs. Bruce W.Bell. tabs illus Countermeasures 2:24-27 May '76

C^3: How we got here--where are we? CDR Peter S. Roder. illus Signal 30:7-10 Jul '76

C^3 in century 21. James S.McLeod. illus tabs Signal 30:39-40 Jul '76

C^3 mobility in management of crisis. Donald J.Yockey. illus Signal 31:14-15+ Nov-Dec '76

C^3 software myopia. Editorial. Julian S.Lake. illus Countermeasures 2:8+ Dec '76

C^3 system engineering. CAPT George Heffernan. Signal 30:88-89 Aug '76

A command, control and communications overview. Donald H.Rumsfeld. illus Signal 30:34-35+ May-Jun '76

Counterfire! MajGen David E.Ott and Col Donald M. Rhea. illus Army 26:22-26 Jul '76

Data link improves air/ground command and control. Martin Amsler. illus tab Elect Warfare 8:111+ Sep-Oct '76

The E-4 airborne command post. W.L.Shockley. illus (Also cutaway) Countermeasures 2:34-36 Jul '76

Electronic warfare and smart weapons. Edgar E.Ulsamer. illus Aerosp Intl 12:18+ Jul-Aug '76

The evolving role of C^3 in crisis management. BrigGen Lawrence E.Adams. Signal 30:59-61 Aug '76

Fleet commanders: Afloat or ashore? VADM Ray Peet, Ret and Michael E.Melich. illus US Nav Inst Proc 102:25-33 Jun '76

The initial voice switched network: First step toward the NICS (NATO Integrated Communications System). Leo I.Barker, Jr and Jerry M.Dressner. illus Signal 30:6-12 Feb '76

COMMAND AND CONTROL SYSTEMS - Continued

The INtegrated TActical Communications System (INTACS) study. William M.Mannel. illus tabs Signal 30:19-27 Jul '76

Joint ops: An exercise in frustration. Capt J.T.Reynolds. illus Aerosp Safety 32:16-19 Oct '76

Jungle communications. illus AF Times 37:38 Oct 18 '76

Military/government perspectives on communications-electronics. illus Signal 30:17-19+ May-Jun '76

A modular surface ship bridge control system. Joseph G.Dimmick. illus US Nav Inst Proc 102:98-100 Sep '76

The NATO program for rationalization and standardization. Norman Gray. illus Signal 30:80-81+ May-Jun '76

NATO satellite communications: Past, present, future. LtGen Harold A.Kissinger. illus Signal 30: 53-57 Mar '76

The Naval Command and Control System (NCCS). CAPT Frank R.Fahland. illus Signal 30:79-83 Aug '76

Naval command, control and communications C^3 architecture. CAPT Frank M.Snyder. illus Signal 30:76-79 Aug '76

Navy C^3 in transition. (Panel discussion, AFCEA, Washington, June 9, 1976) CAPT Frank M.Snyder and others. illus Signal 30:74-89 Aug '76

A Navy satellite communications system. VADM Jon L.Boyes. Signal 30:5+ Mar '76

New automated command and control systems for the French Army. H.-J.Jung. illus Intl Def Rev 9: 453-457 Jun '76

New data handling technology in air defence. J.W. Sutherland. illus Intl Def Rev 9:616-618 Aug '76

The Spanish Territorial Command Network. Maj Tommy H.Berggren. illus Signal 31:31-34 Sep '76

The tactical command post dilemma: Bigger does not mean better. Maj Don R.Alexander. illus Army 26:18-23 Mar '76

Trends in Soviet military technology. Charles DeVore. tabs illus Signal 30:47-50 Jul '76

Troop control in combat. Col P.Simchenkov. Soviet Mil Rev No. 1:14-15+ Jan '76

WWMCCS in transition: A Navy view. VADM Jon L. Boyes. Signal 30:72-73 Aug '76

WWMCCS in transition: An Air Force view. BrigGen Van C.Doubleday. Signal 30:70-71 Aug '76

WWMCCS in transition: An Army view. MajGen Thomas M.Rienzi. Signal 30:67-70 Aug '76

What we get for our DOD telecommunications $. LtGen Lee M.Paschall. illus Signal 30:6-8 Jan '76

What's missing is the dialogue. (Interview with AFCEA's Tom Campobasso) illus Govt Exec 8: 45-46 Dec '76

History

Tannenburg: A lesson in command and control. LtCol Thomas G.Adcock. illus Signal 30:36-39 Apr '76

COMMAND AND CONTROL SYSTEMS – Continued

Study and Teaching

Communication in troop control. LtCol G. Kondakov. Soviet Mil Rev No.3:18-19 Mar '76

(E-3A simulator installed at Tinker AFB, Okla) Signal 31:102 Oct '76

COMMAND AND GENERAL STAFF COLLEGE

Curricula

Work-settings: A focus for the future Command and General Staff College. Maj James B. Channon. illus Mil Rev 56:74-87 May '76

COMMAND POSTS

See also
Advanced Airborne Command Post
National Emergency Airborne Command Post

The tactical command post dilemma: Bigger does not mean better. Maj Don R. Alexander. illus Army 26:18-23 Mar '76

COMMANDING OFFICERS

Admiral H. Kent Hewitt, U.S. Navy. John Clagett. illus Nav War Col Rev pt 1, Preparing for high command. 28:72-86 Summer '75; pt 2, High command. 28:60-86 Fall '75

Advice to commanders: Problems can lead to drugs. AF Times 37:4 Oct 11 '76

CATTS (Combined Arms Tactical Training Simulator)--a new approach to command training. R.E. Sansom and LtCol R.C. Dickson. illus Countermeasures 2:24+ Jun '76

Command at sea--the ultimate specialty. CAPT William J. Holland, Jr. illus US Nav Inst Proc 102: 18-23 Dec '76

Command influence and military justice. Capt C.H. Morrison, Jr. MarCor Gaz 60:37-43 Feb '76

Commander's independent actions. Col L. Yeremeyev. Soviet Mil Rev No.10:34-35 Oct '76

Distribution of AFOSI reports of investigation. TIG Brief 28:11 Aug 27 '76

Freedom of Information and Privacy Act releases regarding AFOSI investigations. TIG Brief 28:11 Aug 27 '76

Personnel quality force management. TIG Brief 28:10 Feb 13 '76

Taking care of our people. (Security police force) MajGen Thomas M. Sadler. TIG Brief 28:3 Apr 23 '76

12 nav(igator)s command flying units. AF Times 37:4 Aug 2 '76

The unit commander as a safety program director. LtCol Alan D. Miedrich. illus Interceptor 18:26-28 Jun '76

What AFOSI does for commanders. TIG Brief 28:9 Dec 3 '76

COMMANDOS

See also
Air Commandos

COMMANDS

See also specific commands by name, e.g.,
Strategic Air Command

COMMANDS – Continued

Directories

(Army) command and staff (1976 directory). pors Army 26:131-143 Oct '76

COMMENDATIONS see Awards, Decorations, etc

COMMERCE

Australia

The vulnerability of Australia's maritime trade. A.W. Grazebrook. illus tabs NATO's Fifteen Nations 20:40-45+ Dec '75-Jan '76

China (People's Republic)

Communist China and oil business. Niu Sien-chong. NATO's Fifteen Nations 21:90-91+ Apr-May '76

Rhodesia

The influence of transnational actors on the enforcement of sanctions against Rhodesia. Harry R. Strack. illus Nav War Col Rev 28:52-64 Spring '76

Russia

The new Soviet maritime strategy--and the lack of an effective U.S. counter-strategy. RADM George H. Miller, Ret. illus Sea Power 19:17-20 May '76

United States

Agricultural freedom and national strength. Earl L. Butz. Persp in Def Mgt No.24:13-18 Winter '75-'76

Are we running out of metals? Simon D. Strauss. Persp in Def Mgt No.24:19-31 Winter '75-'76

CBEMA (Computer and Business Equipment Manufacturers Assoc) and GSA (General Services Administration): A dialogue on how government hurts itself (because of its own procurement and contracting practices). C.W. Borklund. illus Govt Exec 8:24+ May '76

Cargo preference: Prescription for an ailing industry. Donald C. Leavens. illus tabs Sea Power 19: 26-30 Jun '76

FMS (Foreign Military Sales) is only one export control. (Interview with Maurice Mountain) Govt Exec 8:20-21 Dec '76

FMS (Foreign Military Sales): "No more giving it away." Interview. LtGen Howard Fish. illus tabs Govt Exec 8:19+ Dec '76

Military sales overseas. S. Stanley Katz. illus Natl Def 60:446-448 May-Jun '76

Statistics

Cargo preference: Prescription for an ailing industry. Donald C. Leavens. illus tabs Sea Power 19: 26-30 Jun '76

COMMISSARIES

Air Force--U.S.

Air Force Commissary Service. TIG Brief 28:14 Feb 27 '76

(Air Force Commissary Service) Interview. MajGen Daniel L. Burkett. illus Review 56:15-16 Jul-Aug '76

Air Force commissary system (Air Force Commissary Service) begins to take shape under (MajGen Daniel L.) Burkett. Review 55:23 Mar-Apr '76

128

COMMISSARIES - Continued

Air Force--U.S. - Cont'd

BXs, comstores: Credit cards (and) centralized control. Interviews. LtGen Charles E. Buckingham and MajGen Daniel L. Burkett. illus AF Times 37:19+ Nov 8 '76

Comstores centralized under agency (Air Force Commissary Service). Ron Sanders. AF Times 36:3 Jan 19 '76

4 colonels to head comstore offices. AF Times 36:8 Jun 7 '76

(Gen Daniel) Burkett on AFCOMS (Air Force COMmissarieS). illus Review 56:39-40+ Sep-Oct '76

(JSC Chairman Gen George S.) Brown criticizes Times newspapers (in testimony before House Armed Services Committee). AF Times 36:3 Feb 9 '76

(Major) General (Daniel L.) Burkett heads new (Air Force) Commissary Service. AF Times 36:3 Feb 23 '76

Poor quality (meat) forced on comstores. Andy Plattner. AF Times 36:25+ May 3 '76

Shoddy meat tactics revealed. AF Times 36:12 Feb 9 '76

Stores 'here to stay,' AFCOMS chief says. Interview. MajGen Daniel L. Burkett. AF Times 37:2 Sep 6 '76

A talk with the commander of AFCOMS. Interview. MajGen Daniel L. Burkett. illus AF Engrg & Svcs Qtr 17:14-17 Nov '76

Organization

Centralized commissary concept (Air Force COMmissary Service (AFCOMS)). CMSgt Donald M. Leach. illus chart map AF Engrg & Svcs Qtr 17: 2-5 May '76

Armed Forces--U.S.

AAFES, comstore merger would mean higher prices. Andy Plattner. AF Times 36:3 Feb 16 '76

Accord reached on (com) store closing. Ron Sanders. AF Times 37:20 Nov 22 '76

CHAMPUS, store curbs fought, draft fight lost on Capitol Hill. Officer 52:5 Apr '76

A commentary on the European resale system. Wayne E. Dorsett. illus Review 56:19-20 Jul-Aug '76

Commissaries in Europe got bad meat, DOD says. Andy Plattner. AF Times 37:4 Oct 4 '76

Commissaries OK for now. AF Times 36:3 Jul 5 '76

Commissary store operations appropriated fund support. Table only. Review 55:16 Jan-Feb '76

DOD paper explains plan on commissaries. AF Times 36:48 Feb 9 '76

DOD pushes store closings. AF Times 36:4 Mar 15 '76

DOD to appeal 'bag-boy' minimum (wages). AF Times 37:4 Dec 6 '76

Defense again asks increase in commissary store prices. Officer 52:10 Mar '76

Direct Commissary Support System. RADM John C. Shepard. Review 56:41 Jul-Aug '76

COMMISSARIES - Continued

Armed Forces--U.S. - Cont'd

HASC (House Armed Services Committee) comstore hearings. H.R. Kaplan. illus Review 56:42-44 Jul-Aug '76

Hot line suggested for beefs on food. Andy Plattner. AF Times 37:2 Aug 2 '76

House panel (Armed Services Committee) again supports stores. AF Times 36:2 Mar 29 '76

Improving the commissary system. (Address, ALA Eastern Regional Seminar, Fort Lee, Va, April 1976) William M. Powell. illus Review 56:46-48+ Jul-Aug '76

A look at the budget: What's ahead for ALA members. Tony Upton. tab Review 55:16-18 Jan-Feb '76

Move to erase store $$ wins (by) 45-44 Senate vote. Phil Stevens. AF Times 37:2 Aug 16 '76

Move to pay bag boys could hike store costs. Randy Shoemaker. AF Times 37:2 Nov 15 '76

New regs in effect for kin of retirees (in Korea). AF Times 36:20 May 10 '76

Panel (House Armed Services Investigations) warned subsidy cut could kill commissaries. AF Times 36:12 Jun 21 '76

Partial store closing OK'd--3-year fund phaseout. Phil Stevens. AF Times 36:3 Jan 5 '76

Pay boost advocate supports stores' end. (Interview with Sen John Culver) AF Times 36:18 Jan 12 '76

(Pres) Ford nixes junior EM aid; phaseout of store subsidies asked. Randy Shoemaker. AF Times 37:3 Dec 27 '76

(Pres) Ford signs DOD (FY 1977 Defense Authorization) Bill; stores question open. AF Times 36:8 Jul 26 '76

(Pres) Ford signs $104 billion defense bill. AF Times 37:9 Oct 4 '76

Prospects darken for commissaries. Officer 52:4+ Aug '76

(Rep Bill) Nichols advises saving on stores: An interview. AF Times 36:8 Feb 16 '76

Retiree store limit studied. Phil Stevens. AF Times 37:28 Aug 9 '76

"Returnables" required by EPA would cost too much--DOD. Review 55:21-24 Nov-Dec '75

Senate curbs commissaries in passing money bill--many other Congress actions. Officer 52:4+ Sep '76

Senate OKs money bill, comstore fund fight set. tab AF Times 37:6 Aug 23 '76

Senate unit (Appropriations Committee) okays full stores funding. Phil Stevens. AF Times 37:4 Aug 2 '76

Senate votes 5-year stageout of commissary staff subsidy. Officer 52:8 Jan '76

Shift on stores seems certain. AF Times 36:19 Jan 5 '76

Store subsidies scored by (Pres) Ford. AF Times 36:2 Feb 2 '76

Stores, BX funds okayed. Phil Stevens. AF Times 37:3 Sep 13 '76

COMMISSARIES - Continued

Armed Forces--U.S. - Cont'd

2 on Hill (Sens John Culver and Henry Bellmon) attack comstore funds. AF Times 37:2 Aug 9 '76

What senators said about (com)stores. AF Times 37:8+ Aug 23 '76

Army--U.S.

The 'mess sergeant' goes shopping. Capt John M. Campbell. illus Army Log 8:24-27 Jul-Aug '76

Plastic police (ration control card). Sgt1C Floyd Harrington. illus tab Soldiers 31:37-40 Nov '76

Navy--U.S.

Beef falsely graded, suit says. AF Times 37:10 Dec 13 '76

Statistics

Market data report: Navy commissary stores sales for Fiscal Year 1976. Tables only. Review 56:77-80 Sep-Oct '76

Market data report: Navy commissary stores sales for second quarter Fiscal Year 1976. Tables only. Review 55:57-60 Jan-Feb '76

COMMISSIONS, MILITARY

(AF) officer accessions up from last year. AF Times 37:6 Nov 8 '76

DOD seeks extra commissioning outlet. AF Times 36:28 Jun 21 '76

846 named for Regular AF--875 offered Career Reserve. AF Times 37:23+ Oct 11 '76

Health officers named RegAF. Lee Ewing. AF Times 37:22 Nov 1 '76

Nonrated officers get Reg(ular) AF break. AF Times 36:4 Jul 26 '76

Statistics

871 (Reserve) officers named Regular (by) last 3-year board. AF Times 36:14 Jun 14 '76

COMMON MARKET see European Economic Community

COMMUNICATIONS (GENERAL)

Are you communicating? TIG Brief 28:18 Apr 9 '76

The art of listening. illus MAC Flyer 23:3-5 Oct '76

Ask for it clearly. (Multiservice acquisition) LtCol Donald M.Keith and Charles A.McCarthy. illus Army Log 8:14-16 Jul-Aug '76

Attention to health/safety matters. TIG Brief 28:5-6 Feb 27 '76

Back to basics II: The ability to communicate. (Address, National Council of Teachers of English, Philadelphia, March 25, 1976) Charles R.Cyr. (Reprinted from Vital Speeches, Sep 15, 1976) Educ J 19:29-33 Winter '76

Communication: The key element to prisoner of war survival. LtCol Bobby D.Wagnon. illus tab AU Rev 27:33-46 May-Jun '76

Communications: A necessity for sound DCAS/contractor relationship. E.V.Francis. Review 55:31+ Mar-Apr '76

Conflict in organizations: Good or bad? LtCol Russell Pierre, Jr and Maj Jerome G.Peppers, Jr, Ret. AU Rev 28:69-79 Nov-Dec '76

COMMUNICATIONS (GENERAL) - Continued

In defense of language standards. Argus J.Tresidder. MarCor Gaz 60:51-56 Apr '76

"Interoperability"--the now challenge in Europe. Maj Gary F.Ramage. illus USA Avn Dig 22:26-29 Aug '76

KIA: The English language; or, the only thing we have to fear is obfuscation itself. W.J.Farquharson. illus tab AF Times, Times Magazine sup: 26-27 Feb 9 '76

Management and communication: MBO/R (Management By Objectives/Results). TIG Brief 28:15 Sep 10 '76

Management by objectives. TIG Brief 28:4 Nov 19 '76

Military talk. Maj Bill Wallisch. illus AU Rev 27:56-60 Mar-Apr '76

The team: Operations and maintenance. Majs James D.Stetson, III and Warren D.Johnson. illus Navigator 23:29-30 Winter '76

Teams get out and talk to troops in keeping with (Gen David C.) Jones' policy. Lee Ewing. AF Times 36:12+ May 3 '76

Tickets to good communication. Argus J.Tresidder. illus MarCor Gaz pt 1, The fourteen commandments. 60:56-58 Nov '76; pt 2, Organizing ideas. 60:49-53 Dec '76

Vendor communication. TIG Brief 28:9 Sep 24 '76

What communications gap? Marv Davis. Translog 7:3 Nov '76

What do you hear? Capt Jerry E.Walker. Aerosp Safety 32:5 Aug '76

Women's language: A new bend in the double bind. 2dLt Katie Cutler. illus AU Rev 27:73-79 Jul-Aug '76

History

Two hundred years of communications. Edward A. Havens. illus Signal 31:33-35 Nov-Dec '76

COMMUNICATIONS, MILITARY

See also
Liaison
Radio Communications

AFCS and AF resource management. BrigGen Rupert H.Burris. illus AF Compt 10: back cover Jan '76

Air defense in Reforger. LtCol Joseph J.Heinlein, Jr. illus Air Def Mag, pp 16-21, Apr-Jun '76

A better horse for Paul Revere: National command and control communications. Thomas C.Reed. illus Strat Rev 4:25-32 Summer '76

C-E/ATC (Communications-Electronics/Air Traffic Control) service from a user's point of view. TIG Brief 28:8 Aug 13 '76

Communications-electronics digest, monthly review of developments. Regular feature in issues of Signal

Communications in a tactical airborne force. Col S.Vasilyev. map Soviet Mil Rev No.4:26-28 Apr '76

The evolving role of C^3 in crisis management. BrigGen Lawrence E.Adams. Signal 30:59-61 Aug '76

COMMUNICATIONS SYSTEMS, MILITARY - Continued

United States - Cont'd

They get the message. (Technical controllers keep communications equipment operating at the technical control facility, Andrews AFB, Md) Maj Michael F.Weber and Capt Stephen O.Manning. illus Airman 20:21-23 Dec '76

COMMUNISM

Catalyst of historical progress. Y.Tarabrin. Soviet Mil Rev No.10:2-4 Oct '76

Dangerous doctrine. G.Apalin. Soviet Mil Rev No.1: 44-45 Jan '76

Detente: Soviet policy and purpose. John Erickson. Strat Rev 4:37-43 Spring '76

Ideology and war. Capt A.Skrylnik. Soviet Mil Rev No.7:14-16 Jul '76

Africa

New horizons. Vasily Yefremov. Soviet Mil Rev No.10:46-47 Oct '76

Asia

Trouble in the Far East: Quemoy still waging war of words; the domino theory--alive and well. Fred Reed. AF Times 36:10-11 Mar 1 '76

Asia, Southeastern

A reconsideration of the domino theory. John Baylis. Royal Air Forces Qtr 15:277-287 Winter '75

The USSR-DRV-PRC triangle in Southeast Asia. Donald E.Weatherbee. illus Parameters 6, No.1: 71-86 '76

Cambodia

Political change in wartime: The Khmer Krahom revolution in southern Cambodia, 1970-1974. Kenneth M.Quinn. illus maps charts Nav War Col Rev 28: 3-31 Spring '76

China (People's Republic)

Mao Tse-tung and original sin. Richard Clutterbuck. Army Qtr 106:142-148 Apr '76

The politics of the Chinese People's Republic Navy. LT David G.Muller, Jr. illus Nav War Col Rev 28:32-51 Spring '76

Republican China. Jerry Kamstra. illus Countermeasures pt 1, The death of a dynasty. 2:24-26+ Jul '76; pt 2, Birth of modern China. 2:22-23 Aug '76

Cuba

Guarding the gains of socialism. (20th anniversary of the Revolutionary Armed Forces of Cuba) Maj I. Garbuzov. illus Soviet Mil Rev No.12:43-45 Dec '76

Germany (Democratic Republic)

The effect of detente on professionalism and political control in the East German Army. Dale R.Herspring. illus Nav War Col Rev 28:10-20 Winter '76

Indonesia

Gestapu--ten years after. Capt L.K.Burgess. illus Nav War Col Rev 28:65-75 Winter '76

Russia

Clausewitz and Soviet politico-military strategy. BrigGen Antonio Pelliccia. NATO's Fifteen Nations 20:18-21+ Dec '75-Jan '76; Digest.) Mil Rev 56:23-33 Aug '76

COMMUNISM - Continued

Russia - Cont'd

Democracy in action. (25th Congress of the CPSU and the development of the political system of Soviet society) Y.Todorsky. Soviet Mil Rev No.8:2-5 Aug '76

For the sake of peace and socialism. (The 25th CPSU Congress, Feb 24-March 5, 1976) Soviet Mil Rev No.4:2-5 Apr '76

The Peace Programme (adopted by the 25th CPSU Congress, Feb 1976), a contribution to the weal of mankind. Y.Tarabrin. illus Soviet Mil Rev No.3: 7-10 Mar '76

Political controls within the structure of the Soviet Armed Forces--some problems? Pilot Officer R.G.Smith. Royal Air Forces Qtr 16:45-49 Spring '76

A revolution must be able to defend itself. (Nov 7, 1976, 59th anniversary of the Great October Socialist Revolution) Col V.Zubarev. Soviet Mil Rev No.11:2-4 Nov '76

Vanguard of the Soviet people. (Communist Party) Col V.Soldatov. Soviet Mil Rev No.1:2-5 Jan '76

With the Party, with the people. Col A.Korkeshkin. Soviet Mil Rev No.2:4-6 Feb '76

Woman and socialism (in the USSR). LtCol Marina Popovich. illus Soviet Mil Rev No.3:43-46 Mar '76

History

Bolshevik ideas on the military's role in modernization. William E.Odom. Armed Forces & Soc 3: 103-120 Fall '76

The vital power of socialism. Col A.Pozmogov. illus Soviet Mil Rev No.4:8-10 Apr '76

COMMUNITY COLLEGE OF THE AIR FORCE

CCAF (Community College of the Air Force). illus Air Reservist 28:12 Apr '76

CCAF (Community College of the Air Force) on road to awarding degrees. Len Famiglietti. AF Times 36:2 Jul 26 '76

CCAF may change to all-Service. Len Famiglietti. AF Times 36:8 Jul 19 '76

(Civilian) educators urge CCAF degrees. AF Times 37:2 Dec 13 '76

Community College of the Air Force registrations: Getting the word out! TIG Brief 28:3 Nov 19 '76

Decision on CCAF granting degrees. Len Famiglietti. AF Times 37:4 Dec 27 '76

Educators to review CCAF (Community College of the AF) plan (for anticipated awarding of associate degrees). AF Times 37:22 Aug 23 '76

Job training could earn CCAF (Community College of the AF) credit. AF Times 36:7 Jun 14 '76

COMMUNITY RELATIONS
Here is entered material on the relations between a base and its neighboring community.

Base access and the first amendment: The rights of civilians on military installations. Maj Alan C. Stine. AF Law Rev 18:18-32 Fall '76

Base tours: Public communication. TIG Brief 28:16 Oct 22 '76

COMMUNITY RELATIONS - Continued

COMPRESSORS

COMPTROLLER GENERAL OF THE UNITED STATES see General Accounting Office

COMPTROLLERS

COMPTROLLERS - Continued

Directories

Education and Training

COMPTROLLERS - Continued

Education and Training - Cont'd

Professional Military Comptroller Course (at Air University, Maxwell AFB, Ala). Col Hugh S.Austin. illus AF Compt 10:20-21 Oct '76

Professional Military Comptroller Course (at Institute for Professional Development, Air University, Maxwell AFB, Ala). Col Hugh S.Austin. illus AF Compt 10:22-23 Apr '76

Professional Military Comptroller Course (at Institute for Professional Development, Air University, Maxwell AFB, Ala). Maj Jackson E.Rendleman. tabs illus AF Compt 10:30-32 Jan '76

3780 Technical Training Group, USAF School of Applied Aerospace Sciences. Col John A.Humphries, Jr. illus chart AF Compt 10:22-23 Oct '76

Statistics

The Air Force comptroller family: Personnel authorized Air Force-wide. Tables only. AF Compt 10: 46-47 Jan '76

The Air Force comptroller family: Personnel authorized Air Force-wide. Tables only. AF Compt 10: 28-29 Oct '76

COMPUTERS

Computers alive? Hoyt W.Huggins. illus AU Rev 27: 24-32 May-Jun '76

Aeronautical Applications

Air traffic control automation (in Italy, Sweden, Netherlands). Dan Boyle. illus Interavia 31:155-159 Feb '76

Latest FAA innovations (Radar Beacon Code System, Conflict Alert System) for safety, convenience. illus MAC Flyer 23:22-23 Apr '76

Astronautical Applications
See Computers--Space Flight Applications

Business Applications

The Automated Clearing House (ACH)--a new delivery system. James H.Jarrell. illus Armed Forces Compt 21:4-5 Apr '76

Bar coding. Beverly B.Joyce. illus Army Log 8:2-5 Jul-Aug '76

EFTS (Electronic Funds Transfer System)--alive and well at the USAF Accounting & Finance Center. Thomas D.Kronoveter. illus Armed Forces Compt 21:6-7 Apr '76

Electronic Funds Transfer System (EFTS). Tom D. Kronoveter. illus AF Compt 10:6-7 Jul '76

Electronic Funds Transfer Systems (EFTS). illus Armed Forces Compt 21:28-29 Jan '76

Recurring Federal payments and EFTS (Electronic Funds Transfer System) at the U.S. Treasury. Les W.Plumly. illus Armed Forces Compt 21: 2-3 Apr '76

Selecting a project management technique. Maj Robert P.Klaver. illus tabs Def Mgt J 12:53-60 Apr '76

Communication Applications

C^3 in century 21. James S.McLeod. illus tabs Signal 30:39-40 Jul '76

CONUS weather service communications upgrade. TIG Brief 28:10 Sep 24 '76

COMPUTERS - Continued

Communication Applications - Cont'd

Data processing + data communications = telecomputing: Equation for maximum productivity. Glenn E.Penisten. illus Signal 30:34-37 Jan '76

A milestone in the development of data management systems for WWMCCS. Frank R.Dirnbauer and others. illus Signal 30:34-37 Jul '76

Reprogrammable simulators respond quickly to EW/SIGINT changes. Terry E.Bibbens. illus tabs Elect Warfare 8:65-68+ Nov-Dec '76

Technical telecommunications forces and trends that have affected and are affecting the confluence of automatic data processing and telecommunications. Thomas Yium and others. illus tabs Signal 30:28-35 Feb '76

Technology: Its impact on the 1980s. Joseph A.Boyd. illus tabs Signal 30:50-54 May-Jun '76

A time for transition for naval communications. CAPT Milton J.Schultz, Jr. illus map Signal 30: 84-87 Aug '76

WWMCCS ADP: A promise fulfilled. Herbert B. Goertzel and Col James R.Miller. illus Signal 30:57-63 May-Jun '76

What we get for our DOD telecommunications $. LtGen Lee M.Paschall. illus Signal 30:6-8 Jan '76

Winds of change in communications and computers. Theodore D.Puckorius. illus Signal 31:18-22 Sep '76

Educational Applications

Computer Assisted Instruction (CAI): How "Herbie" can help students and government. illus Govt Exec 8:40-41 Feb '76

How about a modern safety program? LCDR Russ Harrison. illus Approach 22:24-25 Nov '76

Instructional technology in the Department of Defense, now and in the future. M.Richard Rose. illus tab AU Rev 27:11-23 May-Jun '76

Engineering Applications

Base Engineer Automated Management System (BEAMS). TIG Brief 28:10 Dec 17 '76

Computers cut energy costs in buildings. Phil Deakin. illus tab Govt Exec 8:33+ May '76

Programming sense into resource constraints. John E.Burke and Capt Hugh A.Shaffer. illus tabs Mil Engr 68:460-461 Nov-Dec '76

Errors

Vendor communication. TIG Brief 28:9 Sep 24 '76

Government Applications

Computer crimes uncovered (by General Accounting Office). Jim Parker. AF Times 36:20 May 31 '76

Congress & budgets: The computer takes hold. illus Govt Exec 8:60-61 May '76

EFTS (Electronic Funds Transfer System)--alive and well at the USAF Accounting & Finance Center. Thomas D.Kronoveter. illus Armed Forces Compt 21:6-7 Apr '76

Electronic Funds Transfer System (EFTS). Tom D. Kronoveter. illus AF Compt 10:6-7 Jul '76

COMPUTERS - Continued

Government Applications - Cont'd

Logistics management in municipalities. (Burbank, Calif) Robert N. Carlton. illus chart Log Spectrum 10:22-25+ Summer '76

NCO is key figure in (AF) software library. illus AF Times 36:28 May 10 '76

New milestones in geodesy. (National Geodetic Survey) RADM Allen L. Powell. illus map Mil Engr 68:22-24 Jan-Feb '76

Now, a way to get at those grants and loans. (Federal Domestic Assistance Program Retrieval Systems) Spencer B. Child. illus Govt Exec 8:26+ Mar '76

A positive look at the Federal computer mess. Ernest C. Baynard. Govt Exec 8:28+ Sep '76

Recurring Federal payments and EFTS (Electronic Funds Transfer System) at the U.S. Treasury. Les W. Plumly. illus Armed Forces Compt 21: 2-3 Apr '76

Small cities (like Redondo Beach, Calif) & computers: It can be done. illus Govt Exec 8:55-56+ Dec '76

Systems approach to administrative support (in Transportation Dept's Office of Contracts and Procurement). Govt Exec 8:54+ Sep '76

Costs

Government can cut DP (Data Processing) costs in half. (Interview with Computer Sciences Corp's Vincent R. Grillo, Jr) illus tab Govt Exec 8:52+ Nov '76

Why not buy ADP (Automatic Data Processing) solutions, instead of problems. Vincent R. Grillo, Jr. illus Govt Exec 8:56-58 Nov '76

Law Enforcement Applications

The Air Force law enforcement terminal system. TIG Brief 28:15 Apr 9 '76

Small cities (like Redondo Beach, Calif) & computers: It can be done. illus Govt Exec 8:55-56+ Dec '76

The vital role of the computer in controlling crime. Clarence M. Kelley. illus Signal 30:12-15 Apr '76

Laws and Regulations

A positive look at the Federal computer mess. Ernest C. Baynard. Govt Exec 8:28+ Sep '76

Medical Applications

Algorithm for analyses of saccadic eye movements using a digital computer. Robert W. Baloh and others. illus tabs Aviation, Space & Envmt Med 47:523-527 May '76

Computerized (military) med setup to link Services by '82. AF Times 37:8 Aug 30 '76

Military Applications

AIREP's--how they work for you. illus MAC Flyer 23:10-12 Apr '76

The Administrative Center: Air Force makes it (word processing) work! John F. Judge. illus Govt Exec 8:39+ Sep '76

Advances in automatic testing. O. T. Carver. illus Countermeasures 2:39-41+ Jun '76

COMPUTERS - Continued

Military Applications - Cont'd

Advances in semiconductor memories. illus Countermeasures 2:32-33 Jun '76

Bar coding. Beverly B. Joyce. illus Army Log 8:2-5 Jul-Aug '76

CATTS (Combined Arms Tactical Training Simulator)--a new approach to command training. R. E. Sansom and LtCol R. C. Dickson. illus Countermeasures 2:24+ Jun '76

Computer Assisted Instruction (CAI): How "Herbie" can help students and government. illus Govt Exec 8:40-41 Feb '76

DAIS (Digital Avionics Information System) computers developed. illus Countermeasures 2:54 Jul '76

Electronics: Key military 'force multiplier.' Malcolm R. Currie. illus AF Mag 59:39-45 Jul '76

Exploitation of computers. TIG Brief 28:13-14 Feb 27 '76

Federal cataloging in the seventies. H. Melvin Silver. illus Log Spectrum 10:9-10 Spring '76

Hanscom (AFB, Mass) weather system to use microcomputers. AF Times 37:25 Aug 9 '76

Improving the man-machine interface. Bill Walsh. illus Countermeasures 2:53-55 Jun '76

Keeping up with ADP (Automatic Data Processing). SqLdr R. B. Lloyd. Royal Air Forces Qtr 16:165-169 Summer '76

Liquid crystals: The daylight survivable display. Glen F. Ingle. illus tabs Elect Warfare 8:55-56+ Sep-Oct '76

MCF: A Military Computer Family for computer-based systems. LtCol Alan B. Salisbury. illus Signal 30:42-45 Jul '76

Microprocessors in military systems. Rob Walker. illus Countermeasures 2:28-32 May '76

Naval weapon system automation with the WSA4. J. R. Harper. illus Intl Def Rev 9:795-797 Oct '76

New concept in data system development. Nancy Ito. illus AF Compt 10:40-41 Jul '76

New data handling technology in air defence. J. W. Sutherland. illus Intl Def Rev 9:616-618 Aug '76

Performance Analysis and Technical Evaluation (PATE) and Nuclear Safety Cross-Check Analysis (NSCCA). TIG Brief 28:8 Aug 27 '76

SAM-D tactical operations simulator. Capt James L. Hubbard. illus Air Def Mag, pp 26-29, Jan-Mar '76

Shaping tomorrow's soldier. (Field training exercises) SP5 Ed Aber. illus Soldiers 31:19-20 Jun '76

Strategic pulse: Electronic warfare in the current strategic environment. David Harvey. illus Def & For Aff Dig No. 5:4-5+ '76

System Capability-Over-Requirement Evaluation (SCORE). MajGen Richard L. Harris. illus tabs Def Mgt J 12:46-52 Apr '76

The USAF Academy B-6700 management decision. LtCol Jerry B. Smith. illus tabs AF Compt 10:44-47 Jul '76

COMPUTERS - Continued

Military Applications - Cont'd

(USAF) switch to computer logistics. AF Times 36:41 Jan 5 '76

Personnel Applications

AF to purify stored data on ethnics. AF Times 36:9 Apr 19 '76

IG complaint data collection system. TIG Brief 28: 5-6 Jul 2 '76

Security Measures

Computer crimes uncovered (by General Accounting Office). Jim Parker. AF Times 36:20 May 31 '76

Space Flight Applications

Satellite computer developments. Countermeasures 2:23 Dec '75-Jan '76

Study and Teaching

DOD Computer Institute. TIG Brief 28:16 May 21 '76

Traffic Control Applications

Latest FAA innovations (Radar Beacon Code System, Conflict Alert System) for safety, convenience. illus MAC Flyer 23:22-23 Apr '76

Transportation Applications

The computer: The computer: The comp; triumph or terror for transportation manager. Col Alan D. Wheeler. illus Def Trans J 32:12-18+ Feb '76

Standard port system. LtCol Arthur G. Neil, Jr. illus Army Log 8:30-32 May-Jun '76

CONDUCT, MILITARY

See also
Americans in Foreign Countries
Standards of Conduct

"I am the two-headed ogre." RADM Bruce Keener III. illus US Nav Inst Proc 102:38-45 Apr '76

Military ethics in a changing world. MajGen Robert N. Ginsburgh, Ret. illus AU Rev 27:2-10 Jan-Feb '76

Soviet military ethics. Maj A. Grishin. Soviet Mil Rev No. 12:34-35 Dec '76

Unfitness: New name but aim is the same. AF Times 37:8 Aug 30 '76

CONFEDERATE AIR FORCE

Rebels over the Rockies. Capt David V. Froehlich. illus Interceptor 18:16-19 Aug '76

Rebels with a cause. (Confederate Air Force is dedicated to finding, restoring, preserving and flying World War II airplanes) LtCol Fred A. Meurer. illus Airman 20:24-31 Feb '76

CONFERENCES, COMMUNICATION

(AFCEA's 30th Annual Convention Program, Washington, June 8-10, 1976) illus Signal 30:10-15 May-Jun '76

(30th Annual AFCEA Convention Report, Washington, June 8-10, 1976) illus Signal 30: entire issue Aug '76

U.S. preparation for the World Administrative Radio Conference 1979. Jack E. Weatherford. illus charts Signal 30:17-19 Apr '76

CONFERENCES, MEDICAL

Minutes of 1976 Business Meeting, Aerospace Medical Association (Bal Harbour, Fla, May 11, 1976). illus Aviation, Space & Envmt Med 47:1130-1134 Oct '76

23d International Congress of Aviation and Space Medicine, Acapulco, Mexico (Sep 29-Oct 2, 1975); 5th Soviet Congress on Aerospace Medicine, Kaluga, USSR (Oct 21-25, 1975)--informal report. J. Harold Brown. illus Aviation, Space & Envmt Med 47: 103-105 Jan '76

CONFERENCES, MILITARY

(AFA Convention, Washington, Sep 19-21, 1976: 30th anniversary highlights) illus Air Reservist 28: 16-17 Nov '76

AFA's Statement of Policy for 1976-77 (and 2 policy papers adopted at the 30th National Convention, Washington, Sep 20, 1976). AF Mag 59:26-33 Nov '76

AFA's Thirtieth Anniversary Convention (Washington, Sep 19-23, 1976). Don Steele. illus AF Mag 59:56-63 Nov '76

AFA's 30th Anniversary Convention (Washington, Sep 19-23, 1976): A window on USAF's new challenges. Edgar Ulsamer. illus AF Mag 59:22-25 Nov '76

Adjutants General Association Conference (Williamsburg, Va, April 1976). Natl Guardsman 30:34-36 Jun '76

The challenge of safety. (Report on 1975 SAC Safety Seminar, Carswell AFB, Tex) Maj Richard W. Blatter. illus Combat Crew 26:8-11 Jan '76

500 Daedalians meet founders at convention (Pensacola, Fla, May 1976). illus AF Times 36:21 Jun 14 '76

(In series of management conferences Army Guard commanders told to) bite the bullet. Bruce P. Hargreaves. illus Natl Guardsman 30:22-25 May '76

(Military) 'Bill of Rights' backed to protect benefits; (Gen David C.) Jones warns on Soviets (at Air Force Assoc National Convention, Washington, Sep 19-22, 1976). Lee Ewing. illus AF Times 37:21 Oct 4 '76

(NGAUS) 97th General Conference resolutions: Where matters stand. Natl Guardsman 30:28-34 Jul '76

The (NGAUS) 98th General Conference (Washington, Aug 30-Sep 1, 1976). illus Natl Guardsman 30: 10-16+ Oct '76

Navy League Convention, Boston, May 18-21, 1976. illus Sea Power 19:22-34 Jul '76

The 1976 Air Commanders Conference. Bruce P. Hargreaves. illus Natl Guardsman 30:44-48 Mar '76

(ROA 50th National Convention, Bal Harbour, Fla, June 29-July 2, 1976) illus Officer 9: entire issue Sep '76

ROA lists wants at (50th Annual) Convention (Bal Harbour, Fla, June 29-July 2, 1976). Don Hirst. AF Times 36:10 Jul 26 '76

ROA scores DOPMA, up-or-out, age bias (at 50th Annual Convention, Bal Harbour, Fla, June 29-July 2, 1976). Don Hirst. AF Times 36:16 Jul 19 '76

(Report on NGAUS 98th General Conference, Washington, Aug 30-Sep 1, 1976) illus Air Reservist 28:8-9+ Oct '76

CONFERENCES, MILITARY - Continued

(Reports of (ROA) Bicentennial Mid-Winter Conference, Washington, Feb 19-20, 1976) illus Officer
52:13-14+ Apr '76

6,000 attend AUSA event: World power balance gets
major attention at '76 Annual Meeting (Washington,
Oct 11-13, 1976) illus Army 26:36-38+ Nov '76

TROA views benefits issue; (Gen George S.) Brown
decries 'contract attitude' (at TROA 23d Biennial
Convention, Philadelphia, Sep 14-17, 1976). Bruce
Callander. AF Times 37:25 Oct 4 '76

CONFLICT OF INTERESTS

Conflict of interest: Proxmire alleges 10 broke laws.
AF Times 36:32 Apr 19 '76

DOD clarifies 'conflict' (of interest) policy. Randy
Shoemaker. AF Times 36:19 Feb 16 '76

Reports of Defense related employment. TIG Brief
28:15 Feb 13 '76

600 retired officers reported holding jobs with DOD
contractors. AF Times 36:40 Feb 2 '76

2 (top-level Pentagon officials) scored for 'conflict'
(of interest impropriety). AF Times 36:6
Mar 29 '76

Who speaks for the people? Editorial. John T. Hayward. Govt Exec 8:11-12 Jun '76

CONGRESS--U.S.

See also
Laws and Legislation

(AF) personnel program best in Pentagon, (SecAF)
Reed says (in news conference). AF Times 36:3
Mar 8 '76

(Air, Army) Guard, agencies (NASA and CIA) ask
malpractice protection. Ann Gerow. AF Times
36:26 Mar 15 '76

Airpower in the news. Regular feature in issues of
Air Force Magazine

Alcohol abuse efforts pushed (by House Appropriations Committee). AF Times 36:4 Jun 21 '76

Another (Naval) Reserve study! (But this one, ordered by the Senate Armed Services Committee,
promises much) Officer 52:19+ Aug '76

Assignments change makeup of military affairs committees. Army 26:12 Apr '76

The attempt to kill the B-1. LtGen Ira C. Eaker, Ret.
AF Times 36:13+ Jun 21 '76

Backing the President. Phil Stevens. AF Times 37:14
Oct 18 '76

Big new tax law opens IRAs (Individual Retirement
Accounts) to Reservists but curbs disability tax
breaks. Officer 52:17 Nov '76

Bill to ban (military) unions introduced in House. AF
Times 36:3 Mar 29 '76

Bill would ban unionization (of the Armed Services).
AF Times 36:4 Mar 15 '76

Bill would ensure legal aid. AF Times 36:4 Jun 7 '76

Bill would thaw top pay--boost to civilian workers.
AF Times 36:16 Mar 8 '76

CNO (ADM James L. Holloway III) stresses Reserve
importance to 'Hill' staffs. illus Officer 52:22-23
Jul '76

CONGRESS--U.S.- Continued

Cheating at West Point stirs up squalls on Hill. AF
Times 37:12 Sep 20 '76

Commissaries OK for now. AF Times 36:3 Jul 5 '76

Comparing pay, examining benefits--fringes under
fire in House harangue. tab AF Times 36:16
Mar 8 '76

Congress & budgets: The computer takes hold. illus
Govt Exec 8:60-61 May '76

The Congress and intelligence. Lawrence Griswold.
Sea Power 19:31-34 Jun '76

Congress and the political guidance of weapons procurement. Jonathan E. Medalia. illus Nav War Col
Rev 28:12-31 Fall '75

Congress approves four major veterans bills. Officer
52:16 Nov '76

Congress okays B-1 go-ahead. AF Times 36:3
Jul 12 '76

Congress seen almost certain to end 1% add-on to
retired COL raises. tab Officer 52:26 Aug '76

Congress should stay out of tactical military decisions. Interview. Barry M. Goldwater. Armed
Forces J Intl 113:25 Mar '76

Congress split on money bill. Phil Stevens. AF
Times 36:2 Jun 7 '76

Congress: Too much time off? Phil Stevens. AF
Times 37:21 Oct 25 '76

Congress views B-1 delay, new ship mix as major
hardware issues in new budget. Armed Forces J
Intl 113:5 Jun '76

Congressional demands for American troop withdraw-
als from Western Europe: The past as prologue.
Phil Williams and Scott D. Sagan. RUSI J for Def
Studies 121:52-56 Sep '76

Construction bill veto tied to closing limit. AF Times
36:6 Jul 19 '76

DOPMA action up to Senate. Andy Plattner. AF
Times 37:21 Nov 22 '76

DOPMA amendments fail; bill heads for House vote.
Phil Stevens. AF Times 36:6 Jun 21 '76

DOPMA approaching final action in House. AF Times
36:3 May 31 '76

DOPMA deadline looms in Senate: Proposal for grade
relief waiting in wings. Lee Ewing. AF Times
37:4 Aug 30 '76

DOPMA headed for House floor. AF Times 36:31
Jul 26 '76

DOPMA looks dead this year. Lee Ewing. AF Times
37:4 Sep 20 '76

Defense Appropriations Bill moves: House votes money for comstores, B-1. AF Times 36:4 Jun 28 '76

Defense Appropriations Bill moves: Senate committee
(Appropriations Defense Subcommittee) makes
major cuts. Phil Stevens. AF Times 36:4
Jun 28 '76

Defense Authorization Bill: House-passed measure
calls for high spending. AF Times 36:3 Apr 26 '76

Defense Authorization Bill: Senate Panel (Armed Services Committee) votes deep benefits cuts. Phil
Stevens. AF Times 36:3 Apr 26 '76

CONGRESS--U.S. - Continued

Explaining the 'A' (authorization and appropriations) bills: Setting limits, supplying funds. tab AF Times 36:4 Jun 21 '76

Favor curried on Hill for athletes: (AF Academy Athletic) Association spent thousands recruiting for Academy. Andy Plattner. AF Times 36:33 May 24 '76

Ford wins Hill fight over closing (military) bases. AF Times 37:53 Sep 6 '76

Goldwater illustrates, assails congressional 'privileges of the Hill.' (Address, National Space Club, Washington, Feb 4, 1976) Barry Goldwater. illus Armed Forces J Intl 113:23-25 Mar '76; Condensation. AF Mag 59:11 Apr '76; Condensation. Officer 52:8-9 Apr '76

HASC (House Armed Services Committee) comstore hearings. H.R.Kaplan. illus Review 56:42-44 Jul-Aug '76

Hearings on improving aid to widows opened (by House Armed Services Compensation Subcommittee). AF Times 37:4 Aug 9 '76

Hill can prohibit base union acts. Lee Ewing. AF Times 36:2 May 24 '76

Hill delays survivor plan action. AF Times 37:54 Sep 6 '76

Hill fight: People, weapons. Phil Stevens. AF Times 36:3 Jun 14 '76

Hill group (Members of Congress for Peace through Law) would slash manpower $$. Andy Plattner. AF Times 36:23 Jun 7 '76

Hill levels guns at unions. Andy Plattner. AF Times 37:4 Dec 27 '76

Hill made few major DOD cuts: 6-year budget review. AF Times 37:25 Nov 1 '76

Hill OKs state withholding (taxes). AF Times 37:2 Sep 27 '76

Hill raids cut aides to 396. AF Times 36:40 Jun 21 '76

Hill to weigh more retiree benefits. AF Times 37:4 Nov 22 '76

Hill unit (House Armed Services Committee's Military Compensation Subcommittee) writes new DOPMA bill. AF Times 36:12 Jun 7 '76

(House Armed Services Committee) members scold (SecDef) Rumsfeld. Phil Stevens. AF Times 36:25 Feb 9 '76

House OKs amendment on base closing policy. AF Times 37:6 Oct 4 '76

House okays bill to improve SBP (Survivor Benefits Program). AF Times 37:2 Oct 4 '76

House panel (Appropriations Committee) wants training planes full (and AF crews to fly some aircraft now contracted to airlines). Len Famiglietti. AF Times 36:17 Jun 21 '76

House panel (Armed Services Committee) again supports stores. AF Times 36:2 Mar 29 '76

House panel (Armed Services Committee) rejects extra $$ for Navy. AF Times 37:6 Sep 20 '76

House panel (Armed Services Military Compensation Subcommittee) approves change in SBP laws. Phil Stevens. AF Times 37:20 Aug 16 '76

CONGRESS--U.S.- Continued

House panel (Armed Services Military Compensation Subcommittee) OKs DOPMA. AF Times 36:7 Jun 14 '76

House panel (Civil Service Committee) opposes 5% cap. Randy Shoemaker. AF Times 36:4 Mar 8 '76

House panel (Select Committee on Missing Persons in Southeast Asia) gives up on Indochina MIAs. M.L. Craver. AF Times 37:5 Dec 27 '76

House (Post Office and Civil Service) Committee begins hearings on mail delays. AF Times 37:30 Oct 4 '76

House ready to vote on killing kicker. AF Times 37:2 Aug 9 '76

House/Senate conferees set for bitter battle (over naval ship construction for FY 1977). tab Sea Power 19:12-13 Jun '76

House unit (Armed Services Committee) acts to cut Social Security offset. AF Times 37:57 Sep 13 '76

How GAO assists the Congress on budgetary matters. Ellsworth H. Morse, Jr. illus Armed Forces Compt 21:6-10 Jan '76

In the (military pay) crunch it'll be up to Congress. Bruce Callander. AF Times 37:4 Oct 18 '76

(Income) tax bill faces House, Senate fight. AF Times 36:14 Jun 28 '76

The intelligence shake-up. LtGen Ira C. Eaker, Ret. AF Times 36:13-14 Mar 15 '76

(JSC Chairman Gen George S.) Brown criticizes Times newspapers (in testimony before House Armed Services Committee). AF Times 36:3 Feb 9 '76

Job restriction added to DOPMA. AF Times 37:4 Sep 27 '76

Joint unit (House-Senate conference committee) agrees to kill 1% kicker, (but provides for) semiannual COL raise. AF Times 37:3 Sep 27 '76

Key (military) $$ bills still in works. AF Times 37:3 Sep 20 '76

The kings on the Hill: Their good life gets better while you pay the bill. Richard C. Barnard. illus AF Times, Times Magazine sup:6-11 May 3 '76

Large-scale changes coming in military trade legislation. F. Clifton Berry, Jr. Armed Forces J Intl 113:12 Feb '76

Leave selling curbed; DOD bill stalls. AF Times 36:9 Jan 5 '76

Leave selling faces $ cut: Congress eyes 45-day limit. Phil Stevens. AF Times 36:3 Apr 5 '76

(Lt)Gen (Daniel O. Graham) says DIA got CIA treatment. AF Times 36:2 Mar 8 '76

Malpractice bill appears stalled. AF Times 37:27 Sep 13 '76

Many congressional actions impact on Services. Officer 52:5+ Jun '76

Marianas commonwealth status approved; DOD eyes air base. AF Times 36:20 Mar 8 '76

(Military) construction bill passes Senate. AF Times 36:36 Jun 14 '76

Move to erase store $$ wins (by) 45-44 Senate vote. Phil Stevens. AF Times 37:2 Aug 16 '76

CONGRESS--U.S. - Continued

Move to kill $ $ for Med U (Uniformed Services University of Health Sciences) fails (in Senate). AF Times 36:2 Jul 12 '76

The next budget and the new Congress: Changes in both. L. Edgar Prina. illus Sea Power 19:8-9 Dec '76

1976 national security voting index. tabs Def Trans J 32:30+ Apr '76

'76-'79 group med students get tax relief (on scholarship payments). AF Times 37:26 Oct 18 '76

The 94th Congress: What it did and didn't do. AF Times 37:20 Oct 18 '76

OFPP (Office of Federal Procurement Policy) one year later: A look ahead. Interview. Hugh E. Witt. illus Govt Exec 8:16+ Feb '76

Panel (House Armed Services Investigation Subcommittee) may call commanders to testify on arms losses. Ron Sanders. AF Times 36:6 Feb 2 '76

Panel (House Armed Services Investigations) warned subsidy cut could kill commissaries. AF Times 36:12 Jun 21 '76

Panel (Senate Armed Services Committee) approves officer grade relief. (Added to bill to improve financial status of Soldiers' and Airmen's Home) AF Times 37:4 Sep 27 '76

Panel (Senate Armed Services Committee) moves to put more pay into BAQ. AF Times 36:3 May 31 '76

Pay panel (President's Panel on Federal Compensation) submits changes; far-reaching effects seen. Randy Shoemaker. AF Times 36:2 Jan 5 '76

People programs get boost from House (Appropriations) Committee. AF Times 36:4+ Jun 21 '76

President (Ford) accuses Congress of driving up defense costs. AF Times 37:4 Sep 6 '76

Prospects darken for commissaries. Officer 52:4+ Aug '76

ROA endorses bill making survivor improvements. Officer 52:5 Sep '76

(Rep Bill) Chappell, Manpower Commission, ROA point way to strong Total Force. Editorial. Officer 52:4+ Jun '76

(Rep Les) Aspin bills would overhaul pay. Phil Stevens. AF Times 37:4 Oct 18 '76

Retiring Hebert fires final salvos. Interview. F. Edward Hebert. illus AF Times 36:23 Jul 26 '76

Senate curbs commissaries in passing money bill--many other Congress actions. Officer 52:4+ Sep '76

(Senate) hearings on honor code: Inflexible system held root of problem. AF Times 36:50 Jul 5 '76

Senate panel (Armed Services Committee) guts SBP bill. Phil Stevens. AF Times 37:2 Oct 11 '76

Senate panel (Armed Services Committee) OKs DOD (FY 1977 Defense Authorization) Bill. Phil Stevens. AF Times 36:3 May 24 '76

Senate unit (Appropriations Committee) okays full stores funding. Phil Stevens. AF Times 37:4 Aug 2 '76

(Sen Barry) Goldwater hits lawmakers' goodies. Phil Stevens. AF Times 36:3 Feb 16 '76

CONGRESS--U.S. - Continued

(Sen Barry) Goldwater's 'Hill hypocrite' speech (on congressional and military fringe benefits). AF Times 36:31-32+ Mar 15 '76

(Sen Sam) Nunn blasts career bill: DOPMA passage slowed. Phil Stevens. AF Times 37:3 Aug 23 '76

(Sen Sam) Nunn explains bill delay (on) per diem raise. AF Times 36:39 Mar 8 '76

(Sen William) Proxmire: 41 for B-1, 26 against. AF Times 36:14 Mar 1 '76

'Shock wave' effect (from Senate investigation) hiked beef prices. AF Times 36:12 Jun 14 '76

Stores: DOD must cut costs--Authorization Bill goes to President. AF Times 36:3 Jul 12 '76

Survivor Benefits Bill passes in cliff-hanger: Many other bills approved. Officer 52:6+ Nov '76

Trailer, pension bills for vets move on Hill. AF Times 36:6 Jul 5 '76

2 on Hill (Sens John Culver and Henry Bellmon) attack comstore funds. AF Times 37:2 Aug 9 '76

200 years of financial management. Allen Schick. Armed Forces Compt 21:4-7 Jul '76

Vastly improved survivor benefit plan nears vote--many other congressional actions. Officer 52:4+ Oct '76

The week in Congress. Regular feature in some issues of Air Force Times

What senators said about (com)stores. AF Times 37:8+ Aug 23 '76

Who speaks for the people? Editorial. John T. Hayward. Govt Exec 8:11-12 Jun '76

Why Congress wants reform in the regulatory agencies. Interview. Charles H. Percy. illus Govt Exec 8:52+ Jun '76

History

The Continental Congress: Management by committee and board. H. James Henderson. illus Def Mgt J 12:3-6 Jul '76

Organization

The Congressional Budget Office: The logistics of budget, program, and finance. Ronald G. Bishop. illus tab charts Log Spectrum 10:26-32 Winter '76

CONGRESSIONAL MEDAL OF HONOR see Medal of Honor

CONSOLIDATED NAVY ELECTRONIC WARFARE SCHOOL

The Navy's new EW school (Consolidated Navy Electronic Warfare School): Off to a good start on the Florida coast. LCDR H. J. Scarborough. illus tabs Elect Warfare 8:85-86+ Sep-Oct '76

CONSTITUTION

United States

Base access and the first amendment: The rights of civilians on military installations. Maj Alan C. Stine. AF Law Rev 18:18-32 Fall '76

CONSTRUCTION see Building and Construction

CONSULTANTS

Alcohol consultant (National Council on Alcoholism) hired (by AF). AF Times 36:10 Jul 5 '76

CONSUMERS

Consumer Product Safety Act: Working to protect you. TIG Brief 28:9 Apr 9 '76

Credit cards: Handle with care. Donna Peterson. illus AF Times 37:31 Dec 20 '76

DOD begins new consumer push. AF Times 37:53 Oct 25 '76

Industry in the U.S.: The facts don't match the image. illus Govt Exec 8:30+ Feb '76

Two CPIs (Consumer Price Index) next year--how index is figured. Fred Reed. AF Times 37:6 Dec 13 '76

CONTAINER SHIPS see Ships, Transport

CONTAINERS

Air Force packaging. (AFR 71-9) TIG Brief 28:9 Jun 4 '76

An aircraft engine container can be a bomb. TIG Brief 28:4 Dec 17 '76

Balloons tested for containership offload. Dan Hall. illus Translog 7:1-4 Apr '76

Bringing air freight into the intermodal age. Russell T. Daly. illus Def Trans J 32:18-20+ Jun '76

Delivery assurance. William E. Billion. illus tab Army Log 8:10-12 Mar-Apr '76

EPA (Environmental Protection Agency)'s mandatory deposit rule: Tempest in a pop bottle. illus Govt Exec 8:38-39 Feb '76

The future: An industry view. Joseph A. Austin. (Adapted from Sealift, Aug 1976) illus Translog 7:4-5+ Nov '76

Intermodal technology as seen by Lykes Brothers. illus Def Trans J 32:28+ Jun '76

Long-term storage of ammunition. Howard M. Weiner. illus Army Log 8:34-36 Jul-Aug '76

Packaging of Air Force items for depot-level repair. TIG Brief 28:5 Feb 13 '76

Prime BEEF in Europe. Maj Charles F. Kreis. illus AF Engrg & Svcs Qtr 17:28-30 May '76

"Returnables" required by EPA would cost too much--DOD. Review 55:21-24 Nov-Dec '75

The role of intermodality. Alfred E. Perlman. Def Trans J 32:6-11 Feb '76

When ammo goes to sea. Eric R. Jackson and William F. Ernst. illus tab Translog 7:6+ Nov '76

CONTRACTED SERVICES

Audio-visual transfer (to civilian contractors) weighed. AF Times 36:13 Jun 14 '76

Base maintenance contracts: A different approach. Capt George E. Ehnert. illus AF Engrg & Svcs Qtr 17:15-17 May '76

Contract KP--ATC (Air Training Command)'s asset. James L. Skiles. illus AF Engrg & Svcs Qtr 17: 23-24 Aug '76

Contract services: Too many or too few? Lloyd K. Moseman II. Govt Exec 8:30+ Jan '76

Contracting out: "Great potential." Govt Exec 8:28 Nov '76

Determination of responsibility of prospective contractors. TIG Brief 28:11-12 Oct 22 '76

CONTRACTED SERVICES - Continued

Federal wage regulations and service contracts. Capt Derrick R. Franck. AF Law Rev 18:17-34 Summer '76

Government can cut DP (Data Processing) costs in half. (Interview with Computer Sciences Corp's Vincent R. Grillo, Jr) illus tab Govt Exec 8:52+ Nov '76

Government: Wrong kind of competition. John F. Judge. illus Govt Exec 8:16+ May '76

Mortuary affairs. TIG Brief 28:8 Apr 9 '76

Plan would cut 1500 remote slots (for support people). AF Times 36:6 May 17 '76

Remote sites losing 1600 support jobs. (Food service, maintenance and transportation jobs will be filled by civilian contractors) AF Times 36:30 Jul 12 '76

Remote support (tours) eyed for cuts. (To be replaced by contracted services) AF Times 36:2 Mar 8 '76

Transportation: Monitoring COPARS (Contractor Operated PARts Stores). TIG Brief 28:3-4 May 21 '76

Units weigh support personnel cut (at remote sites). AF Times 36:17 Apr 5 '76

Violations of the public trust in connection with contractor-operated parts stores. TIG Brief 28:6-7 Jan 30 '76

Why Bedek (Aviation Division of Israel Aircraft Industries) is bidding for U.S. government aircraft service contract work. illus Govt Exec 8:31-32 May '76

Why not buy ADP (Automatic Data Processing) solutions, instead of problems. Vincent R. Grillo, Jr. illus Govt Exec 8:56-58 Nov '76

CONTRACTS, GOVERNMENT

Defense industry news. Regular feature in issues of International Defense Review

Major defense contracts--value over $1 million. Regular feature in issues of International Defense Review

Methodology

Can contract methodology improve product reliability? Robert F. Trimble. illus Def Mgt J 12:20-23 Apr '76

United States

See also
Defense Contract Administration Services

Aerospace: Capital shortage--artificial environment. Paul Thayer. illus Govt Exec 8:36-37 Feb '76

Award fee contracting--the total approach is important. TIG Brief 28:15 Jan 16 '76

CBEMA (Computer and Business Equipment Manufacturers Assoc) and GSA (General Services Administration): A dialogue on how government hurts itself (because of its own procurement and contracting practices). C. W. Borklund. illus Govt Exec 8:24+ May '76

Can contract methodology improve product reliability? Robert F. Trimble. illus Def Mgt J 12:20-23 Apr '76

Communications: A necessity for sound DCAS/contractor relationship. E. V. Francis. Review 55:31+ Mar-Apr '76

CONTRACTS, GOVERNMENT - Continued

United States - Cont'd

Contractor participation in aircraft accident investigations. TIG Brief 28:10 Aug 27 '76

DOD revamping its profit policies for defense contractors: Profit '76 revisited. Dale R. Babione. illus tabs Def Mgt J 12:41-46 Oct '76

Defense industry: Is the foundation crumbling? tab Govt Exec 8:19 Mar '76

Delivery assurance. William E. Billion. illus tab Army Log 8:10-12 Mar-Apr '76

Designing for life cycle cost. William H. Boden. illus tabs Def Mgt J 12:29-37 Jan '76

Disclosure of information by contractors. TIG Brief 28:12 Sep 10 '76

Evaluating nonmajor procurements. Robert F. Williams. Army Log 8:33-35 May-Jun '76

Export releases for CONUS contractor shipments. TIG Brief 28:4 Nov 5 '76

Faith restored--the F-15 program. Maj Gilbert B. Guarino and others. illus AU Rev 27:63-77 Jan-Feb '76

GSA: Effectiveness through increased communications. (Interview with Jack Eckerd) illus Govt Exec 8:18+ Oct '76

Government contracts: Recent developments in depreciation and rental costs. Capt B. Alan Dickson. AF Law Rev 18:94-102 Summer '76

A growing Federal absurdity. (Small business and government supply contract regulations) Ernest Baynard. Govt Exec 8:40-44 Dec '76

Lawton Chiles and spending reforms: Is it for real this time? (Interview with chairman, Senate Subcommittee on Federal Spending Practices) C.W. Borklund. illus Govt Exec 8:12+ Feb '76

Maintainability--a shared responsibility. Hartley I. Starr. Natl Def 60:360-363 Mar-Apr '76

Management leverage: A new concept in military procurement. Col Ronald Terry. Persp in Def Mgt No. 24:79-89 Winter '75-'76

The military looks and listens to industry: The telecommunications equipment acquisition process. R. Leffler. illus Log Spectrum 10:23-28 Fall '76

OFPP (Office of Federal Procurement Policy) one year later: A look ahead. Interview. Hugh E. Witt. illus Govt Exec 8:16+ Feb '76

Price Negotiation Memorandum (PNM). TIG Brief 28:4 Oct 22 '76

Procurement elements--how do these fit together? Maj W.R. Montgomery. illus Log Spectrum 10: 13-16 Winter '76

(Requests for information) data called wrongly held up (by Hq). AF Times 37:5 Dec 27 '76

600 retired officers reported holding jobs with DOD contractors. AF Times 36:40 Feb 2 '76

Source selection and contracting approach to life cycle cost management. BrigGen J. W. Stansberry. Def Mgt J 12:19-22 Jan '76

Technical Representatives of the Contracting Officer (TRCO). TIG Brief 28:12 Oct 22 '76

Techniques for a multifaceted discipline. Don Earles. illus tabs Def Mgt J 12:38-47 Jan '76

Truth in negotiations. Emanuel Kintisch. Natl Def 61:118-121 Sep-Oct '76

CONTRACTS, GOVERNMENT - Continued

United States - Cont'd

Types of government contracts. LtCol Anthony P. Ingrao. tabs AF Law Rev 18:63-86 Spring '76

USAF EW program matrix. Table only. Elect Warfare 7:41 May-Jun '75

Warranties as a life cycle cost management tool. C.R. Knight. tabs Def Mgt J 12:23-28 Jan '76

Warranties: Your money and mine. TIG Brief 28:17 Sep 10 '76

What suppliers don't know can hurt them. (Defense Construction Supply Center Buyers/Suppliers Symposium, Columbus, Ohio, 1975) E.V. Francis. illus Review 55:30+ Nov-Dec '75

What's happening in electronics at ESD: A checklist of major electronics projects. Table only. AF Mag 59:58-60 Jul '76

Why not more straight commercial buying? Eberhardt Rechtin. illus Govt Exec 8:46-48+ Oct '76

Costs

Compensation: Reasonableness is the yardstick. Ray W. Dellas. illus Govt Exec 8:42-43 Oct '76

Cost overruns: The defense industry view. Earl A. Molander. tabs Persp in Def Mgt No.24:98-104 Winter '75-'76

A tool for managers of small contracts (Cost/Schedule Status Report (C/SSR)). TIG Brief 28:16 Nov 19 '76

CONVERSION see Ships--Conversion

COOPERATION see International Cooperation; Interservice Cooperation

COPYING PROCESSES

Image transfer of classified information. TIG Brief 28:19 Mar 12 '76

CORNING, Duane L.

Equal pay for equal service. MajGen Duane L. Corning. por Natl Guardsman 30:1 Jul '76

CORPORATIONS, INTERNATIONAL

After the Bicentennial: The end of an era? Maj Barry M. Meuse. illus tab AU Rev 27:2-12 Jul-Aug '76

A forecast for the 70's and 80's. Anthony J. Wiener. Persp in Def Mgt No.24:1-12 Winter '75-'76

Global corporations and the American economy. Ronald Muller. Persp in Def Mgt No.24:43-55 Winter '75-'76

The hot button (at IBM) is EEOC (Equal Employment Opportunity Commission). Govt Exec 8:15 Dec '76

The influence of transnational actors on the enforcement of sanctions against Rhodesia. Harry R. Strack. illus Nav War Col Rev 28:52-64 Spring '76

Multinational coproduction programs: New programs and corporate memory. TIG Brief 28:10 Dec 17 '76

CORRESPONDENCE, MILITARY

Preparing and Processing Correspondence (AFR 10-1). TIG Brief 28:19 Oct 8 '76

'Privileged' status of internal correspondence. TIG Brief 28:18 Mar 26 '76

CORRESPONDENCE, MILITARY - Continued

Use of Address Indicating Groups (AIGs) for intra-command correspondence. TIG Brief 28:21 Dec 17 '76

CORRESPONDENCE SCHOOLS AND COURSES

ACSC Associate Programs revision. TIG Brief 28:6 Aug 27 '76

Correspondence courses can save training dollars. TIG Brief 28:8 Sep 24 '76

Educational shopping center. (Army Training Support Center, Fort Eustis, Va, brings "one-stop shopping" to Army's Non-Resident Instruction (NRI) programs) SSgt Zack Richards. illus Soldiers 31: 50-51 Mar '76

CORROSION

Aircraft corrosion control. TIG Brief 28:14 Aug 27 '76

Aircraft washing versus touchup painting. TIG Brief 28:20 Dec 3 '76

Corrosion and fatigue: Problems in life cycle costing. Maj Thomas K. Moore. tabs illus Def Mgt J 12:48-53 Jan '76

Corrosion control features for Air Force facilities. TIG Brief 28:4 Dec 3 '76

Corrosion control of reciprocating aircraft engines. TIG Brief 28:8 Jun 18 '76

In Guam they (B-52s) rust. Capt John B. Taylor. illus Airman 20:8 Jan '76

CORTRIGHT, Edgar M.

Edgar Cortright (retires as director of Langley Research Center). Dave Dooling. por Spaceflight 18: 150-151 Apr '76

COSMONAUTICS see Space Flight

COSMONAUTS see Astronauts

COST ACCOUNTING STANDARDS BOARD

Cost Accounting Standards Board (CASB). Capt R. L. Smith. illus AF Compt 10:3-5 Jul '76

COST ANALYSIS

See also
Economic Analysis
Output Measurement

AFSC's cost accounting system. Gary W. Amlin. tab illus AF Compt 10:8-9 Jan '76

Compensation: Reasonableness is the yardstick. Ray W. Dellas. illus Govt Exec 8:42-43 Oct '76

Cost realism. TIG Brief 28:13 Jul 2 '76

Ground launch missile mishaps. TIG Brief 28:6 Feb 13 '76

An operations cost index: Answer to the question "how much more?" (CONUS vs overseas cost differences) Capt Willard L. Mason. illus tabs AU Rev 27:61-71 Mar-Apr '76

Price Negotiation Memorandum (PNM). TIG Brief 28:4 Oct 22 '76

COST AND STANDARD OF LIVING

Army costs out benefit losses. Gene Famiglietti. AF Times 36:2 Mar 1 '76

CSC sets new cost-of-living rates in U.S. areas o'seas. AF Times 37:12 Dec 6 '76

COST AND STANDARD OF LIVING - Continued

Congress seen almost certain to end 1% add-on to retired COL raises. tab Officer 52:26 Aug '76

Joint unit (House-Senate conference committee) agrees to kill 1% kicker, (but provides for) semi-annual COL raise. AF Times 37:3 Sep 27 '76

(Retirees) COL hikes: No sweat on 'trigger.' AF Times 37:8 Nov 15 '76

What's going on about pay--COLA trouble. AF Times 36:3 May 24 '76

Statistics

Two CPIs (Consumer Price Index) next year--how index is figured. Fred Reed. AF Times 37:6 Dec 13 '76

COST CONTROL

AFSC's cost accounting system. Gary W. Amlin. tab illus AF Compt 10:8-9 Jan '76

The Army: Electronics vs dwindling budgets. illus Govt Exec 8:37+ Jan '76

Comment (on costing). John J. Bennett. illus Def Mgt J 12:1-4 Jan '76

Continuing emphasis on acquisition cost reduction. TIG Brief 28:15 Jul 2 '76

Design to cost. John J. Bennett. illus tabs Comdrs Dig: entire issue Aug 12 '76

Design-to-cost and its impact on weapons systems. Maj Jerry E. Knotts. illus Elect Warfare 8:91+ Sep-Oct '76

Design to cost models: Helping program managers manage programs. Richard H. Anderson and Thomas E. Dixon. tabs illus Def Mgt J 12:65-71 Jan '76

Design to price: An experiment in (electronic warfare) procurement. RADM Julian S. Lake III, Ret. Countermeasures 2:67-68 Nov '76

Designing to cost on the XM1. Robert P. Erickson and John W. Wosina. illus Govt Exec 8:38+ May '76

FLight Information Publications (FLIPs). TIG Brief 28:21 Sep 24 '76

Fourth generation field support. (Address, Long Island Chapter SOLE Symposium, Long Island, NY, May 12, 1976) Michael D. Basch. illus tabs Log Spectrum 10:17-20 Winter '76

I dreamed we went nowhere in our solid gold airplane. (Based upon remarks, National Security Industrial Assoc, Absecon, NJ, June 23, 1975) O. C. Boileau. Def Mgt J 12:5-9 Jan '76

Improve your resource management program. TIG Brief 28:18 Jul 16 '76

MCF: A Military Computer Family for computer-based systems. LtCol Alan B. Salisbury. illus Signal 30:42-45 Jul '76

(Maintenance) records are dollars. TIG Brief 28:14 Nov 5 '76

Management of integrated logistics. (Address, Long Island Chapter SOLE Symposium, Long Island, NY, May 12, 1976) Lawrence M. Mead, Jr. illus Log Spectrum 10:5-6+ Winter '76

Managing downstream weapons acquisition costs. Russell R. Shorey. illus tabs Def Mgt J 12:10-18 Jan '76

COST CONTROL - Continued

The military looks and listens to industry: The telecommunications equipment acquisition process. R.Leffler. illus Log Spectrum 10:23-28 Fall '76

Modernizing and cutting costs. (Remarks, National Security Industrial Assoc luncheon, Los Angeles, July 23, 1976) Gen William J.Evans. AF Plcy Ltr for Comdrs: Sup No. 10:2-8 Oct '76

The obstacles to effective design-to-cost. Raymond Kendall. Govt Exec 8:24-25 Oct '76

PROMS (PROcurement Management System). Robert F.Williams and Capt Robert J.Walker. tabs Army Log 8:2-6 Nov-Dec '76

Procurement elements--how do these fit together? Maj W.R.Montgomery. illus Log Spectrum 10: 13-16 Winter '76

Why DOD emphasizes reliability & maintainability in testing. Jacques S.Gansler. illus Comdrs Dig 19: entire issue Dec 23 '76

Why its contestants think AMST is a good deal for the government. (Interview with AF program manager, LtCol Dave Englund) illus Govt Exec 8:43-44+ Apr '76

COST EFFECTIVENESS

See also
Efficiency

ATCA (Advanced Tanker Cargo Aircraft)--key to global mobility. Edgar Ulsamer. illus (Also cutaway) map AF Mag 59:20-25 Apr '76

AWACS: Can it cut out ground clutter on Capitol Hill? illus tab Govt Exec 8:16-17 Mar '76

The Army: Electronics vs dwindling budgets. illus Govt Exec 8:37+ Jan '76

Army stock fund: A friend indeed. Raymond R.Nelson. Army Log 8:32-33 Nov-Dec '76

Army stock fund: Friend or foe. Col John R.Brinton. illus tab Army Log 8:2-5 Mar-Apr '76

Audio-visual transfer (to civilian contractors) weighed. AF Times 36:13 Jun 14 '76

Avionics proliferation: A life cycle cost perspective. Russell M.Genet and Thomas D.Meitzler. tabs Def Mgt J 12:60-64 Jan '76

CBEMA (Computer and Business Equipment Manufacturers Assoc) and GSA (General Services Administration): A dialogue on how government hurts itself (because of its own procurement and contracting practices). C.W.Borklund. illus Govt Exec 8:24+ May '76

Centralized commissary concept (Air Force COMmissary Service (AFCOMS)). CMSgt Donald M. Leach. illus chart map AF Engrg & Svcs Qtr 17: 2-5 May '76

Comment (on costing). John J.Bennett. illus Def Mgt J 12:1-4 Jan '76

Compensation: Reasonableness is the yardstick. Ray W.Dellas. illus Govt Exec 8:42-43 Oct '76

Computers cut energy costs in buildings. Phil Deakin. illus tab Govt Exec 8:33+ May '76

Contract KP--ATC (Air Training Command)'s asset. James L.Skiles. illus AF Engrg & Svcs Qtr 17: 23-24 Aug '76

Contract services: Too many or too few? Lloyd K. Moseman II. Govt Exec 8:30+ Jan '76

COST EFFECTIVENESS - Continued

Contracting out: "Great potential." Govt Exec 8:28 Nov '76

Corrosion and fatigue: Problems in life cycle costing. Maj Thomas K.Moore. tabs illus Def Mgt J 12:48-53 Jan '76

Cost for decision making: A synopsis. LtCol Eugene O.Poindexter. illus tabs Armed Forces Compt 21: 16-23 Jan '76

Cost overruns: The defense industry view. Earl A. Molander. tabs Persp in Def Mgt No.24:98-104 Winter '75-'76

DCA commercial communications policy. LtCol Albert J.Edmonds. Signal 30:95-98 Aug '76

Delivery assurance. William E.Billion. illus tab Army Log 8:10-12 Mar-Apr '76

Designing for life cycle cost. William H.Boden. illus tabs Def Mgt J 12:29-37 Jan '76

Energy monitoring control systems. Capt Robert E. Dant. illus tab AF Engrg & Svcs Qtr 17:25-28 Aug '76

Equipment maintainability--design in, don't add on. BrigGen William E.Eicher. illus Natl Def 60:353-355 Mar-Apr '76

Evaluating nonmajor procurements. Robert F.Williams. Army Log 8:33-35 May-Jun '76

The FFG-7 integrated logistics support program. (Address, Long Island Chapter, SOLE, April 24, 1976) RADM E.J.Otth. Log Spectrum 10:34-35+ Fall '76

Facsimile: Legal status. Charles W.Savory. illus tab Signal 30:33-35 Apr '76

Federal Supply Service commissioner Wallace H. Robinson, Jr. Interview. illus Govt Exec 8:23 Oct '76

Forecasting the impact of base level programs. LtCol Norbert W.Frische. illus tabs AF Compt 10:34-37 Jul '76

Fuel and energy conservation program (at Subic Bay, Philippines). CAPT Joseph A.D.Emidio. illus tabs Mil Engr 68:387-389 Sep-Oct '76

GPO: Aggressively marketing their unique services. (Interview with Thomas F.McCormick) illus Govt Exec 8:19-20 Jan '76

GSA: Effectiveness through increased communications. (Interview with Jack Eckerd) illus Govt Exec 8:18+ Oct '76

GSA seeks wider base of suppliers. H.R.Kaplan. illus Review 55:45-48+ Mar-Apr '76

Going to film (government micrographics): It's now up to the agencies. (Interview with John D.Livsey) John F.Judge. illus Govt Exec 8:15+ Jan '76

Government can cut DP (Data Processing) costs in half. (Interview with Computer Sciences Corp's Vincent R.Grillo, Jr) illus tab Govt Exec 8:52+ Nov '76

Government: Wrong kind of competition. John F. Judge. illus Govt Exec 8:16+ May '76

I dreamed we went nowhere in our solid gold airplane. (Based upon remarks, National Security Industrial Assoc, Absecon, NJ, June 23, 1975) O.C. Boileau. Def Mgt J 12:5-9 Jan '76

Industry feedback on life cycle cost. John J.Bennett. Def Mgt J 12:38 Oct '76

COST EFFECTIVENESS - Continued

Is the U.S. losing its investment (in space)? John F. Judge. illus Govt Exec 8:21+ Mar '76

Lawton Chiles and spending reforms: Is it for real this time? (Interview with chairman, Senate Subcommittee on Federal Spending Practices) C.W. Borklund. illus Govt Exec 8:12+ Feb '76

Life cycle cost. TIG Brief 28:4 Feb 13 '76

Life cycle cost: An NSIA (National Security Industrial Assoc) review. A.M. Frager. Def Mgt J 12:39-40 Oct '76

Life cycle cost is here to stay. TIG Brief 28:4 Mar 12 '76

The logic in logistics. Joseph J. Addison. illus charts Log Spectrum pt 1, 9:4-9 Winter '75; pt 2, 10:3-6+ Spring '76; pt 3, 10:14-17 Summer '76

MAC 'new look' ORI. BrigGen Edward J. Nash. tab TIG Brief 28:3-4 Aug 27 '76

The MTMC realignment program. David R. Goodmon. Translog 7:2-5 Feb '76

Maintainability--a shared responsibility. Hartley I. Starr. Natl Def 60:360-363 Mar-Apr '76

Maintenance in the Navy. Robert Emsworth. illus Natl Def 60:356-358 Mar-Apr '76

Maintaining a modern force. (Remarks, National Security Industrial Assoc, Absecon, NJ, June 28, 1976) MajGen Charles F. Minter, Sr. AF Plcy Ltr for Comdrs: Sup No. 9:13-19 Sep '76

Making retrograde cost effective. (Air Force materiel used in Southeast Asia) LtCol Barry W. Jenkins. illus AF Engrg & Svcs Qtr 17:26-27 May '76

Managing downstream weapons acquisition costs. Russell R. Shorey. illus tabs Def Mgt J 12:10-18 Jan '76

Managing major end items. John P. McCormick. illus tab Army Log 8:31-33 Jul-Aug '76

The military looks and listens to industry: The telecommunications equipment acquisition process. R. Leffler. illus Log Spectrum 10:23-28 Fall '76

The Military Sealift Command's build and charter program for nine sealift-class tankers. Scott C. Truver. illus tabs Nav War Col Rev 28:32-44 Fall '75

Models a key to air force life cycle cost implementation. 1stLt Dwight E. Collins. tabs Def Mgt J 12:54-59 Jan '76

New inventory analysis techniques. James J. Eder. illus Log Spectrum 10:29-33 Fall '76

The obstacles to effective design-to-cost. Raymond Kendall. Govt Exec 8:24-25 Oct '76

An operations cost index: Answer to the question "how much more?" (CONUS vs overseas cost differences) Capt Willard L. Mason. illus tabs AU Rev 27:61-71 Mar-Apr '76

Paying only your fair share. (Joint Utility Service Boards (JUSBs)) Leon E. McDuff. illus AF Engrg & Svcs Qtr 17:35-37 Aug '76

Performance purchasing: A rising state & local tide. Govt Exec 8:22+ Sep '76

Small cities (like Redondo Beach, Calif) & computers: It can be done. illus Govt Exec 8:55-56+ Dec '76

COST EFFECTIVENESS - Continued

Solar energy applications. Capts Anthony Eden and Michael A. Aimone. tabs illus map AF Engrg & Svcs Qtr 17:29-33 Aug '76

Source selection and contracting approach to life cycle cost management. BrigGen J.W. Stansberry. Def Mgt J 12:19-22 Jan '76

Standardized EW software--a method of improving life cycle costs. Harvey I. Hylton. Elect Warfare 7:43-44+ May-Jun '75

System safety: The key to lower cost of ownership. LtGen Donald G. Nunn. TIG Brief 28:2 Feb 13 '76

Systems approach to administrative support (in Transportation Dept's Office of Contracts and Procurement). Govt Exec 8:54+ Sep '76

Techniques for a multifaceted discipline. Don Earles. illus tabs Def Mgt J 12:38-47 Jan '76

Testing Army materiel. MajGen Patrick W. Powers. illus Army Log 8:28-31 Nov-Dec '76

Toward flexible definitive designs. Capt Michael J. Burrill. illus AF Engrg & Svcs Qtr 17:26-31 Nov '76

UMTA (Urban Mass Transportation Administration): Controlling the costs. John F. Judge. illus Govt Exec 8:18-20 Jul '76

UTTAS: Low cost of ownership from the start. Interview. MajGen Jerry B. Lauer. illus Govt Exec 8:48-50 Apr '76

Warranties as a life cycle cost management tool. C.R. Knight. tabs Def Mgt J 12:23-28 Jan '76

Why airlift isn't free. Gen Paul K. Carlton. tab illus Army Log 8:2-6 Jan-Feb '76

Why Bedek (Aviation Division of Israel Aircraft Industries) is bidding for U.S. government aircraft service contract work. illus Govt Exec 8:31-32 May '76

Why its contestants think AMST is a good deal for the government. (Interview with AF program manager, LtCol Dave Englund) illus Govt Exec 8:43-44+ Apr '76

Why not buy ADP (Automatic Data Processing) solutions, instead of problems. Vincent R. Grillo, Jr. illus Govt Exec 8:56-58 Nov '76

Why not more straight commercial buying? Eberhardt Rechtin. illus Govt Exec 8:46-48+ Oct '76

Winds of change in communications and computers. Theodore D. Puckorius. illus Signal 31:18-22 Sep '76

Word processing: How to save $700 million a year. (Interview with Ron Companion, Installation Officer at Fort Benning, Ga) Govt Exec 8:52+ Dec '76

COST OF LIVING see Cost and Standard of Living

COST REDUCTION PROGRAM

See also
Resources Conservation Program

COUNCIL OF MUTUAL ECONOMIC ASSISTANCE

Soviet oil in the 1980s: Shortage or surplus? R. Rockingham Gill. tabs RUSI J for Def Studies 121:73-77 Jun '76

COUNSELING

(AF) counseling jobs erased. AF Times 36:6 Jun 7 '76

Counseling: A face to face confrontation. Capt Charles M. Shane. Educ J 19:9-10 Winter '76

Palace Dollar (comptroller career counseling) today. Capt Benjamin Lester, Jr. illus AF Compt 10:33 Jan '76

Sunday every day. Janet Hake. illus Soldiers 31:28-31 Oct '76

COUNTERINSURGENCY

Intelligence and insurgency. Capt A.C.Bevilacqua. illus MarCor Gaz 60:40-46 Jan '76

Vietnam intervention: Systematic distortion in policymaking. Jeffrey Race. Armed Forces & Soc 2: 377-396 Spring '76

COUNTERINTELLIGENCE

The AFOSI Intelligence Information Report (IIR). illus TIG Brief 28:12 Jan 16 '76

Military intelligence: A fight for identity. Col Leonard A. Spirito and Maj Marc B. Powe. Army 26: 14-21 May '76

COUNTERMEASURES

See also
Electronic Countermeasures

Acoustic countermeasures in the undersea environment. Owen Flynn. illus tabs Elect Warfare 8: 62-64+ Sep-Oct '76

COURAGE

Flying steels will. LtCol Y. Besschyotnov. Soviet Mil Rev No. 12:30-31 Dec '76

A study of the anatomy of fear and courage in war. LtCol A.T.A.Browne, Ret. Army Qtr 106:297-303 Jul '76

COURT OF CLAIMS

Dual comp suit (by) 700 retired officers asks millions. Lee Ewing. AF Times 37:10 Aug 2 '76

Two wives granted MIA status trials. AF Times 36:6 Jul 26 '76

U.S. Court (of Claims) nixes War II back pay. AF Times 36:26 Jul 12 '76

COURT OF MILITARY APPEALS

CMA (Court of Military Appeals) ruling could mean stiffer hard drug terms. AF Times 37:22 Aug 9 '76

Early hearings due imprisoned (AF) members. Ann Gerow. AF Times 36:2 Feb 9 '76

Haircut regs get hearing in Court (of Military Appeals). AF Times 36:18 Mar 15 '76

NCO conviction upset: Court (of Military Appeals) cautions JAGs. AF Times 37:24 Nov 8 '76

Penalties limited on drug offenses (by Court of Military Appeals). AF Times 36:24 Jul 19 '76

Right to hold trial limited by CMA. AF Times 37:33 Oct 18 '76

Ruling limits drug sniffers (drug-detection dogs). illus AF Times 37:11 Nov 8 '76

Shakedown searches ruled illegal (by Court of Military Appeals). AF Times 37:8 Oct 25 '76

COURT OF MILITARY APPEALS - Continued

The Supreme Court and its impact on the Court of Military Appeals. (Adapted from lecture, Homer Ferguson Conference on Appellate Advocacy, Washington, May 20, 1976) Capt Scott L. Silliman. AF Law Rev 18:81-93 Summer '76

Will CMA review cadet cheating? AF Times 37:9 Aug 30 '76

COURT OF MILITARY REVIEW

Air Force

CMR asks rehearing in EM's heroin case. AF Times 37:26 Dec 13 '76

NCO spy (MSgt Raymond G. DeChamplain) retried, convicted. AF Times 36:20 Mar 29 '76

Narcotics sentence (for airman) reduced. AF Times 37:20 Aug 23 '76

2 drug rulings upheld (by AF Court of Military Review). AF Times 37:17 Oct 25 '76

COURTS

United States

Appearance of Air Force personnel as expert witnesses. TIG Brief 28:21 Dec 17 '76

Court voids 'gag' rule. AF Times 36:32 Jun 7 '76

High court (Supreme Court) frees (military) honor code data. AF Times 36:2 May 3 '76

Military law in the 1970's: The effects of Schlesinger v Councilman (decision in the Supreme Court). Capt H. Michael Bartley. AF Law Rev 17:65-78 Winter '75

The military defense counsel's use of scientific evidence and expert witnesses. Maj William M. McKenna III. AF Law Rev 18:48-65 Fall '76

No politicking on base, Supreme Court rules. Ann Gerow. AF Times 36:8 Apr 5 '76

Political campaigning on Air Force bases. TIG Brief 28:15 Jun 18 '76

Right to counsel tossed out (by Supreme Court). AF Times 36:8 Apr 5 '76

Right to oust homosexuals upheld (by U.S. District Court). Rose Sterling. AF Times 37:29 Aug 2 '76

Ruling may end hair fight: High court (Supreme Court) decision on police reg could apply to military. Phil Stevens. AF Times 36:3 Apr 19 '76

Sticky court suit could affect raise (for civilian workers and the military). AF Times 36:2 Jan 19 '76

The Supreme Court and its impact on the Court of Military Appeals. (Adapted from lecture, Homer Ferguson Conference on Appellate Advocacy, Washington, May 20, 1976) Capt Scott L. Silliman. AF Law Rev 18:81-93 Summer '76

Supreme Court to rule on Navy VRB (Variable Reenlistment Bonuses) suit. AF Times 37:45 Dec 20 '76

COURTS-MARTIAL

See also
Court of Military Review
Military Justice
Uniform Code of Military Justice

Court-martial rate drops to all-time low. AF Times 37:4 Aug 30 '76

Hearing regarding pretrial confinement. TIG Brief 28:18 Mar 12 '76

COURTS-MARTIAL - Continued

The McClure affair. (The jury found Marine SSgt Harold Bronson innocent in death of Pvt Lynn McClure) Joseph E. Revell. illus AF Times, Times Magazine sup:6-12+ Dec 13 '76

NCO conviction upset: Court (of Military Appeals) cautions JAGs. AF Times 37:24 Nov 8 '76

Pot convictions: 5-year maximum. AF Times 37:2 Nov 1 '76

Right to counsel tossed out (by Supreme Court). AF Times 36:8 Apr 5 '76

COVERDALE, Robert F.

Our jumpin' general. (BrigGen Robert F. Coverdale spends his 45th birthday learning to parachute jump in order to better understand his units' support of airborne operations) Capt Bill Campbell. Airman 20:35-36 May '76

CRASH BARRIER see Airplanes, Military--Arresting Gear

CRAWFORD, Albert B.

Combat applications of radar. MajGen A. B. Crawford, Jr and Michael A. Fanuele. por Signal 31: 16-19 Oct '76

CREATIVITY

Is staff thinking too conventional? SqLdr R. G. M. Sivewright. Royal Air Forces Qtr 16:279-283 Autumn '76

CREDIT

BX credit plan boosted. Andy Plattner. AF Times 36:3 Jul 26 '76

BXs, comstores: Credit cards (and) centralized control. Interviews. LtGen Charles E. Buckingham and MajGen Daniel L. Burkett. illus AF Times 37:19+ Nov 8 '76

Control of U.S. government national credit cards by vehicle operations. TIG Brief 28:14 Jul 2 '76

Credit cards: Handle with care. Donna Peterson. illus AF Times 37:31 Dec 20 '76

Extensive credit use brings new (USAF) policies. Ron Sanders. AF Times 36:20 Apr 26 '76

Plastic police (ration control card). Sgt1C Floyd Harrington. illus tab Soldiers 31:37-40 Nov '76

Poll shows most want BX credit (cards). Andy Plattner. AF Times 37:20 Sep 27 '76

CRIMES AND MISDEMEANORS

See also
Fraud
Prisoners and Prisons

Americans & overseas law. illus Comdrs Dig 19: entire issue Feb 12 '76

Are your antirobbery procedures workable? TIG Brief 28:12 Sep 10 '76

Barracks thieves. MSgt Nat Dell. illus Soldiers 31: 22-24 Jan '76

CMA (Court of Military Appeals) ruling could mean stiffer hard drug terms. AF Times 37:22 Aug 9 '76

Cargo security conferees stress industry/shipper controls (at National Cargo Security Conference, Washington, March 30-31, 1976). Col H. I. Pitchford. Translog 7:6-7 May '76

Central (reporting) system to list crimes. Ron Sanders. AF Times 37:2 Sep 20 '76

CRIMES AND MISDEMEANORS - Continued

Children homicides (among AF families) decline. AF Times 36:13 Jun 14 '76

Corona Lock versus terrorist activities. TIG Brief 28:14 Jan 30 '76

Correct disposition of incident reports and violation notices. TIG Brief 28:15 Oct 22 '76

Court-martial rate drops to all-time low. AF Times 37:4 Aug 30 '76

Crime fighting in Oceanside (Calif). Richard C. Barnard. illus AF Times, Times Magazine sup:6-10 Mar 22 '76

Crimes in hostilities. Maj W. Hays Parks. illus tab MarCor Gaz pt 1, 60:16-22 Aug '76; pt 2, 60:33-39 Sep '76

Effective analysis can help prevent crime. TIG Brief 28:16 Oct 8 '76

Entrapment in military law. Capt Kenneth M. Murchison. AF Law Rev 18:57-75 Summer '76

Gottcha! (Personnel Control Facility and the National Crime Information Center) Sgt1C Floyd Harrington. illus tab map Soldiers 31:51-53 Feb '76

How to protect personal property. TIG Brief 28:9-10 Apr 23 '76

Indebtedness of separated members resulting from reporting of leave transactions after separation. TIG Brief 28:15 Jan 30 '76

Intense new SP drive seeks to curb crime. AF Times 36:12 Jun 28 '76

Is (new) base housing (at Bolling AFB, DC) burglarproof? Ron Sanders. AF Times 36:4 Apr 12 '76

NCO conviction upset: Court (of Military Appeals) cautions JAGs. AF Times 37:24 Nov 8 '76

Narcotics sentence (for airman) reduced. AF Times 37:20 Aug 23 '76

Panel (House Armed Services Investigation Subcommittee) may call commanders to testify on arms losses. Ron Sanders. AF Times 36:6 Feb 2 '76

Penalties limited on drug offenses (by Court of Military Appeals). AF Times 36:24 Jul 19 '76

Pot convictions: 5-year maximum. AF Times 37:2 Nov 1 '76

Probe of 'theft ring' still on at (AF) Academy. AF Times 37:12 Sep 20 '76

Prompt reporting of lost/stolen firearms and nonnuclear munitions. (AFR 125-37) TIG Brief 28:4 Jan 30 '76

Rape! (Potential victims include every female soldier and dependent in the Army) Sgt JoAnn Mann. illus Soldiers 31:6-10 Feb '76

Rape, a report: Why the Services' methods for dealing with rape are part of the problem. Marianne Lester. AF Times, Times Magazine sup:4-8+ Jan 26 '76

Reg will require bases to adopt (anti-) crime policy. Ron Sanders. AF Times 36:4 Jan 12 '76

Reporting threats against the President of the United States or against presidential candidates. TIG Brief 28:11 Nov 5 '76

Right to hold trial limited by CMA. AF Times 37:33 Oct 18 '76

Risk management: Bonding of security alarm companies. TIG Brief 28:13 Jul 16 '76

CRIMES AND MISDEMEANORS - Continued

SPs get latitude in probing crime. Ron Sanders. AF Times 36:12 Mar 15 '76

SPs get warning on criminals' ploys (to get around security systems). AF Times 37:18 Aug 9 '76

"Send in the special team." (Port Pilferage Prevention and Detection Team) Capt William C. Fluty. illus Translog 7:6+ Dec '76

2 drug rulings upheld (by AF Court of Military Review). AF Times 37:17 Oct 25 '76

The vital role of the computer in controlling crime. Clarence M. Kelley. illus Signal 30:12-15 Apr '76

Ways to cut weapon losses asked (by DOD). AF Times 36:24 Jun 21 '76

Weapons loss (in 10 years) put at 18,500. AF Times 36:10 May 3 '76

Statistics

AWOL figures drop in FY 76. tab AF Times 37:18 Sep 20 '76

CRISIS MANAGEMENT

C^3 mobility in management of crisis. Donald J. Yockey. illus Signal 31:14-15+ Nov-Dec '76

Crisis decisionmaking in Israel: The case of the October 1973 Middle East War. Maj Robert H. McKenzie-Smith. illus Nav War Col Rev 29:39-52 Summer '76

Crisis in relocation planning. (Denver NDTA chapter undertaking emergency evacuation planning exercises) John W. Billheimer. Def Trans J 32:20+ Apr '76

Detente and the Yom Kippur War: From crisis management to crisis prevention? Phil Williams. Royal Air Forces Qtr 16:227-233 Autumn '76

The evolving role of C^3 in crisis management. BrigGen Lawrence E. Adams. Signal 30:59-61 Aug '76

The Mayaguez incident--crisis management. LtCol Donald E. Carlile. illus Mil Rev 56:3-14 Oct '76

NATO's military preparedness. FAdm Peter Hill-Norton. RUSI J for Def Studies 121:2+ Jun '76

CROOCH, Dorven K.

Do more with less: Job enrichment may be the answer. Maj D. K. Crooch. AU Rev 27:55-61 May-Jun '76

CRUISERS

The antisubmarine cruiser "Kiev." illus Soviet Mil Rev No. 11:22-23 Nov '76

CRYPTOGRAPHY

Cryptology. Kirk H. Kirchhofer. illus tabs Intl Def Rev pt 1, Users, principles and methods. 9:281-286 Apr '76; pt 2, The unbreakable system. 9:389-394 Jun '76; pt 3, Crypto communication. 9:585-590 Aug '76

Secure voice communication: Cryptophony. Kirk H. Kirchhofer. illus tabs Intl Def Rev 9:761-767 Oct '76

CUBA

Foreign Relations

Chile: Fascism and militarism. G. Spersky. Soviet Mil Rev No. 7:59-60 Jul '76

CUBA - Continued

Foreign Relations - Cont'd
Russia

Cuba: Russia's foreign legion. Col Robert Debs Heinl, Jr, Ret. illus Sea Power 19:44-45 Mar '76

United States

The U.S. presence in Guantanamo. Martin J. Scheina. illus Strat Rev 4:81-88 Spring '76

CUBAN CRISIS, 1962

The Cuban missile crisis and Soviet naval development: Myths and realities. LCDR Harlan K. Ullman. tabs Nav War Col Rev 28:45-56 Winter '76

The Cuban missile crisis: Soviet view. Capt Ralph D. Crosby, Jr. illus tab map Mil Rev 56:58-70 Sep '76

CURRERI, Anthony R.

Curreri: Doctors U(niversity) is cheaper (than alternative costs of providing the military with doctors). Interview. Anthony R. Curreri. por AF Times 36:2 Jul 5 '76

CURRIE, Malcolm R.

Comparing American & Soviet defense: How does U.S. technology stack up with USSR? Malcolm R. Currie. Comdrs Dig 19: entire issue Jun 17 '76

Electronic warfare's role in future conflicts. Malcolm R. Currie. Comdrs Dig 19: entire issue Dec 9 '76

Electronics: Key military 'force multiplier.' Malcolm R. Currie. por AF Mag 59:39-45 Jul '76

Future tactical missiles. Malcolm R. Currie. Natl Def 61:32-35 Jul-Aug '76

Readiness and national survival. (Address, Air Force Assoc Symposium, Los Angeles, Oct 22, 1976) Malcolm R. Currie. AF Ploy Ltr for Comdrs: Sup No. 12:14-21 Dec '76

Soviet R&D at "critical mass": "Sobering assessment" troubles DOD research chief. Benjamin F. Schemmer. Armed Forces J Intl 113:12-13 Mar '76

CUSHMAN, Robert E., Jr

The Marine Corps today: Asset or anachronism? Gen Robert E. Cushman, Jr, Ret. Intl Sec 1:123-129 Fall '76

CUSTIS, Donald L.

Single Medical Corps urged. Interview. VADM Donald L. Custis. AF Times 36:16 Jun 7 '76

CUSTOMER SERVICE

Single vendor integrity. Cary A. Moore. illus Log Spectrum 10:13-15+ Spring '76

CUSTOMS (TARIFF) see Tariff

CUSTOMS, MILITARY

See also
Traditions, Military

Genesis. (Custom of saluting the flag at colors aboard ship) CAPT Edgar K. Thompson, Ret. US Nav Inst Proc 102:70 Feb '76

CUSTOMS SERVICE

Drug program (Project Commando Plug) under review: Team visits PACAF bases. MSgt Dave Sheeder. AF Times 36:21 Jun 28 '76

Drug smuggling in Bangkok: AF-Army team helps crack ring. AF Times 36:39 Apr 12 '76

NORAD gear makes $6 million 'haul' (in) smuggled items. AF Times 36:16 Feb 16 '76

Night riders. (NORAD radar at Luke AFB, Ariz, and Customs Service planes at Davis-Monthan AFB, Ariz, aid in the Customs Service fight against smuggling) Capt John B. Taylor. illus Airman 20: 42-48 Sep '76

CUSTOMS SERVICE - Continued

Small dogs proving worth (for detection duty). AF Times 36:61 May 24 '76

History

The first Federal customs. CDR Roger P. Vance. illus US Nav Inst Proc 102:46-53 Mar '76

CYBERNETICS

Computers alive? Hoyt W. Huggins. illus AU Rev 27: 24-32 May-Jun '76

CYPRUS

Ringed with a lake of fire: Cyprus 1976. Penelope Tremayne. Army Qtr 106:101-107 Jan '76

D

DANTES see Defense Activity for Non-Traditional Educational Support

DARCOM see Army Materiel Development and Readiness Command

DARPA see Defense Advanced Research Projects Agency

DCAS see Defense Contract Administration Services

DEW see Distant Early Warning Systems

DDR&E see Defense Research and Engineering

D-Day, 1944 see Normandy Campaign, 1944

DIS see Defense Investigative Service

DMA see Defense Mapping Agency

DOPMS see Defense Officer Personnel Management System

DSCS see Defense Satellite Communications Systems

DALTON, James E.

Air Reserve Personnel Center. por AF Mag 59:104 May '76

DAMAGES see Claims

DAMS

Oversize dry dock passes Chittenden Locks (Seattle). Col Raymond J. Eineigl and others. illus maps Mil Engr 68:83-85 Mar-Apr '76

Slurry trench construction (on Tennessee-Tombigbee Waterway). Carroll D. Winter. illus map tab Mil Engr 68:437-440 Nov-Dec '76

Stairway of water (Mississippi River). Capt William J. Diehl, Jr. illus Soldiers 31:49 Jun '76

Maintenance and Repair

Bankhead Lock failure. John A. Perdue. illus map Mil Engr 68:462-464 Nov-Dec '76

Outlet repairs at Dworshak Dam (Idaho). Ernest K. Schrader and Richard A. Kaden. illus tab Mil Engr 68:254-259 May-Jun '76

Stilling basin repairs at Dworshak Dam (Idaho). Ernest K. Schrader and Richard A. Kaden. illus Mil Engr 68:282-286 Jul-Aug '76

DANGEROUS MATERIALS see Hazardous Substances

DARUGH, David G.

Motor vehicle claims. Capt David G. Darugh. AF Law Rev 18:103-107 Summer '76

DATA PROCESSING SYSTEMS see Electronic Data Processing Systems

DAVIDSON, Phillip B., Jr

Revitalizing a beaten unit. (Story of MajGen John Pope of the Union Army shows what not to do; Field Marshal Montgomery's command of British 8th Army in Africa, 1942, demonstrates what should be done) LtGen Phillip B. Davidson, Jr, Ret. Army 26:43-45 Jan '76

DAVIES, Isaiah

(Brig)Gen Isaiah Davies--in '21 bomb tests. obit AF Times 37:18 Sep 27 '76

DAVIS, Bennie L.

Davis: Pay comparable to civilian. Interview. MajGen B.L. Davis. AF Times 36:4 Mar 1 '76

DAVIS, William V., Jr

A long trail with no dust. (Dole Race to Honolulu, 1927) VADM W.V. Davis, Jr, Ret. por Aerosp Hist 22:181-184 Dec '75

DEAN, Merrell E.

Managerial styles. LtCol Merrell E. Dean. AU Rev 27:41-46 Mar-Apr '76

DEANE, John R., Jr

A new way of doing business. (Army Materiel Development and Readiness Command) Interview. Gen John R. Deane, Jr. por Soldiers 31:21-24 Jun '76

Progress in the midst of change: From AMC to DARCOM. Gen John R. Deane, Jr. por Army 26:78-80+ Oct '76

DEATH see Life and Death

DEBTOR AND CREDITOR

CG (Comptroller General) clarifies rules on collecting debts. AF Times 37:24 Sep 27 '76

DECEPTION IN WARFARE

Soviet air defense concepts. LtCol Thomas E. Bearden, Ret. illus Air Def Mag, pp 6-11, Jan-Mar '76

DECISION MAKING

See also
Economic Analysis
Problem Solving

About aborts. Capt Dick Morrow. illus tab Aerosp Safety 32:6-7 Oct '76; TAC Attack 16:4-6 Oct '76

Born to fly. LtCol Robert T. Howard, Ret. illus Combat Crew 26:4-7 Feb '76

Cost for decision making: A synopsis. LtCol Eugene O. Poindexter. illus tabs Armed Forces Compt 21:16-23 Jan '76

Crisis decisionmaking in Israel: The case of the October 1973 Middle East War. Maj Robert H. McKenzie-Smith. illus Nav War Col Rev 29:39-52 Summer '76

The decision. LtCol James A. Learmonth. Aerosp Safety 32:5 Oct '76

Decisions and disaster. Norman F. Dixon. illus RUSI J for Def Studies 121:50-53 Jun '76

Environmental planning and the decision process. MajGen Robert C. Thompson. tab Mil Engr 68:11-13 Jan-Feb '76

Foresight and intuition in battle. Col V. Login. Soviet Mil Rev No. 8:13-15 Aug '76

Location logistics. (Address, seminar sponsored by Utah Air Force Assoc, Society of Logistics Engineers and Weber State College, May 10, 1975) Col Nathan H. Mazer, Ret. Log Spectrum 10:11-12 Spring '76

The Mayaguez incident--crisis management. LtCol Donald E. Carlile. illus Mil Rev 56:3-14 Oct '76

DECISION MAKING - Continued

A method for conceptualizing combat theory. Chantee Lewis. illus tabs Nav War Col Rev 28:45-56 Fall '75

The pilot as a decision-maker. Maj Joe A. Tillman. illus TAC Attack 16:20-21 Apr '76

A practitioner's guide to systems analysis. Col Larry N. Tibbetts. illus Nav War Col Rev 28:21-33 Winter '76

A proposal on sound decisions: A revised commander's estimate. Col William S.Hollis. illus tabs Mil Rev 56:41-52 Dec '76

Tooth-to-tail: A conceptual void. illus tab Army Log 8:33-37 Mar-Apr '76

Your opinion counts. Darryl D.McEwen. illus Soldiers 31:6-9 Dec '76

DECOMPRESSION

Application of hyperbaric oxygen therapy in a case of prolonged cerebral hypoxia following rapid decompression. Paul J.Sheffield and Jefferson C. Davis. tab Aviation, Space & Envmt Med 47:759-762 Jul '76

Biochemistry and hematology of decompression sickness: A case report. Michael J. Jacey and others. illus tabs Aviation, Space & Envmt Med 47:657-661 Jun '76

Blood viscosity in man following decompression: Correlations with hematocrit and venous gas emboli. Tom S.Neuman and others. illus tab Aviation, Space & Envmt Med 47:803-807 Aug '76

Denitrogenation interruptions with air. Julian P. Cooke. tabs Aviation, Space & Envmt Med 47:1205-1209 Nov '76

Effect of physical activity of airline flight attendants on their time of useful consciousness in a rapid decompression. Douglas E.Busby and others. tabs Aviation, Space and Envmt Med 47:117-120 Feb '76

Hematologic changes in man during decompression: Relations to overt decompression sickness and bubble scores. Robert F.Goad and others. tabs Aviation, Space & Envmt Med 47:863-867 Aug '76

Incidence of decompression sickness in Navy low-pressure chambers. R.Bason and others. tabs Aviation, Space & Envmt Med 47:995-997 Sep '76

Injectable agent for the treatment of air emboli-induced paraplegia in rats. Pava Popovic and others. tab Aviation, Space & Envmt Med 47:1073-1075 Oct '76

Intracardial bubbles during decompression to altitude in relation to decompression sickness in man. U.I. Balldin and P. Borgström. tab Aviation, Space and Envmt Med 47:113-116 Feb '76

Mechanism of lung damage in explosive decompression. E. D. L. Topliff. illus tabs Aviation, Space & Envmt Med 47:517-522 May '76

Protection of airline flight attendants from hypoxia following rapid decompression. Douglas E.Busby and others. illus tabs Aviation, Space & Envmt Med 47:942-944 Sep '76

DECORATIONS OF HONOR see Awards, Decorations, etc

DEFECTION

Korea (Democratic People's Republic)

The freedom flight of Kum Suk No (in a MIG-15 to Kimpo AB near Seoul, 1953). Capt John B.Taylor. illus Airman 20:38-40 Jan '76

DEFENSE (MILITARY SCIENCE) see Attack and Defense (Military Science)

DEFENSE ACTIVITY FOR NON-TRADITIONAL EDUCATIONAL SUPPORT

Bootstrappers lose school breaks (and some tighter controls may be coming for students under DANTES). Len Famiglietti. AF Times 37:12 Nov 29 '76

DANTES seeks specialized civilian exams. AF Times 36:26 Mar 22 '76

DEFENSE ADVANCED RESEARCH PROJECTS AGENCY

The role of DARPA (Defense Advanced Research Projects Agency). George H.Heilmeier. illus map Comdrs Dig 19: entire issue Oct 7 '76

DEFENSE ATOMIC SUPPORT AGENCY see Defense Nuclear Agency

DEFENSE CIVIL PREPAREDNESS AGENCY

Crisis in relocation planning. (Denver NDTA chapter undertaking emergency evacuation planning exercises) John W.Billheimer. Def Trans J 32:20+ Apr '76

Relocation plan drafted in case of nuclear war. M.L. Craver. AF Times 37:18 Nov 15 '76

DEFENSE COMMUNICATIONS AGENCY

Command, control and technology. LtGen Lee M. Paschall. illus Countermeasures 2:39-40+ Jul '76

DCA commercial communications policy. LtCol Albert J.Edmonds. Signal 30:95-98 Aug '76

DCA management of DOD multiplex. MajGen James M.Rockwell and Maj Gordon W.Arbogast. illus Signal 31:11+ Sep '76

Military communications: The 'what' is much tougher than the 'how.' C. W. Borklund. illus Govt Exec 8:21+ Jun '76

DEFENSE COMMUNICATIONS SYSTEM

A command, control and communications overview. Donald H.Rumsfeld. illus Signal 30:34-35+ May-Jun '76

Command, control and technology. LtGen Lee M. Paschall. illus Countermeasures 2:39-40+ Jul '76

DCS (Defense Communications System) channel packing system. Col Clifford O. C.Henning, Jr and Maj Gordon W.Arbogast. illus Signal 31:10-13 Nov-Dec '76

DEFENSE COMMUNITY SERVICE PROGRAM

See also
Civil Action Program
It takes heart. (AFR 514th Military Airlift Wg, Mc-Guire AFB, NJ, wins AFR Annual Community Award) illus Air Reservist 28:6-7 Apr '76

DEFENSE CONSTRUCTION SUPPLY CENTER

What suppliers don't know can hurt them. (Defense Construction Supply Center Buyers/Suppliers Symposium, Columbus, Ohio, 1975) E.V.Francis. illus Review 55:30+ Nov-Dec '75

DEFENSE CONTRACT ADMINISTRATION SERVICES

Communications: A necessity for sound DCAS/con-
tractor relationship. E.V.Francis. Review 55:31+
Mar-Apr '76

Delivery assurance. William E. Billion. illus tab
Army Log 8:10-12 Mar-Apr '76

Taking a "forward look" in Defense contract administration. John H. Kunsemiller. tabs Def Mgt J 12:
56-59 Oct '76

DEFENSE CONTRACTS see Contracts, Government

DEFENSE DEPT

Australia

Electronic warfare and the new Australian defence
organization. (Summary of address, Southwest
Crows Chapter, Las Cruces, NM, Feb 1, 1975)
R.G.Gillis. illus Elect Warfare 7:36 May-Jun '75

Great Britain

Sights lowered: The United Kingdom's defense effort
1975-84. (1974 Defence Review) David Greenwood.
(Reprinted from Royal Air Forces Quarterly, Autumn 1975) illus Mil Rev 56:34-46 Mar '76

Russia

Organization

Soviet aerospace forces: Continuity and contrast. Col
William F. Scott, Ret. illus charts AF Mag 59:38-
47 Mar '76

United States

(Airlift) transportation in support of American embassies. TIG Brief 28:9 Jun 4 '76

BrigGen Marks retires; served as Ass't Sec'y, Air
Force (Financial Management). AF Compt 10:7
Oct '76

A change of command: Signing up the new CinC. Army 26:4+ Dec '76

DOD against unions. AF Times 37:8 Oct 18 '76

DOD agrees to free new data on MIAs. AF Times
36:12 Jun 7 '76

DOD aids film men; Senator (Patrick J. Leahy) gets
the story. AF Times 37:30 Nov 29 '76

DOD begins new consumer push. AF Times 37:53
Oct 25 '76

DOD fights cut in o'seas BXs. Randy Shoemaker. AF
Times 37:2 Sep 6 '76

DOD hits (OMB) report on Dr recruiting. AF Times
37:12 Nov 29 '76

DOD political guidelines remain same. Ann Gerow.
AF Times 36:14 Mar 8 '76

DOD pushes store closings. AF Times 36:4
Mar 15 '76

DOD rebuked (by GAO) for paying some unnecessary
BAQ. AF Times 36:18 Jul 26 '76

DOD revamping its profit policies for defense contractors: Profit '76 revisited. Dale R. Babione.
illus tabs Def Mgt J 12:41-46 Oct '76

DOD to appeal 'bag-boy' minimum (wages). AF
Times 37:4 Dec 6 '76

DEFENSE DEPT - Continued

United States - Cont'd

DOD to control health care? AF Times 37:4
Dec 13 '76

DOD to justify health job merger (Health Affairs into
Manpower and Reserve Affairs). AF Times 36:21
Jul 5 '76

DOD wants limits on Privacy Act--computer add-ons
could boost cost to $74.6 million. AF Times 36:22
Feb 2 '76

Defense (Dept) fights widening of benefits for veterans. AF Times 36:61 Jun 21 '76

The Defense energy conservation investment program. Col Vito D.Stipo. illus tab Mil Engr 68:
111-112 Mar-Apr '76

Defense highlights. Regular feature in issues of
National Defense

Defense in struggle over (overseas) goods shipping.
Interview. Paul H.Riley. AF Times 36:4 Jul 12 '76

Defense posture needs fortifying, says (SecDef Donald H.) Rumsfeld. Len Famiglietti. AF Times
36:17 Feb 16 '76

Department of Defense human goals. AF Plcy Ltr for
Comdrs: Sup No.2:9 Feb '76

Ex-USAF officer back as Secretary. (Thomas C.
Reed confirmed to replace John L.McLucas as
Secretary of the Air Force) Officer 52:22 Feb '76

For the common defense: Secretary (of Defense)
Rumsfeld must stand fast for adequate preparedness. illus Natl Def 60:264-265 Jan-Feb '76

A force second to none: The FY 1977 Defense budget.
Terence E.McClary. illus tab Armed Forces
Compt 21:16-19 Apr '76

Group (Defense Manpower Commission) faults DOD
personnel management. AF Times 36:27 Mar 8 '76

An introspective analysis of DOD manpower management. David P.Taylor. tabs Def Mgt J 12:2-8
Oct '76

(John J.) Bennett and (David R.) Macdonald join Navy
Secretariat. Ellen R.Davis. illus Sea Power 19:14
Oct '76

Managing for Defense. Robert S.McNamara. Def
Mgt J 12:67-74 Jul '76

Manpower aide named. (Juanita Ashcraft to be Asst
SecDef AF for Manpower and Reserve Affairs)
illus AF Times 37:8 Aug 2 '76

The military and national purpose. (Farewell remarks, Pentagon, Nov 10, 1975) James R.Schle-
singer. illus AF Mag 59:13-14 Jan '76; Nav War
Col Rev 28:57-59 Fall '75

New Air Force Secretary: Thomas C.Reed is well
qualified to meet the current problems. illus Natl
Def 60:428-429 May-Jun '76

New DOD explosives hazard classification system.
TIG Brief 28:9 Aug 27 '76

New duty in Defense (Deputy SecDef): Robert Ellsworth will supervise intelligence and foreign operations. illus Natl Def 60:346-347 Mar-Apr '76

New health unit (Defense Dept Health Council) to
mesh all Services' programs. Andy Plattner.
AF Times 37:22 Dec 27 '76

DEFENSE MANPOWER COMMISSION - Continued

DMC (Defense Manpower Commission) asks annuities hike. Randy Shoemaker. AF Times 36:3 May 10 '76

DMC (Defense Manpower Commission) urges pay changes, standby draft, retirement reforms. Sea Power 19:29-30 May '76

DOD to consider pay switch: Comparability to competitive. (Defense Manpower Commission's recommendation) Bob Schweitz. AF Times 36:10 Jun 28 '76

(Defense Manpower Commission) report supports ban on women in combat. AF Times 36:6 May 3 '76

Despite pitfalls, recruiters have done well, DMC (Defense Manpower Commission) says. AF Times 36:20 May 17 '76

Group (Defense Manpower Commission) faults DOD personnel management. AF Times 36:27 Mar 8 '76

(Imputed) retired 'contribution' scored. Bob Schweitz. AF Times 36:6 Feb 2 '76

Major pay shakeup asked: (Defense Manpower Commission) report covers broad field. AF Times 36:4 Apr 26 '76

Major pay shakeup asked: Salary plan backed. Randy Shoemaker. tab AF Times 36:4 Apr 26 '76

Merged pilot training pushed (by Defense Manpower Commission). AF Times 36:3 May 3 '76

NCO key to union threat: Board (Defense Manpower Commission) suggests hard line against organizing. Lee Ewing. AF Times 36:3 May 3 '76

New method of comparing (U.S.-Soviet strength) advised (by Defense Manpower Commission). AF Times 36:38 May 31 '76

New raise mechanism asked (by Defense Manpower Commission). Randy Shoemaker. AF Times 36:3 May 3 '76

People, the Navy's most critical resource. Curtis W.Tarr and CAPT Paul C.Keenan, Jr, Ret. illus US Nav Inst Proc 102:45-51 Nov '76

(Rep Bill) Chappell, Manpower Commission, ROA point way to strong Total Force. Editorial. Officer 52:4+ Jun '76

Salary plan seen in pay switch. Phil Stevens. AF Times 36:3 Mar 8 '76

Solution on pay not easy. AF Times 36:27 May 10 '76

X factor vs comparability: Comparison with civilian pay ignores hazards. Randy Shoemaker. AF Times 36:3 Mar 15 '76

DEFENSE MAPPING AGENCY TOPOGRAPHIC CENTER

A new point positioning system (Analytical Photogrammetric Positioning System (APPS)). Donald L.Light and William H.Revell. illus Mil Engr 68: 442-444 Nov-Dec '76

DEFENSE MARKETS AND MARKETING see Markets and Marketing

DEFENSE NUCLEAR AGENCY

DNA's (Defense Nuclear Agency) business: Thinking the unthinkable. Edgar Ulsamer. illus AF Mag 59: 50-54 Sep '76

DEFENSE OFFICER PERSONNEL MANAGEMENT SYSTEM

AF sweats grade relief (Defense Officer Personnel Management Act)--again. AF Times 36:18 May 24 '76

Another extension for grade relief? DOPMA deadline looms. AF Times 36:13 Jan 26 '76

Army group (Promotion Research Committee) challenging DOPMA. AF Times 36:6 Feb 23 '76

Army officers attack DOPMA. AF Times 36:4 May 10 '76

DOPMA action up to Senate. Andy Plattner. AF Times 37:21 Nov 22 '76

DOPMA amendments fail; bill heads for House vote. Phil Stevens. AF Times 36:6 Jun 21 '76

DOPMA approaching final action in House. AF Times 36:3 May 31 '76

DOPMA deadline looms in Senate: Proposal for grade relief waiting in wings. Lee Ewing. AF Times 37:4 Aug 30 '76

DOPMA headed for House floor. AF Times 36:31 Jul 26 '76

DOPMA looks dead this year. Lee Ewing. AF Times 37:4 Sep 20 '76

DOPMA Q&A. AF Times 37:27 Dec 13 '76

Hike to major now takes 12 years (and other recent developments in officer promotion policy and programs reflect slower promotions in effort to bring the officer promotion system into line with DOPMA). Lee Ewing. AF Times 36:4 Jul 5 '76

Hill unit (House Armed Services Committee's Military Compensation Subcommittee) writes new DOPMA bill. AF Times 36:12 Jun 7 '76

House panel (Armed Services Military Compensation Subcommittee) OKs DOPMA. AF Times 36:7 Jun 14 '76

Job restriction added to DOPMA. AF Times 37:4 Sep 27 '76

Major hikes face six-month delay (and other promotion variations projected). Lee Ewing. AF Times 36:4 May 17 '76

Personnel shops told to publicize DOPMA. AF Times 36:25 Feb 2 '76

(Sen Sam) Nunn blasts career bill: DOPMA passage slowed. Phil Stevens. AF Times 37:3 Aug 23 '76

Services review DOPMA language. AF Times 36:16 Mar 22 '76

1625 named for regular O-5. Lee Ewing. AF Times 36:17+ Jul 19 '76

DEFENSE PERSONNEL SUPPORT CENTER

Hot line suggested for beefs on food. Andy Plattner. AF Times 37:2 Aug 2 '76

Poor quality (meat) forced on comstores. Andy Plattner. AF Times 36:25+ May 3 '76

DEFENSE RESEARCH AND ENGINEERING

R&D emphasis on reliability. Robert N.Parker. Def Mgt J 12:19 Apr '76

DEFENSE SATELLITE COMMUNICATIONS SYSTEM

Command, control and technology. LtGen Lee M. Paschall. illus Countermeasures 2:39-40+ Jul '76

Defense satellite communications in the 1980s. illus tabs Countermeasures 2:46-48+ Dec '75-Jan '76

DEFENSE SUPPLY AGENCY

See also entries under sub-agencies, e.g., Defense Personnel Support Center

DSA adding role in food services. AF Times 37:36 Dec 6 '76

Direct Commissary Support System. RADM John C. Shepard. Review 56:41 Jul-Aug '76

New troubles hamper (Defense Supply Agency) meat buying. AF Times 37:12 Dec 20 '76

Vaughan: DSA's new director speaks his mind. Interview. LtGen Woodrow W. Vaughan. illus Review 55:19+ Jan-Feb '76

DEFENSE SUPPLY ASSOCIATION see American Logistics Association

DEFENSES

See also
Air Defenses
Civil Defense
Deterrence

International defense digest. Regular feature in issues of International Defense Review

Africa

History

African armies in historical and contemporary perspectives: The search for connections. Rene Lemarchand. J Pol & Mil Sociol 4:261-275 Fall '76

Alaska

The pipe (line, Exercise Jack Frost). Sgt1C Floyd Harrington. illus Soldiers 31:30-34 Nov '76

Arabian Peninsula

Arabesque. (The Arabian Peninsula) Leigh Johnson. illus Def & For Aff Dig No. 4:32-38+ '76

Australia

Australia: Defence planner's teaser. Brig F.V.Speed. map Army Qtr 106:359-365 Jul '76

Australia's defence dilemma. Brig F.W.Speed. tab Army Qtr 106:92-100 Jan '76

The vulnerability of Australia's maritime trade. A.W.Grazebrook. illus tabs NATO's Fifteen Nations 20:40-45+ Dec '75-Jan '76

Canada

Canadian defence policy, 1945-1976. Reginald H.Roy. illus tab Parameters 6, No.1:60-70 '76

China (People's Republic)

China's evolving national security requirements. R.D.M.Furlong. illus map tab Intl Def Rev 9: 557-562+ Aug '76

Europe

The influence of navies on the European Central Front. Comdr Hans Garde. illus maps US Nav Inst Proc 102:160-175 May '76

DEFENSES - Continued

Europe, Western

The Channel Command, sea highway to Europe. Comdr Joseph M. Palmer, Ret. illus map chart US Nav Inst Proc 102:176-189 May '76

European security: Helsinki to Vienna. Colin Gordon. RUSI J for Def Studies 121:34-36+ Sep '76

A new American defensive doctrine for Europe? Harold C. Deutsch. illus Parameters 6, No. 1:18-34 '76

The nuclear land battle. Col Marc Geneste, Ret. illus Strat Rev 4:79-85 Winter '76

Precision guided munitions: Implications for detente. BrigGen Edward B.Atkeson. illus tabs Parameters 5, No.2:75-87 '76

War with Russia in Europe would find U.S. sorely outnumbered. Col Robert D.Heinl, Jr, Ret. illus Sea Power 19:33-34 Aug '76

Weapons technology. AVM S. W. B. Menaul, Ret. Royal Air Forces Qtr 15:271-274 Winter '75

Western European collateral damage from tactical nuclear weapons. S.T.Cohen and W.R.Van Cleave. tab RUSI J for Def Studies 121:32-38 Jun '76

France

French defense planning: The future in the past. Gen Pierre M.Gallois, Ret. Intl Sec 1:15-31 Fall '76

Germany (Federal Republic)

A new self-confidence in the Bundeswehr. Richard Cox. RUSI J for Def Studies 120:58-61 Dec '75

Great Britain

Britain at the crossroads. Comdr Joseph Palmer. illus tabs Sea Power 19:33-39 Sep '76

British defence policy--a critical analysis. George Younger. RUSI J for Def Studies 121:15-22 Mar '76

Doctrine and the soldier. Colin Gordon. RUSI J for Def Studies 121:38-45 Jun '76

Open your eyes and wish. ACM Christopher Foxley-Norris. Army Qtr 106:149-153 Apr '76

Putting the great back into Great Britain? (Interview with Geoffrey Pattie, MP) illus Def & For Aff Dig No. 8-9:32-33+ '76

The Royal Navy--its contribution to national and Western defence. Adm Terence Lewin. RUSI J for Def Studies 121:3-4+ Sep '76

Sights lowered: The United Kingdom's defense effort 1975-84. (1974 Defence Review) David Greenwood. (Reprinted from Royal Air Forces Quarterly, Autumn 1975) illus Mil Rev 56:34-46 Mar '76

Israel

Israeli defense capability. Irvine J.Cohen. Natl Def 60:271-273 Jan-Feb '76

Israel's changing Military Posture. Charles Wakebridge. Mil Rev 56:3-7 Jun '76

Two years after: The Israel Defence Forces (IDF), 1973-75. Martin van Creveld. RUSI J for Def Studies 121:29-34 Mar '76

Costs

The burden of defense on the Israeli economy. Patrick W. Murphy. illus tabs Def & For Aff Dig No. 4: 46-51 '76

DEFENSES - Continued

Japan

Is Japan on the way to super-power status? Niu Sienchong. NATO's Fifteen Nations 20:34-39 Dec '75-Jan '76

Korea (Republic)

Korea and U.S. policy in Asia. illus tabs Def Monitor 5: entire issue Jan '76

NATO

Air interdiction in a European future war: Doctrine or dodo? WgComdr Alan Parkes. AU Rev 27:16-18 Sep-Oct '76

Air power and NATO options. (1st prize, Gordon Shephard Memorial Trophy Essay Competition, 1975) Air Commodore M.J. Armitage. Royal Air Forces Qtr 16:17-23 Spring '76

Airfield defense--the British approach. R. Pengelley. illus Intl Def Rev 8:832-834 Dec '75

Allied team. (Brigade 76 will deploy to Europe to gain combat proficiency in its North Atlantic Treaty Organization role) MSgt Dick Larsen. illus map Soldiers 31:6-10 Mar '76

Apprehension without fear. Interview. Gen Alexander M. Haig, Jr. illus NATO's Fifteen Nations 21: 18-21+ Feb-Mar '76

The best defense is ... Majs Walter P. Lang, Jr and John N. Taylor. illus Mil Rev 56:12-22 Aug '76

Britain at the crossroads. Comdr Joseph Palmer. illus tabs Sea Power 19:33-39 Sep '76

Coalition warfare. Robert W. Komer. illus Army 26: 28-32 Sep '76

Inflexibility in NATO's flexible response. Maj Donald F. Borden. illus maps Mil Rev 56:26-41 Jan '76

Military support for NATO political strategy. Maj Edward A. Corcoran. illus Mil Rev 56:37-43 Aug '76

NATO ... 'A viable, healthy deterrent.' Interview. Gen Alexander M. Haig, Jr. illus Army 26:12+ Aug '76

NATO defensive concepts. Maj A.E. Hemesley. illus Armor 85:25-26 Nov-Dec '76

The NATO program for rationalization and standardization. Norman Gray. illus Signal 30:80-81+ May-Jun '76

NATO's military preparedness. FAdm Peter Hill-Norton. RUSI J for Def Studies 121:2+ Jun '76

NATO's tender watery flanks. Joseph Palmer. illus Sea Power 19:34-39 Mar '76

The need for offensive operations on land. (Trench Gascoigne Prize Essay, 1975) Maj R.S. Evans. RUSI J for Def Studies 121:28-33 Sep '76

Putting it together with R-S-1 in U.S. Army, Europe. Gen George S. Blanchard. illus Army 26:52-54+ Oct '76

Red runs the Rubicon: Turbulent Italy faces new troubles, NATO could lose its Mediterranean anchor. Lawrence Griswold. illus map Sea Power 19:20-24 Mar '76

SACEUR's subcommanders take the floor: Northern European Command after 25 years. Gen John Sharp. illus NATO's Fifteen Nations 21:68-74 Feb-Mar '76

DEFENSES - Continued

NATO - Cont'd

SACEUR's subcommanders take the floor: The ACE Mobile Force. MajGen John Groven. illus NATO's Fifteen Nations 21:106-113 Feb-Mar '76

SACEUR's subcommanders take the floor: The central region of ACE. Gen Karl Schnell. illus NATO's Fifteen Nations 21:76-82+ Feb-Mar '76

SACEUR's subcommanders take the floor: The southern region. ADM Stansfield Turner. illus chart NATO's Fifteen Nations 21:86-94 Feb-Mar '76

The southern flank of NATO: Problems of the southern region in the post-1973 October War period. ADM Means Johnston, Jr. illus Mil Rev 56:22-29 Apr '76

Soviet tactical doctrine and capabilities and NATO's strategic defense. Capt Eugene D. Bétit. illus tabs Strat Rev 4:95-107 Fall '76

Spain and the defense of NATO. CAPT R.A. Komorowski, Ret. illus map tabs US Nav Inst Proc 102:190-203 May '76

Tactical nuclear warfare and NATO: Viable strategy or dead end? LtGen Arthur S. Collins, Jr, Ret. illus NATO's Fifteen Nations 21:72-74+ Jun-Jul '76

A tactical triad for deterring limited war in Western Europe. LtCol Thomas C. Blake, Jr. illus AU Rev 27:8-15 Sep-Oct '76

The United States and the defence of Western Europe. Capt D.H. Humphries. Army Qtr 106:211-219 Apr '76

U.S. readiness--reality or myth? Capt John P. Baker. illus Armor 85:26-29 Mar-Apr '76

Warsaw Pact amphib ops in Northern Europe. Graham H. Turbiville. illus MarCor Gaz 60:20-27 Oct '76

What's an MBFR (Mutual and Balanced Force Reduction)? Donald L. Clark. illus chart AU Rev 27:51-64 Jul-Aug '76

Who needs nuclear tacair? Col David L. Nichols. illus AU Rev 27:15-25 Mar-Apr '76

Costs

Indices of NATO defense expenditure, current and constant prices. London's International Institute for Strategic Studies. Table only. AF Mag 59:97 Dec '76

Russia

Comparing Soviet and American defense efforts. Les Aspin. tabs NATO's Fifteen Nations 21:34-36+ Jun-Jul '76

Military economics in the USSR. William T. Lee. illus AF Mag 59:48-51 Mar '76

Scientific progress and defensive potential. MajGen I. Anureyev. Soviet Mil Rev No. 2:13-15 Feb '76

U.S. defense perspectives. Donald H. Rumsfeld. illus tabs Comdrs Dig 19: entire issue Aug 26 '76

Costs

CIA says Soviet defense spending is double earlier estimates. tab Armed Forces J Intl 113:8 Jul '76

Estimates of Soviet defense spending: What they mean. (Message to major commands, March 22, 1976) MajGen George J. Keegan, Jr. AF Plcy Ltr for Comdrs: Sup No. 6:26-27 Jun '76

DEFENSES - Continued

Yugoslavia

Yugoslavia's defense: The logic of politics. Axel Hörhager. illus map chart Intl Def Rev 9:733-738 Oct '76

DEGREES, ACADEMIC

(Civilian) educators urge CCAF degrees. AF Times 37:2 Dec 13 '76

DMC (Defense Manpower Commission) report: BA (degree) usually enough for 4-star rank. AF Times 36:23 May 10 '76

Decision on CCAF granting degrees. Len Famiglietti. AF Times 37:4 Dec 27 '76

Educators to review CCAF (Community College of the AF) plan (for anticipated awarding of associate degrees). AF Times 37:22 Aug 23 '76

99 degrees awarded at AFIT School (of Systems and Logistics). AF Times 36:18 Jul 19 '76

DEL MAR, Henry R.

(DOD transportation system) (Excerpts from address, NDTA Forum, Boston, Sep 1976) Gen Henry R. Del Mar. por Translog 7:1-2+ Dec '76

DEMOCRACY

After the Bicentennial: The end of an era? Maj Barry M. Meuse. illus tab AU Rev 27:2-12 Jul-Aug '76

Do Americans understand democracy? Henry F. Graff. Persp in Def Mgt No.24:69-77 Winter '75-'76

Who speaks for the people? Editorial. John T. Hayward. Govt Exec 8:11-12 Jun '76

DEMOCRATIC REPUBLIC OF VIETNAM see Vietnam (Democratic Republic)

DEMONSTRATIONS (PROTEST)

Mobilizing people for collective political action. (Paper, American Sociological Assoc, San Francisco, Aug 1975) Kenneth L. Wilson and Anthony M. Orum. J Pol & Mil Sociol 4:187-202 Fall '76

DEMOTION

Air Force--U.S.

E-4 Sgt status can be removed. AF Times 37:10 Nov 29 '76

3-tier: New rules on getting busted. AF Times 36:10 Jun 28 '76

National Guard--Air Force--U.S.

ANG to demote surplus E-9s: Nonactive-duty units affected. AF Times 36:16 Jan 19 '76

DENTAL CARE

Medical/dental care for USAFR/ANG personnel. TIG Brief 28:17 Oct 22 '76

DENTAL CORPS

Air Force

Management of medical (materiel) excesses. TIG Brief 28:6 Mar 12 '76

DENTAL CORPS - Continued

Air Force - Cont'd

Medic officers face hike delay. Lee Ewing. AF Times 37:4 Sep 13 '76

Medical/dental supervisors' responsibilities for mobilization augmentees. TIG Brief 28:10 Jul 16 '76

New reg (DOD Directive 1320.7) forces O-6 board shift. AF Times 37:4 Sep 13 '76

Quarterly inventory of precious metal records. TIG Brief 28:10 Jul 16 '76

75 MC/DC officers picked for lieutenant colonel hikes. AF Times 37:6 Nov 22 '76

DEPENDENCY AND INDEMNITY COMPENSATION see Survivors Rights and Benefits

DEPENDENTS, MILITARY

See also
Children, Military
Wives, Military

Airmen home basing assignments. TIG Brief 28:17 Feb 27 '76

DOD would lift CHAMPUS bars. AF Times 36:2 Apr 19 '76

(Dept of) Defense can fire (foreign school bus) drivers abroad. AF Times 37:10 Sep 13 '76

Dependent travel to establish a bona fide residence. TIG Brief 28:15 Jan 30 '76

Garnishment actions rise for actives. AF Times 37:6 Oct 25 '76

Garnishment policies detailed. AF Times 36:12+ Apr 12 '76

"Help me learn English!" (AF programs for foreign born dependents) Capt Stephen O. Manning III. illus Airman 20:35-37 Mar '76

Kin can purchase space required. Len Famiglietti. AF Times 37:2 Dec 20 '76

Long fight on MIA status goes on. AF Times 36:29 Jun 14 '76

Medical care for fliers' dependents. TIG Brief 28:9 Jul 16 '76

New regs in effect for kin of retirees (in Korea). AF Times 36:20 May 10 '76

State order on garnishment backed. Lee Ewing. AF Times 36:4 Mar 29 '76

Statistics

Some statistics on manpower. tabs AF Times 37:26 Sep 13 '76

DEPLOYMENT

Air Force

Flexibility--a state of mind. Gen Richard H. Ellis and LtCol Frank B. Horton III. illus Strat Rev 4: 26-36 Winter '76

Tanker task force operations (at Loring AFB, Me). Col Kenneth M. Patterson. illus map Combat Crew 27:4-7+ Jul '76

DEPLOYMENT - Continued

Armed Forces

Hell on wheels. (Air Force and Army's 2d Armored Division (Brigade 75) train in West Germany for NATO support) MSgt Harold D. Newcomb. illus Airman 20:8-12 Apr '76

Korean killings prompt switch in alert methods. AF Times 37:4 Aug 30 '76

Reforger movement plans readied. Translog 7:13 Jul '76

Reforger 76: A MTMC first. illus Translog 7:2-4 Aug-Sep '76

Reforger 76 is history. illus Translog 7:7 Dec '76

"Return the forces to Germany"--(Reforger) 76. LtCol Gary Sorensen. illus Def Trans J 32:6-8+ Oct '76

Army

101st (Airborne Division (Air Assault)) in Reforger 76. Col Larry J. Baughman and Maj Robert E. Jones, Jr. illus maps USA Avn Dig 22:2-3+ Dec '76

Airlift is key to commuter Army (in Reforger 75). Translog 7:16-17 Mar '76; Mil Engr 68:308 Jul-Aug '76

Get ready--get set--go!!! LtCol John A.G.Klose. illus USA Avn Dig 22:6-7+ Dec '76

Reforger load-out. illus Army Log 8:24-27 Nov-Dec '76

National Guard--Air Force

(Operation) Coronet Sprint. (Two weeks of hard work by 180 Air Guardsmen of the 117th Tactical Reconnaissance Wg, Birmingham, Ala) 1stLt Gregory Hodges. illus Air Reservist 28:8-9 Jun '76

Reserve Forces--Armed Forces

General (Henry) Mohr stresses wartime need of rapid shift of Reserves to Europe. illus Officer 52:10 Dec '76

DEPOTS, SUPPLY

Army

Bar coding. Beverly B.Joyce. illus Army Log 8:2-5 Jul-Aug '76

Battle tanks $1.33 a lb. (Anniston, Ala, Army Depot) LtCol Tom Hamrick, Ret. illus Army 26:30-35 Jun '76

Learning by doing. Maj Hardy W.Bryan III. illus Army Log 8:34-37 Nov-Dec '76

DEPUY, William E.

Introspection is key in sweeping revision of (TRADOC's) training methods. Gen William E. DePuy. por Army 26:61+ Oct '76

DESERT OPERATIONS

Bold Eagle '76. illus USAF Ftr Wpns Rev, p 17, Spring '76

Study and Teaching

Desert lab. (Visit by Natick Development Center (Mass) personnel to 3d Armored Cavalry Regiment near El Paso, Tex) Capt Sam Closkey. illus Soldiers 31:38-41 May '76

DESERTION, MILITARY

Best and worst clemency records revealed. Ann Gerow. AF Times 36:12 Jan 26 '76

Deserter discharges could be upgraded (by AF Discharge) Réview Board. AF Times 36:12 Jan 26 '76

Gottcha! (Personnel Control Facility and the National Crime Information Center) Sgt1C Floyd Harrington. illus tab map Soldiers 31:51-53 Feb '76

DESIGN TO COST CONCEPT see Cost Control

DESTROYERS

(Advanced Spruance-class destroyer) Signal 31:86 Nov-Dec '76

The FFG-7 integrated logistics support program. (Address, Long Island Chapter, SOLE, April 24, 1976) RADM E.J.Otth. Log Spectrum 10:34-35+ Fall '76

HMS Sheffield, a ship for the 80s. Col Norman L. Dodd. illus US Nav Inst Proc 102:95-97 Feb '76

Missile boats: The modern destroyers. Frank Uhlig, Jr. illus Sea Power 19:17-18 Sep '76

USS Spruance (DD-963). illus US Nav Inst Proc 102: 61-69 Feb '76

DETECTION EQUIPMENT

ASW: The deterrent. F.Glenn Peters. illus Elect Warfare 8:49-50+ Jul-Aug '76

The acoustical pinger. Maj Tony Helbling, Jr. illus Aerosp Safety 32:21 Jun '76

Advanced data link aids Army commander. Arthur R. Gandy. illus map Signal 31:6-9 Sep '76

Battlefield surveillance. Charles Latour. illus NATO's Fifteen Nations 20:62-65+ Dec '75-Jan '76

Combat applications of radar. MajGen A.B.Crawford, Jr and Michael A.Fanuele. illus Signal 31: 16-19 Oct '76

Electronic warfare and smart weapons. Edgar E.Ulsamer. illus Aerosp Intl 12:18+ Jul-Aug '76

First TRAM (Target Recognition and Attack Multisensor) system undergoes navy testing. illus Countermeasures 2:47 Mar '76

Improved maintenance inspection (with neutron-radiography). Maj Vincent G.Ripoll. illus USA Avn Dig 22:44-45 Mar '76

Intercept probability and intercept time. B.R.Hatcher. illus tabs Elect Warfare 8:95+ Mar-Apr '76

Internal security equipment. illus tabs Intl Def Rev 9:820-823 Oct '76

Intrusion detection alarms. TIG Brief 28:19 Sep 24 '76

Military aircraft navigation and attack systems. John Marriott. illus NATO's Fifteen Nations 21:58-61+ Aug-Sep '76

No place to hide. illus Countermeasures 2:58-60 Dec '75-Jan '76

Radar application within the USAF. BrigGen Phillip N.Larsen. illus Signal 31:46-47+ Oct '76

Sub detection. Bill Walsh. illus Countermeasures 2: 6-7+ Apr '76

DETECTION EQUIPMENT - Continued

TRAM (Target Recognition Attack Multi-sensor)
makes A-6E world's most advanced EO aircraft.
illus Elect Warfare 8:75-76+ May-Jun '76

Track back, smack back. Bill Walsh. illus tab Countermeasures 2:18-21+ Aug '76

DETERRENCE

ALCM (Air-Launched Cruise Missile). Govt Exec
8:16 Jun '76

Arms control and world order. Hedley Bull. Intl Sec
1:3-16 Summer '76

The B-1: Strategic deterrence into the twenty-first
century. MajGen Abner B.Martin. illus tabs AU
Rev 27:2-14 Mar-Apr '76

The B-1: The right solution. (Remarks, Council of
World Affairs, Dallas, April 15, 1976) Thomas C.
Reed. AF Pley Ltr for Comdrs: Sup No.6:2-9
Jun '76

The case for the B-1 bomber. John F.McCarthy, Jr.
illus tabs Intl Sec 1:78-97 Fall '76

Comparing American & Soviet defense: How does
U.S. technology stack up with USSR? Malcolm R.
Currie. illus tab Comdrs Dig 19: entire issue
Jun 17 '76

Conventional forces as deterrent. LtGen Daniel O.
Graham, Ret. illus Army 26:18-22 Jun '76

Defense Department report--FY 77. (Statement before House Armed Services Committee, Washington, Jan 27, 1976) Donald H.Rumsfeld. AF Plcy
Ltr for Comdrs: Sup No.4:2-12 Apr '76

The evolution of American policy towards the Soviet
Union. (Gustav Pollak Lecture, Harvard Univer-
sity, April 13, 1976) James R.Schlesinger. Intl
Sec 1:37-48 Summer '76

The future and the strategic mission. (Excerpt from
address, 57th Defense Preparedness Meeting,
American Defense Preparedness Assoc, Los Angeles, Oct 15, 1975) MajGen Andrew B.Anderson,
Jr. Natl Def 60:286 Jan-Feb '76

Future concepts of air power. (Excerpt from address, 57th Defense Preparedness Meeting, American Defense Preparedness Assoc, Los Angeles,
Oct 15, 1975) LtGen John W.Pauly. Nat Def 60:
284 Jan-Feb '76

GAO slams strategic airlift "requirements" and programs. Armed Forces J Intl 113:14 Jul '76

A holocaust for Happy Valley? Henry Young. illus US
Nav Inst Proc 102:52-61 Nov '76

The impact of technology on U.S. deterrent forces.
Gen William J.Evans. illus Strat Rev 4:40-47
Summer '76

In Korea, 'single-minded emphasis on deterrence.'
Gen Richard G.Stilwell. illus Army 26:68-70+
Oct '76

M-X, a new dimension in strategic deterrence. LtGen
Alton D.Slay. illus AF Mag 59:44-49 Sep '76

Military concepts for political objectives. LtCol Joel
J.Snyder, Ret. illus AU Rev 27:55-62 Jan-Feb '76

NATO ... 'A viable, healthy deterrent.' Interview.
Gen Alexander M.Haig, Jr. illus Army 26:12+
Aug '76

DETERRENCE - Continued

NATO: How credible a deterrent? Gen T.R.Milton,
Ret. AF Mag 59:28-33 Jun '76

The new "nuclear options" in military strategy. Maj
Donald A.Mahley. illus Mil Rev 56:3-7 Dec '76

New threats to the nuclear balance: A challenge for
arms control. (Remarks, Town Hall of California,
Los Angeles, Aug 31, 1976) Fred C.Ikle. AF Plcy
Ltr for Comdrs: Sup No.11:14-20 Nov '76

The nuclear land battle. Col Marc Geneste, Ret.
illus Strat Rev 4:79-85 Winter '76

Nuclear war--the life-and-death issues. Edgar Ulsamer. illus AF Mag 59:57-59 Jan '76

Operations research shall inherit the earth. Maj Robert W.Chandler. AU Rev 27:57-61 Sep-Oct '76

Peace is our profession. (Remarks, Truman Lecture
and Fine Arts Series, Westminster College, Fulton, Mo, April 24, 1976) Gen Russell E.Dougher-
ty. AF Plcy Ltr for Comdrs: Sup No.7:15-23
Jul '76

Readiness and national survival. (Address, Air Force
Assoc Symposium, Los Angeles, Oct 22, 1976)
Malcolm R.Currie. AF Plcy Ltr for Comdrs: Sup
No.12:14-21 Dec '76

SALT II's gray-area weapon systems. (Report on
AFA's Symposium on "Tomorrow's Strategic Options," Vandenberg AFB, Calif, April 28-29,
1976) Edgar Ulsamer. illus AF Mag 59:80-82+
Jul '76

The strategic conflict. James Constant. illus tabs
Countermeasures pt 1, 2:32-36+ Mar '76; pt 2,
2:26-30+ Apr '76

The strategic cruise missile: What it means! John T.
Hayward. Govt Exec 8:56 Jun '76

Tac nukes and deterrence. Gen T.R.Milton, Ret. AF
Mag 59:25 Aug '76

A tactical triad for deterring limited war in Western
Europe. LtCol Thomas C.Blake, Jr. illus AU Rev
27:8-15 Sep-Oct '76

The United States, NATO and the decade ahead. Col
Robert W.Kochenour. illus Mil Rev 56:14-24
Jul '76

Weapons technology. AVM S.W.B.Menaul, Ret. Royal Air Forces Qtr 15:271-274 Winter '75

Who needs nuclear tacair? Col David L.Nichols.
illus AU Rev 27:15-25 Mar-Apr '76

DIGITAL COMMUNICATIONS see Digital Equipment

DIGITAL EQUIPMENT

Airborne data link: A weight-watcher's delight.
(Army In-flight DAta Transmission System
(AIDATS)) illus Elect Warfare 8:51+ Nov-Dec '76

Automation in military air traffic control. Bill
Walsh. illus Countermeasures 2:40-41 Apr '76

Binary beam IFM (Instantaneous Frequency Measurement): Multiple discriminators improve frequency resolution. Marc Smirlock. illus tab Elect
Warfare 8:83-84+ May-Jun '76

Command, control and technology. LtGen Lee M.
Paschall. illus Countermeasures 2:39-40+ Jul '76

DISCHARGES, RELEASES, AND SEPARATIONS

DISCHARGES, RELEASES, AND SEPARATIONS
Continued

See also
Reduction in Force
Retirement

Air Force

Admin(istrative) discharge: Proof burden shift. AF Times 36:34 May 3 '76

Child problem can lead to involuntary discharge. AF Times 37:8 Aug 16 '76

Deadline extended on officer early outs. AF Times 36:4 Jul 26 '76

Deserter discharges could be upgraded (by AF Discharge) Review Board. AF Times 36:12 Jan 26 '76

Drop in exits could force out more officers. tabs AF Times 36:3 Mar 22 '76

Drug rehab must before discharge. AF Times 37:6 Nov 8 '76

EM early outs extended a year--surplus first termers eligible. Bruce Callander. AF Times 36:2 Apr 26 '76

EM must solve re-up equation. Bruce Callander. AF Times 37:14 Nov 29 '76

Early outs end; some not okayed. Bruce Callander. AF Times 36:2 Jun 14 '76

Early outs limited to first termers. AF Times 36:2 Jan 19 '76

'Early outs' may avert need for RIF. AF Times 36:4 Jan 26 '76

Early outs okayed for holiday period. AF Times 37:6 Nov 22 '76

Early outs set for FY 77: Palace Furlough plan extended. Lee Ewing. AF Times 36:3 May 17 '76

Early release skills for May identified. AF Times 36:21 Feb 23 '76

Leave selling: New wrinkles. AF Times 37:4 Aug 23 '76

More early releases ordered: Voluntary medical rollback would affect 350 officers. AF Times 36:4 Feb 9 '76

Not all first-term EM to get early outs. AF Times 36:8 Mar 1 '76

Obese members face discharge. Len Famiglietti. AF Times 36:2 Jul 12 '76

Officer early outs reopen. Lee Ewing. AF Times 37:3 Dec 6 '76

Right to oust homosexuals upheld (by U.S. District Court). Rose Sterling. AF Times 37:29 Aug 2 '76

Ruling on (Reserve line) officers: Early out can't go career. AF Times 36:4 Apr 5 '76

(SecAF Thomas C.) Reed turns down (TSgt Leonard P.) Matlovich appeal. AF Times 36:26 May 10 '76

Some bases too liberal with quick discharges. AF Times 37:26 Dec 13 '76

3000 EM may leave early. AF Times 36:4 Jan 12 '76

Unfitness: New name but aim is the same. AF Times 37:8 Aug 30 '76

Laws and Regulations

Rules on admin(istrative) discharges changed. Lee Ewing. AF Times 36:4 Apr 19 '76

Armed Forces

DOD defines 'marginal' EM--3 grounds for release. Randy Shoemaker. AF Times 36:4 Feb 23 '76

Exit physicals made optional. Lee Ewing. AF Times 36:2 Mar 15 '76

Social implications of the clemency discharge. William A. Pearman. tabs J Pol & Mil Sociol 4:309-316 Fall '76

DISCIPLINE, MILITARY

Advice to commanders: Problems can lead to drugs. AF Times 37:4 Oct 11 '76

Clemency, transfer, and parole of Air Force prisoners at the United States Disciplinary Barracks (Fort Leavenworth, Kans). Capt Jeffrey W. Cook. AF Law Rev 18:101-107 Fall '76

Complaint evaluation and disciplinary action. LtGen Donald G. Nunn. TIG Brief 28:2 Jun 18 '76

Gottcha! (Personnel Control Facility and the National Crime Information Center) Sgt1C Floyd Harrington. illus tab map Soldiers 31:51-53 Feb '76

"I am the two-headed ogre." RADM Bruce Keener III. illus US Nav Inst Proc 102:38-45 Apr '76

Military discipline and the (Disciplinary) Regulations (of the USSR Armed Forces). Col N. Arisov. Soviet Mil Rev No. 10:14-16 Oct '76

Military justice--a reinforcer of discipline. LtCol Robert S. Poydasheff. illus Nav War Col Rev 28:76-92 Winter '76

New Armed Forces (Interior Service) Regulations. MajGen Z. Averyanov. Soviet Mil Rev No. 3:15-17 Mar '76

One last word on discipline. LtGen R. M. Hoban. illus Combat Crew 27:3+ Oct '76

The regulations and commander's initiative. MajGen A. Zyryanov. illus Soviet Mil Rev No. 2:26-27 Feb '76

Some bases too liberal with quick discharges. AF Times 37:26 Dec 13 '76

USS Constellation flare-up: Was it mutiny? CAPT Paul B. Ryan, Ret. illus US Nav Inst Proc 102:46-53 Jan '76

DISEASES

Death in a flyer due to acute epiglottitis and septicemia caused by Haemophilus influenza type B. Leonard W. Johnson, Jr. tab Aviation, Space and Envmt Med 47:187-191 Feb '76

Determination of regional pulmonary mechanics using a scintillation camera. R. C. Brown and others. illus tabs Aviation, Space & Envmt Med 47:231-237 Mar '76

Exercise in an hypoxic environment as a screening test for ischaemic heart disease. Purshottam Kumar Khanna and others. tabs Aviation, Space & Envmt Med 47:1114-1117 Oct '76

Flu shots (for military) planned for Oct: Active duty troops to get priority. George Marker. AF Times 37:26 Aug 30 '76

Infection control. TIG Brief 28:11-12 Jun 4 '76

DISEASES - Continued

Study of the microbiological environment within long- and medium-range Canadian Forces aircraft. A. J. Clayton and others. illus tabs Aviation, Space & Envmt Med 47:471-482 May '76

Transportation in commercial aircraft of passengers having contagious diseases. Michel Perin. Aviation, Space & Envmt Med 47:1109-1113 Oct '76

War of the microbes. SSgt John Savard. illus Soldiers 31:13-16 Sep '76

World War I's silent killer. (Influenza epidemic of 1918) LtCol Kenneth Kay, Ret. illus Army 26:40-46 Apr '76

DISLOCATION ALLOWANCES

Ruling (by General Accounting Office) hits dislocation $ $. AF Times 37:8 Nov 22 '76

'Year' for DLA (DisLocation Allowance) is 15 months. AF Times 37:3 Nov 15 '76

DISPENSARIES

All-purpose clinic (at Fort Bliss, Tex). Sgt1C Floyd Harrington. illus Soldiers 31:31-33 Dec '76

DISPLAY SYSTEMS

An advanced long-range radar for military and civilian applications. James E. Dalmas. illus Signal 31:76-81 Oct '76

F-16. Capt George S. Gennin. illus (Also cutaways) tab USAF Ftr Wpns Rev, pp 1-8, Spring '76

Flight deck design--technology--money. illus Interavia 31:640-642 Jul '76

Head-up displays. Stefan Geisenheyner. illus Aerosp Intl 12:8+ Jul-Aug '76

Liquid crystals: The daylight survivable display. Glen F. Ingle. illus tabs Elect Warfare 8:55-56+ Sep-Oct '76

Naval weapon system automation with the WSA4. J. R. Harper. illus Intl Def Rev 9:795-797 Oct '76

Optimization of crew effectiveness in future cockpit design: Biomedical implications. Siegfried J. Gerathewohl. illus tab Aviation, Space & Envmt Med 47:1182-1187 Nov '76

Radar electro-optical display improvements. L. Wesley Hopper. illus tabs Countermeasures 2:96+ Sep '76

A revolutionary all-weather HUD (Head-Up Display). (Thomson-CSF TC 125) Douglas Chopping. illus Interavia 31:548-549 Jun '76

Safety razor's edge? Maj Robert P. Bateman. illus Aerosp Safety 32:2-4 Mar '76

Visual elements in flight simulation. John Lott Brown. Aviation, Space & Envmt Med 47:913-924 Sep '76

DISSENTERS

Mobilizing people for collective political action. (Paper, American Sociological Assoc, San Francisco, Aug 1975) Kenneth L. Wilson and Anthony M. Orum. J Pol & Mil Sociol 4:187-202 Fall '76

The need for dissent. Interview. VADM William P. Mack, Ret. illus AF Times, Times Magazine sup: 20-24+ Jan 12 '76

Tolerating honest dissent. LtCol F. N. Van Sant. MarCor Gaz 60:44-45 Feb '76

DISTANT EARLY WARNING SYSTEMS

Raven on the 'cap. (109th Tactical Airlift Group of the Air National Guard flies resupply missions to DEW-Line sites in Greenland) Maj Terry A. Arnold. illus Airman 20:2-8 Nov '76

DIVERS AND DIVING

Associations between psychological factors and pulmonary toxicity during intermittent oxygen breathing at 2 ATA. Robert J. Biersner and others. tab Aviation, Space and Envmt Med 47:173-176 Feb '76

Hematologic changes in man during decompression: Relations to overt decompression sickness and bubble scores. Robert F. Goad and others. tab Aviation, Space & Envmt Med 47:863-867 Aug '76

Indirect evidence for arterial chemoreceptor reflex facilitation by face immersion in man. Sigmund B. Strømme and Arnoldus Schytte Blix. tab illus Aviation, Space & Envmt Med 47:597-599 Jun '76

Occupational differences between conventional and saturation divers. Robert J. Biersner and others. tabs Aviation, Space & Envmt Med 47:29-32 Jan '76

Serum uric acid, cholesterol, and psychological moods throughout stressful naval training. Richard H. Rahe and others. tabs Aviation, Space & Envmt Med 47:883-888 Aug '76

Technique for electrocardiographic monitoring of working divers. P. F. Hoar and others. illus Aviation, Space & Envmt Med 47:667-671 Jun '76

Use of H_2 as an inert gas during diving: Pulmonary function during H_2-O_2 breathing at 7.06 ATA. James H. Dougherty, Jr. tabs Aviation, Space & Envmt Med 47:618-626 Jun '76

What EEG criteria for diving fitness? J. Corriol and others. illus tabs Aviation, Space & Envmt Med 47:868-872 Aug '76

DIVORCE see Marriage and Divorce

DIXON, Robert J.

The future and Tactical Air Command. (Remarks, American Defense Preparedness Assoc Meeting, Los Angeles, Oct 15, 1975) Gen Robert J. Dixon. AF Plcy Ltr for Comdrs: Sup No. 2:10-21 Feb '76; Condensation. Natl Def 60:285 Jan-Feb '76

"Our" Air Force and its future. (Remarks, ROA National Convention, Bal Harbour, Fla, June 29-July 2, 1976) Gen Robert J. Dixon. por Air Reservist 28:4-6 Aug-Sep '76

Tactical Air Command. por AF Mag 59:77-79 May '76

DOCKS

Oversize dry dock passes Chittenden Locks (Seattle). Col Raymond J. Eineigl and others. illus maps Mil Engr 68:83-85 Mar-Apr '76

DOCTORS see Physicians

DOCTRINE

Air Force--Great Britain

Some thoughts about air power. ACM Andrew Humphrey. illus Hawk No. 37:5-7+ Jul '76

DOCTRINE - Continued

Air Force--Poland

History

The operational doctrine of the Polish Air Force in World War II: A thirty-year perspective. Michael A. Peszke. illus chart Aerosp Hist 23:140-147 Sep '76

Air Force--U.S.

Air interdiction in a European future war: Doctrine or dodo? WgComdr Alan Parkes. AU Rev 27:16-18 Sep-Oct '76

The thread of doctrine. LtGen John W. Pauly. illus AU Rev 27:2-10 May-Jun '76

What is aerospace doctrine? AF Plcy Ltr for Comdrs: Sup No. 1:29-30 Jan '76

Armed Forces--Great Britain

Doctrine and the soldier. Colin Gordon. RUSI J for Def Studies 121:38-45 Jun '76

Armed Forces--Russia

Clausewitz and Soviet politico-military strategy. BrigGen Antonio Pelliccia. NATO's Fifteen Nations 20:18-21+ Dec '75-Jan '76; Digest. Mil Rev 56:23-33 Aug '76

The Soviet antitank debate. Phillip A. Karber. (Reprinted from Survival, May-June 1976) illus Mil Rev 56:67-76 Nov '76; Armor 85:10-14 Nov-Dec '76

Soviet logistic support for ground operations. Graham H. Turbiville. (Reprinted from RUSI Journal for Defence Studies, Sep 1975) illus Mil Rev 56:29-39 Jul '76

Soviet military thought. Joseph D. Douglass, Jr. illus AF Mag 59:88-91 Mar '76

Soviet tactical doctrine and capabilities and NATO's strategic defense. Capt Eugene D. Bétit. illus tabs Strat Rev 4:95-107 Fall '76

The Soviet view. (Excerpts from Soviet publications as examples of official pronouncement important to an appraisal of U.S. interests) Regular feature in issues of Strategic Review

With the Party, with the people. Col A. Korkeshkin. Soviet Mil Rev No. 2:4-6 Feb '76

History

The origins of Soviet military doctrine. R. H. Baker. RUSI J for Def Studies 121:38-43 Mar '76

Armed Forces--U.S.

Evolution of the U.S. military doctrine. MajGen P. Sergeyev and Col V. Trusenkov. Soviet Mil Rev No. 11:52-54 Nov '76

Army--U.S.

Air defense: The Excalibur of the corps and division commanders. Col Russell W. Parker and LtCol Joseph W. House. illus Air Def Mag, pp 29-33, Apr-Jun '76

Counterfire! MajGen David E. Ott and Col Donald M. Rhea. illus Army 26:22-26 Jul '76

A dissenting view of the next war. Capt Andrew J. Bacevich, Jr. illus Armor 85:41-43 Sep-Oct '76

DOCTRINE - Continued

Army--U.S. - Cont'd

Forward ho! The Delta Troop myth. LtCol William P. Gillette. tab Armor 85:45-46 Jan-Feb '76

Needed now: An antiarmor doctrine. Capt Timothy R. O'Neill. illus Armor 85:18-24 Jan-Feb '76

Tooth-to-tail: A conceptual void. illus tab Army Log 8:33-37 Mar-Apr '76

Marine Corps--U.S.

Return to a maritime-based national strategy for the Marine Corps. E. W. Girard. illus tabs MarCor Gaz 60:38-45 Nov '76

DODDS, Joseph B.

Auditor General. BrigGen Joseph B. Dodds. por AF Compt 10:18-19 Oct '76

Notes from the Auditor General. BrigGen Joseph B. Dodds. por AF Compt 10:18-19 Jul '76

DOGS

Drug program (Project Commando Plug) under review: Team visits PACAF bases. MSgt Dave Sheeder. AF Times 36:21 Jun 28 '76

GAO OKs Army's dog experiments. AF Times 37:29 Sep 20 '76

Mondo Cane (USAF SP Academy's Military Dog Studies Branch). Capt Larry J. Myers. illus Soldiers 31:13-16 May '76

New facilities for Air Force working dogs. TIG Brief 28:18 Dec 3 '76

North to Nome. (TSgt Steve Fee represents Elmendorf AFB, Alas, in the Iditarod dog sled race) SSgt Joe Cardoza. illus Airman 20:30-34 May '76

Proficiency training of military dog teams. TIG Brief 28:21 Feb 13 '76

Ruling limits drug sniffers (drug-detection dogs). illus AF Times 37:11 Nov 8 '76

Small dogs do well (sniffing out drugs and explosives). AF Times 37:6 Dec 6 '76

Small dogs proving worth (for detection duty). AF Times 36:61 May 24 '76

Small sniffers (dogs) go to bases for training. AF Times 36:17 Feb 23 '76

Use of drug detector dogs. TIG Brief 28:12 Aug 13 '76

DOMESTIC ACTION PROGRAM see Defense Community Service Program

DOOLITTLE, James H.

B-25s over Tokyo, 18 April 1942. MSgt Dave Sylva. Aerosp Safety 32:14-17+ Apr '76

Jimmy Doolittle--the first 80 years. Barrett Tillman. por Am Avn Hist Soc J 21:297-306 Winter '76

DOUBLEDAY, Van C.

WWMCCS in transition: An Air Force view. BrigGen Van C. Doubleday. Signal 30:70-71 Aug '76

DOUGHERTY, Russell E.

(Combat crew officers' careers) Gen Russell E. Dougherty. por Combat Crew 27:3+ Jul '76; TIG Brief 28:2-4 Aug 13 '76

DOUGHERTY, Russell E. - Continued

'Doing our country's thing.' Gen Russell E. Dougherty. TIG Brief 28:1-2 Jan 30 '76

Human relations. (Remarks, Midlands Chapter, National Conference of Christians and Jews, Omaha, June 13, 1976) Gen Russell E. Dougherty. AF Plcy Ltr for Comdrs: Sup No. 9:6-12 Sep '76

It won't just happen. Gen Russell E. Dougherty. por Combat Crew 26:3+ Jan '76

Make service your profession. (Address, Air Force Engineering and Services Conference, Homestead AFB, Fla, Dec 1975) Gen Russell E. Dougherty. por AF Engrg & Svcs Qtr 17:6-12 May '76

Ours is an honorable profession. Gen Russell E. Dougherty. (Reprinted from Combat Crew, May 1975) Combat Crew 27:8-11 Mar '76

Peace is our profession. (Remarks, Truman Lecture and Fine Arts Series, Westminster College, Fulton, Mo, April 24, 1976) Gen Russell E. Dougherty. AF Plcy Ltr for Comdrs: Sup No. 7:15-23 Jul '76

SAC chief extended a year (and other general officer news announced). AF Times 37:3 Aug 16 '76

Strategic Air Command. por AF Mag 59:74-76 May '76

Utilization of Air Force women (or ... 'rediscovering the wheel'). Gen Russell E. Dougherty. TIG Brief 28:2 Mar 26 '76

What does the nation want of its military? (Remarks, 1976 Air Force Sergeants Assoc Convention, Kansas City, Mo, July 25, 1976) Gen Russell E. Dougherty. AF Plcy Ltr for Comdrs: Sup No. 11:20-30 Nov '76

DRAFT, MILITARY see Military Service, Compulsory

DRIESSNACK, Hans H.

Meet BrigGen Hans H. Driessnack, DCS/Comptroller, Hq Air Force Systems Command. por AF Compt 10:11 Apr '76

DRILL

The DI (Drill Instructor) mystique, sows' ears and a delicate imponderable. Col Robert D. Heinl, Jr, Ret. illus Sea Power 19:37-39 Jun '76

DRONES

See also
Remotely Piloted Vehicles
Targets, Aerial

Missilex: Flailex or safex? LT Ross Burgess. illus Approach 22:18-20 Jul '76

Unmanned aircraft: New answers and new problems. Air Commodore M. J. Armitage. illus Royal Air Forces Qtr 16:208-221 Autumn '76

DRUEN, Walter D., Jr

Air Force Military Personnel Center. por AF Mag 59:97-98 May '76

DRUG ADDICTS

Alcohol inaction charged (by General Accounting Office). AF Times 36:31 May 3 '76

Alcoholism today. AVM P. J O'Connor. Royal Air Forces Qtr 15:319-320 Winter '75

DRUG ADDICTS - Continued

Rehabilitation

See also
Rehabilitation

ANG/Res can't bar ex-drug user. AF Times 36:6 Feb 16 '76

Alcohol abuse efforts pushed (by House Appropriations Committee). AF Times 36:4 Jun 21 '76

Alcohol consultant (National Council on Alcoholism) hired (by AF). AF Times 36:10 Jul 5 '76

The alcohol problem and what the Army is doing about it. E. A. Lawrence. illus Army 26:23-27 Aug '76

Andrews (AFB, Md) gets Alcohol (Treatment) Center. AF Times 36:4 Jun 14 '76

Bottled in booze. Darryl D. McEwen. illus Soldiers 31:47-48 Aug '76

Civilian drug and alcohol abuse control program. TIG Brief 28:10-11 Sep 10 '76

Don't ignore the problem drinker--lessons learned. TIG Brief 28:3-4 Jun 4 '76

Drug rehab must before discharge. AF Times 37:6 Nov 8 '76

Experts to examine alcohol problem. Len Famiglietti. AF Times 36:2 May 10 '76

New alcohol abuse control measures implemented. TIG Brief 28:5-6 Oct 22 '76

Pot still tops drugs in use. AF Times 36:8 Jan 5 '76

Recovered alcoholics get help: Discrimination fought. Len Famiglietti. AF Times 37:61 Sep 20 '76

Statistics

Pot still tops drugs in use. AF Times 36:8 Jan 5 '76

DRUGS

Advice to commanders: Problems can lead to drugs. AF Times 37:4 Oct 11 '76

Alcohol won't push drug program aside. AF Times 37:61 Oct 4 '76

CMA (Court of Military Appeals) ruling could mean stiffer hard drug terms. AF Times 37:22 Aug 9 '76

CMR (Court of Military Review) asks rehearing in EM's heroin case. AF Times 37:26 Dec 13 '76

Drug program (Project Commando Plug) under review: Team visits PACAF bases. MSgt Dave Sheeder. AF Times 36:21 Jun 28 '76

Drug smuggling in Bangkok: AF-Army team helps crack ring. AF Times 36:39 Apr 12 '76

86 in jail abroad on drugs. Fred Reed. AF Times 37:16 Dec 6 '76

Hq urges commanders to continue drug tests. AF Times 37:12 Dec 20 '76

How pot affects driving. AF Times 37:31 Aug 23 '76

Management of controlled drugs in the emergency room. TIG Brief 28:19 Dec 3 '76

Marijuana smoking and cold tolerance in man. Joel M. Hanna and others. illus tabs Aviation, Space & Envmt Med 47:634-639 Jun '76

DRUGS - Continued

NORAD gear makes $6 million 'haul' (in) smuggled items. AF Times 36:16 Feb 16 '76

Narcotics sentence (for airman) reduced. AF Times 37:20 Aug 23 '76

Penalties limited on drug offenses (by Court of Military Appeals). AF Times 36:24 Jul 19 '76

Pot convictions: 5-year maximum. AF Times 37:2 Nov 1 '76

Prevention of experimental motion sickness by scopolamine absorbed through the skin. Ashton Graybiel and others. illus tabs Aviation, Space & Envmt Med 47:1096-1100 Oct '76

Ruling limits drug sniffers (drug-detection dogs). illus AF Times 37:11 Nov 8 '76

Security Police Investigations (AFR 125-21). TIG Brief 28:8 Apr 23 '76

Simulated flying performance after marihuana intoxication. David S. Janowsky and others. illus tabs Aviation, Space and Envmt Med 47:124-128 Feb '76

Small dogs do well (sniffing out drugs and explosives). AF Times 37:6 Dec 6 '76

Small dogs proving worth (for detection duty). AF Times 36:61 May 24 '76

Small sniffers (dogs) go to bases for training. AF Times 36:17 Feb 23 '76

2 drug rulings upheld (by AF Court of Military Review). AF Times 37:17 Oct 25 '76

Use of drug detector dogs. TIG Brief 28:12 Aug 13 '76

Laws and Regulations

Military law in the 1970's: The effects of Schlesinger v Councilman (decision in the Supreme Court). Capt H. Michael Bartley. AF Law Rev 17:65-78 Winter '75

Testing

Airborne testing of three antimotion sickness preparations. W. H. Johnson and others. tabs Aviation, Space & Envmt Med 47:1214-1216 Nov '76

DRY DOCKS see Docks

DUAL-BASING see Deployment

DUAL COMPENSATION

Dual comp suit (by) 700 retired officers asks millions. Lee Ewing. AF Times 37:10 Aug 2 '76

400 (retired Regular military and naval officers) challenge dual comp. Lee Ewing. AF Times 36:3 Mar 22 '76

DUIN, Robert A.

(Procurement program for the Coast Guard's Non-Appropriated Fund Activities) Interview. RADM Robert A. Duin. por Review 55:83-84 May-Jun '76

DUTIES (TARIFF) see Tariff

DUTY AND RESPONSIBILITY, MILITARY

Active duty service commitment. TIG Brief 28:13 Jan 30 '76

'Doing our country's thing.' Gen Russell E. Dougherty. TIG Brief 28:1-2 Jan 30 '76

1st Sgt nice guy. Richard C. Barnard. illus AF Times, Times Magazine sup:4-7+ Dec 20 '76

Middle management involvement. TIG Brief 28:17 May 7 '76

Reg (AFR 39-6) spells out noncom duties. AF Times 36:8 Jun 21 '76

Safety is everyone's responsibility. BrigGen George C. Cannon, Jr. illus Interceptor 18:14-15 May '76

Technical Representatives of the Contracting Officer (TRCO). TIG Brief 28:12 Oct 22 '76

What are you (squadron commanders and supervisors) doing for Green 16? LtCol Murphy Neal Jones. illus Aerosp Safety 32:2-4 Jun '76

E

E F T S see Electronic Funds Transfer System

E S S A see Environmental Science Services Administration

EAKER, Ira C.

The Air Corps' 1926 Pan American flight. LtGen Ira C. Eaker, Ret. AF Mag 59:114+ Sep '76

Airline industry in jeopardy. LtGen Ira C. Eaker, Ret. AF Times 36:17-18 Jul 12 '76

And how good is the MIG-25? LtGen Ira C. Eaker, Ret. AF Times 37:13-14 Oct 4 '76

The attempt to kill the B-1. LtGen Ira C. Eaker, Ret. AF Times 36:13+ Jun 21 '76

The fate of the B-1 bomber. LtGen Ira C. Eaker, Ret. AF Times 37:13-14 Oct 11 '76

The intelligence shake-up. LtGen Ira C. Eaker, Ret. AF Times 36:13-14 Mar 15 '76

Israel solves a hijacking. LtGen Ira C. Eaker, Ret. AF Times 36:13-14 Jul 26 '76

Meeting the Russian threat. LtGen Ira C. Eaker, Ret. AF Times 37:17-18 Sep 6 '76

Military manpower problems. LtGen Ira C. Eaker, Ret. AF Times 37:13-14 Sep 20 '76

Most critical issue: U.S. security. LtGen Ira C. Eaker, Ret. AF Times 37:13-14 Nov 1 '76

NATO defenders still undaunted. LtGen Ira C. Eaker, Ret. AF Times 37:13-14 Nov 15 '76

(New Air and) Space Museum: By, for Americans. LtGen Ira C. Eaker, Ret. AF Times 36:13-14 Jul 19 '76

A new naval policy emerging? LtGen Ira C. Eaker, Ret. AF Times 36:11-12 May 3 '76

The new Pacific doctrine. LtGen Ira C. Eaker, Ret. AF Times 36:13+ Jan 5 '76

On pardons for draft dodgers. LtGen Ira C. Eaker, Ret. AF Times 37:13-14 Sep 27 '76

Our clear and present danger. LtGen Ira C. Eaker, Ret. AF Times 37:13-14 Oct 18 '76

The U.S. and Russian Navies. LtGen Ira C. Eaker, Ret. AF Times 37:13-14 Aug 23 '76

U.S. election: Russian reaction. LtGen Ira C. Eaker, Ret. AF Times 37:13-14 Dec 27 '76

What we learned from MIG (25). LtGen Ira C. Eaker, Ret. AF Times 37:13-14 Oct 25 '76

Who shall run U.S. Navy. LtGen Ira C. Eaker, Ret. AF Times 36:17+ Jun 14 '76

Why Russia wants Angola. LtGen Ira C. Eaker, Ret. AF Times 36:13+ Jan 19 '76

EARTHQUAKES see Disasters

ECOLOGY see Environment

ECONOMIC AID TO FOREIGN COUNTRIES

Israel

The burden of defense on the Israeli economy. Patrick W. Murphy. illus tabs Def & For Aff Dig No. 4: 46-51 '76

ECONOMIC AID TO FOREIGN COUNTRIES - Continued

Latin America

Dependence, exploitation and economic growth. Albert Szymanski. tabs J Pol & Mil Sociol 4:53-65 Spring '76

Spain

The Spanish connection: A wider U.S. commitment in the making. maps tabs Def Monitor 5: entire issue Feb '76

Thailand

Post Vietnam: U.S. and Thailand. Maj Merrill L. Bartlett. illus map MarCor Gaz 60:24-29 Jan '76

ECONOMIC ANALYSIS

Are the cities saveable? illus Govt Exec 8:18-20+ Nov '76

Jacksonville (Fla): Consolidation is no panacea. illus chart Govt Exec 8:24-26+ Nov '76

Off-base buying: What impact does this have on the town? Capt Randall B. King. illus tabs AF Compt 10:26-27 Jan '76

Strategic economic intelligence: A systems approach. Maj R. Carl Moor, Jr. illus Mil Rev 56:47-51 Oct '76

Weights and balances. Capt Tim Traub. Translog 7: 4-6 Jan '76

ECONOMIC DEVELOPMENT

Arabesque. (The Arabian Peninsula) Leigh Johnson. illus Def & For Aff Dig No. 4:32-38+ '76

Dependence, exploitation and economic growth. Albert Szymanski. tabs J Pol & Mil Sociol 4:53-65 Spring '76

ECONOMICS

Economic strategy. Regular feature in issues of Defense & Foreign Affairs Digest

Fetch the age of gold. A. Ranney Johnson. illus Def & For Aff Dig No. 8-9:74-77 '76

A forecast for the 70's and 80's. Anthony J. Wiener. Persp in Def Mgt No. 24:1-12 Winter '75-'76

Global corporations and the American economy. Ronald Muller. Persp in Def Mgt No. 24:43-55 Winter '75-'76

EDUCATION

Guam

Guam HEW-school rejected (by U.S. Office of Education). AF Times 37:50 Sep 27 '76

Guam schools 'inadequate'; separate system sought. Lee Ewing. AF Times 36:3 Mar 8 '76

Schools on Guam prod PCS change. Lee Ewing. AF Times 37:3 Aug 9 '76

United States

Career transition course (offered by Catholic University) teaches retirees to survive. M. L. Craver. AF Times 37:12 Nov 8 '76

Education supplement. AF Times 36:20p sup opposite p 30 Mar 15 '76; 36:16p sup opposite p 26 Jul 19 '76; 37:16p sup opposite p 28 Nov 8 '76

400 schools using AF-type courses. AF Times 37:32 Aug 9 '76

EDUCATION - Continued

United States - Cont'd

Fund boost backed for GI schooling. Larry Carney. AF Times 37:2 Sep 13 '76

GI Bill benefit boosted 8 percent; Flight training funds not raised. Larry Carney. AF Times 37:4 Nov 1 '76

GI school aid up, time cut. Larry Carney. AF Times 37:3 Oct 18 '76

House hearings: GI Bill cheating--$1 billion. AF Times 36:25 May 17 '76

House seen passing pay-in school bill. Larry Carney. AF Times 37:8 Sep 20 '76

President signs law; GI Bill benefits increased. MarCor Gaz 60:3 Dec '76

2 more GI Bill items (correspondence courses and flight training) face Ford budget ax. AF Times 36:8 Feb 2 '76

VA (education) allowance raise, pay-in plan proposed. Larry Carney. AF Times 36:18 Jul 19 '76

History

Educate the freedman. Soldiers 31:18 Feb '76

EDUCATION (DEPENDENTS)

(Dept of) Defense can fire (foreign school bus) drivers abroad. AF Times 37:10 Sep 13 '76

Dependents schools in Europe: A disorganized system in danger of flunking. Richard C. Barnard. illus AF Times, Times Magazine sup pt 1, pp 8-12+, Oct 18 '76; pt 2, pp 18-22+, Nov 1 '76

Guam HEW-school rejected (by U.S. Office of Education). AF Times 37:50 Sep 27 '76

Guam schools 'inadequate'; separate system sought. Lee Ewing. AF Times 36:3 Mar 8 '76

The kids who go TDY. (London Central High School is a dorm school for junior and senior high school military dependents) MSgt Harold Newcomb. illus Airman 20:44-48 Apr '76

More o'seas (dependents) may walk to school. AF Times 37:25 Aug 23 '76

Schools on Guam prod PCS change. Lee Ewing. AF Times 37:3 Aug 9 '76

EDUCATION, MILITARY see Education, Technical; Education and Training

EDUCATION, SCIENTIFIC

See also
Medical Education Program

EDUCATION, TECHNICAL

See also
Medical Education Program
Mobile Training Units
Retraining Program

Professionalism through logistics education and training. Ben S. Blanchard. illus tabs Log Spectrum 10: 28-33 Summer '76

EDUCATION, TECHNICAL - Continued

Air Force--U.S.

See also
Community College of the Air Force

(AF) peer-instructed grads graded as job-ready. AF Times 37:10 Dec 27 '76

Army--U.S.

Logistics training asset--community colleges. Capt B. D. Sullivan. illus Army Log 8:28-29 May-Jun '76

National Guard--Air Force--U.S.

Volk-Alpena connection. (Air Traffic Control (ATC) training programs at ANG bases in Michigan and Wisconsin) Capt D. T. Davis. illus Air Reservist 27:10-11 Feb '76

Navy--U.S.

See also
Consolidated Navy Electronic Warfare School
Naval Training Centers

The LSO Phase One School. LCDR Mick Sumnick. illus Approach 22:14 Sep '76

Russia

Fruitful cooperation. (Interview with Nikolai Sofinsky) Vasily Yefremov. illus Soviet Mil Rev No. 2; 45-47 Feb '76

EDUCATION AND NATIONAL DEFENSE

Warriors and scholars: Fellow professionals in hard times. Bruce M. Russett. Nav War Col Rev 28:87-91 Fall '75

EDUCATION AND TRAINING

See also
On-the-Job Training
Retraining Program
Training Aids
    also specific types of centers and schools, e. g.,
Engineer Centers and Schools
Management Centers and Schools
Medical Centers and Schools
Officer Candidate Schools
Transportation Centers and Schools
    also subdivision under specific subjects, e. g.,
Pilots--Education and Training

Air Force--Germany(Federal Republic)

The Luftwaffe + twenty. (German pilots train at Luke AFB, Ariz) LtCol Fred A. Meurer. illus Airman 20:2-8 Aug '76

Air Force--Great Britain

Dominie--trainer for the backroom boys. (No. 6 Flying Training School, RAF Finningley) (Flying with the RAF today, no. 8) Philip J. Birtles. illus Air Pict 38:358-360 Sep '76

Instructor on a Jet Provost. (Flying with the R.A.F. today, no. 10) J. D. R. Rawlings. illus Air Pict 38: 480-482 Dec '76

Air Force--Russia

(Soviet) Air Force engineers' school (Yakov Alksnis Higher Aviation Engineering School, Riga). Col N. Konkov. illus Soviet Mil Rev No. 7:42-43 Jul '76

EDUCATION AND TRAINING - Continued

Air Force--U.S.

See also
Air Command and Staff College
Air Force Academy
Air Force Institute of Technology
Air Training Command
Air War College
Airman Education and Commissioning Program
Community College of the Air Force
Fighter Weapons School
Flight Training
Minuteman Education Program
Missile Training
Officer Training School
Squadron Officer School
   also subdivision Education and Training under
the following subjects,

Air Crews   Navigators
Astronauts   Pilots

(Air) Staff TRAining plan (ASTRA) open. AF Times
37:33 Sep 27 '76

Care in selecting MTIs (Military Training Instructors) paying off. AF Times 36:4 Jun 7 '76

Educational deferments. TIG Brief 28:3 Nov 5 '76

400 schools using AF-type courses. AF Times 37:32
Aug 9 '76

Individual Training; Inspection Guide C. TIG Brief
28:6p addendum Jan 30 '76

Learning--despite the instructor. Capt Charles Austin. illus tab AU Rev 27:72-78 Mar-Apr '76

NCO training gets classroom push. AF Times 36:19
Jun 28 '76

OTSL (SAC's Operations Training Support Laboratory) training topics. Regular feature in some issues
of Combat Crew starting with May '76

Professional identity in a plural world: The focus of
junior officer education in the U.S. Air Force.
BrigGen John E. Ralph. illus AU Rev 27:11-25
Jan-Feb '76

Professionalism. LtGen Raymond B. Furlong. TIG
Brief 28:2 Mar 12 '76

Rules of war detailed in training package. AF Times
37:41 Nov 1 '76

SPs to take new 'get tough' drills. AF Times 36:9
Feb 23 '76

Sports camps slated--dates, locations later. Len Famiglietti. AF Times 37:6 Sep 27 '76

TDY funding for short course students: Try centralized control! LtCol Norman E.Qualtrough. illus
AF Compt 10:30-31 Apr '76

Training: A new concept. (Caramate II audiovisual
teaching machine) Capt Robert S.Klinger. illus
tab Combat Crew 27:16-19 Mar '76

Training denied some first shirts. AF Times 36:11
Jul 12 '76

Using good sense in stress training. TIG Brief 28:12
Dec 17 '76

Costs

Training (cost-reducing) study ordered by C/S (Gen
David C.Jones). AF Times 36:2 May 31 '76

Armed Forces

Costs

DOD lowers charges for foreign trainees. AF Times
37:10 Nov 1 '76

EDUCATION AND TRAINING - Continued

Armed Forces--Canada

Professionalism and the Canadian military. LtCol
J.H.Pocklington. AU Rev 27:34-40 Mar-Apr '76

Armed Forces--Great Britain

The Joint Warfare Establishment. AVM F.S.S.Hazlewood. (Reprinted from Royal Air Forces Quarterly, Autumn 1975) Army Qtr 106:161-170 Apr '76

Armed Forces--NATO

The Joint Warfare Establishment. AVM F.S.S.Hazlewood. (Reprinted from Royal Air Forces Quarterly, Autumn 1975) Army Qtr 106:161-170 Apr '76

Armed Forces--Russia

Competence in method--the commander: A pedagogue
and educator. LtGen L.Kuznetsov. Soviet Mil Rev
No.11:17-19 Nov '76

Ideological education of servicemen. Maj A.Rybin.
Soviet Mil Rev No.9:46-48 Sep '76

The military profession in the USSR. Harriet Fast
Scott. illus tabs AF Mag 59:76-81 Mar '76

The moral strength of the Soviet soldier. Col V.Mikheyev. Soviet Mil Rev No.6:30-31 Jun '76

The Soviet military machine; Morale, muscles, and
megatons. Col Robert D.Heinl, Jr, Ret. illus Sea
Power 19:31-34 May '76

Training facilities at military schools. Col S.Mutsynov. Soviet Mil Rev No.11:26-27 Nov '76

Armed Forces--U.S.

See also
Industrial College of the Armed Forces
National War College

AF, Navy look at sharing systems training data. AF
Times 36:32 Feb 23 '76

Crimes in hostilities. Maj W.Hays Parks. illus tab
MarCor Gaz pt 1, 60:16-22 Aug '76; pt 2, 60:33-39
Sep '76

Education supplement. AF Times 36:20p sup opposite
p 30 Mar 15 '76; 36:16p sup opposite p 26
Jul 19 '76; 37:16p sup opposite p 28 Nov 8 '76

Instructional technology in the Department of Defense, now and in the future. M.Richard Rose.
illus tab AU Rev 27:11-23 May-Jun '76

Interservice Training (AFR 50-18). TIG Brief 28:15
Mar 26 '76

Costs

Military Manpower Training Report (MMTR). Maj
J.L.Finan. illus AF Compt 10:30-31+ Jul '76

Army--Russia

A battery on exercise. Lt V.Yusupdjanov. illus Soviet Mil Rev No.1:19-20 Jan '76

Maturing of soldiers: Experience in work with young
soldiers (missilemen) of the Air Defence Forces.
LtCol V.Selyodkin. Soviet Mil Rev No.8:36-37
Aug '76

Methods used in educating Soviet soldiers. Col N.
Fedenko. Soviet Mil Rev No.11:34-36 Nov '76

Psychological steeling of tankmen. Maj M.Rudachenko. Soviet Mil Rev No.1:30-31 Jan '76

EDUCATION AND TRAINING - Continued

Soviet night operations. Arthur W. McMaster III. illus tabs USA Avn Dig 22:2-3+ Jan '76

The Soviet soldier. Maj Joseph C. Liberti. illus Infantry 66:37-41 Jan-Feb '76

Troop control in combat. Col P. Simchenkov. Soviet Mil Rev No. 1:14-15+ Jan '76

A r m y - - S w i t z e r l a n d

Military service and social change in Switzerland. Hanspeter Kriesi. tabs Armed Forces & Soc 2: 218-226 Winter '76

A r m y - - U. S.

See also
Armor--Education and Training
Armored Centers and Schools
Army Air Defense School
Army Aviation Centers and Schools
Army Field Artillery School
Army War College
Command and General Staff College
Military Academy, West Point, NY

AMC schools--the other Army school system. illus Army Log 8:10-14 Jan-Feb '76

Air defense in the 2d Infantry Division. (Fit-to-fight (Pro-Life) program) illus Air Def Mag, pp 20-23, Jan-Mar '76

Airborne--and then some. (Airborne School, Fort Benning, Ga, has first female instructors) LtCol Floyd A. Frost. illus Soldiers 31:30 Dec '76

All in one. (One Station Unit Training (OSUT)) SSgt John Savard. illus Soldiers 31:36-40 Oct '76

The artillery raid, air assault style. LtCol Albert E. Wolfgang and Capt Ronald E. Spears. illus Fld Arty J 44:22-28 May-Jun '76

As it is. (Basic training today) Darryl D. McEwen. illus Soldiers 31:49-51 Jul '76

11th Aviation Group (Combat) aviation training in USAREUR. Capt Eric R. Kunz. illus USA Avn Dig 22:2-3+ Aug '76

The buck stops here. Maj Alexander P. Shine. illus Infantry 66:23-26 Nov-Dec '76

Capstone (Warrant Officer Senior Course (WOSC), Fort Rucker, Ala) is back. Sgt1C Floyd Harrington. illus Soldiers 31:11-13 Jun '76

EISPE (Expert Infantryman Squad and Platoon Evaluation). MajGen Joseph C. McDonough. illus tabs Infantry 66:19-22 Nov-Dec '76

EPMS (Enlisted Personnel Management System): What it's all about. SGM Nat Dell. illus Soldiers 31:8-11 Sep '76

For E4s only. (PNCOC/CA, Primary NonCommissioned Officer's Course/Combat Arms) Sgt1C Floyd Harrington. illus Soldiers 31:10-12 Oct '76

Forging the main link. LtCol Serge P. C. Demyanenko. illus Fld Arty J 44:40-44 May-Jun '76

Introspection is key in sweeping revision of (TRADOC's) training methods. Gen William E. DePuy. illus Army 26:61+ Oct '76

The lessons were not just military: What the Army taught me. Charles R. Murrah. Army 26:32-33 Nov '76

EDUCATION AND TRAINING - Continued

Logistics training asset--community colleges. Capt B. D. Sullivan. illus Army Log 8:28-29 May-Jun '76

MPs behind bars. (Correctional specialist course, Army Military Police School, Fort McClellan, Ala) Jerry Hill. illus Soldiers 31:18-20 Nov '76

The next one will be a squad leader's war. Capt Robert B. Killebrew. illus Army 26:22-25 Dec '76

Realistic training at any price? Arnold R. Lambert. illus USA Avn Dig 22:35-36 Jun '76

Shaping tomorrow's soldier. (Field training exercises) SP5 Ed Aber. illus Soldiers 31:19-20 Jun '76

TDY funding for short course students: Try centralized control! LtCol Norman E. Qualtrough. illus AF Compt 10:30-31 Apr '76

3-phase training makes the difference. (Basic combat training at Fort Knox, Ky) CMSgts Haywood F. Wren and Dana D. Brookover. illus Army 26:29-31+ Aug '76

Toward a more congenial training environment. LtCol Frank A. Partlow, Jr. Fld Arty J 44:13-16 May-Jun '76

Trainers, rise up: Hostile training environment. Capt Lee Baxter. illus Fld Arty J 44:16-20 Jan-Feb '76; Condensation. Armor 85:46-47 Jul-Aug '76

Training at -70° F. (Army's Northern Warfare Training Center (NWTC), Fort Greely, Alas) Sgt1C Floyd Harrington. illus Soldiers 31:46-48 Nov '76

Training devices become "big business." LtCol Theodore S. May, Ret. illus Mil Rev 56:79-84 Sep '76

Training points the way. LtGen Robert M. Shoemaker. illus USA Avn Dig 22:2-3+ Jul '76

Training tankers to think. (1st Cav Div, Fort Hood, Tex) Richard C. Barnard. illus AF Times, Times Magazine sup:4-8 Jun 14 '76

Turn-on to life. (Pro Life program at Fort Dix, NJ) SSgt Zack Richards. illus Soldiers 31:18-20 Sep '76

The U. S. Infantry: Training then and now. SSgt Jerry Van Slyke and Jane Beachner. illus Infantry 66: 40-46 Jul-Aug '76

WACs in combat. Joseph E. Revell. illus tab AF Times, Times Magazine sup pt 1, If the Army expects women to fight, why aren't they trained like men? 36:10-14+ Feb 9 '76; pt 2, Does the nation want women to have an equal right to die on the battlefield? 36:10-16+ Feb 23 '76

Costs

Professionalism in Army Aviation and budgetary constraints. BrigGen Charles E. Canedy. illus USA Avn Dig 22:1-3 Jun '76

Directories

(Army) schools and centers. Army 26:136 Oct '76

History

As it was. (Recruit training during WW I) Darryl D. McEwen. illus tab Soldiers 31:46-48 Jul '76

EDUCATION AND TRAINING - Continued

Marine Corps--U.S.

See also
Marine Corps Development and Education Command

Academia in direct support. (The Adjunct Faculty, composed of selected Marine Corps Reserve officers, occupying civilian academic positions, as adjunct to the military staff at Marine Corps Command and Staff College) Col George M. Van Sant and Maj Allan R. Millet. illus MarCor Gaz 60:31-38 Aug '76

Computer Assisted Instruction (CAI): How "Herbie" can help students and government. illus Govt Exec 8:40-41 Feb '76

The DI (Drill Instructor) mystique, sows' ears and a delicate imponderable. Col Robert D. Heinl, Jr, Ret. illus Sea Power 19:37-39 Jun '76

Emphasis on professionalism for a new generation of Marines. Gen Louis H. Wilson. illus Sea Power 19:24-29 Jan '76

The final coordination line. Maj M. R. Janay. MarCor Gaz 60:50-51 Jan '76

New training center. (Marine Corps Air-Ground Combat Training Center, 29 Palms, Calif) MarCor Gaz 60:4 Jan '76

Real training now for combat. Maj Gary E. Todd. MarCor Gaz 60:52-55 Sep '76

Recruit training: Challenging and tough. (Adapted from statement before House Armed Services Committee Sub-committee on Recruiting and Recruit Training) Gen Louis H. Wilson. MarCor Gaz 60:2-4 Aug '76

Recruit training, one piece of the puzzle. LtCol T.C. Dolson. illus MarCor Gaz 60:23-34 Mar '76

Taking the highground. Sgt John Galt. illus MarCor Gaz 60:26-32 Sep '76

National Guard--Air Force--U.S.

The enemy fired needles. (Security police from NM ANG and USAF's 4900th Security Police Sq, Kirtland AFB, NM, complete Corona Lock, AF's Combat Air Base Defense Course) illus Natl Guardsman 30:37 Jan '76

The great Minnesota/Arizona cactus caper. Capt Neal Gendler. illus Natl Guardsman 30:30-31 May '76

(Operation) Coronet Sprint. (Two weeks of hard work by 180 Air Guardsmen of the 117th Tactical Reconnaissance Wg, Birmingham, Ala) 1stLt Gregory Hodges. illus Air Reservist 28:8-9 Jun '76

National Guard--Army--U.S.

In Guard, Army partnership, the key is mutual respect. LtCol Raymond E. Bell, Jr. illus Army 26:24-26 Jan '76

The 'Ohio solution': Dynamic new training spurs Guardsmen. Maj Martin C. Froebel. illus Army 26:49-51 Mar '76

Navy--U.S.

See also
Naval War College

Improving the man-machine interface. Bill Walsh. illus Countermeasures 2:53-55 Jun '76

Reserve Forces--Armed Forces--U.S.

ROA (Executive Director Gen J. Milnor Roberts) tells senators (Manpower and Personnel Subcommittee of the Senate Armed Services Committee) world will see U.S. Reserve cuts as weakening. Officer 52:4 Apr '76

Two out of thirty. Maj Howard C. Race. illus Infantry 66:27-29 Nov-Dec '76

EDUCATION AND TRAINING - Continued

Reserve Forces--Army--Great Britain

A role for the uncommitted Reserve? LtCol Michael Burkham. RUSI J for Def Studies 121:43-45 Sep '76

The training of General Reserve battalions of the TAVR (Territorial Army Volunteer Reserve). Maj M. J. Dudding. illus RUSI J for Def Studies 120: 23-26 Dec '75

Reserve Forces--Army--U.S.

Can the Reserve Components make it? LtCol Benjamin L. Abramowitz. illus tab Mil Rev 56:58-64 May '76

Desk to desk. (USAR Research and Development Officer Career Program) Col James L. Wohlfahrt. illus Army Log 8:6-7 Jul-Aug '76

ILC (Instructional Learning Center): A success story. (Unique application of audio-visual techniques, personalized additional instruction and assistance and a practical field application, all in one package, to improve readiness of Reserve Component units in Army Readiness Region I) Col Edward P. Metzner. Fld Arty J 44:53-54 Jul-Aug '76

Learning by doing. Maj Hardy W. Bryan III. illus Army Log 8:34-37 Nov-Dec '76

Reserve training upgrade at MTMCEA (Military Traffic Management Command Eastern Area). Capt Mike Fillmore. illus Translog 7:16-18 Dec '76

Reserve Forces--Marine Corps--U.S.

Top level school for senior Reserves (National Defense University's Defense Strategy Seminar). LtCol Carl R. Venditto. MarCor Gaz 60:60-61 Oct '76

Reserve Officers Training Corps--Army--U.S.

Working vacation. (ROTC summer training) LtCol Don Kington. illus Soldiers 31:45-48 Jun '76

EDUCATION AND TRAINING, OFF-DUTY

Air Force--U.S.

CCAF (Community College of the Air Force). illus Air Reservist 28:12 Apr '76

Correspondence courses can save training dollars. TIG Brief 28:8 Sep 24 '76

Educational deferments. TIG Brief 28:3 Nov 5 '76

Making the mark with missiles. Capt Robert G.H. Carroll. illus tab AF Mag 59:50-54 Jun '76

Voluntary in-service educational opportunities: Air Force policies--individual goals. Armand J. Galfo. illus AU Rev 27:26-33 Mar-Apr '76

Armed Forces--U.S.

Education supplement. AF Times 36:20p sup opposite p 30 Mar 15 '76; 36:16p sup opposite p 26 Jul 19 '76; 37:16p sup opposite p 28 Nov 8 '76

Off-campus education questioned. Len Famiglietti. AF Times 37:18 Dec 6 '76

PREP (PRe-discharge Education Program) expires end of October. AF Times 37:4 Nov 1 '76

SOC (Servicemen's Opportunity College) schools: Latest listing. AF Times 36:33 Jul 19 '76

Strategy seminars (at Naval War College to) offer graduate credit. AF Times 37:2 Aug 9 '76

EDUCATION AND TRAINING, OFF-DUTY- Continued

Armed Forces--U.S. - Cont'd

362 schools in SOC (Serviceman's Opportunity College); grad programs eyed. AF Times 37:35 Nov 29 '76

Army--U.S.

Educational shopping center. (Army Training Support Center, Fort Eustis, Va, brings "one-stop shopping" to Army's Non-Resident Instruction (NRI) programs) SSgt Zack Richards. illus Soldiers 31: 50-51 Mar '76

Marine Corps--U.S.

Send more Marines to school. GySgt Jimmy Carl Harris. MarCor Gaz 60:61-62 Jun '76

EDUCATION-WITH-INDUSTRY PROGRAM see Training-with-Industry Program

EDUCATIONAL LEVEL OF MILITARY PERSONNEL

DMC (Defense Manpower Commission) report: BA (degree) usually enough for 4-star rank. AF Times 36:23 May 10 '76

Send more Marines to school. GySgt Jimmy Carl Harris. MarCor Gaz 60:61-62 Jun '76

Voluntary in-service educational opportunities: Air Force policies--individual goals. Armand J.Galfo. illus AU Rev 27:26-33 Mar-Apr '76

EDUCATIONAL TECHNOLOGY

Instructional technology in the Department of Defense, now and in the future. M.Richard Rose. illus tab AU Rev 27:11-23 May-Jun '76

Never for knowledge alone. (Defense Language Institute's teaching methods) Ted R.Sturm. illus Airman 20:16-20 May '76

EFFECTIVENESS REPORTS

Air Force

Advisory review board won't be given old OERs. AF Times 37:2 Aug 30 '76

Chaplain OERs now controlled. AF Times 36:31 Apr 12 '76

Correction of officer and airman evaluation reports. TIG Brief 28:21 Jan 16 '76

A 50/50 chance of being passed over. Capt W.E. Thompson. AF Engrg & Svcs Qtr 17:21-22 Feb '76

Headquarters study: New OER plan works, brings few surprises. Lee Ewing. tab AF Times 36:4 Jan 19 '76

I am a three, or how I learned to stop worrying and love the new OER system. Maj Mark Wynn. AU Rev 27:43-46 Sep-Oct '76

Lieutenant colonel effectiveness report results. tabs AF Plcy Ltr for Comdrs: Sup No.4:26-29 Apr '76

Lieutenant colonel selectee OER data. tab AF Times 37:3 Nov 29 '76

Most lieutenant colonel choices had top-box OER. Lee Ewing. tabs AF Times 36:10 Feb 2 '76

New OER OK, but needs work. Lee Ewing. AF Times 37:4 Sep 27 '76

OER plan believed misjudged: New and old not the same. Lee Ewing. AF Times 36:17 Mar 29 '76

OER: Problems, progress. Lee Ewing. AF Times 37:3 Sep 6 '76

EFFECTIVENESS REPORTS - Continued

Air Force - Cont'd

OER reviewers begin seminars. AF Times 37:2 Nov 22 '76

Performance evaluation and productivity. TIG Brief 28:18 Apr 9 '76

Performance new OER key. Lee Ewing. AF Times 37:3 Nov 29 '76

Army

Writing a readable OER. Col John C.Bahnsen, Jr and Maj R.William Highlander. illus Armor 85:26-28 Jul-Aug '76

History

Army scorecards (then and now). Sgt JoAnn Mann. illus Soldiers 31:20-21 Jul '76

EFFICIENCY

Small cities (like Redondo Beach, Calif) & computers: It can be done. illus Govt Exec 8:55-56+ Dec '76

Word processing: How to save $700 million a year. (Interview with Ron Companion, Installation Officer at Fort Benning, Ga) Govt Exec 8:52+ Dec '76

Your opinion counts. Darryl D.McEwen. illus Soldiers 31:6-9 Dec '76

EFFICIENCY RATINGS see Airman Performance Reports; Effectiveness Reports

EGYPT

Return to Egypt. (USS Barnstable County, first U.S. ship to enter the Suez Canal since the 1967 Six-Day War) CDR J.M.Lang. illus US Nav Inst Proc 102:98-100 Feb '76

Foreign Relations

Israel

U.S. early warning system in the Sinai is begun. F.Clifton Berry, Jr. illus Armed Forces J Intl 113:25 Feb '76

History

The Faluja pocket (1st Palestinian War, 1948). David Nicolle. map Army Qtr pt 1, The Egyptian advance. 105:440-448+ Oct '75; pt 2, The Black Panther of Faluja. 106:333-350 Jul '76

EICHER, William E.

Equipment maintainability--design in, don't add on. BrigGen William E.Eicher. Natl Def 60:353-355 Mar-Apr '76

EISEMAN, Ben

Border war: China vs India. RADM Ben Eiseman. MarCor Gaz 60:19-25 Sep '76

EISENHOWER, Dwight D.

The military-industrial complex: What President Eisenhower really said. (Farewell radio and television address to the American people, Jan 17, 1961) AF Plcy Ltr for Comdrs: Sup No.7:29-32 Jul '76

EJECTION

See also
Parachute Jumping

The decision. LtCol James A.Learmonth. Aerosp Safety 32:5 Oct '76

EJECTION - Continued

More on the ejection decision. TIG Brief 28:8
Mar 26 '76

The rise of the ejection survival rate. Rudolph C.
Delgado. illus Aerosp Safety 32:6-7 Apr '76

Too late, too hot to survive. LCDR C.J.Sutherland.
illus Approach 21:18-19 May '76

EJECTION EQUIPMENT

Birdstrikes ... and the ejection seat. Michael R.
Grost. illus TAC Attack 16:4-6 Jan '76

Egress news for the T-bird (T-33). LtCol Everett
R.Patterson. illus Interceptor 18:5-7 Feb '76

Parachute techniques for aircrews. Maj Allan R.
Homstead. illus TAC Attack 16:4-9 Feb '76

Problem egress accident items. TIG Brief 28:6
Jul 16 '76

The rise of the ejection survival rate. Rudolph C.
Delgado. illus Aerosp Safety 32:6-7 Apr '76

Super-search progress report. (Another look at life
support equipment development) LtCol Lee Crock.
illus Interceptor 18:8-11 Sep '76

Maintenance and Repair

FOD in the F-4 egress system. Michael Grost. illus
Aerosp Safety 32:8-9 Jan '76

ELECTIONS

See also
Voting

Electing the President. tab Soldiers 31:38-39 Sep '76

No panic at Pentagon over (President-elect Jimmy)
Carter's victory. Paul Smith. AF Times 37:20
Nov 15 '76

The power tables: Significant elections and changes
in governments in the past year. Regular feature
in some issues of Defense & Foreign Affairs Digest

U.S. election: Russian reaction. LtGen Ira C.Eaker,
Ret. AF Times 37:13-14 Dec 27 '76

ELECTRIC EQUIPMENT

See also
Generators, Electric

Car devices cut (electrically ignited crash) fires,
tests show. AF Times 36:25 Mar 1 '76

Maintenance and Repair

Infrared scanning techniques. ("Hot spots" in your
overhead electrical distribution lines?) Don Lyne.
illus AF Engrg & Svcs Qtr 17:18-20 Feb '76

Underground electrical system testing: A review.
Capt Michael A.Aimone. illus tabs AF Engrg &
Svcs Qtr 17:33-35 May '76

ELECTRIC POWER

Infrared scanning techniques. ("Hot spots" in your
overhead electrical distribution lines?) Don Lyne.
illus AF Engrg & Svcs Qtr 17:18-20 Feb '76

The night the world died (at Clark AB, RP). illus Approach 22:6-7 Oct '76

ELECTRIC POWER PLANTS

Chemical engineering aids solar energy. Talbot A.
Chubb. illus tab Mil Engr 68:456-458 Nov-Dec '76

ELECTRICITY

(Electrical fixtures) grounded or not grounded. TIG
Brief 28:6 Oct 22 '76

Static electricity during winter months. TIG Brief
28:6 Feb 27 '76

ELECTROMAGNETIC COMPATIBILITY

Electronic warfare--a key to combat survival. G.S.
Sundaram. illus tabs Intl Def Rev 9:51-54 Feb '76

Radio frequencies: Check before you buy. TIG Brief
28:3 Dec 3 '76

ELECTRONIC AIDS TO NAVIGATION

Air traffic management and tactical instruments.
Capt Lewis D.Ray. illus USA Avn Dig 22:22-23+
Mar '76

Planning a tactical instrument flight. Capt Lewis D.
Ray. illus USA Avn Dig 22:11-13 Jan '76

ELECTRONIC COUNTERMEASURES

AN/ALE-39 countermeasures dispenser systems detailed. illus Elect Warfare 7:30-31 Nov-Dec '75

AN/ALQ-123: IRCM (InfraRed CounterMeasures) pioneer. Roger C.Farmer. illus Elect Warfare 7:
33-35+ Nov-Dec '75

Artful dodger of the 1980s. Bill Walsh. illus Countermeasures 2:42-43+ Nov '76

Combatting voice jamming. Capt Benjamin L.Hardin.
illus Interceptor 18:20-23 Sep '76

Digital control for effective power management. John
F.Moran and Charles B.Balser. illus tabs Elect
Warfare 7:55+ Nov-Dec '75

EF-111A (tactical jamming aircraft) designated 'major system.' illus Elect Warfare 8:19 Jul-Aug '76

Electron bombarded semiconductors for fast rise
time modulators. Bruce Bell. illus tab Countermeasures 2:43-46+ Aug '76

Electronic warfare and smart weapons. Edgar E.Ul-
samer. illus Aerosp Intl 12:18+ Jul-Aug '76

Gallery of Soviet aerospace weapons: Reconnaissance,
ECM, and early warning aircraft. illus AF Mag
59:99 Mar '76

Jamming calculations for FM voice communications.
Lawrence E.Follis. illus tabs Elect Warfare 8:
33+ Nov-Dec '75

Jamming of FM tactical communications. Capt Robert D.Rood. illus tab Mil Rev 56:58-65 Feb '76

New hardware. Regular feature in issues of Countermeasures

Philosophy of ECCM utilization. (Comment on interview with Joseph Saloom, Electronic Warfare,
Sep-Oct 1974) Stephen L.Johnston. Elect Warfare
7:59-61 May-Jun '75

Pods vs internal (ECM). Bill Walsh. illus tab Countermeasures 2:16-17+ Feb '76

Threats and ECM techniques. R.Loomis. illus tabs
Intl Def Rev 9:55-58 Feb '76

When the target employs jamming. Col Y.Lyakhov.
illus Soviet Mil Rev No.6:23-25 Jun '76

ELECTRONIC DATA PROCESSING SYSTEMS

See also
Air Force Data Automation Agency
Computers
Digital Equipment

ELECTRONIC EQUIPMENT (AIRCRAFT) - Continued

Avionics equipment reliability: An elusive objective.
LtGen Robert T. Marsh. illus tabs Def Mgt J 12:
24-29 Apr '76

Electronic warfare and smart weapons. Edgar E. Ulsamer. illus Aerosp Intl 12:18+ Jul-Aug '76

Flexible multimission avionics. illus Countermeasures 2:25-26+ Nov '76

German aerospace electronics--the big four domi-
nate. Dan Boyle. illus Interavia 31:342-345
Apr '76

New hardware. Regular feature in issues of Countermeasures

Typical airborne EW equipment. illus Intl Def Rev 9:
64-66 Feb '76

Who's who in helicopter avionics? illus Interavia 31:
48-50 Jan '76

Maintenance and Repair

Handling Inertial Measurement Units (IMUs). TIG
Brief 28:14 Nov 5 '76

ELECTRONIC EQUIPMENT (SPACE VEHICLES)

German aerospace electronics--the big four domi-
nate. Dan Boyle. illus Interavia 31:342-345
Apr '76

ELECTRONIC EQUIPMENT, MINIATURE

Electronically-scanned phased array augments EW
power management. O.B.Mitchell. illus Elect
Warfare 7:24-26+ May-Jun '75

Fundamentals of integrated circuits: Integrated cir-
cuit component technology. Saul Zatz. illus Countermeasures 2:22-23+ Oct '76

Laboratory testing of microprocessor-based systems. David A.Curtis and Stephen Swerling. illus
tab Countermeasures 2:22+ Dec '76

Microprocessors in military systems. Rob Walker.
illus Countermeasures 2:28-32 May '76

An overview of MIL-M-38510 (microcircuit). Bob
Berryman. illus tabs Countermeasures 2:54+
Sep '76

U.S. military microcircuit activity: Monthly status
report. Regular features in issues of Countermeasures starting with Oct 1976

ELECTRONIC FUNDS TRANSFER SYSTEM

EFTS (Electronic Funds Transfer System)--alive
and well at the USAF Accounting & Finance Center. Thomas D.Kronoveter. illus Armed Forces
Compt 21:6-7 Apr '76

Electronic Funds Transfer System (EFTS). Tom D.
Kronoveter. illus AF Compt 10:6-7 Jul '76

Electronic Funds Transfer Systems (EFTS). illus
Armed Forces Compt 21:28-29 Jan '76

ELECTRONIC INDUSTRY AND TRADE

Communications-electronics digest, monthly review
of developments. Regular feature in issues of
Signal

Industrial roundup. Regular feature in some issues
of Interavia

Microwave power tube survey. tabs Countermeasures
2:24+ Mar '76

ELECTRONIC INDUSTRY AND TRADE - Continued

Strategic pulse: Electronic warfare in the current
strategic environment. David Harvey. illus Def &
For Aff Dig No. 5:4-5+ '76

View from the top. (Interviews with outstanding exec-
utives in the electronic field) Regular feature in
issues of Countermeasures

Directories

The 1976 AFCEA sustaining and group member capabilities directory. illus Signal 30:54-111 Jan '76

France

Naval systems from Thomson-CSF. R.Meller. illus
tab Intl Def Rev 9:847-851 Oct '76

Germany (Federal Republic)

German aerospace electronics--the big four domi-
nate. Dan Boyle. illus Interavia 31:342-345
Apr '76

Great Britain

Aerospace electronics--wait and see in an unstable
situation. Dan Boyle. illus Interavia 31:805-806
Sep '76

Aerospace (equipment). John Marriott. illus tabs
NATO's Fifteen Nations 21:35-39+ Apr-May '76

Electronics. John Marriott. illus NATO's Fifteen
Nations 21:53-55+ Apr-May '76

Sweden

Swedish industry looks ahead. Dan Boyle. illus Interavia 31:131-134 Feb '76

United States

CBEMA (Computer and Business Equipment Manufacturers Assoc) and GSA (General Services Administration): A dialogue on how government hurts
itself (because of its own procurement and contracting practices). C. W.Borklund. illus Govt
Exec 8:24+ May '76

The hot button (at IBM) is EEOC (Equal Employment
Opportunity Commission). Govt Exec 8:15 Dec '76

An industry perspective on satellites. Henry E.
Hockeimer and others. illus Signal 30:60-74
Mar '76

Industry report and survey: A report on the microwave component market. illus tab Countermeasures 2:33-40+ Aug '76

The military looks and listens to industry: The telecommunications equipment acquisition process.
R.Leffler. illus Log Spectrum 10:23-28 Fall '76

A prescription for progress. James R.McNitt. illus
Signal 30:20-22 Feb '76

Rockwell Autonetics group moves into new markets.
J. Philip Geddes. illus Interavia 31:550-552 Jun '76

Semiconductor devices and circuits in military applications. Helmut F.Wolf. illus tabs Countermeasures 2:59-60+ Sep '76

Telecommunications. Betsy Ancker-Johnson. illus
Signal 30:10-12+ Jan '76

USAF EW program matrix. Table only. Elect Warfare
7:41 May-Jun '75

The U.S. general aviation market--a decade of solid
growth is forecast. illus tabs Interavia 31:567-569
Jun '76

ELECTRONIC WARFARE - Continued

Air electronic warfare. RADM Julian S. Lake, Ret
and LCDR Richard V. Hartman, Ret. illus US Nav
Inst Proc 102:42-49 Oct '76

Airborne EW equipment--a mature military asset.
Harry F. Eustace. illus Intl Def Rev 9:59-63
Feb '76

Army EW--current U.S. concepts. Harry F. Eustace.
illus Intl Def Rev 9:429-432 Jun '76

At last: 10 years of EW and Crow Caws. (A multiple
index of Electronic Warfare magazine and its pre-
decessor Crow Caws) Elect Warfare 8:61+ Jul-
Aug '76

The EW Center and the Air Force. BrigGen Kenneth
D. Burns. TIG Brief 28:2 Nov 5 '76

EW in anti-ship missile defense? Julian S. Lake III.
illus Countermeasures 2:6+ Oct '76

Electronic environments. Regular feature in issues
of Defense & Foreign Affairs Digest

Electronic warfare. TIG Brief 28:7-8 Jan 16 '76

Electronic warfare. W. J. Norris. illus RUSI J for
Def Studies 120:54-58 Dec '75

Electronic warfare. Maj Harold W. Whitten. illus
MarCor Gaz 60:38-42 May '76

Electronic warfare--a key to combat survival. G. S.
Sundaram. illus tabs Intl Def Rev 9:51-54 Feb '76

Electronic warfare: A view from the Hill. (Remarks,
Southwestern Crow Club, Fort Bliss, Tex, Jan 31,
1976) Joseph M. Montoya. illus Elect Warfare 8:
109-110 Mar-Apr '76

Electronic warfare and smart weapons. Edgar E. Ulsamer. illus Aerosp Intl 12:18+ Jul-Aug '76

Electronic warfare at sea. G. S. Sundaram. illus Intl
Def Rev 9:217-220 Apr '76

Electronic warfare in tactical air operations: A new
approach. SqLdr A. P. Slinger. illus Hawk No. 37:
35-40 Jul '76

Electronic warfare review. Regular feature in issues
of Electronic Warfare

Electronic warfare's role in future conflicts. Malcolm R. Currie. illus Comdrs Dig 19: entire issue
Dec 9 '76

Electronics: Key military 'force multiplier.' Malcolm R. Currie. illus AF Mag 59:39-45 Jul '76

Electronics, pivot of USAF's technological strength:
A new era in electronic warfare. Edgar Ulsamer.
illus AF Mag 59:46-50 Jul '76

Ground-based electronic warfare. G. S. Sundaram.
illus Intl Def Rev 9:425-428 Jun '76

The growing threat: New challenges for the EW community. Ronald T. Pretty. illus Elect Warfare 8:
43+ Mar-Apr '76

Is EW still a Pentagon stepchild? Harry F. Eustace.
illus Elect Warfare 8:28-29+ Jul-Aug '76

Modern shipboard EW: The key to survival. illus
Countermeasures 2:35-37+ Feb '76

Naval systems from Thomson-CSF. R. Meller. illus
tab Intl Def Rev 9:847-851 Oct '76

Needed: A new family of EW systems. Edgar Ulsamer. illus AF Mag 59:27-31 Feb '76

ELECTRONIC WARFARE - Continued

Reprogrammable simulators respond quickly to
EW/SIGINT changes. Terry E. Bibbens. illus tabs
Elect Warfare 8:65-68+ Nov-Dec '76

Ships' EW: Better than ever ... but is it good enough?
Richard Davis. illus tab Elect Warfare 8:41-43+
May-Jun '76

Simulators in electronic warfare. G. S. Sundaram.
illus tab Intl Def Rev 9:591-594 Aug '76

Strategic pulse: Electronic warfare in the current
strategic environment. David Harvey. illus Def &
For Aff Dig No. 5:4-5+ '76

TAC navigators: Meeting the challenge. Maj Ronald
E. Schulz. illus Navigator 23:10-14 Spring '76

Tac air--history's most potent fighting machine.
Edgar Ulsamer. illus AF Mag 59:22-26 Feb '76

Tac air, member of the (combined arms) team supporting the supersoldier. LtCol William H. Rees.
illus Infantry 66:16-23 May-Jun '76

Typical airborne EW equipment. illus Intl Def Rev 9:
64-66 Feb '76

Typical naval EW equipment. illus Intl Def Rev 9:221-
225 Apr '76

A U.S. view of naval EW. Harry F. Eustace. illus
Intl Def Rev 9:226-228+ Apr '76

Bibliography

A complete bibliography: Soviet literature on radar
and EW. Stephen L. Johnston. Elect Warfare pt 1,
Subject listing. 8:43-44+ Sep-Oct '76

Costs

Air EW--they have forgotten again! RADM Julian S.
Lake III, Ret. illus Countermeasures 2:14+
Nov '76

Directories

Who's who in ASD (Aeronautical Systems Division)
EW, Wright-Patterson AFB, Ohio. Table only.
Elect Warfare 7:49-51 May-Jun '75

Who's who in the USAF Foreign Technology Division
(FTD). Table only. Elect Warfare 7:65 May-
Jun '75

History

Electronic warfare--a key to combat survival. G. S.
Sundaram. illus tabs Intl Def Rev 9:51-54 Feb '76

Study and Teaching

Improving the man-machine interface. Bill Walsh.
illus Countermeasures 2:53-55 Jun '76

The Navy's new EW school (Consolidated Navy Elec-
tronic Warfare School): Off to a good start on the
Florida coast. LCDR H. J. Scarborough. illus tabs
Elect Warfare 8:85-86+ Sep-Oct '76

"Tally ho" reality--not MQF. Maj Dick Taylor. illus
USAF Ftr Wpns Rev, pp 20-22, Fall '76

Australia

Electronic warfare and the new Australian defence
organization. (Summary of address, Southwest
Crows Chapter, Las Cruces, NM, Feb 1, 1975)
R. G. Gillis. illus Elect Warfare 7:36 May-Jun '75

ELECTRONICS

See also
Avionics

Electronics: Key military 'force multiplier.' Malcolm R. Currie. illus AF Mag 59:39-45 Jul '76

Industrial luncheon address (AFCEA, Washington, June 10, 1976). Gen Fred C. Weyand. illus Signal 30:40-43 Aug '76

1976 major project listing: USAF Electronic Systems Division, Air Force Systems Command. Intl Def Rev 9:712-713 Oct '76

What's happening in electronics at ESD: A checklist of major electronics projects. Table only. AF Mag 59:58-60 Jul '76

ELECTRO-OPTICS

Army EW--current U.S. concepts. Harry F. Eustace. illus Intl Def Rev 9:429-432 Jun '76

A case for smart weapons. LtCol Frank C. Regan, Jr. illus tabs MarCor Gaz 60:31-35 May '76

Electronics: Key military 'force multiplier.' Malcolm R. Currie. illus AF Mag 59:39-45 Jul '76

Electro optical EW seen key to new developments. Harvey Rinn and Joseph Savino. illus Elect Warfare 7:21-22 Nov-Dec '75

Electro-optical search & discovery. illus Countermeasures 2:13-14+ Mar '76

Head-up displays. Stefan Geisenheyner. illus Aerosp Intl 12:8+ Jul-Aug '76

Radar electro-optical display improvements. L. Wesley Hopper. illus tabs Countermeasures 2:96+ Sep '76

TRAM (Target Recognition Attack Multi-sensor) makes A-6E world's most advanced EO aircraft. illus Elect Warfare 8:75-76+ May-Jun '76

U.S. EO (Electro-Optics) and IRCM (InfraRed CounterMeasures) budget outlined. Tables only. Elect Warfare 7:24+ Nov-Dec '75

Window to the world: EVS (Electro-optical Viewing System) and the navigator. 1stLt James R. McDonald. illus Navigator 23:25-26 Summer '76

Directories

Who's who in EOEW (Electro-Optical Electronic Warfare). Table only. Elect Warfare 7:26 Nov-Dec '75

ELLIS, Billy J.

Readiness. (Remarks, Jolly Green Pilots Assoc reunion, Eglin AFB, Fla, April 24, 1976) MajGen Billy J. Ellis. AF Plcy Ltr for Comdrs: Sup No. 7: 2-6 Jul '76

ELLIS, Richard H.

Flexibility--a state of mind. Gen Richard H. Ellis and LtCol Frank B. Horton III. por Strat Rev 4:26-36 Winter '76

Staff assistance visits and the IG. Gen R. H. Ellis. TIG Brief 28:1-2 May 21 '76

United States Air Forces in Europe. por AF Mag 59: 80-81 May '76

ELLSWORTH, Robert F.

Capabilities and courage. Robert F. Ellsworth. Natl Def 61:29-31 Jul-Aug '76

ELLSWORTH, Robert F. - Continued

Conference speakers. (Excerpts from addresses, NGAUS 98th General Conference, Washington, Aug 30-Sep 1, 1976) por Natl Guardsman 30: 23-27 Oct '76

Erroneous doctrines misshaping perceptions of U.S. defense needs. (Excerpts from address, Montgomery, Ala, Jan 26, 1976) Robert Ellsworth. Armed Forces J Intl 113:29 Feb '76

F-16: Fighter procurement essential to Iranian Air Force modernization. Robert Ellsworth. por Comdrs Dig 19: entire issue Oct 21 '76

Military force and political influence in an age of peace. Robert Ellsworth. por Strat Rev 4:5-11 Spring '76

Military intelligence--streamlined, centralized, civilianized. Interview. Robert F. Ellsworth. por AF Mag 59:26-30 Aug '76

New duty in Defense (Deputy SecDef): Robert Ellsworth will supervise intelligence and foreign operations. por biog Natl Def 60:346-347 Mar-Apr '76

The strategic significance of the Northern Marianas. Robert Ellsworth. Comdrs Dig 19: entire issue Jan 22 '76

Why we need the total force. (Remarks, National Guard Assoc Conference, Washington, Aug 30, 1976) Robert Ellsworth. AF Plcy Ltr for Comdrs: Sup No. 12:8-13 Dec '76

EMERGENCY POWERS see War and Emergency Powers

EMERGING NATIONS see States, New

EMOTIONS

See also
Fear
Panic

Method for determining pilot stress through analysis of voice communication. Isao Kuroda and others. illus tabs Aviation, Space & Envmt Med 47:528-533 May '76

Prolactin, thyrotropin, and growth hormone release during stress associated with parachute jumping. Gordon L. Noel and others. illus Aviation, Space & Envmt Med 47:543-547 May '76

Time bomb (stress). Capt Allan R. Sweeny. illus Aerosp Safety 32:26-28 Jun '76

EMPLOYMENT

See also
Moonlighting

Anatomy of a job search. Ralph Lewis. illus MarCor Gaz 60:40-47 Jul '76

Civilian employment. TIG Brief 28:16 Mar 26 '76

400 (retired Regular military and naval officers) challenge dual comp. Lee Ewing. AF Times 36:3 Mar 22 '76

Government jobs scarce o'seas. AF Times 37:23 Sep 6 '76

Job hunters forum. I. Norman Johansen. Regular feature in some issues of Air Force Times starting with January 19, 1976

Oversea recruitment and rotation. TIG Brief 28: 19-20 Apr 9 '76

Reports of Defense related employment. TIG Brief 28:15 Feb 13 '76

EMPLOYMENT - Continued

600 retired officers reported holding jobs with DOD contractors. AF Times 36:40 Feb 2 '76

Social implications of the clemency discharge. William A. Pearman. tabs J Pol & Mil Sociol 4:309-316 Fall '76

Transportation career forecast. Chester Levine and others. tab Def Trans J pt 1, Outlook. 32:18-20+ Oct '76

ENERGY see Force and Energy

ENERGY CONSERVATION

Army meets the fuel crisis. LtCol Robert R. Bachmann. illus tabs Natl Def 60:436-438 May-Jun '76

Civil transport technology up to 2000: NASA believes fuel consumption is the major consideration. J. Philip Geddes. illus tabs Interavia 31:419-421 May '76

Computers cut energy costs in buildings. Phil Deakin. illus tab Govt Exec 8:33+ May '76

Conserving our energy resources. TIG Brief 28:13 Mar 12 '76

The Defense energy conservation investment program. Col Vito D. Stipo. illus tab Mil Engr 68: 111-112 Mar-Apr '76

Energy monitoring control systems. Capt Robert E. Dant. illus tab AF Engrg & Svcs Qtr 17:25-28 Aug '76

Fuel and energy conservation program (at Subic Bay, Philippines). CAPT Joseph A. D'Emidio. illus tabs Mil Engr 68:387-389 Sep-Oct '76

Fuel conservation and security police vehicle patrols. TIG Brief 28:18 Dec 3 '76

More power for sea power. LT Larry A. Lukens. illus tabs map Natl Def 60:439-443 May-Jun '76

No more yet no less (action in implementing energy conservation practices). Roman A. Metz. illus tab AF Engrg & Svcs Qtr 17:13-15 Aug '76

Nuclear power development: Will facts win out over unfounded fear? illus Govt Exec 8:46+ May '76

Solar energy applications. Capts Anthony Eden and Michael A. Aimone. tabs illus map AF Engrg & Svcs Qtr 17:29-33 Aug '76

(Vehicle) fuel conservation program. TIG Brief 28:16 Jan 16 '76

ENERGY CRISIS

Army meets the fuel crisis. LtCol Robert R. Bachmann. illus tabs Natl Def 60:436-438 May-Jun '76

Can government create a private sector? (Interview with Robert L. Hirsch, Assistant Administrator for Solar, Geothermal and Advanced Energy Systems, Energy Research & Development Administration) John F. Judge. illus Govt Exec 8:15+ Aug '76

Conserving our energy resources. TIG Brief 28:13 Mar 12 '76

Fuel and energy conservation program (at Subic Bay, Philippines). CAPT Joseph A. D'Emidio. illus tabs Mil Engr 68:387-389 Sep-Oct '76

More power for sea power. LT Larry A. Lukens. illus tabs map Natl Def 60:439-443 May-Jun '76

No more yet no less (action in implementing energy conservation practices). Roman A. Metz. illus tab AF Engrg & Svcs Qtr 17:13-15 Aug '76

ENERGY CRISIS - Continued

Nuclear power for defense. Capt Anthony V. Nida. tabs Natl Def 60:432-435 May-Jun '76

ENERGY POLICY

United States

Can government create a private sector? (Interview with Robert L. Hirsch, Assistant Administrator for Solar, Geothermal and Advanced Energy Systems, Energy Research & Development Administration) John F. Judge. illus Govt Exec 8:15+ Aug '76

Nuclear power: A time for decision. James D. Hessman. illus tab Sea Power 19:18-23 Apr '76

ENERGY RESEARCH

Army meets the fuel crisis. LtCol Robert R. Bachmann. illus tabs Natl Def 60:436-438 May-Jun '76

Can government create a private sector? (Interview with Robert L. Hirsch, Assistant Administrator for Solar, Geothermal and Advanced Energy Systems, Energy Research & Development Administration) John F. Judge. illus Govt Exec 8:15+ Aug '76

Development of the Satellite Solar Power Station (SSPS). Peter E. Glaser. illus tabs Spaceflight 18:198-208 Jun '76

More power for sea power. LT Larry A. Lukens. illus tabs map Natl Def 60:439-443 May-Jun '76

Nuclear power development: Will facts win out over unfounded fear? illus Govt Exec 8:46+ May '76

Nuclear power for defense. Capt Anthony V. Nida. tabs Natl Def 60:432-435 May-Jun '76

ENERGY RESEARCH AND DEVELOPMENT ADMINISTRATION

Can government create a private sector? (Interview with Robert L. Hirsch, Assistant Administrator for Solar, Geothermal and Advanced Energy Systems, Energy Research & Development Administration) John F. Judge. illus Govt Exec 8:15+ Aug '76

ENERGY RESOURCES see Power Resources

ENGINEER CENTERS AND SCHOOLS

Air Force

(Soviet) Air Force engineers' school (Yakov Alksnis Higher Aviation Engineering School, Riga). Col N. Konkov. illus Soviet Mil Rev No. 7:42-43 Jul '76

ENGINEERING

See also specific types of engineering, e.g., Aeronautical Engineering Civil Engineering Military Engineering

Craftsmen all: The Corps of Royal Electrical and Mechanical Engineers. Col Norman L. Dodd, Ret. illus Mil Engr 68:361-364 Sep-Oct '76

An engineering brief for the 1980's. Charles J. Merdinger. illus Mil Engr 68:212-214 May-Jun '76

Engineering requirements for the year 2000. Lev Zetlin. Mil Engr 68:215-217 May-Jun '76

The lower Mississippi Valley. MajGen Francis P. Koisch. illus map tabs Mil Engr 68:290-293 Jul-Aug '76

ENGINEERING - Continued

History

Two centuries of engineering accomplishments. Donald C. Bentley. illus Mil Engr 68:204-206 May-Jun '76

ENGINEERING RESEARCH

Chemical engineering aids solar energy. Talbot A. Chubb. illus tab Mil Engr 68:456-458 Nov-Dec '76

Geotechnical engineering in the coastal zone. CDR Gordon W. Callender, Jr. illus tabs Mil Engr 68: 366-370 Sep-Oct '76

The Waterways Experiment Station. LtCol Robert K. Hughes. illus Mil Engr 68:374-379 Sep-Oct '76

ENGINEERS

See also specific types of engineers, e.g., Aeronautical Engineers
Flight Engineers

Keynote address, 56th Annual Meeting of the Society of American Military Engineers (Arlington, Va, April 28-May 1, 1976). ADM Ben Moreell, Ret. illus Mil Engr 68:294-297 Jul-Aug '76

Air Force

Environmental planning and the decision process. MajGen Robert C. Thompson. tab Mil Engr 68: 11-13 Jan-Feb '76

A 50/50 chance of being passed over. Capt W.E. Thompson. AF Engrg & Svcs Qtr 17:21-22 Feb '76

Palace Blueprint: Six years later. LtCol Marvin T. Howell. illus tabs AF Engrg & Svcs Qtr 17:31-32+ May '76

Prime BEEF in Europe. Maj Charles F. Kreis. illus AF Engrg & Svcs Qtr 17:28-30 May '76

Remote assignments: On the decline. Maj Richard L. Brown. illus tabs AF Engrg & Svcs Qtr 17:22-25 Nov '76

Requiem for an engineer, MajGen Frank G. Barnes. illus AF Engrg & Svcs Qtr 17:13+ Nov '76

Organization

Make service your profession. (Address, Air Force Engineering and Services Conference, Homestead AFB, Fla, Dec 1975) Gen Russell E. Dougherty. illus AF Engrg & Svcs Qtr 17:6-12 May '76

Armed Forces

History

Sword, shovel, and compass. Leland R. Johnson. illus Mil Engr 68:158-165 May-Jun '76

Army

The Army's facilities engineering operations. BrigGen Walter O. Bachus. illus tabs chart Mil Engr 68:94-97 Mar-Apr '76

Bankhead Lock failure. John A. Perdue. illus map Mil Engr 68:462-464 Nov-Dec '76

Bridging the generations. (Replicas of the famous bridge at Concord, Mass, are spanning the Anacostia River in Washington to the new Children's Islands Park) Sgt Deb Notah. illus Soldiers 31: 18-21 Dec '76

Craftsmen all: The Corps of Royal Electrical and Mechanical Engineers. Col Norman L. Dodd, Ret. illus Mil Engr 68:361-364 Sep-Oct '76

ENGINEERS - Continued

Army - Cont'd

Geotechnical engineering in the coastal zone. CDR Gordon W. Callender, Jr. illus tabs Mil Engr 68: 366-370 Sep-Oct '76

Guatemala: Helping hand. SSgt Zack Richards. illus Soldiers 31:14-17 Aug '76

New Chief of Engineers (LtGen John W. Morris). illus Mil Engr 68:400 Sep-Oct '76

Salvage of the (Great Lakes freighter) Sidney E. Smith. Maj Thomas J. Woodall. illus Mil Engr 68:448-451 Nov-Dec '76

Stairway of water (Mississippi River). Capt William J. Diehl, Jr. illus Soldiers 31:49 Jun '76

The Waterways Experiment Station. LtCol Robert K. Hughes. illus Mil Engr 68:374-379 Sep-Oct '76

History

America's first Chief Engineer (Col Richard Gridley). Raleigh B. Buzzaird. (Reprinted from Military Engineer, Dec 1947) illus map Mil Engr 68:31-36 Jan-Feb '76

Engineering for people: 200 years of Army public works. Roy Gordon. illus Mil Engr 68:180-185 May-Jun '76

Passing 200 and still climbing. (Army Corps of Engineers) LtGen William C. Gribble, Jr. illus Mil Engr 68:6-10 Jan-Feb '76

Washington's favorite engineer (BrigGen Rufus Putnam). Raleigh B. Buzzaird. illus Mil Engr 68:298-301 Jul-Aug '76

Washington's last Chief Engineer, Etienne Bechet, Sieur de Rochefontaine. Raleigh B. Buzzaird. (Reprinted from Military Engineer, March-April 1953) illus map Mil Engr 68:452-455 Nov-Dec '76

Washington's most brilliant engineer (Chevalier Louis Le Bègue Du Portail). Raleigh B. Buzzaird. illus maps Mil Engr 68:104-110 Mar-Apr '76

Organization

FORSCOM engineers: The first 1,000 days. Col Alvin G. Rowe. illus tab Mil Engr 68:445-447 Nov-Dec '76

Coast Guard

Varied challenges for Coast Guard engineers. RADM Malcolm E. Clark. illus map Mil Engr 68:18-21 Jan-Feb '76

Zero base management system. CDR Walter E. Peterson. Mil Engr 68:371-373 Sep-Oct '76

History

Coast Guard public works. Jeffrey P. High. illus Mil Engr 68:194-197 May-Jun '76

Navy

The shipboard engineering crisis. LT Walter E.W. Ruska. illus chart US Nav Inst Proc 102:101-103 Jan '76

History

Navy public works--1776-1976. Judith Johnston. illus Mil Engr 68:186-193 May-Jun '76

Reserve Forces--Air Force

Mission to Tortugas. (Restoration of historical lighthouse by a team of Reservists from 915th Civil Engineering Flt, Homestead AFB, Fla) TSgt Dan Doherty. illus Air Reservist 28:8-9 Jul '76

ENGINEERS - Continued

Reserve Forces--Air Force - Cont'd

Never a dull moment. (USAF Reserve Civil Engineers work at restoring the Fort Jefferson National Monument 65 miles west of the Florida coast) TSgt Dan Doherty. illus Airman 20:42-47 Aug '76

ENGINES

See also specific types of engines, e.g., Jet Engines
also subdivision Engines under specific subjects, e.g.,
Airplanes, Fighter--Engines
Automobiles--Engines
Helicopters, Military--Engines
Rockets--Engines

General Electric's view of the engine market. illus tabs Interavia 31:180-182 Feb '76

Hazards of operating internal combustion engine-powered equipment in enclosed munitions storage facilities. TIG Brief 28:6 Sep 24 '76

Maintenance and Repair

Synthetic oil? SGM Nat Dell. illus Soldiers 31:19-22 Oct '76

ENLISTED MEN

See also
Airmen
Noncommissioned Officers
Soldiers

'Catch-up' program eyed for minorities. Andy Plattner. AF Times 36:2 Jun 28 '76

DOD defines 'marginal' EM--3 grounds for release. Randy Shoemaker. AF Times 36:4 Feb 23 '76

'Dogrobber' flap (about enlisted aides) nothing new. AF Times 37:31 Sep 13 '76

EM clothing allowances to vary by Service. AF Times 37:39 Oct 4 '76

EM on BAS charged higher meal rates. AF Times 37:3 Oct 25 '76

Enlisted TDY pay: Question of equity. AF Times 36:2 Jun 28 '76

(Pres) Ford nixes junior EM aid; phaseout of store subsidies asked. Randy Shoemaker. AF Times 37:3 Dec 27 '76

Time in service for EM hikes to rise. illus AF Times 37:12 Sep 13 '76

ENLISTMENT see
Recruiting and Enlistment
Reenlistment

ENTEBBE RAID, 1976

Entebbe and after. ACM Christopher Foxley-Norris. Army Qtr 106:397-401 Oct '76

Israel solves a hijacking. LtGen Ira C.Eaker, Ret. AF Times 36:13-14 Jul 26 '76

ENVIRONMENT

See also
Pollution

Arousing environmental stresses can improve performance, whatever people say. E.C.Poulton. tabs Aviation, Space & Envmt Med 47:1193-1204 Nov '76

ENVIRONMENT - Continued

Basing the new Air Force weapon systems: A potential for problems. Maj John G.Terino. illus map AU Rev 27:65-72 Jul-Aug '76

Environmental management. (Remarks, Energy, Environment & Ethics Seminar, National Assoc of Environmental Professionals, Washington, Nov 5, 1975) MajGen Robert C.Thompson. AF Plcy Ltr for Comdrs: Sup No.2:22-26 Feb '76

Environmental planning and the decision process. MajGen Robert C.Thompson. tab Mil Engr 68: 11-13 Jan-Feb '76

The pipe (line, Exercise Jack Frost). Sgt1C Floyd Harrington. illus Soldiers 31:30-34 Nov '76

Protecting nature's balance. (Ecological research at Aberdeen Proving Ground, Md) Frank Bender. illus Soldiers 31:42-44 Apr '76

Reservists fill detective's role (as) environmental health technicians (at Dobbins AFB, Ga). illus AF Times 36:41 Apr 19 '76

The Trading Post (Kans) event. (AF Weapons Laboratory studies the effect of simulated nuclear explosions on different types of soil) MSgt Harold Newcomb. illus Airman 20:14-17 Mar '76

Laws and Regulations

Federal compliance with state environmental procedures. Capt William S.Niehaus. AF Law Rev 18: 1-17 Fall '76

The judge advocate and the action-forcing provisions of the National Environmental Policy Act. Maj Charles A.Brothers. AF Law Rev 18:1-16 Summer '76

ENVIRONMENTAL PROTECTION AGENCY

EPA (Environmental Protection Agency)'s mandatory deposit rule: Tempest in a pop bottle. illus Govt Exec 8:38-39 Feb '76

Federal compliance with state environmental procedures. Capt William S.Niehaus. AF Law Rev 18: 1-17 Fall '76

Foundries in dilemma. Debbie C.Tennison. illus tabs Natl Def 60:453-458 May-Jun '76

Laws to aid foundries. Debbie C.Tennison. illus Natl Def 61:131-134 Sep-Oct '76

The national stream quality accounting network. Joseph S.Cragwall, Jr. illus map tabs Mil Engr 68: 25-27 Jan-Feb '76

"Returnables" required by EPA would cost too much--DOD. Review 55:21-24 Nov-Dec '75

ENVIRONMENTAL PROTECTION RESEARCH

See also related subjects, e.g.,
Clothing, Protective
Desert Operations

Chemist, biologist, engineer, detective (Air Force Reserve environmental health technician). Chris Scheer. illus Air Reservist 28:6-7 Jun '76

Contemporary forum of cooperative planning. (Air Installation Compatible Use Zone) Gary D.Vest. illus maps AF Engrg & Svcs Qtr 17:9-12 Aug '76

The future environment. LCDR Jacob D.Dumelle. Mil Engr 68:304-305 Jul-Aug '76

Maintaining defense efficiency with minimal impact on man & environment. illus tabs Comdrs Dig 19: entire issue Nov 4 '76

ENVIRONMENTAL PROTECTION RESEARCH -
Continued

Passing 200 and still climbing. (Army Corps of Engineers) LtGen William C.Gribble, Jr. illus Mil
Engr 68:6-10 Jan-Feb '76

Protecting nature's balance. (Ecological research at
Aberdeen Proving Ground, Md) Frank Bender.
illus Soldiers 31:42-44 Apr '76

The Waterways Experiment Station. LtCol Robert K.
Hughes. illus Mil Engr 68:374-379 Sep-Oct '76

ENVIRONMENTAL SCIENCE SERVICES ADMINISTRA-
TION

See also
National Oceanic and Atmospheric Administration

ENVIRONMENTAL SERVICES

USAF Environmental Health and Radiological Health
Laboratories. TIG Brief 28:19 Feb 13 '76

EQUAL EMPLOYMENT OPPORTUNITY see Equal Opportunity

EQUAL OPPORTUNITY

(AF) equal opportunity Affirmative Actions Plan
(AAP). TIG Brief 28:12 Feb 27 '76

Black soldier update. MSgt Nat Dell. illus Soldiers
31:6-10 Jan '76

'Catch-up' program eyed for minorities. Andy Plattner. AF Times 36:2 Jun 28 '76

EEO: For the states, a reporting nightmare. John
M.Proctor. tab Govt Exec 8:35-36 Nov '76

EO action plan: 19 objectives. AF Times 37:4
Dec 20 '76

EOT (Equal Opportunity and Treatment) and HRE
(Human Relations Education) review. TIG Brief
28:13-14 Mar 26 '76

The hot button (at IBM) is EEOC (Equal Employment
Opportunity Commission). Govt Exec 8:15 Dec '76

(Joy M.) Bishop: Civilian women's role (in Federal
Women's Program (FWP)). Interview. illus AF
Times 36:8 Mar 1 '76

New drive for ethnic equality starts. AF Times 37:23
Aug 23 '76

No plan to trim EO jobs. H.Minton Francis. AF
Times 37:4 Oct 25 '76

Recovered alcoholics get help: Discrimination fought.
Len Famiglietti. AF Times 37:61 Sep 20 '76

Women must have full opportunity: DACOWITS (Defense Advisory Committee On Women In The Services) testimony (by Pat Leeper, representing the
National Organization for Women (NOW)). Ann
Gerow. AF Times 36:9 May 17 '76

EQUIPMENT

See also subdivision Equipment under specific
subjects, e.g.,
Helicopters, Military--Equipment
Middle East War, 1973--Equipment

Weapons, vehicles, equipment. Regular feature in
issues of International Defense Review

Air Force--Germany (Federal Republic)

The West German Air Force re-equips for the 1980s.
Rudi Meller. illus tab Interavia pt 1, Combat
strength increases under cost pressures. 31:320-
322+ Apr '76; pt 2, 31:459-461 May '76

EQUIPMENT - Continued

Air Force--U.S.

'The Air Force Nuclear Safety Certification Program,' (AFR 122-3). TIG Brief 28:6 Dec 3 '76

Are you or your commander in this situation? (Custodian Authorization/Custody Receipt Listing
(CA/CRL)) TIG Brief 28:11 Jul 16 '76

Nuclear safety certified equipment list. TIG Brief
28:7 May 21 '76

Prime BEEF in Europe. Maj Charles F.Kreis. illus
AF Engrg & Svcs Qtr 17:28-30 May '76

26 wings (AF) goal: 1700 planes needed. Len Famiglietti. AF Times 36:19 May 3 '76

Maintenance and Repair

Maintaining a modern force. (Remarks, National Security Industrial Assoc, Absecon, NJ, June 28,
1976) MajGen Charles F.Minter, Sr. AF Plcy Ltr
for Comdrs: Sup No.9:13-19 Sep '76

Significant historical data processing (AFTO
Form 95). TIG Brief 28:12 Jul 16 '76

Armed Forces--Great Britain

Miscellaneous (defence equipments and services).
John Marriott. illus tab NATO's Fifteen Nations
21:66-69 Apr-May '76

Armed Forces--NATO

Standardisation and defence in NATO. Gardiner L.
Tucker. RUSI J for Def Studies 121:7-8+ Mar '76

A twenty one jewel watch: Mutual logistic support in
NATO. CDR Eugene F.Coughlin. illus Def Trans J
32:12-14+ Apr '76

Armed Forces--Russia

The ever-expanding umbrella. LtCol Arthur D.
McQueen. tab illus Air Def Mag, pp 8-17, Jul-
Sep '76

Armed Forces--U.S.

GAO report: O'seas aid causes U.S. arms shortage.
AF Times 36:10 Jan 19 '76

Army--Great Britain

Exhibitions

The British Army Equipment Exhibition (Aldershot,
June 21-25, 1976). illus Intl Def Rev 9:637-639
Aug '76

The British Army Equipment Exhibition (Aldershot,
June 21-25, 1976). Charles Latour. illus NATO's
Fifteen Nations 21:34-41 Aug-Sep '76

The British Army Equipment Exhibition (Aldershot,
June 21-23, 1976: A preview). illus tab Intl Def
Rev 9:253-258 Apr '76

Maintenance and Repair

Craftsmen all: The Corps of Royal Electrical and
Mechanical Engineers. Col Norman L.Dodd, Ret.
illus Mil Engr 68:361-364 Sep-Oct '76

Army--Russia

Soviet logistics: How good is it? Capts William R.
Hotze and Terry L.Schott. illus tab Army Log 8:
18-21 Mar-Apr '76

Army--Sweden

New Swedish cross-country logistics vehicles. Colin
E.Howard. illus tab Intl Def Rev 9:826-828 Oct '76

ETHICS - Continued

Cohesion and disintegration in the American Army (in Vietnam): An alternative perspective. Paul L. Savage and Richard A.Gabriel. tabs Armed Forces & Soc 2:340-376 Spring '76

The ethics of intelligence activities. Col Barrie P. Masters. illus tab Natl Sec Aff Forum No. 24:39-47 Spring-Summer '76

The Honor Code. (Statement, Subcommittee on Manpower and Personnel, Committee on Armed Services, U.S. Senate, June 22, 1976) LtGen James R.Allen. AF Plcy Ltr for Comdrs: Sup No. 10: 27-31 Oct '76

Military ethics in a changing world. MajGen Robert N.Ginsburgh, Ret. illus AU Rev 27:2-10 Jan-Feb '76

Military justice--a reinforcer of discipline. LtCol Robert S.Poydasheff. illus Nav War Col Rev 28: 76-92 Winter '76

On fostering integrity. Maj William E.Gernert III. AU Rev 27:62-67 Sep-Oct '76

Soviet military ethics. Maj A.Grishin. Soviet Mil Rev No. 12:34-35 Dec '76

'Standards of Conduct, ' AFR 30-30. TIG Brief 28:11 Jun 4 '76

Standards of conduct for Morale, Welfare, and Recreation (MWR) personnel. TIG Brief 28:5-6 Aug 27 '76

Trust and confidence revisited: Commentary on the (Marine) Corps. Col J.W.Duncan. MarCor Gaz 60:60-62 Nov '76

What the captain really means. (A survey on Air Force ethics and standards made at Squadron Officer School and resulting recommendations) Maj Peter Henderson. illus AU Rev 27:96-101 Jan-Feb '76

ETHIOPIA

Making the most of it. (Dr (LtCol) Jaroslav K.Richter of MacDill AFB, Fla, likes to be where the action is) 1stLt Katie Cutler. illus Airman 20: 20-23 Oct '76

EUROPE

European security: Soviet preferences and priorities. John Erickson. Strat Rev 4:37-43 Winter '76

Foreign Relations

The Helsinki agreement and self-determination. Stefan Korbonski. illus Strat Rev 4:48-58 Summer '76

EUROPE, WESTERN

Foreign Relations

Security makes strange bedfellows: NATO's problems from a minimalist perspective. Ken Booth. RUSI J for Def Studies 120:3-4+ Dec '75

China (People's Republic)

The Sino-West European connection. Maj Alfred Biegel. illus Mil Rev 56:68-78 Jan '76

United States

A new American defensive doctrine for Europe? Harold C.Deutsch. illus Parameters 6, No. 1:18-34 '76

Politics and Government

France and Britain: European powers and members of NATO. Jean Houbert. Royal Air Forces Qtr 15:289-300+ Winter '75

EUROPEAN COMMAND, ALLIED see Allied Command Europe

EUROPEAN ECONOMIC COMMUNITY

The United States and the defence of Western Europe. Capt D.H.Humphries. Army Qtr 106:211-219 Apr '76

EVACUATION, CIVILIAN

Angola--a last look? John Wegg. illus Air Pict 38: 96-98 Mar '76

Crisis in relocation planning. (Denver NDTA chapter undertaking emergency evacuation planning exercises) John W.Billheimer. Def Trans J 32:20+ Apr '76

Crowded decks. (Air America and ARVN pilots land Hueys with Vietnamese refugees on tiny decks of destroyer escorts Cook and Kirk during evacuation of Saigon) AW3 John P.Pieper. illus Approach 21: 18-21 Mar '76

Frequent Wind. MajGen Richard E.Carey and Maj D.A.Quinlan. maps illus MarCor Gaz pt 1, Organization and assembly (of 9th Marine Amphibious Brigade). 60:16-24 Feb '76; pt 2, Planning. 60: 35-45 Mar '76; pt 3, Execution. 60:35-45 Apr '76

The new nuclear strategy: Battle of the dead? maps Def Monitor 5: entire issue Jul '76

Operation Eagle Pull. (Emergency evacuation of American citizens and designated aliens from Cambodia, 1975) Col Sydney H.Batchelder, Jr and Maj D.A.Quinlan. illus MarCor Gaz 60:47-60 May '76

EVACUATION, MILITARY

Frequent Wind. MajGen Richard E.Carey and Maj D.A.Quinlan. maps illus MarCor Gaz pt 1, Organization and assembly (of 9th Marine Amphibious Brigade). 60:16-24 Feb '76; pt 2, Planning. 60: 35-45 Mar '76; pt 3, Execution. 60:35-45 Apr '76

Operation Eagle Pull. (Emergency evacuation of American citizens and designated aliens from Cambodia, 1975) Col Sydney H.Batchelder, Jr and Maj D.A.Quinlan. illus MarCor Gaz 60:47-60 May '76

EVACUATION OF CASUALTIES

See also
Aeromedical Evacuation

EVANS, William J.

Air Force Systems Command. por AF Mag 59:60-61 May '76

(Excerpt from) Keynote Address (57th Defense Preparedness Meeting, American Defense Preparedness Assoc, Los Angeles, Oct 15, 1975). Gen William J.Evans. Natl Def 60:283 Jan-Feb '76

The impact of technology on U.S. deterrent forces. Gen William J.Evans. por Strat Rev 4:40-47 Summer '76

Modernizing and cutting costs. (Remarks, National Security Industrial Assoc luncheon, Los Angeles, July 23, 1976) Gen William J.Evans. AF Plcy Ltr for Comdrs: Sup No. 10:2-8 Oct '76

Technological investment and payoff. (Remarks, AFA/SAC 9th Annual Missile Combat Competition, Vandenberg AFB, Calif, April 29, 1976) Gen William J.Evans. AF Plcy Ltr for Comdrs: Sup No. 7: 7-14 Jul '76

Bold Eagle - Cont'd

Exercise Bold Eagle (76). AF Times 36:31 Mar 1 '76

A "real world" transportation challenge: Exercise Bold Eagle '76. Maj Eldon T. Rippee. illus Translog 7:2-6 May '76

Brave Shield

Brave Shield XIII. LtCol Don Rosenkranz. illus Air Reservist 27:8-9 Feb '76

Brave Shield XIV. illus Air Reservist 28:6 Oct '76

Brave Shield XV. AF Times 37:33 Oct 18 '76

Compass Sight, 1 of a kind. (New relay type of intelligence-gathering system) MSgt Dom Cardonita. AF Times 37:34 Nov 8 '76

Exercise Brave Shield. AF Times 37:31 Sep 20 '76

The Hawk and the clamshell. Capt Dave Hawkins. illus Air Def Mag, pp 18-22, Jul-Sep '76

Crested Cap

Tanker task force operations (at Loring AFB, Me). Col Kenneth M. Patterson. illus map Combat Crew 27:4-7+ Jul '76

Firex

Ammo supply in rapid deployment. LtCol Robert P. Jones. illus Army Log 8:30-32 Jan-Feb '76

Jack Frost

14,000 taking part in Alaska Exercise Jack Frost. illus AF Times 36:38 Feb 2 '76

The pipe (line, Exercise Jack Frost). Sgt1C Floyd Harrington. illus Soldiers 31:30-34 Nov '76

Realistic exercise (Jack Frost 76) tests Alaska pipeline defense. Armed Forces J Intl 113:28 Jan '76

Red Flag

(F-15) Eagle makes bow (during Red Flag III). AF Times 36:38 Mar 29 '76

Readiness through realism. LtCol James Glaza. illus Air Reservist 28:8-9 Aug-Sep '76

Realistic Red Flag (VIII). Capt John V. Alexander. illus AF Times 37:43 Oct 25 '76

Red Flag. illus USAF Ftr Wpns Rev, p 17, Spring '76

Red Flag. MSgt Robert Foster. illus Air Reservist 28:10 Jun '76

Red Flag VI. AF Times 37:30 Aug 23 '76

Red Flag: Getting caught in a washer. T. J. Coats. AF Times 37:35 Nov 22 '76

Red Flag mirrors war in desert near Nellis (AFB, Nev). AF Times 36:18 Jan 5 '76

Red Flag (or how to fight the elements and live to tell about it). Capt Ronald E. Vivion. illus TAC Attack 16:20-22 Dec '76

Survival: Red Flag. Capt Ronald E. Vivion. illus Aerosp Safety pt 1, 32:16-19 Dec '76

Reforger

Air defense in Reforger. LtCol Joseph J. Heinlein, Jr. illus Air Def Mag, pp 16-21, Apr-Jun '76

101st (Airborne Division (Air Assault)) in Reforger 76. Col Larry J. Baughman and Maj Robert E. Jones, Jr. illus maps USA Avn Dig 22:2-3+ Dec '76

Reforger - Cont'd

Airlift is key to commuter Army (in Reforger 75). Translog 7:16-17 Mar '76; Mil Engr 68:308 Jul-Aug '76

Attack. (4th Battalion (Attack Helicopter), 77th Field Artillery) Capts Michael E. Sloniker and Gary R. Sosnowski. illus USA Avn Dig 22:4-5+ Dec '76

Get ready--get set--go!!! LtCol John A. G. Klose. illus USA Avn Dig 22:6-7+ Dec '76

Reforger load-out. illus Army Log 8:24-27 Nov-Dec '76

Reforger movement plans readied. Translog 7:13 Jul '76

Reforger 76: A MTMC first. illus Translog 7:2-4 Aug-Sep '76

Reforger 76 is history. illus Translog 7:7 Dec '76

(Reforger tests new tactical automatic telephone central office--AN/TTC-38) illus Signal 30:86 Jul '76

"Return the forces to Germany"--(Reforger) 76. LtCol Gary Sorensen. illus Def Trans J 32:6-8+ Oct '76

A terrific job in Europe (Project Team IV, the SOTAS (Stand-Off Target Acquisition System). illus USA Avn Dig 22:10 Dec '76

SAREX

SAREX keeps Osan units in shape. Sgt Larry Finney. AF Times 36:26 May 17 '76

SAREX 76: Canada versus U.S. illus AF Times 37:28 Nov 1 '76

Solid Shield

Tiny craft play big role in drill. illus AF Times 36:31 Jun 7 '76

Triad

Airdrop tops (three-nation (Australia, New Zealand, U.S.) Exercise) Triad. AF Times 36:38 Mar 29 '76

EXHIBITIONS see subdivision Exhibitions under specific specific subjects, e.g., Aviation--Exhibitions

EXPLOSIVE ORDNANCE DISPOSAL

Demilitarization facility. Frits H. Fenger. illus tab Mil Engr 68:86-87 Mar-Apr '76

Home on the range. Maj John N. P. Reisbick. illus TAC Attack 16:8-9 Jan '76

Rocky Mountain haven. (Rocky Mountain Arsenal (RMA)) Darryl D. McEwen. illus Soldiers 31:49-51 Aug '76

EXPLOSIVES AND EXPLOSIONS

Bombs and bomb beaters. LtCol S. G. Styles, Ret. illus tabs Intl Def Rev 9:817-819 Oct '76

DOD Explosives Safety Board surveys. TIG Brief 28:5 Jul 16 '76

A new ball game: Arms shipment security rules. Capt Paul L. Govekar, Jr. tabs Translog 7:16-17+ Oct '76

New DOD explosives hazard classification system. TIG Brief 28:9 Aug 27 '76

FAA see Federal Aviation Administration

FAMCAMPS see Recreation

FBI see Federal Bureau of Investigation

FORSCOM see Forces Command

FABYANIC, Thomas A.

Manpower trends in the British all-volunteer force. LtCol Thomas A.Fabyanic. Armed Forces & Soc 2:553-572 Summer '76

FACSIMILE TRANSMISSION

Facsimile: Legal status. Charles W.Savory. illus tab Signal 30:33-35 Apr '76

Use of AUTOVON for graphics, facsimile, and data service. TIG Brief 28:10 Jun 18 '76

FASTENERS
Here are entered articles on various types of fasteners, e.g., bolts and nuts, washers, pin connectors, etc.

Tamper detection seals for railcars/large containers. TIG Brief 28:13-14 Apr 9 '76

FATIGUE

Air operations and circadian performance rhythms. Karl E.Klein and others. illus tabs Aviation, Space & Envmt Med 47:221-230 Mar '76

A Christmas story. (Plain of Jars, Dec 1970) Capt Craig W.Duehring. illus TAC Attack 16:18-19 Dec '76

Crew rest. illus Approach 21:24-25 Jun '76

Effects of time zone changes on performance and physiology of airline personnel. F.S.Preston and others. illus tabs Aviation, Space & Envmt Med 47:763-769 Jul '76

Fatigue. LtCol David H.Karney and Patsy Thompson. illus tabs USA Avn Dig 22:28-34 Feb '76

Fatigue, a tiring subject. Maj Lowell A.Schuknecht, Jr. illus MAC Flyer 23:12-13 Jan '76

Flight limits and crew rest. LtCol David H.Karney. illus tab USA Avn Dig 22:38-39 Dec '76

The four horsemen of the apocalypse (illness, boredom, fatigue, unfitness). CDR A.F.Wells. illus Approach 21:10-11 May '76

Not up to par. illus Approach 21:12-13 Mar '76

Operational aspects of stress and fatigue. Maj William C.Wood. illus tabs USA Avn Dig 22:30-33 Sep '76

Physiological index as an aid in developing airline pilot scheduling patterns. Stanley R.Mohler. illus map tabs Aviation, Space & Envmt Med 47:238-247 Mar '76

So now you're an instructor pilot! Maj Donald E.Yarbrough. illus Aerosp Safety 32:2-4 Aug '76

Stress and fatigue. LtCol John J.Treanor. illus tab USA Avn Dig 22:8+ Nov '76

FATIGUE IN METALS see Strains and Stresses

FEAR

Self-possession. (Some forms and methods used in the Soviet Armed Forces to educate this quality in military personnel) Col V.Grebnev. Soviet Mil Rev No.7:47-48 Jul '76

FEAR - Continued

A study of the anatomy of fear and courage in war. LtCol A.T.A.Browne, Ret. Army Qtr 106:297-303 Jul '76

FEDERAL AID

Legitimacy and government control of the production of academic social knowledge. Michael Useem. tabs J Pol & Mil Sociol 4:217-232 Fall '76

Now, a way to get at those grants and loans. (Federal Domestic Assistance Program Retrieval Systems) Spencer B.Child. illus Govt Exec 8:26+ Mar '76

Performance purchasing: A rising state & local tide. Govt Exec 8:22+ Sep '76

FEDERAL ASSISTANCE PROGRAMS see Federal Aid

FEDERAL AVIATION ADMINISTRATION

Air commerce: Stimulated or damned. A.Scott Crossfield. illus tabs Govt Exec 8:31-32+ Dec '76

Big mother can kill you. Capt Marshall Hydorn. illus TAC Attack 16:10-11 Jan '76

Energy savings: The FAA. (Automation of environmental control in 20 Air Route Traffic Control Centers) illus Govt Exec 8:15+ Mar '76

FAA acts to cut down on near misses in air. AF Times 36:10 Jan 5 '76

The FAA Military Competency Examination. Edward A.Ewell. USA Avn Dig 22:28-29 Apr '76

Latest FAA innovations (Radar Beacon Code System, Conflict Alert System) for safety, convenience. illus MAC Flyer 23:22-23 Apr '76

New FAA control on (private) pilot tests asked (in GAO report). AF Times 36:23 Apr 12 '76

No evidence of (military pilot) intercepts (on civilian planes), says FAA. Ron Sanders. AF Times 36:11 Feb 16 '76

The U.S. air traffic control and navigation equipment market--continuing growth foreseen. tabs Interavia 31:462-463 May '76

FEDERAL BUREAU OF INVESTIGATION

The vital role of the computer in controlling crime. Clarence M.Kelley. illus Signal 30:12-15 Apr '76

FEDERAL COMMUNICATIONS COMMISSION

Anti-trust and over-regulation: "Ma Bell" strikes back. illus Govt Exec 8:38-39 Jun '76

The complexities of seeking a (telecommunications) policy. (Interview with John Eger) John F.Judge. illus Govt Exec 8:40+ Jun '76

FEDERAL MARITIME COMMISSION

Regulatory agencies: Are they promoters or inhibitors to intermodalism. C.Everhard. Def Trans J 32:22-26 Aug '76

FEDERAL SUPPLY SERVICE

Federal Supply Service commissioner Wallace H. Robinson, Jr. Interview. illus Govt Exec 8:23 Oct '76

FEDERAL TELECOMMUNICATIONS SYSTEM see Communications Systems--United States

FELLOWSHIPS see Scholarships and Fellowships

FERRYING OF AIRCRAFT

Hours of terror. Maj John O'Connor. illus MAC
Flyer 23:3-5 Feb '76

Red stars over America. (Delivering U.S. aircraft
to Russia via an Alaska-Siberian route, under the
Lend-Lease Act, during WW II) Capt Stephen O.
Manning III. illus Airman 20:35-37 Apr '76

FIELD ARTILLERY see Artillery, Field

FIGHTER UNITS

318th FIS (Fighter Interceptor Sq) Hughes Trophy
winners. illus Interceptor 18:10-11 Mar '76

A new home for TAC fighters ... Moody AFB (Ga).
LtCol Bill Ardern. illus TAC Attack 16:10-11
Feb '76

Readiness through realism. LtCol James Glaza. illus
Air Reservist 28:8-9 Aug-Sep '76

Red Flag: Getting caught in a washer. T.J.Coats.
AF Times 37:35 Nov 22 '76

The Voodoo (Oregon's 142d Fighter Interceptor Gp)
revenge (wins the 1976 Aerospace Defense Command's Weapons Loading Competition). illus Natl
Guardsman 30:4-5 Jul '76

Women and the 185th (Tactical Fighter Gp). Maj
Lloyd Bach. illus Air Reservist 28:4-5 May '76

History

The ending of World War II. (History of the 547th
Night Fighter Sq) LtCol Paul H.Baldwin, Ret.
illus Aerosp Hist 23:136-139 Sep '76

FIGHTER WEAPONS AND GUNNERY MEETS

Air Force

Coming: William Tell 1976 (Tyndall AFB, Fla,
Oct 31-Nov 21) tabs Interceptor 18:6-7 Aug '76

The competitive spirit of '76. (Aerospace Defense
Command 1976 Weapons Loading Competition,
Tyndall AFB, Fla) Capt Robert J.Perry. illus
Interceptor 18:5-9 Jul '76

The number '1' team (in 1976 William Tell Weapons
Loading Competition). illus Air Reservist 28:11
Aug-Sep '76

The Voodoo (Oregon's 142d Fighter Interceptor Gp)
revenge (wins the 1976 Aerospace Defense Command's Weapons Loading Competition). illus Natl
Guardsman 30:4-5 Jul '76

FIGHTER WEAPONS SCHOOL

Ph.D. for fighter pilots (at USAF's Fighter Weapons
School). Maj Lester D.Alford. illus AF Mag 59:
50-53 Oct '76

FINANCE

See also
Auditing

Air Force--U.S.

See also
Air Force Accounting and Finance Center

Air Force comptroller objectives. LtGen Charles E.
Buckingham. illus Armed Forces Compt 21:20-22
Apr '76

FINANCE - Continued

Air Force--U.S. - Cont'd

A message from the Comptroller of the Air Force.
LtGen C.E.Buckingham. illus AF Compt 10:2-4
Jan '76

Notes from the Auditor General. BrigGen Joseph B.
Dodds. illus AF Compt 10:18-19 Jul '76

Notes from the Director of Accounting & Finance.
MajGen Lucius Theus. illus AF Compt 10:16-17
Jul '76

Notes from the Director of Budget. MajGen C.C.
Blanton. illus AF Compt 10:12-13 Jul '76

Notes from the Director of Management Analysis.
Col C.T.Spangrud. illus AF Compt 10:14-15
Jul '76

Resource management team at base level? Why not?
Maj D.J.Herrington. illus AF Compt 10:30-31
Oct '76

Organization

Auditor General. BrigGen T.G.Bee. chart illus AF
Compt 10:28-29 Jan '76

Auditor General. BrigGen Thomas G.Bee. illus
chart AF Compt 10:18-19 Apr '76

Auditor General. BrigGen Joseph B.Dodds. illus
chart AF Compt 10:18-19 Oct '76

The comptroller organization--U.S. Air Force. illus
chart AF Compt 10:24-25 Jan '76

The comptroller organization--U.S. Air Force.
illus chart AF Compt 10:24-25 Apr '76

The comptroller organization--U.S. Air Force. illus
chart AF Compt 10:24-25 Oct '76

Directorate of Accounting & Finance. MajGen L.
Theus. illus chart AF Compt 10:20-21 Jan '76

Directorate of Accounting & Finance. MajGen Lucius
Theus. illus chart AF Compt 10:16-17 Apr '76

Directorate of Accounting & Finance. MajGen Lucius
Theus. illus chart AF Compt 10:16-17 Oct '76

Directorate of Budget. MajGen C.C.Blanton. chart
illus AF Compt 10:16-17 Jan '76

Directorate of Budget. MajGen C.C.Blanton. illus
chart AF Compt 10:12-13 Apr '76

Directorate of Budget. MajGen C.C.Blanton. illus
chart AF Compt 10:12-13 Oct '76

Directorate of Management Analysis. Col C.T.Span-
grud. chart illus tabs AF Compt 10:18-19 Jan '76

Directorate of Management Analysis. Col C.T.Span-
grud. illus chart AF Compt 10:14-15 Apr '76

Directorate of Management Analysis. Col C.T.Span-
grud. illus chart AF Compt 10:14-15 Oct '76

SAF/FM organization. (SecAF/Financial Management) illus chart AF Compt 10:29 Jan '76

SAF/FM organization. (SecAF/Financial Management) Chart only. AF Compt 10:10 Apr '76

SAF/FM organization. (SecAF/Financial Management) Chart only. AF Compt 10:7 Oct '76

FINANCE - Continued

Armed Forces--U.S.

See also
Joint Uniform Military Pay System

Resource management: A view from the top. (Panel discussion, American Society of Military Comptrollers National Symposium, Arlington, Va, May 26, 1976) Fred P. Wacker and others. illus Armed Forces Compt 21:20-26 Jul '76

Army--U.S.

Financial management--division to battalion contracts. LtCol Thomas W. Cassada. illus Mil Rev 56:42-46 Jan '76

Managing the Army's money, '76. LtGen John A. Kjellstrom. illus tabs Army 26:91-93+ Oct '76

Review, surveillance and self-examination: A special interview on Army funding problems. Hadlai A. Hull. illus Armed Forces Compt 21:2-5 Jan '76

History

Keepin' the money comin'. (Army pay through the years) Sgt JoAnn Mann. illus Soldiers 31:17 Jul '76

Navy--U.S.

Reflections on an approach to financial management. Gary D. Penisten. illus Armed Forces Compt 21: 12-14 Jan '76

United States

History

200 years of financial management. Allen Schick. Armed Forces Compt 21:4-7 Jul '76

FINGERPRINTING

Need for good fingerprinting techniques. TIG Brief 28:16 Jul 2 '76

FIRE CONTROL

Here is entered material on the control of weapon fire. For control of forest, house and similar fires **see** Fires and Fire Prevention.

Consumer notice: Please read FAAO (Field Artillery Aerial Observer) team article thoroughly prior to entering combat. Fld Arty J 44:50-54 Nov-Dec '76

Destruction of artillery batteries. Col V. Rudakov. Soviet Mil Rev No. 10:22-23 Oct '76

Lasers in reconnaissance and gunfire control. MajGen V. Vetrov and Col N. Sokolov. illus Soviet Mil Rev No. 1:25-27 Jan '76

Red Team AO (Aerial Observer) training. Capt Gary N. Grubb. illus Fld Arty J 44:22-23 Nov-Dec '76

U.S. field artillery in Vietnam. MajGen David E. Ott. (Extracts from "Field Artillery Monograph") illus tabs maps Fld Arty J pt 1, The field artillery adviser. 43:23-29 Jan-Feb '75; pt 2, In order to win. 43:15-22 May-Jun '75; pt 3, Field artillery mobility. 43:9-16 Jul-Aug '75, 43:46-51 Sep-Oct '75; pt 4, The field artillery buildup: 1967 combat operations. 43:29-34 Nov-Dec '75; pt 5, The hot war: 1968, the Tet offensive. 44:27-31 Jan-Feb '76; pt 5, The hot war: The Battle of Khe Sanh. 44:44-48 Mar-Apr '76; pt 5, The hot war: 1968-69, A Shau Valley. 44:53-57 May-Jun '76; pt 5, The hot war: Operations and raids. 44:37-43 Jul-Aug '76; pt 6, Vietnamization: FA assistance programs. 44: 10-17 Sep-Oct '76; pt 6, Vietnamization: Operations into Cambodia. 44:13-18 Nov-Dec '76

FIRE CONTROL EQUIPMENT

Attack T(hunder)-stick style. Capt John C. Morrissey. (Reprinted from Fighter Weapons Newsletter, Dec 1967) illus USAF Ftr Wpns Rev, pp 21-27, Summer '76

In search of the illusive green ball. Maj Richard M. Stroud. illus Fld Arty J 44:7-9 Jan-Feb '76

Initial pipper position and tracking. Capt Alexander H.C. Harwick. (Reprinted from USAF Fighter Weapons Review, Fall 1972) illus tab USAF Ftr Wpns Rev, pp 2-10, Summer '76

Let's get serious about dive toss. Capt Robert H. Baxter. (Reprinted from USAF Fighter Weapons Newsletter, Sep 1970) illus tab USAF Ftr Wpns Rev, pp 28-34, Summer '76

Mk 86 (shipboard) weapon control system. illus Countermeasures 2:12-15 Oct '76

Naval systems from Thomson-CSF. R. Meller. illus tab Intl Def Rev 9:847-851 Oct '76

Naval weapon system automation with the WSA4. J.R. Harper. illus Intl Def Rev 9:795-797 Oct '76

Night tactical evaluation. Col John H. Weckerling. illus Armor 85:45-46 May-Jun '76

The Polaris method (of obtaining accurate direction for the firing battery). Lt James G. Taphorn. tab illus Fld Arty J 44:8-12 Jul-Aug '76

Reduce your (fire control system) budget, yet buy more. Capt Edward A. Bryla. tab Armor 85:15 Nov-Dec '76

Scope interpretation. Sgt Edward A. Ranzenbach. illus tabs Combat Crew 27:14-17 Jul '76

Tank fire and gun control systems. R.M. Ogorkiewicz. illus tabs Intl Def Rev 9:70-74 Feb '76

Tank fire control. MajGen Bennett L. Lewis. illus tabs Countermeasures 2:42-45 Oct '76

The threat to air assault operations. Capt Daniel W. Henk. illus USA Avn Dig 22:6-7+ Feb '76

True magic for the artilleryman. (A shell homing in automatically on a target with the help of laser technology devices) John S. Phillip. illus Aerosp Intl 12:22-24 Jan-Feb '76

The U.S. Army Firefinder System. Maj Jay R. Hern. illus Signal 31:72+ Oct '76

FIRE DIRECTION CENTER

Battalion FDC--Cav style. Capt Eric C. Deets. illus Fld Arty J 44:38-40 Nov-Dec '76

U.S. field artillery in Vietnam. MajGen David E. Ott. (Extracts from "Field Artillery Monograph") illus tabs maps Fld Arty J pt 1, The field artillery adviser. 43:23-29 Jan-Feb '75; pt 2, In order to win. 43:39-45 Mar-Apr '75; pt 3, Field artillery mobility. 43:15-22 May-Jun '75; pt 4, The buildup. 43: 9-16 Jul-Aug '75, 43:46-51 Sep-Oct '75; pt 4, The field artillery buildup: 1967 combat operations. 43:29-34 Nov-Dec '75; pt 5, The hot war: 1968, the Tet offensive. 44:27-31 Jan-Feb '76; pt 5, The hot war: The Battle of Khe Sanh. 44:44-48 Mar-Apr '76; pt 5, The hot war: 1968-69, A Shau Valley. 44:53-57 May-Jun '76; pt 5, The hot war: Operations and raids. 44:37-43 Jul-Aug '76; pt 6, Vietnamization: FA assistance programs. 44: 10-17 Sep-Oct '76; pt 6, Vietnamization: Operations into Cambodia. 44:13-18 Nov-Dec '76

FIREARMS **see** Small Arms

FIREPOWER

FIST (Fire Support Team)! Responses. LtCol William F. Muhlenfeld and others. illus Fld Arty J 44: 16-21+ Jul-Aug '76

Firepower. (Address, V Corps Artillery Firepower Conference, Giessen, Germany, March 19, 1976) BrigGen Albert B. Akers. Fld Arty J 44:17-21+ May-Jun '76

Flexible firepower. (Fuses for airborne rockets) Steve Kimmel. illus (Also cutaways) Natl Def 60: 444-445 May-Jun '76

Troops and fire support. BrigGen Richard C. Schulze. MarCor Gaz 60:47-48 Jan '76

Study and Teaching

SAM-D tactical operations simulator. Capt James L. Hubbard. illus Air Def Mag, pp 26-29, Jan-Mar '76

FIRES AND FIRE PREVENTION

See also
Airplanes in Fire Fighting
   also subdivision under specific subjects, e.g.,
Airplanes--Fires and Fire Prevention
Airplanes, Military--Fires and Fire Prevention
Ships--Fires and Fire Prevention

Bases receive message on fighting nuclear fire. AF Times 36:6 Mar 1 '76

Car devices cut (electrically ignited crash) fires, tests show. AF Times 36:25 Mar 1 '76

Facility and a method for evaluation of thermal protection. A. M. Stoll and others. illus tab Aviation, Space & Envmt Med 47:1177-1181 Nov '76

Fire! SSgt Zack Richards. illus Soldiers 31:13 Oct '76

Fire prevention program. TIG Brief 28:17 Jan 16 '76

Fire protection and life safety. Lawrence G. Adams. illus tab Mil Engr 68:91-93 Mar-Apr '76

Got a HFEWS (Home Fire Early Warning System)? Maj James M. Fredregill. illus TAC Attack 16:9 Mar '76

It'll never happen, but ... (Battery fire at a missile launch control center) Capt Tom Luisi. illus Combat Crew 27:14-15 May '76

Nomex protection, a 50-50 proposition. Capt Michael E. Humphreys. illus MAC Flyer 23:7-8 Jan '76

Oil and fuel spills. TIG Brief 28:15 Feb 13 '76

Potential hazards of a nuclear weapon accident. TIG Brief 28:8 Feb 13 '76; Correction. TIG Brief 28:8 Jul 2 '76

Equipment

The P-15--soon to be the largest production crash-fire vehicle in existence. illus tab AF Engrg & Svcs Qtr 17:24-25 May '76

FIRING RANGES see Bombing and Gunnery Ranges

FIRST AID

See also
Artificial Respiration

(Automobile) crash: Then what? (Reprinted from Family Safety, Fall 1974) illus TAC Attack 16: 18-19 Mar '76

FIRST AID - Continued

Bugs and bites. illus TAC Attack 16:16-17 Mar '76

Idealized inflight airline medical kit: A committee report. Stanley R. Mohler and others. Aviation, Space & Envmt Med 47:1094-1095 Oct '76

Medical aspects of survivability. LtCol David H. Karney and Patsy Thompson. illus USA Avn Dig pt 1, Lifesaving emergency medical aid. 22:40-45 May '76; pt 2, Medical problems in a prolonged survival situation. 22:28-31 Jun '76

Survival. illus Approach 21:22-23 Jan '76

FISH, Howard M.

FMS (Foreign Military Sales): "No more giving it away." Interview. LtGen Howard Fish. por Govt Exec 8:19+ Dec '76

The Security Assistance Program. (Statement before Committee on International Relations, House of Representatives, Nov 12, 1975) LtGen H. M. Fish. AF Plcy Ltr for Comdrs: Sup No. 1:18-22 Jan '76

FISH INDUSTRY AND TRADE

The big patrol: Coast Guard gears up to monitor new fisheries zone. L. Edgar Prina. illus Sea Power 19:8-10 Sep '76

The Coast Guard and fisheries law enforcement. LT Eugene R. Fidell. illus tab US Nav Inst Proc 102: 70-75 Mar '76

Great Britain

The 1975-6 cod war (between Britain and Iceland). John Marriott. illus map tabs RUSI J for Def Studies 121:45-51 Sep '76

Iceland

Codfish war threatens NATO's northern flank. Gen T. R. Milton, Ret. AF Mag 59:40 Apr '76

The 1975-6 cod war (between Britain and Iceland). John Marriott. illus map tabs RUSI J for Def Studies 121:45-51 Sep '76

United States

NACOA (National Advisory Committee on Oceans and Atmosphere) says 'urgent action' needed on economic (resource) zone. illus Sea Power 18:26-28 Dec '75

FISHES

Jaws II. (Fishing follies) Maj Art Ivins. illus TAC Attack 16:4-8 Mar '76

FLAG OFFICERS

Russia

Naval Kremlinology. CAPT William H. J. Manthorpe, Jr. illus tab US Nav Inst Proc 102:70-72 Jan '76

United States

Admiral H. Kent Hewitt, U.S. Navy. John Clagett. illus Nav War Col Rev pt 1, Preparing for high command. 28:72-86 Summer '75; pt 2, High command. 28:60-86 Fall '75

Star status: Army, Navy, Air Force, Marines. Regular feature in some issues of Armed Forces Journal International

FLAG OFFICERS - Continued

United States - Cont'd

Directories

Flag and general officers of the naval services; officers of flag rank of the U.S. Navy, U.S. Coast Guard, and NOAA, and general officers of the U.S. Marine Corps on active duty as of January 1, 1976. illus US Nav Inst Proc 102:213-244 May '76

FLAGS

History

Proud heritage. (U.S. flag) Betty Woolley. illus Countermeasures 2:51 Jul '76

FLAME THROWERS

Inferno! A history of American flamethrowers. Capt John W. Mountcastle. illus Armor 85:21-25 Mar-Apr '76

FLEET, 6th

Aboard the USS "John F. Kennedy." Brian M. Service. illus tab Air Pict 38:168-173 May '76

FLEET, 7th

Ready power for peace--the U.S. Seventh Fleet. VADM George P. Steele II, Ret. illus tab US Nav Inst Proc 102:24-30 Jan '76

FLEET MARINE FORCE--Marine Corps--U.S. see Marine Corps--U.S.

FLIGHT, LOW-ALTITUDE

"Above the best" but below the threat. Capt Lewis D. Ray. illus USA Avn Dig 22:19-23 Feb '76

Air traffic management and tactical instruments. Capt Lewis D. Ray. illus USA Avn Dig 22:22-23+ Mar '76

Are you NOE and lost? Garvin L. Holman. illus USA Avn Dig 22:8-12 Mar '76

Cockpit design for night NOE (Nap-Of-the-Earth). J.H. Emery. illus USA Avn Dig 22:6-7 Jan '76

Consumer notice: Please read FAAO (Field Artillery Aerial Observer) team article thoroughly prior to entering combat. Fld Arty J 44:50-54 Nov-Dec '76

F-111 terrain following radar. Maj John Phillips. (Reprinted from USAF Fighter Weapons Newsletter, March 1969) illus USAF Ftr Wpns Rev, pp 11-13, Summer '76

Increased responsibility for Army aviators. BrigGen Charles E. Canedy. illus USA Avn Dig 22:1+ Nov '76

Low level techniques. Capt Gary A. Voellger. illus Navigator 23:12-15 Winter '76

Military low flying--why and where? Air Commodore P. B. Hine. Royal Air Forces Qtr 16:253-256 Autumn '76

The new (battlefield) dead-man's curve. Col William R. Ponder. tabs USA Avn Dig 22:6-7 Mar '76

Red Team AO (Aerial Observer) training. Capt Gary N. Grubb. illus Fld Arty J 44:22-23 Nov-Dec '76

A study of crew workload in low-level tactical fighter aircraft. WgComdr W.J. Wratten. Royal Air Forces Qtr 16:119-121+ Summer '76

FLIGHT, LOW-ALTITUDE - Continued

Terrain flight international. (Survey of 9 NATO nations and 3 Army agencies) Capt Don A. Mynard. illus USA Avn Dig 22:30-34 Aug '76

Study and Teaching

Cerebrations: Night attack helicopter training. Maj William E. Whitworth. illus tabs USA Avn Dig 22: 4-5+ Jan '76

Night terrain flight training in USAREUR. Maj George R. Miller. illus USA Avn Dig 22:8-11 Aug '76

FLIGHT ATTENDANTS see Cabin Crews

FLIGHT CONTROL SYSTEMS

DLC (Direct Lift Control) is here, finally! LCDR George Webb. tab illus Approach 21:1-3 Jun '76

GCA slow roll. illus Approach 21:5 Jun '76

Optimization of crew effectiveness in future cockpit design: Biomedical implications. Siegfried J. Gerathewohl. illus tab Aviation, Space & Envmt Med 47:1182-1187 Nov '76

Overcontrol: Commanded or uncommanded? Col Neil L. Eddins. illus tabs TAC Attack 16:10-14 Sep '76

FLIGHT ENGINEERS

Flight engineers fear cutback--AF says no move under way. AF Times 36:7 Mar 8 '76

FLIGHT INFORMATION
Here are entered articles on services provided for the purpose of giving advice and information useful for the safe and efficient conduct of flights.

See also related subjects, e.g.,
Flight Path
Weather Forecasting

Automated information processing system under development for Flight Service Stations. Bruce C. Abernethy. illus Combat Crew 27:12-15 Nov '76

FLight Information Publications (FLIPs). TIG Brief 28:21 Sep 24 '76

From mission order to instrument takeoff. CW2 Joel E. Warhurst. USA Avn Dig 22:12-14 Sep '76

General Flight Rules (AFR 60-16). TIG Brief 28: 13-14 Dec 3 '76

FLIGHT INSTRUMENTS see Aeronautical Instruments

FLIGHT NURSES

A call from mother. (Capt Joyce Stauffer is followed on a typical mission as a MAC flight nurse) TSgt David B. Drachlis. illus Airman 20:43-45 Oct '76

Flight nursing. Regular feature in some issues of Aviation, Space and Environmental Medicine

(Maj Betty Vierra the recipient of) first annual E. A. Hoefly Award. illus Aviation, Space & Envmt Med 47:798 Jul '76

Those were the days. (Flight nurses from World War II compare training, equipment, and experiences with today's AF flight nurses) Airman 20: 45 Oct '76

FLIGHT PATH

Comprehensive (formerly master) Plan Tabs and TERminal instrument Procedures (TERPs). TIG Brief 28:13 Nov 19 '76

FLIGHT PATH - Continued

DLC (Direct Lift Control) is here, finally! LCDR George Webb. tab illus Approach 21:1-3 Jun '76

Descent decisions. Capt Mike C. Kostelnik. illus tabs TAC Attack 16:12-14 Oct '76

How to prevent undershoot or landing short accidents. TIG Brief 28:9 Oct 22 '76

Reviewing the fine print. Capt M.C. Kostelnik. illus TAC Attack 16:22-24 Jul '76

Something new for the LAMPS program. (GSI, Glide Slope Indicator) illus Approach 22:10-11 Nov '76

FLIGHT PAY

Fly duty credit rules, flight pay changes due. AF Times 36:6 Apr 19 '76

Flying EM closer to career status: Mixed blessing. Bruce Callander. AF Times 36:2 May 17 '76

Ford signs 120-day notice order (for) grounded EM fliers. AF Times 37:10 Aug 9 '76

Key changes (in AFR 35-13) give fliers new break. AF Times 36:27 May 24 '76

2 plans aim at cutting flight time. Lee Ewing. AF Times 36:3 Jun 21 '76

FLIGHT PLAN

Alternate to what? CAPT J.E. Russ. illus Approach 22:8-10 Jul '76

Winter flying ... seasonal work. Capt John E. Richardson. Aerosp Safety 32:9 Dec '76

FLIGHT RECORDERS

The acoustical pinger. Maj Tony Helbling, Jr. illus Aerosp Safety 32:21 Jun '76

FLIGHT RECORDS
Here are entered articles on the logs and reports of a flight. For articles on record flying time for a given distance see Aviation Records

The first aerial voyage in America. (A Frenchman, Jean Pierre Blanchard, Philadelphia, Jan 9, 1793). Douglas H. Robinson. Am Avn Hist Soc J 21:3 Spring '76

I was there: Wright flight, 1910. Joseph R. McQuilkin. illus Am Avn Hist Soc J 21:199 Fall '76

Logging flying time. TIG Brief 28:19 Jul 16 '76

1929: Refueling proves practical--log of the 'Question Mark.' illus AF Times 36:23+ Jan 12 '76

FLIGHT SIMULATORS

Catching up with today. (New methods and equipment for training USAF navigators at Mather AFB, Calif) Ted R. Sturm. illus Airman 20:39-43 Apr '76

The coming payoffs of improved flight simulators. John L. Allen. illus tab Comdrs Dig 19: entire issue Jul 29 '76

Limit simulators, top official says. Len Famiglietti. AF Times 37:10 Aug 30 '76

A major step forward in simulation. illus Interavia 31:1174 Dec '76

A new approach to flight simulator acceptance. (CH-47 Chinook cargo helicopter simulator) LtCol Robert L. Catron. illus USA Avn Dig 22: 2-3+ Apr '76

FLIGHT SIMULATORS - Continued

Pilots' ground training. Col V. Andrianov. Soviet Mil Rev No. 6:20-22 Jun '76

SFTS (Synthetic Flight Training System): The shape of things to come. CW2 Thomas K. Equels. illus tab USA Avn Dig 22:13-17 Apr '76

Simulated flying performance after marihuana intoxication. David S. Janowsky and others. illus tabs Aviation, Space and Envmt Med 47:124-128 Feb '76

Simulator emergency procedure training. Capt Bernard R. Smith, Jr. TAC Attack 16:8-9 Oct '76

Simulators. Anchard F. Zeller. illus Aerosp Safety 32:1-4 Oct '76

Simulators in flight training: A pilot's view. LCDR C.A. Wheal. illus US Nav Inst Proc 102:50-57 Oct '76

Tactical training in the SFTS (Synthetic Flight Training System). Maj Elmer E. Curbow and MSgt Thomas McGuire. illus USA Avn Dig 22:18-19 Apr '76

The USAF Instrument Flight Center: Anachronism or instrument flight pacesetter for the future? Maj Jimmie L. Coombes. illus AU Rev 27:62-71 May-Jun '76

Visual elements in flight simulation. John Lott Brown. Aviation, Space & Envmt Med 47:913-924 Sep '76

FLIGHT SURGEONS

Aeromedical safety operations: A new concept in aviation accident prevention and investigation. CDR A.F. Wells. illus Approach 21:18-21 Jun '76

The flight surgeon. Col Daniel T. Sanders. illus USA Avn Dig 22:3+ Oct '76

Flight surgeon. CAPT Charles C. Yanquell, Ret. illus US Nav Inst Proc 102:46-59 Sep '76

Medical aspects of aircraft accident boards. Capt Gene R. Beaty. AF Law Rev 18:33-47 Fall '76

More than a doctor. (Specially trained flight surgeons) LtCol David H. Karney. illus USA Avn Dig 22:36-39 Oct '76

FLIGHT TRAINING

See also
Pilots--Education and Training

Air Force--U.S.

Board to tap women (for undergraduate pilot training) in July. AF Times 36:10 Jan 19 '76

Greater emphasis placed on use of flight trainers. AF Times 36:22 May 10 '76

House panel (Appropriations Committee) wants training planes full (and AF crews to fly some aircraft now contracted to airlines). Len Famiglietti. AF Times 36:17 Jun 21 '76

Lomcevak (46th Flying Training Sq, Peterson Fld, Colo). Capt Eugene W. Bricker. illus Interceptor 18:8-12 Feb '76

Armed Forces--U.S.

Limit simulators, top official says. Len Famiglietti. AF Times 37:10 Aug 30 '76

Army--U.S.

History

Flight training marks 65 years of growth. AF Times 36:24 Apr 12 '76

FLIGHTS, FAMOUS AND HISTORIC

The Air Corps' 1926 Pan American flight. LtGen Ira C. Eaker, Ret. illus map AF Mag 59:114+ Sep '76

The first aerial voyage in America. (A Frenchman, Jean Pierre Blanchard, Philadelphia, Jan 9, 1793) Douglas H. Robinson. Am Avn Hist Soc J 21:3 Spring '76

A long trail with no dust. (Dole Race to Honolulu, 1927) VADM W. V. Davis, Jr, Ret. illus Aerosp Hist 22:181-184 Dec '75

Never a 'Question Mark.' (Spaatz Trophy, given to SAC by TAC to be awarded to best tanker unit each year, in honor of historic flight of the Question Mark in 1929, which stayed in the air nearly 7 days and proved that in-flight refueling was practical) Maj Jay B. Welsh. illus Airman 20: 24-29 Mar '76

1929: Refueling proves practical--log of the 'Question Mark.' illus AF Times 36:23+ Jan 12 '76

'Question Mark' 'refuelers' honored: Two Air Force pioneers (BrigGens Ross G. Hoyt, Ret, and Joseph G. Hopkins, Ret) awarded DFCs nearly half a century after their key role in a world record endurance flight. illus AF Mag 59:22 Jul '76

With the Byrd North Pole expedition. E. J. "Pete" Demas. illus Am Avn Hist Soc J 21:4-8 Spring '76

FLOODS see Disasters

FLUTTER see Vibration

FLYING
This heading is used for popular, nontechnical articles on the pleasures of flying.

Light aircraft flying can be fun. Capt Marty Steere. illus TAC Attack 16:6-7 Jul '76

FLYING BOATS see Seaplanes

FLYING CLUBS see Aero Clubs

FLYING SAFETY

See also
Airplanes, Military--Safety Measures
Helicopters, Military--Safety Measures
Mountain Flying

The A-7: One aircraft or two? LCDR Ken Sanger. illus Approach 21:10-11 Jun '76

The ABC (Actions, Briefings, Coordination) for flying professionals. Col Richard C. Jones. illus TAC Attack 16:12-15 Dec '76

The ABC's of safety involvement. LtCol Jay M. Strayer. illus MAC Flyer 23:16-19 Apr '76

AIREP's--how they work for you. illus MAC Flyer 23:10-12 Apr '76

About aborts. Capt Dick Morrow. illus tab Aerosp Safety 32:6-7 Oct '76; TAC Attack 16:4-6 Oct '76

Air commerce: Stimulated or damned. A. Scott Crossfield. illus tabs Govt Exec 8:31-32+ Dec '76

Aircraft empathy. illus Aerosp Safety 32:10-12 Aug '76

Alternate to what? CAPT J. E. Russ. illus Approach 22:8-10 Jul '76

Another big vote for NATOPS (Naval Air Training and Operating Procedures Standardization). CAPT I. Patch. illus Approach 21:12-13 Feb '76

FLYING SAFETY - Continued

Big mother can kill you. Capt Marshall Hydorn. illus TAC Attack 16:10-11 Jan '76

Breakaway after tanking. illus Approach 22:16-17 Oct '76

Carelessness, incapacity, or neglect. illus MAC Flyer 23:9-11 Jun '76

Cockpit UNs (UNaccountables). illus Approach 22: 24-25 Oct '76

A commander speaks to his aviators on aviation safety. MajGen Eivind H. Johansen. illus USA Avn Dig 22:2-4 Nov '76

Control & supervision and flying. Col Paul M. Davis. illus Aerosp Safety 32:19-21 Aug '76

The controller and weather. David D. Thomas. illus MAC Flyer 23:18-20 Jan '76

Crew rest. illus Approach 21:24-25 Jun '76

Critical 11 minutes. (Takeoff plus 3 and landing minus 8) Maj John R. Dockendorff. illus Combat Crew 27:4-7 May '76; Aerosp Safety 32:2-5 Sep '76

DI (Decision Irreversibility). LtCol Gerald B. Hurst. illus TAC Attack 16:12-14 Feb '76

The depths of distraction. LtCol Robert J. Brun. illus Aerosp Safety 32:3 Jul '76

Engine hot, reaction cool. LCDR P. L. Leum. illus Approach 22:26-27 Dec '76

Flight safety. (Trans from a Russian publication) illus USA Avn Dig 22:40-41 Mar '76

Flight violation! LT Dave McPherson. illus Approach 22:12-13 Jul '76

Fly smart! Capt Donald K. Fenno. illus Aerosp Safety 32:26-27 Dec '76

Food sanitation and air safety. A. S. R. Peffers. Aviation, Space & Envmt Med 47:1107-1108 Oct '76

General Flight Rules (AFR 60-16). TIG Brief 28: 13-14 Dec 3 '76

Ground Proximity Warning Systems (GPWS)--will they survive the enthusiasm? Dan Boyle. Interavia 31:852-854 Sep '76

Hangar flying. Maj John R. Spey. illus Aerosp Safety 32:10-11 Feb '76

Hazy daze. (Altitude myopia: Visual deception in the air) illus MAC Flyer 23:9-10 Feb '76; Interceptor 5:18-19 May '76

He hit a what? Maj Thomas R. Allocca. illus Aerosp Safety 32:12-13 Feb '76

Helicopter SVFR (Special VFR). Capt William A. Battey. illus Approach 22:24-27 Aug '76

Hold the ice, please. Maj Philip M. McAtee. illus Aerosp Safety 32:23-25 Dec '76

How about a modern safety program? LCDR Russ Harrison. illus Approach 22:24-25 Nov '76

Ice and airfoils. (Reprinted from F-5 Technical Digest, Jan 1976) illus Aerosp Safety 32:26-27 Feb '76

Is Danny O'Keefe qualified ... yet? Capt Richard L. Cecil. illus MAC Flyer 23:18-21 Dec '76

Is safety really paramount? LCDR Frank Stauts. illus Approach 22:14-15 Oct '76

FLYING SAFETY - Continued

The launch. (Complacency in the cockpit) LCDR Bob Jones. illus Approach 22:24-25 Dec '76

Learning by doing. Capt Robert M. Hail. illus Aerosp Safety 32:10-13 Dec '76

Lessons learned (in Naval Aviation). LT C.F.Wise. illus Approach 21:7-8 Nov '75

Light aircraft flying can be fun. Capt Marty Steere. illus TAC Attack 16:6-7 Jul '76

New FAA control on (private) pilot tests asked (in GAO report). AF Times 36:23 Apr 12 '76

No new causes. Capt James P. Bloom. illus Aerosp Safety 32:8-9 Jun '76

One of the finest pilots in the squadron. illus Approach 22:16-18 Aug '76; Combat Crew 27:8-10 Oct '76

Ops topics. Regular feature in issues of _Aerospace Safety_

Overcontrol: Commanded or uncommanded? Col Neil L. Eddins. illus tabs TAC Attack 16:10-14 Sep '76

Pilots: Be suspicious! illus Approach 22:10-11 Sep '76

Raindrops keep falling. MAC Flyer 23:11 Feb '76

Safe and on time. Capt Bruce L. Gumble. illus MAC Flyer 23:6-9 Sep '76

Safety is no accident--the first commandment: Guidelines for light aircraft pilots. tab illus Interavia 31:233-234 Mar '76

The second time around. Maj Jack Spey. illus Aerosp Safety 32:16-18 Aug '76

Situation awareness: One key to safety. Capt Larry Kanaster. illus Aerosp Safety 32:14-15 Dec '76

A slight case of the blues. (Hypoxic passenger) illus MAC Flyer 23:19 Jun '76

Something new for the LAMPS program. (GSI, Glide Slope Indicator) illus Approach 22:10-11 Nov '76

Sunday afternoon cu(mulonimbus). Maj Orlen L. Brownfield. illus MAC Flyer 23:3-5 Apr '76

Supervisor of Flying regulation (AFR 60-2). TIG Brief 28:8 May 21 '76

Supervisor Of Flying (SOF) program. (AFR 60-2) TIG Brief 28:14 Dec 3 '76

Talking of safety. Douglas H. Chopping. illus tabs Interavia pt 1, 31:1074-1075 Nov '76

Terrain flight international. (Survey of 9 NATO nations and 3 Army agencies) Capt Don A. Mynard. illus USA Avn Dig 22:30-34 Aug '76

Thunderstorm? Cumulonimbus? Maj Herbert Weigl, Jr. illus Aerosp Safety 32:1 Sep '76

Time bomb (stress). Capt Allan R. Sweeny. illus Aerosp Safety 32:26-28 Jun '76

A trace of disaster. LtCol Robert J. Brun. illus Aerosp Safety 32:17 Feb '76

Twelve o'clock low. Maj Orlen L. Brownfield. illus MAC Flyer 23:18-19 Mar '76

A WW (Weather Warning) by any other name. LT Paul J. Derocher, Jr. illus Approach 21:12-14 Nov '75

FLYING SAFETY - Continued

Walking a tightrope. (Flying a helicopter into icing conditions) Ted Kontos. illus USA Avn Dig 22:38-41 Feb '76

Weather report. illus MAC Flyer 23:10-12 Aug '76

(What is cockpit discipline?) What it isn't. Maj Albert R. Barbin, Jr. illus MAC Flyer 23:14-15 Apr '76

What's your approach plate IQ? LT Bob Harler. illus Approach 22:10-12 Oct '76

Who are you calling student? Capt Charles E. Bailey. illus Combat Crew 27:8-10 Dec '76

Winter flying ... seasonal work. Capt John E. Richardson. Aerosp Safety 32:9 Dec '76

FLYING SAUCERS see Unidentified Flying Objects

FLYING STATUS

Fliers assured on-time top rates (under pending changes to AFR 35-13). AF Times 36:5 Mar 29 '76

Flight Status Selection Board. LtCol Kenneth R. Town. tab MarCor Gaz 60:43-46 May '76

Flying EM closer to career status: Mixed blessing. Bruce Callander. AF Times 36:2 May 17 '76

Key changes (in AFR 35-13) give fliers new break. AF Times 36:27 May 24 '76

100-250 pilots (rated supplement withdrawals) going back to flying status. Lee Ewing. AF Times 37:12 Nov 22 '76

FLYING TIME
Here are entered articles on time spent in flying by an individual pilot to maintain his proficiency rating. For articles on record flying time for a given distance, see Aviation Records.

Cut fly time and costs, GAO says. Bruce Callander. tab AF Times 37:12 Aug 16 '76

Minimum flight time. LtCol Kenneth R. Town. illus tabs MarCor Gaz 60:35-39 Jan '76

2 plans aim at cutting flight time. Lee Ewing. AF Times 36:3 Jun 21 '76

FLYNN, John P.

Front seats in history. (MajGen John Flynn recalls the Vietnam POW experience and how the AF returnees were integrated back into the personnel system) LtCol Fred A. Meurer. por Airman 20:24-29 Sep '76

FOG AND FOG DISPERSAL

Severe clear. CW2 Jon L. Osgood. illus USA Avn Dig 22:42-43 Feb '76

FOOD

See also
Nutrition
Rations

Blood fat and the fighter pilot. LCDR Gary Smith. illus tabs Approach 22:18-22 Sep '76

Meat buying: Good is good enough, GAO study suggests. AF Times 36:8 May 31 '76

Sausage firm (in Southern California) indicted. AF Times 36:9 Jul 19 '76

Survival: Food. SSgt Charles R. Teagarden. illus Aerosp Safety pt 1, Nutrition and survival rations. 32:17-19 Jul '76; pt 2, Subsistence off the land. 32:13-15 Aug '76; pt 3, Food preparation. 32:14-16 Sep '76

FOOD - Continued

Costs

Higher food costs for those on BAS? Ron Sanders. AF Times 36:2 Jun 21 '76

Meal charges to drop. AF Times 37:9 Dec 13 '76

'Shock wave' effect (from Senate investigation) hiked beef prices. AF Times 36:12 Jun 14 '76

Inspection

Abuses (in procurement of fresh meat for European commissaries) reported. AF Times 36:9 Jul 19 '76

Beef falsely graded, suit says. AF Times 37:10 Dec 13 '76

Commissaries in Europe got bad meat, DOD says. Andy Plattner. AF Times 37:4 Oct 4 '76

Food sanitation and air safety. A.S.R.Peffers. Aviation, Space & Envmt Med 47:1107-1108 Oct '76

Hot line suggested for beefs on food. Andy Plattner. AF Times 37:2 Aug 2 '76

How vendors get past inspection: Meat cheating. Andy Plattner. AF Times 36:24 Apr 26 '76

Lack of competition a problem: Military meat buying. Andy Plattner. AF Times 36:17+ May 10 '76

Meat witnesses cite bribery. Andy Plattner. AF Times 36:4 May 24 '76

Poor quality (meat) forced on comstores. Andy Plattner. AF Times 36:25+ May 3 '76

Quality assurance provisions in Blanket Purchase Agreements (BPAs). TIG Brief 28:13 Jun 4 '76

Subsistence quality assurance in veterinary-origin inspection. TIG Brief 28:5 Mar 26 '76

They shoot horses, don't they? (Army veterinarians do spend some time working with animals but still keep close watch on other veterinary medical activities) Janet Hake. illus Soldiers 31:32-35 Mar '76

Tighter rein put on (meat) procurement. AF Times 36:8 May 31 '76

Preservation

Balloonists sample food and air aloft. AF Times 37:23 Sep 6 '76

Gastronautics--chowing down in flight. Maj Orlen L. Brownfield. illus MAC Flyer 23:18-19 Feb '76

Reg tightened on food handlers: Potato salad out. AF Times 36:16 Jun 14 '76

Supply

Agricultural freedom and national strength. Earl L. Butz. Persp in Def Mgt No.24:13-18 Winter '75-'76

Food as a factor in U.S.-USSR relations. Joseph W. Willett. illus Natl Sec Aff Forum No.24:33-37 Spring-Summer '76

The food weakness. (State of the Soviets) Ellis Tenant. illus tabs Def & For Aff Dig No.6:11-14 '76

New troubles hamper (Defense Supply Agency) meat buying. AF Times 37:12 Dec 20 '76

Testing

Food samples slated for balloon journey--taste tests to reveal flight effects. Ron Sanders. illus AF Times 36:24 Feb 23 '76

FOOD AND DRUG ADMINISTRATION

Management training: AMA (American Management Associations) courses show results. illus Govt Exec 8:38-39 Mar '76

FOOD SERVICE

See also
In-Flight Meal Service

Air Force

ALA salutes the National Restaurant Association on the Hennessy (Trophy) at 20. illus Review 55:33-34+ Mar-Apr '76

Catering to customer desires. (Modular fast food program) Capt Thomas J.Padgett. illus AF Engrg & Svcs Qtr 17:18-20 Aug '76

Contract KP--ATC (Air Training Command)'s asset. James L.Skiles. illus AF Engrg & Svcs Qtr 17: 23-24 Aug '76

Food service--200 years of advancement. Lt Dennis A.Bossen. illus AF Engrg & Svcs Qtr 17:14-16 Feb '76

GAO seen favoring a la carte. AF Times 36:16 Jun 14 '76

A look at the big picture in U.S. Air Force food service management. Interview. BrigGen William D. Gilbert. illus Review 55:27-29 Mar-Apr '76

Loring (AFB, Maine) food plan permanent. AF Times 37:13 Sep 6 '76

(Loring AFB) Maine food test extended. AF Times 36:22 Feb 23 '76

Loring (AFB, Maine): Pay-as-you-go (food service) may stay. Ron Sanders. AF Times 37:10 Aug 23 '76

RAF Chicksands (Eng), Kadena AB (Okinawa) take firsts in Hennessy contest. illus AF Engrg & Svcs Qtr 17:22 Aug '76

Reg tightened on food handlers: Potato salad out. AF Times 36:16 Jun 14 '76

SAC food service. Maj Frank Dooley. illus Review 55:27-30+ Jan-Feb '76

Strictly gourmet. (AF dining hall (Priory Arms) at RAF Chicksands, Eng) SSgt Bruce D.Hoffman. illus Airman 20:19-21 Jan '76

Armed Forces

DSA (Defense Supply Agency) adding role in food services. AF Times 37:36 Dec 6 '76

EM on BAS charged higher meal rates. AF Times 37:3 Oct 25 '76

New basic meal charges detailed. AF Times 37:8 Oct 18 '76

History

Food service--200 years of advancement. Lt Dennis A.Bossen. illus AF Engrg & Svcs Qtr 17:14-16 Feb '76

Army

Dining in style. (Army's new facilities) Sgt JoAnn Mann. illus Soldiers 31:34-35 Jun '76

The 'mess sergeant' goes shopping. Capt John M. Campbell. illus Army Log 8:24-27 Jul-Aug '76

History

Continental Army logistics: Food supply. illus Army Log 8:24-28 Jan-Feb '76

FOOD SERVICE - Continued

Army - Cont'd

History - Cont'd

Fire cakes to French fries. Sgt JoAnn Mann. illus Soldiers 31:18-19 Jul '76

Marine Corps

Marine Corps to upgrade food services. AF Times 37:2 Oct 25 '76

FORCE AND ENERGY

An energy perspective on the evolution of weapons systems technology. Capt Timothy G. Larsen. Educ J 19:28-29 Fall '76

FORCES COMMAND

In U.S. Forces Command: 'Total Army' readiness. Gen Bernard W. Rogers. illus Army 26:30-32+ Oct '76

Total force. LtCol James E. Witek. tab Soldiers 31: 43-46 Aug '76

Directories

Forces Command. Army 26:135 Oct '76

Organization

FORSCOM engineers: The first 1,000 days. Col Alvin G. Rowe. illus tab Mil Engr 68:445-447 Nov-Dec '76

FORD, Gerald R., Jr

Backing the President. Phil Stevens. AF Times 37:14 Oct 18 '76

Conference speakers. (Excerpts from addresses, NGAUS 98th General Conference, Washington, Aug 30-Sep 1, 1976) por Natl Guardsman 30: 23-27 Oct '76

Ford promises strong Guard (in address to NGAUS 98th General Conference, Washington, Aug 30-Sep 1, 1976). AF Times 37:10 Sep 13 '76

Ford signs 120-day notice order (for) grounded EM fliers. AF Times 37:10 Aug 9 '76

Ford wins Hill fight over closing (military) bases. AF Times 37:53 Sep 6 '76

The new Pacific doctrine. LtGen Ira C. Eaker, Ret. AF Times 36:13+ Jan 5 '76

'76 money bill goes to (Pres) Ford. AF Times 36:4 Feb 9 '76

President accuses Congress of driving up defense costs. AF Times 37:4 Sep 6 '76

(Pres) Ford asks AF cut of 13,000. tab AF Times 36:4 Feb 2 '76

(Pres) Ford nixes junior EM aid; phaseout of store subsidies asked. Randy Shoemaker. AF Times 37:3 Dec 27 '76

(Pres) Ford okays new medal for superior service (Defense Superior Service Medal). AF Times 36:2 Feb 23 '76

(Pres) Ford signs $104 billion defense bill. AF Times 37:9 Oct 4 '76

(Pres) Ford signs procurement bill: Hits Congress for shipbuilding cuts. L. Edgar Prina. Sea Power 19:7-10 Aug '76

FORD, Gerald R., Jr - Continued

President (Ford) urges repeal of (1%) 'kicker.' Randy Shoemaker. AF Times 36:3 Apr 5 '76

Store subsidies scored by (Pres) Ford. AF Times 36:2 Feb 2 '76

The Sunday morning massacre: A murder-suicide? Aaron Latham. (Reprinted from New York, Dec 22, 1975) por Armed Forces J Intl 113:18-25 Jan '76

2 more GI Bill items (correspondence courses and flight training) face Ford budget ax. AF Times 36:8 Feb 2 '76

FOREIGN AID see Economic Aid to Foreign Countries; Military Aid to Foreign Countries; Technical Aid to Foreign Countries

FOREIGN AREA SPECIALIST PROGRAM see Area Specialist Programs

FOREIGN LEGION

The ultimate battle. (French Foreign Legion action at Camerone, Mexico, 1863) SP4 Robert G. Fuller. illus Soldiers 31:50-53 Sep '76

FOREIGN NATIONALS IN THE ARMED FORCES

Our tempest-tost. (Air Force immigrants) MSgt Harold Newcomb. illus Airman 20:34-39 Jul '76

FOREIGN OBJECT DAMAGE

FOD: A management problem. Col Samuel Huser. illus tabs TAC Attack 16:24-27 Sep '76

FOD in the F-4 egress system. Michael Grost. illus Aerosp Safety 32:8-9 Jan '76

FOD prevention: Everybody's business. TIG Brief 28:3 Jan 16 '76

Foreign Object Damage (FOD). tab TIG Brief 28:9 May 7 '76

Foreign Object Damage (FOD). TIG Brief 28:6 Sep 10 '76

Fuel tank Foreign Object Damage (FOD). TIG Brief 28:11-12 Jul 2 '76

One problem too many. illus Approach 21:24-26 Jan '76

Things that go bump in the flight. Maj Joe Tillman. illus TAC Attack 16:26-28 Aug '76

X-ray for FOD. TIG Brief 28:13 Aug 27 '76

You and your toolbox. Sgt1C Jerry E. Mills. illus USA Avn Dig 22:30-35 Dec '76

FOREIGN RELATIONS

For general foreign relations of a country, look under the name of the country, e.g., United States--Foreign Relations. For foreign relations of one country with another, look under either country, e.g., United States--Foreign Relations--Latin America; Latin America--Foreign Relations--United States.

See also
International Relations

FOREIGN SCIENCE AND TECHNOLOGY CENTER see Army Foreign Science and Technology Center

FOREIGN SERVICE see Diplomatic and Consular Service

FOREIGN TECHNOLOGY DIVISION

Directories

Who's who in the USAF Foreign Technology Division (FTD). Table only. Elect Warfare 7:65 May-Jun '75

FORMATION FLYING

Linked pairs. Capts Daniel J.Gibson and John G. Swanson. illus USAF Ftr Wpns Rev, pp 31-36, Fall '76

Study and Teaching

Dissimilar aircraft engagements. Capt Maurice B. Johnston, Jr. (Reprinted from USAF Fighter Weapons Newsletter, March 1968) illus USAF Ftr Wpns Rev, pp 14-17+, Summer '76

FORMOSA see China (Republic)

FORMS, MILITARY

Prepaid postage on change of mailing address cards and other forms (limited by AF). TIG Brief 28:8 Sep 10 '76

Record of Emergency Data (DD Form 93). TIG Brief 28:15 Mar 26 '76

Significant historical data processing (AFTO Form 95). TIG Brief 28:12 Jul 16 '76

FORRESTER, Eugene P.

Is enemy us? (Condensed from address, Texas Assoc of Broadcasters, Dallas, Sep 16, 1976) MajGen Eugene P.Forrester. Army 26:6-8 Nov '76

FORTIFICATIONS

History

Fortress West Point: 19th century concept in an 18th century war. Col Dave R.Palmer. illus map Mil Engr 68:171-174 May-Jun '76

The rock (Alcatraz). Capt John D.Anderson. illus Soldiers 31:45-48 Apr '76

FORTS see Army Posts

FORWARD AIR CONTROLLERS

Forward air control in the Korean War. Maj Tim Cline. illus Am Avn Hist Soc J 21:257-262 Winter '76

Tac air, member of the (combined arms) team supporting the supersoldier. LtCol William H.Rees. illus Infantry 66:16-23 May-Jun '76

Tally on the FAC (Forward Air Controller). Capt Duane Tway. illus TAC Attack 16:4-6 Nov '76

Tiny craft play big role in drill (Exercise Solid Shield). illus AF Times 36:31 Jun 7 '76

FORWARD OBSERVER

Consumer notice: Please read FAAO (Field Artillery Aerial Observer) team article thoroughly prior to entering combat. Fld Arty J 44:50-54 Nov-Dec '76

FIST (Fire Support Team)! BrigGen Paul F.Pearson. illus tabs Fld Arty J 44:7-12 May-Jun '76

FIST (Fire Support Team)! Responses. LtCol William F.Muhlenfeld and others. illus Fld Arty J 44: 16-21+ Jul-Aug '76

Forward observer effectiveness. Col Paul F.Pearson. tab Fld Arty J 44:24-26 Jan-Feb '76

Red Team AO (Aerial Observer) training. Capt Gary N.Grubb. illus Fld Arty J 44:22-23 Nov-Dec '76

History

My beautiful balloon: Evolution--the FO. Ronald W. Shin. illus Fld Arty J 44:9-12 Nov-Dec '76

FRANCE

France. Def & For Aff Dig No.10:29-31+ '76

Foreign Policy

France and Britain: European powers and members of NATO. Jean Houbert. Royal Air Forces Qtr 15:289-300+ Winter '75

FRANCIS, H. Minton

No plan to trim EO jobs. H.Minton Francis. AF Times 37:4 Oct 25 '76

FRAUD

Bad checks hurt prices, profits. Andy Plattner. AF Times 37:2 Sep 6 '76

Bad checks: Losses by commands. AF Times 37:28 Sep 13 '76

Computer crimes uncovered (by General Accounting Office). Jim Parker. AF Times 36:20 May 31 '76

OSI program aims at fighting fraud. AF Times 37:11 Dec 20 '76

Packing, crating, and household goods fraud indications. TIG Brief 28:17-18 Sep 24 '76

Reporting fraud indicators. TIG Brief 28:9 Nov 19 '76

Shippers (of household goods) accused of fraud. Ron Sanders. AF Times 37:8 Oct 4 '76

Unintended bad check not actionable. AF Times 36:6 Mar 8 '76

FREEDOM OF INFORMATION

Defense public information policy. (Memorandum, Jan 26, 1976) Donald H.Rumsfeld. AF Plcy Ltr for Comdrs: Sup No.4:31-32 Apr '76

Distribution of AFOSI reports of investigation. TIG Brief 28:11 Aug 27 '76

The Freedom of Information Act: An analysis. Review 55:17+ Nov-Dec '75

Freedom of Information and Privacy Act releases regarding AFOSI investigations. TIG Brief 28:11 Aug 27 '76

Guidance on release of information under the Privacy Act. AF Plcy Ltr for Comdrs: Sup No.7:26-27 Jul '76

High court (Supreme Court) frees (military) honor code data. AF Times 36:2 May 3 '76

'Info Act' report leaves some gaps. Ann Gerow. AF Times 36:12 Mar 22 '76

Intelligence secrecy and security in a free society. William E.Colby. Intl Sec 1:3-14 Fall '76

Is enemy us? (Condensed from address, Texas Assoc of Broadcasters, Dallas, Sep 16, 1976) MajGen Eugene P.Forrester. illus Army 26:6-8 Nov '76

Maintaining special security files. TIG Brief 28:9 Dec 17 '76

Medical aspects of aircraft accident boards. Capt Gene R.Beaty. AF Law Rev 18:33-47 Fall '76

'Privileged' status of internal correspondence. TIG Brief 28:18 Mar 26 '76

Release of information contained in military personnel records. TIG Brief 28:20 Jul 16 '76

Release of information on military pay records. TIG Brief 28:12 Jun 18 '76

FUND RAISING

AF Assistance Fund seeks new ideas. AF Times 36:12 May 24 '76

Assistance fund drive sets $1.4 million goal. AF Times 37:18 Dec 20 '76

(Bob) Hope salute tied to USO fund drive. illus AF Times 36:23 May 17 '76

USO passing hat for funds. AF Times 36:24 Jun 21 '76

Welfare 'haves' can aid 'have nots.' AF Times 36:10 Jun 7 '76

FURLONG, Raymond B.

Air University. por AF Mag 59:64-65 May '76

The military and the media. (Remarks, Air War College Media-Military Symposium '76, Maxwell AFB, Ala, March 29, 1976) LtGen Raymond B. Furlong. AF Plcy Ltr for Comdrs: Sup No.6:19-2: Jun '76

Professionalism. LtGen Raymond B. Furlong. TIG Brief 28:2 Mar 12 '76

FUSES, ORDNANCE

The development of the proximity fuze. Capt Geoffrey Bennett. illus RUSI J for Def Studies 121:57-62 Mar '76

Flexible firepower. (Fuses for airborne rockets) Steve Kimmel. illus (Also cutaways) Natl Def 60: 444-445 May-Jun '76

Fuzing in 1776. Ronald O. Nitzsche. illus Natl Def 61:54-55 Jul-Aug '76

Kongsberg's NVT (Norwegian Variable Time) proximity fuzes for mortar bombs and artillery shells. P. Simonsen. illus tab Intl Def Rev 8:919-922 Dec '75

Remote set fuzing for 2.75-inch rocket. Alexander Janushevich. illus (Also cutaway) USA Avn Dig 22: 6-7+ Apr '76

History

Antipersonnel shrapnel rounds. Capt John R. deTreville. illus (Also cutaways) Fld Arty J 44:24-28 Mar-Apr '76

FUTURE

See also
War, Future

Aerospace defense. (Remarks, American Defense Preparedness Assoc, Los Angeles, Oct 15, 1975) Gen Daniel James, Jr. AF Plcy Ltr for Comdrs: Sup No.1:2-10 Jan '76; Condensation. Natl Def 60: 289 Jan-Feb '76

Africa's future armies: Age of experiment. Maj P.G. Francis. Army Qtr 106:324-332 Jul '76

The Air Force and national security: 1976 and beyond. (Remarks, Air Force Assoc, Mobile Chapter, Mobile, Ala, March 27, 1976) LtGen John W. Pauly. AF Plcy Ltr for Comdrs: Sup No.6:10-18 Jun '76

The air transport customer in 1980. tab Interavia 31: 143-144 Feb '76

The B-1: Strategic deterrence into the twenty-first century. MajGen Abner B.Martin. illus tabs AU Rev 27:2-14 Mar-Apr '76

Boeing's view of future air transport growth. illus tabs Interavia 31:626 Jul '76

FUTURE - Continued

C^3 in century 21. James S. McLeod. illus tabs Signal 30:39-40 Jul '76

Civil transport technology up to 2000: NASA believes fuel consumption is the major consideration. J. Philip Geddes. illus tabs Interavia 31:419-421 May '76

The coup against entropy. Aidan M.G. Moore. illus tabs Spaceflight 18:126-129 Apr '76

An engineering brief for the 1980's. Charles J. Merdinger. illus Mil Engr 68:212-214 May-Jun '76

Engineering requirements for the year 2000. Lev Zetlin. Mil Engr 68:215-217 May-Jun '76

The evolution of military satellite communications systems. Frederick E. Bond and CDR William H. Curry, Jr. illus tabs Signal 30:39-40+ Mar '76

(Excerpt from) Keynote Address (57th Defense Preparedness Meeting, American Defense Preparedness Assoc, Los Angeles, Oct 15, 1975). Gen William J. Evans. Natl Def 60:283 Jan-Feb '76

Extra-terrestrial communities. illus tabs Spaceflight 18:130-134 Apr '76

A fleet for the future: Some modest suggestions. Norman Polmar. illus tabs Sea Power 19:12-17 Apr '76

Forces for the future. (Remarks, Lancaster Chamber of Commerce, Lancaster, Calif, Feb 6, 1976) Thomas C. Reed. AF Plcy Ltr for Comdrs: Sup No.4:16-20 Apr '76

A forecast for the 70's and 80's. Anthony J. Wiener. Persp in Def Mgt No.24:1-12 Winter '75-'76

The future and Tactical Air Command. (Remarks, American Defense Preparedness Assoc Meeting, Los Angeles, Oct 15, 1975) Gen Robert J. Dixon. AF Plcy Ltr for Comdrs: Sup No.2:10-21 Feb '76; Condensation. Natl Def 60:285 Jan-Feb '76

The future and the strategic mission. (Excerpt from address, 57th Defense Preparedness Meeting, American Defense Preparedness Assoc, Los Angeles, Oct 15, 1975) MajGen Andrew B. Anderson, Jr. Natl Def 60:286 Jan-Feb '76

Future combat vehicles. William F. Banks. Natl Def 60:274-275 Jan-Feb '76

Future concepts of air power. (Excerpt from address, 57th Defense Preparedness Meeting, American Defense Preparedness Assoc, Los Angeles, Oct 15, 1975) LtGen John W. Pauly. Nat Def 60: 284 Jan-Feb '76

The future environment. LCDR Jacob D. Dumelle. Mil Engr 68:304-305 Jul-Aug '76

Future military preparedness. (Address, Naval Academy Graduation Ceremonies, Annapolis, June 2, 1976) Donald H. Rumsfeld. AF Plcy Ltr for Comdrs: Sup No.8:2-7 Aug '76

The future of tactical Air Forces. (Remarks, Graduation Ceremonies, 82d Flying Training Wg, Williams AFB, Ariz, June 12, 1976) LtGen Sanford K. Moats. AF Plcy Ltr for Comdrs: Sup No.8: 17-22 Aug '76

Future tactical missiles. Malcolm R. Currie. illus Natl Def 61:32-35 Jul-Aug '76

Guarding against technological surprise. George H. Heilmeier. AU Rev 27:2-7 Sep-Oct '76

FUTURE - Continued

In the Tricentennial year 2076. (Artist Robert T. McCall illustrates possible items of the future and creates space mural for the new National Air and Space Museum) Robert K. Ruhl. illus Airman 20: 24-33 Jul '76

Industry and defense. (Excerpt from address, 57th Defense Preparedness Meeting, American Defense Preparedness Assoc, Los Angeles, Oct 15, 1975) R. Anderson. Natl Def 60:287 Jan-Feb '76

The INtegrated TActical Communications System (INTACS) study. William M. Mannel. illus tabs Signal 30:19-27 Jul '76

Keynote address, 56th Annual Meeting of the Society of American Military Engineers (Arlington, Va, April 28-May 1, 1976). ADM Ben Moreell, Ret. illus Mil Engr 68:294-297 Jul-Aug '76

Lockheed world air traffic report, 1976-1985. J. Philip Geddes. illus map tabs Interavia 31: 623-625 Jul '76

Looking beyond the space shuttle. Dave Dooling. illus Spaceflight pt 1, 18:68-69 Feb '76; pt 2, 18:227 Jun '76; pt 3, 18:367-368+ Oct '76

The Marine Corps in 1985. Peter A. Wilson. illus US Nav Inst Proc 102:31-38 Jan '76

Military airlift and the future. (Excerpt from address, 57th Defense Preparedness Meeting, American Defense Preparedness Assoc, Los Angeles, Oct 15, 1975) Gen Paul K. Carlton. Natl Def 60: 288 Jan-Feb '76

A military elite in transition: Air Force leaders in the 1980s. (Research undertaken at Air Command and Staff College) LtCol Franklin D. Margiotta. tabs Armed Forces & Soc 2:155-184 Winter '76

NASA operational communications. Charles A. Taylor. illus maps tabs Signal 30:91-95 Aug '76

NASA's goal: Keeping the U.S. Number One in aeronautics. Alan M. Lovelace. illus AF Mag 59:36-40 Feb '76

Outlook for space. Dave Dooling. Spaceflight pt 1, 18:422-425 Dec '76

Research horizons: Where the Air Force ought to be going. Col James E. Strub. illus AU Rev 28:16-25 Nov-Dec '76

Space in the Air Force future. (Remarks, American Defense Preparedness Assoc, Oct 15, 1975) Thomas W. Morgan. AF Plcy Ltr for Comdrs: Sup No. 2:2-8 Feb '76; Condensation. Natl Def 60:290 Jan-Feb '76

FUTURE - Continued

Tank for the 1980's (XM1 main battle tank). illus Natl Def 60:364-365 Mar-Apr '76

Technology and strategy: Precision guided munitions and other highly sophisticated weapons will increase the effectiveness of the nuclear threat. Michael L. Nacht. Natl Def 61:199-202 Nov-Dec '76

Technology and the future. Earl C. Joseph. illus Armed Forces Compt 21:8-9 Jul '76

Technology: Its impact on the 1980s. Joseph A. Boyd. illus tabs Interavia 31:50-54 May-Jun '76

Tools and civilization. Lynn T. White, Jr. Persp in Def Mgt No. 24:33-42 Winter '75-'76; Condensation. Fld Arty J 44:44-47 Sep-Oct '76

Two hundred years of communications. Edward A. Havens. illus Signal 31:33-35 Nov-Dec '76

Two tracks to new worlds. Michael A. G. Michaud. illus tab Spaceflight 18:2-6+ Jan '76

The uncertain market for commercial aircraft to 1990: A McDonnell Douglas survey. J. Philip Geddes. illus tabs Interavia 31:350-354 Apr '76

The U.S. Air Force--systems of the future. (Excerpts from talks, Luncheon and Seminar Sessions, 57th Defense Preparedness Meeting, American Defense Preparedness Assoc, Los Angeles, Oct 15, 1975) illus Natl Def 60:283-290 Jan-Feb '76

The U.S. Infantry: The future. illus Infantry 66:36-39 Jul-Aug '76

U.S. military strategy for the eighties. Gen Andrew J. Goodpaster, Ret. illus Natl Sec Aff Forum No. 24:1-12 Spring-Summer '76

WWMCCS ADP: A promise fulfilled. Herbert B. Goertzel and Col James R. Miller. illus Signal 30:57-63 May-Jun '76

War, peace, and society in the 1980's: A historian's view. Richard A. Preston. illus Nav War Col Rev 28:34-44 Winter '76

The West German Air Force re-equips for the 1980s. Rudi Meller. illus tab Interavia pt 1, Combat strength increases under cost pressures. 31:320-322+ Apr '76; pt 2, 31:459-461 May '76

The world environment and U.S. military policy for the 1970s and 1980s. ADM Thomas H. Moorer, Ret and Alvin J. Cottrell. tab Strat Rev 4:56-65 Spring '76

G

G C A see Ground-Controlled Approach

G C I see Ground-Controlled Interception

GAMES, THEORY OF

See also
War Games

GARD, Robert G., Jr

(Army personnel problems) Interview. MajGen Robert Gard. Fld Arty J 44:35-37 Nov-Dec '76

GAS TURBINES (AIRCRAFT)

More power to you! Clarence J. Carter. illus USA Avn Dig 22:40-43 Sep '76

Turbine blade manufacture for modern aircraft powerplants. Werner Niefer. illus tabs Interavia 31: 238-240 Mar '76

U.S. small turbine review. Irwin Stambler. illus (Also cutaway) tabs Interavia 31:440-443 May '76

Maintenance and Repair

Health Indication Test (HIT). Clarence J. Carter. USA Avn Dig 22:35 Mar '76

GASES

See also
Hydrogen
Oxygen

Chlorine hazard. TIG Brief 28:5 Feb 27 '76; Addendum: Use of protective masks for chlorine maintenance. TIG Brief 28:7 Jun 18 '76

Compressed gas cylinders: Are you sure of the contents? TIG Brief 28:5 Jul 16 '76

Denitrogenation interruptions with air. Julian P. Cooke. tabs Aviation, Space & Envmt Med 47: 1205-1209 Nov '76

GASES, ASPHYXIATING AND POISONOUS

See also
Carbon Monoxide

GASES IN WARFARE see Chemical-Biological Warfare

GAYLER, Noel A.

Maintaining U.S. military strength in the Pacific. ADM Noel Gayler. por Comdrs Dig 19: entire issue May 13 '76

GENERAL ACCOUNTING OFFICE

The academies five: Compliments and criticism (by General Accounting Office). illus Sea Power 18:28 Dec '75

All-vol recruit same as previous (according to a study by the General Accounting Office). AF Times 36:15 Mar 29 '76

C-5 flaws (largely wing modification) to cost $1.5 billion. (GAO report) AF Times 36:35 Jan 19 '76

CG (Comptroller General) clarifies rules on collecting debts. AF Times 37:24 Sep 27 '76

Care of handicapped children under CHAMPUS hit by GAO. AF Times 37:8 Nov 15 '76

Computer crimes uncovered (by General Accounting Office). Jim Parker. AF Times 36:20 May 31 '76

GENERAL ACCOUNTING OFFICE - Continued

A critical look. (Critique of the GAO's report on the XM-1 procurement program) Sen Robert Taft, Jr and William S. Lind. tab Armor 85:40-42 Nov-Dec '76

Cut fly time and costs, GAO says. Bruce Callander. tab AF Times 37:12 Aug 16 '76

DOD rebuked (by GAO) for paying some unnecessary BAQ. AF Times 36:18 Jul 26 '76

(Dept of) Defense can fire (foreign school bus) drivers abroad. AF Times 37:10 Sep 13 '76

$$ savings seen in comm(unications facilities) merger (a General Accounting Office report has said). AF Times 37:25 Aug 9 '76

Experts to examine alcohol problem. Len Famiglietti. AF Times 36:2 May 10 '76

GAO cites SEA fuel rip-off. Don Hirst. AF Times 36:10 Apr 12 '76

GAO: Consider recreation as 'pay.' tab AF Times 36:30 May 24 '76

GAO finds Reserves building needlessly. AF Times 37:57 Nov 29 '76

GAO lauds AAFES for Vietnam pullout. AF Times 37:2 Oct 18 '76

GAO: 'Lift ability is overestimated. AF Times 36:40 Jul 12 '76

GAO OKs Army's dog experiments. AF Times 37:29 Sep 20 '76

GAO report hits cost of recruit ads. AF Times 36:34 May 3 '76

GAO report; O'seas aid causes U.S. arms shortage. AF Times 36:10 Jan 19 '76

GAO: Rising costs threaten strength. AF Times 37:21 Dec 6 '76

GAO seen favoring a la carte. AF Times 36:16 Jun 14 '76

GAO slams strategic airlift "requirements" and programs. Armed Forces J Intl 113:14 Jul '76

GAO wants to keep uneconomical household (goods) plan. AF Times 37:4 Aug 16 '76

Health school (Uniformed Services University of the Health Sciences) too costly, GAO reports. Ann Gerow. AF Times 36:8 May 24 '76

How GAO assists the Congress on budgetary matters. Ellsworth H. Morse, Jr. illus Armed Forces Compt 21:6-10 Jan '76

Meat buying: Good is good enough, GAO study suggests. AF Times 36:8 May 31 '76

New FAA control on (private) pilot tests asked (in GAO report). AF Times 36:23 Apr 12 '76

O'seas banks (for American servicemen) cost U.S. $$. Andy Plattner. AF Times 36:4 Jan 5 '76

Pay-as-you-go retirement full of pitfalls, GAO says. Randy Shoemaker. AF Times 36:3 Mar 22 '76

People vs hardware: Tough nut for Carter (administration). AF Times 37:6 Dec 6 '76

Rules for selecting homes eased: Retirees after Aug 1 affected. AF Times 37:11 Dec 6 '76

GENERAL ACCOUNTING OFFICE - Continued

Ruling (by General Accounting Office) hits dislocation
$$. AF Times 37:8 Nov 22 '76

(Service) academy drop outs explained (by General
Accounting Office). Andy Plattner. AF Times 36:4
Mar 15 '76

Survey (by GAO) costs troops Social Security money.
AF Times 37:8 Dec 13 '76

Uniform Dr pay asked--GAO cites haphazard system
(in the Federal government). AF Times 37:26
Oct 25 '76

Women getting better job chances (General Account-
ing Office reports, but) strength still a problem.
AF Times 36:17 May 31 '76

GENERAL OFFICERS

Air Force--U.S.

(Brigadier) General (George M.) Wentsch (and oth-
ers) on USAF two star list., illus Translog 7:19
Feb '76

Generals on the move. (Title varies) Regular feature
in some issues of Air Force Times

Managerial careers of Air Force generals: A test of
the Janowitz convergence hypothesis. Arnold Kan-
ter. tabs J Pol & Mil Sociol 4:121-133; Comment.
Kurt Lang. 4:141-143; Comment. Thomas C.Pad-
gett. 4:145-146; Reply to comments by Lang and
Padgett. Arnold Kanter. 4:147-149 Spring '76

SAC chief (Gen Russell E.Dougherty) extended a
year (and other general officer news announced).
AF Times 37:3 Aug 16 '76

Senior staff changes. Regular feature in issues of
Air Force Magazine

34 to pin on second star. AF Times 37:10 Dec 13 '76

29 permanent brigadier generals, 30 major generals
selected. AF Times 36:22 Jan 19 '76

Which generals have how many aides and where. Ta-
ble only. AF Times 36:40 Jun 21 '76

Armed Forces--NATO

Former SACEURs: The 25th anniversary of SHAPE
and Allied Command Europe. Gen Matthew B.
Ridgway and others. illus NATO's Fifteen Nations
21:36-39 Feb-Mar '76

Armed Forces--U.S.

Star status: Army, Navy, Air Force, Marines. Regu-
lar feature in some issues of Armed Forces Jour-
nal International

Army--Germany

History

The Hutier legend. Laszlo M.Alfoldi. illus Param-
eters 5, No.2:69-74 '76

Army--Great Britain

History

The ranker general, Major-General Sir Gerald Far-
rell Boyd. Derek Boyd. Army Qtr 106:440-448+
Oct '76

Army--Russia

General of the Army (Ivan) Chernyakhovsky. MajGen
N.Konstantinov. illus Soviet Mil Rev No.6:42-43
Jun '76

GENERAL OFFICERS - Continued

Army--U.S.

General officer changes. Regular feature in News
Call section of some issues of Army

The Vietnam War in retrospect: The Army generals'
views. Douglas Kinnard. tabs J Pol & Mil Sociol
4:17-28 Spring '76

Directories

Senior Army officers in special assignments. Army
26:138 Oct '76

History

George Washington's first generals. James B.
Deerin. illus Natl Guardsman 30:2-6 Apr '76

Marine Corps--U.S.

CMC lists (general officer) reassignments. MarCor
Gaz 60:2 May '76

One, two-star selections. MarCor Gaz 60:2 Mar '76

Retirements, reassignment. MarCor Gaz 60:2 Jun '76

Directories

Flag and general officers of the naval services; offi-
cers of flag rank of the U.S. Navy, U.S. Coast
Guard, and NOAA, and general officers of the
U.S. Marine Corps on active duty as of January 1,
1976. illus US Nav Inst Proc 102:213-244 May '76

National Guard--Air Force--U.S.

ANG generals move up. AF Times 36:4 Feb 9 '76

GENERAL PURPOSE FORCES

China (People's Republic)

USSR, Pact, and PRC General Purpose Force capa-
bilities. illus Comdrs Dig 19: entire issue
Apr 29 '76

Russia

USSR, Pact, and PRC General Purpose Force capa-
bilities. illus Comdrs Dig 19: entire issue
Apr 29 '76

United States

The artificial crisis of American security. illus tabs
Def Monitor pt 1 (Military balance between U.S.
and USSR) 5: entire issue May '76; pt 2, How much
for defense? 5: entire issue Jun '76

Coalition warfare. Robert W.Komer. illus Army 26:
28-32 Sep '76

Defense hearings underway: Rumsfeld details plans
for new weapons. tabs Officer 52:5+ Mar '76

Future military preparedness. (Address, Naval
Academy Graduation Ceremonies, Annapolis,
June 2, 1976) Donald H.Rumsfeld. AF Plcy Ltr
for Comdrs: Sup No.8:2-7 Aug '76

The future of tactical Air Forces. (Remarks, Grad-
uation Ceremonies, 82d Flying Training Wg, Wil-
liams AFB, Ariz, June 12, 1976) LtGen Sanford
K.Moats. AF Plcy Ltr for Comdrs: Sup No.8:
17-22 Aug '76

JCS Chairman's Posture Statement. (Statement be-
fore House Armed Services Committee, Washing-
ton, Jan 27, 1976) Gen George S.Brown. tabs AF
Plcy Ltr for Comdrs: Sup No.4:13-15 Apr '76

GENERAL PURPOSE FORCES - Continued

United States - Cont'd

A tactical triad for deterring limited war in Western Europe. LtCol Thomas C. Blake, Jr. illus AU Rev 27:8-15 Sep-Oct '76

U.S. General Purpose Forces: A need for modernization. Gen George S. Brown. illus tab Comdrs Dig 19: entire issue May 27 '76

Who needs nuclear tacair? Col David L. Nichols. illus AU Rev 27:15-25 Mar-Apr '76

Warsaw Pact

USSR, Pact, and PRC General Purpose Force capabilities. illus Comdrs Dig 19: entire issue Apr 29 '76

GENERAL SERVICES ADMINISTRATION

See also
Federal Supply Service

CBEMA (Computer and Business Equipment Manufacturers Assoc) and GSA (General Services Administration): A dialogue on how government hurts itself (because of its own procurement and contracting practices). C. W. Borklund. illus Govt Exec 8:24+ May '76

GSA: Effectiveness through increased communications. (Interview with Jack Eckerd) illus Govt Exec 8:18+ Oct '76

GSA seeks wider base of suppliers. H. R. Kaplan. illus Review 55:45-48+ Mar-Apr '76

A growing Federal absurdity. (Small business and government supply contract regulations) Ernest Baynard. Govt Exec 8:40-44 Dec '76

A positive look at the Federal computer mess. Ernest C. Baynard. Govt Exec 8:28+ Sep '76

Winds of change in communications and computers. Theodore D. Puckorius. illus Signal 31:18-22 Sep '76

GENERATORS, ELECTRIC

Emergency power generators. TIG Brief 28:11 Nov 19 '76

Power cables too short on MD-3 generators. TIG Brief 28:3-4 Jul 16 '76

Power generation the easy way. illus Aerosp Intl 12: 42-43 Jul-Aug '76

Study and Teaching

Emergency power generators. TIG Brief 28:11 Nov 19 '76

GEODESY

New milestones in geodesy. (National Geodetic Survey) RADM Allen L. Powell. illus map Mil Engr 68:22-24 Jan-Feb '76

Surveys for engineering and science. (From "Survey of the Coast" to National Ocean Survey) RADM Allen L. Powell. illus Mil Engr 68:198-201 May-Jun '76

GEOLOGICAL SURVEY

The national stream quality accounting network. Joseph S. Cragwall, Jr. illus map tabs Mil Engr 68: 25-27 Jan-Feb '76

GEOLOGY

The Trading Post (Kans) event. (AF Weapons Laboratory studies the effect of simulated nuclear explosions on different types of soil) MSgt Harold Newcomb. illus Airman 20:14-17 Mar '76

GEOPOLITICS

Hemispheric denial: Geopolitical imperatives and Soviet strategy. BrigGen Edward B. Atkeson. maps illus Strat Rev 4:26-36 Spring '76

GERM WARFARE see Chemical-Biological Warfare

GERMANY

History

The Waffen SS: A social psychological perspective. George M. Kren and Leon H. Rappoport. Armed Forces & Soc 3:87-102 Fall '76

GERMANY (DEMOCRATIC REPUBLIC)

Politics and Government

The effect of detente on professionalism and political control in the East German Army. Dale R. Herspring. illus Nav War Col Rev 28:10-20 Winter '76

GERMANY (FEDERAL REPUBLIC)

Official military history in the Federal Republic of Germany. Friedrich Forstmeier. chart illus Aerosp Hist 23:124-127 Sep '76

Description and Travel

Bernkastel's Burgermeister. (The major of a nearby town is a friend to Americans based at Hahn AB, Germany) MSgt Yuen-Gi Yee. illus Airman 20: 17-19 Oct '76

Politics and Government

Action and reaction: West Germany and the Baader-Meinhof guerrillas. Maj John D. Elliott. illus Strat Rev 4:60-67 Winter '76

Social Life and Customs

Study and Teaching

Making Kontakt. (Strengthening German-American relations) Capt Larry J. Myers. illus Soldiers 31: 10-13 Aug '76

GHANA

Politics and Government

The military in Ghanaian politics. S. J. Baynham. Army Qtr 106:428-439 Oct '76

GIBSON, John H.

Retired (BrigGen John H. Gibson) starts Texas air school (for commercial pilots, Ava Flight Academy). por AF Times 36:32 Jan 26 '76

GIFTS

Receipt and disposition of foreign gifts. TIG Brief 28:19 Nov 19 '76

'Standards of Conduct,' AFR 30-30. TIG Brief 28:11 Jun 4 '76

What you must do about a foreign gift. M. L. Craver. AF Times 37:2 Dec 6 '76

GRAHAM, Daniel O. - Continued

The Soviet military budget controversy. LtGen Daniel O.Graham, Ret. AF Mag 59:33-37 May '76

GRAHAM, Erwin M., Jr

The dynamism of Army combat logistics. MajGen Erwin M.Graham, Jr. Mil Rev 56:65-75 Apr '76

GRAVITY

Perception of static orientation in a constant gravito-inertial environment. C.C.Ormsby and L.R.Young. illus tabs Aviation, Space and Envmt Med 47:159-164 Feb '76

The story of G. CDR A.F.Wells. illus Approach 22: 22-23 Nov '76

GREAT BRITAIN

Description and Travel

In search of ancient navigators. (Stonehenge--an ancient observatory?) MSgt Harold D.Newcomb. illus Airman 20:10-13 Feb '76

Foreign Policy

France and Britain: European powers and members of NATO. Jean Houbert. Royal Air Forces Qtr 15:289-300+ Winter '75

Putting the great back into Great Britain? (Interview with Geoffrey Pattie, MP) illus Def & For Aff Dig No.8-9:32-33+ '76

Foreign Relations

Far East--History

The Royal Navy and the Far Eastern problem, 1931-1941. Paul Haggie. Army Qtr 106:402-414 Oct '76

Hong Kong

The Crown Colony of Hong Kong. Col Norman L. Dodd, Ret. illus Mil Rev 56:37-46 Oct '76

Iceland

A final appraisal of the British occupation of Iceland, 1940-42. Donald F.Bittner. maps RUSI J for Def Studies 120:45-53 Dec '75

History

From Lexington to Cuddalore: British strategy in the War of American Independence. Maj David Curtis Skaggs. illus map Mil Rev 56:41-55 Apr '76

The war Britain lost: An analysis of the reasons for Britain's defeat in the War of American Independence. Michael Hayes. RUSI J for Def Studies 121: 38-42 Sep '76

GREECE

The Aegean Sea dispute. Capt Thomas J.McCormick, Jr. maps illus Mil Rev 56:90-96 Mar '76

Foreign Relations

NATO

The Greek disentanglement: An interim report. Penelope Tremayne. RUSI J for Def Studies 120:61-64 Dec '75

Turkey

Ringed with a lake of fire: Cyprus 1976. Penelope Tremayne. Army Qtr 106:101-107 Jan '76

Politics and Government

The Greek disentanglement: An interim report. Penelope Tremayne. RUSI J for Def Studies 120:61-64 Dec '75

GREENE, Wallace M., Jr

The bombing 'pause': Formula for failure. Gen Wallace M.Greene, Ret. por AF Mag 59:36-39 Apr '76

GREENLIEF, Francis S.

The budget--a grim outlook. MajGen Francis S. Greenlief, Ret. Natl Guardsman 30:15 Jan '76

GRENADES

Engineering miracle in munition design. (40-mm grenade round) Victor Lindner. illus tabs Natl Def 60:294-297 Jan-Feb '76

GRIBBLE, William C., Jr

Passing 200 and still climbing. (Army Corps of Engineers) LtGen William C.Gribble, Jr. Mil Engr 68: 6-10 Jan-Feb '76

GRIDS

Navigation North of Seventy. 1stLt David J.Haney. illus map Navigator 23:5-10 Summer '76

GRIEVANCE PROCEDURES

Attention to health/safety matters. TIG Brief 28:5-6 Feb 27 '76

Complaint evaluation and disciplinary action. LtGen Donald G.Nunn. TIG Brief 28:2 Jun 18 '76

Complaints processing: How you can help. TIG Brief 28:3 Feb 27 '76

IG complaint data collection system. TIG Brief 28: 5-6 Jul 2 '76

'The Inspector General Complaint System,' AFR 123-11. TIG Brief 28:5-6 Nov 19 '76

Reg (AFR 123-11) changes to ease general (USAF) gripe system. AF Times 36:10 Mar 8 '76

Request mast: Tail wags dog. LtCol Richard H.Esau, Jr. MarCor Gaz 60:53-54 Jan '76

GROOME, Thomas M., Jr

Groome on marriage breakdowns. Interview. Ch(BrigGen) Thomas M.Groome, Jr. por AF Times 36:12 Jul 26 '76

GROSS NATIONAL PRODUCT

Comparisons of defence expenditures 1973-76. London's International Institute for Strategic Studies. Table only. AF Mag 59:95 Dec '76

GROUND-CONTROLLED APPROACH

Automation in military air traffic control. Bill Walsh. illus Countermeasures 2:40-41 Apr '76

GCA slow roll. illus Approach 21:5 Jun '76

Radar-directed routing and terminal arrival depiction. LT Daniel E.Graham. illus maps Approach 21:1-4 May '76

Surveillance radar approach Minimum Descent Altitude (MDA) for circling approaches. TIG Brief 28:8 Nov 19 '76

Terminal Precision Approach Control Program (TPACP). TIG Brief 28:12 Aug 27 '76

What's your approach plate IQ? LT Bob Harler. illus Approach 22:10-12 Oct '76

GROUND-CONTROLLED INTERCEPTION

Ground controlled interception training simulators. Norman W.Emmott. illus Signal 30:36-40 Feb '76

GROUND CREWS

(AF) heading off jet mechanic loss. AF Times 37:6 Dec 27 '76

"Super troop." (Pressure on the men who repair airplanes) Capt Milton G.Schellhase. illus MAC Flyer 23:8-9 Dec '76

To his credit. (A1C Bert Jackson has the best aircraft maintenance record at RAF Lakenheath, Eng) Maj Mark R.Foutch. illus Airman 20:32-34 Apr '76

GROUND EFFECT MACHINES see Air Cushion Vehicles

GROUND FORCES

Helicopters and land force tactics. Col M.Belov. illus Soviet Mil Rev No.12:22-24 Dec '76

Helicopters used by ground troops. Col M.Belov. illus Soviet Mil Rev No.4:30-31+ Apr '76

Soviet logistic support for ground operations. Graham H.Turbiville. (Reprinted from RUSI Journal for Defence Studies, Sep 1975) illus Mil Rev 56:29-39 Jul '76

U.S. General Purpose Forces: A need for modernization. Gen George S.Brown. illus tab Comdrs Dig 19: entire issue May 27 '76

GROUND SAFETY

See also
Seat Belts

Bicycle safety. 1stLt Martin J.Robinowich. illus TAC Attack 16:24-25 Mar '76

Car devices cut (electrically ignited crash) fires, tests show. AF Times 36:25 Mar 1 '76

Down to earth: Ground safety quotes and notes. Regular feature in some issues of TAC Attack

Moody maze saves lives (at Moody AFB, Ga). Capt Bob Revell. illus tab TAC Attack 16:12-13 Mar '76

Motorcycles--no second chance. Capt George C. Neiss. illus TAC Attack 16:10-11 Mar '76

Power cables too short on MD-3 generators. TIG Brief 28:3-4 Jul 16 '76

'Unclear' clear zone. TIG Brief 28:3 Feb 13 '76

GROUND SUPPORT see Close Air Support

GROUND-SUPPORT EQUIPMENT

See also
Airplanes, Military--Ground-Support Equipment
Helicopters, Military--Ground-Support Equipment

The ever-expanding umbrella. LtCol Arthur D. McQueen. tab illus Air Def Mag, pp 8-17, Jul-Sep '76

Military satellite communications terminals. Col Fred M.Knipp and Joseph A.Buegler. illus Signal 30:12-16+ Mar '76

GUATEMALA

Earthquake! (USAF aids Guatemala with airlift, reconnaissance, and communications) MSgt Harold Newcomb and SSgt Ken Peterson. illus Airman 20: 8-13 Jun '76

Guatemala: Helping hand. SSgt Zack Richards. illus Soldiers 31:14-17 Aug '76

GUATEMALA - Continued

Guatemala: 210th Aviation Battalion comes through again in disaster relief. CW2 Larry R.Santure. illus USA Avn Dig 22:4-5+ Jul '76

Making the most of it. (Dr (LtCol) Jaroslav K.Richter of MacDill AFB, Fla, likes to be where the action is) 1stLt Katie Cutler. illus Airman 20: 20-23 Oct '76

Operation Wagonmaster. ("D" Company (Wagonmasters), 34th Support Battalion, 6th Cavalry Brigade (Air Combat), in disaster relief operation in Guatemala) Maj Terry N.Rosser. illus USA Avn Dig 22:6-7+ Jul '76

Supply airlift after quake (in) Guatemala. illus AF Times 36:26 Mar 8 '76

The view from a U-2. (The 349th Strategic Reconnaissance Sq from Davis-Monthan AFB, Ariz, flies over Guatemala to survey and describe earthquake damage) Capt Robert W.Gaskin. illus Airman 20:14-15 Jun '76

GUERRILLA WARFARE

The essence of future guerrilla warfare: Urban combat. Thomas M.Schlaak. illus MarCor Gaz 60: 18-26 Dec '76

The guerrilla problem in retrospect. George H.Quester. (Reprinted from Military Affairs, Dec 1975) Mil Rev 56:44-55 Aug '76

Transnational terrorism. Charles A.Russell. illus AU Rev 27:26-35 Jan-Feb '76

History

"Arranging the minds of men": T.E.Lawrence as a theorist of war. Anthony Burton. map Army Qtr 106:51-58 Jan '76

Asia, Southeastern

GCMA (Groupements de Commandos Mixtes Aéroportés)/GMI (Groupement Mixte d'Intervention): A French experience in Indochina. Maj John D.Howard. illus map Mil Rev 56:76-81 Apr '76

Germany (Federal Republic)

Action and reaction: West Germany and the Baader-Meinhof guerrillas. Maj John D.Elliott. illus Strat Rev 4:60-67 Winter '76

Ireland, Northern

Northern Ireland's 'Twilight War': Frustrating duty for British troops. Col James B.Deerin, Ret. illus map Army 26:14-21 Dec '76

Middle East

Israel and the Fedayeen: Persistence or transformation. Maj Bard E.O'Neill. illus Strat Rev 4:89-101 Spring '76

GUIDED MISSILES see Missiles

GUNBOATS see Warships

GUNNERY

Safety Measures

Ricochets. LtCol Jim Learmonth. illus tab Aerosp Safety 32:16-17 Jan '76

GUNNERY - Continued

Study and Teaching

Changes in tank gunnery. MajGen John W.McEnery. tabs Armor 85:8-10 May-Jun '76

Reduce your (fire control system) budget, yet buy more. Capt Edward A.Bryla. tab Armor 85:15 Nov-Dec '76

Revive the telescope. Capt Everette L.Roper, Jr. illus tabs Armor 85:23-24 Sep-Oct '76

'We didn't come just to qualify.' (Tank Crew Qualification Course (TCQC)) Capt Robert E.Harry. illus Armor 85:30-34 Mar-Apr '76

GUNNERY, AERIAL

See also
Fighter Weapons and Gunnery Meets

Missilex: Flailex or safex? LT Ross Burgess. illus Approach 22:18-20 Jul '76

Range assessing device. LtCol Ross Whistler. illus tabs USAF Ftr Wpns Rev, pp 20-25, Spring '76

Three point assessing (of target circles on gun camera film). LtCol Joseph Y.Whistler. illus USAF Ftr Wpns Rev, pp 1-8, Fall '76

History

The Texas pinball machine. (Frangible bullet combat training device) Capt John D.Edgar. illus AF Mag 59:57-61 Aug '76

Study and Teaching

TC 1-4: Aircrew gunnery accuracy = staying power + survivability. Rush R.Wicker. illus USA Avn Dig 22:24-25 Jan '76

The Texas pinball machine. (Frangible bullet combat training device) Capt John D.Edgar. illus AF Mag 59:57-61 Aug '76

GUNNERY RANGES see Bombing and Gunnery Ranges

GUNS

See also
Machine Guns

Assault gun in the Marine Corps? Capt Ronald J. Brown. illus MarCor Gaz 60:53-54 Oct '76

GUNS - Continued

Automatic cannon technology. Gary W.Fischer. illus Natl Def 61:192-194 Nov-Dec '76

The long range guns. Stanley Goddard and Allan S. Chace. tabs Natl Def 60:299-303 Jan-Feb '76

NATO's new MBT "gun" will be 3 new guns. Benjamin F.Schemmer. illus Armed Forces J Intl 113:12 Apr '76

New guns for the Navy. illus Natl Def 61:195-198 Nov-Dec '76

Rheinmetall's 120 mm smooth bore gun--tank armament of the future. R.Meller. illus tabs Intl Def Rev 9:619-624 Aug '76

The surface Navy today: Prospects and problems. Col Robert D.Heinl, Jr, Ret. illus Sea Power 19:27-32 Oct '76

The Tampella 155 mm gun-howitzer. LtCol P.Crèvecoeur, Ret. illus tabs Intl Def Rev 9:662-663 Aug '76

Tank killer team (Air Force A-10 ground-attack aircraft mounting the powerful GAU-8/A 30-mm gun system). Col Robert G.Dilger. illus Natl Def 61: 190-191 Nov-Dec '76

GUNSHIPS

Equipment

Remote set fuzing for 2.75-inch rocket. Alexander Janushevich. illus (Also cutaway) USA Avn Dig 22: 6-7+ Apr '76

Russia

The Soviet Mi-24 (Hind) combat helicopter. Alexander Malzeyev. illus tabs Intl Def Rev 8:879-881 Dec '75

United States

Attack. (4th Battalion (Attack Helicopter), 77th Field Artillery) Capts Michael E.Sloniker and Gary R. Sosnowski. illus USA Avn Dig 22:4-5+ Dec '76

Bell's new YAH-63 (AAH) Advanced Attack Helicopter. illus tab Interavia 31:251-254 Mar '76

Guns A Go-Go (ACH-47 helicopter gunship). LCDR Donald A.Mohr. illus USA Avn Dig 22:8-13 Jun '76

GUNSIGHTS see Fire Control Equipment

HSC see Army Health Services Command

HAIG, Alexander M., Jr

Apprehension without fear. Interview. Gen Alexander M. Haig, Jr. por NATO's Fifteen Nations 21: 18-21+ Feb-Mar '76

(Gen Alexander) Haig paints bleak picture of European situation. Col Robert D. Heinl, Jr, Ret. por Sea Power 19:22-24 Dec '76

NATO ... 'A viable, healthy deterrent.' Interview. Gen Alexander M. Haig, Jr. por Army 26:12+ Aug '76

HAILS, Robert E.

A challenge to logistics managers. LtGen Robert E. Hails. TIG Brief 28:2 Jul 2 '76

The metrication program. LtGen Robert E. Hails. TIG Brief 28:2 Dec 3 '76

HANDICAPPED

Aide to the disabled (LtCol E. A. Richmond). Steve Stevens. illus Soldiers 31:41-43 Mar '76

Care of handicapped children under CHAMPUS hit by GAO. AF Times 37:8 Nov 15 '76

Easy access for handicapped urged: Changes proposed in building law. AF Times 37:46 Sep 13 '76

Handicapped getting help in infancy (at Vandenberg AFB, Calif). Donna Peterson. illus AF Times 37:37+ Dec 6 '76

One from the many. (SSgt Tom Jones of McConnell AFB, Kans, welcomes a deaf boy into the Boy Scout troop he leads) TSgt Tom Dwyer and CMSgt Joe Stockton. illus Airman 20:31-32 Aug '76

HANDLING OF MATERIALS see Materials Handling

HANGARS

History

Rebuilt Wright. (Volunteers from Squadron Officer School at Maxwell AFB, Ala, build a replica of the Wright brothers' 1910 hangar) Irene P. Barrett. illus Airman 20:20 Nov '76

HARBORS see Ports

HASDORFF, James C.

Sources in aerospace history: The USAF oral history collection (at Albert F. Simpson Historical Research Center, Maxwell AFB, Ala). James C. Hasdorff. por Aerosp Hist 23:103-104 Jun '76

HAWAII

Description and Travel

Hale Koa holiday. LtCol James Witek and SP5 Ed Aber. illus Soldiers 31:11-16 Feb '76

Living with Madam Pele's fury. (Military residents of Kilauea Military Camp share Hawaii's Big Island with the legend of Madam Pele, said to be the goddess of the island's active volcano, Kilauea) MSgt James McDermid. illus Airman 20:30-33 Oct '76

HAZARDOUS DUTY PAY see Incentive Pay

HAZARDOUS MATERIALS see Hazardous Substances

HAZARDOUS SUBSTANCES

Chlorine hazard. TIG Brief 28:5 Feb 27 '76; Addendum: Use of protective masks for chlorine maintenance. TIG Brief 28:7 Jun 18 '76

Lithium batteries. TIG Brief 28:7 Mar 12 '76

Transportation

Air shipment of hazardous material. (Address, Philadelphia Chapter 2, SOLE, March 1976) Morton Spiegel. Log Spectrum 10:26-27 Summer '76

HEADQUARTERS AIR FORCE RESERVE

Air Force Reserve. illus tab AF Mag 59:100-101 May '76

HEADQUARTERS COMMAND--AIR FORCE

Headquarters Command, USAF. illus AF Mag 59:68 May '76

Manpower and organization. TIG Brief 28:21 Mar 26 '76

HEALTH AND HYGIENE

See also
Diseases
Nutrition
Physical Fitness

Animal bites: Everyone's concern. TIG Brief 28:14 Oct 8 '76

Attention to health/safety matters. TIG Brief 28:5-6 Feb 27 '76

Chemist, biologist, engineer, detective (Air Force Reserve environmental health technician). Chris Scheer. illus Air Reservist 28:6-7 Jun '76

Food sanitation and air safety. A.S.R. Peffers. Aviation, Space & Envmt Med 47:1107-1108 Oct '76

In the name of man. (Public health service in the Soviet Union) V. Ryvkin. illus Soviet Mil Rev No. 7: 52-55 Jul '76

Military service hygiene. ColGen D. Kuvshinsky. Soviet Mil Rev No. 12:38-39 Dec '76

Occupational safety and health programs. TIG Brief 28:3 Jan 30 '76

Reservists fill detective's role (as) environmental health technicians (at Dobbins AFB, Ga). illus AF Times 36:41 Apr 19 '76

Shipment of samples to USAF Environmental and Radiological Health labs. TIG Brief 28:12 Nov 5 '76

USAF Environmental Health and Radiological Health Laboratories. TIG Brief 28:19 Feb 13 '76

HEALTH SERVICES COMMAND see Army Health Services Command

HEARING

Cycle helmets given ear-eye test. AF Times 37:53 Aug 23 '76

Evaluating the ability of aircrew personnel to hear speech in their operational environments. C.E. Williams and others. tabs Aviation, Space and Envmt Med 47:154-158 Feb '76

Hearing under stress. III: The effect of external auditory meatal pressure on speech discrimination. G.L. Whitehead and others. tabs Aviation, Space & Envmt Med 47:308-309 Mar '76

HEARING - Continued

Hearing under stress. IV: A speech delivery communication system for utilization in high ambient noise environments. G. L. Whitehead and others. tab Aviation, Space & Envmt Med 47:811-812 Aug '76

Hypoxia and auditory thresholds. P. R. Burkett and Wallace F. Perrin. tabs Aviation, Space & Envmt Med 47:649-651 Jun '76

Long-duration exposure to intermittent noises. Daniel L. Johnson and others. tabs Aviation, Space & Envmt Med 47:987-990 Sep '76

Turning JP (Jet Propulsion) into noise. LTJG David M. Tyler. illus Approach 22:26 Nov '76

HEART

Acquired bundle branch block and its response to exercise testing in asymptomatic aircrewmen: A review with case reports. James E. Whinnery and Victor Froelicher, Jr. illus tabs Aviation, Space & Envmt Med 47:1217-1225 Nov '76

Blood fat and the fighter pilot. LCDR Gary Smith. illus tabs Approach 22:18-22 Sep '76

Bradycardia induced by negative acceleration. (Test for standard lap belt) James A. Kenneay and others. illus Aviation, Space & Envmt Med 47: 483-484 May '76

CPR (CardioPulmonary Resuscitation) ... it could save your life or that of someone else! Chris Scheer. illus Air Reservist 28:15 Nov '76

Cardiac output during human sleep. J. C. Miller and S. M. Horvath. tabs Aviation, Space & Envmt Med 47:1046-1051 Oct '76

Cardiac pathology associated with high sustained $+G_z$. I: Subendocardial hemorrhage. R. R. Burton and W. F. MacKenzie. illus tabs Aviation, Space & Envmt Med 47:711-717 Jul '76

Cardiac pathology associated with high sustained $+G_z$. II: Stress cardiomyopathy. W. F. MacKenzie and others. illus tab Aviation, Space & Envmt Med 47:718-725 Jul '76

Cardiovascular function during sustained $+G_z$ stress. Howard H. Erickson and others. illus tab Aviation, Space & Envmt Med 47:750-758 Jul '76

Care of patients after cardiac catheterization. Mary M. Thomas and Michael R. Longo, Jr. tabs Aviation, Space and Envmt Med 47:192-198 Feb '76

Changes in clinical cardiologic measurements associated with high $+G_z$ stress. Kent K. Gillingham and Phelps P. Crump. illus tabs Aviation, Space & Envmt Med 47:726-733 Jul '76

Diet + exercise (for atherosclerosis). Nathan Pritikin and Edward Carlstrom. illus Army 26:42-46 Jun '76

ECG monitoring of heart failure and pilot load/overload by the Vesla seat pad. C. W. Sem-Jacobsen. illus Aviation, Space & Envmt Med 47:441-444 Apr '76

Effect of sequential anti-G suit inflation on pulmonary capillary blood flow in man. Raymond Begin and others. illus tabs Aviation, Space & Envmt Med 47:937-941 Sep '76

Electronic stethoscope with frequency shaping and infrasonic recording capabilities. Ernest S. Gordon and John M. Lagerwerff. illus tab Aviation, Space & Envmt Med 47:312-316 Mar '76

HEART - Continued

Evaluation of electrocardiograms on rated fliers. TIG Brief 28:15 Oct 8 '76

Exercise in an hypoxic environment as a screening test for ischaemic heart disease. Purshottam Kumar Khanna and others. tabs Aviation, Space & Envmt Med 47:1114-1117 Oct '76

Heart biochemical responses 14 days after $+G_z$ acceleration. R. T. Dowell and others. illus tab Aviation, Space & Envmt Med 47:1171-1173 Nov '76

High altitude, indigenous origin, and continuous cardiac monitoring. Sara A. Barton and others. tabs Aviation, Space & Envmt Med 47:592-596 Jun '76

Indirect evidence for arterial chemoreceptor reflex facilitation by face immersion in man. Sigmund B. Strømme and Arnoldus Schytte Blix. illus tab Aviation, Space & Envmt Med 47:597-599 Jun '76

Instrumentation for the rhesus monkey as a cardiovascular analog for man during air-combat maneuvering acceleration. Howard H. Erickson and John R. Ritzman. illus tabs Aviation, Space & Envmt Med 47:1153-1158 Nov '76

Of heart attacks and belly aches (for pilots only). Anchard F. Zeller. Aerosp Safety 32:20-21 Feb '76

Paroxysmal and chronic atrial fibrillation in airman certification. Douglas E. Busby and Audie W. Davis. tabs Aviation, Space and Envmt Med 47:185-186 Feb '76

Prolonged visual loss and bradycardia following deceleration from +6 G_z acceleration: A case report. John S. Kirkland and James A. Kennealy. illus Aviation, Space & Envmt Med 47:310-311 Mar '76

Technique for electrocardiographic monitoring of working divers. P. F. Hoar and others. illus Aviation, Space & Envmt Med 47:667-671 Jun '76

Use of pilot heart rate measurement in flight evaluation. Alan H. Roscoe. illus tabs Aviation, Space & Envmt Med 47:86-90 Jan '76

HEAT

Acclimation processes by daily exercise stints at temperate conditions followed by short heat exposures. Eliezer Kamon. tabs Aviation, Space & Envmt Med 47:20-25 Jan '76

Facility and a method for evaluation of thermal protection. A. M. Stoll and others. illus tab Aviation, Space & Envmt Med 47:1177-1181 Nov '76

(Temperature) going up! Ted Kontos. illus USA Avn Dig 22:34-37 May '76

Physiological Effects

Effectiveness of four water-cooled undergarments and a water-cooled cap in reducing heat stress. George F. Fonseca. tabs Aviation, Space & Envmt Med 47:1159-1164 Nov '76

Evaluation of a face cooling device integrated with the standard HGU-type USAF flight helmet. Abbott T. Kissen and others. illus tabs Aviation, Space & Envmt Med 47:1188-1192 Nov '76

Head and neck cooling by air, water, or air plus water in hyperthermia. Abbott T. Kissen and others. illus tabs Aviation, Space & Envmt Med 47:265-271 Mar '76

Heat and simulated high altitude: Effects on biochemical indices of stress and performance. Ralph P. Francesconi and others. tabs Aviation, Space & Envmt Med 47:548-552 May '76

HEAT - Continued

Physiological Effects - Cont'd

Heat stroke: A review. Shlomo Shibolet and others. illus tabs Aviation, Space & Envmt Med 47:280-301 Mar '76

Identification of an apprehension effect on physiological indices of thermal strain. M.H.Harrison and C.Saxton. tabs Aviation, Space & Envmt Med 47: 950-953 Sep '76

"In the good ol' summertime ..." LtCol Harold Andersen. illus TAC Attack 16:14-15 Jul '76

Measurement of change in plasma volume during heat exposure and exercise. M.H.Harrison and R.J. Edwards. tabs Aviation, Space & Envmt Med 47: 1038-1045 Oct '76

Medical aspects of survivability. LtCol David H. Karney and Patsy Thompson. illus USA Avn Dig pt 1, Lifesaving emergency medical aid. 22:40-45 May '76; pt 2, Medical problems in a prolonged survival situation. 22:28-31 Jun '76

Physiological effects of solar heat load in a fighter cockpit. Sarah A.Nunneley and Loren G.Myhre. illus tabs Aviation, Space & Envmt Med 47:969-973 Sep '76

Potassium losses in sweat under heat stress. M.S. Malhotra and others. tabs Aviation, Space & Envmt Med 47:503-504 May '76

Simple reaction time during exercise, heat exposure, and heat acclimation. E.Shvartz and others. tabs Aviation, Space & Envmt Med 47:1168-1170 Nov '76

(Temperature) going up! Ted Kontos. illus USA Avn Dig 22:34-37 May '76

HEATING SYSTEMS

Solar energy applications. Capts Anthony Eden and Michael A.Aimone. tabs illus map AF Engrg & Svcs Qtr 17:29-33 Aug '76

Work begins on solar energy BX at Kirtland (AFB, NM). AF Times 37:4 Nov 8 '76

Work to start in Fall on solar BXs. AF Times 36:61 Apr 19 '76

Costs

Computers cut energy costs in buildings. Phil Deakin. illus tab Govt Exec 8:33+ May '76

Testing

Air Force Academy solar energy program. Maj M.W.Nay, Jr and Lt W.A.Tolbert. illus tab AF Engrg & Svcs Qtr 17:23-27 Feb '76

Solar home saves on gas (in test at (AF) Academy). AF Times 37:37 Aug 9 '76

HÉBERT, F. Edward

ROA honors a staunch friend. (F.Edward Hébert chosen Minute Man of the Year) Officer 52:8-9 Nov '76

Respected legislator: F.Edward Hébert. por Review 56:25 Jul-Aug '76

Retiring Hébert fires final salvos. Interview. F.Edward Hébert. por AF Times 36:23 Jul 26 '76

HEGENBERGER, Albert F.

(Eight aviation pioneers (Clarence D.Chamberlin, John H.Glenn, Jr, George W.Goddard, Albert F. Hegenberger, Edwin A.Link, Sanford A.Moss, William A.Patterson, Nathan F.Twining) to be enshrined in Aviation Hall of Fame, July 24, 1976) por AF Mag 59:29-30 Jul '76

HEISER, Joseph M., Jr

Vietnam logistics: Past is prologue? LtGen Joseph M.Heiser, Jr, Ret. Def Mgt J 12:74-80 Jul '76

HELICOPTER INDUSTRY AND TRADE

Aiming for new (aviation) markets (to support offshore oil field work). Richard S.Page. illus Aerosp Intl 12:34-37 Mar-Apr '76

The world's current helicopters--1976. Tables only. Interavia 31:68-71 Jan '76

Europe, Western

European helicopter manufacturers--pushing new products and new technologies. illus tab Interavia 31:27-31 Jan '76

European prospects in the helicopter field. illus tabs Interavia 31:635-639 Jul '76

France

The AS.350 Ecureuil: A new 5/6-seat helicopter from Aérospatiale. Bob Salvy. illus tabs Interavia 31: 476-478 May '76

A profile of Aerospatiale. John Marriott. illus NATO's Fifteen Nations 20:80-84 Dec '75-Jan '76

A royal performance: SA.360 Dauphin flight report. Douglas H.Chopping. illus Interavia 31:32-34 Jan '76

Great Britain

Aerospace (equipment). John Marriott. illus tabs NATO's Fifteen Nations 21:35-39+ Apr-May '76

The UK airframe industry. Derek Wood. illus Interavia 31:802-803 Sep '76

United States

Bell YAH-63. illus (Also cutaway) USA Avn Dig 22:4+ May '76

Bell's new YAH-63 (AAH) Advanced Attack Helicopter. illus tab Interavia 31:251-254 Mar '76

Hughes YAH-64. illus USA Avn Dig 22:5+ May '76

NBAA helicopter report. Frank McGuire. illus Interavia 31:1034 Nov '76

UTTAS: The helicopter of the 1980s? Mark Lambert. illus US Nav Inst Proc 102:128-130 Oct '76

UTTAS (Utility Tactical Transport Aircraft System) YUH-60A (Sikorsky Aircraft). illus (Also cutaways) USA Avn Dig 22:2+ May '76

UTTAS (Utility Tactical Transport Aircraft System) YUH-61A (Boeing-Vertol Co). illus USA Avn Dig 22:3+ May '76

The U.S. helicopter scene--guarded optimism among American manufacturers. illus Interavia 31:39-43 Jan '76

HELICOPTER TYPE

Only U. S. military helicopters are entered under
type. For helicopters of other countries see entries
under specific categories, e.g., Helicopters, Mili-
tary--Great Britain.

AH-1

AH-1S avionics. Peter Boxman. illus USA Avn Dig
22:42-45 Nov '76

Cockpit design for night NOE (Nap-Of-the-Earth).
J.H.Emery. illus USA Avn Dig 22:6-7 Jan '76

Crowded decks. (Air America and ARVN pilots land
Hueys with Vietnamese refugees on tiny decks of
destroyer escorts Cook and Kirk during evacuation
of Saigon) AW3 John P.Pieper. illus Approach 21:
18-21 Mar '76

How to get out of a snake in six milliseconds. (Evolu-
tion of emergency egress hardware in the Huey
Cobra) James M.Boen. illus Approach 21:6-9
Dec '75

A matter of confidence. (Canopy removal system in
the AH-1 Cobra) Arnold R.Lambert. illus USA
Avn Dig 22:32-34 Jan '76

The TOW Cobra anti-tank helicopter--more mobile
firepower for the U.S. Army in Europe. R.Meller.
illus tabs Intl Def Rev 8:882-886 Dec '75

CH-46

First military landing. (A CH-46 lands on a LHA-1,
Tarawa, first in a new class of amphibious assault
ships) illus MarCor Gaz 60:8 Feb '76

Testing

Sea Knights begin trials. illus MarCor Gaz 60:6
Sep '76

CH-47

History

Guns A Go-Go (ACH-47 helicopter gunship). LCDR
Donald A. Mohr. illus USA Avn Dig 22:8-13 Jun '76

Study and Teaching

A new approach to flight simulator acceptance.
(CH-47 Chinook cargo helicopter simulator)
LtCol Robert L.Catron. illus USA Avn Dig 22:
2-3+ Apr '76

HH-53

Pave Low III (modified Sikorsky HH-53 for night
rescue capability). AF Mag 59:18 Feb '76

Iroquois

See UH-1

Kiowa

See OH-58

LAMPS

See SH-2

Nighthawk

See UH-1

OH-58

New OH-58 engine. Merle A.Clapsaddle. illus USA
Avn Dig 22:15 Oct '76

HELICOPTER TYPE - Continued

SH-2

Something new for the LAMPS program. (GSI, Glide
Slope Indicator) illus Approach 22:10-11 Nov '76

When you gotta bingo, you gotta go! illus Approach
21:5 May '76

SH-3

Black nights and glassy seas. LCDR Bill Roop. illus
Approach 22:28-29 Dec '76

Helo in the water! Helo in the water! LT Thomas P.
Pocklington. illus Approach 22:12-14 Nov '76

Sea King

See SH-3

Sea Knight

See CH-46

UH-1

Ditching the Huey. CW4 John L.Nicol. illus USA Avn
Dig 22:44-46 Oct '76

Get ready--get set--go!!! LtCol John A.G.Klose.
illus USA Avn Dig 22:6-7+ Dec '76

Night Hawk Training Test. illus USA Avn Dig pt 1,
The overview. CW2 David R.Heaton. 21:1-3+
Dec '75; pt 2, The procedures. CW2 Douglas V.
Joyce. 22:21-23 Jan '76

T700: The Army's engine of the 80s. tab illus (Also
cutaways) USA Avn Dig 22:1+ May '76

A terrific job in Europe (Project Team IV, the SOTAS
(Stand-Off Target Acquisition System). illus USA
Avn Dig 22:10 Dec '76

Three bladed Huey. Maj Ralph E.Riddle, Jr. illus
USA Avn Dig 22:38-39 Nov '76

Study and Teaching

SFTS (Synthetic Flight Training System): The shape
of things to come. CW2 Thomas K.Equels. illus
tab USA Avn Dig 22:13-17 Apr '76

Tactical training in the SFTS (Synthetic Flight Train-
ing System). Maj Elmer E.Curbow and MSgt
Thomas McGuire. illus USA Avn Dig 22:18-19
Apr '76

YAH-63

Bell YAH-63. illus (Also cutaway) USA Avn Dig 22:4+
May '76

Bell's new YAH-63 (AAH) Advanced Attack Helicopter. illus tab Interavia 31:251-254 Mar '76

YAH-64

Hughes YAH-64. illus USA Avn Dig 22:5+ May '76

YUH-60

UTTAS: The helicopter of the 1980s? Mark Lambert.
illus US Nav Inst Proc 102:128-130 Oct '76

UTTAS (Utility Tactical Transport Aircraft System)
YUH-60A (Sikorsky Aircraft). illus (Also cutaways) USA Avn Dig 22:2+ May '76

HELICOPTER TYPE - Continued

YUH-61

UTTAS: The helicopter of the 1980s? Mark Lambert. illus US Nav Inst Proc 102:128-130 Oct '76

UTTAS (Utility Tactical Transport Aircraft System) YUH-61A (Boeing-Vertol Co). illus USA Avn Dig 22:3+ May '76

HELICOPTERS

Aiming for new (aviation) markets (to support offshore oil field work). Richard S. Page. illus Aerosp Intl 12:34-37 Mar-Apr '76

The 1976 Reading (Pa) Show--better than ever. Howard Levy. illus Interavia 31:703-706 Aug '76

Accidents
See Accidents, Air; Accidents, Ground (Aircraft)

Characteristics

The world's current helicopters--1976. Tables only. Interavia 31:68-71 Jan '76

Control
See Flight Control Systems

Electronic Equipment
See Electronic Equipment (Aircraft)

Equipment

Who's who in helicopter avionics? illus Interavia 31: 48-50 Jan '76

Inspection

See also
Preflight Inspections

Instruments
See Aeronautical Instruments

Lift Capability

Flying the Bell 214B big lifter. Douglas H. Chopping. illus Interavia 31:46-47 Jan '76

Maintenance and Repair
See Aircraft Maintenance

Manufacture
See Helicopter Industry and Trade

Piloting

Study and Teaching

Training helicopter pilots at Oxford (Air Training School). illus Interavia 31:51-52 Jan '76

Refueling

See also
In-Flight Refueling

Safety Measures

See also
Flying Safety

A review of helicopter IFR (Instrument Flight Rules) operational considerations: The U.S. viewpoint. Glen A. Gilbert. illus maps tabs Interavia 31:709-713 Aug '76

HELICOPTERS - Continued

France

The AS.350 Ecureuil: A new 5/6-seat helicopter from Aérospatiale. Bob Salvy. illus tabs Interavia 31: 476-478 May '76

A royal performance: SA.360 Dauphin flight report. Douglas H. Chopping. illus Interavia 31:32-34 Jan '76

Great Britain

Study and Teaching

Training helicopter pilots at Oxford (Air Training School). illus Interavia 31:51-52 Jan '76

Norway

Offshore Stavanger. (Operations of Helikopter Service A/S) John C. Cook. illus tab Air Pict 38:228-230 Jun '76

Russia

Helicopters doing civilian jobs. illus Soviet Mil Rev No. 12:20-21 Dec '76

United States

Flying the Bell 214B big lifter. Douglas H. Chopping. illus Interavia 31:46-47 Jan '76

Exhibitions

The 1976 Helicopter Assoc of America meeting (and exhibition). J. Philip Geddes. illus Interavia 31: 207-210 Mar '76

History

Helicopter rescue: The early years. Merle Olmsted. illus tab Am Avn Hist Soc J 21:112-117 Summer '76

HELICOPTERS, EXPERIMENTAL see Aircraft, Experimental

HELICOPTERS, GUNSHIP see Gunships

HELICOPTERS, LOCAL SERVICE

The helicopter: Candidate for urban problems. Thomas R. Stuelpnagel. illus Govt Exec 8:36-37 Jul '76

Offshore Stavanger. (Operations of Helikopter Service A/S) John C. Cook. illus tab Air Pict 38:228-230 Jun '76

HELICOPTERS, MILITARY

See also entries on U.S. military helicopters by model designation under the specific type, e.g., Helicopter Type--AH-1

Accidents
See Accidents, Air; Accidents, Ground (Aircraft)

Armament

Automatic cannon technology. Gary W. Fischer. illus Natl Def 61:192-194 Nov-Dec '76

Cost-efficient anti-tank helos. illus Aerosp Intl 12: 20-22+ May-Jun '76

Blades

The wings of a helicopter. Maj Robert L. Gardner. illus Aerosp Safety 32:8-9 Mar '76

Canopies

How to get out of a snake in six milliseconds. (Evolution of emergency egress hardware in the Huey Cobra) James M.Boen. illus Approach 21:6-9 Dec '75

A matter of confidence. (Canopy removal system in the AH-1 Cobra) Arnold R.Lambert. illus USA Avn Dig 22:32-34 Jan '76

Characteristics

Bell YAH-63. illus (Also cutaway) USA Avn Dig 22:4+ May '76

Gallery of Soviet aerospace weapons: Helicopters. illus AF Mag 59:102-103 Mar '76

Gallery of USAF weapons: Helicopters. illus AF Mag 59:120+ May '76

Hughes YAH-64. illus USA Avn Dig 22:5+ May '76

The Soviet Mi-24 (Hind) combat helicopter. Alexander Malzeyev. illus tabs Intl Def Rev 8:879-881 Dec '75

UTTAS: The helicopter of the 1980s? Mark Lambert. illus US Nav Inst Proc 102:128-130 Oct '76

UTTAS (Utility Tactical Transport System) YUH-60A (Sikorsky Aircraft). illus (Also cutaways) USA Avn Dig 22:2+ May '76

UTTAS (Utility Tactical Transport Aircraft System) YUH-61A (Boeing-Vertol Co). illus USA Avn Dig 22:3+ May '76

The world's current helicopters--1976. Tables only. Interavia 31:68-71 Jan '76

Cockpits

Cockpit design for night NOE (Nap-Of-the-Earth). J.H.Emery. illus USA Avn Dig 22:6-7 Jan '76

Combat Evaluation

Army aircraft survivability. Maj N.I.Patla. illus tab USA Avn Dig 22:7+ Nov '76

Guns A Go-Go (ACH-47 helicopter gunship). LCDR Donald A.Mohr. illus USA Avn Dig 22:8-13 Jun '76

Control
See Flight Control Systems

Design

Cockpit design for night NOE (Nap-Of-the-Earth). J.H.Emery. illus USA Avn Dig 22:6-7 Jan '76

Ditching

Ditching the Huey. CW4 John L.Nicol. illus USA Avn Dig 22:44-46 Oct '76

Electronic Equipment
See Electronic Equipment (Aircraft)

Emergency Procedures

Autorotation. illus MAC Flyer 23:11-14 May '76

Black nights and glassy seas. LCDR Bill Roop. illus Approach 22:28-29 Dec '76

Helo in the water! Helo in the water! LT Thomas P. Pocklington. illus Approach 22:12-14 Nov '76

How to get out of a snake in six milliseconds. (Evolution of emergency egress hardware in the Huey Cobra) James M.Boen. illus Approach 21:6-9 Dec '75

Emergency Procedures - Cont'd

Mountain flying. illus Approach 21:16-17 Nov '75

A point of view: Underwater egress from helicopters. LT Mariner G.Cox. illus Approach 21:16-18 Feb '76

Engines
See also
Gas Turbines (Aircraft)

New OH-58 engine. Merle A.Clapsaddle. illus USA Avn Dig 22:15 Oct '76

T700: The Army's engine of the 80s. tab illus (Also cutaways) USA Avn Dig 22:1+ May '76

Equipment

Omera-Segid's Heracles modular radar. illus Interavia 31:73 Jan '76

Fuel Systems

When you gotta bingo, you gotta go! illus Approach 21:5 May '76

Ground-Support Equipment

Airmobility for air defense. Capt Bob Messmore. illus Air Def Mag, pp 28-31, Jul-Sep '76

Ice Prevention

A problem with ice. (Engine inlet icing) LtCol Charles R.Barr. illus Aerosp Safety 32:26-27 Mar '76

Severe clear. CW2 Jon L.Osgood. illus USA Avn Dig 22:42-43 Feb '76

Walking a tightrope. (Flying a helicopter into icing conditions) Ted Kontos. illus USA Avn Dig 22:38-41 Feb '76

Inspection

See also
Preflight Inspections

Improved maintenance inspection (with neutron-radiography). Maj Vincent G.Ripoll. illus USA Avn Dig 22:44-45 Mar '76

The wings of a helicopter. Maj Robert L.Gardner. illus Aerosp Safety 32:8-9 Mar '76

Instruments
See Aeronautical Instruments

Landing and Takeoff

Autorotation. illus MAC Flyer 23:11-14 May '76

The gap that must be bridged. (Tactical instrument flight--will you be ready?) CW2 Alvin T.Kyle, Jr. illus USA Avn Dig 22:4-5+ Aug '76

Helo in the water! Helo in the water! LT Thomas P. Pocklington. illus Approach 22:12-14 Nov '76

Helos: No two landings are alike. LCDR Allen K. Mears. illus Approach 21:4 Jun '76

"P" stands for practice, not prang. Maj Robert L. Gardner. illus Aerosp Safety 32:20-22 Jul '76

Serious shortcomings. Maj William C.Childree. tab illus USA Avn Dig 22:28-30 Jul '76

Something new for the LAMPS program. (GSI, Glide Slope Indicator) illus Approach 22:10-11 Nov '76

HELICOPTERS, MILITARY - Continued

United States - Cont'd

Gallery of USAF weapons: Helicopters. illus AF Mag 59:120+ May '76

Get ready--get set--go!!! LtCol John A. G. Klose. illus USA Avn Dig 22:6-7+ Dec '76

Hangar talk for aeroscouts. CW2 Homer E. Shuman. illus Armor 85:48-49 May-Jun '76

The planes we (ANG/AFR) fly. Pictorial. Air Reservist 27:12-13 Dec '75-Jan '76

The "Real Cav" (4th Sq, 9th Cavalry). MSgt Wayne E. Hair. illus USA Avn Dig 22:24-25 Mar '76

UTTAS: Low cost of ownership from the start. Interview. MajGen Jerry B. Lauer. illus Govt Exec 8: 48-50 Apr '76

UTTAS: The helicopter of the 1980s? Mark Lambert. illus US Nav Inst Proc 102:128-130 Oct '76

Value of U.S. helicopter exports continues to increase. illus tab Armed Forces J Intl 113:11 Jan '76

History

The banana flies again. (Surplus H-21 has re-united crew for maintenance and first "civilian" flight) illus Airman 20:48 Jan '76

HELICOPTERS IN BUSINESS

The '75 NBAA (National Business Aircraft Assoc) show (New Orleans, Oct 29-31, 1975). illus Interavia 31:75-78 Jan '76

Transair France: Business aviation in action. illus Interavia 31:1004-1005 Oct '76

HELICOPTERS IN MEDICAL SERVICE

See also
MAST (Military Assistance to Safety and Traffic)

Aeromedical transportation for infants and children. Burton H. Harris and others. illus tab USA Avn Dig 22:12-14 Oct '76

Helicopter aviation medicine. Col Rapheal J. DiNapoli. illus tab USA Avn Dig 22:2+ Oct '76

HELICOPTERS IN RESCUE WORK

See also
MAST (Military Assistance to Safety and Traffic)

Black nights and glassy seas. LCDR Bill Roop. illus Approach 22:28-29 Dec '76

Guatemala: 210th Aviation Battalion comes through again in disaster relief. CW2 Larry R. Santure. illus USA Avn Dig 22:4-5+ Jul '76

Mission: Typhoon mopup (on the island of Mauritius). LTs Brad Winstead and Mike Willoughby. illus Approach 21:1-3 Feb '76

Operation Wagonmaster. ("D" Company (Wagonmasters), 34th Support Battalion, 6th Cavalry Brigade (Air Combat), in disaster relief operation in Guatemala) Maj Terry N. Rosser. illus USA Avn Dig 22:6-7+ Jul '76

Pave Low III (modified Sikorsky HH-53 for night rescue capability). AF Mag 59:18 Feb '76

Survival. illus Approach 21:22-23 Jan '76

The United States Air Force in West New Guinea 1962-1963--help for the United Nations. LtCol Nick P. Apple. illus Aerosp Hist 22:212-217 Dec '75

HELICOPTERS IN RESCUE WORK - Continued

History

Helicopter rescue: The early years. Merle Olmsted. illus tab Am Avn Hist Soc J 21:112-117 Summer '76

HELMETS

Army tries out new helmet (at Fort Benning, Ga): 'Pot' to be out, 'Fritz' in? illus Army 26:57 Sep '76

Avionic developments steal Farnborough Air Show. illus tab Elect Warfare 8:19-20+ Nov-Dec '76

Cycle helmets given ear-eye test. AF Times 37:53 Aug 23 '76

Evaluation of a face cooling device integrated with the standard HGU-type USAF flight helmet. Abbott T. Kissen and others. illus tab Aviation, Space & Envmt Med 47:1188-1192 Nov '76

Repeal of helmet laws (for motorcyclists) causing concern. AF Times 37:30 Nov 15 '76

Simulated instrument hood. LT James R. Porter. illus Approach 21:8-9 May '76

Turning JP (Jet Propulsion) into noise. LTJG David M. Tyler. illus Approach 22:26 Nov '76

HENNESSEY, John J.

Strategy and readiness. Gen John J. Hennessey. por Strat Rev 4:44-48 Fall '76

HENRY, Richard C.

The space shuttle and Vandenberg Air Force Base. MajGen R. C. Henry and Maj Aubrey B. Sloan. AU Rev 27:19-26 Sep-Oct '76

HEWITT, H. Kent

Admiral H. Kent Hewitt, U.S. Navy. John Clagett. Nav War Col Rev pt 1, Preparing for high command. 28:72-86 Summer '75; pt 2, High command. 28:60-86 Fall '75

Skipper of the Eagle: Rehearsal for greatness. LCDR John H. Clagett, Ret. US Nav Inst Proc 102:58-65 Apr '76

HIGHWAYS see Roads

HIJACKING OF AIRCRAFT see Airplane Hijacking

HILL, James E.

Alaskan Air Command. por AF Mag 59:66-67 May '76

HISTORY

See also
Military History
  also subdivision History under specific subjects

How will history judge us? (Admiral Raymond A. Spruance Lecture, Naval War College, Oct 29, 1975) Barbara W. Tuchman. Nav War Col Rev 28: 3-11 Fall '75; Comment. LCDR Edwin R. Linz. Nav War Col Rev 29:104-107 Summer '76

HOBAN, Richard M.

One last word on discipline. LtGen R. M. Hoban. por Combat Crew 27:3+ Oct '76

HOFFMANN, Martin R.

Army (Secretary Martin R. Hoffmann) outlines plan to readmit (West Point) cadets. Phil Stevens. AF Times 37:8 Sep 6 '76

HOFFMANN, Martin R. - Continued

Return to airborne country. (SecArmy Martin R. Hoffmann visits Fort Bragg, NC) SP4 Jack Frear. por Soldiers 31:52-53 Jan '76

Secretary (of the Army Martin R.) Hoffmann joins (Field Artillery OCS) Hall of Fame. por Fld Arty J 44:45-46 May-Jun '76

Taking stock of the Army on nation's Bicentennial. Martin R. Hoffmann. por Army 26:8-9+ Oct '76

HOLLERS, James P.

(Brig)Gen Hollers, wartime ROA president, noted San Antonio civic leader, dies. por obit Officer 52:47-48 Jul '76

HOLLOWAY, James L., III

(ADM) Holloway/(Gen) Jones cooperation pact raises difficult questions. L. Edgar Prina. Sea Power 19: 34-36 Jan '76

(ADM James L.) Holloway discusses future needs; VTOL, Tomahawk head weapons list. L. Edgar Prina. Sea Power 19:9-10 May '76

CNO stresses Reserve importance to 'Hill' staffs. por Officer 52:22-23 Jul '76

Tides and currents in the Pacific: Long-term maritime implications. ADM James L. Holloway III. por Strat Rev 4:33-39 Summer '76

The U.S. Navy: A Bicentennial appraisal. ADM James L. Holloway III. por US Nav Inst Proc 102:18-24 Jul '76

HOLM, Jeanne M.

New look in government: (Maj)Gen Holm (Special Assistant to the President for Women) leads the way to greater participation by women. por Natl Def 61:22-23 Jul-Aug '76

HOME LOANS see Loans, Home

HONG KONG

The Crown Colony of Hong Kong. Col Norman L. Dodd, Ret. illus Mil Rev 56:37-46 Oct '76

HONOR SYSTEM

The (AF) Academy honor system. Gen T. R. Milton, Ret. AF Mag 59:86 Jul '76

Army (Secretary Martin R. Hoffmann) outlines plan to readmit (West Point) cadets. Phil Stevens. AF Times 37:8 Sep 6 '76

Cheating at West Point stirs up squalls on Hill. AF .Times 37:12 Sep 20 '76

High court (Supreme Court) frees (military) honor code data. AF Times 36:2 May 3 '76

(Senate) hearings on honor code: Inflexible system held root of problem. AF Times 36:50 Jul 5 '76

Some attitudes on honor code (at West Point): Survey report. Phil Stevens. AF Times 36:14 Jul 19 '76

Will CMA (Court of Military Appeals) review cadet cheating? AF Times 37:9 Aug 30 '76

HONORS see Awards, Decorations, etc

HOOPER, Edwin B.

Developing naval concepts: The early years, 1815-42. VADM Edwin B. Hooper, Ret. Def Mgt J 12:19-24 Jul '76

HOPKINS, Joseph G.

'Question Mark' 'refuelers' honored: Two Air Force pioneers (BrigGens Ross G. Hoyt, Ret, and Joseph G. Hopkins, Ret) awarded DFCs nearly half a century after their key role in a world record endurance flight. por AF Mag 59:22 Jul '76

HOSPELHORN, Cecil W.

(AAFES, Army and Air Force Exchange Service) Interview. MajGen C. W. Hospelhorn. por Review 55: 45-46+ May-Jun '76

Army & Air Force Exchange Service briefing to Air Force Staff Council. MajGen C. W. Hospelhorn. por Review 55:53-54+ Mar-Apr '76

Centralized distribution. MajGen C. W. Hospelhorn. Army Log 8:12-15 May-Jun '76; Review 55:51-52 May-Jun '76

HOSPITALS

See also
Dispensaries

Air Force--U.S.

AF hospital specialties available. Table only. AF Times 36:4 Jun 14 '76

Blood transfusion. TIG Brief 28:17 Oct 22 '76

Care of patients after cardiac catheterization. Mary M. Thomas and Michael R. Longo, Jr. tabs Aviation, Space and Envmt Med 47:192-198 Feb '76

Infection control. TIG Brief 28:11-12 Jun 4 '76

Management of controlled drugs in the emergency room. TIG Brief 28:19 Dec 3 '76

Management of emergency services in medical facilities. TIG Brief 28:8 Feb 27 '76

Medical aspects of third party liability. TIG Brief 28:10 Feb 27 '76

Medical committees as management tools. TIG Brief 28:5-6 Apr 9 '76

Medical Deficiency Analysis System (DAS). TIG Brief 28:15-16 Mar 12 '76

Medical facility committee effectiveness. TIG Brief 28:18 Nov 19 '76

Medical institutional planning. TIG Brief 28:15 Dec 17 '76

Medical methods improvement program. TIG Brief 28:17 Dec 17 '76

Medical Service: Inspection Guide E. TIG Brief pt 1, Medical units and activities on active duty, A-E. 28:6p addendum Apr 23 '76; pt 1, F-I. 28:4p addendum May 7 '76; pt 1, J. 28:6p addendum May 21 '76; pt 1, K. 28:6p addendum Jun 4 '76; pt 1, L. 28:6p addendum Jun 18 '76; pt 1, M: Veterinary service. pt 2, Air Reserve Forces medical units or activities. 28:4p addendum Jul 2 '76; pt 1, M, Supplement 1. 28, addendum:7 Aug 27 '76

Outpatient records: Do you have a maintenance system? TIG Brief 28:9-10 Feb 27 '76

Report of patients: Workload audits. TIG Brief 28:16 Dec 17 '76

Self-inspection programs within medical facilities. TIG Brief 28:5 Feb 13 '76

(USAF) ward clerk program. TIG Brief 28:7-8 Jul 16 '76

HOUSING - Continued

United States - Cont'd

Rules for selecting homes eased: Retirees after Aug 1 affected. AF Times 37:11 Dec 6 '76

HOVERCRAFT see Air Cushion Vehicles

HOYT, Ross G.

Flying the early birds: The Curtiss Hawks. BrigGen Ross G. Hoyt, Ret. AF Mag 59:68-69 Oct '76

Flying the early birds: The SE-5. BrigGen Ross G. Hoyt, Ret. AF Mag 59:110-111 Sep '76

'Question Mark' 'refuelers' honored: Two Air Force pioneers (BrigGens Ross G. Hoyt, Ret, and Joseph G. Hopkins, Ret) awarded DFCs nearly half a century after their key role in a world record endurance flight. por AF Mag 59:22 Jul '76

HUGHES, Howard R.

Howard Hughes, 70. obit AF Times 36:40 Apr 19 '76

HUGHES AIRCRAFT CO

A profile of the Hughes Aircraft Company. John Marriott. illus NATO's Fifteen Nations 21:86-88 Aug-Sep '76

HULL, Hadlai A.

Review, surveillance and self-examination: A special interview on Army funding problems. Hadlai A. Hull. por Armed Forces Compt 21:2-5 Jan '76

HUMAN ENGINEERING

Human factors: A vital part of system safety. TIG Brief 28:7 Jul 2 '76

Human factors engineering. TIG Brief 28:5 Jan 16 '76

Monument to people oriented construction (Air Force Accounting and Finance Center, Lowry AFB, Colo). Maj Peter LoPresti and William L. Kollman. illus AF Engrg & Svcs Qtr 17:7-10 Nov '76

Testing human factors. Ward A. Harris. illus Army Log 8:20-23 Nov-Dec '76

HUMAN GOALS

Department of Defense human goals. AF Plcy Ltr for Comdrs: Sup No. 2:9 Feb '76

HUMAN RELATIONS

(AF) equal opportunity Affirmative Actions Plan (AAP). TIG Brief 28:12 Feb 27 '76

Black soldier update. MSgt Nat Dell. illus Soldiers 31:6-10 Jan '76

Chaplain visitations. TIG Brief 28:13 Aug 13 '76

Complaints processing: How you can help. TIG Brief 28:3 Feb 27 '76

Conflict in organizations: Good or bad? LtCol Russell Pierre, Jr and Maj Jerome G. Peppers, Jr, Ret. AU Rev 28:69-79 Nov-Dec '76

Control & supervision and flying. Col Paul M. Davis. illus Aerosp Safety 32:19-21 Aug '76

EOT (Equal Opportunity and Treatment) and HRE (Human Relations Education) review. TIG Brief 28:13-14 Mar 26 '76

HUMAN RELATIONS - Continued

Eliminating the wife error. Jackie Starmer. (Adapted from MATS Flyer, Aug 1963) illus Interceptor 18: 5-7 Apr '76; Adaptation. Approach 21:24-26 Nov '75

Goal: Individual awareness. (Air Force Reserve's social actions program) illus Air Reservist 27:12 Mar '76

How a manager gets the job done: Leadership, the common thread. (Remarks, 27th Industrial Engineering Conference for Management and Supervision, West Virginia University, Morgantown, April 5, 1976) MajGen Frank J. Simokaitis. AF Plcy Ltr for Comdrs: Sup No. 6:22-25 Jun '76

Human relations. (Remarks, Midlands Chapter, National Conference of Christians and Jews, Omaha, June 13, 1976) Gen Russell E. Dougherty. AF Plcy Ltr for Comdrs: Sup No. 9:6-12 Sep '76

Human relations council. TIG Brief 28:22 Jul 16 '76

Managerial inconsistency: Attitudes vs behavior. Norman L. Warden and Fred Burrell. illus tab Armed Forces Compt 21:28-30 Apr '76

The people mix. Maj James M. Alford. AU Rev 27: 72-74 May-Jun '76

Personnel quality force management. TIG Brief 28:10 Feb 13 '76

Responding to HumRel. 2dLt Andrew J. Franklin. MarCor Gaz 60:70-71 May '76

The squad. (From desk to squad duty for a few days, by request, to become a better leader) Col Dandridge M. Malone. illus Army 26:12-16+ Feb '76

Turbulence and teamwork. LtGen K. L. Tallman. TIG Brief 28:2 Aug 27 '76

Visibility. TIG Brief 28:14 Oct 22 '76

When Daddy comes home: How to cope with children who are hurt and angry because Daddy's been away. Marianne Lester. illus AF Times, Times Magazine sup:8-11 Sep 20 '76

Study and Teaching

A common value of survival. Col John R. Love. illus MarCor Gaz 60:45-46 Feb '76

Force-fed human relations. Capt J. P. Sureau. MarCor Gaz 60:50-51 Sep '76

HUMAN RELIABILITY

Cutting the accident bill. Maj Thomas R. Allocca. illus Aerosp Safety 32:25-27 Nov '76

HRP (Human Reliability Program): Be aware. TIG Brief 28:19 Feb 13 '76

HRP (Human Reliability Program) disqualifications under annual review. AF Times 37:10 Aug 23 '76

Health records and the human reliability program. TIG Brief 28:13 Oct 8 '76

High-risk jobs listed in reg (AFR 35-99). AF Times 37:21 Dec 13 '76

Human-factor-caused mishaps: A subject of continuing concern. TIG Brief 28:6 Dec 3 '76

Human reliability program. TIG Brief 28:5 Aug 13 '76

Human reliability program; AFR 35-99 revision. TIG Brief 28:5 Apr 9 '76

IN-FLIGHT REFUELING - Continued

Hangar flying: How to stop chasing airspeed with throttles. illus Combat Crew 27:14-15 Mar '76

On speed: 245-265 KIAS (Knots Indicated Air Speed). Capt Dwayne Hicks. illus Combat Crew 27:12-13 Mar '76

Tanker task force operations (at Loring AFB, Me). Col Kenneth M. Patterson. illus map Combat Crew 27:4-7+ Jul '76

"Thanks, tank(er crew)." L.I. Wilson. illus Aerosp Hist 23:65-70 Jun '76

Three little words ... breakaway, breakaway, breakaway. SMSgt Billy G. Hall. illus Combat Crew 27: 4-5 Aug '76

Working with SAC. Capt Marc Epstein. illus Air Reservist 28:6 Jul '76

History

Never a 'Question Mark.' (Spaatz Trophy, given to SAC by TAC to be awarded to best tanker unit each year, in honor of historic flight of the Question Mark in 1929, which stayed in the air nearly 7 days and proved that in-flight refueling was practical) Maj Jay B. Welsh. illus Airman 20: 24-29 Mar '76

1929: Refueling proves practical--log of the 'Question Mark.' illus AF Times 36:23+ Jan 12 '76

'Question Mark' 'refuelers' honored: Two Air Force pioneers (BrigGens Ross G. Hoyt, Ret, and Joseph G. Hopkins, Ret) awarded DFCs nearly half a century after their key role in a world record endurance flight. illus AF Mag 59:22 Jul '76

"Thanks, tank(er crew)." L.I. Wilson. illus Aerosp Hist 23:65-70 Jun '76

Study and Teaching

Hangar Flying: Central Flight Instructors Course. illus Combat Crew 27:16-18 Jun '76

IN-SERVICE TRAINING see On-the-Job Training

INACTIVATION OF INSTALLATIONS AND UNITS

Air Force

Base shakeups to cost jobs: 7500 military, 3000 civilian. Len Famiglietti. AF Times 36:2 Mar 22 '76

Caring enough. (USAF's military personnel offices work hard to solve problems arising from suspension of U.S. military operations in Turkey) MSgt Fred Harrison. Airman 20:48 Feb '76

4 alternate bases (UPT sites) studied for closing. Ron Sanders. AF Times 37:8 Sep 27 '76

Hearings end on shutdown: Kincheloe (AFB, Mich) too old. AF Times 37:26 Dec 6 '76

Impact statements issued on proposed shutdowns (at) Kincheloe (AFB, Mich) and Loring (AFB, Maine). AF Times 37:32 Oct 4 '76

Costs

Making retrograde cost effective. (Air Force materiel used in Southeast Asia) LtCol Barry W. Jenkins. illus AF Engrg & Svcs Qtr 17:26-27 May '76

Armed Forces

DOD eying plan to ease home sales loss. AF Times 37:4 Sep 6 '76

INACTIVATION OF INSTALLATIONS AND UNITS - Continued

Armed Forces - Cont'd

Ford wins Hill fight over closing (military) bases. AF Times 37:53 Sep 6 '76

House OKs amendment on base closing policy. AF Times 37:6 Oct 4 '76

(Military) construction bill passes Senate. AF Times 36:36 Jun 14 '76

Army

Safeguard (Ballistic Missile Defense System) Center to close. illus AF Times 36:41 Mar 1 '76

INCENTIVE PAY

See also
Flight Pay

Be choosy on special pay, manpower group (Defense Manpower Commission) says. AF Times 36:27 May 10 '76

INCOME

Compensation: Reasonableness is the yardstick. Ray W. Dellas. illus Govt Exec 8:42-43 Oct '76

INDIA

Foreign Relations

China (People's Republic)

Border war: China vs India. RADM Ben Eiseman. illus MarCor Gaz 60:19-25 Sep '76

Russia

Ever strengthening cooperation. (5th anniversary, Soviet-Indian Treaty of Peace, Friendship and Cooperation) V. Yefremov. Soviet Mil Rev No. 8:47-48 Aug '76

Politics and Government

Revolution and tradition in the Middle East, Africa, and South Asia. Marcus W. Franda. illus Natl Sec Aff Forum No. 24:23-31 Spring-Summer '76

INDIAN OCEAN REGION

The vulnerability of Australia's maritime trade. A. W. Grazebrook. illus tabs NATO's Fifteen Nations 20:40-45+ Dec '75-Jan '76

The vulnerability of the West in the Southern Hemisphere. Patrick Wall. illus tab Strat Rev 4:44-50 Winter '76

The world environment and U.S. military policy for the 1970s and 1980s. ADM Thomas H. Moorer, Ret and Alvin J. Cottrell. tab Strat Rev 4:56-65 Spring '76

Strategic Importance

From Moscow, South by Southeast. Maj William G. Hanne. illus map tab Mil Rev 56:47-55 Jan '76

New look down under as (Malcolm) Fraser backs U.S./Australian naval cooperation. L. Edgar Prina. illus Sea Power 19:37-38 Feb '76

The Transkei: Key to U.S. naval strategy in the Indian Ocean. Maj Wesley A. Groesbeck. illus map Mil Rev 56:18-24 Jun '76

INDONESIA

Economic Conditions

Indonesia. A.Ranney Johnson. illus tabs Def & For
Aff Dig No. 7:32-36 '76

Economic Policy

Indonesia. A.Ranney Johnson. illus tabs Def & For
Aff Dig No. 7:32-36 '76

Foreign Relations

Malaysia--History

The confrontation in Borneo. Brig E. D.Smith. Army
Qtr pt 1, The revolt in Brunei leads to "confrontation." 105:479-483 Oct '75; pt 2, The incursions
of the undeclared war. 106:30-36 Jan '76

History

The United States Air Force in West New Guinea
1962-1963--help for the United Nations. LtCol
Nick P.Apple. illus Aerosp Hist 22:212-217
Dec '75

Politics and Government

Gestapu--ten years after. Capt L.K.Burgess. illus
Nav War Col Rev 28:65-75 Winter '76

INDUSTRIAL COLLEGE OF THE ARMED FORCES

See also
National Defense University

Industrial College briefs. Regular feature in issues
of Perspectives in Defense Management

War, Industrial Colleges to admit ANG, AFRes. AF
Times 36:12 Jun 14 '76

INDUSTRIAL MOBILIZATION see Mobilization,
Industrial

INDUSTRIAL PLANNING

See also
Industry and Defense

Industrial Preparedness Planning. (AFR 78-13) TIG
Brief 28:17 Feb 13 '76

Location logistics. (Address, seminar sponsored by
Utah Air Force Assoc, Society of Logistics Engi-
neers and Weber State College, May 10, 1975) Col
Nathan H.Mazer, Ret. Log Spectrum 10:11-12
Spring '76

INDUSTRIAL RELATIONS see Labor-Management
Relations

INDUSTRIAL SECURITY see Security, Industrial

INDUSTRY

See also
Industrial Planning
Mobilization, Industrial
also specific kinds of industry, e.g.,
Aerospace Industry and Trade
Aircraft Industry and Trade
Electronic Industry and Trade
Fish Industry and Trade
Helicopter Industry and Trade
Missile Industry and Trade
Petroleum Industry and Trade

Economic strategy. Regular feature in issues of Defense & Foreign Affairs Digest

INDUSTRY - Continued

Great Britain

The British defence industry. John Marriott. illus
tabs NATO's Fifteen Nations 21:21+ Apr-May '76

British defence procurement: Organisation and practice. E.C.Cornford. NATO's Fifteen Nations 21:
23-26 Apr-May '76

The (defence products) industry. John Marriott. illus
tab NATO's Fifteen Nations 21:29-31 Apr-May '76

Miscellaneous (defence equipments and services).
John Marriott. illus tab NATO's Fifteen Nations
21:66-69 Apr-May '76

Vulcan's forge. David Harvey. illus Def & For Aff
Dig No. 8-9:18-21+ '76

Directories

Principal firms in British defence industry. Table
only. NATO's Fifteen Nations 21:68-69 Apr-
May '76

Russia

Confident growth. (Tatar Autonomous Soviet Socialist
Republic) F. Tabeyev. illus Soviet Mil Rev No. 3:
11-14 Mar '76

The feat goes on. (Uralmash Engineering Works in
Sverdlovsk) illus Soviet Mil Rev No. 5:8-11 May '76

Steady strides ahead. G.Alexeyev. tab illus Soviet
Mil Rev No. 6:7-9 Jun '76

Tank and tractor alike. V.Semyonov. illus Soviet Mil
Rev No. 2:10-12 Feb '76

Singapore

The Singapore military/industrial scene. R.B.Pen-
gelley. illus tab Intl Def Rev 9:657-660 Aug '76

United States

How private enterprise is committing "subtle suicide." illus Govt Exec 8:56-57 May '76

Industry in the U.S.: The facts don't match the image. illus Govt Exec 8:30+ Feb '76

Location logistics. (Address, seminar sponsored by
Utah Air Force Assoc, Society of Logistics Engi-
neers and Weber State College, May 10, 1975) Col
Nathan H.Mazer, Ret. Log Spectrum 10:11-12
Spring '76

Rockwell's (Donn L.) Williams: "We do it to ourselves." illus Govt Exec 8:29+ Feb '76

INDUSTRY AND DEFENSE

Aerospace: Capital shortage--artificial environment.
Paul Thayer. illus Govt Exec 8:36-37 Feb '76

Are we running out of metals? Simon D.Strauss.
Persp in Def Mgt No. 24:19-31 Winter '75-'76

The British defence industry. John Marriott. illus
tabs NATO's Fifteen Nations 21:21+ Apr-May '76

British defence procurement: Organisation and practice. E.C.Cornford. NATO's Fifteen Nations 21:
23-26 Apr-May '76

(Collier Trophy awarded by National Aeronautic
Assoc to David S.Lewis, chief executive officer
of General Dynamics Corp, and to USAF-industry
team that produced the F-16) illus Natl Def 61:
102-103 Sep-Oct '76

INDUSTRY AND DEFENSE - Continued

Conventional weapons. John Marriott. illus NATO's Fifteen Nations 21:62+ Apr-May '76

Cost overruns: The defense industry view. Earl A. Molander. tabs Persp in Def Mgt No.24:98-104 Winter '75-'76

DOD revamping its profit policies for defense contractors: Profit '76 revisited. Dale R. Babione. illus tabs Def Mgt J 12:41-46 Oct '76

The (defence products) industry. John Marriott. illus tab NATO's Fifteen Nations 21:29-31 Apr-May '76

Defense industry: Is the foundation crumbling? tab Govt Exec 8:19 Mar '76

Defense industry news. Regular feature in issues of International Defense Review

Electronics. John Marriott. illus NATO's Fifteen Nations 21:53-55+ Apr-May '76

Engineering miracle in munition design. (40-mm grenade round) Victor Lindner. illus tabs Natl Def 60:294-297 Jan-Feb '76

Fighting vehicles. John Marriott. illus NATO's Fifteen Nations 21:59-60 Apr-May '76

Foreign military sales: An $11 billion market for the U.S. Charles De Vore. illus Signal 30:38-43 Jan '76

Foundries and the OSHA Act: Problems and some solutions. Debbie C. Tennison. illus Natl Def 61:56-59 Jul-Aug '76

Foundries in dilemma. Debbie C. Tennison. illus tabs Natl Def 60:453-458 May-Jun '76

The foundry industry--Achilles' heel of defense? Debbie C. Tennison. illus tab Natl Def 60:366-369 Mar-Apr '76

Giddap, GIDEP (Government-Industry Data Exchange Program). TIG Brief 28:7 Jan 16 '76

Industry and defense. (Excerpt from address, 57th Defense Preparedness Meeting, American Defense Preparedness Assoc, Los Angeles, Oct 15, 1975) R. Anderson. Natl Def 60:287 Jan-Feb '76

Industry feedback on life cycle cost. John J. Bennett. Def Mgt J 12:38 Oct '76

An industry perspective on satellites. Henry E. Hockeimer and others. illus Signal 30:60-74 Mar '76

Life cycle cost: An NSIA (National Security Industrial Assoc) review. A. M. Frager. Def Mgt J 12:39-40 Oct '76

Maintainability--a shared responsibility. Hartley I. Starr. Natl Def 60:360-363 Mar-Apr '76

Major defense contracts--value over $1 million. Regular feature in issues of International Defense Review

The military-industrial complex: What President Eisenhower really said. (Farewell radio and television address to the American people, Jan 17, 1961) AF Plcy Ltr for Comdrs: Sup No.7:29-32 Jul '76

The military looks and listens to industry: The telecommunications equipment acquisition process. R. Leffler. illus Log Spectrum 10:23-28 Fall '76

Miscellaneous (defence equipments and services). John Marriott. illus tab NATO's Fifteen Nations 21:66-69 Apr-May '76

INDUSTRY AND DEFENSE - Continued

Navy shipbuilding dispute rages on. James D. Hessman. illus Sea Power 19:15-18 Aug '76

Navy shipbuilding problems reach critical stage. illus Sea Power 19:13-14 Jul '76

Principal firms in British defence industry. Table only. NATO's Fifteen Nations 21:68-69 Apr-May '76

Procurement for Defense. Eberhardt Rechtin. Natl Def 61:122-124 Sep-Oct '76

Putting the great back into Great Britain? (Interview with Geoffrey Pattie, MP) illus Def & For Aff Dig No. 8-9:32-33+ '76

R&D emphasis on reliability. Robert N. Parker. Def Mgt J 12:19 Apr '76

The Singapore military/industrial scene. R.B. Pengelley. illus tab Intl Def Rev 9:657-660 Aug '76

Swedish industry looks ahead. Dan Boyle. illus Interavia 31:131-134 Feb '76

Tank and tractor alike. V. Semyonov. illus Soviet Mil Rev No.2:10-12 Feb '76

USAF's crusade to streamline industrial production. Edgar Ulsamer. illus AF Mag 59:62-67 Oct '76

Warships. John Marriott. illus NATO's Fifteen Nations 21:47-50 Apr-May '76

Whatever happened to mutual trust and respect? Clyde A. Parton. illus Natl Def 60:268-270 Jan-Feb '76

INDUSTRY AND STATE

Aerospace: Capital shortage--artificial environment. Paul Thayer. illus Govt Exec 8:36-37 Feb '76

Airline deregulation: Will it make the dominos fall faster? C.W. Borklund. illus tabs Govt Exec 8:38-40+ Jul '76

Anti-trust and over-regulation: "Ma Bell" strikes back. illus Govt Exec 8:38-39 Jun '76

British aerospace--the future. tab Air Pict 38:267 Jul '76

CBEMA (Computer and Business Equipment Manufacturers Assoc) and GSA (General Services Administration): A dialogue on how government hurts itself (because of its own procurement and contracting practices). C.W. Borklund. illus Govt Exec 8:24+ May '76

The complexities of seeking a (telecommunications) policy. (Interview with John Eger) John F. Judge. illus Govt Exec 8:40+ Jun '76

The (defence products) industry. John Marriott. illus tab NATO's Fifteen Nations 21:29-31 Apr-May '76

The hot button (at IBM) is EEOC (Equal Employment Opportunity Commission). Govt Exec 8:15 Dec '76

How America is becoming a regulated society. (Interview with Rep Steven D. Symms) illus Govt Exec 8:34-35 Aug '76

Industry in the U.S.: The facts don't match the image. illus Govt Exec 8:30+ Feb '76

Mass transit: What government needs to do to attract high technology industry. illus Govt Exec 8:10+ Nov '76

Nationalizing the British aerospace industry: When, how and for how long? Derek Wood. illus Interavia 31:799-800 Sep '76

INFORMATION STORAGE AND RETRIEVAL SYSTEMS

See also
Electronic Data Processing Systems
Management Information Systems
Microforms

NCO is key figure in (AF) software library. illus AF Times 36:28 May 10 '76

Now, a way to get at those grants and loans. (Federal Domestic Assistance Program Retrieval Systems) Spencer B. Child. illus Govt Exec 8:26+ Mar '76

SP automation would speed (AF) file retrieval. AF Times 37:12 Nov 1 '76

INFRARED DETECTORS

Battlefield surveillance. Charles Latour. illus NATO's Fifteen Nations 20:62-65+ Dec '75-Jan '76

First TRAM (Target Recognition and Attack Multisensor) system undergoes navy testing. illus Countermeasures 2:47 Mar '76

Infrared scanning techniques. ("Hot spots" in your overhead electrical distribution lines?) Don Lyne. illus AF Engrg & Svcs Qtr 17:18-20 Feb '76

Is EW still a Pentagon stepchild? Harry F. Eustace. illus Elect Warfare 8:28-29+ Jul-Aug '76

TRAM (Target Recognition Attack Multi-sensor) makes A-6E world's most advanced EO aircraft. illus Elect Warfare 8:75-76+ May-Jun '76

INFRARED EQUIPMENT

AN/ALQ-123; IRCM (InfraRed CounterMeasures) pioneer. Roger C. Farmer. illus Elect Warfare 7: 33-35+ Nov-Dec '75

Army EW--current U.S. concepts. Harry F. Eustace. illus Intl Def Rev 9:429-432 Jun '76

Atmospheric transmissometer for military system performance evaluation. Frederic M. Zweibaum and Thomas F. McHenry. tabs illus Countermeasures 2:27-29+ Jun '76

Electro optical EW seen key to new developments. Harvey Rinn and Joseph Savino. illus Elect Warfare 7:21-22 Nov-Dec '75

Infrared aerial photography. Howard Beauchamp. illus Countermeasures 2:40-41 Mar '76

Infrared comes of age in the world of electronic warfare. Dave Fitzpatrick. illus Elect Warfare 7:38-40+ Nov-Dec '75

New infrared missile developed. Countermeasures 2: 47 Mar '76

U.S. EO (Electro-Optics) and IRCM (InfraRed CounterMeasures) budget outlined. Tables only. Elect Warfare 7:24+ Nov-Dec '75

INFRARED PHOTOGRAPHY see Photography, Infrared

INLAND NAVIGATION see Waterways

INSECTS

Bugs and bites. illus TAC Attack 16:16-17 Mar '76

INSIGNIA

See also -
Airplanes, Military--Insignia

Space insignia. C. M. Hempsell. illus Spaceflight 18: 151+ Apr '76

INSIGNIA - Continued

Air Force--U.S.

Insignia changes offered: Top NCOs would get new stripes. Bruce Callander. illus AF Times 36:3 Jul 19 '76

Lower-grade insignia: Who's what? AF Times 36:6 Jun 14 '76

New stripes for top EM: Commands study NCO change. Bruce Callander. illus AF Times 36:2 Apr 5 '76

Revision (of AFR 35-13) tightens rules on badges. AF Times 36:27 May 24 '76

Armed Forces--U.S.

Heraldry Institute: Eagle and lion No. One. Gregory Simpkins. AF Times 37:34 Sep 27 '76

The patch game. SSgt Zack Richards. illus Soldiers 31:50-52 Nov '76

Army--U.S.

"Follow Me": The story of a patch. Arnold Tilden. (Reprinted from Infantry, Nov-Dec 1965) illus Infantry 66:47-49 Jul-Aug '76

History

Bars, stars & General Washington. Donald C. Wright. illus Soldiers 31:17 Feb '76

Marine Corps--U.S.

Informal recognition for lower enlisted ranks. ("Top Quality Marine" patch) MarCor Gaz 60:10 Oct '76

INSPECTION

See also
Airplanes, Military--Inspection
Food--Inspection

Air Force

Air Force AFRT (Air Force Radio and Television) Broadcast Management: Inspection Guide D-1. TIG Brief 28:2p addendum Feb 27 '76

Air Force Chaplain Service: Inspection Guide H. TIG Brief 28:2p addendum Dec 3 '76

Air Force Chaplain Service inspection model. TIG Brief 28:10 Dec 3 '76

Another look at Operational Readiness Inspections (ORIs). TIG Brief 28:22 Sep 24 '76

Ants and elephants (management effectiveness inspection). TIG Brief 28:5 Nov 5 '76

Base inspection questionnaire on people problems. TIG Brief 28:5 Jun 18 '76

Command Inspection System (CIS) inspections. TIG Brief 28:5 Dec 17 '76

Comptroller: Inspection Guide G. TIG Brief sec I-IV, 28:5p addendum Oct 22 '76; sec V-VI, 28:5p addendum Nov 5 '76

Inspectors are management consultants. TIG Brief 28:6 Nov 5 '76

Inspector's viewpoint (formerly ORI). Regular feature in issues of Interceptor

MAC 'new look' ORI. BrigGen Edward J. Nash. tab TIG Brief 28:3-4 Aug 27 '76

INSTRUMENT FLYING - Continued

Comprehensive (formerly master) Plan Tabs and TERminal instrument Procedures (TERPs). TIG Brief 28:13 Nov 19 '76

Danger area--look out. Maj Jack Spey. illus Aerosp Safety 32:8-9 Sep '76

Descent decisions. Capt Mike C.Kostelnik. illus tabs TAC Attack 16:12-14 Oct '76

Flight violation! LT Dave McPherson. illus Approach 22:12-13 Jul '76

From mission order to instrument takeoff. CW2 Joel E.Warhurst. USA Avn Dig 22:12-14 Sep '76

The gap that must be bridged. (Tactical instrument flight--will you be ready?) CW2 Alvin T.Kyle, Jr. illus USA Avn Dig 22:4-5+ Aug '76

Good ol' VFR. Capt Kenneth D.Van Meter. illus Interceptor 18:12-13 Oct '76

IFR minimum altitudes. Capt John L.Wilson. illus Combat Crew pt 1, 27:26-27 May '76; pt 2, 27: 22-24 Jun '76

Lost ... on a circling approach. Maj Brian C.Bernet. illus Aerosp Safety 32:22-23 Mar '76

The new (battlefield) dead-man's curve. Col William R.Ponder. tabs USA Avn Dig 22:6-7 Mar '76

The night the world died (at Clark AB, RP). illus Approach 22:6-7 Oct '76

Planning a tactical instrument flight. Capt Lewis D. Ray. illus USA Avn Dig 22:11-13 Jan '76

Radar-directed routing and terminal arrival depiction. LT Daniel E.Graham. illus maps Approach 21:1-4 May '76

A review of helicopter IFR (Instrument Flight Rules) operational considerations: The U.S. viewpoint. Glen A.Gilbert. illus maps tabs Interavia 31:709-713 Aug '76

A revolutionary all-weather HUD (Head-Up Display). (Thomson-CSF TC 125) Douglas Chopping. illus Interavia 31:548-549 Jun '76

Visibility--to land or not to land. Capt John L.Wilson. illus Combat Crew pt 1, 27:22-23 Aug '76; pt 2, The runway environment. 27:18-20 Sep '76; pt 3, The rules. 27:26-27 Oct '76; pt 4, Going visual. 27:20-21 Nov '76; pt 5, Techniques. 27:14-15 Dec '76

Study and Teaching

The IFC (Instrument Flight Center) approach. Regular feature in issues of Aerospace Safety

One love. (Sgt Tom Theobald of Chanute AFB, Ill, is ATC's Instructor of the Year) Milene Wells. illus Airman 20:41-42 Oct '76

Simulated instrument hood. LT James R.Porter. illus Approach 21:8-9 May '76

The USAF Instrument Flight Center: Anachronism or instrument flight pacesetter for the future? Maj Jimmie L.Coombes. illus AU Rev 27:62-71 May-Jun '76

What's your approach plate IQ? LT Bob Harler. illus Approach 22:10-12 Oct '76

INSTRUMENT LANDING SYSTEMS see Automatic Landing Systems

INSTRUMENT PANELS

Cockpit design for night NOE (Nap-Of-the-Earth). J.H.Emery. illus USA Avn Dig 22:6-7 Jan '76

INSTRUMENTATION

Crowded electronic sky demands accurate instrumentation. Hilliard F.Penfold. illus Signal 30: 65-70 May-Jun '76

INSTRUMENTS

See also specific kinds of instruments, e.g.,
Aeronautical Instruments   Recording Instruments
Altimeters   Sensors
Navigation Instruments   Sextants
Periscopes   Telescopes

INSURANCE

(Air, Army) Guard, agencies (NASA and CIA) ask malpractice protection. Ann Gerow. AF Times 36:26 Mar 15 '76

CHAMPUS payments pose problems. Andy Plattner. AF Times 37:19 Sep 13 '76

Health insurance switch (from CHAMPUS) would cost. AF Times 37:4 Sep 20 '76

IRA (Individual Retirement Accounts) not for (active) military. AF Times 36:24 Jun 28 '76

It's your move and your money. Sgt1C Floyd Harrington. illus tab Soldiers 31:6-11 Apr '76

Malpractice bill appears stalled. AF Times 37:27 Sep 13 '76

(Marine Corps Association) Group Annuity Plan. Ira U.Cobleigh. MarCor Gaz 60:15-18 Sep '76

You and the 'other guy.' (A discussion of auto insurance) LtCol Harry A.Grab, Jr. illus Airman 20: 30-34 Mar '76

INSURANCE, LIFE

88 insurance firms accredited (overseas). AF Times 37:31 Oct 11 '76

Legislative actions include many veterans bills. Officer 52:8-9 Aug '76

Life insurance as a function of estate planning for the middle income military member. Maj Mell J. Lacy. tabs AF Law Rev 17:1-49 Winter '75

Life insurance increase eyed (among other) Reserve incentives. AF Times 37:10 Aug 16 '76

A matter of life and death. SSgt John Savard. illus tab Soldiers 31:40-44 Sep '76

INSURGENCY

Intelligence and insurgency. Capt A.C.Bevilacqua. illus MarCor Gaz 60:40-46 Jan '76

Transnational terrorism. Charles A.Russell. illus AU Rev 27:26-35 Jan-Feb '76

Why the British lost the war: The American Revolution in modern perspective. Robert Detweiler. illus MarCor Gaz 60:18-24 Jul '76

INTEGRATED LOGISTIC SUPPORT

The FFG-7 integrated logistics support program. (Address, Long Island Chapter, SOLE, April 24, 1976) RADM E.J.Otth. Log Spectrum 10:34-35+ Fall '76

INTELLIGENCE, MILITARY - Continued

United States - Cont'd

Military intelligence: A fight for identity. Col Leonard A. Spirito and Maj Marc B. Powe. Army 26: 14-21 May '76

Military intelligence--streamlined, centralized, civilianized. Interview. Robert F. Ellsworth. chart illus AF Mag 59:26-30 Aug '76

Organization

Military intelligence--streamlined, centralized, civilianized. Interview. Robert F. Ellsworth. chart illus AF Mag 59:26-30 Aug '76

INTERCEPTION OF AIRCRAFT see Airplanes, Military --Interception

INTERCEPTION OF MISSILES see Missiles--Interception

INTERCONTINENTAL BALLISTIC MISSILES see Missiles

INTERDICTION

Air interdiction in a European future war: Doctrine or dodo? WgComdr Alan Parkes. AU Rev 27:16-18 Sep-Oct '76

A tactical triad for deterring limited war in Western Europe. LtCol Thomas C. Blake, Jr. illus AU Rev 27:8-15 Sep-Oct '76

Who needs nuclear tacair? Col David L. Nichols. illus AU Rev 27:15-25 Mar-Apr '76

INTERNATIONAL AIR TRANSPORT ASSOCIATION

Pillars of world air transport. (Member airlines of International Air Transport Assoc plus some 50 major non-members) Table only. Interavia 31: 939-954 Oct '76

The state of the air transport industry--by some of its leading personalities. illus Interavia 31:923-926+ Oct '76

Talking of safety. Douglas H. Chopping. illus tabs Interavia pt 1, 31:1074-1075 Nov '76

Upholding the IATA tariff structure: The long arm of the compliance law. illus Interavia 31:1146-1147 Dec '76

INTERNATIONAL CIVIL AVIATION ORGANIZATION

MLS (Microwave Landing Systems): Breakthrough in landing systems. John L. McLucas. illus AF Mag 59:66-68+ Jul '76

INTERNATIONAL COOPERATION

See also
Aircraft Industry and Trade--International Aspects
Aviation, Commercial--International Aspects
Nuclear Power--International Aspects
Space--International Aspects
Technology--International Cooperation

Artillery projects of the future. Karl Heinz Bodlien. (Trans from Soldat und Technik, Aug 1974) illus tabs Fld Arty J 44:10-15 Jan-Feb '76

Defence of North Sea energy sources: The military aspects of the problem. Patrick Wall. illus map NATO's Fifteen Nations 21:78-83 Apr-May '76

Fruitful cooperation. (Interview with Nikolai Sofinsky) Vasily Yefremov. illus Soviet Mil Review No. 2: 45-47 Feb '76

INTERNATIONAL COOPERATION - Continued

The Global Atmospheric Research Programme (GARP): GARP Atlantic Tropical Experiment (GATE). B.J. Mason. Royal Air Forces Qtr 16: 35-40 Spring '76

The NATO program for rationalization and standardization. Norman Gray. illus Signal 30:80-81+ May-Jun '76

Project Kiwi One--new dimensions in underwater sound. David G. Browning and Richard W. Bannister. illus maps US Nav Inst Proc 102:104-105 Jan '76

A twenty one jewel watch: Mutual logistic support in NATO. CDR Eugene F. Coughlin. illus Def Trans J 32:12-14+ Apr '76

U.S. preparation for the World Administrative Radio Conference 1979. Jack E. Weatherford. illus charts Signal 30:17-19 Apr '76

INTERNATIONAL CORPORATIONS see Corporations, International

INTERNATIONAL LAW

The Aegean Sea dispute. Capt Thomas J. McCormick, Jr. maps illus Mil Rev 56:90-96 Mar '76

Americans & overseas law. illus Comdrs Dig 19: entire issue Feb 12 '76

Civilian combat casualties: Our moral and legal responsibilities. Maj S.P. Mehl. illus MarCor Gaz 60:43-46 Oct '76

(Implications of the 3d Law of the Sea Conference) illus Def & For Aff Dig No. 5:28-29+ '76

International law and the Air Force. (Address, Society of International Law, New York, Oct 29, 1975) John L. McLucas. AF Law Rev 18:76-80 Summer '76

LOS (Law Of the Sea) '76: Constitution or chaos for the world's oceans? New York meeting may be last chance for a world Law of the Sea Treaty. Merle Macbain. illus Sea Power 19:14-19 Mar '76

The law of the sea: An analysis of the scientific justifications for boundary extensions in South America. Capt Donald G. Rehkopf, Jr. AF Law Rev 18: 35-56 Summer '76

Legitimated interposition and international law: Accepted violations of the law of nations. Capt Burrus M. Carnahan. AF Law Rev 17:79-84 Winter '75

New LOS (Law Of the Sea) conference: The U.N.'s final try? Sea Power 19:9-11 Dec '76

The possible effects on maritime operations of any future convention of the law of the sea. Adm Edward Ashmore. illus Nav War Col Rev 29:3-11 Fall '76

Punishment of aerial piracy--a new development. Robert-Louis Perret. illus Interavia 31:545 Jun '76

A survey of the international law of naval blockade. Sally V. and W. Thomas Mallison, Jr. illus map US Nav Inst Proc 102:44-53 Feb '76

Tides and currents in the Pacific: Long-term maritime implications. ADM James L. Holloway III. illus Strat Rev 4:33-39 Summer '76

Study and Teaching

Crimes in hostilities. Maj W. Hays Parks. illus tab MarCor Gaz pt 1, 60:16-22 Aug '76; pt 2, 60:33-39 Sep '76

INTERNATIONAL LAW - Continued

Study and Teaching - Cont'd

Rules of war detailed in training package. AF Times 37:41 Nov 1 '76

INTERNATIONAL LOGISTICS NEGOTIATIONS see Arms Sales

INTERNATIONAL MONETARY FUND

Fetch the age of gold. A. Ranney Johnson. illus Def & For Aff Dig No. 8-9:74-77 '76

INTERNATIONAL POLITICS

An assessment of peace research. J. David Singer. Intl Sec 1:118-137 Summer '76

Capabilities and control in an interdependent world. James N. Rosenau. Intl Sec 1:32-49 Fall '76

Dangerous doctrine. G. Apalin. Soviet Mil Rev No. 1: 44-45 Jan '76

Military concepts for political óbjectives. LtCol Joel J. Snyder, Ret. illus AU Rev 27:55-62 Jan-Feb '76

A reconsideration of the domino theory. John Baylis. Royal Air Forces Qtr 15:277-287 Winter '75

Where do we go from here? CAPT John E. Green-backer, Ret. illus US Nav Inst Proc 102:18-24 Jun '76

INTERNATIONAL RELATIONS

See also subdivision Foreign Relations under names of countries

Africa strategy. Gregory Copley. illus Def & For Aff Dig No. 3:6-9+ '76

America's future: The third century. Barry M. Gold-water. illus Strat Rev 4:8-15 Winter '76

The balancing of L. I. Brezhnev. Lawrence Griswold. illus Sea Power 18:11-16 Dec '75

Dawn of freedom for Angola. M. Zenovich. illus Sovi-et Mil Rev No. 5:46-48 May '76

A forecast for the 70's and 80's. Anthony J. Wiener. Persp in Def Mgt No. 24:1-12 Winter '75-'76

Foreign policies at risk: Some problems of managing naval power. Ken Booth. illus Nav War Col Rev 29:3-15 Summer '76

France and Britain: European powers and members of NATO. Jean Houbert. Royal Air Forces Qtr 15:289-300+ Winter '75

The geostrategic triangle of North-East Asia. Niu Sien-chong. NATO's Fifteen Nations 21:68+ Aug-Sep '76

Helsinki and military détente. (Conference on Securi-ty and Cooperation in Europe) Col O. Ivanov. Sovi-et Mil Rev No. 8:44-46 Aug '76

Kissinger on the security of the democracies and East-West relations. (Excerpts from lecture, In-ternational Institute for Strategic Studies, London, June 25, 1976) Henry A. Kissinger. Intl Def Rev 9:533-535 Aug '76

Mission to Mecca: The cruise of the Murphy. (U.S. destroyer brings Arabian king from Mecca to Great Bitter Lake in Suez Canal, to meet with Pres Franklin Roosevelt after Yalta Conference, 1945, and deals successfully with seemingly un-surmountable problems, both diplomatic and prag-matic) CAPT John S. Keating, Ret. illus US Nav Inst Proc 102:54-63 Jan '76

INTERNATIONAL RELATIONS - Continued

NATO and détente. LtCol N. Chaldymov. illus Soviet Mil Rev No. 2:42-44 Feb '76

The National Guard in a changing world. Dana Adams Schmidt. illus tabs Natl Guardsman 30:8-12 Apr '76

New horizons of the peace programme. (25th CPSU Congress) Soviet Mil Rev No. 6:2-4 Jun '76

The Peace Programme (adopted by the 25th CPSU Congress, Feb 1976), a contribution to the weal of mankind. Y. Tarabrin. illus Soviet Mil Rev No. 3: 7-10 Mar '76

Problems of nuclear free zones--the Nordic exam-ple. LtCol Jay C. Mumford. illus Mil Rev 56:3-10 Mar '76

Resource control strategy. Anthony Harrigan. illus Natl Def 60:350-352 Mar-Apr '76

The scrambled geometry of the new Pacific: West of the Dateline and East of India. Lawrence Gris-wold. illus Sea Power 19:24-29 Apr '76

Sidelight on post-détente Southeast Asia. WgComdr Maharaj K. Chopra, Ret. Mil Rev 56:11-22 Mar '76

The South Atlantic: A new order emerging. Richard E. Bissell. illus Sea Power 19:11-13 Oct '76

South East Asia now. Brig F. W. Speed. Army Qtr 106:226-235 Apr '76

The thin bread line. David Harvey. illus Def & For Aff Dig No. 7:6-9+ '76

INTERNATIONAL SECURITY see Security, International

INTERPLANETARY FLIGHT see Space Flight
also space flights to specific planets. e. g.,
Space Flight to Mars
Space Flight to the Moon
Space Flight to Venus

INTERROGATION

The Luftwaffe's master interrogator (Hanns Scharff). Royal D. Frey. illus AF Mag 59:68-71 Jun '76

INTERSERVICE COOPERATION

AF, Navy look at sharing systems training data. AF Times 36:32 Feb 23 '76

(ADM) Holloway/(Gen) Jones cooperation pact raises difficult questions. L. Edgar Prina. illus Sea Power 19:34-36 Jan '76

Air-Land Forces Application (ALFA). Air Def Mag, p 37, Apr-Jun '76

Air transport in the northern provinces (of South Vietnam). Col Ray L. Bowers. illus MarCor Gaz 60:39-49 Jun '76

Airlift problems pose threat to our security. Edito-rial. Officer 52:6+ Jan '76

Another Army "Navy" game (Azores). SSgt Virgil L. Laning. illus Translog 7:16-20 Jan '76

A bluewater interface and the Running Mates pro-gram: Navy/Merchant Marine officer exchange program offers benefits to each. James D. Hess-man. illus Sea Power 19:20-22 Jun '76

Collateral mission support (agreement between U.S. Navy and Air Force): An economic and operational necessity. LCDR Brent Baker. illus US Nav Inst Proc 102:93-95 Feb '76

INTERSERVICE COOPERATION - Continued

Combined Army and Navy operations. Capt G. Ammon. illus Soviet Mil Rev No. 3:48-50 Mar '76

Drug smuggling in Bangkok: AF-Army team helps crack ring. AF Times 36:39 Apr 12 '76

Float like a dandelion. (AF 7th Weather Sq, Operating Location C, trains with 1st Battalion, 10th Special Forces Gp, at Bad Toelz, Germany) MSgt Harold Newcomb. illus Airman 20:2-6 Mar '76

Helicopters and land force tactics. Col M. Belov. illus Soviet Mil Rev No. 12:22-24 Dec '76

Interservice navigator training at Mather (AFB, Calif). Capt Hector M. Acosta. illus Navigator 23:27-28 Summer '76

Interservice Training (AFR 50-18). TIG Brief 28:15 Mar 26 '76

Joint Logistics Commanders: Interservice cooperation improves support. Marvin Wilson, Jr. Army Log 18:14-15 Mar-Apr '76

The Joint Warfare Establishment. AVM F.S.S. Hazlewood. (Reprinted from Royal Air Forces Quarterly, Autumn 1975) Army Qtr 106:161-170 Apr '76

The Marines are looking for a few good navigators. Capt Daniel O. Pyne. illus Navigator 23:29-30 Summer '76

Meeting the Russian threat. LtGen Ira C. Eaker, Ret. AF Times 37:17-18 Sep 6 '76

Merged pilot training pushed (by Defense Manpower Commission). AF Times 36:3 May 3 '76

Needed: A new family of EW systems. Edgar Ulsamer. illus AF Mag 59:27-31 Feb '76

A new look at control of the seas. MajGen Robert N. Ginsburgh, Ret. Strat Rev 4:86-89 Winter '76

Pact expands AF role in backing Navy in war. AF Times 36:26 Apr 12 '76

Paying only your fair share. (Joint Utility Service Boards (JUSBs)) Leon E. McDuff. illus AF Engrg & Svcs Qtr 17:35-37 Aug '76

A "remotely nearby" test facility (Hill/Wendover/ Dugway (H/W/D) Test Range Complex, Utah). Col Alfred L. Atwell. illus map Log Spectrum 10: 7-12+ Winter '76

Santa Fe/TI: 'The core issue'--new report (by the Transportation Institute) recommends increased Navy/Merchant Marine cooperation and coordination. James D. Hessman. illus tab Sea Power 19: 15-16 Jul '76

Single Medical Corps urged. Interview. VADM Donald L. Custis. AF Times 36:16 Jun 7 '76

Tac air, member of the (combined arms) team supporting the supersoldier. LtCol William H. Rees. illus Infantry 66:16-23 May-Jun '76

"Thanks, tank(er crew)." L.I. Wilson. illus Aerosp Hist 23:65-70 Jun '76

Token minority. (Army instructors at other Service academies) Darryl D. McEwen. illus Soldiers 31: 52-53 Aug '76

The unsung art of sharing shortages. (Joint Logistics Commanders (JLC)) C.W. Borklund. illus Govt Exec 8:19-20+ Apr '76

INTERSTATE COMMERCE COMMISSION

Regulatory agencies: Are they promoters or inhibitors to intermodalism. C. Everhard. Def Trans J 32:22-26 Aug '76

Shipper support ... and how to get it. Herbert Paige. Translog 7:16-18 Feb '76

INTERVENTION

Cuba: Russia's foreign legion. Col Robert Debs Heinl, Jr, Ret. illus Sea Power 19:44-45 Mar '76

"Farewell the tranquil mind": Security and stability in the post-Vietnam era. Col Lloyd J. Matthews. illus map Parameters 5, No.2:2-13 '76

Soviet airborne forces: Increasingly powerful factor in the equation. Graham H. Turbiville. illus Army 26:18-24+ Apr '76

The Soviet intervention in Angola: Intentions and implications. Peter Vanneman and Martin James. tabs Strat Rev 4:92-103 Summer '76

Vietnam intervention: Systematic distortion in policymaking. Jeffrey Race. Armed Forces & Soc 2: 377-396 Spring '76

INVENTORIES

Army stock fund: A friend indeed. Raymond R. Nelson. Army Log 8:32-33 Nov-Dec '76

Army stock fund: Friend or foe. Col John R. Brinton. illus tab Army Log 8:2-5 Mar-Apr '76

Fourth generation field support. (Address, Long Island Chapter SOLE Symposium, Long Island, NY, May 12, 1976) Michael D. Basch. illus tabs Log Spectrum 10:17-20 Winter '76

Management of medical (materiel) excesses. TIG Brief 28:6 Mar 12 '76

New inventory analysis techniques. James J. Eder. illus Log Spectrum 10:29-33 Fall '76

Preparation of 463L pallet and net control report. TIG Brief 28:11 Mar 12 '76

Quarterly inventory of precious metal records. TIG Brief 28:10 Jul 16 '76

Stockpile Emergency Verification (SEV). TIG Brief 28:8 Jun 18 '76

Supplemental inventory research checklist. TIG Brief 28:4 Nov 5 '76

INVESTMENTS

(Air Force) Academy Athletic Association: Investment losses held high. Andy Plattner. AF Times 36:29 May 17 '76

(Conference on Capital Investment in Transportation (NDTA-sponsored), Chicago, March 11, 1976) reports on outlook. illus Def Trans J 32:38-39+ Apr '76

Investing for beginners: 'Low risk' investing for a little profit vs 'high risk' investing for a big profit. Don G. Campbell. illus tab AF Times, Times Magazine sup:6-9 Nov 29 '76

ION PROPULSION

Ion engines from Farnborough. Robert Edgar. illus tab Spaceflight 18:144-145 Apr '76

IONOSPHERE see Atmosphere, Upper

JUMPS see Joint Uniform Military Pay System

JACKSON, Henry M.

Senator Jackson declassifies Schlesinger SALT testimony, awaits Kissinger reply to August letter (concerning Soviet deployment of the SS-19 missile). Armed Forces J Intl 113:8 Jan '76

JACKSONVILLE, FLA

Jacksonville (Fla): Consolidation is no panacea. illus chart Govt Exec 8:24-26+ Nov '76

JAMES, Daniel, Jr

Aerospace defense. (Remarks, American Defense Preparedness Assoc, Los Angeles, Oct 15, 1975) Gen Daniel James, Jr. AF Plcy Ltr for Comdrs: Sup No.1:2-10 Jan '76; Condensation. Natl Def 60: 289 Jan-Feb '76

Aerospace Defense Command. por AF Mag 59:54-55 May '76

JAPAN

Economic Conditions

Is Japan on the way to super-power status? Niu Sien-chong. NATO's Fifteen Nations 20:34-39 Dec '75-Jan '76

Foreign Policy

The geostrategic triangle of North-East Asia. Niu Sien-chong. NATO's Fifteen Nations 21:68+ Aug-Sep '76

Is Japan on the way to super-power status? Niu Sien-chong. NATO's Fifteen Nations 20:34-39 Dec '75-Jan '76

Japan: Another threat. Brig F.W.Speed. Army Qtr 106:483-487 Oct '76

U.S. policy alternatives in Asia. Robert A.Scalapino. illus Parameters 5, No.2:14-24 '76

Foreign Relations

Korea

Japan's security interests in Korea. Nathan White. (Digested from Asian Survey, April 1976) Mil Rev 56:28-35 Nov '76

History

Japan: Another threat. Brig F.W.Speed. Army Qtr 106:483-487 Oct '76

Strategic Importance

Asia. Philip Paisley and Leigh Johnson. illus tab Def & For Aff Dig No.5:18-19+ '76

Is Japan on the way to super-power status? Niu Sien-chong. NATO's Fifteen Nations 20:34-39 Dec '75-Jan '76

JEFFERSON, Thomas

Economy before preparedness. (Jefferson's policy) Forrest C.Pogue. Def Mgt J 12:14-18 Jul '76

JET ENGINES

See also
Gas Turbines (Aircraft)

CFM56 engine still looking for an aircraft. Michael Brown. illus tabs Interavia 31:847-849 Sep '76

JET ENGINES - Continued

Civil transport technology up to 2000; NASA believes fuel consumption is the major consideration. J.Philip Geddes. illus tabs Interavia 31:419-421 May '76

Hurricane in a barrel. LtCol Robert J.Brun. illus Aerosp Safety 32:24-25 May '76

A problem with ice. (Engine inlet icing) LtCol Charles R.Barr. illus Aerosp Safety 32:26-27 Mar '76

Quiet and efficient (jet) engines for tomorrow. Richard S.Page. illus Aerosp Intl 12:12-13+ Jan-Feb '76

Rolls-Royce pushing for RB.211 orders. illus tabs Interavia 31:177-180 Feb '76

Rolls-Royce status report. Derek Wood. illus Interavia 31:804 Sep '76

SNECMA M.53 status report. Marc Grangier. illus Interavia 31:409 May '76

The TFE731 (turbofan engine) goes from strength to strength. illus tabs Interavia 31:18 Jan '76

Ten-ton (jet engine) competition. Mark E.Berent. tab illus Aerosp Intl 12:36+ Jul-Aug '76

Characteristics

Jane's All the World's Aircraft Supplement. Regular feature in issues of Aerospace International; some issues of Air Force Magazine

Quiet and efficient (jet) engines for tomorrow. Richard S.Page. illus Aerosp Intl 12:12-13+ Jan-Feb '76

Maintenance and Repair

Engine inflight monitoring. LtCol James L.Pettigrew and CMSgt Robert M.McCord. illus tabs Combat Crew 27:8-13 Jul '76

Starters

Be prepared! SqLdr Mark Perrett. Aerosp Safety 32:3 Jan '76

JOB ANALYSIS

Job enrichment--Ogden (Air Logistics Center) style. MajGen Edmund A.Rafalko. illus tabs AU Rev 28: 46-53 Nov-Dec '76

JOHANSEN, Eivind H.

A commander speaks to his aviators on aviation safety. MajGen Eivind H.Johansen. por USA Avn Dig 22:2-4 Nov '76

JOHNSON, John B.

Naval Reserve cuts threaten all Reserves. RADM John Johnson. Officer 52:16-17 Mar '76

1975 events, 1976 portents pose serious challenges to (Navy) Reservists. RADM John B.Johnson. por Officer 52:20-21+ Feb '76

JOHNSON, Lyndon B.

AFJ's bum dope on LBJ's farewell. Col John G. Jameson, Jr. por Armed Forces J Intl 113:20-21 Apr '76

The day the President got conned: (Lyndon Johnson) saying goodbye to the wrong troops (at Fort Bragg, NC, Feb 16, 1968). Benjamin F.Schemmer. por Armed Forces J Intl 113:26-28 Feb '76

JOHNSON SPACE CENTER see Lyndon B. Johnson Space
Center

JOHNSTON, Means, Jr

The southern flank of NATO: Problems of the south-
ern region in the post-1973 October War period.
ADM Means Johnston, Jr. Mil Rev 56:22-29
Apr '76

JOINT CHIEFS OF STAFF

Joint Chiefs. Photo only. AF Times 36:16 Mar 1 '76

Narrow vote confirms JCS chief (Gen George Brown)
for 2d term. illus AF Times 36:26 Jul 19 '76

JOINT FORCES

This term applies to forces of one country only. For
information on forces of two or more allied countries
see Combined Forces.

Great Britain

The Joint Warfare Establishment. AVM F. S. S. Hazlewood. (Reprinted from Royal Air Forces Quarterly, Autumn 1975) Army Qtr 106:161-170 Apr '76

JOINT OPERATIONS

This term applies to operations of one country only.
For information on operations of two or more allied
countries see Combined Operations.
See also specific exercises and/or operations by
name.

Ammo supply in rapid deployment. LtCol Robert P.
Jones. illus Army Log 8:30-32 Jan-Feb '76

Bold Eagle '76. illus USAF Ftr Wpns Rev, p 17,
Spring '76

Brave Shield XIII. LtCol Don Rosenkranz. illus Air
Reservist 27:8-9 Feb '76

Brave Shield XIV. illus Air Reservist 28:6 Oct '76

Brave Shield XV. AF Times 37:33 Oct 18 '76

Exercise Bold Eagle (76). AF Times 36:31 Mar 1 '76

Exercise Brave Shield. AF Times 37:31 Sep 20 '76

14,000 taking part in Alaska Exercise Jack Frost.
illus AF Times 36:38 Feb 2 '76

Hell on wheels. (Air Force and Army's 2d Armored
Division (Brigade 75) train in West Germany for
NATO support) MSgt Harold D. Newcomb. illus
Airman 20:8-12 Apr '76

Joint ops: An exercise in frustration. Capt J. T. Reynolds. illus Aerosp Safety 32:16-19 Oct '76

A "real world" transportation challenge: Exercise
Bold Eagle '76. Maj Eldon T. Rippee. illus Translog 7:2-6 May '76

Tiny craft play big role in drill (Exercise Solid
Shield). illus AF Times 36:31 Jun 7 '76

What is aerospace doctrine? AF Plcy Ltr for Comdrs:
Sup No. 1:29-30 Jan '76

Study and Teaching

The Joint Warfare Establishment. AVM F. S. S. Hazlewood. (Reprinted from Royal Air Forces Quarterly, Autumn 1975) Army Qtr 106:161-170 Apr '76

JOINT UNIFORM MILITARY PAY SYSTEM

Air Force JUMPS--the payoff is now! Cols James D.
Suver, Ret and Ray L. Brown, Ret. AF Compt 10:
32-33 Jul '76

Validating basic pay for medical officers. TIG Brief
28:17 Apr 9 '76

JONES, David C.

(ADM) Holloway/(Gen) Jones cooperation pact raises
difficult questions. L. Edgar Prina. Sea Power 19:
34-36 Jan '76

JONES, David C. - Continued

Air Chief tells aides B-1 is vital. por Officer 52:18
May '76

Air Force Chief of Staff's FY 1977 Posture State-
ment. (Statement before House Committee on
Armed Services, Washington, Jan 29, 1976) Gen
David C. Jones. AF Plcy Ltr for Comdrs: Sup
No. 3:23-40 Mar '76

Bending the Chief's ear. (AF Personnel Management
Teams (PMT Air Staff teams) discuss the AF life
with members, and then work with the Chief of
Staff to solve problems) MSgt Fred Harrison.
Airman 20:36-37 Jan '76

The cutting edge: Combat capability. Gen David C.
Jones. por AF Mag 59:48-50+ May '76

Jones on records of officers--Regulars 'generally
better.' Lee Ewing. AF Times 36:3 Mar 1 '76

(Military) 'Bill of Rights' backed to protect benefits;
(Gen) Jones warns on Soviets (at Air Force Assoc
National Convention, Washington, Sep 19-22,
1976). Lee Ewing. por AF Times 37:21 Oct 4 '76

No new officer RIF this FY (according to Chief of
Staff, Gen David C.) Jones. Lee Ewing. AF Times
36:2 Feb 16 '76

Setting reasonable rules. Interview. Gen David C.
Jones. por AF Times 36:4 May 3 '76

Soviet threat and national strategic choices. (Remarks, Air Force Assoc luncheon, Washington,
Sep 21, 1976) Gen David C. Jones. AF Plcy Ltr
for Comdrs: Sup No. 11:8-13 Nov '76

The Soviet threat and U.S. strategic alternatives.
(Address, AFA National Convention, Washington,
Sep 19-23, 1976) Gen David C. Jones. por AF Mag
59:38-41 Nov '76

Teams get out and talk to troops in keeping with
Jones' policy. Lee Ewing. AF Times 36:12+
May 3 '76

Training (cost-reducing) study ordered by C/S. AF
Times 36:2 May 31 '76

JUDGE ADVOCATE GENERAL

Air Force

Appearance of Air Force personnel as expert witnesses. TIG Brief 28:21 Dec 17 '76

JAG (MajGen Harold R. Vague) allows attorneys some
off-duty practice. AF Times 37:2 Oct 4 '76

Medical aspects of third party liability. TIG Brief
28:10 Feb 27 '76

When the law's at your door. (The JAG's office at
Plattsburg AFB, NY, tries to keep the commu-
nity advised of legal services available) Capt John
B. Taylor. illus Airman 20:32-34 Jun '76

JUDGES

Challenging the military judge for cause. Maj Ludolf
R. Kuhnell. AF Law Rev 17:50-64 Winter '75

The waiver doctrine: Is it still viable? Maj John E.
Hilliard. AF Law Rev 18:45-62 Spring '76

JUDICIAL SYSTEMS see Courts

JUPITER (PLANET)

Discovering Jupiter. (Jupiter Science Symposium,
NASA's Ames Research Center, Mountain View,
Calif, 1976) illus tabs Spaceflight pt 1, 18:438-
447 Dec '76

K

KOREAN WAR, 1950-1953 - Continued

Campaigns and Battles

Operation Chromite: A study of generalship. (Korea, 1950) Capt James P.Totten. illus Armor 85:33-38 Nov-Dec '76

Naval Operations, American

First through the Suez Canal. (Marines travel 8200 miles from Mediterranean to Kobe, Japan, then to land on Inchon, 1950) Col Maurice E.Roach, Ret. MarCor Gaz 60:46-48 Aug '76

Peace and Mediation

The 1953 cease-fire in Korea. James H. Toner. illus Mil Rev 56:3-13 Jul '76

KOSYGIN, Aleksei N.

Grand construction programme. (Excerpt from report to the 25th CPSU Congress, "Guidelines for the Development of the National Economy of the USSR for 1976-1980") A. N. Kosygin. Soviet Mil Rev No. 5:2-4 May '76

KRULAK, Victor H.

Panama: Strategic pitfall. LtGen V.H.Krulak, Ret. Strat Rev 4:68-71 Winter '76

KUHNELL, Ludolf R., III

Challenging the military judge for cause. Maj Ludolf R. Kuhnell. AF Law Rev 17:50-64 Winter '75

LABOR-MANAGEMENT RELATIONS

United States

Adversary partnership: Trends in labor-management relations. Thomas Kennedy. Persp in Def Mgt No.24:57-67 Winter '75-'76

Is military unionization an idea whose time has come? LT John E.Kane and others. illus tab US Nav Inst Proc pt 1, 102:36-44 Nov '76; pt 2, 102: 24-28 Dec '76

Major changes in Federal labor-management relations program. TIG Brief 28:17-18 Mar 12 '76

LABOR SUPPLY see Manpower

LABOR UNIONS

See also
Military Unions

Adversary partnership: Trends in labor-management relations. Thomas Kennedy. Persp in Def Mgt No.24:57-67 Winter '75-'76

A conversation with Paul Hall (President of the Seafarers International Union of North America): Maritime labor--the ally within. Interview. illus Sea Power 19:11-16 Feb '76

(David P.) Taylor says unions have little chance. AF Times 37:26 Nov 1 '76

Federal wage regulations and service contracts. Capt Derrick R.Franck. AF Law Rev 18:17-34 Summer '76

Major changes in Federal labor-management relations program. TIG Brief 28:17-18 Mar 12 '76

The military and labor union organizations in Germany. Bernhard Fleckenstein. Armed Forces & Soc 2:495-515 Summer '76

Own labor group (within the American Federation of Government Employees) seen for military: No early recruiting expected. AF Times 37:6 Nov 29 '76

Sticky court suit could affect raise (for civilian workers and the military). AF Times 36:2 Jan 19 '76

Union (American Federation of Government Employees) to accept military. AF Times 37:3 Oct 4 '76

Union (American Federation of Government Employees) weighs military drive. Lee Ewing. AF Times 37:2 Oct 11 '76

Union (American Federation of Government Employees) won't act till at least Feb. Lee Ewing. AF Times 37:4 Dec 20 '76

Union's (American Federation of Government Employees) chiefs want military. Lee Ewing. AF Times 36:3 Jun 28 '76

LABORATORIES

See also specific types of laboratories, e.g., Aeronautical Laboratories also laboratories by name, e.g., Air Force Avionics Laboratory Air Force Weapons Laboratory Army Aeromedical Research Laboratory Naval Research Laboratory

Optical exposure--a look at the horizon. (Refinement in laser technology at Army's Harry Diamond Laboratories) Steve Kimmel. illus USA Avn Dig 22: 24-27 Nov '76

LABORATORIES - Continued

Shipment of samples to USAF Environmental and Radiological Health labs. TIG Brief 28:12 Nov 5 '76

Solution seeks a problem. (Army's Harry Diamond Labs conduct research on use of lasers in optical fuzes, target designators, and other devices) Edward A.Brown. illus Natl Def 61:112-113 Sep-Oct '76

USAF Environmental Health and Radiological Health Laboratories. TIG Brief 28:19 Feb 13 '76

USAF's crusade to streamline industrial production. Edgar Ulsamer. illus AF Mag 59:62-67 Oct '76

The Waterways Experiment Station. LtCol Robert K. Hughes. illus Mil Engr 68:374-379 Sep-Oct '76

LAKE, Julian S.

Air EW--they have forgotten again! RADM Julian S. Lake III, Ret. Countermeasures 2:14+ Nov '76

Air electronic warfare. RADM Julian S.Lake, Ret and LCDR Richard V.Hartman, Ret. por US Nav Inst Proc 102:42-49 Oct '76

Design to price: An experiment in (electronic warfare) procurement. RADM Julian S.Lake III, Ret. Countermeasures 2:67-68 Nov '76

LAND BRIDGE see Railroads

LAND WARFARE

The Marine Corps in 1985. Peter A.Wilson. illus US Nav Inst Proc 102:31-38 Jan '76

The need for offensive operations on land. (Trench Gascoigne Prize Essay, 1975) Maj R.S.Evans. RUSI J for Def Studies 121:28-33 Sep '76

The nuclear land battle. Col Marc Geneste, Ret. illus Strat Rev 4:79-85 Winter '76

LANDING CRAFT

A battalion in a seaborne landing. Col A.Akimov. illus maps Soviet Mil Rev No.3:22-24 Mar '76

LVA (Landing Vehicles Assault) project underway. illus MarCor Gaz 60:6 Mar '76

LANDING GEAR see Airplanes, Military--Landing Gear

LANDING OPERATIONS see Amphibious Operations

LANDS, PUBLIC see Property, Government

LANGUAGE AND LANGUAGES

In defense of language standards. Argus J.Tresidder. MarCor Gaz 60:51-56 Apr '76

"Interoperability"--the now challenge in Europe. Maj Gary F.Ramage. illus USA Avn Dig 22:26-29 Aug '76

KIA: The English language; or, the only thing we have to fear is obfuscation itself. W.J.Farquharson. illus tab AF Times, Times Magazine sup: 26-27 Feb 9 '76

Study and Teaching

Back to basics II: The ability to communicate. (Address, National Council of Teachers of English, Philadelphia, March 25, 1976) Charles R.Cyr. (Reprinted from Vital Speeches, Sep 15, 1976) Educ J 19:29-33 Winter '76

LAWS AND LEGISLATION

Can patients die natural death? (California law) AF Times 37:2 Dec 6 '76

The Congressional Budget Office: The logistics of budget, program, and finance. Ronald G.Bishop. illus tab charts Log Spectrum 10:26-32 Winter '76

Consumer Product Safety Act: Working to protect you. TIG Brief 28:9 Apr 9 '76

Evolution of a law: (National Guard Assoc of) Illinois grass-roots effort succeeds (providing enlisted Illinois Guardsmen with scholarships to state colleges and universities). illus Natl Guardsman 30: 14-15 Feb '76

The Freedom of Information Act: An analysis. Review 55:17+ Nov-Dec '75

Law to increase (civilian) housing (around military bases) never used. AF Times 36:4 Mar 29 '76

Legislative actions include many veterans bills. Officer 52:8-9 Aug '76

New (Federal income) tax reform law: A few quirks. Randy Shoemaker. AF Times 37:3 Oct 18 '76

Newest Veterans Housing Act provides variety of new, liberalized benefits. Officer 52:12 Jan '76

94th Congress is history--many last-minute actions affect Reserves. Officer 52:12-13+ Dec '76

Pay changes on 'plus side.' Bruce Callander. illus AF Times 37:21 Nov 1 '76

President signs law; GI Bill benefits increased. MarCor Gaz 60:3 Dec '76

Status of legislation (of interest to Service personnel). Table only. AF Times 36:22 Apr 12 '76

U.S. arms sales: Congress steps on the brake. Henry T.Simmons. illus Interavia 31:987-988 Oct '76

The U.S. goes metric. H.R.Kaplan. illus tab Review 55:33-37 Jan-Feb '76

The week in Congress. Regular feature in some issues of Air Force Times

What the 50,000 call-up bill means to you (Reserves). Officer 52:5 Feb '76

LAWYERS

JAG (MajGen Harold R.Vague) allows attorneys some off-duty practice. AF Times 37:2 Oct 4 '76

The military defense counsel's use of scientific evidence and expert witnesses. Maj William M. McKenna III. AF Law Rev 18:48-65 Fall '76

Right to counsel tossed out (by Supreme Court). AF Times 36:8 Apr 5 '76

The waiver doctrine: Is it still viable? Maj John E. Hilliard. AF Law Rev 18:45-62 Spring '76

LAYTON, Edwin T.

24 Sentai--Japan's commerce raiders. RADM Edwin T.Layton, Ret. por US Nav Inst Proc 102:53-61 Jun '76

LEADERSHIP

See also
Command

Alienation and participation: A replication comparing leaders and the "mass." D.Duane Braun. tabs J Pol & Mil Sociol 4:245-259 Fall '76

LEADERSHIP - Continued

Assessing the Assessment Center: New dimensions in leadership. Maj Peter Henderson. illus AU Rev 27:47-54 May-Jun '76

Cohesion and disintegration in the American Army (in Vietnam): An alternative perspective. Paul L. Savage and Richard A.Gabriel. tabs Armed Forces & Soc 2:340-376 Spring '76

Commander and leader: The Army officer as meritocrat. Dennis E.Showalter. illus Mil Rev 56:80-89 Nov '76

The commander's creative activity. LtGen L.Kuznetsov. Soviet Mil Rev No.8:16-18 Aug '76

Commander's independent actions. Col L.Yeremeyev. Soviet Mil Rev No.10:34-35 Oct '76

Dissidence is not a virtue. ADM Arleigh A.Burke, Ret. illus US Nav Inst Proc 102:78-79 Apr '76

Do Americans understand democracy? Henry F. Graff. Persp in Def Mgt No.24:69-77 Winter '75-'76

A fifty-yard line view of leadership. (Remarks, Graduation Ceremonies of the Strategic Air Command Noncommissioned Officer Academy, Barksdale AFB, La, Sep 24, 1976) LtGen Bryan M. Shotts. AF Plcy Ltr for Comdrs: Sup No.12:22-27 Dec '76

How a manager gets the job done: Leadership, the common thread. (Remarks, 27th Industrial Engineering Conference for Management and Supervision, West Virginia University, Morgantown, April 5, 1976) MajGen Frank J.Simokaitis. AF Plcy Ltr for Comdrs: Sup No.6:22-25 Jun '76

The Infantry leader: Mentally tough. illus Infantry 66:30-32 Jan-Feb '76

The Infantry leader: Physically fit. LtCol Robert B. Simpson. illus Infantry 66:27-29 Jan-Feb '76

The Infantry leader: Spiritually aware. Ch(Maj) Walter C.Tucker. illus Infantry 66:33-36 Jan-Feb '76

The Infantry leader: Tactically and technically proficient. illus Infantry 66:20-26 Jan-Feb '76

Influence of technology upon leadership. LT A.M. Petruska. illus US Nav Inst Proc 102:64-67 Aug '76

Introspection (on professional development)--and some reflections on the way it was. Col Gustav J. Gillert, Jr. illus Mil Rev 56:36-41 Nov '76

Leadership. TIG Brief 28:13 Nov '76

A leadership action plan. CDR Robert C.Powers. illus US Nav Inst Proc 102:72-74 Feb '76

Leadership failures. Maj M.T.Hopgood, Jr. illus MarCor Gaz 60:23-30 Aug '76

Leadership: The theory behind the principles. Maj Thomas U.Wall. illus US Nav Inst Proc 102:72-77 Dec '76

Managerial styles. LtCol Merrell E.Dean. illus AU Rev 27:41-46 Mar-Apr '76

Military leadership. Capt E.F.Carlson. (Reprinted from US Nav Inst Proc, Nov 1937) illus US Nav Inst Proc 102:66 Jan '76

The navigator: An inflight commander. Capt Michael A.Niziol. illus Navigator 23:22-23 Summer '76

New leadership for a new Air Force. Col Harold P. Knutty. illus AU Rev 27:78-84 Jan-Feb '76

Outcomes, essences, and individuals. LT Thomas B. Grassey. illus US Nav Inst Proc 102:72-75 Jul '76

LEADERSHIP - Continued

Paper prisons. (Prize Essay, 1976) 1stLt Lawrence P. Hebron. illus US Nav Inst Proc 102:76-78 Jun '76

The people mix. Maj James M. Alford. AU Rev 27: 72-74 May-Jun '76

Responding to HumRel. 2dLt Andrew J. Franklin. MarCor Gaz 60:70-71 May '76

Self-discipline and standards: A commitment to excellence. (Programs at Florida State University) Capt Richard A. Zucker. Educ J 19:11-12 Winter '76

Small unit leader. CSGM W.J.Cronin. Infantry 66: 50-51 Jan-Feb '76

Spirit of America. (Remarks, Commissioning Ceremonies, Texas A&M, Dec 13, 1975) LtGen John W. Roberts. AF Plcy Ltr for Comdrs: Sup No. 4: 21-25 Apr '76

The squad. (From desk to squad duty for a few days, by request, to become a better leader) Col Dandridge M. Malone. illus Army 26:12-16+ Feb '76

Turn-on to life. (Pro Life program at Fort Dix, NJ) SSgt Zack Richards. illus Soldiers 31:18-20 Sep '76

U.S. Army Europe ... 'Sense of excitement.' Interview. Gen George S. Blanchard. illus Army 26:13+ Aug '76

War and peace and promotion. Capt Peter D. Weddle. illus Army 26:24-28 Jun '76

What is a good leader? Capt Eddie J. Miles, Jr. Educ J 19:27-28 Winter '76

Why America needs a ruling class: Common men don't make uncommon leaders. CAPT Jack Caldwell, Ret. illus AF Times, Times Magazine sup:10-12 Jun 28 '76

Study and Teaching

Air Force Air University adds new units (USAF Leadership and Management Development Center, located at Maxwell AFB, Ala, and the Air Force Logistics Management Center, located at Gunter AFS, Ala). Review 55:9 Nov-Dec '75

Air University gets two new units (USAF Leadership and Management Development Center, Maxwell AFB, Ala, and Air Force Logistics Management Center, Gunter AFS, Ala). Contact, p 6, Winter '76

Assessing the Assessment Center: New dimensions in leadership. Maj Peter Henderson. illus AU Rev 27:47-54 May-Jun '76

E-4s' teachers begin training (at Leadership and Management Development Center, Maxwell AFB, Ala). Len Famiglietti. AF Times 36:2 Mar 8 '76

Force-fed human relations. Capt J.P.Sureau. MarCor Gaz 60:50-51 Sep '76

Forging the future force (at Squadron Officer School). Ted R.Sturm. illus Airman 20:18-22 Mar '76

Leadership program lacking. Capt Robert MacPherson. MarCor Gaz 60:48-50 Feb '76

The lessons were not just military: What the Army taught me. Charles R.Murrah. Army 26:32-33 Nov '76

NCO (Leadership) School (Langley AFB, Va) trains professionals. SSgt Linda Henggeler. AF Times 36:37 Jul 12 '76

LEADERSHIP - Continued

Study and Teaching - Cont'd

New Air University units (USAF Leadership and Management Development Center, Maxwell AFB, Ala, and Air Force Logistics Management Center, Gunter AFS, Ala). AF Pley Ltr for Comdrs: Sup No. 2:26 Feb '76

The psychology of enthusiasm. Maj Gerald A. Fabisch. Educ J 19:34-35 Fall '76

LEARNING

How to study and take tests. Gen Bruce C.Clarke, Ret. illus Soldiers 31:31-33 Apr '76

LEARNING CENTERS see Instructional Materials Centers

LEAVE, MILITARY

Emergency leave orders for oversea travel. TIG Brief 28:15-16 Dec 3 '76

Expensive, cheap leave tallied. AF Times 37:27 Nov 1 '76

Leave selling curbed; DOD bill stalls. AF Times 36:9 Jan 5 '76

Leave selling faces $ cut: Congress eyes 45-day limit. Phil Stevens. AF Times 36:3 Apr 5 '76

Leave selling: New wrinkles. AF Times 37:4 Aug 23 '76

No easing of leave-selling in sight. AF Times 36:3 Mar 15 '76

Oct 1 change simplifies leave request procedure. AF Times 36:30 Jun 21 '76

Policy allows sale of excess leave. AF Times 37:8 Sep 6 '76

(Pres) Ford signs $104 billion defense bill. AF Times 37:9 Oct 4 '76

Waiting to cash in leave could save $. AF Times 37:31 Aug 30 '76

LEBANON

Linkage politics and coercive diplomacy: A comparative analysis of two Lebanese crises. Paul H.B. Godwin and Lewis B. Ware. illus AU Rev 28:80-89 Nov-Dec '76

U.S. intervention in Lebanon, 1958. LtCol Margaret M.Bodron. illus Mil Rev 56:66-76 Feb '76

Foreign Policy

Linkage politics and coercive diplomacy: A comparative analysis of two Lebanese crises. Paul H.B. Godwin and Lewis B.Ware. illus AU Rev 28:80-89 Nov-Dec '76

LEGAL AID

See also
Lawyers

Bill would ensure legal aid. AF Times 36:4 Jun 7 '76

When the law's at your door. (The JAG's office at Plattsburg AFB, NY, tries to keep the community advised of legal services available) Capt John B.Taylor. illus Airman 20:32-34 Jun '76

LEGION OF MERIT

(BrigGen Albert G.Peterson, president of ROA, retires from the active Reserve, receives Legion of Merit) illus Officer 52:14 May '76

LEGISLATION see Laws and Legislation

LENIN, Vladimir I.

Clausewitz and Soviet politico-military strategy.
BrigGen Antonio Pelliccia. NATO's Fifteen Nations 20:18-21+ Dec '75-Jan '76; Digest. Mil Rev
56:23-33 Aug '76

Force of Lenin's ideas. LtCol V. Amelchenko. Soviet
Mil Rev No.3:2-4 Mar '76

Moving pages. (Visitors Book in the Kremlin Lenin
memorial museum) LtCol L. Rakovsky. por Soviet Mil Rev No.3:5-6 Mar '76

LETCHER, John S.

ABC's of getting promoted. BrigGen John S. Letcher,
Ret. MarCor Gaz 60:57-59 Apr '76

LEWIS RESEARCH CENTER

Lewis Research Center. Mike Howard. Spaceflight
18:142-143 Apr '76

LIABILITY

(Air, Army) Guard, agencies (NASA and CIA) ask
malpractice protection. Ann Gerow. AF Times
36:26 Mar 15 '76

Malpractice bill appears stalled. AF Times 37:27
Sep 13 '76

Malpractice bill would aid Guard; no shift in filing
malpractice suits. AF Times 37:8 Oct 11 '76

Medical aspects of third party liability. TIG Brief
28:10 Feb 27 '76

Personal liability for official acts. LtCol Garrett W.
Palmer. AF Law Rev 18:85-100 Fall '76

LIAISON

USAFA (U.S. Air Force Academy)'s liaison officers.
illus AF Mag 59:62-63 Jan '76

LIBRARIES

Air Force

(AF) libraries held vital to bases. AF Times 36:18
Mar 29 '76

Army

Field artilleryman's library (Morris Swett Library,
Army Field Artillery School, Fort Sill, Okla).
LtCol James H. Byrn. illus Fld Arty J 44:36-38
Mar-Apr '76

LIBYA

Foreign Relations

Russia

Soviet arms aid to Libya. Roger F. Pajak. illus Mil
Rev 56:82-87 Jul '76

LIDDELL HART, Basil H.

Basil Liddell Hart: Much to say to the 'Army of '76.'
MajGen George B. Pickett, Jr, Ret. por Army 26:
29-33 Apr '76

Liddell Hart's influence on Israeli military theory
and practice. Brian Bond. RUSI J for Def Studies
121:83-89 Jun '76

LIFE AND DEATH

Can patients die natural death? (California law) AF
Times 37:2 Dec 6 '76

LIFE CYCLE COSTING see Cost Effectiveness

LIFE INSURANCE see Insurance, Life

LIFE ON OTHER PLANETS see Extraterrestrial Life

LIGHT

Effect of pre-adapting spectral stimuli on visual responses. Gloria Twine Chisum. illus tabs Aviation, Space & Envmt Med 47:739-745 Jul '76

How high the moon--how bright the night? Garvin L.
Holman. illus tabs USA Avn Dig 22:6-9+ Sep '76

What is a laser? illus Natl Def 61:106-107 Sep-
Oct '76

LIGHT AIRBORNE MULTI-PURPOSE SYSTEM see
Helicopter Type--SH-2

LIGHTERS see Barges

LIGHTING

See also
Airplanes, Military--Lighting
Airports--Landing Aids
Helicopters, Military--Lighting

New approaches to office design. illus AF Engrg &
Svcs Qtr 17:6-10 Feb '76

Night aircraft maintenance. Maj Ted A. Cimral and
Capt L. Allyn Noel. illus USA Avn Dig 22:8-10
Apr '76

Night flying without feathers. Capt Glenn Wendt.
Interceptor 18:14-15 Jun '76

Night tactical evaluation. Col John H. Weckerling.
illus Armor 85:45-46 May-Jun '76

The night the world died (at Clark AB, RP). illus Approach 22:6-7 Oct '76

Visibility--to land or not to land. Capt John L. Wilson. illus Combat Crew pt 1, 27:22-23 Aug '76;
pt 2, The runway environment. 27:18-20 Sep '76;
pt 3, The rules. 27:26-27 Oct '76; pt 4, Going visual. 27:20-21 Nov '76; pt 5, Techniques. 27:
14-15 Dec '76

LIGHTNING

No time to gamble. map illus Interceptor 18:5-9
May '76

LIGHTSHIPS

History

Destination nowhere: Twilight of the lightship. LT
Richard D. White, Jr. illus US Nav Inst Proc 102:
64-69 Mar '76

LIMITED WAR

Options in using nuclear weapons. (Remarks, Air
Force Assoc Symposium, Vandenberg AFB, Calif,
April 28, 1976) LtGen John W. Pauly. AF Plcy Ltr
for Comdrs: Sup No.10:15-23 Oct '76

U.S. on dangerous course. (Interview with Sidney D.
Drell) M.L. Craver. AF Times 37:11 Dec 27 '76

History

Force levels and limited war. Steven T. Ross. Nav
War Col Rev 28:91-96 Fall '75

LINCOLN, Abraham

A patient for Dr Leale. (Young Union Army surgeon attends dying Pres Lincoln after shooting at Ford's Theater) Donald C. Wright. Army 26:41-45 Aug '76

LINDBERGH, Charles A.

The search for Leon Klink (Lindbergh's barnstorming partner). Jack Keasler. por Am Avn Hist Soc J 21:92-100 Summer '76

LINK, Edwin A.

(Eight aviation pioneers (Clarence D. Chamberlin, John H. Glenn, Jr, George W. Goddard, Albert F. Hegenberger, Edwin A. Link, Sanford A. Moss, William A. Patterson, Nathan F. Twining) to be enshrined in Aviation Hall of Fame, July 24, 1976) por AF Mag 59:29-30 Jul '76

LISTENING

The art of listening. illus MAC Flyer 23:3-5 Oct '76

LOADING AND UNLOADING

See also
Airplanes, Military--Loading and Unloading
Ships--Loading and Unloading

Lifting device accidents. TIG Brief 28:9-10 Jan 16 '76

LOANS, HOME

GI housing loans still are available. Larry Carney. AF Times 37:6 Dec 6 '76

Newest Veterans Housing Act provides variety of new, liberalized benefits. Officer 52:12 Jan '76

Trailer, pension bills for vets move on Hill. AF Times 36:6 Jul 5 '76

LOENING, Grover C.

Memories of Grover Loening. Robert E. McMinn. por Aerosp Hist 23:202-206 Dec '76

LOGAIR

Shipment of samples to USAF Environmental and Radiological Health labs. TIG Brief 28:12 Nov 5 '76

LOGISTICS

See also
Integrated Logistic Support
Movement Control
Transportation, Military
also subdivision under specific wars, e.g.,
World War II--Logistics

The Annals of the Society of Logistics Engineers. Regular feature in some issues of Logistics Spectrum

Fourth generation field support. (Address, Long Island Chapter SOLE Symposium, Long Island, NY, May 12, 1976) Michael D. Basch. illus tabs Log Spectrum 10:17-20 Winter '76

· Location logistics. (Address, seminar sponsored by Utah Air Force Assoc, Society of Logistics Engineers and Weber State College, May 10, 1975) Col Nathan H. Mazer, Ret. Log Spectrum 10:11-12 Spring '76

The logic in logistics. Joseph J. Addison. illus charts Log Spectrum pt 1, 9:4-9 Winter '75; pt 2, 10: 3-6+ Spring '76; pt 3, 10:14-17 Summer '76

LOGISTICS - Continued

Logistics management in municipalities. (Burbank, Calif) Robert N. Carlton. illus chart Log Spectrum 10:22-25+ Summer '76

Modern logistics: A professional's profession. CAPT Carl L. Henn, Ret. illus Log Spectrum 10:18-21+ Summer '76

Priorities and emphases for logistics, 1976-78. (Letter to Asst SecDef John J. Bennett) VADM Thomas R. Weschler, Ret. illus Nav War Col Rev 29:16-29 Summer '76

Soviet logistic support for ground operations. Graham H. Turbiville. (Reprinted from RUSI Journal for Defence Studies, Sep 1975) illus Mil Rev 56:29-39 Jul '76

Soviet logistics: How good is it? Capts William R. Hotze and Terry L. Schott. illus tab Army Log 8: 18-21 Mar-Apr '76

The thin bread line. David Harvey. illus Def & For Aff Dig No. 7:6-9+ '76

History

The Army of Lord Cornwallis: A study of logistics inadequacies. James L. Carpenter, Jr. illus map Log Spectrum 10:5-13 Fall '76

Historical logistics. Hugh Hodgins. illus Log Spectrum 10:14-15 Fall '76

Looking back. Col Jeptha W. Dennis, Jr. illus Log Spectrum 10:16-18+ Fall '76

"Old wine in new bottles." Harold L. Rubenstein. illus Log Spectrum 10:40-42 Fall '76

Study and Teaching

Professionalism through logistics education and training. Ben S. Blanchard. illus tabs Log Spectrum 10: 28-33 Summer '76

Air Force

AFLC steps up USAF's combat readiness. Edgar Ulsamer. illus AF Mag 59:63-67 Jun '76

A challenge to logistics managers. LtGen Robert E. Hails. TIG Brief 28:2 Jul 2 '76

Early logistics planning (of support requirements). TIG Brief 28:16 Sep 10 '76

Maintaining a modern force. (Remarks, National Security Industrial Assoc, Absecon, NJ, June 28, 1976) MajGen Charles F. Minter, Sr. AF Plcy Ltr for Comdrs: Sup No. 9:13-19 Sep '76

Military logistics: Assurance of mission accomplishment. LtCol Fred Gluck, Ret. illus Log Spectrum 10:19-22 Fall '76

Priority of nuclear logistic movement support. TIG Brief 28:10 Nov 19 '76

Significant historical data processing (AFTO Form 95). TIG Brief 28:12 Jul 16 '76

(USAF) switch to computer logistics. AF Times 36:41 Jan 5 '76

Study and Teaching

Address, ACSC Logistics Education Symposium, Maxwell AFB, Ala, 17 Feb 1976. MajGen Gerald J. Post. Log Spectrum 10:34-36 Spring '76

LOGISTICS - Continued

Air Force - Cont'd

Study and Teaching - Cont'd

Air Force Air University adds new units (USAF Leadership and Management Development Center, located at Maxwell AFB, Ala, and the Air Force Logistics Management Center, located at Gunter AFS, Ala). Review 55:9 Nov-Dec '75

Air University gets two new units (USAF Leadership and Management Development Center, Maxwell AFB, Ala, and Air Force Logistics Management Center, Gunter AFS, Ala). Contact, p 6, Winter '76

Armed Forces

Ask for it clearly. (Multiservice acquisition) LtCol Donald M.Keith and Charles A.McCárthy. illus Army Log 8:14-16 Jul-Aug '76

Joint Logistics Commanders: Interservice cooperation improves support. Marvin Wilson, Jr. Army Log 18:14-15 Mar-Apr '76

New inventory analysis techniques. James J.Eder. illus Log Spectrum 10:29-33 Fall '76

A "real world" transportation challenge: Exercise Bold Eagle '76. Maj Eldon T.Rippee. illus Translog 7:2-6 May '76

A strategic logistics force: An answer to the exploitation of the developing nations. BrigGen Winfield S.Scott, Ret. illus Strat Rev 4:68-75 Fall '76

A twenty one jewel watch: Mutual logistic support in NATO. CDR Eugene F.Coughlin. illus Def Trans J 32:12-14+ Apr '76

The unsung art of sharing shortages. (Joint Logistics Commanders (JLC)) C.W.Borklund. illus Govt Exec 8:19-20+ Apr '76

(Us logisticians) (Address, American Logistics Assoc Annual Convention, Miami Beach, Sep 13-15, 1976) LtGen W.W.Vaughan. illus Review 56:33 Sep-Oct '76

Army

Achilles' heel. (ASL, Authorized Stockage List, immobility) Maj Walter A.Bawell. illus Army Log 8:17-19 Sep-Oct '76

Ammo supply in rapid deployment. LtCol Robert P. Jones. illus Army Log 8:30-32 Jan-Feb '76

Army railroading: Tele-train to Trident missile. Dan Hall. illus Translog 7:2-5 Jun '76

Army stock fund: Friend or foe. Col John R.Brinton. illus tab Army Log 8:2-5 Mar-Apr '76

The dynamism of Army combat logistics. MajGen Erwin M.Graham, Jr. illus Mil Rev 56:65-75 Apr '76

Equipment maintainability--design in, don't add on. BrigGen William E.Eicher. illus Natl Def 60:353-355 Mar-Apr '76

Lifting the fog around ILS. illus Army Log 8:14-16 Nov-Dec '76

A maintenance perspective. LtCols Clifford L.Wollard and Garry A.Scharberg. illus Army Log 8:17-19 Nov-Dec '76

Managing logistics in the field. LtCol William C. Banze and Miles S.Abbott. illus Army Log 8:2-5 May-Jun '76

LOGISTICS - Continued

Army - Cont'd

Managing major end items. John P.McCormick. illus tab Army Log 8:31-33 Jul-Aug '76

Managing your logistics career: Here's how OPMD (Officer Personnel Management Directorate) does it. Maj Frank Cunningham III. Army Log 8:12-13 Nov-Dec '76

The new short war strategy. Gen James H.Polk, Ret. (Reprinted from Strategic Review, Summer 1975) Mil Rev 56:58-64 Mar '76

Service support for the Armored Cavalry Regiment (ACR). George R.Albert. illus Armor 85:27-29 May-Jun '76

Supply base camouflage. Capt John M.Forbes, Jr. illus Army Log 8:20-22 May-Jun '76

Tech supply--move 'em out. (1st Cavalry Division's 27th Maintenance Battalion's Operation First Team Logistics) Capt Daniel M.Smith. Translog 7:6-7 Oct '76

The up-load exercise. (Planning for combat battalion ammunition supply points in the European environment) Capt Keith E.Predmore. illus Fld Arty J 44:33-36 May-Jun '76

History

Challenging the logistics status quo during the Civil War. James A.Huston. illus Def Mgt J 12:25-33 Jul '76

Continental Army logistics: An overview. illus Army Log 8:12-13 Jul-Aug '76

Continental Army logistics: Clothing supply. illus Army Log 8:28-32 Mar-Apr '76; Def Trans J 32:28-30+ Oct '76

Continental Army logistics: Food supply. illus Army Log 8:24-28 Jan-Feb '76

Continental Army logistics: Transportation. (Reprinted from Army Logistician, Nov-Dec 1975) illus map Def Trans J 32:28-31 Aug '76

Organization

Combat oriented general support: A conceptual view of how the general support of the Army in the field can be operated. LtCols James R.Stivison and Richard M.Wangenheim. illus Army Log 8:20-23 Jan-Feb '76

Study and Teaching

AMC schools--the other Army school system. illus Army Log 8:10-14 Jan-Feb '76

Logistics training asset--community colleges. Capt B.D.Sullivan. illus Army Log 8:28-29 May-Jun '76

Training of logistics units. LtCol James Bickley and Capt Kenneth J.Utecht, Jr. illus Army Log 8:8-11 Jul-Aug '76

National Guard--Army

(Army) Guard aviation logistics. Capt Arthur W. Ries. illus Army Log 8:8-11 Nov-Dec '76

Navy

The FFG-7 integrated logistics support program. (Address, Long Island Chapter, SOLE, April 24, 1976) RADM E.J.Otth. Log Spectrum 10:34-35+ Fall '76

LONG RANGE NAVIGATION see Loran

LORAN

(New precise Loran system) Signal 30:143 Jan '76

Testing

Dynamic testing of airborne Loran navigation receivers. Robert P. Bartlett. illus tabs Countermeasures 2:87-89 Sep '76

LOW-ALTITUDE FLYING see Flight, Low-Altitude

LOYALTY

Tolerating honest dissent. LtCol F.N.Van Sant. MarCor Gaz 60:44-45 Feb '76

LUBRICATION AND LUBRICANTS

General aviation fuel--which is right? Maj Philip M. McAtee. illus tab Aerosp Safety 32:6-7 Nov '76

Potluck lubrication. TIG Brief 28:3 Jan 16 '76

Synthetic oil? SGM Nat Dell. illus Soldiers 31:19-22 Oct '76

Unsatisfactory wheel bearing grease. TIG Brief 28:7 Oct 8 '76

Vital life fluid. (Oil analysis program) Patsy Thompson. illus USA Avn Dig 22:36-40 Aug '76

LUNAR VEHICLES see Moon Vehicles

LUNN, Robert J.

Major General Lunn is new Fort Bliss commander. por Air Def Mag, pp 4-5, Apr-Jun '76

LURIE, Phillip J.

AFCEA Chapter Man of the Month (Maj Phillip J. Lurie, DCS/Communications-Electronics, Air University, Maxwell AFB, Ala). por Signal 30:50 Feb '76

LYNDON B.JOHNSON SPACE CENTER

Lyndon B.Johnson Space Center. Mike Howard. illus Spaceflight 18:108-109 Mar '76

LYNN, James T.

Conference speakers. (Excerpts from addresses, NGAUS 98th General Conference, Washington, Aug 30-Sep 1, 1976) por Natl Guardsman 30: 23-27 Oct '76

LYON, Herbert A.

Weather probability forecasts: A cost-saving technique in space launch and missile test operations. MajGen Herbert A.Lyon, Ret, and LtCol Lynn L. LeBlanc. AU Rev 27:45-54 Jan-Feb '76

LYON, William

AFRES/ANG--best shape ever. Interviews. MajGens John J.Pesch and William Lyon. por AF Mag 59: 55-59 Jun '76

Air Force Reserve. por AF Mag 59:100-101 May '76

M A A G see Military Assistance Advisory Group

M A C see Military Airlift Command

M A S T (Military Assistance to Safety and Traffic)

MAST: New dimension in life-saving. MSgt Nat Dell.
illus Soldiers 31:46-49 Feb '76

The MAST program. illus USA Avn Dig 22:8-11+
Oct '76

M I L P E R C E N see Army Military Personnel Center

M L S see Microwave Landing Systems

M S C see Military Sealift Command

M T M C see Military Traffic Management Command

MacARTHUR, Douglas

Operation Chromite: A study of generalship. (Korea,
1950) Capt James P.Totten. Armor 85:33-38 Nov-
Dec '76

McBRIDE, William V.

The Air Staff--a view from the top. Interview. Gen
William V.McBride. por AF Mag 59:26-29 Apr '76

Three words or less. (Adapted from speech, Outstanding Airman banquet, Air Force Assoc Convention, Washington, Sep 15, 1975) Gen William
V.McBride. por Airman 20:9-10 Jan '76

McCLARY, Terence E.

A force second to none: The FY 1977 Defense budget.
Terence E.McClary. por Armed Forces Compt
21:16-19 Apr '76

McCLELLAN, John L.

Conference speakers. (Excerpts from addresses,
NGAUS 98th General Conference, Washington,
Aug 30-Sep 1, 1976) por Natl Guardsman 30:
23-27 Oct '76

MACDONALD, David R.

(John J.) Bennett and (David R.) Macdonald join Navy
Secretariat. Ellen R.Davis. por Sea Power 19:14
Oct '76

McDONOUGH, Joseph C.

EISPE (Expert Infantryman Squad and Platoon Evaluation). MajGen Joseph C.McDonough. Infantry 66:
19-22 Nov-Dec '76

McENERY, John W.

Changes in tank gunnery. MajGen John W.McEnery.
por Armor 85:8-10 May-Jun '76

McGOVERN, George

Talk to Hanoi, McGovern advises. AF Times 36:38
Apr 19 '76

MACHINE GUNS

MAG-58: The new coax(ially mounted machinegun for
U.S. tanks). LtCol Robert W.DeMont. illus Armor
85:52-54 Sep-Oct '76

The U.S. choice of a coaxial tank machine gun. LtCol
P.Crevecoeur, Ret. illus tabs Intl Def Rev 9:770-
772 Oct '76

Wild bore: The hunt for an elusive new NATO rifle
caliber. Def & For Aff Dig No.6:16+ '76

MACK, William P.

The need for dissent. Interview. VADM William P.
Mack, Ret. por AF Times, Times Magazine sup:
20-24+ Jan 12 '76

McLUCAS, John L.

(AF) Secretary McLucas's farewell message. AF
Mag 59:21 Jan '76

International law and the Air Force. (Address, Society of International Law, New York, Oct 29, 1975)
John L.McLucas. AF Law Rev 18:76-80 Summer '76

MLS (Microwave Landing Systems): Breakthrough in
landing systems. John L.McLucas. AF Mag 59:
66-68+ Jul '76

New horizons for radar. John L.McLucas. por Signal
31:65-67 Oct '76

McNAMARA, Robert S.

Managing for Defense. Robert S.McNamara. Def
Mgt J 12:67-73 Jul '76

MADDOX, William J.,Jr

Hail and farewell. (MajGen James C.Smith succeeds
MajGen William J.Maddox, Jr, as commander of
Army Aviation Center, Fort Rucker, Ala) por USA
Avn Dig 22:48-49 Jul '76

MAGNESIUM see Metals

MAGNETOMETERS

Sub detection. Bill Walsh. illus Countermeasures 2:
6-7+ Apr '76

MAHAN, Alfred T.

Alfred Thayer Mahan speaks for himself. James A.
Field, Jr. Nav War Col Rev 29:47-60 Fall '76

Sea power--Teddy's "big stick." (Alfred Mahan's
influence on Theodore Roosevelt and U.S. history)
CAPT Guy Cane. por US Nav Inst Proc 102:40-48
Aug '76

MAINTENANCE AND REPAIR

See also
Aircraft Maintenance
Missile Maintenance
also subdivision Maintenance and Repair under
specific subjects

Correction of Source, Maintenance, and Recover-
ability (SMR) codes. TIG Brief 28:12 Jul 2 '76

Defective Parts and Components Control Program
(DPCCP). TIG Brief 28:11 Jul 2 '76

Field maintenance. TIG Brief 28:9 Jan 30 '76

The logic in logistics. Joseph J.Addison. illus charts
Log Spectrum pt 1, 9:4-9 Winter '75; pt 2, 10:
3-6+ Spring '76; pt 3, 10:14-17 Summer '76

Maintainability--a shared responsibility. Hartley I.
Starr. Natl Def 60:360-363 Mar-Apr '76

Maintenance management policy. (AFM 66-1) TIG
Brief 28:11 Mar 26 '76

Management of repair cycle assets. TIG Brief 28:6
Mar 26 '76

Materiel control: Serving maintenance and supply.
TIG Brief 28:8 May 7 '76

Organizational maintenance. TIG Brief 28:10
Jan 30 '76

MAINTENANCE AND REPAIR - Continued

Parts ordering for repair cycle assets. TIG Brief 28:8 Oct 8 '76

The repair cycle. TIG Brief 28:9 Oct 8 '76

Shipping of reparables (to repair facilities) incomplete. TIG Brief 28:8 Jun 4 '76

Organization

A maintenance perspective. LtCols Clifford L.Wollard and Garry A.Scharberg. illus Army Log 8: 17-19 Nov-Dec '76

MAINTENANCE MANAGEMENT see Maintenance and Repair

MALAYSIA

Foreign Relations

Indonesia--History

The confrontation in Borneo. Brig E.D.Smith. Army Qtr pt 1, The revolt in Brunei leads to "confrontation." 105:479-483 Oct '75; pt 2, The incursions of the undeclared war. 106:30-36 Jan '76

Strategic Importance

Asia. Philip Paisley and Leigh Johnson. illus tab Def & For Aff Dig No.5:18-19+ '76

MALOY, Frederick L.

Air Force Data Automation Agency. por AF Mag 59: 93-94 May '76

MAN

Comparative muscular strength of men and women: A review of the literature. Lloyd L.Laubach. illus tabs Aviation, Space & Envmt Med 47:534-542 May '76

MANAGEMENT

See also
Personnel Administration

Another look at MBO (Management By Objectives). Ronald L.Adolphi. illus tab Armed Forces Compt 21:24-27 Apr '76

Conflict in organizations: Good or bad? LtCol Russell Pierre, Jr and Maj Jerome G.Peppers, Jr, Ret. AU Rev 28:69-79 Nov-Dec '76

Give MBO/R (Management By Objectives/Results) a chance. TIG Brief 28:19 Dec 17 '76

How a manager gets the job done: Leadership, the common thread. (Remarks, 27th Industrial Engineering Conference for Management and Supervision, West Virginia University, Morgantown, April 5, 1976) MajGen Frank J.Simokaitis. AF Plcy Ltr for Comdrs: Sup No.6:22-25 Jun '76

MBO (Management By Objectives): Problems noted. TIG Brief 28:5-6 Sep 24 '76

Management and communication: MBO/R (Management By Objectives/Results). TIG Brief 28:15 Sep 10 '76

Management by objectives ... a practical approach. Capt Howard H.Miller. Air Def Mag, pp 48-50, Jul-Sep '76

Management By Objectives/Results (MBO/R) checklist. TIG Brief 28:9 Jun 18 '76

Management information requirements. TIG Brief 28:7 Sep 10 '76

MANAGEMENT - Continued

Managerial inconsistency: Attitudes vs behavior. Norman L.Warden and Fred Burrell. illus tab Armed Forces Compt 21:28-30 Apr '76

Managerial styles. LtCol Merrell E.Dean. illus AU Rev 27:41-46 Mar-Apr '76

The response of organisations to change. Bernard Barry. illus tab RUSI J for Def Studies 120:33-41 Dec '75

Study and Teaching

Can academic management research be profitable? LtCol Ronald R.Calkins. illus AU Rev 27:47-55 Mar-Apr '76

Defense Systems Management School. illus tab Comdrs Dig 19:4-12 Jan 8 '76

Management training: AMA (American Management Associations) courses show results. illus Govt Exec 8:38-39 Mar '76

MANAGEMENT, MILITARY

See also
Resource Management
Single Manager System
Supervision
Supply Management
Weapon Systems Management

Air Force resource management: Blending systems with skills. MajGen Jack I.Posner. tabs illus Def Mgt J 12:23-31 Oct '76

Ants and elephants (management effectiveness inspection). TIG Brief 28:5 Nov 5 '76

Command Inspection System (CIS) inspections. TIG Brief 28:5 Dec 17 '76

Company management by objective. Capt Thomas M. Tobin. illus Army Log 8:8-10 Sep-Oct '76

Control and management of information requirements: A look at the SAC approach. Maj Thomas M.Caldwell. illus AF Compt 10:6-7 Jan '76

Disaster preparedness. TIG Brief 28:3 Feb 27 '76

Do more with less: Job enrichment may be the answer. Maj D.K.Crooch. illus AU Rev 27:55-61 May-Jun '76

Early, effective planning: The guide for achievement. TIG Brief 28:20 Sep 10 '76

Financial management--division to battalion contracts. LtCol Thomas W.Cassada. illus Mil Rev 56:42-46 Jan '76

Group (Defense Manpower Commission) faults DOD personnel management. AF Times 36:27 Mar 8 '76

How does the (AF) Chief (of Staff) keep on target? Management by objectives. Lee Ewing. AF Times 36:10 Jan 26 '76

(In series of management conferences Army Guard commanders told to) bite the bullet. Bruce P.Hargreaves. illus Natl Guardsman 30:22-25 May '76

'The Inspector General Complaint System,' AFR 123-11. TIG Brief 28:5-6 Nov 19 '76

Inspectors are management consultants. TIG Brief 28:6 Nov 5 '76

A look at the big picture in U.S. Air Force food service management. Interview. BrigGen William D. Gilbert. illus Review 55:27-29 Mar-Apr '76

MANAGEMENT, MILITARY - Continued

MBO (Management By Objectives): Update 76--results so far right on target. Capt Robert J. Courter, Jr. illus AF Engrg & Svcs Qtr 17:3-6 Aug '76

Management and command--possible confusion today? LtGen John W. Roberts. TIG Brief 28:2 Jul 16 '76

Management by objectives. TIG Brief 28:4 Nov 19 '76

Management by objectives ... a practical approach. Capt Howard H. Miller. Air Def Mag, pp 48-50, Jul-Sep '76

Management leverage: A new concept in military procurement. Col Ronald Terry. Persp in Def Mgt No.24:79-89 Winter '75-'76

Management, supervision, and other old proverbs. TIG Brief 28:10 Jun 4 '76

Managerial careers of Air Force generals: A test of the Janowitz convergence hypothesis. Arnold Kanter. tabs J Pol & Mil Sociol 4:121-133; Comment. Kurt Lang. 4:141-143; Comment. Thomas C.Padgett. 4:145-146; Reply to comments by Lang and Padgett. Arnold Kanter. 4:147-149 Spring '76

Manpower and organization. TIG Brief 28:21 Mar 26 '76

Middle management involvement. TIG Brief 28:17 May 7 '76

Military contributions to organization theory: Unity of effort, cohesiveness, flexibility. Maj James K. McCollum, Ret. tabs illus Mil Rev 56:65-76 Mar '76

Mission effectiveness & base livability: A hypothesis. Lester H.Henriksen and Gary D.Vest. illus AF Engrg & Svcs Qtr 17:2-6 Nov '76

New inventory analysis techniques. James J.Eder. illus Log Spectrum 10:29-33 Fall '76

Nuclear capability inspections: Some thoughts. TIG Brief 28:4 Jun 18 '76

An operations cost index: Answer to the question "how much more?" (CONUS vs overseas cost differences) Capt Willard L.Mason. illus tabs AU Rev 27:61-71 Mar-Apr '76

PROMS (PROcurement Management System). Robert F.Williams and Capt Robert J.Walker. tabs Army Log 8:2-6 Nov-Dec '76

Personnel quality force management. TIG Brief 28:10 Feb 13 '76

Reflections on an approach to financial management. Gary D.Penisten. illus Armed Forces Compt 21: 12-14 Jan '76

Resource management: A view from the top. (Panel discussion, American Society of Military Comptrollers National Symposium, Arlington, Va, May 26, 1976) Fred P.Wacker and others. illus Armed Forces Compt 21:20-26 Jul '76

Safety program management: What's new? TIG Brief 28:6 Jun 4 '76

Self-inspection programs. TIG Brief 28:3-4 May 7 '76

The thin bread line. David Harvey. illus Def & For Aff Dig No.7:6-9+ Jul '76

A tool to fight race problem. AF Times 36:25 May 10 '76

Tooth-to-tail: A conceptual void. illus tab Army Log 8:33-37 Mar-Apr '76

MANAGEMENT, MILITARY - Continued

Tough and ready--"to keep the peace ... to deter war." Interview. Army Chief of Staff, Gen Fred C.Weyand. illus Soldiers 31:31-34 Feb '76

Your opinion counts. Darryl D.McEwen. illus Soldiers 31:6-9 Dec '76

Study and Teaching

Defense Systems Management School. illus tab Comdrs Dig 19:4-12 Jan 8 '76

Learning depends upon the learner! (Seminar sponsored by MTMC) Tory Billard. illus Translog 7: 7-8 Nov '76

MANAGEMENT ANALYSIS

Directorate of Management Analysis. Col C.T.Spangrud. chart illus tabs AF Compt 10:18-19 Jan '76

Directorate of Management Analysis. Col C.T.Spangrud. illus chart AF Compt 10:14-15 Apr '76

Directorate of Management Analysis. Col C.T.Spangrud. illus chart AF Compt 10:14-15 Oct '76

Notes from the Director of Management Analysis. Col C.T.Spangrud. illus AF Compt 10:14-15 Jul '76

MANAGEMENT CENTERS AND SCHOOLS

Air Force

Air Force Air University adds new units (USAF Leadership and Management Development Center, located at Maxwell AFB, Ala, and the Air Force Logistics Management Center, located at Gunter AFS, Ala). Review 55:9 Nov-Dec '75

Air University gets two new units (USAF Leadership and Management Development Center, Maxwell AFB, Ala, and Air Force Logistics Management Center, Gunter AFS, Ala). Contact, p 6, Winter '76

E-4s' teachers begin training (at Leadership and Management Development Center, Maxwell AFB, Ala). Len Famiglietti. AF Times 36:2 Mar 8 '76

New Air University units (USAF Leadership and Management Development Center, Maxwell AFB, Ala, and Air Force Logistics Management Center, Gunter AFS, Ala). AF Pley Ltr for Comdrs: Sup No.2:26 Feb '76

Army

AMC schools--the other Army school system. illus Army Log 8:10-14 Jan-Feb '76

Defense Dept

DOD Computer Institute. TIG Brief 28:16 May 21 '76

Defense Systems Management School. illus tab Comdrs Dig 19:4-12 Jan 8 '76

MANAGEMENT IMPROVEMENT

See also
Automation
Cost Effectiveness
Efficiency
Output Measurement
Resource Management

The Administrative Center: Air Force makes it (word processing) work! John F.Judge. illus Govt Exec 8:39+ Sep '76

Air Force documentation management program. TIG Brief 28:20 Mar 12 '76

MANAGEMENT IMPROVEMENT - Continued

Another look at MBO (Management By Objectives).
Ronald L.Adolphi. illus tab Armed Forces Compt
21:24-27 Apr '76

Ants and elephants (management effectiveness inspection). TIG Brief 28:5 Nov 5 '76

Base Engineer Automated Management System
(BEAMS). TIG Brief 28:10 Dec 17 '76

The Bicentennial challenge: The management revolution. Donald Ogilvie. illus Armed Forces Compt
21:10-14 Jul '76

A Bicentennial look at the bureacracy. George S.
Odiorne. illus Armed Forces Compt 21:16-17
Jul '76

CV safety problems: (USS) America's approach. CDR
S.P.Dunlap. illus Approach 21:12-15 May '76

Can academic management research be profitable?
LtCol Ronald R.Calkins. illus AU Rev 27:47-55
Mar-Apr '76

Catering to customer desires. (Modular fast food
program) Capt Thomas J.Padgett. illus AF Engrg
& Svcs Qtr 17:18-20 Aug '76

Centralized commissary concept (Air Force COM-
missary Service (AFCOMS)). CMSgt Donald M.
Leach. illus chart map AF Engrg & Svcs Qtr 17:
2-5 May '76

A challenge to logistics managers. LtGen Robert E.
Hails. TIG Brief 28:2 Jul 2 '76

Chapel management personnel. TIG Brief 28:16
Jul 16 '76

Committee approach to quality force management.
TIG Brief 28:19 Mar 26 '76

Company management by objective. Capt Thomas M.
Tobin. illus Army Log 8:8-10 Sep-Oct '76

Compensation: Reasonableness is the yardstick. Ray
W.Dellas. illus Govt Exec 8:42-43 Oct '76

Early, effective planning: The guide for achievement. TIG Brief 28:20 Sep 10 '76

Effective plans and scheduling: Cure for most panic
situations. TIG Brief 28:7 Aug 13 '76

Energy monitoring control systems. Capt Robert E.
Dant. illus tab AF Engrg & Svcs Qtr 17:25-28
Aug '76

1st shirts to work more with troops. Bruce Callander.
AF Times 36:4 Jun 28 '76

Food service--200 years of advancement. Lt Dennis
A.Bossen. illus AF Engrg & Svcs Qtr 17:14-16
Feb '76

Fourth generation field support. (Address, Long
Island Chapter SOLE Symposium, Long Island,
NY, May 12, 1976) Michael D.Basch. illus tabs
Log Spectrum 10:17-20 Winter '76

Give MBO/R (Management By Objectives/Results) a
chance. TIG Brief 28:19 Dec 17 '76

Government: Wrong kind of competition. John F.
Judge. illus Govt Exec 8:16+ May '76

Handling the high cost of personnel. Col R.W.Hag-
auer. tabs Govt Exec 8:24+ Aug '76

Human resources management as an accident prevention tool. Robert A.Alkov. illus Approach 22:
26-29 Jul '76

MANAGEMENT IMPROVEMENT - Continued

Inspectors are management consultants. TIG Brief
28:6 Nov 5 '76

Job enrichment--Ogden (Air Logistics Center) style.
MajGen Edmund A.Rafalko. illus tabs AU Rev 28:
46-53 Nov-Dec '76

Lifting the fog around ILS. illus Army Log 8:14-16
Nov-Dec '76

The logic in logistics. Joseph J.Addison. illus charts
Log Spectrum pt 1, 9:4-9 Winter '75; pt 2, 10:
3-6+ Spring '76; pt 3, 10:14-17 Summer '76

Logistics management in municipalities. (Burbank,
Calif) Robert N.Carlton. illus chart Log Spectrum
10:22-25+ Summer '76

MBO (Management By Objectives): Problems noted.
TIG Brief 28:5-6 Sep 24 '76

MBO (Management By Objectives):Update 76--results
so far right on target. Capt Robert J.Courter, Jr.
illus AF Engrg & Svcs Qtr 17:3-6 Aug '76

The MTMC realignment program. David R.Goodmon.
Translog 7:2-5 Feb '76

A maintenance perspective. LtCols Clifford L.Wol-
lard and Garry A.Scharberg. illus Army Log 8:
17-19 Nov-Dec '76

Make service your profession. (Address, Air Force
Engineering and Services Conference, Homestead
AFB, Fla, Dec 1975) Gen Russell E.Dougherty.
illus AF Engrg & Svcs Qtr 17:6-12 May '76

Management and communication: MBO/R (Management By Objectives/Results). TIG Brief 28:15
Sep 10 '76

Management by objectives. TIG Brief 28:4 Nov 19 '76

Management by objectives ... a practical approach.
Capt Howard H.Miller. Air Def Mag, pp 48-50,
Jul-Sep '76

Management By Objectives/Results (MBO/R) checklist. TIG Brief 28:9 Jun 18 '76

Management leverage: A new concept in military
procurement. Col Ronald Terry. Persp in Def
Mgt No.24:79-89 Winter '75-'76

Management training: AMA (American Management
Associations) courses show results. illus Govt
Exec 8:38-39 Mar '76

Managing by exception in space systems operation--
the Four Grand experience. Col Gerald J.Win-
chell. illus tab Def Mgt J 12:64-68 Oct '76

Managing logistics in the field. LtCol William C.
Banze and Miles S.Abbott. illus Army Log 8:2-5
May-Jun '76

Managing technical activities and the future. Vincent
P.Luchsinger. illus Armed Forces Compt 21:
18-19 Jul '76

Medical institutional planning. TIG Brief 28:15
Dec 17 '76

Medical methods improvement program. TIG Brief
28:17 Dec 17 '76

Mission area planning helps spend dollars wisely.
TIG Brief 28:19 Dec 17 '76

Mission effectiveness & base livability: A hypothesis.
Lester H.Henriksen and Gary D.Vest. illus AF
Engrg & Svcs Qtr 17:2-6 Nov '76

MANAGEMENT IMPROVEMENT - Continued

New inventory analysis techniques. James J. Eder. illus Log Spectrum 10:29-33 Fall '76

Now, a way to get at those grants and loans. (Federal Domestic Assistance Program Retrieval Systems) Spencer B. Child. illus Govt Exec 8:26+ Mar '76

The obstacles to effective design-to-cost. Raymond Kendall. Govt Exec 8:24-25 Oct '76

Office of Federal Procurement Policy. Hugh E. Witt. illus Signal 30:17-19 Feb '76

PROMS (PROcurement Management System). Robert F. Williams and Capt Robert J. Walker. tabs Army Log 8:2-6 Nov-Dec '76

Participatory management. TIG Brief 28:19 Dec 3 '76

Paying only your fair share. (Joint Utility Service Boards (JUSBs)) Leon E. McDuff. illus AF Engrg & Svcs Qtr 17:35-37 Aug '76

Performance purchasing: A rising state & local tide. Govt Exec 8:22+ Sep '76

Pumping new technology into local buying practices. Robert M. Belmonte. tabs Govt Exec 8:21-23+ Jan '76

'Quality' study sparks personnel changes: AFMIG (AF Management Improvement Group), year later. Bruce Callander. AF Times 37:2 Aug 23 '76

Recruiting Service's Management Emphasis Program. TIG Brief 28:12 Jun 18 '76

Reflections on an approach to financial management. Gary D. Penisten. illus Armed Forces Compt 21: 12-14 Jan '76

Security policy performance during ORIs. TIG Brief 28:16 Nov 5 '76

Self-inspection: A fresh look at the original approach. TIG Brief 28:8 Dec 3 '76

Small cities (like Redondo Beach, Calif) & computers: It can be done. illus Govt Exec 8:55-56+ Dec '76

Systems approach--a technique for logistics managers. Neil O. Knarr. illus Army Log 8:12-13 Sep-Oct '76

Systems approach to administrative support (in Transportation Dept's Office of Contracts and Procurement). Govt Exec 8:54+ Sep '76

Taking a "forward look" in Defense contract administration. John H. Kunsemiller. tabs Def Mgt J 12: 56-59 Oct '76

A talk with the commander of AFCOMS. Interview. MajGen Daniel L. Burkett. illus AF Engrg & Svcs Qtr 17:14-17 Nov '76

U.S. aeronautical R&D: Seeking effective policies and leadership. A. Scott Crossfield. illus tabs Govt Exec 8:38-39+ Nov '76

Visibility. TIG Brief 28:14 Oct 22 '76

Why Bedek (Aviation Division of Israel Aircraft Industries) is bidding for U.S. government aircraft service contract work. illus Govt Exec 8:31-32 May '76

Why not more straight commercial buying? Eberhardt Rechtin. illus Govt Exec 8:46-48+ Oct '76

Word processing: How to save $700 million a year. (Interview with Ron Companion, Installation Officer at Fort Benning, Ga) Govt Exec 8:52+ Dec '76

MANAGEMENT IMPROVEMENT - Continued

A workable Program Measurement System (PMS) under the National Labor Relations Board. Richard J. Shakman and Joel C. Anderson. Def Mgt J 12:60-63 Oct '76

Zero base management system. CDR Walter E. Peterson. Mil Engr 68:371-373 Sep-Oct '76

MANAGEMENT INFORMATION SYSTEMS

Congress & budgets: The computer takes hold. illus Govt Exec 8:60-61 May '76

Control and management of information requirements: A look at the SAC approach. Maj Thomas M. Caldwell. illus AF Compt 10:6-7 Jan '76

Data processing and the Reserve components. BrigGen H. W. Meetze and Maj J. Steiger. illus Army Log 8:20-23 Sep-Oct '76

Magnifying inner space. Janet Hake. illus Soldiers 31:45-48 Sep '76

Marine Corps Exchange Service Management Information System (MIS). Spencer C. Jones. illus Review 55:77-78 May-Jun '76

Small cities (like Redondo Beach, Calif) & computers: It can be done. illus Govt Exec 8:55-56+ Dec '76

Systems approach to administrative support (in Transportation Dept's Office of Contracts and Procurement). Govt Exec 8:54+ Sep '76

Zero base management system. CDR Walter E. Peterson. Mil Engr 68:371-373 Sep-Oct '76

Costs

Government can cut DP (Data Processing) costs in half. (Interview with Computer Sciences Corp's Vincent R. Grillo, Jr) illus tab Govt Exec 8:52+ Nov '76

Study and Teaching

DOD Computer Institute. TIG Brief 28:16 May 21 '76

MANEUVERS

See also
Combined Operations
Joint Operations
War Games
    also specific exercises and/or operations by name

Air Force--U.S.

Exercises. Regular feature in some issues of Air Force Times

Armed Forces--NATO

Canberras to Europe. 1stLt Norman B. Hutcherson. illus Interceptor 18:8-9 Dec '76

Army--Russia

The "Sever" manoeuvres. illus Soviet Mil Rev No. 10: 17-19 Oct '76

Army--U.S.

11th Aviation Group (Combat) aviation training in USAREUR. Capt Eric R. Kunz. illus USA Avn Dig 22:2-3+ Aug '76

MANEUVERS - Continued

Marine Corps

Warsaw Pact

Warsaw Pact amphib ops in Northern Europe. Graham H. Turbiville. illus MarCor Gaz 60:20-27 Oct '76

Navy--Russia

Okean-75. LCDRs Bruce W. Watson and Margurite A. Walton. illus map US Nav Inst Proc 102:93-97 Jul '76

MANN, Chris C.

Ability, not sex, concerns (Human Resources' chief) Mann. Interview. BrigGen Chris C. Mann. por AF Times 36:4 Jan 26 '76

MANNED SPACECRAFT CENTER see Lyndon B. Johnson Space Center

MANPOWER

United States

Costs

Compensation: Reasonableness is the yardstick. Ray W. Dellas. illus Govt Exec 8:42-43 Oct '76

MANPOWER, MILITARY
For strength of the Services see subdivision Statistics under the respective Service, e.g., Air Force--United States--Statistics.

See also
Military Service, Compulsory
Military Service, Voluntary
Personnel

Mobilization
See Mobilization, Military

Statistics

Comparisons of military manpower 1972-76. London's International Institute for Strategic Studies. Table only. AF Mag 59:96 Dec '76

Great Britain

Manpower trends in the British all-volunteer force. LtCol Thomas A. Fabyanic. tabs Armed Forces & Soc 2:553-572 Summer '76

United States

Air Force resource management: Blending systems with skills. MajGen Jack I. Posner. tabs illus Def Mgt J 12:23-31 Oct '76

Are 2 million members enough? Bruce Callander. AF Times 37:14 Sep 27 '76

A careful look at defense manpower. Gen Bruce Palmer, Jr, Ret and Curtis W. Tarr. illus Mil Rev 56:3-13 Sep '76

DMC (Defense Manpower Commission) urges pay changes, standby draft, retirement reforms. Sea Power 19:29-30 May '76

Defense budget, 1977: A 'serious effort' at restraint. illus tabs Eric C. Ludvigsen. Army 26:12-17 Mar '76

FY 77 proposed Defense budget. illus tabs Comdrs Dig 19: entire issue Feb 26 '76

Group (Defense Manpower Commission) faults DOD personnel management. AF Times 36:27 Mar 8 '76

MANPOWER, MILITARY - Continued

United States - Cont'd

Hill made few major DOD cuts: 6-year budget review. AF Times 37:25 Nov 1 '76

An introspective analysis of DOD manpower management. David P. Taylor. tabs Def Mgt J 12:2-8 Oct '76

Medics expect good year, despite manpower pinch. AF Times 36:8 Jul 5 '76

Men, myths, and machines, or, "All the ships at sea." Douglas M. Johnston. illus tabs Def Mgt J 12:17-22 Oct '76

Military manpower problems. LtGen Ira C. Eaker, Ret. AF Times 37:13-14 Sep 20 '76

Military Manpower Training Report (MMTR). Maj J. L. Finan. illus AF Compt 10:30-31+ Jul '76

Costs

Comparing pay, examining benefits--fringes under fire in House harangue. tab AF Times 36:16 Mar 8 '76

GAO: Rising costs threaten strength. AF Times 37:21 Dec 6 '76

Hill group (Members of Congress for Peace through Law) would slash manpower $$. Andy Plattner. AF Times 36:23 Jun 7 '76

Human factor is paramount. (Defense Manpower Commission report) Eric C. Ludvigsen. illus Army 26: 38-40 Jun '76

Statistics

Manpower malaise hits the AFROTC. Ed Gates. AF Mag 59:73 Feb '76

MANPOWER, TECHNICAL

See also
Engineers

Reserve Forces--Air Force--U.S.

Chemist, biologist, engineer, detective (Air Force Reserve environmental health technician). Chris Scheer. illus Air Reservist 28:6-7 Jun '76

MANSFIELD, Michael J.

Senator Mansfield and the NATO alliance: A reappraisal of policy and objectives. Scott D. Sagan. Royal Air Forces Qtr 16:129-137 Summer '76

(Sen Mike) Mansfield says quit Korea. AF Times 37:9 Dec 27 '76

MANSTEIN, Erich von

(Field Marshall Erich von) Manstein's winter miracle (Jan-March 1943). Capt Ronald J. Brown. por Armor 85:18-21 Nov-Dec '76

MAO, Tsê-tung

Mao Tse-tung and original sin. Richard Clutterbuck. Army Qtr 106:142-148 Apr '76

Republican China. Jerry Kamstra. por Countermeasures pt 1, The death of a dynasty. 2:24-26+ Jul '76; pt 2, Birth of modern China. 2:22-23 Aug '76

MAPS AND MAPPING

Airborne hydrographic surveying. Clifford J. Crandall. illus Mil Engr 68:102-103 Mar-Apr '76

MAPS AND MAPPING - Continued

Are you NOE and lost? Garvin L. Holman. illus USA Avn Dig 22:8-12 Mar '76

Digital stereo mapping. Dale J. Panton. illus Countermeasures 2:12+ May '76

Geodesy, mapping, oceanography: Current surveying and mapping news. Regular feature in issues of Military Engineer

The U. S. -Soviet map gap. LtCol Walter H. Parsons III. illus map Army 26:36-39 Aug '76

Equipment

A new point positioning system (Analytical Photogrammetric Positioning System (APPS)). Donald L. Light and William H. Revell. illus Mil Engr 68: 442-444 Nov-Dec '76

MARGIOTTA, Franklin D.

A military elite in transition: Air Force leaders in the 1980s. (Research undertaken at Air Command and Staff College) LtCol Franklin D. Margiotta. Armed Forces & Soc 2:155-184 Winter '76

MARIANAS

Marianas commonwealth status approved; DOD eyes air base. AF Times 36:20 Mar 8 '76

Strategic Importance

The strategic significance of the Northern Marianas. Robert Ellsworth. illus maps Comdrs Dig 19: entire issue Jan 22 '76

MARINE CORPS

Biography

The destiny of Pete Ellis. Col David H. Wagner. illus MarCor Gaz 60:50-55 Jun '76

O'Bannon and company. Trudy J. Sundberg. illus MarCor Gaz 60:35-39 Jul '76

Brigades, Divisions, etc

United States

Bigger role for U.S. Marines in sea control operations. MarCor Gaz 60:4 Sep '76

Frequent Wind. MajGen Richard E. Carey and Maj D. A. Quinlan. maps illus MarCor Gaz pt 1, Organization and assembly (of 9th Marine Amphibious Brigade). 60:16-24 Feb '76; pt 2, Planning. 60: 35-45 Mar '76; pt 3, Execution. 60:35-45 Apr '76

Operation Eagle Pull. (Emergency evacuation of American citizens and designated aliens from Cambodia, 1975) Col Sydney H. Batchelder, Jr and Maj D. A. Quinlan. illus MarCor Gaz 60:47-60 May '76

VMFA-323 wins 2d Hanson Award (for best Fighter Attack Sq of the Year). MarCor Gaz 60:4 Dec '76

WestPac Afloat Battalion (concept). LtCol Wallace M. Greene III. illus MarCor Gaz 60:33-36 Feb '76

United States--History

The imperialistic mercenaries (33d Company, 3d Regiment). W. M. Ancker. MarCor Gaz 60:60-62 Mar '76

MARINE CORPS - Continued

Great Britain

History

Royal Marines: Soldiers from the sea. Col T. J. Saxon, Jr, Ret. illus MarCor Gaz 60:35-42 Oct '76

Russia

Visiting the Marines. G. Shutov. illus Soviet Mil Rev No. 12:58-59 Dec '76

United States

Brookings (Institution) defense study (Where Does the Marine Corps Go from Here?). LtCol W. R. Ball. MarCor Gaz 60:7-9 Mar '76

Commandant's (Gen Louis W. Wilson's) Okinawa interview. MarCor Gaz 60:4+ Jul '76

Corps' high standards will continue. (From address, Navy League, San Diego, Calif) Gen Louis H. Wilson. MarCor Gaz 60:2 Dec '76

Crime fighting in Oceanside (Calif). Richard C. Barnard. illus AF Times, Times Magazine sup:6-10 Mar 22 '76

The DI (Drill Instructor) mystique, sows' ears and a delicate imponderable. Col Robert D. Heinl, Jr, Ret. illus Sea Power 19:37-39 Jun '76

Emphasis on professionalism for a new generation of Marines. Gen Louis H. Wilson. illus Sea Power 19:24-29 Jan '76

The first 12 months--a special report from CMC. Interview. Gen Louis H. Wilson. illus MarCor Gaz 60:2+ Oct '76

A flexible military posture. Gen Louis H. Wilson. illus Strat Rev 4:7-13 Fall '76

Foreign policy and the Marine Corps. Maj W. Hays Parks. illus US Nav Inst Proc 102:18-25 Nov '76

Hard thinking on new ideas. Col R. C. Shreckengost. MarCor Gaz 60:53-54 Aug '76

I am a Marine! GySgt John H. Lofland III. MarCor Gaz 60:22-23 Nov '76

Leadership failures. Maj M. T. Hopgood, Jr. illus MarCor Gaz 60:23-30 Aug '76

The McClure affair. (The jury found Marine SSgt Harold Bronson innocent in death of Pvt Lynn McClure) Joseph E. Revell. illus AF Times, Times Magazine sup:6-12+ Dec 13 '76

The Marine Corps in 1985. Peter A. Wilson. illus US Nav Inst Proc 102:31-38 Jan '76

The Marine Corps today: Asset or anachronism? Gen Robert E. Cushman, Jr, Ret. Intl Sec 1:123-129 Fall '76

The Marine team: Men and women working together. Col Margaret A. Brewer. illus MarCor Gaz 60:18-25 Apr '76

Spirit of '76: 'The troops are looking good.' (A briefing to Congress) Gen Louis H. Wilson. illus tabs MarCor Gaz 60:11-22 Mar '76

(The state of the seas, 1976) illus tabs Sea Power 19: 7-20+ Jan '76

Today's Marine Corps: Stepping out smartly. James W. Canan. illus Sea Power 19:14-18 Nov '76

Troops and fire support. BrigGen Richard C. Schulze. MarCor Gaz 60:47-48 Jan '76

MARINE CORPS - Continued

United States - Cont'd

USMC memorial in Colorado. MarCor Gaz 60:6 Dec '76

U.S. Marine Corps radar requirements. Col H.L. Fogarty and LtCol L.S.Fry. illus Signal 31:36-39 Oct '76

Vital tool for our nation. (Amphibious forces) Capt Wayne S.Keck. MarCor Gaz 60:50-51 Aug '76

Withdraw from Okinawa. Maj S.K.McKee. illus MarCor Gaz 60:50-51 Feb '76

History

Cover reproductions. (14 Continental Marine scenes to commemorate the Bicentennial) Maj Charles Waterhouse. MarCor Gaz no.1, "The First Recruits, December 1775." 59: outside covers Jan '75; no.2, "Landing at New Providence, 3 March 1776." 59: outside covers Feb '75; no.3, "A Marine Lieutenant Dies, 6 April 1776." 59: outside covers Mar '75; no.4, "Defeat on Lake Champlain, 13 October 1776." 59: outside covers Apr '75; no.5, "Marines with Washington at Princeton, 3 January 1777." 59: outside covers May '75; no.6, "The Evacuation of Billingsport, 2 October 1777." 59: outside covers Jun '75; no.7, "Flag Raising at New Providence, 28 January 1778." 59: outside covers Jul '75; no.8, "Willing's Marine Expedition, February 1778." 59: outside covers Aug '75; no.9, "Launching of the Whitehaven Raid, 22 April 1778." 59: outside covers Sep '75; no.10, "John Adams Reviews Jones' Marines, 13 May 1779." 59: outside covers Oct '75; no.11, "Fighting Tops." 59: outside covers Nov '75; no.12, "Assault at Penobscot." 59: outside covers Dec '75; no.13, "Ohio River Row Galley, Summer 1782." 60: outside covers Jan '76; no.14, "Mustering Out, 1 April 1783." 60: outside covers Feb '76

The daring sloop Providence. Charles R.Smith. illus MarCor Gaz 60:25-28 Jul '76

The first birthday ball. Jane Redicker. illus MarCor Gaz 60:24-27 Nov '76

First through the Suez Canal. (Marines travel 8200 miles from Mediterranean to Kobe, Japan, then to land on Inchon, 1950) Col Maurice E.Roach, Ret. MarCor Gaz 60:46-48 Aug '76

I remember ... Gen Lemuel C.Shepherd, Jr, Ret. illus MarCor Gaz 60:28-29 Nov '76

John Philip Sousa is enshrined (by Hall of Fame for Great Americans). MarCor Gaz 60:6 Nov '76

Marines are special Americans. Robert Leader. MarCor Gaz 60:62-63 Mar '76

Marines in Panama 1856-1976. Capt J.H.Reynolds. illus MarCor Gaz 60:28-34 Oct '76

O'Bannon and company. Trudy J.Sundberg. illus MarCor Gaz 60:35-39 Jul '76

Our pre-colonial experience. Col Brooke Nihart, Ret. illus MarCor Gaz 60:29-34 Jul '76

Who is this Marine? (James W.Taylor, the Marine with the bandaged hand in the well-known Battle of Tarawa photograph) Robert Sherrod. illus MarCor Gaz 60:30-34 Jan '76

Organization

Assault by sea. Frank Uhlig, Jr. illus MarCor Gaz 60:18-20 Jun '76

MARINE CORPS - Continued

United States - Cont'd

Organization - Cont'd

New department for Corps (Operations and Training). MarCor Gaz 60:4 Jun '76

Tank company FMF (Fleet Marine Force). Capt Maxwell O.Johnson. illus MarCor Gaz 60:33-38 Jun '76

Warsaw Pact

Warsaw Pact amphib ops in Northern Europe. Graham H.Turbiville. illus MarCor Gaz 60:20-27 Oct '76

MARINE CORPS ASSOCIATION

(Marine Corps Association) Group Annuity Plan. Ira U.Cobleigh. MarCor Gaz 60:15-18 Sep '76

MARINE CORPS AVIATION

Affordability vs requirements. LtCol R.R.Powell. MarCor Gaz 60:23-25 May '76

Air transport in the northern provinces (of South Vietnam). Col Ray L.Bowers. illus MarCor Gaz 60:39-49 Jun '76

Brookings (Institution) defense study (Where Does the Marine Corps Go from Here?). LtCol W.R.Ball. MarCor Gaz 60:7-9 Mar '76

A case for smart weapons. LtCol Frank C.Regan, Jr. illus tabs MarCor Gaz 60:31-35 May '76

Electronic warfare. Maj Harold W.Whitten. illus MarCor Gaz 60:38-42 May '76

Flight Status Selection Board. LtCol Kenneth R. Town. tab MarCor Gaz 60:43-46 May '76

How much can we afford? LtCol W.C.Ryan. illus MarCor Gaz 60:25-30 May '76

Marine Aviation: A constrained requirement. LtGen Thomas H.Miller, Jr. illus MarCor Gaz 60:18-22 May '76

Marine Aviation: Looking up (straight up). John Rhea. illus Sea Power 19:9-13 Nov '76

The Marine Corps in 1985. Peter A.Wilson. illus US Nav Inst Proc 102:31-38 Jan '76

The Marine Corps today: Asset or anachronism? Gen Robert E.Cushman, Jr, Ret. Intl Sec 1:123-129 Fall '76

The Marines are looking for a few good navigators. Capt Daniel O.Pyne. illus Navigator 23:29-30 Summer '76

Minimum flight time. LtCol Kenneth R. Town. illus tabs MarCor Gaz 60:35-39 Jan '76

A step forward with Harrier. Capt A.H.Boquet. illus MarCor Gaz 60:59-61 Apr '76

VMFA-323 wins 2d Hanson Award (for best Fighter Attack Sq of the Year). MarCor Gaz 60:4 Dec '76

V/STOL close air support in the U.S. Marine Corps. Col Stanley P.Lewis. illus US Nav Inst Proc 102: 113-116 Oct '76

History

'Pappy' Boyington flies again (in TV series, Baa Baa Black Sheep). illus MarCor Gaz 60:4 Nov '76

MARINE CORPS BASES

Panama

Marines in Panama 1856-1976. Capt J.H.Reynolds. illus MarCor Gaz 60:28-34 Oct '76

United States
Marine Corps bases are entered by name and location as given by the U.S. Organization Chart Service's U.S. Military and Government Installation Directory.

Camp Pendleton, Calif

Crime fighting in Oceanside (Calif). Richard C.Barnard. illus AF Times, Times Magazine sup:6-10 Mar 22 '76

The hand of hope. (Vietnamese refugee camp at Camp Pendleton, Calif) Maj Patrick L.Townsend. illus US Nav Inst Proc 102:38-45 Sep '76

MARINE CORPS DEVELOPMENT AND EDUCATION COMMAND

Academia in direct support. (The Adjunct Faculty, composed of selected Marine Corps Reserve officers, occupying civilian academic positions, as adjunct to the military staff at Marine Corps Command and Staff College) Col George M. Van Sant and Maj Allan R.Millet. illus MarCor Gaz 60:31-38 Aug '76

MARINE CORPS SCHOOLS, QUANTICO, VA see
Marine Corps Development and Education Command

MARINE RESOURCES

The law of the sea: An analysis of the scientific justifications for boundary extensions in South America. Capt Donald G.Rehkopf, Jr. AF Law Rev 18: 35-56 Summer '76

NAGOA (National Advisory Committee on Oceans and Atmosphere) says 'urgent action' needed on economic (resource) zone. illus Sea Power 18:26-28 Dec '75

Next year: A national oceanic policy? James D.Hessman. illus Sea Power 19:15-18 Oct '76

Offshore technology. Regular feature in issue of Military Engineer

The UN, LOS (Law Of the Sea), and sea treasures. James D.Hessman. illus Sea Power 19:12-14 Aug '76

MARITIME ADMINISTRATION

See also
Merchant Marine--U.S.

A healthier, more prosperous, and more productive U.S. Merchant Marine. Robert J.Blackwell. illus Sea Power 19:30-33 Jan '76

MARITIME LAW

The Coast Guard and fisheries law enforcement. LT Eugene R.Fidell. illus tab US Nav Inst Proc 102: 70-75 Mar '76

Covenants without the sword? Control of the seas. (International conventions and enforcible law) Elizabeth Young. Armed Forces & Soc 2:305-325 Winter '76

Enforcement of the 1973 Marine Pollution Convention. LT Douglas H.Williams. illus US Nav Inst Proc 102:39-45 Dec '76

MARITIME LAW - Continued

(Implications of the 3d Law of the Sea Conference) illus Def & For Aff Dig No.5:28-29+ '76

LOS (Law Of the Sea) '76: Constitution or chaos for the world's oceans? New York meeting may be last chance for a world Law of the Sea Treaty. Merle Macbain. illus Sea Power 19:14-19 Mar '76

The law of the sea: An analysis of the scientific justifications for boundary extensions in South America. Capt Donald G.Rehkopf, Jr. AF Law Rev 18: 35-56 Summer '76

The law of the sea: An Army perspective. Maj Ronald P.Cundick. illus Mil Rev 56:50-55 Mar '76

Malacca and the law. Joel Evan Marsh and LTJG Bruce J.Janigian. US Nav Inst Proc 102:101-102 Feb '76

Men o'war. Joseph Fama. illus Def & For Aff Dig No.6:26-31 '76

NACOA (National Advisory Committee on Oceans and Atmosphere) says 'urgent action' needed on economic (resource) zone. illus Sea Power 18:26-28 Dec '75

New LOS (Law Of the Sea) conference: The U.N.'s final try? Sea Power 19:9-11 Dec '76

The 1975-6 cod war (between Britain and Iceland). John Marriott. illus map tabs RUSI J for Def Studies 121:45-51 Sep '76

'Offshore tapestry'--co-ordination and control. FltLt J.A.Cowan. Royal Air Forces Qtr 16:41-44 Spring '76

Tides and currents in the Pacific: Long-term maritime implications. ADM James L.Holloway III. illus Strat Rev 4:33-39 Summer '76

The UN, LOS (Law Of the Sea), and sea treasures. James D.Hessman. illus Sea Power 19:12-14 Aug '76

MARKETS AND MARKETING

Market data report. (Ships stores afloat recorded sales of $54,137,412 during Fiscal Year 1975, which ended on June 30, 1975) tab Review 55:36 Nov-Dec '75

Market data report: Navy commissary stores sales for Fiscal Year 1976. Tables only. Review 56:77-80 Sep-Oct '76

Market data report: Navy commissary stores sales for second quarter Fiscal Year 1976. Tables only. Review 55:57-60 Jan-Feb '76

MARKS, Leonard, Jr

BrigGen Marks retires; served as Ass't Sec'y, Air Force (Financial Management). por AF Compt 10:7 Oct '76

MARKSMANSHIP

ATC, SAC split gun honors (in Worldwide Security Police Marksmanship matches at Vandenberg AFB, Calif). Ron Sanders. AF Times 37:24 Oct 18 '76

Individual Training: Inspection Guide C. TIG Brief 28:6p addendum Jan 30 '76

The other 'Doc' Holliday. (TSgt Daniel E.Holliday is NCOIC of the firing range at Moody AFB, Ga) Maj Norm Guenther. illus Airman 20:14 Oct '76

Practice makes perfect. (Marksmanship matches, clubs, and awards) Sgt1C Floyd Harrington. illus Soldiers 31:42-44 Jun '76

MARKSMANSHIP - Continued

Woman shooter (Cpl Jamie M.Trombley) wins Cup Match at Camp Perry (Ohio). MarCor Gaz 60:4 Nov '76

Study and Teaching

BMT may start soon with modified M-16s. AF Times 37:8 Nov 29 '76

Fort Jackson's gun-totin' WACs are very at home on the range. LtCol Tom Hamrick, Ret. illus Army 26:26-30 Feb '76

Moving targets. LtCol Paul L.Davis. Infantry 66: 11-12 May-Jun '76

MARRIAGE AND DIVORCE

Garnishment policies detailed. AF Times 36:12+ Apr 12 '76

Groome on marriage breakdowns. Interview. Ch(BrigGen) Thomas M.Groome, Jr. illus AF Times 36:12 Jul 26 '76

Retired money eyed as divorce pay. AF Times 37:11 Oct 18 '76

Singles lib. (Are the unmarried discriminated against?) Darryl D.McEwen. illus tabs Soldiers 31:6-10 May '76

State order on garnishment backed. Lee Ewing. AF Times 36:4 Mar 29 '76

MARS (PLANET)

See also
Space Flight to Mars

Mars polar ice sample return mission. Robert L. Staehle. illus tabs Spaceflight pt 1, 18:383-390 Nov '76

Mars: The historical perspective. Steven J.Hynes. illus Spaceflight 18:81-83 Mar '76

The puzzle of the Martian soil. Richard S.Lewis. illus Spaceflight 18:391-395 Nov '76

Viking: Lander science equipment. David Baker. illus (Also cutaways) Spaceflight pt 1, 18:211-213 Jun '76; pt 2, 18:241-245 Jul-Aug '76

Viking: Orbiter science equipment. David Baker. illus (Also cutaway) Spaceflight 18:124-125 Apr '76

Viking: The Orbiter. David Baker. illus Spaceflight 18:84-86 Mar '76

The voyages of Viking. illus Spaceflight pt 1, Why explore? Gerald A.Soffen and others. 18:78-80 Mar '76; pt 2, Is there life on Mars? Richard S. Young and Harold P.Klein. 18:118-123 Apr '76; pt 3, Viking: The Lander. David Baker. 18:158-161. Looking at Mars--inside and out. Hugh H. Kieffer and others. 18:162-164+ May '76; pt 4, The chemistry of Mars. Priestly Toulmin III and others. 18:209-211 Jun '76; pt 5, The landing sites. 18:238-240 Jul-Aug '76

MARSCHALL, Albert R.

The Bethesda project (National Naval Medical Center and Uniformed Services University of the Health Sciences). RADM A.R.Marschall. Mil Engr 68: 14-17 Jan-Feb '76

MARSH, Robert T.

Avionics equipment reliability: An elusive objective. LtGen Robert T.Marsh. Def Mgt J 12:24-29 Apr '76

MARSHALL, Samuel L.A.

Tank warrior in the Golan. BrigGen S.L.A.Marshall, Ret. por Mil Rev 56:3-12 Jan '76

MARTIN, George E.

Henry Wong and the 'Gunnel's' chicken. MajGen George E.Martin, Ret. Army 26:26 May '76

MASS TRANSPORTATION see Transportation

MATERIALS

Arkansas Nuclear One. Harlan T.Holmes. illus Mil Engr 68:287-289 Jul-Aug '76

Chances good for no-iron fatigues. Don Hirst. AF Times 37:36 Dec 13 '76

Crew protection (from birdstrikes which penetrate some portion of the cockpit enclosure). LtCol Frank B.Pyne. illus Aerosp Safety 32:24-25 Mar '76

Good news for aircrews. (Nomex winter-weight flight jacket (CWU/45/P)) Capt Kenneth M.Lewis. illus MAC Flyer 23:20 Aug '76

Materials report. Regular feature in some issues of National Defense

The medium girder bridge. LtCol C.Hartington, Ret. illus Mil Engr 68:306-307 Jul-Aug '76

Nomex protection, a 50-50 proposition. Capt Michael E.Humphreys. illus MAC Flyer 23:7-8 Jan '76

Outlet repairs at Dworshak Dam (Idaho). Ernest K. Schrader and Richard A.Kaden. illus tab Mil Engr 68:254-259 May-Jun '76

Slurry trench construction (on Tennessee-Tombigbee Waterway). Carroll D.Winter. illus map tab Mil Engr 68:437-440 Nov-Dec '76

Stilling basin repairs at Dworshak Dam (Idaho). Ernest K.Schrader and Richard A.Kaden. illus Mil Engr 68:282-286 Jul-Aug '76

Testing

Fire protection and life safety. Lawrence G.Adams. illus tab Mil Engr 68:91-93 Mar-Ap: '76

MATERIALS HANDLING

See also
Containers
Hazardous Substances--Transportation
Packing for Shipment

Do you have a transportability problem item? Herbert F.Coen. illus tabs Translog 7:13-16 Apr '76

Handling Inertial Measurement Units (IMUs). TIG Brief 28:14 Nov 5 '76

Learning by doing. Maj Hardy W.Bryan III. illus Army Log 8:34-37 Nov-Dec '76

Preparation of 463L pallet and net control report. TIG Brief 28:11 Mar 12 '76

Shipment of samples to USAF Environmental and Radiological Health labs. TIG Brief 28:12 Nov 5 '76

MAURITIUS

Mission: Typhoon mopup (on the island of Mauritius). LTs Brad Winstead and Mike Willoughby. illus Approach 21:1-3 Feb '76

MAYAGUEZ INCIDENT, 1975

Air mission Mayaguez. Capt John B.Taylor. illus Airman 20:39-47 Feb '76

Flexibility--a state of mind. Gen Richard H.Ellis and LtCol Frank B.Horton III. illus Strat Rev 4: 26-36 Winter '76

For extraordinary heroism ... (USAF recipients of medals of heroism for action during Mayaguez incident) illus Airman 20:44-45 Feb '76

(Maj Robert W.) Undorf wins Mackay Trophy for role in Mayaguez rescue. AF Times 37:31 Oct 25 '76

The Mayaguez incident--crisis management. LtCol Donald E.Carlile. illus Mil Rev 56:3-14 Oct '76

"Mayday" for the Mayaguez. CDR J.A.Messegee and others. illus map US Nav Inst Proc 102:93-111 Nov '76

MEADE, Henry J.

Strengthening Air Force family life. Ch(MajGen) Henry J.Meade. TIG Brief 28:2 Dec 17 '76

MEASUREMENT see Weights and Measures

MECHANIZED FORCES see Armor

MEDAL OF HONOR

All day's tomorrows. (AF Maj George E.Day earns Medal of Honor by escaping from North Vietnam in 1967; he is recaptured and held prisoner until 1973) Robert K.Ruhl. illus Airman 20:24-26+ Nov '76

(BrigGen Charles E.) Yeager receives Congressional Medal. illus AF Times 37:45 Dec 20 '76

A common value of survival. Col John R.Love. illus MarCor Gaz 60:45-46 Feb '76

'I'll try, Sir.' (West Point plebe, Calvin P.Titus, wins Medal of Honor for scaling Tartar Wall during Boxer Rebellion) Col R.C.Burns, Ret. illus Army 26:55-56 Jun '76

3 POWs, 1 rescuer (LT Thomas R.Norris, Capt Lance P.Sijan, Col George E.Day, RADM James B.Stockdale) earn Medal of Honor. illus Armed Forces J Intl 113:34 Mar '76

Two former POWs (Col George E.Day; Capt Lance P.Sijan, who died in prison camp) win Medal of Honor. AF Times 36:12 Mar 15 '76

MEDALS see Awards, Decorations, etc

MEDICAL AND SANITARY AFFAIRS

Armed Forces

Flu shots (for military) planned for Oct: Active duty troops to get priority. George Marker. AF Times 37:26 Aug 30 '76

Army

They shoot horses, don't they? (Army veterinarians do spend some time working with animals but still keep close watch on other veterinary medical activities) Janet Hake. illus Soldiers 31:32-35 Mar '76

MEDICAL CENTERS AND SCHOOLS

Air Force

Lackland's 'bank' (USAF Central Eye Bank at Wilford Hall Medical Center) offers most precious asset. illus AF Times 37:25 Oct 25 '76

MEDICAL CENTERS AND SCHOOLS - Continued

Air Force - Cont'd

Wilford Hall (Medical Center, Lackland AFB, Tex) due major facelift. AF Times 36:22 Jul 12 '76

Armed Forces

The Bethesda project (National Naval Medical Center and Uniformed Services University of the Health Sciences). RADM A.R.Marschall. illus Mil Engr 68:14-17 Jan-Feb '76

Curreri: Doctors U(niversity) is cheaper (than alternative costs of providing the military with doctors). Interview. Anthony R.Curreri. illus AF Times 36:2 Jul 5 '76

Health school (Uniformed Services University of the Health Sciences) too costly, GAO reports. Ann Gerow. AF Times 36:8 May 24 '76

Medical school (Uniformed Services University of the Health Sciences) cancels plans for third building. AF Times 36:21 Mar 22 '76

Move to kill $$ for Med U (Uniformed Services University of Health Sciences) fails (in Senate). AF Times 36:2 Jul 12 '76

32 ready to start med school (Uniformed Services University of the Health Sciences) classes. AF Times 37:6 Nov 1 '76

Army

Modern medical center (Dwight David Eisenhower Army Medical Center, Fort Gordon, Ga). SP5 Manuel Gomez. illus Soldiers 31:22-25 Nov '76

Navy

The Bethesda project (National Naval Medical Center and Uniformed Services University of the Health Sciences). RADM A.R.Marschall. illus Mil Engr 68:14-17 Jan-Feb '76

MEDICAL CORPS

Air Force--U.S.

Efforts fail to boost dwindling MD ranks. Ann Gerow. AF Times 36:10 Apr 26 '76

'Emergency physician' set up as specialty. AF Times 37:4 Aug 9 '76

Medic officers face hike delay. Lee Ewing. AF Times 37:4 Sep 13 '76

Medics expect good year, despite manpower pinch. AF Times 36:8 Jul 5 '76

More early releases ordered: Voluntary medical rollback would affect 350 officers. AF Times 36:4 Feb 9 '76

New reg (DOD Directive 1320.7) forces O-6 board shift. AF Times 37:4 Sep 13 '76

Off-duty employment. Contact, pp 8-9, Fall '76

PA doing more of doctor's work. M.L.Craver. AF Times 37:4 Oct 25 '76

75 MC/DC officers picked for lieutenant colonel hikes. AF Times 37:6 Nov 22 '76

USAF medicare on the mend. Ed Gates. illus AF Mag 59:52-56 Jan '76

Validating basic pay for medical officers. TIG Brief 28:17 Apr 9 '76

MEDICAL CORPS - Continued

Armed Forces--U.S.

Debate growing over doctor bonus. Phil Stevens. AF Times 37:12 Aug 9 '76

New reg (DOD Directive 1320.7) seen speeding hikes in health field. AF Times 36:6 Jul 26 '76

Single Medical Corps urged. Interview. VADM Donald L. Custis. AF Times 36:16 Jun 7 '76

Army--U.S.

Extra pair of hands (physician assistant). Janet Hake. illus Soldiers 31:6-9 Oct '76

Navy--U.S.

Aeromedical safety operations: A new concept in aviation accident prevention and investigation. CDR A.F. Wells. illus Approach 21:18-21 Jun '76

FY 77 PA (Physician Assistants) training cut by Navy. AF Times 36:8 Mar 8 '76

MEDICAL EDUCATION PROGRAM

Health professions scholarship supplement. Contact, 5p sup following p 12, Fall '76

Health professions scholarship supplement. Contact, 9p sup following p 10, Winter '76

Medical program (Medical, Dental and Veterinary Education Program for Air Force Officers) being phased out. Rose Sterling. AF Times 36:10 Jul 19 '76

'76-'79 group med students get tax relief (on scholarship payments). AF Times 37:26 Oct 18 '76

(Service academy) cadets can opt for med school. AF Times 36:3 Apr 26 '76

MEDICAL EQUIPMENT AND SUPPLIES

Dental Service's silver reclamation responsibilities. TIG Brief 28:4 Jan 16 '76

ECG monitoring of heart failure and pilot load/overload by the Vesla seat pad. C. W. Sem-Jacobsen. illus Aviation, Space & Envmt Med 47:441-444 Apr '76

Electronic stethoscope with frequency shaping and infrasonic recording capabilities. Ernest S. Gordon and John M. Lagerwerff. illus tab Aviation, Space & Envmt Med 47:312-316 Mar '76

Idealized inflight airline medical kit: A committee report. Stanley R. Mohler and others. Aviation, Space & Envmt Med 47:1094-1095 Oct '76

Improving hospital logistics support. Wilbur J. Balderson. illus Army Log 8:18-21 Jul-Aug '76

Management of medical (materiel) excesses. TIG Brief 28:6 Mar 12 '76

Medical materiel technicians assigned to Reserve Forces medical units. TIG Brief 28:11 Jun 18 '76

Medical supply customer training. TIG Brief 28:15 Aug 13 '76

MEDICAL EXAMINATIONS

Acquired bundle branch block and its response to exercise testing in asymptomatic aircrewmen: A review with case reports. James E. Whinnery and Victor Froelicher, Jr. illus tabs Aviation, Space & Envmt Med 47:1217-1225 Nov '76

MEDICAL EXAMINATIONS - Continued

Aircrew medical standards and their application in the Royal Australian Air Force. Roy L. DeHart and others. tabs Aviation, Space & Envmt Med 47: 70-76 Jan '76

Dear Doc. Maj William Sullivan. MAC Flyer 23: 18-19 Aug '76

Evaluation of electrocardiograms on rated fliers. TIG Brief 28:15 Oct 8 '76

Exercise in an hypoxic environment as a screening test for ischaemic heart disease. Purshottam Kumar Khanna and others. tabs Aviation, Space & Envmt Med 47:1114-1117 Oct '76

Exit physicals made optional. Lee Ewing. AF Times 36:2 Mar 15 '76

Paroxysmal and chronic atrial fibrillation in airman certification. Douglas E. Busby and Audie W. Davis. tabs Aviation, Space and Envmt Med 47:185-186 Feb '76

Preemployment and periodic physical examination of airline pilots at the Mayo Clinic, 1939-1974. Robert R. Orford and Earl T. Carter. tabs Aviation, Space and Envmt Med 47:180-184+ Feb '76

MEDICAL RESEARCH

Diet + exercise (for atherosclerosis). Nathan Pritikin and Edward Carlstrom. illus Army 26:42-46 Jun '76

U.S. Army Aeromedical Research Laboratory. Col Robert W. Bailey. illus USA Avn Dig 22:4-5+ Oct '76

War of the microbes. SSgt John Savard. illus Soldiers 31:13-16 Sep '76

MEDICAL SERVICE

See also
Dental Corps	Medical Service Corps
Flight Surgeons	Nurse Corps
Medical Corps	Veterinary Corps

Air Force--Australia

Aircrew medical standards and their application in the Royal Australian Air Force. Roy L. DeHart and others. tabs Aviation, Space & Envmt Med 47: 70-76 Jan '76

Air Force--U.S.

Blood transfusion. TIG Brief 28:17 Oct 22 '76

Handicapped getting help in infancy (at Vandenberg AFB, Calif). Donna Peterson. illus AF Times 37:37+ Dec 6 '76

Management of emergency services in medical facilities. TIG Brief 28:8 Feb 27 '76

MedEvac 001. LCDRs H.K. Barnhill and H.W. Benter. illus Approach 21:1-3 Dec '75

Medical board responsibility. TIG Brief 28:18 Jan 16 '76

Medical care for fliers' dependents. TIG Brief 28:9 Jul 16 '76

Medical Deficiency Analysis System (DAS). TIG Brief 28:15-16 Mar 12 '76

Medical/dental supervisors' responsibilities for mobilization augmentees. TIG Brief 28:10 Jul 16 '76

Medical disaster plans. TIG Brief 28:9-10 Jul 16 '76

(Medical) malpractice claims seen at high level. AF Times 36:26 Jun 14 '76

MEDICAL SERVICE - Continued

Air Force--U.S. - Cont'd

Medical Service: Inspection Guide E. TIG Brief pt 1, Medical units and activities on active duty, A-E. 28:6p addendum Apr 23 '76; pt 1, F-I. 28:4p addendum May 7 '76; pt 1, J. 28:6p addendum May 21 '76; pt 1, K. 28:6p addendum Jun 4 '76; pt 1, L. 28:6p addendum Jun 18 '76; pt 1, M: Veterinary service. pt 2, Air Reserve Forces medical units or activities. 28:4p addendum Jul 2 '76; pt 1, M, Supplement 1. 28, addendum:7 Aug 27 '76

Pet control, or the owner should pay. TIG Brief 28:14 Sep 10 '76

Three-year minimum initial term of service for officers. TIG Brief 28:15 Apr 23 '76

USAF medicare on the mend. Ed Gates. illus AF Mag 59:52-56 Jan '76

Statistics

USAF medicare on the mend. Ed Gates. illus AF Mag 59:52-56 Jan '76

Armed Forces--Russia

Military service hygiene. ColGen D. Kuvshinsky. Soviet Mil Rev No. 12:38-39 Dec '76

Armed Forces--U.S.

Computerized (military) med setup to link Services by '82. AF Times 37:8 Aug 30 '76

DOD to control health care? AF Times 37:4 Dec 13 '76

DOD to justify health job merger (Health Affairs into Manpower and Reserve Affairs). AF Times 36:21 Jul 5 '76

Malpractice bill would aid Guard; no shift in filing malpractice suits. AF Times 37:8 Oct 11 '76

Costs

CHAMPUS to lose doctors--shift to Medicare rates seen costing patients more. Ann Gerow. AF Times 36:3 Feb 23 '76

Organization

New health unit (Defense Dept Health Council) to mesh all Services' programs. Andy Plattner. AF Times 37:22 Dec 27 '76

Army--U.S.

All-purpose clinic (at Fort Bliss, Tex). Sgt1C Floyd Harrington. illus Soldiers 31:31-33 Dec '76

HSC (Health Services Command) outlines cutbacks in medical care. tabs AF Times 37:28 Dec 13 '76

Medics, door-to-door. (MObile MEdical Teams (MOMET) at Fort Leonard Wood, Mo) Sgt JoAnn Mann. illus Soldiers 31:24-25 Oct '76

National Guard--Air Force--U.S.

Medical/dental care for USAFR/ANG personnel. TIG Brief 28:17 Oct 22 '76

Reserve Forces--Air Force--U.S.

Maintenance of Reserve Forces health records. TIG Brief 28:11 Jun 18 '76

Medical/dental care for USAFR/ANG personnel. TIG Brief 28:17 Oct 22 '76

MEDICAL SERVICE - Continued

Reserve Forces--Armed Forces--U.S.

(Air, Army) Guard, agencies (NASA and CIA) ask malpractice protection. Ann Gerow. AF Times 36:26 Mar 15 '76

Russia

In the name of man. (Public health service in the Soviet Union) V. Ryvkin. illus Soviet Mil Rev No. 7: 52-55 Jul '76

United States

(Air, Army) Guard, agencies (NASA and CIA) ask malpractice protection. Ann Gerow. AF Times 36:26 Mar 15 '76

MEDICAL SERVICE CORPS

Air Force--U.S.

(USAF) ward clerk program. TIG Brief 28:7-8 Jul 16 '76

Reserve Forces--Air Force--U.S.

Decentralization of publications within Reserve forces medical units. TIG Brief 28:3 Apr 9 '76

Medical materiel technicians assigned to Reserve Forces medical units. TIG Brief 28:11 Jun 18 '76

MEDICARE

Big CHAMPUS cost cut ahead. Ann Gerow. AF Times 36:4 Mar 8 '76

CHAMPUS appeal procedures ordered. Andy Plattner. AF Times 37:4 Sep 20 '76

CHAMPUS changes still coming (so's info now). Officer 52:10 Jun '76

CHAMPUS clears up child abuse cases. Ann Gerow. AF Times 36:20 Jun 21 '76

CHAMPUS: Confusing but helpful. Andy Plattner. AF Times 37:6 Aug 30 '76

CHAMPUS delay hits Southwest. Andy Plattner. AF Times 37:2 Oct 18 '76

CHAMPUS options widened. AF Times 37:33 Aug 23 '76

CHAMPUS payments pose problems. Andy Plattner. AF Times 37:19 Sep 13 '76

CHAMPUS reg outlines claim appeal procedure. AF Times 37:3 Nov 8 '76

CHAMPUS relaxes 40-mile policy. AF Times 36:4 Jul 26 '76

CHAMPUS seeks emergency $$. AF Times 36:10 May 10 '76

CHAMPUS, store curbs fought, draft fight lost on Capitol Hill. Officer 52:5 Apr '76

CHAMPUS switch (Medicare charge system) confuses users. AF Times 36:22 Mar 29 '76

CHAMPUS to lose doctors--shift to Medicare rates seen costing patients more. Ann Gerow. AF Times 36:3 Feb 23 '76

CHAMPUS wasn't always DOD's fall guy. AF Times 36:10 Mar 22 '76

Care of handicapped children under CHAMPUS hit by GAO. AF Times 37:8 Nov 15 '76

DOD held lax on CHAMPUS data. Ann Gerow. AF Times 36:4 Mar 29 '76

MEDICARE - Continued

DOD would lift CHAMPUS bars. AF Times 36:2 Apr 19 '76

Families should pay (CHAMPUS) for coverage: (Les) Aspin charge. AF Times 36:10 Mar 22 '76

Filing CHAMPUS claim is complex, but vital. Andy Plattner. AF Times 37:6+ Sep 6 '76

Health insurance switch (from CHAMPUS) would cost. AF Times 37:4 Sep 20 '76

Memo tells what CHAMPUS will cover in family planning. Andy Plattner. AF Times 37:4 Dec 13 '76

Military care comes first: 40-mile CHAMPUS rule. AF Times 36:3 Feb 23 '76

More decisions affect Medicare. Officer 52:4+ Aug '76

('77) budget to shut USPHS (U.S. Public Health Service) hospitals and add new CHAMPUS curbs. Officer 52:10 Mar '76

Option under CHAMPUS: Study urges use of outside plans. AF Times 36:10 Mar 15 '76

Senate, House votes combine to assure new CHAMPUS cuts. Officer 52:8 Jan '76

Some eye care suggested under CHAMPUS. AF Times 36:4 Feb 16 '76

Southwest contractor changed: CHAMPUS developments. AF Times 37:20 Dec 6 '76

Study (by Defense, Office of Management and Budget and Dept of Health, Education and Welfare) calls for CHAMPUS shakeup. Ann Gerow. AF Times 36:4 Feb 16 '76

Travelers subject to CHAMPUS rules. AF Times 36:2 May 24 '76

USAF medicare on the mend. Ed Gates. illus AF Mag 59:52-56 Jan '76

Costs

USAF medicare on the mend. Ed Gates. illus AF Mag 59:52-56 Jan '76

MEDICINE

See also
Aviation Medicine
Military Medicine
Space Medicine

The military defense counsel's use of scientific evidence and expert witnesses. Maj William M. McKenna III. AF Law Rev 18:48-65 Fall '76

MEDITERRANEAN FLEET see Fleet, 6th

MEDITERRANEAN REGION

The world environment and U.S. military policy for the 1970s and 1980s. ADM Thomas H.Moorer, Ret and Alvin J.Cottrell. tab Strat Rev 4:56-65 Spring '76

Strategic Importance

NATO's tender watery flanks. Joseph Palmer. illus Sea Power 19:34-39 Mar '76

Red runs the Rubicon: Turbulent Italy faces new troubles, NATO could lose its Mediterranean anchor. Lawrence Griswold. illus map Sea Power 19:20-24 Mar '76

SACEUR's subcommanders take the floor: The southern region. ADM Stansfield Turner. illus chart NATO's Fifteen Nations 21:86-94 Feb-Mar '76

MEDITERRANEAN REGION - Continued

Strategic Importance - Cont'd

Sea of uncertainty (Eastern Mediterranean). illus Def & For Aff Dig pt 1. Gregory Copley. No.12-No.1: 4-7+ '75-'76; pt 2. Leigh Johnson and Gregory Copley. No.2:6-8+ '76

MEETZE, H.W.

Data processing and the Reserve components. BrigGen H.W.Meetze and Maj J.Steiger. Army Log 8:20-23 Sep-Oct '76

MELNER, Sinclair L.

The role of air defense. BrigGen Sinclair L.Melner. Air Def Mag, pp 24-25, Apr-Jun '76

MEMORIALS

See also
Cemeteries, National
Unknown Soldier

Fortress on the Bug (Brest, Belorussia). LtCol N. Yelshin. illus Soviet Mil Rev No.6:39-41 Jun '76

The message of the Minuteman. Col William T.Coffey. illus Natl Guardsman 30:22-23 Jul '76

Tie a yellow ribbon. (Memorial at McConnell AFB, Kans, honors five AF flyers from Kansas who were casualties in Southeast Asia) illus Airman 20: inside back cover Nov '76

USMC memorial in Colorado. MarCor Gaz 60:6 Dec '76

MENTAL HEALTH

See also
Psychiatry

MERCENARIES (SOLDIERS) see Mercenary Troops

MERCENARY TROOPS

See also
Foreign Legion

Former GIs reported fighting in Rhodesia. AF Times 37:21 Dec 27 '76

MERCHANT MARINE

The AMVER (Automated Mutual-assistance VEssel Rescue) system. LT Walter McDougall. illus US Nav Inst Proc 102:106-108 Mar '76

Russia

Pressure builds for (Merchant Marine) 'fair share' legislation. James D.Hessman. illus Sea Power 19:19-22 Aug '76

The Soviet merchant fleet. CDR Richard T.Ackley, Ret. illus tabs US Nav Inst Proc 102:27-37 Feb '76

United States

See also
Maritime Administration

A bluewater interface and the Running Mates program: Navy/Merchant Marine officer exchange program offers benefits to each. James D.Hessman. illus Sea Power 19:20-22 Jun '76

Cargo preference: Prescription for an ailing industry. Donald C.Leavens. illus tabs Sea Power 19: 26-30 Jun '76

MERCHANT MARINE - Continued

United States - Cont'd

A conversation with Paul Hall (President of the Sea-
farers International Union of North America):
Maritime labor--the ally within. Interview. illus
Sea Power 19:11-16 Feb '76

Getting it all together (at Mormacsun launching in San
Diego): Congress and a cargo plan, shipbuilders
and ship operators, the sea services and the Merchant Marine. illus Sea Power 19:30 Feb '76

A healthier, more prosperous, and more productive
U.S. Merchant Marine. Robert J.Blackwell. illus
Sea Power 19:30-33 Jan '76

The Navy begins a new approach to modern maritime
defense: Strengthening the link between U.S. naval
forces and the American Merchant Marine. (Reserve Merchant Ship Defense System (RMSDS))
James J.Mulquin. illus Sea Power 19:25-29
Mar '76

The new Soviet maritime strategy--and the lack of an
effective U.S. counter-strategy. RADM George H.
Miller, Ret. illus Sea Power 19:17-20 May '76

New support for cargo preference. L.Edgar Prina.
illus Sea Power 19:30-33 Mar '76

Pressure builds for (Merchant Marine) 'fair share'
legislation. James D.Hessman. illus Sea Power
19:19-22 Aug '76

Santa Fe/TI: 'The core issue'--new report (by the
Transportation Institute) recommends increased
Navy/Merchant Marine cooperation and coordination. James D.Hessman. illus tab Sea Power 19:
15-16 Jul '76

(Seapower) Address, NDTA, New York, April 21,
1976) ADM Elmo R.Zumwalt, Jr, Ret. illus Def
Trans J 32:34-36 Jun '76

Solving the sealift shortage. L.Edgar Prina. illus
Sea Power 19:19-26 Oct '76

(The state of the seas, 1976) illus tabs Sea Power 19:
7-20+ Jan '76

USMER (U.S.-Flag MERchant Vessel Locator Filing
System): Following the U.S. "Flags." CDR Rich-
ard E.Johe. illus US Nav Inst Proc 102:102-103
Dec '76

U.S. Merchant Marine--for commerce and defense.
RADM John D.Chase. illus tabs US Nav Inst Proc
102:130-145 May '76

History

The banana Navy. (United Fruit Co's Great White
Fleet) CAPT Robert Carl, Ret. illus US Nav Inst
Proc 102:55-67 Dec '76

MERCY MISSIONS

Airlifts to Turkish quake victims end. illus AF
Times 37:22 Dec 13 '76

Earthquake. (Soldiers from Army Southern European
Task Force assist in Italy, May 1946) Maj Patricia
Whelan. illus Soldiers 31:6-7 Sep '76

Earthquake! (USAF aids Guatemala with airlift, reconnaissance, and communications) MSgt Harold
Newcomb and SSgt Ken Peterson. illus Airman 20:
8-13 Jun '76

Earthquake (northern Italy, May 6, 1976). LtCol Arthur P.Hahn. illus map AF Engrg & Svcs Qtr 17:
18-21 Nov '76

MERCY MISSIONS - Continued

Guatemala: Helping hand. SSgt Zack Richards. illus
Soldiers 31:14-17 Aug '76

Guatemala: 210th Aviation Battalion comes through
again in disaster relief. CW2 Larry R.Santure.
illus USA Avn Dig 22:4-5+ Jul '76

Mission: Typhoon mopup (on the island of Mauritius).
LTs Brad Winstead and Mike Willoughby. illus
Approach 21:1-3 Feb '76

Operation Wagonmaster. ("D" Company (Wagonmasters), 34th Support Battalion, 6th Cavalry Brigade
(Air Combat), in disaster relief operation in Guatemala) Maj Terry N.Rosser. illus USA Avn Dig
22:6-7+ Jul '76

MERKLING, Richard E.

Seeking failure-free systems. MajGen Richard E.
Merkling. AU Rev 27:41-50 Jul-Aug '76

METAL WORK

Light metal castings. Hans-G.Lülfing. illus Aerosp
Intl 12:40-41 May-Jun '76

Scrap metal recycled into tools. illus Fld Arty J 44:
29-30 May-Jun '76

METALS

Are we running out of metals? Simon D.Strauss.
Persp in Def Mgt No.24:19-31 Winter '75-'76

Foundries in dilemma. Debbie C.Tennison. illus
tabs Natl Def 60:453-458 May-Jun '76

Gold plated traffic. Donald T.Isaacs. illus Translog
7:13-15 Jan '76

Laws to aid foundries. Debbie C.Tennison. illus
Natl Def 61:131-134 Sep-Oct '76

Quarterly inventory of precious metal records. TIG
Brief 28:10 Jul 16 '76

Working titanium alloys. Aerosp Intl 12:56 Mar-
Apr '76

METEOROLOGICAL STATIONS see Weather Stations

METEOROLOGY

See also
Climatic Research
Weather

METHODOLOGY

See also subdivision Methodology under specific
subjects

METRIC SYSTEM see Weights and Measures

MEUSE, Barry M.

After the Bicentennial: The end of an era? Maj Barry
M.Meuse. AU Rev 27:2-12 Jul-Aug '76

MEXICO

History

The ultimate battle. (French Foreign Legion action
at Camerone, Mexico, 1863) SP4 Robert G.Ful-
ler. illus Soldiers 31:50-53 Sep '76

MICHAELIS, Frederick H.

Is inflation a new malady in defense planning? (Remarks, Annual National Conference Banquet, Assoc of Old Crows, San Diego, Calif, Sep 24, 1975) ADM Frederick H.Michaelis. por Elect Warfare 7:63-64+ Nov-Dec '75

MICROFICHE see Microforms

MICROFILM see Microforms

MICROFORMS

Going to film (government micrographics): It's now up to the agencies. (Interview with John D. Livsey) John F.Judge. illus Govt Exec 8:15+ Jan '76

Magnifying inner space. Janet Hake. illus Soldiers 31:45-48 Sep '76

MICRONESIA

Strategic Importance

The strategic significance of the Pacific Islands: A new debate begins. Allan W.Cameron. (Condensed from Orbis, Fall 1975) map Mil Rev 56:19-28 Oct '76

MICROWAVE LANDING SYSTEMS

Germany's MLS proposal. Guenter Blaschke. illus Aerosp Intl 12:6-8+ May-Jun '76

MLS: Breakthrough in landing systems. John L. McLucas. illus AF Mag 59:66-68+ Jul '76

Microwave landing system. John G.Leyden. illus tab USA Avn Dig 22:4-5+ Sep '76

(Microwave Scanning Beam Landing System--MSBLS) Signal 31:82 Nov-Dec '76

Terminal Precision Approach Control Program (TPACP). TIG Brief 28:12 Aug 27 '76

The UK's MLS entry. illus Aerosp Intl 12:14-16 May-Jun '76

MICROWAVES

Binary beam IFM (Instantaneous Frequency Measurement): Multiple discriminators improve frequency resolution. Marc Smirlock. illus tab Elect Warfare 8:83-84+ May-Jun '76

DIA (Defense Intelligence Agency): Communists study microwaves as weapons. AF Times 37:3 Dec 6 '76

Electronics: Key military 'force multiplier.' Malcolm R.Currie. illus AF Mag 59:39-45 Jul '76

High-altitude carbon monoxide. (First microwave observations of carbon monoxide in upper atmospheres of Earth, Venus and Mars) Spaceflight 18:196 May '76

Industry report and survey: A report on the microwave component market. illus tab Countermeasures 2:33-40+ Aug '76

The maturing of digital microwave radio. Kerry R. Fox and John F.Beckerich. illus tabs Signal 30: 6-11 Apr '76

Microwave power tube survey. tabs Countermeasures 2:24+ Mar '76

Millimeter wave power tube developments. Mike Cunningham. illus tabs Countermeasures 2:34-36+ Jun '76

MICROWAVES - Continued

Spin tuned magnetrons for frequency agile radars. illus tab Countermeasures 2:52-55 Mar '76

MIDDENDORF, John W., II

American maritime strategy and Soviet naval expansion. J.William Middendorf II. por Strat Rev 4: 16-25 Winter '76

European odyssey: A NATO tour with Navy Secretary Middendorf. James D.Hessman. por Sea Power 19:14-21 Dec '76

(The Navy): Unknown events, disturbing trends, and a rebuilding of strength. J.William Middendorf II. por Sea Power 19:7-13 Jan '76

Travels with the Secretary (of the Navy). L.Edgar Prina. por Sea Power 19:17-20 Feb '76

MIDDLE EAST

Doomed to peace. Béchir Ben Yahmed. (Digested from Foreign Affairs, Oct 1975) Mil Rev 56:39-44 Feb '76

Materials control and peace: The Middle East. Dennis Chaplin. RUSI J for Def Studies 121:34-37 Mar '76

Middle East oil and military balance of power. Col Irving Heymont, Ret. illus Mil Rev 56:70-76 Jul '76

Nuclear terrorism and the Middle East. Capt Augustus R.Norton. illus Mil Rev 56:3-11 Apr '76

The psychology of Middle East peace. Nahum Goldmann. (Digested from Foreign Affairs, Oct 1975) Mil Rev 56:31-39 Feb '76

History

The Faluja pocket (1st Palestinian War, 1948). David Nicolle. map Army Qtr pt 1, The Egyptian advance. 105:440-448+ Oct '75; pt 2, The Black Panther of Faluja. 106:333-350 Jul '76

Politics and Government

Revolution and tradition in the Middle East, Africa, and South Asia. Marcus W.Franda. illus Natl Sec Aff Forum No.24:23-31 Spring-Summer '76

Strategic Importance

Linkage politics and coercive diplomacy: A comparative analysis of two Lebanese crises. Paul H.B. Godwin and Lewis B.Ware. illus AU Rev 28:80-89 Nov-Dec '76

Soviet policy toward the Middle East since the October 1973 Arab-Israeli War. Robert O.Freedman. illus Nav War Col Rev 29:61-103 Fall '76

MIDDLE EAST CRISIS, 1967

See also
Arab-Israeli Conflict, 1967-
Middle East War, 1973

MIDDLE EAST WAR, 1973

See also
Arab-Israeli Conflict, 1967-
Middle East Crisis, 1967

Air war: Middle East--a report from the International Symposium on the Military Aspects of the Arab-Israeli Conflict, Jerusalem, 12-17 October 1975. Jeffrey Greenhut. illus Aerosp Hist 23:21-23 Mar '76

A call from the wilderness. Maj Donald J.Alberts. illus AU Rev 28:35-45 Nov-Dec '76

MIDDLE EAST WAR, 1973 - Continued

Crisis decisionmaking in Israel: The case of the October 1973 Middle East War. Maj Robert H. McKenzie-Smith. illus Nav War Col Rev 29:39-52 Summer '76

Detente and the Yom Kippur War: From crisis management to crisis prevention? Phil Williams.
Royal Air Forces Qtr 16:227-233 Autumn '76

The Israeli Air Force. Zeev Schiff. illus map AF
Mag 59:31-38 Aug '76

The October War: Burying the blitzkrieg. Jeffrey
Record. illus Mil Rev 56:19-21 Apr '76

The Syrian side of the hill. Charles Wakebridge. map
illus Mil Rev 56:20-30 Feb '76

Tac air, member of the (combined arms) team supporting the supersoldier. LtCol William H. Rees.
illus Infantry 66:16-23 May-Jun '76

A tank myth or a missile mirage? Charles Wakebridge. illus Mil Rev 56:3-11 Aug '76

Tank warrior in the Golan. BrigGen S. L. A. Marshall, Ret. illus Mil Rev 56:3-12 Jan '76

The War of Atonement--and its lessons. Maj T. P.
Toyne Sewell. Army Qtr 106:67-71 Jan '76

Equipment

Tank warrior in the Golan. BrigGen S. L. A. Marshall, Ret. illus Mil Rev 56:3-12 Jan '76

Tanks in the Middle East. Jac Weller. illus Mil Rev
56:11-23 May '76

Weapon systems: Gabriel. Mark Hewish. illus US
Nav Inst Proc 102:101 Jul '76

MILITARISM

African armies in historical and contemporary perspectives: The search for connections. Rene Lemarchand. J Pol & Mil Sociol 4:261-275 Fall '76

Chile: Fascism and militarism. G. Spersky. Soviet
Mil Rev No. 7:59-60 Jul '76

Clausewitz and Soviet politico-military strategy.
BrigGen Antonio Pelliccia. NATO's Fifteen Nations 20:18-21+ Dec '75-Jan '76; Digest. Mil Rev
56:23-33 Aug '76

MILITARY ACADEMIES

See also
Noncommissioned Officers Academies
Preparatory Schools

The professional study of war. Keith R. Simpson.
RUSI J for Def Studies 120:27-31 Dec '75

Russia

A solid foundation. (Opochetsk Higher AA Missile
School of Air Defence Forces) LtCol V. Lutsenko.
illus Soviet Mil Rev No. 8:23-24 Aug '76

Training facilities at military schools. Col S. Muts-
ynov. Soviet Mil Rev No. 11:26-27 Nov '76

United States

See also Service academies by name, e. g.,
Air Force Academy
Military Academy, West Point, NY

The academies five: Compliments and criticism (by
General Accounting Office). illus Sea Power 18:28
Dec '75

MILITARY ACADEMIES - Continued

United States - Cont'd

Academy teachers: Put civilians in place of military,
(Sen John) Glenn advises. Len Famiglietti. AF
Times 36:8 Jun 14 '76

Academy women raising standards (according to
academy officials speaking at DACOWITS, Defense
Advisory Committee On Women In The Services,
Meeting, Washington, Nov 14-18, 1976). M. L.
Craver. AF Times 37:2 Nov 29 '76

Naval Academy faculty called 'worst' (of the three by
DepSecDef William P. Clements). AF Times 36:12
Apr 5 '76

(Senate) hearings on honor code: Inflexible system
held root of problem. AF Times 36:50 Jul 5 '76

(Service academy) cadets can opt for med school. AF
Times 36:3 Apr 26 '76

(Service) academy drop outs explained (by General
Accounting Office). Andy Plattner. AF Times 36:4
Mar 15 '76

Token minority. (Army instructors at other Service
academies) Darryl D. McEwen. illus Soldiers 31:
52-53 Aug '76

MILITARY ACADEMY, WEST POINT, NY

Army (Secretary Martin R. Hoffmann) outlines plan to
readmit (West Point) cadets. Phil Stevens. AF
Times 37:8 Sep 6 '76

Cheating at West Point stirs up squalls on Hill. AF
Times 37:12 Sep 20 '76

Some attitudes on honor code (at West Point): Survey
report. Phil Stevens. AF Times 36:14 Jul 19 '76

West Point bound. (Students at the United States Military Academy Preparatory School) Capt Peter D.
Weddle. illus Soldiers 31:21-23 Apr '76

Will CMA (Court of Military Appeals) review cadet
cheating? AF Times 37:9 Aug 30 '76

Women at West Point. Darryl D. McEwen. illus Soldiers 31:28-31 Jun '76

History

Washington's last Chief Engineer, Etienne Bechet,
Sieur de Rochefontaine. Raleigh B. Buzzaird. (Reprinted from Military Engineer, March-April
1953) illus map Mil Engr 68:452-455 Nov-Dec '76

MILITARY AID TO FOREIGN COUNTRIES

GAO report: O'scas aid causes U.S. arms shortage.
AF Times 36:10 Jan 19 '76

The Security Assistance Program. (Statement before
Committee on International Relations, House of
Representatives, Nov 12, 1975) LtGen H. M. Fish.
AF Plcy Ltr for Comdrs: Sup No. 1:18-22 Jan '76

Angola

The Soviet intervention in Angola: Intentions and implications. Peter Vanneman and Martin James.
tabs Strat Rev 4:92-103 Summer '76

Egypt

Materials control and peace: The Middle East. Dennis
Chaplin. RUSI J for Def Studies 121:34-37 Mar '76

Iraq

Soviet military aid to Iraq and Syria. Roger F. Pajak.
illus Strat Rev 4:51-59 Winter '76

MILITARY AID TO FOREIGN COUNTRIES -Continued

Israel

The burden of defense on the Israeli economy. Patrick W. Murphy. illus tabs Def & For Aff Dig No. 4: 46-51 '76

Korea (Republic)

American nuclear weapons in South Korea. Table only. Def Monitor 5:5 Jan '76

Korea and U.S. policy in Asia. illus tabs Def Monitor 5: entire issue Jan '76

U.S. military assistance and sales to Korea (1971-76). Table only. Def Monitor 5:7 Jan '76

Libya

Soviet arms aid to Libya. Roger F. Pajak. illus Mil Rev 56:82-87 Jul '76

Russia

Red stars over America. (Delivering U.S. aircraft to Russia via an Alaska-Siberian route, under the Lend-Lease Act, during WW II) Capt Stephen O. Manning III. illus Airman 20:35-37 Apr '76

Spain

The Spanish connection: A wider U.S. commitment in the making. maps tabs Def Monitor 5: entire issue Feb '76

Syria

Soviet military aid to Iraq and Syria. Roger F. Pajak. illus Strat Rev 4:51-59 Winter '76

Vietnam (Democratic Republic)

Lessons of Vietnam. Col O. Ivanov. Soviet Mil Rev No. 4:44-46 Apr '76

MILITARY AIRLIFT COMMAND

See also
Aerospace Rescue and Recovery Service

Accident statistics for 1975. Maj Russell L. Cayler. tabs MAC Flyer 23:6-7 Apr '76

Airlift is key to commuter Army (in Reforger 75). Translog 7:16-17 Mar '76; Mil Engr 68:308 Jul-Aug '76

Airlift problems pose threat to our security. Editorial. Officer 52:6+ Jan '76

Bolling (AFB, DC), Andrews (AFB, Md) join MAC. AF Times 36:27 Jul 19 '76

Flight engineers fear cutback--AF says no move under way. AF Times 36:7 Mar 8 '76

House panel (Appropriations Committee) wants training planes full (and AF crews to fly some aircraft now contracted to airlines). Len Famiglietti. AF Times 36:17 Jun 21 '76

In the barrel. (Military airlift managers, referred to as barrelmasters, respond to worldwide demands) TSgt Tom Dwyer. illus Airman 20:36-39 Jun '76

The MAC line revisited. LtCol John W. Ray. illus MAC Flyer 23:14-15 Jan '76

MAC 'new look' ORI. BrigGen Edward J. Nash. tab TIG Brief 28:3-4 Aug 27 '76

MAC not joking about security. TIG Brief 28:15 May 7 '76

MILITARY AIRLIFT COMMAND - Continued

MAC passenger terminals toughen security. TIG Brief 28:16 Apr 9 '76

MAC's (Gen Paul K.) Carlton asks 'airlift partnership.' AF Times 37:36 Dec 6 '76

Military airlift and the future. (Excerpt from address, 57th Defense Preparedness Meeting, American Defense Preparedness Assoc, Los Angeles, Oct 15, 1975) Gen Paul K. Carlton. Natl Def 60: 288 Jan-Feb '76

Military Airlift Command. tab illus charts AF Mag 59:69-71 May '76

The other side of the coin. (Many non-flying personnel were necessary for Operation Coin Alaska, airlift supply operation from Elmendorf AFB to AF and Navy installations on the North Slope) TSgt Tom Dwyer. illus Airman 20:38-42 May '76

Priority of nuclear logistic movement support. TIG Brief 28:10 Nov 19 '76

System safety--expanding the user's role. Gen Paul K. Carlton. TIG Brief 28:2 Jun 4 '76

Triple Deuce leads the way. (Two C-5's at Dover AFB, Del, compete in a Lead the Force program of accelerated use of the planes in order to prepare for maintenance needs in other C-5's) Maj Jim Gibson. illus Airman 20:20-23 Aug '76

Why airlift isn't free. Gen Paul K. Carlton. tab illus Army Log 8:2-6 Jan-Feb '76

History

History of MAC. illus Navigator 23:15-19 Spring '76

Organization

MAC Associates ... a vital role. MSgt Gerald H. Smith. illus Air Reservist 28:12-13 Nov '76

MILITARY ART AND SCIENCE

See also
Attack and Defense (Military Science)
Deception in Warfare
Interdiction
Strategy
Surprise in Warfare
Tactics

Basil Liddell Hart: Much to say to the 'Army of '76.' MajGen George B. Pickett, Jr, Ret. illus Army 26:29-33 Apr '76

A battery on exercise. Lt V. Yusupdjanov. illus Soviet Mil Rev No. 1:19-20 Jan '76

Craftsmen in armor: The hobo (MajGen Percy Hobart) and der schnelle Heinz (Gen Heinz Guderian). Kenneth Macksey. illus Armor 85:36-40 Jan-Feb '76

Flex that military mind. ACM Christopher Foxley-Norris. Army Qtr 106:23-29 Jan '76

The genetics of the battlefield. Maj George M. Hall. illus Mil Rev 56:47-55 Nov '76

Historical logistics. Hugh Hodgins. illus Log Spectrum 10:14-15 Fall '76

Military science as an important factor of defence potential. LtGen M. Gareyev. Soviet Mil Rev No. 12:15-17 Dec '76

Organisation of a march. MajGen A. Zyryanov. Soviet Mil Rev No. 6:18-19+ Jun '76

MILITARY ART AND SCIENCE - Continued

Scharnhorst to Schlieffen: The rise and decline of
German military thought. Herbert Rosinski. Nav
War Col Rev 29:83-103 Summer '76

The War of Atonement--and its lessons. Maj T.P.
Toyne Sewell. Army Qtr 106:67-71 Jan '76

History

Sun Pin: China's other master of war. Maj W.H.P.J.
Fitzsimons. Army Qtr 106:287-290 Jul '76

MILITARY ASSISTANCE ADVISORY GROUP

Consider the low echelon advisor. WO1 Frederick V.
Leppien. illus Mil Rev 56:18-19 Feb '76

On going native: A discussion. Maj Robert V. Bran-
son. illus tab Mil Rev 56:13-25 Jan '76

Vietnam (Republic)

U.S. field artillery in Vietnam. MajGen David E.Ott.
(Extracts from "Field Artillery Monograph") illus
tabs maps Fld Arty J pt 1, The field artillery adviser. 43:23-29 Jan-Feb '75; pt 2, In order to win.
43:39-45 Mar-Apr '75; pt 3, Field artillery mobility. 43:15-22 May-Jun '75; pt 4, The buildup. 43:
9-16 Jul-Aug '75, 43:46-51 Sep-Oct '75; pt 4, The
field artillery buildup: 1967 combat operations.
43:29-34 Nov-Dec '75; pt 5, The hot war: 1968,
the Tet offensive. 44:27-31 Jan-Feb '76; pt 5, The
hot war: The Battle of Khe Sanh. 44:44-48 Mar-
Apr '76; pt 5, The hot war: 1968-69, A Shau Valley. 44:53-57 May-Jun '76; pt 5, The hot war:
Operations and raids. 44:37-43 Jul-Aug '76; pt 6,
Vietnamization: FA assistance programs. 44:
10-17 Sep-Oct '76; pt 6, Vietnamization: Operations into Cambodia. 44:13-18 Nov-Dec '76

MILITARY ASSISTANCE PROGRAM

See also
Security Assistance Program

MILITARY ASSISTANCE TO SAFETY AND TRAFFIC
see MAST

MILITARY BASES

See also
Air Bases
Army Posts
Inactivation of Installations and Units
Marine Corps Bases

United States

Base access and the first amendment: The rights of
civilians on military installations. Maj Alan C.
Stine. AF Law Rev 18:18-32 Fall '76

MILITARY BASES, AMERICAN

Pacific Region

The strategic significance of the Pacific Islands: A
new debate begins. Allan W. Cameron. (Condensed
from Orbis, Fall 1975) map Mil Rev 56:19-28
Oct '76

Turkey

No change seen in Turkey bases. AF Times 37:20
Oct 18 '76

MILITARY CEREMONIES, HONORS AND SALUTES

In tribute to the Yanks. (British Sea Scout group
honors seven particular Americans on Remembrance Sunday, England's annual day of honor for
British and American dead of WW II) LtCol Steve
Hinderliter. illus Airman 20:41-43 Nov '76

MILITARY CEREMONIES, HONORS AND SALUTES -
Continued

21 seconds, 21 steps. Sgt1C Floyd Harrington. illus
Soldiers 31:29-32 Jul '76

When the (USAF Honor) Guard's up. TSgt Tom
Dwyer. illus Airman 20:2-7 Feb '76

MILITARY CIVIC ACTION see Civic Action Program

MILITARY-CIVIL RELATIONS

African armies in historical and contemporary perspectives: The search for connections. Rene Lemarchand. J Pol & Mil Sociol 4:261-275 Fall '76

Army in a multi-ethnic society: The case of Nkrumah's Ghana, 1957-1966. (Condensed from paper,
African Studies Assoc 17th Annual Meeting, Chicago, Oct 30-Nov 2, 1974) J. 'Bayo Adekson. tab
Armed Forces & Soc 2:251-272 Winter '76

Base access and the first amendment: The rights of
civilians on military installations. Maj Alan C.
Stine. AF Law Rev 18:18-32 Fall '76

Civil-military relations in Yugoslavia, 1971-1975.
Robert W. Dean. Armed Forces & Soc 3:17-58
Fall '76

Congress should stay out of tactical military decisions. Interview. Barry M. Goldwater. Armed
Forces J Intl 113:25 Mar '76

A difference in perspective (between military and political leaders). Frederick H. Hartmann. illus Nav
War Col Rev 28:65-74 Spring '76

Efficiency, responsibility, and equality in military
staffing: The ethnic dimension in comparative perspective. (Demography of military institutions in
Burma and Malaysia) James F. Guyot. Armed
Forces & Soc 2:291-304 Winter '76

The military and social adaptation. Col Richard M.
Jennings, Ret. illus Strat Rev 4:72-78 Winter '76

The military in Ghanaian politics. S.J. Baynham.
Army Qtr 106:428-439 Oct '76

Military institutions and citizenship in western soci-
eties. Morris Janowitz. Armed Forces & Soc 2:
185-204 Winter '76

Military intelligence: A fight for identity. Col Leonard A. Spirito and Maj Marc B. Powe. Army 26:
14-21 May '76

The performance of military and civilian governments in South America, 1948-1967. R. Neal Tan-
nahill. tabs J Pol & Mil Sociol 4:233-244 Fall '76

Personal perceptions of the Vietnam War. CAPT
John C. MacKercher, Ret. Natl Sec Aff Forum
No. 24:6p addendum Spring-Summer '76

A perspective of the military and the media. Carl J.
Migdail. illus Nav War Col Rev 28:2-9 Winter '76

Portugal: Problems and prospects in the creation of
a new regime. Thomas C. Bruneau. illus tabs Nav
War Col Rev 29:65-82 Summer '76

The present state and development of sociology of
the military. George A. Kourvetaris and Betty A.
Dobratz. tabs J Pol & Mil Sociol 4:67-105
Spring '76

Profession and society: Young military officers look
outward. James Clotfelter and B. Guy Peters.
tabs J Pol & Mil Sociol 4:39-51 Spring '76

Public confidence in the U.S. military. David R.
Segal and John D. Blair. tabs Armed Forces &
Soc 3:3-11 Fall '76

MILITARY-CIVIL RELATIONS - Continued

The relevance of civilian-based defense to U.S. security interests. BrigGen Edward B.Atkeson. tab illus Mil Rev pt 1, 56:24-32 May '76; pt 2, 56:45-55 Jun '76

The role of the Services in support of foreign policy. J.K.Holloway, Jr. illus tabs US Nav Inst Proc 102:65-81 May '76

Taxation of Federal instrumentalities incident to state regulation of intoxicants: The Mississippi Tax Commission case. Capt Edward C.Hooks. AF Law Rev 18:1-23 Spring '76

U.S. defense transportation goals. Paul J.Hyman. illus Def Trans J 32:6-8+ Jun '76

Warriors and scholars: Fellow professionals in hard times. Bruce M.Russett. Nav War Col Rev 28:87-91 Fall '75

What does the nation want of its military? (Remarks, 1976 Air Force Sergeants Assoc Convention, Kansas City, Mo, July 25, 1976) Gen Russell E.Dougherty. AF Plcy Ltr for Comdrs: Sup No. 11:20-30 Nov '76

When is deception necessary? RADM Wycliffe D. Toole, Jr. (Excerpted from U.S. Naval Institute Proceedings, Dec 1975) AF Times 36:14 Jan 12 '76

MILITARY CONFERENCES see Conferences, Military

MILITARY CORRESPONDENCE see Correspondence, Military

MILITARY DEPENDENTS see Dependents, Military

MILITARY EDUCATION see Education, Scientific; Education, Technical; Education and Training

MILITARY ENGINEERING

Engineer support of a march. Col P.Diky. Soviet Mil Rev No.10:20-21 Oct '76

The French PAA (Pont Automoteur d'Accompagnement) self-propelled bridging vehicle. illus tab Intl Def Rev 9:302-305 Apr '76

The medium girder bridge. LtCol C.Hartington, Ret. illus Mil Engr 68:306-307 Jul-Aug '76

Offshore technology. Regular feature in issues of Military Engineer

Passing 200 and still climbing. (Army Corps of Engineers) LtGen William C.Gribble, Jr. illus Mil Engr 68:6-10 Jan-Feb '76

The Waterways Experiment Station. LtCol Robert K. Hughes. illus Mil Engr 68:374-379 Sep-Oct '76

History

Fortress West Point: 19th century concept in an 18th century war. Col Dave R.Palmer. illus map Mil Engr 68:171-174 May-Jun '76

Military engineers at Yorktown, 1781. James N.Haskett. illus map Mil Engr 68:175-179 May-Jun '76

Surveys for engineering and science. (From "Survey of the Coast" to National Ocean Survey) RADM Allen L.Powell. illus Mil Engr 68:198-201 May-Jun '76

Sword, shovel, and compass. Leland R.Johnson. illus Mil Engr 68:158-165 May-Jun '76

Washington's favorite engineer (BrigGen Rufus Putnam). Raleigh B.Buzzaird. illus Mil Engr 68:298-301 Jul-Aug '76

MILITARY ENGINEERING - Continued

History - Cont'd

Washington's last Chief Engineer, Etienne Bechet, Sieur de Rochefontaine. Raleigh B.Buzzaird. (Reprinted from Military Engineer, March-April 1953) illus map Mil Engr 68:452-455 Nov-Dec '76

MILITARY EXPORT SALES see Arms Sales

MILITARY HISTORY

See also subdivision History under specific Services

"Arranging the minds of men": T.E.Lawrence as a theorist of war. Anthony Burton. map Army Qtr 106:51-58 Jan '76

Craftsmen in armor: The hobo (MajGen Percy Hobart) and der schnelle Heinz (Gen Heinz Guderian). Kenneth Macksey. illus Armor 85:36-40 Jan-Feb '76

Force levels and limited war. Steven T.Ross. Nav War Col Rev 28:91-96 Fall '75

History + symbolism = morale. (Organizational History Branch, Center of Military History) Robert K.Wright, Jr. Translog 7:14-15+ Aug-Sep '76

How will history judge us? (Admiral Raymond A. Spruance Lecture, Naval War College, Oct 29, 1975) Barbara W.Tuchman. Nav War Col Rev 28:3-11 Fall '75; Comment. LCDR Edwin R.Linz. Nav War Col Rev 29:104-107 Summer '76

Official military history in the Federal Republic of Germany. Friedrich Forstmeier. chart illus Aerosp Hist 23:124-127 Sep '76

The study of military history. Maj T.L.Gatchel. illus MarCor Gaz 60:58-59 Mar '76

Tannenburg: A lesson in command and control. LtCol Thomas G.Adcock. illus Signal 30:36-39 Apr '76

The Union Brigade at Waterloo: Reply to a challenge. MajGen G.N.Wood. illus Army Qtr 106:59-66 Jan '76

Winning the West. Col Robert M.Stegmaier, Ret. maps illus Fld Arty J pt 1, 44:52-54 Mar-Apr '76; pt 2, 44:37-39 May-Jun '76; pt 3, 44:53-54 Jul-Aug '76; pt 4, 44:38-41 Sep-Oct '76; pt 5, 44:58-61 Nov-Dec '76

Methodology

Sources in aerospace history: The USAF oral history collection (at Albert F.Simpson Historical Research Center, Maxwell AFB, Ala). James C. Hasdorff. illus Aerosp Hist 23:103-104 Jun '76

Unit history ("corporate memory"). TIG Brief 28:8 Aug 13 '76

Study and Teaching

The future of studying the past: Informal minutes of a military history workshop (Fort Leavenworth, Kans, 1976). Col James F.Ransone, Jr. illus Mil Rev 56:22-27 Nov '76

Military history: The Army's pivotal study. Warren W.Hassler, Jr. illus Mil Rev 56:29-33 Oct '76

MILITARY JUSTICE

Challenging the military judge for cause. Maj Ludolf R.Kuhnell. AF Law Rev 17:50-64 Winter '75
Command influence and military justice. Capt C.H. Morrison, Jr. MarCor Gaz 60:37-43 Feb '76
The military defense counsel's use of scientific evidence and expert witnesses. Maj William M. McKenna III. AF Law Rev 18:48-65 Fall '76

MILITARY JUSTICE - Continued

Military justice--a reinforcer of discipline. LtCol
Robert S.Poydasheff. illus Nav War Col Rev 28:
76-92 Winter '76

Military justice: Fair and efficient. MajGen Wilton B
Persons, Jr. illus Army 26:116-118+ Oct '76

MILITARY LAW

Russia

Armed Forces Regulations as a mirror of (Soviet)
military build-up. Gen Y.Maltsev. Soviet Mil Rev
No.6:10-12 Jun '76

Law of Army life (in Soviet Armed Forces). LtCol
V.Aidarov. illus Soviet Mil Rev No.11:40-43
Nov '76

Military discipline and the (Disciplinary) Regulations
(of the USSR Armed Forces). Col N.Arisov. Soviet Mil Rev No.10:14-16 Oct '76

New Armed Forces (Interior Service) Regulations.
MajGen Z.Averyanov. Soviet Mil Rev No.3:15-17
Mar '76

United States

See also
Court of Military Appeals
Courts-Martial
Military Justice
Uniform Code of Military Justice

Are you just government property? An interview with
two civil liberties lawyers who think military service should not mean fewer freedoms. illus AF
Times, Times Magazine sup:14-18 Apr 5 '76

Entrapment in military law. Capt Kenneth M.Murchi-
son. AF Law Rev 18:57-75 Summer '76

Military law in the 1970's: The effects of Schlesinger
v Councilman (decision in the Supreme Court).
Capt H.Michael Bartley. AF Law Rev 17:65-78
Winter '75

(Military law) seminars help dispel myths about AF
law. AF Times 36:4 Jul 19 '76

Nonappropriated funds: A unique area of military
law. Capt Kenneth M.Murchison. Educ J 19:23-27
Fall '76

The waiver doctrine: Is it still viable? Maj John E.
Hilliard. AF Law Rev 18:45-62 Spring '76

MILITARY LIFE

See also
Seamanship

As it is. (Basic training today) Darryl D.McEwen.
illus Soldiers 31:49-51 Jul '76

Basics quizzed at Lackland (AFB, Tex) reveal ideas
on prevailing issues. Bruce Callander. AF Times
37:10 Sep 6 '76

Board (Defense Manpower Commission) calls for
ending piecemeal changes (in personnel policies).
AF Times 36:8 May 3 '76

Chaplains' goal: Stronger families. AF Times 37:10
Nov 22 '76

DOD begins new consumer push. AF Times 37:53
Oct 25 '76

Eliminating the wife error. Jackie Starmer. illus
Approach 21:24-26 Nov '75

Family separation top (AF) gripe. AF Times 37:18
Aug 23 '76

MILITARY LIFE - Continued

Feminism challenging wives' role? Problems in long
separations. AF Times 37:27 Nov 22 '76

Law of Army life (in Soviet Armed Forces). LtCol
V.Aidarov. illus Soviet Mil Rev No.11:40-43
Nov '76

Learning to fly in the Air Force. LtCol Wayne Goodson. illus AU Rev 27:35-40 Jul-Aug '76

Mission effectiveness & base livability: A hypothesis.
Lester H.Henriksen and Gary D.Vest. illus AF
Engrg & Svcs Qtr 17:2-6 Nov '76

Mothers in army green. Martha Falls. illus Soldiers
31:45-46 Oct '76

New rules to limit moves: Boon to family. Randall
Shoemaker. AF Times 36:3 Jan 19 '76

Quality-of-life survey: Spouses like service more
than mates do--family separation top gripe.
Bruce Callander and others. tabs AF Times 36:4+
Mar 22 '76

'Quality' study sparks personnel changes: AFMIG
(AF Management Improvement Group), year later.
Bruce Callander. AF Times 37:2 Aug 23 '76

Service life improving. Interview. MajGen Robert C.
Thompson. AF Times 37:22 Oct 18 '76

Setting reasonable rules. Interview. Gen David C.
Jones. illus AF Times 36:4 May 3 '76

Singles lib. (Are the unmarried discriminated
against?) Darryl D.McEwen. illus tabs Soldiers
31:6-10 May '76

The squad. (From desk to squad duty for a few days,
by request, to become a better leader) Col Dandridge M.Malone. illus Army 26:12-16+ Feb '76

Strengthening Air Force family life. Ch(MajGen) Henry J.Meade. TIG Brief 28:2 Dec 17 '76

Trends in the structure of army families. David R.
Segal and others. J Pol & Mil Sociol 4:135-139
Spring '76

Waiting (Navy) wives. Kathleen P.O'Beirne. illus
US Nav Inst Proc 102:28-37 Sep '76

History

An Army wife remembers. (Fort Sill at the turn of
the century) Grace Paulding. illus Soldiers 31:40-
41 Jul '76

As it was. (Recruit training during WW I) Darryl D.
McEwen. illus tab Soldiers 31:46-48 Jul '76

Brown shoes and campaign hats. (Army life in the
'20's and '30's) Eve E.Simmons. illus Army 26:
46-49 Sep '76

Forty miles a day on beans & hay. (Soldier's life on
the 1876 frontier) LtCol Wilfred L.Ebel. illus
Soldiers 31:36-39 Jul '76

"I like sogering first rate." (From letters of a Civil
War soldier) LtCol Robert W.Frost. illus Soldiers
31:25-28 Jul '76

They would endure. (Life in the Continental Army,
based on the diary of an enlisted man, Aaron Barlow) Capts Duncan A.Carter and Michael S.Lan-
caster. illus Soldiers 31:6-9 Jul '76

MILITARY MANPOWER see Manpower, Military

MILITARY POLICE - Continued

SPs to take new 'get tough' drills. AF Times 36:9 Feb 23 '76

Security police. (Air Force Reserve's Weapon Systems Security units) Capt Tom Treband. illus Air Reservist 28:10-11 May '76

Security Police Investigations (AFR 125-21). TIG Brief 28:8 Apr 23 '76

Security policy performance during ORIs. TIG Brief 28:16 Nov 5 '76

60 women enter SP test. AF Times 37:8 Sep 13 '76

Skill (security specialist) opened to females. AF Times 36:11 Apr 12 '76

Small dogs proving worth (for detection duty). AF Times 36:61 May 24 '76

Spang(dahelm AB, Germany) SPs test skills under 'fire.' TSgt Bill Zink. illus AF Times 37:21 Aug 9 '76

Specialty skill determination. TIG Brief 28:12 Aug 13 '76

TV cameras may assist base perimeter sentries. AF Times 36:21 Feb 23 '76

Taking care of our people. (Security police force) MajGen Thomas M.Sadler. TIG Brief 28:3 Apr 23 '76

'They flat love the MPs in this town': Fort McClellan and Anniston, Ala and the Army's only law enforcement academy. LtCol Tom Hamrick, Ret. illus Army 26:34-39 Dec '76

Tougher ORIs to foster more SP involvement. AF Times 37:24 Nov 15 '76

Use of drug detector dogs. TIG Brief 28:12 Aug 13 '76

Visitor controls and the Privacy Act of 1974. TIG Brief 28:16 Mar 26 '76

Equipment

Security police equipment monitoring activity. TIG Brief 28:15 Feb 27 '76

Testing

W-P (Wright-Patterson AFB, Ohio) unit to test SP gear. AF Times 36:8 Jan 19 '76

MILITARY POLICY

Africa

African armies in historical and contemporary perspectives: The search for connections. Rene Lemarchand. J Pol & Mil Sociol 4:261-275 Fall '76

Australia

Australia: Defence planner's teaser. Brig F.V.Speed map Army Qtr 106:359-365 Jul '76

Australia's defence dilemma. Brig F.W.Speed. tab Army Qtr 106:92-100 Jan '76

Canada

Canadian defence policy, 1945-1976. Reginald H.Roy. illus tab Parameters 6, No.1:60-70 '76

China (Republic)

Asia. Philip Paisley and Leigh Johnson. illus tab Def & For Aff Dig No.5:18-19+ '76

France

French defense planning: The future in the past. Gen Pierre M.Gallois, Ret. Intl Sec 1:15-31 Fall '76

MILITARY POLICY - Continued

Great Britain

Britain at the crossroads. Comdr Joseph Palmer. illus tabs Sea Power 19:33-39 Sep '76

British defence policy--a critical analysis. George Younger. RUSI J for Def Studies 121:15-22 Mar '76

Doctrine and the soldier. Colin Gordon. RUSI J for Def Studies 121:38-45 Jun '76

Sights lowered: The United Kingdom's defense effort 1975-84. (1974 Defence Review) David Greenwood. (Reprinted from Royal Air Forces Quarterly, Autumn 1975) illus Mil Rev 56:34-46 Mar '76

Israel

Israel's changing Military Posture. Charles Wakebridge. Mil Rev 56:3-7 Jun '76

Liddell Hart's influence on Israeli military theory and practice. Brian Bond. maps RUSI J for Def Studies 121:83-89 Jun '76

Japan

Asia. Philip Paisley and Leigh Johnson. illus tab Def & For Aff Dig No.5:18-19+ '76

Malaysia

Asia. Philip Paisley and Leigh Johnson. illus tab Def & For Aff Dig No.5:18-19+ '76

NATO

NATO and détente. LtCol N.Chaldymov. illus Soviet Mil Rev No.2:42-44 Feb '76

Putting it together with R-S-1 in U.S. Army, Europe. Gen George S.Blanchard. illus Army 26:52-54+ Oct '76

Philippines (Republic)

Asia. Philip Paisley and Leigh Johnson. illus tab Def & For Aff Dig No.5:18-19+ '76

Russia

The Nordic balance. Col Arthur E.Dewey. illus map Strat Rev 4:49-60 Fall '76

The Northern Theater: Soviet capabilities and concepts. John Erickson. map Strat Rev 4:67-82 Summer '76

Soviet airborne forces: Increasingly powerful factor in the equation. Graham H.Turbiville. illus Army 26:18-24+ Apr '76

The Soviet antitank debate. Phillip A.Karber. (Reprinted from Survival, May-June 1976) illus Mil Rev 56:67-76 Nov '76; Armor 85:10-14 Nov-Dec '76

Soviet tactical doctrine and capabilities and NATO's strategic defense. Capt Eugene D.Bétit. illus tabs Strat Rev 4:95-107 Fall '76

History

The origins of Soviet military doctrine. R.H.Baker. RUSI J for Def Studies 121:38-43 Mar '76

Thailand

Asia. Philip Paisley and Leigh Johnson. illus tab Def & For Aff Dig No.5:18-19+ '76

United States

Air Force Chief of Staff's FY 1977 Posture Statement. (Statement before House Committee on Armed Services, Washington, Jan 29, 1976) Gen David C.Jones. AF Plcy Ltr for Comdrs: Sup No.3:23-40 Mar '76

MILITARY POWER - Continued

United States

Air Force Chief of Staff's FY 1977 Posture Statement. (Statement before House Committee on Armed Services, Washington, Jan 29, 1976) Gen David C.Jones. AF Plcy Ltr for Comdrs: Sup No.3:23-40 Mar '76

Capabilities and courage. Robert F.Ellsworth. Natl Def 61:29-31 Jul-Aug '76

Comparing Soviet and American defense efforts. Les Aspin. tabs NATO's Fifteen Nations 21:34-36+ Jun-Jul '76

Defense Department report--FY 77. (Statement before House Armed Services Committee, Washington, Jan 27, 1976) Donald H.Rumsfeld. AF Plcy Ltr for Comdrs: Sup No.4:2-12 Apr '76

A force second to none: The FY 1977 Defense budget. Terence E.McClary. illus tab Armed Forces Compt 21:16-19 Apr '76

Forces for the future. (Remarks, Lancaster Chamber of Commerce, Lancaster, Calif, Feb 6, 1976) Thomas C.Reed. AF Plcy Ltr for Comdrs: Sup No.4:16-20 Apr '76

A holocaust for Happy Valley? Henry Young. illus US Nav Inst Proc 102:52-61 Nov '76

JCS Chairman's Posture Statement. (Statement before House Armed Services Committee, Washington, Jan 27, 1976) Gen George S.Brown. tabs AF Plcy Ltr for Comdrs: Sup No.4:13-15 Apr '76

Maintaining U.S. military strength in the Pacific. ADM Noel Gayler. illus Comdrs Dig 19: entire issue May 13 '76

The military balance today. Donald H.Rumsfeld. illus tabs Comdrs Dig 19: entire issue Mar 11 '76

Military force and political influence in an age of peace. Robert Ellsworth. illus Strat Rev 4:5-11 Spring '76

Peace is our profession. (Remarks, Truman Lecture and Fine Arts Series, Westminster College, Fulton, Mo, April 24, 1976) Gen Russell E.Dougherty. AF Plcy Ltr for Comdrs: Sup No.7:15-23 Jul '76

Preserving a balance of power. (Address, Reuters 125th anniversary dinner, New York, March 10, 1976) Donald H.Rumsfeld. AF Plcy Ltr for Comdrs: Sup No.5:2-9 May '76

Serving the people: The need for military power. Gen Fred C.Weyand, Ret and LtCol Harry G.Summers, Jr. illus Mil Rev 56:8-18 Dec '76

Strategic Forces: How America & the Soviets compare. Gen George S.Brown. illus tabs Comdrs Dig 19: entire issue Apr 15 '76

The United States: A military power second to none? Gen Maxwell D.Taylor, Ret. Intl Sec 1:49-55 Summer '76

U.S. defense perspectives. Donald H.Rumsfeld. illus tabs Comdrs Dig 19: entire issue Aug 26 '76

(U.S./USSR military balance) illus tabs Armed Forces J Intl pt 1, U.S./USSR military balance shifts in favor of Russia. Benjamin F.Schemmer. 113:18+ Mar '76; pt 2, Scope of and reasons behind U.S./USSR force asymmetries. 113:23-26+ Apr '76; pt 3 (Summary) 113:24-28 May '76

Statistics

Defense budget, 1977: A 'serious effort' at restraint. illus tabs Eric C.Ludvigsen. Army 26:12-17 Mar '76

MILITARY RESEARCH see Research and Development also specific kinds of research, e.g., Space Research

MILITARY SEA TRANSPORTATION SERVICE see Military Sealift Command

MILITARY SEALIFT COMMAND

The Military Sealift Command's build and charter program for nine sealift-class tankers. Scott C. Truver. illus tabs Nav War Col Rev 28:32-44 Fall '75

A Navy success: Support ships manned by civilian crews. LCDR Paul Stillwell. illus Armed Forces J Intl 113:26+ Jul '76

Solving the sealift shortage. L.Edgar Prina. illus Sea Power 19:19-26 Oct '76

MILITARY SERVICE, COMPULSORY

Switzerland

Military service and social change in Switzerland. Hanspeter Kriesi. tabs Armed Forces & Soc 2: 218-226 Winter '76

United States

AUSA opposes Selective Service cuts. illus Army 26: 60-61 Mar '76

America in World War II: How limitless was the manpower pool? Byron V.Pepitone. illus tabs Def Mgt J 12:47-54 Jul '76

CHAMPUS, store curbs fought, draft fight lost on Capitol Hill. Officer 52:5 Apr '76

Dangers cited in gutting of Selective Service: ROA, congressmen protest. Officer 52:22 Mar '76

On pardons for draft dodgers. LtGen Ira C.Eaker, Ret. AF Times 37:13-14 Sep 27 '76

MILITARY SERVICE, VOLUNTARY

Great Britain

Manpower trends in the British all-volunteer force. LtCol Thomas A.Fabyanic. tabs Armed Forces & Soc 2:553-572 Summer '76

United States

All-vol recruit same as previous (according to a study by the General Accounting Office). AF Times 36:15 Mar 29 '76

The American volunteer soldier: Will he fight? A provisional attitudinal analysis. Col Charles W. Brown and Charles C.Moskos, Jr. illus tabs Mil Rev 56:8-17 Jun '76

A careful look at defense manpower. Gen Bruce Palmer, Jr, Ret and Curtis W.Tarr. illus Mil Rev 56:3-13 Sep '76

Combat readiness on a shoestring. (Army augmentation units) Anthony J.Daniels. illus Army 26: 49-51 Apr '76

Despite pitfalls, recruiters have done well, DMC (Defense Manpower Commission) says. AF Times 36:20 May 17 '76

Human factor is paramount. (Defense Manpower Commission report) Eric C.Ludvigsen. illus Army 26: 38-40 Jun '76

Military manpower problems. LtGen Ira C.Eaker, Ret. AF Times 37:13-14 Sep 20 '76

On pardons for draft dodgers. LtGen Ira C.Eaker, Ret. AF Times 37:13-14 Sep 27 '76

MILITARY SERVICE, VOLUNTARY - Continued

United States - Cont'd

Profession and society: Young military officers look outward. James Clotfelter and B.Guy Peters. tabs J Pol & Mil Sociol 4:39-51 Spring '76

Racial composition in the all-volunteer force. Morris Janowitz and Charles C.Moskos, Jr. tabs Armed Forces & Soc 1:109-123 Nov '74; Reply: Race and the all-volunteer system. Alvin J. Schneider and John Sibley Butler. 2:421-432 Spring '76; Comment (on Schneider and Butler's reply). Morris Janowitz and Charles C.Moskos, Jr. 2:433-434 Spring '76

Sustaining the volunteer Army: A manpower headache. LtGen Harold G.Moore. illus tabs Def Mgt J 12: 9-16 Oct '76

MILITARY SERVICE AS A PROFESSION

See also
Career Program

As it is. (Basic training today) Darryl D.McEwen. illus Soldiers 31:49-51 Jul '76

Future military preparedness. (Address, Naval Academy Graduation Ceremonies, Annapolis, June 2, 1976) Donald H.Rumsfeld. AF Plcy Ltr for Comdrs: Sup No.8:2-7 Aug '76

Introspection (on professional development)--and some reflections on the way it was. Col Gustav J. Gillert, Jr. illus Mil Rev 56:36-41 Nov '76

Learning to fly in the Air Force. LtCol Wayne Goodson. illus AU Rev 27:35-40 Jul-Aug '76

A military elite in transition: Air Force leaders in the 1980s. (Research undertaken at Air Command and Staff College) LtCol Franklin D.Margiotta. tabs Armed Forces & Soc 2:155-184 Winter '76

The military ethic. Col William L.Hauser. illus Strat Rev 4:76-86 Fall '76

Military ethics in a changing world. MajGen Robert N.Ginsburgh, Ret. illus AU Rev 27:2-10 Jan-Feb '76

The military profession in the USSR. Harriet Fast Scott. illus tabs AF Mag 59:76-81 Mar '76

Mothers in army green. Martha Falls. illus Soldiers 31:45-46 Oct '76

The naval profession: Challenge and response, 1870-1890 and 1950-1970. Lawrence C.Allin. Nav War Col Rev 28:75-90 Spring '76

Ours is an honorable profession. Gen Russell E. Dougherty. (Reprinted from Combat Crew, May 1975) illus Combat Crew 27:8-11 Mar '76

The present role of the American soldier. Maj Robert F.Helms II. illus Mil Rev 56:12-18 Apr '76

The present state and development of sociology of the military. George A.Kourvetaris and Betty A. Dobratz. tabs J Pol & Mil Sociol 4:67-105 Spring '76

Profession and society: Young military officers look outward. James Clotfelter and B.Guy Peters. tabs J Pol & Mil Sociol 4:39-51 Spring '76

Professional identity in a plural world: The focus of junior officer education in the U.S. Air Force. BrigGen John E.Ralph. illus AU Rev 27:11-25 Jan-Feb '76

Professionalism and the Canadian military. LtCol J.H.Pocklington. AU Rev 27:34-40 Mar-Apr '76

MILITARY SERVICE AS A PROFESSION - Continued

Promises--or "perceptions?" (Erosion of promised military entitlements) MajGen Herbert G.Sparrow, Ret. Armed Forces J Intl 113:14+ May '76

Times are perilous for 'contractual rights.' Army 26:6-8 Jan '76

Warriors and scholars: Fellow professionals in hard times. Bruce M.Russett. Nav War Col Rev 28:87-91 Fall '75

MILITARY TRAFFIC MANAGEMENT AND TERMINAL SERVICE see Military Traffic Management Command

MILITARY TRAFFIC MANAGEMENT COMMAND

Another Army "Navy" game (Azores). SSgt Virgil L. Laning. illus Translog 7:16-20 Jan '76

CERS (Carrier Evaluation and Reporting System) testing moves into second phase. Translog 7:14+ Jun '76

DISREP (Discrepency In Shipment REPort, SF 361) system is ITO's 'Man Friday.' LtCol B.E.Greenfield. Translog 7:5 Oct '76

GAO wants to keep uneconomical household (goods) plan. AF Times 37:4 Aug 16 '76

JPPSOWA (Joint Personal Property Shipping Office, WAshington): Service, economy, success. Tory Billard. illus Translog 7:13-15 Mar '76

Key points in shipping your car. Don Hirst. AF Times 37:36 Aug 30 '76

Learning depends upon the learner! (Seminar sponsored by MTMC) Tory Billard. illus Translog 7: 7-8 Nov '76

MTMC and the total Army. Dan Hall. illus Translog 7:3-5 Dec '76

MTMC assumes Europe ports on July 1, 1976. illus Translog 7:14 Jul '76

(MTMC Awards) for Excellence in Traffic Management (made during NDTA's 31st Annual Forum, 1976). illus Translog 7:1-3 Oct '76

The MTMC realignment program. David R.Goodmon. Translog 7:2-5 Feb '76

(MTMC) suggesters save over $750,000. Dan Hall. illus Translog 7:18-19 May '76

Outport insight. Debbi Dunstan and Donna Orsini. illus Translog 7:1-3+ Jan '76

Railroads for national defense--an overview; legislation proposed. illus Translog 7:8 Jun '76

Rate filing test (for shipments) set for Germany. Translog 7:16+ Jun '76

Rating system aims to reward movers. AF Times 36:2 May 17 '76

Reforger 76: A MTMC first. illus Translog 7:2-4 Aug-Sep '76

Reserve training upgrade at MTMCEA (Military Traffic Management Command Eastern Area). Capt Mike Fillmore. illus Translog 7:16-18 Dec '76

"Return the forces to Germany"--(Reforger) 76. LtCol Gary Sorensen. illus Def Trans J 32:6-8+ Oct '76

Directories

Military Traffic Management Command. Army 26:138 Oct '76

MILTON, Theodore R. - Continued

Tac nukes and deterrence. Gen T.R.Milton, Ret. AF
Mag 59:25 Aug '76

Tankers, task forces, and terrorism. Gen T.R.Mil-
ton, Ret. AF Mag 59:108 Sep '76

MINERALS

See also
Ocean Mining

Satellite monitors strip mines. Spaceflight 18:364
Oct '76

MINES AND MINE LAYING

Scatterable mines. Maj Charles L.Belitz. Infantry
66:45-46 Jan-Feb '76

MINING, OCEAN see Ocean Mining

MINORITIES

See also
Race Relations
also specific groups, e.g.,
Blacks in the Armed Forces
Eskimos

AF to purify stored data on ethnics. AF Times 36:9
Apr 19 '76

'Catch-up' program eyed for minorities. Andy Plattner. AF Times 36:2 Jun 28 '76

In the Air Force who you are doesn't matter, what
counts is how well you do your job. illus Air Reservist 28:12 May '76

Man in the OD turban (SSgt Paramjit Sibia). Barbara
Sorensen. illus Soldiers 31:12 Sep '76

Middle class Mexican Americans and political power
potential: A dilemma. Raymond H.C.Teske, Jr
and Bardin H.Nelson. tabs J Pol & Mil Sociol 4:
107-119 Spring '76

New (AF) programs to accent Spanish-speaking culture. Len Famiglietti. AF Times 36:2 Feb 9 '76

New drive for ethnic equality starts. AF Times 37:23
Aug 23 '76

MINTER, Charles F., Sr

Maintaining a modern force. (Remarks, National Security Industrial Assoc, Absecon, NJ, June 28,
1976) MajGen Charles F.Minter, Sr. AF Plcy Ltr
for Comdrs: Sup No.9:13-19 Sep '76

MINUTEMAN EDUCATION PROGRAM

Making the mark with missiles. Capt Robert G.H.
Carroll. illus tab AF Mag 59:50-54 Jun '76

MISSILE BASES

See also
Missile Sites

United States

Making the mark with missiles. Capt Robert G.H.
Carroll. illus tab AF Mag 59:50-54 Jun '76

MISSILE COMBAT COMPETITIONS

Blanchard Trophy winner: Malmstrom (AFB, Mont,
341st Strategic Missile) Wing top SAC unit (in
1976 Missile Combat Competition). illus AF
Times 36:34 May 17 '76

Competition: A fundamental part of readiness (Olympic Arena '76). BrigGen S.H.Sherman, Jr. illus
Combat Crew 27:12-13 Apr '76

MISSILE COMBAT COMPETITIONS - Continued

Olympic Arena '76. MajGen John W.Burkhart. illus
Combat Crew 27:4-5 Apr '76

Olympic Arena 76: Competition highlights. Maj Don
Green. illus Combat Crew 27:4-7+ Jun '76

Olympic Arena trophy winners. illus tab Combat
Crew 27:28-29 Jun '76

Wings in competition (for Blanchard Trophy in Olympic Arena '76). illus Combat Crew 27:6-7+ Apr '76

MISSILE COMMAND

(At a cost of $40 million, the Army's Missile Com-
mand at Huntsville, Ala, has developed a new Advanced Simulation Center capable of testing any
missile known today or foreseen for the future)
illus Countermeasures 2:10 Jul '76

MISSILE CREWS

See also
Missile Training

(Combat crew officers' careers) Gen Russell E.Dou-
gherty. illus Combat Crew 27:3+ Jul '76; TIG
Brief 28:2-4 Aug 13 '76

It'll never happen, but ... (Battery fire at a missile
launch control center) Capt Tom Luisi. illus Combat Crew 27:14-15 May '76

Making the mark with missiles. Capt Robert G.H.
Carroll. illus tab AF Mag 59:50-54 Jun '76

Olympic Arena 76: Competition highlights. Maj Don
Green. illus Combat Crew 27:4-7+ Jun '76

Wings in competition (for Blanchard Trophy in Olympic Arena '76). illus Combat Crew 27:6-7+ Apr '76

The "young" professional SAC crew force. MajGen
A.B.Anderson, Jr. illus Combat Crew 26:3+
Feb '76

MISSILE DEFENSE

See also
Missiles--Interception
Safeguard ABM System

Effective military technology for the 1980s. Richard
L.Garwin. illus tabs Intl Sec 1:50-77 Fall '76

Seawolf/GWS25, the Royal Navy's anti-missile missile system. illus tabs Intl Def Rev 9:789-794
Oct '76

The strategic conflict. James Constant. illus tabs
Countermeasures pt 1, 2:32-36+ Mar '76; pt 2,
2:26-30+ Apr '76

Strategic vulnerability: The balance between prudence
and paranoia. John D.Steinbruner and Thomas M.
Garwin. illus tabs Intl Sec 1:138-181 Summer '76

MISSILE INDUSTRY AND TRADE

Europe, Western

Weapon systems: Martel (Anglo-French air-to-surface missile). Mark Hewish. illus US Nav Inst
Proc 102:112 Nov '76

France

A profile of Aerospatiale. John Marriott. illus
NATO's Fifteen Nations 20:80-84 Dec '75-Jan '76

Great Britain

Aerospace (equipment). John Marriott. illus tabs
NATO's Fifteen Nations 21:35-39+ Apr-May '76

MISSILE INDUSTRY AND TRADE - Continued

Great Britain - Cont'd

UK guided weapons--the next move. Rupert Pengel-ley. illus Interavia 31:823 Sep '76

United States

Manufacturing the Maverick. J.Philip Geddes. illus tabs Interavia 31:1091-1092 Nov '76

Roland meets the challenge. Robert L.Roderick. illus Natl Def 61:39-42 Jul-Aug '76

MISSILE MAINTENANCE

Condition status reporting. TIG Brief 28:4 Apr 9 '76

Maintenance participation provides innovative action (in Olympic Arena '76). MajGen T.M.Ryan, Jr. illus Combat Crew 27:8-9 Apr '76

Type 3 (nuclear weapons) trainers used during train-ing operations and inspections. TIG Brief 28:20 Dec 3 '76

Wings in competition (for Blanchard Trophy in Olym-pic Arena '76). illus Combat Crew 27:6-7+ Apr '76

MISSILE RANGES see Missile Test Centers

MISSILE SITES

See also
Missile Bases

SPs call for check on nuclear security. AF Times 37:6 Aug 16 '76

MISSILE TEST CENTERS

Duels in the sun: Yuma ACMR (Air Combat Maneu-vering Range) saves planes, pilots. L.Edgar Prina. illus Sea Power 18:25-26 Dec '75

MISSILE TRAINING

At maximum range. A.Polyakov. Soviet Mil Rev No. 1:21-22 Jan '76

Improved Hawk Simulator AN/TPQ-29. C.F.Nolan. illus Countermeasures 2:33-34+ Oct '76

Maturing of soldiers: Experience in work with young soldiers (missilemen) of the Air Defence Forces. LtCol V.Selyodkin. Soviet Mil Rev No.8:36-37 Aug '76

Top Hand. Maj Rich Scredon and Capt Victor D.Bras illus Combat Crew 27:12-14 Oct '76

MISSILE TYPE

See also
Missiles

ALCM

ALCM (Air-Launched Cruise Missile). Govt Exec 8:16 Jun '76

The air-launched cruise missile. J.Philip Geddes. tabs illus (Also cutaways) Interavia 31:580-583 Jun '76; Adaptation. Intl Def Rev 9:370-374 Jun '76

The cruise missile: A weapon in search of a mission. illus (Also cutaway) Def Monitor 5: entire issue Sep '76

Cruise missile: Double insurance for defense. Rob-ert N.Parker. illus Comdrs Dig 19: entire issue Sep 23 '76

Tomahawk and ALCM: Cruise missile decision pend-ing. John Rhea. illus Sea Power 19:25-28 Dec '76

MISSILE TYPE - Continued

ALCM - Cont'd

Testing

ALCM in flight tests. illus (Also cutaway) Counter-measures 2:37-38 Jul '76

(The Air Force is conducting flight tests on the newly developed Air Launched Cruise Missile (ALCM) at White Sands Missile Range, NM) Countermeasures 2:10+ Jul '76

ASMS

See Aegis

Aegis

Backfire problems and the Aegis mix. L.Edgar Prina. illus Sea Power 19:19-21 Sep '76

HELLFIRE

HELLFIRE (HELicopter Launched FIRE) designated AAH (Advanced Attack Helicopter) missile. Capt Mark Robison. illus USA Avn Dig 22: inside back cover May '76

Harpoon

Versatile Harpoon. Stefan Geisenheyner. illus (Also cutaway) tab Aerosp Intl 12:16-18+ Mar-Apr '76

Hawk

The Hawk and the clamshell. Capt Dave Hawkins. illus Air Def Mag, pp 18-22, Jul-Sep '76

Improved Hawk Simulator AN/TPQ-29. C.F.Nolan. illus Countermeasures 2:33-34+ Oct '76

Lance

In search of the illusive green ball. Maj Richard M. Stroud. illus Fld Arty J 44:7-9 Jan-Feb '76

Lance ASP (Annual Service Practice) in Crete. LtCol John A.Raymond and others. illus Fld Arty J 44: 55-56 Jul-Aug '76

The time has come. LtCol Wilson A.Shoffner. illus tab Fld Arty J 44:46-53 Jan-Feb '76

Testing

Lance testing in the European environment. LtCol Justin LaPorte. maps Fld Arty J 44:44-45 Jul-Aug '76

Maverick

Manufacturing the Maverick. J.Philip Geddes. illus tabs Interavia 31:1091-1092 Nov '76

New infrared missile developed. Countermeasures 2:47 Mar '76

Minuteman

Clear to launch. Capts Manuel Torres and Mike Hen-shaw. illus Combat Crew 27:16-19 Apr '76

It'll never happen, but ... (Battery fire at a missile launch control center) Capt Tom Luisi. illus Com-bat Crew 27:14-15 May '76

Minuteman nuclear safety critical components. TIG Brief 28:4 Apr 23 '76

Performance Analysis and Technical Evaluation (PATE) and Nuclear Safety Cross-Check Analysis (NSCCA). TIG Brief 28:8 Aug 27 '76

SELM (Simulated Electronic Launch Minuteman) test. 1stLt Thomas L.Roush. illus Combat Crew 27: 8-9+ Aug '76

Top Hand. Maj Rich Scredon and Capt Victor D.Bras. illus Combat Crew 27:12-14 Oct '76

MISSILES - Continued

Characteristics - Cont'd

Seawolf/GWS25, the Royal Navy's anti-missile missile system. illus tabs Intl Def Rev 9:789-794 Oct '76

Strategic missile forces. Gen George S. Brown. illus Natl Def 61:36-38+ Jul-Aug '76

Three new Soviet air-to-air missiles in service. illus tabs Intl Def Rev 9:400 Jun '76

Versatile Navy weapon (Standard anti-aircraft missile). Robert M. Kemp. illus tabs Natl Def 61:44-47 Jul-Aug '76

Components

Minuteman nuclear safety critical components. TIG Brief 28:4 Apr 23 '76

Reliability

Reporting major missile component failures. TIG Brief 28:10 Aug 13 '76

Countermeasures
See Missiles--Defenses

Design

Roland meets the challenge. Robert L. Roderick. illus Natl Def 61:39-42 Jul-Aug '76

Fuels
See Propellants

Guidance and Control

A case for smart weapons. LtCol Frank C. Regan, Jr. illus tabs MarCor Gaz 60:31-35 May '76

Rockwell Autonetics group moves into new markets. J. Philip Geddes. illus Interavia 31:550-552 Jun '76

True magic for the artilleryman. (A shell homing in automatically on a target with the help of laser technology devices) John S. Phillip. illus Aerosp Intl 12:22-24 Jan-Feb '76

Interception

Beehive: An innovative approach to employment. Maj Eugene D. Colgan. illus tabs Armor 85:20-22 Sep-Oct '76

Launching

Clear to launch. Capts Manuel Torres and Mike Henshaw. illus Combat Crew 27:16-19 Apr '76

Roland II: Has America bought the wrong weapon? John Marriott. illus NATO's Fifteen Nations 20:78-79 Dec '75-Jan '76

Test launches of sea-launched cruise missiles. (Navy's testing of the Tomahawk) illus Armed Forces J Intl 113:28 Mar '76

Top Hand. Maj Rich Scredon and Capt Victor D. Bras. illus Combat Crew 27:12-14 Oct '76

Weather probability forecasts: A cost-saving technique in space launch and missile test operations. MajGen Herbert A. Lyon, Ret, and LtCol Lynn L. LeBlanc. illus tabs AU Rev 27:45-54 Jan-Feb '76

Will Minuteman work? Simulation testing. Eugene M. Del Papa. illus tab Armed Forces J Intl 113:14-15 Jan '76

Testing

SELM (Simulated Electronic Launch Minuteman) test. 1stLt Thomas L. Roush. illus Combat Crew 27:8-9+ Aug '76

MISSILES - Continued

Maintenance and Repair
See Missile Maintenance

Re-entry

Weather probability forecasts: A cost-saving technique in space launch and missile test operations. MajGen Herbert A. Lyon, Ret, and LtCol Lynn L. LeBlanc. illus tabs AU Rev 27:45-54 Jan-Feb '76

Reliability

The TOW weapon system: A reliability case history. Joseph A. Scanlan. tab Def Mgt J 12:35-39 Apr '76

Testing

(At a cost of $40 million, the Army's Missile Command at Huntsville, Ala, has developed a new Advanced Simulation Center capable of testing any missile known today or foreseen for the future) illus Countermeasures 2:10 Jul '76

Test launches of sea-launched cruise missiles. (Navy's testing of the Tomahawk) illus Armed Forces J Intl 113:28 Mar '76

Warheads

Soviet Union modernizes IRBM. Intl Def Rev 9:709+ Oct '76

Europe, Western

The battlefield missile tables. Tables only. Def & For Aff Dig No. 2:15-17 '76

Missile muscle: A report on battlefield missiles. David Harvey. illus Def & For Aff Dig No. 2:12-14+ '76

Roland II: Has America bought the wrong weapon? John Marriott. illus NATO's Fifteen Nations 20:78-79 Dec '75-Jan '76

Weapon systems: Martel (Anglo-French air-to-surface missile). Mark Hewish. illus US Nav Inst Proc 102:112 Nov '76

France

The Exocet anti-ship missiles. tabs illus Intl Def Rev 9:395-399 Jun '76

Naval systems from Thomson-CSF. R. Meller. illus tab Intl Def Rev 9:847-851 Oct '76

Great Britain

Aerospace (equipment). John Marriott. illus tabs NATO's Fifteen Nations 21:35-39+ Apr-May '76

RAF front-line aircraft and missiles, 1st April 1976. Table only. Air Pict 38:175 May '76

Seawolf/GWS25, the Royal Navy's anti-missile missile system. illus tabs Intl Def Rev 9:789-794 Oct '76

UK guided weapons--the next move. Rupert Pengelley. illus Interavia 31:823 Sep '76

Israel

Weapon systems: Gabriel. Mark Hewish. illus US Nav Inst Proc 102:101 Jul '76

NATO

The AIM-9L Super-Sidewinder: NATO standardization in practice. W. Schenk. tab illus (Also cutaway) Intl Def Rev 9:365-369 Jun '76

Russia

The battlefield missile tables. Tables only. Def & For Aff Dig No. 2:15-17 '76

MISSILES - Continued

Russia - Cont'd

The ever-expanding umbrella. LtCol Arthur D. McQueen. tab illus Air Def Mag, pp 8-17, Jul-Sep '76

Future tactical missiles. Malcolm R. Currie. illus Natl Def 61:32-35 Jul-Aug '76

Gallery of Soviet aerospace weapons: Airborne tactical and defence missiles. illus AF Mag 59:105-106 Mar '76

Gallery of Soviet aerospace weapons: Strategic missiles. illus AF Mag 59:103-105 Mar '76

Gallery of Soviet aerospace weapons: Surface-to-air missiles. illus AF Mag 59:106-107 Mar '76

The growing threat: New challenges for the EW community. Ronald T. Pretty. illus Elect Warfare 8: 43+ Mar-Apr '76

Military production in the USSR. (Basic facts on each type of Russian weapon) Tables only. NATO's Fifteen Nations 21:46-47 Jun-Jul '76

A new family of Soviet strategic weapons. Edgar Ulsamer. illus tab AF Mag 59:24-27 Oct '76

A problem guide to SALT II. Colin S. Gray. (Reprinted from Survival, Sep-Oct 1975) Mil Rev 56: 82-89 Apr '76

SA-8: The latest Soviet mobile SAM system. illus Intl Def Rev 8:805-806 Dec '75

Senator (Henry M.) Jackson declassifies Schlesinger SALT testimony, awaits Kissinger reply to August letter (concerning Soviet deployment of the SS-19 missile). Armed Forces J Intl 113:8 Jan '76

Soviet R&D at "critical mass": "Sobering assessment" troubles DOD research chief (Malcolm R. Currie). Benjamin F. Schemmer. tabs Armed Forces J Intl 113:12-13 Mar '76

Soviet Union modernizes IRBM. Intl Def Rev 9:709+ Oct '76

Strategic missile forces. Gen George S. Brown. illus Natl Def 61:36-38+ Jul-Aug '76

Strategic vulnerability: The balance between prudence and paranoia. John D. Steinbruner and Thomas M. Garwin. illus tabs Intl Sec 1:138-181 Summer '76

The surface Navy today: Prospects and problems. Col Robert D. Heinl, Jr, Ret. illus Sea Power 19:27-32 Oct '76

Three new Soviet air-to-air missiles in service. illus tabs Intl Def Rev 9:400 Jun '76

Will the Soviets wage war in space? Edgar Ulsamer. illus AF Mag 59:30-33+ Dec '76

Sweden

The Swedish Air Force: An official history. illus Aerosp Hist 22:218-230 Dec '75

United States

See also
Missile Type

The AIM-9L Super-Sidewinder: NATO standardization in practice. W. Schenk. tab illus (Also cutaway) Intl Def Rev 9:365-369 Jun '76

(The B-1 debate: Authors' responses) Archie L. Wood and John F. McCarthy, Jr. Intl Sec 1:117-122 Fall '76

The battlefield missile tables. Tables only. Def & For Aff Dig No. 2:15-17 '76

MISSILES - Continued

United States - Cont'd

Cruise missile: Double insurance for defense. Robert N. Parker. illus Comdrs Dig 19: entire issue Sep 23 '76

Effective military technology for the 1980s. Richard L. Garwin. illus tabs Intl Sec 1:50-77 Fall '76

Future tactical missiles. Malcolm R. Currie. illus Natl Def 61:32-35 Jul-Aug '76

Ivan's edge is our bureaucracy. (Interview with John L. McDaniel) illus Armed Forces J Intl 113:16+ Jul '76

Missiles and astronautics. Regular feature in issues of National Defense

Modernizing the strategic bomber force without really trying: A case against the B-1. Archie L. Wood. Intl Sec 1:98-116 Fall '76

On the technological frontier: Laser-powered rockets and dark satellites. Edgar Ulsamer. tab AF Mag 59:60-64 Apr '76

A problem guide to SALT II. Colin S. Gray. (Reprinted from Survival, Sep-Oct 1975) Mil Rev 56: 82-89 Apr '76

Soviet R&D at "critical mass": "Sobering assessment" troubles DOD research chief (Malcolm R. Currie). Benjamin F. Schemmer. tabs Armed Forces J Intl 113:12-13 Mar '76

The strategic conflict. James Constant. illus tabs Countermeasures pt 1, 2:32-36+ Mar '76; pt 2, 2:26-30+ Apr '76

Strategic missile forces. Gen George S. Brown. illus Natl Def 61:36-38+ Jul-Aug '76

Strategic nuclear balance is not enough. Interview. Gen George Brown. illus tab Govt Exec 8:24-26+ Dec '76

Strategic vulnerability: The balance between prudence and paranoia. John D. Steinbruner and Thomas M. Garwin. illus tabs Intl Sec 1:138-181 Summer '76

Tomahawk and ALCM: Cruise missile decision pending. John Rhea. illus Sea Power 19:25-28 Dec '76

United States--Air Force

ALCM (Air-Launched Cruise Missile). Govt Exec 8:16 Jun '76

Affordability + performance: USAF's R&D goal. Edgar Ulsamer. illus AF Mag 59:31-36 Mar '76

The air-launched cruise missile. J. Philip Geddes. tabs illus (Also cutaways) Interavia 31:580-583 Jun '76; Adaptation. Intl Def Rev 9:370-374 Jun '76

The cruise missile: A weapon in search of a mission. illus (Also cutaway) Def Monitor 5: entire issue Sep '76

DNA's (Defense Nuclear Agency) business: Thinking the unthinkable. Edgar Ulsamer. illus AF Mag 59: 50-54 Sep '76

Department of the Air Force Fiscal Years 1977 and 1978 missile procurement estimates. Table only. AF Plcy Ltr for Comdrs: Sup No. 5:27 May '76

Gallery of USAF weapons: Airborne tactical and defense missiles. illus AF Mag 59:124+ May '76

Gallery of USAF weapons: Strategic missiles. illus AF Mag 59:123-124 May '76

M-X, a new dimension in strategic deterrence. LtGen Alton D. Slay. illus AF Mag 59:44-49 Sep '76

MISSILES - Continued

United States--Air Force - Cont'd

New aircraft and missiles. (Presentation, Senate Appropriations Committee, Washington, March 18, 1976) LtGen Alton D. Slay. tabs AF Plcy Ltr for Comdrs: Sup No. 5:10-28 May '76

Space in the Air Force future. (Remarks, American Defense Preparedness Assoc, Oct 15, 1975) LtGen Thomas W. Morgan. AF Plcy Ltr for Comdrs: Sup No. 2:2-8 Feb '76; Condensation. Natl Def 60:290 Jan-Feb '76

Tac air--history's most potent fighting machine. Edgar Ulsamer. illus AF Mag 59:22-26 Feb '76

United States--Army

Beehive: An innovative approach to employment. Maj Eugene D. Colgan. illus tabs Armor 85:20-22 Sep-Oct '76

Congress gives go-ahead for SAM-D development. Army 26:60 Apr '76

HELLFIRE (HELicopter Launched FIRE) designated AAH (Advanced Attack Helicopter) missile. Capt Mark Robison. illus USA Avn Dig 22: inside back cover May '76

Lance ASP (Annual Service Practice) in Crete. LtCol John A. Raymond and others. illus Fld Arty J 44: 55-56 Jul-Aug '76

Lance testing in the European environment. LtCol Justin LaPorte. maps Fld Arty J 44:44-45 Jul-Aug '76

Missile muscle: A report on battlefield missiles. David Harvey. illus Def & For Aff Dig No. 2: 12-14+ '76

Roland II: Has America bought the wrong weapon? John Marriott. illus NATO's Fifteen Nations 20: 78-79 Dec '75-Jan '76

Roland meets the challenge. Robert L. Roderick. illus Natl Def 61:39-42 Jul-Aug '76

Stinger. Col David Green. illus USAF Ftr Wpns Rev, pp 14-17, Fall '76

The time has come. LtCol Wilson A. Shoffner. illus tab Fld Arty J 44:46-53 Jan-Feb '76

United States--Navy

The cruise missile: A weapon in search of a mission. illus (Also cutaway) Def Monitor 5: entire issue Sep '76

The sea launched cruise missile. J. Philip Geddes. illus (Also cutaway) Interavia 31:260-264 Mar '76; Intl Def Rev 9:198-202 Apr '76

The strategic cruise missile: What it means! John T. Hayward. Govt Exec 8:56 Jun '76

The surface Navy today: Prospects and problems. Col Robert D. Heinl, Jr, Ret. illus Sea Power 19:27-32 Oct '76

Test launches of sea-launched cruise missiles. (Navy's testing of the Tomahawk) illus Armed Forces J Intl 113:28 Mar '76

Versatile Navy weapon (Standard anti-aircraft missile). Robert M. Kemp. illus tabs Natl Def 61:44-47 Jul-Aug '76

Weapon systems: Phoenix. Mark Hewish. illus US Nav Inst Proc 102:142 Oct '76

MISSILES, ANTI-AIRCRAFT

At maximum range. A. Polyakov. Soviet Mil Rev No. 1:21-22 Jan '76

Gallery of Soviet aerospace weapons: Surface-to-air missiles. illus AF Mag 59:106-107 Mar '76

SA-8: The latest Soviet mobile SAM system. illus Intl Def Rev 8:805-806 Dec '75

Stinger. Col David Green. illus USAF Ftr Wpns Rev, pp 14-17, Fall '76

The threat to air assault operations. Capt Daniel W. Henk. illus USA Avn Dig 22:6-7+ Feb '76

Versatile Navy weapon (Standard anti-aircraft missile). Robert M. Kemp. illus tabs Natl Def 61:44-47 Jul-Aug '76

Weapon systems: Sea Dart. Mark Hewish. illus US Nav Inst Proc 102:101 Sep '76

MISSILES, ANTISHIP

Backfire problems and the Aegis mix. L. Edgar Prina. illus Sea Power 19:19-21 Sep '76

Cruise missile: The ship killer. CAPT William J. Ruhe, Ret. illus US Nav Inst Proc 102:45-52 Jun '76

EW in anti-ship missile defense? Julian S. Lake III. illus Countermeasures 2:6+ Oct '76

The Exocet anti-ship missiles. tabs illus Intl Def Rev 9:395-399 Jun '76

Popguns vs cruise missiles. R. J. Quallen. illus tab US Nav Inst Proc 102:97-100 Jul '76

Versatile Harpoon. Stefan Geisenheyner. illus (Also cutaway) tab Aerosp Intl 12:16-18+ Mar-Apr '76

Weapon system: Exocet. Mark Hewish. illus US Nav Inst Proc 102:102 Jun '76

Weapon systems: Gabriel. Mark Hewish. illus US Nav Inst Proc 102:101 Jul '76

Weapon systems: Otomat. Mark Hewish. illus US Nav Inst Proc 102:98 Aug '76

History

German remotely piloted bombs (WW II). Charles H. Bogart. illus US Nav Inst Proc 102:62-68 Nov '76

MISSILES, ANTITANK

The battlefield missile tables. Tables only. Def & For Aff Dig No. 2:15-17 '76

Beehive: An innovative approach to employment. Maj Eugene D. Colgan. illus tabs Armor 85:20-22 Sep-Oct '76

Cost-efficient anti-tank helos. illus Aerosp Intl 12: 20-22+ May-Jun '76

Destroying armor. Edited by Infantry Magazine Staff. illus Infantry 66:35-42 Sep-Oct '76

HELLFIRE (HELicopter Launched FIRE) designated AAH (Advanced Attack Helicopter) missile. Capt Mark Robison. illus USA Avn Dig 22: inside back cover May '76

The HOT (Haut subsonique Optiquement Téléguidé) missile system--long arm of the anti-tank forces. illus tabs Intl Def Rev 8:887-892 Dec '75

Missile muscle: A report on battlefield missiles. David Harvey. illus Def & For Aff Dig No. 2: 12-14+ '76

MONEY - Continued

Checks To Financial Organizations (CTFO) program and innocent NonSufficient Funds (NSF) checks. TIG Brief 28:18 Feb 13 '76; Correction. 28:12 Mar 26 '76

Fetch the age of gold. A. Ranney Johnson. illus Def & For Aff Dig No. 8-9:74-77 '76

Recurring Federal payments and EFTS (Electronic Funds Transfer System) at the U.S. Treasury. Les W. Plumly. illus Armed Forces Compt 21: 2-3 Apr '76

Unintended bad check not actionable. AF Times 36:6 Mar 8 '76

MONTGOMERY, Bernard L. Montgomery, 1st Viscount

Field-Marshal Viscount Montgomery of Alamein. obit Army Qtr 106:154-160 Apr '76

Revitalizing a beaten unit. (Story of MajGen John Pope of the Union Army shows what not to do; Field Marshal Montgomery's command of British 8th Army in Africa, 1942, demonstrates what should be done) LtGen Phillip B. Davidson, Jr, Ret. Army 26:43-45 Jan '76

MOON

See also
Space Flight to the Moon

How bright the moon--how bright the night? Garvin L. Holman. illus tabs USA Avn Dig 22:6-9+ Sep '76

MOON BASES

Two tracks to new worlds. Michael A. G. Michaud. illus tab Spaceflight 18:2-6+ Jan '76

MOON VEHICLES

Lunar roving vehicles, models 1901, 1915 and 1918. Mitchell R. Sharpe. illus (Also cutaway) Spaceflight 18:56-58 Feb '76

MOONLIGHTING

Off-duty employment. Contact, pp 8-9, Fall '76

MOORE, Harold G.

On pay and benefits, a 'balanced approach.' LtGen Harold G. Moore. por Army 26:100-102+ Oct '76

Sustaining the volunteer Army: A manpower headache LtGen Harold G. Moore. Def Mgt J 12:9-16 Oct '76

MOORER, Joseph P.

U.S. naval strategy of the future. VADM Joseph P. Moorer. por Strat Rev 4:72-80 Spring '76

MOORER, Thomas H.

The world environment and U.S. military policy for the 1970s and 1980s. ADM Thomas H. Moorer, Ret and Alvin J. Cottrell. Strat Rev 4:56-65 Spring '76

MORALE

Base inspection questionnaire on people problems. TIG Brief 28:5 Jun 18 '76

Board (Defense Manpower Commission) calls for ending piecemeal changes (in personnel policies). AF Times 36:8 May 3 '76

Cohesion and disintegration in the American Army (in Vietnam): An alternative perspective. Paul L. Savage and Richard A. Gabriel. tabs Armed Forces & Soc 2:340-376 Spring '76

MORALE - Continued

(David P.) Taylor on benefits: Piecemeal cuts hurt morale. AF Times 36:3 Feb 16 '76

Flying steels will. LtCol Y. Besschyotnov. Soviet Mil Rev No. 12:30-31 Dec '76

Morale shifts worry (Asst SecDef William) Brehm. AF Times 36:11 Feb 23 '76

'Reports' on benefit cuts held damaging to morale. AF Times 37:3 Dec 20 '76

Teams get out and talk to troops in keeping with (Gen David C.) Jones' policy. Lee Ewing. AF Times 36:12+ May 3 '76

Tuning in the (crew member) awareness frequency. 1stLt Alfred Nickerson. illus MAC Flyer 23:8-9 Apr '76

MOREELL, Ben

Keynote address, 56th Annual Meeting of the Society of American Military Engineers (Arlington, Va, April 28-May 1, 1976). ADM Ben Moreell, Ret. por Mil Engr 68:294-297 Jul-Aug '76

MORGAN, Thomas W.

The pervasive importance of USAF's space mission. Interview. LtGen Thomas W. Morgan. por AF Mag 59:46-50 Jan '76

Space in the Air Force future. (Remarks, American Defense Preparedness Assoc, Oct 15, 1975) LtGen Thomas W. Morgan. AF Plcy Ltr for Comdrs: Sup No. 2:2-8 Feb '76; Condensation. Natl Def 60:290 Jan-Feb '76

MOROCCO

The Green March (1975). C. G. White. Army Qtr 106: 351-358 Jul '76

MORRIS, John W.

New Chief of Engineers (LtGen John W. Morris). por Mil Engr 68:400 Sep-Oct '76

MORSE, Ellsworth H., Jr

How GAO assists the Congress on budgetary matters. Ellsworth H. Morse, Jr. por Armed Forces Compt 21:6-10 Jan '76

MOSS, Sanford A.

(Eight aviation pioneers (Clarence D. Chamberlin, John H. Glenn, Jr, George W. Goddard, Albert F. Hegenberger, Edwin A. Link, Sanford A. Moss, William A. Patterson, Nathan F. Twining) to be enshrined in Aviation Hall of Fame, July 24, 1976) por AF Mag 59:29-30 Jul '76

MOTELS see Hotels and Motels

MOTHBALL FLEET

The mothball fleet: Dwindling, dilapidated and doubtful. Paul Stillwell. illus Armed Forces J Intl 113: 35+ Mar '76

MOTHBALLING see Mothball Fleet

MOTION PICTURES

DOD aids film men; Senator (Patrick J. Leahy) gets the story. AF Times 37:30 Nov 29 '76

MOTION SICKNESS

Airborne testing of three antimotion sickness preparations. W. H. Johnson and others. tabs Aviation, Space & Envmt Med 47:1214-1216 Nov '76

MOTORCYCLES AND BICYCLES - Continued

Motorcycles--no second chance. Capt George C. Neiss. illus TAC Attack 16:10-11 Mar '76

New guidance on the use and control of Off-Road Vehicles (ORV). TIG Brief 28:17 Jan 16 '76

The "Real Cav" (4th Sq, 9th Cavalry). MSgt Wayne E.Hair. illus USA Avn Dig 22:24-25 Mar '76

Repeal of helmet laws (for motorcyclists) causing concern. AF Times 37:30 Nov 15 '76

Wheels of danger. (Dirt-biking at Fort Hood, Tex) SP5 Manuel Gómez. illus Soldiers 31:42-46 Dec '76

Study and Teaching

Motorcycles--no second chance. Capt George C. Neiss. illus TAC Attack 16:10-11 Mar '76

MOUNTAIN FLYING

Mountain flying. illus Approach 21:16-17 Nov '75

MOUNTAIN OPERATIONS

How strongly do you feel about life? Your survival gear and SAR preparation will probably tell. LTJG Kim A.King. illus Approach 21:18-21 Nov '75; Aerosp Safety 32:22-24 Jan '76

In the depth of defences. LtCol A.Tkalenko. map Soviet Mil Rev No. 4:22-23 Apr '76

Training at -70° F. (Army's Northern Warfare Training Center (NWTC), Fort Greely, Alas) Sgt1C Floyd Harrington. illus Soldiers 31:46-48 Nov '76

Study and Teaching

An advanced detachment in mountains. Col V.Petrov. map Soviet Mil Rev No. 8:26-28 Aug '76

Taking the highground. Sgt John Galt. illus MarCor Gaz 60:26-32 Sep '76

MOUNTAIN SICKNESS see Altitude, Influence of

MOVEMENT CONTROL
Here are entered articles on planning and control of movement of troops and supplies.

See also
Deployment

Managing logistics in the field. LtCol William C. Banze and Miles S.Abbott. illus Army Log 8:2-5 May-Jun '76

Movement of military impedimenta by common carriers. (AFR 75-5) TIG Brief 28:12 Mar 26 '76

MOVING see Household Effects

MULTINATIONAL CORPORATIONS see Corporations, International

MUNITIONS

Corona Lock. TIG Brief 28:16 Oct 8 '76

'Corona Lock' works. AF Times 37:24 Oct 18 '76

Engineering miracle in munition design. (40-mm grenade round) Victor Lindner. illus tabs Natl Def 60:294-297 Jan-Feb '76

Foreign military sales: An $11 billion market for the U.S. Charles De Vore. illus Signal 30:38-43 Jan '76

Hazards of operating internal combustion engine-powered equipment in enclosed munitions storage facilities. TIG Brief 28:6 Sep 24 '76

Home on the range. Maj John N.P.Reisbick. illus TAC Attack 16:8-9 Jan '76

MUNITIONS - Continued

New guns for the Navy. illus Natl Def 61:195-198 Nov-Dec '76

NonNuclear Munitions Safety Group (NNMSG). TIG Brief 28:15 Sep 24 '76

Prompt reporting of lost/stolen firearms and nonnuclear munitions. (AFR 125-37) TIG Brief 28:4 Jan 30 '76

RR-141 chaff. TIG Brief 28:13 Jul 2 '76

Stockpile Emergency Verification (SEV). TIG Brief 28:8 Jun 18 '76

War reserve materiel spares for munitions support. TIG Brief 28:13 Apr 9 '76

Maintenance and Repair

Munitions maintenance. TIG Brief 28:12 Apr 23 '76

Use of training units during inspections. TIG Brief 28:16 Feb 13 '76

MUNITIONS LOADING COMPETITIONS

The competitive spirit of '76. (Aerospace Defense Command 1976 Weapons Loading Competition, Tyndall AFB, Fla) Capt Robert J.Perry. illus Interceptor 18:5-9 Jul '76

Giant Sword '76: Best of the best. (Strategic Air Command's Munitions Loading Competition) illus tab Combat Crew 27:11-13 Dec '76

Giant Sword '76 (Ellsworth AFB, SD, Sep 27-Oct 6, 1976). illus Combat Crew 27:12-15 Sep '76

The number '1' team (in 1976 William Tell Weapons Loading Competition). illus Air Reservist 28:11 Aug-Sep '76

The Voodoo (Oregon's 142d Fighter Interceptor Gp) revenge (wins the 1976 Aerospace Defense Command's Weapons Loading Competition). illus Natl Guardsman 30:4-5 Jul '76

MURCHISON, Kenneth M.

Entrapment in military law. Capt Kenneth M.Murchison. AF Law Rev 18:57-75 Summer '76

Nonappropriated funds: A unique area of military law. Capt Kenneth M.Murchison. Educ J 19:23-27 Fall '76

MURPHY, James S.

The evolution of the general staff concept. MajGen James Murphy. Def Mgt J 12:34-39 Jul '76

MUSEUMS

Museum news. Regular feature in some issues of Aerospace Historian

Air Force--U.S.

The Air Force Museum. LtCol Lee Crock. illus Interceptor 18:5-9 Oct '76

Maintaining the Air Force sense of history. TIG Brief 28:21 Sep 10 '76

Project Museum: A first status report (on a Museum of Navigation Arts and Sciences, Mather AFB, Calif). Capt James P.Mallery. illus Navigator 23:31 Summer '76

The wives' way. (Volunteer tour guides, members of the Wright-Patterson AFB Officers' Wives Club, tell school children about items on display at the Air Force Museum) Capt John B.Taylor and R.E. Baughman. illus Airman 20:19-20 Sep '76

MUSEUMS - Continued

Army--U.S.

Army Transportation Museum (Fort Eustis, Va) near completion. illus Translog 7:18-19 Apr '76

Army Transportation Museum opens. illus Translog 7:5-7 Aug-Sep '76

Souvenirs of history. (Army Intelligence Museum and Fort Huachuca Historical Museum, Fort Huachuca, Ariz) Janet Hake. illus Soldiers 31:42-44 Oct '76

Directories

U.S. Army museums. Soldiers 31:44 Oct '76

National Guard--Armed Forces--U.S.

The Heritage Gallery. illus tab Natl Guardsman 30: 6-7 Feb '76

Heritage Gallery making progress. illus tabs Natl Guardsman 30:20-22 Mar '76

(Heritage Gallery) sneak preview brings rave reviews. illus Natl Guardsman 30:6-7 Aug-Sep '76

The National Guard Heritage Gallery: A status report on development, incorporation, funding and construction. illus tabs Natl Guardsman 30:22-29 Jan '76

Navy--Japan

Mikasa: Japan's memorial battleship. William M. Powers. illus US Nav Inst Proc 102:69-77 Apr '76

Navy--Russia

Search for the heroic. (Northern Fleet Museum) Col P. Altunin. illus Soviet Mil Rev No. 12:36-37 Dec '76

Navy--U.S.

The new U.S. Naval Aviation Museum, Pensacola, Florida. Pictorial. Aerosp Hist 23:214-216 Dec '7

Russia

Moving pages. (Visitors Book in the Kremlin Lenin memorial museum) LtCol L. Rakovsky. illus Soviet Mil Rev No. 3:5-6 Mar '76

United States

America's new Air and Space Museum. William P. Schlitz. illus tab AF Mag 59:42-48 Aug '76

MUSEUMS - Continued

United States - Cont'd

The collector. (Col Farley L. Berman, Ret, has most unusual and complete individually owned collection of weapons in America in Anniston, Ala) Sgt1C Floyd Harrington. illus Soldiers 31:14-18 Oct '76

Guarding the victory at Silver Hill (Md, the Smithsonian's National Air and Space Museum Preservation and Restoration Facility). Lawrence Noriega and Ronald Carriker. illus Aerosp Hist 23:28-35 Mar '76

History of the National Air and Space Museum. Dave Dooling. illus Spaceflight 18:249-262 Jul-Aug '76

In the Tricentennial year 2076. (Artist Robert T. McCall illustrates possible items of the future and creates space mural for the new National Air and Space Museum) Robert K. Ruhl. illus Airman 20: 24-33 Jul '76

The National Air and Space Museum. Gyo Obata. illus Mil Engr 68:279-281 Jul-Aug '76

A nautical observance of the Bicentennial from sea to shining sea; a monumental itinerary. (Operation Sail and the International Naval Review) Col Brooke Nihart, Ret. illus Sea Power 19:21-28 May '76

(New Air and) Space Museum: By, for Americans. LtGen Ira C. Eaker, Ret. AF Times 36:13-14 Jul 19 '76

New (National) Air and Space Museum Bicentennial opening: History of flight comes alive. illus AF Times 36:33 Jul 5 '76

"One nation, indivisible ..." (The American Freedom Train builds unity and patriotism within its visitors) Ted R. Sturm. illus Airman 20:18-23 Jul '76

MUSIC, MILITARY

See also
Bands (Music)

The General (Daniel Butterfield) wrote a bugle call ("Taps," 1862). Franklin Winters. illus Army 26:31 Nov '76

Gospel-singing soldiers. (Martin Luther King Singers, Fort Lewis, Wash) Sgt JoAnn Mann. illus Soldiers 31:33-35 May '76

NASA see National Aeronautics and Space Administration

NATO see North Atlantic Treaty Organization

NATO INTEGRATED COMMUNICATIONS SYSTEM

The initial voice switched network: First step toward the NICS (NATO Integrated Communications System). Leo I. Barker, Jr and Jerry M. Dressner. illus Signal 30:6-12 Feb '76

NATO satellite communications: Past, present, future. LtGen Harold A. Kissinger. illus Signal 30: 53-57 Mar '76

NDTA see National Defense Transportation Association

NEACP see National Emergency Airborne Command Posts

NGAUS see National Guard Association

NICS see NATO Integrated Communications System

NOAA see National Oceanic and Atmospheric Administration

NORAD see North American Air Defense Command

NAP-OF-THE-EARTH FLYING see Flight, Low-Altitude

NAPOLEONIC WARS

The Union Brigade at Waterloo: Reply to a challenge. MajGen G.N.Wood. illus Army Qtr 106:59-66 Jan '76

NASH, Edward J.

MAC 'new look' ORI. BrigGen Edward J.Nash. TIG Brief 28:3-4 Aug 27 '76

NATIONAL AERONAUTICS AND SPACE ADMINISTRATION

Civil transport technology up to 2000: NASA believes fuel consumption is the major consideration. J.Philip Geddes. illus tabs Interavia 31:419-421 May '76

Guide to NASA's research centers. AF Mag 59:158 May '76

Help wanted: Astronaut! (Qualifications and possible careers for the new space shuttle astronauts needed by NASA in 1978) Capt John B. Taylor. illus Airman 20:46-48 Oct '76

Is the U.S. losing its investment (in space)? John F. Judge. illus Govt Exec 8:21+ Mar '76

The NASA budget--FY 1977. David Baker. illus tabs Spaceflight 18:351-355 Oct '76

NASA operational communications. Charles A. Taylor. illus maps tabs Signal 30:91-95 Aug '76

NASA's goal: Keeping the U.S. Number One in aeronautics. Alan M.Lovelace. illus AF Mag 59:36-40 Feb '76

U.S. aeronautical R&D: Seeking effective policies and leadership. A.Scott Crossfield. illus tabs Govt Exec 8:38-39+ Nov '76

NATIONAL BUSINESS AIRCRAFT ASSOCIATION

NBAA business aviation showcase. (29th Annual Meeting, Denver, Sep 14-16, 1976) J.Philip Geddes. illus Interavia 31:1095-1097 Nov '76

The '75 NBAA (National Business Aircraft Assoc) show (New Orleans, Oct 29-31, 1975). illus Interavia 31:75-78 Jan '76

NATIONAL CHARACTERISTICS, AMERICAN

America and its Army: A Bicentennial look at posture and goals. Gen Fred C.Weyand. illus Parameters 6, No.1:2-11 '76

The national purpose: Conflict and creativity. Sam A. Banks. illus Parameters 5, No.2:33-39 '76

NATIONAL CHARACTERISTICS, ISRAELI

Racialist essence of Zionism. V.Sergeyev. Soviet Mil Rev No.10:43-45 Oct '76

NATIONAL CHARACTERISTICS, JAPANESE

Japan: Another threat. Brig F.W.Speed. Army Qtr 106:483-487 Oct '76

NATIONAL COMMUNICATIONS SYSTEM

Standards for government telecommunication systems. Joseph Rose and Marshall L.Cain. illus tab chart Signal 30:23-27 Jan '76

NATIONAL DEFENSE see Defenses

NATIONAL DEFENSE TRANSPORTATION ASSOCIATION

(Conference on Capital Investment in Transportation (NDTA-sponsored), Chicago, March 11, 1976) reports on outlook. illus Def Trans J 32:38-39+ Apr '76

Crisis in relocation planning. (Denver NDTA chapter undertaking emergency evacuation planning exercises) John W.Billheimer. Def Trans J 32:20+ Apr '76

A look at the '76 (31st Annual) Forum (Boston, Sep 26-29, 1976). illus Def Trans J 32:25-47 Dec '76

(MTMC Awards) for Excellence in Traffic Management (made during NDTA's 31st Annual Forum, 1976). illus Translog 7:1-3 Oct '76

Military unit awards. illus Def Trans J 32:65-69+ Oct '76

NDTA talk. Regular feature in issues of Defense Transportation Journal

(1976 NDTA Transportation and Logistics Forum, Boston, Sep 26-29, 1976) illus Def Trans J 32:45-72 Oct '76

NATIONAL DEFENSE UNIVERSITY

The National Defense University: A strategic asset. VADM Marmaduke G.Bayne. illus Strat Rev 4: 23-32 Fall '76

NATIONAL EMERGENCY AIRBORNE COMMAND POST

AFSC's Electronic Systems Division (ESD). illus AF Mag 59:51-57 Jul '76

Diversity our specialty--the 55th Strategic Reconnaissance Wing reports. Capt Sid R.Howard. illus Combat Crew 27:16-17 Oct '76

NATIONAL 'GOALS see National Policy

NATIONAL GUARD

Air Force

AFRES/ANG--best shape ever. Interviews. MajGens John J.Pesch and William Lyon. illus AF Mag 59: 55-59 Jun '76

ANG requests AFROTC grads (under Palace Option). AF Times 36:2 Jul 12 '76

ANG/Res can't bar ex-drug user. AF Times 36:6 Feb 16 '76

NATIONAL GUARD - Continued

Air Force - Cont'd

ANG to demote surplus E-9s: Nonactive-duty units affected. AF Times 36:16 Jan 19 '76

ANG to lift E-9 freeze October 1--some force outs seen. AF Times 36:20 May 24 '76

Air Guard faces changes, (MajGen John J.) Pesch says: 290 recommendations (of the DMC report) scanned (at Air Session, NGAUS 98th General Conference, Washington, Aug 30-Sep 1, 1976). AF Times 37:6 Sep 13 '76

Air National Guard. illus tab AF Mag 59:102-103 May '76

Colorado catastrophe (July 31, 1976). illus Air Reservist 28:10-11 Nov '76

From props to jets. illus Air Reservist 28:8-9 Apr '76

The great Minnesota/Arizona cactus caper. Capt Neal Gendler. illus Natl Guardsman 30:30-31 May '76

Looking forward to new horizons (161st Air Refueling Group, Phoenix, Ariz, receives Spaatz Trophy and AFA's Outstanding Unit Award). SMSgt Louis M. Nicolucci. illus Air Reservist 28:8-9 Nov '76

National Guard Heritage Encampment (Washington, Aug 28-Sep 1, 1976). Paul Lyter. illus Air Reservist 28:12-13 Jul '76

New Palace Chase rules announced. AF Times 36:2 Jun 21 '76

The 1976 Air Commanders Conference. Bruce P. Hargreaves. illus Natl Guardsman 30:44-48 Mar '76

(Operation) Coronet Sprint. (Two weeks of hard work by 180 Air Guardsmen of the 117th Tactical Reconnaissance Wg, Birmingham, Ala) 1stLt Gregory Hodges. illus Air Reservist 28:8-9 Jun '76

Planned budget cuts may hurt Reserves. AF Times 36:11 Jan 5 '76

Progress in our total force policy. James P. Gilligan. illus Air Reservist 28:3 Jul '76

A proud heritage, promising future. Thomas C. Reed. illus Air Reservist 28:2 Jul '76

Raven on the 'cap. (109th Tactical Airlift Group of the Air National Guard flies resupply missions to DEW-Line sites in Greenland) Maj Terry A. Arnold. illus Airman 20:2-8 Nov '76

Roots in the Revolution. (The 193d Tactical Electronic Warfare Gp, Pennsylvania Air Guard, has the same sense of commitment which Washington looked for in his troops) MSgt Harold Newcomb. illus Airman 20:2-7 Jul '76

3800 going Reserve under (Palace) 'Chase.' AF Times 36:3 Jul 5 '76

Unions signing Air Guardsmen. Lee Ewing. AF Times 36:4 May 10 '76

The Voodoo (Oregon's 142d Fighter Interceptor Gp) revenge (wins the 1976 Aerospace Defense Command's Weapons Loading Competition). illus Natl Guardsman 30:4-5 Jul '76

(What you've always wanted to know about the Air National Guard and the Air Force Reserve) illus charts tabs Air Reservist 27: entire issue Dec '75-Jan '76

Women and the 185th (Tactical Fighter Gp). Maj Lloyd Bach. illus Air Reservist 28:4-5 May '76

NATIONAL GUARD - Continued

Air Force - Cont'd

Working with SAC. Capt Marc Epstein. illus Air Reservist 28:6 Jul '76

History

Army Guard has glorious history and Air Guard proved worth even in WW I. illus Officer 52:14 Jul '76

73,050 yesterdays: Excerpts of militia history. Martin Gordon. illus Air Reservist 28:4+ Jul '76

Statistics

AFRES/ANG--best shape ever. Interviews. MajGens John J. Pesch and William Lyon. illus AF Mag 59: 55-59 Jun '76

Armed Forces

The Army as cop. Martin Blumenson. illus Army 26: 50-56 May '76

The budget--a grim outlook. MajGen Francis S. Greenlief, Ret. tab Natl Guardsman 30:15 Jan '76

Civilian (technicians) union to start organizing Guard/ Res. AF Times 36:6 Jan 5 '76

Evolution of a law: (National Guard Assoc of) Illinois grass-roots effort succeeds (providing enlisted Illinois Guardsmen with scholarships to state colleges and universities). illus Natl Guardsman 30: 14-15 Feb '76

1st phase of (Reserve pay system) study starts Sep 1. Paul Smith. AF Times 37:10 Aug 30 '76

Ford promises strong Guard (in address to NGAUS 98th General Conference, Washington, Aug 30-Sep 1, 1976). AF Times 37:10 Sep 13 '76

Freedoms Foundation honors Guard writers, doers. Natl Guardsman 30:37 Apr '76

The Guard & Reserve in the total force program. illus Comdrs Dig 19: entire issue Jan 29 '76

The message of the Minuteman. Col William T. Coffey. illus Natl Guardsman 30:22-23 Jul '76

The National Guard in a changing world. Dana Adams Schmidt. illus tabs Natl Guardsman 30:8-12 Apr '76

Smoke grenades, fireworks and school buses. (Guardsmen handle unusual missions during state active duty) illus Natl Guardsman 30:2-4 Aug-Sep '76

Where NGAUS stands on major issues. Natl Guardsman 30:26-27 Apr '76

Why we need the total force. (Remarks, National Guard Assoc Conference, Washington, Aug 30, 1976) Robert Ellsworth. AF Plcy Ltr for Comdrs: Sup No. 12:8-13 Dec '76

History

Citizen soldiers through the years. illus Officer 52:5+ Jul '76

73,050 yesterdays: Excerpts of militia history. Martin Gordon. illus Air Reservist 28:4+ Jul '76

Army

(Army) Guard aviation logistics. Capt Arthur W. Ries. illus Army Log 8:8-11 Nov-Dec '76

Can the Reserve Components make it? LtCol Benjamin L. Abramowitz. illus tab Mil Rev 56:58-64 May '76

NATIONAL GUARD - Continued

Army - Cont'd

In Guard, Army partnership, the key is mutual respect. LtCol Raymond E. Bell, Jr. illus Army 26: 24-26 Jan '76

(In series of management conferences Army Guard commanders told to) bite the bullet. Bruce P. Hargreaves. illus Natl Guardsman 30:22-25 May '76

The 'Ohio solution': Dynamic new training spurs Guardsmen. Maj Martin C. Froebel. illus Army 26:49-51 Mar '76

Strong new Guard for total force: Dedicated to both missions. MajGen LaVern E. Weber. illus Army 26:45-46+ Oct '76

Those tenacious trouble-shooters at (maintenance branch of) ALC (Aviation Logistics Center, Edgewood Arsenal, Md). Bruce P. Hargreaves. illus tab Natl Guardsman 30:22-25 Apr '76

The village armories in Alaska. LtCol W. F. Gabella and SP5 Byron Wooten. illus Natl Guardsman 30: 26-27 Feb '76

Yuk Yek! You've come a long way, baby! (First all-woman Eskimo Scout class) Maj Wanda T. Banta. illus Natl Guardsman 30:24-25 Jun '76

Directories

National Guard units. Army 26:142 Oct '76

Army

History

Army Guard has glorious history and Air Guard proved worth even in WW I. illus Officer 52:14 Jul '76

The militia in the Revolutionary War. James B. Deerin. map illus Natl Guardsman 30:32p sup opposite p 12 Aug-Sep '76

A nation is born. (At least 14 signers of the Declaration of Independence either had been or were later to become members of the militia) illus Natl Guardsman 30:2-3 Jul '76

Our militia is as old as Jamestown. illus Officer 52:4+ Jul '76

Organization

Total force. LtCol James E. Witek. tab Soldiers 31: 43-46 Aug '76

Statistics

Readiness of all total force jumps. tabs Officer 52:19 Feb '76

NATIONAL GUARD ASSOCIATION

An alternate view: NGAUS Executive Council takes a stand, pro or con, on key issues raised by Defense Manpower Commission report. Natl Guardsman 30:54-55 Aug-Sep '76

Conference resolutions. (NGAUS 98th General Conference, Washington, Aug 30-Sep 1, 1976) Natl Guardsman 30:32-33 Oct '76

Conference speakers. (Excerpts from addresses, NGAUS 98th General Conference, Washington, Aug 30-Sep 1, 1976) illus Natl Guardsman 30: 23-27 Oct '76

Ford promises strong Guard (in address to NGAUS 98th General Conference, Washington, Aug 30-Sep 1, 1976). AF Times 37:10 Sep 13 '76

NATIONAL GUARD ASSOCIATION - Continued

Issues & positions as adopted by the NGAUS Executive Council, January 1976. (Summary of position statements and rationale behind 2d NGAUS "Redbook") illus Natl Guardsman 30:31-41 Mar '76

NGAUS awards program: Criteria for selection. illus Natl Guardsman 30:18-20 Feb '76

The (NGAUS) 98th General Conference (Washington, Aug 30-Sep 1, 1976). illus Natl Guardsman 30: 10-16+ Oct '76

97th General Conference resolutions: Where matters stand. Natl Guardsman 30:28-34 Jul '76

The President reports. (NGAUS 98th General Conference, Washington, Aug 30-Sep 1, 1976) MajGen Richard A. Miller. Natl Guardsman 30:14-16 Oct '76

(Report on NGAUS 98th General Conference, Washington, Aug 30-Sep 1, 1976) illus Air Reservist 28:8-9+ Oct '76

(Sen John C.) Stennis receives Truman Award. illus Natl Guardsman 30:30 Mar '76

Where NGAUS stands on major issues. Natl Guardsman 30:26-27 Apr '76

NATIONAL LIBERATION FRONT OF SOUTH VIETNAM
see Viet Cong

NATIONAL MILITARY COMMAND SYSTEM

See also
Worldwide Military Command and Control System

A command, control and communications overview. Donald H. Rumsfeld. illus Signal 30:34-35+ May-Jun '76

Complex (National Military Command Center) takes world military pulse. Andy Plattner. illus AF Times 36:17 Jul 26 '76

NATIONAL OCEANIC AND ATMOSPHERIC ADMINISTRATION

Directories

Flag and general officers of the naval services; officers of flag rank of the U.S. Navy, U.S. Coast Guard, and NOAA, and general officers of the U.S. Marine Corps on active duty as of January 1, 1976. illus US Nav Inst Proc 102:213-244 May '76

NATIONAL PARK SERVICE

Bridging the generations. (Replicas of the famous bridge at Concord, Mass, are spanning the Anacostia River in Washington to the new Children's Islands Park) Sgt Deb Notah. illus Soldiers 31: 18-21 Dec '76

NATIONAL POLICY

China (People's Republic)

Dangerous doctrine. G. Apalin. Soviet Mil Rev No. 1: 44-45 Jan '76

Iran

The Rapier & mace: Air defense & the art of grand strategy; a study of the Iranian example. Gregory Copley. illus Def & For Aff Dig No. 4:6-11 '76

Japan

Is Japan on the way to super-power status? Niu Sienchong. NATO's Fifteen Nations 20:34-39 Dec '75-Jan '76

NAVAL AVIATION - Continued

United States - Cont'd

Lessons learned (in Naval Aviation). LT C.F.Wise. illus Approach 21:7-8 Nov '75

NATOPS check. LCDR Frank A.Miley. illus Approach 22:22-24 Jul '76

Naval Air Rework Facility, North Island (NAS, Calif) William M.Powers. illus US Nav Inst Proc 102: 62-71 Jun '76

Out-of-control aircraft losses (precipitate conferenc under sponsorship of Naval Safety Center). Approach 21:14 Jan '76

Proficiency flying is terminated. MarCor Gaz 60:2 Dec '76

Survival of the fittest: Five years later. LCDR William W.Turkington. illus tabs US Nav Inst Proc 102:58-65 Oct '76

Top Gun--the Navy's "MIG-killing" school. (Navy Fighter Weapons School, Miramar NAS, Calif) CAPT Andrew Hamilton, Ret. illus US Nav Inst Proc 102:95-97 Jan '76

History

The new U.S. Naval Aviation Museum, Pensacola, Florida. Pictorial. Aerosp Hist 23:214-216 Dec '7(

NAVAL BASES

See also
Air Bases, Naval

NAVAL BASES, AMERICAN

Cuba

The U.S. presence in Guantanamo. Martin J.Scheina. illus Strat Rev 4:81-88 Spring '76

Iceland

Codfish war threatens NATO's northern flank. Gen T.R.Milton, Ret. AF Mag 59:40 Apr '76

Philippines

Fuel and energy conservation program (at Subic Bay, Philippines). CAPT Joseph A.D'Emidio. illus tabs Mil Engr 68:387-389 Sep-Oct '76

Spain

The Spanish connection: A wider U.S. commitment in the making. maps tabs Def Monitor 5: entire issue Feb '76

NAVAL FACILITIES ENGINEERING COMMAND

Pollution control at Navy fire-fighting schools. Floyd C.Hildebrand. illus Mil Engr 68:100-101 Mar-Apr '76

NAVAL LIFE see Military Life

NAVAL MATERIAL COMMAND

See also
Naval Facilities Engineering Command

NAVAL RESEARCH LABORATORY

Radar evolution and innovation at NRL (Naval Research Laboratory). John H.Dunn. illus tab Signal 31:8-13 Oct '76

NAVAL TRAINING CENTERS

Pollution control at Navy fire-fighting schools. Floyd C.Hildebrand. illus Mil Engr 68:100-101 Mar-Apr '76

NAVAL WAR COLLEGE

The 'new' NWC (Naval War College): Professionalism, power projections, CCE (Center for Continuing Education), NEWS (Navy Electronic Warfare Simulator), and WARS (Warfare Analysis and Research System). L.Edgar Prina. illus Sea Power 19:17-21 Jul '76

Strategy seminars (at Naval War College to) offer graduate credit. AF Times 37:2 Aug 9 '76

NAVIGATION

See also specific types of navigation, e.g.,
Radar Navigation
Radio Navigation
Space Navigation

Study and Teaching

Interceptor pilots' navigational training. MajGen V. Kadyshev. Soviet Mil Rev No.11:28-29 Nov '76

Introduction to navigation. LtCol Brian T.Parker. Educ J 19:39-40 Winter '76

NAVIGATION, AIR

Air superiority (F-4) GIB (WSO, Weapon Systems Officer). Capt Roger E.Rosenberg. illus Navigator 23:18-19 Summer '76

Airpath turn. LtCol Andrew Labosky, Jr. illus tabs Navigator 23:14-16 Summer '76

Are you NOE and lost? Garvin L.Holman. illus USA Avn Dig 22:8-12 Mar '76

DR (Dead Reckoning) or DA (Drift Angle)? LTJG C.S.Young. illus Approach 22:15 Sep '76

History

Air navigation: The early years. LtCol William T. Dewey. illus Navigator 23:5-9 Spring '76

NAVIGATION, CELESTIAL

Improving your celestial accuracy. Capts Wayne R. Mathis and Howard W.Brickman. illus tabs Navigator 23:30-31 Spring '76

Star identification. Capt Peter A.Cook. (Reprinted from Navigator, Summer-Fall 1969) illus tabs Navigator pt 1, 23:24-28 Winter '76

Handbooks, Manuals, etc.

Celestial competence (with the Air Almanac). Capt Joseph R.Hamlin. illus Navigator 23:21 Winter '76

NAVIGATION, INERTIAL

And now, a navigator in a box. (The Palletized Inertial Navigation System (PINS) is adding flight course accuracy to some AF tanker flights) MSgt Harold Newcomb. illus Airman 20:16-18 Jun '76

Fine tuning your INS (Inertial Navigation System). LtCol Wallace E.Beebe and Capt Gerald R.J. Heuer. illus Navigator 23:16-20 Winter '76

Inertial navigation means help is on the way. illus MAC Flyer 23:9-10 Mar '76

Military strapdown inertial navigation systems. G.J. Campos. tabs illus (Also cutaway) Countermeasures 2:82-85+ Sep '76

Modern navigational systems. Comdr C.J.Eliot, Ret. illus NATO's Fifteen Nations 20:72-77 Dec '75-Jan '76

PINS (Palletized Inertial Navigation System) in Alaska. Capt William T.Nuzum and Lt Christopher G. Knowles. illus Combat Crew 27:28-29 Nov '76

NAVY - Continued

Bolivia

La Paz lament. (Need for sovereign access to the Pacific) Leigh Johnson. Def & For Aff Dig No. 3: 14-19 '76

China (People's Republic)

The PRC Navy--coastal defense or blue water? CDR Bruce Swanson. illus tabs maps US Nav Inst Proc 102:82-107 May '76

The politics of the Chinese People's Republic Navy. LT David G. Muller, Jr. illus Nav War Col Rev 28:32-51 Spring '76

Great Britain

Britain at the crossroads. Comdr Joseph Palmer. illus tabs Sea Power 19:33-39 Sep '76

Maritime affairs. VADM B. B. Schofield. Regular feature in issues of Army Quarterly and Defence Journal

The Royal Navy--its contribution to national and Western defence. Adm Terence Lewin. RUSI J for Def Studies 121:3-4+ Sep '76

Exhibitions

The 1975 (3d) Royal Navy Equipment Exhibition (Greenwich, Eng, Sep 15-19, 1975). illus Intl Def Rev 8:843-848 Dec '75

History

The captain and the convoy (1779). S. W. Bryant, Jr. illus US Nav Inst Proc 102:69-70 Jul '76

The Royal Navy and the Far Eastern problem, 1931-1941. Paul Haggie. Army Qtr 106:402-414 Oct '76

Sea power in the (American) Revolution. James A. Carr. illus Natl Def 61:125-128 Sep-Oct '76

Iran

The Shah's Navy. John T. Hayward. Govt Exec 8:36+ Oct '76

Japan

History

Mikasa: Japan's memorial battleship. William M. Powers. illus US Nav Inst Proc 102:69-77 Apr '76

NATO

The Channel Command, sea highway to Europe. Comdr Joseph M. Palmer. illus map chart US Nav Inst Proc 102:176-189 May '76

The-influence of navies on the European Central Front. Comdr Hans Garde. illus maps US Nav Inst Proc 102:160-175 May '76

Russia

The antisubmarine cruiser "Kiev." illus Soviet Mil Rev No. 11:22-23 Nov '76

The Cuban missile crisis and Soviet naval development: Myths and realities. LCDR Harlan K. Ullman. tabs Nav War Col Rev 28:45-56 Winter '76

The Gorshkov doctrine: Seapower and the world ocean. L. Edgar Prina. illus Sea Power 19:33-37 Oct '76

The growing threat: New challenges for the EW community. Ronald T. Pretty. illus Elect Warfare 8:43+ Mar-Apr '76

NAVY - Continued

Russia - Cont'd

"Kiev" and her aircraft. illus Air Pict 38:342-343 Sep '76

Kiev and the U.S. carrier controversy. Henry T. Simmons. illus tabs Intl Def Rev 9:741-744 Oct '76

Naval Kremlinology. CAPT William H. J. Manthorpe, Jr. illus tab US Nav Inst Proc 102:70-72 Jan '76

(The Navy): Unknown events, disturbing trends, and a rebuilding of strength. J. William Middendorf II. illus tabs Sea Power 19:7-13 Jan '76

The Northern Theater: Soviet capabilities and concepts. John Erickson. map Strat Rev 4:67-82 Summer '76

Okean-75. LCDRs Bruce W. Watson and Margurite A. Walton. illus map US Nav Inst Proc 102:93-97 Jul '76

The Soviet aircraft carrier. Norman Polmar. illus US Nav Inst Proc 102:138-141 Oct '76

The Soviet military machine: Morale, muscles, and megatons. Col Robert D. Heinl, Jr, Ret. illus Sea Power 19:31-34 May '76

The Soviet Navy in 1975. CAPT William H. J. Manthorpe, Jr. illus tabs US Nav Inst Proc 102:204-212 May '76

The surface Navy today: Prospects and problems. Col Robert D. Heinl, Jr, Ret. illus Sea Power 19:27-32 Oct '76

Thinking about Soviet ASW. Norman Polmar. illus map US Nav Inst Proc 102:108-129 May '76

The U.S. and Russian Navies. LtGen Ira C. Eaker, Ret. AF Times 37:13-14 Aug 23 '76

The vulnerability of the West in the Southern Hemisphere. Patrick Wall. illus tab Strat Rev 4:44-50 Winter '76

History

American maritime strategy and Soviet naval expansion. J. William Middendorf II. illus tabs Strat Rev 4:16-25 Winter '76

Statistics

Arms, men, and military budgets: Some grim facts and sobering conclusions about the present military 'balance.' James D. Hessman. tabs Sea Power 19:14-16 May '76

Soviet Naval strength. tab Elect Warfare 8:69 May-Jun '76

South Africa (Republic)

The South African Navy: Guardian of the ocean crossroads. Col Norman L. Dodd, Ret. illus tab US Nav Inst Proc 102:94-97 Sep '76

United States

See also
Military Sealift Command
    also specific fleets, e.g.,
Fleet, 7th

(ADM James L.) Holloway discusses future needs; VTOL, Tomahawk head weapons list. L. Edgar Prina. illus Sea Power 19:9-10 May '76

Annual Navy Day report (1975). illus Sea Power 18:35 Dec '75

A bluewater interface and the Running Mates program: Navy/Merchant Marine officer exchange program offers benefits to each. James D. Hessman. illus Sea Power 19:20-22 Jun '76

NAVY - Continued

United States - Cont'd

History

Admiral H. Kent Hewitt, U.S. Navy. John Clagett. illus Nav War Col Rev pt 1, Preparing for high command. 28:72-86 Summer '75; pt 2, High command. 28:60-86 Fall '75

American maritime strategy and Soviet naval expansion. J. William Middendorf II. illus tabs Strat Rev 4:16-25 Winter '76

Citizen sailors played key role in every war. illus Officer 52:8+ Jul '76

Developing naval concepts: The early years, 1815-42. VADM Edwin B. Hooper, Ret. illus tab Def Mgt J 12:19-24 Jul '76

Mission to Mecca: The cruise of the Murphy. (U.S. destroyer brings Arabian king from Mecca to Great Bitter Lake in Suez Canal, to meet with Pres Franklin Roosevelt after Yalta Conference, 1945, and deals successfully with seemingly unsurmountable problems, both diplomatic and pragmatic) CAPT John S. Keating, Ret. illus US Nav Inst Proc 102:54-63 Jan '76

The naval profession: Challenge and response, 1870-1890 and 1950-1970. Lawrence C. Allin. Nav War Col Rev 28:75-90 Spring '76

"Old Ironsides": Relevant relic. CDR Tyrone G. Martin. illus US Nav Inst Proc 102:106-109 Sep '76

The (Richmond Pearson) Hobson craze. (Naval officer in the Spanish-American War, commander and survivor of a certifiable suicide mission (sinking of the Merrimac), with matinee idol looks that made him his country's first major sex symbol) Barton C. Shaw. illus US Nav Inst Proc 102:54-60 Feb '76

The sea in the making of America. Clark G. Reynolds. illus US Nav Inst Proc 102:36-51 Jul '76

Skipper of the Eagle (ADM H. Kent Hewitt): Rehearsal for greatness. LCDR John H. Clagett, Ret. illus US Nav Inst Proc 102:58-65 Apr '76

The spirit of '76. (U.S. Navy exhibition at the International Centennial Exposition, Philadelphia, 1876, reveals antiquated equipment and low level of naval technology) LT Richard D. Glasow, Ret. illus US Nav Inst Proc 102:25-35 Jul '76

United States-Soviet naval relations in the 1930's: The Soviet Union's efforts to purchase naval vessels. Thomas R. Maddux. illus Nav War Col Rev 29:28-37 Fall '76

Organization

The surface forces. VADM Robert S. Salzer, Ret. illus US Nav Inst Proc 102:26-35 Nov '76

Statistics

Soviet Naval strength. tab Elect Warfare 8:69 May-Jun '76

NAVY DAY

Annual Navy Day report (1975). illus Sea Power 18:35 Dec '75

Navy Day 1976. illus Sea Power 19:35-41 Dec '76

· NAVY ELECTRONIC WARFARE SCHOOL see Consolidated Navy Electronic Warfare School ·

NAVY EXCHANGES see Exchanges--Navy

NAVY LEAGUE

Declaration of objectives, Navy League of the United States. (Text of resolutions adopted at convention, Boston, May 21, 1976) Sea Power 19:15-17 Jun '76

Meet Mr and Ms Navy Leaguer--1976. tabs Sea Power 19:35-37 May '76

Navy League Convention, Boston, May 18-21, 1976. illus Sea Power 19:22-34 Jul '76

NEEL, Spurgeon H., Jr

A doctor looks at Army Aviation. MajGen Spurgeon Neel. por USA Avn Dig 22:1+ Oct '76

(MajGen) Spurgeon Neel elected to Army Aviation Hall of Fame for pioneering aeromedevac. por Aviation, Space & Envmt Med 47:799 Jul '76

NEGOTIATION

Doomed to peace. Béchir Ben Yahmed. (Digested from Foreign Affairs, Oct 1975) Mil Rev 56:39-44 Feb '76

The 1953 cease-fire in Korea. James H. Toner. illus Mil Rev 56:3-13 Jul '76

The psychology of Middle East peace. Nahum Goldmann. (Digested from Foreign Affairs, Oct 1975) Mil Rev 56:31-39 Feb '76

NEGROES IN THE ARMED FORCES see Blacks in the Armed Forces

NEUTRALITY

Sweden

The security and defence of Sweden. Nils Andrén. illus map RUSI J for Def Studies 121:23-32 Jun '76

Switzerland

Military service and social change in Switzerland. Hanspeter Kriesi. tabs Armed Forces & Soc 2: 218-226 Winter '76

NEWMAN, Aubrey S.

Employ lieutenant years as special time to learn. MajGen A. S. Newman. Army 26:49-50 Dec '76

NEWS MEDIA

Accidents and public information responsibilities. TIG Brief 28:15 Jun 18 '76

DOD recruiting advertising: The 19-million dollar question. Benjamin F. Schemmer. illus tabs Armed Forces J Intl 113:12-13+ Jun '76

Debate on TV: (Rep Les) Aspin vs (Col George) Hennrikus. illus AF Times 37:16+ Dec 13 '76

Is enemy us? (Condensed from address, Texas Assoc of Broadcasters, Dallas, Sep 16, 1976) MajGen Eugene P. Forrester. illus Army 26:6-8 Nov '76

The military and the media. (Remarks, Air War College Media-Military Symposium '76, Maxwell AFB, Ala, March 29, 1976) LtGen Raymond B. Furlong. AF Plcy Ltr for Comdrs: Sup No. 6:19-21 Jun '76

News--or views? Harry M. Zubkoff. illus Strat Rev 4:104-110 Summer '76

Personal perceptions of the Vietnam War. CAPT John C. MacKercher, Ret. Natl Sec Aff Forum No. 24:6p addendum Spring-Summer '76

A perspective of the military and the media. Carl J. Migdail. illus Nav War Col Rev 28:2-9 Winter '76

NEWS MEDIA - Continued

The Sunday morning massacre: A murder-suicide?
Aaron Latham. (Reprinted from New York,
Dec 22, 1975) illus Armed Forces J Intl 113:18-25
Jan '76

Who speaks for the people? Editorial. John T.Hay-
ward. Govt Exec 8:11-12 Jun '76

NEWSPAPERS

Commercial enterprise newspaper operations. TIG
Brief 28:20 Dec 17 '76

(JSC Chairman Gen George S.) Brown criticizes
Times newspapers (in testimony before House
Armed Services Committee). AF Times 36:3
Feb 9 '76

NIEHAUS, William S.

Federal compliance with state environmental procedures. Capt William S.Niehaus. AF Law Rev 18:
1-17 Fall '76

NIGERIA

Economic Conditions

Nigeria: African super-state. Leigh Johnson. illus
maps tabs Def & For Aff Dig No.8-9:44-45+ '76

Politics and Government

Nigeria: African super-state. Leigh Johnson. illus
maps tabs Def & For Aff Dig No.8-9:44-45+ '76

NIGHT FIGHTING

The ending of World War II. (History of the 547th
Night Fighter Sq) LtCol Paul H.Baldwin, Ret.
illus Aerosp Hist 23:136-139 Sep '76

In the still of the night. LtCol Billy A.Lyles. illus
Air Def Mag, pp 40-41, Apr-Jun '76

Night fighting capabilities. Maj William G.Privette.
illus tabs Armor 85:43-47 Mar-Apr '76

Night tactical evaluation. Col John H.Weckerling.
illus Armor 85:45-46 May-Jun '76

Soviet night operations. Arthur W.McMaster III.
illus tabs USA Avn Dig 22:2-3+ Jan '76

Equipment

Eyes that see in the night. David M.Clementz. illus
MarCor Gaz 60:54-55 Jul '76

Night fighting capabilities. Maj William G.Privette.
illus tabs Armor 85:43-47 Mar-Apr '76

Night tactical evaluation. Col John H.Weckerling.
illus Armor 85:45-46 May-Jun '76

NIGHT FLYING

Black nights and glassy seas. LCDR Bill Roop. illus
Approach 22:28-29 Dec '76

The case of mistaken identity. Rush R.Wicker. illus
USA Avn Dig 22:24-25 Apr '76

Death at the ramp. illus Approach 21:26-27 Feb '76

The enemy is a man who (will try to kill you before
you see him). Capt Nelson Cobleigh. illus USAF
Ftr Wpns Rev, pp 23-30, Fall '76

How high the moon--how bright the night? Garvin L.
Holman. illus tabs USA Avn Dig 22:6-9+ Sep '76

Midnight mass divert. LT John Stevenson. illus Approach 22:2-5 Dec '76

NIGHT FLYING - Continued

Night flight. Capt Richard P.Keida. illus Aerosp
Safety 32:18-19 Apr '76

Night flying without feathers. Capt Glenn Wendt.
Interceptor 18:14-15 Jun '76

"No joy." Maj Jack Spey. illus Aerosp Safety 32:
10-11 Jun '76

On a night mission. (Pilot's courage and skill helped
to save a supersonic missile-carrying plane)
LtCol A.Sorokin. illus Soviet Mil Rev No.1:36-38
Jan '76

Paddles to pilots, what now? LT Randy Leddy. illus
tab Approach 22:18-19 Dec '76

Pave Low III (modified Sikorsky HH-53 for night rescue capability). AF Mag 59:18 Feb '76

Something new for the LAMPS program. (GSI, Glide
Slope Indicator) illus Approach 22:10-11 Nov '76

Equipment

Cockpit design for night NOE (Nap-Of-the-Earth).
J.H.Emery. illus USA Avn Dig 22:6-7 Jan '76

Study and Teaching

101st Aviation Group night flying. Capt Peter L.
Wyro. illus USA Avn Dig 22:8-10 Jan '76

Cerebrations: Night attack helicopter training. Maj
William E.Whitworth. illus tabs USA Avn Dig 22:
4-5+ Jan '76

Night Hawk Training Test. illus USA Avn Dig pt 1,
The overview. CW2 David R.Heaton. 21:1-3+
Dec '75; pt 2, The procedures. CW2 Douglas V.
Joyce. 22:21-23 Jan '76

Night terrain flight training in USAREUR. Maj
George R.Miller. illus USA Avn Dig 22:8-11
Aug '76

NIMITZ, Chester W.

Admiral Nimitz and the Battle of Midway. E.B.Pot-
ter. por US Nav Inst Proc 102:60-68 Jul '76

NIXON, Richard M.

The enigma of the Nixon Doctrine. Col Larry E.Will-
ner. Persp in Def Mgt No.24:91-95 Winter '75-'76

NOISE

Arousing environmental stresses can improve performance, whatever people say. E.C.Poulton.
tabs Aviation, Space & Envmt Med 47:1193-1204
Nov '76

B-1 gets 'clean' (environmental) rating. AF Times
37:18 Oct 18 '76

Basing the new Air Force weapon systems: A potential for problems. Maj John G.Terino. illus map
AU Rev 27:65-72 Jul-Aug '76

Hearing under stress. IV: A speech delivery communication system for utilization in high ambient
noise environments. G.L.Whitehead and others.
tab Aviation, Space & Envmt Med 47:811-812
Aug '76

How quickly will the aircraft noise problem subside?
M.J.T.Smith. illus tabs Interavia 31:989-991
Oct '76

Long-duration exposure to intermittent noises. Daniel L.Johnson and others. tabs Aviation, Space &
Envmt Med 47:987-990 Sep '76

NOISE - Continued

Panel on Impact of Noise Control on Aircraft Operations. (Papers presented at 1975 Annual Scientific Meeting, Aerospace Medical Assoc) illus tabs Aviation, Space & Envmt Med 47:42-69 Jan '76

Quiet and efficient (jet) engines for tomorrow. Richard S. Page. illus Aerosp Intl 12:12-13+ Jan-Feb '76

Review of the effects of infrasound on man. C. Stanley Harris and others. Aviation, Space & Envmt Med 47:430-434 Apr '76

Turning JP (Jet Propulsion) into noise. LTJG David M. Tyler. illus Approach 22:26 Nov '76

NONAPPROPRIATED FUNDS

(Air Force) Academy Athletic Association: Investment losses held high. Andy Plattner. AF Times 36:29 May 17 '76

Appropriated funds for Morale, Welfare, and Recreation (MWR) activities. TIG Brief 28:15 Nov 19 '76

NAF cost survey ordered by DOD. AF Times 36:2 Jan 12 '76

A new era for nonappropriated funds. John M. Weddle. illus AF Compt 10:4-6 Oct '76

Nonappropriated funds: A unique area of military law. Capt Kenneth M. Murchison. Educ J 19:23-27 Fall '76

Standards of conduct for Morale, Welfare, and Recreation (MWR) personnel. TIG Brief 28:5-6 Aug 27 '76

NONCOMMISSIONED OFFICERS

Air Force--U.S.

Air Force elevates NCO transport training. (Transportation Staff Officer course, Sheppard AFB, Tex) illus Def Trans J 32:32-33 Aug '76

April hike quotas: E-5 in trouble. AF Times 36:9 Mar 22 '76

BTZ (Below-The-Zone) hike dates posted for E-3s. AF Times 37:8 Aug 9 '76

Base-choice plan 1st-shirt incentive. AF Times 37:41 Dec 27 '76

Ceiling stabilized for top 6 (EM grades). AF Times 37:16 Aug 9 '76

Changed admin(istration) field to groom 1st shirts. Len Famiglietti. AF Times 37:6 Oct 11 '76

E-4 sergeant 'ranks' senior airman in E-4. AF Times 37:32 Dec 13 '76

E-4 Sgt status can be removed. AF Times 37:10 Nov 29 '76

E-4 through E-9: 8868 advancing. AF Times 36:3 Jul 26 '76

E-4s' teachers begin training (at Leadership and Management Development Center, Maxwell AFB, Ala). Len Famiglietti. AF Times 36:2 Mar 8 '76

E-8 hike pace rises, E-5 falls. AF Times 36:17 Feb 2 '76

EM hike future looks OK: Quotas for upper noncoms rising in March. Bruce Callander. AF Times 36:3 Mar 1 '76

EM hikes--changes, impact. Bruce Callander. tabs AF Times 37:3 Aug 30 '76

EM hikes mostly in orbit. Bruce Callander. illus AF Times 37:3-4 Nov 22 '76

NONCOMMISSIONED OFFICERS - Continued

Air Force--U.S. - Cont'd

EM promotion picture mostly a gloomy one. Bruce Callander. AF Times 36:2 Jan 19 '76

829 out of 7200 selected for E-9. AF Times 36:6 May 10 '76

Enlisted force structure changes. AF Plcy Ltr for Comdrs: Sup No.5:34-36 May '76

Enlisted promotions back on schedule. Bruce Callander. AF Times 37:2 Sep 27 '76

15 bases to test new APR plan. AF Times 36:9 Feb 2 '76

A fifty-yard line view of leadership. (Remarks, Graduation Ceremonies of the Strategic Air Command Noncommissioned Officer Academy, Barksdale AFB, La, Sep 24, 1976) LtGen Bryan M. Shotts. AF Plcy Ltr for Comdrs: Sup No.12:22-27 Dec '76

1st Sgt nice guy. Richard C. Barnard. illus AF Times, Times Magazine sup:4-7+ Dec 20 '76

First shirts can leave field to retrain after 36 months. AF Times 37:61 Oct 18 '76

1st shirts to work more with troops. Bruce Callander. AF Times 36:4 Jun 28 '76

4-year stabilized tours with ROTC units offered. tab AF Times 37:10 Aug 9 '76

Guide due on 1stSgt manning. Len Famiglietti. AF Times 37:6 Oct 18 '76

Hand-picked E-9s to get key jobs. AF Times 36:4 Jan 12 '76

High NCOs get alert on board-points plan. AF Times 37:16 Aug 9 '76

Hike activity getting back on track. Bruce Callander. AF Times 36:3 Jun 21 '76

Hike picture for EM brightens--in spots. AF Times 37:30 Aug 2 '76

Improving 1st sergeants' effectiveness. (Interview with CMSgt Royce A. Flynn) AF Times 36:31 Feb 23 '76

Insignia changes offered: Top NCOs would get new stripes. Bruce Callander. illus AF Times 36:3 Jul 19 '76

Is WAPS promoting the right people? AF Times 37:29 Aug 23 '76

JOC and EM councils soon to be optional. AF Times 36:2 May 3 '76

Jobs list issued for top E-9s. tabs AF Times 36:16+ May 24 '76

Just who or what ... is an NCO? SMSgt Harold Newcomb. illus Airman 20:2-8 Oct '76

Most new E-8s took Senior NCO course. AF Times 36:12 Jul 19 '76

NCO conviction upset: Court (of Military Appeals) cautions JAGs. AF Times 37:24 Nov 8 '76

NCO (Leadership) School (Langley AFB, Va) trains professionals. SSgt Linda Henggeler. AF Times 36:37 Jul 12 '76

NCO retrainees due $$. AF Times 37:8 Aug 16 '76

NCO status: 'Must' before E-5 hike. AF Times 36:8 Jun 21 '76

NONCOMMISSIONED OFFICERS - Continued

Air Force--U.S. - Cont'd

NCO training gets classroom push. AF Times 36:19 Jun 28 '76

NCOs aiming for top spot to face 2 sets of tests. AF Times 37:2 Dec 27 '76

New hike plan for E-9 studied. AF Times 36:10 May 31 '76

New stripes for top EM: Commands study NCO change. Bruce Callander. illus AF Times 36:2 Apr 5 '76

New 2-step E-4 plan begins June 1. Bruce Callander. AF Times 36:16 Feb 23 '76

1904 NCOs selected for E-8 in '77. tab AF Times 36:8 Jul 12 '76

No hike delay (for E-4s) seen from 2-way split. AF Times 37:6 Oct 4 '76

No new NCOs for one year: 3-tier EM plan launched. Bruce Callander. AF Times 36:6+ May 24 '76

Noncom grades, except for E-6, are on target. AF Times 37:2 Dec 27 '76

Noncom hike cycles facing major change. Bruce Callander. AF Times 36:6 May 31 '76

Outstanding Airmen for 1976. illus AF Times 37:19+ Sep 27 '76

Outstanding Airmen (of 1976). illus Airman 20:11-14 Dec '76

Phase I NCO PME a must for E-4s. AF Times 37:2 Dec 6 '76

Point-board OK for E-8, 9. Bruce Callander. AF Times 37:3 Aug 2 '76

Quality breeds quality. TIG Brief 28:21 Jul 16 '76

Quotas issued for below-zone hikes: 1242 to make E-4. AF Times 36:6 Feb 16 '76

Reg (AFR 39-6) spells out noncom duties. AF Times 36:8 Jun 21 '76

Revamping the enlisted structure. Ed Gates. tab AF Mag 59:39-41 Aug '76

Rules preclude 3-tier 'slips.' Bruce Callander. AF Times 36:25 Jun 14 '76

Senior NCOs to get direct BAS payments. Bruce Callander. AF Times 36:6 Feb 9 '76

7542 picked for E-6, 7 promotions. AF Times 36:17+ Feb 9 '76

Some bonus skills dropped, a few added. AF Times 36:3 Jun 7 '76

Some NCOs to fill higher-level jobs. AF Times 37:57 Nov 29 '76

Some skills tests lifted until Dec. AF Times 37:6 Aug 30 '76

Statistics on E-6, 7 selections. tab AF Times 37:17 Aug 9 '76

Switch to three-tier (system) includes cushioners. Bruce Callander. AF Times 36:1+ Jun 7 '76

TIG (Time In Grade) schedule set for E-8s, 9s. Bruce Callander. AF Times 37:2 Dec 6 '76

Test scores--big factor in (NCO promotion) point plan. AF Times 37:3 Nov 22 '76

Three-tier setup and how it works. tab AF Times 36:10 May 31 '76

NONCOMMISSIONED OFFICERS - Continued

Air Force--U.S. - Cont'd

3-tier structure: New EM lineup begins June 1. AF Times 36:3 Mar 1 '76

3-tier system takes hold. AF Times 37:3 Nov 22 '76

Top NCOs getting retraining bid. AF Times 37:8 Aug 2 '76

Top NCOs moving to shortage skills. Bruce Callander. AF Times 37:2 Dec 13 '76

Training denied some first shirts. AF Times 36:11 Jul 12 '76

2811 NCOs going up Sep 1. AF Times 37:3 Aug 23 '76

USAF's finest. (12 Outstanding Airmen for 1976) Maj Terry A. Arnold. illus AF Mag 59:47-49 Nov '76

What's good about switching skills. AF Times 37:19 Aug 9 '76

Armed Forces--U.S.

(Deputy DefSec William P.) Clements speaks on NCOs. Gene Famiglietti. AF Times 36:61 May 24 '76

NCO key to union threat: Board (Defense Manpower Commission) suggests hard line against organizing. Lee Ewing. AF Times 36:3 May 3 '76

Army--U.S.

(Army personnel problems) Interview. MajGen Robert Gard. Fld Arty J 44:35-37 Nov-Dec '76

Charlie's place. (SSgt Charles R.Reed, NCOIC of Wackernheim Range near Mainz, West Germany) Lt Michael A. Bartell and SP4 Kregg P.J.Jorgenson. illus Army 26:22-25 Nov '76

EM career notes. Regular feature in issues of Infantry

Enlisted career news. Regular feature in issues of Air Defense Magazine

For E4s only. (PNCOC/CA, Primary NonCommissioned Officer's Course/Combat Arms) Sgt1C Floyd Harrington. illus Soldiers 31:10-12 Oct '76

NCO reclassification. Fld Arty J 44:34-35 Sep-Oct '76

The new gunnery sergeant. SGM Harvey M. McBride. illus Fld Arty J 44:8-9 Sep-Oct '76

The next one will be a squad leader's war. Capt Robert B.Killebrew. illus Army 26:22-25 Dec '76

Quality, training and motivation. SMA William G. Bainbridge. illus Army 26:27-29 Oct '76

Marine Corps--U.S.

Is the Corps losing its backbone? 1stLt Ronald B. Helle. MarCor Gaz 60:65-67 Nov '76

National Guard--Air Force--U.S.

ANG to demote surplus E-9s: Nonactive-duty units affected. AF Times 36:16 Jan 19 '76

ANG to lift E-9 freeze October 1--some force outs seen. AF Times 36:20 May 24 '76

(Air National) Guard picks 71 for hike to E-9. AF Times 37:10 Nov 22 '76

Reserve Forces--Air Force--U.S.

Hikes open to Reserve EM. AF Times 37:2 Dec 27 '76

NORTH ATLANTIC TREATY ORGANIZATION -
Continued

The North Atlantic Treaty. London's International
Institute for Strategic Studies. illus tabs AF Mag
59:54-61 Dec '76

North European oil: Implications for NATO nations.
LtCol Henrik O. Lunde. illus map tab Parameters
6, No. 1:87-96 '76

Red runs the Rubicon: Turbulent Italy faces new
troubles, NATO could lose its Mediterranean anchor. Lawrence Griswold. illus map Sea Power
19:20-24 Mar '76

SHAPE: A silvered shield--twenty-five years in the
service of peace and security. Morris Honick.
illus NATO's Fifteen Nations 21:48-52+ Feb-
Mar '76

Security makes strange bedfellows: NATO's problems from a minimalist perspective. Ken Booth.
RUSI J for Def Studies 120:3-4+ Dec '75

Senator Mansfield and the NATO alliance: A reap-
praisal of policy and objectives. Scott D. Sagan.
Royal Air Forces Qtr 16:129-137 Summer '76

South Africa: NATO's unwelcome ally. Charles Latour. illus map tab NATO's Fifteen Nations 21:
58-64+ Jun-Jul '76

The southern flank of NATO: Problems of the south-
ern region in the post-1973 October War period.
ADM Means Johnston, Jr. illus Mil Rev 56:22-29
Apr '76

Spain and the defense of NATO. CAPT R. A. Komorowski, Ret. illus map tabs US Nav Inst Proc 102:190-
203 May '76

Standardisation and defence in NATO. Gardiner L.
Tucker. RUSI J for Def Studies 121:7-8+ Mar '76

Tac air--history's most potent fighting machine.
Edgar Ulsamer. illus AF Mag 59:22-26 Feb '76

The theatre balance between NATO and the Warsaw
Pact. London's International Institute for Strategic
Studies. tabs AF Mag 59:98-106 Dec '76

A twenty one jewel watch: Mutual logistic support in
NATO. CDR Eugene F. Coughlin. illus Def Trans J
32:12-14+ Apr '76

USAF's new Soviet awareness program. Edgar Ulsamer. AF Mag 59:38-42 May '76

The United States, NATO and the decade ahead. Col
Robert W. Kochenour. illus Mil Rev 56:14-24
Jul '76

Foreign Relations

United States

Dove in the cockpit: Peace in today's Europe. Maj
Edd D. Wheeler. illus tabs AU Rev 27:36-44 Jan-
Feb '76

History

SHAPE--those were the days. Gen Robert J. Wood,
Ret. illus Army 26:42-47 Dec '76

NORTH SEA REGION

Strategic Importance

North European oil: Implications for NATO nations.
LtCol Henrik O. Lunde. illus map tab Parameters
6, No. 1:87-96 '76

The Northern Theater: Soviet capabilities and concepts. John Erickson. map Strat Rev 4:67-82
Summer '76

NORTH VIETNAM see Vietnam (Democratic Republic)

NORTHWEST AIRLINES, INC

History

The aircraft history of Northwest Airlines. David
Galbraith. illus map tabs Am Avn Hist Soc J 21:
241-256 Winter '76

Northwest Orient. M. J. Hardy. illus tabs Air Pict
pt 1, Formation; through WW II. 38:489-493
Dec '76

NORTHWEST PASSAGE see Arctic Regions

NORWAY

Foreign Relations

Russia

The Nordic balance. Col Arthur E. Dewey. illus map
Strat Rev 4:49-60 Fall '76

Strategic Importance

SACEUR's subcommanders take the floor: Northern
European Command after 25 years. Gen John
Sharp. illus NATO's Fifteen Nations 21:68-74
Feb-Mar '76

NUCLEAR BOMBS

Who will have the bomb? Thomas C. Schelling. Intl
Sec 1:77-91 Summer '76

NUCLEAR ENERGY PLANTS
Here are entered articles on the facilities and means
used in the production of electrical power by use of
nuclear energy.

United States

Arkansas Nuclear One. Harlan T. Holmes. illus Mil
Engr 68:287-289 Jul-Aug '76

Nuclear power: A time for decision. James D. Hessman. illus tab Sea Power 19:18-23 Apr '76

Nuclear power development: Will facts win out over
unfounded fear? illus Govt Exec 8:46+ May '76

NUCLEAR POWER

Superfuels. Bob Parkinson. tabs Spaceflight 18:348-
350 Oct '76

Economic Aspects

Nuclear power: A time for decision. James D. Hessman. illus tab Sea Power 19:18-23 Apr '76

Nuclear power for defense. Capt Anthony V. Nida.
tabs Natl Def 60:432-435 May-Jun '76

International Aspects

Nuclear futures for sale: To Brazil from West Germany, 1975. William W. Lowrance. Intl Sec 1:
147-166 Fall '76

Nuclear strategy: The debate moves on. Colin S. Gray.
RUSI J for Def Studies 121:44-50 Mar '76

Who will have the bomb? Thomas C. Schelling. Intl
Sec 1:77-91 Summer '76

NUCLEAR POWER PLANTS

See also
Nuclear Reactors

Nuclear power for defense. Capt Anthony V. Nida.
tabs Natl Def 60:432-435 May-Jun '76

NUCLEAR REACTORS

Nuclear futures for sale: To Brazil from West Germany, 1975. William W. Lowrance. Intl Sec 1: 147-166 Fall '76

NUCLEAR RESEARCH

Nuclear technology in support of our strategic options. MajGen Edward B. Giller, Ret. tab AU Rev 28:26-34 Nov-Dec '76

NUCLEAR TEST BAN

A comprehensive test ban: Everybody or nobody. Donald G. Brennan. Intl Sec 1:92-117 Summer '76

NUCLEAR WARFARE

DNA's (Defense Nuclear Agency) business: Thinking the unthinkable. Edgar Ulsamer. illus AF Mag 59: 50-54 Sep '76

Detente and reality. R. J. Rummel. illus tabs Strat Rev 4:33-43 Fall '76

The new nuclear strategy: Battle of the dead? maps Def Monitor 5: entire issue Jul '76

The nuclear land battle. Col Marc Geneste, Ret. illus Strat Rev 4:79-85 Winter '76

Nuclear strategy: The debate moves on. Colin S. Gray. RUSI J for Def Studies 121:44-50 Mar '76

Nuclear war--the life-and-death issues. Edgar Ulsamer. illus AF Mag 59:57-59 Jan '76

Options in using nuclear weapons. (Remarks, Air Force Assoc Symposium, Vandenberg AFB, Calif, April 28, 1976) LtGen John W. Pauly. AF Plcy Ltr for Comdrs: Sup No. 10:15-23 Oct '76

Relocation plan drafted in case of nuclear war. M.L. Craver. AF Times 37:18 Nov 15 '76

Strategic vulnerability: The balance between prudence and paranoia. John D. Steinbruner and Thomas M. Garwin. illus tabs Intl Sec 1:138-181 Summer '76

TNFs (Theater Nuclear Forces): Critical U.S. defense requirements. illus Comdrs Dig 19: entire issue Jul 1 '76

Tactical nuclear warfare and NATO: Viable strategy or dead end? LtGen Arthur S. Collins, Jr, Ret. illus NATO's Fifteen Nations 21:72-74+ Jun-Jul '76

U.S. on dangerous course. (Interview with Sidney D. Drell) M. L. Craver. AF Times 37:11 Dec 27 '76

War survival in Soviet strategy. Foy D. Kohler. AF Mag 59:90-92+ Sep '76

Western European collateral damage from tactical nuclear weapons. S. T. Cohen and W. R. Van Cleave. tab RUSI J for Def Studies 121:32-38 Jun '76

Medical Aspects

Radiation battlefield casualties--credible!! Capt Arnold S. Warshawsky. illus tabs Mil Rev 56:3-10 May '76

NUCLEAR WEAPONS

See also
Missiles
Nuclear Bombs

NATO and the dawn of new technology. Stefan T. Possony. illus tab Def & For Aff Dig pt 1, No. 10: 15-17+ '76; pt 2, No. 11:18-20+ '76

Nuclear terrorism and the Middle East. Capt Augustus R. Norton. illus Mil Rev 56:3-11 Apr '76

NUCLEAR WEAPONS - Continued

Nuclear war--the life-and-death issues. Edgar Ulsamer. illus AF Mag 59:57-59 Jan '76

Problems of nuclear free zones--the Nordic example. LtCol Jay C. Mumford. illus Mil Rev 56:3-10 Mar '76

Revised procedures for nuclear accident, incident, deficiency reporting. (AFR 127-4) TIG Brief 28:5 Mar 12 '76

SALT II's gray-area weapon systems. (Report on AFA's Symposium on "Tomorrow's Strategic Options," Vandenberg AFB, Calif, April 28-29, 1976) Edgar Ulsamer. illus AF Mag 59:80-82+ Jul '76

Western European collateral damage from tactical nuclear weapons. S. T. Cohen and W. R. Van Cleave. tab RUSI J for Def Studies 121:32-38 Jun '76

Who will have the bomb? Thomas C. Schelling. Intl Sec 1:77-91 Summer '76

International Control

See also
Nuclear Test Ban

Nuclear terrorism and the escalation of international conflict. Forrest R. Frank. illus Nav War Col Rev 29:12-27 Fall '76

On the objectives of arms control. Bernard Brodie. Intl Sec 1:17-36 Summer '76

Maintenance and Repair

(AF) tips on nuclear gear. AF Times 36:43 Jan 5 '76

Does your nuclear weapon stockpile meet prescribed standards? TIG Brief 28:6 Apr 9 '76

Lapse of Limited Life Component (LLC) exchange certification (-1A maintenance). TIG Brief 28:14 Aug 13 '76

Nuclear capability inspections: Some thoughts. TIG Brief 28:4 Jun 18 '76

What's the status of your nuclear weapon maintenance program? TIG Brief 28:7 Feb 13 '76

Study and Teaching

Type 3 (nuclear weapons) trainers used during training operations and inspections. TIG Brief 28:20 Dec 3 '76

Safety Measures

AFR 122-9, 'The Nuclear Safety Cross-Check Analysis and Certification Program for Weapon Systems Software.' TIG Brief 28:5 Oct 8 '76

'The Air Force Nuclear Safety Certification Program,' (AFR 122-3). TIG Brief 28:6 Dec 3 '76

Air Force nuclear surety program. illus TIG Brief 28:5-6 Apr 23 '76

The applicability of nuclear weapon system safety rules. TIG Brief 28:6 Dec 17 '76

B-52 nuclear weapon system safety study completed. TIG Brief 28:10 Aug 27 '76

Bases receive message on fighting nuclear fire. AF Times 36:6 Mar 1 '76

HRP (Human Reliability Program): Be aware. TIG Brief 28:19 Feb 13 '76

HRP (Human Reliability Program) disqualifications under annual review. AF Times 37:10 Aug 23 '76

NUCLEAR WEAPONS - Continued

Safety Measures - Cont'd

Handling nuclear weapons. TIG Brief 28:6 May 21 '76

Human reliability program; AFR 35-99 revision. TIG Brief 28:5 Apr 9 '76

Intrusion detection alarms. TIG Brief 28:19 Sep 24 '76

Judgment and the two-man concept. TIG Brief 28:14 Sep 24 '76

Management controls of the nuclear safety program. TIG Brief 28:13 Sep 24 '76

Minuteman nuclear safety critical components. TIG Brief 28:4 Apr 23 '76

The NWSSG (Nuclear Weapon System Safety Group), major commands, and you. TIG Brief 28:8 Nov 19 '76

Nuclear capability inspections: Some thoughts. TIG Brief 28:4 Jun 18 '76

Nuclear safety certified equipment list. TIG Brief 28:7 May 21 '76

Nuclear weapon system safety rule changes. TIG Brief 28:9 Aug 13 '76

Nuclear weapon system safety rules. TIG Brief 28:6 Apr 23 '76

Operation of vehicles loaded with or towing nuclear weapons. TIG Brief 28:15-16 Sep 24 '76

Performance Analysis and Technical Evaluation (PATE) and Nuclear Safety Cross-Check Analysis (NSCCA). TIG Brief 28:8 Aug 27 '76

Potential hazards of a nuclear weapon accident. TIG Brief 28:8 Feb 13 '76; Correction. TIG Brief 28:8 Jul 2 '76

Priority of nuclear logistic movement support. TIG Brief 28:10 Nov 19 '76

Revised nuclear safety regulations. (AFR 122-4 and AFR 122-5) TIG Brief 28:5 Jan 30 '76

Safety Analysis Summary (SAS). TIG Brief 28:11-12 Apr 9 '76

Safety awards: USAF Nuclear Safety Certificates. TIG Brief 28:6 Jun 4 '76

Security requirements for Limited Life Component (LLC) shipments. TIG Brief 28:19 Sep 24 '76

Two-man team qualification. TIG Brief 28:3 Apr 9 '76

Statistics

Nuclear delivery vehicles, comparative strengths and characteristics: A, United States and Soviet Union; B, Other NATO and Warsaw Pact countries. London's International Institute for Strategic Studies. Tables only. AF Mag 59:92-94 Dec '76

Study and Teaching

SAC nuclear safety training. TIG Brief 28:5 May 7 '76

China (People's Republic)

China's nuclear strategy and U.S. reactions in the "post-détente" era. William T. Tow. illus Mil Rev 56:80-90 Jun '76

France

French defense planning: The future in the past. Gen Pierre M. Gallois, Ret. Intl Sec 1:15-31 Fall '76

NUCLEAR WEAPONS - Continued

NATO

Air power and NATO options. (1st prize, Gordon Shephard Memorial Trophy Essay Competition, 1975) Air Commodore M.J.Armitage. Royal Air Forces Qtr 16:17-23 Spring '76

Problem and paradox, tactical nuclear weapons in NATO. LtCol L.R.Gaboury and Thomas H.Etzold. illus MarCor Gaz 60:46-50 Apr '76

TNFs (Theater Nuclear Forces): Critical U.S. defense requirements. illus Comdrs Dig 19: entire issue Jul 1 '76

Tac nukes and deterrence. Gen T.R.Milton, Ret. AF Mag 59:25 Aug '76

Who needs nuclear tacair? Col David L.Nichols. illus AU Rev 27:15-25 Mar-Apr '76

Russia

Measuring the strategic nuclear balance. tabs AF Mag 59:106-107 Dec '76

United States

(AF) recruits could get nuclear jobs. Ron Sanders. AF Times 37:4 Oct 18 '76

American nuclear weapons in South Korea. Table only. Def Monitor 5:5 Jan '76

Corona Lock. TIG Brief 28:16 Oct 8 '76

DNA's (Defense Nuclear Agency) business: Thinking the unthinkable. Edgar Ulsamer. illus AF Mag 59: 50-54 Sep '76

Measuring the strategic nuclear balance. tabs AF Mag 59:106-107 Dec '76

The new "nuclear options" in military strategy. Maj Donald A.Mahley. illus Mil Rev 56:3-7 Dec '76

Nuclear capability inspection exercise scenarios. TIG Brief 28:7 Oct 22 '76

Nuclear non-proliferation: U.S. Defense policy today. Donald R.Cotter. illus Comdrs Dig 19: entire issue Nov 25 '76

Nuclear technology in support of our strategic options. MajGen Edward B.Giller, Ret. tab AU Rev 28:26-34 Nov-Dec '76

The Nuclear Weapon Security Review Group (NWSRG). TIG Brief 28:14 Dec 17 '76

Options in using nuclear weapons. (Remarks, Air Force Assoc Symposium, Vandenberg AFB, Calif, April 28, 1976) LtGen John W.Pauly. AF Plcy Ltr for Comdrs: Sup No.10:15-23 Oct '76

Security classification policy on terminology for nuclear weapons storage locations. TIG Brief 28:13 Jul 16 '76

Stockpile Emergency Verification (SEV). TIG Brief 28:8 Jun 18 '76

Tac nukes and deterrence. Gen T.R.Milton, Ret. AF Mag 59:25 Aug '76

NUNN, Donald G.

Complaint evaluation and disciplinary action. LtGen Donald G. Nunn. TIG Brief 28:2 Jun 18 '76

System safety: The key to lower cost of ownership. LtGen Donald G.Nunn. TIG Brief 28:2 Feb 13 '76

NURSE CORPS

Air Force--U.S.

See also
Flight Nurses

Care of patients after cardiac catheterization. Mary M. Thomas and Michael R. Longo, Jr. tabs Aviation, Space and Envmt Med 47:192-198 Feb '76

New nurses get o'sea opportunity. AF Times 36:2 Jul 19 '76

PA doing more of doctor's work. M.L. Craver. AF Times 37:4 Oct 25 '76

Armed Forces--U.S.

Participatory management. TIG Brief 28:19 Dec 3 '76

NURSES AND NURSING

See also
Flight Nurses

Professional territoriality: A study of the expanded role of the nurse. Regina L. Monnig. Aviation, Space & Envmt Med 47:773-776 Jul '76

NUTRITION

See also
Flight Nurses

Slim down or ship out ... I got slim. Col Albert J. Brown. illus Army 26:35-39 Apr '76

Think when losing weight. TIG Brief 28:18 Dec 17 '76

O

OFFICE OF SPECIAL INVESTIGATIONS - Continued

OSI program aims at fighting fraud. AF Times 37:11 Dec 20 '76

Reporting fraud indicators. TIG Brief 28:9 Nov 19 '76

Reporting threats against the President of the United States or against presidential candidates. TIG Brief 28:11 Nov 5 '76

Requesting AFOSI investigations and safeguarding, handling, and releasing information from AFOSI reports. TIG Brief 28:13 Feb 13 '76

What AFOSI does for commanders. TIG Brief 28:9 Dec 3 '76

OFFICE OF TELECOMMUNICATIONS POLICY

The complexities of seeking a (telecommunications) policy. (Interview with John Eger) John F. Judge. illus Govt Exec 8:40+ Jun '76

OFFICE OF THE DIRECTOR OF DEFENSE RESEARCH AND ENGINEERING see Defense Research and Engineering

OFFICER CANDIDATE SCHOOLS

Armed Forces

DOD seeks extra commissioning outlet. AF Times 36:28 Jun 21 '76

Army

Women in Infantry OCS (Fort Benning, Ga). illus Mil Rev 56:93 Sep '76

Marine Corps

Is OCS too ambitious? Capt E.V. Kelley, Jr. illus MarCor Gaz 60:56-58 Jun '76

OFFICER EFFECTIVENESS REPORT see Effectiveness Reports

OFFICER TRAINING SCHOOL

8 OTS classes listed for FY 77. Len Famiglietti. AF Times 36:2 Apr 19 '76

9 (career) fields for OTS grads. AF Times 36:8 Feb 2 '76

OTS age limit raised. AF Times 36:20 May 24 '76

OFFICERS

See also
Commanding Officers
Flag Officers
General Officers

Air Force--U.S.

Active duty service commitment. TIG Brief 28:13 Jan 30 '76

(Air) Staff TRAining plan (ASTRA) open. AF Times 37:33 Sep 27 '76

Another extension for grade relief? DOPMA deadline looms. AF Times 36:13 Jan 26 '76

Breakdown of (promotion) board results. AF Times 36:4 Jun 7 '76

Career information (Signal Corps and Air Force personnel). Regular feature in some issues of Signal

Colonel retirements drop, fewer PCS moves seen. AF Times 37:10 Oct 4 '76

(Combat crew officers' careers) Gen Russell E. Dougherty. illus Combat Crew 27:3+ Jul '76; TIG Brief 28:2-4 Aug 13 '76

OFFICERS - Continued

Air Force--U.S. - Cont'd

Deadline extended on officer early outs. AF Times 36:4 Jul 26 '76

Delay in Senate sets O-6 hikes back a bit. Lee Ewing. AF Times 36:4 Jan 5 '76

Don't broaden careers by PCS, commands told. (Use base-level cross-training) AF Times 36:3 Jan 19 '76

Early outs set for FY 77: Palace Furlough plan extended. Lee Ewing. AF Times 36:3 May 17 '76

87 make colonel, 24 get two stars. AF Times 36:4 Feb 23 '76

The FSO (Flight Safety Officer). LtCol David E. Raley. illus Aerosp Safety 32:15-17 Mar '76

Field-grade hikes going up 32 percent. Lee Ewing. AF Times 36:2 Feb 23 '76

Field grades (promotion) record best August in years. AF Times 37:17 Aug 2 '76

448 officers tagged for Sep 1 promotion. AF Times 37:22 Sep 6 '76

(Gen David C.) Jones on records of officers--Regulars 'generally better.' Lee Ewing. AF Times 36:3 Mar 1 '76

Headquarters study: New OER plan works, brings few surprises. Lee Ewing. tab AF Times 36:4 Jan 19 '76

Hike to major now takes 12 years (and other recent developments in officer promotion policy and programs reflect slower promotions in effort to bring the officer promotion system into line with DOPMA). Lee Ewing. AF Times 36:4 Jul 5 '76

JOC and EM councils soon to be optional. AF Times 36:2 May 3 '76

June hike quota set at 789. AF Times 36:8 Jun 7 '76

Lieutenant colonel effectiveness report results. tabs AF Plcy Ltr for Comdrs: Sup No.4:26-29 Apr '76

Lieutenant colonel selectee OER data. tab AF Times 37:3 Nov 29 '76

Long-tour shift set for officers. Lee Ewing. AF Times 36:2 Apr 26 '76

MPC (Military Personnel Center) withdraws control of SEIs (Special Experience Identifiers) from commands. AF Times 37:8 Dec 6 '76

Medic officers face hike delay. Lee Ewing. AF Times 37:4 Sep 13 '76

A military elite in transition: Air Force leaders in the 1980s. (Research undertaken at Air Command and Staff College) LtCol Franklin D. Margiotta. tabs Armed Forces & Soc 2:155-184 Winter '76

More early releases ordered: Voluntary medical rollback would affect 350 officers. AF Times 36:4 Feb 9 '76

Most lieutenant colonel choices had top-box OER. Lee Ewing. tabs AF Times 36:10 Feb 2 '76

New colonels offered procurement training. AF Times 37:6 Oct 25 '76

New guide for officers: Reg (AFR 36-23) answers many career questions. AF Times 36:32 Jul 12 '76

New reg (DOD Directive 1320.7) forces O-6 board shift. AF Times 37:4 Sep 13 '76

OFFICERS - Continued

Air Force--U.S. - Cont'd

No new officer RIF this FY (according to Chief of
Staff, Gen David C.) Jones. Lee Ewing. AF Times
36:2 Feb 16 '76

O-5s can cross-train in new fields. AF Times 37:26
Sep 20 '76

Officer career management directory. Contact,
pp 7-8, Winter '76

Officer scientific field overhauled. AF Times 37:12
Aug 30 '76

Officers get choice of when to update career statement. AF Times 36:4 Mar 29 '76

Officers told to shape up (in presenting a good physical appearance). Len Famiglietti. AF Times 36:2
Jan 19 '76

Officers who apply for CRS (Career Reserve Status)
must qualify for retirement. AF Times 37:3
Dec 6 '76

101 named for (Senior and Intermediate Service)
Schools. AF Times 36:10 May 24 '76

Only temporary O-6s can make permanent. tab AF
Times 36:6 Mar 8 '76

O'sea choice eased for officers. AF Times 37:8
Dec 6 '76

Palace Blueprint: Six years later. LtCol Marvin T.
Howell. illus tabs AF Engrg & Svcs Qtr 17:31-32+
May '76

Panel (Senate Armed Services Committee) approves
officer grade relief. (Added to bill to improve financial status of Soldiers' and Airmen's Home)
AF Times 37:4 Sep 27 '76

Pilots did well in lieutenant colonel results. AF
Times 37:28 Nov 22 '76

Professional identity in a plural world: The focus of
junior officer education in the U.S. Air Force.
BrigGen John E.Ralph. illus AU Rev 27:11-25
Jan-Feb '76

Rated supplement list issued. tabs AF Times 37:26+
Nov 15 '76

'Selection,' 'promotion' mean different things. AF
Times 37:6 Dec 20 '76

75 MC/DC officers picked for lieutenant colonel
hikes. AF Times 37:6 Nov 22 '76

1625 named for regular O-5. Lee Ewing. AF Times
36:17+ Jul 19 '76

3403 temporary O-3s picked. AF Times 37:10+
Oct 11 '76

375 picked for Senior (Service) Schools. AF Times
37:32 Nov 29 '76

2749 selected for regular captain. tab AF Times
37:16+ Sep 20 '76

2294 making temporary lieutenant colonel. AF Times
37:6+ Nov 15 '76

What the captain really means. (A survey on Air
Force ethics and standards made at Squadron Of-
ficer School and resulting recommendations) Maj
Peter Henderson. illus AU Rev 27:96-101 Jan-
Feb '76

Why O-5s missed permanent O-6. Lee Ewing. AF
Times 36:4 Jun 7 '76

Air Force--U.S. - Cont'd

Statistics

(AF) officer accessions up from last year. AF Times
37:6 Nov 8 '76

Rated--nonrated distribution by grade. Table only.
AF Times 36:52 Mar 1 '76

Armed Forces--Canada

Officer career profile in the Canadian forces. LtCol
Robert S.Riley. illus tabs Mil Rev 56:45-55
Feb '76

Armed Forces--U.S.

See also
Defense Officer Personnel Management System

DOD eyeing ways to cut top ranks (of very senior officers and civilians in the Services). AF Times
36:4 Jul 12 '76

New reg (DOD Directive 1320.7) seen speeding hikes
in health field. AF Times 36:6 Jul 26 '76

No plan to trim EO jobs. H.Minton Francis. AF
Times 37:4 Oct 25 '76

Senior officials lose (pay) raise (this year). Phil
Stevens. AF Times 37:3 Sep 27 '76

Strategy seminars (at Naval War College to) offer
graduate credit. AF Times 37:2 Aug 9 '76

Three-year minimum initial term of service for officers. TIG Brief 28:15 Apr 23 '76

Why America needs a ruling class: Common men don't
make uncommon leaders. CAPT Jack Caldwell,
Ret. illus AF Times, Times Magazine sup:10-12
Jun 28 '76

History

21 soldier, sailor Presidents--only 2 careerists.
Maj John C.Reynolds. tab Officer 52:45 Jul '76

Army--U.S.

(Army personnel problems) Interview. MajGen Robert Gard. Fld Arty J 44:35-37 Nov-Dec '76

Aviation as a specialty. LtCol B.H.Freeman. USA
Avn Dig 22:16-18 Oct '76

Bars to stars. Regular feature in issues of Air Defense Magazine

Career information (Signal Corps and Air Force personnel). Regular feature in some issues of Signal

Career patterns for field artillery company grade officers. LtCol Richard L.Reynard. illus Fld Arty J
44:42-44 Nov-Dec '76

Cohesion and disintegration in the American Army
(in Vietnam): An alternative perspective. Paul L.
Savage and Richard A.Gabriel. tabs Armed Forces
& Soc 2:340-376 Spring '76

Employ lieutenant years as special time to learn.
MajGen A.S.Newman. illus Army 26:49-50 Dec '76

Managing your logistics career: Here's how OPMD
(Officer Personnel Management Directorate) does
it. Maj Frank Cunningham III. Army Log 8:12-13
Nov-Dec '76

Motivation in the grade of colonel, U.S. Army. Col
George E.Taylor. illus Mil Rev 56:80-88 Oct '76

OFFICERS - Continued

Army--U.S. - Cont'd

Officers career notes. Regular feature in issues of Infantry

War and peace and promotion. Capt Peter D. Weddle. illus Army 26:24-28 Jun '76

Marine Corps--U.S.

Col F.E.Petersen Jr is first Black Group (Marine Combat Crew Readiness Training Gp (MCCRTG)-20), CO. illus MarCor Gaz 50:3 Jan '76

Compiling the slate; a discussion of the officer assignment process and how it works for you. Col Benjamin B.Skinner. tabs illus MarCor Gaz 60: 25-32 Feb '76

1976 colonel selectees, statistical analysis. tab MarCor Gaz 60:6 May '76

Trust and confidence revisited: Commentary on the Corps. Col J.W.Duncan. MarCor Gaz 60:60-62 Nov '76

National Guard--Air Force--U.S.

War, Industrial Colleges to admit ANG, AFRes. AF Times 36:12 Jun 14 '76

Navy--U.S.

A bluewater interface and the Running Mates program: Navy/Merchant Marine officer exchange program offers benefits to each. James D.Hessman. illus Sea Power 19:20-22 Jun '76

Command at sea--the ultimate specialty. CAPT William J.Holland, Jr. illus US Nav Inst Proc 102: 18-23 Dec '76

"The easiest job in the squadron." (Safety Officer) LCDR L.E.Gardiner. illus Approach 21:26-27 Dec '75

Surface warfare officers: The need for professionalism. CDR Raymond J.Hart. illus US Nav Inst Proc 102:38-44 Jun '76

Survival of the fittest: Five years later. LCDR William W.Turkington. illus tabs US Nav Inst Proc 102:58-65 Oct '76

Reserve Forces--Air Force--U.S.

Decision on RIF expected in Oct--1100 Reservists? AF Times 37:8 Sep 27 '76

598 in Reserves win permanent O-3. AF Times 37:40 Oct 11 '76

(Maj)Gen (Richard) Bodycombe new AFR Vice Cmdr; other officers receive new assignments. illus Officer 52:19 Dec '76

More early releases ordered: Voluntary medical rollback would affect 350 officers. AF Times 36:4 Feb 9 '76

RIFed Reserve officers out in cold on tax break. AF Times 37:8 Dec 20 '76

Reserve officers get break on extensions. Lee Ewing. AF Times 36:4 Apr 5 '76

Ruling on (Reserve line) officers: Early out can't go career. AF Times 36:4 Apr 5 '76

USAFA (U.S. Air Force Academy)'s liaison officers. illus AF Mag 59:62-63 Jan '76

War, Industrial Colleges to admit ANG, AFRes. AF Times 36:12 Jun 14 '76

OFFICERS - Continued

Reserve Forces--Armed Forces--NATO

CIOR (Interallied Confederation of Reserve Officers) organizes Reserve officers of NATO countries. illus Officer 52:39 Jul '76

Copenhagen CIOR Congress was memorable event. illus tab Officer 52:14-16 Oct '76

Guard and Reserve Olympians compete in Denmark ... CIOR. Maj Dennis Keegan. illus Air Reservist 28:4-5 Oct '76

Sleep like a bear, run like a deer: Army and Air Guardsmen battle NATO teams in Reserve (CIOR) olympics. Maj Dennis Keegan. illus Natl Guardsman 30:44-45 Oct '76

Reserve Forces--Army--U.S.

Two out of thirty. Maj Howard C.Race. illus Infantry 66:27-29 Nov-Dec '76

OFFSHORE OIL WELL DRILLING see Oil Well Drilling

OIL see
Lubrication and Lubricants
Petroleum
Petroleum Industry and Trade

OIL WELL DRILLING

Aiming for new (aviation) markets (to support offshore oil field work). Richard S.Page. illus Aerosp Intl 12:34-37 Mar-Apr '76

Defence of North Sea energy sources: The military aspects of the problem. Patrick Wall. illus map NATO's Fifteen Nations 21:78-83 Apr-May '76

Geodesy, mapping, oceanography: Current surveying and mapping news. Regular feature in issues of Military Engineer

Guarding Britain's liquid gold. (North Sea oil) Stefan Geisenheyner. illus AF Mag 59:31-33 Jan '76

North European oil: Implications for NATO nations. LtCol Henrik O.Lunde. illus map tab Parameters 6, No.1:87-96 '76

Offshore technology. Regular feature in issues of Military Engineer

OILERS (SHIPS)

See also
Tankers

A Navy success: Support ships manned by civilian crews. LCDR Paul Stillwell. illus Armed Forces J Intl 113:26+ Jul '76

OKINAWA

Withdraw from Okinawa. Maj S.K.McKee. illus MarCor Gaz 60:50-51 Feb '76

OLDFIELD, Barney

A "might have been"--Operation Eclipse. (Airborne operations to Berlin which, by not being carried out, lost the initiative in Berlin for the West) Col Barney Oldfield, Ret. Armed Forces J Intl 113:20+ May '76

OMEGA

An automatic Omega navigation system for submarines. Brian Greenberg. illus RUSI J for Def Studies 121:76-81 Mar '76

OPERATIONAL TEST AND EVALUATION - Continued

Will Minuteman work? Simulation testing. Eugene M.Del Papa. illus tab Armed Forces J Intl 113: 14-15 Jan '76

OPERATIONS, MILITARY

Operations: Inspection Guide F. TIG Brief pt 1, Sections I-VI. 28:6p addendum Aug 13 '76; pt 2, Sections VII-IX. 28:7p addendum Aug 27 '76; Supplement 1. 28:2p addendum Oct 8 '76

Organisation of a march. MajGen A. Zyryanov. Soviet Mil Rev No.6:18-19+ Jun '76

OPERATIONS ORDERS see Orders

OPTICS

See also
Lasers

Fiber optics and Naval Aviation. William M.Powers. illus US Nav Inst Proc 102:135-136 Oct '76

Fundamentals of fiber optics. illus Countermeasures 2:6-7+ Mar '76

Technology: Its impact on the 1980s. Joseph A.Boyd. illus tabs Signal 30:50-54 May-Jun '76

ORDER OF DAEDALIANS

500 Daedalians meet founders at convention (Pensacola, Fla, May 1976). illus AF Times 36:21 Jun 14 '76

ORDERS

Air Force

Administrative transfer orders. TIG Brief 28:16 Oct 22 '76

Emergency leave orders for oversea travel. TIG Brief 28:15-16 Dec 3 '76

ORDNANCE

The Tampella 155 mm gun-howitzer. LtCol P.Crevecoeur, Ret. illus tabs Intl Def Rev 9:662-663 Aug '76

Ultrasonic welding process for detonable materials. Florence R.Meyer. illus Natl Def 60:291-293 Jan-Feb '76

ORGANIZATION

See also subdivision under specific subjects, e.g., Army--U.S.--Organization

Military contributions to organization theory: Unity of effort, cohesiveness, flexibility. Maj James K. McCollum, Ret. tabs illus Mil Rev 56:65-76 Mar '76

The response of organisations to change. Bernard Barry. illus tab RUSI J for Def Studies 120:33-41 Dec '75

OTT, David E.

Counterfire! MajGen David E.Ott and Col Donald M. Rhea. Army 26:22-26 Jul '76

Win the first battle! MajGen David E.Ott. Natl Def 60:276-278 Jan-Feb '76

OTTH, Edward J.

The FFG-7 integrated logistics support program. (Address, Long Island Chapter, SOLE, April 24, 1976) RADM E.J.Otth. Log Spectrum 10:34-35+ Fall '76

OUTPUT MEASUREMENT

Contract services: Too many or too few? Lloyd K. Moseman II. Govt Exec 8:30+ Jan '76

Word processing: How to save $700 million a year. (Interview with Ron Companion, Installation Officer at Fort Benning, Ga) Govt Exec 8:52+ Dec '76

A workable Program Measurement System (PMS) under the National Labor Relations Board. Richard J.Shakman and Joel C.Anderson. Def Mgt J 12:60-63 Oct '76

OVERALL EFFICIENCY INDEX see Effectiveness Reports--Army

OVERSEAS DUTY

Airmen can choose o'seas tour sites--year longer required. Bruce Callander. AF Times 36:24 Mar 15 '76

Airmen home basing assignments. TIG Brief 28:17 Feb 27 '76

Catalytic converter confusion. Tory Billard. illus Translog 7:13-15 May '76

Defense in struggle over (overseas) goods shipping. Interview. Paul H.Riley. AF Times 36:4 Jul 12 '76

(Dept of) Defense can fire (foreign school bus) drivers abroad. AF Times 37:10 Sep 13 '76

Emergency leave orders for oversea travel. TIG Brief 28:15-16 Dec 3 '76

GAO wants to keep uneconomical household (goods) plan. AF Times 37:4 Aug 16 '76

Government jobs scarce o'seas. AF Times 37:23 Sep 6 '76

In-place COTs (Consecutive Overseas Tours) set for split-tour areas. AF Times 37:4 Oct 4 '76

Key points in shipping your car. Don Hirst. AF Times 37:36 Aug 30 '76

Long-tour people can be released: Conditions outlined. AF Times 37:6 Sep 27 '76

Long-tour shift set for officers. Lee Ewing. AF Times 36:2 Apr 26 '76

More o'seas (dependents) may walk to school. AF Times 37:25 Aug 23 '76

New nurses get o'sea opportunity. AF Times 36:2 Jul 19 '76

New rules hit shipping of overseas 'goodies,' but singles get weight rise. Lee Ewing. tab AF Times 37:4 Aug 16 '76

O'sea choice eased for officers. AF Times 37:8 Dec 6 '76

O'sea choice sweetened. AF Times 37:3 Nov 15 '76

Regs on travel o'seas detailed. AF Times 37:30 Sep 13 '76

Restrictions (on POVs) vary in host countries. Translog 7:16 May '76

SEIs (Special Experience Identifiers) to match members, jobs. Lee Ewing. AF Times 37:2 Oct 25 '76

Europe, Western

Berlin: A tale of two cities. Capt Larry J.Myers. illus Soldiers 31:14-17 Nov '76

OVERSEAS DUTY - Continued

Europe, Western - Cont'd

Dependents schools in Europe: A disorganized system in danger of flunking. Richard C. Barnard. illus AF Times, Times Magazine sup pt 1, pp 8-12+, Oct 18 '76; pt 2, pp 18-22+, Nov 1 '76

Germany (Federal Republic)

Allied team. (Brigade 76 will deploy to Europe to gain combat proficiency in its North Atlantic Treaty Organization role) MSgt Dick Larsen. illus map Soldiers 31:6-10 Mar '76

Hell on wheels. (Air Force and Army's 2d Armored Division (Brigade 75) train in West Germany for NATO support) MSgt Harold D. Newcomb. illus Airman 20:8-12 Apr '76

Making Kontakt. (Strengthening German-American relations) Capt Larry J. Myers. illus Soldiers 31: 10-13 Aug '76

Great Britain

The kids who go TDY. (London Central High School is a dorm school for junior and senior high school military dependents) MSgt Harold Newcomb. illus Airman 20:44-48 Apr '76

A Yank in the RAF. (AF exchange officer flies the V/STOL Harrier) Capt Dennis A. Guyitt. illus Airman 20:38-41 Mar '76

Greenland

Raven on the 'cap. (109th Tactical Airlift Group of the Air National Guard flies resupply missions to DEW-Line sites in Greenland) Maj Terry A. Arnold. illus Airman 20:2-8 Nov '76

Guam

Guam HEW-school rejected (by U.S. Office of Education). AF Times 37:50 Sep 27 '76

Guam schools 'inadequate'; separate system sought. Lee Ewing. AF Times 36:3 Mar 8 '76

Schools on Guam prod PCS change. Lee Ewing. AF Times 37:3 Aug 9 '76

Hawaii

Living with Madam Pele's fury. (Military residents of Kilauea Military Camp share Hawaii's Big Island with the legend of Madam Pele, said to be the goddess of the island's active volcano, Kilauea) MSgt James McDermid. illus Airman 20:30-33 Oct '76

Japan

POVs face tough controls in Japan (because of emission standards). Don Hirst. AF Times 36:16 Jul 5 '76

Korea (Republic)

Incident in Korea. Pictorial. AF Times 37:15 Sep 6 '76

Korean killings prompt switch in alert methods. AF Times 37:4 Aug 30 '76

The last outpost (Republic of Korea). TSgt Tom Dwyer. illus Airman 20:40-44 Jun '76

The link in North Korea. (Life of AF SSgt Pedro Rodriguez in the Joint Security Area) TSgt Tom Dwyer. illus Airman 20:45-48 Jun '76

OVERSEAS DUTY - Continued

Korea (Republic) - Cont'd

The Panmunjom incident--and the aftermath. illus Army 26:71-72+ Oct '76

Plastic police (ration control card). Sgt1C Floyd Harrington. illus tab Soldiers 31:37-40 Nov '76

Radar keeps watch. (Det 2, 51st Composite Wg (Tactical), Mangilsan, Korea) Sgt Larry Finney. illus AF Times 36:34 Jan 19 '76

Scotland

Haggis and pumpkin pie. (USAF communications site personnel and dependents become part of Scottish community at Mormond Hill, near Fraserburgh) MSgt Harold Newcomb. illus Airman 20:44-48 May '76

Thailand

Thailand (military personnel) cut continuing. AF Times 36:3 Apr 26 '76

Turkey

Caring enough. (USAF's military personnel offices work hard to solve problems arising from suspension of U.S. military operations in Turkey) MSgt Fred Harrison. Airman 20:48 Feb '76

No change seen in Turkey bases. AF Times 37:20 Oct 18 '76

TUSLOG chief: Turkey good tour. Interview. MajGen William H. Ginn, Jr. AF Times 37:61 Oct 4 '76

Turkey at Christmas. SP4 Tom Anderson. illus Soldiers 31:47-50 Dec '76

Turkey for Christmas. Sara Anne VanderClute. illus Army 26:31-33 Dec '76

OXYGEN

Associations between psychological factors and pulmonary toxicity during intermittent oxygen breathing at 2 ATA. Robert J. Biersner and others. tab Aviation, Space and Envmt Med 47:173-176 Feb '76

Quality control of breathing air/oxygen. TIG Brief 28:14 Jun 18 '76

A slight case of the blues. (Hypoxic passenger) illus MAC Flyer 23:19 Jun '76

OXYGEN EQUIPMENT

Biomedical aspects of oxygen regulator performance. I: Static characteristics. Paul J. Zalesky and Ronald D. Holden. illus tabs Aviation, Space & Envmt Med 47:485-494 May '76

Biomedical aspects of oxygen regulator performance. II: Dynamic characteristics. Paul J. Zalesky and others. illus tabs Aviation, Space & Envmt Med 47:495-502 May '76

Economical oxygen-delivery system. Robert M. Olson. illus tab Aviation, Space & Envmt Med 47:449-451 Apr '76

Hypoxia. Maj Brian C. Bernet. Aerosp Safety 32:25 Mar '76

Quality control of breathing air/oxygen. TIG Brief 28:14 Jun 18 '76

PACAF see Pacific Air Forces

PCS see Permanent Change of Station

PPBS see Planning-Programming-Budgeting System

PACE, Frank, Jr

Frank Pace, former Army Secretary, is named to receive (George Catlett) Marshall Medal. por Army 26:11 Jun '76

PACIFIC AIR FORCES

See also
Air Force, 13th

Drug program (Project Commando Plug) under review: Team visits PACAF bases. MSgt Dave Sheeder. AF Times 36:21 Jun 28 '76

Pacific Air Forces. tab illus chart AF Mag 59:72-73 May '76

PACIFIC COMMAND

Maintaining U.S. military strength in the Pacific. ADM Noel Gayler. illus Comdrs Dig 19: entire issue May 13 '76

PACIFIC FLEET see Fleet, 7th

PACIFIC ISLANDS

An island for the birds: How the fearless gooney bird won the second Battle of Midway. Emily Watson Hallin. illus AF Times, Times Magazine sup: 14-17 Mar 22 '76

PACIFIC REGION

Tides and currents in the Pacific: Long-term maritime implications. ADM James L. Holloway III. illus Strat Rev 4:33-39 Summer '76

Strategic Importance

The geostrategic triangle of North-East Asia. Niu Sien-chong. NATO's Fifteen Nations 21:68+ Aug-Sep '76

Maintaining U.S. military strength in the Pacific. ADM Noel Gayler. illus Comdrs Dig 19: entire issue May 13 '76

New (U.S. Pacific) doctrine in pursuit of old goals. Capt B. Rodionov and Col S. Yashin. Soviet Mil Rev No. 8:49-51 Aug '76

The scrambled geometry of the new Pacific: West of the Dateline and East of India. Lawrence Griswold. illus Sea Power 19:24-29 Apr '76

The strategic significance of the Northern Marianas. Robert Ellsworth. illus maps Comdrs Dig 19: entire issue Jan 22 '76

PACIFISM

The relevance of civilian-based defense to U.S. security interests. BrigGen Edward B. Atkeson. tab illus Mil Rev pt 1, 56:24-32 May '76; pt 2, 56:45-55 Jun '76

PACIOLI, Luca

Luca Pacioli. 1stLt William A. Bernstein. AF Compt pt 1, The father of accounting. 10:44-45 Apr '76; pt 2, The accounting writer. 10:42-44 Jul '76; pt 3, The method of Venice. 10:44-46 Oct '76

PACKAGING see Containers

PACKING FOR SHIPMENT

Delivery assurance. William E. Billion. illus tab Army Log 8:10-12 Mar-Apr '76

Packaging of Air Force items for depot-level repair. TIG Brief 28:5 Feb 13 '76

Packing, crating, and household goods fraud indications. TIG Brief 28:17-18 Sep 24 '76

Prime BEEF in Europe. Maj Charles F. Kreis. illus AF Engrg & Svcs Qtr 17:28-30 May '76

Shipping of reparables (to repair facilities) incomplete. TIG Brief 28:8 Jun 4 '76

PACTS see Treaties and Alliances

PAINTS

Aircraft washing versus touchup painting. TIG Brief 28:20 Dec 3 '76

PALESTINE

History

The Faluja pocket (1st Palestinian War, 1948). David Nicolle. map Army Qtr pt 1, The Egyptian advance. 105:440-448+ Oct '75; pt 2, The Black Panther of Faluja. 106:333-350 Jul '76

PALMER, Bruce, Jr

A careful look at defense manpower. Gen Bruce Palmer, Jr, Ret and Curtis W. Tarr. por Mil Rev 56:3-13 Sep '76

PANAMA

Economic Conditions

The Panama Canal: Past and present in perspective. Virginia Prewett. illus tab Sea Power 19:23-31 Aug '76

History

Marines in Panama 1856-1976. Capt J.H. Reynolds. illus MarCor Gaz 60:28-34 Oct '76

The Panama Railroad--predecessor to the Canal. Col Wil Ebel. illus Translog 7:14-15+ Nov '76

PANAMA CANAL

The military value of the Panama Canal. illus map Comdrs Dig 19:2-7 Mar 25 '76

The Panama Canal: Old myths and new realities. illus tabs maps Def Monitor 5: entire issue Aug '76

The Panama Canal: Past and present in perspective. Virginia Prewett. illus tab Sea Power 19:23-31 Aug '76

Panama Canal: Primary issue (in 1976 presidential primary campaign). AF Times 36:14 Jun 7 '76

Panama: Strategic pitfall. LtGen V.H. Krulak, Ret. Strat Rev 4:68-71 Winter '76

Statement of principles (between the United States of America and the Republic of Panama). Comdrs Dig 19: back cover Mar 25 '76

(U.S.) Navy doesn't rank first in use of Panama Canal. AF Times 37:26 Sep 6 '76

Strategic Importance

The military value of the Panama Canal. illus map Comdrs Dig 19:2-7 Mar 25 '76

PANAMA CANAL - Continued

Strategic Importance - Cont'd

The Panama Canal: Old myths and new realities.
illus tabs maps Def Monitor 5: entire issue
Aug '76

PAN AMERICAN WORLD AIRWAYS, INC

Is PanAm seeing the end of the tunnel? Klaus Höhle.
illus tab Interavia 31:619-621 Jul '76

PANIC

Planning an airport disaster drill. Marvin B. Hays
and others. Aviation, Space & Envmt Med 47:556-
560 May '76

PANMUNJOM INCIDENT, 1976

Incident in Korea. Pictorial. AF Times 37:15
Sep 6 '76

Korean killings prompt switch in alert methods. AF
Times 37:4 Aug 30 '76

Murder at Panmunjom. Army 26:9 Sep '76

The Panmunjom incident--and the aftermath. illus
Army 26:71-72+ Oct '76

PARACHUTE JUMPING

Float like a dandelion. (AF 7th Weather Sq, Oper-
ating Location C, trains with 1st Battalion, 10th
Special Forces Gp, at Bad Toelz, Germany) MSgt
Harold Newcomb. illus Airman 20:2-6 Mar '76

Free fall. Capt Harvey A. Teston, Jr. illus Army 26:
27-29 Dec '76

Jumpfest! (1976 World Invitational Military Jumpfest,
Hurlburt Field, Fla) SSgt Bill Stephenson. illus
Airman 20:44-48 Nov '76

Jumpfest '76 (Hurlburt Fld, Fla). illus Air Reservist
28:11 Jun '76

Our jumpin' general. (BrigGen Robert F. Coverdale
spends his 45th birthday learning to parachute
jump in order to better understand his units' support of airborne operations) Capt Bill Campbell.
illus Airman 20:35-36 May '76

Prolactin, thyrotropin, and growth hormone release
during stress associated with parachute jumping.
Gordon L. Noel and others. illus Aviation, Space
& Envmt Med 47:543-547 May '76

Sky masters. (Free-falling appeals to all ages, and
Army's Golden Knights win 8 of 10 international
parachuting records) SSgts Zack Richards and
Glen E. Horn. tab illus Soldiers 31:38-42 Aug '76

Study and Teaching

And now--the (parachuting) balloon. Capt Marshall
L. Helena. Infantry 66:13-14 May-Jun '76

Parachute techniques for aircrews. Maj Allan R.
Homstead. illus TAC Attack 16:4-9 Feb '76

PARACHUTES

Your best guarantee. (Parachutes) Capt Demmy
Devenger. illus Combat Crew 27:8-9+ May '76

PARAMILITARY FORCES

Netherlands

Koninklijke Marechaussee: The Royal Netherlands
Marechaussee "Zonder Vrees en Zonder Blaam."
LtCol J. N. Cormack. Army Qtr 106:291-296
Jul '76

PARATROOPS

The airborne mystique. Maj James K. McCollum,
Ret. illus Mil Rev 56:16-21 Nov '76

Airdrop tops (three-nation (Australia, New Zealand,
U.S.) Exercise) Triad. AF Times 36:38
Mar 29 '76

'Drop in' troops: Fast and flexible. Maj James K.
McCollum, Ret. illus Army 26:40-44 Sep '76

The myth and reality of the paratrooper in the Algerian War. John E. Talbott. Armed Forces & Soc
3:69-86 Fall '76

History

Last of the first. (Gen Melvin Zais, last member on
active duty of the original parachute battalion or-
ganized at Fort Benning, Ga, Oct 1940) LtCol
James E. Witek. illus Soldiers 31:11 Nov '76

PASCHALL, Lee M.

WWMCCS in transition: A WWMCCS system engineer
view. LtGen Lee M. Paschall. Signal 30:64-66
Aug '76

What we get for our DOD telecommunications $.
LtGen Lee M. Paschall. por Signal 30:6-8 Jan '76

PASSPORTS

(AF) members asked to lie to get travel visas: OSI
investigation. Ron Sanders. AF Times 37:6
Nov 1 '76

Nonduty travel to Communist-controlled countries by
USAF civilian and military members. TIG Brief
28:8 Oct 22 '76

PATENTS

Government R&D funding: A dismal example of mismanagement. (Comment on "Federal Funding of
Civilian R&D," a study by Arthur D. Little, Inc)
tab Govt Exec 8:49-50 Jun '76

PATHFINDERS

The 11th Pathfinder Platoon (Airborne). 2dLt Michael J. Whitehead. illus USA Avn Dig 22:12
Aug '76

PATRIOTISM

Honoring America. (Remarks, Armed Forces Day
luncheon, Battle Creek, Mich, May 14, 1976)
LtGen W. Y. Smith. AF Pley Ltr for Comdrs: Sup
No. 8:13-16 Aug '76

Learning to fly in the Air Force. LtCol Wayne Goodson. illus AU Rev 27:35-40 Jul-Aug '76

A military force in a democracy. (Address, Twin
Cities Federal Executive Board Bicentennial Cele-
bration, Twin Cities, Minn, July 1, 1976) Gen
George S. Brown. AF Plcy Ltr for Comdrs: Sup
No. 9:2-5 Sep '76

Perceiving the challenge. (Remarks, 3d Annual Reunion, B-58 Hustler Assoc, Fort Worth, Tex,
July 3, 1976) Gen Paul K. Carlton. AF Pley Ltr
for Comdrs: Sup No. 10:8-15 Oct '76

Spirit of America. (Remarks, Commissioning Ceremonies, Texas A&M, Dec 13, 1975) LtGen John
W. Roberts. AF Pley Ltr for Comdrs: Sup No. 4:
21-25 Apr '76

PATROL BOATS

Employment plan for U.S. Navy PHMs. LCDR Rod-
ney P. Rempt. illus US Nav Inst Proc 102:93-96
Jun '76

PATROL BOATS - Continued

Men o'war. Joseph Fama. illus Def & For Aff Dig
No.6:26-31 '76

The small ships. James D.Hessman. illus Sea Power
19:13-16 Sep '76

PATTERSON, William A.

(Eight aviation pioneers (Clarence D.Chamberlin,
John H.Glenn, Jr, George W.Goddard, Albert F.
Hegenberger, Edwin A.Link, Sanford A.Moss,
William A.Patterson, Nathan F.Twining) to be en-
shrined in Aviation Hall of Fame, July 24, 1976)
por AF Mag 59:29-30 Jul '76

PATTON, George S., Jr

George S.Patton's student days at the Army War College. Martin Blumenson. por Parameters 5, No.2:
25-32 '76

Patton and the Hammelburg Mission (to attempt to
liberate POWs). LtCol Frederick E.Oldinsky. por
Armor 85:13-18 Jul-Aug '76

PAULY, John W.

The Air Force and national security: 1976 and beyond. (Remarks, Air Force Assoc, Mobile Chapter, Mobile, Ala, March 27, 1976) LtGen John W.
Pauly. AF Plcy Ltr for Comdrs: Sup No.6:10-18
Jun '76

Future concepts of air power. (Excerpt from address, 57th Defense Preparedness Meeting, American Defense Preparedness Assoc, Los Angeles,
Oct 15, 1975) LtGen John W.Pauly. Nat Def 60:
284 Jan-Feb '76

Options in using nuclear weapons. (Remarks, Air
Force Assoc Symposium, Vandenberg AFB, Calif,
April 28, 1976) LtGen John W.Pauly. AF Plcy Ltr
for Comdrs: Sup No.10:15-23 Oct '76

A strategic concept for defense. LtGen John W.
Pauly and Capt Michael O.Wheeler. por Strat Rev
4:83-91 Summer '76

The thread of doctrine. LtGen John W.Pauly. AU
Rev 27:2-10 May-Jun '76

PAVEMENTS

Runway surface hazards. Capt Dannie O.Burk. illus
tabs Aerosp Safety 32:8-11 Nov '76

What every pilot should know about PFC (Porous
Friction Course). Capt Richard E.Simmons. illus
MAC Flyer 23:10-11 Nov '76

PAY, ALLOWANCES, ETC

See also pay and/or allowances by name, e.g.,
Bonuses   Proficiency Pay
Clothing Allowances   Quarters Allowances
Dislocation Allowances   Retirement Pay
Dual Compensation   Subsistence Allowances
Flight Pay   Travel Pay
Incentive Pay

Air Force--U.S.

Air Force JUMPS--the payoff is now! Cols James D.
Suver, Ret and Ray L.Brown, Ret. AF Compt 10:
32-33 Jul '76

Checks To Financial Organizations (CTFO) program
and innocent NonSufficient Funds (NSF) checks.
TIG Brief 28:18 Feb 13 '76; Correction. 28:12
Mar 26 '76

Child support push starting. AF Times 36:8
Mar 8 '76

PAY, ALLOWANCES, ETC - Continued

Air Force--U.S. - Cont'd

Current USAF pay and allowances. Table only. Contact, p 9, Winter '76

Garnishment actions rise for actives. AF Times 37:6
Oct 25 '76

Indebtedness of separated members resulting from
reporting of leave transactions after separation.
TIG Brief 28:15 Jan 30 '76

Pay changes on 'plus side.' Bruce Callander. illus
AF Times 37:21 Nov 1 '76

Release of information on military pay records. TIG
Brief 28:12 Jun 18 '76

Validating basic pay for medical officers. TIG Brief
28:17 Apr 9 '76

Armed Forces--Great Britain

Manpower trends in the British all-volunteer force.
LtCol Thomas A.Fabyanic. tabs Armed Forces &
Soc 2:553-572 Summer '76

Armed Forces--Russia

The military profession in the USSR. Harriet Fast
Scott. illus tabs AF Mag 59:76-81 Mar '76

Pay boost for the Armed Forces, pay schedule for
Army civilian employees, effective October 1,
1976. Tables only. Soldiers 31:28-29 Nov '76

Armed Forces--U.S.

See also
Joint Uniform Military Pay System

Board (Commission on Executive, Legislative and
Judicial Salaries) expected to ask for big VIP
raise. Don Mace. AF Times 37:4 Nov 22 '76

Board (Defense Pay Study Group) favors salary system. Randy Shoemaker. AF Times 36:3 May 17 '76

Comparing pay, examining benefits--fringes under
fire in House harangue. tab AF Times 36:16
Mar 8 '76

Compensation situation: Many developments. Officer
52:10 Jan '76

Council (Advisory Committee on Federal Pay) urges
(Pres) Ford to OK 6% raise. AF Times 37:3
Sep 27 '76

DOD to consider pay switch: Comparability to competitive. (Defense Manpower Commission's recommendation) Bob Schweitz. AF Times 36:10
Jun 28 '76

(David P.) Taylor on benefits: Piecemeal cuts hurt
morale. AF Times 36:3 Feb 16 '76

Davis: Pay comparable to civilian. Interview.
MajGen B.L.Davis. AF Times 36:4 Mar 1 '76

Dedicated men grind pay data. (Members of 3d Quadrennial Review of Military Compensation) AF
Times 36:28 Jul 19 '76

(Deputy DefSec William P.) Clements on pay, benefits: Restraints could encourage unions. AF Times
36:10 Feb 23 '76

(Donald) Rumsfeld: 'Modification' of pay--salary system rejected. Randy Shoemaker. AF Times 37:4
Dec 6 '76

Drill pay, allowances and per diem increased and
other actions affect pay. tabs Officer 52:7 Nov '76

310

Armed Forces--U.S. - Cont'd

(Federal employee) unions attack raise methods.
Randy Shoemaker. AF Times 37:2 Aug 30 '76

5.4% raise projected. AF Times 37:3 Dec 20 '76

5.16% Oct 1 raise studied. AF Times 36:3 Jul 19 '76

4.83% raise Oct 1 sure(?). AF Times 37:3 Sep 13 '76

4.83% raise: Special military twists. Randy Shoemaker. AF Times 37:3 Oct 11 '76

Future pay boosts face fight. Randall Shoemaker.
illus AF Times 36:3 Feb 2 '76

GAO: Consider recreation as 'pay.' tab AF Times
36:30 May 24 '76

Garnishment policies detailed. AF Times 36:12+
Apr 12 '76

Grab state tax, panel (Senate Finance Committee)
says. AF Times 36:3 Jun 7 '76

House panel (Civil Service Committee) opposes 5%
cap. Randy Shoemaker. AF Times 36:4 Mar 8 '76

Human factor is paramount. (Defense Manpower Commission report) Eric C. Ludvigsen. illus Army 26:
38-40 Jun '76

In cash & in kind. Bruce Callander. illus tabs AF
Times pt 1, 36:22 Jul 19 '76; pt 2, 36:26 Jul 26 '76;
pt 3, 37:38 Aug 2 '76; pt 4, 37:34 Aug 9 '76; pt 5,
Marrieds and singles: How much to pay them.
37:28 Aug 16 '76; pt 6, BAS: How rates were developed. 37:26 Aug 23 '76; pt 7, Benefits mean
cutting costs. 37:34 Aug 30 '76; pt 8, Retirement:
Benefits good despite Congress. 37:28 Sep 6 '76;
pt 9, File of personal papers should be kept current. 37:45 Sep 13 '76; pt 10, Can system be
changed? 37:28 Sep 20 '76

In the (military pay) crunch it'll be up to Congress.
Bruce Callander. AF Times 37:4 Oct 18 '76

Major pay shakeup asked: (Defense Manpower Commission) report covers broad field. AF Times
36:4 Apr 26 '76

Major pay shakeup asked: Salary plan backed. Randy
Shoemaker. tab AF Times 36:4 Apr 26 '76

Military $$ called better than civilian. AF Times
37:8 Nov 15 '76

Military manpower problems. LtGen Ira C. Eaker,
Ret. AF Times 37:13-14 Sep 20 '76

Military pay matters face seasonal crunch. AF
Times 37:2 Oct 4 '76

Morale shifts worry (Asst SecDef William) Brehm.
AF Times 36:11 Feb 23 '76

New pay raise indexes sought. Randy Shoemaker. AF
Times 36:3 Apr 19 '76

New raise mechanism asked (by Defense Manpower
Commission). Randy Shoemaker. AF Times 36:3
May 3 '76

No pay hike cap, but ... Randy Shoemaker. AF
Times 37:3 Aug 16 '76

OMB: Next pay raise 6.5%. (Estimate may be off)
AF Times 37:4 Dec 6 '76

Pay: Freeze or 16% raise? Randy Shoemaker. AF
Times 36:3 Mar 29 '76

Pay not depressed for retirement $$: (3d Quadrennial Review of Military Compensation). AF Times
36:57 Jul 12 '76

Armed Forces--U.S. - Cont'd

Pay plan profits low ranks. Randy Shoemaker. AF
Times 36:3 Apr 12 '76

Pay raise: BAQ rebate doubtful. Randy Shoemaker.
AF Times 37:3 Aug 9 '76

Pay raise: Only 4.83 percent seen. Randy Shoemaker. AF Times 37:4 Aug 23 '76

Pay raise shift, 'salary' under study. Randy Shoemaker. AF Times 36:4 Feb 9 '76

Pay study, 3d Quadrennial Review (of Military Compensation), on thin ice. Randy Shoemaker. AF
Times 37:4 Nov 22 '76

Raise in 'salary' varies by grade. tabs AF Times
37:4 Nov 8 '76

Real 'purchasing power' of monthly pay in 1975 dollars (May 13, 1908-Oct 1, 1975). Table only. AF
Times 36:16 May 17 '76

(Rep Les) Aspin bills would overhaul pay. Phil Stevens. AF Times 37:4 Oct 18 '76

Rocky: 5% cap (on pay increases for federal and military workers) OK at present. Donna Peterson.
illus AF Times 36:39 Feb 9 '76

'Salary' bill readied for Hill (by Rep Les Aspin). tab
AF Times 37:4 Nov 29 '76

Salary concept is gaining. Randall Shoemaker. AF
Times 36:3 Jan 12 '76

Salary plan seen in pay switch. Phil Stevens. AF
Times 36:3 Mar 8 '76

(Sen Barry) Goldwater hits lawmakers' goodies. Phil
Stevens. AF Times 36:3 Feb 16 '76

Senior officials lose (pay) raise (this year). Phil
Stevens. AF Times 37:3 Sep 27 '76

Service heads ask more BAS, BAQ, but oppose salary. Officer 52:6 Dec '76

Services hit salary plan. Randy Shoemaker. AF
Times 37:3 Oct 25 '76

Singles lib. (Are the unmarried discriminated
against?) Darryl D. McEwen. illus tabs Soldiers
31:6-10 May '76

Solution on pay not easy. AF Times 36:27 May 10 '76

State order on garnishment backed. Lee Ewing. AF
Times 36:4 Mar 29 '76

Temporary housing cash supported in PCS survey.
AF Times 37:14 Oct 4 '76

Times are perilous for 'contractual rights.' Army
26:6-8 Jan '76

What 4.83 percent raise means to you. Table only.
AF Times 37:3 Oct 11 '76

What Senate Appropriations Committee says you
make. tab Officer 52:11 Jan '76

What's going on about pay--COLA trouble. AF Times
36:3 May 24 '76

X factor vs comparability: Comparison with civilian
pay ignores hazards. Randy Shoemaker. AF Times
36:3 Mar 15 '76

History

Monthly pay rates at each raise point in this century
(May 13, 1908-Oct 1, 1975). Table only. AF
Times 36:16 May 17 '76

PAY, ALLOWANCES, ETC - Continued

Army--U.S.

On pay and benefits, a 'balanced approach.' LtGen Harold G. Moore. illus tabs Army 26:100-102+ Oct '76

U.S. Court (of Claims) nixes War II back pay. AF Times 36:26 Jul 12 '76

Your army pay: What's it worth? MSgt Nat Dell. illus tabs Soldiers 31:6-10 Jun '76

History

Keepin' the money comin'. (Army pay through the years) Sgt JoAnn Mann. illus Soldiers 31:17 Jul '76

National Guard--Armed Forces--U.S.

Equal pay for equal service. MajGen Duane L. Corning. illus Natl Guardsman 30:1 Jul '76

New daily drill pay rates for Guard, Reserve. Table only. AF Times 37:22 Oct 18 '76

Reserve Forces--Air Force--U.S.

Dobbins AFB (Ga) pays the Air Force Reserves. Chris J. Scheer. illus AF Compt 10:32-33 Apr '76

Reserve Forces--Armed Forces--U.S.

Big changes eyed in compensation--Res/Guard study group. Interview. RADM Richard G. Altmann, Ret. AF Times 37:31 Nov 29 '76

Broad study of Reserve compensation launched. Officer 52:8 Oct '76

Drill pay, allowances and per diem increased and other actions affect pay. tabs Officer 52:7 Nov '76

Equal pay for equal service. MajGen Duane L. Corning. illus Natl Guardsman 30:1 Jul '76

1st phase of (Reserve pay system) study starts Sep 1. Paul Smith. AF Times 37:10 Aug 30 '76

New daily drill pay rates for Guard, Reserve. Table only. AF Times 37:22 Oct 18 '76

Reserve Compensation (System Study) group enlists ROA support. Officer 52:4+ Dec '76

PEACE

An assessment of peace research. J. David Singer. Intl Sec 1:118-137 Summer '76

Dove in the cockpit: Peace in today's Europe. Maj Edd D. Wheeler. illus tabs AU Rev 27:36-44 Jan-Feb '76

The feasibility of increasing the efficiency of United Nations forces. (Andover Prize Essay) LtCol M. Saleh. illus Hawk No. 37:29-31+ Jul '76

For the sake of peace and socialism. (The 25th CPSU Congress, Feb 24-March 5, 1976) Soviet Mil Rev No. 4:2-5 Apr '76

Strategy for lasting peace. LtCol Harold V. Ely. illus Mil Rev 56:58-66 Nov '76

PEARL HARBOR, 1941

The other side of the island: USS Utah at Pearl Harbor. LT Michael S. Eldredge. illus US Nav Inst Proc 102:52-54 Dec '76

USCGC Taney: Still in service 35 years later. Carl and Nell Kraft. illus US Nav Inst Proc 102:50-51 Dec '76

PEARL HARBOR, 1941 - Continued

USS Colorado: The 'other' battleship. Grahame F. Shrader. illus US Nav Inst Proc 102:46-47 Dec '76

Under water at Pearl Harbor. CAPT Charles J. Merdinger, Ret. illus US Nav Inst Proc 102:48-49 Dec '76

PEARSON, Paul F.

FIST (Fire Support Team)! BrigGen Paul F. Pearson. Fld Arty J 44:7-12 May-Jun '76

PEET, Raymond E.

Fleet commanders: Afloat or ashore? VADM Ray Peet, Ret and Michael E. Melich. por US Nav Inst Proc 102:25-33 Jun '76

PEOPLE-TO-PEOPLE PROGRAM

It began with cows. (USAF veterinarians from Lajes AB have worked with the people of Terceira in the Azores since 1949 to improve dairy and other farm production) Maj Angelo Cerchione, Ret. illus Airman 20:34-38 Aug '76

PEPPERS, Jerome G., Jr

Conflict in organizations: Good or bad? LtCol Russell Pierre, Jr and Maj Jerome G. Peppers, Jr, Ret. AU Rev 28:69-79 Nov-Dec '76

PERCY, Charles H.

Why Congress wants reform in the regulatory agencies. Interview. Charles H. Percy. por Govt Exec 8:52+ Jun '76

PERFORMANCE REPORTS see Airman Performance Reports: Effectiveness Reports

PERIODICALS

See also
Newspapers

United States

History

From pulp to slick. Herm Schreiner. illus Am Avn Hist Soc J no. 1, 20:212-214 Fall '75; no. 2, 21: 145-147 Summer '76

PERISCOPES

Television search via periscope. Lee R. Couts. illus Countermeasures 2:58+ Nov '76

PERMANENT CHANGE OF STATION

'INTRO' (Individualized Newcomer TReatment and Orientation) aids sponsor program. TIG Brief 28:19 Apr 9 '76

Making a military move: 10-cents a mile rate OK'd for those using own car. Randall Shoemaker. AF Times 36:4 Mar 1 '76

Making a military move: Trailer allowance hike gets push by Defense. AF Times 36:4 Mar 1 '76

PCS claim revision due. AF Times 36:4 May 10 '76

PCS mileage pay up to 10¢. Randy Shoemaker. AF Times 37:3 Nov 8 '76

Taming PCS turbulence. Ed Gates. AF Mag 59:121 Mar '76

Temporary housing cash supported in PCS survey. AF Times 37:14 Oct 4 '76

Temporary lodging allowance. TIG Brief 28:4 Mar 26 '76

PERMANENT CHANGE OF STATION - Continued

Travel money being boosted. Randy Shoemaker. AF Times 37:3 Sep 20 '76

PERSONAL AFFAIRS

See also
Wills

PERSONAL APPEARANCE

Beard permission won by chaplain. Ron Sanders. AF Times 36:6 Jul 26 '76

Haircut regs get hearing in Court (of Military Appeals). AF Times 36:18 Mar 15 '76

Obese members face discharge. Len Famiglietti. AF Times 36:2 Jul 12 '76

(Rep Patricia) Schroeder again hits rule against long hair. AF Times 36:8 Feb 9 '76

Ruling may end hair fight: High court (Supreme Court) decision on police reg could apply to military. Phil Stevens. AF Times 36:3 Apr 19 '76

Standards of grooming and appearance. TIG Brief 28:8 Jan 30 '76

PERSONAL EQUIPMENT

See also items by name, e.g.,
Clothing, Protective   Parachutes
Helmets   Survival Equipment

Internal security equipment. illus tabs Intl Def Rev 9:820-823 Oct '76

Life support update. Regular feature in some issues of TAC Attack starting with Apr 1976

Night aircraft maintenance. Maj Ted A. Cimral and Capt L. Allyn Noel. illus USA Avn Dig 22:8-10 Apr '76

Testing

Desert lab. (Visit by Natick Development Center (Mass) personnel to 3d Armored Cavalry Regiment near El Paso, Tex) Capt Sam Closkey. illus Soldiers 31:38-41 May '76

PERSONAL PROPERTY see Household Effects

PERSONNEL
For strength of the Services see subdivision Statistics under the respective Services, e.g., Air Force-- United States--Statistics.

See also
Manpower, Military
Retention of Military Personnel

Air Force--U.S.

(AF) personnel program best in Pentagon, (SecAF) Reed says (in news conference). AF Times 36:3 Mar 8 '76

AF to purify stored data on ethnics. AF Times 36:9 Apr 19 '76

The Air Force comptroller family: Personnel authorized Air Force-wide. Tables only. AF Compt 10: 46-47 Jan '76

The Air Force comptroller family: Personnel authorized Air Force-wide. Tables only. AF Compt 10: 28-29 Oct '76

Air Force resource management: Blending systems with skills. MajGen Jack I. Posner. tabs illus Def Mgt J 12:23-31 Oct '76

PERSONNEL - Continued

Air Force--U.S. - Cont'd

Appearance of Air Force personnel as expert witnesses. TIG Brief 28:21 Dec 17 '76

Base inspection questionnaire on people problems. TIG Brief 28:5 Jun 18 '76

Centralized rehabilitation of personnel. (3415th Special Training Sq, Lowry AFB, Colo) TIG Brief 28:17 Jul 2 '76

The cutting edge: Combat capability. Gen David C. Jones. illus tab AF Mag 59:48-50+ May '76

Lackland (AFB, Tex) Reception Center. TIG Brief 28:3 Jun 18 '76

New (AF) programs to accent Spanish-speaking culture. Len Famiglietti. AF Times 36:2 Feb 9 '76

New (INTRO, Individualized Newcomer TReatment and Orientation program) system acquaints members with bases. AF Times 37:6 Nov 8 '76

Nonduty travel to Communist-controlled countries by USAF civilian and military members. TIG Brief 28:8 Oct 22 '76

On your side. Interview. LtGen Kenneth L. Tallman. illus Airman 20:16-19 Apr '76

People come first, says (SecAF) Reed on tour. AF Times 36:10 Feb 9 '76

SEIs (Special Experience Identifiers) to match members, jobs. Lee Ewing. AF Times 37:2 Oct 25 '76

(SecAF Thomas C.) Reed calls for 'people' aid. Lee Ewing. AF Times 36:3 Feb 9 '76

(SecAF Thomas C. Reed lists 5 conclusions about the Air Force in recent news conference at the Pentagon) illus Air Reservist 28:13 May '76; AF Compt 10:24-25 Jul '76

Setting reasonable rules. Interview. Gen David C. Jones. illus AF Times 36:4 May 3 '76

Teams get out and talk to troops in keeping with (Gen David C.) Jones' policy. Lee Ewing. AF Times 36:12+ May 3 '76

Three words or less. (Adapted from speech, Outstanding Airman banquet, Air Force Assoc Convention, Washington, Sep 15, 1975) Gen William V. McBride. illus Airman 20:9-10 Jan '76

Costs

Handling the high cost of personnel. Col R. W. Hagauer. tabs Govt Exec 8:24+ Aug '76

Armed Forces--Cuba

Racial and ethnic relations in the Cuban Armed Forces: A non-topic. Jorge I. Dominguez. tabs Armed Forces & Soc 2:273-290 Winter '76

Armed Forces--Ghana

Army in a multi-ethnic society: The case of Nkrumah's Ghana, 1957-1966. (Condensed from paper, African Studies Assoc 17th Annual Meeting, Chicago, Oct 30-Nov 2, 1974) J. 'Bayo Adekson. tab Armed Forces & Soc 2:251-272 Winter '76

Armed Forces--U.S.

Advocate of people programs. Interview. David P. Taylor. AF Times 37:14 Nov 15 '76

PERSONNEL - Continued

Armed Forces--U.S. - Cont'd

Board (Defense Manpower Commission) calls for ending piecemeal changes (in personnel policies). AF Times 36:8 May 3 '76

Army--Italy

The Italian Army: Some notes on recruitment. Gianfranco Pasquino. tabs Armed Forces & Soc 2:205-217 Winter '76

Army--U.S.

(Army personnel problems) Interview. MajGen Robert Gard. Fld Arty J 44:35-37 Nov-Dec '76

People with a capital P. MajGen Paul T.Smith. illus Army 26:123-124+ Oct '76

Sustaining the volunteer Army: A manpower headache. LtGen Harold G.Moore. illus tabs Def Mgt J 12: 9-16 Oct '76

Marine Corps--U.S.

Job satisfaction. LtCol D.J.Norris. MarCor Gaz 60: 40-43 Sep '76

Marines and alcohol. Maj H.J.Sage. MarCor Gaz 60:32-39 Dec '76

Navy--U.S.

"I am the two-headed ogre." RADM Bruce Keener III. illus US Nav Inst Proc 102:38-45 Apr '76

Is military unionization an idea whose time has come? LT John E.Kane and others. illus tab US Nav Inst Proc pt 1, 102:36-44 Nov '76; pt 2, 102: 24-28 Dec '76

People, the Navy's most critical resource. Curtis W.Tarr and CAPT Paul C.Keenan, Jr, Ret. illus US Nav Inst Proc 102:45-51 Nov '76

PERSONNEL ADMINISTRATION

Ability, not sex, concerns (Human Resources' chief) Mann. Interview. BrigGen Chris C.Mann. illus AF Times 36:4 Jan 26 '76

Advocate of people programs. Interview. David P. Taylor. AF Times 37:14 Nov 15 '76

Air Force resource management: Blending systems with skills. MajGen Jack I.Posner. tabs illus Def Mgt J 12:23-31 Oct '76

Are you communicating? TIG Brief 28:18 Apr 9 '76

Assessing the Assessment Center: New dimensions in leadership. Maj Peter Henderson. illus AU Rev 27:47-54 May-Jun '76

Bending the Chief's ear. (AF Personnel Management Teams (PMT Air Staff teams) discuss the AF life with members, and then work with the Chief of Staff to solve problems) MSgt Fred Harrison. illus Airman 20:36-37 Jan '76

Board (Defense Manpower Commission) calls for ending piecemeal changes (in personnel policies). AF Times 36:8 May 3 '76

CV safety problems: (USS) America's approach. CDR S.P.Dunlap. illus Approach 21:12-15 May '76

Civilian work force in DOD: Diverse and enormous. Carl W.Clewlow. illus Def Mgt J 12:32-37 Oct '76

Committee approach to quality force management. TIG Brief 28:19 Mar 26 '76

PERSONNEL ADMINISTRATION - Continued

Do more with less: Job enrichment may be the answer. Maj D.K.Crooch. illus AU Rev 27:55-61 May-Jun '76

EPMS (Enlisted Personnel Management System): What it's all about. SGM Nat Dell. illus Soldiers 31:8-11 Sep '76

A 50/50 chance of being passed over. Capt W.E. Thompson. AF Engrg & Svcs Qtr 17:21-22 Feb '76

1st Sgt nice guy. Richard C.Barnard. illus AF Times, Times Magazine sup:4-7+ Dec 20 '76

Group (Defense Manpower Commission) faults DOD personnel management. AF Times 36:27 Mar 8 '76

Handling the high cost of personnel. Col R.W.Hagauer. tabs Govt Exec 8:24+ Aug '76

Horror stories! (AF enlisted personnel job placement explained) Capt John B.Taylor. illus Airman 20: 24-28 Apr '76

How does the (AF) Chief (of Staff) keep on target? Management by objectives. Lee Ewing. AF Times 36:10 Jan 26 '76

Human reliability program. TIG Brief 28:5 Aug 13 '76

Human reliability program; AFR 35-99 revision. TIG Brief 28:5 Apr 9 '76

Human resources management as an accident prevention tool. Robert A.Alkov. illus Approach 22: 26-29 Jul '76

Industrial accident investigations. TIG Brief 28:14 Apr 9 '76

'The Inspector General Complaint System,' AFR 123-11. TIG Brief 28:5-6 Nov 19 '76

An introversal analysis of DOD manpower management. David P.Taylor. tabs Def Mgt J 12:2-8 Oct '76

Job satisfaction. LtCol D.J.Norris. MarCor Gaz 60: 40-43 Sep '76

Lackland (AFB, Tex) Reception Center. TIG Brief 28:3 Jun 18 '76

Leadership. TIG Brief 28:13 Nov 5 '76

No plan to trim EO jobs. H.Minton Francis. AF Times 37:4 Oct 25 '76

On your side. Interview. LtGen Kenneth L.Tallman. illus Airman 20:16-19 Apr '76

Palace Blueprint: Six years later. LtCol Marvin T. Howell. illus tabs AF Engrg & Svcs Qtr 17:31-32+ May '76

The people mix. Maj James M.Alford. AU Rev 27: 72-74 May-Jun '76

Performance evaluation and productivity. TIG Brief 28:18 Apr 9 '76

Personnel Management: Inspection Guide B-4. TIG Brief pt 1, 27:7p addendum Dec 5 '75; pt 2, 27:6p addendum Dec 19 '75; Supplement 1, 28:22 Jan 16 '76; Supplement 2, 28:16 Jan 30 '76

Personnel quality force management. TIG Brief 28:10 Feb 13 '76

'Quality' study sparks personnel changes: AFMIG (AF Management Improvement Group), year later. Bruce Callander. AF Times 37:2 Aug 23 '76

Readiness in personnel. TIG Brief 28:15 Nov 19 '76

PERSONNEL ADMINISTRATION - Continued

Self-inspection: A fresh look at the original approach. TIG Brief 28:8 Dec 3 '76

Supervising supervisors. TIG Brief 28:17 Jul 16 '76

Teams get out and talk to troops in keeping with (Gen David C.) Jones' policy. Lee Ewing. AF Times 36:12+ May 3 '76

Turbulence and teamwork. LtGen K.L.Tallman. TIG Brief 28:2 Aug 27 '76

Two-man team qualification. TIG Brief 28:3 Apr 9 '76

Visibility. TIG Brief 28:14 Oct 22 '76

A workable Program Measurement System (PMS) under the National Labor Relations Board. Richard J.Shakman and Joel C.Anderson. Def Mgt J 12:60-63 Oct '76

PERSONNEL CLASSIFICATION

Air Force--U.S.

(AF) heading off jet mechanic loss. AF Times 37:6 Dec 27 '76

(AF) recruits could get nuclear jobs. Ron Sanders. AF Times 37:4 Oct 18 '76

Air Force resource management: Blending systems with skills. MajGen Jack I.Posner. tabs illus Def Mgt J 12:23-31 Oct '76

Admin EM conversion Jan 1. AF Times 37:12 Dec 6 '76

Base-choice plan 1st-shirt incentive. AF Times 37:41 Dec 27 '76

Changed admin(istration) field to groom 1st shirts. Len Famiglietti. AF Times 37:6 Oct 11 '76

Early release skills for May identified. AF Times 36:21 Feb 23 '76

80 skills identified for EM retraining. AF Times 36:18 Jan 19 '76

Horror stories! (AF enlisted personnel job placement explained) Capt John B.Taylor. illus Airman 20: 24-28 Apr '76

Jobs list issued for top E-9s. tabs AF Times 36:16+ May 24 '76

MPC (Military Personnel Center) withdraws control of SEIs (Special Experience Identifiers) from commands. AF Times 37:8 Dec 6 '76

Major career overhaul set for EM. AF Times 36:6+ Mar 15 '76

NCO retrainees due $$. AF Times 37:8 Aug 16 '76

New factor ("special experience identifiers") added in EM assignments. Bruce Callander. AF Times 36:6 Jul 12 '76

New Palace Chase rules announced. AF Times 36:2 Jun 21 '76

New steps taken to match people, jobs. AF Times 37:2 Nov 8 '76

9 (career) fields for OTS grads. AF Times 36:8 Feb 2 '76

Officer scientific field overhauled. AF Times 37:12 Aug 30 '76

Palace Chase cancels 3 skills. AF Times 37:42 Nov 15 '76

PERSONNEL CLASSIFICATION - Continued

Air Force--U.S. - Cont'd

Personnel must meet prerequisite qualifications before retraining is approved. TIG Brief 28:15 Jul 16 '76

Physical profile factor 'X.' TIG Brief 28:20 Sep 24 '76

Rated supplement list issued. tabs AF Times 37:26+ Nov 15 '76

Reg (AFR 39-4) gives details on job switching. AF Times 37:26 Nov 1 '76

SEIs (Special Experience Identifiers) to match members, jobs. Lee Ewing. AF Times 37:2 Oct 25 '76

SP solving supervisor shortages. AF Times 37:9 Dec 20 '76

SRBs cut, retrainees protected. Bruce Callander. AF Times 36:4 Mar 8 '76

Screening for selected HRP (Human Reliability Program)/PRP (Personnel Reliability Program) jobs. TIG Brief 28:4 Jul 16 '76

60 women enter SP test. AF Times 37:8 Sep 13 '76

Some bonus skills dropped, a few added. AF Times 36:3 Jun 7 '76

Some NCOs to fill higher-level jobs. AF Times 37:57 Nov 29 '76

Some skills tests lifted until Dec. AF Times 37:6 Aug 30 '76

Special Experience Identifiers (SEIs). TIG Brief 28:3 Sep 10 '76

Specialty skill determination. TIG Brief 28:12 Aug 13 '76

Statistics on E-6, 7 selections. tab AF Times 37:17 Aug 9 '76

Strength, skill, top EM problems: Pieces in TOPCAP puzzle. Bruce Callander. AF Times 36:6 Jan 26 '76

10,000 EM get 'job reservations.' AF Times 36:23 Mar 1 '76

3800 going Reserve under (Palace) 'Chase.' AF Times 36:3 Jul 5 '76

Top NCOs moving to shortage skills. Bruce Callander. AF Times 37:2 Dec 13 '76

Training change opens 200 skills. Len Famiglietti. AF Times 36:4 Apr 5 '76

27 skills set for Zone-B (6-10 years' service) bonuses. Bruce Callander. tabs AF Times 36:8 Apr 19 '76

Army--U.S.

Army Mine Planter Service "warranted officers.' ' LtCol Lawrence P.Crocker, Ret. Fld Arty J 44: 36-37 Sep-Oct '76

Aviation as a specialty. LtCol B.H.Freeman. USA Avn Dig 22:16-18 Oct '76

Capstone (Warrant Officer Senior Course (WOSC), Fort Rucker, Ala) is back. Sgt1C Floyd Harrington. illus Soldiers 31:11-13 Jun '76

Desk to desk. (USAR Research and Development Officer Career Program) Col James L.Wohlfahrt. illus Army Log 8:6-7 Jul-Aug '76

EPMS (Enlisted Personnel Management System): What it's all about. SGM Nat Dell. illus Soldiers 31:8-11 Sep '76

PHYSICAL FITNESS - Continued

Turn-on to life. (Pro Life program at Fort Dix, NJ) SSgt Zack Richards. illus Soldiers 31:18-20 Sep '76

Winning the war on weight. Dennis R. Brightwell. illus tabs USA Avn Dig 22:6-7+ Oct '76

PHYSICALLY HANDICAPPED see Handicapped

PHYSICIANS

CHAMPUS to lose doctors--shift to Medicare rates seen costing patients more. Ann Gerow. AF Times 36:3 Feb 23 '76

Can patients die natural death? (California law) AF Times 37:2 Dec 6 '76

Cutback in government Dr benefits asked. AF Times 37:31 Nov 15 '76

DOD hits (OMB) report on Dr recruiting. AF Times 37:12 Nov 29 '76

Debate growing over doctor bonus. Phil Stevens. AF Times 37:12 Aug 9 '76

Efforts fail to boost dwindling MD ranks. Ann Gerow. AF Times 36:10 Apr 26 '76

Making the most of it. (Dr (LtCol) Jaroslav K. Richter of MacDill AFB, Fla, likes to be where the action is) 1stLt Katie Cutler. illus Airman 20: 20-23 Oct '76

Malpractice bill would aid Guard; no shift in filing malpractice suits. AF Times 37:8 Oct 11 '76

A patient for Dr Leale. (Young Union Army surgeon attends dying Pres Lincoln after shooting at Ford's Theater) Donald C. Wright. illus Army 26:41-45 Aug '76

Physician productivity. TIG Brief 28:16 Mar 12 '76

Salaries and Wages

Uniform Dr pay asked--GAO cites haphazard system (in the Federal government). AF Times 37:26 Oct 25 '76

PHYSIOLOGICAL RESEARCH

See also
Aviation--Physiological Aspects
Space Flight--Physiological Aspects

Acclimation processes by daily exercise stints at temperate conditions followed by short heat exposures. Eliezer Kamon. tabs Aviation, Space & Envmt Med 47:20-25 Jan '76

Are biorhythms a waste of time? Maj John H. Wolcott and others. (Reprinted from TAC Attack, Nov 1975) illus tabs MAC Flyer 23:11-15 Mar '76

Changes in glucose, insulin, and growth hormone levels associated with bedrest. Joan Vernikos-Danellis and others. tabs Aviation, Space & Envmt Med 47:583-587 Jun '76

Comparison of the subjective intensity of sinusoidal, multifrequency, and random whole-body vibration. Richard W. Shoenberger. illus tabs Aviation, Space & Envmt Med 47:856-862 Aug '76

Effect of ethyl alcohol on ionic calcium and prolactin in man. Jerry M. Earll and others. tab Aviation, Space & Envmt Med 47:808-810 Aug '76

Head and neck cooling by air, water, or air plus water in hyperthermia. Abbott T. Kissen and others. illus tabs Aviation, Space & Envmt Med 47:265-271 Mar '76

PHYSIOLOGICAL RESEARCH - Continued

Heart biochemical responses 14 days after $+G_z$ acceleration. R. T. Dowell and others. illus tab Aviation, Space & Envmt Med 47:1171-1173 Nov '76

High altitude, indigenous origin, and continuous cardiac monitoring. Sara A. Barton and others. tabs Aviation, Space & Envmt Med 47:592-596 Jun '76

Increased 2, 3-diphosphoglycerate during normocapnic hypobaric hypoxia. Allen Cymerman and others. tabs Aviation, Space & Envmt Med 47:1069-1072 Oct '76

Interrelation of atmospheric ozone and cholecalciferol (vitamin D_3) production in man. J. F. Leach and others. illus tabs Aviation, Space & Envmt Med 47:630-633 Jun '76

Pulmonary gas exchange in acute mountain sickness. John R. Sutton and others. tabs Aviation, Space & Envmt Med 47:1032-1037 Oct '76

Review of the effects of infrasound on man. C. Stanley Harris and others. Aviation, Space & Envmt Med 47:430-434 Apr '76

Simple reaction time during exercise, heat exposure, and heat acclimation. E. Shvartz and others. tabs Aviation, Space & Envmt Med 47:1168-1170 Nov '76

Vestibular habituation in flightcrew. P. Pialoux and others. illus Aviation, Space & Envmt Med 47: 302-307 Mar '76

PICKETT, George B., Jr

Basil Liddell Hart: Much to say to the 'Army of '76.' MajGen George B. Pickett, Jr, Ret. Army 26:29-33 Apr '76

PIERRE, Russell, Jr

Conflict in organizations: Good or bad? LtCol Russell Pierre, Jr and Maj Jerome G. Peppers, Jr, Ret. AU Rev 28:69-79 Nov-Dec '76

PILOT ERROR

The "brakes" of naval air. illus Approach 21:19 Feb '76

Cross-validation study of the personality aspects of involvement in pilot-error accidents. Michael G. Sanders and others. tabs Aviation, Space and Envmt Med 47:177-179 Feb '76

Cutting the accident bill. Maj Thomas R. Allocca. illus Aerosp Safety 32:25-27 Nov '76

DI (Decision Irreversibility). LtCol Gerald B. Hurst. illus TAC Attack 16:12-14 Feb '76

Death at the ramp. illus Approach 21:26-27 Feb '76

The decision. LtCol James A. Learmonth. Aerosp Safety 32:5 Oct '76

Flight violation! LT Dave McPherson. illus Approach 22:12-13 Jul '76

Fly your own jet! LTJG D. A. Abner. illus Approach 21:29 Dec '75

Hazy daze. (Altitude myopia: Visual deception in the air) illus MAC Flyer 23:9-10 Feb '76; Interceptor 5:18-19 May '76

A mistake in flight. Col V. Pokrovsky. Soviet Mil Rev No. 1:28-29 Jan '76

No letup (in unintentional wheels-up landings). illus tab Approach 21:10-12 Jan '76

Nugget nightmare. illus Approach 22:18-20 Nov '76

POLITICS - Continued

Political campaigning on Air Force bases. TIG Brief 28:15 Jun 18 '76

The power tables: Significant elections and changes in governments in the past year. Regular feature in some issues of Defense & Foreign Affairs Digest

Readers' survey. (How they feel about this year's elections and whether they plan to vote or support candidates for Federal offices) tab AF Times 36:8 May 17 '76

Status inconsistency and Democratic Party preference: A replication and critique. Phillip A.Salopek and Christopher K.Vanderpool. tab J Pol & Mil Sociol 4:29-38 Spring '76

POLK, James H.

The new short war strategy. Gen James H.Polk, Ret. (Reprinted from Strategic Review, Summer 1975) Mil Rev 56:58-64 Mar '76

POLLUTION

See also
Environment

B-1 gets 'clean' (environmental) rating. AF Times 37:18 Oct 18 '76

Balloonists sample food and air aloft. AF Times 37:23 Sep 6 '76

Catalytic converter confusion. Tory Billard. illus Translog 7:13-15 May '76

The Coast Guard: New missions, increased capabilities, always ready. ADM Owen W.Siler. illus Sea Power 19:14-20 Jan '76

Dirty work missions: The USCG strike force. illus Sea Power 19:11-13 Dec '76

Foundries in dilemma. Debbie C.Tennison. illus tabs Natl Def 60:453-458 May-Jun '76

The future environment. LCDR Jacob D.Dumelle. Mil Engr 68:304-305 Jul-Aug '76

Maintaining defense efficiency with minimal impact on man & environment. illus tabs Comdrs Dig 19: entire issue Nov 4 '76

The national stream quality accounting network. Joseph S.Cragwall, Jr. illus map tabs Mil Engr 68: 25-27 Jan-Feb '76

Oil and fuel spills. TIG Brief 28:15 Feb 13 '76

POVs face tough controls in Japan (because of emission standards). Don Hirst. AF Times 36:16 Jul 5 '76

Pollution, political pressures put USCG in double jeopardy. L.Edgar Prina. illus Sea Power 19: 8-11 Jun '76

USAF Environmental Health and Radiological Health Laboratories. TIG Brief 28:19 Feb 13 '76

The U.S. Coast Guard and the control of oceanic pollution. CDR Hugh D.Williams. illus tab chart US Nav Inst Proc 102:146-159 May '76

Laws and Regulations

Enforcement of the 1973 Marine Pollution Convention. LT Douglas H.Williams. illus US Nav Inst Proc 102:39-45 Dec '76

POPE, John

Revitalizing a beaten unit. (Story of MajGen John Pope of the Union Army shows what not to do; Field Marshal Montgomery's command of British 8th Army in Africa, 1942, demonstrates what should be done) LtGen Phillip B.Davidson, Jr, Ret. Army 26:43-45 Jan '76

POPULATION

United States

Military moves: Big impact on U.S. population shifts. AF Times 36:22 May 17 '76

PORTS

Andean tract. A.Ranney Johnson. illus Def & For Aff Dig No.3:20-23 '76

Another Army "Navy" game (Azores). SSgt Virgil L. Laning. illus Translog 7:16-20 Jan '76

Export releases for CONUS contractor shipments. TIG Brief 28:4 Nov 5 '76

La Paz lament. (Need for sovereign access to the Pacific) Leigh Johnson. Def & For Aff Dig No.3: 14-19 '76

The MTMC realignment program. David R.Goodmon. Translog 7:2-5 Feb '76

Outport insight. Debbi Dunstan and Donna Orsini. illus Translog 7:1-3+ Jan '76

PORTUGAL

Politics and Government

Portugal: Problems and prospects in the creation of a new regime. Thomas C.Bruneau. illus tabs Nav War Col Rev 29:65-82 Summer '76

POSNER, Jack I.

Air Force resource management: Blending systems with skills. MajGen Jack I.Posner. Def Mgt J 12: 23-31 Oct '76

POST, Gerald J.

Address, ACSC Logistics Education Symposium, Maxwell AFB, Ala, 17 Feb 1976. MajGen Gerald J.Post. Log Spectrum 10:34-36 Spring '76

POST EXCHANGES see Exchanges

POSTAGE STAMPS

History

Putting his stamp on it. (Maj Claude Greathouse has become an expert on the stamps of the Confederate States of America) Walter N.Lang. illus Airman 20:40 Nov '76

POSTAL SERVICE

APO patrons cite mail drawbacks: Complaints from Europe. AF Times 37:30 Oct 4 '76

Delays in receipt of mail. TIG Brief 28:13 Sep 10 '76

European mail (delivery) plan draws Army fire. AF Times 37:10 Sep 27 '76

House (Post Office and Civil Service) Committee begins hearings on mail delays. AF Times 37:30 Oct 4 '76

POSTAL SERVICE - Continued

Prepaid postage on change of mailing address cards and other forms (limited by AF). TIG Brief 28:8 Sep 10 '76

Transmission of classified information to foreign addressees. TIG Brief 28:19 Jan 16 '76

Word processing: Training method eases the transition. (New keyboard training system in U.S. Postal Service) Govt Exec 8:40 Jan '76

Costs

The Postal Service: Myth and nostalgia collide with economic reality. C.W.Borklund. illus tabs Govt Exec 8:12+ Sep '76

History

The aircraft history of Western Air Lines. William T.Larkins. illus tabs Am Avn Hist Soc J 21:9-23 Spring '76

POWELL, Allen L.

New milestones in geodesy. (National Geodetic Survey) RADM Allen L.Powell. Mil Engr 68:22-24 Jan-Feb '76

Surveys for engineering and science. (From "Survey of the Coast" to National Ocean Survey) RADM Allen L.Powell. Mil Engr 68:198-201 May-Jun '76

POWER PLANTS see Nuclear Power Plants

POWER RESOURCES

Army meets the fuel crisis. LtCol Robert R.Bachmann. illus tabs Natl Def 60:436-438 May-Jun '76

Can government create a private sector? (Interview with Robert L.Hirsch, Assistant Administrator for Solar, Geothermal and Advanced Energy Systems, Energy Research & Development Administration) John F.Judge. illus Govt Exec 8:15+ Aug '76

Communist China and oil business. Niu Sien-chong. NATO's Fifteen Nations 21:90-91+ Apr-May '76

Defence of North Sea energy sources: The military aspects of the problem. Patrick Wall. illus map NATO's Fifteen Nations 21:78-83 Apr-May '76

More power for sea power. LT Larry A.Lukens. illus tabs map Natl Def 60:439-443 May-Jun '76

Nuclear power: A time for decision. James D.Hessman. illus tab Sea Power 19:18-23 Apr '76

Nuclear power for defense. Capt Anthony V.Nida. tabs Natl Def 60:432-435 May-Jun '76

Their energy--our crisis. C.Sharp Cook. illus US Nav Inst Proc 102:28-32 Aug '76

POWER SOURCES see

Electric Power	Power Resources
Generators, Electric	Solar Energy
Nuclear Power Plants	

PRAYER AND PRAYERS

'Those were the times, Lord ...' (Invocation for Freedom Train's visit to F.E.Warren AFB, Wyo) Ch(Maj) Eugene T.Jarcynski. Airman 20: inside back cover Feb '76

PRECISION GUIDED MUNITIONS

Is EW still a Pentagon stepchild? Harry F.Eustace. illus Elect Warfare 8:28-29+ Jul-Aug '76

PRECISION GUIDED MUNITIONS - Continued

Precision guided munitions: Implications for detente. BrigGen Edward B.Atkeson. illus tabs Parameters 5, No.2:75-87 '76

Technology and strategy: Precision guided munitions and other highly sophisticated weapons will increase the effectiveness of the nuclear threat. Michael L.Nacht. Natl Def 61:199-202 Nov-Dec '76

PREFLIGHT INSPECTIONS

Aircraft weight and balance. Maj John E.Freitas. illus TAC Attack 16:10-12 Aug '76

From mission order to instrument takeoff. CW2 Joel E.Warhurst. USA Avn Dig 22:12-14 Sep '76

Trust (aircraft forms and the Exceptional Release (ER)). Capt Philip M.McAtee. illus Aerosp Safety 32:6 Sep '76

PREGNANCY

Pregnancy as an assignment limitation. TIG Brief 28:6 Jan 16 '76

Pregnant stewardess--should she fly? Paul Scholten. Aviation, Space & Envmt Med 47:77-81 Jan '76

PREJUDICES, RACIAL see Race Relations

PREPARATORY SCHOOLS

Enlisted women have route to (Air Force) Academy (Preparatory School). Contact, p 6, Winter '76

First 10 women enroll at (AF) Academy Prep School. illus AF Times 36:11 Jan 26 '76

West Point bound. (Students at the United States Military Academy Preparatory School) Capt Peter D. Weddle. illus Soldiers 31:21-23 Apr '76

PREPAREDNESS

See also
Air Defenses
Civil Defense
Defenses

Air-Land Forces Application (ALFA). Air Def Mag, p 37, Apr-Jun '76

Coalition warfare. Robert W.Komer. illus Army 26: 28-32 Sep '76

Emergency checklists. TIG Brief 28:9-10 Jul 2 '76

For the common defense: Secretary (of Defense) Rumsfeld must stand fast for adequate preparedness. illus Natl Def 60:264-265 Jan-Feb '76

Future military preparedness. (Address, Naval Academy Graduation Ceremonies, Annapolis, June 2, 1976) Donald H.Rumsfeld. AF Pley Ltr for Comdrs: Sup No.8:2-7 Aug '76

Industrial luncheon address (AFCEA, Washington, June 10, 1976). Gen Fred C.Weyand. illus Signal 30:40-43 Aug '76

MOBDES (MOBilization DESignee): Modern Minutemen. LtCol John X.Loughran III. illus Air Reservist 28:18 Nov '76

A military force in a democracy. (Address, Twin Cities Federal Executive Board Bicentennial Celebration, Twin Cities, Minn, July 1, 1976) Gen George S.Brown. AF Plcy Ltr for Comdrs: Sup No.9:2-5 Sep '76

NATO's military preparedness. FAdm Peter Hill-Norton. RUSI J for Def Studies 121:2+ Jun '76

PROBABILITIES

Intercept probability and intercept time. B.R.Hatcher. illus tabs Elect Warfare 8:95+ Mar-Apr '76

The new (battlefield) dead-man's curve. Col William R.Ponder. tabs USA Avn Dig 22:6-7 Mar '76

PROBLEM SOLVING

Forging the future force (at Squadron Officer School). Ted R.Sturm. illus Airman 20:18-22 Mar '76

MBO (Management By Objectives): Update 76--results so far right on target. Capt Robert J.Courter, Jr. illus AF Engrg & Svcs Qtr 17:3-6 Aug '76

PROCUREMENT

See also
Purchasing
Weapons Procurement

Air Force--U.S.

Designing for life cycle cost. William H.Boden. illus tabs Def Mgt J 12:29-37 Jan '76

Procurement planning. TIG Brief 28:17 Sep 10 '76

Quality control of breathing air/oxygen. TIG Brief 28:14 Jun 18 '76

Shoddy meat tactics revealed. AF Times 36:12 Feb 9 '76

Source selection. TIG Brief 28:13-14 Apr 23 '76

Tamper detection seals for railcars/large containers. TIG Brief 28:13-14 Apr 9 '76

A tool for managers of small contracts (Cost/Schedule Status Report (C/SSR)). TIG Brief 28:16 Nov 19 '76

Using Qualified Products Lists (QPLs). TIG Brief 28:11 Oct 22 '76

Costs

Cost realism. TIG Brief 28:13 Jul 2 '76

Study and Teaching

New colonels offered procurement training. AF Times 37:6 Oct 25 '76

Armed Forces--U.S.

Abuses (in procurement of fresh meat for European commissaries) reported. AF Times 36:9 Jul 19 '76

Ask for it clearly. (Multiservice acquisition) LtCol Donald M.Keith and Charles A.McCarthy. illus Army Log 8:14-16 Jul-Aug '76

Hot line suggested for beefs on food. Andy Plattner. AF Times 37:2 Aug 2 '76

How vendors get past inspection: Meat cheating. Andy Plattner. AF Times 36:24 Apr 26 '76

Lack of competition a problem: Military meat buying. Andy Plattner. AF Times 36:17+ May 10 '76

Meat witnesses cite bribery. Andy Plattner. AF Times 36:4 May 24 '76

Poor quality (meat) forced on comstores. Andy Plattner. AF Times 36:25+ May 3 '76

Sausage firm (in Southern California) indicted. AF Times 36:9 Jul 19 '76

'Shock wave' effect (from Senate investigation) hiked beef prices. AF Times 36:12 Jun 14 '76

Truth in negotiations. Emanuel Kintisch. Natl Def 61:118-121 Sep-Oct '76

PROCUREMENT - Continued

Armed Forces--U.S. - Cont'd

History

Military procurement during World War II: From battleships to blankets. Dale Birdsell. illus tab Def Mgt J 12:55-61 Jul '76

Army--U.S.

PROMS (PROcurement Management System). Robert F.Williams and Capt Robert J.Walker. tabs Army Log 8:2-6 Nov-Dec '76

Testing Army materiel. MajGen Patrick W.Powers. illus Army Log 8:28-31 Nov-Dec '76

Whatever happened to mutual trust and respect? Clyde A.Parton. illus Natl Def 60:268-270 Jan-Feb '76

Defense Construction Supply Center--U.S.

What suppliers don't know can hurt them. (Defense Construction Supply Center Buyers/Suppliers Symposium, Columbus, Ohio, 1975) E.V.Francis. illus Review 55:30+ Nov-Dec '75

Defense Dept--U.S.

Buying commercial: Why not? Richard A.Stimson and Marilyn S.Barnett. illus Def Mgt J 12:47-55 Oct '76

Can contract methodology improve product reliability? Robert F.Trimble. illus Def Mgt J 12:20-23 Apr '76

Meat buying: Good is good enough, GAO study suggests. AF Times 36:8 May 31 '76

Procurement for Defense. Eberhardt Rechtin. Natl Def 61:122-124 Sep-Oct '76

Radio frequencies: Check before you buy. TIG Brief 28:3 Dec 3 '76

Tighter rein put on (meat) procurement. AF Times 36:8 May 31 '76

Types of government contracts. LtCol Anthony P. Ingrao. tabs AF Law Rev 18:63-86 Spring '76

What's missing is the dialogue. (Interview with AFCEA's Tom Campobasso) illus Govt Exec 8: 45-46 Dec '76

Why not more straight commercial buying? Eberhardt Rechtin. illus Govt Exec 8:46-48+ Oct '76

Winds of change in communications and computers. Theodore D.Puckorius. illus Signal 31:18-22 Sep '76

Costs

Compensation: Reasonableness is the yardstick. Ray W.Dellas. illus Govt Exec 8:42-43 Oct '76

Study and Teaching

Procurement mix review slated. (Inventory of federal procurement courses and training to be examined by Federal Procurement Institute) AF Times 37:35 Aug 30 '76

Navy--U.S.

Navy shipbuilding dispute rages on. James D.Hessman. illus Sea Power 19:15-18 Aug '76

Navy shipbuilding problems reach critical stage. illus Sea Power 19:13-14 Jul '76

PROCUREMENT - Continued

Navy--U.S. - Cont'd

Costs

The Military Sealift Command's build and charter program for nine sealift-class tankers. Scott C. Truver. illus tabs Nav War Col Rev 28:32-44 Fall '75

Transportation Dept--U.S.

Systems approach to administrative support (in Transportation Dept's Office of Contracts and Procurement). Govt Exec 8:54+ Sep '76

United States

Buying commercial: OFPP (Office of Federal Procurement Policy) asking, "Why not?" Govt Exec 8:35 Jul '76

CBEMA (Computer and Business Equipment Manufacturers Assoc) and GSA (General Services Administration): A dialogue on how government hurts itself (because of its own procurement and contracting practices). C.W.Borklund. illus Govt Exec 8:24+ May '76

GSA: Effectiveness through increased communications. (Interview with Jack Eckerd) illus Govt Exec 8:18+ Oct '76

GSA seeks wider base of suppliers. H.R.Kaplan. illus Review 55:45-48+ Mar-Apr '76

A growing Federal absurdity. (Small business and government supply contract regulations) Ernest Baynard. Govt Exec 8:40-44 Dec '76

Lawton Chiles and spending reforms: Is it for real this time? (Interview with chairman, Senate Subcommittee on Federal Spending Practices) C.W. Borklund. illus Govt Exec 8:12+ Feb '76

Management leverage: A new concept in military procurement. Col Ronald Terry. Persp in Def Mgt No.24:79-89 Winter '75-'76

OFPP (Office of Federal Procurement Policy) one year later: A look ahead. Interview. Hugh E.Witt. illus Govt Exec 8:16+ Feb '76

Office of Federal Procurement Policy. Hugh E.Witt. illus Signal 30:17-19 Feb '76

Performance purchasing: A rising state & local tide. Govt Exec 8:22+ Sep '76

A positive look at the Federal computer mess. Ernest C.Baynard. Govt Exec 8:28+ Sep '76

Procurement elements--how do these fit together? Maj W.R.Montgomery. illus Log Spectrum 10: 13-16 Winter '76

Procurement: Wrecking free enterprise? C.W.Borklund. illus Govt Exec pt 1, Survey shows government "wrecking" free enterprise. 7:28-29+ Oct '75; pt 2, Who's best at "wrecking free enterprise?" 7:57+ Nov '75; pt 3, How industry loses in the halls of government. 7:15+ Dec '75; pt 4, Energy savings: One place government lags industry badly. 8:11+ Jan '76; pt 5, How government discourages industry growth. 8:24+ Feb '76

Pumping new technology into local buying practices. Robert M.Belmonte. tabs Govt Exec 8:21-23+ Jan '76

Single vendor integrity. Cary A.Moore. illus Log Spectrum 10:13-15+ Spring '76

Truth in negotiations. Emanuel Kintisch. Natl Def 61:118-121 Sep-Oct '76

PRODUCTION see Industry

PROFESSIONAL MILITARY EDUCATION see Staff Colleges

PROFESSIONAL READING

Soviet military thought. Joseph D.Douglass, Jr. illus AF Mag 59:88-91 Mar '76

PROFESSIONALISM

See also
Military Service as a Profession

The ABC (Actions, Briefings, Coordination) for flying professionals. Col Richard C.Jones. illus TAC Attack 16:12-15 Dec '76

Basil Liddell Hart: Much to say to the 'Army of '76.' MajGen George B.Pickett, Jr, Ret. illus Army 26:29-33 Apr '76

Cohesion and disintegration in the American Army (in Vietnam): An alternative perspective. Paul L. Savage and Richard A.Gabriel. tabs Armed Forces & Soc 2:340-376 Spring '76

Commander and leader: The Army officer as meritocrat. Dennis E.Showalter. illus Mil Rev 56:80-89 Nov '76

'Doing our country's thing.' Gen Russell E.Dougherty. TIG Brief 28:1-2 Jan 30 '76

Modern logistics: A professional's profession. CAPT Carl L.Henn, Ret. illus Log Spectrum 10:18-21+ Summer '76

New leadership for a new Air Force. Col Harold P. Knutty. illus AU Rev 27:78-84 Jan-Feb '76

One last word on discipline. LtGen R.M.Hoban. illus Combat Crew 27:3+ Oct '76

Perceiving the challenge. (Remarks, 3d Annual Reunion, B-58 Hustler Assoc, Fort Worth, Tex, July 3, 1976) Gen Paul K.Carlton. AF Plcy Ltr for Comdrs: Sup No.10:8-15 Oct '76

Professional territoriality: A study of the expanded role of the nurse. Regina L.Monnig. Aviation, Space & Envmt Med 47:773-776 Jul '76

Professionalism. LtGen Raymond B.Furlong. TIG Brief 28:2 Mar 12 '76

Professionalism through logistics education and training. Ben S.Blanchard. illus tabs Log Spectrum 10: 28-33 Summer '76

Self-discipline and standards: A commitment to excellence. (Programs at Florida State University) Capt Richard A.Zucker. Educ J 19:11-12 Winter '76

The way we were. WO1 Burton E.Crockett. illus USA Avn Dig 22:35-37 Feb '76

Who are you calling student? Capt Charles E.Bailey. illus Combat Crew 27:8-10 Dec '76

The "young" professional SAC crew force. MajGen A.B.Anderson, Jr. illus Combat Crew 26:3+ Feb '76

PROFICIENCY PAY

Management of Special Duty Assignment Proficiency Pay (SDAPP). TIG Brief 28:22 Sep 10 '76

Pro pay: How it came and went. Bruce Callander. AF Times 36:14 Apr 19 '76

Proficiency flying is terminated. MarCor Gaz 60:2 Dec '76

Air Force--U.S. - Cont'd

(Combat crew officers' careers) Gen Russell E. Dougherty. illus Combat Crew 27:3+ Jul '76; TIG Brief 28:2-4 Aug 13 '76

Delay in Senate sets O-6 hikes back a bit. Lee Ewing. AF Times 36:4 Jan 5 '76

E-3s promoted Oct 1975 eligible for BTZ hike. AF Times 37:2 Nov 15 '76

E-8 hike pace rises, E-5 falls. AF Times 36:17 Feb 2 '76

EM hike future looks OK: Quotas for upper noncoms rising in March. Bruce Callander. AF Times 36:3 Mar 1 '76

EM hikes--changes, impact. Bruce Callander. tabs AF Times 37:3 Aug 30 '76

EM hikes mostly in orbit. Bruce Callander. illus AF Times 37:3-4 Nov 22 '76

EM promotion picture mostly a gloomy one. Bruce Callander. AF Times 36:2 Jan 19 '76

Enlisted promotions back on schedule. Bruce Callander. AF Times 37:2 Sep 27 '76

Fewer EM face hike delays. AF Times 37:9 Sep 6 '76

Field grades (promotion) record best August in years. AF Times 37:17 Aug 2 '76

A 50/50 chance of being passed over. Capt W.E. Thompson. AF Engrg & Svcs Qtr 17:21-22 Feb '76

Generals on the move. (Title varies) Regular feature in some issues of Air Force Times

High NCOs get alert on board-points plan. AF Times 37:16 Aug 9 '76

Hike activity getting back on track. Bruce Callander. AF Times 36:3 Jun 21 '76

Hike picture for EM brightens--in spots. AF Times 37:30 Aug 2 '76

Hike to major now takes 12 years (and other recent developments in officer promotion policy and programs reflect slower promotions in effort to bring the officer promotion system into line with DOPMA). Lee Ewing. AF Times 36:4 Jul 5 '76

Junior E-3s due below-zone hikes. Bruce Callander. AF Times 36:50 Feb 2 '76

Lower-grade insignia: Who's what? AF Times 36:6 Jun 14 '76

Major hikes face six-month delay (and other promotion variations projected). Lee Ewing. AF Times 36:4 May 17 '76

Medic officers face hike delay. Lee Ewing. AF Times 37:4 Sep 13 '76

Most lieutenant colonel choices had top-box OER. Lee Ewing. tabs AF Times 36:10 Feb 2 '76

Most new E-8s took Senior NCO course. AF Times 36:12 Jul 19 '76

NCO status: 'Must' before E-5 hike. AF Times 36:8 Jun 21 '76

NCOs aiming for top spot to face 2 sets of tests. AF Times 37:2 Dec 27 '76

Navigators (recalled in '71) fared well. AF Times 36:23 Jul 12 '76

New hike plan for E-9 studied. AF Times 36:10 May 31 '76

Air Force--U.S. - Cont'd

New reg (DOD Directive 1320.7) forces O-6 board shift. AF Times 37:4 Sep 13 '76

1904 NCOs selected for E-8 in '77. tab AF Times 36:8 Jul 12 '76

No hike delay (for E-4s) seen from 2-way split. AF Times 37:6 Oct 4 '76

No new NCOs for one year: 3-tier EM plan launched. Bruce Callander. AF Times 36:6+ May 24 '76

Noncom grades, except for E-6, are on target. AF Times 37:2 Dec 27 '76

Noncom hike cycles facing major change. Bruce Callander. AF Times 36:6 May 31 '76

Only temporary O-6s can make permanent. tab AF Times 36:6 Mar 8 '76

Phase I NCO PME a must for E-4s. AF Times 37:2 Dec 6 '76

Pilots did well in lieutenant colonel results. AF Times 37:28 Nov 22 '76

Point-board OK for E-8, 9. Bruce Callander. AF Times 37:3 Aug 2 '76

Revamping the enlisted structure. Ed Gates. tab AF Mag 59:39-41 Aug '76

Rules preclude 3-tier 'slips.' Bruce Callander. AF Times 36:25 Jun 14 '76

'Selection,' 'promotion' mean different things. AF Times 37:6 Dec 20 '76

Senior airman: New E-4 title. Bruce Callander. AF Times 36:3 Jan 12 '76

Senior staff changes. Regular feature in issues of Air Force Magazine

75 MC/DC officers picked for lieutenant colonel hikes. AF Times 37:6 Nov 22 '76

Some skills tests lifted until Dec. AF Times 37:6 Aug 30 '76

Switch to three-tier (system) includes cushioners. Bruce Callander. AF Times 36:1+ Jun 7 '76

TIG (Time In Grade) schedule set for E-8s, 9s. Bruce Callander. AF Times 37:2 Dec 6 '76

Test scores--big factor in (NCO promotion) point plan. AF Times 37:3 Nov 22 '76

Three-tier setup and how it works. tab AF Times 36:10 May 31 '76

1200 making special E-4. Bruce Callander. AF Times 36:3 Jan 5 '76

29 permanent brigadier generals, 30 major generals selected. AF Times 36:22 Jan 19 '76

2294 making temporary lieutenant colonel. AF Times 37:6+ Nov 15 '76

Why O-5s missed permanent O-6. Lee Ewing. AF Times 36:4 Jun 7 '76

Statistics

April hike quotas: E-5 in trouble. AF Times 36:9 Mar 22 '76

Breakdown of (promotion) board results. AF Times 36:4 Jun 7 '76

E-4 through E-9: 8868 advancing. AF Times 36:3 Jul 26 '76

PROMOTION - Continued

Air Force--U.S. - Cont'd

Statistics - Cont'd

829 out of 7200 selected for E-9. AF Times 36:6 May 10 '76

87 make colonel, 24 get two stars. AF Times 36:4 Feb 23 '76

Field-grade hikes going up 32 percent. Lee Ewing. AF Times 36:2 Feb 23 '76

448 officers tagged for Sep 1 promotion. AF Times 37:22 Sep 6 '76

June hike quota set at 789. AF Times 36:8 Jun 7 '76

Quotas issued for below-zone hikes: 1242 to make E-4. AF Times 36:6 Feb 16 '76

7542 picked for E-6, 7 promotions. AF Times 36:17+ Feb 9 '76

1625 named for regular O-5. Lee Ewing. AF Times 36:17+ Jul 19 '76

Statistics on E-6, 7 selections. tab AF Times 37:17 Aug 9 '76

34 to pin on second star. AF Times 37:10 Dec 13 '76

3403 temporary O-3s picked. AF Times 37:10+ Oct 11 '76

2811 NGOs going up Sep 1. AF Times 37:3 Aug 23 '76

2749 selected for regular captain. tab AF Times 37:16+ Sep 20 '76

Armed Forces--U.S.

'Catch-up' program eyed for minorities. Andy Plattner. AF Times 36:2 Jun 28 '76

New reg (DOD Directive 1320.7) seen speeding hikes in health field. AF Times 36:6 Jul 26 '76

Star status: Army, Navy, Air Force, Marines. Regular feature in some issues of Armed Forces Journal International

Time in service for EM hikes to rise. illus AF Times 37:12 Sep 13 '76

Army--U.S.

Employ lieutenant years as special time to learn. MajGen A.S.Newman. illus Army 26:49-50 Dec '76

The "Peter Principle" and Army promotions. Capt Ronald W.Carter. Army 26:52-53 Mar '76

Promotion is the name of the game. Sustainer. illus Mil Rev 56:11-15 Nov '76

War and peace and promotion. Capt Peter D. Weddle. illus Army 26:24-28 Jun '76

Marine Corps--U.S.

ABC's of getting promoted. BrigGen John S. Letcher, Ret. MarCor Gaz 60:57-59 Apr '76

1976 colonel selectees, statistical analysis. tab MarCor Gaz 60:6 May '76

One, two-star selections. MarCor Gaz 60:2 Mar '76

Stairway to the stars. LtCol C.M.Lively. MarCor Gaz 60:47-51 Oct '76

National Guard--Air Force--U.S.

ANG generals move up. AF Times 36:4 Feb 9 '76

PROMOTION - Continued

National Guard--Air Force--U.S. - Cont'd

ANG to lift E-9 freeze October 1--some force outs seen. AF Times 36:20 May 24 '76

Statistics

(Air National) Guard picks 71 for hike to E-9. AF Times 37:10 Nov 22 '76

Navy--U.S.

Survival of the fittest: Five years later. LCDR William W.Turkington. illus tabs US Nav Inst Proc 102:58-65 Oct '76

Reserve Forces--Air Force--U.S.

Hikes open to Reserve EM. AF Times 37:2 Dec 27 '76

ROPA lieutenant colonel hikes: Result analyzed. tab AF Times 37:22+ Aug 30 '76

Statistics

846 named for Regular AF--875 offered Career Reserve. AF Times 37:23+ Oct 11 '76

598 in Reserves win permanent O-3. AF Times 37:40 Oct 11 '76

PROPAGANDA

America's Vigilantes and the Great War, 1916-1918. John Carver Edwards. Army Qtr 106:277-286 Jul '76

The Pentagon propaganda machine. LtCol V. Amelchenko. Soviet Mil Rev No.12:48-50 Dec '76

Trouble in the Far East: Quemoy still waging war of words; the domino theory--alive and well. Fred Reed. AF Times 36:10-11 Mar 1 '76

PROPELLANTS

Propellent recovery nets $145,000 savings. AF Times 36:32 Feb 2 '76

Superfuels. Bob Parkinson. tabs Spaceflight 18:348-350 Oct '76

PROPERTY, GOVERNMENT

Are you or your commander in this situation? (Custodian Authorization/Custody Receipt Listing (CA/CRL)) TIG Brief 28:11 Jul 16 '76

Disposal office saves AF $$. Amn Mark Issacs. AF Times 36:25 Feb 9 '76

Maintaining the Air Force sense of history. TIG Brief 28:21 Sep 10 '76

Making retrograde cost effective. (Air Force materiel used in Southeast Asia) LtCol Barry W.Jenkins. illus AF Engrg & Svcs Qtr 17:26-27 May '76

Maintenance and Repair

The Army's facilities engineering operations. BrigGen Walter O.Bachus. illus tabs chart Mil Engr 68:94-97 Mar-Apr '76

PROPULSION SYSTEMS

See also
Boosters
　also specific types of propulsion, e.g.,
Ion Propulsion
Rocket Propulsion

PROTOCOL

White gloves and the aide's aide. Elizabeth B. Libbey. illus Army 26:33-36 Jul '76

PROXMIRE, William

Conflict of interest: Proxmire alleges 10 broke laws. AF Times 36:32 Apr 19 '76

Proxmire: 41 for B-1, 26 against. AF Times 36:14 Mar 1 '76

PSYCHIATRY

Psychotherapy and return to flying duties. Carl B. Steinbacher and Carlos J. G. Perry. tabs Aviation, Space & Envmt Med 47:770-772 Jul '76

PSYCHOLOGICAL RESEARCH

Alpha index and personality traits of pilots. Jan Terelak. tab Aviation, Space and Envmt Med 47: 133-136 Feb '76

Associations between psychological factors and pulmonary toxicity during intermittent oxygen breathing at 2 ATA. Robert J. Biersner and others. tab Aviation, Space and Envmt Med 47:173-176 Feb '76

Psychologic and psychophysiologic response to 105 days of social isolation. Don A. Rockwell and others. illus tabs Aviation, Space & Envmt Med 47: 1087-1093 Oct '76

PSYCHOLOGICAL WARFARE

See also
Vietnamese Conflict, 1957-1975--Psychological Aspects
War--Psychological Aspects

Boris Nikolayevich Ponomarev: Run silent, run deep. Stefan Possony. illus Def & For Aff Dig No. 11: 6-9+ '75

Fighting for people's minds--ideological inroads of imperialism in the developing countries. Col P. Tarutta. Soviet Mil Rev No. 1:41-43 Jan '76

Psychological strategy. Regular feature in some issues of Defense & Foreign Affairs Digest

The state of the Soviets. Gregory Copley. illus Def & For Aff Dig No. 6:6-9+ '76

The TAC role in special operations. BrigGen William J. Holton, Ret. illus AU Rev 28:54-68 Nov-Dec '76

PSYCHOLOGY

See also
Behaviorism (Psychology)
Motivation (Psychology)

PUBLIC INFORMATION

See also
Office of Information--Air Force

Accidents and public information responsibilities. TIG Brief 28:15 Jun 18 '76

Countering the Pentagon line. (Center for Defense Information) Interview. RADM Gene La Rocque, Ret. AF Times 36:28+ Jan 26 '76

Greener on the inside. (William I. Greener, Asst SecDef for Public Affairs, is a retired AF lieutenant colonel) LtCol Fred A. Meurer. illus Airman 20:21-23 Sep '76

'Info Act' report leaves some gaps. Ann Gerow. AF Times 36:12 Mar 22 '76

PUBLIC INFORMATION - Continued

(JSC Chairman Gen George S.) Brown criticizes Times newspapers (in testimony before House Armed Services Committee). AF Times 36:3 Feb 9 '76

The military and the media. (Remarks, Air War College Media-Military Symposium '76, Maxwell AFB, Ala, March 29, 1976) LtGen Raymond B. Furlong. AF Plcy Ltr for Comdrs: Sup No. 6:19-21 Jun '76

A perspective of the military and the media. Carl J. Migdail. illus Nav War Col Rev 28:2-9 Winter '76

Sidle: Keeping the public informed. Interview. MajGen Winant Sidle. AF Times 36:16 Mar 1 '76

Wartime information mission. TIG Brief 28:16 Jul 16 '76

When is deception necessary? RADM Wycliffe D. Toole, Jr. (Excerpted from U. S. Naval Institute Proceedings, Dec 1975) AF Times 36:14 Jan 12 '76

Youth information officers of the Federal Armed Forces. Capt Jurgen Conze. illus NATO's Fifteen Nations 21:49-56 Aug-Sep '76

PUBLIC LANDS see Property, Government

PUBLIC OPINION

See also
Vietnamese Conflict, 1957-1975--Public Opinion

American public opinion and American national security. Col Thomas I. Dickson, Jr, Ret. illus Mil Rev 56:77-81 Jul '76

How private enterprise is committing "subtle suicide." illus Govt Exec 8:56-57 May '76

Military unions opposed by 82% (in poll by Public Service Research Council). tab AF Times 36:10 Jun 21 '76

Public confidence in the U.S. military. David R. Segal and John D. Blair. tabs Armed Forces & Soc 3:3-11 Fall '76

Social implications of the clemency discharge. William A. Pearman. tabs J Pol & Mil Sociol 4:309-316 Fall '76

PUBLIC RELATIONS
For material on the relations between a base and its neighboring community see Community Relations.

Air Force

Public speaking program responsibilities. TIG Brief 28:11 Dec 3 '76

Armed Forces

(Service) women's TV tour bargain for Pentagon. AF Times 36:18 Jan 5 '76

Sidle: Keeping the public informed. Interview. MajGen Winant Sidle. AF Times 36:16 Mar 1 '76

PUBLIC SPEAKING

Deciding on a speech subject. (Guidelines for Air Force commanders) AF Plcy Ltr for Comdrs: Sup No. 2:21 Feb '76

Public speaking program responsibilities. TIG Brief 28:11 Dec 3 '76

PUBLIC SPEAKING - Continued

Talk talk--a series of ideas to improve your presentations. Laurence E. Olewine. illus Armed Forces Compt pt 1, 17:14-15+ Fall '72; pt 2, 18:30-31 Winter '73; pt 3, 18:8-9+ Spring '73; pt 4, 18: 28-29 Summer '73; pt 5, 18:24-25+ Fall '73; pt 6, 19:20-21 Winter '74; pt 7, 19:18-19 Spring '74; pt 8, 19:16-17 Summer '74; pt 9, 19:14-15 Fall '74; pt 10, 20:22-23 Winter '75; pt 11, 20:26-27 Apr '75; pt 12, 20:24-25 Fall '75; pt 13, 21:24-25 Jan '76

PUBLIC UTILITIES

Can government create a private sector? (Interview with Robert L. Hirsch, Assistant Administrator for Solar, Geothermal and Advanced Energy Systems, Energy Research & Development Administration) John F. Judge. illus Govt Exec 8:15+ Aug '76

Rental won't include meters (for utilities). AF Times 37:3 Oct 4 '76

Costs

Paying only your fair share. (Joint Utility Service Boards (JUSBs)) Leon E. McDuff. illus AF Engrg & Svcs Qtr 17:35-37 Aug '76

PUBLICATIONS, MILITARY

See also
Regulations
Standing Operating Procedure
Technical Orders

United States

Decentralization of publications within Reserve forces medical units. TIG Brief 28:3 Apr 9 '76

PUBLICATIONS, MILITARY - Continued

United States - Cont'd

FLight Information Publications (FLIPs). TIG Brief 28:21 Sep 24 '76

New horizons revisited. Maj Clifford Thomas. illus USA Avn Dig 22:18-20 Nov '76

Regulatory inconsistencies. TIG Brief 28:5 Feb 27 '76

PUBLISHERS AND PUBLISHING

GPO: Aggressively marketing their unique services. (Interview with Thomas F. McCormick) illus Govt Exec 8:19-20 Jan '76

PUEBLO INCIDENT, 1968

Principles of command, guidelines of conduct: First report on ADM Hyland's endorsement to the Pueblo inquiry (1969). DeWitt James Griffin. Sea Power 19:31-36 Feb '76

PURCHASING

New awards for procurement research. AF Times 36:11 Jan 5 '76

Quality assurance provisions in Blanket Purchase Agreements (BPAs). TIG Brief 28:13 Jun 4 '76

PUTNAM, Rufus

Washington's favorite engineer (BrigGen Rufus Putnam). Raleigh B. Buzzaird. por Mil Engr 68:298-301 Jul-Aug '76

QUALITY CONTROL

Abuses (in procurement of fresh meat for European commissaries) reported. AF Times 36:9 Jul 19 '76

Beef falsely graded, suit says. AF Times 37:10 Dec 13 '76

Buying commercial: Why not? Richard A. Stimson and Marilyn S. Barnett. illus Def Mgt J 12:47-55 Oct '76

CERS (Carrier Evaluation and Reporting System) testing moves into second phase. Translog 7:14+ Jun '76

Commissaries in Europe got bad meat, DOD says. Andy Plattner. AF Times 37:4 Oct 4 '76

DOD begins new consumer push. AF Times 37:53 Oct 25 '76

Defective Parts and Components Control Program (DPCCP). TIG Brief 28:11 Jul 2 '76

Help from the field for the Technical Order Improvement System (TOIS). TIG Brief 28:5 Sep 10 '76

Hot line suggested for beefs on food. Andy Plattner. AF Times 37:2 Aug 2 '76

How vendors get past inspection: Meat cheating. Andy Plattner. AF Times 36:24 Apr 26 '76

Lack of competition a problem: Military meat buying. Andy Plattner. AF Times 36:17+ May 10 '76

Maintainability for Air Force systems. Capt Ned H. Criscimagna. illus Log Spectrum 10:19-23+ Spring '76

Meat buying: Good is good enough, GAO study suggests. AF Times 36:8 May 31 '76

Meat witnesses cite bribery. Andy Plattner. AF Times 36:4 May 24 '76

Medical facility committee effectiveness. TIG Brief 28:18 Nov 19 '76

The national stream quality accounting network. Joseph S. Cragwall, Jr. illus map tabs Mil Engr 68: 25-27 Jan-Feb '76

On-the-Job Training (OJT) quality. TIG Brief 28:10 Oct 8 '76

Performance Analysis and Technical Evaluation (PATE) and Nuclear Safety Cross-Check Analysis (NSCCA). TIG Brief 28:8 Aug 27 '76

Poor quality (meat) forced on comstores. Andy Plattner. AF Times 36:25+ May 3 '76

Quality assurance provisions in Blanket Purchase Agreements (BPAs). TIG Brief 28:13 Jun 4 '76

Quality control is everybody's business. TIG Brief 28:13 Jun 18 '76

Quality control of breathing air/oxygen. TIG Brief 28:14 Jun 18 '76

Sausage firm (in Southern California) indicted. AF Times 36:9 Jul 19 '76

QUALITY CONTROL - Continued

Subsistence quality assurance in veterinary-origin inspection. TIG Brief 28:5 Mar 26 '76

Using Qualified Products Lists (QPLs). TIG Brief 28:11 Oct 22 '76

What's the status of your nuclear weapon maintenance program? TIG Brief 28:7 Feb 13 '76

QUARTERMASTER CORPS

United States

History

Challenging the logistics status quo during the Civil War. James A. Huston. illus Def Mgt J 12:25-33 Jul '76

Continental Army logistics: Transportation. (Reprinted from Army Logistician, Nov-Dec 1975) illus map Def Trans J 32:28-31 Aug '76

QUARTERS ALLOWANCES

Army costs out benefit losses. Gene Famiglietti. AF Times 36:2 Mar 1 '76

Audit finds many paid wrong rent. AF Times 36:2 Jun 28 '76

BAQ rebate sure, (David P.) Taylor says. AF Times 37:3 Sep 6 '76

Bolling (AFB, DC) EM rooms valued at $50. Ron Sanders. AF Times 37:21 Nov 29 '76

DOD rebuked (by GAO) for paying some unnecessary BAQ. AF Times 36:18 Jul 26 '76

DOD reviewing fair-rental idea. Fred Reed. AF Times 37:12 Nov 22 '76

(DefSec Donald) Rumsfeld to evaluate rental proposal. Randy Shoemaker. AF Times 37:4 Sep 27 '76

Fair market rental favored. Randy Shoemaker. AF Times 37:3 Nov 1 '76

Panel (Senate Armed Services Committee) moves to put more pay into BAQ. AF Times 36:3 May 31 '76

Pay plan profits low ranks. Randy Shoemaker. AF Times 36:3 Apr 12 '76

Pay raise: BAQ rebate doubtful. Randy Shoemaker. AF Times 37:3 Aug 9 '76

Pay raise shift, 'salary' under study. Randy Shoemaker. AF Times 36:4 Feb 9 '76

Rental charges for inadequate quarters. TIG Brief 28:16 Jun 18 '76

Rental charges for inadequate quarters. TIG Brief 28:4 Sep 10 '76

Rental won't include meters (for utilities). AF Times 37:3 Oct 4 '76

Temporary lodging allowance. TIG Brief 28:4 Mar 26 '76

QUESTIONNAIRES see Surveys

RADAR STATIONS - Continued

RAF Fylingdales and the USAF spacetrack system. SqLdr D.J. Nicholson. illus Royal Air Forces Qtr 15:333-336 Winter '75

Radar keeps watch. (Det 2, 51st Composite Wg (Tactical), Mangilsan, Korea) Sgt Larry Finney. illus AF Times 36:34 Jan 19 '76

The Sirocco meteorological sounding station. illus tab Intl Def Rev 9:433-435 Jun '76

RADIATION

Interrelation of atmospheric ozone and cholecalciferol (vitamin D_3) production in man. J.F. Leach and others. illus tabs Aviation, Space & Envmt Med 47:630-633 Jun '76

Radiation battlefield casualties--credible!! Capt Arnold S. Warshawsky. illus tabs Mil Rev 56:3-10 May '76

Safety Measures

The saga of the Humble Hummer (E-2). LT Cam Place. illus Approach 22:6-8 Dec '76

RADIO ASTRONOMY

See also
Satellites, Artificial--Astronomical Applications
Telescopes, Radio

NASA contemplates radio search for extra-terrestrial intelligence. Robert Sheaffer. illus tab Spaceflight 18:343-347 Oct '76

RADIO BROADCASTING

Air Force AFRT (Air Force Radio and Television) Broadcast Management: Inspection Guide D-1. TIG Brief 28:2p addendum Feb 27 '76

Putting on AIRS (Army Information Radio Service). SSgt John Savard. illus Soldiers 31:44-47 May '76

RADIO COMMUNICATIONS

An advanced, versatile HF-SSB communication system. Fred Finder and Zvi Rosner. illus tab Signal 30:102-105 May-Jun '76

Combatting voice jamming. Capt Benjamin L. Hardin. illus Interceptor 18:20-23 Sep '76

Communication in troop control. LtCol G. Kondakov. Soviet Mil Rev No. 3:18-19 Mar '76

Communications in a recce party. LtCol V. Usmanov. illus Soviet Mil Rev No. 12:25-26 Dec '76

HF/SSB (Single Side-Band) tactical communications equipment (from Thomson-CSF). illus tab Intl Def Rev 9:485-487 Jun '76

Hand held communicator. Salvatore Amoroso. illus tabs Countermeasures 2:14+ Dec '76

Huff-Duff vs the U-boat. illus Elect Warfare 8:71+ May-Jun '76

Jamming calculations for FM voice communications. Lawrence E. Follis. illus tabs Elect Warfare 8:33+ Nov-Dec '76

Jamming of FM tactical communications. Capt Robert D. Rood. illus tab Mil Rev 56:58-65 Feb '76

The maturing of digital microwave radio. Kerry R. Fox and John F. Beckerich. illus tabs Signal 30:6-11 Apr '76

RADIO COMMUNICATIONS - Continued

On the Santa Fe Trail. (Operating Location Alpha Bravo, a high-frequency radio site in eastern Colorado, operated by Aerospace Defense Command) SMSgt Harold Newcomb. illus Airman 20:11-14 Nov '76

Sound of silence. Capt Nicholas J. Hinch. Combat Crew 27:6-7 Nov '76

U.S. preparation for the World Administrative Radio Conference 1979. Jack E. Weatherford. illus charts Signal 30:17-19 Apr '76

The Warlock. (Complete remote radio system supporting 101st Airborne Division (Air Assault) Artillery during tactical operations) illus Fld Arty J 44:48-50 May-Jun '76

History

C^3: How we got here--where are we? CDR Peter S. Roder. illus Signal 30:7-10 Jul '76

Terminology

Roger means everything but negative. Capt Gregory Ulrich. illus Aerosp Safety 32:5 May '76

RADIO CORP OF AMERICA

RCA and radar. (Evolving technology in the real world) Joseph C. Volpe. illus Signal 31:40-45 Oct '76

RADIO COUNTERMEASURES see Electronic Countermeasures

RADIO EQUIPMENT

HF/SSB (Single Side-Band) tactical communications equipment (from Thomson-CSF). illus tab Intl Def Rev 9:485-487 Jun '76

Radio frequencies: Check before you buy. TIG Brief 28:3 Dec 3 '76

Versatile King Radio 10-waypoint RNAV. Douglas Chopping. illus Interavia 31:659 Jul '76

Maintenance and Repair

Designing for life cycle cost. William H. Boden. illus tabs Def Mgt J 12:29-37 Jan '76

RADIO FREQUENCY

Crowded electronic sky demands accurate instrumentation. Hilliard F. Penfold. illus Signal 30:65-70 May-Jun '76

HF/SSB (Single Side-Band) tactical communications equipment (from Thomson-CSF). illus tab Intl Def Rev 9:485-487 Jun '76

Hand held communicator. Salvatore Amoroso. illus tabs Countermeasures 2:14+ Dec '76

Jamming calculations for FM voice communications. Lawrence E. Follis. illus tabs Elect Warfare 8:33+ Nov-Dec '76

Radio frequencies: Check before you buy. TIG Brief 28:3 Dec 3 '76

RADIO NAVIGATION

Versatile King Radio 10-waypoint RNAV. Douglas Chopping. illus Interavia 31:659 Jul '76

RADIOACTIVITY

Holloman (AFB, NM) balloonists end Project Ashcan (with the successful recovery of their fifth atmospheric sampling package of radioactive waste). AF Times 36:40 May 17 '76

RADIOLOGICAL WARFARE see Nuclear Warfare

RAFALKO, Edmund A.

Job enrichment--Ogden (Air Logistics Center) style.
MajGen Edmund A. Rafalko. AU Rev 28:46-53
Nov-Dec '76

RAILROADS

Is this the end of the line for TRS (Transportation
Railway Service)? Can the nation afford it? C.J.
Schwendiger. illus Def Trans J 32:8+ Dec '76

Equipment

Maintenance and Repair

Reserve rails. SSgt Doug Grow. illus Translog 7:7-8
Jan '76

History

The bridge at kilometer 111 (China). Bonnie Baker
Quinby and Capt G. William Quinby. illus Mil Engr
68:88-90 Mar-Apr '76

Panama

History

The Panama Railroad--predecessor to the Canal. Col
Wil Ebel. illus Translog 7:14-15+ Nov '76

Russia

Soldiers at BAM (Baikal-AMur railway line). Capt
L. Yakutin. Pictorial. Soviet Mil Rev No. 12:32-33
Dec '76

United States

Nostalgia rides the rails for the Bicentennial. (American Freedom Train) Dan Hall. illus tab Translog
7:14-18 Jul '76

"One nation, indivisible ..." (The American Freedom Train builds unity and patriotism within its
visitors) Ted R. Sturm. illus Airman 20:18-23
Jul '76

A right to survive. Kenneth L. Vore. illus Def
Trans J 32:6-8 Apr '76

History

Army railroading: Tele-train to Trident missile.
Dan Hall. illus Translog 7:2-5 Jun '76
The great locomotive chase (Andrews Raid of 1862).
Tory Billard. illus Translog 7:13+ Aug-Sep '76

Laws and Regulations

Railroads for national defense--an overview; legislation proposed. illus Translog 7:8 Jun '76

RAIN

Raindrops keep falling. MAC Flyer 23:11 Feb '76

When it rains. Capt Guy P. Sumpter. illus Aerosp
Safety 32:12-13 Apr '76

RALPH, John E.

Professional identity in a plural world: The focus of
junior officer education in the U.S. Air Force.
BrigGen John E. Ralph. AU Rev 27:11-25 Jan-
Feb '76

RANK

Air Force

AF sweats grade relief (Defense Officer Personnel
Management Act)--again. AF Times 36:18
May 24 '76

RANK - Continued

Air Force - Cont'd

E-4 sergeant 'ranks' senior airman in E-4. AF
Times 37:32 Dec 13 '76

E-4 Sgt status can be removed. AF Times 37:10
Nov 29 '76

EM grade overhaul begins June 1. AF Times 36:6
Apr 26 '76

EM hikes--changes, impact. Bruce Callander. tabs
AF Times 37:3 Aug 30 '76

Enlisted force structure changes. AF Plcy Ltr for
Comdrs: Sup No. 5:34-36 May '76

New stripes for top EM: Commands study NCO
change. Bruce Callander. illus AF Times 36:2
Apr 5 '76

New 2-step E-4 plan begins June 1. Bruce Callander.
AF Times 36:16 Feb 23 '76

No new NCOs for one year: 3-tier EM plan launched.
Bruce Callander. AF Times 36:6+ May 24 '76

Panel (Senate Armed Services Committee) approves
officer grade relief. (Added to bill to improve financial status of Soldiers' and Airmen's Home)
AF Times 37:4 Sep 27 '76

Rules preclude 3-tier 'slips.' Bruce Callander. AF
Times 36:25 Jun 14 '76

Switch to three-tier (system) includes cushioners.
Bruce Callander. AF Times 36:1+ Jun 7 '76

3-tier: New rules on getting busted. AF Times 36:10
Jun 28 '76

Three-tier setup and how it works. tab AF Times
36:10 May 31 '76

3-tier structure: New EM lineup begins June 1. AF
Times 36:3 Mar 1 '76

3-tier system takes hold. AF Times 37:3 Nov 22 '76

Armed Forces

Statistics

Some statistics on manpower. tabs AF Times 37:26
Sep 13 '76

RATED PERSONNEL see Aeronautical Ratings

RATINGS

See also
Aeronautical Ratings
Effectiveness Reports

Air Force

Terminology

What do the ratings mean? TIG Brief 28:3-4 Jul 2 '76

Army

War and peace and promotion. Capt Peter D. Weddle.
illus Army 26:24-28 Jun '76

RATIONS

Plastic police (ration control card). Sgt1C Floyd
Harrington. illus tab Soldiers 31:37-40 Nov '76

History

Fire cakes to French fries. Sgt JoAnn Mann. illus
Soldiers 31:18-19 Jul '76

READINESS COMMAND

Bold Eagle '76. illus USAF Ftr Wpns Rev, p 17, Spring '76

Brave Shield XIII. LtCol Don Rosenkranz. illus Air Reservist 27:8-9 Feb '76

Brave Shield XIV. illus Air Reservist 28:6 Oct '76

Brave Shield XV. AF Times 37:33 Oct 18 '76

Exercise Bold Eagle (76). AF Times 36:31 Mar 1 '76

Exercise Brave Shield. AF Times 37:31 Sep 20 '76

14,000 taking part in Alaska Exercise Jack Frost. illus AF Times 36:38 Feb 2 '76

A "real world" transportation challenge: Exercise Bold Eagle '76. Maj Eldon T. Rippee. illus Trans- log 7:2-6 May '76

READING, PROFESSIONAL see Professional Reading

READING, REMEDIAL see Remedial Reading

READING AND BOOKS see Books and Reading

RECONNAISSANCE

Ambush (reconnaissance). Maj V. Yatsenko. illus map Soviet Mil Rev No. 5:20-22 May '76

Communications in a recce party. LtCol V. Usmanov. illus Soviet Mil Rev No. 12:25-26 Dec '76

Intercept probability and intercept time. B. R. Hatcher. illus tabs Elect Warfare 8:95+ Mar-Apr '76

Lasers in reconnaissance and gunfire control. MajGen V. Vetrov and Col N. Sokolov. illus Soviet Mil Rev No. 1:25-27 Jan '76

The military characteristics of reconnaissance and surveillance. George F. Steeg. illus tabs Elect Warfare 8:71+ Sep-Oct '76

Observation (reconnaissance). Maj Y. Khatyushin. illus map Soviet Mil Rev No. 5:17-19 May '76

The "Real Cav" (4th Sq, 9th Cavalry). MSgt Wayne E. Hair. illus USA Avn Dig 22:24-25 Mar '76

Reconnaissance in strength. Col B. Antsiz. illus Soviet Mil Rev No. 5:23-24 May '76

Soviet reconnaissance. RUSI J for Def Studies pt 1. P. H. Vigor. 120:41-45 Dec '75; pt 2. Chris Don-nelly. 121:68-75 Mar '76

Tactical reconnaissance. Col R. Trofimov. illus So-viet Mil Rev No. 5:13-16 May '76

Equipment

The reconnaissance dilemma. SSgt Peter L. Bunce. illus Armor 85:18-20 Mar-Apr '76

RECONNAISSANCE, AERIAL

See also
Vietnamese Conflict, 1957-1975--Reconnaissance Operations

Advanced data link aids Army commander. Arthur R. Gandy. illus map Signal 31:6-9 Sep '76

The aerial (International) Ice Patrol: No more Titan-ics! LTJG Stephen R. Osmer. illus US Nav Inst Proc 102:102-106 Mar '76

Air Force sensors. William C. Eppers, Jr. illus (Also cutaway) Natl Def 61:210-213 Nov-Dec '76

Battlefield surveillance. (Army's In-flight DAta Transmission System (AIDATS)) illus Counter-measures 2:12 Jun '76

RECONNAISSANCE, AERIAL - Continued

Compass Sight, 1 of a kind. (New relay type of intel-ligence-gathering system) MSgt Dom Cardonita. AF Times 37:34 Nov 8 '76

Diversity our specialty--the 55th Strategic Recon-naissance Wing reports. Capt Sid R. Howard. illus Combat Crew 27:16-17 Oct '76

Hangar talk for aeroscouts. CW2 Homer E. Shuman. illus Armor 85:48-49 May-Jun '76

The view from a U-2. (The 349th Strategic Recon-naissance Sq from Davis-Monthan AFB, Ariz, flies over Guatemala to survey and describe earthquake damage) Capt Robert W. Gaskin. illus Airman 20:14-15 Jun '76

Equipment

Airborne data link: A weight-watcher's delight. (Army In-flight DAta Transmission System (AIDATS)) illus Elect Warfare 8:51+ Nov-Dec '76

History

From bailing wire to the SR-71: 1st Strategic Recon Sq one of oldest air units. illus AF Times 36:42 May 17 '76

RECORDING INSTRUMENTS

See also
Flight Recorders

The Aircraft Structural Integrity Program (ASIP). TIG Brief 28:17 Feb 13 '76

RECORDS

See also
Correspondence, Military
Forms, Military

Air Force

AF to purify stored data on ethnics. AF Times 36:9 Apr 19 '76

Amendment of Personnel Records--Recording Basic Identifying Data (AFR 35-22). TIG Brief 28:11 May 7 '76

DOD wants limits on Privacy Act--computer add-ons could boost cost to $74.6 million. AF Times 36:22 Feb 2 '76

A 50/50 chance of being passed over. Capt W. E. Thompson. AF Engrg & Svcs Qtr 17:21-22 Feb '76

Health records and the human reliability program. TIG Brief 28:13 Oct 8 '76

(Maintenance) records are dollars. TIG Brief 28:14 Nov 5 '76

Privacy Act checklist. TIG Brief 28:11-12 Feb 27 '76

Release of information contained in military person-nel records. TIG Brief 28:20 Jul 16 '76

Release of information on military pay records. TIG Brief 28:12 Jun 18 '76

Releasing information from and providing access to personnel records. TIG Brief 28:12 May 7 '76

SP automation would speed (AF) file retrieval. AF Times 37:12 Nov 1 '76

Armed Forces

'Personal' records pruned. AF Times 36:22 Feb 2 '76

Weapons loss (in 10 years) put at 18,500. AF Times 36:10 May 3 '76

RECORDS - Continued

Reserve Forces--Air Force--U.S.

Maintenance of Reserve Forces health records. TIG Brief 28:11 Jun 18 '76

RECORDS CENTERS

Air Force

Sources in aerospace history: The USAF oral history collection (at Albert F.Simpson Historical Research Center, Maxwell AFB, Ala). James C. Hasdorff. illus Aerosp Hist 23:103-104 Jun '76

RECORDS MANAGEMENT PROGRAM

Air Force

Air Force documentation management program. TIG Brief 28:20 Mar 12 '76

Outpatient records: Do you have a maintenance system? TIG Brief 28:9-10 Feb 27 '76

Army

Magnifying inner space. Janet Hake. illus Soldiers 31:45-48 Sep '76

RECREATION

Appropriated funds for Morale, Welfare, and Recreation (MWR) activities. TIG Brief 28:15 Nov 19 '76

Are you a good sport? (Sports/recreation accidents) Maj Roger A. Huntington. TAC Attack 16:14-15 Mar '76

Base commanders told to evaluate rec areas. AF Times 37:27 Aug 30 '76

Commanders to get guide on (new off-base) recreation (sites). AF Times 36:9 Jul 12 '76

GAO: Consider recreation as 'pay.' tab AF Times 36:30 May 24 '76

Golf and bowling pay recreation bills. Len Famiglietti. AF Times 37:2 Sep 13 '76

Hale Koa holiday. LtCol James Witek and SP5 Ed Aber. illus Soldiers 31:11-16 Feb '76

Jaws II. (Fishing follies) Maj Art Ivins. illus TAC Attack 16:4-8 Mar '76

New (AF) programs to accent Spanish-speaking culture. Len Famiglietti. AF Times 36:2 Feb 9 '76

USO: After 35 years, it's still the place to go. Marianne Lester. illus AF Times, Times Magazine sup:6-9 Apr 5 '76

Where to camp. Bob Gibson. illus tab AF Times, Times Magazine sup:22+ May 17 '76

RECRUITING AND ENLISTMENT

See also
Reenlistment

Air Force--U.S.

(AF) recruiters: Full involvement. AF Times 36:24 Feb 2 '76

(AF) recruits could get nuclear jobs. Ron Sanders. AF Times 37:4 Oct 18 '76

The Air Force Recruiter Assistance Program (AFRAP). TIG Brief 28:13 Dec 17 '76

Budget cramps recruiters' style: 'Improving economy' seen as drawback. Len Famiglietti. AF Times 37:12 Oct 25 '76

RECRUITING AND ENLISTMENT - Continued

Air Force--U.S. - Cont'd

Care in selecting MTIs (Military Training Instructors) paying off. AF Times 36:4 Jun 7 '76

The con is gone. (USAF recruiters try to give an accurate picture of AF life) Interview. MajGen Andrew P.Iosue. illus Airman 20:29-31 Apr '76

First-term airman recruiter assistance program. TIG Brief 28:15 Nov 5 '76

'Guaranteed base of choice' recruiting option. TIG Brief 28:19-20 Mar 26 '76

Horror stories! (AF enlisted personnel job placement explained) Capt John B. Taylor. illus Airman 20:24-28 Apr '76

Improved security clearance procedures. TIG Brief 28:16 May 7 '76

New weight standards for women enlistees. Table only. AF Times 36:10 Mar 8 '76

Physical profile factor 'X.' TIG Brief 28:20 Sep 24 '76

Quality breeds quality. TIG Brief 28:21 Jul 16 '76

REcruiter/Customer Awareness Program (RECAP). TIG Brief 28:11-12 Jan 30 '76

Recruiters get more base help. AF Times 37:13 Dec 20 '76

Recruiting Service's Management Emphasis Program. TIG Brief 28:12 Jun 18 '76

Revamping the enlisted structure. Ed Gates. tab AF Mag 59:39-41 Aug '76

Support for recruiting. TIG Brief 28:15 Jun 4 '76

'Tell it like it is' in Air Force recruiting and advertising. TIG Brief 28:19-20 Feb 27 '76

Three-year minimum initial term of service for officers. TIG Brief 28:15 Apr 23 '76

Truthful recruiting pays off. AF Times 37:19 Sep 13 '76

What you see is what you get: An essay on recruiting and retention. Col Richard A. Mason and others. Educ J 19:5-11 Fall '76

Armed Forces--Germany (Federal Republic)

Youth information officers of the Federal Armed Forces. Capt Jürgen Conze. illus NATO's Fifteen Nations 21:49-56 Aug-Sep '76

Armed Forces--U.S.

About face for ROTC. Debbie C.Tennison. illus Natl Def 61:48-50 Jul-Aug '76

All-vol recruit same as previous (according to a study by the General Accounting Office). AF Times 36:15 Mar 29 '76

'Catch-up' program eyed for minorities. Andy Plattner. AF Times 36:2 Jun 28 '76

DOD recruiting advertising: The 19-million dollar question. Benjamin F.Schemmer. illus tabs Armed Forces J Intl 113:12-13+ Jun '76

Despite pitfalls, recruiters have done well, DMC (Defense Manpower Commission) says. AF Times 36:20 May 17 '76

GAO report hits cost of recruit ads. AF Times 36:34 May 3 '76

REDUCTION IN FORCE - Continued

Naval Reserve cuts threaten all Reserves. RADM John Johnson. tab Officer 52:16-17 Mar '76

No new officer RIF this FY (according to Chief of Staff, Gen David C.) Jones. Lee Ewing. AF Times 36:2 Feb 16 '76

Personnel cuts linked to (buying) arms (and doing research). AF Times 36:22 Mar 1 '76

Planned budget cuts may hurt Reserves. AF Times 36:11 Jan 5 '76

(Pres) Ford asks AF cut of 13,000. tab AF Times 36:4 Feb 2 '76

RIFed Reserve officers out in cold on tax break. AF Times 37:8 Dec 20 '76

ROA (Executive Director Gen J. Milnor Roberts) tells senators (Manpower and Personnel Subcommittee of the Senate Armed Services Committee) world will see U.S. Reserve cuts as weakening. Officer 52:4 Apr '76

A status report on Mutual and Balanced Forced Reductions (MBFRs). Rembert van Delden. NATO's Fifteen Nations 21:20-21 Aug-Sep '76

What's an MBFR (Mutual and Balanced Force Reduction)? Donald L. Clark. illus chart AU Rev 27:51-64 Jul-Aug '76

REED, Thomas C.

(AF) personnel program best in Pentagon, (SecAF) Reed says (in news conference). AF Times 36:3 Mar 8 '76

The B-1: The right solution. (Remarks, Council of World Affairs, Dallas, April 15, 1976) Thomas C. Reed. AF Plcy Ltr for Comdrs: Sup No.6:2-9 Jun '76

A better horse for Paul Revere: National command and control communications. Thomas C. Reed. por Strat Rev 4:25-32 Summer '76

Ex-USAF officer back as Secretary. (Thomas C. Reed confirmed to replace John L. McLucas as Secretary of the Air Force) Officer 52:22 Feb '76

Forces for the future. (Remarks, Lancaster Chamber of Commerce, Lancaster, Calif, Feb 6, 1976) Thomas C. Reed. AF Plcy Ltr for Comdrs: Sup No.4:16-20 Apr '76

(JSC Chairman Gen George S.) Brown criticizes Times newspapers (in testimony before House Armed Services Committee). AF Times 36:3 Feb 9 '76

Keynote luncheon address (AFCEA, Washington, June 8, 1976). Thomas C. Reed. por Signal 30: 19-23 Aug '76

Lead on, Mr Secretary! (SecAF Thomas C. Reed discusses his job and the Air Force as a whole) Interview. por Airman 20:2-7 Jun '76

Modernization and the military balance. (Address, AFA National Convention, Washington, Sep 19-23, 1976) Thomas C. Reed. por AF Mag 59:34-37 Nov '76

New Air Force Secretary: Thomas C. Reed is well qualified to meet the current problems. por biog Natl Def 60:428-429 May-Jun '76

New uses of electronic communication. (Remarks, Armed Forces Communications and Electronics Assoc, Washington, June 8, 1976) Thomas C. Reed. AF Plcy Ltr for Comdrs: Sup No.8:8-12 Aug '76

People come first, says (SecAF) Reed on tour. AF Times 36:10 Feb 9 '76

REED, Thomas C. - Continued

The promised land. Thomas C. Reed. por AF Mag 59: 45-47 May '76

A proud heritage, promising future. Thomas C. Reed. por Air Reservist 28:2 Jul '76

(SecAF) Reed calls for 'people' aid. Lee Ewing. AF Times 36:3 Feb 9 '76

(SecAF) Reed slaps at congressional critic (of B-1). (From address, Air Force Assoc National Convention, Washington, Sep 19-22, 1976) por AF Times 37:21 Oct 4 '76

(SecAF) Reed turns down (TSgt Leonard P.) Matlovich appeal. AF Times 36:26 May 10 '76

(SecAF Thomas C.) Reed lists 5 conclusions about the Air Force in recent news conference at the Pentagon) por Air Reservist 28:13 May '76; AF Compt 10:24-25 Jul '76

Secretary of the Air Force's Air Force authorization request. (Statement before House Committee on Armed Services, Washington, Jan 29, 1976) Thomas C. Reed. AF Plcy Ltr for Comdrs: Sup No.3:2-23 Mar '76

Secretary Reed: Air Reserve vital to USAF mission. por Officer 52:19 May '76

Strategic Force modernization. (Remarks, Air Force Assoc luncheon, Washington, Sep 22, 1976) Thomas C. Reed. AF Plcy Ltr for Comdrs: Sup No.11: 2-8 Nov '76

The telecommunications revolution. (Remarks, Comstock Club, Sacramento, Calif, Nov 17, 1975) Thomas C. Reed. AF Plcy Ltr for Comdrs: Sup No.1:11-17 Jan '76

Thomas C. Reed, USAF's new Secretary. Claude Witze. por AF Mag 59:32-34 Feb '76

USAF in the forefront of the C^3 revolution. Thomas C. Reed. AF Mag 59:62-65 Jul '76

REENLISTMENT

Air Force--U.S.

EM must solve re-up equation. Bruce Callander. AF Times 37:14 Nov 29 '76

Early out means bonus payback (when reenlisting). AF Times 37:10 Sep 20 '76

1st termers must plan ahead for retraining bonus. AF Times 36:16 Jun 21 '76

Job-finding opens re-up door: Chance for retraining. Bruce Callander. AF Times 36:12 May 10 '76

Job reservation no guarantee: Warning to airmen. AF Times 37:46 Sep 13 '76

Low AQE (Airman Qualifying Examination) scorers urged to try again. Bruce Callander. AF Times 36:3 Jul 5 '76

Many first termers can't get re-up $$. AF Times 36:30 Jul 5 '76

Reconsideration of favorable selective reenlistment program decisions. TIG Brief 28:6 Sep 10 '76

SRBs cut, retrainees protected. Bruce Callander. AF Times 36:4 Mar 8 '76

Some bonus skills dropped, a few added. AF Times 36:3 Jun 7 '76

Some can retrain for 2d re-up $$. Bruce Callander. AF Times 36:5 Mar 29 '76

Some 1st termers to miss re-up $$. AF Times 37:10 Sep 20 '76

RESEARCH AND DEVELOPMENT - Continued

Air Force--U. S. - Cont'd

The technological case for a supersonic cruise aircraft. (Advanced Supersonic Technology/Supersonic Cruise Aircraft Research (AST/SCAR) program) Edgar Ulsamer. illus AF Mag 59:34-39 Jun '76

Technological investment and payoff. (Remarks, AFA/SAC 9th Annual Missile Combat Competition, Vandenberg AFB, Calif, April 29, 1976) Gen William J. Evans. AF Plcy Ltr for Comdrs: Sup No. 7: 7-14 Jul '76

History

Air Force research in retrospect. Col Robert M. Detweiler. illus AU Rev 28:2-15 Nov-Dec '76

Armed Forces--Russia

Scientific progress and defensive potential. MajGen I. Anureyev. Soviet Mil Rev No. 2:13-15 Feb '76

Soviet R&D at "critical mass": "Sobering assessment" troubles DOD research chief (Malcolm R. Currie). Benjamin F. Schemmer. tabs Armed Forces J Intl 113:12-13 Mar '76

Technological investment and payoff. (Remarks, AFA/SAC 9th Annual Missile Combat Competition, Vandenberg AFB, Calif, April 29, 1976) Gen William J. Evans. AF Plcy Ltr for Comdrs: Sup No. 7: 7-14 Jul '76

Armed Forces--U. S.

Military spinoff. (Technology transfer from military R&D to wide range of civilian problems: Fire and safety, environment, transportation, law enforcement, etc) Martha P. Smith. RUSI J for Def Studies 121:53-57 Mar '76

Costs

U.S. EO (Electro-Optics) and IRCM (InfraRed CounterMeasures) budget outlined. Tables only. Elect Warfare 7:24+ Nov-Dec '75

Army--U. S.

Army aircraft survivability. Maj N.I. Patla. illus tab USA Avn Dig 22:7+ Nov '76

The Army: Electronics vs dwindling budgets. illus Govt Exec 8:37+ Jan '76

Defense budget, 1977: A 'serious effort' at restraint. illus tabs Eric C. Ludvigsen. Army 26:12-17 Mar '76

Desk to desk. (USAR Research and Development Officer Career Program) Col James L. Wohlfahrt. illus Army Log 8:6-7 Jul-Aug '76

Flexible firepower. (Fuses for airborne rockets) Steve Kimmel. illus (Also cutaways) Natl Def 60: 444-445 May-Jun '76

New developments. Regular feature in issues of National Defense

Optical exposure--a look at the horizon. (Refinement in laser technology at Army's Harry Diamond Laboratories) Steve Kimmel. illus USA Avn Dig 22: 24-27 Nov '76

Solution seeks a problem. (Army's Harry Diamond Labs conduct research on use of lasers in optical fuzes, target designators, and other devices) Edward A. Brown. illus Natl Def 61:112-113 Sep-Oct '76

RESEARCH AND DEVELOPMENT - Continued

Defense Dept--Russia

A case in point: Patriot's progress. tab Armed Forces J Intl 113:18 Jul '76

Ivan's edge is our bureaucracy. (Interview with John L. McDaniel) illus Armed Forces J Intl 113:16+ Jul '76

Defense Dept--U. S.

"Captive think tanks" revisited: Rebuttal to rebuttal. James R. Craig. Armed Forces J Intl 113:42+ Mar '76

A case in point: Patriot's progress. tab Armed Forces J Intl 113:18 Jul '76

Comparing American & Soviet defense: How does U.S. technology stack up with USSR? Malcolm R. Currie. illus tab Comdrs Dig 19: entire issue Jun 17 '76

Effective military technology for the 1980s. Richard L. Garwin. illus tabs Intl Sec 1:50-77 Fall '76

(Excerpt from) Keynote Address (57th Defense Preparedness Meeting, American Defense Preparedness Assoc, Los Angeles, Oct 15, 1975). Gen William J. Evans. Natl Def 60:283 Jan-Feb '76

Instructional technology in the Department of Defense, now and in the future. M. Richard Rose. illus tab AU Rev 27:11-23 May-Jun '76

Ivan's edge is our bureaucracy. (Interview with John L. McDaniel) illus Armed Forces J Intl 113:16+ Jul '76

The obstacles to effective design-to-cost. Raymond Kendall. Govt Exec 8:24-25 Oct '76

On the technological frontier: Laser-powered rockets and dark satellites. Edgar Ulsamer. tab AF Mag 59:60-64 Apr '76

R&D emphasis on reliability. Robert N. Parker. Def Mgt J 12:19 Apr '76

The role of DARPA (Defense Advanced Research Projects Agency). George H. Heilmeier. illus map Comdrs Dig 19: entire issue Oct 7 '76

Soviet R&D at "critical mass": "Sobering assessment" troubles DOD research chief (Malcolm R. Currie). Benjamin F. Schemmer. tabs Armed Forces J Intl 113:12-13 Mar '76

History

Air Force research in retrospect. Col Robert M. Detweiler. illus AU Rev 28:2-15 Nov-Dec '76

Federal Aviation Administration--U. S.

The U. S. air traffic control and navigation equipment market--continuing growth foreseen. tabs Interavia 31:462-463 May '76

National Aeronautics and Space Administration--U. S.

Civil transport technology up to 2000: NASA believes fuel consumption is the major consideration. J. Philip Geddes. illus tabs Interavia 31:419-421 May '76

The technological case for a supersonic cruise aircraft. (Advanced Supersonic Technology/Supersonic Cruise Aircraft Research (AST/SCAR) program) Edgar Ulsamer. illus AF Mag 59:34-39 Jun '76

RESEARCH AND DEVELOPMENT - Continued

National Aeronautics and Space Administration--U.S. - Cont'd

U.S. aeronautical R&D: Seeking effective policies and leadership. A.Scott Crossfield. illus tabs Govt Exec 8:38-39+ Nov '76

Navy--U.S.

Booster shot for the high speed Navy: Technological successes, and a 3K green light from DOD. James D.Hessman. illus Sea Power 19:23-25 Jun '76

History

To America--with pride. (Civilian applications of naval research) CDR Robert P.Brewer, Ret and JOCM William J.Miller. illus US Nav Inst Proc 102:52-59 Jul '76

Russia

DIA (Defense Intelligence Agency): Communists study microwaves as weapons. AF Times 37:3 Dec 6 '76

Trends in Soviet military technology. Charles De-Vore. illus tabs Signal 30:47-50 Jul '76

United States

Evaluative research: Progress through experimentation. E.William Sarsfield. illus Govt Exec 8:33+ Mar '76

Government R&D funding: A dismal example of mismanagement. (Comment on "Federal Funding of Civilian R&D," a study by Arthur D. Little, Inc) tab Govt Exec 8:49-50 Jun '76

Guarding against technological surprise. George H. Heilmeier. AU Rev 27:2-7 Sep-Oct '76

Industry and defense. (Excerpt from address, 57th Defense Preparedness Meeting, American Defense Preparedness Assoc, Los Angeles, Oct 15, 1975) R.Anderson. Natl Def 60:287 Jan-Feb '76

Costs

Legitimacy and government control of the production of academic social knowledge. Michael Useem. tabs J Pol & Mil Sociol 4:217-232 Fall '76

RESEARCH CENTERS

"Captive think tanks" revisited: Rebuttal to rebuttal. James R.Craig. Armed Forces J Intl 113:42+ Mar '76

Guide to NASA's research centers. AF Mag 59:158 May '76

Setting the record straight about CNA (Center for Naval Analyses). (Comments on "Captive 'think tanks'--DOD's $265-million hobby horse?" by James R.Craig, Armed Forces J Intl, Dec 1975) Arnold B.Moore. tab Armed Forces J Intl 113: 26-27 Jan '76

RESERVATIONS, AIRPLANE see Airlines--Passenger Service

RESERVE FORCES

Air Force--U.S.

AFRES/ANG--best shape ever. Interviews. MajGens John J.Pesch and William Lyon. illus AF Mag 59: 55-59 Jun '76

ANG/Res can't bar ex-drug user. AF Times 36:6 Feb 16 '76

RESERVE FORCES - Continued

Air Force--U.S. - Cont'd

Air Force Reserve. illus tab AF Mag 59:100-101 May '76

The Air Force Reserve navigator in the "total force." Gerald Cantwell. illus Navigator 23:23-26 Spring '76

Career Reserve Status. (AFR 36-14) TIG Brief 28:12 Jan 30 '76

Colorado catastrophe (July 31, 1976). illus Air Reservist 28:10-11 Nov '76

A friendly persuader. (MSgt Redelle Powell, recruiter for the 459th Tactical Airlift Wg (Reserve) at Andrews AFB, Md) MSgt Jerry Smith. illus Airman 20:11-13 Oct '76

From props to jets. illus Air Reservist 28:8-9 Apr '76

(Gen David C.) Jones on records of officers--Regulars 'generally better.' Lee Ewing. AF Times 36:3 Mar 1 '76

Goal: Individual awareness. (Air Force Reserve's social actions program) illus Air Reservist 27:12 Mar '76

It takes heart. (AFR 514th Military Airlift Wg, McGuire AFB, NJ, wins AFR Annual Community Award) illus Air Reservist 28:6-7 Apr '76

Life insurance increase eyed (among other) Reserve incentives. AF Times 37:10 Aug 16 '76

MAC Associates ... a vital role. MSgt Gerald H. Smith. illus Air Reservist 28:12-13 Nov '76

(Maj)Gen (Richard) Bodycombe new AFR Vice Cmdr; other officers receive new assignments. illus Officer 52:19 Dec '76

Medical/dental supervisors' responsibilities for mobilization augmentees. TIG Brief 28:10 Jul 16 '76

Medical materiel technicians assigned to Reserve Forces medical units. TIG Brief 28:11 Jun 18 '76

M(obilization) a(ugmentee) Reserves get new role. AF Times 37:6 Aug 9 '76

Never a dull moment. (USAF Reserve Civil Engineers work at restoring the Fort Jefferson National Monument 65 miles west of the Florida coast) TSgt Dan Doherty. illus Airman 20:42-47 Aug '76

New Palace Chase rules announced. AF Times 36:2 Jun 21 '76

Officers who apply for CRS (Career Reserve Status) must qualify for retirement. AF Times 37:3 Dec 6 '76

Outstanding (Air Force Reservists) Mobilization Augmentees. illus Air Reservist 28:8-9 May '76

Planned budget cuts may hurt Reserves. AF Times 36:11 Jan 5 '76

Progress in our total force policy. James P.Gilligan. illus Air Reservist 28:3 Jul '76

A proud heritage, promising future. Thomas C.Reed. illus Air Reservist 28:2 Jul '76

Readiness through realism. LtCol James Glaza. illus Air Reservist 28:8-9 Aug-Sep '76

Reserve flyers serve nation in war and peace. illus Officer 52:15 Jul '76

Air Force--U.S.-- Cont'd

Reservists fill detective's role (as) environmental health technicians (at Dobbins AFB, Ga). illus AF Times 36:41 Apr 19 '76

Reservists restore a rare one (Martin B-10 bomber). illus AF Times 37:55 Dec 13 '76

Reservists to join active unit in (347th Tactical Fighter Wg) test. AF Times 36:28 Jun 21 '76

Secretary (Thomas C.) Reed: Air Reserve vital to USAF mission. illus Officer 52:19 May '76

Security police. (Air Force Reserve's Weapon Systems Security units) Capt Tom Treband. illus Air Reservist 28:10-11 May '76

3800 going Reserve under (Palace) 'Chase.' AF Times 36:3 Jul 5 '76

(What you've always wanted to know about the Air National Guard and the Air Force Reserve) illus charts tabs Air Reservist 27: entire issue Dec '75- Jan '76

History

73,050 yesterdays: Excerpts of militia history. Martin Gordon. illus Air Reservist 28:4+ Jul '76

Organization

Reserves getting numbered AFs. AF Times 37:12 Oct 11 '76

Statistics

AFRES/ANG--best shape ever. Interviews. MajGens John J.Pesch and William Lyon. illus AF Mag 59: 55-59 Jun '76

Armed Forces--NATO

At CIOR Brussels meeting (Jan 29-Feb 1, 1976) SACEUR Haig, NATO's Luns, others participate. Col Harold A.Veazey. illus Officer 52:11 Apr '76

CIOR (Interallied Confederation of Reserve Officers) organizes Reserve officers of NATO countries. illus Officer 52:39 Jul '76

Armed Forces--U.S.

Are America's Reserve Forces the "keystone" of national security? Defense panel (Defense Manpower Commission) says yea and nay. Natl Guardsman 30:8-11 Jun '76

Better use of Reserve by Services sought (by Defense Manpower Commission). AF Times 36:14 May 3 '76

Big changes eyed in compensation--Res/Guard study group. Interview. RADM Richard G.Altmann, Ret. AF Times 37:31 Nov 29 '76

Bill allows President more call-up power (for Reserves). AF Times 36:53 May 10 '76

Budget ups hardware but degrades personnel. tabs Officer 52:4+ Mar '76

Civilian (technicians) union to start organizing Guard/ Res. AF Times 36:6 Jan 5 '76

DOD bares plans for Reserves. AF Times 36:23 Mar 22 '76

1st phase of (Reserve pay system) study starts Sep 1. Paul Smith. AF Times 37:10 Aug 30 '76

Flux in Reserve causes concern. AF Times 37:2 Nov 22 '76

Armed Forces--U.S. - Cont'd

GAO finds Reserves building needlessly. AF Times 37:57 Nov 29 '76

The Guard & Reserve in the total force program. illus Comdrs Dig 19: entire issue Jan 29 '76

IRA (Individual Retirement Accounts) clause due for push in both House, Senate. (Interview with Congressman James R.Jones and Capt Frank Manson) illus Officer 52:11 Feb '76

MOBDES (MOBilization DESignee): Modern Minutemen. LtCol John X.Loughran III. illus Air Reservist 28:18 Nov '76

(Maj)Gen (W.Stanford) Smith reviews 20 years of Reserve gains. Officer 52:10+ Dec '76

ROA (Executive Director Gen J.Milnor Roberts) tells senators (Manpower and Personnel Subcommittee of the Senate Armed Services Committee) world will see U.S. Reserve cuts as weakening. Officer 52:4 Apr '76

(Rep Bill) Chappell, Manpower Commission, ROA point way to strong Total Force. Editorial. Officer 52:4+ Jun '76

(Reserve Forces) Policy Board makes hard-hitting report: Adequate personnel, equipment vital to total force success. Officer 52:4 Jan '76

Reserves fare well in both construction bills. tab Officer 52:5+ Aug '76

Senate (Armed Services) Committee bill permits 90-day active duty call up. AF Times 36:16 Jan 5 '76

What the 50,000 call-up bill means to you (Reserves). Officer 52:5 Feb '76

History

Citizen soldiers through the years. illus Officer 52:5+ Jul '76

Army--Great Britain

A role for the uncommitted Reserve? LtCol Michael Burkham. RUSI J for Def Studies 121:43-45 Sep '76

The training of General Reserve battalions of the TAVR (Territorial Army Volunteer Reserve). Maj M.J.Dudding. illus RUSI J for Def Studies 120: 23-26 Dec '75

Army--U.S.

Bold thinking is needed to revitalize the Ready Reserve. Col T.G.Westerman and LtCol Wayne C. Knudson. illus Army 26:34-38 May '76

Can the Reserve Components make it? LtCol Benjamin L.Abramowitz. illus tab Mil Rev 56:58-64 May '76

Combat readiness on a shoestring. (Army augmentation units) Anthony J.Daniels. illus Army 26: 49-51 Apr '76

Data processing and the Reserve components. BrigGen H.W.Meetze and Maj J.Steiger. illus Army Log 8:20-23 Sep-Oct '76

(Prepared address, ROA Mid-Winter Conference, Washington, Feb 20, 1976) MajGen Henry Mohr. illus Officer 52:18-19 Apr '76

A "real world" transportation challenge: Exercise Bold Eagle '76. Maj Eldon T.Rippee. illus Translog 7:2-6 May '76

RESERVE OFFICERS ASSOCIATION OF THE U.S. -
Continued

ROA scores DOPMA, up-or-out, age bias (at 50th
Annual Convention, Bal Harbour, Fla, June 29-
July 2, 1976). Don Hirst. AF Times 36:16
Jul 19 '76

ROA's mandates (adopted in 1976 National Convention) provide program for action. Officer 52:
14-15+ Dec '76

(Raymond) Webster (from Office of SecDef) reviews
Naval Reserve situation (at ROA Meeting, Biloxi,
Miss, Oct 30-Nov 1, 1975). illus Officer 52:24-25
Jan '76

(RADM W.S.) Schwob tells ROA CGR (Coast Guard
Reserve) looking good (at Biloxi, Miss, Meeting,
Oct 30-Nov 1, 1975). illus Officer 52:25 Jan '76

(Reports of Bicentennial Mid-Winter Conference,
Washington, Feb 19-20, 1976) illus Officer 52:
13-14+ Apr '76

(Rep Bill) Chappell, Manpower Commission, ROA
point way to strong Total Force. Editorial. Officer 52:4+ Jun '76

Reserve Compensation (System Study) group enlists
ROA support. Officer 52:4+ Dec '76

Reserve officers rap unionization. AF Times 36:8
Mar 8 '76

34 resolutions (adopted by 1976 National Convention)
urge actions to strengthen security. Officer 52:
29-31 Sep '76

Weyand: Full circle. (Gen Fred C. Weyand accepts
"Minute Man Hall of Fame" award at ROA Na-
tional Convention, Bal Harbour, Fla, June 29-
July 2, 1976) Officer 9:21+ Sep '76

Directories

ROA directory, 1976-1977. illus Officer 52:17-24
Oct '76

History

The history of ROA: 55 years of work for national security. Col John T. Carlton. illus Officer 52:24-25+
Jul '76

RESERVE OFFICERS TRAINING CORPS

Air Force

AFROTC airman scholarship and commissioning program. TIG Brief 28:6 Aug 13 '76

AFROTC testing 3dLt program. AF Times 37:18
Oct 4 '76

ANG requests AFROTC grads (under Palace Option).
AF Times 36:2 Jul 12 '76

An aerospace defense game for AS 100 (at Oregon
State). LtCol Charles F. Wilhelm. illus tab Educ J
19:13-20 Winter '76

Degree-holding EM can vie for AECP. AF Times
37:10 Nov 15 '76

Effort to block UPT for '76 grads fails. Len Famiglietti. AF Times 36:3 Jun 7 '76

Enlivening American Defense Policy (ADP). Maj Larry B. Atkinson. tab Educ J 19:36-38 Winter '76

4-year stabilized tours with ROTC units offered. tab
AF Times 37:10 Aug 9 '76

Introduction to navigation. LtCol Brian T. Parker.
Educ J 19:39-40 Winter '76

RESERVE OFFICERS TRAINING CORPS - Continued

Air Force - Cont'd

Manpower malaise hits the AFROTC. Ed Gates. AF
Mag 59:73 Feb '76

Only top (AFROTC) grads will get UPT. Len Famiglietti. AF Times 36:2 Mar 1 '76

The psychology of enthusiasm. Maj Gerald A. Fabisch. Educ J 19:34-35 Fall '76

ROTCers get UPT (Undergraduate Pilot Training)
break. Len Famiglietti. AF Times 36:2 Apr 26 '76

Self-discipline and standards: A commitment to excellence. (Programs at Florida State University)
Capt Richard A. Zucker. Educ J 19:11-12 Winter '76

Some ideas about influencing attitudes. Capt Lee G.
Borts. Educ J 19:21-23 Winter '76

2980 officers FY 78 quota for AFROTC. AF Times
36:9 Apr 5 '76

21 AFROTC schools saved. Len Famiglietti. AF
Times 36:4 Jun 28 '76

21 AFROTC units put on probation, 11 to close. Len
Famiglietti. AF Times 36:26 Mar 15 '76

What you see is what you get: An essay on recruiting
and retention. Col Richard A. Mason and others.
Educ J 19:5-11 Fall '76

Armed Forces

About face for ROTC. Debbie C. Tennison. illus Natl
Def 61:48-50 Jul-Aug '76

Freedoms (Foundation) Awards honor ROA, ROTC
members. Officer 52:31 Jul '76

150 ROTC units face closing. Andy Plattner. AF
Times 36:4 Feb 23 '76

ROTC cadet attitudes: A product of socialization or
self-selection? James E. Dorman. tabs J Pol &
Mil Sociol 4:203-216 Fall '76

The ROTC in 1976. J. Glenn Sartori. illus Mil Engr
68:380-383 Sep-Oct '76

History

Army, Air Force and Navy ROTC units form training
ground for officers (1777-1976). Officer 52:36
Jul '76

Statistics

Army, Air Force and Navy ROTC units form training
ground for officers (1777-1976). Officer 52:36
Jul '76

Army

Black ROTC scholarships to be dispersed (in effort
to involve a wider range of schools). Army 26:57
Sep '76

The civilian military college. Maj. John D. Kraus, Jr.
illus Mil Rev 56:77-87 Aug '76

Jr ROTC goes to summer camp. illus Army 26:50-51
Sep '76

History

An 'ROTC' unit (Alabama Corps of Cadets) fought as
such, trained troops. Col Paul R. O'Mary. Officer
52:36 Jul '76

RESERVES see Reserve Forces

RESOURCE MANAGEMENT

AFCS and AF resource management. BrigGen Rupert H. Burris. illus AF Compt 10: back cover Jan '76

Air Force resource management: Blending systems with skills. MajGen Jack I. Posner. tabs illus Def Mgt J 12:23-31 Oct '76

Are we running out of metals? Simon D. Strauss. Persp in Def Mgt No. 24:19-31 Winter '75-'76

A Bicentennial look at the bureacracy. George S. Odiorne. illus Armed Forces Compt 21:16-17 Jul '76

Fuels management. TIG Brief 28:20 Feb 13 '76

Improve your resource management program. TIG Brief 28:18 Jul 16 '76

Logistics management in municipalities. (Burbank, Calif) Robert N. Carlton. illus chart Log Spectrum 10:22-25+ Summer '76

Managing technical activities and the future. Vincent P. Luchsinger. illus Armed Forces Compt 21: 18-19 Jul '76

Mission area planning helps spend dollars wisely. TIG Brief 28:19 Dec 17 '76

Oil embargoes: Creating the cushion. John F. Judge. illus Govt Exec 8:46+ Nov '76

Planning, programming, and budgeting: A search for a management philosopher's stone. Maj Lorentz A. Feltes. illus AU Rev 27:85-95 Jan-Feb '76

Programming sense into resource constraints. John E. Burke and Capt Hugh A. Shaffer. illus tabs Mil Engr 68:460-461 Nov-Dec '76

Resource control strategy. Anthony Harrigan. illus Natl Def 60:350-352 Mar-Apr '76

Resource management: A view from the top. (Panel discussion, American Society of Military Comptrollers National Symposium, Arlington, Va, May 26, 1976) Fred P. Wacker and others. illus Armed Forces Compt 21:20-26 Jul '76

Resource management team at base level? Why not? Maj D. J. Herrington. illus AF Compt 10:30-31 Oct '76

Resource management training. TIG Brief 28:4 Feb 27 '76

Study and Teaching

A cram course in resource management for commanders (recommended for Air University Institute for Professional Development). Maj George J. C. Fries. illus AF Compt 10:42-43 Apr '76

RESOURCES CONSERVATION PROGRAM

Only a couple of hundred pounds. (Fuel conservation) Capt Thomas F. King. illus Combat Crew 26:19-21 Feb '76

RESPIRATION

See also
Artificial Respiration

Pulmonary function evaluation during the Skylab and Apollo-Soyuz missions. C. F. Sawin and others. illus tabs Aviation, Space and Envmt Med 47:168-172 Feb '76

RESPIRATORY ORGANS

Changes in pulmonary volumes with relocation to 1,600 m following acute translocation to 4,300 m. J. G. Dramise and others. tabs Aviation, Space & Envmt Med 47:261-264 Mar '76

Determination of regional pulmonary mechanics using a scintillation camera. R. C. Brown and others. illus tabs Aviation, Space & Envmt Med 47:231-237 Mar '76

Effects of the frequency content in complex air shock waves on lung injuries in rabbits. Carl-Johan Clemedson and Arne Jönsson. tabs Aviation, Space & Envmt Med 47:1143-1152 Nov '76

Mechanism of lung damage in explosive decompression. E. D. L. Topliff. illus tabs Aviation, Space & Envmt Med 47:517-522 May '76

RETENTION OF MILITARY PERSONNEL

"I am the two-headed ogre." RADM Bruce Keener III. illus US Nav Inst Proc 102:38-45 Apr '76

Life insurance increase eyed (among other) Reserve incentives. AF Times 37:10 Aug 16 '76

What you see is what you get: An essay on recruiting and retention. Col Richard A. Mason and others. Educ J 19:5-11 Fall '76

RETIRED MILITARY PERSONNEL

(AF) survey reveals retirees active in base functions. AF Times 36:8 Jan 19 '76

Better break for retirees strongly backed by panel (retired activities workshop held in April at Randolph AFB, Tex). AF Times 37:12 Aug 2 '76

Bringing them back right. (Several AF bases have programs for keeping retirees informed on AF projects and activities) illus Airman 20: inside back cover Mar '76

Career transition course (offered by Catholic University) teaches retirees to survive. M. L. Craver. AF Times 37:12 Nov 8 '76

Dual comp suit (by) 700 retired officers asks millions. Lee Ewing. AF Times 37:10 Aug 2 '76

400 (retired Regular military and naval officers) challenge dual comp. Lee Ewing. AF Times 36:3 Mar 22 '76

More decisions affect Medicare. Officer 52:4+ Aug '76

New regs in effect for kin of retirees (in Korea). AF Times 36:20 May 10 '76

Old soldiers never die ... some just run for office. LtCol Tom Hamrick, Ret. illus Army 26:29-31+ Mar '76

145,000 are 'double dippers.' AF Times 37:3 Nov 8 '76

142,000 retirees hold Federal jobs. AF Times 37:2 Nov 15 '76

1-year rule eased on retiree travel. AF Times 36:11 May 24 '76

Promises--or "perceptions?" (Erosion of promised military entitlements) MajGen Herbert G. Sparrow, Ret. Armed Forces J Intl 113:14+ May '76

Retiree store limit studied. Phil Stevens. AF Times 37:28 Aug 9 '76

Retiree tax break urged (by TROA). AF Times 36:3 May 10 '76

RETIRED MILITARY PERSONNEL - Continued

Rules for selecting homes eased: Retirees after Aug 1 affected. AF Times 37:11 Dec 6 '76

600 retired officers reported holding jobs with DOD contractors. AF Times 36:40 Feb 2 '76

Social Security for Service people and veterans. Officer 52:35-36 Oct '76

RETIRED OFFICERS ASSOCIATION

TROA views benefits issue; (Gen George S.) Brown decries 'contract attitude' (at TROA 23d Biennial Convention, Philadelphia, Sep 14-17, 1976). Bruce Callander. AF Times 37:25 Oct 4 '76

RETIREMENT

See also
Discharges, Releases, and Separations

Air Force--U.S.

Be prompt on 7-day option on retirement. AF Times 36:8 Apr 26 '76

Better break for retirees strongly backed by panel (retired activities workshop held in April at Randolph AFB, Tex). AF Times 37:12 Aug 2 '76

Colonel retirements drop, fewer PCS moves seen. AF Times 37:10 Oct 4 '76

EM exit options changed. AF Times 36:11 May 24 '76

Generals on the move. (Title varies) Regular feature in some issues of Air Force Times

Officers who apply for CRS (Career Reserve Status) must qualify for retirement. AF Times 37:3 Dec 6 '76

Retirement 'lock-in' waiver extended to Sep 1. AF Times 36:4 May 3 '76

SAC chief (Gen Russell E. Dougherty) extended a year (and other general officer news announced). AF Times 37:3 Aug 16 '76

Senior staff changes. Regular feature in issues of Air Force Magazine

Statistics

January retirements total 1286. AF Times 36:38+ Mar 8 '76

Armed Forces--U.S.

Exit physicals made optional. Lee Ewing. AF Times 36:2 Mar 15 '76

New group (special congressional task force) probes pensions. AF Times 36:19 Feb 16 '76

Retirement supplement. AF Times 36:24p sup opposite p 32 Apr 12 '76; 37:24p sup opposite p 30 Sep 13 '76

Star status: Army, Navy, Air Force, Marines. Regular feature in some issues of Armed Forces Journal International

Why is retirement rate rising? Lee Ewing. AF Times 36:16+ Apr 26 '76

Marine Corps--U.S.

Retirements, reassignment. MarCor Gaz 60:2 Jun '76

National Guard--Air Force--U.S.

ANG to lift E-9 freeze October 1--some force outs seen. AF Times 36:20 May 24 '76

RETIREMENT - Continued

Reserve Forces--Armed Forces--U.S.

IRA (Individual Retirement Accounts) clause due for push in both House, Senate. (Interview with Congressman James R. Jones and Capt Frank Manson) illus Officer 52:11 Feb '76

RETIREMENT PAY

Army costs out benefit losses. Gene Famiglietti. AF Times 36:2 Mar 1 '76

Big new tax law opens IRAs (Individual Retirement Accounts) to Reservists but curbs disability tax breaks. Officer 52:17 Nov '76

Congress seen almost certain to end 1% add-on to retired COL raises. tab Officer 52:26 Aug '76

Cost-sharing pension eyed: Present system called too expensive. Randy Shoemaker. AF Times 36:3 Jan 26 '76

DMC (Defense Manpower Commission) asks annuities hike. Randy Shoemaker. AF Times 36:3 May 10 '76

Debate on TV: (Rep Les) Aspin vs (Col George) Henrikus. illus AF Times 37:16+ Dec 13 '76

Dual comp suit (by) 700 retired officers asks millions. Lee Ewing. AF Times 37:10 Aug 2 '76

EM being misled on retired pay, (Rep Les) Aspin's claim. AF Times 36:3 Jan 26 '76

Few advantages and many drawbacks in delaying first retirement check. Col A. H. Humphreys. Officer 52:25 Jun '76

5.4 percent pay boost due retirees March 1. AF Times 36:22 Feb 2 '76

Hill to weigh more retiree benefits. AF Times 37:4 Nov 22 '76

House ready to vote on killing kicker. AF Times 37:2 Aug 9 '76

IRA (Individual Retirement Accounts) clause due for push in both House, Senate. (Interview with Congressman James R. Jones and Capt Frank Manson) illus Officer 52:11 Feb '76

IRA (Individual Retirement Accounts) not for (active) military. AF Times 36:24 Jun 28 '76

(Imputed) retired 'contribution' scored. Bob Schweitz. AF Times 36:6 Feb 2 '76

In the (military pay) crunch it'll be up to Congress. Bruce Callander. AF Times 37:4 Oct 18 '76

Joint unit (House-Senate conference committee) agrees to kill 1% kicker, (but provides for) semiannual COL raise. AF Times 37:3 Sep 27 '76

Most retirees to lose unemployment dollars. AF Times 37:26 Nov 1 '76

New group (special congressional task force) probes pensions. AF Times 36:19 Feb 16 '76

94th Congress is history--many last-minute actions affect Reserves. Officer 52:12-13+ Dec '76

145,000 are 'double dippers.' AF Times 37:3 Nov 8 '76

Pay-as-you-go retirement full of pitfalls, GAO says. Randy Shoemaker. AF Times 36:3 Mar 22 '76

Pay not depressed for retirement $$: (3d Quadrennial Review of Military Compensation). AF Times 36:57 Jul 12 '76

(Pension) funds 'time bomb' cited by (Sen Thomas) Eagleton. AF Times 36:3 Jan 26 '76

RETIREMENT PAY - Continued

Pension system under (Rep Les) Aspin fire. AF Times 36:8 Apr 12 '76

President (Ford) urges repeal of (1%) 'kicker.' Randy Shoemaker. AF Times 36:3 Apr 5 '76

Recomp: Still not much prospect. Lee Ewing. AF Times 36:49 Apr 19 '76

(Rep Les) Aspin bills would overhaul pay. Phil Stevens. AF Times 37:4 Oct 18 '76

(Rep Les) Aspin continues attack on retiree pay. AF Times 37:10 Dec 20 '76

Retired money eyed as divorce pay. AF Times 37:11 Oct 18 '76

Retired pay reform: Aspin answers critics again. AF Times 37:11 Oct 11 '76

Retiree tax break urged (by TROA). AF Times 36:3 May 10 '76

(Retirees) COL hikes: No sweat on 'trigger.' AF Times 37:8 Nov 15 '76

Retirees get 5.4% raise in March but next raises may drop 1% add-on. Officer 52:27 Mar '76

Retirees to get option (to have pay sent directly to banks electronically). AF Times 36:33 Apr 12 '76

Why (Rep Les) Aspin wants to change (military retirement) system. AF Times 37:28-29 Sep 6 '76

Wilson on retirement benefits. (Interview with Rep Bob Wilson) illus AF Times 36:23 Mar 22 '76

RETRAINING PROGRAM

Air Force

Base-choice plan 1st-shirt incentive. AF Times 37:41 Dec 27 '76

80 skills identified for EM retraining. AF Times 36:18 Jan 19 '76

First shirts can leave field to retrain after 36 months. AF Times 37:61 Oct 18 '76

Job-finding opens re-up door: Chance for retraining. Bruce Callander. AF Times 36:12 May 10 '76

Low AQE (Airman Qualifying Examination) scorers urged to try again. Bruce Callander. AF Times 36:3 Jul 5 '76

NCO retrainees due $$. AF Times 37:8 Aug 16 '76

New colonels offered procurement training. AF Times 37:6 Oct 25 '76

O-5s can cross-train in new fields. AF Times 37:26 Sep 20 '76

Personnel must meet prerequisite qualifications before retraining is approved. TIG Brief 28:15 Jul 16 '76

Reg (AFR 39-4) gives details on job switching. AF Times 37:26 Nov 1 '76

SRBs cut, retrainees protected. Bruce Callander. AF Times 36:4 Mar 8 '76

Some can retrain for 2d re-up $$. Bruce Callander. AF Times 36:5 Mar 29 '76

Strength, skill, top EM problems: Pieces in TOPCAP puzzle. Bruce Callander. AF Times 36:26 Jan 26 '76

Top NCOs getting retraining bid. AF Times 37:8 Aug 2 '76

Top NCOs moving to shortage skills. Bruce Callander. AF Times 37:2 Dec 13 '76

RETRAINING PROGRAM - Continued

Air Force - Cont'd

Training change opens 200 skills. Len Famiglietti. AF Times 36:4 Apr 5 '76

What's good about switching skills. AF Times 37:19 Aug 9 '76

REVENUE SHARING

Are the cities saveable? illus Govt Exec 8:18-20+ Nov '76

Jacksonville (Fla): Consolidation is no panacea. illus chart Govt Exec 8:24-26+ Nov '76

REVETMENTS

Gabions control erosion. illus Mil Engr 68:28-29 Jan-Feb '76

REVIEWS, MILITARY see Military Ceremonies, Honors and Salutes

REVOLUTIONARY WAR--U.S.

Airmen of foot. (A volunteer troupe at Offutt AFB, Nebr, modeled after the 2d Maryland Regiment of Foot, reenacts battles of the Revolutionary War) MSgt Harold Newcomb. illus Airman 20:42-47 Jan '76

America's first Chief Engineer (Col Richard Gridley). Raleigh B. Buzzaird. (Reprinted from Military Engineer, Dec 1947) illus map Mil Engr 68:31-36 Jan-Feb '76

The Army of Lord Cornwallis: A study of logistics inadequacies. James L. Carpenter, Jr. illus map Log Spectrum 10:5-13 Fall '76

Background of freedom. (South Carolina in the Revolutionary War) Maj Jamie W. Walton. illus Mil Rev 56:56-57 Aug '76

The battle at Moore's Creek Bridge (NC). James D. Deerin. illus Natl Guardsman 30:2-5 Feb '76

The Battle of Fort Washington: One of the worst American defeats of the Revolutionary War. Bruce P. Hargreaves. illus map Natl Guardsman 30:2-5 Nov '76

Bayonets at midnight. (Battle of Stoney Point, 1779) 2dLt John L. Clarke. illus map Mil Rev 56:42-46 Nov '76

The Boston Massacre. Cecil B. Currey. Mil Rev 56:56-57 Oct '76

Bunker Hill. Col John H. Mason and Walter F. Mackie. illus Mil Engr 68:166-170 May-Jun '76

Cantankerous commander (artillery officer John Lamb during the American Revolution). Fairfax Downey. illus Natl Def 61:214-216 Nov-Dec '76

Continental Army logistics: An overview. illus Army Log 8:12-13 Jul-Aug '76

Continental Army logistics: Clothing supply. illus Army Log 8:28-32 Mar-Apr '76; Def Trans J 32: 28-30+ Oct '76

Continental Army logistics: Food supply. illus Army Log 8:24-28 Jan-Feb '76

Continental Army logistics: Transportation . (Reprinted from Army Logistician, Nov-Dec 1975) illus map Def Trans J 32:28-31 Aug '76

The Continental Congress: Management by committee and board. H. James Henderson. illus Def Mgt J 12:3-6 Jul '76

Contributors to the cause: Many valiant women helped blaze freedom's trail. Janet Hake. illus Soldiers 31:15-16 Jul '76

REVOLUTIONS - Continued

Theoretical and methodological problems in the analysis of governmental coercion and collective violence. David Snyder. illus J Pol & Mil Sociol 4: 277-293 Fall '76

RHODESIA

Former GIs reported fighting in Rhodesia. AF Times 37:21 Dec 27 '76

Economic Conditions

The influence of transnational actors on the enforcement of sanctions against Rhodesia. Harry R. Strack. illus Nav War Col Rev 28:52-64 Spring '76

Foreign Relations

The influence of transnational actors on the enforcement of sanctions against Rhodesia. Harry R. Strack. illus Nav War Col Rev 28:52-64 Spring '76

Politics and Government

The influence of transnational actors on the enforcement of sanctions against Rhodesia. Harry R. Strack. illus Nav War Col Rev 28:52-64 Spring '76

RICKOVER, Hyman G.

Who shall run U.S. Navy. LtGen Ira C. Eaker, Ret. AF Times 36:17+ Jun 14 '76

RIDGWAY, Matthew B.

Former SACEURs: The 25th anniversary of SHAPE and Allied Command Europe. Gen Matthew B. Ridgway and others. por NATO's Fifteen Nations 21:36-39 Feb-Mar '76

RIENZI, Thomas M.

WWMCCS in transition: An Army view. MajGen Thomas M. Rienzi. Signal 30:67-70 Aug '76

RIFLES

BMT may start soon with modified M-16s. AF Times 37:8 Nov 29 '76

M16 vs AK (Avtomat Kalashnikov, Automatic Rifle): Which is better? Capt Jack T. Kornfeld. illus tabs Infantry 66:38-41 Nov-Dec '76

Practice makes perfect. (Marksmanship matches, clubs, and awards) Sgt1C Floyd Harrington. illus Soldiers 31:42-44 Jun '76

Wild bore: The hunt for an elusive new NATO rifle caliber. Def & For Aff Dig No.6:16+ '76

RILEY, Paul H.

Defense in struggle over (overseas) goods shipping. Interview. Paul H. Riley. AF Times 36:4 Jul 12 '76

RIOT CONTROL

The Army as cop. Martin Blumenson. illus Army 26: 50-56 May '76

Equipment

The AT105 series: A new family of internal security vehicles from Britain. illus tabs Intl Def Rev 9: 824-825 Oct '76

Internal security equipment. illus tabs Intl Def Rev 9:820-823 Oct '76

Training

Riot strategy switched (by SPs). AF Times 36:24 Jul 12 '76

RIOTS

Mobilizing people for collective political action. (Paper, American Sociological Assoc, San Francisco, Aug 1975) Kenneth L. Wilson and Anthony M. Orum. J Pol & Mil Sociol 4:187-202 Fall '76

Theoretical and methodological problems in the analysis of governmental coercion and collective violence. David Snyder. illus J Pol & Mil Sociol 4: 277-293 Fall '76

RISNER, Robinson

Day after the night. (Former POW reflects on his experiences) Interview. BrigGen Robinson Risner. por Airman 20:30-34 Sep '76

RIVER CROSSING, MILITARY see Stream Crossing, Military

RIVERINE OPERATIONS

See also
Vietnamese Conflict, 1957-1975 --Riverine Operations

RIVERO, Horacio, Jr

Spain: Free World asset. ADM Horacio Rivero, Ret. por Strat Rev 4:66-71 Spring '76

RIVERS see Waterways

ROADS

Night flight. Capt Richard P. Keida. illus Aerosp Safety 32:18-19 Apr '76

ROBERTS, James M., Jr

ROA (Executive Director Gen J. Milnor Roberts) tells senators (Manpower and Personnel Subcommittee of the Senate Armed Services Committee) world will see U.S. Reserve cuts as weakening. Officer 52:4 Apr '76

ROBERTS, John W.

Air Training Command. por AF Mag 59:62-63 May '76

Management and command--possible confusion today? LtGen John W. Roberts. TIG Brief 28:2 Jul 16 '76

Spirit of America. (Remarks, Commissioning Ceremonies, Texas A&M, Dec 13, 1975) LtGen John W. Roberts. AF Plcy Ltr for Comdrs: Sup No. 4: 21-25 Apr '76

ROCKEFELLER, Nelson A.

Rocky: 5% cap (on pay increases for federal and military workers) OK at present. Donna Peterson. por AF Times 36:39 Feb 9 '76

ROCKET BOOSTERS see Boosters

ROCKET PROPULSION

History

William Moore: A pioneer in the theory of rocket dynamics. Frank H. Winter and Mitchell R. Sharpe. illus Spaceflight 18:179-182 May '76

ROCKETS

See also
Missiles

ROCKETS - Continued

Engines

A decade on ... A retrospective look at major space achievements. David Baker. illus Spaceflight pt 1, Gemini. 16:174+ May '74; pt 2, Ranger 7. 16:276 Jul '74; pt 3, Mariner 4. 16:418 Nov '74; pt 4, Voskhod 2. 17:197 May '75; pt 5, F-1: The clustered giant. 17:234 Jun '75; pt 6, NASA EVA-1 (Extra-Vehicular Activity): The first of 39. 17:331-332 Aug-Sep '75; pt 7, The Russian-Venus probes. 17:446 Dec '75; pt 8, Gemini 8: First docking, first abort. 18:153 Apr '76; pt 9, Surveyor on the moon. 18:228 Jun '76; pt 10, Orbiters to the moon. 18:291 Jul-Aug '76

Ion engines from Farnborough. Robert Edgar. illus tab Spaceflight 18:144-145 Apr '76

Soviet rocket engines--some new details. Anthony Kenden. illus tabs Spaceflight 18:223-226 Jun '76

Fuels·
See Propellants

Launching

We need an MRL (Multiple Rocket Launcher). LtCol W.H.Rees. Fld Arty J pt 1, An airman's view. 44:30-34 Nov-Dec '76

Reliability

We need an MRL (Multiple Rocket Launcher). LtCol W.H.Rees. Fld Arty J pt 1, An airman's view. 44:30-34 Nov-Dec '76

Brazil

Brazilian Army artillery rockets. Ronaldo S.Olive. illus Intl Def Rev 9:435-436 Jun '76

Germany

History

The first field artillery guided missile system (the German V-2 rocket). Capt Benjamin D.King. illus map Fld Arty J 44:57-60 Jul-Aug '76

Russia

Soviet rocket engines--some new details. Anthony Kenden. illus tabs Spaceflight 18:223-226 Jun '76

United States

Flexible firepower. (Fuses for airborne rockets) Steve Kimmel. illus (Also cutaways) Natl Def 60: 444-445 May-Jun '76

Remote set fuzing for 2.75-inch rocket. Alexander Janushevich. illus (Also cutaway) USA Avn Dig 22: 6-7+ Apr '76

ROCKETS, SOUNDING

Japan

Sounding rockets used by ISAS (Institute of Space and Aeronautical Sciences, University of Tokyo). Table only. Spaceflight 18:103 Mar '76

ROCKWELL, James M.

DCA (Defense Communications Agency) management of DOD multiplex. MajGen James M.Rockwell and Maj Gordon W.Arbogast. Signal 31:11+ Sep '76

ROCKWELL INTERNATIONAL CORP

Evolution of the space shuttle. David Baker. illus (Also cutaways) tabs Spaceflight pt 1, 15:202-210 Jun '73; pt 2, 15:264-268 Jul '73; pt 3, 15:344-352 Sep '73; pt 4, 18:304-326+ Sep '76

ROGERS, Bernard W.

Gen Rogers named to succeed (Gen Fred C.) Weyand as Army Chief of Staff. Army 26:9-10 Sep '76

In U.S. Forces Command: 'Total Army' readiness. Gen Bernard W.Rogers. por Army 26:30-32+ Oct '76

New (Army) Chief of Staff. por Soldiers 31:2 Oct '76

New Army Chief of Staff: General Rogers brings vision and experience to this high office. por Natl Def 61:186-187 Nov-Dec '76

ROGERS, Felix M.

AFLC (Air Force Logistics Command): A delicate balance. Gen Felix M.Rogers. por Review 55:39+ Jan-Feb '76

Air Force Logistics Command. por AF Mag 59:58-59 May '76

The Logistics Command job. (Remarks, Iron Gate Chapter, Air Force Assoc, New York, Sep 29, 1976) Gen F.Michael Rogers. AF Plcy Ltr for Comdrs: Sup No.12:2-8 Dec '76

ROLES AND MISSIONS

Air Force--Great Britain

CINCUKAIR (Commander-IN-Chief United Kingdom AIR Forces): ACE's new one. illus NATO's Fifteen Nations 20:53-60 Dec '75-Jan '76

Air Force--U.S.

(ADM) Holloway/(Gen) Jones cooperation pact raises difficult questions. L.Edgar Prina. illus Sea Power 19:34-36 Jan '76

An active force for peace. LtGen James M.Keck. illus Combat Crew 27:3 Dec '76

Aerospace defense. (Remarks, American Defense Preparedness Assoc, Los Angeles, Oct 15, 1975) Gen Daniel James, Jr. AF Plcy Ltr for Comdrs: Sup No.1:2-10 Jan '76; Condensation. Natl Def 60: 289 Jan-Feb '76

The Air Force story. MSgt Dave Sylva. illus Aerosp Safety 32:4-9 Jul '76

Air interdiction in a European future war: Doctrine or dodo? WgComdr Alan Parkes. AU Rev 27:16-18 Sep-Oct '76

Continuity (of operations) planning. TIG Brief 28:11 Apr 23 '76

Flexibility--a state of mind. Gen Richard H.Ellis and LtCol Frank B.Horton III. illus Strat Rev 4: 26-36 Winter '76

Make service your profession. (Address, Air Force Engineering and Services Conference, Homestead AFB, Fla, Dec 1975) Gen Russell E.Dougherty. illus AF Engrg & Svcs Qtr 17:6-12 May '76

Mission effectiveness & base livability: A hypothesis. Lester H.Henriksen and Gary D.Vest. illus AF Engrg & Svcs Qtr 17:2-6 Nov '76

A new look at control of the seas. MajGen Robert N. Ginsburgh, Ret. Strat Rev 4:86-89 Winter '76

"Our" Air Force and its future. (Remarks, ROA National Convention, Bal Harbour, Fla, June 29-July 2, 1976) Gen Robert J.Dixon. illus Air Reservist 28:4-6 Aug-Sep '76

Pact expands AF role in backing Navy in war. AF Times 36:26 Apr 12 '76

ROLES AND MISSIONS - Continued

Air Force--U.S. - Cont'd

Space in the Air Force future. (Remarks, American Defense Preparedness Assoc, Oct 15, 1975) LtGen Thomas W. Morgan. AF Plcy Ltr for Comdrs: Sup No. 2:2-8 Feb '76; Condensation. Natl Def 60:290 Jan-Feb '76

Who needs nuclear tacair? Col David L. Nichols. illus AU Rev 27:15-25 Mar-Apr '76

Army--U.S.

Tough and ready--"to keep the peace ... to deter war." Interview. Army Chief of Staff, Gen Fred C. Weyand. illus Soldiers 31:31-34 Feb '76

Coast Guard--U.S.

The big patrol: Coast Guard gears up to monitor new fisheries zone. L. Edgar Prina. illus Sea Power 19:8-10 Sep '76

The Coast Guard: New missions, increased capabilities, always ready. ADM Owen W. Siler. illus Sea Power 19:14-20 Jan '76

The Coast Guard's personality: A product of changing roles and missions. LCDR Gary Russell, Ret. illus US Nav Inst Proc 102:38-45 Mar '76

Dirty work missions: The USCG strike force. illus Sea Power 19:11-13 Dec '76

The expanding Coast Guard mission. ADM O. W. Siler. illus Def Trans J 32:6-8+ Aug '76

Varied challenges for Coast Guard engineers. RADM Malcolm E. Clark. illus map Mil Engr 68:18-21 Jan-Feb '76

Marine Corps--U.S.

Brookings (Institution) defense study (Where Does the Marine Corps Go from Here?). LtCol W. R. Ball. MarCor Gaz 60:7-9 Mar '76

Emphasis on professionalism for a new generation of Marines. Gen Louis H. Wilson. illus Sea Power 19:24-29 Jan '76

Foreign policy and the Marine Corps. Maj W. Hays Parks. illus US Nav Inst Proc 102:18-25 Nov '76

Hard thinking on new ideas. Col R. C. Shreckengost. MarCor Gaz 60:53-54 Aug '76

Spirit of '76: 'The troops are looking good.' (A briefing to Congress) Gen Louis H. Wilson. illus tabs MarCor Gaz 60:11-22 Mar '76

Today's Marine Corps: Stepping out smartly. James W. Canan. illus Sea Power 19:14-18 Nov '76

Vital tool for our nation. (Amphibious forces) Capt Wayne S. Keck. MarCor Gaz 60:50-51 Aug '76

Navy--Russia

The Gorshkov doctrine: Seapower and the world ocean. L. Edgar Prina. illus Sea Power 19:33-37 Oct '76

Navy--U.S.

(ADM) Holloway/(Gen) Jones cooperation pact raises difficult questions. L. Edgar Prina. illus Sea Power 19:34-36 Jan '76

Can the Navy rebuild the U.S. fleet? John T. Hayward. Govt Exec 8:27+ Jul '76

A new look at control of the seas. MajGen Robert N. Ginsburgh, Ret. Strat Rev 4:86-89 Winter '76

ROLES AND MISSIONS - Continued

Navy--U.S. - Cont'd

Pact expands AF role in backing Navy in war. AF Times 36:26 Apr 12 '76

Reserve Forces--Army--Great Britain

A role for the uncommitted Reserve? LtCol Michael Burkham. RUSI J for Def Studies 121:43-45 Sep '76

Reserve Forces--Navy--U.S.

Another (Naval) Reserve study! (But this one, ordered by the Senate Armed Services Committee, promises much) Officer 52:19+ Aug '76

ROOSEVELT, Franklin D.

F.D.R. and the great War Department feud: (Harry H.) Woodring vs (Louis A.) Johnson. Keith D. McFarland. por Army 26:36-42 Mar '76

ROOSEVELT, Theodore

Sea power--Teddy's "big stick." (Alfred Mahan's influence on Theodore Roosevelt and U.S. history) CAPT Guy Cane. por US Nav Inst Proc 102:40-48 Aug '76

ROTATION

Army--U.S.

Hell on wheels. (Air Force and Army's 2d Armored Division (Brigade 75) train in West Germany for NATO support) MSgt Harold D. Newcomb. illus Airman 20:8-12 Apr '76

RULE OF THE ROAD AT SEA see Safety at Sea

RUMSFELD, Donald H.

Additional benefits sought (by DefSec Donald Rumsfeld). Randy Shoemaker. AF Times 37:3 Dec 20 '76

Budget keeps Rumsfeld busy. AF Times 36:10 Jan 12 '76

A command, control and communications overview. Donald H. Rumsfeld. por Signal 30:34-35+ May-Jun '76

Crisis: (DefSec) Rumsfeld and benefits. Randy Shoemaker. AF Times 37:4 Nov 29 '76

(DefSec Donald) Rumsfeld gives go-ahead on B-1: Carter could block it. Lee Ewing. AF Times 37:4 Dec 13 '76

(DefSec) Rumsfeld to evaluate rental proposal. Randy Shoemaker. AF Times 37:4 Sep 27 '76

Defense Department report--FY 77. (Statement before House Armed Services Committee, Washington, Jan 27, 1976) Donald H. Rumsfeld. AF Plcy Ltr for Comdrs: Sup No. 4:2-12 Apr '76

Defense hearings underway: Rumsfeld details plans for new weapons. Officer 52:5+ Mar '76

Defense posture needs fortifying, says (SecDef Donald H.) Rumsfeld. Len Famiglietti. AF Times 36:17 Feb 16 '76

Defense public information policy. (Memorandum, Jan 26, 1976) Donald H. Rumsfeld. AF Plcy Ltr for Comdrs: Sup No. 4:31-32 Apr '76

For the common defense: Secretary (of Defense) Rumsfeld must stand fast for adequate preparedness. por Natl Def 60:264-265 Jan-Feb '76

Future military preparedness. (Address, Naval Academy Graduation Ceremonies, Annapolis, June 2, 1976) Donald H. Rumsfeld. AF Plcy Ltr for Comdrs: Sup No. 8:2-7 Aug '76

RUMSFELD, Donald H. - Continued

(House Armed Services Committee) members scold (SecDef) Rumsfeld. Phil Stevens. AF Times 36:25 Feb 9 '76

The military balance today. Donald H. Rumsfeld. por Comdrs Dig 19: entire issue Mar 11 '76

The new SecDef: Donald H. Rumsfeld. L. Edgar Prina. Sea Power 18:17-18 Dec '75

Political prelude to a no-win scenario. James D. Hessman and Vincent C. Thomas. por Sea Power 18:23-24 Dec '75

Preserving a balance of power. (Address, Reuters 125th anniversary dinner, New York, March 10, 1976) Donald H. Rumsfeld. AF Pley Ltr for Comdrs: Sup No. 5:2-9 May '76

Rumsfeld: 'Modification' of pay--salary system rejected. Randy Shoemaker. AF Times 37:4 Dec 6 '76

Rumsfeld--1, Press--0 in initial outing. (Excerpts from press conference with DefSec Rumsfeld, Dec 22, 1975) F. Clifton Berry, Jr. por Armed Forces J Intl 113:6-7 Jan '76

The Sunday morning massacre: A murder-suicide? Aaron Latham. (Reprinted from New York, Dec 22, 1975) por Armed Forces J Intl 113:18-25 Jan '76

U.S. defense in an era of détente. (Acceptance address, Washington, Nov 20, 1975) Donald H. Rumsfeld. por AF Mag 59:15 Jan '76

U.S. defense perspectives. Donald H. Rumsfeld. por Comdrs Dig 19: entire issue Aug 26 '76

"The United States should possess a military capability second to none." Donald H. Rumsfeld. por Comdrs Dig 19:2-4 Jan 8 '76

RUNWAYS

Aircraft tire damage due to grooved runways. illus Approach 21:16-17 Mar '76

How to prevent runway directional control accidents. TIG Brief 28:9-10 Nov 5 '76

Reviewing the fine print. Capt M. C. Kostelnik. illus TAC Attack 16:22-24 Jul '76

Ride the foam. illus Aerosp Safety 32:2-4 Apr '76

Runway foaming ... an extinct species. CDR R. C. Gibson. illus tab Approach 22:3-5 Aug '76

Runway surface hazards. Capt Dannie O. Burk. illus tabs Aerosp Safety 32:8-11 Nov '76

'Unclear' clear zone. TIG Brief 28:3 Feb 13 '76

Visibility--to land or not to land. Capt John L. Wilson. illus Combat Crew pt 1, 27:22-23 Aug '76; pt 2, The runway environment. 27:18-20 Sep '76; pt 3, The rules. 27:26-27 Oct '76; pt 4, Going visual. 27:20-21 Nov '76; pt 5, Techniques. 27: 14-15 Dec '76

What every pilot should know about PFC (Porous Friction Course). Capt Richard E. Simmons. illus MAC Flyer 23:10-11 Nov '76

RUSHWORTH, Robert A.

Air Force Test and Evaluation Center. por AF Mag 59:96-97 May '76

RUSSIA

R. U. S. I. /R. M. A. S. Research Centre bulletin. (Précis, abstracts, or translations of whole articles from the Soviet press) Regular feature in issues of RUSI Journal for Defence Studies

RUSSIA - Continued

Economic Conditions

CIA's Soviet market forecast: Mixed. Edgar Ulsamer. AF Mag 59:64-68 Nov '76

Confident growth. (Tatar Autonomous Soviet Socialist Republic) F. Tabeyev. illus Soviet Mil Rev No. 3: 11-14 Mar '76

The food weakness. (State of the Soviets) Ellis Tenant. illus tabs Def & For Aff Dig No. 6:11-14 '76

Grand construction programme. (Excerpt from report to the 25th CPSU Congress, "Guidelines for the Development of the National Economy of the USSR for 1976-1980") A. N. Kosygin. Soviet Mil Rev No. 5:2-4 May '76

A land transformed beyond recognition (Kirghiz Soviet Socialist Republic). Akhmatbek Suyumbayev. illus Soviet Mil Rev No. 1:6-7+ Jan '76

Ossetia transformed. (Interview with Mikhail Gatsirovich Tsagarayev) Col M. Zimenkov. illus Soviet Mil Rev No. 7:8-11 Jul '76

The Soviet approach to détente. Peter Wiles. (Reprinted from NATO Review, Oct 1975) illus Mil Rev 56:28-33 Jun '76

Economic Policy

CIA's Soviet market forecast: Mixed. Edgar Ulsamer. AF Mag 59:64-68 Nov '76

Confident growth. (Tatar Autonomous Soviet Socialist Republic) F. Tabeyev. illus Soviet Mil Rev No. 3: 11-14 Mar '76

Development of (Soviet) transport (in 10th 5-year-plan period, 1976-1980). G. Alexeyev. illus Soviet Mil Rev No. 8:6-8 Aug '76

The food weakness. (State of the Soviets) Ellis Tenant. illus tabs Def & For Aff Dig No. 6:11-14 '76

The good of man, the primary goal. G. Alexeyev. tabs Soviet Mil Rev No. 12:12-13 Dec '76

Grand construction programme. (Excerpt from report to the 25th CPSU Congress, "Guidelines for the Development of the National Economy of the USSR for 1976-1980") A. N. Kosygin. Soviet Mil Rev No. 5:2-4 May '76

Science in the service of economy. G. Alexeyev. illus Soviet Mil Rev No. 11:8-9 Nov '76

Scientific progress and defensive potential. MajGen I. Anureyev. Soviet Mil Rev No. 2:13-15 Feb '76

Steady strides ahead. G. Alexeyev. tab illus Soviet Mil Rev No. 6:7-9 Jun '76

(USSR) farming prospects (under the 10th five-year plan). G. Alexeyev. illus Soviet Mil Rev No. 7:6-7 Jul '76

Foreign Economic Relations

Foreign economic ties of the USSR. (Interview with Vladimir Alkhimov) illus Soviet Mil Rev No. 9:50-52 Sep '76

Foreign Policy

The balancing of L. I. Brezhnev. Lawrence Griswold. illus Sea Power 18:11-16 Dec '75

The Brezhnev report (to the 25th CPSU Congress): The meaning of words. Charles T. Baroch. illus Strat Rev 4:118-120 Summer '76

Detente and the Yom Kippur War: From crisis management to crisis prevention? Phil Williams. Royal Air Forces Qtr 16:227-233 Autumn '76

RUSSIA - Continued

Foreign Policy - Cont'd

European security: Soviet preferences and priorities. John Erickson. Strat Rev 4:37-43 Winter '76

The Helsinki agreement and self-determination. Stefan Korbonski. illus Strat Rev 4:48-58 Summer '76

Helsinki and military détente. (Conference on Security and Cooperation in Europe) Col O.Ivanov. Soviet Mil Rev No.8:44-46 Aug '76

Lasting peace and security for Asia. Y.Lugovskoi. Soviet Mil Rev No.7:56-58 Jul '76

Nearing the climacteric 1976. A.H.S.Candlin. Army Qtr 106:194-203 Apr '76

A new American defensive doctrine for Europe? Harold C.Deutsch. illus Parameters 6, No.1:18-34 '76

New horizons of the peace programme. (25th CPSU Congress) Soviet Mil Rev No.6:2-4 Jun '76

The Peace Programme (adopted by the 25th CPSU Congress, Feb 1976), a contribution to the weal of mankind. Y.Tarabrin. illus Soviet Mil Rev No.3: 7-10 Mar '76

The scrambled geometry of the new Pacific: West of the Dateline and East of India. Lawrence Griswold. illus Sea Power 19:24-29 Apr '76

The Soviet view of navies in peacetime. Uri Ra'anan. illus Nav War Col Rev 29:30-38 Summer '76

The state of the Soviets. Gregory Copley. illus Def & For Aff Dig No.6:6-9+ '76

Foreign Relations

For the sake of peace and socialism. (The 25th CPSU Congress, Feb 24-March 5, 1976) Soviet Mil Rev No.4:2-5 Apr '76

The Soviet approach to détente. Peter Wiles. (Reprinted from NATO Review, Oct 1975) illus Mil Rev 56:28-33 Jun '76

Africa

Africa strategy. Gregory Copley. illus Def & For Aff Dig No.3:6-9+ '76

Angola

Dawn of freedom for Angola. M.Zenovich. illus Soviet Mil Rev No.5:46-48 May '76

The Soviet intervention in Angola: Intentions and implications. Peter Vanneman and Martin James. tabs Strat Rev 4:92-103 Summer '76

Why Russia wants Angola. LtGen Ira C.Eaker, Ret. AF Times 36:13+ Jan 19 '76

Asia

Lasting peace and security for Asia. Y.Lugovskoi. Soviet Mil Rev No.7:56-58 Jul '76

Asia, Southeastern

The USSR-DRV-PRC triangle in Southeast Asia. Donald E.Weatherbee. illus Parameters 6, No.1: 71-86 '76

China (People's Republic)

Peking and Soviet-Chinese relations. I.Alexandrov. Soviet Mil Rev No.9:55-58 Sep '76

The Soviet military machine: Morale, muscles, and megatons. Col Robert D.Heinl, Jr, Ret. illus Sea Power 19:31-34 May '76

RUSSIA - Continued

Foreign Relations - Cont'd

Cuba

Cuba: Russia's foreign legion. Col Robert Debs Heinl, Jr, Ret. illus Sea Power 19:44-45 Mar '76

India

Ever strengthening cooperation. (5th anniversary, Soviet-Indian Treaty of Peace, Friendship and Cooperation) V.Yefremov. Soviet Mil Rev No.8:47-48 Aug '76

Indian Ocean Region

From Moscow, South by Southeast. Maj William G. Hanne. illus tab map Mil Rev 56:47-55 Jan '76

Iraq

Soviet military aid to Iraq and Syria. Roger F.Pajak. illus Strat Rev 4:51-59 Winter '76

Libya

Soviet arms aid to Libya. Roger F.Pajak. illus Mil Rev 56:82-87 Jul '76

Middle East

Conflict in the Middle East. (Conclusions, lessons and opinions) K.Vologdin. Soviet Mil Rev No.6: 44-46 Jun '76

Soviet military aid to Iraq and Syria. Roger F.Pajak. illus Strat Rev 4:51-59 Winter '76

Soviet policy toward the Middle East since the October 1973 Arab-Israeli War. Robert O.Freedman. illus Nav War Col Rev 29:61-103 Fall '76

Norway

The Nordic balance. Col Arthur E.Dewey. illus map Strat Rev 4:49-60 Fall '76

Syria

Soviet military aid to Iraq and Syria. Roger F.Pajak. illus Strat Rev 4:51-59 Winter '76

United States

American-Soviet relations: Informal remarks. Helmut Sonnenfeldt. illus Parameters 6, No.1:12-17 '76

"Detente" in Soviet strategy. G.M.Bailly-Cowell. NATO's Fifteen Nations 20:86-90 Dec '75-Jan '76

Erroneous doctrines misshaping perceptions of U.S. defense needs. (Excerpts from address, Montgomery, Ala, Jan 26, 1976) Robert Ellsworth. Armed Forces J Intl 113:29 Feb '76

SALT: Time to quit. Colin S.Gray. illus Strat Rev 4:14-22 Fall '76

U.S.-Soviet detente: The nature of the relationship and Soviet aims. Col Don O.Stovall. illus Natl Sec Aff Forum No.24:13-22 Spring-Summer '76

War survival in Soviet strategy. Foy D.Kohler. AF Mag 59:90-92+ Sep '76

Vietnam (Democratic Republic)

Lessons of Vietnam. Col O.Ivanov. Soviet Mil Rev No.4:44-46 Apr '76

Politics and Government

The balancing of L.I.Brezhnev. Lawrence Griswold. illus Sea Power 18:11-16 Dec '75

Boris Nikolayevich Ponomarev: Run silent, run deep. Stefan Possony. illus Def & For Aff Dig No.11: 6-9+ '75

RUSSIA - Continued

Politics and Government - Cont'd

Democracy in action. (25th Congress of the CPSU and the development of the political system of Soviet society) Y. Todorsky. Soviet Mil Rev No. 8:2-5 Aug '76

Grand construction programme. (Excerpt from report to the 25th CPSU Congress, "Guidelines for the Development of the National Economy of the USSR for 1976-1980") A. N. Kosygin. Soviet Mil Rev No. 5:2-4 May '76

Political controls within the structure of the Soviet Armed Forces--some problems? Pilot Officer R.G.Smith. Royal Air Forces Qtr 16:45-49 Spring '76

The Soviet approach to détente. Peter Wiles. (Reprinted from NATO Review, Oct 1975) illus Mil Rev 56:28-33 Jun '76

RUSSIA - Continued

Politics and Government - Cont'd

The Soviet view of navies in peacetime. Uri Ra'anan. illus Nav War Col Rev 29:30-38 Summer '76

Social Conditions

A land transformed beyond recognition (Kirghiz Soviet Socialist Republic). Akhmatbek Suyumbayev. illus Soviet Mil Rev No. 1:6-7+ Jan '76

RYAN, Michael P.

Brookings study in error, says (MajGen) Ryan; the Marine Corps Reserve is ready. por Officer 52:16 May '76

RYAN, Thomas M., Jr

Maintenance participation provides innovative action (in Olympic Arena '76). MajGen T.M.Ryan, Jr. Combat Crew 27:8-9 Apr '76

S

S A B M I S (Strategic Antiballistic Missile Intercept System) see Missile Defense

S A C see Strategic Air Command

SACEUR see Allied Command Europe

SALT see Arms Control

SAMSO see Space and Missile Systems Organization

SAMTEC see Space and Missile Test Center

SAR see Search and Rescue

SES see Air Cushion Vehicles

SHAPE see Supreme Headquarters Allied Powers in Europe

SOF see Special Operations Force

SOLE see Society of Logistics Engineers

STOL see Airplanes, V/STOL

SABOTAGE

AFR 205-57 ("Reporting and Investigating Espionage, Sabotage, Terrorism and Subversion") is applicable to all USAF personnel. TIG Brief 28:6 May 7 '76

Reporting and Investigating Espionage, Sabotage, Terrorism, and Subversion. (AFR 205-57) Contact, p 2, Spring '76

SADLER, Thomas M.

Taking care of our people. (Security police force) MajGen Thomas M. Sadler. TIG Brief 28:3 Apr 23 '76

SAFEGUARD ABM SYSTEM

Safeguard (Ballistic Missile Defense System) Center to close. illus AF Times 36:41 Mar 1 '76

SAFETY AT SEA

The Coast Guard: New missions, increased capabilities, always ready. ADM Owen W. Siler. illus Sea Power 19:14-20 Jan '76

Searching for icebergs. (Coast Guard and International Ice Patrol work to prevent another Titanic disaster) Marianne Lester. illus AF Times, Times Magazine sup:10-14+ Jul 12 '76

SAFETY MEASURES see
Flying Safety
Ground Safety
Water Safety
   also subdivision Safety Measures under specific subjects, e.g.,
Aircraft Carriers--Safety Measures
Airplanes--Safety Measures
Airplanes, Military--Safety Measures
Gunnery--Safety Measures
Helicopters--Safety Measures

Helicopters, Military--Safety Measures
Missiles--Safety Measures
Nuclear Weapons--Safety Measures
Radar--Safety Measures
Ships--Safety Measures

SAFETY PROGRAMS

One man's battle against OSHA (Occupational Safety and Health Administration). Raymond J. Larson. Govt Exec 8:36 Jan '76

SAFETY PROGRAMS - Continued

Air Force

The ABC's of safety involvement. LtCol Jay M. Strayer. illus MAC Flyer 23:16-19 Apr '76

Additional duty safety training. TIG Brief 28:5 May 7 '76

Air Force nuclear surety program. illus TIG Brief 28:5-6 Apr 23 '76

Attention to health/safety matters. TIG Brief 28:5-6 Feb 27 '76

The challenge of safety. (Report on 1975 SAC Safety Seminar, Carswell AFB, Tex) Maj Richard W. Blatter. illus Combat Crew 26:8-11 Jan '76

The cost of noncompliance. TIG Brief 28:3 Jul 16 '76

The FSO (Flight Safety Officer). LtCol David E. Raley. illus Aerosp Safety 32:15-17 Mar '76

Feedback and USAF accident board recommendations. Maj T. R. Allocca. illus Aerosp Safety 32:18-19 Jun '76

High-speed, low-level training routes. TIG Brief 28:8 May 21 '76

Home on the range. Maj John N. P. Reisbick. illus TAC Attack 16:8-9 Jan '76

Human-factor-caused mishaps: A subject of continuing concern. TIG Brief 28:6 Dec 3 '76

Moody maze saves lives (at Moody AFB, Ga). Capt Bob Revell. illus tab TAC Attack 16:12-13 Mar '76

Motherhood, apple pie and safety. LtCol Richard B. Durant. illus Aerosp Safety 32:12-13 Jan '76

NonNuclear Munitions Safety Group (NNMSG). TIG Brief 28:15 Sep 24 '76

Occupational safety and health programs. TIG Brief 28:3 Jan 30 '76

SAC nuclear safety training. TIG Brief 28:5 May 7 '76

Safety Analysis Summary (SAS). TIG Brief 28:11-12 Apr 9 '76

Safety awards (presented to Alaskan Air Command and Air Training Command in recognition of the most effective accident prevention programs during 1975). TIG Brief 28:10 Apr 9 '76

Safety awards: USAF Nuclear Safety Certificates. TIG Brief 28:6 Jun 4 '76

Safety is everyone's business. Capt Jerry I. Grabeklis. illus Combat Crew 27:20-21 Mar '76

Safety program management: What's new? TIG Brief 28:6 Jun 4 '76

Son of a ruddy duck. (Fleagle, an accident-prone bird drawn by Stan Hardison, teaches safety to TAC Attack readers) MSgt Harold Newcomb. illus Airman 20:12-16 Aug '76

The supervisor and hazard reporting. TIG Brief 28:11 Apr 9 '76

A supervisor's responsibility. TIG Brief 28:4 Jan 30 '76

System safety engineering programs. (AFR 127-8) TIG Brief 28:8 Mar 12 '76

Traffic safety education. TIG Brief 28:12 Sep 24 '76

The unit commander as a safety program director. LtCol Alan D. Miedrich. illus Interceptor 18:26-28 Jun '76

SAFETY PROGRAMS - Continued

Armed Forces

DOD Explosives Safety Board surveys. TIG Brief 28:5 Jul 16 '76

Army

Rocky Mountain haven. (Rocky Mountain Arsenal (RMA)) Darryl D. McEwen. illus Soldiers 31:49-51 Aug '76

To your health! Ted Kontos. illus USA Avn Dig 22: 32-35 Jul '76

The vanishing yellow helmet. LtCol Jon Porter. illus tab Fld Arty J 44:12-17 Mar-Apr '76

Navy

Aeromedical safety operations: A new concept in aviation accident prevention and investigation. CDR A.F.Wells. illus Approach 21:18-21 Jun '76

The air wing duty safety officer. LCDR L.G.Mullin, Jr. illus Approach 22:10-11 Dec '76

Another big vote for NATOPS (Naval Air Training and Operating Procedures Standardization). CAPT I.Patch. illus Approach 21:12-13 Feb '76

CV safety organization--reality or lip service. CDR H.A.Petrich. illus tab Approach 21:1-4 Jan '76

CV safety problems: (USS) America's approach. CDR S.P.Dunlap. illus Approach 21:12-15 May '76

Crew rest. illus Approach 21:24-25 Jun '76

"The easiest job in the squadron." (Safety Officer) LCDR L.E.Gardiner. illus Approach 21:26-27 Dec '75

How about a modern safety program? LCDR Russ Harrison. illus Approach 22:24-25 Nov '76

Is safety really paramount? LCDR Frank Stauts. illus Approach 22:14-15 Oct '76

Lessons learned (in Naval Aviation). LT C.F.Wise. illus Approach 21:7-8 Nov '75

NATOPS (Naval Air Training and Operating Procedures Standardization) training: A total approach. LT Frederick D.Hansen. illus Approach 21:18-21 Dec '75

SAILING

The Navy needs more sailors. LCDR John B.Bonds. illus US Nav Inst Proc 102:38-43 Feb '76

SAILPLANES see Gliders

SALARIES see Income
    also subdivision Salaries and Wages under specific subjects, e.g.,
    Civilian Employees--U.S.--Salaries and Wages

SALUTES, MILITARY see Military Ceremonies, Honors and Salutes

SALVAGE

Nimrod Spar: Clearing the Suez Canal (of 10 wrecks). CAPT J.Huntly Boyd, Jr. illus map tab US Nav Inst Proc 102:18-26 Feb '76

Salvage of the (Great Lakes freighter) Sidney E. Smith. Maj Thomas J.Woodall. illus Mil Engr 68:448-451 Nov-Dec '76

VLCC aground: Everybody's problem. (International cooperation in refloating Shell VLCC tanker Metula, aground in the Strait of Magellan in 1974) CDR James A.Atkinson. illus US Nav Inst Proc 102:95-99 Mar '76

SALZER, Robert S.

The surface forces. VADM Robert S.Salzer, Ret. US Nav Inst Proc 102:26-35 Nov '76

SATELLITES, ARTIFICIAL

See also
Space Stations

Astronomical Applications

Russia's 'Orion' space observatories. (Interview with Grigor Gurzadian) illus Spaceflight 18:74 Feb '76

Communication Applications

See also
Air Force Satellite Communications Systems
Tactical Satellite Communications

(Advanced communications satellite--Satcom I) Signal 30:70 Feb '76

C^3 system engineering. CAPT George Heffernan. Signal 30:88-89 Aug '76

A command, control and communications overview. Donald H.Rumsfeld. illus Signal 30:34-35+ May-Jun '76

Communication services provided by environmental satellites. Joseph Fortuna. illus tabs Signal 30: 28-31 Apr '76

Defense satellite communications in the 1980s. illus tabs Countermeasures 2:46-48+ Dec '75-Jan '76

The ELF (Extremely Low Frequency) revolution: Satellites, Seafarer to change the face of Navy communications. John Rhea. illus Sea Power 19:41-44 Jul '76

The evolution of military satellite communications systems. Frederick E.Bond and CDR William H. Curry, Jr. illus tabs Signal 30:39-40+ Mar '76

First maritime (telecommunications) satellite (Marisat). Spaceflight 18:216-217 Jun '76

(405B program experimental satellite laser communications system) Signal 30:75 Feb '76

An industry perspective on satellites. Henry E. Hockeimer and others. illus Signal 30:60-74 Mar '76

MARISAT (MARitime SATellites): Launching a new era in marine communications. Charles DeVore. Signal 30:36 Mar '76

Military satellite communications terminals. Col Fred M.Knipp and Joseph A.Buegler. illus Signal 30:12-16+ Mar '76

NATO satellite communications: Past, present, future. LtGen Harold A.Kissinger. illus Signal 30: 53-57 Mar '76

(NATO-IIIA communications satellite began operations, July 1976) Signal 31:76 Sep '76

A Navy satellite communications system. VADM Jon L.Boyes. Signal 30:5+ Mar '76

Operational considerations for tactical satellite communications systems. Maj John M.Kuhn. illus Signal 30:29-31 Mar '76

The pervasive importance of USAF's space mission. Interview. LtGen Thomas W.Morgan. illus AF Mag 59:46-50 Jan '76

RCA Satcom system update. Philip Schneider. illus Signal 30:52-55 Jul '76

(Satcom II launched) map Signal 30:150 May-Jun '76

SATELLITES, ARTIFICIAL - Continued

Communication Applications - Cont'd

Satellite communications at the Goddard Space Flight
Center. John F. Clark and William N. Redisch. tab
illus Signal 30:46-52 Mar '76

Technology: Its impact on the 1980s. Joseph A. Boyd.
illus tabs Signal 30:50-54 May-Jun '76

Telecommunications: The leading edge of defense effectiveness. Donald R. Beall. illus Signal 30:16-21
Jan '76

A time for transition for naval communications.
CAPT Milton J. Schultz, Jr. illus map Signal 30:
84-87 Aug '76

Venus-Earth space communication line functioning.
LtCol N. Kharitonov. Soviet Mil Rev No. 2:38
Feb '76

Testing

(First FLTSATCOM (FLeeT SATellite COMmunications) satellite assembled in an operational config-
uration) Signal 30:90 Mar '76

Detection

See also
Space Detection and Tracking System

Earth Sciences Applications

Earth resources management: The role of the Fucino
ground station. illus map Interavia 31:886-887
Sep '76

Landsat: A routine problem-solving tool for naval
officers. Bruce H. Needham. illus tabs US Nav
Inst Proc 102:94-97 Aug '76

Satellite monitors strip mines. Spaceflight 18:364
Oct '76

Senator Moss pushes info satellite system. (Conden-
sation of address, U.S. Senate, Washington,
Aug 9, 1976) Frank Moss. AF Times 37:18+
Aug 30 '76

Educational Applications

Instructional technology in the Department of Defense, now and in the future. M. Richard Rose.
illus tab AU Rev 27:11-23 May-Jun '76

Launching

Chronology

Japanese satellites successfully launched. Table only.
Spaceflight 18:105 Mar '76

NASA satellite launch programme for 1976. Table
only. Interavia 31:204 Mar '76

Satellite digest; a monthly listing of all known satellites and spacecraft. Table only. Spaceflight 18:
32-33 Jan '76; 18:72 Feb '76; 18:110-111 Mar '76;
18:152 Apr '76; 18:192 May '76; 18:229-230 Jun '76;
18:297-298 Jul-Aug '76; 18:337-338 Sep '76; 18:374
Oct '76; 18:411 Nov '76; 18:448-449 Dec '76

USSR's 1975 recon/survey flights. Table only. Elect
Warfare 8:107 Mar-Apr '76

Meteorological Applications

See also
Space Project--Nimbus

Army Aviation applications of meteorological satellites. Willis L. Webb. illus USA Avn Dig 22:1-3+
Sep '76

SATELLITES, ARTIFICIAL - Continued

Meteorological Applications - Cont'd

(First operational geostationary satellite for meteorological use) Signal 30:147 Jan '76

Managing by exception in space systems operation--
the Four Grand experience. Col Gerald J. Win-
chell. illus tab Def Mgt J 12:64-68 Oct '76

(Transportable weather satellite receiving terminal)
Signal 30:86 Jul '76

Weather probability forecasts: A cost-saving tech-
nique in space launch and missile test operations.
MajGen Herbert A. Lyon, Ret, and LtCol Lynn L.
LeBlanc. illus tabs AU Rev 27:45-54 Jan-Feb '76

Navigation Applications

ATC systems for tomorrow. Dale Milford. illus
Aerosp Intl 12:26-28+ Mar-Apr '76

Modern navigational systems. Comdr C. J. Eliot, Ret.
illus NATO's Fifteen Nations 20:72-77 Dec '75-
Jan '76

NAVSTAR technology. David Holmes. illus tab Countermeasures 2:27-28+ Dec '76

Satellite navigation. (Tri-Service NAVSTAR Global
Positioning Systems (GPS)) illus tab Countermeasures 2:6-7+ Dec '75-Jan '76

Satellite navigation: Multiplying the North Star. (Reprinted from Skyline, Spring 1975) illus Navigator
23:27-29 Spring '76

Oceanographic Applications

Landsat: A routine problem-solving tool for naval
officers. Bruce H. Needham. illus tabs US Nav
Inst Proc 102:94-97 Aug '76

Orbits

Orbits of Soviet deep space probes. Phillip S. Clark.
illus tabs Spaceflight pt 1, 18:139-141 Apr '76;
pt 2, 18:188-189 May '76

Scientific Uses

See also
Satellites, Artificial--Astronomical Applications
Satellites, Artificial--Meteorological Applications
Satellites, Artificial--Oceanographic Applications
also specific satellites under project name,
e.g.,
Space Project--Mariner

COS B--ESA (European Space Agency) off the ground.
Robert Edgar. illus Spaceflight 18:28-30 Jan '76

Communication services provided by environmental
satellites. Joseph Fortuna. illus tabs Signal 30:
28-31 Apr '76

Development of the Satellite Solar Power Station
(SSPS). Peter E. Glaser. illus tabs Spaceflight
18:198-208 Jun '76

Outlook for space. Dave Dooling. Spaceflight pt 1,
18:422-425 Dec '76

Satellite communications at the Goddard Space Flight
Center. John F. Clark and William N. Redisch. tab
illus Signal 30:46-52 Mar '76

Skylab experiment results. Robert Edgar. illus tabs
Spaceflight 18:59-67 Feb '76

Viking: Orbiter science equipment. David Baker. illus
(Also cutaway) Spaceflight 18:124-125 Apr '76

Viking: The Orbiter. David Baker. illus Spaceflight
18:84-86 Mar '76

SATELLITES, ARTIFICIAL - Continued

Tracking

See also
Space Detection and Tracking System

Scope detects space objects by sun glints. illus AF Times 36:38 May 17 '76

Europe, Western

The space business--has Europe a chance? Dan Boyle. illus tab Interavia 31:647-650 Jul '76

India

India joins the space club. H.P. Mama. illus Interavia 31:376-377 Apr '76

Japan

Japanese satellites successfully launched. Table only. Spaceflight 18:105 Mar. '76

Russia

Soviet space activities in 1975. Charles S. Sheldon II. illus tabs AF Mag 59:82-87 Mar '76

SCANDINAVIA

Problems of nuclear free zones--the Nordic example. LtCol Jay C. Mumford. illus Mil Rev 56:3-10 Mar '76

SCHARNHORST, Gerhard J.D. von

Scharnhorst to Schlieffen: The rise and decline of German military thought. Herbert Rosinski. Nav War Col Rev 29:83-103 Summer '76

SCHLESINGER, James R.

Defense lists Secretary's total force actions. (Text of SecDef James R. Schlesinger's decisions on total force) Officer A. The total force. C. Total force program guidance: 1. General. 2. The manpower mobilization system. 51:7-8 Dec '75; C-3 (Army Reserve and Guard). 52:15-16 Jan '76; (Naval and Air Force Reserves) 52:8+ Feb '76

The evolution of American policy towards the Soviet Union. (Gustav Pollak Lecture, Harvard University, April 13, 1976) James R. Schlesinger. Intl Sec 1:37-48 Summer '76

The military and national purpose. (Farewell remarks, Pentagon, Nov 10, 1975) James R. Schlesinger. por AF Mag 59:13-14 Jan '76; Nav War Col Rev 28:57-59 Fall '75

Political prelude to a no-win scenario. James D. Hessman and Vincent C. Thomas. por Sea Power 18:23-24 Dec '75

The Sunday morning massacre: A murder-suicide? Aaron Latham. (Reprinted from New York, Dec 22, 1975) por Armed Forces J Intl 113:18-25 Jan '76

SCHLIEFFEN, Alfred von

Scharnhorst to Schlieffen: The rise and decline of German military thought. Herbert Rosinski. Nav War Col Rev 29:83-103 Summer '76

SCHOLARSHIPS AND FELLOWSHIPS

AFROTC airman scholarship and commissioning program. TIG Brief 28:6 Aug 13 '76

Black ROTC scholarships to be dispersed (in effort to involve a wider range of schools). Army 26:57 Sep '76

SCHOLARSHIPS AND FELLOWSHIPS - Continued

Degree-holding EM can vie for AECP. AF Times 37:10 Nov 15 '76

Evolution of a law: (National Guard Assoc of) Illinois grass-roots effort succeeds (providing enlisted Illinois Guardsmen with scholarships to state colleges and universities). illus Natl Guardsman 30: 14-15 Feb '76

Health professions scholarship supplement. Contact, 5p sup following p 12, Fall '76

Health professions scholarship supplement. Contact, 9p sup following p 10, Winter '76

Health school (Uniformed Services University of the Health Sciences) too costly, GAO reports. Ann Gerow. AF Times 36:8 May 24 '76

Medical program (Medical, Dental and Veterinary Education Program for Air Force Officers) being phased out. Rose Sterling. AF Times 36:10 Jul 19 '76

'76-'79 group med students get tax relief (on scholarship payments). AF Times 37:26 Oct 18 '76

Tax bites holders of scholarships: Relief may be on the way. Lee Ewing. AF Times 36:4 Apr 12 '76

SCHOOL OF MILITARY SCIENCES, OFFICER see Officer Training School

SCHULZE, Richard C.

Troops and fire support. BrigGen Richard C. Schulze. MarCor Gaz 60:47-48 Jan '76

SCHWOB, William S.

(RADM W.S.) Schwob tells ROA CGR (Coast Guard Reserve) looking good (at Biloxi, Miss, Meeting, Oct 30-Nov 1, 1975). por Officer 52:25 Jan '76

SCIENCE

The military defense counsel's use of scientific evidence and expert witnesses. Maj William M. McKenna III. AF Law Rev 18:48-65 Fall '76

Science in the service of economy. G. Alexeyev. illus Soviet Mil Rev No. 11:8-9 Nov '76

SCIENCE FICTION

Lunar roving vehicles, models 1901, 1915 and 1918. Mitchell R. Sharpe. illus (Also cutaway) Spaceflight 18:56-58 Feb '76

SCIENTIFIC RESEARCH

Military Applications

Air Force research in retrospect. Col Robert M. Detweiler. illus AU Rev 28:2-15 Nov-Dec '76

United States

Discovering Jupiter. (Jupiter Science Symposium, NASA's Ames Research Center, Mountain View, Calif, 1976) illus tabs Spaceflight pt 1, 18:438-447 Dec '76

(New weather radar system to be installed on the Antarctica Peninsula) Signal 31:84 Nov-Dec '76

SCOTLAND

Description and Travel

Haggis and pumpkin pie. (USAF communications site personnel and dependents become part of Scottish community at Mormond Hill, near Fraserburgh) MSgt Harold Newcomb. illus Airman 20:44-48 May '76

SCOTT, Winfield S., III

A strategic logistics force: An answer to the exploitation of the developing nations. BrigGen Winfield S.Scott, Ret. por Strat Rev 4:68-75 Fall '76

SEA-BASED MISSILE DEFENSE SYSTEM see Missile Defense

SEA CADETS

Sea cadets. Regular feature in some issues of Sea Power

SEA CONTROL

(ADM) Holloway/(Gen) Jones cooperation pact raises difficult questions. L.Edgar Prina. illus Sea Power 19:34-36 Jan '76

Bigger role for U.S. Marines in sea control operations. MarCor Gaz 60:4 Sep '76

Meeting the Russian threat. LtGen Ira C.Eaker, Ret. AF Times 37:17-18 Sep 6 '76

A new look at control of the seas. MajGen Robert N. Ginsburgh, Ret. Strat Rev 4:86-89 Winter '76

Pact expands AF role in backing Navy in war. AF Times 36:26 Apr 12 '76

Today's Marine Corps: Stepping out smartly. James W.Canan. illus Sea Power 19:14-18 Nov '76

Why V/STOL? CAPT Gerald G.O'Rourke, Ret. illus US Nav Inst Proc 102:39-45 Jan '76

SEA CONTROL SHIPS

Men o'war. Joseph Fama. illus Def & For Aff Dig No.6:26-31 '76

SEA POWER

Africa strategy. Gregory Copley. illus Def & For Aff Dig No.3:6-9+ '76

Alfred Thayer Mahan speaks for himself. James A. Field, Jr. illus Nav War Col Rev 29:47-60 Fall '76

Foreign policies at risk: Some problems of managing naval power. Ken Booth. illus Nav War Col Rev 29:3-15 Summer '76

The foreword to Jane's (Fighting Ships 1976-77). Capt John Moore, Ret. Sea Power 19:24-32 Sep '76

(The Navy): Unknown events, disturbing trends, and a rebuilding of strength. J.William Middendorf II. illus tabs Sea Power 19:7-13 Jan '76

The possible effects on maritime operations of any future convention of the law of the sea. Adm Edward Ashmore. illus Nav War Col Rev 29:3-11 Fall '76

The Soviet view of navies in peacetime. Uri Ra'anan. illus Nav War Col Rev 29:30-38 Summer '76

Tides and currents in the Pacific: Long-term maritime implications. ADM James L.Holloway III. illus Strat Rev 4:33-39 Summer '76

Where do we go from here? CAPT John E.Greenbacker, Ret. illus US Nav Inst Proc 102:18-24 Jun '76

Great Britain

Britain at the crossroads. Comdr Joseph Palmer. illus tabs Sea Power 19:33-39 Sep '76

Iran

The Shah's Navy. John T.Hayward. Govt Exec 8:36+ Oct '76

SEA POWER - Continued

Russia

American maritime strategy and Soviet naval expansion. J.William Middendorf II. illus tabs Strat Rev 4:16-25 Winter '76

The Cuban missile crisis and Soviet naval development: Myths and realities. LCDR Harlan K.Ullman. tabs Nav War Col Rev 28:45-56 Winter '76

From Moscow, South by Southeast. Maj William G. Hanne. illus tab map Mil Rev 56:47-55 Jan '76

The Gorshkov doctrine: Seapower and the world ocean. L.Edgar Prina. illus Sea Power 19:33-37 Oct '76

A new look at control of the seas. MajGen Robert N. Ginsburgh, Ret. Strat Rev 4:86-89 Winter '76

New look at sea power. (Interview with Capt John Moore) Debbie C.Tennison. illus Natl Def 61: 203-204 Nov-Dec '76

The Nordic balance. Col Arthur E.Dewey. illus map Strat Rev 4:49-60 Fall '76

Santa Fe/TI: 'The core issue'--new report (by the Transportation Institute) recommends increased Navy/Merchant Marine cooperation and coordination. James D.Hessman. illus tab Sea Power 19: 15-16 Jul '76

Superpowers at sea: A debate. ADM Worth H.Bagley, Ret and RADM Gene R.LaRocque, Ret. Intl Sec 1:56-76 Summer '76

The surface Navy today: Prospects and problems. Col Robert D.Heinl, Jr. Ret. illus Sea Power 19:27-32 Oct '76

The U.S. and Russian Navies. LtGen Ira C.Eaker, Ret. AF Times 37:13-14 Aug 23 '76

The vulnerability of the West in the Southern Hemisphere. Patrick Wall. illus tab Strat Rev 4:44-50 Winter '76

United States

American maritime strategy and Soviet naval expansion. J.William Middendorf II. illus tabs Strat Rev 4:16-25 Winter '76

Can the Navy rebuild the U.S. fleet? John T.Hayward. Govt Exec 8:27+ Jul '76

New look at sea power. (Interview with Capt John Moore) Debbie C.Tennison. illus Natl Def 61: 203-204 Nov-Dec '76

Santa Fe/TI: 'The core issue'--new report (by the Transportation Institute) recommends increased Navy/Merchant Marine cooperation and coordination. James D.Hessman. illus tab Sea Power 19: 15-16 Jul '76

(Seapower) (Address, NDTA, New York, April 21, 1976) ADM Elmo R.Zumwalt, Jr, Ret. illus Def Trans J 32:34-36 Jun '76

(Sen Robert) Taft proposes long-range 'advanced technology' shipbuilding plan. L.Edgar Prina. tab illus Sea Power 19:31-34 Apr '76

Sen (Robert) Taft urges massive naval buildup, paid for by land forces overhaul, cuts. Benjamin F. Schemmer. Armed Forces J Intl 113:19+ Apr '76

Superpowers at sea: A debate. ADM Worth H.Bagley, Ret and RADM Gene R.LaRocque, Ret. Intl Sec 1:56-76 Summer '76

The surface Navy today: Prospects and problems. Col Robert D.Heinl, Jr, Ret. illus Sea Power 19:27-32 Oct '76

SEA POWER - Continued

United States - Cont'd

U.S. Merchant Marine--for commerce and defense. RADM John D.Chase. illus tabs US Nav Inst Proc 102:130-145 May '76

Weapons a warship make. John T.Hayward. Govt Exec 8:8+ Dec '76

History

The sea in the making of America. Clark G.Reynolds. illus US Nav Inst Proc 102:36-51 Jul '76

Sea power--Teddy's "big stick." (Alfred Mahan's influence on Theodore Roosevelt and U.S. history) CAPT Guy Cane. illus US Nav Inst Proc 102:40-48 Aug '76

SEALIFT

Forcible entry: A lost art? Col James R.Sherman. illus tabs Mil Rev 56:14-20 Sep '76

House panel (Appropriations Committee) scores 9.7-billion dollar airlift hodge-podge. tab Armed Forces J Intl 113:14-15 Jul '76

Reforger 76: A MTMC first. illus Translog 7:2-4 Aug-Sep '76

Reforger 76 is history. illus Translog 7:7 Dec '76

"Return the forces to Germany"--(Reforger) 76. LtCol Gary Sorensen. illus Def Trans J 32:6-8+ Oct '76

Solving the sealift shortage. L.Edgar Prina. illus Sea Power 19:19-26 Oct '76

SEAMANSHIP

Army goes to sea. SSgt James M.Boersema. illus Soldiers 31:35-37 Apr '76

The Navy needs more sailors. LCDR John B.Bonds. illus US Nav Inst Proc 102:38-43 Feb '76

SEAPLANES

A Sandringham returns. Peter J.Bish. illus Air Pict 38:444-445 Nov '76

History

The Catalina patrol bomber. George T.Mundorff. illus Aerosp Hist 23:217-221 Dec '76

SEARCH AND RESCUE

The AMVER (Automated Mutual-assistance VEssel Rescue) system. LT Walter McDougall. illus US Nav Inst Proc 102:106-108 Mar '76

Evasion and escape--still a stepchild. Capt Joseph A. McGrath, Jr. illus AU Rev 27:47-56 Sep-Oct '76

"For those in peril ..." (Search and rescue of submersibles) W.Robert Bryant. illus US Nav Inst Proc 102:105-108 Apr '76

How strongly do you feel about life? Your survival gear and SAR preparation will probably tell. LTJG Kim A.King. illus Approach 21:18-21 Nov '75; Aerosp Safety 32:22-24 Jan '76

Little Charlie Hill is missing! (Idaho CAP aids in search for lost 20-month-old child) Laura Tangley. illus Airman 20:22-23 Apr '76

'Offshore tapestry'--co-ordination and control. FltLt J.A.Cowan. Royal Air Forces Qtr 16:41-44 Spring '76

Proceed to assist ... the Belknap ablaze. CDR Robert C.Powers. illus US Nav Inst Proc 102:100-103 Aug '76

SEARCH AND RESCUE - Continued

Red Flag mirrors war in desert near Nellis (AFB, Nev). AF Times 36:18 Jan 5 '76

Red Flag (or how to fight the elements and live to tell about it). Capt Ronald E.Vivion. illus TAC Attack 16:20-22 Dec '76

Survival. illus Approach 21:22-23 Jan '76

Survival: Red Flag. Capt Ronald E.Vivion. illus Aerosp Safety pt 1, 32:16-19 Dec '76

"They are all gone." (Story of a tragic event in the history of the U.S. Life-Saving Service, 1880) MSTC Dennis L.Noble. illus US Nav Inst Proc 102:92-94 Mar '76

The United States Air Force in West New Guinea 1962-1963--help for the United Nations. LtCol Nick P.Apple. illus Aerosp Hist 22:212-217 Dec '75

History

The life-savers: "For those in peril on the sea." (History of the U.S. Life-Saving Service through the 1800s until it became part of the new Coast Guard in 1915) Robert Frank Bennett. illus US Nav Inst Proc 102:54-63 Mar '76

Study and Teaching

SAREX keeps Osan units in shape. Sgt Larry Finney. AF Times 36:26 May 17 '76

SAREX 76: Canada versus U.S. illus AF Times 37:28 Nov 1 '76

SEASICKNESS see Motion Sickness

SEAT BELTS

Bradycardia induced by negative acceleration. (Test for standard lap belt) James A.Kennealy and others. illus Aviation, Space & Envmt Med 47: 483-484 May '76

SEATTLE

Are the cities saveable? illus Govt Exec 8:18-20+ Nov '76

SECURITY, INDUSTRIAL

Automated security systems (for access control to secure areas). Robert Colten and James M.Kaye. illus Countermeasures 2:38+ Feb '76

Can pot smoker be cleared? Matter of security. Ron Sanders. AF Times 37:6 Dec 27 '76

Cargo security conferees stress industry/shipper controls (at National Cargo Security Conference, Washington, March 30-31, 1976). Col H.I.Pitchford. Translog 7:6-7 May '76

Disclosure of information by contractors. TIG Brief 28:12 Sep 10 '76

Keeping cargo secure. Tory Billard. illus Translog 7:13-15 Feb '76

SECURITY, INTERNATIONAL

Arms control and world order. Hedley Bull. Intl Sec 1:3-16 Summer '76

Cohesion and competition in the Atlantic Community: Implications for security. Col William F.Burns. illus Parameters 6, No.1:35-47 '76

European security: Helsinki to Vienna. Colin Gordon. RUSI J for Def Studies 121:34-36+ Sep '76

SECURITY, INTERNATIONAL - Continued

How will history judge us? (Admiral Raymond A. Spruance Lecture, Naval War College, Oct 29, 1975) Barbara W. Tuchman. Nav War Col Rev 28: 3-11 Fall '75; Comment. LCDR Edwin R. Linz. Nav War Col Rev 29:104-107 Summer '76

Kissinger on the security of the democracies and East-West relations. (Excerpts from lecture, International Institute for Strategic Studies, London, June 25, 1976) Henry A. Kissinger. Intl Def Rev 9:533-535 Aug '76

Nuclear terrorism and the escalation of international conflict. Forrest R. Frank. illus Nav War Col Rev 29:12-27 Fall '76

Superpowers at sea: A debate. ADM Worth H. Bagley, Ret and RADM Gene R. LaRocque, Ret. Intl Sec 1:56-76 Summer '76

SECURITY, MILITARY

See also
Defense Investigative Service

AFR 205-57 ("Reporting and Investigating Espionage, Sabotage, Terrorism and Subversion") is applicable to all USAF personnel. TIG Brief 28:6 May 7 '76

Answering the (ancillary transportation) protection question. Capt Paul L. Govekar, Jr. Translog 7:8+ Aug-Sep '76

Automated security systems (for access control to secure areas). Robert Colten and James M. Kaye. illus Countermeasures 2:38+ Feb '76

Corona Lock. TIG Brief 28:16 Oct 8 '76

'Corona Lock' works. AF Times 37:24 Oct 18 '76

Followup reports for breaches of security. (AFR 205-1) TIG Brief 28:21 Feb 13 '76

High-risk jobs listed in reg (AFR 35-99). AF Times 37:21 Dec 13 '76

Improved security clearance procedures. TIG Brief 28:16 May 7 '76

MAC passenger terminals toughen security. TIG Brief 28:16 Apr 9 '76

MOTBY (Military Ocean Terminal, BaYonne) security forces: Unique. Arthur Stewart. illus Translog 7:1-2+ Nov '76

The Nuclear Weapon Security Review Group (NWSRG). TIG Brief 28:14 Dec 17 '76

Panel (House Armed Services Investigation Subcommittee) may call commanders to testify on arms losses. Ron Sanders. AF Times 36:6 Feb 2 '76

Priority of nuclear logistic movement support. TIG Brief 28:10 Nov 19 '76

Reduction in DOD investigative resources. TIG Brief 28:15 Oct 22 '76

Risk management: Bonding of security alarm companies. TIG Brief 28:13 Jul 16 '76

SPs call for check on nuclear security. AF Times 37:6 Aug 16 '76

SPs get warning on criminals' ploys (to get around security systems). AF Times 37:18 Aug 9 '76

Safeguarding information subject to the Privacy Act of 1974. TIG Brief 28:20 Nov 19 '76

Security leaks may be only a phone call away. Ron Sanders. AF Times 36:6 Apr 5 '76

Security requirements for Limited Life Component (LLC) shipments. TIG Brief 28:19 Sep 24 '76

SECURITY, MILITARY - Continued

Special assignment airlift mission. TIG Brief 28:15 Feb 27 '76

TV cameras may assist base perimeter sentries. AF Times 36:21 Feb 23 '76

Transmission of classified information to foreign addressees. TIG Brief 28:19 Jan 16 '76

SECURITY, NATIONAL

See also
Security, International

The Air Force and national security: 1976 and beyond. (Remarks, Air Force Assoc, Mobile Chapter, Mobile, Ala, March 27, 1976) LtGen John W. Pauly. AF Plcy Ltr for Comdrs: Sup No. 6:10-18 Jun '76

Airlift problems pose threat to our security. Editorial. Officer 52:6+ Jan '76

American public opinion and American national security. Col Thomas I. Dickson, Jr, Ret. illus Mil Rev 56:77-81 Jul '76

Are America's Reserve Forces the "keystone" of national security? Defense panel (Defense Manpower Commission) says yea and nay. Natl Guardsman 30:8-11 Jun '76

Are we running out of metals? Simon D. Strauss. Persp in Def Mgt No. 24:19-31 Winter '75-'76

The artificial crisis of American security. illus tabs Def Monitor pt 1 (Military balance between U.S. and USSR) 5: entire issue May '76; pt 2, How much for defense? 5: entire issue Jun '76

Assault on military institutions. Gen T.R. Milton, Ret. AF Mag 59:30 Jan '76

Defense posture needs fortifying, says (SecDef Donald H.) Rumsfeld. Len Famiglietti. AF Times 36:17 Feb 16 '76

Enlivening American Defense Policy (ADP). Maj Larry B. Atkinson. tab Educ J 19:36-38 Winter '76

The ethics of intelligence activities. Col Barrie P. Masters. illus tab Natl Sec Aff Forum No. 24:39-47 Spring-Summer '76

'Farewell the tranquil mind": Security and stability in the post-Vietnam era. Col Lloyd J. Matthews. illus map Parameters 5, No. 2:2-13 '76

Forces for the future. (Remarks, Lancaster Chamber of Commerce, Lancaster, Calif, Feb 6, 1976) Thomas C. Reed. AF Plcy Ltr for Comdrs: Sup No. 4:16-20 Apr '76

Foreign policy and national security. (From address, World Affairs Council and Southern Methodist University, Dallas, March 22, 1976) Henry A. Kissinger. Intl Sec 1:182-191 Summer '76

The military and national purpose. (Farewell remarks, Pentagon, Nov 10, 1975) James R. Schlesinger. illus AF Mag 59:13-14 Jan '76; Nav War Col Rev 28:57-59 Fall '75

A military force in a democracy. (Address, Twin Cities Federal Executive Board Bicentennial Celebration, Twin Cities, Minn, July 1, 1976) Gen George S. Brown. AF Plcy Ltr for Comdrs: Sup No. 9:2-5 Sep '76

Military intelligence: A fight for identity. Col Leonard A. Spirito and Maj Marc B. Powe. Army 26: 14-21 May '76

Most critical issue: U.S. security. LtGen Ira C. Eaker, Ret. AF Times 37:13-14 Nov 1 '76

1976 national security voting index. tabs Def Trans J 32:30+ Apr '76

SECURITY, NATIONAL - Continued

Perils of the Vietnam syndrome. Gen T.R. Milton, Ret. AF Mag 59:29 Mar '76

Readiness and national survival. (Address, Air Force Assoc Symposium, Los Angeles, Oct 22, 1976) Malcolm R. Currie. AF Plcy Ltr for Comdrs: Sup No. 12:14-21 Dec '76

The relevance of civilian-based defense to U.S. security interests. BrigGen Edward B. Atkeson. tab illus Mil Rev pt 1, 56:24-32 May '76; pt 2, 56:45-55 Jun '76

The safety of the Republic: Can the tide be turned? Eugene V. Rostow. illus Strat Rev 4:12-25 Spring '76

Soviet threat and national strategic choices. (Remarks, Air Force Assoc luncheon, Washington, Sep 21, 1976) Gen David C. Jones. AF Plcy Ltr for Comdrs: Sup No. 11:8-13 Nov '76

USAF in the forefront of the C^3 revolution. Thomas C. Reed. illus AF Mag 59:62-65 Jul '76

U.S. military strategy for the eighties. Gen Andrew J. Goodpaster, Ret. illus Natl Sec Aff Forum No. 24:1-12 Spring-Summer '76

U.S. national security policy, 1950-1973--a quantitative description. Charles W. Kegley, Jr and Pamela A. Holcomb. tab Armed Forces & Soc 2:573-594 Summer '76

Zumwalt: Public misled on defense. (Excerpts from remarks, Democratic National Convention, New York, July 13, 1976) ADM Elmo R. Zumwalt, Jr, Ret. illus AF Times 37:26 Sep 6 '76

SECURITY ASSISTANCE PROGRAM

FMS (Foreign Military Sales) is only one export control. (Interview with Maurice Mountain) Govt Exec 8:20-21 Dec '76

FMS (Foreign Military Sales): "No more giving it away." Interview. LtGen Howard Fish. illus tabs Govt Exec 8:19+ Dec '76

Military assistance program and foreign military sales. (Statement before House Committee on International Relations, Nov 11, 1975) William P. Clements, Jr. AF Plcy Ltr for Comdrs: Sup No. 2:27-31 Feb '76

The Security Assistance Program. (Statement before Committee on International Relations, House of Representatives, Nov 12, 1975) LtGen H.M. Fish. AF Plcy Ltr for Comdrs: Sup No. 1:18-22 Jan '76

SECURITY CLASSIFICATION

Accidents and public information responsibilities. TIG Brief 28:15 Jun 18 '76

DOD agrees to free new data on MIAs. AF Times 36:12 Jun 7 '76

Disclosure of information by contractors. TIG Brief 28:12 Sep 10 '76

Image transfer of classified information. TIG Brief 28:19 Mar 12 '76

Improved security clearance procedures. TIG Brief 28:16 May 7 '76

Maintaining special security files. TIG Brief 28:9 Dec 17 '76

Marking of foreign restricted messages. TIG Brief 28:16 Apr 9 '76

Safeguarding information subject to the Privacy Act of 1974. TIG Brief 28:20 Nov 19 '76

SECURITY CLASSIFICATION - Continued

Security classification policy on terminology for nuclear weapons storage locations. TIG Brief 28:13 Jul 16 '76

'Special access' problems. TIG Brief 28:19 Mar 12 '76

Transmission of classified information to foreign addressees. TIG Brief 28:19 Jan 16 '76

Unauthorized security markings and unorthodox terms. TIG Brief 28:13 Aug 27 '76

SECURITY POLICE see Military Police

SEGREGATION

See also
Blacks in the Armed Forces
Race Relations

SEITZ, John A.

What do you know about military banks? BrigGen John A. Seitz, Ret. por Armed Forces Compt 21: 8-9 Apr '76

SEMICONDUCTOR DEVICES

Advances in semiconductor memories. illus Countermeasures 2:32-33 Jun '76

Electron bombarded semiconductors for fast rise time modulators. Bruce Bell. illus tab Countermeasures 2:43-46+ Aug '76

Protection: An essential design element. William T. Craven. illus Signal 31:30-31 Nov-Dec '76

Semiconductor devices and circuits in military applications. Helmut F. Wolf. illus tabs Countermeasures 2:59-60+ Sep '76

Technology: Its impact on the 1980s. Joseph A. Boyd. illus tabs Signal 30:50-54 May-Jun '76

SENIOR SERVICE SCHOOLS see Staff Colleges

SENSORS

ASW: The deterrent. F. Glenn Peters. illus Elect Warfare 8:49-50+ Jul-Aug '76

Air Force sensors. William C. Eppers, Jr. illus (Also cutaway) Natl Def 61:210-213 Nov-Dec '76

Battlefield surveillance. Charles Latour. illus NATO's Fifteen Nations 20:62-65+ Dec '75-Jan '76

First TRAM (Target Recognition and Attack Multisensor) system undergoes navy testing. illus Countermeasures 2:47 Mar '76

The government communications planning program. LtCol James Jenkins. Signal 30:98-100 Aug '76

TRAM (Target Recognition Attack Multi-sensor) makes A-6E world's most advanced EO aircraft. illus Elect Warfare 8:75-76+ May-Jun '76

Tactical sensors for the Army. Maj John P. Bulger. illus Natl Def 60:279-281 Jan-Feb '76

Window to the world: EVS (Electro-optical Viewing System) and the navigator. 1stLt James R. McDonald. illus Navigator 23:25-26 Summer '76

SENTINEL ABM SYSTEM

See also
Safeguard ABM System

SEPARATION FROM MILITARY SERVICE see Discharges, Releases, and Separations

SERVICE SCHOOLS see Staff Colleges

SHIPPING - Continued

United States

CERS (Carrier Evaluation and Reporting System) testing moves into second phase. Translog 7:14+ Jun '76

Can the Navy rebuild the U.S. fleet? John T. Hayward. Govt Exec 8:27+ Jul '76

Cargo preference: Prescription for an ailing industry. Donald C. Leavens. illus tabs Sea Power 19: 26-30 Jun '76

Cargo security conferees stress industry/shipper controls (at National Cargo Security Conference, Washington, March 30-31, 1976). Col H.I. Pitchford. Translog 7:6-7 May '76

Carrier selection: How one military shipper selects a carrier. illus Def Trans J 32:36-37 Oct '76

DISREP (Discrepency In Shipment REPort, SF 361) system is ITO's 'Man Friday.' LtCol B.E. Greenfield. Translog 7:5 Oct '76

Defense in struggle over (overseas) goods shipping. Interview. Paul H. Riley. AF Times 36:4 Jul 12 '76

Drive on to test shipping weights. Len Famiglietti. AF Times 37:8 Nov 22 '76

Easing of HHG (HouseHold Goods) weight limits seen. AF Times 37:3 Dec 13 '76

Export releases for CONUS contractor shipments. TIG Brief 28:4 Nov 5 '76

GAO wants to keep uneconomical household (goods) plan. AF Times 37:4 Aug 16 '76

Gold plated traffic. Donald T. Isaacs. illus Translog 7:13-15 Jan '76

A healthier, more prosperous, and more productive U.S. Merchant Marine. Robert J. Blackwell. illus Sea Power 19:30-33 Jan '76

New rules hit shipping of overseas 'goodies,' but singles get weight rise. Lee Ewing. tab AF Times 37:4 Aug 16 '76

Pressure builds for (Merchant Marine) 'fair share' legislation. James D. Hessman. illus Sea Power 19:19-22 Aug '76

Shipper support ... and how to get it. Herbert Paige Translog 7:16-18 Feb '76

Solving the sealift shortage. L. Edgar Prina. illus Sea Power 19:19-26 Oct '76

U.S. Merchant Marine--for commerce and defense. RADM John D. Chase. illus tabs US Nav Inst Proc 102:130-145 May '76

Costs

Rate filing test (for shipments) set for Germany. Translog 7:16+ Jun '76

History

The first Federal customs. CDR Roger P. Vance. illus US Nav Inst Proc 102:46-53 Mar '76

SHIPS

See also specific types of ships, e.g.,
Icebreakers   Patrol Boats
Landing Craft   Tanlers
Lightships .   Warships
Oilers (Ships)

SHIPS - Continued

Armament

New guns for the Navy. illus Natl Def 61:195-198 Nov-Dec '76

Popguns vs cruise missiles. R.J. Quallen. illus tab US Nav Inst Proc 102:97-100 Jul '76

Seawolf/GWS25, the Royal Navy's anti-missile missile system. illus tabs Intl Def Rev 9:789-794 Oct '76

Weapons a warship make. John T. Hayward. Govt Exec 8:8+ Dec '76

Conversion

Cinderella carriers. (Conversion of merchant ships into aircraft carriers in WW II) CAPT Robert L. Evans, Ret. illus US Nav Inst Proc 102:52-61 Aug '76

Design

Freeboard problems--1938. Philip Sims. illus US Nav Inst Proc 102:79 Jan '76

Exhibitions

A nautical observance of the Bicentennial from sea to shining sea; a monumental itinerary. (Operation Sail and the International Naval Review) Col Brooke Nihart, Ret. illus Sea Power 19:21-28 May '76

Fires and Fire Prevention

Study and Teaching

Pollution control at Navy fire-fighting schools. Floyd C. Hildebrand. illus Mil Engr 68:100-101 Mar-Apr '76

Loading and Unloading

Balloons tested for containership offload. Dan Hall. illus Translog 7:1-4 Apr '76

Equipment

2d Logistics-Over-The-Shore (LOTS) test held at (Fort) Story (Va), April 21-26 (1976). illus Translog 7:13+ Jun '76

Mothballing
See Mothball Fleet

Safety Measures

Texaco Oklahoma: Another Bermuda Triangle victim? LT Michael R. Adams. illus map US Nav Inst Proc 102:109-110 Mar '76

Laws and Regulations--History

A case of calculated mischief. (History of steamboat inspection and safety legislation) CDR Robert Frank Bennett. illus US Nav Inst Proc 102:76-83 Mar '76

United States

Forcible entry: A lost art? Col James R. Sherman. illus tabs Mil Rev 56:14-20 Sep '76

Salvage of the (Great Lakes freighter) Sidney E. Smith. Maj Thomas J. Woodall. illus Mil Engr 68:448-451 Nov-Dec '76

The small ships. James D. Hessman. illus Sea Power 19:13-16 Sep '76

Equipment

First maritime (telecommunications) satellite (Marisat). Spaceflight 18:216-217 Jun '76

SHIPS - Continued

United States - Cont'd

History

USCGC Taney: Still in service 35 years later. Carl and Nell Kraft. illus US Nav Inst Proc 102:50-51 Dec '76

SHIPS, AUXILIARY see Auxiliary Ships

SHIPS, CARGO see Ships, Transport

SHIPS, CONTAINER see Ships, Transport

SHIPS, NUCLEAR POWERED

United States

House panel (Armed Services Committee) increases SCN (Ship Construction, Navy) funding: Nuclear power advocates gain ground. L. Edgar Prina. illus Sea Power 19:7-11 Apr '76

SHIPS, TRANSPORT

The AMVER (Automated Mutual-assistance VEssel Rescue) system. LT Walter McDougall. illus US Nav Inst Proc 102:106-108 Mar '76

Russia

The Soviet merchant fleet. CDR Richard T. Ackley, Ret. illus US Nav Inst Proc 102:27-37 Feb '76

United States

A conversation with Paul Hall (President of the Seafarers International Union of North America): Maritime labor--the ally within. Interview. illus Sea Power 19:11-16 Feb '76

Intermodal technology as seen by Lykes Brothers. illus Def Trans J 32:28+ Jun '76

The Navy begins a new approach to modern maritime defense: Strengthening the link between U.S. naval forces and the American Merchant Marine. (Reserve Merchant Ship Defense System (RMSDS)) James J. Mulquin. illus Sea Power 19:25-29 Mar '76

Pressure builds for (Merchant Marine) 'fair share' legislation. James D. Hessman. illus Sea Power 19:19-22 Aug '76

Sea-Land's new sweethearts: The SL-7s. LT G.S. Marton. illus US Nav Inst Proc 102:99-101 Jun '76

History

The banana Navy. (United Fruit Co's Great White Fleet) CAPT Robert Carl, Ret. illus US Nav Inst Proc 102:55-67 Dec '76

SHIP'S STORES see Exchanges--Navy

SHOCK WAVES

Effects of the frequency content in complex air shock waves on lung injuries in rabbits. Carl-Johan Clemedson and Arne Jönsson. tabs Aviation, Space & Envmt Med 47:1143-1152 Nov '76

SHOEMAKER, Robert M.

Training points the way. LtGen Robert M. Shoemaker. USA Avn Dig 22:2-3+ Jul '76

SHORE PATROL see Military Police

SHORT TAKEOFF AND LANDING see Airplanes, V/STOL

SHOTTS, Bryan M.

A fifty-yard line view of leadership. (Remarks, Graduation Ceremonies of the Strategic Air Command Noncommissioned Officer Academy, Barksdale AFB, La, Sep 24, 1976) LtGen Bryan M. Shotts. AF Plcy Ltr for Comdrs: Sup No. 12:22-27 Dec '76

SIDLE, Winant

(Maj)Gen Sidle named AUSA executive. por Army 26:8 Jan '76

Sidle: Keeping the public informed. Interview. MajGen Winant Sidle. AF Times 36:16 Mar 1 '76

SIGHT

See also
Eyes

The case of mistaken identity. Rush R. Wicker. illus USA Avn Dig 22:24-25 Apr '76

Night flying without feathers. Capt Glenn Wendt. Interceptor 18:14-15 Jun '76

Prolonged visual loss and bradycardia following deceleration from +6 G_z acceleration: A case report. John S. Kirkland and James A. Kennealy. illus Aviation, Space & Envmt Med 47:310-311 Mar '76

Readability of approach charts as a function of visual acuity, luminance, and printing format. K.W. Welsh and others. illus tabs Aviation, Space & Envmt Med 47:1027-1031 Oct '76

To see or not to see: Visual acuity of pilots involved in midair collisions. Leonard C. Ryan and others. illus Combat Crew 27:8-10 Sep '76

SIGNAL CORPS

Career information (Signal Corps and Air Force personnel). Regular feature in some issues of Signal

History

Getting the message. illus Soldiers 31:28-31 Mar '76

SIGNALS AND SIGNALING

C^3: How we got here--where are we? CDR Peter S. Roder. illus Signal 30:7-10 Jul '76

The "in-close" waveoff: An LSO's (Landing Signal Officer) point of view. LCDR George Webb and others. illus Approach 21:6-9 Feb '76

SILER, Owen W.

The Coast Guard: New missions, increased capabilities, always ready. ADM Owen W. Siler. Sea Power 19:14-20 Jan '76

The expanding Coast Guard mission. ADM O.W. Siler. Def Trans J 32:6-8+ Aug '76

Tradition of excellence, time of change. ADM Owen W. Siler. por US Nav Inst Proc 102:34-37 Mar '76

SILLIMAN, Scott L.

The Supreme Court and its impact on the Court of Military Appeals. (Adapted from lecture, Homer Ferguson Conference on Appellate Advocacy, Washington, May 20, 1976) Capt Scott L. Silliman. AF Law Rev 18:81-93 Summer '76

SILVER

Dental Service's silver reclamation responsibilities. TIG Brief 28:4 Jan 16 '76

SLAY, Alton D.

M-X, a new dimension in strategic deterrence. LtGen Alton D.Slay. AF Mag 59:44-49 Sep '76

New aircraft and missiles. (Presentation, Senate Appropriations Committee, Washington, March 18, 1976) LtGen Alton D.Slay. AF Plcy Ltr for Comdrs: Sup No.5:10-28 May '76

SLEEP

Air operations and circadian performance rhythms. Karl E.Klein and others. illus tabs Aviation, Space & Envmt Med 47:221-230 Mar '76

Cardiac output during human sleep. J.C.Miller and S.M.Horvath. tabs Aviation, Space & Envmt Med 47:1046-1051 Oct '76

Effects of time zone changes on performance and physiology of airline personnel. F.S.Preston and others. illus tabs Aviation, Space & Envmt Med 47:763-769 Jul '76

Psychomotor test performance and sleep patterns of aircrew flying transmeridional routes. Leslie Buck. illus tabs Aviation, Space & Envmt Med 47: 979-986 Sep '76

SMALL ARMS

See also
Rifles

Converting rifle to shotgun. MGySgt J.P.Driver, Ret. illus MarCor Gaz 60:45-46 Aug '76

A firearms treasure. (Collection of Col Farley L. Berman, Ret, Anniston, Ala) BrigGen Robert L. Bergquist. illus Natl Def 60:378-381 Mar-Apr '76

Firing the multi-purpose hand gun. MGySgt J.P. Driver, Ret. MarCor Gaz 60:46-47 Sep '76

Foreign weapons. Regular feature in issues of National Defense

The new British Infantry (4.85 mm) weapons system. illus tab Intl Def Rev 9:768-769 Oct '76

Prompt reporting of lost/stolen firearms and nonnuclear munitions. (AFR 125-37) TIG Brief 28:4 Jan 30 '76

Small arms: Big problems. TIG Brief 28:6 May 21 '76

SMALL BUSINESS

Foundries and the OSHA Act: Problems and some solutions. Debbie C.Tennison. illus Natl Def 61:56-59 Jul-Aug '76

A growing Federal absurdity. (Small business and government supply contract regulations) Ernest Baynard. Govt Exec 8:40-44 Dec '76

OFPP (Office of Federal Procurement Policy) one ·year later: A look ahead. Interview. Hugh E.Witt. illus Govt Exec 8:16+ Feb '76

SMITH, James C.

Hail and farewell. (MajGen James C.Smith succeeds MajGen William J.Maddox, Jr, as commander of Army Aviation Center, Fort Rucker, Ala) por USA Avn Dig 22:48-49 Jul '76

SMITH, Lynn D.

Our neglected civil defenses. BrigGen Lynn D. Smith, Ret. Army 26:12-20 Jul '76

SMITH, Paul T.

People with a capital P. MajGen Paul T.Smith. por Army 26:123-124+ Oct '76

SMITH, W.Stanford

(Maj)Gen Smith reviews 20 years of Reserve gains. Officer 52:10+ Dec '76

RFPB (Reserve Forces Policy Board) rejuvenated. MajGen W.Stanford Smith. Natl Guardsman 30:32-33 Apr '76

SMITH, William Y.

Honoring America. (Remarks, Armed Forces Day luncheon, Battle Creek, Mich, May 14, 1976) LtGen W.Y.Smith. AF Plcy Ltr for Comdrs: Sup No.8:13-16 Aug '76

SMOKE

Pollution control at Navy fire-fighting schools. Floyd C.Hildebrand. illus Mil Engr 68:100-101 Mar-Apr '76

Support fire and maneuver with smoke. Maj Kirk L. Lewis. illus Fld Arty J 44:45-49 Nov-Dec '76

SMUGGLING see Customs Service

SOARING see Gliding and Soaring

SOCIAL ACTIONS PROGRAM

(AF) equal opportunity Affirmative Actions Plan (AAP). TIG Brief 28:12 Feb 27 '76

(AF) social action heads for Phase III. AF Times 36:6 Jan 5 '76

Alcohol abuse and deglamorization. TIG Brief 28:12 Oct 8 '76

Centralized rehabilitation of personnel. (3415th Special Training Sq, Lowry AFB, Colo) TIG Brief 28:17 Jul 2 '76

Civilian drug and alcohol abuse control program. TIG Brief 28:10-11 Sep 10 '76

Friends are for the making. (1stLt William Baird teaches unique and useful human relations course for German employees at Bitburg AB, Germany) MSgt Yuen-Gi Yee. illus Airman 20:16-17 Nov '76

Goal: Individual awareness. (Air Force Reserve's social actions program) illus Air Reservist 27:12 Mar '76

SOCIAL CHANGE

Evaluative research: Progress through experimentation. E.William Sarsfield. illus Govt Exec 8:33+ Mar '76

Global corporations and the American economy. Ronald Muller. Persp in Def Mgt No.24:43-55 Winter '75-'76

How private enterprise is committing "subtle suicide." illus Govt Exec 8:56-57 May '76

How will history judge us? (Admiral Raymond A. Spruance Lecture, Naval War College, Oct 29, 1975) Barbara W.Tuchman. Nav War Col Rev 28: 3-11 Fall '75; Comment. LCDR Edwin R.Linz. Nav War Col Rev 29:104-107 Summer '76

The military and social adaptation. Col Richard M. Jennings, Ret. illus Strat Rev 4:72-78 Winter '76

Occupational mobility and political behavior: Some unresolved issues. Joseph Lopreato and others. J Pol & Mil Sociol 4:1-15 Spring '76

Tools and civilization. Lynn T.White, Jr. Persp in Def Mgt No.24:33-42 Winter '75-'76; Condensation. Fld Arty J 44:44-47 Sep-Oct '76

SOCIAL CHANGE - Continued

Trends in the structure of army families. David R. Segal and others. J Pol & Mil Sociol 4:135-139 Spring '76

War, peace, and society in the 1980's: A historian's view. Richard A. Preston. illus Nav War Col Rev 28:34-44 Winter '76

SOCIAL PROBLEMS AND THE MILITARY

A military elite in transition: Air Force leaders in the 1980s. (Research undertaken at Air Command and Staff College) LtCol Franklin D. Margiotta. tabs Armed Forces & Soc 2:155-184 Winter '76

New (AF) programs to accent Spanish-speaking culture. Len Famiglietti. AF Times 36:2 Feb 9 '76

A perspective of the military and the media. Carl J. Migdail. illus Nav War Col Rev 28:2-9 Winter '76

The present state and development of sociology of the military. George A. Kourvetaris and Betty A. Dobratz. tabs J Pol & Mil Sociol 4:67-105 Spring '76

Racial and ethnic relations in the armed forces: An introductory note (for) Symposium on Racial and Ethnic Relations in the Armed Forces. (Papers by Douglas L. Wheeler and others, edited by Kenneth W. Grundy) Armed Forces & Soc 2:227-304 Winter '76

SOCIAL SCIENCES

Legitimacy and government control of the production of academic social knowledge. Michael Useem. tabs J Pol & Mil Sociol 4:217-232 Fall '76

SOCIAL SECURITY

House unit (Armed Services Committee) acts to cut Social Security offset. AF Times 37:57 Sep 13 '76

Life insurance as a function of estate planning for the middle income military member. Maj Mell J. Lacy. tabs AF Law Rev 17:1-49 Winter '75

Military/SS (Social Security): New questions raised. AF Times 36:22 May 24 '76

Social Security for Service people and veterans. Officer 52:35-36 Oct '76

(Social Security tax) withholding increase. AF Times 37:3 Oct 18 '76

Social Security to rise June 1. AF Times 36:16 May 10 '76

Survey (by GAO) costs troops Social Security money. AF Times 37:8 Dec 13 '76

SOCIETY OF LOGISTICS ENGINEERS

The Annals of the Society of Logistics Engineers. Regular feature in some issues of Logistics Spectrum

Modern logistics: A professional's profession. CAPT Carl L. Henn, Ret. illus Log Spectrum 10:18-21+ Summer '76

Professionalism through logistics education and training. Ben S. Blanchard. illus tabs Log Spectrum 10: 28-33 Summer '76

The role of SOLE. Carl L. Henn. (Reprinted from "Selected Readings in Logistics," 1972) illus Log Spectrum 10:38-39+ Fall '76

History

SOLE's ten years: Its aspirations, its accomplishments, and its future. Robert N. Johns and others. illus Log Spectrum 10:5-13+ Summer '76

SOCIOLOGY

Alienation and participation: A replication comparing leaders and the "mass." D. Duane Braun. tabs J Pol & Mil Sociol 4:245-259 Fall '76

Development of sociology of militaria in Yugoslavia. Anton Bebler. tabs Armed Forces & Soc 3:59-68 Fall '76

The present state and development of sociology of the military. George A. Kourvetaris and Betty A. Dobratz. tabs J Pol & Mil Sociol 4:67-105 Spring '76

SOILS

The puzzle of the Martian soil. Richard S. Lewis. illus Spaceflight 18:391-395 Nov '76

SOLAR ENERGY

Air Force Academy solar energy program. Maj M. W. Nay, Jr and Lt W. A. Tolbert. illus tab AF Engrg & Svcs Qtr 17:23-27 Feb '76

Can government create a private sector? (Interview with Robert L. Hirsch, Assistant Administrator for Solar, Geothermal and Advanced Energy Systems, Energy Research & Development Administration) John F. Judge. illus Govt Exec 8:15+ Aug '76

Chemical engineering aids solar energy. Talbot A. Chubb. illus tab Mil Engr 68:456-458 Nov-Dec '76

Development of the Satellite Solar Power Station (SSPS). Peter E. Glaser. illus tabs Spaceflight 18:198-208 Jun '76

Solar energy applications. Capts Anthony Eden and Michael A. Aimone. tabs illus map AF Engrg & Svcs Qtr 17:29-33 Aug '76

Solar home saves on gas (in test at (AF) Academy). AF Times 37:37 Aug 9 '76

Work begins on solar energy BX at Kirtland (AFB, NM). AF Times 37:4 Nov 8 '76

Work to start in Fall on solar BXs. AF Times 36:61 Apr 19 '76

SOLDIERS

United States

Army travel breaks urged (by Gen Fred C. Weyand). Don Hirst. AF Times 37:21 Nov 1 '76

EM career notes. Regular feature in issues of Infantry

EPMS (Enlisted Personnel Management System): What it's all about. SGM Nat Dell. illus Soldiers 31:8-11 Sep '76

Enlisted career news. Regular feature in issues of Air Defense Magazine

History

Brown shoes and campaign hats. (Army life in the '20's and '30's) Eve E. Simmons. illus Army 26: 46-49 Sep '76

He never missed his aim. (Timothy Murphy, the American Revolution's hero in the ranks) Col John B. B. Trussell, Jr, Ret. illus maps Parameters 6, No. 1:48-59 '76

The private (Nathanael Greene)'s strategy. LtCol Fred Grenier. illus Soldiers 31:42-43 May '76

SOLDIERS' HOME

50¢ bite for (Soldiers' and Airmen's) 'Home' still iffy. Lee Ewing. AF Times 37:2 Nov 8 '76

SOLDIERS' HOME - Continued

Panel (Senate Armed Services Committee) approves officer grade relief. (Added to bill to improve financial status of Soldiers' and Airmen's Home) AF Times 37:4 Sep 27 '76

SONAR

Acoustic countermeasures in the undersea environment. Owen Flynn. illus tabs Elect Warfare 8: 62-64+ Sep-Oct '76

Simrad (searchlight) sonars for naval vessels. Capt I.W.Storvik. illus Intl Def Rev 9:798-800 Oct '76

Sonar and the USS Monitor. Bill Walsh. illus map Countermeasures 2:32-33 Apr '76

SOUND

Review of the effects of infrasound on man. C.Stanley Harris and others. Aviation, Space & Envmt Med 47:430-434 Apr '76

SOUNDING ROCKETS see Rockets, Sounding

SOUTH AFRICA (REPUBLIC)

Apartheid: Shadow over South Africa. Capt Jacques A.Rondeau. illus map US Nav Inst Proc 102:18-27 Sep '76

The new Africa. Gregory Copley. illus Def & For Aff Dig No. 2:18-21+ '76

South Africa: Some misconceptions. Maj John Selby. Army Qtr 106:204-210 Apr '76

History

Colenso: The first battle of the early Tugela River Campaign (1899). 1stLt David M.Crane. maps illus Mil Rev 56:77-91 Feb '76

Strategic Importance

Apartheid: Shadow over South Africa. Capt Jacques A.Rondeau. illus map US Nav Inst Proc 102:18-27 Sep '76

South Africa: NATO's unwelcome ally. Charles Latour. illus map tab NATO's Fifteen Nations 21: 58-64+ Jun-Jul '76

The South African Navy: Guardian of the ocean cross roads. Col Norman L.Dodd, Ret. illus tab US Nav Inst Proc 102:94-97 Sep '76

The strategic position of South Africa. Editorial. RUSI J for Def Studies 121:1-2 Sep '76

The vulnerability of the West in the Southern Hemisphere. Patrick Wall. illus tab Strat Rev 4:44-50 Winter '76

SOUTHERN COMMAND

Navy and Air Force components of Southern Command to close. AF Plcy Ltr for Comdrs: Sup No.1:17 Jan '76

TAC sets up (USAF Southern Air Division (USAFSO)) in Canal Zone (territory formerly covered by Southern Command). AF Times 36:2 Jan 12 '76

SOVIET UNION see Russia

SPAATZ, Carl A.

Insight to airpower: The life of General Spaatz. Kenneth Crawford. (Reprinted from Washington Post, July 15, 1974) obit biog AF Plcy Ltr for Comdrs: Sup No.7:33-38 Jul '76

SPAATZ, Carl A. - Continued

Never a 'Question Mark.' (Spaatz Trophy, given to SAC by TAC to be awarded to best tanker unit each year, in honor of historic flight of the Question Mark in 1929, which stayed in the air nearly 7 days and proved that in-flight refueling was practical) Maj Jay B.Welsh. por Airman 20:24-29 Mar '76

SPACE

Commercial Applications

Cities in the sky. Kenneth W.Gatland. illus Spaceflight 18:7-9 Jan '76

Extra-terrestrial communities. illus tabs Spaceflight 18:130-134 Apr '76

Two tracks to new worlds. Michael A.G.Michaud. illus tab Spaceflight 18:2-6+ Jan '76

International Aspects

Getting aboard Spacelab. Kenneth W.Gatland. illus Spaceflight 18:302-303 Sep '76

The legacy of Viking--a taste of things to come. Arthur C.Clarke. illus Spaceflight 18:429-431 Dec '76

Legal achievements in space. Cyril E.S.Horsford. illus Spaceflight 18:73 Feb '76

Payloads for the shuttle. Robert Edgar. illus tabs Spaceflight 18:327-330 Sep '76

Trail into the future. (15th anniversary of the 1st manned space flight) LtGen V.Shatalov. illus Soviet Mil Rev No.4:11-13 Apr '76

Military Applications

See also
Space Warfare

Space in the Air Force future. (Remarks, American Defense Preparedness Assoc, Oct 15, 1975) LtGen Thomas W.Morgan. AF Plcy Ltr for Comdrs: Sup No.2:2-8 Feb '76; Condensation. Natl Def 60:290 Jan-Feb '76

Scientific Applications

See also
Satellites, Artificial--Scientific Uses

A new concept in planetary probes--the Mars penetrator. illus tabs Spaceflight 18:432-434 Dec '76

SPACE AND MISSILE SYSTEMS ORGANIZATION

Space in the Air Force future. (Remarks, American Defense Preparedness Assoc, Oct 15, 1975) LtGen Thomas W.Morgan. AF Plcy Ltr for Comdrs:Sup No.2:2-8 Feb '76; Condensation. Natl Def 60:290 Jan-Feb '76

SPACE AND MISSILE TEST CENTER

Clear to launch. Capts Manuel Torres and Mike Henshaw. illus Combat Crew 27:16-19 Apr '76

Weather probability forecasts: A cost-saving technique in space launch and missile test operations. MajGen Herbert A.Lyon, Ret and LtCol Lynn L. LeBlanc. illus tabs AU Rev 27:45-54 Jan-Feb '76

SPACE BIOLOGY

Viking: Lander science equipment. David Baker. illus (Also cutaways) Spaceflight pt 1, 18:211-213 Jun '76; pt 2, 18:241-245 Jul-Aug '76

SPACE BIOLOGY - Continued

The voyages of Viking. illus Spaceflight pt 1, Why explore? Gerald A.Soffen and others. 18:78-80 Mar '76; pt 2, Is there life on Mars? Richard S. Young and Harold P.Klein. 18:118-123 Apr '76; pt 3, Viking: The Lander. David Baker. 18:158-161. Looking at Mars--inside and out. Hugh H. Kieffer and others. 18:162-164+ May '76; pt 4, The chemistry of Mars. Priestly Toulmin III and others. 18:209-211 Jun '76; pt 5, The landing sites. 18:238-240 Jul-Aug '76

SPACE CLOTHING

See also
Pressure Suits

SPACE COMMUNICATIONS

See also
Satellites, Artificial--Communication Applications

Calling M13 on 12.6 cm: Do you read? A.T.Lawton. illus Spaceflight 18:10-12 Jan '76

NASA contemplates radio search for extra-terrestrial intelligence. Robert Sheaffer. illus tab Spaceflight 18:343-347 Oct '76

NASA operational communications. Charles A.Taylor. illus maps tabs Signal 30:91-95 Aug '76

SPACE CREWS

See also
Astronauts

Behavioral control as a tool in evaluating the functional state of cosmonauts in flight. O.G.Gazenko and others. illus tab Aviation, Space & Envmt Med 47:1226-1227 Nov '76

Opening the door: The beginning of EVA (Extra-Vehicular Activity). James E.Oberg. illus Spaceflight 18:168-175 May '76

SPACE DEFENSES

Aerospace defense. (Remarks, American Defense Preparedness Assoc, Los Angeles, Oct 15, 1975) Gen Daniel James, Jr. AF Plcy Ltr for Comdrs: Sup No.1:2-10 Jan '76; Condensation. Natl Def 60: 289 Jan-Feb '76

SPACE DETECTION AND TRACKING SYSTEM

RAF Fylingdales and the USAF spacetrack system. SqLdr D.J.Nicholson. illus Royal Air Forces Qtr 15:333-336 Winter '75

SPACE FLIGHT

See also
Space Vehicles

Missiles and astronautics. Regular feature in issues of National Defense

Space report. Regular feature in issues of Spaceflight

Commercial Applications
See Space--Commercial Applications

Exhibitions

Moscow and the Soviet Space Pavilion. John Boyes. illus Spaceflight 18:292-293 Jul-Aug '76

SPACE FLIGHT - Continued

History

A decade on ... A retrospective look at major space achievements. David Baker. illus Spaceflight pt 1, Gemini. 16:174+ May '74; pt 2, Ranger 7. 16:276 Jul '74; pt 3, Mariner 4. 16:418 Nov '74; pt 4, Voskhod 2. 17:197 May '75; pt 5, F-1: The clustered giant. 17:234 Jun '75; pt 6, NASA EVA-1 (Extra-Vehicular Activity): The first of 39. 17: 331-332 Aug-Sep '75; pt 7, The Russian-Venus probes. 17:446 Dec '75; pt 8, Gemini 8: First docking, first abort. 18:153 Apr '76; pt 9, Surveyor on the moon. 18:228 Jun '76; pt 10, Orbiters to the moon. 18:291 Jul-Aug '76

International Aspects
See Space--International Aspects

Manned Flights

Two tracks to new worlds. Michael A.G.Michaud. illus tab Spaceflight 18:2-6+ Jan '76

Statistics

Soviet space activities in 1975. Charles S.Sheldon II. illus tabs AF Mag 59:82-87 Mar '76

Manned Flights, American

See also specific projects by name, e.g., Space Project--Skylab

See also specific manned projects by name, e.g., Space Project--Apollo-Soyuz Space Project--Gemini

A decade on ... A retrospective look at major space achievements. David Baker. illus Spaceflight pt 1, Gemini. 16:174+ May '74; pt 2, Ranger 7. 16:276 Jul '74; pt 3, Mariner 4. 16:418 Nov '74; pt 4, Voskhod 2. 17:197 May '75; pt 5, F-1: The clustered giant. 17:234 Jun '75; pt 6, NASA EVA-1 (Extra-Vehicular Activity): The first of 39. 17:331-332 Aug-Sep '75; pt 7, The Russian-Venus probes. 17:446 Dec '75; pt 8, Gemini 8: First docking, first abort. 18:153 Apr '76; pt 9, Surveyor on the moon. 18:228 Jun '76; pt 10, Orbiters to the moon. 18:291 Jul-Aug '76

Opening the door: The beginning of EVA (Extra-Vehicular Activity). James E.Oberg. illus Spaceflight 18:168-175 May '76

Trail into the future. (15th anniversary of the 1st manned space flight) LtGen V.Shatalov. illus Soviet Mil Rev No.4:11-13 Apr '76

Manned Flights, Russian

See also
Space Project--Apollo-Soyuz

The cosmonauts. Gordon R.Hooper. illus Spaceflight pt 1, 17:58-59 Feb '75; pt 2, 17:116-117 Mar '75; pt 3, 17:129-130 Apr '75; pt 4, 17:189-190 May '75; pt 5, 17:236-237 Jun '75; pt 6, 17:274-275 Jul '75; pt 7, 17:333-334 Aug-Sep '75; pt 8, 17:365 Oct '75; pt 9, 17:403-404 Nov '75; pt 10, 17:443-445 Dec '75; pt 11, 18:26-27 Jan '76

Opening the door: The beginning of EVA (Extra-Vehicular Activity). James E.Oberg. illus Spaceflight 18:168-175 May '76

Trail into the future. (15th anniversary of the 1st manned space flight) LtGen V.Shatalov. illus Soviet Mil Rev No.4:11-13 Apr '76

SPACE PROJECT - Continued

Viking - Cont'd

On the golden plains of Mars: First Viking report from the Jet Propulsion Laboratory. Richard S. Lewis. illus Spaceflight pt 1, 18:356-364 Oct '76

The puzzle of the Martian soil. Richard S. Lewis. illus Spaceflight 18:391-395 Nov '76

Viking: Lander science equipment. David Baker. illus (Also cutaways) Spaceflight pt 1, 18:211-213 Jun '76; pt 2, 18:241-245 Jul-Aug '76

The Viking landing sites. Robert Edgar. maps Spaceflight 18:30-31 Jan '76

Viking: Looking for life on Mars. illus tab Interavia 31:570-571 Jun '76

Viking: Orbiter science equipment. David Baker. illus (Also cutaway) Spaceflight 18:124-125 Apr '76

Viking: The Orbiter. David Baker. illus Spaceflight 18:84-86 Mar '76

The voyages of Viking. illus Spaceflight pt 1, Why explore? Gerald A. Soffen and others. 18:78-80 Mar '76; pt 2, Is there life on Mars? Richard S. Young and Harold P. Klein. 18:118-123 Apr '76; pt 3, Viking: The Lander. David Baker. 18:158-161. Looking at Mars--inside and out. Hugh H. Kieffer and others. 18:162-164+ May '76; pt 4, The chemistry of Mars. Priestly Toulmin III and others. 18:209-211 Jun '76; pt 5, The landing sites 18:238-240 Jul-Aug '76

Watching and listening as Viking scratches the Mars surface. Irving Brown. illus Signal 30:30-32 Jul '76

What exploration is all about. Michael B. McElroy and others. illus Spaceflight 18:246-248 Jul-Aug '76

SPACE RACE

See also
Space--International Aspects

SPACE RESEARCH

See also
Space--International Aspects
Space Medicine
Space Programs
also projects under specific name, e.g.,
Space Project--Apollo-Soyuz

Aerospace review. Regular feature in issues of Aerospace International

Is the U.S. losing its investment (in space)? John F. Judge. illus Govt Exec 8:21+ Mar '76

Space report. Regular feature in issues of Spaceflight

What exploration is all about. Michael B. McElroy and others. illus Spaceflight 18:246-248 Jul-Aug '76

Russia

Orbits of Soviet deep space probes. Phillip S. Clark. illus tabs Spaceflight pt 1, 18:139-141 Apr '76; pt 2, 18:188-189 May '76

Russia's 'Orion' space observatories. (Interview with Grigor Gurzadian) illus Spaceflight 18:74 Feb '76

SPACE RESEARCH - Continued

United States--National Aeronautics and Space Administration

Edgar Cortright (retires as director of Langley Research Center). Dave Dooling. illus Spaceflight 18:150-151 Apr '76

Extra-terrestrial communities. illus tabs Spaceflight 18:130-134 Apr '76

Mars polar ice sample return mission. Robert L. Staehle. illus tabs Spaceflight pt 1, 18:383-390 Nov '76

NASA contemplates radio search for extra-terrestrial intelligence. Robert Sheaffer. illus tab Spaceflight 18:343-347 Oct '76

On the golden plains of Mars: First Viking report from the Jet Propulsion Laboratory. Richard S. Lewis. illus Spaceflight pt 1, 18:356-364 Oct '76

Outlook for space. Dave Dooling. Spaceflight pt 1, 18:422-425 Dec '76

Viking: Lander science equipment. David Baker. illus (Also cutaways) Spaceflight pt 1, 18:211-213 Jun '76; pt 2, 18:241-245 Jul-Aug '76

The voyages of Viking. illus Spaceflight pt 1, Why explore? Gerald A. Soffen and others. 18:78-80 Mar '76; pt 2, Is there life on Mars? Richard S. Young and Harold P. Klein. 18:118-123 Apr '76; pt 3, Viking: The Lander. David Baker. 18:158-161. Looking at Mars--inside and out. Hugh H. Kieffer and others. 18:162-164+ May '76; pt 4, The chemistry of Mars. Priestly Toulmin III and others. 18:209-211 Jun '76; pt 5, The landing sites. 18:238-240 Jul-Aug '76

SPACE SHUTTLES see Space Transporters

SPACE STATIONS

See also
Space Project--Skylab

Cities in the sky. Kenneth W. Gatland. illus Spaceflight 18:7-9 Jan '76

Extra-terrestrial communities. illus tabs Spaceflight 18:130-134 Apr '76

Getting aboard Spacelab. Kenneth W. Gatland. illus Spaceflight 18:302-303 Sep '76

Missions to Salyut 4. Gordon R. Hooper. illus (Also cutaway) Spaceflight pt 1, 17:219-225 Jun '75; pt 2, 18:13-18 Jan '76

Outlook for space. Dave Dooling. Spaceflight pt 1, 18:422-425 Dec '76

Payloads for the shuttle. Robert Edgar. illus tabs Spaceflight 18:327-330 Sep '76

Russia's 'Orion' space observatories. (Interview with Grigor Gurzadian) illus Spaceflight 18:74 Feb '76

The Soyuz-Salyut programme: Soviet achievements and hopes. Eduard A. Konstantin. illus tab Interavia 31:741-743 Aug '76

Two tracks to new worlds. Michael A. G. Michaud. illus tab Spaceflight 18:2-6+ Jan '76

Design

Manned orbital facility. Phillip J. Parker. illus tab Spaceflight 18:426-428+ Dec '76

SPACE STATIONS - Continued

Design - Cont'd

Missions to Salyut 4. Gordon R. Hooper. illus (Also cutaway) Spaceflight pt 1, 17:219-225 Jun '75; pt 2, 18:13-18 Jan '76

SPACE TAXIS see Space Transporters

SPACE TRANSPORTERS

After Viking, the space shuttle approaches readiness. J. Philip Geddes. illus Interavia 31:969-971 Oct '76

Astronaut positions open for space shuttle flights. illus AF Times 37:18 Sep 20 '76

A chronology of the space shuttle. David Baker. illus tab Spaceflight 1962-Dec 17, 1971. 15:210-214 Jan '73; Jan 13-Aug 4, 1972. 15:268-270 Jul '73; Aug 7, 1972-Apr 18, 1973. 15:312-314+ Aug '73; Apr 1973-Dec 20, 1974. 17:335-337 Aug-Sep '75; Jan 17-Jun 11, 1975. 18:23-25 Jan '76; Jun 16-Sep 1975. 18:294-296+ Jul-Aug '76; Sep-Dec 1975. 18:365-366 Oct '76

A closer look at the space shuttle Orbiter. illus Interavia 31:1170-1171 Dec '76

Evolution of the space shuttle. David Baker. illus (Also cutaways) tabs Spaceflight pt 1, 15:202-210 Jun '73; pt 2, 15:264-268 Jul '73; pt 3, 15:344-352 Sep '73; pt 4, 18:304-326+ Sep '76

Help wanted: Astronaut! (Qualifications and possible careers for the new space shuttle astronauts needed by NASA in 1978) Capt John B. Taylor. illus Airman 20:46-48 Oct '76

Looking beyond the space shuttle. Dave Dooling. illus -Spaceflight pt 1, 18:68-69 Feb '76; pt 2, 18:227 Jun '76; pt 3, 18:367-368+ Oct '76

(Microwave Scanning Beam Landing System--MSBLS) Signal 31:82 Nov-Dec '76

Payloads for the shuttle. Robert Edgar. illus tabs Spaceflight 18:327-330 Sep '76

The pervasive importance of USAF's space mission. Interview. LtGen Thomas W. Morgan. illus AF Mag 59:46-50 Jan '76

Rockwell International's Shuttle Orbiter. (Design profile, no. 28) Maurice Allward. illus tab Air Pict 38:432-436 Nov '76

The space shuttle and Vandenberg Air Force Base. MajGen R. C. Henry and Maj Aubrey B. Sloan. illus map AU Rev 27:19-26 Sep-Oct '76

Space shuttle economics and U.S. defence potentialities. Klaus Heiss. illus tabs Interavia 31:1071-1073 Nov '76

Space shuttle: High-flying Yankee ingenuity. Edgar Ulsamer. illus tab AF Mag 59:98-100+ Sep '76

Two tracks to new worlds. Michael A. G. Michaud. illus tab Spaceflight 18:2-6+ Jan '76

History

Evolution of the space shuttle. David Baker. illus (Also cutaways) tabs Spaceflight pt 1, 15:202-210 Jun '73; pt 2, 15:264-268 Jul '73; pt 3, 15:344-352 Sep '73; pt 4, 18:304-326+ Sep '76

SPACE VEHICLES

See also
Satellites, Artificial
Space Stations
Space Transporters
    also space vehicles under project name, e.g.,
Space Project--Skylab

SPACE VEHICLES - Continued

Detection

See also
Space Detection and Tracking System

Electronic Equipment

See Electronic Equipment (Space Vehicles)

Landing

Landing systems for space vehicles. Karl O. Brauer. illus tab Spaceflight 18:47-53 Feb '76

Launching

Weather probability forecasts: A cost-saving technique in space launch and missile test operations. MajGen Herbert A. Lyon, Ret, and LtCol Lynn L. LeBlanc. illus tabs AU Rev 27:45-54 Jan-Feb '76

Rendezvous and Docking

The genesis of orbital rendezvous. H. E. Ross. illus Spaceflight 18:185-186 May '76

Missions to Salyut 4. Gordon R. Hooper. illus (Also cutaway) Spaceflight pt 1, 17:219-225 Jun '75; pt 2, 18:13-18 Jan '76

Tracking

See also
Space Detection and Tracking System

SPACE WARFARE

Will the Soviets wage war in space? Edgar Ulsamer. illus AF Mag 59:30-33+ Dec '76

SPAIN

Foreign Relations

United States

The Spanish Territorial Command Network. Maj Tommy H. Berggren. illus Signal 31:31-34 Sep '76

Politics and Government

Iberian metamorphosis. Leigh Johnson. illus tabs Def & For Aff Dig No. 11:26-35 '76

Spain in 1975: Evolution or sharp break. Guy Hermet. (Trans and condensed from Défense nationale, Aug-Sep 1975) Mil Rev 56:2+ Jun '76

Statistics

Spain. (Demographics) tabs Def & For Aff Dig No. 11: 31-35 '76

Strategic Importance

Iberian metamorphosis. Leigh Johnson. illus tabs Def & For Aff Dig No. 11:26-35 '76

Spain and the defense of NATO. CAPT R. A. Komorowski, Ret. illus map tabs US Nav Inst Proc 102:190-203 May '76

Spain: Free World asset. ADM Horacio Rivero, Ret. illus Strat Rev 4:66-71 Spring '76

The Spanish connection: A wider U.S. commitment in the making. maps tabs Def Monitor 5: entire issue '76

SPANISH-AMERICAN WAR, 1898

The (Richmond Pearson) Hobson craze. (Naval officer in the Spanish-American War, commander and survivor of a certifiable suicide mission (sinking of the Merrimac), with matinee idol looks that made him his country's first major sex symbol) Barton C. Shaw. illus US Nav Inst Proc 102: 54-60 Feb '76

SPRUANCE, William W.

The will to live. (From address, 1975 SAC Safety Conference, Carswell AFB, Tex) BrigGen William W.Spruance. por Combat Crew 26:16-21 Jan '76

SQUADRON OFFICER SCHOOL

Forging the future force (at Squadron Officer School). Ted R.Sturm. illus Airman 20:18-22 Mar '76

Rebuilt Wright. (Volunteers from Squadron Officer School at Maxwell AFB, Ala, build a replica of the Wright brothers' 1910 hangar) Irene P.Barrett. illus Airman 20:20 Nov '76

What the captain really means. (A survey on Air Force ethics and standards made at Squadron Officer School and resulting recommendations) Maj Peter Henderson. illus AU Rev 27:96-101 Jan-Feb '76

STAFF COLLEGES

Air Force--U.S.

See also colleges by name, e.g.,
Air Command and Staff College
Air War College

375 picked for Senior (Service) Schools. AF Times 37:32 Nov 29 '76

Armed Forces

Enhance your potential through PME. LtCol Marvin T.Howell. illus tabs AF Engrg & Svcs Qtr 17:33-37 Nov '76

Intermediate (Service) Schools to get 634 officers. AF Times 36:21 Mar 8 '76

214 selected for FY 77 Senior Service Schools. AF Times 36:25 Feb 23 '76

Armed Forces--U.S.

See also colleges by name, e.g.,
Industrial College of the Armed Forces
National Defense University
National War College

(Defense) group seeks to improve quality of Staff Colleges. AF Times 36:8 Feb 23 '76

82 placed on list for Senior (Service) Schools. AF Times 36:17 Mar 22 '76

101 named for (Senior and Intermediate Service) Schools. AF Times 36:10 May 24 '76

Army--U.S.

See also
Army War College
Command and General Staff College

Navy--U.S.

See also
Naval War College

NATO

The NATO School (SHAPE). Capt Terry L.Heyns. illus NATO's Fifteen Nations 21:49-56 Jun-Jul '76

STAFFS, MILITARY

See also
Air Staff
Army General Staff
Joint Chiefs of Staff

STAMPS, POSTAGE see Postage Stamps

STANDARD OF LIVING see Cost and Standard of Living

STANDARDIZATION

AF, Navy look at sharing systems training data. AF Times 36:32 Feb 23 '76

The AIM-9L Super-Sidewinder: NATO standardization in practice. W.Schenk. tab illus (Also cutaway) Intl Def Rev 9:365-369 Jun '76

Artillery projects of the future. Karl Heinz Bodlien. (Trans from Soldat und Technik, Aug 1974) illus tabs Fld Arty J 44:10-15 Jan-Feb '76

Buying commercial: Why not? Richard A.Stimson and Marilyn S.Barnett. illus Def Mgt J 12:47-55 Oct '76

CV safety problems: (USS) America's approach. CDR S.P.Dunlap. illus Approach 21:12-15 May '76

Coming: A North Atlantic Common Defense Market. Thomas A.Callaghan, Jr. illus map Countermeasures 2:24+ Aug '76

Exporting & importing: A two sided view. Wallace W. Orr. tabs Countermeasures 2:50-51+ Aug '76

Federal cataloging in the seventies. H.Melvin Silver. illus Log Spectrum 10:9-10 Spring '76

Fundamental changes in NATO's standardization policy. Gen T.R.Milton, Ret. AF Mag 59:35 Feb '76

GSE (Ground Support Equipment): From yellow to dark green. TIG Brief 28:13 Apr 23 '76

The Leopard 2AV German hope for a standard NATO tank. illus tabs Intl Def Rev 9:111-114 Feb '76

MBT Leopard 2 AV for NATO? G.M.Bailly-Cowell. illus tabs NATO's Fifteen Nations 21:19-26+ Jun-Jul '76

The metrication program. LtGen Robert E.Hails. TIG Brief 28:2 Dec 3 '76

NATO equipment standardization--the German view. illus Intl Def Rev 9:563-568 Aug '76

NATO must standardize. Maj Patrick Wall, Ret. (Reprinted from Navy International, May 1976) tabs Mil Rev 56:58-63 Dec '76

The NATO program for rationalization and standardization. Norman Gray. illus Signal 30:80-81+ May-Jun '76

NATO: Standardization for improved combat capability. MajGen Richard C.Bowman. illus Comdrs Dig 19: entire issue Sep 9 '76

NATO's new MBT "gun" will be 3 new guns. Benjamin F.Schemmer. illus Armed Forces J Intl 113:12 Apr '76

New DOD explosives hazard classification system. TIG Brief 28:9 Aug 27 '76

New explosives hazard classification/compatibility and fire symbol systems. TIG Brief 28:6 Feb 27 '76

Roland II: Has America bought the wrong weapon? John Marriott. illus NATO's Fifteen Nations 20: 78-79 Dec '75-Jan '76

Single vendor integrity. Cary A.Moore. illus Log Spectrum 10:13-15+ Spring '76

Standard port system. LtCol Arthur G.Neil, Jr. illus Army Log 8:30-32 May-Jun '76

Standardisation and defence in NATO. Gardiner L. Tucker. RUSI J for Def Studies 121:7-8+ Mar '76

STRATEGIC FORCES

Russia

The impact of technology on U.S. deterrent forces. Gen William J.Evans. illus Strat Rev 4:40-47 Summer '76

Measuring the strategic nuclear balance. tabs AF Mag 59:106-107 Dec '76

Soviet R&D at "critical mass": "Sobering assessment" troubles DOD research chief (Malcolm R. Currie). Benjamin F.Schemmer. tabs Armed Forces J Intl 113:12-13 Mar '76

Strategic Forces: How America & the Soviets compare. Gen George S.Brown. illus tabs Comdrs Dig 19: entire issue Apr 15 '76

Strategic vulnerability: The balance between prudence and paranoia. John D.Steinbruner and Thomas M. Garwin. illus tabs Intl Sec 1:138-181 Summer '76

(U.S./USSR military balance) illus tabs Armed Forces J Intl pt 1, U.S./USSR military balance shifts in favor of Russia. Benjamin F.Schemmer. 113:18+ Mar '76; pt 2, Scope of and reasons behind U.S./USSR force asymmetries. 113:23-26+ Apr '76; pt 3 (Summary) 113:24-28 May '76

United States

The Air Force and national security: 1976 and beyond. (Remarks, Air Force Assoc, Mobile Chapter, Mobile, Ala, March 27, 1976) LtGen John W. Pauly. AF Pley Ltr for Comdrs: Sup No.6:10-18 Jun '76

The artificial crisis of American security. illus tabs Def Monitor pt 1 (Military balance between U.S. and USSR) 5: entire issue May '76; pt 2, How much for defense? 5: entire issue Jun '76

The B-1: A national imperative. Francis P.Hoeber. Strat Rev 4:111-117 Summer '76

The B-1: The right solution. (Remarks, Council of World Affairs, Dallas, April 15, 1976) Thomas C. Reed. AF Pley Ltr for Comdrs: Sup No.6:2-9 Jun '76

The case for the B-1 bomber. John F.McCarthy, Jr. illus tabs Intl Sec 1:78-97 Fall '76

Defense hearings underway: Rumsfeld details plans for new weapons. tabs Officer 52:5+ Mar '76

Foreign policy and national security. (From address, World Affairs Council and Southern Methodist University, Dallas, March 22, 1976) Henry A.Kissinger. Intl Sec 1:182-191 Summer '76

The impact of technology on U.S. deterrent forces. Gen William J.Evans. illus Strat Rev 4:40-47 Summer '76

Measuring the strategic nuclear balance. tabs AF Mag 59:106-107 Dec '76

Modernization and the military balance. (Address, AFA National Convention, Washington, Sep 19-23, 1976) Thomas C.Reed. illus AF Mag 59:34-37 Nov '76

Modernizing the strategic bomber force without really trying: A case against the B-1. Archie L.Wood. Intl Sec 1:98-116 Fall '76

Options in using nuclear weapons. (Remarks, Air Force Assoc Symposium, Vandenberg AFB, Calif, April 28, 1976) LtGen John W.Pauly. AF Pley Ltr for Comdrs: Sup No.10:15-23 Oct '76

STRATEGIC FORCES - Continued

United States - Cont'd

Soviet R&D at "critical mass": "Sobering assessment" troubles DOD research chief (Malcolm R. Currie). Benjamin F.Schemmer. tabs Armed Forces J Intl 113:12-13 Mar '76

Strategic Force modernization. (Remarks, Air Force Assoc luncheon, Washington, Sep 22, 1976) Thomas C.Reed. AF Pley Ltr for Comdrs: Sup No.11: 2-8 Nov '76

Strategic Forces: How America & the Soviets compare. Gen George S.Brown. illus tabs Comdrs Dig 19: entire issue Apr 15 '76

Strategic vulnerability: The balance between prudence and paranoia. John D.Steinbruner and Thomas M. Garwin. illus tabs Intl Sec 1:138-181 Summer '76

(U.S./USSR military balance) illus tabs Armed Forces J Intl pt 1, U.S./USSR military balance shifts in favor of Russia. Benjamin F.Schemmer. 113:18+ Mar '76; pt 2, Scope of and reasons behind U.S./USSR force asymmetries. 113:23-26+ Apr '76; pt 3 (Summary) 113:24-28 May '76

STRATEGIC IMPORTANCE see as subdivision under specific country and geographical area

STRATEGY

See also as a subdivision under specific wars, e.g.,
Vietnamese Conflict, 1957-1975--Strategy
World War II--Strategy

A difference in perspective (between military and political leaders). Frederick H.Hartmann. illus Nav War Col Rev 28:65-74 Spring '76

Economic strategy. Regular feature in issues of Defense & Foreign Affairs Digest

En clair: A monthly report on strategic news. Regular feature in issues of Defense & Foreign Affairs Digest

Military concepts for political objectives. LtCol Joel J.Snyder, Ret. illus AU Rev 27:55-62 Jan-Feb '76

NATO defensive concepts. Maj A.E.Hemesley. illus Armor 85:25-26 Nov-Dec '76

Nuclear strategy: The debate moves on. Colin S.Gray. RUSI J for Def Studies 121:44-50 Mar '76

Psychological strategy. Regular feature in some issues of Defense & Foreign Affairs Digest

Strategic pulse: Electronic warfare in the current strategic environment. David Harvey. illus Def & For Aff Dig No.5:4-5+ '76

Strategy and society. Correlli Barnett. RUSI J for Def Studies 121:11-19 Sep '76

War survival in Soviet strategy. Foy D.Kohler. AF Mag 59:90-92+ Sep '76

Asia

Asia. Philip Paisley and Leigh Johnson. illus tab Def & For Aff Dig No.5:18-19+ '76

Australia

The vulnerability of Australia's maritime trade. A.W.Grazebrook. illus tabs NATO's Fifteen Nations 20:40-45+ Dec '75-Jan '76

Germany

History

Scharnhorst to Schlieffen: The rise and decline of German military thought. Herbert Rosinski. Nav War Col Rev 29:83-103 Summer '76

Great Britain

Strategy and society. Correlli Barnett. RUSI J for Def Studies 121:11-19 Sep '76

Iran

The Rapier & mace: Air defense & the art of grand strategy; a study of the Iranian example. Gregory Copley. illus Def & For Aff Dig No. 4:6-11 '76

Israel

Liddell Hart's influence on Israeli military theory and practice. Brian Bond. maps RUSI J for Def Studies 121:83-89 Jun '76

NATO

Inflexibility in NATO's flexible response. Maj Donald F. Borden. illus maps Mil Rev 56:26-41 Jan '76

Military support for NATO political strategy. Maj Edward A. Corcoran. Mil Rev 56:37-43 Aug '76

NATO and the dawn of new technology. Stefan T. Possony. illus tab Def & For Aff Dig pt 1, No. 10: 15-17+ '76; pt 2, No. 11:18-20+ '76

The need for offensive operations on land. (Trench Gascoigne Prize Essay, 1975) Maj R. S. Evans. RUSI J for Def Studies 121:28-33 Sep '76

Security makes strange bedfellows: NATO's problems from a minimalist perspective. Ken Booth. RUSI J for Def Studies 120:3-4+ Dec '75

The southern flank of NATO: Problems of the southern region in the post-1973 October War period. ADM Means Johnston, Jr. illus Mil Rev 56:22-29 Apr '76

Tactical nuclear warfare and NATO: Viable strategy or dead end? LtGen Arthur S. Collins, Jr, Ret. illus NATO's Fifteen Nations 21:72-74+ Jun-Jul '76

A tactical triad for deterring limited war in Western Europe. LtCol Thomas C. Blake, Jr. illus AU Rev 27:8-15 Sep-Oct '76

Who needs nuclear tacair? Col David L. Nichols. illus AU Rev 27:15-25 Mar-Apr '76

Russia

Africa strategy. Gregory Copley. illus Def & For Aff Dig No. 3:6-9+ '76

The best defense is ... Majs Walter P. Lang, Jr and John N. Taylor. illus Mil Rev 56:12-22 Aug '76

Boris Nikolayevich Ponomarev: Run silent, run deep. Stefan Possony. illus Def & For Aff Dig No. 11: 6-9+ '75

Clausewitz and Soviet politico-military strategy. BrigGen Antonio Pelliccia. NATO's Fifteen Nations 20:18-21+ Dec '75-Jan '76; Digest. Mil Rev 56:23-33 Aug '76

"Detente" in Soviet strategy. G. M. Bailly-Cowell. NATO's Fifteen Nations 20:86-90 Dec '75-Jan '76

Detente: Soviet policy and purpose. John Erickson. Strat Rev 4:37-43 Spring '76

Russia - Cont'd

A dilemma in studying Soviet tactics. LtCol George F. Steger. illus Mil Rev 56:76-79 Jun '76

The Helsinki agreement and self-determination. Stefan Korbonski. illus Strat Rev 4:48-58 Summer '76

Hemispheric denial: Geopolitical imperatives and Soviet strategy. BrigGen Edward B. Atkeson. maps illus Strat Rev 4:26-36 Spring '76

A holocaust for Happy Valley? Henry Young. illus US Nav Inst Proc 102:52-61 Nov '76

NATO: A view from the East. Maj Geoffrey H. Kleb. illus tabs map Mil Rev 56:3-10 Nov '76

The new Soviet maritime strategy--and the lack of an effective U.S. counter-strategy. RADM George H. Miller, Ret. illus Sea Power 19:17-20 May '76

Soviet Civil Defense--upsetting the strategic balance. Editorial. John L. Frisbee. AF Mag 59:4 Aug '76

Soviet ground forces and the conventional mode of operations. John Erickson. RUSI J for Def Studies 121:45-49 Jun '76

The Soviet threat and U.S. strategic alternatives. (Address, AFA National Convention, Washington, Sep 19-23, 1976) Gen David C. Jones. illus AF Mag 59:38-41 Nov '76

The Soviet view. (Excerpts from Soviet publications as examples of official pronouncement important to an appraisal of U.S. interests) Regular feature in issues of Strategic Review

The state of the Soviets. Gregory Copley. illus Def & For Aff Dig No. 6:6-9+ '76

United States

The airborne division and a strategic concept. Col Fletcher K. Ware. illus tabs Mil Rev 56:23-33 Mar '76

The dimensions of current U.S. military strategy. LtCol C. R. Nelson. illus tabs Mil Rev 56:88-92 Aug '76

The future and the strategic mission. (Excerpt from address, 57th Defense Preparedness Meeting, American Defense Preparedness Assoc, Los Angeles, Oct 15, 1975) MajGen Andrew B. Anderson, Jr. Natl Def 60:286 Jan-Feb '76

GAO slams strategic airlift "requirements" and programs. Armed Forces J Intl 113:14 Jul '76

A holocaust for Happy Valley? Henry Young. illus US Nav Inst Proc 102:52-61 Nov '76

The impact of technology on U.S. deterrent forces. Gen William J. Evans. illus Strat Rev 4:40-47 Summer '76

Keynote luncheon address (APGEA, Washington, June 8, 1976). Thomas C. Reed. illus Signal 30: 19-23 Aug '76

Latin America: Military-strategic concepts. LtCol John Child. maps AU Rev 27:27-42 Sep-Oct '76

M-X, a new dimension in strategic deterrence. LtGen Alton D. Slay. illus AF Mag 59:44-49 Sep '76

Military force and political influence in an age of peace. Robert Ellsworth. illus Strat Rev 4:5-11 Spring '76

Military intelligence: A fight for identity. Col Leonard A. Spirito and Maj Marc B. Powe. Army 26: 14-21 May '76

STRATEGY - Continued

United States - Cont'd

Missile muscle: A report on battlefield missiles. David Harvey. illus Def & For Aff Dig No.2: 12-14+ '76

The new "nuclear options" in military strategy. Maj Donald A.Mahley. illus Mil Rev 56:3-7 Dec '76

The new nuclear strategy: Battle of the dead? maps Def Monitor 5: entire issue Jul '76

The new short war strategy. Gen James H.Polk, Ret. (Reprinted from Strategic Review, Summer 1975) Mil Rev 56:58-64 Mar '76

Nuclear technology in support of our strategic options. MajGen Edward B.Giller, Ret. tab AU Rev 28:26-34 Nov-Dec '76

Options in using nuclear weapons. (Remarks, Air Force Assoc Symposium,. Vandenberg AFB, Calif, April 28, 1976) LtGen John W.Pauly. AF Plcy Ltr for Comdrs: Sup No. 10:15-23 Oct '76

The present role of the American soldier. Maj Robert F.Helms II. illus Mil Rev 56:12-18 Apr '76

Readiness and national survival. (Address, Air Force Assoc Symposium, Los Angeles, Oct 22, 1976) Malcolm R.Currie. AF Plcy Ltr for Comdrs:Sup No.12:14-21 Dec '76

The relevance of civilian-based defense to U.S. security interests. BrigGen Edward B.Atkeson. tab illus Mil Rev pt 1, 56:24-32 May '76; pt 2, 56:45-55 Jun '76

Resource control strategy. Anthony Harrigan. illus Natl Def 60:350-352 Mar-Apr '76

Soviet threat and national strategic choices. (Remarks, Air Force Assoc luncheon, Washington, Sep 21, 1976) Gen David C.Jones. AF Plcy Ltr for Comdrs: Sup.No.11:8-13 Nov '76

The Soviet threat and U.S. strategic alternatives. (Address, AFA National Convention, Washington, Sep 19-23, 1976) Gen David C.Jones. illus AF Mag 59:38-41 Nov '76

A strategic concept for defense. LtGen John W. Pauly and Capt Michael O.Wheeler. illus Strat Rev 4:83-91 Summer '76

The strategic conflict. James Constant. illus tabs Countermeasures pt 1, 2:32-36+ Mar '76; pt 2, 2:26-30+ Apr '76

Strategy and readiness. Gen John J.Hennessey. illus Strat Rev 4:44-48 Fall '76

Technology and strategy: Precision guided munitions and other highly sophisticated weapons will increase the effectiveness of the nuclear threat. Michael L.Nacht. Natl Def 61:199-202 Nov-Dec '76

U.S. military strategy for the eighties. Gen Andrew J.Goodpaster, Ret. illus Natl Sec Aff Forum No.24:1-12 Spring-Summer '76

The United States, NATO and the decade ahead. Col Robert W.Kochenour. illus Mil Rev 56:14-24 Jul '76

U.S. policy alternatives in Asia. Robert A.Scalapino. illus Parameters 5, No.2:14-24 '76

WestPac Afloat Battalion (concept). LtCol Wallace M.Greene III. illus MarCor Gaz 60:33-36 Feb '76

STRATEGY, AIR

Who needs nuclear tacair? Col David L.Nichols. illus AU Rev 27:15-25 Mar-Apr '76

Great Britain

History

The RAF and counter-force strategy before World War II. Malcolm Smith. RUSI J for Def Studies 121:68-73 Jun '76

NATO

The viability of offensive air support in the next decade. Gary Tobin. illus Intl Def Rev 9:361-364 Jun '76

United States

Is TacAir dead? CAPT Gerald G.O'Rourke, Ret. illus US Nav Inst Proc 102:34-41 Oct '76

STRATEGY, NAVAL

Foreign policies at risk: Some problems of managing naval power. Ken Booth. illus Nav War Col Rev 29:3-15 Summer '76

The naval profession: Challenge and response, 1870-1890 and 1950-1970. Lawrence C.Allin. Nav War Col Rev 28:75-90 Spring '76

Where do we go from here? CAPT John E.Greenbacker, Ret. illus US Nav Inst Proc 102:18-24 Jun '76

NATO

The Royal Navy--its contribution to national and Western defence. Adm Terence Lewin. RUSI J for Def Studies 121:3-4+ Sep '76

Russia

Foreign policies at risk: Some problems of managing naval power. Ken Booth. illus Nav War Col Rev 29:3-15 Summer '76

The Gorshkov doctrine: Seapower and the world ocean. L.Edgar Prina. illus Sea Power 19:33-37 Oct '76

Kiev and the U.S. carrier controversy. Henry T. Simmons. illus tabs Intl Def Rev 9:741-744 Oct '76

The role of the Kiev in Soviet naval operations. LCDR William R.Hynes. illus Nav War Col Rev 29:38-46 Fall '76

The Soviet view of navies in peacetime. Uri Ra'anan. illus Nav War Col Rev 29:30-38 Summer '76

Superpowers at sea: A debate. ADM Worth H.Bagley, Ret and RADM Gene R.LaRocque, Ret. Intl Sec 1:56-76 Summer '76

The vulnerability of the West in the Southern Hemisphere. Patrick Wall. illus tab Strat Rev 4:44-50 Winter '76

History

American maritime strategy and Soviet naval expansion. J.William Middendorf II. illus tabs Strat Rev 4:16-25 Winter '76

United States

Admiral Ernest J.King and the strategy for victory in the Pacific. Clark G.Reynolds. illus Nav War Col Rev 28:57-64 Winter '76

STRATEGY, NAVAL - Continued

United States - Cont'd

American maritime strategy and Soviet naval expansion. J.William Middendorf II. illus tabs Strat Rev 4:16-25 Winter '76

A flexible military posture. Gen Louis H. Wilson. illus Strat Rev 4:7-13 Fall '76

Kiev and the U.S. carrier controversy. Henry T. Simmons. illus tabs Intl Def Rev 9:741-744 Oct '76

Return to a maritime-based national strategy for the Marine Corps. E.W.Girard. illus tabs MarCor Gaz 60:38-45 Nov '76

Superpowers at sea: A debate. ADM Worth H.Bagley, Ret and RADM Gene R.LaRocque, Ret. Intl Sec 1:56-76 Summer '76

Tactical development in the fleet. (Prize Essay, 1976) CAPT Robert H.Smith, Ret. illus US Nav Inst Proc 102:18-23 Apr '76

The Transkei: Key to U.S. naval strategy in the Indian Ocean. Maj Wesley A.Groesbeck. illus map Mil Rev 56:18-24 Jun '76

U.S. naval strategy of the future. VADM Joseph P. Moorer. illus tab Strat Rev 4:72-80 Spring '76

The world environment and U.S. military policy for the 1970s and 1980s. ADM Thomas H.Moorer, Ret and Alvin J.Cottrell. tab Strat Rev 4:56-65 Spring '76

History

American maritime strategy and Soviet naval expansion. J.William Middendorf II. illus tabs Strat Rev 4:16-25 Winter '76

Sea power--Teddy's "big stick." (Alfred Mahan's influence on Theodore Roosevelt and U.S. history) CAPT Guy Cane. illus US Nav Inst Proc 102:40-48 Aug '76

The U.S. Navy and the problem of oil in a future war The outline of a strategic dilemma, 1945-1950. David Alan Rosenberg. illus Nav War Col Rev 29: 53-64 Summer '76

STRATOSPHERE see Atmosphere, Upper

STREAM CROSSING, MILITARY

(Water barriers in combination with obstructions considerably influence the character of combat operations of attacking subunits) 1. Crossing a water obstacle; 2. Dash to a river; 3. Supporting motorised Infantry; 4. Air defence of an advanced detachment; 5. Pontoniers; 6. Raising offensive enthusiasm; 7. Exploit at crossing; 8. An Army forces a crossing. illus maps Soviet Mil Rev No.7: 17-41 Jul '76

STRESS (PHYSIOLOGY)

Arousing environmental stresses can improve performance, whatever people say. E.C.Poulton. tabs Aviation, Space & Envmt Med 47:1193-1204 Nov '76

Fatigue. LtCol David H.Karney and Patsy Thompson. illus tabs USA Avn Dig 22:28-34 Feb '76

Flight-induced changes in human amino acid excretion. James P.Ellis, Jr and others. tabs Aviation, Space & Envmt Med 47:1-8 Jan '76

Flight limits and crew rest. LtCol David H.Karney. illus tab USA Avn Dig 22:38-39 Dec '76

STRESS (PHYSIOLOGY) - Continued

Head and neck cooling by air, water, or air plus water in hyperthermia. Abbott T.Kissen and others. illus tabs Aviation, Space & Envmt Med 47:265-271 Mar '76

Hearing under stress. III: The effect of external auditory meatal pressure on speech discrimination. G.L.Whitehead and others. tabs Aviation, Space & Envmt Med 47:308-309 Mar '76

Heat and simulated high altitude: Effects on biochemical indices of stress and performance. Ralph P. Francesconi and others. tabs Aviation, Space & Envmt Med 47:548-552 May '76

Heat stroke: A review. Shlomo Shibolet and others. illus tabs Aviation, Space & Envmt Med 47:280-301 Mar '76

Instrumentation for the rhesus monkey as a cardiovascular analog for man during air-combat maneuvering acceleration. Howard H.Erickson and John R.Ritzman. illus tabs Aviation, Space & Envmt Med 47:1153-1158 Nov '76

Method for determining pilot stress through analysis of voice communication. Isao Kuroda and others. illus tabs Aviation, Space & Envmt Med 47:528-533 May '76

Operational aspects of stress and fatigue. Maj William C.Wood. illus tabs USA Avn Dig 22:30-33 Sep '76

Prolactin, thyrotropin, and growth hormone release during stress associated with parachute jumping. Gordon L.Noel and others. illus Aviation, Space & Envmt Med 47:543-547 May '76

Prolonged visual loss and bradycardia following deceleration from +6 G_z acceleration: A case report. John S.Kirkland and James A.Kennealy. illus Aviation, Space & Envmt Med 47:310-311 Mar '76

Responses of the autonomic nervous system during acclimatization to high altitude in man. M.S.Malhotra and others. tabs Aviation, Space & Envmt Med 47:1076-1079 Oct '76

Self-possession. (Some forms and methods used in the Soviet Armed Forces to educate this quality in military personnel) Col V.Grebnev. Soviet Mil Rev No.7:47-48 Jul '76

Serum uric acid, cholesterol, and psychological moods throughout stressful naval training. Richard H.Rahe and others. tabs Aviation, Space & Envmt Med 47:883-888 Aug '76

Stress and fatigue. LtCol John J.Treanor. illus tab USA Avn Dig 22:8+ Nov '76

Stress in air traffic controllers: Effects of ARTS-III. C.E.Melton and others. illus tabs Aviation, Space & Envmt Med 47:925-930 Sep '76

Time bomb (stress). Capt Allan R.Sweeny. illus Aerosp Safety 32:26-28 Jun '76

Using good sense in stress training. TIG Brief 28:12 Dec 17 '76

STRESSES see Strains and Stresses

STRIKE COMMAND see Readiness Command

STUDY, METHOD OF

How to study and take tests. Gen Bruce C.Clarke, Ret. illus Soldiers 31:31-33 Apr '76

SUBMARINE WARFARE

See also
Antisubmarine Warfare

SUBMARINES

See also
Submersible Vehicles

Anti-submarine warfare: The envious siege of wat'ry Neptune. illus Def & For Aff Dig No.8-9:60-63+ '76

Equipment

An automatic Omega navigation system for submarines. Brian Greenberg. illus RUSI J for Def Studies 121:76-81 Mar '76

Indian Ocean Region

The vulnerability of Australia's maritime trade. A.W.Grazebrook. illus tabs NATO's Fifteen Nations 20:40-45+ Dec '75-Jan '76

Russia

(The Navy): Unknown events, disturbing trends, and a rebuilding of strength. J.William Middendorf II. illus tabs Sea Power 19:7-13 Jan '76

United States

History

A brief history of the Submarine Force. D.J.Bishop. (Condensed from Fathom, Spring 1975) illus Countermeasures 2:24-25 Dec '75-Jan '76

SUBMERSIBLE VEHICLES

"For those in peril ..." (Search and rescue of submersibles) W.Robert Bryant. illus US Nav Inst Proc 102:105-108 Apr '76

SUBSISTENCE ALLOWANCES

EM on BAS charged higher meal rates. AF Times 37:3 Oct 25 '76

Food service--200 years of advancement. Lt Dennis A.Bossen. illus AF Engrg & Svcs Qtr 17:14-16 Feb '76

Higher food costs for those on BAS? Ron Sanders. AF Times 36:2 Jun 21 '76

(Loring AFB) Maine food test extended. AF Times 36:22 Feb 23 '76

Meal charges to drop. AF Times 37:9 Dec 13 '76

New basic meal charges detailed. AF Times 37:8 Oct 18 '76

Senior NCOs to get direct BAS payments. Bruce Callander. AF Times 36:6 Feb 9 '76

SUBVERSIVE ACTIVITIES

AFR 205-57 ("Reporting and Investigating Espionage, Sabotage, Terrorism and Subversion") is applicable to all USAF personnel. TIG Brief 28:6 May 7 '76

Boris Nikolayevich Ponomarev: Run silent, run deep. Stefan Possony. illus Def & For Aff Dig No.11: 6-9+ '75

Joining KKK not prohibited. AF Times 37:2 Dec 13 '76

Reporting and Investigating Espionage, Sabotage, Terrorism, and Subversion. (AFR 205-57) Contact, p 2, Spring '76

SUEZ CANAL

Nimrod Spar: Clearing the Suez Canal (of 10 wrecks). CAPT J.Huntly Boyd, Jr. illus map tab US Nav Inst Proc 102:18-26 Feb '76

Return to Egypt. (USS Barnstable County, first U.S. ship to enter the Suez Canal since the 1967 Six-Day War) CDR J.M.Lang. illus US Nav Inst Proc 102:98-100 Feb '76

SUGGESTION PROGRAMS

Air Force suggestion program. TIG Brief 28:17 Dec 3 '76

(MTMC) suggesters save over $750,000. Dan Hall. illus Translog 7:18-19 May '76

SUKHOI, Pavel O.

Sukhoi: Pioneer Soviet aircraft designer. Jean P.Alexander. por Air Pict 38:136-139 Apr '76

SUN

(Air Force worldwide solar network) Signal 30:152 May-Jun '76

SUPERIOR PERFORMANCE PAY see Proficiency Pay

SUPERPORTS see Ports

SUPERSONIC FLIGHT

See also
Airplanes, Bomber (Supersonic)
Airplanes, Supersonic
Airplanes, Transport (Supersonic)

SUPERVISION

Attention to health/safety matters. TIG Brief 28:5-6 Feb 27 '76

Civilian training to meet Air Force needs. TIG Brief 28:15 Jul 16 '76

Control & supervision and flying. Col Paul M.Davis. illus Aerosp Safety 32:19-21 Aug '76

Effective performance of employees. TIG Brief 28:12 May 21 '76

How to define training requirements for OJT. TIG Brief 28:12 Dec 17 '76

Leadership. TIG Brief 28:13 Nov 5 '76

Management, supervision, and other old proverbs. TIG Brief 28:10 Jun 4 '76

Medical/dental supervisors' responsibilities for mobilization augmentees. TIG Brief 28:10 Jul 16 '76

On-the-job training. TIG Brief 28:13 Oct 22 '76

The people mix. Maj James M.Alford. AU Rev 27: 72-74 May-Jun '76

Performance evaluation and productivity. TIG Brief 28:18 Apr 9 '76

Supervising supervisors. TIG Brief 28:17 Jul 16 '76

The supervisor and hazard reporting. TIG Brief 28:11 Apr 9 '76

Supervisor of Flying regulation (AFR 60-2). TIG Brief 28:8 May 21 '76

Supervisor Of Flying (SOF) program. (AFR 60-2) TIG Brief 28:14 Dec 3 '76

A supervisor's responsibility. TIG Brief 28:4 Jan 30 '76

SUPREME HEADQUARTERS ALLIED POWERS IN
EUROPE - Continued

History - Cont'd

SHAPE--those were the days. Gen Robert J.Wood,
Ret. illus Army 26:42-47 Dec '76

SURFACE EFFECT SHIPS see Air Cushion Vehicles

SURPLUS PROPERTY

The banana flies again. (Surplus H-21 has re-united
crew for maintenance and first "civilian" flight)
illus Airman 20:48 Jan '76

Disposal office saves AF $$. Amn Mark Issacs. AF
Times 36:25 Feb 9 '76

Making retrograde cost effective. (Air Force materi-
el used in Southeast Asia) LtCol Barry W.Jenkins.
illus AF Engrg & Svcs Qtr 17:26-27 May '76

SURPRISE IN WARFARE

Ambush (reconnaissance). Maj V.Yatsenko. illus map
Soviet Mil Rev No.5:20-22 May '76

Reconnaissance in strength. Col B.Antsiz. illus Sovi-
et Mil Rev No.5:23-24 May '76

Roving AA (Anti-Aircraft) subunits and ambushes.
Col V.Subbotin. Soviet Mil Rev No.2:24-25 Feb '76

Soviet reconnaissance. RUSI J for Def Studies pt 1.
P.H.Vigor. 120:41-45 Dec '75; pt 2. Chris Don-
nelly. 121:68-75 Mar '76

Speed in attack. Col V.Ustyuzhnikov. Soviet Mil Rev
No.2:20-21 Feb '76

SURVEILLANCE

Airborne warning--it's worth the price. LtCol Lowell
Davis. illus (Also cutaway) Natl Def 60:374-377
Mar-Apr '76

Battlefield surveillance. Charles Latour. illus
NATO's Fifteen Nations 20:62-65+ Dec '75-Jan '76

Battlefield surveillance. (Army's In-Flight DAta
Transmission System (AIDATS)) illus Counter-
measures 2:12 Jun '76

Guarding Britain's liquid gold. (North Sea oil) Stefan
Geisenheyner. illus AF Mag 59:31-33 Jan '76

The military characteristics of reconnaissance and
surveillance. George F.Steeg. illus tabs Elect
Warfare 8:71+ Sep-Oct '76

SURVEYING

Geodesy, mapping, oceanography: Current surveying
and mapping news. Regular feature in issues of
Military Engineer

Surveys for engineering and science. (From "Survey
of the Coast" to National Ocean Survey) RADM Al-
len L.Powell. illus Mil Engr 68:198-201 May-
Jun '76

SURVEYING BY AIR

Airborne hydrographic surveying. Clifford J.Cran-
dall. illus Mil Engr 68:102-103 Mar-Apr '76

SURVEYS

Base inspection questionnaire on people problems.
TIG Brief 28:5 Jun 18 '76

Basics quizzed at Lackland (AFB, Tex) reveal ideas
on prevailing issues. Bruce Callander. AF Times
37:10 Sep 6 '76

Being Number One nation: Primacy and detente. Col
Anthony L.Wermuth, Ret. illus tabs Parameters
5, No.2:54-68 '76

SURVEYS - Continued

Family separation top (AF) gripe. AF Times 37:18
Aug 23 '76

A military elite in transition: Air Force leaders in
the 1980s. (Research undertaken at Air Command
and Staff College) LtCol Franklin D.Margiotta.
tabs Armed Forces & Soc 2:155-184 Winter '76

Military unions opposed by 82% (in poll by Public Ser-
vice Research Council). tab AF Times 36:10
Jun 21 '76

Quality-of-life survey: Spouses like service more
than mates do--family separation top gripe.
Bruce Callander and others. tabs AF Times 36:4+
Mar 22 '76

Race-relation efforts pay off: Survey charts prog-
ress. Len Famiglietti. AF Times 36:4 May 24 '76

Readers' survey. (How they feel about this year's
elections and whether they plan to vote or support
candidates for Federal offices) tab AF Times 36:8
May 17 '76

Some attitudes on honor code (at West Point): Survey
report. Phil Stevens. AF Times 36:14 Jul 19 '76

Survey says (military Service) members deserve new
contract. AF Times 36:6 Jun 7 '76

Terrain flight international. (Survey of 9 NATO na-
tions and 3 Army agencies) Capt Don A.Mynard.
illus USA Avn Dig 22:30-34 Aug '76

The Vietnam War in retrospect: The Army generals'
views. Douglas Kinnard. tabs J Pol & Mil Sociol
4:17-28 Spring '76

What the captain really means. (A survey on Air
Force ethics and standards made at Squadron Of-
ficer School and resulting recommendations) Maj
Peter Henderson. illus AU Rev 27:96-101 Jan-
Feb '76

SURVIVAL

See also
Civil Defense
Evasion and Escape

Escape. LtCol Charles L.Pocock, Jr. illus Aerosp
Safety 32:10-11 Jul '76

Killer of the unprepared. (Hypothermia) Sgt Allan L.
Bobst. illus tab Aerosp Safety 32:20-21 Nov '76

Medical aspects of survivability. LtCol David H.Kar-
ney and Patsy Thompson. illus USA Avn Dig pt 1,
Lifesaving emergency medical aid. 22:40-45
May '76; pt 2, Medical problems in a prolonged
survival situation. 22:28-31 Jun '76

Ordeal. Scott McIntire. (Reprinted from Interceptor,
Feb 1974) illus Interceptor 18:5-9 Jan '76

A point of view: Underwater egress from helicopters.
LT Mariner G.Cox. illus Approach 21:16-18
Feb '76

Red Flag mirrors war in desert near Nellis (AFB,
Nev). AF Times 36:18 Jan 5 '76

Red Flag (or how to fight the elements and live to tell
about it). Capt Ronald E.Vivion. illus TAC Attack
16:20-22 Dec '76

The rise of the ejection survival rate. Rudolph C.
Delgado. illus Aerosp Safety 32:6-7 Apr '76

Survival. illus Approach 21:22-23 Jan '76

Survival: Food. SSgt Charles R.Teagarden. illus
Aerosp Safety pt 1, Nutrition and survival rations.
32:17-19 Jul '76; pt 2, Subsistence off the land.
32:13-15 Aug '76; pt 3, Food preparation 32:
14-16 Sep '76

SURVIVAL - Continued

Survival: Water. SSgt Charles R. Teagarden. illus
Aerosp Safety 32:22-24 Oct '76

Survival: Your way out. SSgt Robert J. Paetz. illus
Aerosp Safety 32:12-13 Jun '76

The will to live. (From address, 1975 SAC Safety
Conference, Carswell AFB; Tex) BrigGen William
W. Spruance. illus Combat Crew 26:16-21 Jan '76

SURVIVAL EQUIPMENT

How strongly do you feel about life? Your survival
gear and SAR preparation will probably tell. LTJG
Kim A. King. illus Approach 21:18-21 Nov '75;
Aerosp Safety 32:22-24 Jan '76

Life support update. Regular feature in some issues
of TAC Attack starting with Apr 1976

Light aircraft flying can be fun. Capt Marty Steere.
illus TAC Attack 16:6-7 Jul '76

Ordeal. Scott McIntire. (Reprinted from Interceptor,
Feb 1974) illus Interceptor 18:5-9 Jan '76

Passenger assistance in emergencies. LtCol Robert
J. Brun. illus Aerosp Safety 32:9 Feb '76

A point of view: Underwater egress from helicopters·
LT Marine G. Cox. illus Approach 21:16-18
Feb '76

Red Flag (or how to fight the elements and live to tell
about it). Capt Ronald E. Vivion. illus TAC Attack
16:20-22 Dec '76

Stateside survival. illus USA Avn Dig 22:36-37
Dec '76

Super-search progress report. (Another look at life
support equipment development) LtCol Lee Crock.
illus Interceptor 18:8-11 Sep '76

Survival: Red Flag. Capt Ronald E. Vivion. illus
Aerosp Safety pt 1, 32:16-19 Dec '76

The Ventile antiexposure suit: It's great! LCDR Gary
Smith and LT Bob Brich. illus tab Approach 22:
1-5 Oct '76

SURVIVAL TRAINING

Army SERE (Survival, Evasion, Resistance and Es-
cape) training--yes or no, what, where and who.
Capt Ronald J. Jeffers. illus USA Avn Dig 22:34-36
Sep '76

A point of view: Underwater egress from helicopters.
LT Mariner G. Cox. illus Approach 21:16-18
Feb '76

Red Flag (or how to fight the elements and live to tell
about it). Capt Ronald E. Vivion. illus TAC Attack
16:20-22 Dec '76

Survival: Red Flag. Capt Ronald E. Vivion. illus
Aerosp Safety pt 1, 32:16-19 Dec '76

SURVIVORS RIGHTS AND BENEFITS

Children are due full SBP annuity. AF Times 37:61
Oct 18 '76

Clause can speed will settlement. AF Times 37:10
Dec 20 '76

DIC (Dependency and Indemnity Compensation) payments: $260 to $712. tab AF Times 37:21
Dec 13 '76

Extension of tax breaks sought: Benefits for MIA
families. AF Times 37:25 Sep 20 '76

Few advantages and many drawbacks in delaying first
retirement check. Col A. H. Humphreys. Officer
52:25 Jun '76

SURVIVORS RIGHTS AND BENEFITS - Continued

Hearings on improving aid to widows opened (by
House Armed Services Compensation Subcommittee). AF Times 37:4 Aug 9 '76

Hill delays survivor plan action. AF Times 37:54
Sep 6 '76

House okays bill to improve SBP (Survivor Benefits
Program). AF Times 37:2 Oct 4 '76

House panel (Armed Services Military Compensation
Subcommittee) approves change in SBP laws. Phil
Stevens. AF Times 37:20 Aug 16 '76

House unit (Armed Services Committee) acts to cut
Social Security offset. AF Times 37:57 Sep 13 '76

Life insurance as a function of estate planning for the
middle income military member. Maj Mell J.
Lacy. tabs AF Law Rev 17:1-49 Winter '75

Nation-wide concern (with benefits enjoyed in the Soviet Union by war invalids and families of servicemen killed in the war). Soviet Mil Rev No. 4:42-43
Apr '76

ROA endorses bill making survivor improvements.
Officer 52:5 Sep '76

SBP still open to some. AF Times 37:53 Nov 22 '76

Senate panel (Armed Services Committee) guts SBP
bill. Phil Stevens. AF Times 37:2 Oct 11 '76

Survivor Benefits Bill passes in cliff-hanger: Many
other bills approved. Officer 52:6+ Nov '76

3 groups struggle with MIA (status) problem. AF
Times 36:19 May 31 '76

Trailer, pension bills for vets move on Hill. AF
Times 36:6 Jul 5 '76

Vastly improved survivor benefit plan nears vote--
many other congressional actions. Officer 52:4+
Oct '76

Vets to get pension increase Jan 1. AF Times 37:25
Oct 18 '76

When it comes to survivor benefits ... help's at
hand. TSgt Tom Dwyer. illus tabs Airman 20:
36-39 Oct '76

SWEDEN

Foreign Policy

The security and defence of Sweden. Nils Andrén.
illus map RUSI J for Def Studies 121:23-32 Jun '76

Politics and Government

National defense and citizen participation in Sweden:
The citizen army in an open society. William J.
Stover. Nav War Col Rev 28:97-99 Fall '75

SWITCHING SYSTEMS

The initial voice switched network: First step toward
the NICS (NATO Integrated Communications System). Leo I. Barker, Jr and Jerry M. Dressner.
illus Signal 30:6-12 Feb '76

A milestone in the development of data management
systems for WWMCCS. Frank R. Dirnbauer and
others. illus Signal 30:34-37 Jul '76

Ptarmigan--a secure area communications system
for the British Army. illus tabs Intl Def Rev 9:
458-461 Jun '76

SWITCHING SYSTEMS - Continued

They get the message. (Technical controllers keep communications equipment operating at the technical control facility, Andrews AFB, Md) Maj Michael F. Weber and Capt Stephen O. Manning. illus Airman 20:21-23 Dec '76

SYSTEMS ANALYSIS

See also
Economic Analysis

Need for system safety analysis. TIG Brief 28:9 Mar 26 '76

New data handling technology in air defence. J.W. Sutherland. illus Intl Def Rev 9:616-618 Aug '76

New inventory analysis techniques. James J. Eder. illus Log Spectrum 10:29-33 Fall '76

A practitioner's guide to systems analysis. Col Larry N. Tibbetts. illus Nav War Col Rev 28:21-33 Winter '76

Systems approach--a technique for logistics managers. Neil O. Knarr. illus Army Log 8:12-13 Sep-Oct '76

SYSTEMS ENGINEERING

C³ system engineering. CAPT George Heffernan. Signal 30:88-89 Aug '76

Designing to cost on the XM1. Robert P. Erickson and John W. Wosina. illus Govt Exec 8:38+ May '76

Equipment maintainability--design in, don't add on. BrigGen William E. Eicher. illus Natl Def 60:353-355 Mar-Apr '76

Human factors: A vital part of system safety. TIG Brief 28:7 Jul 2 '76

The logic in logistics. Joseph J. Addison. illus charts Log Spectrum pt 1, 9:4-9 Winter '75; pt 2, 10: 3-6+ Spring '76; pt 3, 10:14-17 Summer '76

SYSTEMS ENGINEERING - Continued

Maintainability--a shared responsibility. Hartley I. Starr. Natl Def 60:360-363 Mar-Apr '76

Maintainability for Air Force systems. Capt Ned H. Criscimagna. illus Log Spectrum 10:19-23+ Spring '76

Maintenance in the Navy. Robert Emsworth. illus Natl Def 60:356-358 Mar-Apr '76

Need for system safety analysis. TIG Brief 28:9 Mar 26 '76

OT&E safety analyses. TIG Brief 28:14 Nov 19 '76

Operating command's role in system safety. TIG Brief 28:11 Sep 24 '76

R&D emphasis on reliability. Robert N. Parker. Def Mgt J 12:19 Apr '76

Reliability by design, not by chance. Willis J. Willoughby. illus Def Mgt J 12:12-18 Apr '76

Seeking failure-free systems. MajGen Richard E. Merkling. illus tab AU Rev 27:41-50 Jul-Aug '76

Support requirements analysis. Arthur W. Raymond and Kenneth W. Tobin. illus Log Spectrum 10: 24-29 Spring '76

System safety engineering programs. (AFR 127-8) TIG Brief 28:8 Mar 12 '76

System safety--expanding the user's role. Gen Paul K. Carlton. TIG Brief 28:2 Jun 4 '76

System safety: The key to lower cost of ownership. LtGen Donald G. Nunn. TIG Brief 28:2 Feb 13 '76

Why DOD emphasizes reliability & maintainability in testing. Jacques S. Gansler. illus Comdrs Dig 19: entire issue Dec 23 '76

Word processing: How to save $700 million a year. (Interview with Ron Companion, Installation Officer at Fort Benning, Ga) Govt Exec 8:52+ Dec '76

TACTICS, AIR - Continued

Study and Teaching - Cont'd

Prior planning prevents ... Capt Marty Steere. illus
TAC Attack 16:20-22 May '76

Top Gun--the Navy's "MIG-killing" school. (Navy
Fighter Weapons School, Miramar NAS, Calif)
CAPT Andrew Hamilton, Ret. illus US Nav Inst
Proc 102:95-97 Jan '76

Training for combat. (Air Combat Maneuvering Range)
Emile Pettecs-Snider. illus Aerosp Intl 12:40-42
Mar-Apr '76

U.S. Army Aviation Center Tactics Laboratory.
Capt Charles E.Taylor. illus tab USA Avn Dig 22:
8-12 Feb '76

Until the Aggressors come! Capt Neil McCoy. illus
USAF Ftr Wpns Rev, pp 9-13, Fall '76

TAFT, Robert, Jr

(Sen Robert) Taft proposes long-range 'advanced
technology' shipbuilding plan. L.Edgar Prina. por
Sea Power 19:31-34 Apr '76

Sen Taft urges massive naval buildup, paid for by
land forces overhaul, cuts. Benjamin F.Schem-
mer. Armed Forces J Intl 113:19+ Apr '76

TAIWAN see China (Republic)

TALLMAN, Kenneth L.

On your side. Interview. LtGen Kenneth L.Tallman.
por Airman 20:16-19 Apr '76

Turbulence and teamwork. LtGen K.L.Tallman.
TIG Brief 28:2 Aug 27 '76

TANK WARFARE see Armored Warfare

TANKERS

See also
Oilers (Ships)

Getting it all together (at Mormacsun launching in San
Diego): Congress and a cargo plan, shipbuilders
and ship operators, the sea services and the Merchant Marine. illus Sea Power 19:30 Feb '76

The Military Sealift Command's build and charter
program for nine sealift-class tankers. Scott C.
Truver. illus tabs Nav War Col Rev 28:32-44
Fall '75

Pollution, political pressures put USCG in double
jeopardy. L.Edgar Prina. illus Sea Power 19:
8-11 Jun '76

VLCC aground: Everybody's problem. (International
cooperation in refloating Shell VLCC tanker Metula, aground in the Strait of Magellan in 1974)
CDR James A.Atkinson. illus US Nav Inst Proc
102:95-99 Mar '76

TANKS, MILITARY

Tank-automotive news. Regular feature in issues
of National Defense

The tank is dead; Long live the tank. Toby Wrigley.
illus Def & For Aff Dig No.7:18-19+ '76

Armament

Automatic cannon technology. Gary W.Fischer. illus
Natl Def 61:192-194 Nov-Dec '76

Beehive: An innovative approach to employment. Ma;
Eugene D.Colgan. illus tabs Armor 85:20-22 Sep-
Oct '76

TANKS, MILITARY - Continued

Armament - Cont'd

Israel's new 155mm SP gun. Irvine Cohen. illus
Armed Forces J Intl 113:16-17 Mar '76

MAG-58: The new coax(ially mounted machinegun for
U.S. tanks). LtCol Robert W.DeMont. illus Armor
85:52-54 Sep-Oct '76

MBT Leopard 2 AV for NATO? G.M.Bailly-Cowell.
illus tabs NATO's Fifteen Nations 21:19-26+ Jun-
Jul '76

NATO's new MBT "gun" will be 3 new guns. Benjamin F.Schemmer. illus Armed Forces J Intl
113:12 Apr '76

Rheinmetall's 120 mm smooth bore gun--tank armament of the future. R.Meller. illus tabs Intl Def
Rev 9:619-624 Aug '76

The U.S. choice of a coaxial tank machine gun. LtCol
P.Crevecoeur, Ret. illus tabs Intl Def Rev 9:770-
772 Oct '76

Characteristics

Army accepts XM-1 tank prototypes. illus Armed
Forces J Intl 113:13 Feb '76

The combat-improved Chieftain (tank)--first impressions. F.Schreier. illus tabs Intl Def Rev 9:259-
264 Apr '76

A critical look. (Critique of the GAO's report on the
XM-1 procurement program) Sen Robert Taft, Jr
and William S.Lind. tab Armor 85:40-42 Nov-
Dec '76

Improved Chieftain (tank) for Iran. illus (Also cutaway) Intl Def Rev 9:640-642 Aug '76

Latest trends in tank technology. Richard M.Ogorkie-
wicz. illus Armor 85:39-44 May-Jun '76

A less vulnerable M-60 turret. Capt James D.Brown.
illus Armor 85:36-38 May-Jun '76

MBT Leopard 2 AV for NATO? G.M.Bailly-Cowell.
illus tabs NATO's Fifteen Nations 21:19-26+ Jun-
Jul '76

More bangs for fewer buck$. Col Robert J.Icks, Ret.
illus Armor 85:35-39 Mar-Apr '76

A new MICV (Mechanized Infantry Combat Vehicle)
from Yugoslavia. illus tab Intl Def Rev 9:170-172
Apr '76

T-92 (light gun tank development program). illus tab
Armor 85:50-51 Jul-Aug '76

Tank for the 1980's (XM1 main battle tank). illus
Natl Def 60:364-365 Mar-Apr '76

Target identification. Capt Joseph Moore, Jr. illus
USA Avn Dig 22:14-17 Mar '76

XM1 face-off to have strong impact on future ground
forces. Eric C.Ludvigsen. illus tabs Army 26:32-
35 Feb '76

The XM-1 tank program--a status report. R.D.M.
Furlong. tabs illus Intl Def Rev 9:481-484 Jun '76

Design

A good tank misused. (The French Char B) Raymond
Surlemont. illus tab Armor 85:41-43 Jul-Aug '76

A less vulnerable M-60 turret. Capt James D.Brown.
illus Armor 85:36-38 May-Jun '76

More bangs for fewer buck$. Col Robert J.Icks, Ret.
illus Armor 85:35-39 Mar-Apr '76

TANKS, MILITARY - Continued

United States - Cont'd

GM, Chrysler in tight tank race. illus Sea Power 19: 37-38 Jul '76

Hold off the tank fight for a while, Ivan, until we build up. F. Clifton Berry, Jr. tab Armed Forces J Intl 113:8 Apr '76

How to defend outnumbered and win. LtCol David L. Tamminen. (Reprinted from Armor, Nov-Dec 1975) illus tabs Fld Arty J 44:39-43 Mar-Apr '76

A less vulnerable M-60 turret. Capt James D. Brown. illus Armor 85:36-38 May-Jun '76

MAG-58: The new coax(ially mounted machinegun for U.S. tanks). LtCol Robert W. DeMont. illus Armor 85:52-54 Sep-Oct '76

New U.S. MBT candidates said to test out in "dead heat." Armed Forces J Intl 113:18 Apr '76

T-92 (light gun tank development program). illus tab Armor 85:50-51 Jul-Aug '76

The T-95 tank. Nathan N. Shiovitz. illus Armor 85: 25-27 Jan-Feb '76

Tank fire control. MajGen Bennett L. Lewis. illus tabs Countermeasures 2:42-45 Oct '76

Tank for the 1980's (XM1 main battle tank). illus Natl Def 60:364-365 Mar-Apr '76

Tank, supertank, or no tank at all. Maj L. D. Holder. illus Armor 85:41-44 Jan-Feb '76

'The tanks don't roll'--again: XM1 stopped in its tracks. Army 26:11-12 Sep '76

Tanks (for the South Carolina Army Guard). Maj Wanda Banta. illus Natl Guardsman 30:21 Feb '76

The U.S. choice of a coaxial tank machine gun. LtCol P. Crèvecoeur, Ret. illus tabs Intl Def Rev 9:770-772 Oct '76

Upgraded M48A5 tank joins National Guard. Armed Forces J Intl 113:28 Jan '76

XM1 face-off to have strong impact on future ground forces. Eric C. Ludvigsen. illus tabs Army 26:32-35 Feb '76

The XM-1 tank program--a status report. R.D.M. Furlong. tabs illus Intl Def Rev 9:481-484 Jun '76

History

The tank that was ahead of its time. illus Armor 85: 35 Jan-Feb '76

A Yankee inventor (J. Walter Christie) and the military establishment. George F. Hofmann. (Reprinted in part from Military Affairs, Feb 1975) illus Armor 85:13-17+ Mar-Apr '76

Maintenance and Repair

Battle tanks $1.33 a lb. (Anniston, Ala, Army Depot) LtCol Tom Hamrick, Ret. illus Army 26:30-35 Jun '76

Testing

XM1 tank prototypes being tested at Aberdeen. illus Officer 52:14 Mar '76

·Yugoslavia·

A new MICV (Mechanized Infantry Combat Vehicle) from Yugoslavia. illus tab Intl Def Rev 9:170-172 Apr '76

TANZANIA

Foreign Relations

China (People's Republic)

Inroads into East Africa: The People's Republic of China and Tanzania. Maj Michael E. Dash. illus map Mil Rev 56:58-64 Apr '76

Strategic Importance

Inroads into East Africa: The People's Republic of China and Tanzania. Maj Michael E. Dash. illus map Mil Rev 56:58-64 Apr '76

TARGET ACQUISITION

See also
Detection Equipment

Advances in airborne laser systems. illus Countermeasures 2:31 Mar '76

Attack T(hunder)-stick style. Capt John C. Morrissey. (Reprinted from Fighter Weapons Newsletter, Dec 1967) illus USAF Ftr Wpns Rev, pp 21-27, Summer '76

Combat applications of radar. MajGen A. B. Crawford, Jr and Michael A. Fanuele. illus Signal 31: 16-19 Oct '76

Consumer notice: Please read FAAO (Field Artillery Aerial Observer) team article thoroughly prior to entering combat. Fld Arty J 44:50-54 Nov-Dec '76

The enemy is a man who (will try to kill you before you see him). Capt Nelson Cobleigh. illus USAF Ftr Wpns Rev, pp 23-30, Fall '76

First TRAM (Target Recognition and Attack Multisensor) system undergoes navy testing. illus Countermeasures 2:47 Mar '76

Forward observer effectiveness. Col Paul F. Pearson. tab Fld Arty J 44:24-26 Jan-Feb '76

From swords to plowshares and back: A radar system to track combat vehicles. George W. Gerung. illus Signal 31:20-22+ Oct '76

Get the most out of your Q-4 (AN/MPQ-4A radar). Maj Edmund Greenwell. illus Fld Arty J 44:60-61 Mar-Apr '76

Initial pipper position and tracking. Capt Alexander H. C. Harwick. (Reprinted from USAF Fighter Weapons Review, Fall 1972) illus tab USAF Ftr Wpns Rev, pp 2-10, Summer '76

Intercept probability and intercept time. B. R. Hatcher. illus tabs Elect Warfare 8:95+ Mar-Apr '76

Lasers in reconnaissance and gunfire control. MajGen V. Vetrov and Col N. Sokolov. illus Soviet Mil Rev No. 1:25-27 Jan '76

Let's get serious about dive toss. Capt Robert H. Baxter. (Reprinted from USAF Fighter Weapons Newsletter, Sep 1970) illus tab USAF Ftr Wpns Rev, pp 28-34, Summer '76

Light weight laser designator for U.S. Army trials. illus tab Intl Def Rev 9:120 Feb '76

The military characteristics of reconnaissance and surveillance. George F. Steeg. illus tabs Elect Warfare 8:71+ Sep-Oct '76

Modern weapons employment. Capt Arthur Fowler. illus Aerosp Safety 32:5 Nov '76

The new (battlefield) dead-man's curve. Col William R. Ponder. tabs USA Avn Dig 22:6-7 Mar '76

TAXES AND TAXATION - Continued

In cash & in kind. Bruce Callander. illus tabs AF Times pt 1, 36:22 Jul 19 '76; pt 2, 36:26 Jul 26 '76; pt 3, 37:38 Aug 2 '76; pt 4, 37:34 Aug 9 '76; pt 5, Marrieds and singles: How much to pay them. 37:28 Aug 16 '76; pt 6, BAS: How rates were developed. 37:26 Aug 23 '76; pt 7, Benefits mean cutting costs. 37:34 Aug 30 '76; pt 8, Retirement: Benefits good despite Congress. 37:28 Sep 6 '76; pt 9, File of personal papers should be kept current. 37:45 Sep 13 '76; pt 10, Can system be changed? 37:28 Sep 20 '76

(Income) tax bill faces House, Senate fight. AF Times 36:14 Jun 28 '76

Income tax time: What every Guardsman wants to know but might not ask! Jack M. Vaughan. illus Natl Guardsman 30:24-27 Mar '76

New (Federal income) tax reform law: A few quirks. Randy Shoemaker. AF Times 37:3 Oct 18 '76

'76-'79 group med students get tax relief (on scholarship payments). AF Times 37:26 Oct 18 '76

RIFed Reserve officers out in cold on tax break. AF Times 37:8 Dec 20 '76

Retiree tax break urged (by TROA). AF Times 36:3 May 10 '76

7 states ask withholding (income taxes). Andy Plattner. AF Times 37:3 Nov 15 '76

Singles lib. (Are the unmarried discriminated against?) Darryl D. McEwen. illus tabs Soldiers 31:6-10 May '76

(Social Security tax) withholding increase. AF Times 37:3 Oct 18 '76

Special tax section (state and Federal). Andy Plattner and others. AF Times 36:38-40 Feb 16 '76

State income taxes. Darryl D. McEwen. tab Soldiers 31:27-30 Feb '76

State tax withholding expected next year. AF Times 37:2 Sep 13 '76

States give policy on collecting delinquent taxes. Table only. AF Times 37:17 Oct 25 '76

Tax bites holders of scholarships: Relief may be on the way. Lee Ewing. AF Times 36:4 Apr 12 '76

Taxation of Federal instrumentalities incident to state regulation of intoxicants: The Mississippi Tax Commission case. Capt Edward C. Hooks. AF Law Rev 18:1-23 Spring '76

25 states ask for withholding (tax). AF Times 37:4 Dec 20 '76

Withholding tax--February earliest. Lee Ewing. AF Times 37:6 Oct 18 '76

TAYLOR, David P.

Advocate of people programs. Interview. David P. Taylor. AF Times 37:14 Nov 15 '76

BAQ rebate sure, Taylor says. AF Times 37:3 Sep 6 '76

An introspective analysis of DOD manpower management. David P. Taylor. Def Mgt J 12:2-8 Oct '76

Taylor on benefits: Piecemeal cuts hurt morale. AF Times 36:3 Feb 16 '76

Taylor says unions have little chance. AF Times 37:26 Nov 1 '76

TAYLOR, Maxwell D.

The United States: A military power second to none? Gen Maxwell D. Taylor, Ret. Intl Sec 1:49-55 Summer '76

TEACHERS AND TEACHING

See also
Instructor Pilots

Academia in direct support. (The Adjunct Faculty, composed of selected Marine Corps Reserve officers, occupying civilian academic positions, as adjunct to the military staff at Marine Corps Command and Staff College) Col George M. Van Sant and Maj Allan R. Millet. illus MarCor Gaz 60:31-38 Aug '76

Academy teachers: Put civilians in place of military, (Sen John) Glenn advises. Len Famiglietti. AF Times 36:8 Jun 14 '76

Airborne--and then some. (Airborne School, Fort Benning, Ga, has first female instructors) LtCol Floyd A. Frost. illus Soldiers 31:30 Dec '76

Care in selecting MTIs (Military Training Instructors) paying off. AF Times 36:4 Jun 7 '76

Learning--despite the instructor. Capt Charles Austin. illus tab AU Rev 27:72-78 Mar-Apr '76

Naval Academy faculty called 'worst' (of the three by DepSecDef William P. Clements). AF Times 36:12 Apr 5 '76

One love. (Sgt Tom Theobald of Chanute AFB, Ill, is ATC's Instructor of the Year) Milene Wells. illus Airman 20:41-42 Oct '76

The psychology of enthusiasm. Maj Gerald A. Fabisch. Educ J 19:34-35 Fall '76

The term paper: To write or not to write. Martha S. Shull. Educ J 19:6-8 Winter '76

Token minority. (Army instructors at other Service academies) Darryl D. McEwen. illus Soldiers 31:52-53 Aug '76

TECHNICAL AID TO FOREIGN COUNTRIES

FMS (Foreign Military Sales): "No more giving it away." Interview. LtGen Howard Fish. illus tabs Govt Exec 8:19+ Dec '76

Fruitful cooperation. (Interview with Nikolai Sofinsky) Vasily Yefremov. illus Soviet Mil Rev No.2; 45-47 Feb '76

TECHNICAL EDUCATION see Education, Technical

TECHNICAL ORDERS

Aircraft weight and balance. Maj John E. Freitas. illus TAC Attack 16:10-12 Aug '76

Anatomy of a TCTO (Time Compliance Technical Order). Capt Marty Steere. illus TAC Attack 16:20-21 Sep '76

Help from the field for the Technical Order Improvement System (TOIS). TIG Brief 28:5 Sep 10 '76

Significant historical data processing (AFTO Form 95). TIG Brief 28:12 Jul 16 '76

Tech order versus quick checks. TIG Brief 28:16 Apr 23 '76

The technical manual lag: Space age anachronism. Maj R. William Highlander. illus Army 26:42-44 May '76

Who are you calling student? Capt Charles E. Bailey. illus Combat Crew 27:8-10 Dec '76

TECHNICAL PERSONNEL see Manpower, Technical

TECHNOLOGY

TECHNOLOGY - Continued

Telecommunications: The leading edge of defense effectiveness. Donald R. Beall. illus Signal 30:16-21 Jan '76

War, peace, and society in the 1980's: A historian's view. Richard A. Preston. illus Nav War Col Rev 28:34-44 Winter '76

Wheels and tracks. M. G. Bekker. illus tabs Armor 85:15-20 May-Jun '76

Why not more straight commercial buying? Eberhardt Rechtin. illus Govt Exec 8:46-48+ Oct '76

Educational Applications
See Educational Technology

History

American architectural heritage. Edward M. Tower. illus Mil Engr 68:207-209 May-Jun '76

Tools and civilization. Lynn T. White, Jr. Persp in Def Mgt No.24:33-42 Winter '75-'76; Condensation. Fld Arty J 44:44-47 Sep-Oct '76

International Cooperation

Nuclear futures for sale: To Brazil from West Germany, 1975. William W. Lowrance. Intl Sec 1: 147-166 Fall '76

The risky business of technology transfer. Editorial. John L. Frisbee. AF Mag 59:4 Oct '76

TELECOMMUNICATIONS see Communications Systems

TELEMETRY

Electronic stethoscope with frequency shaping and infrasonic recording capabilities. Ernest S. Gordon and John M. Lagerwerff. illus tab Aviation, Space & Envmt Med 47:312-316 Mar '76

The Sirocco meteorological sounding station. illus tab Intl Def Rev 9:433-435 Jun '76

Technique for electrocardiographic monitoring of working divers. P. F. Hoar and others. illus Aviation, Space & Envmt Med 47:667-671 Jun '76

TELEPHONES AND TELEPHONE SERVICE

Abuse of AUTOVON precedence system. TIG Brief 28:20 Jan 16 '76

The complexities of seeking a (telecommunications) policy. (Interview with John Eger) John F. Judge. illus Govt Exec 8:40+ Jun '76

PCM (Pulse Code Modulation) subscriber system provides quick response telephone service to remote training site. Capt Salvatore R. Genova. illus Signal 30:88-90+ May-Jun '76

(Reforger tests new tactical automatic telephone central office--AN/TTC-38) illus Signal 30:86 Jul '76

Security leaks may be only a phone call away. Ron Sanders. AF Times 36:6 Apr 5 '76

Winds of change in communications and computers. Theodore D. Puckorius. illus Signal 31:18-22 Sep '76

Laws and Regulations

Anti-trust and over-regulation: "Ma Bell" strikes back. illus Govt Exec 8:38-39 Jun '76

TELESCOPES

Revive the telescope. Capt Everette L. Roper, Jr. illus tabs Armor 85:23-24 Sep-Oct '76

TELESCOPES - Continued

Scope detects space objects by sun glints. illus AF Times 36:38 May 17 '76

TELESCOPES, RADIO

Calling M13 on 12.6 cm: Do you read? A. T. Lawton. illus Spaceflight 18:10-12 Jan '76

A 'red giant' opens its eyes. (USSR's radio-telescope, RATAN 600) Anthony T. Lawton and Kenneth W. Gatland. illus map Spaceflight 18:268-272 Jul-Aug '76

TELEVISION

Automated security systems (for access control to secure areas). Robert Colten and James M. Kaye. illus Countermeasures 2:38+ Feb '76

(Service) women's TV tour bargain for Pentagon. AF Times 36:18 Jan 5 '76

Military Applications

TV cameras may assist base perimeter sentries. AF Times 36:21 Feb 23 '76

Television search via periscope. Lee R. Couts. illus Countermeasures 2:58+ Nov '76

Programs and Programming

Air Force AFRT (Air Force Radio and Television) Broadcast Management: Inspection Guide D-1. TIG Brief 28:2p addendum Feb 27 '76

'Pappy' Boyington flies again (in TV series, Baa Baa Black Sheep). illus MarCor Gaz 60:4 Nov '76

TELEVISION IN ASTRONAUTICS

Viking: Lander science equipment. David Baker. illus (Also cutaways) Spaceflight pt 1, 18:211-213 Jun '76; pt 2, 18:241-245 Jul-Aug '76

Viking: Orbiter science equipment. David Baker. illus (Also cutaway) Spaceflight 18:124-125 Apr '76

TEMPERATURE

See also
Heat

TEMPORARY DUTY

Bootstrappers lose school breaks (and some tighter controls may be coming for students under DANTES). Len Famiglietti. AF Times 37:12 Nov 29 '76

Civilian use of government quarters. TIG Brief 28:13 Dec 17 '76

Contract quarters (when on-base quarters are not available). TIG Brief 28:10 Jun 18 '76

New per diem: Get receipts. Lee Ewing. AF Times 36:3 Jun 14 '76

Official TDY travel outside CONUS. TIG Brief 28:11 Apr 23 '76

TDY funding for short course students: Try centralized control! LtCol Norman E. Qualtrough. illus AF Compt 10:30-31 Apr '76

Use of government facilities during Temporary Duty (TDY). TIG Brief 28:20-21 Apr 9 '76

Use of rental cars. TIG Brief 28:14 May 7 '76

TENANT UNITS

Preaccident planning. TIG Brief 28:4 Sep 10 '76

TEST PILOTS - Continued

Test pilots: Getting their kicks from a plane. Marianne Lester. illus AF Times, Times Magazine
sup:8-12+ Apr 19 '76

Use of pilot heart rate measurement in flight evaluation. Alan H.Roscoe. illus tabs Aviation, Space &
Envmt Med 47:86-90 Jan '76

History

Alex Henshaw (sporting and racing pilot of the 1930s,
and one of the outstanding test-pilots of WW II).
A.M.Spong. illus Air Pict 38:232-236 Jun '76

TESTS AND MEASUREMENTS

DANTES seeks specialized civilian exams. AF
Times 36:26 Mar 22 '76

The FAA Military Competency Examination. Edward
A.Ewell. USA Avn Dig 22:28-29 Apr '76

How to study and take tests. Gen Bruce C.Clarke,
Ret. illus Soldiers 31:31-33 Apr '76

Intelligence test performance of Vietnam prisoners
of war 2 years post-return. Jesse L.Green and
James K.Phillips III. tabs Aviation, Space &
Envmt Med 47:1210-1213 Nov '76

Low AQE (Airman Qualifying Examination) scorers
urged to try again. Bruce Callander. AF Times
36:3 Jul 5 '76

NATOPS check. LCDR Frank A.Miley. illus Approach 22:22-24 Jul '76

NCOs aiming for top spot to face 2 sets of tests. AF
Times 37:2 Dec 27 '76

Some skills tests lifted until Dec. AF Times 37:6
Aug 30 '76

Test scores--big factor in (NCO promotion) point
plan. AF Times 37:3 Nov 22 '76

Testing of civilian employees. TIG Brief 28:13
Jun 18 '76

TEXTILE INDUSTRY AND TRADE

See also
Clothing, Protective
Uniforms

THAILAND

Foreign Policy
Post Vietnam: U.S. and Thailand. Maj Merrill L.
Bartlett. illus map MarCor Gaz 60:24-29 Jan '76

Foreign Relations
Post Vietnam: U.S. and Thailand. Maj Merrill L.
Bartlett. illus map MarCor Gaz 60:24-29 Jan '76

United States
Thailand (military personnel) cut continuing. AF
Times 36:3 Apr 26 '76

Vietnam (Democratic Republic)
The tasks for Thailand's Army and an assessment of
its ability. E.Stuart Kirby. RUSI J for Def Studies
121:50-53 Mar '76

Strategic Importance
Asia. Philip Paisley and Leigh Johnson. illus tab Def
& For Aff Dig No.5:18-19+ '76

THEUS, Lucius

Air Force Accounting and Finance Center. por AF
Mag 59:92 May '76

THEUS, Lucius - Continued

Directorate of Accounting & Finance. MajGen L.
Theus. por AF Compt 10:20-21 Jan '76

Directorate of Accounting & Finance. MajGen Lucius
Theus. por AF Compt 10:16-17 Apr '76

Directorate of Accounting & Finance. MajGen Lucius
Theus. por AF Compt 10:16-17 Oct '76

Notes from the Director of Accounting & Finance.
MajGen Lucius Theus. por AF Compt 10:16-17
Jul '76

THINK TANKS see Research Centers

THOMPSON, Robert C.

Environmental management. (Remarks, Energy, Environment & Ethics Seminar, National Assoc of
Environmental Professionals, Washington, Nov 5,
1975) MajGen Robert C.Thompson. AF Pley Ltr
for Comdrs: Sup No.2:22-26 Feb '76

Environmental planning and the decision process.
MajGen Robert C.Thompson. Mil Engr 68:11-13
Jan-Feb '76

Service life improving. Interview. MajGen Robert C.
Thompson. AF Times 37:22 Oct 18 '76

THOUGHT AND THINKING

See also
Decision Making
Problem Solving
Is staff thinking too conventional? SqLdr R.G.M.
Sivewright. Royal Air Forces Qtr 16:279-283
Autumn '76

THUNDERBIRDS

Brother birds. Capt John B.Taylor. illus Airman
20:24-29 Oct '76

Flying for show: A look at six aerobatic teams from
five nations--they're all good, but different. Richard F.Lord. illus AF Times, Times Magazine
sup:10-15 May 31 '76

T-birds to fly in open house at March (AFB, Calif,
Oct 3, 1976). AF Times 37:9 Oct 4 '76

Thunderbird pilots: 35th reunion (to be held Memorial
Day weekend 1976, marking 35th anniversary of
Southwest Airways' 4 training bases in Arizona).
Don Dwiggins. illus AF Times 36:33 Mar 29 '76

THUNDERSTORMS

Fire and rain. (An inoperative radar, a revised
weather forecast, a communications breakdown)
illus MAC Flyer 23:13-15 Dec '76

No time to gamble. map illus Interceptor 18:5-9
May '76

Thunderstorm? Cumulonimbus? Maj Herbert Weigl,
Jr. illus Aerosp Safety 32:1 Sep '76

THURMOND, Strom

The budget process vs national defense. (Excerpts
from address, American Defense Preparedness
Assoc, Washington, Nov 11, 1975) Strom Thurmond. Natl Guardsman 30:18-19 Jan '76

Conference speakers. (Excerpts from addresses,
NGAUS 98th General Conference, Washington,
Aug 30-Sep 1, 1976) por Natl Guardsman 30:
23-27 Oct '76

(Sen Strom) Thurmond sees union threat. AF Times
37:4 Dec 27 '76

TIME

Effects of time zone changes on performance and physiology of airline personnel. F.S.Preston and others. illus tabs Aviation, Space & Envmt Med 47:763-769 Jul '76

TIMMES, Charles J.

Vietnam summary: Military operations after the cease-fire agreement. MajGen Charles J. Timmes, Ret. Mil Rev pt 1, 56:63-75 Aug '76; pt 2, 56:21-29 Sep '76

TIRES

See also
Airplanes, Military--Tires

Maintenance and Repair

Vehicle tire management. TIG Brief 28:15 Dec 3 '76

TITANIUM see Metals

TOLSON, John J., III

(AUSA) president's report (1976). LtGen John J. Tolson, Ret. por Army 26:48-49 Nov '76

(LtGen John J.Tolson in) Army Aviation Hall of Fame. por USA Avn Dig 22:30 Mar '76

TOOLE, Wycliffe D., Jr

When is deception necessary? RADM Wycliffe D. Toole, Jr. (Excerpted from U.S. Naval Institute Proceedings, Dec 1975) AF Times 36:14 Jan 12 '76

TOOLS

New tools for industry. (Lasers) John F.Ready. illus tabs Natl Def 61:108-111 Sep-Oct '76

Scrap metal recycled into tools. illus Fld Arty J 44: 29-30 May-Jun '76

You and your toolbox. Sgt1C Jerry E.Mills. illus USA Avn Dig 22:30-35 Dec '76

TORPEDOES

Some modern torpedo developments: I. Northrop upgrades the Mark 37 torpedo. II. Westinghouse develops the Freedom Torpedo. III. Torpedo weapon systems from Sweden. illus tabs Intl Def Rev 9: 91-95 Feb '76

Torpedo development in Germany: Present status and future perspectives. Ulrich Ramsauer. illus Intl Def Rev 9:96-100 Feb '76

TOTAL FORCE CONCEPT

AFRES/ANG--best shape ever. Interviews. MajGens John J.Pesch and William Lyon. illus AF Mag 59: 55-59 Jun '76

The Air Force and national security: 1976 and beyond. (Remarks, Air Force Assoc, Mobile Chapter, Mobile, Ala, March 27, 1976) LtGen John W. Pauly. AF Plcy Ltr for Comdrs: Sup No.6:10-18 Jun '76

Are America's Reserve Forces the "keystone" of national security? Defense panel (Defense Manpower Commission) says yea and nay. Natl Guardsman 30:8-11 Jun '76

Bicentennial tories. (Speech, Army Aviation Assoc of America, Williamsburg, Va, March 1976) Barry Goldwater. illus Natl Guardsman 30:28-29 May '76

Brave Shield XIII. LtCol Don Rosenkranz. illus Air Reservist 27:8-9 Feb '76

TOTAL FORCE CONCEPT - Continued

Defense lists Secretary's total force actions. (Text of SecDef James R.Schlesinger's decisions on total force) Officer A. The total force. C. Total force program guidance: 1. General. 2. The manpower mobilization system. 51:7-8 Dec '75; C-3 (Army Reserve and Guard). 52:15-16 Jan '76; (Naval and Air Force Reserves) 52:8+ Feb '76

The Guard & Reserve in the total force program. illus Comdrs Dig 19: entire issue Jan 29 '76

In U.S. Forces Command: 'Total Army' readiness. Gen Bernard W.Rogers. illus Army 26:30-32+ Oct '76

MTMC and the total Army. Dan Hall. illus Translog 7:3-5 Dec '76

(Maj)Gen (W.Stanford) Smith reviews 20 years of Reserve gains. Officer 52:10+ Dec '76

(Operation) Coronet Sprint. (Two weeks of hard work by 180 Air Guardsmen of the 117th Tactical Reconnaissance Wg, Birmingham, Ala) 1stLt Gregory Hodges. illus Air Reservist 28:8-9 Jun '76

"Our" Air Force and its future. (Remarks, ROA National Convention, Bal Harbour, Fla, June 29-July 2, 1976) Gen Robert J.Dixon. illus Air Reservist 28:4-6 Aug-Sep '76

People, the Navy's most critical resource. Curtis W.Tarr and CAPT Paul C.Keenan, Jr, Ret. illus US Nav Inst Proc 102:45-51 Nov '76

Progress in our total force policy. James P.Gilligan. illus Air Reservist 28:3 Jul '76

ROA (Executive Director Gen J.Milnor Roberts) tells senators (Manpower and Personnel Subcommittee of the Senate Armed Services Committee) world will see U.S. Reserve cuts as weakening. Officer 52:4 Apr '76

Readiness of all total force jumps. tabs Officer 52:19 Feb '76

(Rep Bill) Chappell, Manpower Commission, ROA point way to strong Total Force. Editorial. Officer 52:4+ Jun '76

(Reserve Forces) Policy Board makes hard-hitting report: Adequate personnel, equipment vital to total force success. Officer 52:4 Jan '76

Strong new Guard for total force: Dedicated to both missions. MajGen LaVern E.Weber. illus Army 26:45-46+ Oct '76

Total force. LtCol James E.Witek. tab Soldiers 31: 43-46 Aug '76

Why we need the total force. (Remarks, National Guard Assoc Conference, Washington, Aug 30, 1976) Robert Ellsworth. AF Plcy Ltr for Comdrs: Sup No.12:8-13 Dec '76

TOTAL OBJECTIVE PLAN FOR CAREER AIRMAN PERSONNEL see TOPCAP

TOURS OF DUTY

See also
Assignments, Military
Permanent Change of Station
Remote-Isolated Duty
Temporary Duty

Active duty service commitment. TIG Brief 28:13 Jan 30 '76

Airmen already overseas added to 'home-basing.' Bruce Callander. AF Times 36:2 Feb 16 '76

TRANSPORTATION, AIR - Continued

United States

Air transportation: The real issues. A.Scott Crossfield. tab Govt Exec 8:28+ Oct '76

Laws and Regulations

Air shipment of hazardous material. (Address, Philadelphia Chapter 2, SOLE, March 1976) Morton Spiegel. Log Spectrum 10:26-27 Summer '76

TRANSPORTATION, AIR (MILITARY)

See also
Air Cargo
Airdrop
Airlift
Movement Control

Russia
Soviet air transportation--projection of power. Capt Terry L.Schott. illus USA Avn Dig 22:12-16 Jul '76

TRANSPORTATION, MILITARY

See also
Movement Control

Answering the (ancillary transportation) protection question. Capt Paul L.Govekar, Jr. Translog 7:8+ Aug-Sep '76

Army railroading: Tele-train to Trident missile. Dan Hall. illus Translog 7:2-5 Jun '76

(DOD transportation system) (Excerpts from address, NDTA Forum, Boston, Sep 1976) Gen Henry R. Del Mar. illus Translog 7:1-2+ Dec '76

Delivery assurance. William E.Billion. illus tab Army Log 8:10-12 Mar-Apr '76

Do you have a transportability problem item? Herbert F.Coen. illus tabs Translog 7:13-16 Apr '76

Is this the end of the line for TRS (Transportation Railway Service)? Can the nation afford it? C.J. Schwendiger. illus Def Trans J 32:8+ Dec '76

JPPSOWA (Joint Personal Property Shipping Office, WAshington): Service, economy, success. Tory Billard. illus Translog 7:13-15 Mar '76

A look at the '76 (31st Annual) Forum (Boston, Sep 26-29, 1976). illus Def Trans J 32:25-47 Dec '76

Problems of military transportation. Col N.Malyugin. illus Soviet Mil Rev No.3:25-27 Mar '76

The Red Ball Express: Stay on the Ball--keep 'em rolling! (Express motor route kept supplies moving to Gen Patton's 3d Army during closing days of WW II) Tory Billard. illus map Translog 7:14-15+ Oct '76

Reforger load-out. illus Army Log 8:24-27 Nov-Dec '76

Shipper support ... and how to get it. Herbert Paige. Translog 7:16-18 Feb '76

Soviet logistics: How good is it? Capts William R. Hotze and Terry L.Schott. illus tab Army Log 8: 18-21 Mar-Apr '76

Tech supply--move 'em out. (1st Cavalry Division's 27th Maintenance Battalion's Operation First Team Logistics) Capt Daniel M.Smith. Translog 7:6-7 Oct '76

U.S. defense transportation goals. Paul J.Hyman. illus Def Trans J 32:6-8+ Jun '76

TRANSPORTATION, MILITARY - Continued

History

Continental Army logistics: Transportation. (Reprinted from Army Logistician, Nov-Dec 1975) illus map Def Trans J 32:28-31 Aug '76

Laws and Regulations

A new ball game; Arms shipment security rules. Capt Paul L.Govekar, Jr. tabs Translog 7:16-17+ Oct '76

Study and Teaching

Air Force elevates NCO transport training. (Transportation Staff Officer course, Sheppard AFB, Tex) illus Def Trans J 32:32-33 Aug '76

General George Washington's T.O. could learn a lot (at Army Transportation School, Fort Eustis, Va). Rey Aponte. illus Translog 7:2-6 Mar '76

TRANSPORTATION, SEA

See also
Merchant Marine
Military Sealift Command

When ammo goes to sea. Eric R.Jackson and William F.Ernst. illus tab Translog 7:6+ Nov '76

TRANSPORTATION CENTERS AND SCHOOLS

Army

(Army) Transportation Center (Fort Eustis, Va) looks ahead. Translog 7:19-20 Feb '76

General George Washington's T.O. could learn a lot (at Army Transportation School, Fort Eustis, Va). Rey Aponte. illus Translog 7:2-6 Mar '76

TRANSPORTATION CORPS

Army goes to sea. SSgt James M.Boersema. illus Soldiers 31:35-37 Apr '76

Is this the end of the line for TRS (Transportation Railway Service)? Can the nation afford it? C.J. Schwendiger. illus Def Trans J 32:8+ Dec '76

TRANSPORTATION DEPT

See also
Coast Guard
Federal Aviation Administration

Systems approach to administrative support (in Transportation Dept's Office of Contracts and Procurement). Govt Exec 8:54+ Sep '76

UMTA (Urban Mass Transportation Administration): Controlling the costs. John F.Judge. illus Govt Exec 8:18-20 Jul '76

TRANSPORTATION UNITS

See also
Airlift Units

Armed Forces

(NDTA) military unit awards. illus Def Trans J 32: 65-69+ Oct '76

Army

Another Army "Navy" game (Azores). SSgt Virgil L. Laning. illus Translog 7:16-20 Jan '76

Army goes to sea. SSgt James M.Boersema. illus Soldiers 31:35-37 Apr '76

A "real world" transportation challenge: Exercise Bold Eagle '76. Maj Eldon T.Rippee. illus Translog 7:2-6 May '76

TREATIES AND ALLIANCES - Continued

The Panama Canal: Old myths and new realities. illus tabs maps Def Monitor 5: entire issue Aug '76

The Panama Canal: Past and present in perspective. Virginia Prewett. illus tab Sea Power 19:23-31 Aug '76

The Spanish connection: A wider U.S. commitment in the making. maps tabs Def Monitor 5: entire issue Feb '76

Statement of principles (between the United States of America and the Republic of Panama). Comdrs Dig 19: back cover Mar 25 '76

The U.S.-Japanese alliance and stability in Asia. Col Angus M. Fraser, Ret. illus tabs AF Mag 59: 34-39 Jan '76

TRIALS

See also
Courts-Martial

Right to hold trial limited by CMA. AF Times 37:33 Oct 18 '76

The waiver doctrine: Is it still viable? Maj John E. Hilliard. AF Law Rev 18:45-62 Spring '76

TROOP MOVEMENTS see Movement Control

TROOPS, MERCENARY see Mercenary Troops

TROPHIES see Awards, Decorations, etc

TRUCKS AND TRUCKING

... And leave the repairs to us (the dealers). Edwin G. Pipp. illus Army 26:51-52 Jun '76

New Swedish cross-country logistics vehicles. Colin E. Howard. illus tab Intl Def Rev 9:826-828 Oct '76

The Red Ball Express: Stay on the Ball--keep 'em rolling! (Express motor route kept supplies moving to Gen Patton's 3d Army during closing days of WW II) Tory Billard. illus map Translog 7: 14-15+ Oct '76

TRUMAN, Harry S.

Peace is our profession. (Remarks, Truman Lecture and Fine Arts Series, Westminster College, Fulton, Mo, April 24, 1976) Gen Russell E. Dougherty. AF Plcy Ltr for Comdrs: Sup No. 7:15-23 Jul '76

TRUST TERRITORIES

Marianas commonwealth status approved; DOD eyes air base. AF Times 36:20 Mar 8 '76

TURBINES see Gas Turbines (Aircraft)

TURBULENCE

Turbulence technique. John B. Clark. illus tabs Combat Crew 27:10-15+ Aug '76

TURKEY

The Aegean Sea dispute. Capt Thomas J. McCormick, Jr. maps illus Mil Rev 56:90-96 Mar '76

Airlifts to Turkish quake victims end. illus AF Times 37:22 Dec 13 '76

Foreign Policy
Turkey and the West. Neville Brown. RUSI J for Def Studies 121:63-67 Jun '76

Foreign Relations
Turkey and the West. Neville Brown. RUSI J for Def Studies 121:63-67 Jun '76

Greece
Ringed with a lake of fire: Cyprus 1976. Penelope Tremayne. Army Qtr 106:101-107 Jan '76

TURNER, Stansfield

SACEUR's subcommanders take the floor: The southern region. ADM Stansfield Turner. por NATO's Fifteen Nations 21:86-94 Feb-Mar '76

TWINING, Nathan F.

(Eight aviation pioneers (Clarence D. Chamberlin, John H. Glenn, Jr, George W. Goddard, Albert F. Hegenberger, Edwin A. Link, Sanford A. Moss, William A. Patterson, Nathan F. Twining) to be enshrined in Aviation Hall of Fame, July 24, 1976) por AF Mag 59:29-30 Jul '76

TYPHOONS

Mission: Typhoon mopup (on the island of Mauritius). LTs Brad Winstead and Mike Willoughby. illus Approach 21:1-3 Feb '76

Typhoon--December-1944. (Experiences of destroyer escort Robert F. Keller) CAPT Raymond J. Toner, Ret. illus US Nav Inst Proc 102:68-71 Dec '76

U

U N see United Nations

USAFE see Air Forces in Europe

USAREUR see Army, Europe

USO see United Service Organizations

USSR see Russia

UNCONVENTIONAL WARFARE

See also specific types of unconventional warfare, e.g.,
Chemical-Biological Warfare
Counterinsurgency
Guerrilla Warfare
Nuclear Warfare
Psychological Warfare

The strategy of unconventional warfare. Col George
E. Palm r. illus Mil Rev 56:58-62 Aug '76

The TAC role in special operations. BrigGen William J. Holton, Ret. illus AU Rev 28:54-68 Nov-Dec '76

UNDERDEVELOPED AREAS

Aircraft manufacturing in the developing nations: A
question of policy and politics. illus Interavia 31:
1155-1157 Dec '76

Dependence, exploitation and economic growth. Albert Szymanski. tabs J Pol & Mil Sociol 4:53-65
Spring '76

Fighting for people's minds--ideological inroads of
imperialism in the developing countries. Col P.
Tarutta. Soviet Mil Rev No. 1:41-43 Jan '76

Fruitful cooperation. (Interview with Nikolai Sofinsky) Vasily Yefremov. illus Soviet Mil Rev No.2:
45-47 Feb '76

Global corporations and the American economy.
Ronald Muller. Persp in Def Mgt No.24:43-55
Winter '75-'76

A strategic logistics force: An answer to the exploitation of the developing nations. BrigGen Winfield
S.Scott, Ret. illus Strat Rev 4:68-75 Fall '76

UNDERSEA RESEARCH VEHICLES see Submersible
Vehicles

UNDERWATER OPERATIONS

Acoustic countermeasures in the undersea environment. Owen Flynn. illus tabs Elect Warfare 8:
62-64+ Sep-Oct '76

Physiological Aspects

Hematologic changes in man during decompression:
Relations to overt decompression sickness and
bubble scores. Robert F.Goad and others. tabs
Aviation, Space & Envmt Med 47:863-867 Aug '76

Serum uric acid, cholesterol, and psychological
moods throughout stressful naval training. Richard H.Rahe and others. tabs Aviation, Space &
Envmt Med 47:883-888 Aug '76

What EEG criteria for diving fitness? J.Corriol and
others. illus tabs Aviation, Space & Envmt Med
47:868-872 Aug '76

Physiological Effects

Intracardial bubbles during decompression to altitude
in relation to decompression sickness in man.
U.I.Balldin and P.Borgström. tab Aviation, Space
and Envmt Med 47:113-116 Feb '76

Psychological Aspects

Serum uric acid, cholesterol, and psychological
moods throughout stressful naval training. Richard H.Rahe and others. tabs Aviation, Space &
Envmt Med 47:883-888 Aug '76

UNDERWATER PROPULSION see Propulsion Systems

UNDERWATER RESEARCH

See also
Ocean Mining

Project Kiwi One--new dimensions in underwater
sound. David G.Browning and Richard W.Bannister. illus maps US Nav Inst Proc 102:104-105
Jan '76

Underseas notes. Regular feature in issues of National Defense

Physiological Aspects

Indirect evidence for arterial chemoreceptor reflex
facilitation by face immersion in man. Sigmund B.
Strømme and Arnoldus Schytte Blix. illus tab Aviation, Space & Envmt Med 47:597-599 Jun '76

Technique for electrocardiographic monitoring of
working divers. P.F.Hoar and others. illus Aviation, Space & Envmt Med 47:667-671 Jun '76

Use of H_2 as an inert gas during diving: Pulmonary
function during H_2-O_2 breathing at 7.06 ATA.
James H.Dougherty, Jr. tabs Aviation, Space &
Envmt Med 47:618-626 Jun '76

UNIDENTIFIED FLYING OBJECTS

Flying saucers (AF's investigation of UFOs, Project
Blue Book) land at (National) Archives. illus AF
Times 37:21 Aug 9 '76

UNIFICATION OF THE ARMED FORCES

Canada

Professionalism and the Canadian military. LtCol
J.H.Pocklington. AU Rev 27:34-40 Mar-Apr '76

United States

A strategic logistics force: An answer to the exploitation of the developing nations. BrigGen Winfield
S.Scott, Ret. illus Strat Rev 4:68-75 Fall '76

UNIFIED COMMANDS

See also specific unified commands, e.g.,
Pacific Command
Readiness Command
Southern Command

UNIFORM CODE OF MILITARY JUSTICE

Early hearings due imprisoned (AF) members. Ann
Gerow. AF Times 36:2 Feb 9 '76

Individual Training: Inspection Guide C. TIG Brief
28:6p addendum Jan 30 '76

UNIFORMS

Air Force--U.S.

(Air Force Uniform Clothing) Board rules on wearing of women's cap, beret. Ron Sanders. AF
Times 36:2 Mar 1 '76

Exchanges run short of some caps, coats. Ron Sanders. AF Times 37:2 Dec 20 '76

46 ideas on uniform submitted. Ron Sanders. AF
Times 36:4 May 31 '76

New optional Air Force uniform combination approved. TIG Brief 28:17 Feb 27 '76

UNIFORMS - Continued

Air Force--U.S. - Cont'd

Two uniform outfits ruled out: Board studies 18 proposals, OKs some. Ron Sanders. illus AF Times 37:4 Oct 11 '76

Uniform rules change. TIG Brief 28:14 Jul 16 '76

Armed Forces--U.S.

Chances good for no-iron fatigues. Don Hirst. AF Times 37:36 Dec 13 '76

History

Flying gear through the years. illus AF Times 37:21+ Aug 16 '76

Army--U.S.

The green beret: Where it began. Col John W. Frye. illus Army 26:39-41 May '76

History

Continental Army logistics: Clothing supply. illus Army Log 8:28-32 Mar-Apr '76; Def Trans J 32: 28-30+ Oct '76

Marine Corps--U.S.

Commandant's policy on uniforms. Gen Louis H. Wilson, Jr. MarCor Gaz 60:2 May '76

UNIT TRAINS see Railroads

UNITED AIR LINES, INC

United Airlines also in the red. Klaus Höhle. illus tabs Interavia 31:621-622 Jul '76

History

The aircraft history of United Airlines. Barrett Tillman and Matthew Edward Rodina, Jr. illus tabs Am Avn Hist Soc J 21:169-184 Fall '76

UNITED KINGDOM see Great Britain

UNITED NATIONS

The feasibility of increasing the efficiency of United Nations forces. (Andover Prize Essay) LtCol M.Saleh. illus Hawk No.37:29-31+ Jul '76

The Swedish Air Force: An official history. illus Aerosp Hist 22:218-230 Dec '75

The United States Air Force in West New Guinea 1962-1963--help for the United Nations. LtCol Nick P. Apple. illus Aerosp Hist 22:212-217 Dec '75

UNITED NATIONS COMMAND, KOREA

Plastic police (ration control card). Sgt1C Floyd Harrington. illus tab Soldiers 31:37-40 Nov '76

UNITED NATIONS EMERGENCY FORCE

The feasibility of increasing the efficiency of United Nations forces. (Andover Prize Essay) LtCol M.Saleh. illus Hawk No.37:29-31+ Jul '76

UNITED SERVICE ORGANIZATIONS

(Bob) Hope salute tied to USO fund drive. illus AF Times 36:23 May 17 '76

A gathering of patriots: At a USO conference (Philadelphia, 1976) military loyalists yearn for the past and worry about the present. Marianne Lester. illus AF Times, Times Magazine sup:22-24 May 31 '76

UNITED SERVICES ORGANIZATION - Continued

USO: After 35 years, it's still the place to go. Marianne Lester. illus AF Times, Times Magazine sup:6-9 Apr 5 '76

USO passing hat for funds. AF Times 36:24 Jun 21 '76

History

USO: A friend in need. Stanley M. Ulanoff and MSgt Nat Dell. illus Soldiers 31:18-22 Mar '76

UNITED STATES
In official corporate entries United States is usually omitted, e. g. , Air Force Academy; however, it is included in names of nonofficial bodies, e. g. , United States Armor Association.

Defenses
See Defenses--United States

Economic Conditions

The Bicentennial challenge: The management revolution. Donald Ogilvie. illus Armed Forces Compt 21:10-14 Jul '76

The end of the disposable city. Stephen D. Julias. illus Govt Exec 8:44-45+ May '76

How private enterprise is committing "subtle suicide." illus Govt Exec 8:56-57 May '76

Keynote address, 56th Annual Meeting of the Society of American Military Engineers (Arlington, Va, April 28-May 1, 1976). ADM Ben Moreell, Ret. illus Mil Engr 68:294-297 Jul-Aug '76

The National Guard in a changing world. Dana Adams Schmidt. illus tabs Natl Guardsman 30:8-12 Apr '76

Rockwell's (Donn L.) Williams: "We do it to ourselves." illus Govt Exec 8:29+ Feb '76

Economic Policy

See also
Balance of Payments

After the Bicentennial: The end of an era? Maj Barry M. Meuse. illus tab AU Rev 27:2-12 Jul-Aug '76

Agricultural freedom and national strength. Earl L. Butz. Persp in Def Mgt No.24:13-18 Winter '75-'76

The Bicentennial challenge: The management revolution. Donald Ogilvie. illus Armed Forces Compt 21:10-14 Jul '76

Global corporations and the American economy. Ronald Muller. Persp in Def Mgt No.24:43-55 Winter '75-'76

The National Guard in a changing world. Dana Adams Schmidt. illus tabs Natl Guardsman 30:8-12 Apr '76

History

Economy before preparedness. (Jefferson's policy) Forrest C. Pogue. illus Def Mgt J 12:14-18 Jul '76

Foreign Economic Relations

Global corporations and the American economy. Ronald Muller. Persp in Def Mgt No.24:43-55 Winter '75-'76

Europe, Western

Cohesion and competition in the Atlantic Community: Implications for security. Col William F. Burns. illus Parameters 6, No. 1:35-47 '76

UNITED STATES - Continued

Foreign Economic Relations - Cont'd

Iran

Iran: The psychopolitics of arms; the politics of neighborliness. Gregory Copley. illus tab Def & For Aff Dig No.8-9:6-7+ '76

Middle East

Materials control and peace: The Middle East. Dennis Chaplin. RUSI J for Def Studies 121:34-37 Mar '76

Russia

A note on wheat and the Soviet Armed Forces. Harriet Fast Scott. (Reprinted from Strategic Review, Fall 1975) Mil Rev 56:33-35 May '76

Foreign Policy

After the Bicentennial: The end of an era? Maj Barry M.Meuse. illus tab AU Rev 27:2-12 Jul-Aug '76

America's future: The third century. Barry M.Goldwater. illus Strat Rev 4:8-15 Winter '76

Capabilities and courage. Robert F.Ellsworth. Natl Def 61:29-31 Jul-Aug '76

Detente and reality. R.J.Rummel. illus tabs Strat Rev 4:33-43 Fall '76

Detente and the Yom Kippur War: From crisis management to crisis prevention? Phil Williams. Royal Air Forces Qtr 16:227-233 Autumn '76

The enigma of the Nixon Doctrine. Col Larry E.Willner. Persp in Def Mgt No.24:91-95 Winter '75-'76

The evolution of American policy towards the Soviet Union. (Gustav Pollak Lecture, Harvard University, April 13, 1976) James R.Schlesinger. Intl Sec 1:37-48 Summer '76

Evolution of the U.S. military doctrine. MajGen P. Sergeyev and Col V.Trusenkov. Soviet Mil Rev No.11:52-54 Nov '76

"Farewell the tranquil mind": Security and stability in the post-Vietnam era. Col Lloyd J.Matthews. illus map Parameters 5, No.2:2-13 '76

Foreign arms sales: 2 sides to the coin. LtCol David L.Morse. illus tabs Army 26:14-21 Jan '76

Foreign policy and national security. (From address, World Affairs Council and Southern Methodist University, Dallas, March 22, 1976) Henry A.Kissinger. Intl Sec 1:182-191 Summer '76

Foreign policy and the Marine Corps. Maj W.Hays Parks. illus US Nav Inst Proc 102:18-25 Nov '76

The geostrategic triangle of North-East Asia. Niu Sien-chong. NATO's Fifteen Nations 21:68+ Aug-Sep '76

Hill hears 'advice' (from Rep Herbert E.Harris) on foreign pacts. (Read from Washington's farewell address, 1792) AF Times 36:25 Mar 1 '76

Kissinger's grand design: Peace without risk ... the promise cannot be fulfilled. G.Warren Nutter. illus Sea Power 18:19-22 Dec '75

Korea and U.S. policy in Asia. illus tabs Def Monitor 5: entire issue Jan '76

Liberty or detente? James L.Buckley. Natl Def 61: 26-28 Jul-Aug '76

UNITED STATES - Continued

Foreign Policy - Cont'd

Materials control and peace: The Middle East. Dennis Chaplin. RUSI J for Def Studies 121:34-37 Mar '76

Military concepts for political objectives. LtCol Joel J.Snyder, Ret. illus AU Rev 27:55-62 Jan-Feb '76

The National Guard in a changing world. Dana Adams Schmidt. illus tabs Natl Guardsman 30:8-12 Apr '76

Nearing the climacteric 1976. A.H.S.Candlin. Army Qtr 106:194-203 Apr '76

A new American defensive doctrine for Europe? Harold C.Deutsch. illus Parameters 6, No.1:18-34 '76

The new Pacific doctrine. LtGen Ira C.Eaker, Ret. AF Times 36:13+ Jan 5 '76

New (U.S. Pacific) doctrine in pursuit of old goals. Capt B.Rodionov and Col S.Yashin. Soviet Mil Rev No.8:49-51 Aug '76

Peace is our profession. (Remarks, Truman Lecture and Fine Arts Series, Westminster College, Fulton, Mo, April 24, 1976) Gen Russell E.Dougherty. AF Plcy Ltr for Comdrs: Sup No.7:15-23 Jul '76

Perils of the Vietnam syndrome. Gen T.R.Milton, Ret. AF Mag 59:29 Mar '76

A reconsideration of the domino theory. John Baylis. Royal Air Forces Qtr 15:277-287 Winter '75

Rocky: 5% cap (on pay increases for federal and military workers) OK at present. Donna Peterson. illus AF Times 36:39 Feb 9 '76

The role of the Services in support of foreign policy. J.K.Holloway, Jr. illus tabs US Nav Inst Proc 102:65-81 May '76

The safety of the Republic: Can the tide be turned? Eugene V.Rostow. illus Strat Rev 4:12-25 Spring '76

A Senator on involvement in Africa. (Interview with Sen Dick Clark) AF Times 36:16 Jan 26 '76

'Some concerns about this country we love.' (Condensed from address upon acceptance of the George C.Marshall Medal, AUSA 1976 Annual Meeting) Frank Pace, Jr. Army 26:46-47 Nov '76

The South Atlantic: A new order emerging. Richard E.Bissell. illus Sea Power 19:11-13 Oct '76

The United States and the defence of Western Europe. Capt D.H.Humphries. Army Qtr 106:211-219 Apr '76

U.S. policy alternatives in Asia. Robert A.Scalapino. illus Parameters 5, No.2:14-24 '76

The Vietnam War in retrospect: The Army generals' views. Douglas Kinnard. tabs J Pol & Mil Sociol 4:17-28 Spring '76

Where do we go from here? CAPT John E.Greenbacker, Ret. illus US Nav Inst Proc 102:18-24 Jun '76

Foreign Relations

Being Number One nation: Primacy and detente. Col Anthony L.Wermuth, Ret. illus tabs Parameters 5, No.2:54-68 '76

Africa

A Senator on involvement in Africa. (Interview with Sen Dick Clark) AF Times 36:16 Jan 26 '76

UNITED STATES - Continued

UNITED STATES - Continued

Foreign Relations - Cont'd

Foreign Relations - Cont'd

Asia

The U.S.-Japanese alliance and stability in Asia. Col Angus M.Fraser, Ret. illus tabs AF Mag 59: 34-39 Jan '76

U.S. policy alternatives in Asia. Robert A.Scalapino. illus Parameters 5, No.2:14-24 '76

Asia, Eastern

Our stake in Asia. William V.Kennedy. illus Army 26:19-21+ Sep '76

Asia, Southeastern

"Farewell the tranquil mind": Security and stability in the post-Vietnam era. Col Lloyd J.Matthews. illus map Parameters 5, No.2:2-13 '76

China (People's Republic)

China's nuclear strategy and U.S. reactions in the "post-détente" era. William T.Tow. illus Mil Rev 56:80-90 Jun '76

Cuba

The U.S. presence in Guantanamo. Martin J.Scheina. illus Strat Rev 4:81-88 Spring '76

Europe

Dove in the cockpit: Peace in today's Europe. Maj Edd D.Wheeler. illus tabs AU Rev 27:36-44 Jan-Feb '76

Europe, Western

A new American defensive doctrine for Europe? Harold C.Deutsch. illus Parameters 6, No.1:18-34 '76

The United States and the defence of Western Europe. Capt D.H.Humphries. Army Qtr 106:211-219 Apr '76

Iran

F-16: Fighter procurement essential to Iranian Air Force modernization. Robert Ellsworth. illus (Also cutaway) Comdrs Dig 19: entire issue Oct 21 '76

Japan

The U.S.-Japanese alliance and stability in Asia. Col Angus M.Fraser, Ret. illus tabs AF Mag 59: 34-39 Jan '76

Korea (Democratic People's Republic)

Murder at Panmunjom. Army 26:9 Sep '76

Korea (Republic)

Korea and U.S. policy in Asia. illus tabs Def Monitor 5: entire issue Jan '76

Latin America--History

Latin America: Military-strategic concepts. LtCol John Child. maps AU Rev 27:27-42 Sep-Oct '76

Lebanon

Linkage politics and coercive diplomacy: A comparative analysis of two Lebanese crises. Paul H.B. Godwin and Lewis B.Ware. illus AU Rev 28:80-89 Nov-Dec '76

NATO

Fundamental changes in NATO's standardization policy. Gen T.R.Milton, Ret. AF Mag 59:35 Feb '76

Security makes strange bedfellows: NATO's problems from a minimalist perspective. Ken Booth. RUSI J for Def Studies 120:3-4+ Dec '75

Pacific Region

The new Pacific doctrine. LtGen Ira C.Eaker, Ret. AF Times 36:13+ Jan 5 '76

Panama

The military value of the Panama Canal. illus map Comdrs Dig 19:2-7 Mar 25 '76

The Panama Canal: Old myths and new realities. illus tabs maps Def Monitor 5: entire issue Aug '76

The Panama Canal: Past and present in perspective. Virginia Prewett. illus tab Sea Power 19:23-31 Aug '76

Panama Canal: Primary issue (in 1976 presidential primary campaign). AF Times 36:14 Jun 7 '76

Panama: Strategic pitfall. LtGen V.H.Krulak, Ret. Strat Rev 4:68-71 Winter '76

Statement of principles (between the United States of America and the Republic of Panama). Comdrs Dig 19: back cover Mar 25 '76

Russia

American-Soviet relations:Informal remarks. Helmut Sonnenfeldt. illus Parameters 6, No.1:12-17 '76

"Detente" in Soviet strategy. G.M.Bailly-Cowell. NATO's Fifteen Nations 20:86-90 Dec '75-Jan '76

Erroneous doctrines misshaping perceptions of U.S. defense needs. (Excerpts from address, Montgomery, Ala, Jan 26, 1976) Robert Ellsworth. Armed Forces J Intl 113:29 Feb '76

The evolution of American policy towards the Soviet Union. (Gustav Pollak Lecture, Harvard University, April 13, 1976) James R.Schlesinger. Intl Sec 1:37-48 Summer '76

Food as a factor in U.S.-USSR relations. Joseph W. Willett. illus Natl Sec Aff Forum No.24:33-37 Spring-Summer '76

Kissinger's grand design: Peace without risk ... the promise cannot be fulfilled. G.Warren Nutter. illus Sea Power 18:19-22 Dec '75

Liberty or detente? James L.Buckley. Natl Def 61: 26-28 Jul-Aug '76

SALT: Time to quit. Colin S.Gray. illus Strat Rev 4:14-22 Fall '76

U.S. election: Russian reaction. LtGen Ira C.Eaker, Ret. AF Times 37:13-14 Dec 27 '76

U.S.-Soviet detente: The nature of the relationship and Soviet aims. Col Don O.Stovall. illus Natl Sec Aff Forum No.24:13-22 Spring-Summer '76

War survival in Soviet strategy. Foy D.Kohler. AF Mag 59:90-92+ Sep '76

UNITED STATES - Continued

Foreign Relations - Cont'd

Russia--History

United States-Soviet naval relations in the 1930's:
The Soviet Union's efforts to purchase naval vessels. Thomas R. Maddux. illus Nav War Col Rev
29:28-37 Fall '76

Saudi Arabia

Mission to Mecca: The cruise of the Murphy. (U.S.
destroyer brings Arabian king from Mecca to
Great Bitter Lake in Suez Canal, to meet with
Pres Franklin Roosevelt after Yalta Conference,
1945, and deals successfully with seemingly un-
surmountable problems, both diplomatic and prag-
matic) CAPT John S. Keating, Ret. illus US Nav
Inst Proc 102:54-63 Jan '76

Spain

The Spanish connection: A wider U.S. commitment
in the making. maps tabs Def Monitor 5: entire
issue Feb '76

Thailand

Post Vietnam: U.S. and Thailand. Maj Merrill L.
Bartlett. illus map MarCor Gaz 60:24-29 Jan '76

Turkey

No change seen in Turkey bases. AF Times 37:20
Oct 18 '76

Vietnam (Democratic Republic)

Message from Hanoi takes 'hard line' tone. AF
Times 36:10 Apr 26 '76

POW/MIA families oppose aid, trade, with Vietnam.
Bobbe Lindland. Armed Forces J Intl 113:10-11
Feb '76

Talk to Hanoi, McGovern advises. AF Times 36:38
Apr 19 '76

History

Colonial and Revolutionary War origins of American
military policy. Maj John A. Hardaway. illus Mil
Rev 56:77-89 Mar '76

Developing naval concepts: The early years, 1815-42.
VADM Edwin B. Hooper, Ret. illus tab Def Mgt J
12:19-24 Jul '76

Economy before preparedness. (Jefferson's policy)
Forrest C. Pogue. illus Def Mgt J 12:14-18 Jul '76

O'Bannon and company. Trudy J. Sundberg. illus
MarCor Gaz 60:35-39 Jul '76

A patient for Dr Leale. (Young Union Army surgeon
attends dying Pres Lincoln after shooting at Ford's
Theater) Donald C. Wright. illus Army 26:41-45
Aug '76

Winning the West. Col Robert M. Stegmaier, Ret.
maps illus Fld Arty J pt 1, 44:52-54 Mar-Apr '76;
pt 2, 44:37-39 May-Jun '76; pt 3, 44:53-54 Jul-
Aug '76; pt 4, 44:38-41 Sep-Oct '76; pt 5, 44:58-
61 Nov-Dec '76

Exhibitions

Centennial. (America's 1st 100-year celebration)
Marc J. Epstein. illus Soldiers 31:33-35 Jul '76

UNITED STATES - Continued

Politics and Government

America's future: The third century. Barry M. Goldwater. illus Strat Rev 4:8-15 Winter '76

Backing the President. Phil Stevens. AF Times 37:14
Oct 18 '76

The Bicentennial challenge: The management revolution. Donald Ogilvie. illus Armed Forces Compt
21:10-14 Jul '76

Do Americans understand democracy? Henry F.
Graff. Persp in Def Mgt No. 24:69-77 Winter '75-'76

Hill hears 'advice' (from Rep Herbert E. Harris) on
foreign pacts. (Read from Washington's farewell
address, 1792) AF Times 36:25 Mar 1 '76

How America is becoming a regulated society. (Interview with Rep Steven D. Symms) illus Govt Exec
8:34-35 Aug '76

How's (President-elect Jimmy) Carter on defense?
Bruce Callander. AF Times 37:4 Nov 15 '76

Keynote address, 56th Annual Meeting of the Society
of American Military Engineers (Arlington, Va,
April 28-May 1, 1976). ADM Ben Moreell, Ret.
illus Mil Engr 68:294-297 Jul-Aug '76

No panic at Pentagon over (President-elect Jimmy)
Carter's victory. Paul Smith. AF Times 37:20
Nov 15 '76

U.S. election: Russian reaction. LtGen Ira C. Eaker,
Ret. AF Times 37:13-14 Dec 27 '76

What the (political) parties say about defense issues.
AF Times 37:12 Aug 30 '76

Who speaks for the people? Editorial. John T. Hayward. Govt Exec 8:11-12 Jun '76

History

F.D.R. and the great War Department feud: (Harry
H.) Woodring vs (Louis A.) Johnson. Keith D.
McFarland. illus Army 26:36-42 Mar '76

Social Conditions

Evaluative research: Progress through experimentation. E. William Sarsfield. illus Govt Exec 8:33+
Mar '76

How private enterprise is committing "subtle suicide." illus Govt Exec 8:56-57 May '76

Keynote address, 56th Annual Meeting of the Society
of American Military Engineers (Arlington, Va,
April 28-May 1, 1976). ADM Ben Moreell, Ret.
illus Mil Engr 68:294-297 Jul-Aug '76

History

Do Americans understand democracy? Henry F.
Graff. Persp in Def Mgt No. 24:69-77 Winter '75-'76

UNITED STATES ARMY, EUROPE see Army, Europe

UNITED STATES INFORMATION AGENCY

Sports in Africa: A U.S. grass roots involvement.
illus Govt Exec 8:50+ Sep '76

UNIVERSITIES AND COLLEGES

Great Britain

A short account of the East Midlands Universities Air Squadron. Col G. J. Eltringham, Ret. Royal Air Forces Qtr 15:325-330 Winter '75

University (of London Air Squadron) cadet in a bulldog. (Flying with the RAF today, no.7) J.D.R. Rawlings. illus tab Air Pict 38:320-322 Aug '76

United States

The civilian military college. Maj John D. Kraus, Jr. illus Mil Rev 56:77-87 Aug '76

Logistics training asset--community colleges. Capt B. D. Sullivan. illus Army Log 8:28-29 May-Jun '76

150 ROTC units face closing. Andy Plattner. AF Times 36:4 Feb 23 '76

362 schools in SOC (Serviceman's Opportunity College); grad programs eyed. AF Times 37:35 Nov 29 '76

21 AFROTC schools saved. Len Famiglietti. AF Times 36:4 Jun 28 '76

21 AFROTC units put on probation, 11 to close. Len Famiglietti. AF Times 36:26 Mar 15 '76

History

An 'ROTC' unit (Alabama Corps of Cadets) fought as such, trained troops. Col Paul R. O'Mary. Officer 52:36 Jul '76

UNIVERSITY OF NATIONAL DEFENSE see National Defense University

UNKNOWN SOLDIER

21 seconds, 21 steps. Sgt1C Floyd Harrington. illus Soldiers 31:29-32 Jul '76

URBAN MASS TRANSPORTATION see Transportation

URBAN WARFARE

Action and reaction: West Germany and the Baader-Meinhof guerrillas. Maj John D. Elliott. illus Strat Rev 4:60-67 Winter '76

The Battle of Aachen: City fighting tactics. Capt Monte M. Parrish. illus maps Fld Arty J 44:25-30 Sep-Oct '76

Combat-In-Cities (CIC): Does the helicopter have a role? Maj Alexander Woods, Jr. illus USA Avn Dig 22:24-28 Dec '76

The essence of future guerrilla warfare: Urban combat. Thomas M. Schlaak. illus MarCor Gaz 60: 18-26 Dec '76

MOBA (Military Operations in Built-up Areas): Why? What? How? LtCols Robert L. Graham and Ray M. Franklin. illus tabs maps USA Avn Dig 22:1+ Feb '76

Tactical lessons learned ... but where to apply them? LtCol John W. Burbery, Jr. illus Mil Rev 56:25-28 Jul '76

URBANIZATION see Cities and Towns

UTILITIES see Public Utilities

V

VETERANS BENEFITS - Continued

WASPs (Women's Air Force Service Pilots) lose
(medical) benefits round. AF Times 37:17
Sep 27 '76

When it comes to survivor benefits ... help's at
hand. TSgt Tom Dwyer. illus tabs Airman 20:
36-39 Oct '76

VETERANS ORGANIZATIONS

(Jimmy) Carter scored on pardon (at) Legionnaire
convention. AF Times 37:24 Sep 6 '76

Rank and file VFW repeats 'no women.' AF Times
36:17 Jan 19 '76

Vets group (Combined National Veterans' Association
of America) will push harder for benefits. AF
Times 37:17 Dec 6 '76

VETERINARY CORPS

Air Force

It began with cows. (USAF veterinarians from Lajes
AB have worked with the people of Terceira in the
Azores since 1949 to improve dairy and other
farm production) Maj Angelo Cerchione, Ret. illus
Airman 20:34-38 Aug '76

Quality assurance provisions in Blanket Purchase
Agreements (BPAs). TIG Brief 28:13 Jun 4 '76

Subsistence quality assurance in veterinary-origin
inspection. TIG Brief 28:5 Mar 26 '76

Army

They shoot horses, don't they? (Army veterinarians
do spend some time working with animals but still
keep close watch on other veterinary medical activities) Janet Hake. illus Soldiers 31:32-35
Mar '76

VIBRATION

Arousing environmental stresses can improve performance, whatever people say. E.C.Poulton.
tabs Aviation, Space & Envmt Med 47:1193-1204
Nov '76

Comparison of the subjective intensity of sinusoidal,
multifrequency, and random whole-body vibration.
Richard W.Shoenberger. illus tabs Aviation, Space
& Envmt Med 47:856-862 Aug '76

Human response to buffeting in an all-terrain vehicle.
T.M.Fraser and others. tabs Aviation, Space &
Envmt Med 47:9-16 Jan '76

VIET CONG

Trang Bang. Col Arno L.Ponder. illus map Army 26:
32-41 Jan '76

VIETNAM

History

OGMA (Groupements de Commandos Mixtes Aero-
portés)/GMI (Groupement Mixte d'Intervention): A
French experience in Indochina. Maj John D.How-
ard. illus map Mil Rev 56:76-81 Apr '76

Indochina: The history of Vietnam. Jerry Kamstra.
Countermeasures pt 3, 2:16+ Dec '75-Jan '76

VIETNAM (DEMOCRATIC REPUBLIC)

Foreign Relations

France

Long wait seen on accounting for war dead (from
Vietnamese Conflict and French-Indochinese War).
Ann Gerow. AF Times 36:17 Apr 19 '76

VIETNAM (DEMOCRATIC REPUBLIC) - Continued

Foreign Relations - Cont'd

United States

Long wait seen on accounting for war dead (from
Vietnamese Conflict and French-Indochinese War).
Ann Gerow. AF Times 36:17 Apr 19 '76

VIETNAMESE CONFLICT, 1957-1975

(Jimmy) Carter scored on pardon (at) Legionnaire
convention. AF Times 37:24 Sep 6 '76

Lessons of Vietnam. Col O.Ivanov. Soviet Mil Rev
No.4:44-46 Apr '76

Personal perceptions of the Vietnam War. CAPT
John C.MacKercher, Ret. Natl Sec Aff Forum
No.24:6p addendum Spring-Summer '76

Vietnam ... lest we forget. MajGen Thomas W.Bow-
en. illus Army 26:8-9 Apr '76

Vietnam summary: Military operations after the
cease-fire agreement. MajGen Charles J.Tim-
mes, Ret. illus tab maps Mil Rev pt 1, 56:63-75
Aug '76; pt 2, 56:21-29 Sep '76

The Vietnam War in retrospect: The Army generals'
views. Douglas Kinnard. tabs J Pol & Mil Sociol
4:17-28 Spring '76

Aerial Operations

What really happened in the air defense battle of
North Vietnam. LtCol Thomas E.Bearden, Ret.
illus tab Air Def Mag, pp 8-15, Apr-Jun '76

Aerial Operations, American

Air transport in the northern provinces (of South
Vietnam). Col Ray L.Bowers. illus MarCor Gaz
60:39-49 Jun '76

The bombing 'pause': Formula for failure. Gen Wallace M.Greene, Ret. illus AF Mag 59:36-39
Apr '76

A Christmas story. (Plain of Jars, Dec 1970) Capt
Craig W.Duehring. illus TAC Attack 16:18-19
Dec '76

Linebacker II: A firsthand view. Charles K.Hopkins.
illus Aerosp Hist 23:128-135 Sep '76

Vietnam in Europe? (Sir Robert Brooke-Popham
Prize Essay) WgComdr R.W.D.C.Holliday. illus
Hawk No.37:15-20 Jul '76

Airlift Operations

Air transport in the northern provinces (of South
Vietnam). Col Ray L.Bowers. illus MarCor Gaz
60:39-49 Jun '76

Allied Forces, American

Cohesion and disintegration in the American Army
(in Vietnam): An alternative perspective. Paul L.
Savage and Richard A.Gabriel. tabs Armed Forces
& Soc 2:340-376 Spring '76

Crimes in hostilities. Maj W.Hays Parks. illus tab
MarCor Gaz pt 1, 60:16-22 Aug '76; pt 2, 60:33-39
Sep '76

Trang Bang. Col Arno L.Ponder. illus map Army 26:
32-41 Jan '76

VISUAL FLYING - Continued

Keep your eyes on the road! LT Gary W. Garland.
illus Approach 22:6-7 Sep '76

Lost ... on a circling approach. Maj Brian C. Bernet. illus Aerosp Safety 32:22-23 Mar '76

The one you see won't hit you. (Adapted from Flight
Comment, Jul-Aug 1975) illus Interceptor 18:
20-21 May '76

Raindrops keep falling. MAC Flyer 23:11 Feb '76

Reviewing the fine print. Capt M.C. Kostelnik. illus
TAC Attack 16:22-24 Jul '76

The second time around. Maj Jack Spey. illus Aerosp
Safety 32:16-18 Aug '76

To see or not to see: Visual acuity of pilots involved
in midair collisions. Leonard C. Ryan and others.
illus Combat Crew 27:8-10 Sep '76

Twelve o'clock low. Maj Orlen L. Brownfield. illus
MAC Flyer 23:18-19 Mar '76

Visibility--to land or not to land. Capt John L. Wilson. illus Combat Crew pt 1, 27:22-23 Aug '76;
pt 2, The runway environment. 27:18-20 Sep '76;
pt 3, The rules. 27:26-27 Oct '76; pt 4, Going visual. 27:20-21 Nov '76; pt 5, Techniques. 27:14-15
Dec '76

What's your viewpoint (when you're trying to land an
airplane)? illus MAC Flyer 23:7-8 Oct '76

VISUAL FLYING - Continued

Equipment

Window to the world: EVS (Electro-optical Viewing
System) and the navigator. 1stLt James R. McDonald. illus Navigator 23:25-26 Summer '76

VOLUNTARY SERVICE see Military Service, Voluntary

VOTING

Candidates ignore 'military vote.' Bruce Callander.
AF Times 37:10 Oct 25 '76

How commanders can help military members exercise their right to vote. illus tab Comdrs Dig 19:
entire issue Jul 15 '76

Push on for higher voting tally. AF Times 37:8
Oct 18 '76

Readers' survey. (How they feel about this year's
elections and whether they plan to vote or support
candidates for Federal offices) tab AF Times 36:8
May 17 '76

Some ballots may be invalid: Absentee votes. Bruce
Callander. AF Times 37:10 Nov 8 '76

Vote. Janet Hake. tab Soldiers 31:38-41 Apr '76

Voting, banking off (military) privacy list. Ann
Gerow. AF Times 36:2 Mar 1 '76

Voting record lowest in years. AF Times 36:17
Jan 5 '76

W

WAC see Women in the Army

WAF see Women in the Air Force

WAPS see Weighted Airman Promotion System

WWMCCS see Worldwide Military Command and Control System

WAKE TURBULENCE see Turbulence

WAR

See also specific wars by name, e.g.,
Arab-Israeli Conflict, 1967-
Cambodian Conflict, 1973-
Civil War--U.S.
Korean War, 1950-1953
Middle East War, 1973
Napoleonic Wars
Revolutionary War--U.S.
Spanish-American War, 1898´
Vietnamese Conflict, 1957-1975
War of 1812
World War I
World War II

Coalition warfare. Robert W. Komer. illus Army 26:
28-32 Sep '76

Crimes in hostilities. Maj W. Hays Parks. illus tab
MarCor Gaz pt 1, 60:16-22 Aug '76; pt 2, 60:33-39
Sep '76

Ideology and war. Capt A. Skrylnik. Soviet Mil Rev
No. 7:14-16 Jul '76

Ethical Aspects

Civilian combat casualties: Our moral and legal responsibilities. Maj S.P. Mehl. illus MarCor Gaz
60:43-46 Oct '76

Crimes in hostilities. Maj W. Hays Parks. illus tab
MarCor Gaz pt 1, 60:16-22 Aug '76; pt 2, 60:33-39
Sep '76

Laws
See International Law

Political Aspects

An absence of accountability. CDR Roy L. Beavers,
Ret. illus US Nav Inst Proc 102:18-23 Jan '76

America's Vigilantes and the Great War, 1916-1918.
John Carver Edwards. Army Qtr 106:277-286
Jul '76

Clausewitz and Soviet politico-military strategy.
BrigGen Antonio Pelliccia. NATO's Fifteen Nations 20:18-21+ Dec '75-Jan '76; Digest. Mil Rev
56:23-33 Aug '76

Force levels and limited war. Steven T. Ross. Nav
War Col Rev 28:91-96 Fall '75

Making things difficult (British Services). John Terraine. RUSI J for Def Studies 121:57-59 Sep '76

A reconsideration of the domino theory. John Baylis.
Royal Air Forces Qtr 15:277-287 Winter '75

Principles
See Military Art and Science

Psychological Aspects

A study of the anatomy of fear and courage in war.
LtCol A. T. A. Browne, Ret. Army Qtr 106:297-
303 Jul '76

WAR - Continued

Social Aspects

The social incidence of Vietnam casualties: Social
class or race? Gilbert Badillo and G. David Curry. tabs Armed Forces & Soc 2:397-406 Spring '76

Study and Teaching

The professional study of war. Keith R. Simpson.
RUSI J for Def Studies 120:27-31 Dec '75

WAR, FUTURE

Air defense: The Excalibur of the corps and division
commanders. Col Russell W. Parker and LtCol
Joseph W. House. illus Air Def Mag, pp 29-33,
Apr-Jun '76

Air interdiction in a European future war: Doctrine
or dodo? WgComdr Alan Parkes. AU Rev 27:16-18
Sep-Oct '76

A dissenting view of the next war. Capt Andrew J.
Bacevich, Jr. illus Armor 85:41-43 Sep-Oct '76

Effective military technology for the 1980s. Richard
L. Garwin. illus tabs Intl Sec 1:50-77 Fall '76

Electronic warfare's role in future conflicts. Malcolm R. Currie. illus Comdrs Dig 19: entire issue
Dec 9 '76

RPV's in future combat. David Shore. illus tabs Natl
Def 61:205-208 Nov-Dec '76

The U.S. Navy and the problem of oil in a future war:
The outline of a strategic dilemma, 1945-1950.
David Alan Rosenberg. illus Nav War Col Rev 29:
53-64 Summer '76

Win the first battle! MajGen David E. Ott. illus tab
Natl Def 60:276-278 Jan-Feb '76

WAR, LIMITED see Limited War

WAR AND EMERGENCY POWERS

Backing the President. Phil Stevens. AF Times 37:14
Oct 18 '76

WAR AND TECHNOLOGY

Advanced technology in modern war. John H. Morse.
RUSI J for Def Studies 121:8-16 Jun '76

Effective military technology for the 1980s. Richard
L. Garwin. illus tabs Intl Sec 1:50-77 Fall '76

Future combat vehicles. William F. Banks. Natl Def
60:274-275 Jan-Feb '76

NATO and the dawn of new technology. Stefan T. Possony. illus tab Def & For Aff Dig pt 1, No. 10:
15-17+ '76; pt 2, No. 11:18-20+ '76

Nuclear technology in support of our strategic options.
MajGen Edward B. Giller, Ret. tab AU Rev 28:26-
34 Nov-Dec '76

Scientific progress and defensive potential. MajGen
I. Anureyev. Soviet Mil Rev No. 2:13-15 Feb '76

Technology and strategy: Precision guided munitions
and other highly sophisticated weapons will increase the effectiveness of the nuclear threat.
Michael L. Nacht. Natl Def 61:199-202 Nov-Dec '76

U.S. Army Foreign Science and Technology Center.
David Latt. illus USA Avn Dig 22:24-27 Feb '76

Weapons technology. AVM S. W. B. Menaul, Ret. Royal Air Forces Qtr 15:271-274 Winter '75

WARSHIPS - Continued

Russia - Cont'd

Ship air defence. Capt B. Orestov. illus Soviet Mil Rev No. 1:23-24 Jan '76

Ship's inspections and reviews. Capt K. Antonov. Soviet Mil Rev No. 4:20-21 Apr '76

The surface Navy today: Prospects and problems. Col Robert D. Heinl, Jr, Ret. illus Sea Power 19:27-32 Oct '76

United States

Backfire problems and the Aegis mix. L. Edgar Prina. illus Sea Power 19:19-21 Sep '76

A fleet for the future: Some modest suggestions. Norman Polmar. illus tabs Sea Power 19:12-17 Apr '76

House panel (Armed Services Committee) increases SCN (Ship Construction, Navy) funding: Nuclear power advocates gain ground. L. Edgar Prina. illus Sea Power 19:7-11 Apr '76

Men, myths, and machines, or, "All the ships at sea." Douglas M. Johnston. illus tabs Def Mgt J 12:17-22 Oct '76

(Pres) Ford signs procurement bill: Hits Congress for shipbuilding cuts. L. Edgar Prina. illus Sea Power 19:7-10 Aug '76

The shipbuilding debate: What's at stake. Col Robert D. Heinl, Jr, Ret. illus Sea Power 19:35-37 Jul '76

The surface Navy today: Prospects and problems. Col Robert D. Heinl, Jr, Ret. illus Sea Power 19:27-32 Oct '76

Weapons a warship make. John T. Hayward. Govt Exec 8:8+ Dec '76

History

Battlewagon. Col James B. Soper, Ret. illus MarCor Gaz 60:39-42 Aug '76

The daring sloop Providence. Charles R. Smith. illus MarCor Gaz 60:25-28 Jul '76

"Old Ironsides": Relevant relic. CDR Tyrone G. Martin. illus US Nav Inst Proc 102:106-109 Sep '76

Olympian legacy. CDR John D. Alden, Ret. illus US Nav Inst Proc 102:60-67 Sep '76

The other side of the island: USS Utah at Pearl Harbor. LT Michael S. Eldredge. illus US Nav Inst Proc 102:52-54 Dec '76

Sonar and the USS Monitor. Bill Walsh. illus map Countermeasures 2:32-33 Apr '76

USS Colorado: The 'other' battleship. Grahame F. Shrader. illus US Nav Inst Proc 102:46-47 Dec '76

WASHINGTON, George

Hill hears 'advice' (from Rep Herbert E. Harris) on foreign pacts. (Read from Washington's farewell address, 1792) AF Times 36:25 Mar 1 '76

The religion of George Washington: A Bicentennial report. Ch(LtCol) Edwin S. Davis. AU Rev 27:30-34 Jul-Aug '76

6-star rank (General of the Armies) voted for G. Washington. AF Times 37:22 Aug 16 '76

Top rank (General of the Armies) for George Washington. AF Times 37:18 Oct 18 '76

Washington builds an Army. James B. Deerin. por Natl Guardsman 30:6-9 Jan '76

WASHINGTON, DC

Description and Travel

Footloose in the Capital: Greenbacks ... diamonds ... Al Capone. Donna Peterson. illus AF Times 36:31-32 May 31 '76

WASTE DISPOSAL see Refuse and Refuse Disposal

WATER

The national stream quality accounting network. Joseph S. Cragwall, Jr. illus map tabs Mil Engr 68:25-27 Jan-Feb '76

Survival: Water. SSgt Charles R. Teagarden. illus Aerosp Safety 32:22-24 Oct '76

WATER-BASED AIRPLANES see Seaplanes

WATER POLLUTION see Pollution

WATER SAFETY

Jaws II. (Fishing follies) Maj Art Ivins. illus TAC Attack 16:4-8 Mar '76

WATER SUPPLY

The national stream quality accounting network. Joseph S. Cragwall, Jr. illus map tabs Mil Engr 68:25-27 Jan-Feb '76

WATERWAYS

See also
Panama Canal
Suez Canal

Bankhead Lock failure. John A. Perdue. illus map Mil Engr 68:462-464 Nov-Dec '76

The lower Mississippi Valley. MajGen Francis P. Koisch. illus map tabs Mil Engr 68:290-293 Jul-Aug '76

Malacca and the law. Joel Evan Marsh and LTJG Bruce J. Janigian. US Nav Inst Proc 102:101-102 Feb '76

Oversize dry dock passes Chittenden Locks (Seattle). Col Raymond J. Eineigl and others. illus maps Mil Engr 68:83-85 Mar-Apr '76

Slurry trench construction (on Tennessee-Tombigbee Waterway). Carroll D. Winter. illus map tab Mil Engr 68:437-440 Nov-Dec '76

Stairway of water (Mississippi River). Capt William J. Diehl, Jr. illus Soldiers 31:49 Jun '76

Maintenance and Repair

Salvage of the (Great Lakes freighter) Sidney E. Smith. Maj Thomas J. Woodall. illus Mil Engr 68:448-451 Nov-Dec '76

WEAPON SYSTEMS

Air defense: Protecting the power centers. David Harvey. illus Def & For Aff Dig No. 11:4-5+ '76

Defense industry news. Regular feature in issues of International Defense Review

International defense digest. Regular feature in issues of International Defense Review

Modern weapon technology. Regular feature in issues of RUSI Journal for Defence Studies

SALT II's gray-area weapon systems. (Report on AFA's Symposium on "Tomorrow's Strategic Options," Vandenberg AFB, Calif, April 28-29, 1976) Edgar Ulsamer. illus AF Mag 59:80-82+ Jul '76

Weapons technology. AVM S.W.B.Menaul, Ret. Royal Air Forces Qtr 15:271-274 Winter '75

Combat Evaluation

Needed: A new family of EW systems. Edgar Ulsamer. illus AF Mag 59:27-31 Feb '76

Tank killer team (Air Force A-10 ground-attack aircraft mounting the powerful GAU-8/A 30-mm gun system). Col Robert G.Dilger. illus Natl Def 61: 190-191 Nov-Dec '76

Weapon systems support testing. LtCol William L. Lytle. illus Army Log 8:28-30 Jul-Aug '76

Maintenance and Repair

Corrosion and fatigue: Problems in life cycle costing. Maj Thomas K.Moore. tabs illus Def Mgt J 12:48-53 Jan '76

Warranties as a life cycle cost management tool. C.R.Knight. tabs Def Mgt J 12:23-28 Jan '76

Weapon systems support testing. LtCol William L. Lytle. illus Army Log 8:28-30 Jul-Aug '76

Reliability

A DOD approach to establishing weapon system reliability requirements. Martin A.Meth. tabs Def Mgt J 12:2-11 Apr '76

Maintainability--a shared responsibility. Hartley I. Starr. Natl Def 60:360-363 Mar-Apr '76

Maintainability for Air Force systems. Capt Ned H. Criscimagna. illus Log Spectrum 10:19-23+ Spring '76

Maintenance in the Navy. Robert Emsworth. illus Natl Def 60:356-358 Mar-Apr '76

R&D emphasis on reliability. Robert N.Parker. Def Mgt J 12:19 Apr '76

Reliability by design, not by chance. Willis J.Willoughby. illus Def Mgt J 12:12-18 Apr '76

Warranties as a life cycle cost management tool. C.R.Knight. tabs Def Mgt J 12:23-28 Jan '76

Testing

Atmospheric transmissometer for military system performance evaluation. Frederic M.Zweibaum and Thomas F.McHenry. tabs illus Countermeasures 2:27-29+ Jun '76

Improved deficiency reporting during test and evaluation proposed. TIG Brief 28:14 Aug 13 '76

Independent OT&E is here to stay. TIG Brief 28:11 May 21 '76

Weapon systems support testing. LtCol William L. Lytle. illus Army Log 8:28-30 Jul-Aug '76

Germany (Federal Republic)

Torpedo development in Germany: Present status and future perspectives. Ulrich Ramsauer. illus Intl Def Rev 9:96-100 Feb '76

Great Britain

Naval weapon system automation with the WSA4. J.R. Harper. illus Intl Def Rev 9:795-797 Oct '76

Great Britain - Cont'd

Weapon systems: Sea Dart. Mark Hewish. illus US Nav Inst Proc 102:101 Sep '76

Israel

Israeli defense capability. Irvine J.Cohen. Natl Def 60:271-273 Jan-Feb '76

NATO

Coming: A North Atlantic Common Defense Market. Thomas A.Callaghan, Jr. illus map Countermeasures 2:24+ Aug '76

NATO equipment standardization--the German view. illus Intl Def Rev 9:563-568 Aug '76

NATO: Standardization for improved combat capability. MajGen Richard C.Bowman. illus Comdrs Dig 19: entire issue Sep 9 '76

Standardisation and defence in NATO. Gardiner L. Tucker. RUSI J for Def Studies 121:7-8+ Mar '76

XM-1, Leopard II stakes raised; AWACS hostage? illus Armed Forces J Intl 113:14 Apr '76

Russia

The ever-expanding umbrella. LtCol Arthur D. McQueen. tab illus Air Def Mag, pp 8-17, Jul-Sep '76

Gallery of Soviet aerospace weapons. John W.R.Taylor. illus AF Mag 59:93-107 Mar '76

Military production in the USSR. (Basic facts on each type of Russian weapon) Tables only. NATO's Fifteen Nations 21:46-47 Jun-Jul '76

A new family of Soviet strategic weapons. Edgar Ulsamer. illus tab AF Mag 59:24-27 Oct '76

Ominous Soviet trends. Robert Hotz. (Reprinted from Aviation Week & Space Technology, June 28, 1976) AF Plcy Ltr for Comdrs: Sup No.9:19-21 Sep '76

United States

Affordability + performance: USAF's R&D goal. Edgar Ulsamer. illus AF Mag 59:31-36 Mar '76

Air Force Chief of Staff's FY 1977 Posture Statement. (Statement before House Committee on Armed Services, Washington, Jan 29, 1976) Gen David C.Jones. AF Plcy Ltr for Comdrs: Sup No.3:23-40 Mar '76

An antiaircraft tank. Robert E.Stone. Armor 85:29 Jul-Aug '76

The Army's "Big 5": New combat hardware. John Rhea. illus Natl Guardsman 30:10-13 Jan '76

Automatic cannon technology. Gary W.Fischer. illus Natl Def 61:192-194 Nov-Dec '76

B-52 nuclear weapon system safety study completed. TIG Brief 28:10 Aug 27 '76

Better weapons--low cost (with lasers). R.G.Buser. illus Natl Def 61:114-115 Sep-Oct '76

A blueprint for safeguarding the strategic balance. (2d report on AFA's Symposium on "Tomorrow's Strategic Options," Vandenberg AFB, Calif, April 28-29, 1976) Edgar Ulsamer. illus tabs AF Mag 59:68-74 Aug '76

A case for smart weapons. LtCol Frank C.Regan, Jr. illus tabs MarCor Gaz 60:31-35 May '76

WEAPON SYSTEMS - Continued

WEAPON SYSTEMS MANAGEMENT

426

WEAPONS - Continued

United States - Cont'd

Better weapons--low cost (with lasers). R.G.Buser. illus Natl Def 61:114-115 Sep-Oct '76

Gallery of USAF weapons. S.H.H.Young. illus AF Mag 59:111-120+ May '76

Making do and modest progress: (Army) weapons and equipment, 1976. Eric C.Ludvigsen. illus Army 26:145-146+ Oct '76

Panel (House Armed Services Investigation Subcommittee) may call commanders to testify on arms losses. Ron Sanders. AF Times 36:6 Feb 2 '76

Ways to cut weapon losses asked (by DOD). AF Times 36:24 Jun 21 '76

Weapons loss (in 10 years) put at 18,500. AF Times 36:10 May 3 '76

Costs

Better weapons--low cost (with lasers). R.G.Buser. illus Natl Def 61:114-115 Sep-Oct '76

Exhibitions

The 1975 Association of the U.S. Army Show (Washington, Oct 20-22). illus Intl Def Rev 8:927-929 Dec '75

Statistics

Nuclear delivery vehicles, comparative strengths and characteristics: A, United States and Soviet Union; B, Other NATO and Warsaw Pact countries. London's International Institute for Strategic Studies. Tables only. AF Mag 59:92-94 Dec '76

Tables of comparative strengths. London's International Institute for Strategic Studies. Tables only. AF Mag 59:92-97 Dec '76

Trends in U.S. and Soviet weapons inventories & production rates. Tables only. Armed Forces J Intl 113:22 Feb '76

Warsaw Pact

Statistics

Nuclear delivery vehicles, comparative strengths and characteristics: A, United States and Soviet Union; B, Other NATO and Warsaw Pact countries. London's International Institute for Strategic Studies. Tables only. AF Mag 59:92-94 Dec '76

Tables of comparative strengths. London's International Institute for Strategic Studies. Tables only. AF Mag 59:92-97 Dec '76

The theatre balance between NATO and the Warsaw Pact. London's International Institute for Strategic Studies. tabs AF Mag 59:98-106 Dec '76

WEAPONS CONTROLLERS

Air superiority (F-4) GIB (WSO, Weapon Systems Officer). Capt Roger E.Rosenberg. illus Navigator 23:18-19 Summer '76

WEAPONS LOADING COMPETITIONS see Munitions Loading Competitions

WEAPONS PROCUREMENT

See also
Arms Sales

WEAPONS PROCUREMENT - Continued

Defense industry news. Regular feature in issues of International Defense Review

Major defense contracts--value over $1 million. Regular feature in issues of International Defense Review

Air Force--U.S.

Air Force Chief of Staff's FY 1977 Posture Statement. (Statement before House Committee on Armed Services, Washington, Jan 29, 1976) Gen David C.Jones. AF Plcy Ltr for Comdrs: Sup No.3:23-40 Mar '76

Department of the Air Force Fiscal Years 1977 and 1978 aircraft procurement estimates. Table only. AF Plcy Ltr for Comdrs: Sup No.5:26 May '76

Department of the Air Force Fiscal Years 1977 and 1978 missile procurement estimates. Table only. AF Plcy Ltr for Comdrs: Sup No.5:27 May '76

Design-to-cost and its impact on weapons systems. Maj Jerry E.Knotts. illus Elect Warfare 8:91+ Sep-Oct '76

Faith restored--the F-15 program. Maj Gilbert B. Guarino and others. illus AU Rev 27:63-77 Jan-Feb '76

Flexibility--the key to the success of the cost/schedule control system criteria. Majs Gilbert B.Guarino and James J.Lindenfelser. illus tabs AF Compt 10:40-44 Jan '76

Life cycle cost. TIG Brief 28:4 Feb 13 '76

Models a key to air force life cycle cost implementation. 1stLt Dwight E.Collins. tabs Def Mgt J 12:54-59 Jan '76

Multinational coproduction programs: New programs and corporate memory. TIG Brief 28:10 Dec 17 '76

New aircraft and missiles. (Presentation, Senate Appropriations Committee, Washington, March 18, 1976) LtGen Alton D.Slay. tabs AF Plcy Ltr for Comdrs: Sup No.5:10-28 May '76

Personnel cuts linked to (buying) arms (and doing research). AF Times 36:22 Mar 1 '76

Plan and coordinate (with ATC) before you buy off-the-shelf systems. TIG Brief 28:8 Sep 10 '76

The promised land. Thomas C.Reed. illus tab AF AF Mag 59:45-47 May '76

Secretary of the Air Force's Air Force authorization request. (Statement before House Committee on Armed Services, Washington, Jan 29, 1976) Thomas C.Reed. tabs AF Pley Ltr for Comdrs: Sup No.3:2-23 Mar '76

Armed Forces--Great Britain

British defence procurement: Organisation and practice. E.C.Cornford. NATO's Fifteen Nations 21:23-26 Apr-May '76

British policy for defence procurement. G.H.Green. RUSI J for Def Studies 121:20-28 Sep '76

Armed Forces--Israel

Israeli defense capability. Irvine J.Cohen. Natl Def 60:271-273 Jan-Feb '76

428

WEAPONS PROCUREMENT - Continued

WEATHER - Continued

WEBER, LaVern E.

Conference speakers. (Excerpts from addresses, NGAUS 98th General Conference, Washington, Aug 30-Sep 1, 1976) por Natl Guardsman 30: 23-27 Oct '76

Strong new Guard for total force: Dedicated to both missions. MajGen LaVern E.Weber. por Army 26:45-46+ Oct '76

WEIGHTED AIRMAN PROMOTION SYSTEM

Extra hike cycles reduced for airmen. AF Times 36:6 Jul 19 '76

Fewer EM face hike delays. AF Times 37:9 Sep 6 '76

Is WAPS promoting the right people? AF Times 37:29 Aug 23 '76

WAPS nonweighables. TIG Brief 28:6 Feb 13 '76

WEIGHTLESSNESS

Antiorthostatic hypokinesia as a method of weight-lessness simulation. L.I.Kakurin and others. illus tabs Aviation, Space & Envmt Med 47:1083-1086 Oct '76

Changes in glucose, insulin, and growth hormone levels associated with bedrest. Joan Vernikos-Danellis and others. tabs Aviation, Space & Envmt Med 47:583-587 Jun '76

Effect of a 22-day space flight on the lymphoid organs of rats. Galina N.Durnova and others. illus tab Aviation, Space & Envmt Med 47:588-591 Jun '76

Effects of head-down tilt on fluid and electrolyte balance. Ladislav Volicer and others. tabs Aviation, Space & Envmt Med 47:1065-1068 Oct '76

LDH isoenzymes of skeletal muscles of rats after space flight and hypokinesia. V.V.Portugalov and N.V.Petrova. tabs Aviation, Space & Envmt Med 47:834-838 Aug '76

WEIGHTS AND MEASURES

See also
Telemetry

Metric: A measure of the future. Jacki Smith. illus AF Times 37:35-36 Nov 8 '76

Metric switch slow. AF Times 36:48 Feb 23 '76

The metric system--an overview of current status. Benjamin S.Blanchard. Log Spectrum 10:46-48 Fall '76

Metric timetable work begins. AF Times 36:18 May 17 '76

The metrication program. LtGen Robert E.Hails. TIG Brief 28:2 Dec 3 '76

The U.S. goes metric. H.R.Kaplan. illus tab Review 55:33-37 Jan-Feb '76

Equipment

Maintenance and Repair

Maintenance data reporting for Precision Measurement Equipment (PME). TIG Brief 28:3 Oct 22 '76

Precision Measurement Equipment (PME) calibration support. TIG Brief 28:9-10 Sep 24 '76

WELDING

Ultrasonic welding process for detonable materials. Florence R.Meyer. illus Natl Def 60:291-293 Jan-Feb '76

WELFARE OF ARMED FORCES

Appropriated funds for Morale, Welfare, and Recreation (MWR) activities. TIG Brief 28:15 Nov 19 '76

Survey says (military Service) members deserve new contract. AF Times 36:6 Jun 7 '76

Welfare 'haves' can aid 'have nots.' AF Times 36:10 Jun 7 '76

WENTSCH, George M.

(Brigadier) General Wentsch (and others) on USAF two star list. por Translog 7:19 Feb '76

WESCHLER, Thomas R.

Priorities and emphases for logistics, 1976-78. (Letter to Asst SecDef John J.Bennett) VADM Thomas R.Weschler, Ret. por Nav War Col Rev 29:16-29 Summer '76

WEST POINT, NY

History

Fortress West Point: 19th century concept in an 18th century war. Col Dave R.Palmer. illus map Mil Engr 68:171-174 May-Jun '76

WEST POINT, NY MILITARY ACADEMY see Military Academy, West Point, NY

WESTMORELAND, William C.

Westmoreland in Vietnam: Pulverizing the 'Boulder.' Gen William C.Westmoreland, Ret. por Army 26: 36-44 Feb '76

WEYAND, Frederick C.

America and its Army: A Bicentennial look at posture and goals. Gen Fred C.Weyand. por Parameters 6, No.1:2-11 '76

Army travel breaks urged (by Gen Weyand). Don Hirst. AF Times 37:21 Nov 1 '76

Gen (Bernard W.) Rogers named to succeed (Gen Fred C.) Weyand as Army Chief of Staff. Army 26:9-10 Sep '76

'Great progress in very difficult circumstances.' Interview. Gen Fred C.Weyand. por Army 26: 14-16+ Oct '76

Industrial luncheon address (AFCEA, Washington, June 10, 1976). Gen Fred C.Weyand. por Signal 30:40-43 Aug '76

Serving the people: The need for military power. Gen Fred C.Weyand, Ret and LtCol Harry G.Summers, Jr. por Mil Rev 56:8-18 Dec '76

Tough and ready--"to keep the peace ... to deter war." Interview. Army Chief of Staff, Gen Fred C.Weyand. por Soldiers 31:31-34 Feb '76

Vietnam myths and military realities. Gen Fred C. Weyand and LtCol Harry G.Summers, Jr. Armor 85:30-36 Sep-Oct '76

Weyand: Full circle. (Gen Fred C.Weyand accepts "Minute Man Hall of Fame" award at ROA National Convention, Bal Harbour, Fla, June 29-July 2, 1976) Officer 9:21+ Sep '76

WHEELS

See also
Airplanes, Military--Wheels

WILDLIFE CONSERVATION

At home on the range. (Game warden force, Fort Hood, Tex) SGM Nat Dell. illus Soldiers 31:41-43 Nov '76

Of warriors and warblers. (Songbird-versus-tank problem on the Camp Grayling Military Reservation) Paul L. Stewart. illus Army 26:36-39 Sep '76

Rocky Mountain haven. (Rocky Mountain Arsenal (RMA)) Darryl D. McEwen. illus Soldiers 31:49-51 Aug '76

WILLS

Clause can speed will settlement. AF Times 37:10 Dec 20 '76

WILSON, Louis H., Jr

CMC approves increase in women Marine force. MarCor Gaz 60:8 Aug '76

Commandant's policy on uniforms. Gen Louis H. Wilson, Jr. MarCor Gaz 60:2 May '76

Corps' high standards will continue. (From address, Navy League, San Diego, Calif) Gen Louis H. Wilson. MarCor Gaz 60:2 Dec '76

Emphasis on professionalism for a new generation of Marines. Gen Louis H. Wilson. Sea Power 19: 24-29 Jan '76

The first 12 months--a special report from CMC. Interview. Gen Louis H. Wilson. por MarCor Gaz 60:2+ Oct '76

A flexible military posture. Gen Louis H. Wilson. por Strat Rev 4:7-13 Fall '76

(Marine Corps) Commandant's Okinawa interview. MarCor Gaz 60:4+ Jul '76

Recruit training: Challenging and tough. (Adapted from statement before House Armed Services Committee Sub-committee on Recruiting and Recruit Training) Gen Louis H. Wilson. MarCor Gaz 60:2-4 Aug '76

Spirit of '76: 'The troops are looking good.' (A briefing to Congress) Gen Louis H. Wilson. MarCor Gaz 60:11-22 Mar '76

WILSON, Louis L., Jr

Pacific Air Forces. por AF Mag 59:72-73 May '76

WINDS

AF 209, wind 270° at 600 kts. LtCol Roland R. Robinson. illus Interceptor 18:14-15 Apr '76

Low altitude wind shear. illus Aerosp Safety 32:10-13 Sep '76

Low-level wind shear. Maj Shirley M. Carpenter. illus TAC Attack pt 1, 16:4-8 Sep '76; pt 2, Wind shear on final approach. 16:18-22 Oct '76; pt 3, Detecting and coping with wind shear. 16:8-13 Nov '76

Objects in motion: A look at the mechanics of wind shear. illus MAC Flyer 23:12-15 Sep '76

"Stand by for high winds and heavy seas!" illus Approach 22:18-21 Oct '76

Thrice is nice. (Crosswind corrections) Capt M. C. Kostelnik. illus TAC Attack 16:28-30 Dec '76

Wing low--sweet chariot. Capt Ron Langenfeld. illus Combat Crew 27:4-5+ Nov '76

WINDS - Continued

Wind shear: The mystery of the vanishing airspeed. Capt Barry Schiff. (Reprinted from AOPA Pilot, Nov 1975) illus Combat Crew 26:12-15 Feb '76; Interceptor 18:8-13 Jun '76

WIRE

Wire act (helicopter hazard). illus Aerosp Safety 32:5 Jun '76

WITT, Hugh E.

OFPP (Office of Federal Procurement Policy) one year later: A look ahead. Interview. Hugh E. Witt. por Govt Exec 8:16+ Feb '76

WIVES, MILITARY

An Army wife remembers. (Fort Sill at the turn of the century) Grace Paulding. illus Soldiers 31:40-41 Jul '76

Eliminating the wife error. Jackie Starmer. (Adapted from MATS Flyer, Aug 1963) illus Interceptor 18: 5-7 Apr '76; Adaptation. Approach 21:24-26 Nov '75

Feminism challenging wives' role? Problems in long separations. AF Times 37:27 Nov 22 '76

Military wives speak for themselves. Marianne Lester. illus AF Times, Times Magazine sup:6-14+ Nov 1 '76

Quality-of-life survey: Spouses like service more than mates do--family separation top gripe. Bruce Callander and others. tabs AF Times 36:4+ Mar 22 '76

Waiting (Navy) wives. Kathleen P. O'Beirne. illus US Nav Inst Proc 102:28-37 Sep '76

White gloves and the aide's aide. Elizabeth B. Libbey. illus Army 26:33-36 Jul '76

The wives' way. (Volunteer tour guides, members of the Wright-Patterson AFB Officers' Wives Club, tell school children about items on display at the Air Force Museum) Capt John B. Taylor and R. E. Baughman. illus Airman 20:19-20 Sep '76

WOMEN

Comparative muscular strength of men and women: A review of the literature. Lloyd L. Laubach. illus tabs Aviation, Space & Envmt Med 47:534-542 May '76

(Joy M.) Bishop: Civilian women's role (in Federal Women's Program (FWP)). Interview. illus AF Times 36:8 Mar 1 '76

New look in government: (Maj)Gen (Jeanne M.) Holm (Special Assistant to the President for Women) leads the way to greater participation by women. illus Natl Def 61:22-23 Jul-Aug '76

Rank and file VFW repeats 'no women.' AF Times 36:17 Jan 19 '76

Rape! (Potential victims include every female soldier and dependent in the Army) Sgt JoAnn Mann. illus Soldiers 31:6-10 Feb '76

Woman and socialism (in the USSR). LtCol Marina Popovich. illus Soviet Mil Rev No. 3:43-46 Mar '76

Women's language: A new bend in the double bind. 2dLt Katie Cutler. illus AU Rev 27:73-79 Jul-Aug '76

WOMEN - Continued

History

Contributors to the cause: Many valiant women helped blaze freedom's trail. Janet Hake. illus Soldiers 31:15-16 Jul '76

They (women camp followers) also served. Janet Hake. illus Soldiers 31:50-52 Jun '76

Women and the American Revolution. LtCol Gordon Taylor Bratz. illus Mil Rev 56:56-57 Nov '76

Women's role in the American Revolution. Penelope H. Carson. illus Natl Guardsman 30:2-11 May '76

WOMEN IN ASTRONAUTICS

Make way for the women astronauts! Mitchell R. Sharpe. illus Spaceflight 18:418-421 Dec '76

WOMEN IN THE AIR FORCE

United States

(AF) survey shows women rapidly get on track. AF Times 37:33 Aug 23 '76

(AF) women to begin combat courses. Ron Sanders. AF Times 37:42 Nov 15 '76

Ability, not sex, concerns (Human Resources' chief) Mann. Interview. BrigGen Chris C. Mann. illus AF Times 36:4 Jan 26 '76

(Air Force Uniform Clothing) Board rules on wearing of women's cap, beret. Ron Sanders. AF Times 36:2 Mar 1 '76

Blazing equality's trail. (Women wearing stars, eagles, or 8 stripes, excluding the medical people) Ted R. Sturm. illus Airman 20:32-35 Jan '76

Board to tap women (for undergraduate pilot training) in July. AF Times 36:10 Jan 19 '76

C-141 still OK for female pilots. AF Times 37:32 Sep 6 '76

(18) women named to undergo UPT. Len Famiglietti. AF Times 37:30 Aug 2 '76

Enlisted women have route to (Air Force) Academy (Preparatory School). Contact, p 6, Winter '76

Female SPs get combat training. AF Times 36:12 May 10 '76

First 10 women enroll at (AF) Academy Prep School. illus AF Times 36:11 Jan 26 '76

Four officers' daughters nominated for (AF) Academy. AF Times 36:8 Feb 23 '76

The new cadets. (Women enter the USAF Academy as part of the class of 1980) Capt John B. Taylor. illus Airman 20:2-9 Dec '76

New weight standards for women enlistees. Table only. AF Times 36:10 Mar 8 '76

19th woman for UPT. AF Times 37:2 Aug 23 '76

Planes (mostly trainers, transports) listed for women pilots. Len Famiglietti. AF Times 36:11 Apr 12 '76

Pregnancy as an assignment limitation. TIG Brief 28:6 Jan 16 '76

6 women to enter nav(igator) training. AF Times 37:22 Dec 6 '76

WOMEN IN THE AIR FORCE - Continued

United States - Cont'd

6 women will get UNT (Undergraduate Navigator Training). AF Times 36:10 Feb 2 '76

60 women enter SP test. AF Times 37:8 Sep 13 '76

Skill (security specialist) opened to females. AF Times 36:11 Apr 12 '76

Staff women fill model role at the (AF) Academy. illus AF Times 36:41 Jul 12 '76

USAFA prepares for first women cadets. James R. Patterson. illus AF Mag 59:50-54 Apr '76

Utilization of Air Force women (or ... 'rediscovering the wheel'). Gen Russell E. Dougherty. TIG Brief 28:2 Mar 26 '76

WASPs (Women's Air Force Service Pilots) lose (medical) benefits round. AF Times 37:17 Sep 27 '76

Who sez it's a man's world? ? ? MSgt Jerry Bielke. illus Air Reservist 28:5+ Jul '76

Women and the 185th (Tactical Fighter Gp). Maj Lloyd Bach. illus Air Reservist 28:4-5 May '76

Women and their new role in the Air Force. Ed Gates. illus tab AF Mag 59:56-60 Oct '76

Women's language: A new bend in the double bind. 2dLt Katie Cutler. illus AU Rev 27:73-79 Jul-Aug '76

History

How women flew in wartime. Len Famiglietti. illus AF Times 36:34 Apr 26 '76

Statistics

Women and their new role in the Air Force. Ed Gates. illus tab AF Mag 59:56-60 Oct '76

WOMEN IN THE ARMED FORCES

United States

Academy women raising standards (according to academy officials speaking at DACOWITS, Defense Advisory Committee On Women In The Services, Meeting, Washington, Nov 14-18, 1976). M. L. Craver. AF Times 37:2 Nov 29 '76

(Defense Manpower Commission) report supports ban on women in combat. AF Times 36:6 May 3 '76

Females in war? DACOWITS (Defense Advisory Committee On Women On The Services) passes (on combat slots). Ann Gerow. AF Times 36:8 May 10 '76

Rape, a report: Why the Services' methods for dealing with rape are part of the problem. Marianne Lester. AF Times, Times Magazine sup:4-8+ Jan 26 '76

(Service) women's TV tour bargain for Pentagon. AF Times 36:18 Jan 5 '76

Women getting better job chances (General Accounting Office reports, but) strength still a problem. AF Times 36:17 May 31 '76

Women must have full opportunity: DACOWITS (Defense Advisory Committee On Women In The Services) testimony (by Pat Leeper, representing the National Organization for Women (NOW)). Ann Gerow. AF Times 36:9 May 17 '76

WOMEN IN THE ARMED FORCES - Continued

United States - Cont'd

Women's language: A new bend in the double bind. 2dLt Katie Cutler. illus AU Rev 27:73-79 Jul-Aug '76

Would women fight like men in combat? Fred Reed. AF Times 37:8 Dec 27 '76

Statistics

Some statistics on manpower. tabs AF Times 37:26 Sep 13 '76

WOMEN IN THE ARMY

Russia

Girl with a rifle. L. Zabavskaya. illus Soviet Mil Rev No. 4:60-61 Apr '76

United States

Airborne--and then some. (Airborne School, Fort Benning, Ga, has first female instructors) LtCol Floyd A. Frost. illus Soldiers 31:30 Dec '76

An earned right to 'swing sledgehammers': Training women soldiers. LtCol Raymond E. Funderburk. Army 26:10-11 Apr '76

Fort Jackson's gun-totin' WACs are very at home on the range. LtCol Tom Hamrick, Ret. illus Army 26:26-30 Feb '76

Mothers in army green. Martha Falls. illus Soldiers 31:45-46 Oct '76

She keeps 'em rolling. (1stLt Barbara Doornink, tactical truck platoon leader and company motor officer) SSgt Zack Richards. illus Soldiers 31:24-25 Mar '76

WACs in combat. Joseph E. Revell. illus tab AF Times, Times Magazine sup pt 1, If the Army expects women to fight, why aren't they trained like men? 36:10-14+ Feb 9 '76; pt 2, Does the nation want women to have an equal right to die on the battlefield? 36:10-16+ Feb 23 '76

Women at West Point. Darryl D. McEwen. illus Soldiers 31:28-31 Jun '76

Women in Infantry OCS (Fort Benning, Ga). illus Mil Rev 56:93 Sep '76

Yuk Yek! You've come a long way, baby! (First all-woman Eskimo Scout class) Maj Wanda T. Banta. illus Natl Guardsman 30:24-25 Jun '76

WOMEN IN THE MARINE CORPS

United States

CMC (Gen Louis H. Wilson, Jr) approves increase in women Marine force. MarCor Gaz 60:8 Aug '76

The Marine team: Men and women working together. Col Margaret A. Brewer. illus MarCor Gaz 60:18-25 Apr '76

Woman shooter (Cpl Jamie M. Trombley) wins Cup Match at Camp Perry (Ohio). MarCor Gaz 60:4 Nov '76

WOOD, Robert J.
SHAPE--those were the days. Gen Robert J. Wood, Ret. por Army 26:42-47 Dec '76

WORD PROCESSING
The Administrative Center: Air Force makes it (word processing) work! John F. Judge. illus Govt Exec 8:39+ Sep '76

WORD PROCESSING - Continued

Ohio agency (Division of Public Works) creates management support (Transcription) Center. Raymond R. Kohli. illus Govt Exec 8:15-16 Oct '76

Systems approach to administrative support (in Transportation Dept's Office of Contracts and Procurement). Govt Exec 8:54+ Sep '76

Word processing: How to save $700 million a year. (Interview with Ron Companion, Installation Officer at Fort Benning, Ga) Govt Exec 8:52+ Dec '76

Word processing in the RAF. SqLdr D. J. Silk. Royal Air Forces Qtr 16:259-263 Autumn '76

Equipment

Study and Teaching

Word processing: Training method eases the transition. (New keyboard training system in U.S. Postal Service) Govt Exec 8:40 Jan '76

WORK MEASUREMENT see Output Measurement

WORLD POLITICS see International Politics

WORLD WAR I

America's Vigilantes and the Great War, 1916-1918. John Carver Edwards. Army Qtr 106:277-286 Jul '76

Poster war. S. Michael Schnessel. illus Army 26:40-45 Jul '76

World War I's silent killer. (Influenza epidemic of 1918) LtCol Kenneth Kay, Ret. illus Army 26:40-46 Apr '76

Aerial Operations, American

The first (U.S.) kill (in World War I). Barrett Tillman. illus Am Avn Hist Soc J 21:25 Spring '76

Aerial Operations, British

Royal Air Force--Day 1: Activities on the Western Front, 1st April 1918. Norman L.R. Franks. illus tabs Air Pict 38:474-479 Dec '76

Campaigns and Battles

"Arranging the minds of men": T.E. Lawrence as a theorist of war. Anthony Burton. map Army Qtr 106:51-58 Jan '76

The first shots of the Great War: The Anglo-French conquest of Togo, 1914. Eric J. Grove. Army Qtr 106:308-323 Jul '76

Tannenburg: A lesson in command and control. LtCol Thomas G. Adcock. illus Signal 30:36-39 Apr '76

The theoretical evaluation of artillery after World War I. Fred K. Vigman. (Reprinted from Military Affairs, Fall 1952) Fld Arty J 44:21-23+ Jan-Feb '76

Economic Aspects

American industrial mobilization during World War I. MajGen Theodore Antonelli. illus Def Mgt J 12:40-46 Jul '76

Naval Operations, American

Aboard Subchaser 206. Jack Sweetman. illus US Nav Inst Proc 102:69-71 Sep '76

Personal Narratives

As it was. (Recruit training during WW I) Darryl D. McEwen. illus tab Soldiers 31:46-48 Jul '76

WORLD WAR I - Continued

Political Aspects
See War--Political Aspects

Prisoners of War

Sixty years on. (Officer Prisoners of War (1914-18) Dining Club) V.C.Coombs. Royal Air Forces Qtr 16:149-154 Summer '76

Africa

The first shots of the Great War: The Anglo-French conquest of Togo, 1914. Eric J.Grove. Army Qtr 106:308-323 Jul '76

Germany

The Hutier legend. Laszlo M.Alfoldi. illus Parameters 5, No.2:69-74 '76

The political and social foundations of Germany's economic mobilization, 1914-1916. Gerald D. Feldman. Armed Forces & Soc 3:121-145 Fall '76

Great Britain

Anticipating air attack--in defence of Britain. Alfred Gollin. illus Aerosp Hist 23:197-201 Dec '76

WORLD WAR II

America in World War II: How limitless was the man-power pool? Byron V.Pepitone. illus tabs Def Mgt J 12:47-54 Jul '76

Military procurement during World War II: From battleships to blankets. Dale Birdsell. illus tab Def Mgt J 12:55-61 Jul '76

Red stars over America. (Delivering U.S. aircraft to Russia via an Alaska-Siberian route, under the Lend-Lease Act, during WW II) Capt Stephen O. Manning III. illus Airman 20:35-37 Apr '76

Aerial Operations, Allied

The three victories of the bomber offensive (WW II). Marshal Arthur T.Harris, Ret. AF Mag 59:36+ Dec '76

Aerial Operations, American

The Air Force story. MSgt Dave Sylva. illus Aerosp Safety 32:4-9 Jul '76

B-25s over Tokyo, 18 April 1942. MSgt Dave Sylva. illus Aerosp Safety 32:14-17+ Apr '76

The battle at Ormac Bay (Leyte). (A fictional recreation of an actual event) John "Hank" Henry. illus Aerosp Hist 23:86-89+ Jun '76

The Chinese-American Composite Wing (CACW). LtCol Kenneth Kay, Ret. illus AF Mag 59:60-65 Feb '76

Dauntlesses over Midway. Barrett Tillman. illus Am Avn Hist Soc J 21:154-167 Fall '76

Memories of a U.S. 8th AF Bomb Group. 1stLt Tony Fairbairn. illus Air Pict 38:238-240 Jun '76

"Old Leatherface's" bombers. (Chennault's forces included the 308th Bombardment Gp (Heavy) which saw much action in China during WW II) Capt Stephen O. Manning III. illus Airman 20:8-14 Jul '76

Pacific Privateers: VPB-121 in World War II. Joseph C.Woolf. illus Am Avn Hist Soc J 21:118-125 Summer '76

WORLD WAR II - Continued

Aerial Operations, American - Cont'd

Piper Cub goes to war. Devon Francis. illus Am Avn Hist Soc J 21:72-79 Spring '76

Ploesti (Rumania): Group navigator's eye view. Norman M.Whalen. illus maps Aerosp Hist 23:1-6 Mar '76

The raid on Ploesti (Rumania). MSgt Dave Sylva. illus maps Aerosp Safety 32:14-17 Jun '76

Recalling the feats of WW II glider pilots, the "men on silent wings." Carroll Jones. illus AF Times, Times Magazine sup:6+ Oct 18 '76

Three wars and thirty years: The story of Navy Fight-er Squadron III. Barrett Tillman. illus Am Avn Hist Soc J 21:228-239 Winter '76

Aerial Operations, British

The ace. (The first American fighter ace of World War II relives his Aug 27, 1941, mission with RAF No.71 Eagle Sq) LtCol William R.Dunn, Ret. illus AF Mag 59:76-78+ Sep '76

Air operations and the Dieppe raid. John P.Campbell. illus maps Aerosp Hist 23:10-20 Mar '76

Flying Dutchman (Commodore J.E. van der Kop) in the Royal Air Force: Surabaya--2d TAF (Tactical Air Force). Humphrey Wynn. illus Royal Air Forces Qtr 16:51-56 Spring '76

The RAF and the Warsaw uprising. Richard C.Lu-kas. illus Aerosp Hist 22:188-194 Dec '75

The story of the "Ginger" Mitchell Flight (No.226 Sq, RAF, 1944). Christopher Shores and G.E.T. Nichols. illus Air Pict 38:237 Jun '76

Aerial Operations, German

Air intelligence and the Coventry Raid (1940). N.E. Evans. illus RUSI J for Def Studies 121:66-74 Sep '76

German remotely piloted bombs (WW II). Charles H. Bogart. illus US Nav Inst Proc 102:62-68 Nov '76

The Luftwaffe and Malta: A case of "Hercules" chained. Capt Karl W.Koch, Jr. illus Aerosp Hist 23:94-100 Jun '76

Airborne Operations

Last of the first. (Gen Melvin Zais, last member on active duty of the original parachute battalion or-ganized at Fort Benning, Ga, Oct 1940) LtCol James E.Witek. illus Soldiers 31:11 Nov '76

A "might have been"--Operation Eclipse. (Airborne operations to Berlin which, by not being carried out, lost the initiative in Berlin for the West) Col Barney Oldfield, Ret. illus Armed Forces J Intl 113:20+ May '76

Paradrop at the Bukrin bridgehead: An account of the Soviet Dnieper airborne operation. Graham H. Turbiville, Jr. illus maps Mil Rev 56:26-40 Dec '76

Campaigns and Battles

See also
Normandy Campaign, 1944
Pearl Harbor, 1941

436

WORLD WAR II - Continued

Personal Narratives - Cont'd

Friends from foes. (A German pilot and an American pilot meet three times: In battle, after being shot down, and 32 years later) Robert K.Ruhl. illus Airman 20:24-30 Dec '76

Henry Wong and the 'Cunnel's' chicken. MajGen George E.Martin, Ret. illus Army 26:26 May '76

Incident at Foul Bay. (C-47 beached on the west coast of the Red Sea) John F.Ohlinger. illus Aerosp Hist 23:71-74 Jun '76

The Luftwaffe's master interrogator (Hanns Scharff). Royal D.Frey. illus AF Mag 59:68-71 Jun '76

Mission to Mecca: The cruise of the Murphy. (U.S. destroyer brings Arabian king from Mecca to Great Bitter Lake in Suez Canal, to meet with Pres Franklin Roosevelt after Yalta Conference, 1945, and deals successfully with seemingly unsurmountable problems, both diplomatic and pragmatic) CAPT John S.Keating, Ret. illus US Nav Inst Proc 102:54-63 Jan '76

The old indispensables. (Four "jeep" carriers, the first American escort carriers to be involved in combat in WW II, in the North African campaign) CAPT Fitzhugh L.Palmer, Ret. illus US Nav Inst Proc 102:61-63 Aug '76

Ploesti (Rumania): Group navigator's eye view. Norman M.Whalen. illus maps Aerosp Hist 23:1-6 Mar '76

Under water at Pearl Harbor. CAPT Charles J.Merdinger, Ret. illus US Nav Inst Proc 102:48-49 Dec '76

Political Aspects
See War--Political Aspects

Prisoners of War

The Luftwaffe's master interrogator (Hanns Scharff). Royal D.Frey. illus AF Mag 59:68-71 Jun '76

Patton and the Hammelburg Mission (to attempt to liberate POWs). LtCol Frederick E.Oldinsky. illus map Armor 85:13-18 Jul-Aug '76

Strategy
The ending of World War II. (History of the 547th Night Fighter Sq) LtCol Paul H.Baldwin, Ret. illus Aerosp Hist 23:136-139 Sep '76

France

Air operations and the Dieppe raid. John P.Campbell. illus maps Aerosp Hist 23:10-20 Mar '76

French antitank doctrine, 1940: The antidote that failed. Maj Robert A.Doughty. illus Mil Rev 56: 36-48 May '76

The long range guns. Stanley Goddard and Allan S. Chace. tabs Natl Def 60:299-303 Jan-Feb '76

A proposed refuge in Brittany--June 1940. Gen James Marshall-Cornwall. map RUSI J for Def Studies 121:78-82 Jun '76

Germany

The Luftwaffe's master interrogator (Hanns Scharff). Royal D.Frey. illus AF Mag 59:68-71 Jun '76

Patton and the Hammelburg Mission (to attempt to liberate POWs). LtCol Frederick E.Oldinsky. illus map Armor 85:13-18 Jul-Aug '76

WORLD WAR II - Continued

Germany - Cont'd

The Waffen SS: A social psychological perspective. George M.Kren and Leon H.Rappoport. Armed Forces & Soc 3:87-102 Fall '76

Great Britain

Air intelligence and the Coventry Raid (1940). N.E. Evans. illus RUSI J for Def Studies 121:66-74 Sep '76

In tribute to the Yanks. (British Sea Scout group honors seven particular Americans on Remembrance Sunday, England's annual day of honor for British and American dead of WW II) LtCol Steve Hinderliter. illus Airman 20:41-43 Nov '76

A final appraisal of the British occupation of Iceland, 1940-42. Donald F.Bittner. maps RUSI J for Def Studies 120:45-53 Dec '75

A proposed refuge in Brittany--June 1940. Gen James Marshall-Cornwall. map RUSI J for Def Studies 121:78-82 Jun '76

Japan
The silent bombers. (Japanese free balloons in WW II) LtCol Joseph P.Frankoski. illus Air Def Mag, pp 34-36, Apr-Jun '76

Manchuria

The Soviet Manchurian campaign, August 1945: Prototype for the Soviet offensive. Capt Eugene D. Bétit. illus map Mil Rev 56:65-73 May '76

Mediterranean Theater

The Luftwaffe and Malta: A case of "Hercules" chained. Capt Karl W.Koch, Jr. illus Aerosp Hist 23:94-100 Jun '76

Pacific Theater

The battle at Ormac Bay (Leyte). (A fictional recreation of an actual event) John "Hank" Henry. illus Aerosp Hist 23:86-89+ Jun '76

Poland

The RAF and the Warsaw uprising. Richard C.Lukas. illus Aerosp Hist 22:188-194 Dec '75

Rumania

Action at Facuti. (Battle of Targul Frumos, Rumania, 1944) Maj Hans O.Wagner. illus maps Armor 85: 36-38 Jul-Aug '76

Ploesti (Rumania): Group navigator's eye view. Norman M.Whalen. illus maps Aerosp Hist 23:1-6 Mar '76

The raid on Ploesti (Rumania). MSgt Dave Sylva. illus maps Aerosp Safety 32:14-17 Jun '76

Russia

An army in the offensive. (Soviet Armed Forces in WW II) MajGen M.Kiryan. map Soviet Mil Rev No.8:53-55 Aug '76

The battle of Moscow. Marshal A.Vasilevsky. illus map Soviet Mil Rev No.11:10-13 Nov '76

City of courage and glory (Novorossiisk). LtCol G. Nikolayev. illus Soviet Mil Rev No.12:9-11 Dec '76

Combined Army and Navy operations. CaptG.Ammon. illus Soviet Mil Rev No.3:48-50 Mar '76

WORLD WAR II - Continued

Russia - Cont'd

Cooperation of aviation with land forces (in WW II). Col Y.Veraksa. illus Soviet Mil Rev No.10:54-56 Oct '76

Dawn of the great victory. (Battle of Moscow, World War II) Col O.Rzheshevsky. Soviet Mil Rev No.11: 14-16 Nov '76

Fortress on the Bug (Brest, Belorussia). LtCol N. Yelshin. illus Soviet Mil Rev No.6:39-41 Jun '76

The initial period of the War (WW II). MajGen V. Matsulenko. Soviet Mil Rev No.2:48-50 Feb '76

Meeting engagements of tank armies (1941-45). Col Z.Shutov. map Soviet Mil Rev No.12:51-53 Dec '76

Paradrop at the Bukrin bridgehead: An account of the Soviet Dnieper airborne operation. Graham H. Turbiville, Jr. illus maps Mil Rev 56:26-40 Dec '76

Spearhead of the main effort. Marshal Mikhail Katukov. illus map Soviet Mil Rev No.9:16p supplement Sep '76

A tank Army in the offensive (in WW II). Col N.Kobrin. illus Soviet Mil Rev No.1:47-49 Jan '76

The vital power of socialism. Col A.Pozmogov. illus Soviet Mil Rev No.4:8-10 Apr '76

Volgograd--a hero-city. LtCol L.Rakovsky. illus Soviet Mil Rev No.2:8-10 Feb '76

WORLDWIDE MILITARY COMMAND AND CONTROL SYSTEM

A command, control and communications overview. Donald H.Rumsfeld. illus Signal 30:34-35+ May-Jun '76

Command, control and technology. LtGen Lee M. Paschall. illus Countermeasures 2:39-40+ Jul '76

Keynote luncheon address (AFCEA, Washington, June 8, 1976). Thomas C.Reed. illus Signal 30: 19-23 Aug '76

A milestone in the development of data management systems for WWMCCS. Frank R.Dirnbauer and others. illus Signal 30:34-37 Jul '76

Military communications: The 'what' is much tougher than the 'how.' C.W.Borklund. illus Govt Exec 8:21+ Jun '76

New uses of electronic communication. (Remarks, Armed Forces Communications and Electronics Assoc, Washington, June 8, 1976) Thomas C. Reed. AF Pley Ltr for Comdrs: Sup No.8:8-12 Aug '76

Overview of WWMCCS architecture. Irving Luckom. tab illus Signal 30:61-63 Aug '76

WWMCCS ADP: A promise fulfilled. Herbert B. Goertzel and Col James R.Miller. illus Signal 30:57-63 May-Jun '76

WORLDWIDE MILITARY COMMAND AND CONTROL SYSTEM - Continued

WWMCCS in transition. (Panel discussion, AFCEA, Washington, June 8, 1976) BrigGen Lawrence E. Adams and others. illus Signal 30:58-73 Aug '76

WWMCCS in transition: A Navy view. VADM Jon L. Boyes. Signal 30:72-73 Aug '76

WWMCCS in transition: A WWMCCS system engineer view. LtGen Lee M.Paschall. illus Signal 30:64-66 Aug '76

WWMCCS in transition: An Air Force view. BrigGen Van C.Doubleday. Signal 30:70-71 Aug '76

WWMCCS in transition: An Army view. MajGen Thomas M.Rienzi. Signal 30:67-70 Aug '76

USAF in the forefront of the C^3 revolution. Thomas C.Reed. illus AF Mag 59:62-65 Jul '76

WOUNDS AND INJURIES

Animal bites: Everyone's concern. TIG Brief 28:14 Oct 8 '76

Medical aspects of survivability. LtCol David H.Karney and Patsy Thompson. illus USA Avn Dig pt 1, Lifesaving emergency medical aid. 22:40-45 May '76; pt 2, Medical problems in a prolonged survival situation. 22:28-31 Jun '76

WRIGHT, Orville

Orville (Wright) lost the toss but won the flight. AF Times 37:21 Dec 20 '76

The Wright brothers. Charles H.Gibbs-Smith. Royal Air Forces Qtr 15:311-316 Winter '75

WRIGHT, Wilbur

The Wright brothers. Charles H.Gibbs-Smith. Royal Air Forces Qtr 15:311-316 Winter '75

WRITING (COMPOSITION)

See also
Report Writing

The term paper: To write or not to write. Martha S. Shull. Educ J 19:6-8 Winter '76

To military writers: A word from the editor on words. Col Lloyd J.Matthews. illus Mil Rev 56: 33-40 Apr '76

Study and Teaching

Back to basics II: The ability to communicate. (Address, National Council of Teachers of English, Philadelphia, March 25, 1976) Charles R.Cyr. (Reprinted from Vital Speeches, Sep 15, 1976) Educ J 19:29-33 Winter '76

In basket problems: An aid in teaching effective writing. Capt George M.Lauderbaugh. Educ J 19: 24-26 Winter '76

XYZ

X-RAYS

X-ray for FOD. TIG Brief 28:13 Aug 27 '76

YEAGER, Charles E.

(BrigGen Charles E.) Yeager receives Congressional Medal. por AF Times 37:45 Dec 20 '76

President OKs Yeager medal (for) breaking the sound barrier. AF Times 36:11 Jan 12 '76

YOUTH

Germany (Federal Republic)

Youth information officers of the Federal Armed Forces. Capt Jürgen Conze. illus NATO's Fifteen Nations 21:49-56 Aug-Sep '76

United States

How private enterprise is committing "subtle suicide." illus Govt Exec 8:56-57 May '76

ROTC cadet attitudes: A product of socialization or self-selection? James E. Dorman. tabs J Pol & Mil Sociol 4:203-216 Fall '76

YUGOSLAVIA

Civil-military relations in Yugoslavia, 1971-1975. Robert W. Dean. Armed Forces & Soc 3:17-58 Fall '76

Development of sociology of militaria in Yugoslavia. Anton Bebler. tabs Armed Forces & Soc 3:59-68 Fall '76

Foreign Relations

Russia

Yugoslavia's defense: The logic of politics. Axel Hörhager. illus map chart Intl Def Rev 9:733-738 Oct '76

YUGOSLAVIA - Continued

Politics and Government

Yugoslavia's defense: The logic of politics. Axel Hörhager. illus map chart Intl Def Rev 9:733-738 Oct '76

Strategic Importance

Yugoslavia's defense: The logic of politics. Axel Hörhager. illus map chart Intl Def Rev 9:733-738 Oct '76

ZAIS, Melvin

Flanker in focus. (Gen Melvin Zais) Capt Robert P. Dunleavy. por NATO's Fifteen Nations 21:73-76 Apr-May '76

Last of the first. (Gen Melvin Zais, last member on active duty of the original parachute battalion organized at Fort Benning, Ga, Oct 1940) LtCol James E. Witek. por Soldiers 31:11 Nov '76

ZHUKOV, Georgi K.

Marshal Zhukov. (80th birth anniversary) Col I. Ivanov. por obit Soviet Mil Rev No. 11:48-49 Nov '76

ZUMWALT, Elmo R., Jr

High-low. ADM Elmo R. Zumwalt, Jr, Ret. (Reprinted from the author's On Watch: A Memoir) por US Nav Inst Proc 102:46-56 Apr '76

(Seapower) (Address, NDTA, New York, April 21, 1976) ADM Elmo R. Zumwalt, Jr, Ret. por Def Trans J 32:34-36 Jun '76

Zumwalt: Public misled on defense. (Excerpts from remarks, Democratic National Convention, New York, July 13, 1976) ADM Elmo R. Zumwalt, Jr, Ret. por AF Times 37:26 Sep 6 '76

Lightning Source UK Ltd.
Milton Keynes UK
UKHW020806271218
334504UK00008B/500/P